New, Revised & Enlarged

SEVENTEENTH EDITION: 2006

Indian Economy Since Independence

UMA KAPILA, author/editor of several other books, has taught Indian Economy to undergraduate students for forty two years. She recently retired as Reader from the Department of Economics, Miranda House, University of Delhi. Presently she is Senior Editor, Academic Foundation.

An Honours Graduate from Miranda House, University of Delhi and M.A. and Ph.D. from Delhi School of Economics, Dr. Uma Kapila has also served on the Planning Commission Study Group on "Agricultural Strategies in the Eastern Region of India for the Seventh Five Year Plan" (Perspective Planning Division).

Dr. (Mrs.) Uma Kapila is the author of the book *Oilseeds Economy of India* (1982) published by the Institute of Economic Growth. She is also the author of two other textbooks on Indian Economy, one meant for B.Com (H), and the other for B.A.(Pass)/ B.Com.(Pass) / Eco.(Subsidiary). She has also co-edited along with Raj Kapila, a number of books on India's economy, banking and finance. Detailed information on these publications is readily available at the publisher's website: **www.academicfoundation.com**

Indian Economy Since Independence

Edited by Uma Kapila

New, Revised & Enlarged

SEVENTEENTH EDITION 2006

ACADEMIC FOUNDATION

Academic Foundation NEW DELHI

http://www.academicfoundation.com

Seventeenth Edition

© 2006

ACADEMIC FOUNDATION

4772-73 / 23 Bharat Ram Road, (23 Ansari Road),
Darya Ganj, New Delhi - 110 002 (India)
Phones : 23245001 / 02 / 03 / 04
Fax : +91-11-23245005
E-mail : academic@vsnl.com
www.academicfoundation.com

INDIAN ECONOMY SINCE INDEPENDENCE
New, Revised and Enlarged 17th edition : 2006
Uma Kapila (ed.)

ISBN 81-7188-504-7 (Paperback)
(for sale in the Indian subcontinent only)
ISBN 81-7188-505-5 (Hard-cover)

Designed and typeset by Italics India, New Delhi

Printed and bound in India

TO STUDENTS AND TEACHER-COLLEAGUES
who needed reference material at one source

TO THE EMINENT ECONOMISTS AND EXPERTS
whose contributions have been compliled in this volume

AND

TO ALL THOSE
interested in understanding the development of
India's economy in proper perspective

Contents...

PART - I

Planning, Institutional Framework, Constraints and Role of the State

PART - II

Agriculture

PART - III

Industry & Infrastructure

PART - IV

The External Sector

PART - V

Growth & Structural Change Since 1950 and Assessment of the Growth Experience

Preface

The book *Indian Economy Since Independence* was primarily designed to meet the requirements of the syllabus for B.A. (Hons.) students of economics of the University of Delhi. The recommended readings being scattered in various journals, official documents and books, were not easily accessible to students as well as teachers. It was, therefore, strongly felt by many of my teaching colleagues that somebody should compile the essential readings in a book which could be easily available to students and teachers. My work on the edited volume *Indian Economy Since Independence* is, therefore, an humble attempt towards this end.

The publication of the first edition was welcomed by students and teachers alike and encouraging words from my colleagues and senior economists have been a great source of inspiration for me to revise the book every year (now 17th edition), taking into account the requirements of new readings recommended and the new economic literature on various issues facing the Indian Economy as well as the latest policy measures of the Government of India.

The book, which was originally designed for the students of the University of Delhi, is getting popular in other Universities as well and Prof. V.K.R.V. Rao's comments on the book have thus proved correct:

> "...It will be a most unusual kind of text-book for pioneering which you deserve congratulations. I, therefore, send you my good wishes for the success of the publication and its use by students who do Economics Honours not only in the University of Delhi but also other Universities."

A text-book on Indian Economy must take cognisance of the latest developments that take place in the economy from time to time. Accordingly, the present edition (17th edition) has been thoroughly revised by including several new articles and chapters from Reports recommended in the latest reading list.

In response to the feed back from students as well as my colleagues teaching this paper, *editorial notes for each topic/chapter* have been incorporated to facilitate better understanding. In these notes an attempt has been made to highlight the main points in the articles and to update the data on the basis of the latest reports and other official sources. Many a time, where a single topic has more than one paper/article, an attempt has been made to give an integrated view. Also, when any recommended reading is not available for publication, an attempt has been made to cover the same in the editorial notes particularly for the benefit of the students.

In the present edition, the editorial notes for the various sections have been thoroughly revised in the light of the latest data and analysis provided in the RBI Report on Currency and Finance 2003-04, Economic Survey 2004-2005, 12th Finance Commission Report (2005-2010), Foreign Trade Policy 2004-09, Kelkar Task Force on Implementation of the Fiscal Responsibility, Budget Management Act, 2003 (July 2004), Planning Commission's Mid-term Appraisal of the Tenth Five Year Plan (June 2005) and National Rural Employment Guarantee Bill passed in August 2005.

It is hoped that these revisions and additions will prove handy and useful to students and teachers of Indian Economy.

— *Uma Kapila*

October, 2005

Acknowledgements

In an edited volume you need the cooperation of all those whose work you wish to include. I must express my heartfelt gratitude and thanks to the contributors who responded to my request without any reservations; otherwise the publication of this volume would not have been possible. In many cases permission had to be taken from the institutions to which the contributions belonged. I am grateful to these institutions for giving me the permission to include the research papers originally prepared for their organisations.

I am also grateful to the publishers of the Journals who have permitted me to reproduce from their publications. I would like to make special mention of Economic & Political Weekly and Indian Journal of Agricultural Economics. Due acknowledgement is also given in the footnotes at the end of the chapter.

My special thanks to Prof. K.L. Krishna for his essay specially written for the benefit of students and teachers.

I am thankful to my colleagues and senior economists for their kind appreciation of this project and making suggestions from time to time. I am extremely grateful to the authors whose papers have been included in this volume: Prof. K.L. Krishna, Prof. T.N. Srinivasan, Dr. C. Rangarajan, Dr. Ashok Gulati, Dr. Montek S. Ahluwalia, Prof. B.S. Minhas (late), Prof. Pravin Visaria (late), Prof. A. Vaidyanathan, Prof. S.K. Ray, Prof. Jean Dreze, Prof. Angus Deaton, Dr. Kirit S. Parikh, Dr. R. Radhakrishna, Dr. Mihir Rakshit, Dr. S.L. Shetty, Dr. Rip Landes, Prof. R. Nagaraj, Dr. P.D. Jeromi, Dr. V.M Rao and Dr. K.B.L. Mathur.

In the editorial notes, I have drawn liberally from Dr. Rakesh Mohan's paper on Small Industry; Prof. Tendulkar's paper on Export Performance; Prof. Sundaram's paper on Employment and Unemployment in the 90's; and Prof. C.H.H. Rao's paper (Sept., 2005) relating to National Rural Employment Guarantee Bill for which I must express my gratitude.

Needless to say, I owe a lasting debt to my students who provided the real inspiration for undertaking this project and revising it every year.

I must also put on record my gratitude to my institution i.e. Miranda House, for all that I learnt as a student and as a teacher of this premier University College for women.

Lastly, but most important, I am grateful to Academic Foundation for bringing out this altogether completely revised edition well in time for the new academic session.

— *Uma Kapila*

October, 2005

The Contributors

T.N. Srinivasan.................... *Chairman & Professor, Economic Growth Centre, Department of Economics, Yale University, USA.*

C. Rangarajan. .... *Chairman, Prime Minister's Economic Advisory Council; formerly: Chairman, Twelfth Finance Commission; Governor, RBI, Ex-Member, Planning Commission.*

Montek S. Ahluwalia.......... *Dy. Chairman, Planning Commission, Government of India; formerly: Director (EvO) IMF, Washington; Finance Secretary, Government of India.*

Kirit S. Parikh. .... *Member, Planning Commission, New Delhi.*

Mihir Rakshit........................ *Director, Monetary Research Project, Investment Credit Rating Agency (ICRA) Ltd., Kolkata.*

Ashok Gulati .... *Director, Markets, Trade and Institutions Division (MTID), International Food Policy Research Institute, Washington DC, USA.*

Jean Drèze. .... *Hony. Professor, Deptt. of Economics, Delhi School of Economics, Delhi.*

Angus Deaton .... *Professor of Economics & International Affairs, Princeton University, U.S.A.*

R. Radhakrishna. .... *Director, Indira Gandhi Institute of Development Research, Mumbai.*

Contributors Contd...

B.S. Minhas (late). .... *Formerly: Distinguished Scientist Emeritus, Indian Statistical Institute, Delhi, and Member, Planning Commission.*

S.K. Ray. .... *Professor (Retd.), Institute of Economic Growth, Delhi.*

R. Nagaraj. .... *Professor, Indira Gandhi Institute of Development Research, Mumbai.*

Rip Landes. .... *Senior Economist, U.S. Department of Agriculture, Washington.*

K.L. Krishna. .... *Hony. Research Advisor, Centre for Development Economics, Delhi School of Economics, Delhi; formerly: Sr. Consultant, Indian Council for Research on International Economic Relation (ICRIER), New Delhi.*

A. Vaidyanathan. .... *Distinguished Economist and Ex-Member, Planning Commission, Government of India.*

Pravin M. Visaria (late). .... *Former Director, Institute of Economic Growth, Delhi.*

V.M. Rao. .... *Visiting Fellow, Institute for Social & Economic Change, Bangalore.*

P.D. Jeromi. .... *Asstt. Advisor, Deptt. of Economic Analysis & Policy, Reserve Bank of India, Kochi.*

Gangadhar Darbha. .... *Economist, Morgan Stanley, London.*

A. Ganesh Kumar. .... *Associate Professor, Indira Gandhi Institute of Development Research, Mumbai.*

K. Hanumantha Rao. .... *Faculty, National Institute of Rural Development (NIRD), Hyderabad.*

S.L. Shetty............................ *Director, EPW Research Foundation, Mumbai.*

K.B.L. Mathur........................ *Joint Secretary, Ministry of Finance, Government of India, New Delhi.*

C. Ravi.................................. *Faculty, Centre for Economic and Social Studies (CESS), Hyderabad.*

B. Sambi Reddy.................. *Faculty, National Institute of Rural Development (NIRD), Hyderabad.*

Uma Kapila........................... *Reader, (Retd.) Department of Economics, Miranda House, University of Delhi. Presently, Senior Editor, Academic Foundation, New Delhi.*

◆ ◆ ◆ ◆

Part I

Planning, Institutional Framework, Constraints and Role of the State

1

Indian Economy at Independence

Uma Kapila

The pre-independence period was a period of near stagnation for the Indian economy. At the time of independence, Indian economy was caught up in a *vicious circle of poverty* characterized by one of the lowest per capita consumption and income levels among the countries of the world. Low income levels resulted in low levels of saving and capital formation and, therefore, low productivity and low level of income and this vicious circle perpetuated poverty in the country. Further, the size of the market being limited because of low incomes, entrepreneurs had little incentive for making investments in diversified fields and, therefore, the productivity in the economy continued to be low thereby perpetuating low incomes and mass poverty.

Judged in terms of per capita incomes and standard of wellbeing, the Indian economy remained more or less stagnant during the colonial regime. Quoting from the First Five Year Plan document : "This is primarily because the basic conditions under which an economy can continuously expand have been lacking. The impact of modern industrialism in the latter half of the 19th century was felt in this country initially through imports of machine-made goods from abroad which reacted adversely on the traditional pattern of economic life, but did not create the impulse for development along new lines. The transition that followed was characterized not by expansion of industry and a diversification of the economic structure but by a decay of India's traditional arts, crafts and industries and by an increasing pressure of population on land. This retrogression led to a decline in productivity per person engaged in agriculture, the adverse effects of which were perhaps softened to some extent by the shock absorbing capacity of the old institution of the joint family. The result was a continuous increase in underemployment and the growth of an attitude of *pathetic contentment* on the part of the people. In such an environment there could be little economic or social progress. Whatever surpluses might have been available in the system under these conditions were directed to the purchase of imports, partly of better finished products from abroad and partly of equipment for the new transportation system designed primarily in the interests of foreign commerce. The responsibility for promoting modern commerce and industry came to be concentrated in the hands of certain classes in the urban areas, and up to the end of the nineteenth century the only major large-scale industries which had taken root in the country were textiles. Little attention was paid to improvement of agriculture or to the needs of the rural areas."[1]

Indian economy at the time of independence was overwhelmingly rural and agricultural in character with nearly 85 per cent of the population living in villages and deriving their livelihood from agricultural and related pursuits using traditional, low productivity techniques. The backwardness of Indian economy is reflected in its unbalanced occupational structure with 70 per cent of working population engaged in agriculture. Even with this large proportion of population engaged in agriculture, the country was not self-sufficient in food and raw materials for industry. The average availability of food was not only deficient in quantity and quality but also precarious as exhibited in recurrent famines. Illiteracy was as high as 84 per cent; majority of children (60 per cent) in the 6-11 age group did not attend school. Mass communicable diseases were wide-spread and in the absence of a good public health service, mortality rates were very high (27 per thousand). Thus the economy was faced with the problems of mass poverty, ignorance and diseases which were aggravated by the unequal distribution of resources between groups and regions.

Immediately after the attainment of independence, Government's main concern in economic policy was to control persistent and severe inflationary pressures and to alleviate shortages of essential food items which had been aggravated by the partition of the country in 1947. The Industrial Policy Resolution of 1948 marked a fundamental departure from the earlier policy of laissez-faire. According to the new Policy Resolution, the government was to have a major role in initiating and regulating development in one of the key sectors of the economy. The

Directive Principles of State Policy, incorporated in the Constitution, defined the broad objectives of socio-economic policy. They mentioned the right of citizens to an adequate means of livelihood, regulation of ownership and control of the material resources of the country to subserve the common good and the avoidance of concentration of wealth and means of production. Finally, the concept of co-ordinated planning of development programmes under the auspices of the central government, was accepted and the Planning Commission was set up in March 1950 with the following terms of reference:[2]

(1) to make an assessment of the material, capital and human resources of the country, including technical personnel, and investigate the possibilities of augmenting such of these resources as are found to be deficient in relation to the nation's requirement;

(2) to formulate a Plan for the most effective and balanced utilization of the country's resources;

(3) on a determination of priorities, to define the stages in which the plan should be carried out and propose the allocation of resources for the due completion of each stage;

(4) to indicate the factors which are tending to retard economic development, and determine the conditions which, in view of the current social and political situation, should be established for the successful execution of the Plan;

(5) to determine the nature of the machinery which will be necessary for securing the successful implementation of each stage of the Plan in all its aspects;

(6) to appraise, from time to time, the progress achieved in the execution of each stage of the Plan and recommend the adjustments of policy and measures that such appraisal may show to be necessary; and

(7) to make such interim or ancillary recommendations as appear to it to be appropriate either for facilitating the discharge of the duties assigned to it; or, on a consideration of the prevailing economic conditions, current policies, measures and development programmes; or on an examination of such specific problems as may be referred to it for advice by Central or State Governments.

With the formulation of the First Five Year Plan, India embarked upon the programme of planned economic development of the country. The First Five Year Plan covered the period 1951-56 followed by the

Second Plan (1956-61) and the Third Plan (1961-66). After a *Plan Holiday* following the severe impact of exogenous shocks such as hostilities with Pakistan and unprecedented drought for two successive years 1965-66 and 1966-67, the country resumed the Fourth Plan in 1969 covering the period 1969-74. Then came the Fifth Five Year Plan (1974-79) which did not complete its five years because of the change of party in power. With the coming into power of the Janta Party Government, the Sixth Five Year Plan was launched in 1978 covering the period 1978-83. Again, with the change in Government in 1980, the new Sixth Five Year Plan was started, covering the period 1980-85 and followed by the Seventh Plan (1985-90) which was completed by March-end, 1990. The Eighth Five Year Plan, to begin from April, 1990 covering the period 1990-95 could not be finalised and, again, we had two years of annual plans. After a gap of two years, the Eighth Plan was launched in April 1992, covering the period 1992-97 followed by the Ninth Plan in April 1997, covering the period 1997 to 2002 and the Tenth Five Year Plan (2002-2007) launched in April 2002.

Notes

1. Government of India, The First Five Year Plan, 1951-56, p. 28.
2. Ibid.

2

Planning and Role of the State in India

Chapters 2 to 4 are devoted to the issue of planning, its various aspects, economic and social objectives of planning, strategies, constraints and the role of the State.

The launching of the First Five Year Plan in April 1951 initiated a process of development aimed not merely at raising the standards of living of the people but also opening out to them new opportunities for a richer and more varied life. This was sought to be achieved by planning for growth, and social justice.

The First Five Year Plan contains one of the clearest early formulations of the need for planning and of the State's role in it. Planning, it pointed out, involves "acceptance of a clearly defined set of objectives in terms of which to frame overall policies..., formulation of a strategy for promoting the realization of the ends defined..., and working out a rational solution to problems – an attempt to coordinate means and ends".

Structural Constraints and the Development Strategy

"The underlying causes of structural backwardness were perceived as follows. First, the basic constraint on development was seen as being an acute deficiency of material capital, which prevented the introduction of more productive technologies. Secondly, the limitation on the speed of capital accumulation was seen to lie in the low capacity to save. Thirdly, it was assumed that even if the domestic capacity to save could be raised by means of suitable fiscal and monetary policies, there were structural limitations preventing conversion of savings into productive investment. Fourthly, it was assumed that whereas agriculture was subject to secular diminishing returns, industrialization would allow surplus labour currently underemployed in agriculture to be more productively employed in industries which operated according to increasing returns to scale. A Fifth assumption was that if the market mechanism were accorded primacy, this would result in excessive consumption by the upper-income groups, along with relative under-investment in sectors essential to the accelerated development of the economy. Sixthly, while unequal distribution of income was considered to be a 'bad thing', a precipitate transformation of the ownership of productive assets was held to be detrimental to the maximization of production and savings. In other words, there was a tolerance towards income inequality, provided it was not excessive and could be seen to result in a higher rate of growth than would be possible otherwise."

"Given all these perceptions, it was felt that economic theory indicated that the basic questions relating to how much to save, where to invest, and in what forms to invest could be best handled with the help of a plan.

"It will be observed from the above that the Indian planners subscribed to a basically supply-side view of the planning problem. The argument that domestic demand can possibly be a constraint on the growth process was not even mentioned as a hypothesis that needed to be rejected. The reason, presumably, was the belief that with an active state policy on investment, all possible slack in the economic system would be utilized. Statically considered, the argument was right. There was little Keynesian-type unemployment in India in the early fifties. There was consequently justification for concentrating on factors promoting savings or productive accumulation. Indian planners could at that stage maintain that what mattered most was growth in the aggregate level of investment and that, disproportionalities apart, the growth process was unlikely to lose steam so long as public investment was growing at a fast pace. That led them to look into areas where public investment could be more fruitfully deployed, in the long term. There were three major possibilities which could be expected to balance supply with demand along a growing trend line. First, public investment would be concentrated in the area of infrastructure. Secondly, public investment could be directed primarily towards agriculture. Thirdly, public investment could be directed primarily towards industrial development. Indian planners obviously did attempt all three, as any reasonably planner can be expected to do in such situations. The First Five-Year Plan (1950-55) focused on the first two types of investment. At the time of the Second Five-Year Plan (1955-60), however, a major change was brought about. Indian planners operated on the assumption of a low elasticity of export demand accompanied by a system of strict import allocation. Thus, they were in reality operating on the assumption of a nearly closed economy. In such an economy, if savings were to be substantially raised from a low initial level of around 5 per cent in 1950 to 20 per cent in 1975, inter-sectoral consistency over time would demand that the productive capacity of the capital goods sector would have to rise at an accelerated rate to convert growing savings into additional real investment. It was therefore the need to raise the real savings rate that led Indian planners to accord primacy to a faster rate of growth in the capital goods sector, although doubtless there could have been other considerations such as building up defence capability.

"Indian planners ignore the trade option as a major source of growth? The issue was posed at the time the Second Five-Year Plan was formulated. A projection of the balance of trade was attempted in the plan document, and the planners concluded that no significant increase in export earnings in the short run could be expected. However, they recognised that 'it is only after industrialization has proceeded some way that increased production will be reflected in larger export earnings. . . .'

"The argument, briefly, was as follows. The development of a heavy capital goods base over a period of time would lead to the diversification of the export basket in the direction of manufactured goods, including machinery and equipment; while the increase in employment, leading to an expanded demand for consumer goods, would be met by pursuing 'capital-light' methods of production. That this would not enable India to be competitive in the world market for textiles was considered to be a short-term adjustment problem" (S. Chakravarti pp. 9-17).

Role of the State as Visualised in the Fifties

At this time in the early 1950s it was believed that the State could play a significant role both in raising the domestic rate of savings and in putting it to more productive use. Pre-industrial economies are predominantly rural and agricultural in character. They have land tenure systems in which a substantial part of the surplus over subsistence needs of cultivators and farm labourers gets appropriated by a small class of non-cultivating land owners and intermediaries (especially under the zamindari system and other feudal forms of tenure) and used for non-essential consumption. Abolition of such exploitative and socially wasteful land tenure systems could release surplus for productive investment. Land reforms combined with taxation of agriculture (either directly or indirectly by influencing prices of agricultural commodities relative to that of manufactures) are means of exploiting this potential. Both require strong State intervention.

Apart from its role in maintaining law and order, defining and protecting property rights, enforcement of contracts and the like, the State has to take the primary responsibility for providing elementary education, basic health care, safe drinking water and other facilities which are in the nature of basic needs in any civilized society and which, in addition, have beneficial effects on the general level of productivity. The latter effects – which are referred to as external economies – raise questions as to whether the market mechanism can secure the appropriate sharing of costs and benefits. Where externalities (beneficial or otherwise) happen to be significant, direct State intervention is necessary and justified.

Projects (e.g., road networks, major irrigation, steel plants, railways) which call for investments on a scale far beyond the capacity of individual investors and/or are in the nature of natural monopolies (e.g., public utilities) form another category where direct involvement of the State is deemed justifiable. In most cases even if the private sector is allowed to operate, the need for effective mechanisms to define and enforce standards, norms of efficiency, "fair" rate of return on investment and the like is universally accepted. All of this calls for State regulation, though not necessarily direct ownership and operation. During the early phases of Indian planning, given that indigenous industrial entrepreneurs were few in number and had relatively limited resources, the industrialists themselves favoured a large, direct role for the State in many of these activities.

The government can also help development by creating conditions which induce people to save more. Low rates of savings are of course partly a reflection of low levels of income. But those who have relatively large incomes may prefer to spend on current consumption rather than save when there are relatively limited opportunities for investments that offer attractive returns. A relatively stagnant, slow growing economy implies that profitable opportunities for investment are limited. State intervention can help expand such opportunities in several ways.

Public mobilization of idle labour for creating productive assets especially roads, irrigation, land improvement, schools, rural hospitals etc.

increase the potential productivity of private resources and thereby create profitable private investment opportunities. Under certain conditions, increased public expenditure can enlarge the scope for profitable investment by creating additional demand for goods and services. Both these effects are likely to be considerably strengthened if there is a coordinated programme of investments for 'balanced development' ensuring that supplies of key inputs and services grow in step with the demand for them. This aspect is particularly important in the case of activities which are closely inter-related. With a coordinated programme, the risks of shortages or excesses of particular goods or services are substantially reduced. Reduced risks induce business to invest more.

Finally strong State intervention is a logical corollary of the goals of social justice and preventing concentration of power which have been explicitly incorporated among the Directive Principles of State Policy in the Constitution. In addition, the Directive Principles lay emphasis on:

1. Securing to all citizens the right to an adequate means of livelihood;
2. Ensuring that distribution of ownership and control of material resources is regulated in a manner which best serves the common good;
3. Preventing the concentration of wealth and means of production; and
4. Protecting children from being forced to work or being exploited on account of economic necessity.

Though these provisions lacked legal sanction, they do reflect the importance attached to 'social justice' and have shaped the scope and nature of State intervention.

Altogether, as the First Plan put it, whether one thinks of the problem of capital formation or of the introduction of new techniques or of the extension of social services or of the overall realignment of the productive forces and class relationships in society, one inevitably comes to the conclusion that a rapid expansion of the economic and social responsibilities of the State will alone be capable of satisfying the legitimate expectations of the people. This need not involve complete nationalization of the means of production or elimination of private agencies in agriculture or business and industry. It does however mean a progressive widening of the public sector and a reorientation of the private sector to the needs of a planned economy (First Plan).

Evolution of Strategy and Priorities

The First Plan provided an incisive general analysis of the nature of the country's development problem and various options for mobilizing resources and achieving development with more equal distribution. There was special emphasis on the role of mass mobilization of idle rural labour and land reform. But on balance the plan rejected radical solutions (especially in respect of redistribution of existing wealth and incomes). The plan projected, rather optimistically, that savings and investment as a proportion of national income would rise from an estimated 5-6 per cent in the early 1950s to 20 per cent by 1968-69 and stabilize at that level thereafter. Aggregate income was expected to double in approximately twenty years and per capita income in twenty-seven years.

The successful completion of the modest first plan was followed by a very ambitious Second Five-Year Plan. The plan's author, P.C. Mahalanobis, provided an analytical foundation for it with a closed-economy growth model with two sectors, one of which produced consumer goods and the other investment goods, with sector-specific capital as the only factor of production.

The fundamental insight of this model was that the greater the proportion of investment devoted to increasing the capacity of the investment-goods sector, the faster the long-run growth in consumption and investment. In the strategy based on this model, rapid long-run growth was to be achieved without much sacrifice of short-run consumption by concentrating scarce investment in expanding capital-goods-producing (and intermediate-goods-producing) heavy industry. Current consumption demand was to be met by employing abundant labor resources to manufacture consumer goods using labor-intensive methods that required little capital. (Srinivasan & Tendulkar, 2003).

The Second Plan underlined the political constraints on any radical solutions to redressing inequalities and re-emphasized rapid growth and diversification of economic activity through industrialization as essential for achieving and maintaining full employment at a rising level of productivity. It went on to define a coherent overall strategy whose central elements included stepping up the rate of investment (but at a more moderate pace than envisaged in the first plan) and a conscious policy of developing an indigenous heavy industry base (comprising metallurgical, chemical and machine building industries) to lay the foundation for accelerated self-reliant growth, with a leading role for the public sector. Accordingly, the 1956 Industrial Policy Resolution emphasized that the state must play a progressive role in the development of Industries and as the Resolution puts it "the adoption of socialist pattern of society as the national objective, as well as the need for planned and rapid development, require that all industries of basic and strategic importance, or in the nature of public utility services, should be in the public sector. Other industries which are essential and require investment on a scale which only the State, in present circumstances, could provide, have also to be in the public sector. The state has, therefore, to assume direct responsibility for the future development of industries over a wider area." The encouragement of labour-intensive forms of producing mass consumer goods was seen to be a potentially important way of reconciling the conflict between emphasis on heavy industry (which would generate faster growth of income and employment in the long run) and the need to generate adequate jobs for the currently unemployed and underemployed in the transitional period.

The dominant growth orientation articulated in the Mahalanobis strategy of the Second plan continued into the third plan. Thus, the economic growth was expected to take place through the modern industrialization. The industrialization in turn, was expected to be a replica of the same process that had taken place in the historical past in the advanced countries. However, the relatively greater emphasis on the long-term growth in an import-substitution oriented strategy required a modification in the industrialization process. This consisted of a strong accent on the creation of domestic capacity in the direction of producing capital goods to produce more capital goods. In this strategy, the public sector was expected to play a dual role of (a) promoting the growth of infrastructural facilities and the creation of capacity in the basic and heavy industries and (b) reducing the concentration of economic power through the expansion of public ownership of means of production.

An attempt was made with a reasonable success in implementing the long-term growth maximizing Mahalanobis strategy during the Second and the Third Five Year Plans. There was, as a result, a considerable acceleration in public sector investment in infrastructure (roads, railways, major and medium irrigation) and indirectly productive investments in universal intermediates like steel, coal, power and heavy electrical machinery. Although the encouragement to the cottage, village and small scale industries as a means of providing employment as well as expanding the supplies of consumer goods were conceived as part of this strategy, very little was achieved in this regard. Similar was the fate in regard to the policies towards the reduction of inequalities.

As rightly pointed out by Kaushik Basu "the actual policy regime that India followed in its early days of independence was a mixture of the two competing (and almost contradictory) visions. A Soviet-style planning system was developed, but without the state having a monopoly of control over the resources. Capitalism was allowed to flourish, but a large bureaucracy was nurtured. Huge investments were made in basic industries, but at the same time several sectors were protected as belonging to the small-scale sector. Capitalism was criticised but it was also relied upon. Socialism was never practiced, but the rhetoric of socialism was the norm. A burgeoning bureaucracy became the surrogate for socialism". (Basu, 2004)

However, in terms of the aggregate performance, this phase recorded a fairly sustained 8 to 10 per cent compound growth rate of industrial output, 3 to 3.5 per cent compound growth rate in the foodgrains output and around 1.75 per cent growth rate in per capita income. All these growth rates represented a sharp acceleration over the pre-Independence past. A diversified industrial structure came to be established. This was taken to be a success of the planning efforts. Planning was regarded during this period as a "going." (S.D. Tendulkar)

Thus, the first phase spanning roughly over the first three Five Year Plan periods was characterized by fairly sustained growth in per capita incomes, distinct acceleration in public sector investment and in the growth of industrial output. This phase was dominated by the growth oriented development strategy.

Changing Perceptions

The fifties and sixties were marked by relatively strong and stable governments under the control of the Congress both at the Centre and in the states as well as a clear commitment to, and support for planning from the political leadership. The Planning Commission could impart a sense of vision, direction and an integrated overall perspective on the desired course of the economy. This provided a framework in which investment allocations could be decided and the justification for particular projects and programmes could be evaluated. The Commission acquired prestige and began to play an important role in mediating the claims of different ministries, of the Centre vis-a-vis the states and of different states over limited development resources. It also pioneered independent evaluation of the actual working of selected schemes and their impact. According to Tendulkar "whatever success that had been claimed for the growth oriented development strategy of the first phase could be attributed to the credibility of the planning process."

This atmosphere changed dramatically after the drought and the foreign exchange crisis of the mid-sixties. The sudden increase in defence expenditure consequent to the armed conflicts with China and Pakistan and the levelling-off of foreign aid, all in the short span of three years (1962-65), put the economy under severe strain. A crisis occurred when two consecutive droughts hit the country in 1966 and 1967 and real GDP declined in absolute terms.

The sharp deterioration of the economic situation and the security environment highlighted two main weaknesses of the existing strategy, namely, the relative neglect of agriculture and a critical dependence on foreign aid.

The two-year period 1965 and 1966 witnessed the worst drought in recent memory and consequent famines in large parts of north India. At the same time, all aid was cut off to India by the donor countries on account of the Indo-Pakistan War of 1965, including food aid. The consequence was a virtual collapse of the economy, and recourse had to be taken to extraordinary financing from the International Monetary Fund (IMF) and the World Bank, which were accompanied by stiff conditionalities.

This traumatic experience brought food security into the forefront of our policy imperatives, which was further buttressed by the observation that sustained industrialization was not possible without adequate provision of wage-goods. The Fourth Plan, conceived after three years of Plan holiday, therefore, had to have food security as its centre-piece.

The Fifth Plan recognized that growth and industrialization would not necessarily improve the living conditions of the people, particularly the poor. The concepts of "minimum needs" and directed anti-poverty programmes were innovations of this Plan, whatever may have been the success achieved in implementing them effectively. The Fifth Plan also marks the beginning of a period of steady increase in the growth rate of the economy, which continued right through to the Eighth Plan.

The Sixth Plan for the first time recognized that the success of the Mahalanobis heavy industrialization strategy in raising the savings rate of the country had created a situation where excess capacities were becoming evident in certain industries. A shift in the pattern of industrialization, with lower emphasis on heavy industries and more on infrastructure, begins here. The Seventh Plan represents the culmination of this shift. In perspective, it may justifiably be termed as the infrastructure plan. It was also during this period that a reappraisal of the import-substitution strategy begins, and a gradual liberalisation of the Indian economy is initiated.

The Eighth Plan was overtaken by the crisis of 1991, and the economic reforms that came in its wake. The dramatic events and policy initiatives of the two-year plan holiday period between 1990 and 1992 demanded a full reappraisal of the planning methodology, and the Eighth Plan represents the first efforts at planning for a market-oriented economy.

Jean Dreze and Amartya Sen (1995) pointed out "four decades of allegedly 'interventionist' planning did little to make the country literate, provide a wide-based health service, achieve comprehensive land reforms, or end the rampant social inequalities that blight the material prospects of the underprivileged".

Thus, the Eighth Five Year Plan documents states that "in the background of our experience of planning for development over the last forty years and under the strong imperatives for change as they have emerged now, a question is generally asked: what will be the role of planning in future?

The Role of Planning

"When the term 'planning' was, for the first time, officially defined in the First Five Year Plan document the term used was "democratic planning" as distinct from a 'plan based on regimentation'. The centralised planning of the type practised in socialist economies did not exist in India, ever. In practice, the market has determined allocations in a major segment of the economy. Public sector, of course, has expanded with a wide ranging influence on the economic life of the nation. The lack of cost consciousness of the public sector, its increasing ineffectiveness in achieving the targets and depletion of its resources, crippling its ability to carry on its activities without high-cost borrowing have compelled us to define and limit its role and lay down the objective principles of its operations. The process of planning and the pattern of Government activities followed hitherto have dampened people's initiatives and their sense of responsibility towards building the nation. The process of planning needs to be corrected in this respect.

"As a corollary to this, the role of Planning Commission needs to be redefined. It has to play an integrative role in developing a holistic approach to the policy formulation in critical and inter-sectoral areas of human and economic development. The existing multiplicity of agencies is not only wasteful but also counter-productive because of the long repetitive procedures and the diffusion of authority involved. An integrated approach can lead to better results at much lower cost. So far, resource allocation has been the predominant role of the Planning

Commission. This has to change. Instead of looking for mere increases in the Plan outlays the emphasis should be on increases in the efficiency of utilisation of the allocations being made and the prospects of a return on the investments. The Planning in our country still has a large role to play. Planning is needed for creating social infrastructure and for human development. Planning is necessary to take care of the poor and the downtrodden who have little asset endowments to benefit from the natural growth process. Further planning process has to manage the flow of resources across regions for accelerated removal of regional disparties. Certainly there are areas in which markets cannot play an allocative role. Market mechanism is never adequate for protecting environment, forests, and ecology. Planning and market mechanism should be so dovetailed that one is complementary to the other. Market mechanism must serve as an 'efficiency promoting device', while planning will be the larger guiding force, keeping the long term social goals in the perspective" (Ninth Plan Document).

Redefining the Role of State

The Approach Paper to the Tenth Five Year Plan stated that an important aspect of the redefinition of strategy that is needed relates to the role of Government. It is now generally recognized that Government in the past tended to take on too many responsibilities, imposing severe strains on its limited financial and administrative capabilities and also stifling individual initiative. An all pervasive government role may have appeared necessary at a stage where private sector capabilities were undeveloped, but the situation has changed dramatically in this respect. India now has a strong and vibrant private sector. The public sector is much less dominant than it used to be in many critical sectors and its relative position is likely to decline further as government ownership in many existing public sector organizations is expected to decline to a minority. It is clear that industrial growth in future will depend largely upon the performance of the private sector and our policies must therefore provide an environment which is conducive to such growth.

This is not to say that Government has no role to play or only a minimalist role, in promoting development. On the contrary, government has a very important role but a different one from that envisaged in the past. There are many areas, *e.g.* the social sectors, where its role will clearly have to increase. There are other areas, e.g. infrastructure development, where gaps are large and private sector cannot be expected to step in significantly. In these areas the role of government may have to be restructured. It will have to increase in some areas of infrastructure development which are unlikely to attract private investment e.g. rural infrastructure and road development. In others e.g. telecommunications, power, ports, etc., the private sector can play a much larger role provided an appropriate policy framework is in place. Here, the role of the Government needs to change to facilitate such investment as much as possible while still remaining a public sector service provider for quite some time. In all these areas, the role of government as a regulatory ensuring a fair deal for consumers, transparency and accountability, and a level playing field is also extremely important.

Redefining the role of the Government to reflect the changed circumstances facing the economy must be an important aspect of future strategy. This redefinition is necessary both at the Central Government level and also at State Government level.

According to Kaushik Basu "there is need now for India to move more strongly forward with the reforms, allow private firms to enter sectors earlier kept reserved for state-owned enterprises (this is more important than privatisation), open the economy further, and, in particular, allow Indian companies to go for larger acquisitions abroad. But one must be aware that there are no panaceas in economic policy. One has to be prepared for flexibility, to experiment with policy but be ready to adjust, alter, and on occasion even do a U-turn, depending on the evidence coming in. To stick with one policy, unbendingly, is to make the same mistake of policy stubbornness that led India to its present predicament.

Taking the example of openess, he states, while there is need to push ahead with this in today's India, including a further lowering of tariff barriers and even greater mobility of capital, it is not obvious that these reforms, if implemented in the 1960s, would have automatically yielded benefits for the country. There are several laws and institutional features of Indian industry that handicap our domestic producers. For example, there are some industries, such as handicrafts and toys, which are marked as belonging to the small-scale sectors. Large-scale factory production is not permitted in these industries. Imagine what would happen if India suddenly opened up the doors to all imports, without liberalising this sector. Foreign producers would manufacture the same goods in large-scale modern factories, lower their per-unit cost of production, and outcompete the Indian producers, handicapped by the Indian laws. This would still cause gains from trade, true, but may inhibit the future development of Indian industry. Moreover, the free flow of capital could cause destabilising currency crises. And, not surprisingly, prominent econmists such as Jagdish Bhagwati have advised against full convertibility on the capital account for developing countries, observing that "the optimal speed at which one liberalises is not necessarily the fastest" (2002, 90).

The same is true for globalisation, which creates great opportunities, says Kaushik Basu. But to maintain that it has no costs is to make the same mistake of overconfidence that served India so poorly in the past. Globalisation is likely to bring prices of the weaker economies into alignment with prices in the industrialised nations. Given that the price of illiterate labour is close to zero in industrialised nations, this means that the illiterate population of developing nations will tend to become extremely impoverished if there is globalisation without complementary government intervention. According to Basu, "in a country like India where 35 per cent of the people are illiterate, globalisation can contribute to increasing poverty and inequality. It is important to recognise this not in order to thwart globalisation but to prepare for and benefit from it."

The Government, The State and The Market

Although the competing virtues of the market mechanism and governmental action have been much discussed in the literature, the comparative merits of the two forms of economic decision are so thoroughly context-dependent that it makes little sense to espouse a *general* 'pro state' or 'pro market' view. For proper understanding, the distinction between the state and the government may be of some significance. The state is, in many ways, a broader concept, which includes the government, the legislature that votes on public rules, the political system that regulates elections, the role that is given to opposition parties, and the basic political rights that are upheld by the judiciary. A democratic state makes it exceedingly difficult for the ruling government to be unresponsive to the needs and values of the population at large. (Dreze & Sen, 2002)

There is a similar question about the context-dependence of the role of the market mechanism.

The recent history of Asia and Africa provides plentiful examples of market exchanges being used to make profits out of the miseries of millions. There are also cases where the market manages to misjudge the extent of a shortage quite badly, and causes suffering — even chaos — as a result. Thus, to take general 'pro market' view without conditions attached is no less problematic than taking a general 'pro government' view. (Dreze & Sen, 2002)

There is a close interdependence between markets and governance. In particular, the operation and successes of the market mechanism can be deeply influenced by the nature of governmental arrangements and actions that go with it. As Basu puts it "there is no escape from the need for purposive, intelligent action from government. Government or good governance, is a concommitant of efficient markets, not a substitute." (Basu, 2004)

Markets can hardly function in the absence of legal provisions and justiciable rights to property and contractual entitlements. The disastrous results of indiscriminate liberalisation and wholesale privatisation in Russia in the 1990s illustrate the penalities of ignoring the basic recognition that the effective functioning of the market mechanism is highly contingent on adequate institutional foundations.

Also the government may have a major role in initiating and facilitating market-reliant economic growth. We have examples of such successful capitalist countries as Germany and Japan. More recently, the role of the government has received much attention in interpreting the so-called 'East Asian miracle' — the remarkable economic success of the newly industrialising countries in east Asia (in particular South Korea, Taiwan, Hong Kong, Singapore, and more recently China and Thailand).

Public debates — in India as well as elsewhere — are often dominated by one-sided presentations, reflecting either uncritical faith in the market or blind opposition to it. Indeed, there are signs of both 'market mania' and 'market phobia' in the sharp exchanges that characterise debates on this subject. (Dreze & Sen, 2002)

Market mania involves complete faith in the efficiency and other virtues of the market, regardless of context. It calls for indiscriminate deregulation and privatisation. Market mania played a role in Russia's rush towards a market economy in the nineties with its catastrophic results.

In India, a common form of market mania is the notion that radical deregulation is all it would take to 'kick-start the economy'. This belief according to Dreze and Sen is naive in several ways. First, it is based on a narrow reading of the impediments that are holding the Indian economy. The relevant failures go much beyond a lack of market incentives, and also include widespread illiteracy and undernourishment, inadequate infrastructure, the paralysis of the legal system, endemic corruption, dismal public services, to cite a few concerns. Market mania overlooks the lack of preconditions in the Indian economy for the kind of take-off that has followed market-oriented reforms in countries such as China and Vietnam.

Infact there is a deep complementarity between market efficiency and state action. The performance of the market is highly contingent on various forms of state action, from the provision of an adequate legal framework to redistributive policies. One implication of these complementarities is that liberalisation does not necessarily diminish the importance of state action. This applies even to regulation itself, in so far as a relaxation of one type of rules often calls for developing new rules of a different type. For instance, allowing private entry into new sectors (such as medical insurance or electricity distribution), which may be considered as a form of deregulation, calls for an adequate overseeing framework, especially if these sectors have features (e.g. economies of scale, information asymmetries, pervasive externalities) that interfere with the efficiency of the market mechanism. Even in western 'market economies', including the United States, this necessity is well recognised.

Cooperative Action

Besides State intervention and the market mechanism there is the third alternative way of coordinating economic activity i.e. cooperative action.

Development itself opens up new opportunities for social cooperation. The recent expansion of cooperative action on a global scale (involving concerns such as environmental protection, the debt crisis and world peace) is one example of this process.

Just as the state and the market are highly complementary institutions (even though they are often seen in antagonistic terms), a similar relation holds between cooperative action on the one hand and the state or the market on the other. In a democratic society, the priorities and actions of the state depend on organised public demands, and other aspects of a broad political process in which cooperative action plays a crucial part. Conversely, what cooperative action can achieve depends to a considerable extent on the opportunities created through state action, e.g. the level of education in the community, the accountability of government institutions, and the legal framework of civic associations.

Thus, cooperative action and market institutions are often compatible or even complementary. For instance, the efficiency of the market mechanism can be greatly enhanced by cooperative social norms that reduce so-called 'transaction costs'. Indeed, markets can flourish more easily when contracts are not typically broken and do not have to be rescued by litigation.

According to Dreze and Sen, the tendency to concentrate on the negative roles of government has contributed to another bias in the liberalisation debate, namely, the neglect of what can be achieved through cooperative action. This neglect is particularly serious if we acknowledge the wide-ranging nature of the reforms that are required in India, not only in economic matters but also in the social and political domains. There is urgent need not only for more efficient and equitable economic institutions, but also for uprooting corruption, protecting the environment, eradicating caste inequalities, preventing human rights violations, restoring the credibility of the legal system, halting the criminalisation of politics (to cite a few major concerns). These different fields of reforms are no less important than the kinds of 'economic reforms' that have captured most of the attention in the 1990s. They are indeed best seen in an integrated perspective, where the promotion of human freedoms (rather than just the acceleration of economic growth) is the overarching goal. In that perspective, cooperative action acquires a new importance, in so far as it has a major bearing on many of these broader fields of economic and social life where reform is needed. To illustrate, eradicating corruption or protecting the environment are not just matters of sound government policy; they also involve cooperative action of various kinds e.g. public vigilance against bribery and community management of local environmental resources. According to Dreze and Sen, the liberalisation debate in India in its present form is too narrow in at least three respects: (1) over-concentration on the negative roles of government, (2) over-preoccupation with narrowly 'economic' reforms, and (3) neglect of the role of cooperative action in economic and social reform.

References

Basu, Kaushik (ed.), (2004), "India's Emerging Economy: Performance and Prospects in the 1990s and Beyond", Ch 1, Oxford University Press.

Chakravarti, S. (1989), *Development Planning the Indian Experience*, Oxford University Press.

Dreze, J. and A. Sen, (2002), "India: Development and Participation", Ch.2, Oxford University Press.

——— (1995), "India's Economic Development and Social Opportunity", Oxford: Clarendon Press.

Pant, K.C. (2003), *India's Development Scenario: Next Decade and Beyond*, Academic Foundation.

Plan Documents.

Planning Commission, (2005), *Mid-Term Appraisal of the Tenth Five Year Plan*, June 28.

——— (2001), *Approach Paper to the Tenth Five Year Plan*, September.

——— Tenth Five Year Plan (2002-07), December 2002.

Srinivasan, T.N. and Tendulkar, S.D., (2003), "Reintegrating India with the World Economy", Ch. 1 (OUP).

Tendulkar, S.D., (2000-01), *Indian Development Strategy: Compulsion and Constraints* in Uma Kapila (ed.) Indian Economy Since Independence, 2000-01 edition.

Vaidyanathan, A. (1995), *The Indian Economy, Crisis Response and Prospects*, Orient Longman.

——— (2003), *India's Economic Reforms and Development*, Academic Foundation.

3

The Problem of Development

Planning: Economic and Social Aspects

The central objective of planning in India at the present stage is to initiate a process of development which will raise living standards and open out to the people new opportunities for a richer and more varied life. The problem of development of an under developed economy is one of utilizing more effectively the potential resources available to the community, and it is this which involves economic planning. But the economic condition of a country at any given time is a product of the broader social environment, and economic planning has to be viewed as an integral part of a wider process aiming not merely at the development of resources in a narrow technical sense, but at the development of human faculties and the building up of an institutional framework adequate to the needs and aspirations of the people.

An underdeveloped economy is characterized by the co-existence, in greater or less degree, of unutilized or underutilized manpower on the one hand and of unexploited natural resources on the other. This state of affairs may be due to stagnancy of techniques or to certain inhibiting socio-economic factors which prevent the more dynamic forces in the economy from asserting themselves. Corresponding to each stage of development, there tends to grow a certain economic and social stratification which is conducive to the conservation of the gains from the use of known techniques. Such stratification has a part to play in social progress. But, beyond a point, it hampers innovation and change, and its very strength becomes a source of weakness. For development to proceed further, a re-adaptation of social institutions and social relationships thus becomes necessary. In planning for a better economic order, the close interrelation between the technical and social aspects of the process of development has to be continually kept in view. While there is need for concentrating effort on the more immediate problems, planning implies the readiness on the part of the community to view the social process as one whole and to take action designed to shape this process along desired lines over a defined period.

In spite of considerable advance in public thinking on the subject, the acceptance of such an approach to the problems of economic development and social change represents a relatively new phase in policy-making and in administration. Planning involves the acceptance of a clearly defined system of objectives in terms of which to frame over-all policies. It also involves the formulation of a strategy for promoting the realization of the ends defined. Planning is essentially an attempt at working out a rational solution of problems, an attempt to co-ordinate means and ends; it is thus different from the traditional hit-and-miss methods by which 'reforms' and 'reconstruction' are often undertaken. A planned economy has inevitably in view a somewhat wider time-horizon, to which the day-to-day decisions have to be related. And yet, practical policy cannot operate in terms of mere set doctrines; it must satisfy certain pragmatic tests. In spite of the considerable developments in economic and social sciences in the last few decades, our knowledge of human motivation and of social processes is but limited. We cannot always say for certain that a given set of causes will produce a particular, clearly definable, set of results and none other; we do not always know at what rate the effects of a particular change in a part of the system will be transmitted to the other parts of the system. Responses of individuals or of groups of individuals and of classes cannot always be predicted in advance. Even if the conceptual relationships between different aspects of the phenomena under study are clearly understood, there is often the lack of precise statistical data on which to base an assessment of the requirements of a given situation. It follows that a considerable part of the planning authority's task is to assess the significance of some of these indeterminate or partially known factors at work in the life of the community and to recommend policies on the best judgement available. This is particularly so in India today.

The urge to economic and social change under present conditions comes from the fact of poverty and of inequalities in income, wealth and opportunity. The elimination of poverty cannot, obviously, be achieved merely by redistributing existing wealth. Nor can a programme aiming only at raising production remove existing inequalities. The two have to be considered together; only a simultaneous advance along both these lines can create the conditions in which the community can put forth its best efforts for promoting development. The problem, therefore, is not one of merely re-channelling economic activity within the existing socio-economic framework; that framework has itself to be remoulded so as to enable it to accommodate progressively those fundamental urges which express themselves in the demands for the right to work, the right to adequate income, the right to education and to a measure of insurance against old age, sickness and other disabilities. The Directive Principles of State Policy enunciated in Articles 36 to 51 of the Constitution make it clear that for the attainment of these ends, ownership and control of the material resources of the country should be so distributed as best to subserve the common good, and that the operation of the economic system should not result in the concentration of wealth and economic power in the hands of a few. It is in this larger perspective that the task of planning has to be envisaged.

A process of all-round and orderly development, such as is indicated above, must inevitably take time to come into full fruition. Large scale changes in modes of production, in commercial and industrial organization and in the institutional framework of corporate life cannot be seen through within a brief period of four or five years. In the initial stages of development, divergence in the economic and social interests of different sections of the community may create special problems. While this fact has to be recognized, persistent effort must be made to give a new sense of direction and purpose to the community. It is important also to ensure that in the process of development, the forces of growth from within are not stifled by attempts abruptly to superimpose preconceived patterns of life and activity. The strengthening of these inner forces and the creation of new institutions must proceed side by side so as to facilitate rapid advance through a process of interaction. The modern world is changing so rapidly that it is not enough to think in terms of slow changes and marginal adjustments, a minor shake-up here and a little cementing elsewhere. An underdeveloped country which has suffered long from the effects of cramped development desires inevitably to progress rapidly and in many directions; the aim of planning must be to make this possible. Political independence provides the needed opportunity. It is therefore natural that improvement in economic and social conditions through the acceptance of more progressive ideas and through suitable institutional changes is regarded as the practical test for judging the adequacy of the new political system.

The Determinants of Economic Development

The pace of economic development depends on a variety of factors which constitute the psychological and sociological setting within which the economy operates. A major element in this setting is the community's will to progress and its readiness to develop and adopt new and more efficient methods and processes of production. Basically, development involves securing higher productivity all round and this is a function of the degree of technological advance the community is able to make. The problem is not one merely of adopting and applying the processes and techniques developed elsewhere, but of developing new techniques specially suited to local conditions. Modern technology is changing rapidly and no country can hope to maintain a steady pace of advance unless it keeps abreast of current developments. Techniques in turn affect and are affected by economic and social organization. Certain forms of economic and social organization are unsuited to or incapable of absorbing new techniques and utilizing them to the best advantage. To some extent techniques must of course be adapted to economic and social organization, but the latter has also to change in order to accommodate new techniques which need to be applied not merely in one or two isolated lines but in several lines of economic activity so that advance in one line could react on and stimulate advance in others.

These are aspects of the problem of economic development which have to be constantly kept in view. Given these basic conditions of rapid and sustained progress, institutional as well as others, the key to higher productivity and expanding levels of income and employment lies really in stepping up the rate of capital formation. The level of production and the material well-being a community can attain depends, in the main, on the stock of capital at its disposal, *i.e.,* on the amount of land *per capita* and of productive equipment in the shape of machinery, buildings, tools and implements, factories, locomotives, engines, irrigation facilities, power installations and communications. The larger the stock of capital, the greater tends to be the productivity of labour and therefore the volume of commodities and services that can be turned out with the same effort. The productivity of the economy depends on other things also, as for instance the technical efficiency and attitude to work of the labour that handles the available capital equipment. But the stock of capital reflects in a concrete form the technological knowledge that underlies the organized processes of production, and while other factors are important and essential a rapid increase in productivity is conditional upon additions to and improvements in the technological framework implicit in a high rate of capital formation.

The conditions in which economic development was achieved in the course of the last century have naturally differed from country to country, but a common feature of almost all of them is the high rate of capital formation which characterized periods of expansion. In times when the whole capital structure of a country is being transformed, the normal replacement of existing equipment becomes itself to some extent a means for introducing improvements in the technological framework of production, so that, in assessing rates of capital formation achieved, the resources set apart for this purpose must be also regarded as a material factor in determining the tempo of development. For Britain statistics on national income and investment are not available for the first half of the nineteenth century, which was perhaps the most significant period in its economic development, but the available data for 1870-1913 show that net investment in this period was on an average more than 10 per cent of the national income and in prosperous years as much as 15 per cent. In the United States, the rate of capital formation was higher over the years 1869-1913; net investment represented 13 to 16 per cent of the national product while gross investment ranged between 21 and 24 per cent. In Japan, new capital formation in the decade 1900-1909 is estimated to have averaged about 12 per cent of the national income; this rate appears to have risen to 17 per cent in the following decade, though it declined again to 12 per cent in the period 1920-1929. More recently, the U.S.S.R. furnishes an instance of a high rate of investment being achieved as a matter of deliberate State policy and action. The First Five Year Plan of the Soviet Union had a target of net investment amounting to "between a quarter and a third of the national income", the actual achievement was perhaps slightly lower. At any rate, though the Second Five Year Plan envisaged a some what lower ratio of capital formation to national income, it would appear on a fairly conservative estimate that the rate of net investment in the U.S.S.R. in the decade 1928-1938 was of the order of 20 per cent of the national income, if not more.

The data given above are not of a nature which would warrant any firm relationships being deduced between rates of investment and rates of development, nor can they be used for making comparisons as between countries or as between widely separated periods within the same country. Even conceptually, these relationships are very complex. It is virtually impossible to evaluate in quantitative terms the psychological and social forces which have played a part in shaping the pace and pattern of development under different circumstances. Nevertheless, the available evidence, however scanty, may be used for judging broadly the scale of effort involved in relation to the results obtained. In the United Kingdom, a rate of net investment which fluctuated between 10 and 15 per cent of the national income went hand in hand with an increase of over 150 per cent in the national income between 1870 and 1913. In the United States, with a somewhat higher rate of investment, which was accompanied also by large scale immigration and settlement in virgin territory, national income increased nearly five-fold between 1869 and 1913; the increase in *per capita* income in this period is estimated at over 130 per cent. In Japan, with the population growing at an average annual rate of about 1.25 per cent, *per capita* income is estimated to have been doubled between 1878 and 1912; it was doubled again between 1913 and 1938. Varying estimates have been made of the achievements of the Soviet Union in terms of national income, but, taking again a conservative estimate, it would appear that with a rate of net investment of about one-fifth (or probably a little more) of the national income the increase in the national product in the period from 1928 to about 1940 was around 130 per cent.

These relationships are more suggestive than conclusive, but it is fairly obvious that a doubling of *per capita* incomes within a generation or so (that is in 25 to 30 years) required, in most of these countries, a rate of net investment of the order of 12-15 per cent of the national income. More rapid rates of development have required, apart from other things, still higher rates of investment as in the U.S.S.R. It would appear on the whole that, in under developed countries with low standards of living and rapidly increasing population, a rate of growth commensurate with needs cannot be achieved until the rate of capital formation comes up to around 20 per cent of the national income.

Objectives of Planning

In defining the objectives, priorities and techniques of planning in India, it is necessary to bear in mind the scale and dimensions of the problem as well as the basic values which must find expression in the economic and social pattern to be evolved. It is no longer possible to think of development as a process merely of increasing the available supplies of material goods; it is necessary to ensure that simultaneously a steady advance is made towards the realization of wider objectives such as full employment and the removal of economic inequalities. Maximum production, full employment, the attainment of economic equality and social justice which constitute the accepted objectives of planning under present-day conditions are not really so many different ideas but a series of related aims which the country must work for. None of these objectives can be pursued to the exclusion of others; a plan of development must place balanced emphasis on all of these. For instance, even the limited objective of increased production cannot be attained unless the wider objectives of social policy are constantly kept in mind and steadily pursued. On the other hand, equality and social justice will have little content unless the production potential of the community is substantially raised. Development, thus conceived, is a process which calls for effort and sacrifice on the part of the entire body of citizens. For such effort and sacrifice to come forth psychological conditions have to be created which provide an incentive for all to give of their best.

Democratic Planning and Role of the State

The question of the techniques to be adopted for planning is linked up with the basic approach that a community decides to adopt for the realization of its objectives. It is possible to have a plan based on regimentation and on immediate measures for levelling down in the hope ultimately of being able to level up. The basic premise of democratic planning is that society can develop as an integral whole and that the position which particular classes occupy at any given time — a product of various historical forces for which no individual or class as such can be held responsible — can be altered without reliance on class hatreds or the use of violence. The need is to secure that the change is effected quickly and it is the positive duty of the State to promote this through all the measures at its command. The success of such planning no doubt depends on the classes in positions of power and privilege respecting the democratic system and appreciating the rapid changes it calls for.

It is clear that in the transformation of the economy that is called for the State will have to play the crucial role. Whether one thinks of the problem of capital formation or of the introduction of new techniques or of the extension of social services or of the over-all re-alignment of the productive forces and class relationships within society, one comes inevitably to the conclusion that a rapid expansion of the economic and social responsibilities of the State will alone be capable of satisfying the legitimate expectations of the people. This need not involve complete nationalization of the means of production or elimination of private agencies in agriculture or business and industry. It does mean, however, a progressive widening of the public sector and a re-orientation of the private sector to the needs of a planned economy.

Government of India, Planning Commission, The First Five Year Plan, 1951-56, Excerpts from Chapter 1 and Chapter 2.

4

The Tenth Five Year Plan (2002-07)

Objectives, Strategy and Mid-Term Appraisal

The Tenth Five Year Plan, covering the period 2002-03 to 2006-07, represents but another step in the evolution of development planning in India. In the 55 years that have passed since our Independence, the challenges, the imperatives and the capabilities of the nation have undergone profound changes.

Objectives of the Tenth Plan

Traditionally, the level of per capita income has been regarded as a summary indicator of the economic well being of the country, and growth targets have therefore focused on growth in per capita income or per capita GDP.

The Approach Paper had proposed that the Tenth Plan should aim at an indicative target of 8 per cent average GDP growth for the period 2002-07. It is certainly an ambitious target, especially in view of the fact that GDP growth has decelerated to below 6 per cent at present. Even if the deceleration is viewed as a short-term phenomenon, the medium-term performance of the economy over the past several years suggests that the demonstrated growth potential is only about 6.5 per cent. The proposed 8 per cent growth target therefore involves an increase of at least 1.5 percentage points over the recent medium term performance, which is substantial. Nevertheless, the National Development Council (NDC) affirmed its faith in the latent potentialities of the Indian economy by approving the 8 per cent growth target for the Tenth Plan period.

The NDC has approved that, in addition to the 8 per cent growth target, other targets as given in Box 4.1 should also be considered as being central to the attainment of the objectives of the Plan:

These targets reflect the concern that economic growth alone may not lead to the attainment of long-run sustainability and of adequate improvement in social justice. Earlier Plans have had many of these issues as objectives, but in no case were specific targets set. As a result, these were viewed in terms of being desirable but not essential. Thus a 'best endeavour' approach was usually adopted in this regard. In the Tenth Plan, however, these targets are considered to be as central to the planning framework as the growth objective.

BOX – 4.1

Monitorable Targets for the Tenth Plan and Beyond

- Reduction of poverty ratio by 5 percentage points by 2007 and by 15 percentage points by 2012;
- Providing gainful and high-quality employment at least to addition to the labour force over the Tenth Plan period;
- All children in school by 2003; all children to complete 5 years of schooling by 2007;
- Reduction in gender gaps in literacy and wage rates by at least 50 per cent by 2007;
- Reduction in the decadal rate of population growth between 2001 and 2011 to 16.2 per cent;
- Increase in Literacy rates to 75 per cent within the Plan period;
- Reduction of Infant mortality rate (IMR) to 45 per 1000 live births by 2007 and to 28 by 2012;
- Reduction of Maternal mortality ratio (MMR) to 2 per 1000 live births by 2007 and to 1 by 2012;
- Increase in forest and tree cover to 25 per cent by 2007 and 33 per cent by 2012;
- All villages to have sustained access to potable drinking water within the Plan period;
- Cleaning of all major polluted rivers by 2007 and other notified stretches by 2012.

The targets mandated by the NDC at the time of approval of the Approach Paper to the Tenth Five Year Plan are, by and large, consistent with the 8 per cent growth target either through direct linkages that exist or through the resources that are generated by the growth process for more intensive public interventions. At the time of formulation of the Approach Paper, these linkages had been assessed on the basis of economy-wide aggregative trends observed in the past, and it was felt that achievement of even these targets would require concerted efforts. Subsequently, more detailed study and analysis by the Planning Commission have revealed that it may be possible to record even better achievement as far as employment generation and poverty reduction are concerned. The Report of the Special Group on Targeting 10 Million Employment Opportunities Per Year, which was constituted to deliberate upon the Prime Minister's vision, indicated that with appropriate sectoral focus and directed interventions, it would be possible to generate substantially more employment opportunities than arising merely out of the growth process, not only to take care of the additions to the labour force, but also to reduce the backlog of unemployment. Similarly, internal exercises carried out in the Planning Commission revealed that the state-wise break down of the aggregate growth target, which seeks to redress regional imbalances, could lead to even faster reduction in the poverty rate than the assessment made on the basis of the aggregative trends. The Tenth Plan, therefore, seeks to achieve targets in these two areas which go beyond those set by the NDC in the Approach Paper. (Box 4.2).

BOX – 4.2

Employment Generation and Poverty Reduction: Can We Do Better?

The current back-log of unemployment at around 9 per cent, equivalent to 35 million persons, is too high, and every effort needs to be made to not only arrest the rising trend, but to actually reduce it during the Tenth Plan period itself. The Prime Minister's vision of creating 100 million employment opportunities over the next ten years is taken as the basis for targeting the creation of 50 million employment opportunities during the next five years, which is about 14 million higher than the target mandated in the Approach Paper on the basis of additions to labour force during the Plan period. If this target is achieved, the unemployment rate is likely to decline significantly to 5 per cent by the end of the Tenth Plan.

Contd...

...Box 4.2 Contd...

Similarly, the mandated reductions in the poverty rate of 5 percentage points during the Tenth Plan and another 10 percentage points during the Eleventh Plan, as stipulated in the Approach Paper, will still leave more than 11 per cent of the population, or about 130 million people, below the poverty line in 2012. Every effort, therefore, needs to be made to reduce the poverty rate even faster. It is estimated that with a proper sectoral and regional focus, it may be possible to reduce the poverty rate by nearly 7 percentage points over the Tenth Plan period if the growth target of 8 per cent is achieved through the state-wise break down that has been drawn up in consultation with the States.

The Development Strategy

The Tenth Plan provides an opportunity, at the start of the new millennium, to build upon the gains of the past and also to address the weaknesses that have emerged. There is growing impatience in the country at the fact that a large number of our people continue to live in abject poverty and there are alarming gaps in social attainments even after five decades of planning. To meet this challenge squarely, the Tenth Plan must learn from past experience. It must strengthen what has worked well, and at the same time also avoid repeating past mistakes. There must be willingness to modify policies and institutions based on past experience, keeping in mind the changes that have taken place in the Indian economy and in the rest of the world.

An important aspect of the redefinition of strategy that is needed relates to the role of government. This redefinition is necessary both at the Central Government level and also at State Government level. It is now generally recognised that government in the past tended to take on too many responsibilities, imposing severe strains on its limited financial and administrative capabilities and also stifling individual initiative. An all-pervasive Government role may have been necessary at a stage where private sector capabilities were undeveloped, but the situation has changed dramatically in this respect. India now has a strong and vibrant private sector. The public sector is much less dominant than it used to be in many critical sectors and its relative position is likely to decline further as Government ownership in many existing public sector organisations is expected to decline substantially. It is clear that industrial growth in future will depend largely upon the performance of the private sector and our policies must therefore provide an environment which is conducive to such growth.

This is not to say that government has no role to play, or only a minimalist role, in promoting development. On the contrary, Government has a very important role indeed, but a different one from that envisaged in the past. There are many areas, e.g. the social sectors, where its role will clearly have to expand. There are other areas, e.g. infrastructure development, where gaps are large and the private sector cannot be expected to step in significantly. In these areas, the role of Government may have to be expanded and restructured. It will have to expand in some areas of infrastructure development which are unlikely to attract private investment, e.g. rural infrastructure and road development. In others, e.g. telecommunications, power, ports, etc., the private sector can play a much greater role, provided an appropriate policy framework is in place. Here, the role of the government needs to change to facilitate such investment as much as possible while still remaining a public sector service provider for quite some time. In all these areas, the role of the government as a regulator ensuring a fair deal for consumers, transparency and accountability, and a level playing field is also extremely important.

With the growing importance of the private sector in economic matters, and the consequent increase in the sensitivity of the economy to business cycle fluctuations, both the role and the manner of macro-economic management demand a reappraisal. Greater flexibility in fiscal and monetary policies has now become necessary to ensure that the economy is consistently maintained on the feasible growth path. While there has certainly been considerable improvement in the flexibility and sophistication of monetary and exchange rate management in the country, the same cannot be said about the conduct of fiscal policies, which remain rooted in outmoded budgetary procedures. In recent years it has become evident that there are circumstances in which monetary policy alone is ineffective to address macroeconomic developments, and a more sensitive fiscal policy is essential. It is, therefore, imperative that a reformulation of the fiscal management system be undertaken expeditiously to make it more appropriate for the changed context.

The Indian Central Plans have traditionally focused on setting only national targets. However, recent experiences suggest that the performance of different States varies considerably, and cognisance has to be taken of this issue. For example, although the economy as a whole has accelerated, the growth rates of different States have diverged and some of the poorest States have actually seen a deceleration in growth. It is important to recognise that the sharp increase in the growth rate and significant improvement in the social indicators that are being contemplated for the Tenth Plan will be possible only if there is a corresponding improvement in the performance of the relatively laggard States. Indeed, if the higher targets are sought to be achieved simultaneously with the slow progress, as observed in the past, in some of the most populous States, it would necessarily imply a very large increase in inter-State inequality, with serious consequences for regional balance and national harmony.

In order to emphasise the importance of ensuring a balanced development for all States, the Tenth Plan includes a State-wise break-up of the broad developmental targets, including targets for growth rates and social development, which are consistent with the national targets. These State specific targets take into account the needs, potentialities and constraints present in each State and the scope for improvement in their performance, given these constraints. It needs to be emphasised that these State-wise targets are not meant to be a substitute for or to over-ride the process of State Plan formulation. They are more in the nature of indicative guidelines for facilitating planning in the States. It is an unfortunate fact that many States of the Union have de-emphasised the planning process and have allowed their planning systems to degenerate. As a result, many State Plans are not based on any rigorous and analytically meaningful appraisal of resources and capabilities or of the strategies that can be used to accelerate the development process. National targets are often uncritically adopted as State targets, thereby leading to a dysjunction between the planned and the possible.

The presentation of State-wise targets in the national Plan will serve as a catalyst to reinvigorate planning at the State level. There are two dimensions to this. First, the very recognition of the diversities that exist in the country should lead to a similar recognition at the sub-State level. Different districts within a State are at different levels of development and have different capabilities. A State Plan will, therefore, have to recognise these differences, and ensure that the State-wise targets set in the State Plan are consistent with what is planned at the district level. This will require careful consideration of the sectoral pattern of growth and its regional dispersion within the State. It will also focus attention on the nature of reforms that will have to be implemented at the State level to achieve the growth targets set for the States.

The objective of creating a common economic space within the country, which is an essential element of nationhood, depends critically upon the recognition of commonality of interests by the States. This need has gained urgency as external barriers to trade and commerce are in the process of being brought down. Unfortunately, there has been an increasing tendency on the part of a number of States to increase the barriers to internal trade. Such measures are specifically barred by the Constitution, and it is the responsibility of the Central Government to ensure that no policy, which has the effect of abridgement of inter-State trade and commerce, is permitted by the exercise of Article 307 of the Constitution.

BOX – 4.3

Strategy for Equity and Social Justice

- Agricultural development must be viewed as a core element of the Plan, since growth in this sector is likely to lead to the widest spread of benefits especially to the rural poor. The first generation of reforms concentrated on the industrial economy and reforms in the agricultural sector were neglected. This must change in the Tenth Plan.
- The growth strategy of the Tenth Plan must ensure rapid growth of those sectors which are most likely to create gainful employment opportunities and deal with the policy constraints which discourage growth of employment. Particular attention must be paid to the policy environment influencing a wide range of sectors which have a large employment potential. These include sectors such as agriculture in its extended sense, construction, tourism, transport, SSI, retailing, IT and communication-enabled services, and a range of other new services which also need to be promoted through supportive policies.
- There will be a continuing need to supplement the impact of growth with special programmes aimed at special target groups which may not benefit sufficiently from the normal growth process. Such programmes have long been part of our development strategy and they will have to continue in the Tenth Plan as well. However, it is important to ensure that they are effective in achieving their objectives.

It is important to re-emphasise that the equity related objectives of the Plan, which are extremely important, are intimately linked to the growth objective, and attainment of one may not be possible without the attainment of the other. For example, high rates of growth are essential if we want to ensure sufficient expansion of sustainable gainful employment opportunities for our expanding labour force, and a sufficient increase in the incomes of the poor and the disadvantaged. However, this is not just a one-way relationship. It is also true that high growth rates may not be sustainable if they are not accompanied by a dispersion of purchasing power which can provide the demand needed to support the increase in output without having to rely excessively on external markets. The inherent risks and possible consequences of such excessive dependence have become evident from the experiences of the East Asian and Latin American crises. External markets are certainly an extremely important source of demand, and we would emphasise that they need to be tapped much more aggressively for many sectors. However, given the size of the economy and the present relative size of exports, much of the demand needed to support high growth will have to come from the domestic economy itself.

Although growth has strong direct poverty reducing effects, the frictions and rigidities in the Indian economy can make these processes less effective, and the Tenth Plan must therefore be formulated in a manner, which explicitly addresses the need to ensure equity and social justice. A three-pronged strategy for attaining equity and social justice along with high rates of growth is proposed for the Tenth Plan period (see Box 4.3).

Feasibility of 8 per cent Growth

At an aggregate level, any acceleration in growth requires some combination of an increase in gross domestic fixed capital formation and an increase in efficiency of resource use. The latter requires policies, which will increase the productivity of existing resources as well as the efficiency of new investment. There can be little doubt that India cannot hope to achieve an 8 per cent growth, relying entirely, or even largely, on increased investment. With the average incremental capital output ratio (ICOR) in the Eighth and Ninth Plan period amounting to around 4.0, the investment increase needed to achieve a 1.5 percentage point increase in growth is 6 percentage points. While some part of this could come from an increase in foreign direct investments, it is unrealistic to expect this source to contribute more than 1 to 1.5 percentage points. This means that if the entire acceleration in growth has to come from additional investment with an ICOR of 4.0, it would be necessary to increase the investment ratio by 4.5 and 5 percentage points of GDP, which would have to be mobilised through additional domestic savings. An increase of this order in the average rate of domestic savings over the next five years may not be feasible. A substantial part of the additional growth must, therefore, come from increased efficiency and tapping hidden potentialities in the economy.

The principal reason why 8 per cent growth may be feasible in the Tenth Plan is that the scope for realising improvements in efficiency is very large, both in the public sector and in the private sector. However, this improvement in efficiency can only be realised if policies are adopted which ensure such improvement. The Tenth Plan must therefore give high priority to identifying efficiency enhancing policies both at the macro level and also at the sectoral level. These policies will often involve a radical break from past practices and even institutional arrangements. In many cases they will involve policy decisions, which can easily become controversial given the compulsions of competitive politics. The Tenth Plan can only succeed in achieving the targeted 8 per cent growth if sufficient political will is mobilised and a minimum consensus achieved which will enable significant progress to be made in critical areas. If this is not possible then growth will be correspondingly lower.

There is sufficient evidence to suggest that there may be a considerable stock of existing capital assets, which are either lying idle or have never been used to their full potential. Bringing such assets into full productive use can certainly reduce the resource requirements quite dramatically. The first major area of idle capacity is in public infrastructural investment, which has been caused by the tendency to launch too many projects without the requisite financial provision or management capability, leading to a tardy pace of completion and sometimes even abandonment. Such problems are endemic in sectors such as power, roads, railways and irrigation, but are probably present in other sectors as well. It is present as much in central investments as in the State sector. Since completion of such projects and upgradation of existing capital assets will almost invariably be more cost-efficient than starting new projects, it will require a moratorium on launching new projects until at least a minimum number of partially completed projects are brought to completion. There is, however, no reason to believe that the existing set of projects necessarily represent the most desirable or optimum choice of options; therefore, some reprioritisation on sound economic principles becomes necessary.

The second area of idle capacity stock is in the public sector enterprises where financial and managerial problems have prevented adequate investment in balancing and/or upgradation, leading to inadequate utilisation of the capital assets or to the lack of market competitiveness. Prolonged periods of insufficient maintenance expenditures also have similar effects. Mere infusion of fresh funds is unlikely to solve this problem since the roots of the malaise go deeper, and usually lie in the domain of policies and excessive interference in the management of these enterprises. Measures to unlock such potential capacities through institutional change can yield rich dividends to the economy. Operational autonomy of public enterprises has been discussed, and even attempted in some cases, for many years now; but usually to no avail. Privatisation of non-strategic public enterprises thus appears to hold the best alternative promise in this regard.

The third area is in the private sector itself, which accounts for the bulk of the economy and where efficiency is vital. Much depends here on the policy framework. A comprehensive review is needed of policies in different areas to identify constraints to efficiency and optimal utilisation of resources. The Tenth Plan will have to address these issues in a comprehensive manner. However, an over-arching problem is the legal and procedural hurdles, which prevent the transfer of capital assets from non-performing companies to those that would utilise them better. Even if such transfers are effected, the time-lag is usually so substantial that much of the effective value of the capital stock is eroded. This problem also has implications for the willingness of lenders to advance funds to companies. Solution to such problems will require legal and procedural changes for facilitating quick transfer of productive assets so that their idle time is minimised. In particular, bankruptcy and foreclosure laws need to be instituted and made more effective.

Therefore, in order to take advantage of whatever idle capital stock that exists in the economy today for accelerating the growth rate in the Tenth Plan, there are at least three categories of measures as indicated in Box 4.4, that would need to be taken immediately.

Most infrastructure and industrial investments in India take an unconscionable time to come on stream. Much of this arises from the investor-unfriendly laws and non-transparent procedures and clearances that have to be gone through prior to even launching the project, but hurdles can also come up in the course of execution. As a consequence, the gestation lags get lengthened and leaves investible resources locked up for extended periods. One of the reasons why the services sectors have performed much better than the industrial sector in India is that such impediments are less in their case, though not entirely absent. The solution to this problem would have to be sought in identifying and removing unnecessary hurdles to the investment activity.

BOX – 4.4

Measures to Reduce Idle Capital Stock

- Full emphasis to be placed on completion of partially completed or on-going projects and upgradation of existing capital assets before starting new projects.
- Rapid privatisation of Public Sector Enterprises (PSEs), particularly those, which are working well below capacity.
- Legal and procedural changes for facilitating quick transfer of assets, including such measures as repeal of Sick Industrial Companies (Special Provision) Act (SICA), introduction of a bankruptcy law, facilitating foreclosure, accelerating judicial processes, etc:

Reduction in gestation lags of industrial and infrastructural investments, and indeed in all economic activities, through removal of policy and procedural barriers is of the highest importance, since it is central not only to reducing ICORs, but also to unshackling entrepreneurial energies. Although various Governments from time to time have announced 'single window clearance' procedures and 'investor assistance cells', they have rarely been effective. The primary reason for this is that the problem lies not in inadequate coordination, but in fragmented and often arbitrary exercise of the various powers of Government, vested in a number of functionaries at different levels through a complex system of delegation of powers. It is compounded by the fact that neither are the rules and regulations governing entry and operation transparent, nor are they justiciable. Rationalisation of these various rules, notifying them in a comprehensive and transparent manner, assigning accountability of each functionary, and providing administrative and legal recourse in case of *malafide* dilatoriness will be necessary to address this problem. These are issues in governance, and are addressed in some detail in the Tenth Plan.

The efficiency and productivity of various economic activities in India are well below the international standards. Although this is partly on account of the technological gaps that exist, it is also because of the structural infirmities of the economy. As for example, the average level of inventory holdings in India (which is estimated to be around four months of output) is orders of magnitude higher than in other countries of the world (around one month), which results in a large amount of investible resources being kept in reserve for contingencies rather than being put to productive use. The causes of this problem are many, and lie in poor transport infrastructure which complicates logistics management, an inadequate insurance system, and of course in outmoded methods of management, just to name a few. Although the advent of Information Technology has helped to some extent, there is a considerable way to go before international standards are attained.

Finally, the existence of unjustifiably high capital intensity in many sectors is also a cause of grave concern since these resources could have been applied to creating additional capacity. There is no doubt that this is often caused by the excessively rigid labour laws applied to the organised sector, which make it more difficult for the corporate entrepreneur to rationalise labour than to dispose off capital assets when the need arises. It also has a deleterious effect on work ethics and discipline. As a result, the effective cost of labour to the entrepreneur can be many times the nominal wage bill. Therefore, rationalisation of labour laws and regulations, which reduce the implicit cost of labour without affecting the explicit, can release considerable investible resources.

Overstatement of capital costs is not confined to the private sector alone. It is equally prevalent in public investments. There are numerous instances where the capital cost of a public project is significantly higher than equivalent private projects and even by international comparisons. The reasons, however, are different. Poor project management, leading to time and cost over-runs, and corruption are two principal causes. Excessive acquisition of land, over-investment in amenities for employees and at times undue mechanisation are others. These are again issues of institutional design and governance, and solutions to these will have to be found in that context.

The External Sector

The proposed acceleration in the growth rate cannot take place without tapping on the opportunities offered by the international economy in terms of markets, investment and technologies. But in doing so, vulnerabilities have to be identified and addressed. This is particularly important in view of the emerging trends in the international economy which suggest a period of slow-down.

A high rate of GDP growth will necessarily be associated with a high rate of growth of imports. This is particularly true given the extent of dependence on imports of energy and the limited likelihood of expanding domestic energy sources rapidly enough. Liberalisation of imports as required by the World Trade Organisation (WTO) will also have a role to play. In such a situation, sustained high rates of growth of exports will be essential for keeping the current account deficit within manageable limits. Rapid export growth of exports will also be necessary for aggregate demand reasons, since a steady increase in the rate of domestic savings implies that the rate of domestic consumption growth will be less than the rate of growth of output. Therefore, external markets will have to be sought for sustaining high levels of capacity utilisation.

Most importantly, it is necessary to recognise that rapid growth and development will not be possible without greater integration with the international economy. In order to make most of the opportunities available, it is essential that India evolve a positive agenda for its future negotiations at the WTO. Until recently, the strategy has been largely defensive. While this was perfectly appropriate for an inward-looking development strategy, it is not so now. The Indian interventions at the Doha Ministerial demonstrate the much more active and aggressive position that is being taken by India. This approach will have to be strengthened as the process of globalisation gathers momentum in the Indian economy.

MID-TERM APPRAISAL OF THE TENTH FIVE YEAR PLAN (JUNE, 2005)

The Mid-Term Appraisal (MTA) presents a detailed assessment of the performance of the economy as a whole as well as an assessment of performance in individual sectors in comparison with the Tenth Plan targets. The picture emerging from the appraisal is mixed. The economy is doing well in many areas and these gains need to be consolidated but there are also important weaknesses, which, if not corrected could undermine even the current performance level.

An Overview of Performance and Problems

GDP growth has averaged 6.5 per cent in the first three years, which is below the Tenth Plan target of 8.1 per cent but is commendable nonetheless. Growth in 2005-06 is projected to accelerate to 7.6 per cent and could accelerate further if the corrective steps listed in this chapter are implemented speedily. Private corporate sector investment, which had been dormant for several years, appears to have turned around. International perceptions of India are also generally positive creating a favourable climate for foreign direct investment. Inflation had become a serious concern in mid-2004 when there was upward pressure because of the rise in international oil prices, but it has since been brought under control. The external payment position is comfortable with substantial inflows from abroad leading to a more than comfortable build up of foreign exchange reserves.

The Industrial Sector which had a lackluster performance in the first two years of the Tenth Plan period, appears to have turned around in 2004-05 with a growth rate of 8.1 per cent in the first eleven months (April–February, 2004-2005). This marks a distinct improvement over the performance in the first two years. Nevertheless, the average for the first three years is unlikely to exceed 7 per cent, which is much better than the average of 4.5 per cent in the Ninth Plan but well short of the Tenth Plan target of 8.9 per cent. A positive feature of recent industrial performance is the evident increase in competitiveness in many sectors. The success in the IT sector is well known but equally important is that many other manufacturing sectors, pharmaceuticals, biotechnology, automobiles, auto components *etc*. are all showing considerably stronger competitive capability. Fears of Indian industry collapsing under the onslaught of cheap imports have also evaporated and there is much greater confidence in being able to flourish in a more open environment.

These positive features are clearly a source of strength, and the aim of policy should be to consolidate these gains and accelerate growth in the remaining years of the Tenth Plan. However, there are also important signs of weakness which are a cause for concern and call for corrective steps.

Aggregate Growth

The growth performance in the first three years, averaging 6.5 per cent is clearly below the target of 8.1 per cent. Growth in 2005-06 is projected at 7.6 per cent, on the basis of a recovery of the agricultural sector, and this could accelerate further in 2006-07. Even so, the average growth rate in the Tenth Plan period is likely to be below 7.0 per cent, well short of the 8.1 per cent target. An important reason for the lower growth is that investment did not increase in line with available investible resources.

Trends in Agriculture

The objective of accelerating GDP growth to 8 per cent in the years ahead, and achieving a more inclusive spread of benefits, depends critically upon a reversal of recent trends in agriculture where growth has decelerated sharply from 3.2 per cent between 1980-81 and 1995-96 to a trend average of 1.9 per cent subsequently. This deceleration, observed during and after the Ninth Plan period suggests that the problem of rural distress that has surfaced in many parts of the country is grounded in reality. The problem is also not a purely distributional one, reflecting the special problems of small and marginal farmers and land-less labour. In fact the deceleration is general across all crops, and reflects a broad based deceleration in productivity growth. It is essential to reverse this trend and this certainly calls for something more than continuing with "business as usual".

Infrastructure Problems

The Mid-Term appraisal draws pointed attention to the fact that infrastructure inadequacies in both rural and urban areas are a major factor constraining India's growth. This is especially so in the increasingly open economy environment in which we must operate, where the quality of domestic infrastructure impacts on our ability to compete with imports, to penetrate export markets and also to attract FDI.

International Developments

The oil prices on the world market are likely to remain high for some time. Since we depend on imports for more than 70 per cent of our oil needs, this is a potential source of weakness. The impact on Indian economy has been muted so far as the price increases have not been passed on fully to consumers. Because of the ample foreign exchange reserves, the high outgo for oil imports has not created shortage of other imports. However, if the oil prices remain at a high level, sooner or later that will have to be either passed on to the consumers which will push up inflation, or fiscal deficit will have to increase, which may also push up inflation. Uncertainties prevailing in the international economy also present a challenge. Recent forecasts have downgraded the prospects of growth in world trade, which may have knock-on effects on India's exports, and thereby on our growth prospects. The growth projections for the rest of the Plan are based on a 16 per cent growth rate of our exports, which is more than double the projected growth rate of world trade. While this may be feasible, a downturn in the world economy could make this target difficult to achieve. It is estimated that every 1 percentage point reduction in our export growth rate will *ceteris paribus* reduce the growth rate of GDP by 0.2 percentage points.

Social Development

Social sector indicators in education and health show that while there is progress over time, we are lagging far behind the East Asian countries in these areas. Our social indicators are not only lower than the levels in these countries today, but they are lower even in comparison with the levels achieved by these countries twenty five years ago, when they first began to grow rapidly. The social indicators also show disturbing gender gaps, large rural-urban differences and wide variation across states. A significant improvement in all these dimensions is necessary if we want to create the pre-condition for a general improvement in welfare of our population and for genuine equality of opportunity. A basic shift in priorities signalled by the NCMP was the need to give greater importance to social sector expenditures as part of the effort to promote development with social justice. the Tenth Plan specifies monitorable targets for certain indicators of social development in health, education and gender equality. These targets are not identical to the Millennium Development Goals (MDGs) but it is believed that if these targets are met, then the other MDGs are also likely to be achieved. It is a matter of deep concern that at the current pace of progress, it appears unlikely that many of these targets will be met. The solution to these issues lies in the institutional structures through which public intervention in these areas operates.

Employment

The employment situation in the economy presents a serious problem. The MTA projections, using sectoral growth rates and estimated employment elasticities, suggest that the unemployment rate for the economy as a whole, based on the current daily status of employment would have increased from 8.87 per cent in the base year 2001-02 to 9.11 per cent in 2004-05. This projection implies that total employment increased slower than labour force growth. The data on employment in the organised sector presents an even more disturbing picture showing a decline in absolute employment between 2001 and 2003 in both the public sector and the private sector. This suggests that while employment may be increasing in the unorganised sector in response to growth, there is actually a contraction in employment in the organised sector, which is the preferred sector for employment by new entrants to the labour force.

Inequality and Poverty

Related to the inadequate growth in employment is the issue of the impact on poverty in the Tenth Plan period. There has been a great deal of debate on the extent of reduction in poverty in the 1990s with different views depending on the data used and corrections made to take into account the problems of comparability. The consensus view is that while poverty declined, the decline was less than targeted. A firm assessment of performance in the Tenth Plan period will be possible only when the results of the 61st Round of NSS are received.

There are no measures of income inequality based on reliable income surveys. However, some of the features of recent growth raise concerns that inequality may be increasing, most important of which is the fact that per capita agricultural GDP has actually declined although overall per capita GDP has increased at 5 per cent per annum. Another feature of recent developments which has a bearing on inequality is that factor incomes data from the National Accounts show large increases in operating surpluses of the organised sector and of the compensation of employees in this sector while per capita income growth is much less than average amongst the self-employed in the unorganised sector and actually negative amongst employees in agriculture. This would not be a problem if the size of the organised sector were expanding but that does not seem to be the case given employment trends. The moderate improvement in education and health indicators implies that access to more productive employment remains limited, especially in backward regions and amongst disadvantaged groups.

NCMP priorities in the areas of health, education and agriculture offer correctives from the human capabilities and sectoral points of view, and the promise of an Employment Guarantee Act provides a measure of insurance and additional income for the rural poor, and increases their bargaining capacity.

Balanced Regional Development

An issue of increasing concern, is the apparent regional imbalance in development. This concern surfaces in several different ways. One dimension relates to the fact that the inter-State differences in the pace of development are leading to greater imbalance across States. State SDP data are not available beyond the first year of the Tenth Plan period, but several studies have shown that inter-State inequality increased in the 1990s. Some States were able to benefit from the economic reforms and increase their growth rates significantly. Although, it is not true that the richest States benefited the most, some of the poorest and most populous States did decelerate. The concern for imbalance also surfaces at district level. About 150 districts are backward compared to others and need special corrective efforts. Even advanced States have several backward districts which do not share the general dynamism of the State. The case is also made that districts may not be the appropriate basis for analyses on the grounds that parts of a district are often locked into backwardness.

Resources in the Public Sector

The availability of resources in the public sector to meet targeted levels of Plan expenditure is a major area of weakness. Neither the Centre nor the States have been able to mobilise the resources needed to keep outlays in line with Tenth Plan projections and this has led to significant under funding in many sectors. The Central Sector Plan was projected to be 6.4 per cent of GDP in the Tenth Plan against which the achievement in the first four years is only 5.4 per cent. The States plan was expected to be 4.69 per cent of GDP against which the likely achievement in the first four years will not exceed 3.64 per cent. Taking the Centre and the States together, Plan outlays will be lower than expected by 2 percentage points of GDP. This shortfall is despite the fact that both the Centre and the States have relied much more on borrowed resources than was intended, leading to a rise in public debt. The consolidated public debt of the Centre and States taken together is about 80 per cent of GDP, which is among the highest in emerging market economies.

Planning Commission, the Tenth Five Year Plan 2002-07, (December 2002), Vol. 1, Ch. 1 (excerpts).
Mid-Term Appraisal of the Tenth Five Year Plan (2002-07), Planning Commission, June 28, 2005.

5

Resource Mobilisation and Pattern of Plan Financing

Chapters 6, 7 and 8 are devoted to the subject of Resources Constraint facing the Indian Economy: the pattern of plan financing, the fiscal policy and fiscal correction for economic growth.

Pattern of Plan Financing: First Plan to Ninth Plan

The main sources of funds for financing development expenditures contemplated in the plans are grouped under the following heads :

1. Balance from current revenue of government;
2. Surpluses of public enterprises;
3. Borrowings;
4. Additional resource mobilization;
5. External assistance; and
6. Deficit financing.

The balance from current revenue (BCR), that is the excess of government's revenues over non-plan current expenditure (item 1 above) and resources raised additionally through new measures undertaken during a plan period (item 4) together with the surpluses of public sector enterprises (itcm 2) constitute public savings and were expected to be a major source of finance for the Plans, being the least inflationary instrument for raising resources for public investment expenditure. The other domestic source of finance is borrowings and deficit financing (item 3 and 6). The pattern of plan financing as originally contemplated and as it emerged in reality since the First Five Year Plan is set out in Table 5.1.

Looking at the pattern of financing, one finds that plan financing in India depended primarily on domestic sources. External assistance has constituted no more than 12 per cent of the total outlay in the recent plans (4th, 5th, 6th, 7th and 8th plan). While in the Fourth and the Fifth Plan, external assistance contributed about 12 per cent to plan finances, in Sixth Plan 7.7 per cent, in Seventh Plan 9 per cent and in the 8th plan the net inflow from abroad although projected at 6.6 per cent, turned out to be little less than 4 per cent.

The most important sources of financing are "Additional Resource Mobilisation" (ARM) and domestic borrowings. The term ARM represents the resources which the government and the public enterprises at the Centre and in the States (the federating units of the Indian Union) are expected to raise over and above the surplus which their budgets are likely to generate. This surplus is worked out after projecting the current revenues and non-Plan current expenditure in the five years of a given Plan period, assuming normal growth in both revenues and expenditures. The growth rates of revenues of government are derived on the basis of past trends and / or their elasticities with respect to major determinants (e.g., with respect to GDP in the case of income-tax). Similarly, in the case of public enterprises, the growth is worked out on the basis of the existing structure of prices and costs. The ARM figures are based on an assessment of what the governments at the Centre and in the States and the public enterprises run by them can raise through additional efforts such as by raising the tax rates or intensifying collection efforts and cutting down non-Plan expenditures. In the case of public enterprises ARM represents what they can raise by revising their prices upwards or by cutting costs and improving their operational efficiency.

Borrowings, currently the biggest single item of domestic resources for the Plans, are made up of market borrowings, small savings, state provident funds, term loans from financial institutions and miscellaneous capital receipts. Market borrowings come mainly from the subscription primarily by the commercial banks. The commercial banks are required compulsorily to keep a fraction of their deposits in government securities to maintain what is called the statutory liquidity ratio and this has been a major instrument for channelizing the flow of household savings into the public sector. The other sources of borrowings are the small savings schemes designed to garner the savings of the households in the form of

TABLE – 5.1

Financing of Plan Outlay in Public Sector During Five Year Plans

Figs. in (000 Crores)
(In bracket percentage)

	First Plan (1951-1956)		Second Plan (1956-1961)		Third Plan (1961-1966)		Fourth Plan (1969-1974)	
	Original	Actual estimates	Original	Actual estimates	Original	Actual estimates	Original	Actual estimates
Balance from current revenues	5.7[2] (27.55)	6.8 (32.50)	3.5 (7.29)	-5 (-1.09)	5.5 (7.33)	-4.2 (-4.90)	16.7 (10.52)	-2.4 (-1.46)
Public enterprises CPSEs including Railways	1.7 (8.22)	1.2 (5.87)	1.5 (3.13)	1.6 (3.26)	5.5 (7.33)	4.4 (5.07)	22.3 (14.03)	14.3 (8.86)
Borrowings	5.2 (25.04)	6.9 (35.20)	14.5 (30.21)	14.4 (30.84)	19.4 (25.87)	21.1 (24.62)	55.4 (34.84)	68.3 (42.26)
Additional resource mobilisation	—	2.6 (13.27)	8.5 (17.71)	10.5 (22.48)	17.1 (22.80)	28.9 (33.72)	32.0 (20.11)	42.8 (26.49)
External assistance (net)	5.2 (25.18)	1.9 (9.69)	8.0 (16.67)	10.5 (22.48)	22.0 (29.33)	24.2 (28.23)	26.1 (16.42)	20.9 (12.93)
Deficit financing	2.9 (14.02)	3.3 (16.84)	12.0 (25.00)	9.5 (20.34)	5.5 (7.33)	11.3 (13.19)	8.5 (5.35)	20.6 (12.75)
Aggregate resources	20.0 (100.00)	19.7 (100.00)	48.0 (100.00)	46.0 (100.00)	75.0 (100.00)	85.7 (100.00)	159.0 (100.00)	161.6 (100.00)

Contd...

... Table 5.1 Contd...

	Fifth Plan (1974-1979)		Sixth Plan (1980-1985)		Seventh Plan (1985-90)		Eighth Plan (1992-97)		Ninth Plan (1997-02)
	Original	Actual estimates	Original	Actual estimates	Original	Latest estimates	Original	Latest estimates	
Domestic Budgetary resources									
Current revenues	49.0 (12.47)	66.4 (16.30)	144.8 (14.85)	18.9 (1.71)	-52.5 (-2.92)	-12.5 (-7.00)	35.0 (8.06)	-46.25 (12.01)	-14.06 —
Public enterprises CPSEs including Railways	8.5 (2.20)	25.8 (6.35)	94.0 (9.64)	58.1 (5.24)	354.9 (19.72)	140.8 (7.89)	148.2 (34.13)	101.3 (26.34)	340.5 —
Borrowings	110.7 (28.61)	124.2 (30.52)	363.9 (37.32)	459.4 (41.45)	730.6 (40.59)	101.2 (56.68)	202.3 (46.59)	223.7 (58.19)	460.2 —
Additional resource mobilisation	146.9 (37.97)	103.0 (25.30)	213.0 (21.85)	329.7 (29.75)	447.0 (24.83)	313.1 (17.58)	— —	— —	— —
External assistance (net)	58.3 (15.07)	52.1 (12.79)	109.3 (11.21)	85.3 (7.70)	180.0 (10.00)	161.0 (9.03)	287.0 (6.61)	381.1 (9.93)	600.0 —
Deficit financing	13.5 (3.49)	35.6 (8.74)	50.0 (5.13)	156.8 (14.15)	140.0 (7.78)	282.0 (15.82)	200.0 (5.01)	290.0 (7.55)	— —
Aggregate resources	386.9 (100.00)	407.1 (100.00)	975.0 (100.00)	1108.2 (100.00)	1800.0 (100.00)	178.6 (100)	399.0 (100)	384.6 (100)	859.2 —

Source : Planning Commission, January 2001, *Indian Planning Experience: A Statistical Profile*, P.39, Table 4.1.

deposits with post offices which are spread all over the country reaching the far corners of rural areas, state provident funds amd deposits of other financial institutions like the Life Insurance Corporation of India, General Insurance Corporation of India and so on.

The biggest single item of domestic resources for the Plan comprises borrowings viz market borrowings, small savings, state provident funds, term loans from financial institutions and miscellaneou. capital receipts. Borrowings constituted 40 per cent to 58 per cent of plan finances (42 per cent in the 4th plan, 30.5 per cent in the 5th plan, 41.5 per cent in the 6th plan, 58 per cent in the 7th plan and for the 8th plan against the projected figure of 46.5 per cent the actual turned out be 63.1 per cent of the total finances). Amaresh Baghchi points out that as a result of the large shortfalls in budgetary savings and inadequate surpluses of PSU's, the financing of public sector plan outlay had to depend heavily on borrowings. Total domestic borrowings contributed anything between 40 and 60 per cent to plan finances in recent years (6th, 7th and 8th plan) as compared to about one-fifth to one-fourth in most of the earlier Plans. Inadequacy of current revenues to meet even current expenditures has resulted in the use of borrowed funds to meet current expenditures, leading close to what is called an internal debt trap. The main factor responsible for the falling contribution of the Central budget to the financing of the plans is the mounting burden of non-plan expenditure in the form of interest payments and subsidies on food and fertilisers.

Financing the Tenth Plan (MTA)

The size of the Central sector Plan was expected to be 6.44 per cent of GDP and that of the State sector Plan 4.69 per cent. Resources realised are of the order of 5.36 per cent and 3.64 per cent, respectively. In respect of both the Centre and the States, realisation has been short of the targeted level by around 1 per cent. Although Plan expenditure was lower than targeted, dependence on borrowing has been higher than planned at the Central and the State level. It is evident also that States have been under greater stress for Plan financing, due to shortfall in anticipated tax sharing from the Central government, drain on budgetary resources attributable to the power sector deficit and the need to meet fiscal reform targets laid down legislatively or in agreements entered into with the Central government and multilateral agencies.

The Tenth Plan had targeted a public sector outlay of Rs.15,92,300 crore at 2001-02 prices. This was 67.4 per cent higher than Ninth Plan realisations. Of this Rs.15,25,639 crore had been allocated sector-wise in Central, State and UT Plans. In the case of the Centre, the unallocated component was targeted to be raised through internal and extra-budgetary resources (IEBR) of Central public sector undertakings (CPSUs). In the case of States, resources over and above allocations made for the Core Plan were to be raised as own resources.

To achieve the objectives of securing a sustainable debt burden and restricting public sector draft on private savings to a reasonable limit, only 6.6 per cent of the projected increase in resources over Ninth Plan realisations was planned to come from borrowings and the rest from non-debt resources. It was recognised that such a high level of contribution from non-debt resources would be possible only by raising the tax/GDP ratio, increasing user charges, compressing expenditure on administration and establishment and improving the commercial management of public enterprises.

Central Plan Resources

Total Central Plan resources in the first four years are around Rs.5,72,183 crores which is about 62 per cent of the Tenth Plan target, compared with an expected realisation of 78 per cent of the five year target. This implies a shortfall of 16 per cent.

Resource Constraints

The availability of resources in the public sector to meet targeted levels of Plan expenditure is a major area of weakness. Neither the Centre nor the States have been able to mobilise the resources needed to keep outlays in line with Tenth Plan projections and this has led to significant under funding in many sectors. The Central Sector Plan was projected to be 6.4 per cent of GDP in the Tenth Plan against which the achievement in the first four years is only 5.4 per cent. The States plan was expected to be 4.69 per cent of GDP against which the likely achievement in the first four years will not exceed 3.64 per cent. Taking the Centre and the States together, Plan outlays will be lower than expected by 2 percentage points of GDP. This shortfall is despite the fact that both the Centre and the States have relied much more on borrowed resources than was intended, leading to a rise in public debt. The consolidated public debt of the Centre and States taken together is about 80 per cent of GDP, which is among the highest in emerging market economies.

The most important reason for the excessive reliance on debt financing during the Tenth Plan has been the large negative Balance from Current Revenues (BCR). The Tenth Plan had targeted an improvement in BCR from the negative level of 1.98 per cent of GDP in the Ninth Plan to

TABLE – 5.2

Central Plan Resources (2002-03 To 2005-06)

Rs.crores / %

	Item	2002-07 Tenth Plan	Realised 2002-03 to 2005-06	% Realisation (2002-2006)
1.	Balance from current revenues	-6385 -(0.69)	-129825 -(22.69)	
2.	Borrowing including net miscellaneous capital receipts	685185 (74.37)	592103 (103.48)	86.4
3.	Net inflow from abroad (grants & loans excluding external commercial borrowing)	27200 (3.09)	1184 (0.20)	4.4
4.	Gross Budgetary Support (1+2+3)	706000	@487821	69.1
5.	Central assistance for State and UT Plans	300265	@191192	63.7
6.	Gross Budgetary Support for Central Plan (4-5)	405735 (44.04)	296628 (51.84)	73.1
7.	Internal & Extrabudgetary Resources of Central public entreprises	515556 (55.96)	275554 (48.16)	53.4
8	Total Central Plan (6+7)	921291	572183	62.1

Note: Figures in brackets indicate shares of resources in total Central Plan

@ In 2005-06, to implement the recommendations of the Twelfth Finance Commission, the loan component of Central assistance for State and U.T. Plans has not been provided in the Central budget, as States have been given the option of raising it directly from the market. This is reflected in lower borrowings by the Central government. GBS and Central assistance figures include also the loan component of Central assistance (Rs. 24,358 crores at constant prices). market. If this eventuality arises, the Central deficit may be higher than in the Budget Estimates.

around 0.04 per cent. This improvement was to be achieved by increasing Central revenue (net of States' share) from 8.8 per cent of GDP in 2001-02 to 10 per cent in 2006-07 and reducing non Plan revenue expenditure from 10.6 per cent of GDP to around 9.1 per cent for the same period. In terms of realisations, net Central revenues have almost reached the target of around 10 per cent of GDP and non Plan revenue expenditure appears to have fallen to 9.4 per cent in 2005-06 (B.E.).

However, much of the improvement relates to 2004-05 R.E.s and 2005-06 B.E. The average level of non Plan revenue expenditure realised in the first four years is only about half a percentage point lower than the level reached at the end of the Ninth Plan.

The role of external assistance in financing the Plan was very different from that originally envisaged because of an unexpectedly favourable external position. External assistance is availed of both as loans (included in overall borrowings of government) and grants (covered under non-tax revenue receipts). Tenth Plan projections aimed only at a slight reduction of the scale of net inflow from abroad from 0.22 per cent of GDP in the Ninth Plan to around 0.19 per cent. In the first four years of the Tenth Plan, net inflows were negative in the first two years (-0.4 per cent) and are expected to be only 0.4 per cent in 2004-05, due to the conscious policy adopted by government in the first two years to prepay high cost loans keeping in mind the comfortable foreign exchange position. There will be no appreciable increase in net external inflows with reference to GDP in 2005-06 also.

Internal and extra-budgetary resources of Central public sector undertakings were expected to provide more than half (56 per cent) of the resources for the Central Plan during the Tenth Plan. Internal resources cover retained profits and depreciation and extra budgetary resources include borrowings of CPSUs through debentures, bonds, external commercial borrowings and the like. IEBR of Rs.5,15,556 crores were targeted to be raised by CPSUs (by higher operational efficiency particularly in the railways and power sectors) during the Tenth Plan period, of which normally Rs.4,02,134 crore should have been realised during the first four years. Actual realisation is only around half this amount (Rs.2,75,554 crore) In terms of GDP, the shortfall is 0.7 per cent (2.9 per cent realised against the expected level of 3.6 per cent).

It is a matter of concern that the shortfall in IEBR is much higher than that in net budgetary support for the Central Plan. Independent resource generation is the prime test of commercial viability and self sustainability for a PSU. It makes these corporates less dependent on government (in terms of budgetary support and guarantees) for planning and investment decisions and increases their creditworthiness while accessing the capital market. Failure to raise IEBR as targeted during the first four years of the Tenth Plan is a serious matter that must be addressed.

The Fiscal Challenge

The fiscal problem in India has steadily built up from 1980s onwards.

In the early 1980s, there was actually a revenue *surplus* for the states, and for the consolidated accounts of the centre and the states. Both deteriorated sharply through the 1980s. There was a sharp runup of the deficit in the late 1980s, which ended with the BoP crisis of 1991. This was followed by efforts at fiscal caution until 1997, after which the central revenue deficit deteriorated sharply.

This worsening of the deficit came about through a combination of weak tax revenues, a sharp increase in the wage bill, rising interest payments, and rising subsidies.

The steady growth of the Debt/GDP ratio has led to a corresponding growth in interest payments.

TABLE – 5.3

Growth of Interest and Subsidies

	Percent to GDP		Percent to revenue receipts	
	Interest	Subsidies	Interest	Subsidies
1982-83	2.1	0.9	23.1	11.1
1992-93	4.2	1.4	41.9	14.6
2002-03	4.8	1.8	50.8	18.8

Source: Ministry of Finance, Report of Kelkar Task Force on Implementation of Fiscal Responsibility and Budget Management Act, 2003, July, 2004.

In 1982-83, interest and subsidies added up to 34.2 per cent of revenue receipts. In 2002-03, this had doubled to 79.6 per cent. This has increasingly reduced the fiscal space available for the legitimate expenditures of government on the production of public goods. These numerical values understate the extent of this problem, to the extent that the full extent of subsidies is larger than portrayed by these statistics.

In the case of subsidies, there are important problems of measurement. The elements of expenditure which are classified as a 'subsidy' in budget documents are only a subset of the overall subsidies. There are also many other expenditures which are actually subsidies, i.e. narrow transfers to a few households or firms, without any public goods characteristics. Hence, the size of subsidies as seen using the standard budget data substantially understates the actual extent to which the expenditures of government are being devoted to transfers/subsidies instead of being deployed on producing public goods.

Another area where subsidies exist but are not explicitly reported is the issue of 'tax expenditure'. One of the important reasons for the low Tax/GDP ratio is the erosion of the tax base through a large number of exemptions. Such exemptions are fiscally identical to subsidies. That is, *tax revenues foregone are no different from explicit subsidies paid out.*[1]

References

Baghchi, Amaresh, *Fiscal Policy for Financing Development: The Indian Experience,* in (ed) Uma Kapila, Indian Economy Since Independence, 2000-01 edition.

Govt. of India, various Economic Surveys, including 2003-04.

Ministry of Finance (July, 2004), Report of Kelkar Task Force on Implementation of Fiscal Responsibility and Budget Management Act, 2003.

Planning Commission, Mid-term Appraisal of the Tenth Five Year Plan, June 28, 2005.

——— (2001), *Indian Planning Experience: A Statistical Profile.*

——— (Dec. 2002), Tenth Five Year Plan (2002-07).

1. Kelkar Task Force, July 2004.

6

On Correcting Fiscal Imbalances in the Indian Economy

Some Perspectives

Mihir Rakshit

Abstract

The purpose of the paper is to examine the nature of on-going budgetary imbalances in the Indian economy and suggest a programme of fiscal restructuring, keeping the primary objectives of public policy in view. Our analysis suggests that the basic imbalances lie not so much in the overall fiscal deficit, but more in the composition of government expenditure and modes of its financing. Indeed, the nature of fiscal adjustment attempted during the 90s seems to have played a none-too-insignificant role in creating difficulties on both the macroeconomic and budgetary front. The macroeconomic problems are manifested in decline and stagnation of aggregate capital accumulation and saving, large inter-year variations in the growth rate of investment, low agricultural growth along with sharp fluctuations in foodgrains output and inflation, and deceleration of industrial growth during the second half of the 90s. These problems are due in part to the failure of anti-cyclical fiscal policies, and more generally to the inappropriate budgetary stance reflected in a cutback in public investment, inadequate expenditure on education and health, a fall in the tax-GDP ratio, and reliance on high-cost borrowing instruments. The adjustment programme suggested in the paper includes substantial increases in government expenditure on investment, especially in agriculture and infrastructural facilities; roll-back of public consumption expenditure; and enhanced allocation for social sector in general and primary and health services in particular. So far as financing is concerned, we have suggested restoration of the tax-GDP ratio to the level obtaining at the beginning of the 90s; greater reliance on monetised deficit; drastic changes in high-cost instruments of government borrowing; and moderate deployment of instruments like the SLR.

I. Introduction

By common consent the most serious weakness of the Indian macroeconomy in recent years has consisted in the continuing and growing imbalances in the fiscal sphere. This view is also reiterated by the Eleventh Finance Commission (Government of India, 2000) which, under its terms of reference, has recommended a programme of fiscal adjustment and restructuring over the period 2000-2005. It is thus, an opportune moment to take a fresh look at the nature of the fiscal problems confronting the Indian economy and initiate a fruitful debate on the basic issues and policy options, especially since some of the wide-spread and popular perceptions in this regard do not seem to be based on well founded economic reasoning or a close scrutiny of empirical evidence.

In order to motivate the discussion it is useful first to recapitulate the commonly perceived areas of fiscal imbalance that the government has been trying to rectify since the mid-1980s, especially after the adoption of the economic reforms programme in 1991. At the time the programme was introduced the most important troubles were identified to be large fiscal and monetised deficits and the growing debt-GDP ratio. A related area of concern was the proportion of economy's resources appropriated by the public sector and there was a general feeling that downsizing of the government should form an important plank of any fiscal restructuring programme.

Over the last decade the government has been successful, perhaps too successful, in bringing down monetised deficit (see Table 6.1) so that this issue no longer figures prominently in discussions on budgetary policies. In other areas the record of the government is far from satisfactory and has drawn flaks from practically all quarters including the IMF, the World Bank and the Eleventh Finance Commission. An important part of the Commission's report is accordingly devoted to formulating a fiscal correction programme under which, among other things, between 1999-2000 and 2004-05 the fiscal deficit (as a percentage of gross domestic product) is to be brought down[1] from 9.83 to 6.5 per cent, and the debt-GDP ratio from 65.82 to 55 per cent or less[2].

Before commenting on any fiscal reforms programme or offering suggestion in this regard, it is necessary to have a clear idea regarding why and how the current fiscal scenario is worrisome and badly requires corrective steps. Second, it is also important to consider the economic implications of alternative modes of fiscal adjustment so that we are in a position to judge how far they benefit the society at large. The need for going into these basics may be illustrated by the problem one encounters in answering a few obvious questions that arise in this connection. Why, for example, should a 65 per cent debt-GDP ratio be considered too high, remembering that instances abound when some countries often had debt-GDP ratios exceeding 100 per cent, without any apparent clogging of their economic wheels? If public debt does constitute a burden, why should it not be brought down to zero within the shortest possible period? Why target for a fiscal deficit of (say) 6.5 per cent, no more, no less?

In any given situation it is no doubt extremely difficult to assign numerical values to fiscal targets due to informational problems and uncertainty regarding the future course of events impacting on the economy. However, while some element of subjective judgment or hunch is unavoidable in any policy decision, it is imperative to be fully conversant with the major factors and considerations on the basis of which policies should "ideally" be framed. Hence, our foray into some elementary economics while discussing the modalities of fiscal restructuring for the Indian economy.

The discussion in the present paper is organised as follows. There is a widespread belief that the fiscal stance of the government is recent years is unsustainable: not only is the debt-GDP ratio uncomfortably high, but the government's accumulation of financial liability due to large, continuing fiscal deficit poses a serious threat to both the solvency of the Treasury and viability of the economy. In the context of such concerns, in Section II we go into the economic implications of public debt and fiscal deficit, and examine the problem of sustainability of debt-financed government expenditure. Section III focuses on issues relating to optimality. Even if the fiscal stance is sustainable, it can be grossly suboptimal and leave plenty of room for correction. Keeping this consideration in view we discuss in this section some general principles with special reference to the norms for deciding on the scale and composition of government expenditure, and modes of its financing. Section IV assesses the Indian fiscal scenario and offers some guidelines, drawing on the discussion in the earlier two sections. The final section summarises the main conclusions.

II. On the Economic Impact and Sustainability of Debt and Deficit

Sustainability of the fiscal stance is a long-term problem and concerns the way in which budgetary viability may get eroded over time due to financing of government expenditure through borrowing. Fiscal deficit represents the scale of such financing and accumulation of public debt over the year. While examining the sustainability issue we need to consider three inter-related sets of questions. The first is the old one regarding the burden of public debt. The second concerns the problem of whether continuing fiscal deficit leads to an explosion of the debt-GDP ratio. Third, even if there is no such explosion, it is important to examine whether or how debt-financing itself[3] has any deleterious impact on the economic system.

Burden of Public Debt

From a purely accounting viewpoint public debt[4], economists emphasise, do not constitute any net liability of the economy as a whole, since financial assets held by the rest of the economy exactly offset government debt. By the same logic, however large may the interest payments on public debt be, they are nothing but transfers and do not constitute any net diminution in the community's command over goods and services available for consumption or investment. Why do we then worry about the size of the public debt or the interest liability thereon?

One reason is that when interest payments are very large, transfers to holders of government securities from the rest of the community can have an adverse impact on income distribution. Second, given the rates and structure of taxes, larger interest payments imply a higher ratio of private disposable income to gross domestic product. This can seriously distort the pattern of domestic absorption, as private consumption tends to rise at the expense of capital accumulation and provision of public goods and services. The distortionary impact on the economy's use of available goods and services is also likely to be strengthened by operation of the wealth effect (on household consumption), since holders of government securities generally regard them as part of their assets[5].

The adverse consequences of large public debt mentioned above can, one may argue, be avoided through appropriate tax-transfer schemes. However, these schemes themselves cause substantial distortion and misallocation of resources. Indeed, with or without public debt, limited ability of the Treasury to raise revenue without producing large distortions very often makes the government face a Hobson's choice: either it refrains from implementing some urgently required welfare enhancing schemes, or it is forced to borrow in order to finance the programmes. But does not such financing store up troubles for the future when interest obligations of the government may assume enormous proportions? Herein arises the question of sustainability: given the proportion of GDP the government can collect by way of taxes, can it take recourse to borrowing for meeting part of public consumption expenditure as also for interest payments on the growing public debt?

Canonical Views on Sustainability

Before providing an answer to the question in the Indian context, it is useful to summarise the canonical views in this regard[6]:

- For any given tax-GDP ratio, financing part of public consumption expenditure[7] through borrowing is sustainable so long as the interest rate on government borrowing is less than the GDP growth rate. When this condition is satisfied, public debt, revenue deficit and interest payments rise over time; but their values as ratios of gross domestic product stabilise in the long run, and do not go on increasing indefinitely.
- Lowering of tax rates or enhancement of debt-financed government consumption raises the long-run values of the debt-GDP and other ratios, but do not alter the sustainability result.
- Under the canonical scenario one need not worry about the government's inability to provide some essential public services on account of a high ratio of interest payments to tax collections, associated with a large public debt. In this scenario not only are interest payments made through borrowing without any cutback in public consumption, but the problem of government's "inability" to incur such expenditure without raising taxes does not arise so long as the sustainability condition holds.

Some Caveats and Extensions of the Canonical Framework

An important problem with the canonical model is that it assumes the interest rate and growth rate to remain unaffected irrespective of the government's fiscal stance — an assumption that is hard to reconcile with our discussion of the burden of public debt. Given the tax-GDP ratio, larger interest payments on public debt implies a higher ratio of private disposable income to gross domestic product. This (together with a larger wealth effect associated with a higher debt-GDP ratio) tends to raise household consumption. Maintenance of public consumption expenditure under these circumstances would then raise interest rates, reduce investment and hence the growth rate of the economy[8]. It is thus not very difficult to see how a public consumption-GDP ratio larger than some critical value becomes non-viable without an increase in the tax-GDP ratio. Though the general principles for locating the critical value are fairly straight-forward[9], in any actual situation the estimate cannot but be rough and ready and leave substantial scope for disagreement among economists.

Apart from the impact of tax- and public consumption-GDP ratios, it is necessary to recognise other factors having an important bearing on the sustainability issue[10] — factors which are not dealt with in the canonical model. An implicit assumption of the canonical approach is that the base of taxation is GDP, not earnings of private agents. A more reasonable assumption appears to be that it is the ratio of tax collections to total private "income", irrespective of whether it is by way of factor earnings or transfers, that the government finds difficult to raise without producing serious distortions. Under this assumption debt-financing is far less problematic, since sustainability now requires the growth rate to exceed the *post-tax* interest rate. In this case the burden of public debt will also be lighter than what has been suggested in our earlier discussion.

Central Bank holding of Government Securities

In many countries, including India, public debt refers to all financial liabilities of the government, irrespective of to whom they are owed. While examining the sustainability and related issues government securities held by the central bank should not however be included in public debt: the central bank is after all an organ of the state so that there is no government liability corresponding to bonds held by the central bank, nor does the interest paid thereon stand on the same footing as those paid on private holdings of government securities[11]. Such a perspective appears necessary for judging the Indian fiscal scenario since not only is the proportion of "public debt" held by the Reserve Bank not insignificant, but this proportion has undergone considerable changes over time. The scale and temporal behaviour of the official figures for public debt may thus give a wrong impression regarding sustainability of debt financing and other related issues.

Liabilities and Assets

Perhaps the most important difficulty with the canonical approach for assessing fiscal programmes in countries like India arises from neglect of the asset side of the government's balance sheet[12]. Let us consider first how conditions relating to sustainability of debt-financing are affected when the government borrows in order to meet capital expenditure and interest payments, but not for provision of public goods and services[13]. Given the other assumptions of the canonical model, sustainability now requires the growth rate to be higher than the (post-tax) interest rate less the return on assets being accumulated by the government — a much less onerous condition than the canonical one[14]. It is also easy to see that compared with the canonical case loan-financing of public investment will be associated with a lower debt-GDP ratio, higher growth and lighter burden of public debt.

When the government borrows for meeting not only capital, but part of consumption expenditure also[15], it is necessary to take into account the relative importance of the two categories of debt-financed expenditure. To see why, assume that the aggregate debt-financed government consumption cum capital expenditure is fixed as a ratio of gross domestic product. The larger the proportion of this expenditure for purposes of accumulation of assets, the higher will tend to be the growth rate of the economy[16]. Again, the cost of government borrowing (relevant for sustainability) will in the long run be a weighted average of (a) the (post-tax) interest rate, and (b) the (post-tax) interest rate less the return on government investment, the weights being the fractions of debt-financed government expenditure on public consumption and investment respectively. The implication is that, for any given amount of government borrowing for meeting its non-interest expenses, a larger proportion spent on investment will tend to promote budgetary viability through higher growth and lower (net) interest on public debt.

Government Borrowing: Crowding-out and Crowding-in Effects

Our analysis has so far been based on the presumption that government borrowing, irrespective of its purpose, tends to raise interest rates and hence to crowd out private investment. However, if the economy operates with excess capacity, debt-financed government expenditure, it is well known, may generate a crowding-in rather than crowding-out effect: the boost to aggregate demand, capacity utilisation and profits due to expansionary fiscal measures are likely to raise not only current gross domestic product, but also private investment and the long-term growth potential of the economy[17].

What about the interest-rate effect? Note first that crowding-in can materialise despite an increase in interest rates. Second, as we shall see in a few moments, the interest-rate effect is crucially dependent on the type of government borrowing[18]. Third and perhaps the most important, the popular perception regarding the crowding-out process is based on an extremely narrow view of the financial market and ignores the increasingly important role being played by the stock market, mutual or pension funds, and innovation of financial instruments. When an expansionary fiscal policy improves investors' sentiments, there will generally be an increase in the supply of funds to the private sector despite debt-financing by the government[19]. So long as the economy has excess capacity, an increase in government expenditure supported by borrowing may thus raise private capital formation along with household consumption expenditure.

Once the economy has attained full employment, any increase in government consumption or investment, no matter how it is financed, will necessarily reduce private absorption. The usual conclusions in this respect are:

- Both private consumption and investment will decline.
- The greater the reliance on debt financing, the larger will be the fall in private investment[20].
- Even with 100 per cent debt financing, the fall in private capital accumulation will be smaller than the additional investment expenditure by the government.

However, these conclusions abstract from the impact of changes in composition of government expenditure or in modes of borrowing. Government expenditure for extension and improvement of infrastructural facilities, education, health services, law and order, etc. tends to raise prospective profits in the future and the aggregate demand for investment by firms. We, thus, need to distinguish between government disbursements which promote private investment demand[21] and those which do not[22].

So far as modes of government borrowing are concerned, consider first the two polar cases. Instruments like the Statutory Liquidity Ratio (SLR) requirement, to the extent they act as effective constraints, produce a one-to-one financial crowding out. At the other extreme monetised deficit raises aggregate flow of finance, within and outside the banking sector, by a multiple of the deficit. In this case there is financial crowding in, rather than crowding out. In between the two instruments stand various types of government borrowing some of which tend to raise, others lower, availability of finance to the private sector[23].

Our analysis does not suggest that debt-financed government expenditure (under full employment conditions) necessarily crowds in private investment when the budgetary exercise raises firms' investment demand and there is increased availability of finance to the private sector. The reason is that, given the level of full employment output, crowding-in requires a fall in household consumption in excess of the incremental consumption or capital expenditure by the government[24]. This can come about only when the price rise due to increased demand supported by enhanced availability of funds effects a sufficient cutback in private consumption – an outcome that is neither guaranted, nor devoid of its flip side. What is unambiguous is that, both composition of government expenditure and modes of borrowing have an important bearing on the question relating to crowding-in or crowding-out effects.

Fiscal Deficit: Disabusing Some Common Notions

While discussing the sustainability of a budgetary stance we have not referred to fiscal deficit, the centre of attention of all finance ministers and economists. The perceptive reader must have realised that this was not an oversight: our earlier analysis indicates why fiscal deficit is not a very useful concept for judging the short- and long-run impact of the budget and hence of the sustainability of debt-financed government expenditure. However, in view of the extensive (mis)use of the concept in practically all discussions on fiscal reforms, it appears necessary to clarify our position even at the risk of labouring the obvious[25].

Fiscal deficit, as defined in India, is the gap between aggregate government expenditure and the sum of revenue receipts, proceeds from disinvestment in public sector undertakings, recovery of past loans and other non-debt creating receipts. The basic difficulty with the concept, it is not very difficult to appreciate, arises from clubbings of various items of government expenditure and of receipts which do not have the same implications for sustainability[26] of a budgetary programme.

Many Faces of Government Borrowing

Consider first the problems associated with clubbing all categories of government borrowing under the sobriquet, "fiscal deficit". We have already discussed why government securities held by the central bank should not be regarded as a part of public debt, and how monetised deficit produces a financial crowding-in effect. Indeed, apart from the fact that monetised financing of government expenditure does not add to the future interest burden of the government, in a growing economy such financing (called seignorage) upto a point also produces no inflationary impact either[27]. The effects of alternative modes of government borrowing from the public can also differ significantly, as we have emphasised in the previous subsection. No wonder then that fiscal deficit, comprising all kinds of government borrowing over a year, does not on its own indicate the extent or even the sign of financial crowding out.

Disinvestment for Budgetary Nirvana

Much more misleading is the treatment of disinvestment in public sector undertakings (PSUs) and recovery of loans on the same footing as tax collections. Note first that when the government sells PSU shares in the stock market or recovers past loans, there should, other things remaining the same, be some pressure in the financial market – a pressure which in the aggregate need not be less than that created by an identical amount of government borrowing from the public[28]. The crowding-in or crowding-out effect of financing government expenditure through unloading of shares or loan recovery on the one hand and market borrowing on the other may not thus be very different.

Second, unlike tax collections, non-debt creating receipts like disinvestment proceeds reduce future earnings of the government by way of interests and dividends. From the view-point of budgetary viability there can thus be little doubt that reduction of fiscal deficit through disinvestment cannot but be worse than tax financing[29]. Indeed, a cutback in fiscal deficit through disinvestment may well erode rather than promote the long-run viability of the budget, since (a) the government's borrowing rate of interest is lower than that of private agents, and (b) private asset holders tend to be risk averse[30]. This is not to deny that there can be a number of instances where disinvestment, backed by changes in management, incentives and work environment in the undertakings, contributes toward budgetary viability: it is quite possible that the boost to expected profitability and hence prices of the shares are then high enough to offset the impact associated with the higher borrowing rate of, and risk premium demanded by, private investors[31]. However, the first best solution even in this case consists in adoption of measures for promoting profitability, *without disinvestment*. Indeed, from the viewpoint of budgetary viability market borrowing may be a better alternative to disinvestment even when the increase in profitability under the best possible reorganisation without disinvestment is less than what reorganisation with disinvestment can permit[32]. It is only when political and bureaucratic interference, lying at the root of poor performance of public sector undertakings, cannot be removed without disinvestment, should the government opt for this second best measure for promoting sustainability.

The issues related to government disinvestment in public sector undertakings are in fact broader and closely concern the political economy of efficient use and allocation of nation's resources. But these issues are not brought to the fore when the focus is on disinvestment as a means of reducing fiscal deficit; nor does there seem adequate appreciation of the fact that even for promoting the narrower objective of improvement in the government's balance sheet, the measure may turn out to counter-productive.

Government Expenditure

We have already examined how different types of government expenditure — public consumption, investment and transfer — have quite different implications for future receipts of the government. For examining the sustainability of a fiscal stance it is thus necessary to consider the composition of government expenditure, not simply its aggregate. This need is all the more urgent, as we shall see in the next section, for formulating an optimum, and not simply a sustainable, budgetary programme.

III. Budgetary Objectives and Instruments

The root of the sustainability problem, as already emphasised, may be traced to the difficulty the government encounters in collecting enough taxes for promoting its basic social and economic objectives. In order to examine the best way of resolving the problem, given the basic goals of public policy, it is useful to recapitulate first the nature of the optimum budgetary programme when the tax constraint is not operative. Second, we then have to examine how the text-book programme needs to be modified in the presence of the constraint faced by the government.

Budgetary Rules sans Tax Constraint

For discussing the budgetary rules when the tax constraint is not operative, consider first the intermediate objectives[33] of public policies. These objectives are:

(a) optimum distribution of full employment output between consumption and investment;

(b) optimum balance between household and public consumption;

(c) optimum division of investment between the public and the private sector; and

(d) an equitable (post tax-transfer) distribution of income.

The first involves issues relating to inter-temporal and intergenerational distribution of consumption. We ignore the problem for the moment and assume that in this matter the government is guided entirely by the time preference (or its absence) of private economic agents[34]. The budgetary implications of the other objectives may be summarised as follows:

1. An equitable distribution of income implies an optimum tax-transfer scheme. We put this first since estimation of marginal benefits from private and public consumption or investment under the ideal situation presumes an equitable distribution[35].
2. Government expenditure on administration, defence, maintenance of law and order and provision of other public goods are to be fixed at the level where their social benefits at the margin equals the marginal benefit from private consumption[36] (Samuelson, 1954).
3. The equi-marginal principle should also apply in the division of aggregate investment between the public and the private sector. However, this principle refers to the social, not private, return. Thus, while estimating the return on investment, positive or negative externalities have to be taken into account and appropriate taxes or subsidies to be levied for securing optimal composition and level of private investment. For public investment the relevant return needs to include all future incremental gains to the economy irrespective of whether they contribute anything to government coffers.
4. All government consumption expenditure and transfer payments[37] are to be met from revenue receipts of the government, while public investment and net government support to private investment should be financed through borrowing. The text-book principles thus enjoin the government to target for a zero "revenue deficit" and a fiscal deficit no more, no less, than the optimum level of public investment expenditure plus net subsidy on private investment[38].

Before we examine how the above results are modified on account of constraints faced by the government a few observations appear to be in order.

First, the budgetary programme chalked out above does not create any sustainability problem: even when public investment in roads, improvement in environment or setting up broadcasting facilities does not yield any direct return to the Treasury, (non-distortionary) taxes permit the government to service interest payments on borrowings on account of such investment.

Second, given the optimal level of incremental reserve money and total investible funds, monetised deficit implies an equivalent decrease in financial resources available to the private sector. Hence, for framing an optimal budgetary programme monetised and non-monetised borrowing of the government should be put on the same footing, both having the same opportunity cost from the viewpoint of the society as a whole.

Third, government support to human resource development, R&D, etc., should be treated as capital expenditure and financed by borrowing, not taxation[39].

Second Best Budgetary Programmes

High economic costs of tax collection[40] in developing countries require considerable modifications in the principles enunciated above, especially when the government is already saddled with large interest obligations on public debt[41]. The problem in this context lies in devising the most effective means of promoting the basic objectives, given the tax constraint and the current committed expenditure of the government like interest payments. The revised programme, it is not very difficult to see, will (compared with the first best optimum) display a tilt in favour of those budgetary measures which tend to (a) raise future revenue of the government; (b) lighten the burden of interest obligations over time; and (c) reduce the current or future need for government expenditure for promoting the primary goals. Quite clearly, the revisions in fiscal policy will depend not only on the degree of severity of the tax constraint, but also on the relative weights attached to these goals. In order to discuss the nature of revisions in the composition and scale of the budget, it is useful to examine the type of budgetary measures which helps in easing the inter-temporal budget constraint and promotes the main objectives of public policy.

Faced with the revenue constraint it is tempting for the government to scale down all types of expenditure as far as possible in order to contain growth of public debt and future interest liabilities. Since in the short run it is difficult to reduce interest payments as also wages and salaries, expenditure adjustment under the revenue constraint generally takes the form of cutbacks in government's capital expenditure, subsidies, and allocations for social and other sectors which do not form part of the government's committed expenditure. Such an adjustment may appear eminently sensible: distortionary effects of taxes reduce after all the net marginal (social) benefits of all types of government expenditure[42]. However, scaling down government expenditure, with across-the-board cutbacks in different items, may not in fact be optimum. Indeed, even the revised level of government spending in the short run need not necessarily be smaller than in the first best solution. The reason, as we shall see, is that revisions in the expenditure and financing programmes are to be decided on simultaneously, taking into account their impact on easing the inter-temporal budget constraint and the consequent promotion of the primary goals of public policy.

Non-tax Sources of Government Revenue

Let us consider first the alternative sources of non-tax finance and examine their implications for the inter-temporal budget constraint and basic objectives.

Monetised Deficit

We have already indicated how monetised deficit or seignorage can, within limits, promote budgetary viability, but does not have any special role in the ideal situation. When the tax constraint does not permit the government to implement the first best expenditure programme, borrowing from the central bank constitutes the most effective means of easing the constraint and moving closer to the first best solution. Indeed, when the tax constraint is severe and the government is burdened with a large committed expenditure, maximising the seigniorage generally constitutes an optimum policy, provided the inflation associated therewith does not seriously distort the economic system[43]. However, since even the maximum amount of resources the government can extract through monetised deficit is unlikely to be large enough to ease the budget constraint significantly, further adjustments on the financing side are called for.

Borrowing from the Public

Governments in practically all developing countries have often appropriated funds from the financial sector at below market interest rates through instruments like the Statutory Liquidity Ratio (SLR). Though such instruments are inefficient or distortionary under the first best scenario, in the case under consideration, upto a point their use should be welfare enhancing. Borrowing at below market interest rates constitutes, it is true, taxation of financial saving and may induce savers to switch from financial to real assets. However, given the fact that the problem of distributing their saving between physical and financial assets does not arise for the vast majority of economic agents[44], the distortionary effect by way of substitution between the two types of assets is likely to be minor. The main problem with borrowing through SLR and similar devices arises from the increased cost of financial intermediation and its impact on production and private investment. It is these effects which limit the amount of such borrowing under the optimum budgetary programme.

Restructuring Government Expenditure

Considerations of the tax constraint suggest that, other things remaining the same, the revisions in the government's expenditure programme will be along the following lines:

First, compared with the first best solution, more emphasis will be put on capital expenditure than on public consumption. The reason is that such a shift improves the future revenue collection of the government[45], eases the inter-temporal budget constraint and contributes to promotion of social objectives.

Second, similar considerations tilt the balance in favour of those items of public investment whose returns directly accrue to the Treasury, and against capital disbursements that have positive externalities[46].

Third, the second best optimum will be characterised by exercise of some degree of monopoly power[47] upto a point, even though these measures are inefficient under the first best situation.

Fourth, while large externalities militate against public sector investment[48], the fact that it is easier to tax income generated through public enterprises and that their entire profits contribute toward relaxing the government's budget constraint tend to favour investment in the public at the expense of the private sector.

Income Inequality and Poverty

The steps considered above are designed to raise future revenue or reduce the interest burden of the government so that provision of public goods, expenditure for reducing income inequality and poverty, and government support to economic growth can move closer to their optimum levels. Under the revised programme, these steps will be supplemented by measures which reduce the need for current and future expenditure of the government to promote social objectives.

In developing countries most of these measures will be directed toward reducing both current and future pre-tax-transfer income inequality and poverty, given the prohibitive cost of redistributing purchasing power from the richer to the poorer sections of the society. All empirical studies suggest that the incidence of poverty at the national as also regional level is closely dependent on agricultural production, prices of foodgrains, employment, primary education and health. In the context of this relationship, we may distinguish between two sets of measures for reducing the need for direct government intervention aimed at improving income distribution and reducing poverty, the first designed to tackle the short-term, the second the long-term problem.

Food and fertiliser subsidy along with credit facilities to farmers tend to raise production and reduce prices of foodgrains[49]; suitably designed employment guarantee schemes ensure means of subsistence to the indigent groups of society; and supply of potable drinking water along with health services in rural areas[50] reduces the incidence of sickness and disability. All these measures help reducing current poverty and expenses incurred thereon and thus partake of the characteristic of the government's revenue expenditure from the view-point of its objective of poverty elimination[51]. The longer term solution to the problem lies in investment in agriculture, development of infrastructure in rural areas, setting up of microcredit agencies, and rapid expansion of primary education and basic health services.

In order to appreciate how or to what extent these constitute a departure from the ideal programme, a few observations appear to be in order.

First, the current and capital expenditure for poverty elimination are larger here than what is suggested under the first best solution[52]. For example, there is now near unanimity among economists regarding the crucial role of education, health, R&D and a well-functioning financial system in promoting economic growth. Under the revised programme, we may note, allocation of public funds under these heads will be somewhat different from what is optimal in the ideal situation: there is smaller allocation for higher education and other areas which do not directly benefit the poor and more for primary education, supply of potable drinking water, provision of health services in rural and distress areas, research related to agriculture and mass communicable diseases, and extension of micro credit facilities.

Second, larger expenditure on agriculture and other items mentioned above violates the first best principles of allocative efficiency and involves some loss of GDP[53]. But given the enormous informational and implementation difficulties of tax-transfer schemes, it is not difficult to appreciate the need for special steps[54] to reduce income inequality and poverty by tackling the problem at its source, viz., the process of income and employment generation.

Third, while drawing up the fiscal programme for poverty elimination, it is important to weigh the relative efficacy of current expenditure like subsidies on food or agricultural inputs, and of capital expenditure on irrigation, power supply in rural areas or primary education. Given the inter-temporal budget constraint faced by the government, the litmus test of efficacy of a poverty programme consists in the extent to which it leads over time to growth of income earning assets and capability of the disadvantaged, and hence reduces the need for special steps like agricultural subsidy that are otherwise distortionary.

IV. Fiscal Malady in India : Diagnoses and Remedies

Since all observers including the Eleventh Finance Commission regard India's on-going budgetary stance as unsustainable, we first take a critical look at the behaviour of the relevant variables in recent years, and try to identify the positive developments as also the major blemishes in the fiscal system. This provides the necessary backdrop for discussing both the sustainability problem and the efficacy of alternative programmes of fiscal correction.

Sustainability of Fiscal Stance

Table 1 summarises the time profile of the most important indices of the Indian fiscal system during the 1990s. At first sight behaviour of the usual indicators does not seem to suggest that there was a marked deterioration in the fiscal health of country during the reference period. The public debt-GDP ratio did not show any rising trend; in fact but for the rise over the later part of the period, the trend would have been distinctly downward. Behaviour of the fiscal deficit (as a ratio of GDP) was also similar, registering a rapid decline in the earlier phase and rising in the last three years. What may appear decisive, the crucial condition for sustainability of debt-financing, viz., the growth rate of the economy exceeding the interest cost of government borrowing, is also satisfied. While the interest rate on government borrowing was less than 10 per cent throughout[55], the average GDP growth (in nominal) terms was about 14 per cent per annum[56].

Despite having reservations regarding efficacy of the budgetary programme being followed by the government, one may thus be tempted to dismiss fiscal sustainability as a non-issue for the Indian economy. However, the dismissal is perhaps too hasty, based as it is on neglect of some important negative developments. First, as is evident from Table 1, since 1996-97 while the public debt and fiscal deficit ratios have shown a rising trend, the GDP growth rate in relation to the interest rates has tended to move in the opposite direction. It is this reversal of the trend that has caused apprehension in many a quarter regarding the sustainability of mounting debt and deficit.

Indeed, a scrutiny of the more relevant indicators of, and factors contributing to, sustainability of debt-financing[57] reveals a much more unhealthy trend on the fiscal front than what is suggested by the behaviour of public debt, fiscal deficit or even the (overall) growth-interest differential. As we have already noted, the relevant indicator of the burden of government's indebtedness is public debt less the RBI holding of government securities, or what we call public liability (PL). Unlike the (public) debt-GDP ratio, the proportion of PL to gross domestic product showed a steeply rising trend during the 90s, with the ratio registering an increase of nearly 9 percentage points between the beginning and the end of the decade (Table 6.2). The counterpart of this trend was the decline in public debt held by the Reserve Bank (as a ratio of GDP), from 16.6 per cent in 1990-91 to 7.7 per cent in 1999-2000. Thus, stability of the debt-GDP ratio during the 90s is somewhat misleading in judging the sustainability of the budgetary stance or the change required therein.

An indicator closely related to the above is what we call the fiscal gap, which is nothing but the government's incremental financial liability[58] (IFL) less monetised deficit. Fiscal gap (FG) thus represents the yearly increase in government debt to the rest of the economy plus reduction in its financial assets, and hence constitutes, as we have already argued in Section II, a better measure than fiscal deficit of the government's incremental debt burden due to current budgetary measures. As Table 6.2 shows, during 1990-95 fiscal deficit recorded a significant decline, but FG showed a mildly upward trend. Thus, contrary to the widely held belief, the first phase of the reforms programme did not contribute to fiscal health of the economy. Government expenditure (as a ratio of GDP) did decline during this period (Table 6.1); but with its focus on reduction of fiscal and monetised deficits in the face of a decline in revenue receipts, the government apparently lost sight of the troubles it was piling up for the future. There was some fall in FG during 1995-97, but its subsequent increase at a fairly steep rate constitutes a serious weakness of the budgetary programme pursued in recent years.

What about the uses of funds borrowed by the government — a question answer to which is of crucial importance in assessing the viability of the fiscal stance? As we have emphasised in Section II, other things remaining the same, the greater will be the erosion of fiscal viability, the larger the proportion of total borrowing used for bridging

TABLE – 6.1

Fiscal Profile of the Indian Economy

(Figures unless specified otherwise, are as percentage of GDP)

	1990-91	1991-92	1992-93	1993-94	1994-95	1995-96	1996-97	1997-98	1998-99	1999-00
Revenue Receipts	19.7	20.7	20.3	18.0	18.5	18.4	18.1	17.9	16.2	17.8
Of which										
Interest, Profit & Dividend Receipts	1.3	1.8	1.6	1.5	1.3	1.2	1.4	1.4	1.4	
Revenue Expenditure	24.2	24.2	23.6	22.3	22.1	21.6	21.7	22.0	23.2	23.2
Interest Payments	4.7	5.0	5.2	5.0	5.2	5.0	5.1	5.1	5.2	5.7
Social Sector Expenditure	7.7	7.5	7.3	7.2	7.1	7.1	6.8	7.1	7.3	5.1
Capital Receipt	8.7	8.4	7.0	7.7	8.9	6.7	5.6	8.1	9.3	8.5
Fiscal Deficit	10.0	7.4	7.4	8.3	7.1	6.6	6.4	7.3	8.9	9.9
Primary Deficit	5.3	2.4	2.3	3.3	1.9	1.6	1.3	2.2	3.7	4.2
Monetised Deficit	2.8	0.8	0.6	0.1	0.2	1.7	0.2	0.7	1.0	-0.2
Public Debt[1]	65.5	64.5	64.1	65.4	63.3	61.5	60.0	62.1	62.0	65.1
Public Debt held by RBI	16.6	15.2	13.9	11.6	10.0	10.3	9.1	8.9	8.7	7.7
Interest Cost of Govt. Borrowing (per cent)[2]		8.8	9.2	9.5	9.3	9.2	9.7	9.5	9.9	
Incremental Return on Govt. Capital Disbursement (per cent)[3]		11.8	6.3	5.6	4.1	3.9	5.1	4.7	4.9	
Memo Item										
Nominal GDP (growth rate)	15.7	14.5	15.4	14.4	17.9	15.0	13.9	9.8	13.7	

Sources: RBI, Annual Report, Report on Currency & Finance, Handbook of Statistics; Report of the Eleventh Finance Commission

Note : Figures are for Central and State Governments taken together.

1. Public Debt includes internal and external debt and other liabilities. Other Liabilities comprises Small Savings Scheme, PFs etc. & Reserve Funds and Deposits.
2. Interest cost of Govt. Borrowing of a year = Interest payment of the current year/public debt of the previous year.
3. Incremental Return on Govt. Capital Disbursement = Change in Interest, dividend and profits as % of Cumulative Capital Disbursement, both from 1990-91, till the year concerned.

the revenue deficit and the smaller the fraction devoted to capital expenditure. A look at the relative importance of the two uses of borrowings[59] leaves little doubt regarding the unhealthy trend in India's fiscal system during the 90s: over this period while revenue deficit (as a ratio of GDP) went up by 2.2 percentage points, capital expenditure was reduced by about 2.7 percentage points (Table 6.2). There are wider implications of this sharp change in the government's fiscal stance to which we shall presently turn; but let us first indicate its impact on sustainability.

A larger proportion of capital expenditure in relation to revenue deficit reduces the net interest cost of government borrowing. This cost, as already discussed in Section II, is nothing but the weighted average of (a) the borrowing rate and (b) this rate less the (gross) return on government investment, the weights being the ratios of revenue deficit and capital expenditure respectively (to their total). On the basis of the budgetary figures for the Union and State governments taken together we have estimated the government's borrowing rate, incremental return on its capital expenditure and hence net interest cost of government borrowing[60] (Table 6.2). It is this net interest cost which is more relevant than the government's borrowing rate for examining the sustainability of the on-going fiscal stance. According to our estimate throughout the 90s the net interest cost of debt financing showed an uninterrupted rising trend, the rise amounting to more than 2.5 percentage points between 1991-92 and 1998-99. Part of the increase was accounted for by the fall in the return on government's capital expenditure, but the major reason, especially during the later part of the period, lay in changes in relative weights of the two uses of borrowing, as revenue deficits mounted even while capital disbursements were on their downward course[61].

For examining sustainability we need to compare the GDP growth and the net interest cost of government borrowing, or the growth-net interest cost differential. During the reference period this differential came down sharply[62], especially after 1995-96, lending credence to the common refrain that the budgetary correction programme of the government has gone awry in recent years. However, despite the downward trend of the differential, the GDP growth has remained above the net cost of government borrowing. One may also argue that even if the declining trend in capital expenditure in relation to revenue deficit continues unabated, the net cost of borrowing can at most reach the interest rate, which still falls short of the economy's growth rate.

TABLE – 6.2

Indicators of Fiscal Sustainability: 1990-2000

(Figures unless specified otherwise, are as percentage of GDP)

	1990-91	1991-92	1992-93	1993-94	1994-95	1995-96	1996-97	1997-98	1998-99	1999-00
Public Debt	65.5	64.5	64.1	65.4	63.3	61.5	60.0	62.1	62.0	65.1
Fiscal Deficit	10.0	7.4	7.4	8.3	7.1	6.6	6.4	7.3	8.9	9.9
Nominal GDP Growth Rate	15.7	14.5	15.4	14.4	17.9	15.0	13.9	9.8	13.7	
Interest Cost of Govt. Borrowing		8.8	9.2	9.5	9.3	9.2	9.7	9.5	9.9	
Growth-interest Differential		5.7	6.2	4.9	8.6	5.8	4.3	0.3	3.8	
Public Liability[1]	48.9	49.2	50.2	53.8	53.3	51.2	50.9	53.2	53.4	57.4
Incremental Financial Liability (IFL)[2]	10.8	9.5	8.5	9.1	8.5	7.3	7.1	8.0	9.6	
Fiscal Gap[3]	8.0	8.7	7.9	9.0	8.3	5.6	6.9	7.3	8.6	
Revenue Deficit	4.5	3.6	3.4	4.2	3.7	3.2	3.6	4.1	6.3	6.7
Capital Expenditure	6.4	5.9	5.1	4.8	4.9	4.1	3.6	3.9	3.9	
Capital Expenditure as percentage of IFL	58.8	62.6	60.5	53.0	56.9	55.9	49.8	48.4	40.4	
Net Interest Cost of Govt. Borrowing[4]		5.2	5.4	6.5	7.0	7.0	7.1	7.3	8.0	
Growth-Net Interest Cost Differential		9.3	10.0	7.9	10.9	8.0	6.8	2.6	5.7	
Non-Interest Revenue Receipt[5]	18.5	18.9	18.7	16.5	17.2	17.2	16.7	16.5	14.8	
Primary Gap[6]	3.3	3.6	2.7	3.9	3.1	0.6	1.8	2.2	3.4	

Sources: RBI, Annual Report, Report on Currency & Finance, Handbook of Statistics; Report of the Eleventh Finance Commission.

1. Refers to Public Debt & Other Liabilities net of Public Debt held by RBI.
2. Incremental Financial Liability = Capital Disbursement + Revenue Deficit.
3. Fiscal gap = Incremental Financial Liability - Monetised Deficit.
4. Net Interest Cost of Govt. Borrowing = Weight of Capital Expenditure + (Interest cost - Interest return) + Weight of Revenue Deficit + Interest Cost.
5. This is the difference between Revenue Receipts and Interest, Profit & Dividend Receipts.
6. Primary Gap = Fiscal Gap - Interest Payments.

Such optimism concerning the country's fiscal sustainability needs to be moderated in light of two major disquieting trends[63]. First, a positive growth-interest differntial as a sufficient condition for sustainability presumes a constant tax-GDP ratio. In the Indian context the relevant ratio is that between revenue receipts less earnings from government assets[64] and the gross domestic product, or what we call non-interest revenue-GDP ratio (NIRR). This ratio has shown a distinctly downward trend and registered a fall of about 3.5 percentage points during the 1990s (Table 6.2). Remembering that even with a positive growth-interest differential, a falling NIRR tends to raise over time the debt-GDP ratio and interest burden on public debt, the declining trend in government's non-interest revenue must be regarded as a negative development from the viewpoint of budgetary viability.

The second disquieting trend relates to the behaviour of what we call "primary gap", i.e., the difference between the fiscal gap and interest payments of the government. This is nothing but the increase in the government's liability to the public (excluding the Reserve Bank) due to its current budgetary exercise[65], and determines (along with other factors) future course of the government's debt burden[66]: other things remaining the same, the burden will rise over time with an increase in the primary gap-GDP ratio. As Table 6.2 shows, this ratio also recorded a steep rise during the second half of the 90s and suggests that sustainability of debt financing is not guaranteed unless the trend is arrested, if not reversed.

It is not very difficult to have an overall assessment on the basis of Table 6.2 which shows how the main indicators relating to sustainability of debt financing changed during the 90s. There is little doubt that despite, or because of, the reforms measures initiated since 1991, practically all indicators show a deteriorating health of India's fiscal system. The negative developments on the fiscal front, though worrisome, do not nevertheless suggest that the economy is being inexorably pushed to an internal debt trap. However, much more important is the question whether the current fiscal stance, even if sustainable, helps in promoting the basic social and economic objectives, and if not, how best to alter the policy stance.

Fiscal Correction for Promotion of Economic and Social Objectives

In order to judge whether or to what extent budgetary policies have helped or hindered attainment of primary objectives like growth and equity, it is useful to consider first the performance of the economy and identify the positive or negative role of the government in the outcome.

On the basis of behaviour of the two most important macro variables, viz., GDP growth and inflation, one may feel reasonably optimistic regarding the outlook of the Indian economy (Table 6.3). After an initial setback in the first few years since the reforms programme was initiated, the GDP growth picked up and averaged more than 6.5 per cent per annum during 1994-2000. The higher GDP growth in this period was also accompanied with a lower inflation rate than in the earlier years. This happy conjunction of the two most important macroeconomic trends, many an observer feels, augers well for the country's economic performance in the new millennium.

A closer look at Table 6.3 suggests however that the macroeconomic scenario is not that picture perfect. Not only did the average GDP growth over 1997-2000 fall short of the average during the earlier three years, but the performance of both the industrial and agricultural sectors has been quite lackluster. The last four years of the decade saw a distinct deceleration of industrial growth — a trend also confirmed by the current year's data so far. The average agricultural growth over the decade remained low, and what is no less worrisome, showed sharp year-to-year fluctuations. The relatively high GDP growth in recent years has in fact been driven by growth of services. But it is a moot point whether the tertiary sector growth can be maintained in the absence of growth in the other two sectors and adequate back up by way of investment in required fields[67].

There were other developments in the economy which cast doubts on the possibilities of robust growth in the absence of major policy initiatives. The most important of these negative developments were the fall in investment and saving ratios, especially since 1995-96 (Table 6.3). Remembering that the East and South East Asian economies have been saving and investing 35 to 45 per cent of their gross domestic product almost from the beginning of their attempts at industrialisation, and that raising the domestic investment and saving ratios from around 25 per cent to at least 30 per cent was the avowed target of the government in the early 90s, the fall in the two crucial macro variables by 2 percentage points cannot but be regarded as a major failure of government policies pursued over the previous decade.

The failure is also reflected in composition of investment and sources of saving. Note first that despite the perceptible rise in per capita income during the 90s, household saving as a ratio of GDP showed a significant fall over the period. Saving in the private corporate sector did register an increase; but not only has its upward trend been reversed since 1995 and the increase quite insufficient to arrest the downward

TABLE – 6.3

Macroeconomic Indicators of India: 1990-91 to 1999-00

(Figures unless specified otherwise, are as percentage of GDP)

	1990-91	1991-92	1992-93	1993-94	1994-95	1995-96	1996-97	1997-98	1998-99	1999-00
GDP growth rate	5.4	0.8	5.3	6.0	7.0	7.3	7.5	5.0	6.8	6.4
Agricultural growth rate	4.2	-2.0	5.8	3.6	5.3	-0.4	8.8	-1.1	6.5	1.3
Industrial growth rate	7.0	-1.7	4.4	6.9	9.3	12.5	6.6	5.6	4.5	7.8
Inflation rate	10.3	13.7	10.1	8.4	10.9	7.7	6.4	4.8	5.9	3.3
Food price inflation	11.9	20.2	12.3	4.9	9.9	7.4	11.8	3.4	12.7	3.8
Govt Consumption Expenditure (GFCE)	11.5	11.3	11.1	11.2	10.6	10.7	10.6	11.5		
Investment	27.7	23.4	23.9	23.1	26.1	27.2	24.6	26.2	23.4	
Public	10.4	10.0	10.3	8.2	8.8	7.6	6.9	7.2	6.6	
Private Sector	16.1	13.9	14.6	13.0	14.8	18.8	17.1	16.9	15.2	
of which										
Household	11.5	9.4	9.3	7.3	7.9	9.6	9.3	8.3		
Private Corporate	4.6	4.5	5.3	5.7	6.9	9.2	7.7	8.7		
Investment in Agriculture	2.2	2.2	2.2	1.8	2.0	2.0	1.9	2.0		
Investment in Infrastructure	5.9	6.1	6.3	5.8	5.1	5.0	4.8	4.8		
Investment growth rate	12.2	-11.0	12.4	-2.7	19.9	19.6	-1.3	7.7	-21.5	
Saving	24.3	22.9	22.0	22.5	25.0	25.5	23.3	24.7	22.3	
Household	20.5	17.7	17.7	18.4	19.8	18.5	17.1	19.0	18.5	
Private Corporate	2.8	3.2	2.8	3.5	3.5	5.0	4.5	4.3	3.8	
Public Sector	*1.0*	*1.9*	*1.5*	*0.6*	*1.7*	*2.0*	*1.7*	*1.4*	*0.0*	
of which										
Public Sector Undertakings	5.5	5.5	4.9	4.8	5.4	5.2	5.3	5.5	6.3	

Sources : Economic Survey; RBI, Annual Report, Report on Currency & Finance; CMIE.

drift of private saving[68], but the corporates' contribution in this respect has also not been commensurate with the increase in their share in the economy's total capital stock[69]. Nor does the record of the public sector appear quite commendable: it did manage to raise its saving ratio by 1 percentage point over 1990-96, but since then the ratio came down sharply and the sector ended up with zero saving in 1998-99.

A Tale of Private Profligacy and Public Thrift

In order to suggest corrective measures on the fiscal front, it is important to locate the major factors behind the dismal behaviour of the economy's saving ratio. The first point to appreciate in this connection is that, contrary to popular perception, it was private, not pubic, profligacy that lay at the root of the trouble. Government consumption[70] ratio, unlike that in the private sector, did not go up in the reference period. In fact, over the 80s, this ratio went up by more than 2 percentage points, but showed some slide, albeit marginal, during the last decade.

The explanation of the declining trend in aggregate saving seems to lie in two sets of factors. First, over the 90s the tax-GDP ratio came down by more than 3.5 percentage points; government transfer payments by way of interest and subsidies mounted; and out of interest payments, by far the largest item in government's revenue expenditure, an increasing fraction was accruing to the private sector, as monetised deficits came down sharply and government liability to private agents went up by 9 percentage points. The result was a whopping 6 percentage points increase in the ratio of household disposable income to gross domestic product. Such an increase could not but produce a fall in aggregate saving, remembering that private marginal propensity to consume is quite substantial and much larger than that of the government. Thus while public consumption was not responsible for downward drift of the saving ratio, fiscal policies pursued by the government played an important role in inducing the drift.

No less important behind the negative trend in savings was the increasing profligacy of households during the 90s, something which stands in sharp contrast to their behaviour in earlier periods. An increase in household disposable income (at the expense of the government) reduces aggregate saving in the economy; but under normal conditions household saving as a ratio of GDP should rise[71]. The fall of the ratio implies that for every additional rupee households received from the government by way of transfer, they spent more than one rupee on consumption! This pattern of household behaviour stands in sharp contrast to the experience in the 80s: over the period 1981-90, thanks to an increase in the tax-GDP ratio from 15.1 to 17.5 and the government's heavy reliance on monetised deficit to meet the budgetary gap, household disposable income-GDP ratio came down from 81.6 to 79.7 per cent; but even so, household saving as a proportion of gross domestic product recorded an increase of 4.5 percentage points. Over 1990-99 on the other hand the ratio came down from 20.5 to 18.5 per cent though the disposable income-GDP ratio rose steeply, from 80.2 to 85.7 per cent. There was thus a sharp reversal of the earlier trend of household saving and a quantum jump in the private propensity to consume during the 90s. It will take us too far afield to go into the reasons for the jump or to examine to what extent it was induced by government policies themselves[72]. However, the fact remains that in the context of such changes in consumer behaviour, budgetary policies, through their impact on private disposable income, played a major role in driving down the overall saving ratio, instead of raising it to the targetted level.

The 80s and the 90s were marked by contrasting behaviour of public saving as well, but in the opposite direction than that of private saving. During the period 1981-90, the public sector saving declined by nearly 3 percentage points even though there was a rise in the tax-GDP ratio[73]. During the 90s the government on the whole became much more thrifty, especially over 1990-98[74]: despite the fall in the tax-GDP ratio and mounting transfers to the private sector, the period was characterised by an upward trend in public sector saving.

For both analytical and prescriptive purposes it is useful in this regard to consider separately contributions of the two parts of the public sector, viz., Government Administration (and Defence) and public sector undertakings[75] (PSUs). Even though public consumption did not go up during the 90s, the fall in the revenue ratio and substantial transfer payments resulted in large negative savings of Government Administration, as reflected in growing revenue deficits. It was this, rather than the poor performance of public sector undertakings, that accounted for the government's failure to provide a push to the aggregate saving ratio. Indeed, the PSU savings (as a proportional of GDP) after a dip in 1992-93 and 1994-95, has been showing a mildly upward trend since then (Table 6.3), and this, in the context of substantial decline in public sector investment during the reference period, should be regarded as a positive development in operation of this sector, though there is no doubt ample scope for its improvement.

Investment and Public Policies

The decline in aggregate capital formation as a proportion of gross domestic product does not tell the full story of disquieting trends and the government's policy failure in this crucial area. One of the major blemishes of the Indian economy during the 90s consisted in extremely large year-to-year fluctuations in the growth rate of investment (Table 6.3). Such fluctuations not only highten the risk producers face, but also reflect:

(a) lack of stable economic (including policy) environment under which investments can be undertaken on the basis of their long-term returns;

(b) coordination failure in decision making; and

(c) failure of anti-cyclical fiscal and monetary policies.

These deficiencies are inter-related and largely attributable to government policies, or their absence, during the period under consideration. An important reason behind the government's inability to iron out fluctuations and ensure sustained growth in investment and industrial production was its focus on fiscal and monetised deficit, ignoring the fact that what matters for sustainability and allocative efficiency of the budgetary stance is (among other things) the ratios of the relevant variables to full employment rather than actual GDP. Failure of the government to steer the economy close to its full employment growth path implies that private investment can neither be robust nor steady.

The problem on the investment front has been compounded by the on-going and prospective bottlenecks in infrastructural services — a deficiency to which many a commentator has drawn attention. The cutback in government's capital expenditure has taken a heavy toll of investment in infrastructural facilities; nor has the private sector stepped in to fill the void left by the state. The result has been a decline in infrastructural investment, with its ratio to gross domestic product coming down by 1.5 percentage points over 1993-98 (Table 6.3).

Investment in Human Resource Development and Poverty Alleviation

In the context of the huge shortfall of India's indices relating to education and health from those of high performing emerging economies including China, everybody bemoans the low and stagnant social sector expenditure of the government during the last decade (Table 6.3), and emphasises the need for a substantial step-up of public investment in this area, if the country is to enjoy a growth rate of 7 per cent or more on a sustained basis. However, when it comes to suggesting specific steps, there appears to be quite inadequate appreciation of the urgency of the matter: while "desirability" of a cutback in government support to higher education and research has become almost an article of faith in most quarters, the Eleventh Finance Commission has recommended a mere 0.43 percentage point increase for primary education and 0.61 percentage point for the entire social sector between 1999-2000 and 2004-05 — increases which are bound to keep the country lag far behind others in human resource development.

Inadequate investment in primary education and health services will also postpone, as noted in Section III, a lasting resolution of the problems of income inequality and poverty. We have already drawn attention to sharp fluctuations in agricultural growth around a fairly low average during the 90s (Table 6.3). This along with large swings in food price inflation constitutes a major factor behind slow eradication of poverty and its periodic intensity[76]. The source of this trouble is not difficult to trace. The basic reason lies in slowdown in capital accumulation in agriculture. This slowdown started in fact from the 80s and throughout the next decade investment in the sector remained absymally low. The most important factor behind this development was reversal in government policies. As public sector investment was gradually being reduced from the mid-80s, a disproportionate burden of adjustment fell on the agricultural sector. Given the widely observed crowding-in effect of the public on private investment in this sector, it is no wonder, aggregate capital accumulation in agriculture showed a declining trend and performance of the sector, providing source of livelihood for the vast majority of the country's population and determining the incidence of poverty, continues to remain a major source of worry.

Expenditure Priorities and Financing

Before offering our suggestions for fiscal restructuring it is useful to recapitulate the major policy implications of the foregoing analysis. In light of the experience of the Indian economy over the last decade, we have identified the need for:

(i) arresting the slide in aggregate saving and investment, and for their rapid increase;

(ii) stepping up investment in infrastructure and human resource development in order to remove bottlenecks impeding production and capital accumulation in the rest of the economy;

(iii) tackling the problems of mass illiteracy and lack of adequate health services in rural areas on an emergency basis; and

(iv) raising capital accumulation in agriculture and avoiding large year-to-year variations in foodgrains production and prices.

While there is a fair measure of unanimity concerning the needs suggested above, there can be a good deal of disagreement regarding the best way of meeting these needs and the budgetary measures required in this context. Let us first turn to the least controversial of the measures which the fiscal authorities can implement without much difficulty.

Preventing Cyclical Swings and Promoting Growth

One can hardly overemphasise the importance of anti-cyclical fiscal (and monetary) policies for both full utilisation of resources and promotion of investment and growth. However, in the context of sluggish demand producing a sharp deceleration of industrial growth from 1996-97 (Table 6.3), we need to examine whether there are in fact some serious obstacles which have prevented the government in pursing these policies.

Elementary economic logic suggests that, given underutilisation of resources, by increasing its own expenditure, the government also promotes private consumption and investment and helps the economy attain a higher growth trajectory. It is the bugbear of fiscal deficit, it seems, that has held the government back in following an expansionary fiscal programme, even when there is considerable slack in the economy. In terms of our earlier analysis it is not difficult to see how ill-founded the fear is.

First, the increase in fiscal deficit will be significantly less than the rise in government expenditure, as gross domestic product goes up by a multiple of additional government expenditure and the resulting increase in revenue receipts helps meeting part of extra expenses. Second, to the extent government expenditure is on revenue yielding assets and stimulates future growth, current public borrowing need not create future budgetary problems. Third, in the presence of underutilised resources, monetised financing of government expenditure will generally be non-inflationary, nor does such financing raise future debt burden or budgetary difficulties for the exchequer.

Elimination of output gap[77] will enable the government to further economic and social objectives without storing up troubles for the future; but even with no underutilisation of resources, significant changes in the scale and structure of the budget are necessary for removing major impediments to higher growth and elimination of mass poverty.

Expenditure Reforms

Our diagnosis of the ills afflicting the Indian economy calls for substantial increases in government expenditure in quite a few areas. However, since public absorption of resources implies their withdrawal from other uses[78], the nature of restructuring the budget will depend significantly on the efficacy or cost effectiveness of government expenditure[79] in meeting the desired goals. It is the widely held belief regarding the inefficiency and wastage in government's use of resources that makes many an analyst view enhancement of public expenditure with disfavour. Such belief is also one of the main reasons why tax payers may feel little compunction while trying to avoid and evade their dues to the exchequer, nor are such acts of "avoision" regarded as too reprehensible by the general public. Reducing wastage in government expenditure constitutes, to be sure, an important aspect of fiscal correction, but for the present we do not propose to go into these issues while offering our suggestions for expenditure reforms[80].

Consider first the role fiscal policy can play in boosting the level of aggregate capital accumulation in the economy. We have emphasised how and why such a boost requires a substantial step-up in investment in both physical infrastructure and human resource development. Everybody recognises that primary education and basic health services are to be provided by the government and that there is an urgent need for a substantial increase in public expenditure in these areas. In respect of higher education and research there is, it must be recognised, scope for private sector participation. However, given large externalities and significant private risk associated with investment in education and research, the cutback in government expenditure on these items during the 90s appears short-sighted.

So far as physical infrastructure is concerned, it is useful to distinguish between three categories of services. First, in cases like roads, bridges, flood control, canal irrigation and gathering and providing items of information that have important uses for the vast majority of the population, it is not very difficult to see that investment has to be undertaken by the government: the scale of private provisioning of these services, even when possible, will be grossly inadequate and distortionary[81].

Second, both the private and public sector can undertake electricity generation, transport and other activities where externalities are relatively unimportant and beneficiaries can be easily identified and charged for use of services. The only rider here is that private investment is these areas is guided by long-term expectations of future demand, which in its turn depends on how other activities grow in the future. In view of such coordination problems the government has generally to take an active rôle in promotion of such investment either directly or through provision of facilities which, while attracting private investment, should not lead to serious distortions or inefficiencies[82].

Third, for schemes like extension of railways, electricity, telecommunications or other services in some large areas (especially depressed ones), it is possible to levy user charges; but in many of these cases, even when some investment passes the benefit-cost test (for evaluation of large projects), private producers may not be able to break even, or their profits fail to reflect net gains from the investment[83]. Such cases require public support to investment projects, though whether the support should assume the form of direct public investment or of (non-distortionary) inducements to private producers depends on the specifics of the projcct under consideration.

A back-of-the-envelop calculation suggests that if over the next five to six years the investment ratio is to rise from the current rate of about 23.5 per cent to 30 to 31 per cent, the major increase has to be in infrastructure, and the government's financial support in this area needs to go up by 3 to 4 percentage points. This figure needs to be raised by around 1 to 2 percentage points when we bring in the special role of public sector investment in agriculture for a lasting solution to the problem of poverty. Add to that a minimum of 2.5 percentage point increase in education and health, and the additional government expenditure for meeting the objectives of growth and long-term poverty alleviation comes to around 7 percentage points.

What about the scope for economy in government expenditure in other fields? Public consumption as a ratio of gross domestic product did not go up during the 90s. However, the ratio recorded a more than 2 percentage point increase in the 80s and its subsequent stability needs to be judged against the fact that in the process of liberalisation many administrative activities of the government became redundant or lost their earlier importance. There is thus scope for at least a 2 percentage point cutback in public administration without any loss of efficiency.

So far as subsidies are concerned, we have already indicated why their prolonged continuation constitutes a mark of inefficacy of the system in securing the objectives of growth and equity. Except in some exceptional cases[84], public investment in selected areas (like agriculture and backward area development) appears a much more effective means of promoting these objectives than provision of subsidies in various forms[85].

Phased elimination of these items of expenditure should, on the basis of figures for 1998-99, save the government's revenue disbursement by about 0.5 percentage point.

Considerable scope for expenditure reduction, though in the medium and the long run, lies in the sphere of interest payments. However, the process is closely related not only to the size of the gap between government expenditure and total revenue receipts, but also how the gap is financed.

Financing of Government Expenditure

The perception that the heart of the fiscal matter lies in the tax machinery, is amply supported by the Indian experience over the 90s. The declining trend in the household and aggregate saving ratio, mounting public debt and the difficulty of sustaining public investment having large externalities and of expenditure for poverty alleviation – all these may be traced to the government's inability to mop up purchasing power from the private sector. Both for attaining targets relating to aggregate investment and saving and for enabling the government to discharge its other functions effectively, one can hardly overemphasise the need for raising tax collections. The government will be better able to invest in public goods and infrastructure having widespread external effects, the more efficient it is in collecting taxes from the general public. Second, a decline in the tax-GDP ratio tends to raise households' permanent income (and wealth), as there is a jump in expected future disposable income. This not only reduces aggregate saving in the economy (given the differential between the public and household propensity to save), but tends to lower current household saving as well. This perhaps was the main factor behind the household saving paradox noted in Section III and adds to the importance of reversing the trend in the tax-GDP ratio. Remembering that the tax-GDP ratio fell by nearly 3.5 percentage points between 1989-90 and 1999-2000, and that there has been a significant increase in purchasing power in the meanwhile, an increase in the ratio by 4 percentage points during the current quinquennium and by 7 percentage points over the present decade should be feasible and go a long way in reversing the trend in the aggregate saving ratio and easing the government's inter-temporal budget constraint.

Apart from taxation, the other important factor constraining the government's ability to further the basic objectives has been the low and negative returns on public investment in electricity, irrigation and other infrastructural areas. While there is considerable scope for cost cutting in many of these cases, it is also important for the government to earn competitive rates of returns by levying appropriate user changes, where the beneficiaries can be clearly identified. Indeed, to the extent the government is faced with the tax constraint, even some monopoly returns are justified in some cases, remembering that the additional revenue to the government can be employed for raising growth and reducing poverty. However, the first best alternative in these cases, as we have seen, is competitive pricing, and using taxes in order to further distributional objectives. Be that as it may, most observers feel that, in the context of low user charges for most publicly provided private goods, it should not be difficult for the government to raise non-tax revenue by 1 percentage point over the next five years.

The increase in tax and non-tax revenue by 5 percentage points should enable the government to finance the lion's share of additional expenditure under the suggested programme. Indeed, since the enhancements in public absorption are primarily on capital account, the additional receipts will, on the basis of figures for 1999-2000, enable the government to reduce revenue deficits by 6 percentage points. The reduction will in fact amount to a highly respectable 8.5 percentage points if, following the suggestion in Section II, the government's social sector expenditure is treated as capital accumulation. However, for reducing interest burden on public debt, raising aggregate saving to above 30 per cent, and easing the future budget constraint and moving towards the first best alternative, further fiscal restructuring aimed at reducing the cost of government borrowing is of crucial importance.

We have already explained why government reliance on monetised deficit is, within limits, one of the simplest and most effective means of reducing public expenditure when the cost of additional tax collection is prohibitive. Given the fact that monetised deficit was below 1 per cent of GDP over 1996-2000 and that its safe limit is about 2.5 per cent, there can be a 1 percentage point increase in this source of financing without putting too much constraint on the Reserve Bank in its conduct of monetary policy[86].

Second, the government should reduce reliance on tax-free, high-interest borrowing instruments like PPF, NSCs, etc. These modes of financing have raised the interest burden on public debt and the associated increase in government transfer payments has, we have seen, only served to reduce aggregate saving in the economy without promoting distributional objectives[87].

Finally, given the inter-temporal budget constraint, moderate reliance on government borrowing from financial institutions at below market interest rates through requirements like SLR[88] also constitutes a part of a second best programme, provided such borrowing does not put too onerous a burden on the financial sector. Our perception is that requring banks to hold 20 per cent of their unencumbered deposits[89] in government securities at 200 basis points below the market rate will not stand in the way of efficient financial intermediation: remembering that operation of financial institutions depends crucially on investment demand, economic environment and growth, SLR as part of the fiscal reforms programme suggested above should promote rather than impair the health of the country's financial system.

Given the fact that the government's interest obligations currently amount to nearly 6 per cent of GDP, discontinuance of high cost borrowing and turning SLR into an effective instrument should improve the revenue balance of the government by 0.5 to 1.0 percentage point.

Fiscal Restructuring: An Overview

Let us summarise the arithmetic of fiscal restructuring proposed here and indicate how it agrees with and differs from that recommended by the Eleventh Finance Commission (EFC). The changes in the major budgetary items suggested under the EFC and our adjustment programmes are reproduced in Table 6.4. A cursory look at the table shows that there is no disagreement between the two schemes regarding the directions in which the main fiscal parameters are required to be changed[90]. In fact, the extent of scaling down of revenue deficit suggested by the EFC and us are also almost the same. However, a close scrutiny of the table suggests considerable differences in the magnitude of fiscal correction under the two programmes for various items in the revenue and capital budget of the government.

The suggestion in the present paper concerning the overall revenue deficit is quite close to that under the EFC scheme; but the cutback is revenue expenditure is significantly less and the slated receipts substantially larger under our proposal. We have also put much more emphasis on the social sector and suggested steeper cuts in other items of revenue expenditure: the increase in social sector expenditure amounts to 2.5 percentage points in our proposal compared with 0.61 percentage points recommended by the EFC, while the cuts in government administration, interest payments and subsidies under the two programmes total 3.5 and 1.76 percentage points respectively.

TABLE – 6.4

Fiscal Restructuring Programme

(Changes as percentage of Full Employment GDP)

	Our suggestions	Eleventh Finance Commission's recommendations
Revenue Expenditure	-1.0	-2.37
of which		
Social Sector	2.5	0.61
Government Adminstration	-2.0	NA
Interest Payments	-1.0	NA
Subsidies	-0.5	NA
Revenue Receipts	5.0	3.39
of which		
Tax revenue	4.0	2.64
Non-tax revenue	1.0	0.75
Revenue Deficit (conventional)	-6.0	-5.77
Current Deficit (Revenue deficit less social sector expenditure)	-8.5	-6.38
Capital Expenditure (conventional)	4.5	2.44
of which		
Infrastructure (excluding agriculture)	3.5	NA
Agriculture	1.0	NA
Government Investment (including social sector expenditure)	7.0	3.05
Government Borrowing (Fiscal deficit[1])	-1.5	-3.33
of which		
Monetised Deficit	1.0	NA
Fiscal Gap[2]	-2.5	NA

1 : Ignoring Disinvestment
2 : Fiscal gap = Government Borrowing–Monetised Deficit

The most important difference between our and the EFC programme lies in the relative weights attached to increases in saving and capital accumulation, both human and physical. This is reflected first in the substantial gap between adjustments in what we call "current deficit" under the two sets of proposals. The current deficit is nothing but revenue deficit less social sector expenditure, and constitutes a much better index of government's dissaving due to budgetary operations. In view of our emphasis on human resource development and the need for promotion of aggregate saving in the economy, as against the EFC figure of 6.38, we have suggested a cutback in current deficit to the tune of 8.5 percentage points.

Second, the government's (conventionally defined) capital expenditure under our programme is slated to go up by 4.5 and that under the EFC's by 2.44 percentage points. Much larger is the difference in respect of total investment including social sector expenditure: against the 3.05 percentage point increase suggested by the Commission, the increase in our scheme amounts to 7.0 percentage points.

Even though the revenue and current deficits are to fall significantly in our programme, the proposed increases in capital accumulation permit only a 1.5 percentage point fall in government borrowing[91], compared with the much larger cutback at 3.33 percentage points suggested by the EFC. However, in our adjustment programme the "fiscal gap", the more relevant indicator of debt financing, is scheduled to record a not inconsequential 2.5 percentage point decline.

Compared with the restructuring recommended by the Eleventh Finance Commission, our proposals, it seems, are much more drastic in respect of expenditure and taxes, but more moderate regarding fiscal deficit. In the absence of information regarding the estimation procedure behind the Commission's figures, it is difficult to assess the relative efficacy of and implementation problems associated with the two schemes. While there are bound to be differences among economists offering policy prescriptions under a given situation, our plea is that in putting forth the suggestions we have tried to take into account the needs of the economy and the feasibility of the programme in light of macroeconomic and budgetary trends over the last two decades.

V. Conclusions

1. For a given tax-GDP ratio, sustainability of debt financing depends, *a la* Domar, on whether the growth rate of the economy is higher than the government's borrowing rate of interest. Behind the Domar condition, however, lie the more primitive factors like scale of government borrowing for financing public absorption; proportion of consumption and investment in the aggregate expenditure on goods and services by the government; the return on the government's capital expenditure; the extent of monetised deficit; and the patterns of government borrowing from the public. These factors affect sustainability through their impact on the growth rate and/or the net cost of government borrowing.

2. Fiscal deficit is a hybrid concept and not of much significance for judging sustainability of debt financing or the efficacy of the government's budgetary programme for furthering the basic objectives of public policy.

3. In the context of large, pre-existing public debt and the tax constraint faced by the government, not only can the problem of sustainability become quite serious, but the text-book rules regarding the optimal scale and pattern of government expenditure and their modes of financing also require major modifications. The (second best) budgetary programme under the constraint will be characterised by reliance, within limits, on monetised deficit and borrowing through instruments like SLR; greater emphasis on government investment, especially those generating direct returns; and short- as also long-term measures aimed at reduction of pre-tax-transfer income inequality and poverty.

4. Though the Indian scenario does not as yet suggest that the country is heading toward an internal debt trap, there were quite a few disquieting developments during the 90s on both the macroeconomic and fiscal front. The most important of these were decline and stagnation of aggregate investment and saving ratios; low agricultural growth along with sharp year-to-year fluctuations in foodgrains price inflation and output growth; deceleration of industrial growth during the second half of the decade; and decline in the tax-GDP ratio, fall in public investment and rise in revenue deficit.

5. So far as the expenditure side of the budget is concerned, the adjustment programme suggested here includes substantial increases in government expenditure on investment, especially in agriculture and infrastructural facilities; roll-back of public consumption expenditure to the level obtaining in the early 80s; a decline in subsidies that affect current rather than future production and income distribution; and a considerable increase in social sector expenditure in general and primary education and health services in particular. On the financing side, we have suggested restoration of the tax-GDP ratio to its late 80's level; greater reliance on monetised deficit than in the 90s; termination of high cost instruments of government borrowings; and moderate deployment of instruments like SLR.

Notes

1. Unless mentioned otherwise figures relating to fiscal deficit and other variables refer to those of the Union and State governments taken together.
2. We should add that the Finance Commission does not explicitly specify the length of time over which the target for the debt-GDP ratio is to be reached, though it is possible to work this out from other fiscal targets and the Commission's assumptions relating to GDP growth and other trends.
3. As distinguished from the existence of a large public debt.
4. So long as it is not externally held. In the present paper we do not go into the problem of external debt, since it raises a different set of issues.
5. The effect will not operate if households, *a la* the Ricardian equivalence theory, are "rational", take into account the future tax liabilities or cutback in provision of public goods and services on account of interest payments on public debt and put the consumption of their descendents on the same footing as that of their own—conditions which are unlikely to be satisfied in full. See Barro (1974) in this connection.
6. See the Appendix for details of the canonical model and some of its extensions.
7. Public consumption is that part of revenue expenditure of the government which involves use of real resources like labour or material. Hence interest payments and subsidies do not constitute public consumption.
8. An increase in private consumption need not have an adverse impact on growth when the economy has excess capacity. In the Appendix the canonical results are drawn on the assumption of full employment of resources. It is true that long run growth in the neoclassical model is independent of saving or investment ratios; but the result holds only in the very long run. In the intermediate run, spanning a period of upto 20 to 30 years, changes in the investment ratio will have a considerable impact on the economy's growth rate. Note also that the new growth theories have reestablished the (Harrod-Domar) positive association between higher growth and higher investment ratios even in the long run.
9. Given the relevant set of information, one may work out how an increase in the ratio of debt-financed public consumption to GDP affects the interest rate and growth rate, and hence locate the value of the ratio at which the former exceeds the latter.
10. As also the optimality issue, as we shall discuss in the next section.
11. Recall that public debt creates difficulties primarily through its impact on private consumption and distortions due to taxes and transfers, required for its servicing. These effects do not arise unless the expenditure programme of the central bank is not in consonance with the objectives the government seeks to promote. For examining the debt related issues one has in fact to consider the consolidated accounts and balance sheets of all parts of the state sector, including public undertakings.
12. This neglect is however in accord with the assumption that government expenditure is entirely on consumption or transfers.
13. The implication is that government's revenue deficit equals interest payments.
14. In this connection it is important to distinguish between the sustainability condition and the requirement that the net asset of the government, given by the

discounted sum of all future revenue receipts less that of revenue expenses of the government, must not be negative. Note that in the canonical model the net asset position of the government is negative, but the fiscal stance may well be sustainable. Similarly, the government's net asset is negative when the return on public investment is not enough to meet interest charges, but debt-financing of such investment is likely to be sustainable.

15. In addition to loans for interest payments.

16. Note that even when there is some crowding out effect of government borrowing on private investment, the effect will not generally be one-to-one, as we shall presently see. Be that as it may, the relevant point here is that the aggregate investment in the economy will be larger when government absorption takes the form of investment rather than public consumption.

17. Indeed, the salubrious effects of an increase in government expenditure will then be more pronounced with debt- compared with tax-financing.

18. Thus government expenditure financed through credit from the central bank may well reduce the rate of interest. In this case the crowding-in effect is indubitable.

19. The basic point to note here is that when asset holders find shares or other financial instruments more attractive compared with bank deposits, there will be an increase in the flow of funds outside the banking sector, without any decrease in the supply of aggregate bank finance. See Rakshit (1997) for a theory of the flow of funds within and outside the banking system.

20. Even under tax financing, investment tends to fall with an increase in interest rates (remembering that taxes reduce both consumption and private saving). Since borrowing *per se* does not reduce consumption, in this case the rise in interest rates is steeper and the fall in private investment larger.

21. Note that we are talking of intended, not actual investment, which will be governed by the interaction of the real and financial sectors.

22. Or which tend to depress the private propensity to invest.

23. See Rakshit (1997) for a discussion on these issues.

24. Note that compared with public consumption or investment, government disbursements by way of transfer and subsidies are more likely to raise private investment when they raise investment demand and there is financial crowding in.

25. Also relevant in this connection is Rakshit (1991).

26. Or for optimality, as may be seen from our discussion in the next section.

27. The reason is fairly simple. In a growing economy the demand for real balances and hence for reserve money (in real terms) rise over time. This creates scope for some non-inflationary monetised financing of government expenditure.

28. Disinvestment and recovery of loans constitute flow of finance from the rest of the economy to the government; so does government borrowing from the public.

29. To take a simple example, let r be the interest on public debt, i the interest on loans advanced by the government and d the expected average rate of return on (the current market value) of shares proposed to be sold. In this case r-d, r-i, and r respectively indicate the *net* impact on future revenue earnings per year following a unit reduction in fiscal deficit through disinvestment, recovery of loans and tax or non-tax revenue.

30. To see why, let *d* be the expected annual dividend per share, r the government's borrowing rate of interest, *r'(>r)* the interest rate for private agents and $\breve{\partial}$ the risk premium for holding shares (instead of bonds). The sale price per share is then approximated by $d/(r'+\breve{\partial})$ which, when used to cut fiscal deficit, saves the government $d.r/(r'+\breve{\partial})$ in terms of interest payments per year. Note however that, with $r'+\breve{\partial} > r$, the fall in the government's future annual revenue due to disinvestment *per se*, viz., *d*, is higher than the saving in interest payments. Hence the erosion of budgetary viability.

31. Let disinvestment and the accompanying measures raise the dividend per share of the company from *d* to *d**. Following the argument of the previous footnote, under the disinvestment package the government gets $d^{*}/(r+\breve{\partial})$ per share which, when used to reduce fiscal deficit, reduces the government's interest payments per annum by $r.d^{*}/(r'+\breve{\partial})$. Since the government loses *d* per annum by selling one share, the disinvestment package will promote budgetary viability provided $r.d^{*} > (r'+\breve{\partial})d$.

32. Consider the example in the previous footnote. If the measures other than disinvestment raise the rate of dividend to *d**, by not disinvesting, the government earns *d** per share, which is larger than the saving in interest payments through disinvestment, viz., $r.d^{*}/(r'+\breve{\partial})$. It may easily be shown that if the accompanying measures without disinvestment raises the dividend rate to $\hat{d}$, lying between *d* and *d**, it is better not to disinvestment so long as $\hat{d} > r.d^{*}/(r'+\pi)$.

33. Apart from the objective of full employment of resources, which we ignore here. The ultimate goal is promotion of social welfare for which the intermediate targets constitute the means.

34. The implication is that in any period, given the full employment output and the (desired) distribution of income, the private propensity to save is taken to be the optimum.

35. Note that when the distribution is ideal and private agents are taken to be the best judge of their own welfare, except in the case of externalities there is no need for differential investment or consumption taxes (e.g., those on tobacco).

36. The basic economic rationale of government's use of resources in this connection lies in non-excludability in provision of public services and non-rivalry of consumers in the use of these goods. Thus, benefits enjoyed by a person due to peaceful law and order situation does not reduce the extent of such benefits to the person's neighbours. Nor is it possible in a locality to permit only a select few to enjoy such benefits and exclude others.

37. Other than the excess of subsidy over taxes on private investment.

38. The reason is that financing current expenditure through borrowing or capital expenditure through taxes distorts the society's choice between current and future consumption. Note also that an item of expenditure is treated as capital when its benefits accrue in the subsequent periods, not currently. Hence that part of investment subsidy which is not met through taxation of investment should be treated at par with the conventional capital expenditure of the government for deciding on the mode of financing.

39. It is interesting to note that the Union Government has made essentially the same point before the Eleventh Finance Commission.

40. To the extent tax reforms and better administration can reduce these costs, the economy can move closer to the first best solution. Our focus in this subsection is however on the nature of the budgetary programme, given the tax constraint in force.

41. There are other problems like inefficiency of government administration and enterprises that bedevil developing economies like India. Administrative reforms and public sector reforms should no doubt form an important part of fiscal correction; but so long as taxes are not distortionary, inefficiency in other spheres changes the scale and composition of the optimum budget, but not the principles laid down for its formulation.

42. So that the second best optimum levels of all items of government expenditure may be expected to be smaller than their first best counterparts. It may also seem reasonable to start with the adjustable items in the short run and then try to reduce others over time.

43. In a growing economy inflation does not occur until monetised deficit goes beyond some point. After this point (until the seniorage reaches the maximum level) one has to consider the distortionary effects of inflation on the one hand and gains due to easing of the budget constraint on the other.

44. These agents' optimum pattern of asset holding displays corner solution, to use economists' jargon.

45. Because of an increase in GDP growth.

46. The implication, we emphasise, is not total exclusion of such items of investment, but only their smaller scale compared with the ideal situation where these externalities do not produce any tax constraint.

47. By public or private enterprises. In the case of private enterprises, the government will appropriate the surplus by way of license fees, auctions or other devices.

48. Since investments having large externalities or producing public goods add less to government's future revenue than those yielding direct returns, given the problem of taxing income generated elsewhere.

49. Note that we are not considering here public distribution system which requires direct government intervention in distribution of foodgrains.

50. We are referring to current supply of water and health services, not setting up of health centres or installation of new tubewells.

51. The distinction between current and capital expenditure should in principle be based on the basis of whether the expenditure enhances current or future well-being. Note that to the extent current expenditure on employment schemes or health services contributes toward future production or improvement of income distribution, part of the expenditure should be treated as capital disbursement.

52. Recall that under this solution no capital expenditure is involved for meeting income distributional objectives and the entire amount of current expenditure takes the form of income transfer and is financed through taxes.

53. The extent of "inefficieny" or loss of output is not however as large as it may appear at first sight. As students of welfare economics are told at the very beginning, the relative prices characterising conditions of allocative efficiency and all that are by no means sacrosanct and depend on the initial distribution of income earning assets, both tangible and intangible. In the first best solution the relative prices correspond to an equitable income distribution — a far cry from any actual situation. Again, some of the measures under the revised programme

also go against the principle of allocating domestic resources on the basis of border prices of goods (*a la* the theory of comparative advantage), and thus reduce the community's potential levels of consumption and investment. However, unless there is an easy means of income redistribution, "maximisation" at border prices may leave untouched, if not aggravate, the problem of poverty.

54. This is not to suggest that the special steps actually taken in countries like India have been optimal.

55. Ours is an overestimate, since, because of non-availabilty of the required data, new Treasury Bills issued, but retired within the year, do not form part of the denominator, but interest paid thereon is included in the numerator.

56. For checking on the sustainability condition, we need to consider either the nominal values of the interest rate and the growth rate or their real values. Note also that what is relevant for sustainability is the average values over a considerable period of time.

57. As discussed in Section II.

58. IFL is nothing but fiscal deficit plus non-debt creating capital receipts. We have discussed in Section II why such receipts are required to be taken into account for examining sustainability.

59. Borrowings here include monetised deficit and non-debt creating capital receipts.

60. Due to data limitations we have not taken into account interest on borrowing from the public (other than the RBI) separately. But this does not affect our main conclusions.

61. Note that there was no significant upward trend in the government's borrowing rate so that this was not very important behind the rising net interest cost of debt financing. Abstraction from RBI financing, which came down sharply over the reference period, makes the time trend of the estimated net cost of government borrowing less steep; but the conclusion regarding the impact of changes in the relative importance of revenue deficit and capital expenditure is not affected thereby.

62. Short-run changes in the differential may be due to operation of cyclical factors and should not be given undue importance. Thus, in 1991-92 (and also partly in 1994-95), the large growth-net interest cost differential was due primarily to spurt in inflation. What is relevant for sustainability is the long-term trend of the differential.

63. Apart from the problem regarding the prospective growth rate to which we turn in the next subsection.

64. Note that we take into account returns on government assets while estimating the net interest cost of government borrowing.

65. Not to past borrowings.

66. See the Appendix.

67. Note that services are either intermediate inputs or consumption items. In the absence of adequate growth elsewhere in the economy, the tertiary sector cannot but be hit, sooner or later, by a demand constraint, remembering that export of services constitutes a small fraction of the total. Again, to the extent production of services requires inputs from other sectors, there will be supply constraint due to slowdown in the growth of productive capacity in the rest of the economy.

68. Consisting of household and private corporate saving.

69. Note that while both household and public capital accumulation came down sharply over the reference period, investment in the private corporate sector as a proportion of GDP increased by more than 4 percentage points (Table 3).

70. This refers to revenue expenditure of the government less transfer payments like interest and subsidies — items which do not involve absorption of goods and services by the government.

71. The reason is that both the marginal propensity to consume and save are positive fractions.

72. The hypothesis, that the reforms measures, by promoting "consumerism", were responsible for private profligacy, may have some validity, but is extremely difficult to verify.

73. As we have noted elsewhere (Rakshit, 1994), public sector consumption played a no mean role in driving aggregate demand and growth during the 80s.

74. i.e., if we exclude the year 1998-99.

75. Whose accounts do not form part of the government budget.

76. We do not go into the inconclusive debate regarding whether or to what extent poverty fell during the 90s. The important point to note in this connection is that the incidence of poverty can vary widely from one year to another: in years of high agricultural production and low food prices, the poverty ratio goes down; but the opposite happens in the event of harvest failure and high food price inflation.

77. Given by the difference between the full employment and actual output.

78. Remember, we are considering the reforms measures when there is no slack in the economy.

79. In relation to the marginal benefits of using the resources elsewhere.

80. While drawing up the government's expenditure programme, the relative efficacy of private and public use of resources in promoting social and economic goals is no doubt to be taken into account. However, it is by no means clear that government inefficiency justifies lowering of all types of government expenditure. For meeting urgent needs like law and order, prevention of epidemics, promotion of literacy or avoidance of mass starvation and death, larger allocations are required when nothing can be done to reduce the leakage. Quite clearly, as far as possible expenditure programmes need to contain built-in safeguards against wastages.

81. Thus, private production may be sustained through tolls for use of roads and bridges, or through charges for access to information; but the resulting investment and production in these areas will not only be quite suboptimal, but the pattern of resources used for providing the services will also be inefficient.

82. The implication is that the government avoid schemes like guaranteed returns on capital which tend to produce gross inefficiencies in both investment and production.

83. This may be true even when the gain is purely economic, rather than income-distributional or social. The reason is that through pricing producers appropriate only the marginal gain multiplied by the quantity bought, so that users are left with substantial net surpluses when the project is fairly large. This is why extension of railway lines or electricity to some area raises house rents and land

prices in the locality, even though railway fares or electricity charges are fixed entirely on the basis of profitability considerations.

84. We have suggested above how public support may be required to induce private investment in some infrastructural projects.

85. The most controversial in this respect are subsidies on food and fertiliser. There are several factors that need consideration here. First, it is often argued, e.g., by the Planning Commission, that water and fertiliser subsidies have resulted in degradation of the soil and fertility. However, this impact is due primarily to farmers' lack of knowledge or absence of telescopic faculty solution to which lies more in spread of information or awareness than in withdrawal of subsidy. Second, text-book principles do suggest that all input subsidies constitute inefficient means of raising production. The recommended mode for the purpose is output subsidy along with easy availability of all inputs, including credit, at market prices. But devising an effective output subsidy is by no means simple in countries like India. Thus, subsidy on marketed output neither meets the condition for allocative efficiency, not is defensible on distributional grounds, since the scheme leaves out small and marginal farmers producing primarily for self consumption. Third, while input subsidies may raise production, contain food price inflation and help small farmers to some extent, apart from allocative inefficiencey, one has to take into account the opportunity cost of government expenditure on these heads. Compared with public investment in agriculture and rural development, government expenditure on subsidies may appear less efficient in promoting growth and alleviating poverty. However, in an overall restructuring, it is not clear whether or to what extent they are to be reduced immediately, when judged against a variety of government expenditure which are not only inefficient, but have also a negative impact on income distribution.

86. This policy relates to the management of external balance, not macro stabilisation, since we are considering a budgetary programme with no output gap.

87. Apart from the fact that the benefits of these high cost borrowings accrue mostly to income tax payers who form a tiny part of total population, we need to consider the opportunity cost in terms of foregone public investment aimed at poverty alleviation. We have also argued elsewhere (Rakshit, 1991) that these financial instruments do not promote even private saving, since they affect primarily the allocation of saving between different financial assets, rather than their total.

88. Note that the SLR requirement implies a mode of taxation only to the extent bank holding of SLR bonds is in excess of what otherwise would have been held. In India this requirement is no longer an indirect means of taxation, since over the last 6 to 7 years bank holding of SLR securities has exceeded their stipulated minimum.

89. With corresponding changes in the ratios for other financial institutions.

90. Since for quite a few items the figures under the EFC programme are not available, it is difficult to say whether the agreement extends to all major fiscal variables.

91. Since we have not considered disinvestment, standing as it does on a completely different footing from that for ordinary capital receipts, government borrowing would be the same as fiscal deficit, properly defined. In order to make the two figures comparable, we have also ignored disinvestment proceeds implicit in the EFC figures for fiscal adjustment.

References

Barro, R. (1974), "Are Government Bonds Net Wealth?", *Journal of Political Economy* (82), November.

E. Domar (1944), "The 'Burden' of Public Debt and the National Income", *American Economic Review*, Vol 34.

Government of India (2000), *Report of the Eleventh Finance Commission.*

Rakshit, M. (1991), "The Macroeconomic Adjustment Programme: A Critique", *Economic and Political Weekly*, 24 August.

——— (1994), "Issues in Structural Adjustment of the Indian Economy", in Edmar L. Bacha (ed.), *Economics in a Changing World: Development, Trade and Environment* (Macmillan: London).

——— (1997), "Money, Credit and Government Finances in a Developing Economy", published in Bose, Rakshit and Sinha (eds.), *Issues in Economic Theory and Public Policy* (Oxford University Press: New Delhi).

Samuelson, P.A. (1954), "The Pure Theory of Public Expenditure", *Review of Economics and Statistics*, November.

7

Fiscal and Budgetary Developments

(Economic Survey 2004-05)

Fiscal consolidation has been high among the reform priorities of the Government. Recent initiatives include pre-payment of high cost external debt, buyback of high cost domestic debt, introduction of contributory pension scheme for new entrants to Government service, widening of the tax base and phased withdrawal of tax exemptions. The current year marks a watershed in fiscal reforms in more than one way. First, the Fiscal Responsibility and Budget Management (FRBM) Act, 2003 has been operationalised with the notification of rules in July, 2004. Under the provisions of the Act and the rules, the Government is mandated to eliminate revenue deficit by March, 2009 and restrict its borrowings within certain limits. Second, the decision of States to introduce value added tax (VAT) from April 1, 2005 marks the culmination of efforts that began almost a decade ago at reforming the domestic trade taxes. The introduction of State-level VAT would help ameliorate the present cascading nature of taxation of commodities and eventually facilitate the establishment of a national common market for goods and services. The NCMP aims at sustaining an average real GDP growth of 7 to 8 per cent per annum. The operationalisation of FRBM Act and the proposed introduction of VAT are expected to help in creating conditions that are necessary for sustaining the growth of the economy with macro-economic stability as envisaged in the National Common Minimum Programme (NCMP).

Fiscal consolidation, after a promising start in the early 1990s, had started deteriorating since 1997-98. Fiscal deficit, a comprehensive indicator of fiscal health, after declining from 6.6 per cent of GDP in 1990-91 to 4.1 per cent of GDP in 1996-97 started rising continuously to reach 6.2 per cent of GDP in 2001-02 (Table 7.1). Thereafter, it started declining to a level of 4.6 per cent of GDP in 2003-04 (Prov.)[1]. It is budgeted to decline marginally to 4.4 per cent of GDP in 2004-05. Revenue deficit, which in recent years constituted over 70 per cent of fiscal deficit, has followed a similar trend. Rising interest payments, expenditure on subsidies, pay and allowances, and pensions coupled with a near stagnant tax-GDP ratio have mainly contributed to the worsening of the revenue balance. Revenue deficit after reaching a peak of 4.4 per cent of GDP in 2001-02 and remaining at the same level in 2002-03, declined by 0.8 percentage points to 3.6 per cent of GDP in 2003-04 (Prov). With the operationalisation of FRBM Act, fiscal consolidation is expected to gain momentum.

TABLE – 7.1

Trends in Deficits of Central Government

Year	Revenue deficit	Primary deficit	Fiscal deficit	Revenue deficit as per cent of fiscal deficit
	(As per cent of GDP)			
1990-91	3.3	2.8	6.6	49.4
1991-92	2.5	0.7	4.7	52.7
1992-93	2.5	0.6	4.8	51.7
1993-94	3.8	2.2	6.4	59.2
1994-95	3.1	0.4	4.7	64.6
1995-96	2.5	0.0	4.2	59.2
1996-97	2.4	-0.2	4.1	58.2
1997-98	3.1	0.5	4.8	63.5
1998-99	3.8	0.7	5.1	74.8
1999-2000	3.5	0.7	5.4	64.6
2000-01	4.1	0.9	5.7	71.7
2001-02	4.4	1.5	6.2	71.1
2002-03	4.4	1.1	5.9	74.4
2003-04 (Prov.)*	3.6	0.1	4.6	78.0
2004-05 (BE)#	2.5	0.3	4.4	55.4

* Provisional and unaudited as reported by Controller General of Accounts, Department of Expenditure, Ministry of Finance.

\# The ratios to GDP for 2004-05 (BE) are based on CSO's Advance Estimates released in February, 2005.

Note : 1. Ratios to GDP at current market prices.
2. Fiscal deficit excludes transfer of states' share in small savings collections.

Source: Budget documents.

The fiscal health of the State Governments has been equally worrisome. Fiscal consolidation efforts at the State level have not been significant. Five States have so far enacted fiscal responsibility legislations. As a proportion of GDP, fiscal deficit of States after declining from 4.7 per cent in 1999-00 to 4.3 per cent in 2000-01, worsened to 5.1 per cent in 2003-04 Revised Estimates (RE). The fiscal deficit of States is budgeted to come down to 3.6 per cent of GDP in 2004-05. As a proportion of GDP, revenue deficit of States increased from 0.9 per cent in 1990-91 to 2.8 per cent in 1999-2000. After declining to 2.2 per cent of GDP by 2002-03, revenue deficit increased again to 2.6 per cent of GDP in 2003-04 (RE). Revenue deficit of States is placed at 1.4 per cent of GDP in 2004-05 Budget Estimates (BE). The pay revision effected by States, following the Fifth Central Pay Commission's award and its implementation by the Central Government, and declining transfers from the Centre as a proportion of GDP, contributed to the deterioration of State finances. A number of initiatives have been taken by the Centre and the States to remedy the situation. These include medium term fiscal reforms programme, debt swap scheme and lowering of interest on Central loans to States.

Budgetary Developments in 2004-05

The Budget for 2004-05 has been formulated against the backdrop of the commitments made in the NCMP. The Budget has indicated that the Government will follow a 5-year road map to achieve the NCMP objective of bringing about rapid growth with stability and equity. For realising the NCMP objectives of maintaining an average annual growth rate of 7-8 per cent, providing access to quality basic education, assuring 100 days' of employment to the needy, focusing on agriculture and infrastructure, and fiscal consolidation, the Budget for 2004-05 has laid emphasis on enhancing investment, both public and private as well as domestic and foreign. The Budget for 2004-05 has attempted a front-loaded fiscal adjustment by targeting a revenue deficit of 2.5 per cent of GDP as against 3.6 per cent in 2003-04 (RE) and a fiscal deficit of 4.4 per cent of GDP as against 4.8 per cent of GDP in 2003-04 (RE). The reductions in revenue and fiscal deficits budgeted in 2004-05 are more than the minimum reductions stipulated in the rules framed under FRBM Act. The rules stipulate minimum reductions of 0.5 percentage points of GDP in revenue deficit and 0.3 percentage points of GDP in fiscal deficit.

Revenue Receipts

Budget for 2004-05 aims at a front-loaded and revenue led fiscal consolidation. It envisages a 24.6 per cent growth in gross tax revenue to Rs.3,17,733 crore over 2003-04(RE). Non-tax revenue of Rs.75,416 crore budgeted for 2004-05 is marginally lower than the revised estimate of Rs.75,488 crore in 2003-04. (Table 7.2). The higher budgeted growth in gross tax revenue is based on continuing momentum in direct tax collections and concerted efforts proposed for recovery of arrears. Lower non-tax revenue budgeted for 2004-05 is on account of lower dividends and profits assumed for the year. The share of direct taxes is budgeted to improve from 40.6 per cent in 2003-04 (RE) to 43.9 per cent in 2004-05.

TABLE – 7.2

Receipts and Expenditure of the Central Government

	1990-91	1999-00	2000-01	2001-02	2002-03	2003-04 (R.E.)	2003-04@ (Prov.)	2004-05## (B.E.)
				(As per cent of GDP)				
1. Revenue receipts (a+b)	9.7	9.4	9.2	8.9	9.4	9.5	9.5	10.0
(a) Tax revenue (net of States' share)	7.6	6.6	6.5	5.9	6.5	6.8	6.8	7.5
(b) Non-tax revenue	2.1	2.7	2.7	3.0	2.9	2.7	2.8	2.4
2. Revenue expenditure	12.9	12.9	13.3	13.3	13.8	13.1	13.1	12.4
of which:								
(a) Interest payments	3.8	4.7	4.8	4.7	4.8	4.3	4.5	4.2
(b) Major subsidies	1.7	1.2	1.2	1.3	1.7	1.6	1.6	1.4
(c) Defence expenditure	1.9	1.8	1.8	1.7	1.7	1.6	1.5	1.4
3. Revenue deficit (2-1)	3.3	3.5	4.1	4.4	4.4	3.6	3.6	2.5
4. Capital receipts	5.6	6.0	6.4	7.1	7.4	7.7	7.6	5.4
of which:								
(a) Recovery of loans	1.0	0.5	0.6	0.7	1.4	1.2	2.4	0.9
(b) Other receipt (mainly PSU disinvestment)	0.0	0.1	0.1	0.2	0.1	0.5	0.6	0.1
(c) Borrowings and other liabilities	4.6	5.4	5.7	6.2	5.9	4.8	4.6	4.4
5. Capital expenditure	4.4	2.5	2.3	2.7	3.0	4.0	4.0	3.0

Contd....

... *Table 7.2 Contd....*

6. Total expenditure [2+5=6(a)+6(b)]	17.3	15.4	15.6	15.9	16.8	17.2	17.1	15.4
of which:								
(a) Plan expenditure	5.0	3.9	4.0	4.5	4.5	4.4	4.4	4.7
(b) Non-Plan expenditure	12.3	11.5	11.6	11.5	12.3	12.8	12.7	10.7
7. Fiscal deficit [6-1-4(a)-4(b)]	6.6	5.4	5.7	6.2	5.9	4.8	4.6	4.4
8. Primary deficit [7-2(a)=8(a)+8(b)]	2.8	0.7	0.9	1.5	1.1	0.3	0.1	0.3
(a) Primary deficit consumption	1.1	0.8	1.1	1.6	1.6	0.8	-	-0.1
(b) Primary deficit investment	1.7	-0.1	-0.2	-0.1	-0.5	-0.5	-	0.4

@ Provisional and unaudited as reported by Controller General of Accounts, Department of Expenditure, Ministry of Finance

The Ratio of GDP for 2004-05 (BE) are based on CSO's Advance Estimates released in February 2005..

Note : 1. The figures may not add up to the total because of rounding approximations.

2. Primary deficit consumption = Revenue deficit-interest payments+interest receipts + dividend & profits

3. Primary deficit investment = Capital expenditure-interest receipts - Dividend & profits-recovery of loans-other receipts.

4. Figures are exclusive of the transfer of States' share in the small savings collections.

Source: Budget documents.

The tax-GDP ratio of the Centre has been consistently lower than the level of 10.3 per cent achieved in 1991-92. The tax structure continues to be characterised by reliance on commodity taxes, though the share of direct taxes in total tax revenue has been increasing gradually. There has been an improvement in the ratios of personal income tax and corporate income tax to GDP. The improvement is much greater in the case of corporate income tax. Since 1990-91, there has been a conscious effort to reduce the rates of commodity taxes, both customs and excise. In respect of customs, initially the reductions in duty rates were attributable to multilateral trade agreement induced commitments under the aegis of the World Trade Organisation (WTO). The Government's policy is to go beyond the WTO commitments and align customs duty rates gradually to ASEAN levels to make Indian industry internationally competitive. The lower tax-GDP ratio can be attributed to the fall in indirect tax to GDP ratio from 7.9 per cent in 1990-91 to 5.4 per cent in

2003-04 (RE). The ratio is budgeted to improve to 5.7 per cent in 2004-05. Within indirect taxes, the fall in tax-GDP ratio is more distinct in the case of customs duties. In central excise duties, the policy focus has been on reducing dispersion in rates and lowering of rates. This has resulted in a decline in excise to GDP ratio from 4.3 per cent in 1990-91 to 3.3 per cent in 2003-04 (RE). The budget estimates indicate an improvement in this ratio to 3.5 per cent in 2004-05 (Table 7.3). To

TABLE – 7.3

Sources of Tax Revenue

	1990-91 Actuals	1999-2000 Actuals	2000-01 Actuals	2001-02 Actuals	2002-03 Actuals	2003-04 (RE)	2003-04@ (Prov.)	2004-05 (BE)
	Tax revenue as per cent of gross tax revenue							
Direct (a)	19.1	33.7	36.2	37.0	38.4	40.6	41.4	43.9
PIT	9.3	14.9	16.8	17.1	17.0	15.8	16.3	16.0
CIT	9.3	17.9	18.9	19.6	21.3	24.7	25.0	27.8
Indirect (b)	78.4	65.5	62.9	62.1	60.7	58.9	57.9	55.9
Customs	35.9	28.2	25.2	21.5	20.7	19.4	19.1	17.1
Excise	42.6	36.0	36.3	38.8	38.1	36.2	35.7	34.4
Service tax	0.0	1.2	1.4	1.8	1.9	3.3	3.1	4.5
	Tax revenue as per cent of gross domestic product*							
Direct (a)	1.9	3.0	3.3	3.0	3.4	3.7	3.8	4.5
PIT	0.9	1.3	1.5	1.4	1.5	1.5	1.5	1.6
CIT	0.9	1.6	1.7	1.6	1.9	2.3	2.3	2.8
Indirect (b)	7.9	5.8	5.7	5.1	5.3	5.4	5.3	5.7
Customs	3.6	2.5	2.3	1.8	1.8	1.8	1.8	1.7
Excise	4.3	3.2	3.3	3.2	3.3	3.3	3.3	3.5
Service tax	0.0	0.1	0.1	0.1	0.2	0.3	0.3	0.5
Total#	10.1	8.9	9.0	8.2	8.8	9.2	9.2	10.2

@ Figures for 2003-04 are provisional accounts (unaudited) released by the Controller General of Accounts.

* Refers to gross domestic product at current market prices.

\# Includes taxes referred in (a) & (b) and taxes of Union Territories and "other" taxes.

PIT : Personal income tax CIT : Corporation tax

Note : (1) Direct taxes also includes taxes pertaining to expenditure, interest, wealth, gift and estate duty.

(2) The ratios to GDP for 2004-05 (BE) are based on CSO's Advance Estimates released in February, 2005.

Source: Budget documents

enhance indirect tax collections, the main strategy adopted has been the extension of the service tax base. From a modest level of Rs.407 crore in 1994-95, service tax is budgeted to yield a revenue of Rs.14,150 crore in 2004-05.

Expenditure Trends

As a proportion of GDP, aggregate expenditure of the Central Government, after declining almost continuously from 17.3 per cent in 1990-91 to 13.9 per cent in 1996-97, started rising from 1997-98 to reach 17.2 per cent in 2003-04 (RE). It is budgeted to come down to 15.4 per cent in 2004-05. While the level of expenditure is not very high by international comparison, the main problem in public expenditure management has been the poor quality outcomes of such expenditure. Furthermore, the composition of expenditure has deteriorated, with capital expenditure squeezed out by growing revenue expenditure. As a proportion of GDP, revenue expenditure increased from 12.9 per cent in 1990-91 to 13.8 per cent in 2002-03. In contrast, capital expenditure as a proportion of GDP declined from 4.4 per cent to 3.0 per cent in the same period. The year 2003-04 witnessed an improvement in the composition of expenditure with the revenue expenditure-GDP ratio coming down to 13.1 per cent and the ratio of capital expenditure to GDP improving to 4.0 per cent. The compression in the growth of revenue expenditure has been carried forward in the Budget for 2004-05. The revenue expenditure-GDP ratio budgeted for 2004-05 is lower by 0.7 percentage points at 12.4 per cent. A redeeming feature is that the compression is entirely on non-Plan account from 10.3 per cent of GDP in 2003-04 (RE) to 9.5 per cent of GDP in 2004-05. A marginal improvement in Plan revenue expenditure by 0.2 percentage points to 3.0 per cent of GDP is envisaged in 2004-05. The budgeted capital expenditure is lower at 3.0 per cent of GDP. Important components of expenditure are analysed below.

Interest Payments

As a proportion of GDP, interest payments increased from 3.8 per cent in 1990-91, to 4.8 per cent in 2002-03. With the softening of interest rates, the proportion declined to 4.5 per cent in 2003-04 (RE) and is budgeted at 4.2 per cent in 2004-05. The debt build-up, consequent upon high levels of fiscal deficits, has resulted in preemption of a disproportionately large part of revenue receipts by interest outgo. The proportion of interest payments to revenue receipts, which rose from 39.1 per cent in 1990-91 to 53.4 per cent in 2001-02, has been declining in recent years and is budgeted at 41.9 per cent in 2004-05

(BE). The average cost of total internal liabilities, which rose from 8.2 per cent in 1990-91 to 10.3 per cent in 1999-2000, has shown a declining trend in recent years on account of soft interest rates and elongation in the maturity of Government securities. The estimated average cost of internal liabilities in 2004-05 is 8.8 per cent (Table 7.4). Interest expenditure in 2004-05 (BE) includes, for the first time, interest payable on borrowings under the market stabilisation scheme (MSS), for the purpose of absorption of excess liquidity in the system.

TABLE – 7.4

Interest on Outstanding Internal Liabilities of Central Government

	Outstanding internal liabilities	Interest on internal liabilities*	Average cost of borrowings (per cent per annum)
	(Rs. crore)		
1990-91	283033	19664	8.2
1991-92	317714	23892	8.4
1992-93	359654	27546	8.7
1993-94	430623	33017	9.2
1994-95	487682	40034	9.3
1995-96	554984	45631	9.4
1996-97	621438	55255	10.0
1997-98	722962	61527	9.9
1998-99	834551	73519	10.2
1999-00	933000	85741	10.3
2000-01	1047976	94900	10.2
2001-02	1196245	103175	9.8
2002-03	1323704	113238	9.5
2003-04 (RE)	1444104	117332	8.9
2004-05 (BE)	1621245	126870	8.8

* Excludes Rs.313.61 crore and Rs. 4079.62 crore towards premium on account of domestic debt buyback scheme and prepayment of external debt for 2002-03 and 2003-04(RE) respectively.

Note : 1. Average cost of borrowing is the percentage of interest payment in year ' t' to outstanding liabilities in year 't-1'.

2. Outstanding internal liabilities exclude NSSF loans to States, with no interest liability on the part of the Centre.

Source: Budget documents.

Subsidies

As a proportion of total expenditure, subsidies after declining from 12.4 per cent in 1990-91 to 7.5 per cent in 1995-96, maintained a rising trend till 1998-99, when it reached 9.2 per cent. After briefly declining to 8.2 per cent in 1999-2000 and 2000-01, subsidies rose to 10.5 per cent of total expenditure in 2002-03. In 2004-05, subsidies are budgeted to decline to 9.1 per cent of total expenditure. In absolute terms, expenditure on subsidies is budgeted to come down from Rs.44,709 crore in 2003-04 (RE) to Rs.43,516 crore in 2004-05. The undulating pattern observed in the subsidies arises primarily from the expenditure on food subsidies, which is determined increasingly by the minimum support price of foodgrains, operational efficiency of the public distribution system, highly subsidised welfare schemes and special interventions in drought-affected years. The rise in subsidy bill in 2002-03 and 2003-04 was on account of higher allocations for the food for work programme to soften the impact of drought on the poor and enhanced coverage under Antyodya Anna Yojana and other welfare schemes. Furthermore, with the dismantling of the Administered Price Mechanism, petroleum subsidies were brought on to the budget in 2002-03. A part of the decline in major subsidies in the current fiscal is attributable to lower budgetary subsidies in respect of the petroleum sector.

BOX – 7.1

Central Government Subsidies in India

- Subsidies are estimated to be Rs.104,913 crore for 2002-03 and Rs.1,15,825 crore for 2003-04, constituting 4.25 per cent and 4.18 per cent of GDP, respectively. Subsidies on social services constituted 12.8 per cent and 14.1 per cent of total subsidies in 2002-03 and 2003-04, respectively, with the rest accounted for by economic services. An intertemporal comparison, using estimates for earlier years using a similar methodology, reveals a declining trend in total subsidies.
- Subsidies are classified into Merit I, Merit II and Non-Merit categories, based on the perceived desirability in the provision of public services. Merit subsidies as a proportion of total subsidies accounted for 34 per cent and 42 per cent in 2002-03 and 2003-04, respectively.
- The NIPFP study suggests reducing the volume of subsidies relative to revenue receipts, limiting these to only Merit I and Merit II

Contd....

... Box 7.1 Contd....

categories, while eliminating the non-Merit subsidies. It also favours progressively raising the user charges.

- In food subsidies, the study suggests that a large part of the recent problems are attributable to the relatively high minimum support prices (MSPs), exclusive attention to wheat and rice, limited areas of procurement operations and inefficiencies in the operations of the Food Corporation of India.
- The study offers the following suggestions in the case of food subsidies.
  - i) MSPs not to exceed the levels recommended by the Commission on Agricultural Costs and Prices.
  - ii) Reimbursement to FCI based on normative costs and actual quantities involved.
  - iii) Gradual implementation of food stamps scheme, beginning with differential in the issue prices of foodgrains to the poor and non-poor being given in the form of food stamps, redeemable in fair price shops initially and later in all retail shops.
- On the basis of existing studies, the NIPFP study reported that the benefit of fertilizer subsidy is shared between the farmers and the fertilizer industry in the ratio of 62:38. The study suggests decanalising urea imports and providing a flat rate concession that converges into a uniform rate in the medium-term, periodically increasing the farm gate price and issuing tradable coupons to targeted small farm households.
- Petroleum subsidies are found to be non-transparent, regressive in incidence of benefits and not promoting the main objective of increased access to clean fuels. The study suggests the following policy options: reducing the level of subsidies, allowing private sector participation in marketing subsidised products and cash transfers in lieu of subsidy.
- The performance of poor States in implementing major poverty alleviation schemes is found to be deficient.

One of the important commitments made in the NCMP was to target subsidies sharply at the poor and truly needy sections of the society. Budget for 2004-05 promised to lay a blue print for realizing this objective. In pursuance of this commitment, the National Institute of Public Finance and Policy (NIPFP) was asked to prepare a blue print to accomplish the NCMP objective. The NIPFP report estimates the quantum of total subsidies (unrecovered costs in the provision of non-public goods) for the years 2002-03 and 2003-04, and analyses three major explicit subsidies provided by the Government, viz., subsidies on food, fertilizers and petroleum products (LPG for domestic use and kerosene for PDS). Based on the NIPFP study, a report "Central Government Subsidies in India, 2004", was placed in Parliament on December 23, 2004 (Box 7.1).

Government Debt

The persistently high deficits in the last two decades have resulted in substantial build up of debt. Outstanding liabilities of the Central Government, after declining from 55.3 per cent of GDP in 1990-91 to 51.2 per cent in 1998-99, have risen continuously till 2002-03 (Table 7.5). Outstanding liabilities amounted to 62.5 per cent of GDP in 2003-04 (RE) and are budgeted to increase to 63.9 per cent of GDP in 2004-05. Excluding the borrowings under MSS amounting to Rs.60,000 crore, outstanding liabilities constitute 62.0 per cent of GDP in 2004-05 (BE). Outstanding external debt declined continuously from 5.7 per cent of GDP in 1991-92 to 1.7 per cent of GDP in 2003-04 (RE). It is budgeted at Rs.55,084 crore, equivalent to 1.8 per cent of GDP in 2004-05.

The share of debt in total internal liabilities has been increasing over the years. The share, which was 54.4 per cent in 1990-91, increased to 67.7 per cent in 2003-04 (RE). Within debt, the share of market borrowings increased from 45.8 per cent in 1990-91 to 62.2 per cent in 2003-04 (RE). In recent years, banks have been subscribing to Government securities, much beyond the statutory liquidity ratio (SLR) of 25 per cent of their net demand and time liabilities (NDTL). Commercial banks have been parking their surplus liquidity in risk-free Government securities. Such investments amounted to 41.3 per cent of their NDTL by end-March, 2004. The pre-emption of financial resources by the Government has reduced the availability of credit to the private sector. A noteworthy development in the current year is the significant deceleration in investments in Government securities by commercial banks, following a pick up in the demand for credit from the commercial sector and lower market borrowings by the Central government. Commercial banks' investments in Central and State Government securities in the current year (up to January 21, 2005) have increased by 4.9 per cent compared to a growth of 20.1 per cent in the same period last year. Gross and net market borrowings of the Central Government through dated securities are budgeted at Rs.1,49,817 crore and

Rs.1,15,501 crore, respectively, including Rs.25,000 crore under MSS. Actual gross and net market borrowings of the Central government in the current year (up to January 28, 2005) amounted to Rs.1,00,350 crore and Rs.66,034 crore, respectively compared with Rs.1,25,934 crore and Rs.94,032 crore, respectively in the corresponding period last year. When adjusted for borrowings under MSS, gross and net market borrowings in the current year are much lower than the level in 2003-04.

TABLE – 7.5

Outstanding Liabilities of the Central Government

(end-March)

	1990-91	1999-00	2000-01	2001-02	2002-03	2003-04 (RE)	2004-05## (BE)
	(As per cent of GDP)						
1. Internal liabilities	49.8	49.7	52.8	57.0	60.9	60.8	62.1
a) Internal debt	27.1	36.9	38.5	40.2	41.4	41.1	41.6
i) Market borrowings	12.4	18.4	20.5	22.7	25.1	25.5	26.6
ii) Others	14.7	18.5	17.9	17.5	16.3	15.5	15.0
b) Other Internal liabilities	22.7	12.8	14.3	16.8	19.4	19.7	20.6
2. External debt (outstanding)*	5.5	3.0	3.2	3.1	2.4	1.7	1.8
3. Total outstanding liabilities	55.3	52.7	55.9	60.1	63.3	62.5	63.9

* External debt figures represent borrowings by Central Government from external sources and are based upon historical rates of exchange.

\## Including net borrowing of Rs. 60,000 crore under MSS.

Note : 1. Total liabilities excluding Rs. 60,000 crore under MSS is Rs 1986167 crore (62.0 per cent of GDP).
2. The ratios to GDP for 2004-05 (BE) are based on CSO's Advance Estimates released in February, 2005.

Source: 1. Budget documents.
2. Controller of Aid Accounts and Audit.
3. Reserve Bank of India.

The rules framed under the FRBM Act place a limit of 9 per cent of GDP on the additional liabilities that can be assumed by the Central Government in 2004-05. This limit would go down by one percentage point in each subsequent year. Adherence to these limits is expected to bring down the debt burden over the medium term.

Savings and Capital Formation

The economic and functional classification of the Central Government Budget 2004-05, which analyses budgetary transactions of the Centre by economic and functional categories, places the total expenditure at Rs.4,76,171 crore, an increase of 10.8 per cent over 2003-04 (RE). The share of consumption expenditure, which remained in the range of 21 and 23 per cent between 1990-91 and 2003-04, is budgeted to increase to 25.3 per cent in 2004-05. The substantial increase in the share of consumption expenditure is mainly on account of a step up in the provision made for commodities and services from Rs.53,015 crore in 2003-04 (RE) to Rs.72,014 crore in 2004-05. Expenditure on wages, salaries and pensions of the Centre as a proportion of its total expenditure is budgeted at 15.2 per cent in 2004-05 as compared with 15.0 per cent in 2003-04(RE).

Gross capital formation out of budgetary resources of the Central Government, which has been declining steadily, improved marginally to 19.4 per cent of total expenditure in 2003-04 (RE), compared to 19.2 per cent in the previous year (Table 7.6). This has been carried forward in 2004-05, with the share of gross capital formation in total expenditure improving by 1.4 percentage points to 20.8 per cent. Transfer payments, financial investments and loans to the rest of the economy, which supplement the current and capital receipts of other sectors are placed at Rs.3,25,382 crore, constituting 68.3 per cent of total expenditure. The trend of growing dissavings of the Central Government was arrested in 2003-04. Dissavings of the Central government which declined from Rs.81,734 crore in 2002-03 to Rs.76,448 crore in 2003-04 are placed at Rs.65,125 crore in 2004-05 (BE).The reduction in dissavings are mainly in Government administration. As a proportion of GDP, dissavings are placed at 2.8 per cent in 2003-04 (RE) and 2.1 per cent in 2004-05 (BE).

Collection Rates

Following the initiation of tax reforms, the peak rate of basic customs duty has been reduced in a phased manner from 120 per cent in 1990-91 to 20 per cent in 2003-04. The effective rates of customs duties were lower than nominal rates, as there were numerous general and end-use/specific exemptions in the initial years of tax reforms. Collection rate, the ratio of revenue realized from imports to the value of imports, is a comprehensive indicator of the incidence of customs duties, including the incidence of countervailing duties and special additional duties levied on imports. The average collection rate has come down from 47 per cent in 1990-91 to 14 per cent in 2003-04, reflecting the reductions in nominal rates of customs duties as part of tax reforms. Among the commodity groups, the collection rates have declined by over 65 per

TABLE – 7.6

Total Expenditure and Capital Formation by the Central Government and its Financing (As per Economic and Functional Classification of the Central Government Budget)

	1990-91	1999-00	2000-01	2001-02	2002-03	2003-04 (RE)	2004-05$ (BE)
				(As per cent of GDP)			
I. Total expenditure	17.2	15.9	15.7	15.9	16.2	15.6	15.3
II. Gross capital formation out of budgetary resources of Central Government	4.9	3.5	3.2	3.4	3.1	3.0	3.2
(i) Gross capital formation by the Central Government	1.5	1.3	1.1	0.6	0.9	0.9	1.0
(ii) Financial assistance for capital formation in the rest of the economy	3.4	2.1	2.1	2.8	2.2	2.1	2.2
III. Gross saving of the Central Government	-1.8	-2.1	-2.7	-3.4	-3.3	-2.8	-2.1
IV. Gap (II-III)	6.8	5.6	5.9	6.7	6.4	5.8	5.3
Financed by							
a. Draft on other sectors of domestic economy	6.1	5.5	5.5	6.4	6.8	6.1	4.9
(i) Domestic capital receipts	4.1	5.5	5.6	6.5	6.8	6.5	4.5
(ii) Budgetary deficit/draw down of cash balance	2.0	0.0	-0.1	-0.1	0.1	-0.4	0.4
b. Draft on foreign savings	0.7	0.1	0.4	0.3	-0.4	-0.3	0.4

Contd....

... *Table 7.6 Contd....*

	1990-91	1999-00	2000-01	2001-02	2002-03	2003-04 (RE)	2004-05$ (BE)
			(increase over previous year)				
II. Gross capital formation out of budgetary resources of Central Government	2.8	16.9	-0.9	14.8	-0.1	8.3	19.3

$ The ratios to GDP for 2004-05 (BE) are based on CSO's Advance Estimates released in February, 2005.

Notes : (i) Gross capital formation in this table includes loans given for capital formation on a gross basis. Consequently domestic capital receipts include loan repayments to the Central Government.

(ii) Consumption expenditure is the expenditure on wages & salaries and commodities & services for current use.

(iii) Interest payments, subsidies, pension etc. are treated as current transfers.

(iv) Gross capital formation & total expenditure are exclusive of loans to States'/UTs' against States'/UTs' share in the small savings collection.

(v) The figures of total expenditure of the Central Government as per economic and functional classification do not tally with figures given in the Budget documents. In the economic and functional classification, interest transfered to DCUs, loans written off *etc*, are excluded from the current account. In the capital account, expenditure financed out of Railways, Posts & Telecommunications' own funds *etc*, are included.

Source : Ministry of Finance, An Economic and Functional classification of the Central Government Budget-various issues.

cent between 1990-91 and 2003-04 in respect of chemicals, metals, capital goods and petroleum, oil and lubricants (Table 7.7).

TABLE – 7.7

Collection Rates* for Selected Import Groups

(in per cent)

Sl. No.	Commodity Groups	1990-91	1997-98	1998-99	1999-00	2000-01	2001-02	2002-03	2003-04 (Prov.)
1	Food products	47	16	15	15	31	40	30	19
2	POL	34	29	29	23	16	10	11	11
3	Chemicals	92	37	34	36	38	29	28	24
4	Man-made fibres	83	36	49	64	49	31	31	46
5	Paper & newsprint	24	13	11	9	8	6	7	7
6	Natural fibres	20	17	22	24	18	8	10	13
7	Metals	95	44	51	55	48	36	36	32
8	Capital goods	60	41	42	36	36	28	23	19
9	Others	20	15	11	12	12	9	9	8
10	Non POL	51	27	23	22	23	19	17	14
11	Total	47	27	23	22	21	16	15	14

* Collection rate is defined as the ratio of realised import revenue (including additional customs duty/countervailing duty (CVD), and special additional duty) to the value of imports of a commodity.

S.No.1 includes cereals, pulses, tea, milk and cream, fruits, vegetables, animal fats and sugar.

S.No 3 includes chemical elements, compounds, pharmaceuticals, dyeing and colouring materials, plastic and rubber.

S.No.5 includes pulp and waste paper, newsprint, paperboards and manufactures and printed books.

S.No.6 includes raw wool and silk.

S.No.7 includes iron and steel and non-ferrous metals.

S.No.8 includes non-electronic machinery, project imports and electrical machinery.

Source : Department of Revenue, Ministry of Finance

Post Budget Developments

With a view to reducing relatively low priority expenditure and boost non tax revenues, the Ministry of Finance issued "Guidelines on expenditure management-Fiscal prudence and austerity" effective from October 1, 2004. These guidelines stipulate scrutiny of all on-going programmes and schemes and ensuring that all profit making public sector undertakings (PSUs) declare a minimum dividend on equity of 20 per cent or a minimum dividend payout of 20 per cent of post-tax profits, whichever is higher. The guidelines imposed a 10 per cent cut in the budgetary allocations under non-Plan and non-salary expenditure. At the meeting of Finance Minister with the Financial Advisers on October 28, 2004, it was reiterated that only 33 per cent of budgeted expenditure would be permissible in the last quarter of the financial year. Efforts at better cash management in nine high spending Departments/Ministries are being continued. The practice of allowing Central PSUs to park their surplus cash in the Public Account has been dispensed with.

Twelfth Finance Commission (2005-10)

The Twelfth Finance Commission (TFC) was appointed on November 1, 2002 to make recommendations regarding the distribution between the Union and the States of net proceeds of shareable taxes, the principles which should govern the grants-in-aid of the revenues of States from the Consolidated Fund of India and the measures needed to augment the Consolidated Fund of a State to supplement the resources of local bodies in the State on the basis of the recommendations made by the Finance Commission of the State. The terms of reference mandated the Commission to review the state of the finances of the Union and the States and suggest a Plan by which the Governments, collectively and severally, restore budgetary balance, achieve macroeconomic stability and debt reduction along with equitable growth. Furthermore, the Commission was also asked to suggest corrective measures for debt sustainability and to review the Fiscal Reform Facility introduced by the Central Government.

The Commission submitted its report on November 30, 2004 covering the period 2005-10. The recommendations of the Commission include a plan for restructuring of public finances of the Centre and the States through improvement in revenue mobilization and bringing down debt levels, and through enactment of fiscal responsibility legislation by States (Box 7.2). The Commission recommended debt relief to States linked to fiscal reforms, doing away with the present system of Central assistance to State plans in the form of grants and loans and transfer of external assistance to States on the same terms and conditions as attached to such assistance by external funding agencies. The TFC raised the share of States in shareable Central taxes from 29.5 per cent to 30.5 per cent. Total transfers to States recommended by the TFC amount to Rs.7,55,752 crore over the five year period 2005-10. Of this, transfers by way of share in Central taxes and grants-in-aid amount to Rs.6,13,112 crore and Rs.1,42,640 crore, respectively. The total transfers recommended by the TFC are higher by 73.8 per cent over those recommended by the Eleventh Finance Commission (EFC). Within the total transfers, while the share in Central taxes is higher by 62.9 per cent, grants-in-aid recommended by the TFC are higher by 143.5 per cent over those recommended by the EFC.

BOX – 7.2

Recommendations of the Twelfth Finance Commission

Restructuring Public Finances

- Centre and States to improve the combined tax-GDP ratio to 17.6 per cent by 2009-10.
- Combined debt-GDP ratio, with external debt measured at historical exchange rates, to be brought down to 75 per cent by 2009-10.
- Fiscal deficit to GDP targets for the Centre and States to be fixed at 3 per cent.
- Revenue deficit of the Centre and States to be brought down to zero by 2008-09.
- Interest payments relative to revenue receipts to be brought down to 28 per cent and 15 per cent in the case of the Centre and States, respectively.
- States to follow a recruitment policy in a manner so that the total salary bill, relative to revenue expenditure, net of interest payments, does not exceed 35 per cent.
- Each State to enact a fiscal responsibility legislation providing for elimination of revenue deficit by 2008-09 and reducing fiscal deficit to 3 per cent of State Domestic Product.
- The system of on-lending to be brought to an end over time. The long term goal should be to bring down debt-GDP ratio to 28 per cent each for the Centre and the States.

Sharing of Union Tax Revenues

- The share of States in the net proceeds of shareable Central taxes fixed at 30.5 per cent, treating additional excise duties in lieu of sales tax as part of the general pool of Central taxes. Share of States to come down to 29.5 per cent, when States are allowed to levy sales tax on sugar, textiles and tobacco.
- In case of any legislation enacted in respect of service tax, after the notification of the eighty eighth amendment to the Constitution, revenue accruing to a State should not be less than the share that

Contd....

... Box 7.2 Contd....

would accrue to it, had the entire service tax proceeds been part of the shareable pool.

- The indicative amount of overall transfers to States to be fixed at 38 per cent of the Centre's gross revenue receipts.

Local Bodies

- A grant of Rs.20,000 crore for the Panchayati Raj institutions and Rs.5,000 crore for urban local bodies to be given to States for the period 2005-10.
- Priority to be given to expenditure on operation and maintenance (O&M) costs of water supply and sanitation, while utilizing the grants for the Panchayats. At least 50 per cent of the grants recommended for urban local bodies to be earmarked for the scheme of solid waste management through public-private partnership.

Calamity Relief

- The scheme of Calamity Relief Fund (CRF) to continue in its present form with contributions from the Centre and States in the ratio of 75:25. The size of the Fund worked out at Rs.21,333 crore for the period 2005-10.
- The outgo from the Fund to be replenished by way of collection of National Calamity Contingent Duty and levy of special surcharges.
- The definition of natural calamity to include landslides, avalanches, cloud burst and pest attacks.
- Provision for disaster preparedness and mitigation to be part of State Plans and not calamity relief.

Grants-in-aid to States

- The present system of Central assistance for State Plans, comprising grant and loan components, to be done away with, and the Centre should confine itself to extending plan grants and leaving it to States to decide their borrowings.
- Non-plan revenue deficit grant of Rs.56,856 crore recommended to 15 States for the period 2005-10. Grants amounting to Rs.10,172 crore recommended for the education sector to eight States. Grants amounting to Rs.5,887 crore recommended for the health sector for seven States. Grants to education and health sectors are additionalities over and above the normal expenditure to be incurred by States.

Contd....

... Box 7.2 Contd....

- A grant of Rs.15,000 crore recommended for roads and bridges, which is in addition to the normal expenditure of States.
- Grants recommended for maintenance of public buildings, forests, heritage conservation and specific needs of States are Rs. 500 crore, Rs.1,000 crore, Rs.625 crore, and Rs.7,100 crore, respectively.

Fiscal Reform Facility

- With the recommended scheme of debt relief in place, fiscal reform facility not to continue over the period 2005-10.

Debt Relief and Corrective Measures

- Central loans to States contracted till March, 2004 and outstanding on March 31, 2005 amounting to Rs.1,28,795 crore to be consolidated and rescheduled for a fresh term of 20 years, and an interest rate of 7.5 per cent to be charged on them. This is subject to enactment of fiscal responsibility legislation by a State.
- A debt write-off scheme linked to reduction of revenue deficit of States to be introduced. Under this scheme, repayments due from 2005-06 to 2009-10 on Central loans contracted up to March 31, 2004 will be eligible for write-off.
- Central Government not to act as an intermediary for future lending to States, except in the case of weak States, which are unable to raise funds from the market.
- External assistance to be transferred to States on the same terms and conditions as attached to such assistance by external funding agencies.
- All the States to set up sinking funds for amortization of all loans.
- States to set up guarantee redemption funds through earmarked guarantee fees.

Others

- The Centre should share 'profit petroleum' from New Exploration and Licensing Policy (NELP) areas in the ratio of 50:50 with States where mineral oil and natural gas are produced. No sharing of profits in respect of nomination fields and non-NELP blocks.
- Every State to set up a high level committee to monitor the utilization of grants recommended by the TFC.
- Centre to gradually move towards accrual basis of accounting.

Fiscal Outcome 2004-05

With the notification of the FRBM rules, quarterly reviews of Union finances are required to be placed before Parliament, and the monitoring of fiscal outcome has assumed significance. The Mid-year review presented to Parliament in December 2004, contained, inter alia, fiscal performance in the first half of the current financial year. The fiscal performance in the first half of the current year did not fully measure up to the benchmarks laid down in the FRBM rules. Non-debt receipts at 41.8 per cent and fiscal deficit at 38.7 per cent of BE are better than the FRBM benchmarks of 40 per cent and 45 per cent, respectively reflecting an excess of receipts under prepayment of high cost loans by States, relative to BE. Revenue deficit at 78.7 per cent of BE is considerably in excess of FRBM benchmark of 45 per cent. The main reason for the slippage in achieving the FRBM benchmark of revenue deficit is that growth in overall tax revenue in the first half of the year at 20 per cent fell short of the growth of 25 per cent assumed in the Budget. The Mid-Year Review indicated that while the cumulative impact of post-budget duty concessions and additional expenditure commitments could lead to some slippage in meeting the ambitious Budget targets of reducing revenue deficit, the minimum targets prescribed under the FRBM rules would be met.

The Office of the Controller General of Accounts (CGA) has released the Central Government accounts for the first nine months (April-December, 2004) of the current financial year. Gross tax revenue grew by 18.3 per cent in the first nine months of the current financial year, as compared with 12.3 per cent growth recorded in the corresponding period last year and 25 per cent growth envisaged in the BE for 2004-05. As a per cent of BE, gross tax revenue realised was lower at 61.1 per cent compared to 65.3 per cent in the corresponding period last year. The Budget for 2004-05 targeted a growth over 2003-04 (RE) of 34.9 per cent and 18.4 per cent in direct and indirect taxes, respectively. While direct taxes grew by 25.2 per cent in the first nine months of the current financial year, indirect taxes grew by 13.7 per cent. As a proportion of BE, revenue realised from personal income tax and customs in the current financial year was more or less on par with the realisation in the corresponding period last year. Revenue realised from corporate income tax, excise and service tax in the first nine months of the current financial year, as per cent of BE, was lower as compared with the realisations in the corresponding period last year. Non-tax revenue in the first nine months of the current year declined by 8.7 per cent and as a proportion of BE at 62.6 per cent was lower than the realisation in the corresponding period last year (74.2 per cent), mainly reflecting lower interest receipts and dividends and profits.

Revenue expenditure in the first nine months of the current financial year grew by 3.3 per cent compared to 11.5 per cent growth in the same period last year. This was facilitated by a 14 per cent decline in major subsidies, a lower growth in interest payments, and in non-Plan expenditure on capital account. The deceleration in the growth in interest payments is mainly on account of softening of interest rates. The lower growth in non-Plan expenditure on capital account was due to lower redemption of securities issued to NSSF using the proceeds of prepayment of high cost debt by States under the debt swap scheme. Lower growth in Plan expenditure, both revenue and capital, in the first nine months of the current financial year was on account of the delay in the allocation of additional outlay of Rs.10,000 crore due to the presentation of regular Budget for 2004-05 on July 8, 2004.

Revenue deficit amounted to Rs.62,969 crore in the first nine months of the current financial year, a decline of 13.7 per cent in actual terms over corresponding period last year. However, as a proportion of BE, it was higher in the current financial year at 82.7 per cent as against 65.0 per cent recorded in the same period last year, Fiscal deficit amounted to Rs.90,239 crore, a decline of 2.4 per cent over corresponding period last year. As a proportion of BE, fiscal deficit was higher at 65.7 per cent of BE in the first nine months of the current financial year compared to 60.2 per cent last year.

The Fiscal Responsibility Legislation

The FRBM Act, 2003 (as amended), which became effective from July 5, 2004 mandates the Central Government to eliminate revenue deficit by March, 2009 and to reduce fiscal deficit to an amount equivalent to 3 per cent of GDP by March, 2008. The annual targets for fiscal correction were to be specified by rules to be framed under the Act. Accordingly, Government notified the rules under the FRBM Act on July 2, 2004, which came into force on July 5, 2004. The rules made under FRBM Act specify the annual targets for reduction of fiscal and revenue deficits, annual targets for assuming contingent liabilities in the form of guarantees and the total liabilities as a percentage of GDP (Box 7.3). The rules also prescribe the formats for the medium term fiscal policy statement, the fiscal policy strategy statement and the macro-economic framework statement, which are required to be presented to Parliament along with the annual financial statement. Fiscal indicators to be presented in the medium term fiscal policy statement are also prescribed in the rules.

BOX – 7.3

The Fiscal Responsibility and Budget Management Rules, 2004

- Reduction of revenue deficit by an amount equivalent of 0.5 per cent or more of the GDP at the end of each financial year, beginning with 2004-05.
- Reduction of fiscal deficit by an amount equivalent of 0.3 per cent or more of the GDP at the end of each financial year, beginning with 2004-05.
- No assumption of additional liabilities (including external debt at current exchange rate) in excess of 9 per cent of GDP for the financial year 2004-05 and progressive reduction of this limit by at least one percentage point of GDP in each subsequent year.
- No guarantees in excess of 0.5 per cent of GDP in any financial year, beginning with 2004-05.
- Specifies four fiscal indicators to be projected in the medium term fiscal policy statement. These are, revenue deficit as a percentage of GDP, fiscal deficit as a percentage of GDP, tax revenue as percentage of GDP and total outstanding liabilities as percentage of GDP.
- For greater transparency in the budgetary process, rules mandate the Central Government to disclose changes, if any., in accounting standards, policies and practices that have a bearing on the fiscal indicators. The Government is also mandated to submit statements of receivables and guarantees and a statement of assets, at the time of presenting the annual financial statement, latest by Budget 2006-07.
- The rules prescribe the form for the quarterly review of the trends of receipts and expenditures. The rules mandate the Central Government to take appropriate corrective action in case of revenue and fiscal deficits exceeding 45 per cent of the budget estimates, or total non-debt receipts falling short of 40 per cent of the budget estimates at the end of first half of the financial year.

Task Force on Implementation of FRBM Act

Following the enactment of FRBM Act, Government constituted a Task Force headed by Dr. Vijay Kelkar for drawing up the medium term framework for fiscal policies to achieve the FRBM targets. The Task Force was also asked to formulate annual targets indicating the path of adjustment and required policy measures. The Task Force submitted its report in July, 2004. The Task Force recommended a path of fiscal adjustment that is front-loaded and mainly revenue-led, with complementary reform efforts on revenue expenditure and enhanced capital expenditure to counteract the possible contractionary effects of fiscal correction (Box 7.4).

BOX – 7.4

Report of the Task Force on Implementation of the Fiscal Responsibility and Budget Management Act, 2003

Tax Reforms Strategy

- Widening the tax base through removal of exemptions and "grandfathering".
- Few, but low rates to avoid the problems of bracket creep, classification disputes and lobbying for lower rates.
- Enhancing equity of the tax system, both vertical and horizontal.
- Shifting to non-distortionary consumption taxes to enhance efficiency in production and international competitiveness of Indian goods and services.
- Enhancing the neutrality between present and future consumption; forms of organisation; and sources of finance.
- Establishing an effective and efficient compliance system.
- Focus on buoyancy rather than immediate sources of tax revenues.

Tax Measures Proposed

- An All-India goods and services tax (GST), on the basis of a 'grand bargain' with States, whereby States will have the concurrent powers to tax services, subject to certain principles that will help foster a national common market.
- Income tax exemption limit to be increased to Rs.1,00,000.
- A two-tier rate structure of 20 per cent tax for income of Rs.1,00,000 to Rs.4,00,000 and 30 per cent for income above Rs.4,00,000 for individuals and elimination of standard deduction available to the salaried taxpayers.

Contd....

... *Box 7.4 Contd....*

- A reduction in corporate income tax to 30 per cent for domestic companies and a reduction in depreciation rates from 25 per cent to 15 per cent. All tax incentives for existing units to be 'grandfathered' but to be removed for new units.
- A 3-tier customs duty rates of 5, 8 and 10 per cent to bring down tariffs to ASEAN levels.
- *Ad valorem* rates of excise applicable to petroleum products to be converted into specific rates and the threshold exemption limit for small-scale industries to be reduced from Rs.1 crore to Rs.40 lakhs.
- Allocation of a greater portion of expenditure to legitimate public goods by revisiting the classifications of expenditure.
- Empowering panchayats/local bodies through resource transfer.

The Task Force estimated that under the reforms scenario recommended by it, tax-GDP ratio of the Centre would improve from 9.2 per cent in 2003-04 (RE) to 13.2 per cent in 2008-09. Total expenditure is estimated to come down to 14.3 per cent of GDP by 2008-09 from 15.4 per cent of GDP in 2003-04 (RE). A revenue surplus of 0.2 per cent of GDP is estimated in 2008-09. Fiscal deficit is estimated to come down from 4.8 per cent of GDP in 2003-04 to 2.8 per cent of GDP in 2008-09.

Finances of State Governments

Though the fiscal deterioration of States began much later than that of the Centre, the fiscal stress of some of the State Governments is more acute and an important constraint in their development. The revenue account of States has been continuously in deficit since 1987-88. The deterioration in the revenue account of States has been more pronounced from the late nineties. As a proportion of GDP, revenue deficit of States which increased from 0.3 per cent in 1987-88 to 1.1 per cent in 1996-97, shot up to 2.5 per cent in 1998-99, following mainly the revision of pay scales of Government employees. The deficit continued to remain high till 2001-02. In 2002-03, the deficit declined to 2.2 per cent of GDP. Fiscal deficit of States as a proportion of GDP, increased from a level of 3.3 per cent in 1990-91 to 5.1 per cent in 2003-04 (RE). In BE for 2004-05, revenue and fiscal deficits of States are placed at 1.4 per cent and 3.6 per cent of GDP, respectively. As in the case of the Central Government, the quality of expenditure of States has deteriorated, as revealed by the proportion of revenue deficit to fiscal deficit. The share of revenue deficit in fiscal deficit increased from an average of 25.0 per cent in the period 1990-95 to 48.6 per cent in the period 1995-2000, and further to 54.0 per cent in 2002-03. Growing revenue expenditure, particularly wages and salaries and pensions, burden of interest payments, losses of public sector enterprises, particularly power utilities, declining Central transfers as a proportion of GDP and inappropriate user charges have contributed in large measure to this deterioration. The slower growth in revenues in relation to expenditure and ambitious Plan outlays of States compounded the problem. Furthermore, most States resorted to off-budget borrowings, constrained by limitations on raising public debt through the budgetary process.

States have done relatively better than the Centre in terms of raising own tax revenue. The own tax revenue of States increased from an average of 5.4 per cent of GDP in the period 1990-95 to 5.8 per cent of GDP in 2002-03. In contrast, Central transfers declined from 4.9 per cent of GDP to 4.1 per cent of GDP in the same period. The performance of States in mobilizing non-tax revenue has deteriorated. Non-tax revenue to GDP ratio declined from an average of 4.1 per cent in the period 1990-95 to 3.3 per cent in 2002-03. Total expenditure of States increased from an average of 16.0 per cent of GDP in the period 1990-95 to 17.1 per cent of GDP in 2002-03. Within total expenditure, revenue expenditure increased from 12.8 per cent of GDP in 1990-95 to 13.9 per cent of GDP in 2001-02, while capital expenditure, after declining from 3.2 per cent of GDP to 2.7 per cent of GDP in the same period improved to 3.5 per cent of GDP in 2002-03. In revenue expenditure, the rise in interest payments from an average of 1.7 per cent of GDP in the period 1990-95 to 2.8 per cent of GDP in 2002-03 is much sharper (Table 7.8).

Outstanding liabilities of States as a proportion of GDP, which was 18.2 per cent in 1994-95, after initial decline in the next two years, shot up to 29.2 per cent in 2003-04 (RE). It is budgeted at 29.4 per cent in 2004- 05. Till 2002-03, the build-up of outstanding liabilities of State Governments was accounted for significantly by loans from the Centre. The internal debt of States is composed of loans from the Centre, NSSF, market borrowings and negotiated loans from banks and other institutions. In recent years, the share of loans from Central Government is on the decline on account of higher loans from NSSF and higher market borrowings (Table 7.9).

TABLE – 7.8

Receipts and Disbursements of State Governments

	1990-91	1999-2000	2000-01	2001-02	2002-03	2003-04 (RE)	2004-05# (BE)
	(As per cent of GDP)						
I. Total receipts (A+B)	16.0	16.0	16.7	16.5	17.3	19.7	17.8
A. Revenue receipts (1+2)	11.7	10.7	11.4	11.3	11.4	12.0	12.0
1. Tax receipts	7.8	7.6	8.1	7.9	8.1	8.3	8.5
of which:							
State's own tax revenue	5.3	5.3	5.6	5.6	5.8	5.9	6.0
2. Non-tax receipts	3.8	3.1	3.3	3.3	3.3	3.7	3.6
of which:							
Interest receipts	0.4	0.5	0.5	0.4	0.4	0.4	0.4
B. Capital receipts	4.3	5.3	5.3	5.2	5.9	7.7	5.7
of which:							
Recovery of loans & advances	0.3	0.2	0.3	0.3	0.2	0.6	0.2
II. Total disbursements (a+b+c)	16.0	16.2	16.6	16.6	17.1	20.1	17.7
a) Revenue	12.6	13.5	14.0	13.9	13.6	14.6	13.4
b) Capital	2.4	1.9	2.1	2.2	2.9	4.7	3.8
c) Loans and advances	1.0	0.8	0.6	0.5	0.6	0.8	0.5
III. Revenue deficit	0.9	2.8	2.6	2.6	2.2	2.6	1.4
IV. Gross fiscal deficit	3.3	4.7	4.3	4.2	4.1	5.1	3.6

The ratios to GDP for 2004-05 (BE) are based on CSO's Advance Estimates released in February, 2005.

Note : Data are provisional.

Source: Reserve Bank of India.

In addition to build up of debt, another worrisome feature of State finances is the rapid growth in off-budget borrowings. Available data indicate that outstanding guarantees of State Governments which increased from 4.4 per cent of GDP in 1995-96 to 8.1 per cent in 2000-01 declined to 7.5 per cent of GDP in 2002-03. Many of these guarantees have been given to special purpose vehicles, whose liabilities will ultimately revert to State Governments.

TABLE – 7.9

Outstanding Liabilities of States

Year	Total liabilities (Rs crore)	Col (2) as per cent of GDP
1	2	3
1993-94	160075	18.6
1994-95	184530	18.2
1995-96	212224	17.9
1996-97	242867	17.8
1997-98	281211	18.5
1998-99	341981	19.6
1999-2000	420135	21.7
2000-01	498092	23.8
2001-02	586687	25.8
2002-03	686655	27.9
2003-04 (RE)	807131	29.2
2004-05 (BE)#	913103	29.4

The ratios to GDP for 2004-05 (BE) are based on CSO's Advance Estimates released in February, 2005.

Source: Reserve Bank of India.

State Level Reforms

The need for fiscal adjustment has been well recognized by States. Five States have enacted fiscal responsibility legislations till 2003-04. Three more States have indicated that they would be initiating such legislation. A Working Group was constituted by the RBI to evolve draft model fiscal responsibility legislation at the State level. The draft report of the Group is being examined by State Governments.

The Central Government has been taking proactive steps to encourage State level fiscal reforms through provision of incentives. Based on the recommendations of the Eleventh Finance Commission, the Centre initiated a "States Fiscal Reforms Facility (2000-01 to 2004-05)", in the year 2001, to encourage States to undertake fiscal reforms. Under this facility, Medium Term Fiscal Reform Programmes (MTFRPs) are drawn up by States encompassing fiscal reforms, power sector reforms, public sector restructuring and budgetary reforms. A unique feature of MTFRP is that the ownership of reforms and the initiative rest with State Governments.

Interest payment is a major item of revenue expenditure. To reduce the interest burden of States, a debt swap scheme enabling States to swap their high cost Central Government loans bearing a coupon rate of 13 per cent and above with relatively low cost market borrowings and loans from NSSF, was put in place in 2002-03, at the initiative of the Central Government. In 2004-05 (upto December 2004), high cost debt amounting to Rs.34,085 crore has been swapped through market borrowings of Rs.13,781 crore and loans from small savings of Rs.20,304 crore. The cumulative amount of high cost debt swapped up to December 2004 amounted to Rs.92,444 crore. The process of swapping high cost debt under the scheme is complete in respect of 20 states.

The TFC has made far-reaching recommendations on reform of State finances. Debt relief to States is conditional upon the enactment of fiscal responsibility legislation prescribing specific annual targets with a view to eliminating the revenue deficit by 2008-09 and reduction in fiscal deficit by a path to be specified. Consequently, fiscal reform facilitiy would cease at the end of the current financial year. The practice of loan intermediation by the Centre would be restricted to fiscally weak States and all other States have to approach the market directly for raising loans. All States are required to set up sinking funds in Public Account for amortization of all loans and guarantee redemption funds through earmarked guarantee fees, after risk weighting guarantees.

Value Added Tax

An accepted principle of tax policy is that taxes on commodities and services must be based on consumption (on consumers) and not on sales (traders). However, the levy of tax on sales of goods and services has been on traders and not on consumers, as it is relatively easier to tax traders rather than consumers. By allowing input credit for taxes paid on the series of sales from the producer to the ultimate consumer, the objective of tax on the basis of value addition can be achieved. Value Added Tax (VAT) is a multistage sales tax with credit for taxes paid on business purchases. One of the major advantages of VAT over sales tax is that the former is non-cascading. Union excise duties are based on value addition principles through the CENVAT system which allows input credit.

One of the important components of tax reforms initiated since liberalisation relate to introducing State-level Value Added Tax (VAT). The decision to introduce VAT arrived at during the Conference of Chief Ministers of States/UTs held in 1999 was reiterated during the subsequent meetings held in June 2000 and July 2001. An Empowered Committee of State Finance Ministers was also constituted in July 2000 to monitor the process of introduction of VAT. The consensus arrived at to introduce VAT from April 1, 2003 could not be adhered to as States were not fully prepared both in terms of legislative requirements as well as administrative infrastructure required for the purpose. At the meeting of the Empowered Committee (convenor: Dr. Asim Dasgupta) held on June 18, 2004, it was agreed to implement State level VAT from April 1, 2005. This decision has been further reaffirmed in subsequent meetings of the Empowered Committee held on September 23, 2004 and November 2, 2004.

The proposed VAT is a multi-point destination based system of taxation, with tax being levied on value addition at each stage of transaction in the production/distribution chain. Some other salient features of VAT are :

a) Uniform schedule of rates of VAT for all States. This would make the tax system simple and uniform and prevent unhealthy tax competition among States.

b) The provision of input tax credit would help in preventing cascading effect of tax.

c) The provision of self-assessment by dealers would reduce harassment. Small traders with turnover up to Rs.5 lakhs would be exempt from the provisions of VAT.

d) The zero-rating of exports would increase the competitiveness of Indian exports.

Since sales tax/VAT is basically a State subject, the Central Government is playing the role of a facilitator for successful implementation of this significant reform measure. One of the concerns expressed by States in adopting VAT relates to the possible loss of revenue in the initial years. To allay the apprehensions of States and to provide a measure of comfort, the Central Government agreed to compensate the estimated loss on the basis of an agreed formula, on account of the introduction of VAT, to the extent of 100 per cent of the loss in the first year, 75 per cent of the loss in the second year and 50 per cent of the loss in the third year of introduction of VAT.

The Empowered Committee of State Finance Ministers, constituted by the Ministry of Finance, Government of India which has been engaged in the design and introduction of State-level VAT, has come up with a white paper on State-level value added tax on January 17, 2005. The white paper discusses the issues concerning VAT (Box 7.5).

BOX – 7.5

White Paper on State-level VAT

- Introduction of VAT would help avoid cascading nature of sales tax.
- Present multiple rates and taxes can converge into a few rates and a single VAT.
- Transparency in the system of tax administration through simple self-assessments and departmental audit.
- Rationalisation of taxes to result in lower tax burden and higher tax revenues.
- To avoid tax competition, the design of State VAT needs to be harmonized even as the distinctive needs of individual States are recognized.
- State VAT to have two basic rates of 4 per cent and 12.5 per cent and to cover 550 commodities. About 270 commodities will be under 4 per cent rate.
- 46 items, comprising of natural and unprocessed products in unorganized sector, items legally barred from taxation and items having social implications, are exempt from VAT.
- Gold and silver ornaments subject to a special VAT rate of 1 per cent and other commodities to attract a general VAT rate of 12.5 per cent.

Consolidated General Government

The international community evaluates a country's public finances through the concept of Consolidated General Government, which includes all levels of Government. International credit rating agencies base their sovereign ratings on the combined fiscal position of the Centre and States, which in the absence of readily available data on local governments is taken as a good proxy for consolidated general government in India. The combined fiscal deficit, which showed promising decline in the early nineties, worsened subsequently.

Combined fiscal deficit of the Centre and States, as proportion of GDP, declined from 9.4 per cent in 1990-91 to 6.4 per cent in 1996-97, but started increasing to reach 10.0 per cent in 2001-02. Combined fiscal deficit, which is placed at 9.4 per cent of GDP in 2003-04 (RE) is budgeted to decline to 7.9 per cent of GDP in 2004-05. Combined revenue deficit of the Centre and States as a proportion of GDP at 4.2 per cent in 1990-91, composed of 3.3 per cent of the Centre and 0.9 of States worsened to 7.0 per cent in 2001-02, with Centre accounting for 4.4 per cent and States 2.5 per cent. In 2004-05, combined revenue deficit is budgeted to decline to 3.9 per cent of GDP (Table 7.10).

TABLE – 7.10

Combined Receipts and Disbursements of the Central and State Governments

	1990-91	1999-2000	2000-01	2001-02	2002-03	2003-04 (RE)	2004-05$ (BE)
	(As per cent of GDP)						
I. Total receipts (A+B)	26.8	27.7	28.7	28.7	29.7	31.7	29.2
A. Revenue receipts (1+2)	18.6	17.7	18.1	17.6	18.4	19.3	19.7
1. Tax receipts	15.4	14.2	14.6	13.8	14.5	15.1	16.0
2. Non-tax receipts	3.2	3.5	3.5	3.8	3.9	4.2	3.7
of which: Interest receipts	1.1	0.9	0.9	0.8	0.7	0.6	0.7
B. Capital receipts	8.2	10.0	10.5	11.0	11.3	12.5	9.5
of which:							
a) Disinvestment proceeds	0.0	0.1	0.1	0.2	0.1	0.5	0.1
b) Recovery of loans & advances	0.6	0.3	0.5	0.6	0.5	0.8	0.3
II. Total disbursements (a+b+c)	28.8	27.9	28.5	28.7	29.5	32.2	29.2
a) Revenue	22.8	24.0	24.8	24.6	25.0	25.5	23.6
b) Capital	3.9	2.8	2.9	3.0	3.6	5.6	5.0
c) Loans and advances	2.0	1.1	0.9	1.2	0.9	1.0	0.6
III. Revenue deficit	4.2	6.3	6.6	7.0	6.6	6.2	3.9
IV. Gross fiscal deficit	9.4	9.5	9.6	10.0	9.5	9.4	7.9

$ The ratios to GDP for 2004-05 (BE) are based on CSO's Advance Estimates released in February, 2005.

Source: Reserve Bank of India.

Outlook

Fiscal consolidation has remained intractable despite initiatives of successive budgets at reducing deficits, primarily because of lack of accountability in fiscal marksmanship. One of the major factors that necessitated Parliamentary scrutiny of fiscal responsibility through a legislative framework was the fact that in a business-as-usual scenario, fiscal marksmanship would, in view of the large pressures for funds in an emerging economy, is seldom achieved without institutional accountability. The outlook on the fiscal front very much depends on how the credibility of the budgetary process is enhanced. In the medium term, adherence to FRBM targets, given the limitations of expenditure compression, critically hinges upon the success in raising the tax-GDP ratio. The continuance of the growth momentum witnessed in manufacturing and services and deepening of the tax reforms are likely to facilitate this process and thereby help reinforce growth with macroeconomic stability through fiscal consolidation.

The current year marks the beginning of fiscal adjustment mandated under the FRBM Act. The medium-term fiscal adjustment requires a quantum jump in tax revenues. The Budget for 2004-05 aims at an ambitious front-loaded reduction in revenue and fiscal deficit, beyond the mandated minimum reductions. The fiscal adjustment path shown by the Kelkar Task Force is primarily revenue-led. The Kelkar Task Force has arrived at the balance required under the FRBM Act in 2008-09 through progressive increases in the tax-GDP ratio from 9.2 per cent in 2003-04 (Prov.) to 13.17 per cent in 2008-09. Given the near stagnant tax-GDP ratio in the last few years due to tax restructuring, the task appears daunting, but not impossible. Sustaining the reform process in tax and expenditure regimes is a *sine quo non* for achieving the targets set under the FRBM Act. The tax base needs to be widened through increase in the share of services in tax revenues, removal of exemptions that do not conform to the established principles of tax policy, and an enforcement mechanism that is non-discretionary, transparent and effective. The present tax system needs to be further simplified and streamlined. The higher tax revenues have to be realised not through increasing tax rates, but through innovative changes in policies, procedures, laws and dispute settlement mechanism that help overcome the problems associated with the present complex system. Fiscal consolidation cannot be sustained without the active involvement of States, which account for about 39 per cent and 56 per cent of combined revenue receipts and expenditure, respectively. Fiscal reforms at the Centre and States should be complementary. In this context, harmonization of fiscal reforms at the Centre and States assumes critical importance. The TFC has provided a firm basis for such harmonization through linking debt relief for States to fiscal consolidation through FRBM type legislation. While the consensus reached for the proposed introduction of State-level VAT is a welcome step in the move towards harmonizing tax structures across States, establishing a national common market for goods and services for the country as a whole would require carrying forward this process of coordination.

The fiscal adjustment envisaged under the FRBM Act also is critically dependent on sustaining expenditure reforms through containing unproductive expenditure. While it is essential to increase the level of expenditure in social sectors and in building productive capacity in the economy, it is equally important to transform the outlays into better outcomes. The way forward is in fulfilling the NCMP objective of targeting subsidies sharply at the poor, carrying on with pension reforms, maintaining a benign interest regime through lower Government borrowings, effecting a shift in the composition of expenditures in favour of Plan capital expenditure, and reforms in public service delivery. Capacity development of the civil society organisations and civil service reforms, which facilitate a paradigm shift in public service delivery from the current hierarchical model to a more participatory one, are the demand and supply side governance pre-requisites for converting the enhanced outlays into sustained developmental outcomes.

Economic Survey 2004-05, Ch. 2, Public Finance (Excerpts)

8

Demographic Constraint

Interaction between Population Change and Economic Development

In recent years, there has been an increasing focus on the relationship between population growth and economic development. The most difficult problem for such an analysis is to be able to separate cause from effect. Does economic development accelerate or retard population growth or does population growth contribute to or retard economic development? What are the linkages and how strong they are and in what direction do they operate?

Economic Development and Population Growth

The Theory of Demographic Transition

The Theory of Demographic Transition attempts to explain why all contemporary developed nations have more or less passed through the same three stages of population growth. Before their economic modernisation, these countries, for centuries, had stable or very slow growing population as a result of a combination of high birth rate and almost equally high death rate. With economic development resulting in higher incomes, improved public health facilities, there was marked decline in mortality that gradually raised life expectancy from under 40 years to over 60 years. However, the decline in death rate was not immediately accompanied by a decline in fertility. With declining death rate but birth rate not falling correspondingly, these countries passed through stage two, marking the beginning of Demographic Transition i.e. transition from stable or slow growing population to rapidly increasing number. Finally, stage three is reached when the forces and influences of modernisation and economic development cause fertility to decline so that eventually falling birth rate converge with lower death rate leaving little or no population growth.[1] Thus, how does economic development affect population growth can be explained through the theory of demographic transition.

The Micro Economic Theory of Fertility

In recent years, economist have begun to look more closely at the micro economic determinants of family fertility. They have utilised the principles of economy and optimisation to explain family size decisions. In deciding whether or not to have additional children parents are assumed to weigh economic benefits against costs. The principle of benefits are the expected income from child labour usually on the farm and their family support for elderly parents. Balance against these benefits are the two principle elements of costs. (1) The opportunity cost of mother's time, the income she could earn if she were not at home caring for her children. (2) The cost of educating children that is the trade off between having fewer "high quality" high cost, educated children with high income earning potentials versus more "low quality", low cost, uneducated children with much lower earning prospects.

Statistical studies have shown that birth rates among the poor are likely to fall where there is —

(i) An increase in the education of women and consequent change in their role and status.

(ii) An increase in female non-agricultural wage employment opportunities which raises the price or cost of their traditional child bearing activities.

(iii) A rise in family income through increase in direct employment and earning of husband and wife and or redistribution of income and assets from rich to poor.

(iv) a reduction in infant mortality through expanded public health programme and better nutritional status for both parent and child.

(v) The development of old age and social security systems to bridge the economic dependence of parents on their offsprings.

Thus, efforts to make jobs, education and health more broadly available to poverty groups in Third World countries will not only contribute to their income and physical well being but it also can contribute substantially to their motivation for smaller families which is vital to reducing growth rates.

How Does Population Growth Affect Economic Development ?

So far we have tried to analyse the effect of economic development on population growth, now let us examine how does population growth affect economic development? We may begin by asking the question how does population growth affect the Net National Product?

Until recently, the literature of economic demography drew attention to two main relationships through which population growth affect the economy, what we may call (i) the 'saving effect' and (ii) 'composition of investment effect.'[2] The former of these argues that savings are reduced by population growth because of the so called burden of dependency. With high fertility and declining mortality in younger and older age groups, the population acquires an increasing proportion of people in the non-working age groups relative to those of working age. Since all must consume, in the absence of increasing output per worker, saving per head must fall. Even if productivity is increasing, savings are less than they would be with a smaller number of dependents per worker.

The investment argument is like this : with increasing population, a share of investible resources has to be devoted to reproducing for additional people unproductive facilities, duplication of social services which would be unnecessary if population were not growing. A number of studies starting with Coale and Hoover have shown through comparison of high and low fertility paths that there have been greater growth of GNP with the lesser rate of population growth. Robert Cassen has raised doubts on the validity of the above saving and investments effect. He argues, if bulk of savings in poor countries come from small wealthy class whose fertility is low and if cost of additional children are met out of consumption rather than saving, the saving cost of additional children would be quite inconsiderable.

In the macro economic picture, if population growth leads to slower growth of output, then one would expect slower growth of saving but to avoid circularity, the negative effect of population on GNP growth must be established independentally of the saving effect. Similarly, regarding the composition of investment effect, Cassen observes that one important area which has not been incorporated in the existing demographic models is the question of changing composition of the resource costs of producing basic consumption goods, that is food. As long as a society can increase agricultural output by mainly labour using means, the chief resource to feed growing population is provided by the population itself, the capital required is circulating capital, wage good to support the labour force. But a point is reached where required increases in agricultural output necessitated yield improving inputs which are expensive in both capital and foreign exchange. Just as Coale and Hoover model argued that with slower population growth more capital would have been available for raising per worker productivity because of reduced welfare expenditure, similarly Cassen argues that more capital and foreign exchange would have been available from reduction in expenditure devoted to raising agricultural output.

The composition of investment argument according to Cassen is really quite general. Wherever population growth requires increase in production, which in turn require investment, a lesser rate of population growth would release investible funds for use elsewhere. One fails to understand why past models have concentrated on welfare investment. Food production is infact the least postponable of all forms of population related output needs and if agriculture enters a phase of fundamental alteration in production function or in other words changing resource requirements for additional output, this can be a major burden of population growth. India reached this stage since mid 1960's when increases in agricultural output had to be brought out by yield improving technology which is capital intensive instead of increasing acreage. The biggest problem for India if current trend continues is the increasing share of investible surplus that will be taken up by food needs of the growing population.

According to K. Sundaram the implications of growing demographic pressures in India for the process of development in general and the progress towards poverty eradication become clearer once we focus on the labour force consequences of population growth. The sheer magnitude of the addition to work force brings to the fore the capital constraints in raising the productivity of the labour force. The capital requirement of equipping the labour force would be astronomically large.

It will be seen, that the growth rate of labour force is likely to be highest during the Ninth Plan period and only gradually decline thereafter. As a result, any planning over the perspective period will have to have employment generation as its central focus. If adequate work opportunities are not created, there would be growing incidence of unemployment in the country and an increase in the social tensions that arise therefrom.

The labour force expansion also puts direct pressure on the single most important natural resource in a predominantly agrarian economy, namely, land. Admittedly, the effective supply of land can be augmented by the use of reproducible capital. Irrigation is the most obvious example making it possible to increase the gross cropped area. The inadequate expansion of gross cropped area and of the irrigated area reflects the fact that the irrigation system has not expanded even upto the limits of currently known irrigation potential. This again is a manifestation of the inadequacy of capital resources. Further, it may be emphasized that even if currently known irrigation potential is fully utilised, it will leave a good chunk of the net sown area dependent on rain which may or may not be adequate. Thus, the moisture availability may act as an independent constraint on raising agricultural productivity and hence on over-all economic development.

While Sundaram has analysed the implications for growing demographic processes in India for the process of development in general, Pravin Visaria has focussed on the demographic aspects of development. The process of development has brought about a remarkable decline in mortality level from 22.8 during the decade 1951-60 to 10.3 during 1980-90. The decline in birth rate has been from 40.9 to 30.6 for the same period. Of course the decline in the level of fertility has not been large enough to lower the rate of natural increase of the population. According to Pravin Visaria, despite several limitations, the family planning programme has undoubtedly contributed to the observed decline in the total fertility rates and the birth rate. It has also helped to offset the possible increase in marital fertility rates that could have resulted from the decline in mortality and the incidence of widowhood. But for the family planning programme the rate of growth of India's population could have risen sharply as has happened in several African countries where the growth of population has been 3.6 and 3.8 per cent during 1985-90. The population of India's neighbours, Bangladesh and Pakistan, has too been growing at an annual rate of 2.7 to 3.4 per cent. By comparison, India seems to have done better and the rate of growth of population has remained stable at a moderate level.

The level of fertility is an integral aspect of development, universely related to the latter. The classical model of demographic position postulates a link between a desire for fewer children and change in macro developmental variables such as urbanisation, industrialization, literacy and education, and the status and role of women (Coale 1973, Friedman, 1982). A United Nation's study (1963) has added means of communication to the list. Significant changes in these variables subsumed under 'modernisation' do constitute sufficient conditions but there are multiple pathway to the eventual similiarity of the levels of fertility and mortality. There are lessons to be learnt from the experience of Kerala and Tamil Nadu which have already attained the replacement level of fertility (or a net reproduction rate of one) by 1988. An almost universal female literacy and a low level of infant and child mortality and the high status of women are considered crucial in the decline in fertility in Kerala. The decline in fertility in Tamil Nadu has been attributed to support for both increase in the age at marriage and an imaginative programme of information, education and communication (IEC).

Quite apart from the two southern states that have already lowered their fertility below the replacement level, the diversity of situation in India's heterogenous society needs to be taken into account. In a country with over 575,000 villages and 4700 urban centres, the means of modifying traditional behaviour have to be adapted to the local conditions.

The family planning programme in India has already had a considerable impact on the reproduction behaviour of the people. The challenging task ahead requires a certain shift in strategy from the achievement of centrally fixed targets to helping the people to achieve their reproductive goals. People would then realise the advantages of a small family and fertility decline would accelerate sharply.

BOX – 8.1

India's Demographic Achievement

Half a century after formulating the national family welfare programme, India has:

- reduced crude birth rate (CBR) from 40.8 (1951) to 26.4 (1998, SRS);
- halved the infant mortality rate (IMR) from 146 per 1000 live births (1951) to 72 per 1000 live births (1998, SRS);
- quadrupled the couple protection rate (CPR) from 10.4 percent (1971) to 44 percent (1999);
- reduced crude death rate (CDR) from 25 (1951) to 9.0 (1998, SRS);
- added 25 years to life expectancy from 37 years to 62 years;
- achieved nearly universal awareness of the need for and methods of family planning, and
- reduced total fertility rate from 6.0 (1951) to 3.3 (1997, SRS).

National Population Policy–2000

Stabilising population is an essential requirement for promoting sustainable development with more equitable distribution. However, it is as much a function of making reproductive health care accessible and affordable for all, as of increasing the provision and outreach of primary and secondary education, extending basic amenities including sanitation, safe drinking water and housing, besides empowering women and enhancing their employment opportunities, and providing transport and communications.

Objectives of National Population Policy

The immediate objective of the NPP 2000 is to address the unmet needs for contraception, health care infrastructure, and health personnel, and to provide integrated service delivery for basic reproductive and child health care. The medium-term objective is to bring the TFR to replacement levels by 2010, through vigorous implementation of inter-sectoral operational strategies. The long-term objective is to achieve a stable population by 2045, at a level consistent with the requirements of sustainable economic growth, social development, and environmental protection.

TABLE – 8.1

Population Projections

(millions)

Year	2000	2005	2010	2015	2020
Total	1,010	1,093	1,175	1,256	1,331
Under 15	361	368	370	372	373
15-64	604	673	747	819	882
65+	45	51	58	65	76

Source: Report of India Vision 2020 Committee, Planning Commission.

In pursuance of these objectives, the following National Socio-Demographic Goals to be achieved in each case by 2010 are formulated:

BOX – 8.2

National Socio-Demographic Goals for 2010

(1) Address the unmet needs for basic reproductive and child health services, supplies and infrastructure.

(2) Make school education up to age 14 free and compulsory, and reduce drop outs at primary and secondary school levels to below 20 percent for both boys and girls.

(3) Reduce infant mortality rate to below 30 per 1000 live births.

(4) Reduce maternal mortality ratio to below 100 per 100,000 live births.

(5) Achieve universal immunization of children against all vaccine preventable diseases.

(6) Promote delayed marriage for girls, not earlier than age 18 and preferably after 20 years of age.

(7) Achieve 80 percent institutional deliveries and 100 percent deliveries by trained persons.

(8) Achieve universal access to information/counseling, and services for fertility regulation and contraception with a wide basket of choices.

(9) Achieve 100 per cent registration of births, deaths, marriage and pregnancy.

(10) Contain the spread of Acquired Immunodeficiency Syndrome (AIDS), and promote greater integration between the management of reproductive tract infections (RTI) and sexually transmitted infections (STI) and the National AIDS Control Organisation.

(11) Prevent and control communicable diseases.

(12) Integrate Indian Systems of Medicine (ISM) in the provision of reproductive and child health services, and in reaching out to households.

(13) Promote vigorously the small family norm to achieve replacement levels of TFR.

(14) Bring about convergence in implementation of related social sector programs so that family welfare becomes a people centred programme.

If the NPP 2000 is fully implemented, we anticipate a population of 1107 million (110 crores) in 2010, instead of 1162 million (116 crores) projected by the Technical Group on Population Projections.

Census 2001

As per the Population Census of India, 2001, the population of India in March 2001, was 1,027 million, with 531 million males and 496 million females. India is following the demographic transition pattern of all developing countries from initial levels of "high birth rate — high death rate" phase to the intermediate stage of "high birth rate — low death rate" with high rates of population growth, before graduating to the "low birth rate — low death rate" phase. Over the last two decades, while the crude birth rate declined from 33.9 per thousand persons in 1981 to 25 per thousand persons in 2002, the crude death rate also declined from 12.5 per thousand persons in 1981 to 8.1 per thousand persons in 2002 (Table 8.2).

TABLE – 8.2

Selected Health Indicators

(person years)

Sl.No.	Parameter	1951	1981	1991	Current level
1.	Crude Birth Rate (Per 1000 Population)	40.8	33.9	29.5	25.0 (2002*)
2.	Crude Death Rate (Per 1000 Population)	25.1	12.5	9.8	8.1 (2002*)
3.	Total Fertility Rate (TFR) (Per woman)	6.0	4.5	3.6	3.2 (1999)
4.	Maternal Mortality Rate (MMR) (per 100,000 live births) NFHS	NA	NA	437 (1992-93)	407 (1998)
5.	Infant Mortality Rate (IMR) (Per 1000 live births)	146 (1951-61)	110	80	64 (2002*)
6.	Child (0-4 years) Mortality Rate per 1000 children	57.3 (1972)	41.2	26.5	19.5 (2000)
7.	Couple protection Rate (per cent)	10.4 (1971)	22.8	44.1	48.2 (1998-99) NFHS
8.	Life Expectancy at Birth				
	Male	37.2	54.1	59.7 (1991-95)	63.9 (2001-06)
	Female	36.2	54.7	60.9 (1991-95)	66.9 (2001-06)

Note: The dates in the brackets indicate years for which latest information is available.
NFHS: National Family Health Survey NA: Not Available
* Provisional
Source: Ministry of Health & Family Welfare.

In Socio-demographic parameters, in spite of considerable progress over the last two decades the country continues to lag behind several other countries in the region (Table 8.3). To correct this deficiency, the Tenth Plan envisages a reduction in infant Mortality Rate (IMR) to 45 per 1,000 by 2007 and 28 per 1,000 by 2012, reduction in Maternal

Mortality Rate (MMR) to 2 per 1,000 live births by 2007 and 1 per 1,000 live births by 2012 and reduction in decadal growth rate of the population between 2001-2011 to 16.2 per cent. As against the allocation of Rs. 15,120 crore for the Ninth Five Year Plan, the allocation for the Department of Family Welfare is Rs. 27,125 crore for the Tenth Plan. For the Annual Plan 2003-2004, the allocation increased to Rs. 4,930 crore from Rs. 4,150 crore in 2002-03 (RE).

TABLE – 8.3

India's global position in terms of socio-demographic parameters

Country	Life expectancy at birth (years)	Under-five mortality rate (per 1,000 live births)		Infant mortality rate (per 1,000 live births)		Maternal mortality ratio (per 100,000 live births)
	2001	1990	2001	1990	2001	1995
China	70.6	49	39	38	31	60
India	63.3	123	93	80	67	440
Nepal	59.1	145	91	100	66	830
Pakistan	60.4	128	109	96	84	200
Sri Lanka	72.3	23	19	19	17	60
Bangladesh	60.5	144	77	96	51	600
South Asia	62.8	126	96	84	69	427

Source: UNDP, Human Development Report 2003

Among the major states, the states of Kerala and Tamil Nadu have already achieved the replacement level of fertility viz. TFR of 2.1, while the states of Andhra Pradesh, Gujarat, Karnataka, Maharashtra, Orissa, Punjab and West Bengal, having a TFR in the range, of 2.2 to 3.0 are in the direction of achieving the replacement level of fertility. There are a few states, namely, Assam, Haryana and Madhya Pradesh, which are having a TFR in the range of 3.1 to 4.0 while the States of Bihar, Rajasthan and Uttar Pradesh have recorded TFRs in the range of 4.1 to 4.7 as per the Sample Registration System, 1999.

The National Population Stabilisation Fund (NPSF) was renamed and registered as Janasankhya Sthirata Kosh (JSK) in June 2003. The objective of JSK is to facilitate the attainment of the goals of National Population Policy (NPP) 2000. The Fund will support projects, schemes, initiatives and innovative ideas, designed to help population stabilisation both in the Government and voluntary sectors, and provide a window for canalising monies through voluntary contributions from individuals, industry, trade organisations and other legal entities in furtherance of this national cause. A contribution of Rs. 100 crores has been made out of plan budget.

India and World Population

The estimated global population in 2000 was 6055 million. The population of the ten most populous countries of the world is given in Statement 8.1.

The United Nations has estimated that the world population grew at an annual rate of 1.4 per cent during 1990-2000. China registered a much lower annual growth rate of population (one per cent) during 1990-2000, as compared to India (1.9 per cent during 1991-2001). In fact, the growth rate of China is now very much comparable to that of the USA (0.9 per cent).

Although, in terms of population USA ranks third in the world after India, there is a yawning gap of 746 million between the population of these two countries. India accounts for a meagre 2.4 per cent of the world surface area of 135.79 million square kms yet it supports and sustains a whopping 16.7 per cent of the world population. In 1950, China with 22 per cent share of the world population led the scene followed by India, which had a share of 14.2 per cent. It is now estimated that by 2050, India will most likely overtake China to become the most populous country on the earth with 17.2 per cent population living here[1].

References

Michael P. Todaro, Economic Development of the Third World (1983) Longman, P.18.

R.H. Cassen, India, Population, Economy and Society, Ch. 4, p. 221.

K. Sundaram, Demography and Development (1951-2001), Indian Economy Since Independence (2000-01 edition).

Registrar General & Census Commissioner, India, (2001), Census of India, 2001, Series I, Provisional Population Totals paper-I of 2001, March, New Delhi.

1. United Nations Population Division, World Population Prospects: The 1998 Revision.

STATEMENT – 8.1

Population of Selected Countries

Sl.No.	Country	Reference date	Population (in millions)
1	2	3	4
1.	China	01.02.2000	1,277.6
2.	India	01.03.2001	1,027.0
3.	U.S.A.	April, 2000	281.4
4.	Indonesia	01.07.2000	212.1
5.	Brazil	01.07.2000	170.1
6.	Pakistan	01.07.2000	156.5
7.	Russian Fed.	01.07.2000	146.9
8.	Bangladesh	01.07.2000	129.2
9.	Japan	01.10.2000	126.9
10.	Nigeria	01.02.2000	111.5

STATEMENT – 8.2

Population and its growth, India: 1901-2001

Census Years	Population	Decadal Growth		Change in decadal growth		Average annual exponential growth rate (percent)	Progressive growth rate over 1901 (per cent)
		Absolute	Percent	Absolute	Percent		
1	2	3	4	5	6	7	8
1901	238,396,327			-	-	---	---
1911	252,093,390	13,697,063	5.75	-	-	0.56	5.75
1921	251,321,213	-772,177	-0.31	-14,469,240	-6.05	-0.03	5.42
1931	278,977,238	27,656,025	11.00	28,428,202	11.31	1.04	17.02
1941	318,660,580	39,683,342	14.22	12,027,317	3.22	1.33	33.67
1951[1]	361,088,090	42,427,510	13.31	2,744,168	-0.91	1.25	51.47
1961[1]	439,234,771	78,146,681	21.64	35,719,171	8.33	1.96	84.25
1971	548,159,652	108,924,881	24.80	30,778,200	3.16	2.20	129.94
1981[2]	686,329,097	135,169,445	24.66	26,244,564	-0.14	2.22	186.64
1991[3]	843,387,888	163,058,791	23.86	27,889,346	-0.80	2.14	255.03
2001[4]	1,027,015,247	180,627,359	21.34	17,568,568	-2.52	1.93	330.80

Note: 1. In working out 'Decadal Growth' and 'Percentage Decadal Growth' for India 1941-51 and 1951-61 the population of Tuensang district for 1951 (7,025) and the population of Tuensang (83,501) and Mon (5,774) districts for 1961 Census of nagaland state have not been taken into account as the areas were censused for the first time in 1951 and the same are not comparable.

2. The 1981 Census could not be held owing to disturbed conditions prevailing in Assam. Hence the population figures for 1981 of Assam have been worked out by 'interpolation'.

3. The 1991 Census could not be held owing to disturbed conditions prevailing in Jammu and Kashmir. Hence the population figures for 1991 of Jammu and Kashmir have been worked out by 'interpolation'.

STATEMENT – 8.3

Distribution of Population, Sex Ratio, Density and Decadal Growth Rate of Population: 2001

S.No.	India/State/ Union Territory*	Total Population	Percentage Share in Total Population	Sex Ratio (females per 1,000 males)	Density (per sq.km)	Decadal Growth Rate	Literacy Rate (%)		
							Persons	Males	Females
	1	2	3	4	5	6	7	8	9
	India[1,2]	**1,027,015,247**	**100.00**	**933**	**324**	**21.34**	**65.38**	**75.85**	**54.16**
1.	Jammu & Kashmir[2,3]	10,069,917	0.98	900	99	29.04	54.46	65.75	41.82
2.	Himachal Pradesh[4]	6,077,248	0.59	970	109	17.53	77.13	86.02	68.08
3.	Punjab	24,289,296	2.37	874	482	19.76	69.95	75.63	63.55
4.	Chandigarh*	900,914	0.09	773	7,903	40.33	81.76	85.65	76.65
5.	Uttaranchal	8,479,562	0.83	964	159	19.20	72.28	84.01	60.26
6.	Haryana	21,082,989	2.05	861	477	28.06	68.59	79.25	56.31
7.	Delhi*	13,782,976	1.34	821	9,294	46.31	81.82	87.37	75.00
8.	Rajasthan	56,473,122	5.50	922	165	28.33	61.03	76.46	44.34
9.	Uttar Pradesh	166,052,859	16.17	898	689	25.80	57.36	70.23	42.98
10.	Bihar	82,878,796	8.07	921	880	28.43	47.53	60.32	33.57
11.	Sikkim	540,493	0.05	875	76	32.98	69.68	76.73	61.46
12.	Arunachal Pradesh	1,091,117	0.11	901	13	26.21	54.74	64.07	44.24
13.	Nagaland	1,988,636	0.19	909	120	64.41	67.11	71.77	61.92
14.	Manipur	2,388,634	0.23	978	107	30.02	68.87	77.87	59.70
15.	Mizoram	891,058	0.09	938	42	29.18	88.49	90.69	86.13
16.	Tripura	3,191,168	0.31	950	304	15.74	73.66	81.47	65.41
17.	Meghalaya	2,306,069	0.22	975	103	29.94	63.31	66.14	60.41
18.	Assam	26,638,407	2.59	932	340	18.85	64.28	71.93	56.03
19.	West Bengal	80,221,171	7.81	934	904	17.84	69.22	77.58	60.22
20.	Jharkhand	26,909,428	2.62	941	338	23.19	54.13	67.94	39.38

Contd...

...Contd...

1		2	3	4	5	6	7	8	9
21.	Orissa	36,706,920	3.57	972	236	15.94	63.61	75.95	50.97
22.	Chhatisgarh	20,795,956	2.03	990	154	18.06	65.18	77.86	52.40
23.	Madhya Pradesh	60,385,118	5.88	920	196	24.34	64.11	76.80	50.28
24.	Gujarat[5]	50,596,992	4.93	921	258	22.48	69.97	80.50	58.60
25.	Daman & Diu*	158,059	0.02	709	1,411	55.59	81.09	88.40	70.37
26.	Dadra & Nagar Haveli*	220,451	0.02	811	449	59.20	60.03	73.32	42.99
27.	Maharashtra	96,752,247	9.42	922	314	22.57	77.27	86.27	67.51
28.	Andhra Pradesh	75,727,541	7.37	978	275	13.86	61.11	70.85	51.17
29.	Karnataka	52,733,958	5.14	964	275	17.25	67.04	76.29	57.45
30.	Goa	1,343,998	0.13	960	363	14.89	82.32	88.88	75.51
31.	Lakshadweep*	60,595	0.01	947	1,894	17.19	87.52	93.15	81.56
32.	Kerala	31,838,619	3.10	1,058	819	9.42	90.92	94.20	87.86
33.	Tamil Nadu	62,110,839	6.05	986	478	11.19	73.47	82.33	64.55
34.	Pondicherry*	973,829	0.09	1,001	2,029	20.56	81.49	88.89	74.13
35.	Andaman & Nicobar Islands*	356,265	0.03	846	43	26.94	81.18	86.07	75.29

Note:

1. The population of India includes the estimated population of entire Kachchh district, Morvi, Maliya-Miyana and Wankaner talukas of Rajkot district, Jodiya taluka of Jamanagar district of Gujarat State and entire Kinnaur district of Himachal Pradesh where population enumeration of Census of India 2001 could not be conducted due to natural calamities.
2. For working out the density of India and Jammu & Kashmir the entire area and population of those areas of Jammu & Kashmir which are under illegal occupation of Pakistan and China have not been taken into account.
3. While working out the decadal growth of population of Jammu and Kashmir the population figures for 1991 have been worked out by interpolation as 1991 Census could not be held in this State owing to disturbed conditions.
4. Figures shown against Himachal Pradesh have been arrived at after including the estimated figures of entire Kinnaur district of Himachal Pradesh where the population enumeration of Census of India 2001 could not be conducted due to natural calamity.
5. Figures shown against Gujarat have been arrived at after including the estimated figures of entire Kachchh district, Morvi, Maliya-Miyana and Wankaner talukas of Rajkot district, Jodiya taluka of Jamnagar district of Gujarat State where the population enumeration of Census of India 2001 could not be conducted due to natural calamity.

Source: Census of India, 2001, Series I, March 2001.

9

Demographic Aspects of Development

The Indian Experience

Pravin Visaria

A majority of the Indian elite and social scientists regard the large and growing population of the country as its critical problem. Including an estimate for Jammu and Kashmir where the census could not be conducted, the 1991 Census enumerated nearly 846 million persons in the country. India's population is second largest in the world(886 million by mid-1993). More importantly, its average annual rate of growth has remained stable around 2.1-2.2 per cent for nearly three decades now. With the population of China increasing slowly (at about 1.4 per cent per annum), the absolute annual addition to the Indian population exceeds that of the Chinese population. Within about 50 years (depending on the pace of decline in the Indian growth rate), India will become the most populous country of the world.

Prior to independence, intercensal decades showing a rise in the rate of population growth were considered periods of peace and relative prosperity. Also, the acceleration of population growth since 1947 has been a result of the success of various policies to lower the mortality rate. Given the universal preference for a long life, mortality decline has been an important dimension of the gains of development. However, the usual lags in the compensating declines in fertility and birth rates have led to a rise in the rate of natural increase. The factors contributing to the lag between the declines in mortality and fertility include all the determinants of human reproductive behaviour.

To facilitate an understanding of these complex interrelationships, this paper outlines the key characteristics of India's population, the basic determinants of population growth (fertility and mortality) and population projections, and the various factors that limit the effectiveness of policies to accelerate the decline in fertility.

Population Growth in Historical Perspective

Data pertaining to selected population statistics for India since 1901, including the estimated average annual intercensal growth rates, the level of urbanisation or the percentage of urban population, and the sex ratio (males per 1000 females) of the total populations are presented in Table 9.1.

TABLE – 9.1

Key Population Statistics of India, 1901-1991

Census Year	Total population (million)	Average annual growth rate (per cent)	Density (persons per sq km)	Sex ratio (males per 1000 females)	Per cent of urban population
1901	238.3	0.3	77	1029	10.8
1911	252.0	0.6	82	1038	10.3
1921	251.2	N	81	1047	11.2
1931	278.9	1.1	90	1053	12.0
1941	318.5	1.3	103	1058	13.9
1951	361.0	1.3	117	1057	17.3
1961	439.1	2.0	142	1063	18.0
1971	548.2	2.2	178	1075	19.9
1981	683.3	2.2	221	1071	23.3
1991	846.3	2.1	267	1076	25.7
2001	1027		324	933	

The rate of intercensal growth was less than two-thirds of 1 per cent during 1901-11, and in fact, negative during 1911-21. The main factors underlying the slow growth and the decline were the recurrence of epidemics of plague and cholera and of famines and also the influenza epidemic of 1918-19 and its after-effects.

The influenza epidemic is estimated to have killed almost 5 per cent of the total population of the subcontinent, with the death toll totalling between 16 and 20 million. After 1921, a progressive control of cholera and plague epidemics facilitated an acceleration of the rate of population growth between 1 and 1.3 per cent (Davis, 1951). The growth rate was virtually stable during 1931 and 1951, partly because of the Bengal famine of 1942-43, and the dislocation caused by the partition and the subsequent large scale movement of refugees across what suddenly became international borders.

The decline in the mortality level during the past four decades has been truly remarkable. Epidemics have been controlled. The spraying of DDT helped to check the impact of malaria which used to cause fairly long-lasting debility and contributed to high mortality. During the past one and a half decades the resistance to DDT developed by the malaria causing mosquitoes has led to a resurgence of the problem. In spite of this, the average length of life of the population has risen from about 32 years in the 1940s to 55 years during 1981-85, 57 years during 1986-90 and about 60 years during 1992-93. The number of infant deaths during the first year has dropped from about 225-250 per 1000 in the 1940s to about 80 per 1000 in 1990.

The magnitude of change has far exceeded the expectations or at least the anticipations in the early 1950s.[1] Yet, it is far short of the performance of several other Asian countries such as China, Sri Lanka, Thailand, and the Republic of Korea which have reduced infant mortality rates still further (between 20 and 30) and achieved a higher life expectation for their citizens. Only Kerala state in India has attained comparable progress, with an infant mortality rate of 17 in 1990.

Fertility

The trends in birth and death rates in India since 1901 are presented in Table 9.2. The estimates up to 1971 are 'indirect', based on the age distributions of the population enumerated by successive censuses and the intercensal rate of population growth. The sample registration system was started in 1971 to provide annual estimates of vital rates that are reasonably 'reliable' at the all-India level, with a margin of error of no more than about 5 to 10 per cent.

According to these data, the death rate in India began to decline after 1920 and the trend is continuous. The birth rate also seems to show a downward trend from the beginning of this century, but the pace of decline in the birth rate has been much slower than that of the drop in the death rate. This has led to the acceleration of the rate of natural increase. Since net international migration to or from India has been relatively negligible, the rate of natural increase almost equals the growth rate.

In demographic parlance, the birth and death rates shown in Table 9.2 are 'crude rates'. They are influenced by the age distribution of the population.

TABLE – 9.2

Vital Rates per 1000 Population, India, 1901-1990

	Birth rate	Death rate	Rate of natural increase
1901-10	49.2	42.6	6.6
1911-20	48.1	47.2	0.9
1921-30	46.2	36.3	9.9
1931-40	45.2	31.2	14.0
1941-50	39.9	27.4	12.5
1951-60	40.9	22.8	18.1
1961-70	40.0	17.8	22.2
1971-80	37.8	15.4	22.4
1980-82	33.8	12.3	21.5
1988-90	30.6	10.3	20.3

Sources: Davis (1951); India, Registrar General (1954); Jain (1982); Office of the Registrar General, *Sample Registration Bulletin* (various issues).

The underlying fertility rates can be measured in terms of total fertility rate (TFR) or the average number of children born to a woman up to the end of the reproductive cycle. Once again, the indirect estimates based on age data and the intercensal growth rates suggest a TFR of around 6.2 to 6.4 during 1901-31. These values are only a little higher than the estimate of 5.9 given by the National Sample Survey during 1951-52 (second and fourth rounds). Allowing for some understatement of births in a survey, requiring recall of past events, one can interpret the data as suggesting a virtually constant fertility. Between 1951-52 and 1966, the TFR appears to have remained stable around 6.0; some suggest a modest decline of 5 per cent to 5.7. Thereafter, the decline in fertility has accelerated and the TFR in the country as a whole was 5.3 during 1970-72, 4.5 during 1980-82 and 3.9 during 1988-90 (India,

Registrar General, 1993). The later figure indicates a decline of about 42 per cent in fertility over the 30-year period between 1961 and 1989 and 26 per cent between 1971 and 1989. Of course, this decline in the level of fertility has not been large enough to lower the rate of natural increase of the population. Reasons for this relatively slow decline are discussed below.

Age at Marriage

The key determinants of Indian fertility are: (a) the proportion of married in the population and the age at marriage, and (b) marital fertility rates or the number of children born to married women. Traditionally, marriage has been both universal and early in India. Less than 1 per cent of Indian women remain unmarried beyond the age of reproduction (i.e. age 45). Besides, they marry at an early age. The reference here is not merely to the formal ceremony of marriage but to effective marriage or cohabitation. Estimates based on the duration of time spent as single or never-married are summarised in Table 9.3. In 1951, the average age of Indian girls at the time of marriage was less than 16. Though the mean marriage age has risen slowly over the years, even in 1987-88, it was below 19. (Urban girls marry later, at an average age of 20.7 years, than their rural counterparts.)

TABLE – 9.3

Singulate Mean Age at Marriage (Estimated as the Duration of Time Spent as Single) by Sex, 1951 to 1987-88 (Years)

Census/survey year	Men	Women
1951	19.9	15.6
1961	21.3	15.9
1971	22.4	17.2
1981	23.3	18.3
1987-88[a]	23.4	18.7

[a] Based on the 43rd Round of the National Sample Survey.

Source : Data on marital status by age compiled from successive censuses and published as *Social and Cultural Tables* at the all-India level.

A rise in the age at marriage has meant a delay in the beginning of childbearing. Yet, the decline in mortality rate has lowered the proportion of widowed. In the past, when widow remarriage was proscribed, many of the widows were effectively excluded from the group of childbearing women. The fall in the incidence of widowhood, shown in Table 9.4, may partly reflect the reported relaxation of the prohibition of widow remarriage; but the latter is unlikely to be a major effect. In any case, the lower proportions of widowed have partly offset the effect of rise in the age of marriage.

TABLE – 9.4

Percentage of Widowed among Persons Aged 10 and Over

Census	Males	Females
1951	6.8	17.6
1961	5.2	15.5
1971	4.1	12.7
1981	3.3	11.1

Source : Same as Table 9.3.

Marital Fertility

According to the data available from the Sample Registration System, the average number of children born to a married woman by the end of her reproductive period was 5.5 during 1986-88. The estimates for rural and urban areas were: 5.6 and 5.0. For 1971-72, the estimates were 6.9 and 6.0, respectively. Even the latter values are much lower than the biological maximum observed among the Hutterites, a community of German ancestry, settled in north-western United States and Canada, which viewed fertility regulation as sinful and high fertility as a blessing. The average number of children born to Hutterite women married between 1921 and 1930 was 10. Fertility in India has been much lower than that of the Hutterites; it has been restrained by several customary checks on cohabitation, prohibition of widow remarriage and prolonged lactation.

The main determinants of marital fertility are the extent of use of contraception, abortion, and the length of breast-feeding — all of which tend to delay the resumption of menstruation after a delivery (lactational infecundability). Changes in the duration of breast-feeding of infants seem to be small. The use of canned 'baby foods' has allegedly spread in rural areas and is said to be extensive in urban areas. However, the high cost of baby foods effectively limits their use; and it seems most unlikely that the average length of breast-feeding has declined significantly over the past decade or two. The Medical Termination of Pregnancies Act of 1972 has 'legalised' the use of abortion as a means of limiting the family size in the event of a failure of a method of contraception and certain exigencies such as rape, or a risk to the physical or mental health of the mother. Since 1982-83, the annual number of abortions under the Medical Termination of Pregnancies Act has fluctuated between 516,000 and 588,000. The total number of abortions registered under the Act since 1972 has been 6.4 million up to 31 March 1989 (India, Ministry of Health and Family Welfare, 1990). Yet, 'legal' abortions performed essentially in metropolitan or urban areas are presumably only the proverbial tip of an iceberg and a much larger number of induced abortions remain unregistered.

Practice of Contraception

Since 1952, the family planning programme in India has been trying to encourage the spread of contraception on a voluntary basis. For estimating the impact of these efforts, the Indian practice has been to estimate 'effective couple protection' rates, which take into account the presumed efficacy of the method used for preventing conception. The percentage of effectively contracepting couples has increased from 0.2 per cent at the end of 1960 to about 15 per cent at the end of the Fourth Plan (1974), 22 per cent at the end of the Sixth Plan (1980) and 40 per cent at the end of 1990. Prima facie, the increase in the practice of contraception appears quite impressive, particularly during the 1980s. Independent national surveys conducted by the Operations Research Group (ORG) during 1970, 1980 and 1988 have confirmed the increase in the adoption of contraception.[2]

The estimates for different sub-groups of the population are summarised in Table 9.5. The data confirm some widespread hypotheses and also provide a few interesting insights. The use of contraceptives increases with age and educational attainment of the woman, the number of living children and the number of living sons. It is significantly higher among urban couples than among rural couples. However, very few of the childless couples seem to be using modern methods of contraception. Also, while contraceptive use has increased, since 1970, even among couples not having any son, it is much lower than among couples having at least one son. The widespread preference for sons is a major factor retarding contraceptive use. Contrary to widespread belief, even Muslim couples seem to adopt contraception, but less frequently than couples of other religions. Within the ranks of Hindus, the scheduled tribes and scheduled castes lag behind higher caste couples in the use of contraceptives; but the scheduled castes are ahead of the scheduled tribes. These differentials by religion and caste are generally consistent with the known differences among the groups with respect to the level of literacy and education.

TABLE – 9.5

Estimates of Current Contraceptive Use in India by Selected Charateristics of Couples, 1970, 1980 and 1988

Characteristics	All methods			Modern methods		
	1970	1980	1988	1970	1980	1988
Age of wife						
15-24	7	13	20	5	9	15
15-29	14	32	44	9	26	39
30-34	17	45	58	13	37	52
35-39	18	52	66	13	42	58
40-44	17	47	60	11	36	55
All	13	35	45	9	28	40
Education of wife						
Illiterate	10	28	37	7	22	34
Up to primary	21	47	54	15	39	48
Secondary	33	53	58	25	44	49
High School and above	56	61	65	38	47	53
No. of living children						
Nil	2	4	5	2	3	3
One	7	17	24	4	11	17
Two	13	33	49	8	25	42
Three	16	49	61	11	40	56
Four	18	54	62	14	45	58
Five or more	25	51	55	19	42	50
No. of sons						
Nil	5	11	18	3	7	13
One	12	34	44	8	26	37
Two	19	51	64	13	42	59
Three	20	55	62	16	46	58
Four or more	24	51	59	19	42	53
Place of residence						
Urban	27	51	56	21	41	51
Rural	11	31	39	7	25	36
Religion						
Hindu	14	36	46	10	29	41
Muslim	9	23	34	7	18	29
Others	25	48	62	15	39	55
Caste among Hindus						
Scheduled Caste	NA	28	39	NA	22	34
Scheduled Tribe	NA	33	33	NA	28	29
Other caste Hindus	NA	38	49	NA	30	44
No. of children and desire for additional children						
Have no child	2	4	5	2	3	3
Have 1-2 children and want more children	6	11	18	3	7	12
Have 1-2 children and do not want more children	18	60	68	12	46	59
Have 3 or more children and want more children	5	6	9	2	3	6
Have 3 or more children and do not want more children	23	63	69	18	53	64

The number of couples surveyed was 25,330 in 1970, 26,076 in 1980, and 44,918 in 1988.
Sources: Operations Research Group (n.d., 1983, 1990).

Some Critical Questions

A few critical questions can legitimately be raised: (a) Has India, which takes pride in having been the first country in the world to launch a state-run programme for promoting family planning by the people, done as well as other countries of the world in achieving its goals? (b) Is the decline in the birth rate and the rate of natural increase consistent with the reported increase in the percentage of couples effectively protected against the risk of contraception? If not, why not? (c) Have the people recognised the seriousness of the population problem? (d) What can be done to accelerate the decline in the birth rate?

Contraceptive Prevalence in Comparative Terms

In comparative terms, it must be admitted that by 1987, contraceptive prevalence rates (CPR) in several Asian countries such as China, Thailand and Sri Lanka had reached relatively high levels of 74, 66 and 62 and the crude birth rates in these countries had dropped to 21-22 by 1990 (World Bank, 1991). The corresponding CPR in India was 47 at the end of March 1989 and the birth rate in 1990 was 30. (The reference here is not to the effective couple protection rates cited earlier but to the percentage of married women using contraceptives). Even in Bangladesh 32 per cent of the married women were using contraceptives by 1987. The conclusion seems inevitable that India could and should have done better than it has done in promoting contraception. The reasons for the slow progress are discussed below.

Rise in Contraceptive Use and Fall in Birth Rates

Turning to the second question, the decline in the birth rate appears much slower than the increase in contraceptive prevalence rates during the 1980s. An important explanation for this is the overstatement of the number of acceptors of two reversible methods, IUDs and condoms. The overstatement is attributed to the pressure on the health workers to achieve the targets set by the 'higher authorities' at the district and state levels. As a result, the targets and achievement data, which were expected to help improve the management and monitoring of the family planning programme, have become counter-productive. There is a strong case to scrap the practice of prescribing targets for each district, taluka and village, and to encourage the health and family planning personnel to concentrate on helping the couples to achieve their respective reproductive goals.

Second, the acceptance of contraception (particularly sterilisation) is delayed to a time when the couples have already crossed the age of 30.

In 1988-89, the average age of acceptors of sterilisation was above 30. By the time women cross 30, they have completed a major part of their child-bearing. The demographic effect of their sterilisation can only be small.

Despite these limitations, the family planning programme has undoubtedly contributed to the observed decline in the total fertility rate and the birth rate. It has also helped to offset the possible increase in marital fertility rates that could have resulted from the decline in mortality and in the incidence of widowhood. But for the family planning programme, the rate of growth of India's population could have risen sharply, as has happened in several African countries.

During 1985 and 1990, the population of some African countries – Kenya, Tanzania, Uganda and Zambia – is reported to have grown at an annual rate of between 3.6 and 3.8 per cent. (As a result, their population would double in 18 to 19 years.) The population of India's neighbours, Bangladesh and Pakistan, has also been growing at an annual rate of 2.7 to 3.4 per cent (implying a doubling in 20 to 26 years). By comparison, India seems to have done better; and the rate of growth of its population has remained stable at a moderate level.

Recognition of the Population Problem

A basic reason for the slow decline in fertility is the fact that most individual couples do not really associate a worsening of their living conditions with an increase in their family size or the growth of population in the village. They do not perceive many of the adverse implications of continuing population growth because of the several escape routes (such as out migration) open to individual couples or persons but not to the larger group or country as a whole. Further, despite the continuing population growth at the average annual rate of 2 per cent for the past 40 years, the standard of living of the people has indeed improved. According to a 1989 survey of nearly 13,200 households in four districts of Gujarat (two of them with a significant proportion of scheduled tribes), between 64 and 86 per cent of the respondents indicated that 'the living conditions of the people in general' in their village or town had improved. Improvements were perceived with respect to availability of schools, transportation and health care facilities, and decline in maternal as well as infant mortality. A large majority (between 83 and 97 per cent) realised the growth of population in the village or town; but between 39 and 66 per cent of the respondents did not see a link between population growth and living conditions (Visaria, 1990). Prima facie, it seems surprising because the per capita availability of agricultural land in rural areas has steadily declined from 0.64 hectares in 1950-51 to 0.33 in 1985-86 (Central Statistical Organisation, 1991: Table 14). A sceptic may argue that the biases of interviewers can influence the responses to such qualitative questions. Yet, one must not underrate or ignore the value of perceptions of the people ascertained through qualitative questions.

Possible Pathways to a Faster Decline in Fertility

We can focus attention on the presumably objective indicators of the factors influencing the level of fertility, particularly the lags between declines in mortality and fertility. On the basis of the experience of several countries in Europe, North America and East Asia, the classical model of demographic transition postulates a link between a desire for fewer children and changes in macro-developmental variables such as urbanisation, industrialisation, literacy and education, and the status and roles of women (Coale, 1973; Freedman, 1982). A study by the United Nations (1965) has added means of communications to the list. These changes affect the aspirations relating to children, functions of the family and the perceptions of the costs and benefits of children. Empirical research has highlighted the difficulty of establishing threshold levels of different indicators which may constitute the necessary conditions for fertility decline. Significant changes in these variables, subsumed under 'modernisation', do constitute sufficient conditions but there are multiple pathways to the eventual similarty of the levels of fertility and mortality.

As Indian social scientists are concerned about the absence of a decline in the rate of population growth (despite some fall in the birth rate), it is time to consider the level and pace of changes in the macro indicators of development. The level of fertility is 'an integral aspect of development', albeit inversely related to the latter (Srikantan, 1982). The extent to which conscious policies have determined the pace of change is also an important issue. There are lessons to be drawn from the experience of Kerala and Tamil Nadu which have already attained the replacement level of fertility (or a net reproduction rate of one) by 1988. The term 'replacement level of fertility' or a net reproduction rate of one (or unity) implies that as a cohort of women experiences risks of death and bears children according to the particular age pattern observed during the specified period, each woman would give birth, on an average, to only one daughter.

Urbanisation

The level of urbanisation in a country is substantially affected by the specific definitions chosen by the national authorities. In China, for example, the proportion of urban population was reported to have increased from nearly 22 per cent at a time of the 1982 Census to about 53 per cent by mid-1989 (Visaria and Kothari, 1987; World Bank, 1991); but the 1990 Census has reportedly classified only 26 per cent of the population as urban. In Sri Lanka and Thailand, in mid-1989, only 21 to 22 per cent of the population were residents of urban areas. Evidently, therefore, a low level of urbanisation is not *per se* a hindrance to a decline in fertility. The Indian definition of a town has remained unchanged since 1961. The proportion of urban population in India has increased from about 11 per cent in 1901 to 18 per cent in 1951 and to a modest 26 per cent in 1991. (The latter figure is almost the same as China's for 1990). The total urban population in India in 1991 (including Jammu and Kashmir where the cesus was not conducted) was about 218 million. Had it formed a separate country, it would have been the fourth most populous country of the world (after China, India and the USA).

Both birth and death rates tend to be lower in urban than in rural areas of India. But the differences largely offset each other and the urban rate of natural increase was only slightly lower than the rural. There is some indication that net rural-urban migration has increased in absolute magnitude, but its contribution to urban growth during 1961-71, 1971-81, and 1981-91 was only 21, 20, and 29 per cent, respectively. The net reclassification of rural localities as urban accounted for 15, 13, and 9 per cent, respectively, of the urban growth during the three decades (Visaria and Kothari, 1987; India, Census of 1991, 1991b; Visaria, 1993). The 1991 Census data on migration are not yet available. However, it is evident that the decline in the rate of urbanisation during 1981-91, relative to 1971-81, is partly because of a slowing down of the process of reclassification of rural localities as urban.

An explanation lies in the acute shortage of urban housing and the relatively inexpensive transport facilities, which facilitate communication. Policies which encourage the location of new industrial units outside the cities with a population of more than one million and other incentives to develop the backward areas also have a similar effect.

Almost three-fourths of India's population live in over 575,000 villages. Nearly 73 per cent of the villages had a population of less than 1,000 persons each. They accounted for nearly 32 per cent of the rural population of the country in 1981. The average population of a village, which was only 911 in 1981, has increased to about 1091 in 1991. As a result, the percentage of small villages in terms of population and their share of the rural population have both declined. Yet, the dispersal of population raises the cost of providing various services, including education and health, to the people.

In the context of the need to accelerate fertility decline, it does not seem a feasible option to adopt conscious policies to promote urbanisation. The economies of agglomeration need to be recognised and the state policy cannot effectively neutralise them without considerable cost of society. At the same time, the processes underlying urbanisation are not easily amenable to state intervention, particularly in view of the severe resource crunch.

Workforce Participation and Industrialisation

Industrialisation is measured in terms of the proportion of the workforce engaged in the manufacturing sector (sometimes including mining and construction) or in non-agricultural activities. The Second Five-Year Plan of India had envisaged a sharp decline in the percentage of Indian workforce engaged in agricultural activities from nearly 70 per cent in 1956 to about 60 per cent by 1976 (Visaria and Basant, 1993).

Before evaluating the changes in the nature of economic activities, it is essential to examine the worker-population ratios or the labour force participation rates (which show the proportion of people participating or seeking to participate in the process of production of goods and services in the economy). Changes in the procedures of the 1971 and 1981 Censuses with respect to the enumeration of workers have led to a false impression of a decline in the proportion of women participating in economic activities. However, the quinquennial surveys of the NSS beginning with 1972-73 have confirmed the stability of the worker-population ratio of the total population around 41-42 per cent. The figures are around 54 per cent for rural males, 32 to 34 per cent for rural females, 49-51 per cent in urban males and 13-15 per cent for urban females. The estimates relate to the population of all ages taken together. (See Visaria and Minhas, 1991.)

Changes in the sectoral distribution of the workforce are partly a correlate of urbanisation (with only a very small proportion of urban workers engaging in agricultural activities) and partly a result of diversification of rural economic activities due to specialisation. For rural

India, the NSS surveys between 1972-73 and 1987-88 indicate a decline of 9 percentage points (from 83 to 72) in the proportion of male workers engaged in the agricultural sector; the corresponding decline among female workers is about 5 percentage points, from 90 to 85 per cent. Changes in the sectoral distribution of urban workers are similar in relative terms, though the share of the primary sector among them is naturally much smaller than among rural workers.

Overall, the diversification of the sectoral pattern of the workforce has proceeded more slowly than was envisaged in the late 1950s. A large majority of the workers continue to cultivate land although the intensity of cultivation and the use of modern inputs such as improved varieties of seeds, fertilisers and pesticides have increased. These changes have been accompanied by a considerable strengthening of the economic infrastructure in rural areas such as electrification, transport and communication network. However, the impact of these improvements has been rather slow.

A correlate of the observed changes has been an increase in the proportion of employees and a decrease in the proportion of the self-employed in the workforce. The self-employed find it feasible to accommodate their children on the family farm or in the family interprise. Employees, on the other hand, have to worry about remunerative work opportunities for their children. Therefore, an increase in the proportion of employees is likely to raise the percentage of people who are likely to be forced to the assessment of alternative courses of action and should be conductive to accelerating fertility decline. We shall discuss the possible contribution of this process to the demographic transition in Kerala. It is also necessary to recognise the limits of employment planning in the 1990s and the constraints on the capacity of the state to expand employment in the organised sector. The growing pressure of population on land may nevertheless raise the proportion of agricultural labourers in the rural labour force.

Literacy and School Enrolments

Even at the time of independence, India had much lower literacy rates, particularly in the case of women, than Sri Lanka or Thailand. Since independence, the availability of schooling facilities has expanded substantially. According to the Fifth All India Educational Survey of 1985, about 95 per cent of the rural population had access to a primary school within 1 Km and 85 per cent had a middle school within 3 km. (The distances represent the official norms for 'walking distance' for students of primary and middle school, respectively.) However, when a 'habitation' rather than a village was used as the relevant unit, almost 49 per cent of the 979,000 rural habitations, with a population of 117 million (20 per cent) in 1986, did not have a primary school within the habitation (India, Ministry of Education, 1990: 139-40).

Like the previous censuses, the 1991 Census has shown a rapid increase in the literacy rate among women compared to that among men. In spite of this, rural female literacy rate (25 per cent) is only half the male rate of 47 per cent. Besides, there are large inter-state variations. In the four large states in north India (Uttar Pradesh, Bihar, Rajasthan and Madhya Pradesh), which account for one-third (285 million) of the country's population, the (crude) female literacy rate in rural areas was below 20 per cent (the rate was merely 21 per cent in Andhra Pradesh). While the state or society must necessarily provide adequate schooling facilities, we must understand the reasons for the 'low demand' for female literacy. Evidently, the large majority does not seem to share the emphasis of the urban elite on literacy and female education.

Improvements in literacy are a result of the process of attrition of the aged cohorts with high levels of illiteracy and the rising levels of literacy among the relatively larger cohorts of young children who can avail of the growing infrastructure of schooling facilities. Data on school attendance ratios of boys and girls, available from the Ministry of Education, indicate virtually universal school enrolments and high drop-out rates. The alternative estimates based on the 1981 Census and the two large NSS surveys of 1983 and 1987-88 reveal quite a high percentage of the never-enrolled and a relatively low drop-out rate. (Quite likely, formal or nominal school enrolments of many children do not really sink into the minds of their parents or other members of their families.)

Marked rural-urban and inter-state differentials in the current school attendance ratios of boys and girls are presented in Table 9.6. The four large states in north India (LNIS) lag behind the all-India average of school attendance ratios with respect to rural girls only. An important reason appears to be the perceived risk to the safety and security of a young girl when she attends a school at some distance and not merely the need for support in looking after the younger siblings while the mother goes out to work.

This latter fear about safety and security does not seem to be unwarranted in the light of the prevailing law and order conditions in many rural areas of the country. The fear probably depresses a rise in the age of marriage among girls as well. It is not surprising that the average age of marriage among girls in India even in 1987-88 was below 19 years (in Kerala, on the other hand, the mean age at marriage among females was nearly 22 years).

TABLE – 9.6

Percentage of Boys and Girls Aged 5-14 Going to School in 1987-88

State	Boys		Girls	
	5-9	10-14	5-9	10-14
Rural Areas				
All India	52.5	64.3	40.4	52.8
Bihar	33.0	54.6	19.7	28.7
Madhya Pradesh	43.9	61.6	26.3	29.9
Rajasthan	47.8	69.8	25.5	19.2
Uttar Pradesh	45.4	63.8	28.2	30.7
Urban Areas				
All India	73.0	79.9	67.8	71.9
Bihar	53.7	75.0	45.8	64.0
Madhya Pradesh	71.3	88.3	64.5	76.8
Rajasthan	68.3	83.2	54.7	64.0
Uttar Pradesh	58.9	71.3	49.4	60.8

Sources: NSS data based on the 43rd Round, 1987-88, published in *Sarvekshana*, Special No., during 1990 (all-India) and 1992 (state series).

The need for accelerating the rate of the levels of school attendance and literacy among children of school going age is widely recognised. But, the situation is not likely to improve without substantial changes in the quality and content of instruction offered by many of the rural as well as urban schools. The inclusion of population education in the curriculum of schools would also help only if the teachers can hold the interest of their pupils.

The Status of Indian Women

Among the frequently used indicators of the status of women in a society are the sex differentials in life expectancy at birth and child mortality rates, school enrolment ratios, school retention rates and maternal mortality rates. The age at marriage and the worker-population ratios of women are likely to reflect their status as well as roles. A telling index, however, is the sex ratio or the number of males per 1000 females.

Most developed countries have a higher proportion of females in their populations because women are biologically sturdier and live longer than men. In India, however, all the censuses have shown lower proportion of women; women enumerated in the 1991 Census number 31 million less than men. The data shown in Table 9.1 indicate a stability of the sex ratio since 1971 around 93 females per 100 males. Also, Punjab and Haryana with the lowest proportion of women have continued to show an improvement during 1971-91.

Earlier analytical work has shown higher female mortality as the primary cause of the deficit of women in India (Visaria, 1971). The SRS data suggest a narrowing of the differentials adverse to girls, particularly during childhood which contribute more to the deficit of women than maternal mortality. During the 1980s, urban India had also witnessed an emergence of a reprehensible practice of female foeticide following amniocentesis or the identification of the sex of the foetus. But its contribution to the deficit of women in the total population is perhaps exaggerated. Likewise, there seems to be little credible evidence that the sex ratio of births has risen during the 1980s or that the double counting of males has been more in the 1991 Census than in the preceding censuses (Premi, 1991; Rajan *et al.*, 1991: 2963-64).

The situation with respect to some of the other indicators of the status of women has already been noted above. The level of literacy and education as well as the mean age at marriage have been rising and the proportion of widows has been falling since independence. The pace of change is slower than we would like but its direction is certainly right. Some analysts have taken the employment of women or the female worker-population ratio as an indicator of their status. However, as noted earlier, contrary to the widespread belief based on the census data, the NSS surveys have confirmed a stability of the level of work participation by women. Also, a realistic assessment of the role of planning authorities in employment generation does not suggest a significant scope for their raising the volume of work opportunities for women.

Despite the improvements noted above, Indian women face many handicaps and discrimination with regard to nourishment and growth, access to medical care in the event of an illness, choice of spouse, rights of ownership and inheritance, and even freedom of movement and decision-making for routine matters. On all these matters, very large inter-group differences preclude any generalisation. The growing awareness about these problems also augurs well for their solution. An elimination of all discrimination must indeed be our national goal. But given the difficulty of enforcing new social norms through laws or constitutional provisions, the scope for state intervention to raise the status of women in order to accelerate the decline in fertility seems extremely limited.

Infrastructure and Communication

An excellent index of development is the availability of electricity. There has been a rapid expansion of electrification of villages in India. At the end of 1950-51, only 3061 villages had electricity. A major increase began after 1965-66. By March 1993, 84 per cent of Indian villages were 'electrified'(CMIE, 1993: 2-10). However, the percentage of rural households primarily using electricity for lighting their residences was only 15 in 1983 and 27 in 1988-89 (NSSO, 1988, 1990).

India has been rather slow in introducing television in the country. Regular TV transmissions began only in 1965. As recently as 1981, only 24 per cent of the total population of the country had access to television transmissions. The number of TV-relay centres has expanded rapidly from 42 at the end of 1983 to 520 at the end of 1990 and almost 84 per cent of the total population can now view TV programmes. The number of TV sets in use in the country has increased rapidly from 25,000 in March 1971 to 1.5 million in March 1981 and 22.5 million at the end of 1989. However, this increase has been limited due to low income levels; and people preoccupied with earning the means of bare sustenance have little time to watch TV for entertainment. It is likely that the spread of TV would accelerate the process of modernisation of rural India. Imaginative programmes for 'information, education and communication' about family size norms may contribute towards hastening the pace of fertility decline. *Ex ante,* however, their impact is difficult to judge.

Population Projections

The projections of population of India were last revised by a Standing Committee of Experts on Population Projections in 1989. Taking into account the available data on fertility trends, the Committee projected a population of 843.6 million for 1 March 1991, only a little lower than the enumerated population of nearly 846 million (India, Census of 1991, 1991a). The estimate was higher than that given by an Expert Committee (837 million), which had reported earlier in 1987-88 (India, Census of 1981, 1988). Pending the availability of the age distribution of the population enumerated by the 1991 Census, it is difficult to revise the last population projections. It is clear, however, that barring some exceptional development, India's population would certainly exceed 100 crore at the time of the next census in 2001.

The United Nations projections for India envisage that a replacement level of fertility would be attained by AD 2015 (instead of 2006-2011 postulated by the Planning Commission in 1985 while formulating the Seventh Five-Year Plan) (United Nations, 1991: 430-31; Planning Commission, 1985: 281).

The United Nations projections include an adjustment of the base population for net undercount in the census (on the ground that national planners must provide for the needs of people left out from the census count). They estimate a mid-year population of 1,042 million in 2000, 1,224 million in 2010, 1,372 million in 2020, and 1,442 million in 2025.

Beginning with a mid-1990 population of 853 million, the United Nations projections imply an average annual growth rate of 2.0 per cent during 1990-2000, 1.6 per cent during 2000-2010, 1.1 per cent during 2010-20 and 0.5 per cent during 2020-2025. These projections may seem unduly pessimistic and India would certainly do well to accelerate the decline in its rate of population growth. Projections are certainly not predictions; they only highlighted the implications of alternative assumptions. (The United Nations projections envisage high and low variants implying a population of 1567 and 1294 million, respectively, by 2025.)

As we look at these numbers it is important to remember the young age distribution of the Indian population and its in-built momentum of growth. The issue merits some elaboration.

Age Distribution of the Indian Population

It is a well-established fact that the change in the fertility level of a population has a greater impact on its age distribution than the change in mortality. This is so because changes in death rates at different ages tend to be correlated and usually follow the same direction. A change in fertility, on the other hand, has a tangible impact on the size of the birth cohort. When fertility decline is accompanied by mortality decline, the latter partly offsets the effect of the drop in the birth rate; however, the former effect dominates.

The slow decline in the birth rate during the 1980s and the stability of the growth rate during 1981-91 imply that the change in the age distribution of India's population during the past decade has been relatively small. The age distribution of the sample population surveyed by the NSS during 1987-88 resembles closely that of the population enumerated by the 1981 Census. The Indian age distribution continues to be 'young', with children under age 15 forming nearly 38.5 per cent of the total in 1987-88. (The sample registration system has reported a figure of 36.9 per cent for 1990.)

The number of women in the reproductive age group (15-44) is likely to continue to grow for quite some time. As a result, even if the young couples in India decide to have no more than two children, effective immediately, population would continue to increase for around 60 to 70 years; and beginning with a total of at least about 862 million on March 1, 1992, India's population would eventually stabilise at a level about 70 per cent above the current size (at a level of nearly 1,465 million). This seems to be an inevitable result of the momentum of growth built into the young age distribution. Of course, there is no probability of all Indian couples deciding immediately to have no more than two children. Therefore, the actual course of population growth in India is likely to lead to an even larger ultimate population.

The case for urgent action to slow down the rate of population growth is obvious. The Chinese response to a similar exposition of the dynamics of growth of their population was to adopt a 'one-child policy'. Despite the numerous criticism levelled against this policy, the Chinese seem to have been moderately successful in implementing it at least in urban areas. Even if the policy has been relaxed in some areas (or even if it is now abandoned), the Chinese are expected to attain the replacement level of fertility by 1995.

It would be utopian to plead for the adoption of a one-child policy in India. Even the relatively modest coercion applied in the Indian programme during 1975-77 gave a major setback to government's efforts to spread the small family norm in the country. The Indian political structure and leadership do not command the credibility and the strength that come naturally to the Chinese policy-makers.

The Experience of Kerala and Tamil Nadu

The two southern states of Kerala and Tamil Nadu with a population of 84.7 million (10 per cent of the total) in 1991 illustrate the alternative ways of reaching a replacement level of fertility.

In Kerala, with its very low infant and child mortality rate, the adoption of a two-child norm has led to a total fertility rate of 2.0; allowing for mortality, its fertility is below the replacement level.

An almost universal female literacy and a low level of infant and child mortality, and the high status of women, all intrinsically desirable goals, are considered crucial in the decline in fertility in Kerala. However, other important contributory factors include the very high pressure of population density on land and an associated low proportion of rural male workers engaged in agriculture (the lowest, 54 per cent, among the major states according to the 1987-88 survey of the NSS), a very low proportion of the self-employed, and relatively very high rates of open unemployment (the highest in the country). The persistent high level of unemployment has been accompanied by the demonstration by the emigrants to the Middle East of the feasibility of getting out of the vicious circle of poverty. Such a juxtaposition of forces favourable to fertility decline through both delayed marriage and control of marital fertility is not easy to find elsewhere in the country.

The Working Group on Population Policy, appointed by the Planning Commission, had in 1980 suggested that six other states — Andhra Pradesh, Gujarat, Haryana, Maharashtra, Punjab and Tamil Nadu — might attain a net reproduction rate of one by 1991-92. Among these, in Tamil Nadu, high infant and child mortality has led to a below replacement level of fertility in 1988 even with a total fertility rate of 2.5 and a gross reproduction rate of 1.2. The infant mortality rate in Tamil Nadu was 67 in 1990; and its crude female literacy rate according to the 1991 Census was 45 per cent.

The decline in fertility in Tamil Nadu has been attributed to the political support for both an increase in the age at marriage and an imaginative programme of 'information, education and communication'(IEC). The activity was reportedly aided by the involvement of a great social reformer, 'Periyar' Ramaswamy, in creating awareness among the people 'to liberate women from frequent delivery by use of contraception' and 'to delay marriage'. The reformer was the founder of the Dravida Kazhagam from which the DMK that succeeded the Congress to power in Tamil Nadu emerged (see Antony *et al.,* 1989: 219; Antony, 1992). His disciples have carried the message to newly-wed couples as well as others. Yet, as mortality in Tamil Nadu is likely to drop further, Tamil Nadu must lower its TFR to 2.1 to maintain its fertility at the replacement level.

In urban India with a total population of nearly 217 million, the TFR has declined to 2.8. Besides Kerala and Tamil Nadu, urban population of West Bengal (nearing 19 million or 27 per cent of the population of the state) has also reported a TFR of 2.1-2.2 during 1988-90 or a replacement level of fertility. While there is some uncertainty about the level of fertility in urban areas of West Bengal previously, Calcutta urban agglomeration (with a population of 11 million in 1991) accounts for almost 59 per cent of the urban population of the state. The decline in fertility in the Calcutta metropolitan area might, therefore, be an important factor underlying the change in urban West Bengal. Yet, the significance of this change need not be underestimated because Greater Bombay urban agglomeration with a population of 12.6 million accounts for 41 per cent of the urban population of Maharashtra state, but the TFR of urban Maharashtra during 1988-90 was 2.7. (The value 2.7 was 31 per cent below that of 3.9 estimated for 1970-72.)

Policy Shifts Essential for the Tasks Ahead

The replication of the experiences of Kerala and Tamil Nadu elsewhere in the country, particularly in the four large states in north India is a formidable task. The experience so far reveals a few lessons that might be useful in achieving the long-term goals of the country. In brief, they must include:

1. A well designed programme of increasing the efficacy of the large body of health workers for the difficult task of persuading their clientele to modify their reproductive behaviour.
2. A shift from method specific targets relating to the number of acceptors to an emphasis on the evaluation of the change in the birth rate and in infant, child and adult mortality rates with a complete registration of all vital events in all rural and urban areas.
3. The adoption of a scheme of incentives and disincentives to delay marriage and to limit the number of children after marriage.

To elaborate, health workers recruited by the Indian family planning programme are grossly ill-equipped for the difficult task assigned to them. A careful review of their training is essential. Modern management methods can ensure a system of uninhibited feedback and interaction between the workers and their superiors to tackle the difficult situations. The working hours and the methods can also be modified to ensure a less bureaucratic approach with a concern for the basic needs and dignity of the disadvantaged people.

To facilitate the above change, the Indian programme must abandon its indiscriminate and consequently counter-productive emphasis on the achievement of method specific targets of acceptors. Quite apart from the two southern states that have already lowered their fertility below the replacement level, the diversity of situations in India's heterogeneous society needs to be taken into account. In a country with over 575,000 villages and 4,700 urban centres, the means of modifying traditional behaviour have to be adapted to the local conditions. For this purpose, health workers must focus their attention on the level of birth and death rates and strive to register all pregnancies, births, and infant, child and adult deaths. An identification of a pregnancy can be followed by a systematic sequence of ante-natal, intra-natal and post-natal care for both the mother and the child. The result would be a high degree of rapport between the health workers and their clientele. A carefully monitored experiment in some 15-20 target free districts for a period of 5 to 10 years in cooperation with some non-governmental voluntary agencies and researchers deserves a high priority.

Finally, an effective system of 'incentives and disincentives' for lowering the rate of growth of population can make an invaluable contribution. Incentives and disincentives must be used to encourage youth to marry late and to delay and limit their childbearing after marriage. Incentives seem to be difficult to administer without adding to the corruption except in the organised sector of employment; also, given the fiscal crisis faced by the Indian state, their scope is likely to be limited. Therefore, the focus must be on disincentives. Obviously, we cannot penalise children born to what may be called 'improvident' parents; but an environment in which the seriousness of our population problem is fully recognised by everyone must be created. A law may be enacted disqualifying anyone from applying for a job in the government or the public sector if at the time of marriage, the bride was below 21 years of age. Given the large number of aspirants for government and public sector jobs, the proposed law would have the salutary effect of raising the age at marriage. (The organised private sector can also be persuaded to follow a similar policy.) We might also consider whether the right to contest an election and to hold public office can be denied to couples who decide to have more than two children. Such a restriction on the privileges enjoyed by our citizens would have a much wider impact than is usually realised. Of course, the changes mooted above would be more effective in a setting in which the key elements of the classical demographic transition model are favourable to fertility decline.

As Indian policy-makers look ahead, there is no scope for complacency but there is no need for panic either. The second most populous country of the world with widespread poverty, low literacy and relatively high infant and child mortality rates naturally cannot be complacent about what has been achieved so far. Much remains to be done to eliminate from the remote areas of several backward states the extremes of dire poverty such as hunger and acute want. Continuing population growth makes it difficult to achieve these goals. However, it would be erroneous to panic and to take recourse to hasty measures of dubious efficacy involving an excessive degree of 'guidance' or convert direction as to when couples should have children and when they should stop.

The Indian family planning programme has already had a considerable impact on the reproductive behaviour of the people. The level of contraceptive prevalence has risen significantly and fertility has declined substantially. The challenging task ahead requires a certain shift in strategy towards an emphasis on the quality of care and strengthening the rapport between the health workers and the people, particularly in rural areas. If the central concern of the family planning programme shifts from the achievement of centrally fixed targets to helping the people to achieve their reproductive goals, people would indeed realise the advantages of a small family, the contraceptive prevalence would rise further and fertility decline would accelerate sharply. As noted above, a substantial increase in India's population is unavoidable. Our deepest reserves of strength as a society must be harnessed to mitigate the pain of adjustment and adaption to the emerging situation.

Notes

1. The authors of the First Five-Year Plan as well as the Census Commissioner, who conducted the 1951 Census, had envisaged that the growth rate observed during 1941-51 would continue during the 1950s as well (Planning Commission, 1952).
2. The ORG data pertain to the percentage of couples using a method of contraception or 'current contraceptive use' (and non 'effective' use).

References

Antony, T.V. (1992), "Family Planning Programme: A Different Strategy". Unpublished paper presented at a symposium on 'Perspectives on India's Development in the 1990s' organised to commemorate 40 years of partnership between Indian institutions and the Ford Foundation, New Delhi, 28-29 January.

Antony, T.V., Srinivasan, K. and Saxena, P.C. (1989), "Case Studies of Population Policies and Programmes in India" in G.D. Ness and E. Sattar (eds.), *Strategic Management of Population Programme, Management Contributions to Population Programmes Series*, Vol.7. Kuala Lampur: International Committee on the Management of Population Programmes.

Bongaarts, John (1978), "A Framework for Analyzing the Proximate Determinants of Fertility", *Population and Development Review*, Vol.4, No.1, March, p.p. 105-32.

Census of India, (1961), Vol.1, India, Parts II-A (i): *General Population Tables*, 1961 and II-C (i): *Social and Cultural Tables*, 1964.

——— (1971), Series 1, India, Parts II-A (i): *General Population Tables*, 1975 and II-C(ii): *Social and Cultural Tables*, 1977.

——— (1981), Series 1, India, Paper 1 of 1982: *Final Population Tables*; Part II: *Special Report and Tables based on 5 per cent Sample Data*, 1984; Part II-B(i): *Primary Census Abstract: General Population* 1983.

——— (1991), Series 1, India, Paper 2 of 1991: *Provisional Population Totals: Rural-Urban Distribution*.

Central Statistical Organisation (1991), *Selected Socio-Economic Indicators for India*, 1990. New Delhi.

Centre For Monitoring Indian Economy (CMIE) (1993), *Current Energy Scene in India*. Bombay.

Coale, Ansley, J. (1973), "The Demographic Transition" in International Union for the Scientific Study of Population, *International Population Conference*, Vol.1. Liege.

Croll, Elisabeth et al. (eds.). (1985), *China's One-Child Family Policy*. New York: St. Martin's Press.

Davis, Kingsley (1951), *The Population of India and Pakistan*. Princeton, N.J.: Princeton University Press.

Freedman, Ronald (1982), "Fertility Decline: Theories" in John A. Ross (ed.), *International Encyclopedia of Population*. New York: The Free Press.

India, Census of 1981 (1988), *Report of the Expert Committee on the Population Projections*. Occasional Paper No.4. New Delhi: Office of the Registrar General.

India, Census of 1991 (1991a), *Provisional Population Totals*, Paper 1. New Delhi.

——— (1991b), *Provisional Population Totals: Rural-Urban Distribution*. Paper 2. New Delhi.

India, Ministry of Education (1990), *Towards an Enlightened and Human Society: Report of the Committee for Review of National Policy on Education 1986*. New Delhi.

India, Ministry of Health and Family Welfare (1990), *Family Welfare Programme in India: Yearbook*, 1988-89. New Delhi.

India, Office of the Registrar General (1989), *SRS Based Abridged Life Tables* 1981-85. Occasional Paper No.1. New Delhi.

——— (1991), *Sample Registration System* 1988. New Delhi.

India, Registrar General (1954), Census of India, Paper 2 of 1954. *Life Tables* – 1951 Census. New Delhi.

——— (1988), *Sample Registration System*. New Delhi. (Including reports for previous years.)

——— (1993), *Sample Registration System* 1990. New Delhi (forthcoming).

ICSSR (1983), *Social Information of India: Trends and Structure*. New Delhi: Hindustan Publishing Corporation. (The estimates are based on a 1977 paper by V.S. Swamy, entitled 'Vital Rates and Population Growth', prepared as a status paper.)

Jain, S.P. (1982), *Actuarial Report and Life Tables* 1951-61. New Delhi: Office of the Registrar General.

NSSO (1988), "A Note on Source of Drinking Water Energy Used for Cooking and Lighting", *Sarvekshana*, Vol.12, No.2, October-December.

——— (1990), *Report on Housing Condition*. NSS 44th Round (July 1988-June 1989). New Delhi.

Operations Research Group (ORG). n.d. *Family Planning Practices in India: The First All-India survey Report*. Baroda.

——— (1983), *Family Planning Practices in India – Second All-India Survey Report*. Baroda.

——— (1990), *Family Planning Practices in India, Third All-India Survey Report*. Baroda.

Planning Commission (1952), *The First Five Year Plan*. New Delhi.

——— (1985), *Seventh Five Year Plan* 1985-90, Vol.II. New Delhi.

Premi, M.K. (1991), *India's Population: Heading Towards a Billion*. Delhi. B.R. Publishing Corporation.

Rajan, S.I., Misra, U.S. and Navaneetham, K. (1991), "Decline in Sex Ratio: An Alternative Explanation?", *Economic and Political Weekly*, Vol.26, No.51, 21 December.

Srikantan, K. Sivaswamy (1982), "Threshold Hypothesis" in John A. Ross (ed.), *International Encyclopedia of Population*, Vol.1, New York: The Free Press.

United Nations (1965), Department of Economic and Social Affairs, *Population Bulletin of the United Nations*, No.7 (1963).

——— (1991), *World Population Prospects*, 1990. Population Studies No. 120. New York: Department of International Economic and Social Affairs.

Visaria, Pravin (1971), *The Sex Ratio of the Population of India*. Census Monograph No.10. New Delhi: Office of the Registrar General, India.

——— (1990), "Poverty, Development and Change in India: Some Reflections", *The Indian Journal of Social Science*, Vol.3, No.3.

——— (1993), "Urbanization in India: An Overview". Typescript, Gujarat Institute of Development Research, Ahmedabad.

Visaria, Pravin and Basant, Rakesh (1993), "Non-Agricultural Employment in India: Problems and Perspective" (forthcoming).

Visaria, Pravin and Kothari, Devendra. (1987), "Data Base for the Study of Migration and Urbanization in India: A Critical Analysis" in S. Manzoor Alam and Fatima Alikhan (eds.), *Perspectives on Urbanization and Migration: India and USSR*. New Delhi: Allied Publishers.

Visaria, Pravin and Minhas, B.S. (1991), "Evolving an Employment Policy for the 1990s: What do the Data Tell Us?", *Economic and Political Weekly*, Vol.26, No.15, 13 April.

World Bank (1991), *World Development Report*, 1991. New York: Oxford University Press.

Indian Journal of Social Science, Vol.6, No.3, 1993. Was reprinted with permission from the author.

Part II

Agriculture

10

Developments in Indian Agriculture

Major Issues

Chapters 11 to 16 are devoted to Agriculture: the factors affecting production and productivity in Indian agriculture: the institutional factors relating to the land reform measures, the technological factors relating to the technology aspect and modernisation of agriculture, food security and the public distribution system and food and agricultural development policies and Indian agriculture in the new international trade regime.

Reforms in land system in post-independent India are discussed in Ch.11 (S.K. Ray). The technology aspect and policy issues relating to modernisation of Indian agriculture are discussed in Ch.12 (Rao & Jeromi). Farm sector performance and reform agenda are discussed in Ch. 13 (Landes & Gulati) Ch. 14 by Mihir Rakshit provides a critique of Food policy in India. Growth and welfare consequences of rise in MSP are discussed in Ch.15 (Parikh, Kumar & Darbha).

Agriculture is the most important sector of the Indian economy from the perspective of poverty alleviation and employment generation. Agriculture accounts for about 25 per cent of India's national income. The share of agriculture in national income has been declining from 56.5 per cent in 1950-51 to 52.1 per cent in 1960-61, 45.7 per cent in 1970-71, 39.6 per cent in 1980-81, 33 per cent in 1990-91, 25.2 (Provisional) per cent in 1999-2000, 24.2 per cent in 2000-01 (Quick estimates) and 24.3 per cent in 2001-02 (Advance estimates)[1]. While the

1. Central Statistical Organisation.

share of agriculture in national income has been declining, the workforce engaged in agriculture has exhibited only a marginal decline. Data provided by the Census of India reveals that whereas in 1961, 75.9 per cent of total workforce was engaged in agriculture (the absolute number being 143.2 million workers), in 1981 the percentage was 69 and further fell to 63.8 in 1993-94 and 59.9 in 1999-2000. In absolute terms, agriculture provided employment to 238.68 million persons in 1993-94. In 1999-2000 also although the percentage had declined from 63.8 to 59.9, the number of persons employed remained 237.8 million.

Linkage between Agriculture and Industrial Sectors

The linkages between agriculture and industrial sectors, widely recognised in the literature, focus on the role of agriculture as (i) supplier of wage goods to the industrial sector, (ii) provider of raw materials to agro-based industries which have a weight of 21.2 per cent in the Index of Industrial Production (base: 1980-81=100) and weight of 17.6 per cent in the index with base 1993-94=100, and (iii) generator of agricultural income that enables rural demand for industrial products to take place. Empirical tests show that a unit increase in agricultural output would have a positive effect on both industrial production and national income. Rangarajan (1982) estimated that a one per cent increase in agricultural output tends to raise industrial production by 0.5 per cent and augment national income by 0.7 per cent. The experience in the 'eighties and 'nineties also lends support to the thrust of the findings. During the 'eighties, the trend growth rate of 3.2 per cent in agricultural production appeared to have contributed to accelerated industrial production. The decelerated growth rate in agricultural production seems to have impacted on growth of industrial production in the 'nineties.

Indian agriculture has made significant progress during the last five decades in terms of ensuring food security through higher production, diversification (both in terms of crops and regions), absorption of modern technology, and to a limited extent, reduction in poverty. During the last fifty year period from 1950-51 to 1999-2000, agricultural production grew at an annual compound growth rate of 2.7 per cent (foodgrains 2.5 per cent and non-foodgrains 3.0 per cent). As a result, large-scale import of foodgrains and starvation deaths are no more recurring in India. On the contrary, the country could build up a huge buffer stock of foodgrains (now more than the requirement for internal consumption), which is generally considered as a sort of safety net of the economy (along with growth in foreign exchange reserves).

The Institutional Context

It is important, at the very outset, to understand the institutional, demographic and socio-political context within which agricultural growth has been taking place. The prevailing framework had a profound impact on the pattern of agricultural development. This, in turn, has necessitated special strategies and policies for employment generation and poverty removal in rural areas. The thrust of policies, in the first decade of planning (1951-61) was on institutional and agrarian reforms. The two basic objectives of land reforms were (i) to remove such impediments on agricultural production as arise from the character of agrarian structure in rural areas and (ii) to reduce or eliminate exploitation of landless and small cultivators through measures of land redistribution. The main elements of the land reforms measures carried out during this period were:

(i) to abolish intermediaries (such as zamindar and Jagirdars) between the government and the tillers so as to ensure security of tenure to the latter and eventually to make them the owners of land;

(ii) to impose ceilings on the ownership of landholdings and distribute the surplus land among the landless labourers.

The intermediaries were abolished within a few years after independence and the actual tillers accounting for about 40 per cent of the cultivated area became owners. This, according to C.H.H. Rao provided a major incentive for investment and the growth of agriculture in large parts of the country.

As regards the ceiling on land holdings and distribution of surplus land among the landless, there were two rounds of land reform legislation — one in the fifties and another in the early seventies. However, due to numerous exemptions provided in the law and due to the lack of political will, the objective of this reform could not be fulfilled and not much surplus land could be acquired by the government for distribution among the landless. According to G. Parthasarthy, Indian land reform, conceived as a programme of conferment of rights of ownership on tenants and as public distribution of the land of the big owner in favour of the small farmer and the landless has, by and large, been a failure. The only exception to this sad record is the abolition of intermediaries. However, its indirect effects on the agrarian structure have been marked, though the character of these effects has varied depending upon the responses generated in varying situations of tenurial relationships.

The direct effects of the public distribution programmes to alter the structure of ownership holdings and of cultivation holdings were only marginal except in select pockets. The indirect effects were however quite significant. The major indirect effects were in respect of absentee ownership. The quantitative significance of these could not be precisely measured. But there is enough evidence in a number of studies to indicate the varying trends. Broadly speaking, the absentee landowner was of less importance in the early seventies than in the early fifties. His importance waned much more in the dry areas than in the irrigated areas in which land is much more valuable. Transfers of land, under the forewarning impact of tenancy and ceiling legislation, to the resident landowners was on a much larger scale in the dry than in the irrigated areas. The result of shifts in land from the absentee to resident landowner was a decline in tenancy.

The forewarning effects of tenancy and ceiling legislation had also some effects on the structure of ownership holdings among the residents. The greed of the big landowner to acquire more land was kept in restraint, and the transfer of land should have been effected mainly to the middle group, who were below the declared level of ceiling. Decline in tenancy, resulting in transfers of tenanted land at least in part to the owner cultivator groups, resulting in the drift of tenants into landless, combined with demographic pressures and poor absorption of the growing numbers in non-agriculture had led to a rise in the class of rural proletariat even in the absence of expansion of the large farm. Where tenants had not been evicted, tenancy was pushed underground with informal arrangement and security of tenure.

The emerging agrarian structure revealed that less than one-fourth of the rural households controlled more than 70 per cent of the land, another one-third less than 30 per cent and the rest two-fifths, among whom the majority are the landless agricultural labour, depend upon employment of wage labourers. The likely trend is an increase in the number of percentage of wage labourers. Rich peasants preferred to avoid conflicts with labour on wage issues during crucial peak operations and would rather chose to use tractors and other mechanisation devices adding to the poverty of the landless.

According to S.K. Ray, "On balance, there seems to be some reasons to conclude that agrarian reorganisation in India has failed to make any considerable impact on the socio-economic conditions of the working cultivators. Indeed, the record so far is so depressing and frustrating that even an able administrator like Appu, who championed and spent a considerable part of his career in administering land reform programmes noted:

> "Thus the programmes of land reform implemented since Independence did not lead to any significant re-distribution of land, or, the removal of all the obstacles to increasing agricultural production. Of the three programmes considered in this study, the laws for the abolition of intermediary interests were implemented fairly well. But in the case of tenancy reform and ceilings on holdings, the policies adopted were ambivalent and there were large gaps between policy and legislation and between legislation and implementation. We have seen that as result of the implementation of the tenancy laws, tenants became owners of or acquired rights in only about 4 per cent of the operated area. The enforcement of ceilings led to the redistribution of less than 2 per cent of the operated area. Thus these two measures taken together led to the redistribution of only about 6 per cent of the operated area" (Appu, 1995, p.217).

It is against the background of the last four decades experience that the need to reformulate the land policy of India should be considered. Even persons emotionally attached with land reform programmes agree that the scope for improving implementation through legislative measures is now very limited. They point out, the socio-economic and political environment in which these programmes were introduced have changed so dramatically, that it would be almost impossible to carry out the reforms. Appu described the changed environment as follows:

> "...If the political will in favour of meaningful land reform was weak at independence and weaker still later on, it is non-existent today. Land reform has practically disappeared from the agenda of most political parties. This, in my view, is the inevitable consequence of the great changes that have taken place in the social and economic fields. With the abolition of intermediary interests the erstwhile superior tenants belonging mostly to upper and middle castes acquired a higher social status. Rise in agricultural productivity, rising land values and higher incomes from cultivation have added to their economic strength. Substantial landowners who wield great authority in rural India are bitterly opposed to ceilings on agricultural holdings. They are able to have their way because no serious efforts have been made to organise the landless and the land poor and enlist their support in favour of reforms. As for tenancy reform is concerned, there is a certain commonality of interest between all landowners - large, medium, small and even marginal. They are all passionately attached to their land and all of them are opposed to conferring benefits on insecure tenants. In the first round of land reform only the intermediaries were adversely affected. They were few in number and were weak politically. They had also made themselves obnoxious by aligning themselves with the colonial power. So it was easy enough to abolish intermediary interests. And it was done without hurting them much. But injuring the interests of the present class of landowners is an entirely different proposition. No political party that wishes to win elections and come to power can afford to do that. At the time of independence this class of landowners did not wield much political and economic power, and with a modicum of political will the reforms could have been implemented. But now it has become almost impossible to carry out the reforms" (Appu, 1995, pp. 232-233)."

The New Technology

It was becoming clear by the mid-sixties that there was no alternative to technological change in agriculture for achieving self-sufficiency in foodgrains. Even those countries in Asia which could carry out radical land reforms and build up an adequate infrastructure for agriculture had taken to the path of modernizing agriculture. Japan took the lead in this direction and China followed suit even after successfully experimenting with structural changes and mobilization of a growing labour force for capital construction in agriculture.

After the mid-sixties, apart from the introduction of High Yielding Varieties (HYVs) of seeds for wheat and rice, public investment in agriculture was stepped up significantly. The new technology raised the profitability of investment for the farmers. Besides, in agriculture, there is a high complementarity between public and private investment. As a result, the annual gross capital formation in agriculture, public and private combined, at constant prices, rose much faster than in the pre-green revolution period.

This is reflected in the accelerated increase in gross irrigated area. From less than one million hectares per annum during the pre-green revolution period, it increased to about 2.5 million hectares per annum during the Seventies. However, owing to the land constraint, the growth of net sown area slowed down considerably. This explains why, despite the accelerated increase in capital formation and the introduction of new technologies, the growth rate of agricultural output in the post-green revolution period as a whole was broadly the same as in the pre-green revolution period.

Nevertheless, there was a rapid increase in the marketed surpluses of foodgrains and in the stocks held by the government through internal procurement. This is due to the basic changes in the structure of agricultural production witnessed in this period. First, the breakthrough in foodgrains output occurred in the developed regions in the North-West and in certain parts of the South. The consumption of foodgrains was already high in these areas and therefore a considerably larger proportion of additions to output was marketed. Second, the use of labour per unit of output showed a significant decline, which also resulted in the generation of larger foodgrain surpluses from the rural areas.

There are two other factors responsible for the rise in marketed surpluses and availability of foodgrains. The increase in output during this period has been taking place mainly through the increase in yield per hectare. Therefore, there has been a decline in the ratio of seed to output. Second, the rate of urbanization has increased and the average per capita consumption of foodgrains in the urban areas has been significantly lower than in the rural areas.

It is usual to compare the performance in the pre-green revolution period with that in the post-green revolution period as a whole. However, the mid or the late-Seventies mark a definite departure, in several respects, from the trends observed in the early phase of the green revolution. There seems to be some improvement in the growth rate of foodgrains output in the last decade, i.e., 1978-79 to 1988-89, when compared with the first decade of the green revolution. Crops such as rice, pulses and oilseeds, whose growth rates in the first decade of the green revolution had fallen much below those recorded in the pre-green revolution period, are now showing higher growth rates. The acceleration in the growth rates of output of pulses and oilseeds is particularly impressive. The rate of growth of output of pulses between 1978-79 and 1988-89 was 2.32 per cent per annum as compared with 0.27 per cent during 1967-78 and 1977-78. The corresponding figures for oilseeds are 3.86 per cent and 1.39 per cent. There are thus, clear indications that the major inter-crop imbalances in growth, witnessed in the early years of the green revolution, are getting redressed to some extent in the recent period.

Oilseeds and pulses are grown essentially in the rain-fed or unirrigated areas. Even for rice, nearly 60 per cent of the area is rainfed. The recent experience, therefore, suggests that the disparities in growth between the irrigated and rainfed or dry areas may not be as sharp as in the early years of the green revolution. It is also heartening to find that many of the states where poverty is widespread and where the growth of the foodgrains output had slowed down in the first decade of the green revolution, e.g., Assam, Bihar, Orissa, Madhya Pradesh and West Bengal have shown a much better performance in the last decade. Their performance is nearer, or even higher than, the all India average. The growth of rice had slowed down considerably in the Eastern states during the Seventies. All these states have experienced a step-up in the growth of rice during the last decade and some of them have recorded a higher growth than the national average.

This encouraging performance can be attributed to the spread of new technology. The special programmes for the cultivation of rice and oilseeds and the increasing attention given to dry farming and to the less developed states have started yielding results. This is corroborated by the increase in the consumption of fertilizers during the Eighties at a faster rate in the Eastern and Western regions than in the Northern and Southern regions. What is more, fertilizers consumed in the kharif season increased at a much faster rate than in the rabi season, particularly in the Eastern and Western regions, indicating the spread of new technology to the rainfed and environmentally unfavourable areas. There is also evidence of an increase in the share of the Eastern states in the total gross irrigated area of the country.

The gains in foodgrains output in the last decade have come essentially from the improved utilization of the available infrastructure and from the increase in yield per hectare. Already, during the first decade of the green revolution, increase in yield per hectare accounted for as much as 80 per cent of the increase in foodgrains output. During the last decade, there was some decline in the area under foodgrains. The entire output growth in this period can, therefore, be attributed to increase in yield per hectare. This underscores the growing importance of yield-increasing technology.

According to C.H.H. Rao although the growth rate in the foodgrains output seems to have improved because of the impact of new technology, the growth performance has by no means been smooth. The instability or the year-to-year variation in the foodgrains output has increased in the post-green revolution period. Even within this period, the instability in the last decade (1978-79 to 1988-89) was higher than in the preceding decade. The rural poor, particularly in the drought-prone areas and in the remote areas of the country, continue to suffer from fluctuations in employment and income and inadequate availability of foodgrains in years of drought.

Also the growth pattern has not been uniform with a tendency towards deceleration in the 1990s (Table 10.1).

TABLE – 10.1

Trend Growth Rates in the Indices of Area, Production and Yields of Foodgrains, Non-Foodgrains and All Crops during 1970-71 to 2000-01

(per cent)

Period	Foodgrains			Non-Foodgrains			All Crops		
	Area	Production	Yield	Area	Production	Yield	Area	Production	Yield
1	2	3	4	5	6	7	8	9	10
1970-71 to 2000-01	-0.03	2.52	2.13	1.46	3.31	1.66	0.35	2.83	1.93
1970-71 to 1979-80	0.44	1.91	1.06	1.10	2.15	1.00	0.59	1.99	1.03
1980-81 to 1989-90	-0.22	2.81	2.71	1.11	3.70	2.28	0.09	3.13	2.52
1990-91 to 1999-2000	0.07	1.98	1.30	1.29	2.77	1.08	0.41	2.30	1.19

Note : Trend Growth Rates are based on semi-logarithmic function.
Source: Report on Currency & Finance 2000-01.

The yield pattern in case of both foodgrains and non-foodgrains indicates that highest growth in yield levels occurred during the 1980s. Much of the growth in agricultural production in India is yield-driven as the growth in area is marginal; however, Indian agriculture suffers from lower yield levels vis-a-vis major agricultural producers in the world, despite India being one of the largest producers of most of the major crops (Table 10.2). The yield of 6,059 kg per hectare attained in China during 1998 in the production of paddy was more than double that of 2,890 kg per hectare in India. Similarly, wheat yield in China stood at 3,667 kg per hectare in 1998 in comparison with 2,578 kg per hectare in India.

TABLE – 10.2

India's Global Rank in Major Agricultural Crops

Crop	Rank in 2000		
	Area	Production	Yield
1	2	3	4
Rice (Paddy)	1	2	52
Wheat	1	2	38
Coarse Grains	3	4	125
Pulses	1	1	138
Oil Crops (Primary)	2	5	147
Cotton Seed	1	4	77
Jute and Jute Like Fibres	1	1	7
Tea	2	1	13
Coffee (Green)	7	7	14
Sugarcane	2	2	31

Source : Food and Agricultural Organisation.

The Role of Technology in Indian Agriculture

One of the main reasons for the low levels of yield attained in India is the unsatisfactory spread of new technological practices, including cultivation of High Yielding Varieties (HYV) of seeds. The adoption of new technology, mainly the cultivation of HYV seeds requires intensive use of fertilisers and pesticides under adequate and often assured water supply. The use of HYV seeds entails a higher yield risk (as measured by variance in yield) as compared with the traditional seed varieties, in the absence of proper irrigation facilities. The lower spread of new technological practices to a wide variety of crops other than wheat and rice as also across regions could be attributed to the higher yield risk associated with the cultivation of HYV seeds, caused by inadequate spread of irrigation facilities. There is considerable co-movement between the area under HYV seeds and area under irrigation, probably on account of reduction in yield risk due to irrigation facilities.

It is mainly paddy and wheat, which are cultivated under the HYV seeds, while the areas under HYV seeds for other cereal crops are very low and vary across different States of the country. Low growth experienced during the past two decades in the production of coarse cereals (0.5 per cent) and pulses (0.8 per cent) in comparison to rice (2.8 per cent) and wheat (4.0 per cent) is on account of lower adoption of HYV seeds or non-availability of appropriate seeds (apart from the usual dry-land farming accorded to these crops), given the diverse soil and moisture profiles of different parts of the country. The pattern of adoption of HYV seeds across various states has accordingly been disparate (Table 10.3).

TABLE – 10.3

State-wise Coverage of Area Under HYV Seeds for Cereals during 1996-97

(Lakh hectares)

State	Paddy	Wheat	Jowar	Bajra	Maize	Ragi	Total Cereals
1	2	3	4	5	6	7	8
Andhra Pradesh	36.99	0.07	5.99	0.72	3.22	—	46.99
Assam	14.22	1.03	—	—	0.12	—	15.37
Bihar	35.00	25.00	—	—	7.50	—	67.50
Gujarat	5.33	4.10	1.80	7.95	2.11	—	21.29
Haryana	5.15	19.38	—	3.58	0.12	—	28.23
Karnataka	10.16	1.34	14.01	2.70	3.53	10.45	42.19
Kerala	4.00	—	—	—	—	—	4.00
Madhya Pradesh	34.71	30.00	7.88	0.34	5.08	—	78.01
Maharashtra	12.93	7.40	47.91	18.70	2.62	—	89.56
Orissa	30.27	0.15	0.02	—	0.98	—	41.42
Punjab	20.41	32.30	—	0.03	1.47	—	54.21
Rajasthan	0.43	17.42	0.13	20.32	0.24	—	38.54
Tamil Nadu	21.20	—	5.20	1.86	0.69	1.01	29.96
Uttar Pradesh	50.18	88.83	- 4.67	6.04	—	149.72	
West Bengal	44.63	3.51	—	—	—	—	48.14
All India	**333.99**	**237.26**	**82.94**	**60.98**	**37.64**	**11.47**	**764.28**

Source : Ministry of Agriculture, Government of India.

One significant factor limiting the adoption of HYV seeds is the generally low level of irrigation cover for most of the crops as compared with rice and wheat. Nearly 64 per cent of the total cultivated area in the country is rain-fed. In fact, as compared with 79.1 per cent of the total geographical area as drought prone, the irrigation coverage of 38.2 per cent is quite unfavourable. The Ninth Plan document placed the irrigation potential at 139.89 million hectares. With this irrigation potential, the cropping intensity coefficient can be raised up to 149.0 as against the current level of 134.20. It has been found that the states of Rajasthan, Gujarat and Jammu and Kashmir have a higher probability (in excess of 20 per cent) of the incidence of drought in any given year. Moreover, agriculturally important states such as Andhra Pradesh, Uttar Pradesh, Haryana and Punjab have been found to have more than 10 per cent probability of the incidence of drought in any year. Of these, only Punjab has a good irrigation cover, while Haryana has a moderately good irrigation coverage (Table 10.4). Wheat and rice among foodgrains and sugarcane among non-foodgrains enjoy the maximum irrigation

TABLE – 10.4

State-wise Percentage coverage of Irrigated Area Under Principal Crops during 1997-98

(Per cent)

State	Rice	Wheat	Pulses	Total Food-grains	Oil Seeds	Sugarcane	Cotton	All Crops
1	2	3	4	5	6	7	8	9
Andhra Pradesh	96.4	72.7	1.2	55.1	19.7	95.2	18.9	42.5
Bihar	40.4	89.0	2.1	47.8	20.2	30.6	—	46.6
Gujarat	61.2	75.6	10.7	32.2	26.0	100.0	37.7	34.3
Haryana	99.6	98.3	22.5	77.5	70.0	97.9	98.9	78.6
Karnataka	69.2	38.2	3.9	22.5	21.3	100.0	19.3	24.9
Kerala	52.2	—	—	49.3	16.0	100.0	—	14.0
Madhya Pradesh	23.6	69.2	18.5	30.4	5.7	98.6	39.4	25.0
Maharashtra	28.1	69.6	7.3	13.3	11.1	95.0	2.8	14.5
Orissa	36.2	100.0	5.0	26.7	11.0	100.0	—	26.8
Punjab	95.0	94.8	89.8	93.8	62.2	75.1	99.6	91.7
Rajasthan	41.5	94.7	7.7	23.6	43.9	100.0	98.0	29.9
Tamil Nadu	93.2	—	6.4	62.0	40.9	100.0	34.6	53.7
Uttar Pradesh	62.7	91.7	27.7	64.7	39.5	95.0	91.7	65.9
West Bengal	25.9	73.0	4.5	27.6	63.5	30.8	—	27.1
All India	**50.2**	**85.0**	**11.8**	**40.6**	**24.4**	**92.6**	**36.3**	**38.2**

Source : Ministry of Agriculture, Government of India.

coverage across all states. Even in the states with lesser irrigation coverage, such as Karnataka, Madhya Pradesh, Kerala, etc., the irrigation cover for rice and wheat is much higher in comparison with other crops. Thus, in India irrigated area generally tends to be used for the growing of rice and wheat, while the other crops are grown mostly in rain-fed and unirrigated conditions.

In such a scenario, the technological development in terms of the adoption of HYV seeds is mostly limited to the cultivation of rice and wheat on account of higher yield risk imparted by these seeds. It is pertinent to note in this connection that the foodgrains production in 1999-2000 was at a record high of 208.9 million tonnes despite acute drought conditions in the central stretch of India, mainly on account of record production of rice and wheat. Most of the other crops - mainly oilseeds - suffered significant fall in production in that year. This could be indicative of the disproportionate adoption of technology and irrigation benefits, underscoring the need for spreading the irrigation benefits to all crops.

Another important factor affecting the dissemination of modern technology in general and HYV seed technology in particular is the small size of average farms in India. It has been argued that the small size of land holdings limits the adoption of new technology due to reasons other than the scale of operation. Share-cropping, which is generally undertaken by the small and marginal farmers, limits the scope for adoption of new technology as the farmer has to pay a fraction of (generally around half) the production to the land-owner, while the whole cost of adoption of the green revolution inputs such as HYV seeds and fertilisers will have to be borne by the tenant. In such an arrangement, it is imperative that the gains in marginal product due to adoption of these inputs should at least be twice that of the investment for the farmer to break even. Such dramatic increases in production are difficult to come by in the absence of other infrastructural facilities and hence, the scope for adoption of green revolution inputs by the share-cropper is clearly undermined.

The per hectare consumption of fertilisers and pesticides is quite low in India in comparison with international standards and there is a lot of scope for improvement in this sphere. For instance, the per hectare consumption of fertilisers in India at 88.6 kg was much lower than 256.6 kg and 110.4 kg in China and USA, respectively, in 1997-98. The growth in the consumption of fertilisers during the past two decades has also quite varied across different States (Table 10.5). Another factor that is responsible for lower productivity of Indian agriculture is the skewed distribution of N:P:K (Nitrogen : Phosphorus : Potassium) fertiliser mix. Currently, the N:P:K ratio stands at 6.9:2.9:1.0, which is quite skewed in comparison to the optimal mix of 4:2:1. The skewed consumption of fertiliser accentuates the risk of salination and leaching of soil, thus hampering the long-term productivity of the land. This skewed fertiliser consumption pattern is the result of high subsidies extended to the urea producers.

TABLE – 10.5

State-wise Trend Growth Rates of Area Under HYV Seeds and per Hectare Fertiliser Consumption

(per cent)

State	Area under HYV seeds	Per Hectare Fertiliser Consumption
1	2	3
Andhra Pradesh	1.15	6.21
Assam	2.74	10.63
Bihar	2.09	8.03
Gujarat	0.68	5.18
Haryana	1.09	6.80
Himachal Pradesh	2.12	3.97
Jammu & Kashmir	2.16	5.02
Karnataka	5.68	5.27
Kerala	-4.83	3.51
Maharashtra	3.63	7.10
Madhya Pradesh	5.99	8.36
Orissa	6.14	7.40
Punjab	1.77	1.81
Rajasthan	2.72	9.26
Tamil Nadu	1.62	3.54
Uttar Pradesh	3.40	4.53
West Bengal	5.50	6.62
All-India	3.10	5.29

Notes : 1) The growth rates for area under HYV seeds pertain to 1980-81 to 1996-97, and those for per hectare consumption of fertilisers relate to 1980-81 to 1999-2000.

2) Trend Rates are based on semi-logarithmic function.

Source: Reserve Bank of India, Report on Currency & Finance, 2000-01.

Limits to Growth: Some Tentative Evidence

There are some tentative indications about the limits to growth of Indian agriculture. First, the extensive margin of cultivation has already reached a plateau in Indian agriculture. Since the beginning of Green

Revolution in 1967-68, the area under all crops increased only at a rate of 0.4 per cent per annum as against 1.3 per cent during the period prior to Green Revolution (1950-51 to 1966-67). In the case of foodgrains, there was hardly any growth since the beginning of Green Revolution. However, agricultural production has increased by 2.9 per cent per annum. It is improvement in yields (2.0 per cent per annum) that made the production growth possible (Table 10.6).

TABLE – 10.6

Annual Compound Growth Rates of Area, Production and Yield of Crops*

(Per cent per annum)

Crops	Area		Production		Yield	
	1950-66	1967-99	1950-66	1967-99	1950-66	1967-99
a. All Crops	1.3	0.4	2.5	2.9	0.8	2.0
b. Foodgrains	1.1	0.0	2.0	2.6	0.8	2.2
c. Non-Foodgrains	2.0	1.4	3.3	3.3	0.7	1.7

*: Estimates based on semi-log regression equation.

Second, there was a notable deceleration in the rate of growth of agricultural production during the nineties, a fact highlighted by a number of studies in recent times [Mallik (1997), Rao (1998), Thamarajashi, (1999), George (1999) and Pulapare, (2000)]. Table 10.7 reveals that during the nineties the growth of production of all crops decelerated to 2.2 per cent from 3.2 per cent during the eighties. In case of foodgrains production, the trend rate of growth was only 1.8 per cent, which is just about equal to annual population growth. During nineties there was deceleration in the trend growth of yield of all the major crops, except coarse cereals. In view of the deceleration in the growth of area, production and yield of foodgrains, doubts have been expressed about the future growth of foodgrains production. The decline in the growth rates of foodgrains production during the nineties was felt more in case of kharif crops (on account of decline of both area and yield) than rabi crop (on account of the decline in the yield) (George, 1999). Of late, foodgrains production during the rabi season was almost equal to the level of production during the kharif season. This has reduced the dependence of foodgrains production on monsoon and, in turn, imparted some element of stability to agricultural production in India (Reserve Bank of India, 1999). But what is lacking is the growth momentum of the sector. Area wise the deceleration was more in case of the Indo-

Gangetic region, consisting of Punjab, Haryana, Uttar Pradesh, West Bengal and Bihar, which contributed about 61 per cent of total production of rice and wheat in India. The current rate of growth of agricultural production in India is lower than the targeted growth of agricultural crops in the Ninth Five-Year Plan (1997-2002) at 3.82 per cent per annum (agriculture and allied activities, 4.5 per cent) (Planning Commission, 1997a) and 4 per cent contemplated by the recent National Agricultural Policy (Government of India, 2000). Thus, the growth of agricultural production continues to be a matter of concern.

TABLE – 10.7

Trend Growth Rate of Area, Production and Yield of Important Crops*

(Per cent per annum)

	Crops	Area		Production		Yield	
		80's#	90's@	80's#	90's@	80's#	90's@
I.	All Crops	0.1	0.4	3.2	2.2	2.6	1.4
II.	Foodgrains	-0.2	-0.1	2.9	1.8	2.7	1.4
III.	Non-Foodgrains	1.1	1.5	3.8	3.3	2.3	1.4
i.	Rice	0.3	0.5	3.6	1.9	3.2	1.3
ii.	Wheat	0.5	1.7	3.6	3.1	3.1	1.6
iii.	Coarse Cereals	-1.4	-1.8	0.4	0.2	1.7	2.0
iv.	Pulses	-0.1	-0.2	1.5	1.0	1.6	1.7
v.	Oilseeds	2.4	0.8	5.5	3.4	2.9	2.6
vi.	Sugarcane	1.5	1.8	2.7	2.5	1.2	0.7
vii.	Cotton	-1.3	3.3	2.8	1.7	4.1	-2.0

* : Estimates based on semi-log regression equation.

: 80's cover the period 1980-81 to 1989-90.

@ : In case of production, the 90s cover 1990-91 to 1999-2000. In the case of area and yield the 90's cover the period 1990-91 to 1998-99.

Source: Rao and Jeromi, 2000.

Major Factors Affecting the Growth Potential

A number of factors are constraining the growth potential of the sector. Here, we identify four major factors responsible for limiting the growth potential of the sector. They are i) lack of long-term policy perspective, ii) decline of public sector capital formation, iii) inadequate research and development efforts, and more importantly, iv) inefficient management of natural resources like land and water.

i) Lack of Long Term Policy Perspective

On the policy front, there was lack of long-term strategy for agricultural development. One will be surprised to find that only recently the

Government has come out with a national agricultural policy. From the very beginning of the planning process in India, especially from the Second Five Year Plan with the sectoral priorities of Mahalanobis model favouring industry, the emphasis has been placed on industry relative to agriculture (Bhide, et al, 1998). Broadly, the two basic objectives of agricultural policies have been i) self-sufficiency in production and ii) stability in price. As the objective of higher production and thereby achieving self-sufficiency in production (which required incentives through higher prices) is inherently inconsistent with the objective of achieving stability in prices, there was a policy dilemma. The policies followed for agricultural development suffers from a number of weaknesses. First, though there was no significant direct taxation of the sector, agricultural sector has suffered from a typical anti-agricultural bias due to the nature of policies followed in other sectors like industry, trade, exchange rate, etc. (Gulati, 1998). Agricultural policies provided little incentives for the farmers, as the agricultural prices were depressed (Indian farmers received lower price than international prices). As there were numerous controls and restrictions, the sector was disprotected vis-a-vis other sectors of the economy. The restrictions on agricultural exports were believed to be one of the prime reasons for the disprotection of the sector as compared to the industrial sector (Gulati and Pursell, 1990, Singh, 1995, Economic Survey 1996-97, Parikh, 1999). Second, the nature of the policies was inward-looking as it was driven less by comparative advantage. In general, agricultural policies gave little emphasis on agricultural exports as a means of stimulating domestic production (Jeromi, 1997). Third, it has excessive price-based focus than non-price factors like water, infrastructure, research and development (R&D), extension services, etc., which are important determinants of agricultural production in India, a fact highlighted more than three decades back by Dantwala (1967) and recently by Pulapare (2000) and Vaidyanathan (2000). These weaknesses of agricultural policies, inter alia, affected the faster growth of the sector and in creating a sound infrastructure base for future growth.

ii) Neglect of Capital Formation

Lack of long-term perspectives on the development of the sector is clearly reflected in the poor state of capital formation in the sector, which is likely to affect the future growth. In fact, one of the most disquieting developments in the agricultural sector during the last two decades has been the neglect of capital formation, particularly in the public sector. Gross Capital Formation (GCF) in agriculture as per cent of total gross capital formation in the economy, after rising during the

70's, declined during the eighties and nineties. In 1999-2000 it was just 5.8 per cent as against 16.3 per cent in 1980-81. Further, GCF in agricultural as per cent of GDP in agriculture also declined during the last two decades from 10.9 per cent in 1980-81 to 7.0 per cent in 1999-2000. What is more disturbing is the fact that GCF in the agricultural sector by the public sector declined at an annual average rate of 4.0 per cent during the 1980s. As a result, the share of public sector in total capital formation in the sector declined to around 23.0 per cent during the nineties as against 32.0 per cent during the seventies. However, in the private sector, the decline was only marginal during the eighties (-0.1 per cent) and it picked up at a moderate of 6.7 per cent in the nineties (Table 10.8).

TABLE – 10.8

Gross Capital Formation in Agriculture

Year	GCF in Agriculture			GCF as % Of GDP in Agriculture	GCF as % of Total GCF in Economy@
	Public	Private	Total		
	At 1980-81 Prices				
1970-71	789	1996	2785	7.8	14.7
1980-81	1796	2840	4636	10.9	16.3
1990-91	1154	3440	4594	7.5	8.1
	At 1993-94 Prices				
1995-96	4848	10242	15690	6.8	2.9
1996-97	4668	11508	16176	6.4	6.7
1997-98	3979	11974	15753	6.5	5.9
1998-99	3846	12538	16384	6.2	5.9
1999-00**	4668	13988	18656	7.0	5.8
	Annual Average Growth (%)				
1971-79	10.0	7.2	7.9		
1980-89	-4.0	-0.1	-1.5		
1990-99	1.0	6.7	5.0		

Note : @ : Gross Capital Formation adjusted for errors and omissions
** : Provisional.

Source : 1. National Accounts Statistics, various issues, CSO, Government of India.
2. Agricultural Statistics at a Glance, Various Issues, Government of India.
3. Economic Survey 2000-01, Government of India.

According to B.B. Bhattacharya committee on Capital Formation in Indian Agriculture, there has been a long-term deceleration in the share of capital formation in agriculture in GDP at both aggregate and Public Sector level. In fact the shares of GFCF in agriculture and for agriculture in GDP have declined much more sharply in the Public Sector, as would be evident from the Table 10.9.

TABLE – 10.9

Gross Fixed Capital Formation in and for Agriculture at 1993-94 Prices (Public Sector)

(Rs.Crore)

Year	GDP	GFCF		Percent Share in GDP of GFCF	
		in Agriculture	for Agriculture	in Agriculture	for Agriculture
(1)	(2)	(3)	(4)	(5)	(6)
1980-81	401128	7358	9855	1.8	2.5
1985-86	513990	6005	9224	1.2	1.8
1990-91	692871	4871	8706	0.7	1.3
1995-96	899563	5318	9631	0.6	1.1
1999-00	1148442	4637	9902	0.4	0.9

Currently, GFCF for agriculture at 1993-94 prices account for about 12 per cent of aggregate capital formation. As against this, the share of agriculture in GDP is currently about 24 per cent. Clearly there is a strong case to increase the share of agriculture in total capital formation in the economy. Even in the case of Public Sector, the share of agriculture in total Public Sector capital formation has declined over the years.

As agriculture is getting diversified, there is a need to not only augment but also re-structure the pattern of investment in agriculture. Historically, the Public Sector has taken the lead in directing the growth and pattern of agriculture investment. The Committee recommended that immediate steps should be taken to improve capital formation for agriculture in both Public and Private Sectors. Otherwise, it may be difficult to sustain the agriculture growth and rural purchasing power. Currently, irrigation accounts for the bulk of public investment in agriculture (above 90 per cent). The new strategy of agriculture growth and diversification of agriculture from traditional crop cultivation to horticulture etc. would require more investments on cold storage, rural roads, communication, marketing network and facilities, warehouses etc. Simultaneously efforts should be made to revitalize agriculture through introduction of bio-technology and other innovations. This would require substantial increase in investment on research & development for agriculture.

There is a lively debate in the literature on complementarity between public and private sector capital formation in agricultural sector. Here we take the view that public sector investment has a crucial role to play in creating infrastructure in terms of irrigation, roads, markets, storage facilities, rural electrification and technology development. Private sector capital formation is hard to come in these areas. Private sector capital formation is essentially taking place for short-term asset building and it is mainly in the areas of mechanisation, ground levelling, private irrigation, etc. Therefore, public sector capital formation needed to be augmented with a definite content and targeted focus, especially in case of rainfed areas, which lack not only in irrigation facilities, but also in other infrastructural facilities. Here it may be mentioned that public spending in agriculture is a common feature in both the developed and developing countries. In a World Bank study, Blarcom, et al, (1993) found that in case of 40 developing countries, total central government expenditure during 1972 to 1988 formed around 10 per cent of net value of agricultural production. In case of a group of 15 developed countries, it formed around 20 per cent of their net value of agricultural production. The comparative figure for India is far too low.

There is a view among the agricultural economists that the lagged effect of decline of capital formation during the eighties has been one of the major reasons for the decelerated growth of the sector during the nineties (Mahendra Dev, 1998). Therefore, the subdued level of capital formation during the nineties can have an impact on agriculture production in the coming years.

iii) Lagging Research and Development Efforts

Another important factor limiting the growth potential of the sector is the lack of breakthrough in research and development after the green revolution. Perhaps, it may be one of the reasons for the decline of productivity of in the nineties. India compares poorly with the productivity levels in major producing countries. Though India is one among the major producers of agricultural commodities in the world, the yield levels, here, for a number of commodities like paddy, wheat, groundnut, cotton, jute, etc., were far lower than the yield levels in major producing countries and in case of some crops it was even lower than the world average (Table 10.10).

TABLE – 10.10

Yield of Important Crops in Major Producing Countries in 1997 (Kg./ha.)

Country	Paddy Yield	Country	Wheat Yield	Country	Groundnut Yield	Country	Sugarcane Yield	Country	Cotton Yield	Country	Jute Yield
China	6331	China	4087	China	2574	Brazil	69021	China	943	Banga.	1577
Indonesia	4561	France	6530	Nigeria	1124	China	75982	USA	769	China	2517
Pakistan	2827	USA	2673	USA	2828	Thailand	55878	Pakistan	552	Thailand	3548
Philippines	2933	Australia	1712	Indonesia	1519	Mexico	72734	Turkey	1065	Myanmar	939
Thailand	2143	Canada	2128	Sudan	762	Australia	97337	Argentina	368	Brazil	1714
India	2915	India	2654	India	988	India	69737	India	321	India	1830
World	3827	World	2686	World	1273	World	63324	World	584	World	1734
India % Of World	**76.2**		**98.8**		**77.6**		**110.1**		**55.0**		**105.5**

Source: Production Yearbook, Food and Agricultural Organisation, 1997.

India is considered as having the largest public agricultural research establishments in the world (Evenson, et al, 1999). Indian Council of Agricultural Research (ICAR) and agricultural universities constitute the main part of governmental agencies. However, agricultural research in India suffers from several weaknesses like i) uneven progress of varietal improvement across crops and regions, ii) neglect of crop systems research, iii) unimpressive results of local adaptive research, iv) inadequacy of collaborative multi-disciplinary research, v) weak interaction between researchers, extension workers and farmers; vi) excessive centralisation of planning and monitoring, vii) lack of accountability for performance, etc. (Vaidyanathan, 2000). Compared to other countries, India's efforts in research and development, in terms of provision of resources, is insufficient. India is investing only around 0.3 per cent of GDP in agriculture for agricultural research, as against 0.7 per cent in the developing countries and 2-3 per cent in case of developed countries (Evenson, et al, 1999). Expenditure on agricultural research and education accelerated during the post-green revolution period of the 1970s, but slowed down since the mid-80s and it hovered around 0.49 per cent of agricultural GDP in the early 1990s, which was lower than the requirement of 1.0 per cent projected by the ICAR. Further, the level of research expenditure was sub-optimal or significantly lower than desired in states like Bihar, Orissa, Madhya Pradesh, Uttar Pradesh and West Bengal where productivity is low. Crop-wise, research expenditure was low in case of rice, certain coarse cereals, pulses and oilseeds (Pal, et al, 1997).

Since there is hardly any scope for further expansion of area under cultivation, the future production prospects depends largely on the improvements in the yield levels. Here what we need is to break the yield barrier and bridge the gap between the potential and actual yield through research and development (R&D) efforts. ICAR studies reveals that there is vast unexplored technological potential for improvement in the yield of crops. In this context, Swaminathan (1999) noted that the "low yield phenomena" in India should be considered as a "yield reservoir" and it should be treated as an asset for future development of the sector. Exploiting the "yield reservoir", inter alia, require substantial investment and development and deployment of high yielding seed varieties. So far the emphasis has been on the use of HYV seeds, but it loses it vigor with time. Therefore, new varieties need to be developed periodically to expand production possibilities. However, agricultural research established could not come up with improved varieties of seeds, which are suited to different regions of the country, especially in drought prone areas. Therefore, it is imperative for the country to build up a sound agricultural research system, which is responsive to the changing needs and circumstances. As the agricultural growth reduces rural poverty directly, and it fosters the conditions for pro-poor growth in the non-farm sectors, it is imperative to overcome the limits to growth by increase in productivity of the sector.

iv) Rising Soil Degradation and Over-exploitation of Ground Water

Large-scale soil degradation and over-exploitation of ground water are other important factors putting limits on growth of the sector. Around 40 per cent of India's total geographical area are officially estimated as degraded (some other estimates put the figure at 50 per cent). Using the guidelines of the Global Assessment of Soil Degradation (GLASOD), Sehgal and Abrol (1994) estimated the extent of soil degradation in India. The area under degradation is quite large and the severity is high with significant loss of yield in case of around 68 per cent of the total area degraded.

The emergence of rice-wheat crops system in states like Punjab and Haryana, on account of continuous increase in procurement prices, has resulted in overexploitation of natural resource base. An ICAR study found that soil health is deteriorating in Punjab and Haryana and this is a major cause of decline or stagnation in productivity of cereals, particularly of rice and wheat. The study revealed that the organic carbon content in the soils in Punjab and Haryana has declined to 0.2 per cent in 1995 from 0.5 per cent in the sixties. Soils with low phosphorus content have also increased to 73 per cent from only 3.5 per cent in 1975 in Haryana. Similarly, soils with high potash category have scaled down from 91 per cent in 1975 to 62 per cent in 1995. Further, consequent to the decontrol of prices of phosphorus and potash, there was decline in the application of these fertilisers. This caused nutrient imbalance in the soils. Now farmers have to apply more fertilizers to get the same yield as they were getting with less fertilizer 20-30 years ago. In case of ground water, the study found that the rapid increase in the number of tube-wells during last three decades in the region has resulted in over-exploitation of ground water. This decline forces the farmers to lower the pumps further deeper in the wells, which results in the use of irrigation with saline water (A detailed discussion on the emerging crisis in the agricultural sector of Punjab can be found in Chand, 1999).

The irrigation potential in the country has been estimated at 85 million hectares, of which 76 million hectares have been already utilised by 1993-94. The average cost per hectare of irrigation potential created has risen sharply from Rs. 8,620 during the First Five Year Plan to

Rs. 29,587 in the Seventh Five Year Plan at 1980-81 prices. This acts as a constraint to further augmentation of irrigation potential. Even after full utilisation of the irrigation potential, nearly 45 percent of the net cultivated area will have to depend on rainfall. As the present agricultural development strategy in India is centred mainly on the irrigated areas and the yield levels of crops in many irrigated areas are plateauing, there is a growing realisation that agricultural production cannot be increased beyond a point (Planning Commission, 1997b).

Thus, the indications provided by the deceleration in growth of area, production and productivity, over-use of water resources, degradation of soil, decline of capital formation in the public sector, etc., tend to suggest that Indian agriculture is approaching limits to growth in the near future. The estimation of potential output also suggests that the scope for higher growth is limited. To overcome limits to growth and put the agricultural sector on an ambitious growth curve, there is a need to correct the policy bias against agriculture, make higher investments, develop new varieties of seeds, conserve natural resources like land and water and provide incentives to the farmers to adopt modernisation.

Agricultural Price Policy

The objectives of price policy as propounded from time to time are multiple and often conflicting. The price policy was evolved in the context of relative shortage of agricultural products, particularly of foodgrains. Thus we had the overriding objectives of the price policy as achieving self-sufficiency in foodgrains (understood as the availability of adequate foodgrains from domestic production) and protection of consumer from scarcity-induced speculative price rise. As V.S. Vyas points out "the main function of prices, i.e., to act as signals for allocation of resources has been made subservient to income parity and food security objectives."

Apart from the consideration of income transfers, the policy is also directed to increase agricultural production by offering higher 'incentive' prices. A discriminatory price policy can be used to encourage inter-crop shifts in resource use. However, when it comes to aggregate agricultural output, greater reliance has to be placed on 'non-price' factors, e.g., generating and extending more efficient technologies. The available studies clearly bring out that aggregate supply response of agriculture is very weak. Thus, any attempt to use high prices to encourage agricultural production can bring in its wake irreparable distortions in the price structure.

These limitations of price policy are not very often recognised. Also the strength of price policy in affecting desirable shift in cropping pattern fully exploited. As Vyas remarks "in a mixed economy like ours an important objective of the price policy could be to give directions to the cropping pattern not only on the basis of the existing demand supply situation but also to take into account a qualitatively superior crop mix, e.g., to provide a price advantage to nutritionally superior crops or to the crops where the country may have comparative advantage. In fact, in this respect we seem to be regressing. In the 1970s price policy was used as an effective tool to encourage production of crops where superior technology was available." [Vyas 1989]. In recent years we have largely neglected this aspect of price policy.

Further, there has been no clarity on the priority to be assigned among these numerous objectives, or the trade-off involved in pursuing these objectives simultaneously. If we are to go by the public pronouncements, the objectives sought to be achieved by the price policy include, ensuring (i) reasonable prices for the growers, (ii) reasonable prices for the grains released from public distribution system, and (iii) reasonable prices in the open market. A moment's reflection will show that in most of the circumstances these aims conflict with each other. The price policy cannot resolve all conflicts in the society.

It must be recognised that price policy taken by itself is a weak instrument in giving directions to agricultural economy, more so as an instrument of income transfer. While the objective of providing an insurance cover in terms of guaranteed minimum prices to a large section of agricultural producers could be a worthy objective but until and unless required resources are available and administrative machinery is in place, mere announcement of minimum prices for a large number of commodities may not serve any purpose. It may, infact, do more harm with an erosion of the credibility of the government. In view of this it is suggested that the support prices should be applicable only for a limited number of crops. Crops which can be considered as price leaders or the crops, for which technological break through is imminent ought to be covered under the price guaranties. The other crops to be considered for support are the crops grown under high risk environment and there also it should be a transient measure i.e., till a viable crop insurance programme is evolved.

Along with limiting the scope for price policy is the need for a discriminatory and flexible approach to price interventions. By covering a large number of commodities on the one hand and by ensuring minimum prices in the guise of procurement prices on the other, not only government's commitment has enhanced to an unmanageable extent, it has also led to serious distortions in agricultural economy.

V.S. Vyas remarks "the time has come to take a serious look at the scope, instruments and institutions of agricultural price policy. There is a need to recognise that the price policy is a weak instrument for income transfers; our capacity to offer minimum support prices for a large number of commodities is limited; need for dovetailing agriculture and trade policies is urgent. instrument of minimum support prices has to be used sparingly; procurement operations need to be made more business like; CACP should retain its expert character rather than trying to be representative of various interests, FCI should be decentralised and debureaucratised and the states should be made major stakeholders."

Rao and Gulati maintain "the process of economic reforms, and the gradual opening up of Indian agriculture to world markets is likely to turn the terms of trade in favour of agriculture, creating a better incentive environment for agriculture than has been the case in preceding decades. To fully exploit this opportunity, a major reform in supply-side factors is needed as well as a clean sweep to dismantle all export controls on agricultural commodities, including foodgrains. It is these supply-side factors — technology, fertilisers, irrigation, infrastructure, and credit — that raise aggregate supply response and are the prime movers behind accelerated and sustainable growth of Indian agriculture."

Tenth Plan Targets

The National Agriculture Policy (NAP), 2000 envisages a growth rate exceeding 4 per cent per annum in the agriculture sector. The Tenth Plan also targets a 4 per cent growth. The NAP envisaged the following type of growth :

- Growth that is based on efficient use of resources and conserves our soil, water and bio-diversity.
- Growth with equity, i.e., growth which is widespread across regions and covers all farmers.
- Growth that is demand driven and caters to domestic markets as well as maximises benefits from exports of agricultural products in the face of the challenges arising from economic liberalisation and globalisation,
- Growth that is sustainable technologically, environmentally and economically.

For the Ninth Plan , the foodgrains production target was fixed at 234 mt which had to be revised downward to 218 mt considering the performance during the first four years of the Plan. The Working Group on 'Crop Husbandry, Demand and Supply Projections and Agricultural Inputs for the Tenth Plan has estimated a foodgrains requirement of 230 mt at the end of the Plan (2006-2007). On the basis of normative requirement of foodgrains of 182.50 kg/cu/year (167.9 kg cereals and 14.6 kg pulses), as recommended by the National Institute of Nutrition, the demand works out to 221.4 mt considering the anticipated population level of 1135 Million (deflated by a factor 1.0696 to convert into consumption units). However, on the basis of behaviouristic approach, the demand of foodgrains estimated by the Working Group is 236 mt. On the other hand, the supply projection for foodgrains by the end of the terminal year of the Tenth Plan have been projected in the range of 225 mt to 243 mt.

An adequate thrust on maize cultivation could bring a substantial increase in foodgrains production as even with existing area of about 6.5 m ha, an additional production of about 10-13 mt could be achieved. This is on the assumption that 50 per cent of present potential (3.5 - 4 t/ha) of maize is realised. Considering the immense scope in maize, if the production of other coarse cereals (millets and barley) is maintained at the present level, the total coarse cereals production could be increased to about 43 48 mt by 2006-07. Thus, there is possibility to achieve a production level of food grains of about 245-248 mt by the end of the Tenth Plan, with adequate thrust on maize, especially the multiplication of high yielding seeds on a massive scale and adoption of improved production technology. In addition, thrust on commercialisation of hybrid rice on a large scale and application of improved technologies in wheat could further boost the foodgrains production. For the Tenth Plan allocation to the department of Agriculture and Cooperation has been stepped up to Rs. 13200 crore from Rs. 9153.82 crore provided for the Ninth Plan and realization of Rs. 8308 crore.

Strategy and Thrust in the Tenth Plan

Regionally Differentiated Strategy

The Regionally Differentiated Strategy based on agro-climatic conditions and natural resources envisaged for the Ninth Plan, for increasing the pace of growth in every region of the country, will be continued during the Tenth Plan. The three-pronged strategy envisaged for the Ninth Plan to meet the basic food requirements for all will be continued. This strategy involved: (i) increase in overall employment and incomes by raising farm productivity and the growth of other economic activities in the rural areas; (ii) provision of gainful supplementary employment through poverty alleviation schemes; and (iii) distribution of food grains through the public distribution system at subsidised prices to those living below the poverty line.

Sustainable Development of Natural Resources

The biotic pressure on the natural resources, especially land, water and biodiversity, is increasing resulting in their decrease in per capita availability. With the increasing population, the fragmentation of holdings has increased, resulting in smaller and unviable units of land holdings. To address the issue of fragmentation and small holdings, a clear policy with regard to transfer of agricultural land has to be formulated and implemented. The transfer of land has to be made easier to enable the farmers to augment their holdings to viable units. The rationalisation of stamp duty will facilitate the transaction of land. Besides, freedom in leasing of land, both 'leasing in' and 'leasing out' will help generate income for both lessee and lessor/contractor. A legislation needs to be enacted to facilitate the land utilisation by making land transactions easier and facilitating leasing and contract farming. Besides, to increase the productivity of small and marginal holdings, which constitute 78.2 per cent of all holdings and operate about 32.4 per cent of total area, the technologies suited for such holdings have to be developed.

Besides, consolidation of holdings has to be taken up on a priority basis and completed speedily by the States which have not yet taken up the work. The consolidation of holdings in the northern states has shown promising results in terms of per unit area productivity, adoption of production technologies and returns to the farmers. Preparation of land records would also be given emphasis. States would be asked and helped to take up computerisation of all land records.

Out of the estimated area of about 107 m ha of degraded land, 64 m ha are categorised as wastelands. These wastelands and other degraded areas are either un-utilised or under-utilised. Being a common property resource, individuals do not have the right to utilise these lands for any productive purposes. All such lands under the control of Government or panchayats, would be parceled out in viable units and allotted to landless, scheduled caste and scheduled tribe farmers, small and marginal farmers, retired defence personnel and educated rural youth for cultivation. A condition that a a certain percentage of allotted land (say 40 or 50 per cent) must be utilised for tree cover can be stipulated so as to increase the crown area for improving the environmental and ecological conditions. The highly degraded wasteland could exclusively be used for forestry, tree cropping or agro forestry.

BOX – 10.1

Thurst Areas for the Tenth Plan

- Utilisation of wastelands and un-utilised/under-utilised lands.
- Reclamation/development of problem soils/lands.
- Rainwater harvesting and conservation for the development of rainfed areas.
- Development of irrigation, especially minor irrigation.
- Conservation and utilisation of biological resources.
- Diversification to high value crops/activities.
- Increasing cropping intensity.
- Timely and adequate availability of inputs.
- Strengthening of marketing, processing/value addition infrastructure.
- Revamping and modernising the extension systems and encouraging private sector to take up extension services.
- Bridging the gap between research and farmer's yields.
- Cost-effectiveness while increasing productivity.
- Promotion of farming systems approach.
- Promotion of organic farming and utilisation of organic waste.
- Development of eastern and northeastern regions, hill and coastal areas.
- Reforms to introduce proactive policies for the farm sector.

Rainwater harvesting and conservation will continue to get attention so as to increase productivity of rainfed farmlands. Besides, minor irrigation development, which is more cost-effective will also be emphasised, especially in the eastern region where huge groundwater potential has remained unharnessed. Investments in the development of minor irrigation facilities will be enhanced. Besides, the utilisation of under-utilised irrigation potential will be improved by encouraging the conjunctive use of water, adoption of improved on-farm water management practices and also the use of water saving devices such as sprinkler irrigation system, drip irrigation system, etc., especially in the low rainfall areas.

Vast areas are in need of Watershed Development Programmes, which call for urgent attention. Both the Central and State Governments should provide maximum possible budgetary support for the development of degraded rainfed lands on a priority basis. In watershed development there is need to move from the conventional soil conservation approach of safe disposal of run-off to rainwater harvesting and conservation based on indigenous systems and practices. Rainwater conservation and harvesting hold the key for sustainable development of rainfed areas. The watershed development must ensure that the minimum basic water needs of the rural communities in the project areas are met.

With increasing population, land holdings are getting fragmented and becoming unviable. The average size of holdings has decreased from 2.28 ha in 1970-71 to 1.57 ha in 1990-91. To deal with problems of fragmented and small holdings:

- A clear policy regarding transfer of agricultural land has to be implemented.
- Transfer of land has to be made easy to enable the farmers to augment their holdings to viable size units.
- Stamp duty on transactions of land for agriculture to be rationalised.
- Leasing of land and contract farming to be allowed/promoted and made easy which will help generate income for both lessee and lessor/ contractor.
- Legislation needs to be enacted to facilitate land utilisation - transfer, leasing contract farming.
- Technologies suited for small holdings have to be developed to increase the productivity and returns of small holdings.
- States would be asked to take up the consolidation of holdings and computerisation of land records.

While, on the one hand, the per capita availability of land has declined, there are vast areas which are unutilised or under-utilised. If such lands are put to productive uses, the production will increase and millions of farm families will get livelihood support and their income will increase. For utilisation of unutilised/under-utilised degraded/wastelands, States would be persuaded to consider the following:

- Allotment/leasing of Government/panchayat lands for production purposes to landless and weaker sections.

- Providing access to grasses and fodder from forest area and allowing growing of grasses/fodder and medicinal and aromatic plants.
- Wastelands which require huge financial resources for development will be earmarked and used for generating raw material for industry in partnership with the private sector

Sustainable development of natural resources would be given a major thrust through watershed approach and appropriate measures like:

- Formulation of a perspective plan for the development of rainfed/degraded land;
- Implementation of watershed development programme as a single national initiative;
- Thrust on people's participation in planning and execution of field activities in the implementation of the watershed development programme;
- Emphasis on rain water harvesting and conservation;
- Development of minor irrigation, especially in the eastern region having abundance of ground water;
- Promotion of on-farm water management, water-saving technologies and devices for increasing water use efficiency;
- Increasing forest/tree cover to facilitate recharge of ground water;
- Completing irrigation projects expeditiously and ensuring maintenance of canals and other irrigation projects;
- Setting up of water user associations and recovery of water charges so that there is better maintenance; ensuring that there is sufficient water for drinking, agriculture and other uses. Enaction of legislation on use of ground water will be followed up with the States;
- As electricity is an important input for agriculture, effort will be made to link pricing/tariff as a policy reform for providing adequate power;
- Special thrust on research for efficient water utilisation and conservation - promotion of water saving methods and devices such as diggi, drip/sprinkler irrigation;
- Encouraging water conservation and recycling of water by households, urban local bodies and industry.

Public Distribution System (PDS)

The PDS has attracted considerable debate in recent years on the ground that the benefits of PDS are not reaching the poor on account of, inter alia, poor targeting and leakages in the system, despite its restructuring in 1997. It has also been argued that despite the huge food subsidy and the large-scale of intervention, the food security of many households is still marginal or insufficient. In recent years there has been a substantial rise in procurement of foodgrains by the public sector agencies on account of consistent increases in Minimum Support Prices (MSP), despite the recommendations of the Commission for Agricultural Cost and Prices to freeze the same. It is argued that consistent increases in the MSP have distorted relative prices between alternate agricultural activities, land use patterns as well as the consumption of inputs. The stock of foodgrains as on January 1, 2004 was at 24.4 million tonnes as against minimum norm of 16.8 million tonnes for January. (Table 10.11).

TABLE – 10.11

Procurement, Off-take, Stocks and Food Subsidy

Year	Procurement (Million Tonnes)	Off-Take (Million Tonnes)	Stocks (Million Tonnes)	Food Subsidy (Rupees crore)
1	2	3	4	5
1993-94	26.40	18.61	20.54	5537
1994-95	24.99	19.44	26.80	5100
1995-96	22.24	24.35	20.82	5377
1996-97	20.03	25.63	16.41	6066
1997-98	23.82	18.96	18.12	7500
1998-99	24.22	20.73	21.82	8700
1999-00	31.43	23.05	28.91	9200
2000-01	35.43	17.95	44.98	12010
2001-02	41.91	16.15	59.14	17494
2002-03	35.46	45.60	—	24176
2003-04	37.29	45.13	—	25160
2004-05 BE	—	44.4 (Jan.04)	24.4 (Jan.04)	27746
Jan. 2005	31.14	—	21.7	—

B.E : Budget Estimate

Source: Economic Survey 2003-04

Considerable concern regarding the mounting stocks has been expressed of late, as substantial amount of food credit and food subsidy have been required to finance these operations. Food subsidy, which amounted to Rs.6,066 crore in 1996-97, has increased to Rs.21,200 crore in 2002-03. During 1997-98 to 2000-01, the outstanding food credit witnessed a rise from Rs.7,597 crore to Rs.39,991 crore, indicating a phenomenal average annual growth of 51.9 per cent. The share of consumer subsidy in food subsidy has been declining over these years, indicating that much of the increase in food subsidy goes towards carrying costs. Carrying cost of foodgrains increased to Rs.220.35 per quintal in 2000-01 from Rs.158.26 per quintal in 1996-97. Consumer subsidy on rice for below poverty line (BPL) consumers declined to Rs.565.00 per quintal in July 2000 from Rs.589.33 per quintal in 1997-98. Similarly, the consumer subsidy on wheat for BPL consumers decreased to Rs.415.00 per quintal in July 2000 from Rs.536.35 per quintal in 1997-98. Given the present scenario, the effectiveness of food subsidy in supporting the public distribution programme has been questioned.

From the chronic shortage of foodgrains and virtually 'ship-to-mouth' existence in the mid-sixties, India has made considerable strides towards achieving food security. Thanks to the green revolution, the country has not only achieved self-sufficiency in foodgrains, but has become a net exporter. For the first time in the history of independent India, the country has been a net exporter of foodgrains consecutively for the last seven years. What is more, the Food Corporation of India has, by now, accumulated over 60 million tonnes of foodgrains - nearly three times the normal requirement for buffer stocks and the Public Distribution System. There has been a significant decline in the incidence of poverty since the mid-sixties. Even then, according to the latest official estimates, at least 26 per cent of the population or 260 million people were still below the poverty line in the year 1999-2000. This implies that despite the *availability* of foodgrains for meeting the requirements of the entire population, we are still far from generating the necessary purchasing power or effective demand from the poor to satisfy their needs. Since effective food security implies achievement of both *physical and economic access* to food, a large section of our population can still be considered to be suffering from food insecurity despite the bulging stocks of foodgrains with the Food Corporation of India.

Agriculture and Food-security: Progress in the 10th Plan Mid-term Appraisal (June, 2005)

The Tenth Five-Year Plan had targeted gross domestic product (GDP) growth in agriculture and allied sectors at 4 per cent per annum, aiming to reverse a sharp deceleration in the second half of the 1990s - from

3.2 per cent per annum in the period 1980-81 to 1995- 96 to 1.9 per cent per annum during 1996-97 to 2001-02. GDP growth in agriculture and allied sectors during the first three years of the Tenth Plan averages only 1 per cent per annum. The Tenth Plan target of 4 per cent growth is, therefore, far from being realised.

According to Mid-term Appraisal, almost every sector experienced lower growth after 1996-97 than in the previous decade and a half. The magnitude of deceleration was such that although 2003-04 was a year of excellent monsoon and record production, per capita output in that year was less than 1996-97 in every crop sector except horticulture. Underlying this was productivity deceleration across all sectors, implying lower cost reduction through technological progress than earlier. The deceleration coincided with a downturn in world prices, and this impacted domestic farm prices more than in earlier decades because of greater openness. The consequence was that farm incomes became more variable and decelerated more than output in many cases.

Regional Variations

The available data on growth of State Domestic Product (SDP) from agriculture and allied sectors shows that the deceleration observed at the all-India level occurred also for almost every state individually. However, some distinct regional patterns do emerge from district-wise data on production of individual crops:

- In the relatively rich irrigated rice-wheat and wheat-sugarcane regions, although yields decelerated and almost stagnated, income growth did not slow down significantly. This is because of effective implementation of MSP and generous MSP awards throughout the Ninth Plan. There was no crop diversification and area increased further under wheat, rice and sugarcane.
- In high rainfall unirrigated regions mainly growing rice, growth decelerated but yields continued to grow faster than the national average However, since MSP policy was ineffective, farm incomes declined in these regions when it was decided in 2001 to reduce stocks by lowering sales prices and increasing food for work. Nearly a third of crop growth in these regions since mid-1990s has been on account of diversification, mainly towards vegetables.
- The dry and arid regions growing unirrigated coarse cereals, cotton and oilseeds were the most dynamic during 1992-98 when world prices were high. Yield growth was moderate but area increased rapidly and there was very significant diversification from coarse

cereals, pulses and lower valued oilseeds towards cotton, higher value oilseeds and horticulture. However, lower world prices since then have combined with successive droughts to reduce incomes very significantly. These regions, already most vulnerable to monsoon risk, bore the brunt of transmitted world price volatility.

- The other regions affected significantly by world price movements were the plantations and the already diversified coastal regions in the South.

Consumption Demand and Food Security

A consequence of the marked deceleration of agricultural growth has been that food consumption has stagnated since the beginning of the Ninth Plan. This conclusion follows not only from the NAS, which shows per capita real consumption expenditure on all food and beverages lower in 2002-03 and 2003-04 than in 1996-97, (but also from the National Sample Survey which suggests an even larger decline. These data-sets show larger decline in cereals consumption than of other food, so there is some evidence of diversification of the food basket). But the matter of concern is that the decline in cereals consumption is not being made up by increased consumption of other foods. In fact, the National Accounts data shows real per capita consumption lower in 2003-04 than in 1998-99 of cereals, pulses, edible oils, sugar, milk, fruits and vegetables, with consumption higher only of meat, fish and eggs. Moreover, this data shows that prices of all food items, except fruits and vegetables, increased less than the overall price level.

Since per capita GDP grew at about 3.5 per cent per annum during this period, the above is evidence of a major structural weakening of demand impulses that the agricultural sector can expect from the growth of other sectors of the economy. In addition to changes in patterns of consumption due to variations in life-style, this outcome is almost certainly linked to the fact that overall employment growth has been very slow and real agricultural incomes (which still provide a large source of food demand) have been stagnant or declining. From the point of view of planning future agricultural growth, this means that the demand side can no longer be ignored. This implies that it might be difficult to increase agricultural growth while maintaining profitability unless either costs are reduced by enhanced technological progress or definite steps taken to increase demand, for example, through greater exploitation of export prospects and, even more importantly, through policies which aim directly at increasing rural employment and incomes. Furthermore, these outcomes require that the performance of agriculture be viewed in conjunction with the continuing need for food security since recent trends appear to have set back progress in tackling the problem of under-nutrition, where India still lags behind other developing countries.

India's food security system is one of the largest in the world but is confined almost entirely to provisioning cereals. This system comprises the Food Corporation of India (FCI) which implements the MSP for cereals, holds buffer stocks, and delivers grain to a public distribution system (PDS) with a network of about 400,000 fair price shops (FPS). Since its inception after the food shortages of the mid- 1960s, this system has managed to help the country avoid famine, contain food price variability to much less than in world markets and offered enough price support for farmers to nearly triple cereals production. Quite apart from PDS entitlement, this delivered an almost steady decline in real market prices of cereals over the 1970s and 1980s and rising per capita availability. Till 1997, the annual cost of the entire system was less than 0.5 per cent of GDP.

However, the yield deceleration from early 1990s had cost implications that made it more difficult to reconcile producer, consumer and fiscal interests, especially with MSP being used in the early 1990s as an instrument to compensate farmers for cuts in fertilizer subsidy. The system ran into crisis during the Ninth Plan when large MSP increases were continued despite falling world prices and, simultaneously, the PDS was converted from universal to a targeted benefit.

The targeted Public Distribution System (TPDS) was introduced in 1997 in response to the 1990s reversal of the earlier decline in real cereals prices and to meet criticism that PDS did not deliver adequately to the poor. The TPDS replaced the earlier universal PDS entitlements with differential prices for the below poverty line (BPL) population and those above the poverty line (APL). BPL prices were set much lower than earlier uniform prices and, in order to reduce subsidy outgo, APL prices were increased in phases to reach full cost by 2000.

But since MSPs were above market prices, full cost pricing caused the APL to exit PDS, rendering many FPS unviable, while FCI bought almost the entire market arrivals in traditional surplus areas. PDS sales declined from over 19 million tonnes in 1996-97 to less than 12 million tonnes in 2000-01 even as procurement went up from 21 million tonnes to over 37 million tonnes. With exports restrained by low world prices, stocks increased from 18 million tonnes at end of 1997 to 58 million tonnes at end of 2001. The increased cost of stock holding doubled the food subsidy to nearly 1 per cent of GDP. And, most importantly, per capita cereals availability fell 20 per cent between 1997 and 2001, to its lowest level since 1980.

This perverse operation of the system not only reduced consumption, but, at the same time, prices and supplies became less stable and farm incentives were disturbed. As stocks built up, the wholesale price index for cereals increased 31 per cent between 1996-97 and 1999-00, distorting inter-crop parities and inflating money wages at a time when prices of other agricultural commodities were weak. Subsequently, in order to reduce stocks, BPL prices were cut further and quotas increased sharply in 2001-02. But such cheap supplies depressed farm prices of cereals wherever MSP was ineffective and, in particular, paddy prices in eastern India fell below full cost of production

Large exports at BPL prices and the drought of 2002-03 finally brought stocks down to near normal levels at the end of 2003. MSP policy has since been more restrained and procurement has stabilised at about 40 million tonnes. PDS sales have climbed back from 13 million tonnes in 2001 to about 25 million tonnes and total off-take, including for the Food for Work and Mid-Day Meals programmes, is now also about 40 million tonnes. However, this return to balance has been reached with much larger proportion of cereals production being procured and distributed by public agencies than before 1997. Moreover, per unit subsidy is much higher because about 60 per cent of PDS supply is now at BPL prices that are well below MSP and another 20 per cent at even lower prices for the Antyodaya Anna Yojana (AAY). The food distribution system has, therefore, been converted from its price stabilisation role to primarily one of transfer to the poor.

The failure during 1997-2003 of the till then quite effective food security system is a matter of grave concern. Not only were huge costs incurred (exceeding Central Plan outlays on agriculture, irrigation and rural development put together) without delivering food security, but its perverse operation also distorted producer incentives and added to the already increasing uncertainties. The problem arose because the stabilisation objective of the system was overridden by other objectives such as income support to farmers, compensating for input subsidy reduction and targeting consumer subsidies to the poor. An important question, since BPL prices are below costs of production of wheat and rice, is whether differential PDS pricing is the best way of serving the equity objective? With a decision already taken to introduce Employment Guarantee and expand Mid-Day Meals and the Integrated Child Development Services (ICDS), an alternative may be to move rapidly to full all-India coverage of these welfare initiatives and revert simultaneously to uniform PDS pricing (linked to but no less than MSP) and to the original clear-cut and much less expensive objective of stabilising prices at above costs of production. This would of course still leave the question of reaching the urban poor for whom no expansion of employment schemes is yet on the anvil and the old and infirm currently covered by AAY. But these relatively smaller parts of total PDS could either continue or be replaced by an expanded old age and disability pension. The important objective should be to redesign the system so that the food security and poverty alleviation objectives are strengthened and purchasing power of the poor increased so that agricultural demand growth is restored without distorting price incentives for agricultural growth.

In the context of the inadequate domestic demand growth that has been discussed earlier, the slow and uncertain export growth of agri-products is a cause for worry. Although the Foreign Trade Policy 2004-09 has emphasised the importance of agricultural exports and announced a number of measures to boost them, namely, the Special Agricultural Produce Scheme (Vishesh Krishi Upaj Yojana), Funds for Development of Agri Export Zones (AEZ) and relaxation of Export Promotion Capital Goods (EPCG) scheme for AEZ, etc., these do not really address the fundamental problem of competitiveness which essentially depends on higher productivity, better quality and lower cost of exportable agri-products. Apart from agronomic measures for raising productivity, interventions are required for educating farmers to enable them to upgrade their skills to improve the quality of products so that they conform to the strictest sanitary and phyto-sanitary standards.

Major Supply-side Issues

According to Mid-term Appraisal (MTA), although poor performance of agriculture in the Tenth Plan is partly due to poor monsoon and to sluggish implementation outlined earlier, this is largely attributable to longer-term trends. Besides the demand problems, the supply side problems are: declining public investment; failure to carry out essential reforms to conserve water and soil; unabated degradation of natural resources, and weakened support systems due to financial problems of state governments, i.e. unresponsive agricultural research, nearly broken down extension, inadequate seeds production, distribution and regulation etc. There is consensus among experts that steps are needed in several areas to reverse this trend, and that there are also some inherent problems.

APPENDIX TABLE – 10.1

Plan outlay in Agriculture and Allied Sectors

(Rs. crores)

Plans	Total Plan Outlay	Agriculture and Allied sectors	%age of Agriculture & Allied sectors to Total
I Plan (1951-56)*	2378	354	14.9
II Plan (1956-61)*	4500	501	11.3
III Plan (1961-66)	8577	1089	12.7
Annual Plans (1966-69)**	6625	1107	16.7
IV Plan (1969-74)**	15779	2320	14.7
V Plan (1974-79)	39426	4865	12.3
Annual Plan 1979-80	12177	1997	16.4
VI Plan (1980-85)	97500	5695	5.8
VII Plan (1985-90)	180000	10525	5.9
Annual Plan (1990-91)	58369	3405	5.8
Annual Plan (1991-92)	64751	3851	6.0
VIII Plan (1992-97)	434100	22467	5.2
IX Plan (1997-2002)	859200	42462	4.9
X Plan (2002-07)	398890	20668	5.2

* Includes Animal Husbandry, Special Area Programme, Rural Development and Forestry and Wildlife.

** Includes bufferstocks of Rs. 140 crore for 1968-69, Rs. 24 crore for 1969-70, Rs. 50 crore for 1971-72 and Rs. 25 crore for 1972-73 and Rs. 24 crore for 1973-73. Thus the figures for V Plan work out to Rs. 124 crore against the original Plan provision of Rs. 225 crore

Source: Tenth Five Year Plan (1997-2002) Vol.2.

APPENDIX TABLE – 10.2

Composition and Structure of Growth

		Eighth Plan		Ninth Plan		Tenth Plan		Share of GDP (%)	
		Growth Rate(%)	ICOR	Growth Rate(%)	ICOR	Growth Rate(%)	ICOR	2001-02	2006-07
1	Agriculture & Allied activities	4.69	1.59	2.06	4.05	3.97	1.99	24.7	20.5
2	Mining & Quarrying	3.59	10.74	3.81	5.44	4.30	7.99	2.3	1.9
3	Manufacturing	9.77	6.67	3.68	18.37	9.82	7.77	15.3	16.7
4	Elect, Gas & Water Supply	5.50	18.00	6.46	15.43	7.99	14.97	2.8	2.8
5	Construction	3.56	1.74	6.82	1.00	8.34	0.99	6.0	6.1
6	Trade	9.06	0.54	5.86	1.09	9.44	0.91	12.7	13.6
7	Rail Transport	1.95	27.94	4.70	9.87	5.40	14.66	0.9	0.8
8	Other Transport	8.42	4.41	5.63	6.09	7.54	5.37	4.9	4.8
9	Communication	14.31	7.25	17.14	5.28	15.00	8.33	1.7	2.3
10	Financial Services	10.21	2.23	8.93	1.35	11.69	1.56	6.3	7.5
11	Public Administration	3.91	7.82	9.21	4.09	6.43	5.45	6.6	6.1
12	Other Services	6.22	4.19	8.19	3.70	9.26	3.53	15.8	16.8
	Total	**6.54**	**3.43**	**5.35**	**4.53**	**7.93**	**3.58**	**100.0**	**100.0**

Source: Tenth Five Year Plan (2002-07) Vol.1.

References

Jeromi, P.D. (2002), "Is Indian Agriculture Approaching the Limits to Growth" in *Economic Developments in India*, Vol.58, Academic Foundation.

Government of India, Economic Survey 2002-03, 2003-04.

Parthasarthy, G. (2003), "Economic Reforms and Rural Development", Academic Foundation.

Planning Commission (2002), Tenth Five Year Plan 1997-2002.

——— (2005), Mid-term Appraisal of the Tenth Five Year Plan.

Rao, C.H.H. & Gulati, A, "Indian Agriculture: Emerging Perspectives and Policy", *Indian Economy Since Independence* ed. Uma Kapila 2000-01 edition, Academic Foundation.

Report of the Committee on Capital Formation in Indian Agriculture (Chairman, B.B. Bhattacharya).

Reserve Bank of India, Report on Currency and Finance 2001-02.

Vaidyanathan, A., (2003), "India's Economic Reforms and Development", Academic Foundation.

Vyas, V.S. (2003), "Agrarian Structure, Economic Policies & Sustainable Development", Academic Foundation.

Vyas, V.S. and Reddy, Ratna , "Economic Reforms in Indian Agriculture: Recent Experience and Long-term Issues", in *India's Economy in the 21st Century*, Raj Kapila and Uma Kapila, (eds.), 2nd Revised Edition, New Delhi: Academic Foundation, 2002.

11

Reforms in Land System in Post-Independent India

S.K. Ray

At the time of Independence, India inherited a semi-feudal agrarian structure with onerous tenure arrangements over substantial areas. The ownership and control of land was highly concentrated in a relatively few landlords and intermediaries. The principal interest of this controlling group in agriculture was to extract maximum rental from tenants, either in cash or in kind. Often tenants of land under intermediary and landlord control sublet their lands in smaller plots to working cultivators, thus smaller holdings increased. Under this arrangement, economic motivation to develop farm land for increased production or to improve the economic conditions of cultivators was locking. At the same time, working cultivators after paying high rent had no surplus to invest in farm improvement. They had neither resources nor knowledge for increasing agricultural production. Thus the agricultural land resource of India, along with its operators was gradually impoverished because economic motivation tended toward exploitation rather than toward investment and improvement.

With increasing pressure on land the operating land base of many working cultivators was further reduced. Land occupancy rights became increasingly insecure. Often cultivators were continuously shifted from one plot to another according to the whims of superior holders. Land was divided into small fragments, each owned or leased by cultivators whose objective was subsistence. Together then, the size and distribution of land holding, cultivation practices and product sharing, operated concertedly to hold down farm income. Over time, a large number of farms became disincentive-ridden due to size disability. A substantial portion of such cultivators sought to supplement their farm income by working as hired labourers competitive with even poorer landless workers. Independent India thus emerged with serious imbalances in man-land relationship among the three principal groups in the agricultural sector, viz., proprietors, working cultivators and labourers.

Policy Objectives for Structural Reorganisation

Following Independence, land reform as well as the abolition of intermediaries was considered an essential prerequisite for increasing agricultural production and for establishing an egalitarian society. Each of India's Five Year Plans since 1951 had set forth a policy for land reform. The land reform programmes were built around three major types of land reform measures: abolition of intermediary tenures, regulation of size of holding and, settlement and regulation of tenancy. As a result of these programmes, it was hoped that a different set of rights and duties would emerge in which the freedom of each interest would be regulated and some interests considered harmful for progress in agriculture would be eliminated.

Land policy as laid down in the First Five Year Plan can be viewed from two angles: (i) conception of different interests in land, and (ii) the effect of man-land relationship on agricultural production. It was conceived that the freedom with which intermediaries transacted their business had an adverse effect on agricultural production. The First Plan, therefore, set out to regulate the interests of intermediaries, large owners, small and middle owners, tenants-at-will, and landless workers. The Plan recognised the pattern of land occupancy and cultivation as a fundamental issue of national development.

The Second Five Year Plan stated: "The abolition of intermediaries and the protection given to tenants are intended to give the tiller of the soil his rightful place in the agrarian system and by reducing or eliminating the burden he has borne in the past, to provide him with fuller incentives for increasing agricultural production. Similarly, to bring the tenant into direct relation with the State and to put an end to the tenant-landlord nexus are essential steps in the establishment of a stable rural economy" (Government of India, 1956, p. 178). Complementary to these objectives were the policies of land ceilings, consolidation of holdings and encouragement of co-operative joint farming.

The central thesis behind the abolition of intermediaries was that ownership of land be clearly identified with management and operation of land. The owner himself should operate and manage the farm business.

Ceiling on land holdings were designed to offset the extremely uneven distribution of agricultural land. The policy implications of this measure were (i) to meet the land hunger of working cultivators, (ii) to reduce disparity in agricultural incomes, in ownership and in the use of land, and (iii) to increase employment opportunity in the rural sector. At the same time, consolidation of holdings was advocated to consolidate the scattered holdings of individual cultivators to form a single tract susceptible to more efficient management.

While ceiling on holdings and consolidation of plots were planned to increase the land base of the working cultivators, it was argued that reforms through structural changes could be secured only when the actual tillers of the soil were given a fair share of the fruits of their labour. This called for an overall change in the tenurial conditions of cultivators. Tenancy reforms were launched to confirm the rights of occupancy of tenants, secure their possession of tenanted land and also regulate rents on leased land.

But there existed a very large number of very small holdings. This group of minuscule holdings constituted one of the most difficult problems in agricultural reorganisation. The possibility of co-operative farming as a means of overcoming the difficulties presented by tiny holdings was discussed. It was pointed out that if these smaller holdings were grouped into larger units and farmed co-operatively then the advantage of large-scale organisation would become available. Larger financial resources for agricultural development could be provided and the volume of employment increased.

The rationale for co-operative farming grew out of an examination of the man-land ratio and the supposed economies of scale achievable on large-size units, even though there is little evidence to support the contention that greater per capita production will be forthcoming if holdings are pooled and cultivated jointly. Studies of farm management have indicated that the size of the holding and the yield under traditional agriculture are inversely correlated. The statistical basis of this generalisation has been challenged and it is now accepted that it is difficult to generalise from aggregate data that have not been subjected to careful scrutiny. However, it appears that if adjustment is made for differences in soil fertility, and proper yield and income variables are chosen, then there will be a strong general tendency towards constant returns to scale in Indian agriculture. This, along with the natural reluctance of cultivators to give up their newly won rights to land, seriously hindered co-operative farming. The failure of co-operative farming as a policy was tacitly admitted in the Fourth Five Year Plan when no additional programmes were proposed.

The net effect of all these reforms was presumed to loosen the rigidly stratified rural society so that each cultivator in accordance with his capability could find an opportunity to advance. The owner was envisaged to become the manager as well as the operator of his holdings.

The Reform Controversy

From the very beginning, legislative measures for overall agrarian reorganisation faced resistance from several quarters. The subject was widely discussed and debated. Many argued that ceiling and tenancy legislation would in effect infringe upon constitutional guarantees. Others opined that the proposed legislation was an 'eye wash' and did not go far enough.

The adequacy of the underlying economic analysis on which the programmes were based was challenged by several economists.[1] They expressed fear that agricultural production of the country would be seriously affected if larger holdings were reduced to smaller size by the imposition of ceilings. They argued that the smaller the size of holding, the lower the standards of efficiency and manoeuvrability in management. Distribution of land to a large number of cultivators in small holdings would increase the number of small holders and reduce agricultural production. The economic use of machinery and the adoption of modern methods of agriculture would not be easy to obtain for smaller farms; ceilings on holdings could not bring out enough land to meet the land hunger of the working cultivators and agricultural labourers. Further, it was argued that land is property; imposition of a capital levy in the form of ceiling on agricultural holding would be an injustice when similar measures were not simultaneously adopted for other sectors.

For several years both the Union and State Governments remained prisoners of indecision on this issue. Hesitancy on the ceiling issue was reflected in the original draft outline of the First Five Year Plan.

> "On the larger farms, production will fall and, for a period at any rate, on the other farms also, and it may well be that the decline in production may have a serious effect on the well-being and stability of rural society as whole" (quoted by Thorner, 1955, pp. 62-63).

The final version of the First Five Year Plan took a firmer position:

> "From the social aspect, which is not less important than the economic, a policy for land may be considered adequate in the measure in which, now

> and in the coming years, it reduces disparities in wealth and income, eliminates exploitation, provides security for tenant and worker and, finally promises equality of status and opportunity to different sections of the rural population (Government of India, 1953 b, p. 184).

In formulating the land policy towards substantial owners of land, the First Five Year Plan stated:

> "If it were the sole object of policy to reduce the holdings of the larger owners with a view to providing for the landless or for increasing the farms of those who now have uneconomic fragments, the facts at present available suggest that these aims are not likely to be achieved in any substantial measure. The question whether some limit should not be placed on the amount of land that an individual may hold has, therefore, to be answered in terms of general principles rather than in relation to the possible use that could be made of land in excess of any limit that may be set... It appears to us that, in relation to land (as also in other sectors of the economy) individual property in excess of any norm that may be proposed has to be justified in terms of public interest, and not merely on grounds of individual rights or claims. We are, therefore, in favour of the principle that there should be an upper limit to the amount of land that an individual may hold" (Government of India, 1953 b, pp. 187-188).

As a first step towards reorganisation of the land holding system, the Planning Commission suggested a census on land holdings during 1953. The proposal, however, was coldly received by the State Governments. In explaining this, Thorner commented:

> "In many cases this was taken to mean that the imposition of ceilings might be deferred until after the census of land-holding had been completed. It became clear both to opponents and proponents of ceiling limits that the information collected could be used to buttress the arguments of one or the other side. It was also appreciated that the data obtained would depend in larger part on the way the questionnaires were framed" (Thorner, 1955, pp. 62-63).

The Planning Commission schedules of January 1954 for the proposed census of land holdings failed to impress the State Governments until it was diluted further and made acceptable to all the states in November 1954. But even this weakened form of the proposed census of land holdings did not materialise. Only Hyderabad conducted a well designed survey. Uttar Pradesh refused to conduct a census while Kashmir did not participate on the ground that the question of redistribution of land had already been settled. Some states copied the patwari records, some confined the census for holdings of size ten acres and above and some conducted a nominal sample survey only (see Thorner, 1955, pp. 62-63). In his review of the entire episode. Thorner wrote:

> "Based upon the faulty village records and the seriously defective January, 1954, schedules, they may well prove inaccurate and misleading. In retro-

spect the tussle over the census can be seen as yet another phase in the broader controversy over limitations.

While the officials wrangled over schedules and categories, the landlords hastened their steps to forestall the possible effects of ceilings.... the past few years have witnessed a nation-wide wave of displacement of tenants by landlords. There have also been innumerable partitions of family properties, with the aim of making units of ownership appear smaller than they really are so that the landlords will be able to slip under the proposed ceilings. For the same purpose there have been many transfers to relatives outside the immediate family, to caste fellows, and to 'friends' (e.g., the Benami transactions reported, for example, from Travancore). In view of the special consideration urged for efficiently managed farms (the breaking up of which would presumably lead to a fall in output), some large owners have thought it wise to purchase tractors. Since the land reforms typically place the holdings of co-operatives and joint-stock companies outside their purview, more than a few families have transformed themselves into co-operatives; some affluent landlords have organised themselves into corporations for the production and refining sugarcane" (Thorner, 1955, pp. 68-69).

Impact of Structural Reorganisation

Land policy in the First Five Year Plan was thus formulated without sufficient knowledge about the size and distribution of land holdings in the rural sector. A considerable volume of data was collected for the first time in the Eighth Round (1954) of the National Sample Survey (NSS) for size and distribution of land holdings. However, the draft report of the NSS Eighth Round was only submitted to the Union Government in January 1960, nearly six years later. It, therefore, did not serve the purpose of planners to assess the magnitude of the problem involved in structural reorganisation.

Defects in policy planning became conspicuous in the implementation stage of the land reform programme. Legal, administrative and other factors became principal bottlenecks. In the process, the error of doing the right things too slowly became increasingly costly. Policy makers failed to take into account the importance of the time dimension for the success of these reforms. A go-slow programme of implementation failed to make effective impact upon many working cultivators.

Under the Indian Constitution, land reform is a State subject. Apart from the broad principles directly bearing on the distribution of land resources, tenancy relations are under the control of the several states. Consequently, while the main features of the reform legislation in different states are practically identical, there is a wide difference in the scope of the work actually undertaken. The result is that tenancy problems are concentrated in certain states and are not as important in other states.

As a result of a series of investigations and personal observations, it is generally conceded that the reforms are not complete. For example, while rents may be limited by law to one-fourth of the crop in a given state, this law is not enforced in many cases. Furthermore, land ownership can be divided among the members of a joint family so that each member can own his legal share of the land with the result that the total family holding is several times above the legal limit. The large number of evictions, many justified on the grounds of a 'reform' provision which encouraged the right of land resumption for self-cultivation, and the so-called 'voluntary' surrender of land which were especially prevalent during the 1950s give visible evidence that security of tenure is not an accepted fact of life in India.

Under the conditions prevailing before the introduction of the seed-fertiliser technology, some observers have argued that the weaknesses in tenancy, rent control, etc., have not been important constraints on production. However, the problems of land tenancy and ownership have acquired special significance with the technological advances in agriculture. Land cultivated on tenancy or rented arrangements can enable the cultivator to enlarge the scale of his operations to economically justify mechanisation and his own water supply. However, the increased productivity of the high-yielding varieties (HYVs) has also led to a trend of rising rents, or in the absence of income from this source, the reclaiming of land for owner cultivation. As a result, both the returns from, and the security of, rented and leased lands are apparently decreasing.

A cultivator who does not have security of tenure or who must pay a high proportion of output in rents is less likely to invest in land improvements, adopt HYVs or use inputs up to the optimal economic amounts. Therefore, tenants are likely to suffer a relative decline in income compared to owners, as the modern technology becomes more widely spread.

In order to safeguard the interests of the tenants, the Chief Ministers' Conference in July 1967 recommended the following measures:

1. Tenants in cultivating possession of land should not be disturbed and should be given complete security of tenancy by: (i) staying all evictions, (ii) suspending the right of resumption where such right has been given to landowners, and (iii) regulating voluntary surrenders in such a way that landowners do not get an advantage by persuading tenants to surrender their tenancy.

2. The rate of rent should be reduced to the level of one-fourth or one-fifth of the gross produce so that the tenant is in a position to improve his land.
3. Record of tenancy should be prepared as a special operation and maintained up-to-date.
4. Special attention should be given to ensure credit and other facilities to tenants and small holders for increasing agricultural production.

Since the 1967 Chief Ministers' Conference, many more meetings have followed, each pledging faithful implementation of reform measures. But, as the 1978-83 Draft Five Year Plan (Government of India, 1978) observed, the will to implement the policy has been sadly lacking all along.

In a recently completed study, Appu has made a critical appraisal of policy, legislation and implementation of land reforms in India since Independence. He observed that "the significant features of all those laws were the slow pace of legislation, inadequacies in the content of the legislation, the time-consuming procedures laid down and the role of the judiciary in frustrating the the implementation of the enacted laws" (Appu, 1995, p.210). Notwithstanding these serious limitations, Appu was of the opinion that "the implementation of the laws for the Abolition of Intermediary Interests was far more satisfactory than the implementation of the laws enacted in later years for the Reform of Tenancy and the imposition of Ceilings on Agricultural Holdings (Appu, 1995, p.210). He wrote:

> "The most important beneficial result of the reform was that it put an end to the system of parasitic intermediaries and brought some 25 million erstwhile tenants into direct relationship with the state... With the abolition of intermediary interests the principal tenants became owners of the land... The erstwhile principal tenants acquired a higher social and political status leading to a shift in the rural power structure. The most visible demonstration of this shift is the emergence of persons belonging to the upper layers of the so-called backward castes in the leadership of political parties..." (Appu, 1995, pp. 210-211).

On tenancy reform, Appu found that it "...has not put an end to absentee ownership of land nor has it led to the disappearance of tenancies. It has only resulted in tenancies being pushed underground..." (Appu, 1995, p.214). Summing up the performance on this front, he wrote:

> "...Taking country as a whole, by 1992 ownership rights had been conferred on (or tenancy rights had been protected of) some 11 million tenants on 14.4 million acres of land. That constituted no more than 4% of the operated

> area. It is interesting to note that the seven states of Assam, Gujarat, Himachal Pradesh, Karnataka, Kerala, Maharashtra and West Bengal account for 97% of the beneficiaries. Practically no benefits accrued to the tenants in the other states. Even in these seven states tenancy reform led to the large scale eviction of tenants. Except in West Bengal, share-croppers by and large remained beyond the pale of tenancy reform everywhere. Only in West Bengal and Kerala did those in the lowest rungs of the peasant society receive solid benefits on the implementation of tenancy reform. The rights of some 14 lakh share-croppers were protected in West Bengal and in Kerala some 2.84 lakh rural poor, mostly agricultural labourers, became owners of tiny homesteads. As a result of tenancy reform there has been a sharp fall in the area of land under tenancy. From over one-half of the operated area on the eve of the reform, the area under tenancy has come down to about 15% of the operated area now. The tenants acquired ownership rights or were made secure in only about 4% of the operated area. Thus the reform led to the rural poor losing access to some 30% of the operated area" (Appu, 1995, pp. 213-214).

The performance regarding the implementation of ceiling on agricultural holdings has turned out to be more disappointing. Appu observed:

> "....As a result of the implementation of the old and the new laws, by 1992 only about 2 million hectares of surplus land could be distributed to some 4.76 million beneficiaries. Thus the efforts spread over a period of three and a half decades to enforce ceilings and take over surplus land led to the redistribution of less than 2% of the operated area. If we look into the performance of individual states, we find that the area distributed as a percentage of the total area operated is 17.4 for Jammu and Kashmir, 6.36 in West Bengal and 5 in Assam. In all the other states only less than one per cent of the operated area could be distributed. Obviously, the imposition of ceilings and the redistribution of surplus land made no impact on the agrarian structure in most states" (Appu, 1995, p.216).

On balance, there seems to be some reasons to conclude that agrarian reorganisation in India has failed to make any considerable impact on the socio-economic conditions of the working cultivators. Indeed, the record so far is so depressing and frustrating that even an able administrator like Appu, who championed and spent a considerable part of his career in administering land reform programmes noted:

> "Thus the programmes of land reform implemented since Independence did not lead to any significant re-distribution of land, or, the removal of all the obstacles to increasing agricultural production. Of the three programmes considered in this study, the laws for the abolition of intermediary interests were implemented fairly well. But in the case of tenancy reform and ceilings on holdings, the policies adopted were ambivalent and there were large gaps between policy and legislation and between legislation and implementation. We have seen that as result of the implementation of the tenancy laws, tenants became owners of or acquired rights in only about 4% of the operated area. The enforcement of ceilings led to the redistribution of less than 2% of

the operated area. Thus these two measures taken together led to the redistribution of only about 6% of the operated area" (Appu, 1995, p.217).

Emerging Perspectives and Policy Issues

It is against the background of the last four decades experience that the need to reformulate the land policy of India should be considered. Even persons emotionally attached with land reform programmes agree that the scope for improving implementation through legislative measures is now very limited. They point out, the socio-economic and political environment in which these programmes were introduced have changed so dramatically, that it would be almost impossible to carry out the reforms. Appu described the changed environment as follows:

> "...If the political will in favour of meaningful land reform was weak at independence and weaker still later on, it is non-existent today. Land reform has practically disappeared from the agenda of most political parties. This, in my view, is the inevitable consequence of the great changes that have taken place in the social and economic fields. With the abolition of intermediary interests the erstwhile superior tenants belonging mostly to upper and middle castes acquired a higher social status. Rise in agricultural productivity, rising land values and higher incomes from cultivation have added to their economic strength. Substantial landowners who wield great authority in rural India are bitterly opposed to ceilings on agricultural holdings. They are able to have their way because no serious efforts have been made to organise the landless and the land poor and enlist their support in favour of reforms. As for tenancy reform is concerned, there is a certain commonality of interest between all landowners - large, medium, small and even marginal. They are all passionately attached to their land and all of them are opposed to conferring benefits on insecure tenants. In the first round of land reform only the intermediaries were adversely affected. They were few in number and were weak politically. They had also made themselves obnoxious by aligning themselves with the colonial power. So it was easy enough to abolish intermediary interests. And it was done without hurting them much. But injuring the interests of the present class of landowners is an entirely different proposition. No political party that wishes to win elections and come to power can afford to do that. At the time of independence this class of landowners did not wield much political and economic power, and with a modicum of political will the reforms could have been implemented. But now it has become almost impossible to carry out the reforms" (Appu, 1995, pp. 232-233).

Dramatic changes have also taken place in agriculture. A fundamental and dynamic process of change with far-reaching consequences was introduced in Indian agriculture in 1965. This significant development was the introduction of modern scientific inputs of high-yielding seed varieties, controlled irrigation, chemical fertilisers, plant protection and mechanised power in tested management 'packages'.

The deeper significance of a technologically dynamic agriculture is that it provides opportunity to move from subsistence to viable economic farming and creates new potential for accelerated economic growth well beyond the agricultural sector. To exploit fully the potential created by this new environment in Indian agriculture, Dandekar argued that the structure of production should be changed (Dandekar, 1994). He observed with concern:

> "...that the policy-makers did not see that a concomitant change in the relations of production was needed was deplorable. In fact, they thought had the new technology had made even a small farmer viable so that the ceilings on landholdings could be further lowered. They missed two points. First, even with improved productivity, there is a limit to the population a given land can support at a minimum subsistence, the expectation about which itself changes over time, as it should, and leave behind a surplus for investment. Second, a new technology by itself does not change a static agriculture into a dynamic agriculture. It requires that the dynamism be passed on to the farmer, the essence of which is an opportunity to grow as a farmer. A ceiling on his landholding denies him such an opportunity. The same is true of the present tenancy laws which have practically abolished lease market in land" (Dandekar, 1994, p. 372).

Dandekar was forthright in making the policy prescription: "Hence, the *first* (emphasis added) item on the agenda of future agricultural policy should be the existing ceilings on landholdings and tenancy laws; they should be removed altogether or should be relaxed in stages" (Dandekar, 1974, p.373). Dandekar was aware of the criticisms which his policy recommendations might invite but, he dismissed them as ideological hangover bordering on hypocrisy. He wrote:

> "If this is done, enterprising farmers will enlarge their holdings by buying or leasing in lands of small and marginal farmers, for whom it is not worth staying in agriculture. Consequently, landlessness will increase, as will employment of hired labour in agriculture. There is a strong aversion to this development and it is argued that it be avoided at all cost; that the population presently subsisting on agriculture should be held in agriculture and, as far as possible, kept self-employed even if on small and marginal farms. The view is held on two different ideological grounds. One is that self-employment is a value in itself and, whatever be the level of subsistence it may provide, it should be preferred to wage employment whatever be the wage. One would respect this, as one should respect all moral values, were it not for the fact that the exponents of it are almost all salaried and not self-employed persons.

The other ideological ground is that this will lead to 'capitalist' farming, and to inevitable exploitation of labour. The prerequisite condition of capitalist agriculture is that it brings in capital into agriculture which is essential for adoption and exploitation of new technology. If the capital is generated within agriculture, that is, 'surplus value' in Marxian terminology which is at the bottom of what Marx called 'exploitation' of hired labour. But, if the workers would not leave any 'surplus value' behind for ploughing back into production, the economy would stagnate..." (Dandekar, 1994, pp. 373-374).

The strength of Dandekar's argument also contains its weakness. It fails to recognise fully the ground realities of the environment in which the proposed policy changes have to seek acceptance and a fair chance for implementation. True, the crisis that surfaced at the beginning of this decade from the acute domestic and international economic pressure and threatended to destroy the credibility of the country in international financial markets now provides a necessary environment for initiating economic reforms. But, economic compulsion alone is not enough. Social and political compulsions are also important conditioning factors in making the policy environment receptive for change. Unfortunately, those have not yet become conducive to make Dandekar's policy prescription the *first* item on the agenda of future agricultural policy.

Modern technology, be it for agriculture or for industry, is in general labour saving and capital intensive. Indeed, available empirical evidence shows that the employment elasticity of output in agriculture has fallen sharply in the post-new technology period (Bhalla, 1987; Bhalla *et al.*, 1991; Ray, 1992). Consequently, any unrestrained opportunity to grow through modernisation of agriculture can only be at the cost of aggravating further the problem of unemployment. Dandekar's policy prescription is a deliberate attempt to create this situation for promoting growth in agriculture. He was in favour of building up pressure so that those who are not in a position to leave behind any surplus value for ploughing back in agriculture are forced to leave agriculture. But, where would they go? Obviously, not to industry, as it is also supposed to grow with labour saving modern technology. To resolve the dilemma, Dandekar made two suggestions: (i) to implement a minimum support price for labour, that is, "a minimum wage which, if the capitalist farmer would not pay, the government shall pay and employ the labour on worthwhile work"; and (ii) to the extent possible, employ the unemployed "in the creation of the social and physical infrastructure necessary for agricultural development rather in the operation of cultivation" (Dandekar, 1994, p. 374). These are laudable suggestions but, since the governments in India are presently going through acute financial difficulties, it is very difficult to implement them unless efforts are made to open up new avenues for mobilisation of resources.

It would be of interest to visualise the situation if the existing ceiling and tenancy laws were repealed. As agricultural income is not taxed, there would virtually be a beeline to make investments in land. Not only enterprising farmers would start enlarging their holdings by buying or leasing in land; businessmen and moneyed people from other walks of life would also enter agriculture to make smashing profits. A convenient route to convert black money into white would thuus be firmly established. Luxury farm houses would come up to which rich people would retreat to spend holidays and breathe fresh air. Land prices would soar and speculators would have a field day. The problem of uneconomic holdings would no longer remain. Millions of small and marginal farmers would be squeezed out from their small and tiny plots. However, in the absence of employment opportunities elsewhere, they would remain in agriculture and work in the estates of big landowners as tenants or wage labourers. In short, rural India would acquire a modern look closely resembling the U.S. and other developed countries, though it would continue to carry a huge labour force desperately struggling to eke out living directly or indirectly from agriculture.

The social and political costs of giving rural India such a modern look at this juncture need to be examined, especially when the incidence of poverty has still remained very high. Repealing the existing ceiling and tenancy laws would not doubt provide opportunities to enterprising farmers and moneyed people to grow; modernisation of agriculture might progress rapidly; the trickle down effect too might provide a minimum level of subsistence to all to survive. But the distribution of income would become more skewed, the gap between the rich and the poor would further widen, and the social friction would sharply intensify. The tardy progress of policy reforms initiated under economic compulsion has already started sending warning signals. Newspaper reports of the Planning Commission's mid-term appraisal of the Eighth Five Year Plan do not provide an encouraging picture. Social tension arising from the rich becoming richer and the poor poorer has become a matter of serious concern.

Moreover, the intense love of the intellectuals to study the poverty in India has not only emboldened them to speak with moral overtones but it has also in the process encouraged the politicians to make increasingly tall promises. The politics of competitive populism has now spread its tentacles to all political parties. It has made hypocrisy populism has now spread its tentacles to all political parties. It has made hypocrisy an accepted way of political life in India. Therefore, if the lack of political will has made implementation of land reforms legislation difficult, the politics of competitive populism, at least for some time to come, would also not allow withdrawal of these legislations.

It thus appears that the present policy environment is unlikely to permit drastic changes in the existing land reform legislations. Several measures need to be taken before considering such changes. An appropriate first step in this direction would be the imposition of agricultural income tax and agricultural holding tax. These measures fit well in the newly advocated philosophy for market-friendly approach. They can also help to mobilise the much needed resources for employing the unemployed in the creation of social and physical infrastructure for agricultural development. Moreover, a progressive agricultural holding tax may act as a deterrent against formation of large holdings in the future - while at the same time, it may encourage greater efficiency of farmers who insist on retaining their large holdings.

At the same time, several measures should be taken to discourage farming on uneconomic holdings. Innovative schemes, such as the free boring of wells provided in eastern Uttar Pradesh, should be used to encourage small and marginal farmers to consolidate their holdings. However, consolidation of holdings cannot considerably improve the areal extent of uneconomic holdings. Therefore, a floor limit should be imposed on the size of holding. Simultaneously, small and marginal farmers should be allowed to lease in or lease out land with adequate safeguards, so that they could adjust the sizes of their holdings and maintain them above the floor levels.

A plea is being made to relax the ceiling laws in order to encourage corporate sector to enter agriculture for commercial production of high-value and processed agricultural products, and earn thereby valuable foreign exchange for the country. Rather than relaxing the existing ceiling laws, it would be better to consider the command area approach followed by the sugar industry and the area-based contract farming approach adopted by the Pepsi. Both provide an opportunity to earn foreign exchange without any direct involvement of the corporate sector in the production of required agricultural raw materials. The corporate sector should be welcomed as partners in the task for social and economic upliftment of rural India. They should set up agro-processing units in the rural areas and help in diversifying agriculture, encourage contract farming especially among small and marginal farmers by extending extension and marketing facilities, and also develop the required physical infrastructure support in their areas of operation. But their direct involvement in agricultural production should be firmly resisted till the workforce dependent on agriculture declines significantly to a low level.

The nitty-gritty of future agricultural policy should be worked out only after fully recognising the social, political and cultural milieu in which it has to operate. Increasingly sophisticated technologies are now available which can dramatically push up the growth rate of agriculture. However, not all of them are acceptable and desirable in the present Indian situation.

Note

1. For an excellent commentary on the debate and discussion on the subject that followed, see (Dandekar, 1994, pp. 41-88).

References

Appu, P.S. (1995), *Land Reforms in India: A Survey of Policy, Legislation and Implementation*, Land Reforms Unit, Lal Bahadur Shastri National Academy of Administration, Mussoorie, U.P. (mimeo).

Baden-Powell, B.H. (1892), *The Land Systems of British India*, Vol. 1 and 2, Oxford University Press, London.

——— (1896), *The Indian Village Community*, Longmans and Green, London.

Bauer, P.T. and B.S. Yamey (1957), *The Economics of Underdeveloped Countries*, James Nisbet & Co. Ltd., London.

Bhalla, Sheila (1987), "Trends in Employment in Indian Agriculture, Land and Asset Distribution", *Indian Journal of Agricultural Economics*, Vol. 42, No. 4, October-December.

Bhalla, Sheila; Abhijit Sen, Rohini Nayyar and M.D. Sathe (1991), "Study Group on Employment Generation", in Government of India (1991), *Report of the National Commission on Rural Labour*, Vol. II, Ministry of Labour, New Delhi.

Campbell, George (1870), "Tenure of Land in India", in Cobden Club's *The System of Land Tenure in Various Countries*, Macmillan, London.

Dandekar, V.M. (1994), *The Indian Economy: 1947-92, volume 1, Agriculture,* Sage Publications India Pvt. Ltd., New Delhi.

Government of India (1953 a), *Agriculture Legislation in India, Vol. IV - Land Reforms (Abolition of Intermediaries),* Economic and Statistical Advisor, Ministry of Food and Agriculture, New Delhi.

——— (1953 b), *The First Five Year Plan, 1951-56*, Planning Commission, New Delhi.

——— (1956), *Second Five Year Plan*, Planning Commission, New Delhi.

——— (1963), *Progress of Land Reforms*, Planning Commission, New Delhi.

——— (1978), *Draft Five Year Plan 1978-1983*, Planning Commission, New Delhi.

Maine, Henry S. (1876), *Village Communities in the East and West,* 3rd (Author's) Edition, Henry Holt, New York; reprinted in 1993 by Low Price Publications, Delhi.

Neale, W.C. (1962), *Economic Change in Rural India: Land Tenure and Reform in Uttar Pradesh, 1800-1955*, Yale University Press, New Haven and London.

Rao, C.H. Hanumantha and Ashok Gulati (1994), "Indian Agriculture: Emerging Perspectives and Policy Issues", *Economic and Political Weekly*, Vol. 29, No. 53, December 31.

Ray, S.K. (1992), "Development of Irrigation and Its Impact on Pattern of Land Use, Output Growth and Employment Generation", *Journal of Indian School of Political Economy*, Vol.4, No.4, October-December.

Thomer, Daniel (1955), *The Agrarian Prospect of India*, Delhi University Press, Delhi.

Vyas, V.S. (1994), "Agricultural Policies for the Nineties - Issues and Approaches", *Economic and Political Weekly*, Vol. 29, No. 26, June 25.

Indian Journal of Agricultural Economics, Vol. 51, January-June 1996, "*Land System and its Reforms in India*", Part II and III. Reprinted with permission from the author and the editor, Indian Journal of Agricultural Economics.

12

Modernising Indian Agriculture

V.M. Rao & P.D. Jeromi

I

REFORMING POLICYMAKING: AN AGENDA OF PRIORITY TASKS

1.1 Introduction

The arrival of the new millennium has been heralded by numerous vision documents about the long-term prospects of the Indian economy. There is considerable anxiety about the likely course of the agricultural scenario in the country. While science and technology hold promise of plenty, doubts are expressed about our capacity to make productive and wise use of the technological opportunities. We are told that there is enough room for foodgrain production to expand but we cannot be equally sure that the arrangements needed to reach foodgrains to those in distress would be effectively organised. There is good evidence to show that agricultural growth benefits even the poorest but, regrettably, the impact on the poor appears to remain too modest to support a lifestyle meeting the minimum norms of human development like adequate education, health and nutrition.

Development strategy and policies, particularly those focused on agriculture and rural areas, would be a critical factor influencing the agricultural scenario as it actually unfolds in the decades to come. There is a vast literature on agricultural policies in India assessing their performance and suggesting reforms. The central and state governments and the associated bodies engaged in the task of formulation of policies have adequate in-house facilities for high quality policy analyses. It would be presumptuous on the part of two individual researchers like us to seek to prepare a full-fledged policy agenda for the future. This paper is motivated by a far more modest and limited objective. Our attempt is to identify tasks focussing on which could help the government in strengthening the policy-making process itself so that policies gain in relevance, reach and impact on intended beneficiaries.

One has to begin by taking note of the transition which is in progress in the process of policymaking for agriculture and rural areas. The transition has three inter-related dimensions. The first is the move towards decentralisation with the governments at the state and lower levels — particularly those at the grassroots — assuming larger role and responsibility than now for policy choices and their implementation. Decentralisation makes it necessary to have a framework enabling the governments at different levels - from the centre, states to districts and below-to work in a unified manner complementing each other. The second dimension relates to shift of emphasis from the government role as a intervener in the economy to facilitator enabling the different constituents in the economy-markets, business units, user groups, cooperatives etc.— to operate in a smooth and efficient manner. Direct interventions by the government and its taking up functions normally done by other constituents in the economy were unavoidable in the past but over the years the negative features of direct interventions— burgeoning bureaucracy, politicisation of economic decisions, administered prices flouting economic norms etc.— have come to dominate. Also, the other constituents in the economy are now in position to take up functions in which they have comparative advantage over the government. Shifting of emphasis from direct interventions in the economy to the role as a facilitator would be of help in reducing the size of the government and the range of its direct and primary responsibilities. The policy agenda would become trimmer with many heavyweights dropping out and making room for modest and practicable measures. This would be a time-taking process but, happily, the growing burden of deficits and the prospects of bankruptcy might be of help in quickening the pace of the process! It is to underline the uncertainty about what would eventually remain on the policy agenda that we have chosen to focus the paper on tasks and selected policies rather than on the full range of policy agenda. Third, apart from the facilitating role, the government would have to participate more actively in the society's efforts to realise long-term macro objectives like conservation of environment and promotion of human development where the primary responsibility for building up perspectives, institutions and mechanisms must rest on the government.

Our attempt in Part-I of this paper is to identify tasks focussing on which would make the transition described above in the policymaking process fast and smooth and also help the process get oriented towards the long-term goal in development. Section 1.2 describes the goal that we believe to be appropriate for Indian agriculture at the present juncture of its development viz. Modernisation of agriculture in its physical as well as community dimensions. A serious imbalance between these two dimensions has emerged over the post-Independence decades. Section 1.2 takes note of this imbalance and argues that to eliminate the imbalance the government should strive to have quick breakthrough in achieving three objectives:

i) Making agriculture a self-regulating system with government confining itself to a facilitating role in the day-today business and routine operations. However, we do recognise situations in which the government would have to play an interventionist role.

ii) Meeting the challenge of limits to growth imposed by India's land and water resources.

iii) Promoting human development which is a critical ingredient in transforming modernisation as a broad-based development process.

The next three sections in Part-I - sections 1.3, 1.4 and 1.5 - deal in turn with each of these three objectives discussing their current status and the main problems impeding progress.

The priority tasks are identified in the light of this discussion. It needs to be stressed that we have identified the priority tasks without going into their technical, administrative and organisational aspects. There is a rich literature on these issues and lack of information or expertise is hardly a barrier in the way of the policymaker. Second, the tasks identified in the paper do not form a blueprint for the future. Continuing progress towards modernisation of agriculture would need review at intervals to re-identify priority tasks in the light of what has been achieved till then, what remains and how best to move ahead keeping in mind the dynamics of the system. Looking ahead, Section 1.6 argues that the government would have to work towards modernisation of agriculture while remaining preoccupied with many and difficult problems threatening the stability of the Indian society.

1.2. Modernisation of Agriculture: Goals and Objectives

The post-Independence decades have witnessed a veritable transformation in Indian agriculture. What is most readily noticed is the increase in agricultural production, particularly the nearly four-fold rise in the production of foodgrains which saved the country from one of the gravest crises it faced after Independence. The increase in production was made possible by expansion of irrigation, spread of new technology and additions to rural infrastructure like irrigation works, roads, market yards and warehouses. These changes in the physical features of agriculture needed changes in the institutional structure – like new credit institutions, extension agencies, regulated markets, control of moneylenders etc. The cumulative effect of these changes has been reflected in the farmers – their perceptions, attitudes and behaviour – and in the changing features of rural communities such as stratification, diversification, commercialisation and exposure to outside influences. The total process bringing about these wide ranging changes could be described as modernisation of agriculture. In a rural-cum-agriculture-based society like India, the process of modernisation of agriculture through its direct and indirect impacts would be a major determinant of economic status, development and welfare of rural people.

A striking feature of modernisation of agriculture in India is the contrasting scenarios through which it is unfolding. The aggregative physical parameters of agriculture show remarkable achievement. Listed below are a few striking indicators of improvements in the physical aspects of agriculture.

- Between 1949-50 and 1996-97, Index (base 1980-81) of agricultural production increased from 49 to 176, index of foodgrains from 52 to 161 and non-foodgrains from 45 to 201. Index of per hectare yield (all crops) increased from 74 to 149. It may be mentioned that the agricultural scenario has been one of stagnancy in the decades prior to Independence.
- Between 1950-51 and 1994-95, gross cropped area increased from 132 million hectares to 188 million hectares implying a rise in cropping intensity from 111 to 132. Gross irrigated area went up from 23 million hectares to 71 million hectares.
- Between 1950-51 and 1996-97, distribution of improved seeds increased from negligible to 70 lakh quintals. Fertiliser use increased from only 69 thousand tonnes to 14 million tonnes with per hectare fertiliser use going up from negligible to 77 Kgs. Pesticides use increased from 2.4 thousand tonnes to 56

thousand tonnes. Consumption of electricity in agriculture went up from 15200 Million KWH in 1981-82 to 85736 Million KWH in 1995-96.

- Institutional credit (Cooperative Societies, Commercial Banks and Regional Rural banks) was 28653 crores in 1996-97 as compared to 10186 crores in 1989-90.

Source: Agricultural Statistics at a Glance, Government of India, March 1998.

On the other hand and paradoxically, despite the good performance of agriculture, the rural communities in India have poor development indicators. Before taking a look at the indicators, it may be mentioned that UNDP's Human Development Report, 1997 shows that judged by Human Development Index (HDI) India ranks lower (rank 138 out of 175 countries) than Myanmar (rank 131) which figures among "Least Developed Countries"! The development indicators for the rural communities given below are from a recent large scale survey conducted by National Council of Applied Economic Research (Shariff A, 1999).

- "About half the population of rural India is illiterate and suffers from `capability poverty', about 40 per cent have extremely low incomes".
- "Over 50 per cent of Indian population is still vulnerable and cannot afford the cost of education and health care".
- "National policies and programmes during the last half a century have not helped the SCs and STs to emerge from the perennial poverty trap".
- 63 per cent of villages do not have pucca/all weather connecting roads. In some states this is true of over 80 per cent of villages.
- "About one-half of all villages in India do not have any source of protected drinking water".
- "Overall, 88 per cent of all villages in rural India have a primary school within the village (but) about a quarter of villages in Uttar Pradesh, Himachal Pradesh and Orissa do not have even primary schools. Given the relatively poor transport net work in these states, implementing the goal of universal primary education in these states seems remote".
- "Only about 22 per cent of all villages have a (health) sub-centre within the village".

The purpose of this paper is to look at our experiences to seek clues about how modernisation of agriculture could be harnessed for enhancing the economic status and welfare of rural people. It would be helpful to keep the following points in mind as we undertake the search.

- Linking modernisation of agriculture with modernisation of rural India is a critical part of the larger task of nation-building in India. Nation-building is an outcome of numerous socio-economic and political processes at macro, regional and micro levels. The government's development role requires it to influence, regulate and modify these processes, but, in a democratic polity, the government itself would, to an extent, be a product of these processes.
- It is the fundamental responsibility of the government to ensure that its role and actions are guided by a national perspective and by the long term goals and interests of the nation as a whole. This is a difficult role to play for a government in a democratic polity where it has to continually respond to innumerable sectional demands. This is particularly true in India where elections threaten to become an annual chore!.
- The development strategy so far has been centre-dominated with a metropolis-cum-elite bias and a top-down approach in implementation. The recent reforms and the philosophy underlying it favour a market-led strategy with the government playing a facilitating role, to promote growth, to make growth more broad based, to improve the access to growth by the backward and the poor and to provide safetynet to the weak and the vulnerable.

Harnessing modernisation of agriculture for the development of rural areas and people is a distant goal which needs to be approached through a sequence of phases. The first step in preparing an agenda focused on this distant goal is to specify the objectives which would help in identifying the priority tasks forming what may be regarded as the beginning phase for moving towards the long term goal. The priority tasks would depend on the current status of agriculture and the promising directions for taking the next steps. The agenda we are seeking in Part-I of this paper is a modest exercise to prepare a tentative list of priority tasks on the basis of available research studies and policy analyses. Such an agenda would be useful as a discussion document and as a framework which could be filled out and extended through further consultations. Our discussion of agenda is organised around three objectives described below.

(a) Towards a Self-regulating System

A remarkable feature of agriculture is the wide gap between what the technologist gets in the experimental farm and what a farmer gets on his farm and also a wide gap between the "best-practice" farmer and the common run of farmers. The government's interventions through providing subsidies and organising extension services have had an impact only in a few areas with large parts of agriculture remaining barely touched. As a long term goal, the objective should be to have an agricultural system operating through well-organised markets, efficient farmers and a smooth process integrating technology generation, its adoption on farms and optimum production basket for end uses. Such a process would need well-behaved markets providing clear signals for farmer decisions, farmers able and willing to respond to the signals and supply and demand responses occurring with reasonable speed and accuracy. In the real world, the process would be far from smooth as it would be buffeted by succession of shocks and disturbances. We propose the following specific objectives for the government to push the present system towards self-regulation.

i) A national perspective for agriculture compatible with market-led growth, its implications for regional comparative advantages and preferred opportunities; a time frame and a clear set of priorities for investments and creating infrastructures.

ii) Handing over of development functions to Panchayati Raj Institutions (PRIs) as visualised by the recent constitutional amendments. This could become a catalyst in the emergence of grass root level participatory institutions like user groups and beneficiary unions apart from the functions directly undertaken by the PRIs. The chief weakness in the present government role in agriculture is the inability of the top down approach to look after the development functions at the grassroots level which need a system based on devolution, participation and local leadership and initiatives.

iii) Providing an environment for steady improvements in the self-regulating features of the system. Acquiring capabilities to monitor the system and to make corrective interventions.

(b) Overcoming Limits to Growth

The extensive margin of cultivation has already reached its limit in Indian agriculture. In the three decades (1967-68 to 1996-97) since the green revolution began, area under crops increased at a rate of 0.38%

per annum as compared to 3% per annum increase in agricultural production. The rest of increase in production came from improvement in yields. Net area sown increased from 119 million hectares in 1950-57 to 140 million hectares in 1970-71 and has, since then, been fluctuating between 137 million hectares and 143 million hectares. Agricultural growth targeted in the Ninth Plan is 3.8% per annum. It would be a reasonable assumption to make that sustained agricultural growth around 4% per annum would be critical to the future growth of Indian economy. Thus, in the years to come, Indian agriculture would be using up its potential for intensive cultivation. The progress in this direction achieved so far has been by bringing more area under irrigation. Gross Irrigated Area increased from 23 million hectares in 1950-51 to 38 million hectares in 1970-71. By 1994-95, gross irrigated area had gone up to 71 million hectares. Thus, in the green revolution phase, irrigation increased at the rate of 1.4 million hectares per annum as compared to 0.7 million hectares in the preceding decades, 1950-51 to 1970-71. It would be only prudent to visualise that Indian agriculture would be getting close to the limits to growth imposed by its water resources in the coming decades. It could happen that the water constraint becomes operative even as India's population continues to grow though at a diminishing rate. Even the optimistic estimates made by demographers put India's eventual population at a staggering 1500 millions. Apart from the looming threat of reaching the physical limits of land and water resources, Indian agriculture also faces the challenging task of establishing effective arrangements for conservation of resources and protection to environment. The specific objectives suggested by us in this area are:

i) Building up a comprehensive, reliable and periodically updatable information system for land and water resources.

ii) Numerous programmes have been implemented for soil and water conservation without enduring results. These programmes seem to be particularly difficult to implement when the development strategy relies on top-down approach. Conceptually sound principles like development of watersheds in an integrated manner which have fared poorly so far might do better when PRIs take over the grass root level development tasks.

iii. Infrastructures created in the field need to be handled with care and maintained in good condition. It is necessary to encourage formation of informal groups of beneficiaries which could be in a position to do these tasks efficiently and in a cost-effective manner.

iv. Populist policies in relation to land and water are believed to have resulted in serious distortions in the form of restrictions on markets, low administered prices and regressive subsidies. This is an area where the conflict between meeting short term political pressures and long term goals need to be resolved.

(c) Promotion of Human Development

As agriculture becomes self-regulating and the arrangements for ownership and use of land and water conform to the desired norms, conditions will become favourable for the poorer sections in agriculture – forming the hard core poor – to gain opportunities for upward mobility. Ultimately, the development of these sections could be promoted only by creating such opportunities and enabling the poor to actively seek them and benefit from the gains these opportunities provide. The present anti-poverty programmes give only a modest measure of relief to the poor without touching the system which has reduced them to poverty and frustrates their aspirations and efforts to move upwards. While policy makers and researchers spend considerable time and energy to monitor the changes in the proportion of population falling below the poverty line, they do not seem to pay equal attention to the rapid marginalisation which has occurred in recent years of the population depending on agriculture and the widening gap between the per capita income in agriculture and that in other sectors. There are clear indications that the sectors which are growing faster than agriculture do little to relieve the pressure of population on agriculture. The reasons for the low absorption of labour outside agriculture need to be sought in the development strategy influencing the overall growth of the economy and its pattern and composition. This is beyond the scope of this paper but there is substantial potential for expansion of employment in rural areas through diversification of agriculture and the resulting rise in rural incomes and improvements in rural lifestyles. The specific objectives which would be of help in exploiting this potential are the following:

i) Diversification of agriculture creates wide-ranging opportunities for value addition, supplementary activities and additional employment. As the system becomes more self-regulating, more would the endogenous processes stimulate the rural economy by activating the potential for new activities and additional employment. The government would have to play an enabling role to assist the poor in agriculture to participate in the new activities.

ii) Rising rural incomes would expand the demand for goods and services. In addition to rise in income, the rural areas are also getting influenced profoundly by urban lifestyles and by growing rural – urban linkages through markets, migration, commuting and extending urban frontiers. This scenario would have to be kept in mind while choosing the activities for extending initial support and help.

iii) This emerging context would be favourable for acquisition of training and skills by the rural people, particularly the rural poor, to take up new occupations. It may also be expected that in response to rising demand for new goods and services, the supply of facilities for training and for acquisition of skills would expand. The government would have to be watchful to ensure that the facilities match the requirements and remain within the reach of the poor.

The next three sections – sections 1.3 to 1.5 deal with identification of priority tasks in the light of the objectives mentioned above.

1.3 Towards a Self-Regulating System

Independent India inherited an agricultural system not oriented towards growth and development. During the pre-independence decades, rural communities have had a prolonged exposure to monetisation, commercialisation and penetration by markets. But these processes served the interests of the colonial power and of the organised industries. They disrupted the traditional systems which enabled the villages to survive through succession of adversities over the historical past as relatively cohesive communities. With the disruption of the traditional system, the villages had to struggle on their own to adjust to the changing wider world around them. They could neither go back to their erstwhile relative isolation nor quickly linkup with the modernising mainstream society. When Independence came, the villages were in a state of disorientation lacking the pre-requisites - organisation, institutions and native leadership – to participate in the new era of planned development. Ironically, the sections in society which led the freedom movement and which became the new rulers did not have deep enough roots in the village society and were fascinated by development priorities far removed from the Gandhian commitment to villages and the poor.

This was the setting in which the government struggled in Independent India to modernise the agricultural system. We have already described the transformation brought about in agriculture in which the government played a leading and substantive role. Along with the achievements there were also biases resulting in gaps and shortfalls. Large projects which could be handled from the top received priority at the cost of small local level works. When the food crisis came, the green revolution was engineered by pouring in resources and investments in a relatively small but better-off part of Indian agriculture but the much larger poorer part of agriculture and the farming communities subsisting in that part received much less attention than what was needed to modernise the agricultural system as a whole. The Centre played a dominant role in policy making than the states; the PRI tier of government was yet to take shape. As a result, the advantages of top-down approach were reduced while its defects were made worse. It is important to keep in mind the biases mentioned above when considering the role of the government in promoting modernisation of agriculture in the years to come.

Since the focus in this section is on strengthening the self-regulating features of agriculture, let us do a quick stock-taking exercise which would be of help in suggesting the priority tasks to be attended to by the government. We draw on a few recent studies which have looked at the responsiveness of the agricultural system to technological change and to emerging economic opportunities offering better returns as also the resilience of the system in the face of critical weather conditions. There is a large literature on the rationality of farmer's decisions and behaviour. However, our interest here is in the dynamics of the agricultural system as a whole to move ahead and to respond to the challenges it faces.

Response to Technological Change

Reviewing the period of 1980s and beyond, Sawant and Achutan (1995) give the following assessment.

- There has been an upsurge in the aggregate production and productivity in Indian agriculture during the 1980s which cannot be attributed merely to favourable weather. The fact that the contribution of yield improvement has been far more important than that of expansion in area indicates that the process of growth has been technologically more dynamic (as compared to the earlier green revolution years).
- Unlike in the past, yield growth has been more impressive for non-foodgrains than foodgrains and, among the foodgrains, for kharif foodgrains vis-a-vis rabi foodgrains. Acceleration in yield growth occurred in case of rice, maize, other pulses,

rapeseed, sesame, soyabean, rubber, cotton. For many other crops, yield continued to expand at the pre - 1981 rates. The indication, on the whole, is that of a much wider diffusion of technology across crops than in the past.

- Foodgrains output growth picked up in many less developed areas from the central and eastern regions where growth has been sluggish in the early phase of the green revolution. With fairly rapid expansion in productivity of non-foodgrains, growth in agricultural incomes too accelerated in majority of the states in the 1980s. In sum, agricultural growth has become more broad based in recent years.

What explains the performance of agriculture during the 1980s? Sawant and Achutan offer the guess "Many factors associated with the wider adoption of new technology must have contributed".

Optimisation of Resource Use

Looking again at the post-1980 period, S.K. Ray (1998) finds

> "Agricultural growth became more widespread from the early 1980's. Growth rate exceeded 3 per cent in all the regions, ... crop diversification and choice of appropriate technology made by the states in the 1980s reduced significantly the interstate disparities in agricultural growth .... the inter state disparity in overall crop yield levels declined sharply... It appears resource endowments of the regions are reshaping the locational pattern of production ... areas better endowed with assured water supply are progressively moving towards production of rice, wheat and other high-value non-foodgrain crops. Coarse cereals, pulses, oilseeds and some other non-foodgrain crops - which can withstand short dry spells, require less water for production and are amenable for cultivation under drip and sprinkler techniques of irrigation – are increasingly moving towards water scarce areas. The processes of change in locational pattern of production, initiated from the early 1980s, has contributed in making more efficient use of natural resources ... seasonal changes in the pattern of production have improved productivity coefficients of modern technological inputs. In the post - 1985 period, the impact of these mutually reinforcing changes has given a new look to Indian agriculture. It has induced a dynamic process of change on a higher and stabler growth path".

Resilience in the Face of Critical Situations

S.K. Ray's findings on the vulnerability of agriculture to weather conditions give a reassuring picture.

"Another heartening feature of the recent developments in Indian agriculture is that it has become progressively resilient to vagaries of weather. For most of the crops and crop aggregates, sensitivity of output to fluctuations in rainfall has declined. This positive development is all the more impressive as, contrary to the favourable impression given by the meteorologists, our computed crop specific rainfall indices indicate that Indian agriculture did not enjoy a prolonged run of exceptionally favourable weather. In seven out of the ten years ending in 1994-95, rainfall index for all crops production was below normal, four of which were low enough to cause a crisis situation in agriculture. And, yet, unlike earlier years, agricultural output did not record sharp declines".

Recent periods of severe drought provide convincing evidence of the ability of Indian agriculture to withstand the stress created by such critical situations which used to cause widespread devastation in the past (see table 12.1).

TABLE – 12.1

Indices of Area, Production and Yield - All Crops (Base: Triennium Ending 1981-82 = 100)

Year	Area	Production	Yield
1964-65	91.7	76.4	88.3
1965-66*	90.7	63.7	73.2
1966-67*	90.6	63.0	73.6
1967-68	94.6	77.1	86.8
1971-72	95.8	85.2	91.6
1972-73*	92.5	78.2	86.0
1973-74	98.2	86.5	91.1
1986-87	100.3	115.2	112.4
1987-88*	96.0	115.3	114.4
1988-89	103.4	140.0	130.5

Source : Agricultural Statistics at a Glance, Government of India, New Delhi, 1998.

Note : Drought years are indicated by star. Other years in the table may be expected to be free of the effect of drought.

Two points need to be noted in table 1. All the three variables- area, production and yield which bear the brunt of the impact of drought show increase over the three drought episodes. It would be reasonable to interpret this increase as reflecting the improved capabilities of Indian agriculture to counter droughts. Second, in the 1987-88 drought, while there was some decrease in the cropped area, production and yield show no impact of drought at all as compared to the preceding year. As regards the succeeding year, it seems to have been a year of bumper production. However, it must be borne in mind that drought may still have large impact on particular crops and regions. India's war against droughts has to continue though the country would be in a far more comfortable position than before in tiding over the problems caused by droughts.

In view of the responses of the agricultural system noted above, it would be reasonable to conclude that the system has by now (late 1990s) made good progress towards becoming a self-regulating system in the sense of acquiring endogenous capabilities to move along a steady growth path, to gain in efficiency by adjusting to changing conditions and to manage crises like droughts by minimising their adverse effects. The government played an important role in the evolution of the agricultural system in the post-Independence decades. However, the interesting point about the 1980s is that there was a relative lull in the activities of the government. A recent study of capital formation in agriculture shows that in contrast to the continued decline in public sector real capital formation in agriculture during the 1980s, "private sector capital formation continued to rise throughout the decade .... more than compensating the fall in the public sector capital formation" (Mishra and Chand, 1995). The study also showed that "the marginal efficiency of capital increased from 0.15 to 0.28 and further to 0.41 during the time when public capital formation declined". The authors attribute the growth in the private capital formation to the activities of "politically conscious, interest seeking, organised groups of farmers". Thus, the performance of the agricultural system during the 1980s provides a basis for expecting the system to move forward with its own dynamics in the coming years.

Looking ahead to the future evolution of the agricultural system, the role of the government would have to change from direct interventions to helping the system to gather further strength and thrust. The philosophy of liberalisation and globalisation requires that the agricultural system should operate in an environment of free domestic and world markets. The government could play a dual role in the emerging situation: (i) enabling the agricultural system to adjust to the new environment and to benefit from the advantages it confers, and (ii) to protect the agricultural system and the country when the markets become disorderly, get manipulated by a few dominant operators or other governments encroach on our markets and bars our entry to their markets.

The role that the government can play to help the agricultural system operate effectively in the market environment is by building up a planning system appropriate to the changing situation. The new system would have to be indicative in its approach providing a medium-to-long term perspective on the objectives like growth, diversification, new technologies and investment requirements. Indicative planning means presentation of a road map - and not a set of diktats to be obeyed - for guiding decision-making by the different operators in the agricultural system including the farmers. When these operators have only market signals to rely on, they have in effect to grope without any clear idea about where they are headed. In a sense, market signals at best offer clue to what the next few steps could be. Knowledge of indicative plan would make the task of responding to market signals more amenable to systematic decision-making by the operators in the agricultural system. Secondly, the new planning system has to be multi-level in structure so that the planning objectives at the national level get translated into desirable targets at the regional and micro levels and, in turn, decisions and perceptions at these levels flow up as feed back to the apex level. Thirdly, the new system has to be participatory in operation with farmers having a place in the process of formulation and implementation of development programmes.

Some progress has been made so far in assembling the basic building blocks for constructing a planning system with features described above. The building block at the bottom is the PRI institutions which have now a constitutional status and a mandate for undertaking a wide range of development functions including those relating to agriculture. Our concern here is not with the PRI as a whole but only with their responsibility to organise decentralised planning at the district and lower levels. The second building block is the Agro-climatic Regional Planning exercise undertaken by the Planning Commission since 1988 to construct a national level planning perspective for agriculture based on detailed regional studies to assess resource endowments, strategies for balanced development of the region, comparative advantages, choice of priority activities, infrastructure needs and investments. The regional level studies were done by teams of experts from agricultural universities and research institutions. The exercise began with delineation of 15 regions which were in the second step disaggregated into 73 sub regions. The team of experts, representative from the Planning Commission, representatives of the state governments and academics held periodic meetings to discuss the regional and sub-regional studies, improvements needed in the data bases, investment implications and phasing of programmes over time.

The ACRP documentation has now reached a point where operationalisation of the ACRP approach to agriculture-cum-regional planning could commence. It is only through operationalisation that the regional and sub-regional studies and the development design recommended by them could be field-tested and continually updated through feed back from the bottom and evaluations at the regional and national level. Two moves are in progress to operationalise ACRP approach. First, there has been a broad agreement among the states at the time of formulation of the Ninth Five Year Plan that the state plan and the district break downs would incorporate the ACRP strategies and preferred activities and make the necessary provisions for their implementation. Second, it was also the intention that the district planning committee and other bodies provided for in the PRI legislation would be brought into being to change over from sectoral programmes planned and implemented by the line departments headquartered in the state capital to area planning involving integration of sectoral plans.

The quotation below from a recent ACRP document (Guha, 1997) would give a flavour of the work done by the Zonal Planning Team.

"Zonal profiles include detailed descriptions (both quantitative and qualitative) of land and water resources, population, farming systems, support systems to agriculture and allied sectors. These were supplemented with historical information on development patterns, technological and socio-economic issues relevant to integrated development. These profiles were interfaced with perceived regional needs and priorities to work out broad strategies. The ZPTs then worked out specific action plans and programme outlines respective to the revised strategies giving their financial and organisational implications along with the physical targets. ... The zonal exercise was later translated into state-sub-regional agro-climatic plans. In the ACRP state-sub-regional plan, while the basic profiles and strategies were flowing directly out of the zonal exercise, the programmes were refined by state level priorities.... Sample of the output of Zonal Planning Teams is given in the Exhibit below which forms the basis of various activities at different levels".

Exhibit: Issues and Strategies in Different Zones under ACRP

No.	ZONE	Issues	Strategies
1	Western Himalayan	Steep Slopes, Soil Low Ground Water	Rational Land Use, Soils & Water Conservation
2	Eastern Himalayan	High runoff, Chaur lands, Shifting Cultivation	Soil and Water Conservation, Settled farming
3	Lower Gangetic Plains	Floods and Poor Drainage	Reduced Water Conservation in Low Land through Embankments, Gully Controls & Runoff Diversions
4	Middle Gangetic Plains	Water logging and Salinity	Water Resource Management, Conjunctive use of Canal and Ground Water, Soil Amendments
5	Upper Gangetic Plains	Saline-alkaline lands, Water logging in Canal Irrigated areas & Low Cropping Intensity	Land Reclamation through Soil Amendments, Water Scheduling, Introduction of Intensive Cropping Patterns
6	Transgangetic Plains	Saline Land and Saline Ground Water deteriorating Soil Health	Soil and Water Managements, Restriction of heavy duty crops
7	Eastern Plateau & Hills	Undulating Topography, Poor Ground Water Development, Degraded Tanks	Soil and Water Conservation, Ground Water Development and Renovation of Tanks
8	Central Plateau & Hills	Soil Erosion, Low Irrigation Development	Soil and Water Conservation, Development of irrigation and Waste Land Development
9	Western Plateau & Hills	Shallow Soils, Low Irrigation potential and Drought prone areas	Conservation of Rain water, Development of irrigation Encouraging Dryland Horticulture
10	Southern Plateau & Hills	Waste Land, Saline Soils, Low Irrigation, Reduced Tank Potential	Waste Land Development, Encouraging Horticulture, Soil Correction, Restoration of Tanks
11	East Coast Plains & Hills	Soil Salinity, Low Ground Water, Poor Drainage	Treatment of Soils, Rescheduling Canal water, Irrigation development,

Contd...

...Contd...

			Encouraging Brackish Water Fish development
12	West Coast Plains & Hills	High runoff & erosion, Large amount of waste lands, Low Ground Water development	Soil and Water Conservation, Horticulture Development, Ground Water Development
13	Gujarat Plains & Hills	Over Exploitation of Ground Water, Saline Soils, Drought prone areas	Rationalisation of Ground water, Soil Correction, Soil and Water Conservation
14	Western Dry Region	Irregular Rainfall, Shifting Sand Dunes	Rain Water Conservation, Stabilisation of Sand Dunes, Development of Agro-forestry
15	Islands	Undulating topography, High runoff, Low NSA	Soil and Water Conservation, Rain Water Harvesting

When the ACRP approach focussed on the spatial aspects of resources and their potentialities is combined with institutionalisation of the decentralised-cum-participatory planning at the district and lower levels, the agricultural system would not only gain in capacity for self-regulation but it would also have a much stronger thrust on development of rural areas and people which has lagged so far behind the improvement in the physical parameters of agriculture. Smaller and inaccessible villages which have been neglected so far would get an opportunity to enter the mainstream society owing to improvements in infrastructures, accessibility and availability of services. Broad based rural growth and diversification of rural economic activities resulting from area planning would expand the economic space available to the rural poor. The programmes to improve the human development status of the poor would become more effective in terms of both costs and benefits. Updated information on weather and crop conditions, market prices and prospects and extension messages and advice would get communicated more quickly and widely. It would also be reasonable to assume that the handing over of the development tasks to the PRIs – and through them to the local people – would keep in check populist programmes, leakages and wastages characteristic of the present system and bring out the potential among the people for self-reliance, local initiative and leadership.

Unfortunately, ACRP is still lingering at the workshop-cum-seminar stage without any substantial progress towards operationalisation. The essence of the ACRP approach is a basic change in the mode of planning at the state level from the sector-based approach to the region-based approach. In the former, the line departments headquartered at the state capital operate in relative isolation from each other with their departmental perspectives and priorities. Region-based approach, on the other hand, needs perspectives and priorities focussed on areas and their resources. Centralised planning proceeding from the top downwards finds a natural ally in sector-based approach where orders originate at the top and are obeyed at the lower levels. On the other hand, the region-based approach begins at the bottom with an integrated look at an area and the plans get reconciled and readjusted as they move up to state and central levels. Since the planning at the PRI level is still at the experimental stage in a few selected districts, the full operationalisation of ACRP may need considerable time. There is the further barrier that the politicians and the administrators who have worked with the sector-based approach for long years would have to be reoriented for the region-based approach. The latest available ACRP document (ACRPU, March 1999) mentions that "ACRP has been recognised and accepted as the logical planning paradigm at the state, the substate levels. States like Assam, West Bengal, Orissa, Tamil Nadu and Karnataka have internalised ACRP into their planning process. Other states are also showing greater acceptance of the recommendations of ZPTs.... The Planning Commission has made a major contribution in the acceptance of the ACRP approach through prescription and persuasion. This has to continue along with efforts for "acceptance without imposition" at different layers of "formal and informal systems". Simultaneously, preparation of district plan to test out ACRP approach has been undertaken during the VIII Plan as an "innovative experiment by the Planning Commission to combine resource based planning with decentralised planning" (Guha, 1997). A recent study based on the proceedings of a workshop held in Karnataka to discuss the work done in two selected districts in the state reports. "The broad consensus of the workshop was that the two district plans presented (at the workshop) provided ample evidence of the fact that planning from below is a possibility and needs to be pursued more rigorously. The workshop has provided certain guidelines for strengthening the institutionalisation process of the ACRP approach at the decentralised planning level" (Hanumappa, 1997). We identify the following two priority tasks relating to the ACRP approach:

- The constitution of the District Planning Committees (DPC) should be completed as soon as possible and the DPCs should commence the work allotted to them. Even in a state like Karnataka which has been keen to activate and support PRIs, DPCs have not been constituted so far.
- Once the DPCs become active, there will be pressure at the state level to make the necessary changes in the planning system. Meanwhile, internalisation of ACRP into state plans may be completed in all the remaining states.

Even the best of self-regulating agricultural systems could face crises beyond their capacity to manage. War and widespread famines are good illustrations but relatively rare occurrences. Events like sudden market turbulence or dumping of goods from abroad could be more frequent and seriously disruptive. Keeping an eye on the market would need a regularly operating institutional arrangement. Economic invasions from abroad would need continuing vigilance and readiness to respond. Let us first discuss the government role in containing market turbulence. Agricultural markets are notoriously unstable owing to the nature of production conditions, dispersal of agricultural activities over a wide area and long chain of inter linked markets from the producer to consumer/end user. The role of the government to help organised markets develop in an orderly manner is part of the promotion of self-regulating agricultural system already discussed above. Improvements in accessibility to market, improvements in market infrastructure, modernisation of facilities for communication and information flow, rules to ensure free, open and fair market transactions would be some of the important steps to be taken. However, there would still be occasions requiring direct interventions by the government. We have now considerable experience in the strength and weaknesses of the market operations undertaken by the government. Commission for Agricultural Costs and Prices, now over three decades old, regularly monitors the production and marketing of over 20 crops and recommends to the government minimum support prices designed to protect the interests of the producers. Nodal agencies like Food Corporation of India carry out market operations to ensure that the market prices do not fall below the minimum support prices. There are also cases like groundnut and cotton where market operations have been more commercial in nature and have been relatively more effective in getting better returns to producers. The minimum support price operations for rice and wheat are linked with the important issue of food security and public distribution system. The experiences with the government interventions in this area are summarised below.

- CACP recommendations and the resulting operations have benefited primarily rice and wheat owing to their link up with public distribution system. Rice and wheat are supposed to be crops in which India has comparative advantage and, hence, should be India's preferred exports. In the emerging context, PDS operated by PRIs and based on a wider choice of foodgrains including coarse cereals could be a better alternative than the current PDS to ensure food security to the poor, particularly rural poor.
- The practice of announcing minimum support prices has led to politicisation of the price issue and pressures to raise MSP to unrealistic levels. Often MSPs are announced long after the beginning of the sowing season. In the case of poor man's crops like coarse cereals, MSPs are announced without any serious intention to give price support when prices decline below MSP level. This is also true of prices prevailing in backward areas like Eastern Uttar Pradesh. Further, as specifications with respect to quality of the crop purchased by the government agency are often relaxed, farmer become indifferent towards the imperative need to ensure that the output of the market meets the quality norms. Quality consciousness is important for the development of orderly and self-regulating markets.
- Announcing minimum support prices may be a desirable practice from the point of view of farmers but it is an ineffective and costly way of intervening in the market. It weakens the capacity of the government agency to compete with the traders. When prices decline, traders would sell produce to government agency. On the other hand, when prices rise and government agency enters the market as seller to keep the prices in check, traders would purchase and sell later at a higher price. Compared to MSP operations, the market intervention operations of NDDB and Cotton Corporation of India have been more effective.

Looking ahead, the experience gained by CACP and by the nodal agencies like FCI and NAFED is a valuable asset for the government in organising market intervention operations. A clear distinction needs to be made between the objective of helping farmers when nature or market turns against them and the objective of evening out market fluctuations. Stabilising farmers income needs measures like diversification of activities on farm, cooperativisation of storage, processing and marketing where cooperatives would compete with private agencies and crop insurance. It would be futile - as the price policy has shown so far - to expect price support measures undertaken by the government to achieve an objective which needs a combination of a wide range of programmes. The second objective, on the other hand, would be relatively easy to achieve if market intervention operations are undertaken on a commercial basis and not as a bureaucratic response to political pressures. Market intervention operations on a commercial basis would have to be organised with much care and caution. The operations should at least be no-profit-no-loss in financial results if not profit-making. The operations should be undertaken by an autonomous body having sufficient market expertise and, also, freedom to organise its activities as market operators without interference from politicians and bureaucrats. This may seem an extremely difficult arrangement to make. It is not so. We have a number of nodal agencies who have the necessary expertise but not the autonomy for using the expertise. CACP has excellent credentials as a watch dog though much of its energy is now spent in preparing reports which remain largely neglected excepting for their ritualistic use by the government in fixing minimum support prices. If an autonomous organisation is formed bringing together the nodal agencies with CACP acting as a think tank and coordinator, we would be making a confident beginning in organising market intervention operations on a sound basis. This gives us the third priority task in our policy agenda.

- Change over from the MSP operations to market intervention operations undertaken by an autonomous organisation having the necessary market expertise and freedom to operate on commercial principles without political/administrative interference.

We now come to the role of the government in the context of opening up of Indian agriculture to global markets. The prevailing mood in the policy making circles seems to be coloured by "export-optimism". The pendulum might have moved to the other extreme from the earlier "Export-pessimism" and the new mood may be resting on as fragile assumptions as the earlier mood. If exports perform well and globalisation acts as a tonic on Indian agriculture, the role of the government would remain limited to the three priority tasks already identified above. This would be a realistic scenario to look forward to if the world markets are robustly competitive, governments of developed countries play by the rules of the game and international borders facilitate trade and not bar it. However, globalisation has another and not so pretty face where international trade becomes economic warfare between governments rather than gentlemanly game played in well-behaved markets. Engaging in economic warfare with other governments is a challenging task not amenable to easy and readymade solutions. The government would have to remain vigilant, make maximum use of opportunities to negotiate workable arrangements in WTO or in other fora and, if nothing else helps, take appropriate action to counter and pre-empt adverse moves by other governments. Given below are a few glimpses of globalisation as intensification of the economic warfare between the governments.

"We question the basic argument that (international) prices will rise due to reduction in subsidies by the developed world... Implementation of the AOA agreement is carried out in such a fashion that developed countries do not have to reduce their subsidies to any substantial degree.... (with only) a few (large) multinational firms and trading agencies involved in export operations of agricultural commodities, the export market structure is not perfectly competitive... (they) have a status of oligopsonist-cum-oligopolist in the export markets... in imperfectly competitive markets, it is unlikely that price rises will be passed on to the Indian farmer ... trade opportunities are asymmetric because lower international price leads to imports but higher international price does not lead to export due to quality problems. Such weaknesses may also encourage other countries/trade blocks to propose quality criteria, which are difficult to meet by developing countries" (Indian Institute of Management, 1999).

"Indian farm exporters... face rapidly increasing technical barriers to trade or TBT in their traditional export markets like the European Union. TBTs are amongst the most common non-tariff barriers that several countries use to keep imports out. Of late, TBTs are increasingly employed in farm products where instruments like agricultural practices and ecological labelling are being used to control the import of food products. The trend is especially visible in the European Union... The developing countries have long complained that they have had no role at all in setting of international standards which are almost entirely being decided by the developed world and their corporate giants ... most developing countries lack the resources and the technical know-how to participate in the process... The failure of the Seattle Conference means that the disputes between the developed and the developing world cannot be resolved in the near future" (European technical barriers to trade scare Indian farm exporters, Ranvir Nayar, Rediff on the Net, January 6, 2000).

"Free trade did not have a good year in 1999. There was conflict between rich and poor countries over trade measures... conflict also grew during the year between the world's two largest trading blocs, the United States and Europe – replacing the traditional rivalry between the US and Japan. The EU and the US disagreed on whether there should be further liberalisation of agriculture, with a goal of ending all subsidies, which could threaten the EU's common agricultural policy... More serious were the conflicts over the health related issues. The EU refused to import US beef treated with growth hormones... despite a ruling against them in the World Trade Organisation. And there is another dispute looming over the import of genetically modified food, widely produced in the US but widely feared in Europe. Following the collapse of the trade talks, the EU has insisted that GM foods should not be treated as a trade matter but ... as an environmental hazard in the UN's eco-safety protocol negotiations. The growing protectionist pressures in the world were most keenly felt in the United States ... the failure of the world trade talks did nothing to help the credibility of the World Trade Organisation ... the idea that trade rules have the force of law is being challenged within countries who are concerned that the WTO can override their own laws on issues like competition and environmental protection (Body Blow for Free Trade, BBC Business Page, December 25, 1999).

The following priority tasks are identified for the government to help Indian agriculture adjust to globalisation.

- Promotion of exports would need improvements in infrastructure, modernisation of facilities, rationalisation of rules and procedures and a stable export policy rather than the stop-go type familiar in cases like cotton. We expect that these promotional measures would get implemented in the course of adoption of ACRP approach to stimulate agricultural growth.
- As regards conflicts and clashes of interest with other governments given rise to by arrangements like WTO, the government would have to remain vigilant, make maximum use of opportunities to negotiate for mutually beneficial terms and conditions for trade and take appropriate action to counter or pre-empt hostile moves by other governments or large market operators like multinationals.

1.4 Overcoming Limits to Growth

From the supply side, growth of agriculture depends on natural endowments (land and water), reproducible inputs, capital and technological change. A self-regulating agricultural system would be able to look after the reproducible elements and generation of new technologies through research and innovations. The experience over the post-Independence decades with fertiliser growth, mechanisation and new crop varieties developed by our laboratories and research stations reflect well the capabilities of the agricultural system. Owing to policy deficiencies, the system may not have made the optimum use of these capabilities but it would be reasonable to assume that agricultural growth would normally stimulate expansion and improvements in these capabilities and, consequently, would not encounter any serious barrier along this dimension. But this is not true of natural endowments like land, water and environment. While new technologies help natural endowment to produce more and to carry the burden of a growing population, a point must come eventually beyond which the natural endowment would get exhausted and begin to deteriorate. In the case of India, serious deterioration is already evident in natural endowment much before this limiting point owing to absence of policies or wrong policies. A self-regulating agricultural system may find it extremely difficult to correct the cumulative errors of the past nor would it be able to deal with the crisis if population growth gets close to the carrying capacity of India's natural endowments. Hence, the government has to bear the responsibility for ensuring that the natural endowment remains in a healthy state and that population stabilises well before reaching the carrying capacity of these non-reproducible resources. The discussion in this paper is limited to land and water the principal critical items of natural endowments.

It is best to begin by noting that the prospects are pretty grim not so much because of limited availability of land and water as due to the shocking indifference shown by the policymaker in conserving and making judicious use of the natural resources. Professor Y.K.Alagh who has had a long association with agricultural policies as an analyst and policymaker has recently observed:

"Land scarcity will become an acute feature of the Indian agricultural and rural economy and judicious use of land and water will be central to the growth process; India (is) facing for the first time population densities of the East Asian type... It is reasonable to assume that the geographical area of the country or the extensive land frontier for exploitation has reached its limits. This is an important issue the implications of which are not being realised with the urgency they deserve... Organisations, communities, households and individuals will have to grasp this fact and live with it" (Alagh, 1999).

This is a daunting challenge but Alagh finds that policymaking for agriculture does not reflect the sense of urgency needed in responding to the challenge:

"East Asian societies have a concern for land scarcity which has come through decades. This is not happening in India. We are not understanding that the entire expansion of growth has to now come from productivity or increase in cropping intensity. Indian agriculture is facing a lot of problems and it needs priorities of a kind which have not been given" (Alagh, 1997).

Intensification of land use depends critically on availability of water. This is particularly true in India as intensification of land use is being achieved by changing over to "green revolution technology" which needs abundance of water and chemical inputs. The prospects for water appear to be even more scary than that for land. Lester Brown, who is a keen and careful observer of agricultural and food security situation in developing countries, has this assessment about the prospects for water in India.

"Unless India quickly devises an effective strategy to deal with fast spreading water scarcity, it may soon face a decline in life expectancy as reduced irrigation water supplies will badly hit food production... India is one of the main countries where population is outrunning water supply... the projected growth of world population from 6 billion at present to nearly 9 billion by 2050 will exacerbate nearly all environmental problems" (Hindustan Times, January 15, 2000 Note on Worldwatch Institute Annual Report for 2000).

A tell-tale clue to the attitude of the policymaker towards the land and water situation is the poor data base for these critical inputs for growth. It was reported in newspapers sometime back that the estimates made on the basis of remote sensing techniques show a much larger area under cultivation than the area shown by the official land statistics. It is a common experience of rural investigators that land brought under cultivation through encroachment does not figure in land records as "cultivated land" and this could explain the discrepancy revealed by the remote sensing techniques. More important, the land records miss the quality aspect. Areas categorised as "forests", "pastures" or "under tree crops" include areas which are in reality degraded lands not fit for any use. The rural investigators would also be familiar with the divergence between the distribution of ownership and operational holdings as shown by the records and the actual ground level situation. Land reforms, instead of achieving their objective, have had the opposite result of making it extremely difficult to get reliable data on land under tenancy and land held in excess of the level fixed as ceiling on ownership of land. It is indeed strange that the policymaker in a country with chronic land hunger should remain so indifferent to the need for reliable statistics on the present status and future potentialities of its land resources and the extent to which the different socio-economic groups have access to land.

A word about the data situation with respect to irrigation. The post-Independence decades have witnessed an increase in the area under irrigation from 23 million hectares to about 71 million hectares now. However, these are the figures on the land use statistics compiled by the Ministry of Agriculture. According to the Ministry of Water Resources, out of the irrigation potential of 90 million hectares created so far, 80 million hectares have been utilised. Even the experts seem unable to reconcile the gap of 9 million hectares in the two different figures of utilisation of irrigation or explain the gap between the potential created and the extent of its utilisation. Even more strange are the figures being mentioned about the ultimate irrigation potential of the country. Though the figure taken by most of us is 113 million hectares, according to a study in progress in Institute of Economic Growth, the figure has apparently been revised upward recently to 140 million hectares. The study also mentions a still higher figure of 175 million hectares which is believed to include the potential that can be created by inter-basin transfer of water! However, not much is heard about the time frame and investment plans to realise the ultimate irrigation potential.

It may seem baffling that the policymaker does not have with him even minimal basic data on the inputs critical for sustained long term growth in agriculture. Among the developing countries, India has an enviable reputation for the technical capabilities to build up data bases and information systems. Population census and national sample surveys are good examples of these capabilities. There could be two reasons for the sad state of data on land and water resources. First, centralised planning needs aggregate data and has little occasion to make use of detailed ground level data by districts and villages. The latter tend to get neglected e.g. data on crop yields are not available by sub-district level spatial units like blocks and villages. Second, it could also be that the state of data on land and water resources reflects the lack of interest in and concern about agriculture in the policymaker's long term perspective on the Indian economy.

The government would have to play a leading role in improving the data bases and information systems to enable agriculture to cope with the requirements of modernisation. When PRIs become active at the district and lower levels, they would need updated and reliable data on numerous aspects including land and water resources. Since the PRIs, would be collecting these data for their own use, one may expect substantial improvement in the quality, accuracy and timeliness of the data. By the same argument, improvements may also be expected in the data compiled at regional, state and central levels. The multileyel system would also be in a position to make more frequent, extensive and probing use of remote sensing and similar advanced technologies for collection of data and assessment of resources.

If the data base on land is in a poor state, it is only to be expected that the policies for conservation and optimum use of land resources would be handicapped. We present below a few indicators (see table 12.2).

TABLE – 12.2

Land Use Pattern

(Mill.Hectares)

	Item	1950-51	1970-71	1990-91
1.	Total Reported Area	284	304	305
2.	Area Under Forests	40	64	68
3.	Barren and Uncultivable	38	28	21
4.	Under Non-Agricultural Use	9	16	20
5.	Pastures	7	13	12
6.	Under Tree Crops and Groves	20	4	4
7.	Culturable Waste	23	18	15
8.	Other Fallows	17	9	10
9.	Current Fallows	11	11	14
10.	Net Sown Area	119	141	142
11.	Gross Cropped Area	132	166	185

The major trends in land use over the years 1950-51 to 1990-91 have been the following:

- Net sown area increased from 119 million hectares in 1950-51 to 141 million hectares in 1970-71 which, apparently, is the limit of the extensive margin of land.
- Over the period 1950-51 to 1990-91 gross cropped area increased from 132 million hectares to 185 million hectares.

While between 1950-51 and 1970-71, the increase was 34 million hectares, between 1970-71 and 1990-91 – with net area sown remaining at 140 million hectares – gross cropped area increased by only 19 million hectares i.e., a little over half of the increment between 1950-51 to 1970-71.

- Area under forests increased from 40 million hectares to 68 million hectares but most of the increase occurred between 1950-51 and 1970-71. The increase from 1970-71 to 1990-91 was only 4 million hectares. More important, as a recent study notes that "more than 40 per cent of total forest lands have poor tree cover and can roughly be described as degraded forest lands" (Chadha, 1996).
- Area under non-agricultural use expanded from 9 million hectares to 20 million hectares while there was a steep decline in barren and uncultivable land, apparently due mainly to shift to non-agricultural use.
- The categories of land of particular interest are pastures, area under tree crops, culturable waste and fallows. Area under tree crops seem to have practically disappeared while pastures registered good increase between 1950-51 and 1970-71 but there was a slight decline – instead of an increase – between 1970-71 and 1990-91. Culturable waste decreased from 23 million hectares to 15 million hectares but there is no sign of the area having been added to any productive category like pastures, area under tree crops or net area sown. Fallows went down from 28 million hectares from 1950-51 to 20 million hectares in 1970-71 but increased to 24 million hectares in 1990-91 of which nearly two-thirds were current fallows indicative of growing land exhaustion. In 1990-91 nearly 40 million hectares with some potential to contribute to production - almost a third as much as the net area sown – remained out of the production sphere in a country with chronic land hunger!

Policy analyses relating land use reveal a number of weaknesses:

- "much needs to be done to plug in policy deficiencies, implementation weaknesses and for raising the consciousness of the people at large. To put it bluntly, some hard thinking and some unconventional doing are needed.... The question of waste land development technologies has attracted only peripheral attention". (Chadha, 1996)

- Lamenting the absence of any decisive policy intervention, Nadkarni points out that soil conservation is not being adopted even where it is economically profitable for the farmer to do so (Nadkarni and Govindaru 1995). These lands are "Nobody's Child" – neglected by the government as well as farmers owing to absence of arrangement to ensure that the benefits of investments made by the farmer accrue to him.
- As regards forests, Pasha observes "Even after independence, the Government of India largely adopted the policies... of the British. But of late, the continued depletion and degradation of forest resources and the importance of forests to the rural communities forced the Indian policy makers to adopt National Forest Policy Resolution in 1988 which commits itself to the sound management and projection of forests as well as to protect and support the livelihood and farming systems of the local communities" (Pasha, 1999).

When programmes like soil conservation, wasteland reclamation and consolidation of holdings fail to achieve results, it is usual to blame the implementation agency and/or the intended beneficiary of the programme. It is important to realise that land use is influenced by a host of factors like comparative advantage in alternative uses, policy regime for agriculture and farmer's perceptions and attitudes. Hence, when considering improvements in land use, it is not enough to look only at deficiencies of the implementation agencies or lack of interest or motivation on the part of the intended beneficiary.

This point can be illustrated by taking a look at the two major situations in India accounting for a substantial part of the problems in land use viz., the green revolution areas and the semi arid drought prone regions. As regards the green revolution areas, consider the following findings from a study in Haryana on ground water over-exploitation and the consequential land degradation.

"fresh ground water areas witnessed comparatively high rate of ground water exploitation. The over exploitation of ground water in the State has largely been the consequence of more intensive cultivation of land, large scale shift in cropping pattern towards rice-wheat and installation of large number of private tube wells.... The consequences are (i) fall in water table forcing the farmers either to deepen the well or abandon it depending upon the accessibility of financial resources, (ii) adverse effects on equity issue and (iii) abandoning agriculture itself and becoming agricultural and non-agricultural labourers.... The adverse consequences of land degradation due to salinity and water-logging are decline in farm production and income, unemployment and migration, disparities and ecological imbalance..... for sustainable use of ground water based farming systems, we have to conserve the ground water resources and simultaneously explore ways and means for enhancing ground water recharge". (Sharma, et al., 1995).

It may seem from the description above that if only the excessive use of ground water is checked, the situation in the area would return to normalcy. This is not true. The situation is an outcome of an historical process which began in the late sixties in response to the critical food situation faced by the country. The policy maker, very rightly in the circumstances prevailing then, decided to overcome the crisis by an ambitious strategy to secure a breakthrough in the production of rice and wheat to increase the domestic supplies of foodgrains. The strategy relied on supporting the farmer up to the hilt-abundant supplies of water and electricity, subsidised inputs, remunerative prices for the produce, dependable availability of services like credit, research and extension, modernisation of rural infrastructures. In less than a decade the food grain supplies increased enabling the country to eliminate imports and to build up a public distribution system with a country wide spread. The seeds of the present problems in Haryana were sown when the strategy devised to deal with a crisis was not suitably modified when the crisis abated. The situation can now be dealt with only if thoroughgoing reforms are implemented to benefit from the export potential of rice and wheat and to price power, water, and credit to reflect their economic cost and to rationalise public distribution system and the related procurement, storage and distribution of foodgrains. If the reforms are implemented, the problems given rise to by overexploitation of groundwater would be eliminated at the roots. If the reforms are not implemented, the problems would persist irrespective of the attempts made to regulate water use and to treat degraded land.

The second major problem situation we describe is agriculture in the semi-arid drought-prone regions which account for over a half of Indian agriculture. These regions are deteriorating into hardcore poverty areas with low crop yields, stagnant technology, meagre investments and continuing degradation of land base owing to erosion, loss of tree cover and indifference towards conservation of scarce water resources. Governments show little interest in these areas, farmers remain too weak to counter the oppressive poverty and rural communities subsist on periphery cut off from many dimensions of modernisation. Technologies for overcoming degradation of land and loss of water resources are known. This is also true of technologies waiting in laboratories which could substantially raise crop yields. There are instances – regrettably few – of village communities achieving remarkable growth and modernisation through local leadership, self-help and participation by using the programmes and resources made available by the government (Rao and Hanumappa, 1999). NGOs have also some successful cases to their credit. Barring these exceptions, villages remain bypassed with a bewildering variety of schemes being implemented leaving behind nothing more than some dubious records and statistics.

The strategy recommended for improving agriculture in drought prone area is Watershed Development which takes a comprehensive and integrated view of land and water resources in watersheds which are the appropriate units to plan and implement programmes for upgrading and conserving these resources. National Watershed Development Project for Rainfed Agriculture (NWDPRA) taken up in the mid-eighties (GOI, 1985) appears to have been the first major step taken in India to operationalise watershed development strategy. Deshpande and Thimmaiah have recently reviewed the field assessments of the project (Deshpande and Thimmaiah, 1999). They find some impact on yield, employment and shifting towards high value crops. The impact has not been quantified. They note that "the consultation (with the people) during planning stage was totally absent. The plans were prepared without involving them". They do not sound confident about the long-term sustainability of the programme and its eventual takeover by the people belonging to the project area. Hanumappa's findings also are rather disturbing on this score (Hanumappa, 1999). He observes "experience shows that even those watersheds which were initially managed most efficiently have slowly degenerated due to lack of involvement of the participants. One of the reasons for this is the extra care taken by the implementing agencies (mainly government agencies which provided all the required technical and engineering help along with subsidies) and managing the projects from above. In the process participants became mere onlookers than stake holders... Even the efforts to form collective associations and operationalise them have met with poor response". Hanumappa also mentions that NWDRA is targeted to cover only 3 million hectares by the end of the Eighth Plan. It is important to note that even in this experimental phase there is no clear evidence of acceptability of the underlying strategy to the farmers.

Here, again, the influence of the larger agricultural system needs to be borne in mind when looking for reasons for the cumulative neglect of land and water resources in the drought-prone areas. The market environment marked by low and unstable prices add to the woes of farmers facing droughts and scarcities. The policy regime instead of taking a corrective measures makes the situation worse by neglecting infrastructure, investments and institutions. This is evident in the case of oilseeds which were the source of a remarkable breakthrough in agricultural production in the drought-prone areas during the 1980s. A World Bank report points out the "fragmented structure whose inefficiencies are borne by growers who receive lower than international prices at one end of the production chain and consumers who pay higher than international prices at the other" (World Bank, 1997). A recent study by Gulati and Kelley (1999) observes "that farmers are responsive to profits and prices suggests that improvement in crop yield, input and output markets and other infrastructure can bring about efficiencies in agriculture in the SAT (semi arid tropics), notwithstanding some degree of subsistence behaviour... There are several constraints at the micro-level that may not allow farmers to go for the most efficient crop even when price incentives are given. These constraints may range from limited irrigation to lack of marketing or processing facilities, or even lack of farmer's knowledge about the crop.... Government policy formulation would do well to focus on non-price factors ranging from seeds to irrigation for farmers and on dereservation of oilseed processing from small sector for the processors." According to Alagh policymaking should also focus on biotechnology to promote sustainable agricultural growth in future "biotechnology has emerged as one of the most innovative and powerful tools to increase the agricultural productivity on a sustainable basis... (it) can make important contributions to crop, livestock, forestry and fishery development. It holds promise for increasing the productivity, quality, efficient processing and utilisation of products and at the same time reduce reliance on agro-chemicals and other external inputs" (Alagh, 1999).

In the light of the discussion in this section, we identify the following priority tasks in relation to conservation and optimum use of our land and water resources.

i) Building up and maintaining an updated data base on the extent of land and water resources, their location, present status, potentialities, ownership, use, regulation and control. PRIs should be given the primary responsibility for collecting, recording and verifying data. Remote sensing and other advanced technologies should be used to explore the potentialities of the resources and to complement the collection of data at the ground level.

ii) Preparing a detailed perspective plan to extend irrigation as quickly as possible to make full use of the ultimate potential.

iii) Ensuring that the market, institutional and policy environment, are conducive to conservation-oriented and judicious use of land and water resources. Economic sanity should be restored to administered pricing, user charges and government operations like procurement, storage and distribution of foodgrains. Micro-level decision-makers like producers and consumers should get signals consistent with the social objective of conservation and economic use of valuable but scarce resources like land and water.

iv) It is hoped that, given the right environment, schemes for improving degraded lands in green revolution areas and the watershed development strategy in the drought-prone areas would be able to take rapid strides provided the problems of institutional arrangements, procedures and personnel are tackled in right earnest.

v) As we approach the limits of land and water resources, search for a technology appropriate to the emerging situation should be intensified. Experts suggest that biotechnology would be a promising field to explore. Attention must also be paid to technologies available in research stations but not reaching farms.

1.5 Promoting Human Development

The strategy for human development needs to be economy-wide in its scope. Generating productive employment for the growing labour force should be an objective pursued by all sectors. Similarly, eliminating extremes of inequality in the society would only be possible if peaks of wealth and accumulation wherever they occur in the society are taken note of for distributive policies. The approach in this respect has been quite hypocritical. Agricultural and rural sectors were expected to absorb the residual labour while leaving the other sectors free to adopt capital-intensive technologies with meagre labour absorption or permit entry only to the highly skilled. Again, inequality in distribution of land and the economic gap between the haves and have-nots within agriculture and rural area attract considerable policy attention but not the pomp and vulgar show of affluence in the urban enclaves of rich proud of their western lifestyles. Inevitably, agriculture became a "parking lot" of the poor and the marginalised. The purpose of this section is to argue that the marginalisation process in agriculture has now reached a critical stage. While agriculture has a substantial contribution to make to human development, it is important to take note of its growing and oppressive burden which needs to be shifted to other sectors.

We begin by taking note of selected major trends suggesting marginalisation of people in agriculture. Table 12.3 is of help in taking a comparative look at the growth in population and in agriculture in the decades since Independence. The population growth rate shown in Table 3 relates to the decade preceding the year against which it appears. The rate increased steadily from 1.25 per cent per annum in 1941-51 to 2.22 per cent per annum in 1971-81 and came down to 2.11 per cent per annum in 1981-91. There is an expectation of a sharp reduction in the rate to 1.09 per cent per annum in 1991-2000. While this could be an optimistic estimate, one can at least have a fair measure of assurance that the population growth rate which decreased by a modest margin in 1981-91 would continue its downward trend in the years to come. As regards the agricultural growth, a word needs to be said about the periodisation of the post-Independence decades. The period 1949-50 to 1964-65 could be identified as one of agricultural growth through area expansion; as can be seen from table 12.3, the growth rate in area was higher than that in yield during this period. The next period – 1967-68 to 1980-81 is usually reckoned as the green revolution period though it may be appropriate to regard it as the first round of the green revolution. The period is marked by sharp reduction in area expansion and a perceptible upward shift in yields. The first round of the green revolution was confined to only a few crops – rice and wheat being the major beneficiaries – and selected areas like Punjab and Haryana. In the first round, the yield improvement across all the crops was too modest to compensate for the decrease in the rate of area expansion and, as a result, growth rate of production came down from 3.13 per cent per annum during 1949-50 to 1964-65 to 2.38 per cent per annum during 1967-68 to 1980-81. The second round of the green revolution - 1980-81 to 1991-92 - had a more creditable record with the almost entire growth rate of 3.21 per cent coming from improvement in yields. The main point to be noted here is that over the post-Independence decades the agricultural growth rate - and in the last decade even the rate of yield increases – have remained ahead of the population growth rate. Thus, the marginalisation process in agriculture cannot be explained in terms of the Malthusian model alone though population growth would certainly need to be carefully monitored in the years ahead to devise effective brakes on it.

TABLE – 12.3

Population Growth Vs Agricultural Growth

Year	Population Growth		Agricultural Growth (Annual Compound Growth Rate)			
	Total Population	Annual Compound Growth Rate (%)	Period	Area	Yield	Production
1951	361.1	1.25	1949-50 to 1964-65	1.61	1.50	3.13
1961	439.2	1.96	1967-68 to 1980-81	0.54	1.83	2.38
1971	548.2	2.20	1980-81 to 1991-92	0.05	3.16	3.21
1981	685.2	2.22	1949-50 to 1991-92	0.64	2.05	2.70
1991	844.3	2.11				
2000*	987.3	1.09				

Note :

* : Estimated population as on March 1, 2000.

While calculating agricultural growth, years 1965-66 and 1966-67 have been excluded as they were years of serious scarcity.

Source: Agricultural Statistics at a Glance, Government of India, New Delhi, 1998.

Table 12.4 provides two pointers to the marginalisation of workers deriving their livelihood in agriculture. First, over the period 1951-1991, the work force in agriculture almost doubled from 97 million to 185 million; the proportion of rural workers in agriculture to total rural workers declined only marginally from 69 per cent in 1951 to 65 per cent in 1991. More alarming, there was a nearly three-fold increase in the number of agricultural labourers from 27 million in 1951 to 75 million in 1991 and, as a consequence, the proportion of labourers in agricultural workforce increased from 28 per cent in 1951 to 40 per cent in 1991.

This fast pace of casualisation of workforce in agriculture is a very suggestive clue to the marginalisation of those deriving their livelihood in agriculture. Second, the share of agriculture in the national GDP decreased sharply over the period 1951 to 1991 from around 50 per cent to about 25 per cent irrespective of whether a broader or a narrower concept of agriculture is adopted for calculating its GDP share. The implication is that the gap between the per worker GDP in agriculture and that in non-agriculture widened markedly over the post-Independence decades. The widening gap, considered in the context of casualisation of workforce in agriculture mentioned above, appears to provide a clear indication of the marginalisation process operating in agriculture.

TABLE – 12.4

Indicators of Marginalisation of Workers in Agriculture

Year	Population and Workforce (Millions)					
	Total	Rural	Rural Workers			Total Rural Workers
			Cultivators	Agricultural Labourers	Others	
1951	361.1	298.6	69.9 (49.9)	27.3 (19.5)	42.8 (30.6)	140.0 (100.0)
1991	844.3	627.1	110.6 (38.8)	74.6 (26.1)	100.2 (35.1)	285.4 (100.0)

Figures in brackets are percentage to total rural workers.

Source: Agricultural Statistics at a Glance, Govt. of India, New Delhi, 1993.

TABLE – 12.5

Share of Agriculture GDP in Total GDP (at 1980-81 Prices)

(Per cent of Total GDP)

Year	Agriculture, Forestry and Fisheries	Agriculture
1950-51	55.4	48.7
1996-97	26.1	24.4

Source: National Account Statistics of India 1950-51 to 1996-97, EPW, Research Foundation, Mumbai, 1998.

The changing structure of landholdings permits a closer observation of the marginalisation process as it operates over time. In a land-based economy, like the Indian rural economy, access to land and to economic opportunities linked to land-based activities would be a good indicator of the economic status of a household. In such an economy, it would be reasonable to infer marginalisation of cultivators if the structure of land holding has a strong trend towards proliferation of small and marginal farmers who are usually viewed as the principal target groups, along with landless labourers, for the anti-poverty programmes. Even so, the inferences given below based on the National Sample Survey data on land holdings from the different rounds are best viewed as indicative rather than definitive. Table 12.6 shows the percentage of rural households which were "landless" (owning less than 0.002 ha) and "near landless" (owning between 0.002 ha and 0.200 ha).

TABLE – 12.6

Rural Landless Households

Year (Households owning less than 0.002 ha)	Landless (Households owning between 0.002 ha and 0.200 ha)	Near Landless	Total
1960-61	11.68	26.22	37.90
1970-71	9.64	27.78	37.42
1981-82	11.33	28.60	39.93
1991-92	11.25	31.15	42.40

Source: NSS 17th , 26th , 37th and 48th rounds

It is significant to note that the liberalisation era began in India with over 40 per cent of rural households being landless or near landless. The proportion of the latter category shows a modest but steady increase since the beginning of the green revolution in the early seventies. It would be easy to appreciate the significance of this trend when it is considered along with the trend in the distribution of ownership holdings (See Table 12.7).

TABLE – 12.7

Distribution of Owned Holdings

(% of total holdings and total area)

Year	Marginal (<1 ha.)		Small (1 to 2 ha.)		Semi Medium (2 to 4 ha.)		Medium (4 to 10 ha.)		Large (10 ha & above)	
	Holding	Area	Holding	Area	Holding	Area	Holding	Area	Holding	Area
1960-61	60.06	7.59	15.16	12.4	12.86	20.54	9.07	31.23	2.85	28.24
1970-71	62.62	9.76	15.49	14.68	11.4	21.92	7.83	30.75	2.12	22.91
1981-82	66.64	12.22	14.70	16.49	10.78	23.38	6.45	29.83	1.42	18.07
1991-92	69.38	16.93	21.75	33.97	5.06	17.63	2.84	17.64	0.95	13.83

Source: Same as for Table 12.6.

It is worth noting that by the early nineties, over 96 per cent of owned holdings belonged to the size-groups marginal, small and semi-medium i.e., owners ranging between vulnerable to those likely to have only modest potential for viability. More important, over two-thirds of owned land was with the lower three groups with the medium and large owners accounting for less than a third of total land. Around the mid-fifties Professor Dantwala had drawn attention to the feature of the Indian agriculture that while the small and marginal holdings predominated in numbers, large part of land was in the hands of medium and large owners. Thus, apparently, the marginalisation process has brought about a major change in the production structure in agriculture. Much more than before, the small and marginal owners would have to shoulder in future the responsibility for the tasks necessitated by agricultural growth and modernisation.

Would the small and marginal owners have strong enough shoulders to bear this burden? Table 12.7 offers little room for optimism. A disturbing point to note is that the decade of 1981-82 to 1991-92 seems to have witnessed a marked intensification of the marginalisation process – the percentage of small owners increased from 14.70 per cent to 21.75 per cent. Further, the small owners emerged as the size-group with the largest share in total land. The group accounted in 1991-92 for over a third of total land with its share more than doubling over the decade 1981-82 to 1991-92. In contrast, the medium owners who had the largest share in total land at the three earlier time points covered by table 5 suffered a drastic reduction both in numbers and in the share in total land.

As regards the large owners, they were less than one per cent of the total owners in 1991-92 but owned nearly 14 per cent of total land. An interesting, but frankly speculative, inference would be that the changing position of the large owners represents the other side of the marginalisation process i.e., the presence, and possibly growing strength, of a small but dominant and influential group in agriculture. It must be borne in mind that the diminishing proportion of the large owners and reduction in their land share could in part be due to their moving out of agriculture to more lucrative opportunities in other sectors and, also, preference for investment in non-land capital rather than only further addition to size of holding. It may be recalled that the newer opportunities in agriculture depend critically on investments in modern inputs and technologies and not merely on larger and growing size of holding.

Put together, the clues provided by tables 12.6 and 12.7 yield the following scenario of the marginalisation process in agriculture since the beginning of the planning era in India. The era began with substantial landlessness in rural areas. The process instead of being reversed – or even arrested - has continued to operate over the post-Independence decades with landlessness reaching the extent of over 40 per cent in 1991-92. What should cause particular concern is the apparent intensification of the process during the eighties with a noticeable impact on the production structure in which small and marginal owners now account for a half of the total land. At the same time, there is also an indication of the large owners diminishing in proportion but, possibly, gaining in status and dominance through modernising their farming activities. Our political system is already under a severe strain owing to its inability to accommodate the rising expectations of the lower strata in the society, particularly those in the rural areas. Unchecked marginalisation of the poor in agriculture could prove to be the last straw on the back of the camel.

What might explain the paradox of marginalisation of large parts of rural people despite fairly sustained agricultural growth since Independence? It is important to seek an explanation as the sustained potentialities for agricultural growth now being visualised for the coming decades may not by themselves arrest the marginalisation process. We have three promising clues which could help in resolving the paradox. First, urban India and large industries have received far more policy attention during the planning era than rural environs, resources and people. This has been an unfavourable policy context for agriculture. An influential group of economists, including Dr. Manmohan Singh, the former Finance Minister, believe that the overall effect of the policy context has been to disprotect agriculture in India. Second, agricultural growth strategy and policies have benefited limited regions, crops and farmer groups giving rise to a growing dualism in rural India. Disaggregated studies bring out the parlous state in which rainfed regions in India accounting for 70 per cent of area under crops find themselves half-a-century after Independence. Biased agricultural growth spawns persistent and growing regional inequities pushing masses of cultivators to the brink of economic collapse. Third, the unfavourable policy context for the rural people have had the result of creating an institutional vacuum at the ground level making it difficult for the development agencies to reach rural people and to mobilise them for developmental activities. The institutional vacuum at the ground level has also the effect of inhibiting capacities of the rural people to take development initiatives, provide local leadership and build up organisations for collective action to protect their interests. With docile and passive rural communities dispersed over a vast area, the policy making elites have little reason to look beyond their own interests while choosing development strategies and priorities.

The prevailing policy context along with the shift towards liberalisation and globalisation has frightening implications for human development in India. Studies using the Head Count Ratio of poverty (HCR) – reflecting the minimal concept of poverty based on food deprivation – show that poverty diminishes with growth, particularly agricultural growth. There is a near consensus among the academics that liberalisation through its linkage with growth would be a powerful anti-poverty strategy. However, it is not clear that the type of growth that has taken place in India and which is likely to continue in the coming decades would reduce poverty reckoned in terms of multiple deprivation criteria besides food. In fact, the marginalisation process in operation in agriculture is very likely to have an extremely adverse impact on poverty measured in terms of low/diminishing human development.

The priority tasks identified in the preceding two sections would be of some help to the government in focussing the policy regime as a whole on the marginalised people. It is also necessary to repeat the point made at the beginning of this section that promoting human development would need an economy-wide strategy to generate productive employment for the poor and the marginalised and to level down the extremes of inequality. Keeping this overall policy context in mind, one can suggest the following priority tasks to counter the marginalisation process operating in agriculture.

i. Broad based agricultural growth and diversification would stimulate value-adding activities like processing and preparing specialist items with large demand. There would be growth in productive employment opportunities but the workers in agriculture would have to be trained for the new skills and occupations. In the light of the experience gained so far in programmes like Training for Rural Youth for Self Employment (TRYSEM) run by the government and similar activities of NGOs, attempt should be made to look ahead to identify the promising opportunities in different areas and to anticipate in advance the training and other assistance which could help the workers in agriculture to benefit from these emerging employment opportunities.

ii. Rise in rural incomes and the formation of a relatively better off middle strata in the rural communities would generate wide ranging demands for goods and services. The consequential rise in employment opportunities needs to be kept in mind while planning the training and other assistance to be given to the workers in agriculture.

iii. There is a trend towards the rural-urban continuum becoming more connected with quicker and smoother flow of people and goods. This trend needs to be supported so that village economies remaining relatively isolated from the mainstream get more firmly linked with it. Ideally, rural communities should have bustling commuting zone around them for employment, for marketing their products and for purchasing inputs. This would check the flow of migrants to urban slums and flight of talent from villages. It would also help in obtaining a more even and balanced spatial spread of economic and other social activities.

1.6 Getting Oriented to Modernisation: The Prospects Ahead

Modernisation is a society-wide process working through many channels interacting with each other and with the global environment. It is a powerful process bringing about systemic changes-particularly in the traditional and poor societies like India-which individual countries and governments find increasingly difficult to counter. Modernisation brings many benefits but could also cause widespread disruptions and distress. It would be futile for a developing country to try to insulate itself from the process of modernisation. It is an essential ingredient of development and a successful development strategy could very appropriately be defined as the one which adjusts to modernisation maximizing its benefits and minimizing the costs. This is the reason our search for priority tasks has been focused on modernisation of agriculture as the goal of development.

It is evident from the preceding sections that, despite its many achievements in the post-Independence decades, Indian agriculture fails to meet the criterion of modernisation. Human development indices and the indicators of marginalisation of vast numbers in agriculture presented in this paper serve to underline this failure as also the urgent need to orient policy-making towards modernisation. It is our conviction that this cannot be done by only reviewing the existing policies to improve them. The economic reforms being implemented since the beginning of the nineties do recognise the need for a new paradigm for policymaking for development though, as in the past, agriculture tends to remain on sidelines until a crisis knocks on the door. Abundant funds are promised for agriculture but there is no matching readiness on the part of the government to take up tasks which are crucial for modernisation of agriculture but have been grossly neglected so far. A common characteristic of the priority tasks identified in this paper is that they have tons of writings adorning them but the action taken by the government has to be measured in ounces! In social science analysis, it is important to look at government as one constituent in the total society. This is of help in understanding how social milieu helps/ inhibits capacity of governments to undertake tasks relating to goals like modernisation of traditional societies.

Let us begin by taking a look at our experiences in building up Panchayati Raj Institutions (PRIs). PRIs form the foundation of representative and participatory institutions which is of crucial importance in making agriculture self-regulating, overcoming limits to growth and promoting human development. The development functions to be handled by them and the responsibility for area-based planning assigned to them make them a key change agent in the process of modernisation. PRIs occupy a prominent place in Gandhian ideology. The first major report on PRIs was prepared in the fifties followed by many others. However, concrete steps towards empowering PRIs were taken only in the Eighties and they acquired the constitutional status almost a decade later. The long interval between the official recognition of the need to have PRIs (various reports) and concrete action (constitutional amendments in 1993) could be explained by the fact that in the intervening period rural growth and spread of political awareness among rural masses had prepared the ground for a much larger role than before for rural people in policymaking for development. The process of rural areas and people joining the mainstream is still far from complete. The progress of PRIs is bound to help this process which, in turn, would add thrust to activation of PRIs. If the task of building up PRIs gets the priority it deserves, one may expect rapid progress in the next decade or so with a noticeable impact on policymaking for agriculture and rural areas.

Once PRIs become active at the grassroots, a necessary outcome would be the coming into being of a multilevel system linking the plans and decisions of PRIs with those at the top. The ACRP literature referred to in section 1.3 has done some groundwork in this direction but its operationalisation as a multilevel system would become feasible only when the institutional change at the grassroots begins to exert pressure on the centre and the states for substantial devolution of resources and autonomy in their use. In the process, the present division of functions-policy making at the centre and implementation by the governments at the lower tiers-would be replaced by dispersal of policymaking function across tiers of the government from the centre to PRIs. Currently, policy formulation is identified with impressive documents prepared at the top in language elastic enough to reconcile ambitious objectives with modest achievement. In a multilevel system, policies would be shaped by aggregation and adjustments across the different tiers of the government with only broad goals, norms and parameters being formulated at the top reflecting the consensus emerging from hard bargaining across the tiers of the government. The present policy documents prepared at the top could undergo many and substantial changes difficult to foresee now. It is for this reason that we have focused this paper on priority tasks rather than on the policy agenda.

A self-regulating agricultural system would still need selective government interventions to keep it moving towards modernisation. As we have indicated in the preceding sections, interventions would be needed to preserve economic stability, to conserve and make judicious use of critical endowments like land and water and to reach human development to substantial sections of population trapped in poverty. It is unnecessary to repeat the scope and importance of these priority tasks. What is important to note is that the government would be able to focus attention on these tasks only after it gets disentangled from its present numerous interventions of wrong kind motivated by populism, need to appease powerful lobbies and a strong urge to retain-and, if possible, further extend and strengthen-its control over the economy. These wrong kind of interventions are rapidly becoming unsustainable owing to rising economic costs, disenchantment of intended beneficiaries with populism and lobbies getting too numerous and large to be appeased. Simultaneously, pressures would also grow from large constituencies like farmers for the right kind of interventions indicated above. Thus, the emerging context promises some improvement in the government's role as an intervener.

Would the movement towards modernisation of agriculture induced by changing social milieu and different kinds of pressures working on the government be fast and balanced enough to bring about development? It is difficult to be very optimistic on this score. India appears to be on the verge of passing through a succession of crises. It would have to face them relying on very inadequate equipment: weak governance; poor work culture and professional ethics among elites and organised groups; gathering impatience among the lower strata with the social system and its inequities. These features would have to change for the society as a whole to move towards modernisation. The future, indeed, looks grim. But it is not necessarily without hope. Crises often help societies to get rid of accumulated toxicities and regain health and vigour. India could benefit much from such crises!

II

A REVIEW OF CRITICAL POLICY ISSUES

2.1 Introduction

As we have explained in the preface and in Part I of this paper, the purpose of Part II is not to open up for review the entire policy agenda. If it is accepted that the government has to be less interventionist in future, it would follow that the government should choose to take up only the policies consistent with its new role towards agriculture. This raises the tricky question of disengagement from the present policy commitments and transition to the new role. The process of disengagement and transition is likely to be protracted with frequent interruptions occasioned by political wranglings. For the purpose of this paper, we have selected only a few policy areas in which, in our view, the government would have to play an active role for a long time to come.

It is useful, while looking at these policy areas, to keep in mind certain persistent features of policy regimes for agriculture as they have operated so far in India. First, there are abundant findings to show that India shares with many developing countries a strong preference for the development path seeking to promote modern industries at the cost of discriminating against agriculture. Researchers have argued that the policy regime in India from Independence right up to about the early nineties has had the effect of lowering the prices received by the farmers for their output while raising the prices paid by them for inputs purchased from industries [Pursell and Gulati (1993), Singh (1995), Economic Survey (GOI), 1996-97, Parikh (1999)]. A world Bank study covering 18 developing countries over the period 1960- 85 found that there has been an enormous transfer of income out of agriculture estimated at 46 per cent of the gross domestic product originating from agriculture per year over the period of quarter of a century (Schiff and Valdes, 1995). It is easy to imagine the impact of such large income transfer from agriculture on farmer's incentives and capacity to invest and take risks.

Second, between the better-off and the poor in agriculture, the policy regime has favoured the former neglecting the development potential waiting to be tapped in the poorer parts of agriculture. As a result, a dualistic structure has emerged in agriculture with a small but dynamic part aligned with the mainstream economy and polity and a large part languishing with inadequate access to the policymaker and to mainstream opportunities. Third, the policymaker remains far too preoccupied with the problems of the moment and the fire-fighting operations to deal with them; the long term issues like sustainable development and inter-regional and inter temporal equity get neglected. Underlying these features of the policy regime is the development perspective still lingering in Indian policymaking that agriculture is inherently traditional and that modernisation and development come from growth in other sectors. With this view of agriculture, the natural next step is to regard farmers-and rural society in general - as people unwilling to change from the attitudes, perceptions and lifestyle established over generations in the past. Hence, it is the position today that half-a-century after Independence few city dwellers – and the affluent in rural society-would want to live in villages.

Agricultural policies in India have to manoeuvre within the constraints imposed by the features of the policy regime described above. It is not unusual to come across corrective measures in policies recommended over and over again by succession of committees but remaining unimplemented. Unfulfilled targets cause little embarrassment as alibis would be readily available in the past reports. The ingenious invention of measuring programme achievements by expenditures incurred helps progress reports to look impressive and provides basis for demanding increased funds for the next year. This is not to ridicule implementation of policies or the programme personnel. Our intention is only to point out that such weaknesses in implementation are inevitable given the prevailing policy regime. The policy regime affects policies at two levels. Policies formulated at the top without a sense of commitment to the goals which they are expected to achieve tend to be ritualistic. The parameters relating to time-frame, phasing, release of funds and monitoring and evaluation are disregarded with impunity. Delays, lack of coordination and indifference towards mounting costs become rampant. Corruption and leakages spread widely. At the ground level, the personnel finds that their conscientiousness, performance and rapport with the target groups bring neither any appreciation nor rewards. The target groups, in turn, remain cynical and passive. It is, thus, that the policy regime becomes ineffective from the top downwards. Trying to improve the system by looking at only the lower and junior levels may yield some marginal improvements but no major breakthroughs. It is the reforming of the regime described in Part I which would make it possible for more thoroughgoing changes to occur partly through planned improvements and partly as a consequence of pressures from outside. It would be legitimate to expect substantive improvements to occur in the coming years in the policies considered in the sections which follow. The priority tasks identified for these policies could be of help in guiding this process along the right direction.

2.2 Capital Formation

The pace and pattern of agricultural development are largely conditioned by the growth of infrastructural facilities of irrigation, road, market, power, cold storage, etc. Infrastructure plays a critical role on both input and output sides. While on the input front, it helps ensure timely and adequate delivery to farmers, on the output front, it helps integrate local markets with national and international markets. Therefore, an adequate and efficient infrastructure system is essential for realising the potential of the sector. In this context, the experience of China shows that high rate of investment in agriculture can ensure big spurt in agricultural output over a long period (Rao and Gulati, 1994).

However, one of the most disquieting developments in the agricultural sector during the last two decades has been the neglect of capital formation, particularly in the public sector. Gross Capital Formation (GCF) in agriculture as per cent of total gross capital formation in the economy, after rising during the 70's, declined during the eighties and nineties. In 1998-99 it was just 5.5 per cent as against 16.3 per cent in 1980-81. Further, GCF in agriculture as per cent of GDP in agriculture also declined during the last two decades from 10.9 per cent in 1980-81 to 6.2 per cent in 1998-99 (Table 12.8 and Chart 12.1).

What is more disturbing is the fact that GCF in the agriculture sector by the public sector declined at an annual average rate of 4.0 per cent and 1.9 per cent during the 1980s and the 1990s, respectively. As a result, the share of public sector in total capital formation in the sector declined to around 23.0 per cent during the nineties as against 32.0 per cent during the seventies. However, in the private sector, the decline was only marginal during eighties (-0.1 per cent) and it picked up at a moderate of 8.1 per cent in the nineties (Table 12.8 and Chart 12.2).

TABLE – 12.8

Gross Capital Formation in Agriculture

(Rs.Crore)

Year	GCF in Agriculture			GCFA as % of GDP in Agriculture	GCF as % of Total GCF in Economy@
	Public	Private	Total		
		At 1980-81 Prices			
1960-61	589	1079	1668	5.8	13.5
1970-71	789	1996	2785	7.8	14.7
1980-81	1796	2840	4636	10.9	16.3
1990-91	1154	3440	4594	7.5	8.1
1991-92	1002	3727	4729	8.0	9.3
1992-93	1061	4311	5372	8.5	9.4
1993-94	1153	3878	5031	7.7	9.3
1994-95	1316	4940	6256	9.0	8.6
1995-96	1268	5693	6961	10.4	8.2
		At 1993-94 Prices			
1996-97	4689	11921	16610	6.5	6.4
1997-98	4240	12140	16380	6.6	5.5
1998-99p	3876	12581	16457	6.2	5.5
		Annual Average Growth (%)			
1971-79	10.0	7.2	7.9		
1980-89	-4.0	-0.1	-1.5		
1990-98	-1.9	8.1	5.6		

Note: P : Provisional.

@ : Gross Capital Formation adjusted for errors and omissions

GCFA: Gross Capital Formation in Agriculture.

Source : 1. National Accounts Statistics, various issues, CSO, Government of India.

2. Agricultural Statistics at a Glance, Various Issues, Government of India.

CHART – 12.1

Gross Capital Formation in Agriculture as % of GDP Agriculture and Total GCF in the Economy

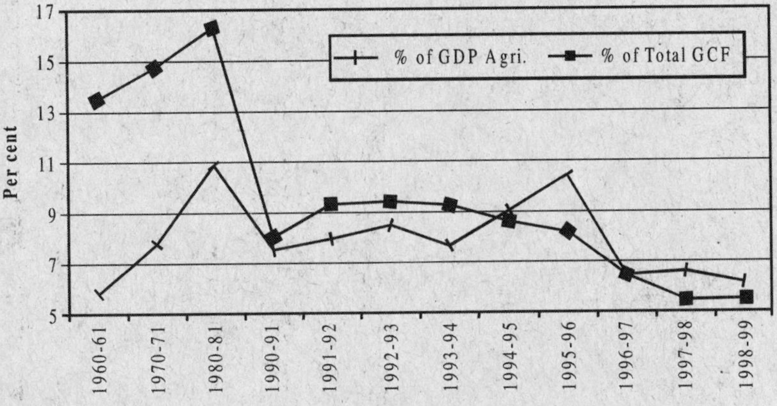

CHART – 12.2

Trends in Capital Formation in Agriculture

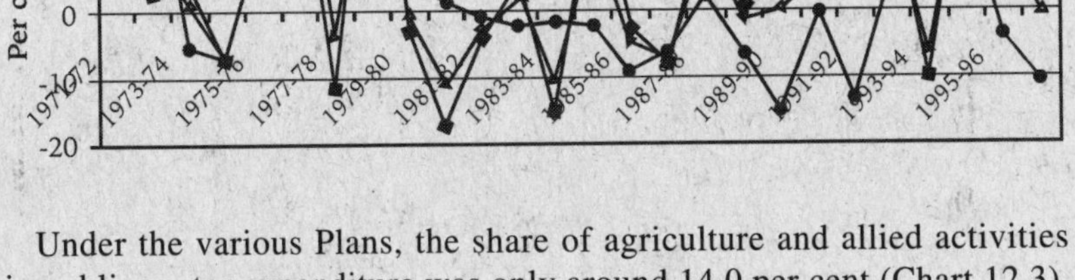

Under the various Plans, the share of agriculture and allied activities in public sector expenditure was only around 14.0 per cent (Chart 12.3). During the Ninth Plan (1997-2002), investment requirement in the agricultural sector is estimated at 1,54,900 crore, of which around 82,200 crore or 42 per cent is expected to come from the public sector (Centre and States) (Planning Commission, 1998). Given the current trends in public sector capital formation, it is doubtful whether the target will be achieved at the end of the Plan period.

There is a view among the agricultural economists that the lagged effect of decline of capital formation during the eighties has been one of the major reasons for the decelerated growth of the sector during the nineties (Mahendra Dev, 1998). Therefore, the subdued level of capital formation during the nineties can have an impact on agriculture production in the coming years. Apart from the sluggishness in capital formation at the national level, there are large inter-regional variations in public investment on rural infrastructure, which probably accounts for differential growth of agriculture in various regions. Bhatia (1999) found that the index of rural infrastructure was the highest in Punjab followed by Kerala, Tamil Nadu and Haryana. However, in case of Rajasthan, Bihar, Madhya Pradesh, Orissa, Uttar Pradesh, West Bengal and Assam it was very low. Further, the study found a strong relationship between rural infrastructural development and level of per hectare yield of foodgrains as also value of output from agriculture. It is, therefore, recommended that development of infrastructure should be given top most priority by national, state and local self-governments. Ideally, we need to evolve a core investment programme for the country and economic criteria should guide in its implementation.

CHART – 12.3

Plan-Wise Share of Agriculture and Allied Activities in Public Sector Expenditure

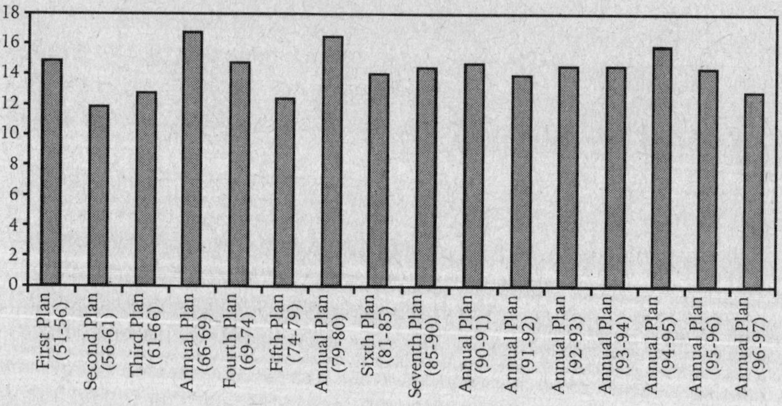

In the literature there is a lively debate on complementarity between public and private sector capital formation in agricultural sector. While Studies by Shetty (1990), Rao (1994), Dhawan and Yadav (1995),

Dhawan (1996a), Dhawan (1996b), Alagh (1997) and Rao (1998) postulate or establish the complementarity between the public and private investment in agriculture, studies of Mishra and Chand (1995), Mishra and Hazell (1996), and Mishra (1998) refuted the existence of complementarity. On this issue, Rao (1998) opined that there is severe underestimation of public investment in agriculture, especially in case of rural electrification, rural roads, etc., which may be responsible for the empirical findings of non-existence of complementarity. Agriculture is basically a private activity in India and, hence, public investment has a crucial role to play in creating infrastructure in terms of irrigation, roads, markets, storage facilities, rural electrification and technology development, besides education and health (Thamarajakshi, 1999). Another view gaining ground in recent times is that the decline of capital formation in the public sector has been compensated by the private sector. Logically, the argument looks sound but its fallacy comes out when one examines the composition of private capital formation. Private sector capital formation is essentially taking place for short-term asset building and it is mainly in the areas of mechanisation, ground levelling, private irrigation, etc. However, public sector capital formation is mainly in the form of construction of dams, roads, marketing yards, rural electrification, etc, where private sector capital formation is hard to come in. Therefore, public sector capital formation needed to be augmented with a definite content and targeted focus, especially in case of rainfed areas, which lack not only in irrigation facilities, but also in other infrastructural facilities.

Here it may be mentioned that public spending in agriculture is a common feature in both the developed and developing countries. In a World Bank study, Blarcom, *et al*, (1993) found that in case of 40 developing countries, an average of 7.5 per cent (including subsidies) of total central government expenditure was allocated to agriculture during the period 1972 to 1988. And it formed around 10 per cent of net value of agricultural production. In case of a group of 15 developed countries, the share of government expenditure was around 3 per cent of total expenditure. However, it formed around 20 per cent of their net value of agricultural production.

Some studies suggests that the decline in the Incremental Capital Output Ratio (ICOR) and the concomitant increase in Marginal Efficiency of Capital (MEC) during the eighties has compensated the decline in capital formation during that decade (Mishra and Chand 1995, Alagh, 1997, Purohit and Reddy, 1999). However, this argument has been questioned by some other studies on the ground that why MEC, which improved during the eighties, deteriorated during the nineties (due to the decelerated growth of agricultural production and accelerated growth of capital formation during the nineties) (Mallik, 1997 and Pulapare, 2000). As the estimation of ICOR and MEC are not very reliable, it is imprudent to conclude that the decline of capital formation has been compensated by improvement in efficiency of use of capital.

Rising subsidies on food, fertilisers, credit, etc., is said to be the factors limiting the growth of public sector investment. In general, subsidies distort resource allocation and hence, it need to be kept at the minimum. Well targeted subsidies for programmes like adoption of improved seeds, mechanisation, irrigation, etc., can play a valuable role in promoting agriculture growth. However, they need to be removed once their original purpose has been met. With the move towards reduction in subsidies on food and fertiliser in the recent Union Budget, Government can redirect the money for capital formation purpose. In fact what is need is prioritisation of the requirement of capital formation in different areas like watershed development, rural electrification, extension services, flood control, etc., where private sector investment is hard to come.

One major step taken for improving capital formation in the public sector is the creation of Rural Infrastructural Development Fund (RIDF) in 1995-96 in NABARD with a corpus of Rs.2000 crore, with the objective of providing funds to State Governments and State owned corporations to enable them to complete various types of rural infrastructure projects. Since 1995-96, the scheme continued in each succeeding years with enhancement of the volume of the fund; the last one being RIDF-VI announced in the Union Budget 2000-01 with a corpus of Rs.4,500 crores. The resources for the fund is contributed by the scheduled commercial banks to the extent of the shortfall the bank may post for meeting the priority sector lending targets. Of course, the creation of RIDF will improve the infrastructural facilities in various states. However, we would like to flag some issues associated with RIDF. First, RIDF is not an additional resource to the agriculture sector. Rather, it is a mechanism through which private sector resources (deposit) are diverted to the public sector. Had the banks met the stipulated target of priority sector lending, the resource flow would have been much more in the sector, especially at the private hands. In other words, RIDF basically involves the transfer of resources from the private sector to the public sector. Therefore, the efficiency in the utilisation of funds by the states may be lower than the efficiency in case of utilisation by the private sector (mainly farmers), had the banks met their priority sector targets. Second, though the NABARD sanctioned the fund to various State Governments, its disbursement is not impressive; only around 37.0 per cent of the sanctioned amount at the end of March 1999. Third, it provided the commercial banks a golden opportunity for parking their funds with ensured return without risk and that made the banks less interested in expanding their priority sector lending.

Based on the above discussion on capital formation, we identify the following priority tasks:

- Capital formation in the public sector should be augmented. Money saved from the reduction in subsidy for agricultural inputs should be utilised for this purpose.
- In view of the resource constraints, capital formation requirements need to be prioritised. As ACRP gets operationalised, it would be possible to do prioritisation in a rational manner.
- Inter-state variations in capital formation need to be reduced by stepping up investments in backward regions.
- Delays in disbursement of funds under RIDF should be eliminated.

2.3 Agricultural Credit

Credit is one of the important supply side factors which contributes to agricultural production. An efficient and effective rural credit delivery system is imperative for providing timely, adequate and equitable access to credit for raising agricultural productivity and incomes. Equitable access to institutional credit is important in the context of relative scarcity of credit and the high cost of informal credit. In India, the emphasis on agricultural credit has continued through progressive institutionalisation for providing timely and adequate credit to farmers at reasonable rates of interest. Broadly, over the years, India has followed three pronged strategy for developing rural credit, viz, i) promotion of institutional structure, ii) directed lending, and iii) concessional or subsidised credit (Rangarajan, 1996).

TABLE – 12.9

Agricultural Credit: Growth, Per cent of GDP Agriculture and Per cent of Private Capital Formation

Period	Loans issued (Per cent per annum)	GDP Agri.* (Per cent per annum)	Loans as % of GDP Agri.	Term Loans as % of Private GCF
1970-71 to 1979-80	16.1	9.2	6.1	42.0
1980-81 to 1989-90	14.0	13.4	9.4	79.9
1990-91 to 1998-99	15.2	15.9	7.7	54.7
1971-72 to 1998-99	14.9	12.6	7.9	60.9

* : At Current prices
GCF: Gross Capital formation.

There has been considerable progress in the above three strategies, especially, we could develop a large institutional network, at different layers, for rural credit. The aggregate loan disbursements for agriculture and allied activities by the co-operatives, commercial banks and Regional Rural Banks (RRBs) together rose by 14.9 per cent per annum during the last three decades (from 1970-71 to 1998-99). However, during the eighties and nineties, the rate of growth slowed down as compared to the seventies (Table 12.9). As a result, per cent of total loans to GDP in agriculture declined during the nineties to 7.7 from 9.4 in the eighties (Chart 12.4). Lower expansion of credit in relation to the requirements for private sector capital formation is also evident. The share of term loans in private sector capital formation declined during the nineties to 54.7 per cent from 79.9 per cent in the eighties (Table 12.9 and Chart 12.5).

Over the years, rural credit system has been suffering from a number of weaknesses like, limited outreach, skewness in the availability of credit in different regions, sectors and sections of the farming community, lower recovery of loans and growing non-performing assets, loss making institutions, etc. In this context, Mujumdar (1999) observed that "It is an irony of economic history that India which was a pioneer in evolving its own brand of institutional framework for rural credit today finds its entire rural credit system in a moribund state" (pp.1577).

CHART – 12.4

Total Loans Disbursed as % of GDP Agri.

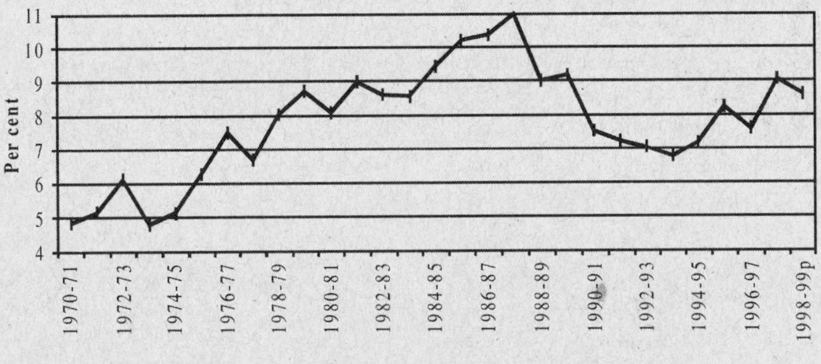

CHART – 12.5

Term Loans As Per cent of Private Capital Formation

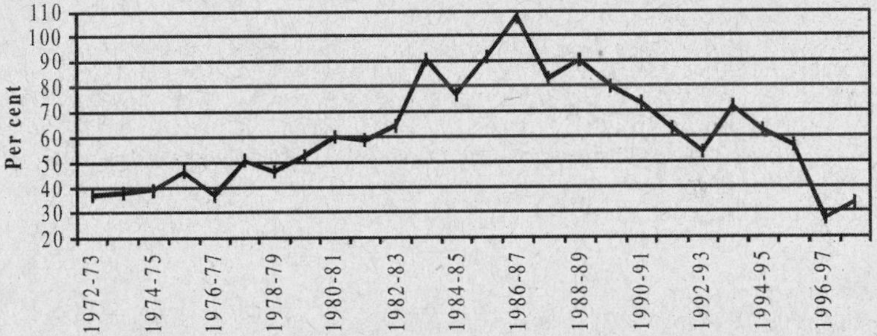

Poor recovery of loans and the consequent rise in non-performing assets (NPA) is a matter of grave concern. There is a general perception that higher NPA of the banking system is mainly on account of the priority sector advances. This is not entirely true as the data show that the share of gross NPAs in the priority sector in the total gross NPAs of the commercial banks is only around 46.4 per cent in 1998 and it in fact declined from the level of 48.3 per cent in 1996. As the priority sector accounts for around 30-32 per cent of net bank credit of the commercial banks, the above share need not be taken as extremely high. In fact, in recent times, NPAs are increasingly occurring on borrowal accounts of industrial sector. The proportion of gross NPA to priority sector advances of the public sector banks was around 23.0 per cent in 1998, which is higher than around 13.0 per cent in case of non-priority advances (Reserve Bank of India, 1999b). Hence, the focus of commercial banks is on recovery of advances. Reports from various parts of the country indicate that forceful recovery of loans by banks is putting undue hardship on the poor and they are even forming associations to fight against the recovery operations of the banks. They argue that when the big industrialists are left free from the repayment of loans, why the poor people are being targeted and harassed. After the write-off of loans under the Agricultural and Rural Debt Relief Scheme, 1990, people are still under the impression that they need not pay back the loans taken from the financial institutions. Therefore, it is essential that people are to be educated about the need to recover loans for recycling the loans.

Despite having a wide network of rural branches in the country and implementation of many schemes and programmes for expansion of credit (targeted lending) for agriculture and rural development, a large number of the very poor people still continue to remain outside the fold of the formal banking system. The All India Debt and Investment Survey 1991-92 shows that during the eighties there was a decline in the share of institutional agencies in cash dues of rural households by 4.6 percentage points to 56.6 per cent as against a rise of 32 percentage points to 61.2 per cent during the seventies. In case of non-cultivators, the share of institutional agencies was only 49.9 per cent in 1991. What is more revealing is the fact that the share of institutional agencies declined at a time when the proportion of rural households reported debt in 1991 increased to 32 per cent from 19.4 per cent in 1981. Thus, the rural households still seem to depend on money lenders, landlords and relatives for a significant par of their credit. In case of non-cultivators, the share of institutional agencies was only 49.9 per cent in 1991. The decline in the institutional outreach during the eighties is mainly on account of decline in the share of co-operatives from 28.6 per cent in 1981 to 18.6 per cent in 1991. Correspondingly, the shares of traders and professional money lenders have increased (Table 12.10 and Chart 12.6). What is more revealing is the fact that the share of institutional agencies declined at a time wnen the proportion of rural households reported debt in 1991 increased to 32 per cent from 19.4 per cent in 1981. It is hard to believe that the outreach could have increased substantially during the nineties given the non-expansion of branch network and cautious attitude followed by the banks on account of financial sector reforms, which focussed on profitability of operations.

CHART – 12.6

Share of Agencies in Outstanding Debt of Rural Households

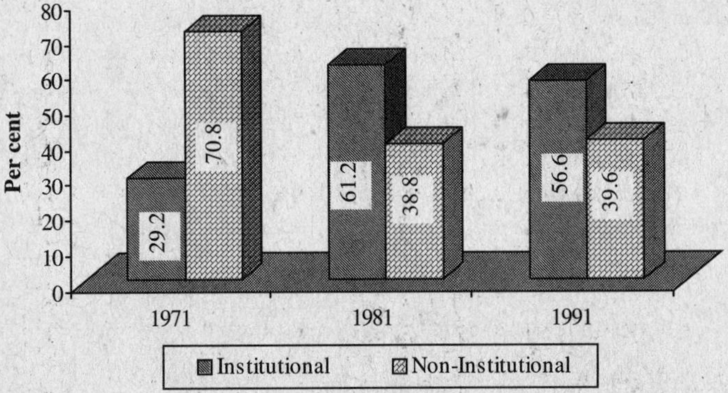

TABLE – 12.10

Agency-wise Per cent of Cash Dues Outstanding in the Rural Households (as on end June)

(Per cent)

Credit Agency	1971	1981	1991
I. Institutional - Total	**29.2**	**61.2**	**56.6**
1. Commercial Banks	2.2	28.0	29.0
2. Co-operatives	20.1	28.6	18.6
3. Government	6.7	4.0	5.7
4. Insurance	0.1	0.3	0.5
5. Provident Fund	0.1	0.3	0.9
6. Others	—	—	1.9
II. Non-Institutional - Total	**70.8**	**38.8**	**39.6**
1. Professional Moneylender	13.8	8.3	9.4
2. Agricultural Moneylender	23.1	8.6	6.3
3. Relatives/Friends	13.8	9.0	6.7
4. Landlords	8.6	4.0	4.0
5. Traders	8.7	3.4	7.1
6. Doctors, Lawyers, etc.	—	—	1.2
7. Other Sources	2.8	4.9	4.9
III. Sources not specified	**—**	**0.6**	**3.8**

Source: All India Debt and Investment Survey, 1991-92, Indebtedness of Rural Households as on 30.6.1991, Report 2 (Part-1), NSS forty-eighth Round, NSSO, GoI, 1997, reported in Reserve Bank of India Bulletin, February 2000.

In this context, a World Bank study carried out in a district in Eastern Rajasthan reveals that the share of institutional agencies in the availment of credit was just 16 per cent among the surveyed people below the poverty line (World Bank, 1995). Further, during the nineties, public sector banks could not meet their agricultural credit target of 18 per cent of net bank credit. Their achievement was only 15.7 per cent during the nineties. The Report of the High-Level Committee on Agricultural Credit Through Commercial Banks (1997) (Chairman: Shri. R.V. Gupta) also found that there is a substantial unfulfilled demand for crop loans, which is being met either by the money lenders or leading to the usage of lower inputs. However, the Committee recommended for non stipulation of credit targets. Once the recommendation is accepted it will make agricultural credit on equal par with credit to other sectors. Given the inherent weakness of the agricultural sector (susceptible to the vagaries of monsoon, operation of the law of diminishing returns and the general policy bias against the sector), it may not be appropriate to treat the sector on equal par with other sectors where returns are much higher than agriculture. Further, if this recommendation is accepted, the Government and the Reserve Bank will be left with no policy instrument for increasing the flow of credit to the agriculture. As informal credit is very costly as compared to the institutional sources and the existing set-up largely serves well-off farmers, the reach of the institution needs to be further improved especially to small and marginal farmers. Credit targeting can ensure the availability of credit to those sections of the society.

Along with credit targeting, concessionality in interest rates has been an instrument for increasing the flow of credit to the agricultural credit. There is a valid reason for following such a policy: "principal justification for charging lower interest rates to certain category of borrowers was that the farm based investment activity in the short-run does not always yield a return which enables regular servicing of loans and at the same time meet the minimum consumption requirements" (Reserve Bank of India (1971). However, the Report of the Committee on the Financial System (1991) suggested that it is timely and adequacy of the credit that is more important than the cost of credit. Subsequently, following the financial sector reforms and de-regulation of interest rates in the economy, the concessional element in agricultural credit has been gradually wiped out. This is done by giving freedom to commercial banks, RRBs and co-operatives to fix their own interest rates on loans of amount. The only stipulation now is in respect of commercial banks that the rate of interest on loans below Rs.2 Lakhs should not exceed the Prime Lending Rate (PLR) of the respective banks. As PLR of banks are decided purely in terms of commercial considerations, the above stipulation does not provide any concessionality in lending to the agriculture sector.

With the rising rural income and agricultural exports, agricultural output mix is likely to undergo radical changes in the coming years which would substantially increase the demands for rural credit. The investment needs for the production of highly income elastic agricultural products such as dairying and livestock, horticulture, farm-forestry and agro forestry, which are more land saving and capital intensive, would rise much faster than before. Similarly, with the liberalisation of agricultural exports, the agriculture sector will be more commercialised and capital intensive, particularly in area like horticulture, floriculture, aquaculture, agro-industries, etc. Since many of the emerging activities are land saving in character, the income earning prospects for small and marginal farmers can be improved by providing requisite credit and technical expertise. Owing to these factors rural credit has to expand at a rate faster than in the recent past.

In this context, the role of micro credit comes into picture. Major reasons for the lack of interest of formal financial institutions in extending rural credit are high transaction cost involved in small loan accounts and poor recovery of loans. As a solution, a new mode of delivery of credit through Self-help Groups (SHGs) and Voluntary Organisations has been emphasised in recent times. In fact, micro credit is considered as the last hope for rural India. The early results of linking SHGs with banks, which launched by NABARD during 1992-93, is very encouraging. By the end of March 1999, 32,995 SHGs have been linked with banks, and credit to the order of Rs. 57 crores has been dispursed However, the linkage programme was highly skewed in respect of regions and institutions. Region-wise, Southern Region accounted for about 65 per cent of the SHGs financed by the NABARD, primarily because of the strong presence of NGOs in that region. In case of northern region, the share was just 1 per cent. Further, 60 per cent of the financing is done through commercial banks and another 35 per cent through RRBs. The share of co-operatives, which has the largest network of branches, was just 4 per cent (NABARD, 1999a). NABARD envisages to cover at least one-third of the rural poor population by the year 2008 through one million SHGs (NABARD, 1999b). Measures are being taken now to bring micro-credit as an integral part of banks' corporate credit plan (Reserve Bank of India, 2000a). Further, in their report, Micro Credit Special Cell in the Reserve Bank, *inter alia*, suggested that 5 per cent of fresh net bank credit (50 per cent of fresh weaker section lending) should be made through micro credit lending procedure in a gradual manner (Reserve Bank of India, 2000b).

From the above discussion on rural credit, the following priority tasks are identified:

- Increase the outreach of the formal financial institutions, especially to the small and marginal farmers.
- Continuation of credit targeting for ensuring adequacy of credit in the agricultural sector
- Progressively link SHGs with formal credit institutions for reducing transaction cost and high loan recovery

2.4 Agricultural Insurance

In the context of increasing commercialisation and globalisation, the scope and relevance of agricultural insurance are not widely understood in India. Crop insurance, which is generally restricted to field crops, is generally considered synonymous with agricultural insurance. However, agricultural insurance covers a wide spectrum of activities like horticulture, plantations, livestock, poultry, aquaculture, sericulture, etc. Further, it extends to the entire production process including post-harvest storage, processing and transportation of produce to the final markets.

Agricultural insurance has many advantages. First, as the agricultural sector is not well organised on institutional lines, it can help agriculture to develop through institutionalised channels and assist in speeding up the process of commercialisation of the sector. Second, agricultural insurance can play a distinct role in securing credit from institutional sources as it provides security to the lending institutions. Third, it provides strength to farmers for a better deal in respect of interest rates in a liberalised interest rate regime. Four, it can ensure better recovery of loans as the credit agency would receive the payment from the insurance company in the event of production risk. Five, crop insurance has relevance for improving agricultural technology as with the security of insurance, farmers might be more willing to experiment with new technology. Six, agricultural insurance is an efficient instrument and an institutionalised mechanism for dealing with problems of natural calamities like drought, flood, etc., rather than providing ad hoc aid or relief measures (UNCATD, 1994).

In a country like India, where agricultural production has been subjected to vagaries of weather and large-scale damages due to attack of pests and diseases, agricultural insurance has to assume the role of a very vital institution for the stable growth of the sector. However, the country has failed miserably in this area as, till recently, the Government did not pay much attention on developing a well-designed agricultural insurance scheme. Suicidal deaths of many farmers in recent years in different parts of the country (especially in Andhra Pradesh and Maharashtra) could have been avoided had there been a well-designed crop insurance scheme. It is true that there had been a crop insurance scheme in India by the name 'Comprehensive Crop Insurance Scheme', which started in 1985. However, it was not comprehensive as its name suggests as its coverage was very limited in terms of crops, areas and sum insured. Table 12.11 shows that the area covered by the scheme is less than one per cent of gross cropped area. However, on account of fixation of premium at unrealistically low levels, the loss ratio was over 300 per cent (average during 1995-96 to 1997-98) in India (higher claims than the premium collected), which is very high in comparison with other developing countries (UNCTAD, 1994).

TABLE – 12.11

Coverage of Comprehensive Crop Insurance Scheme

Season	No. of Farmers Covered (Lakhs)	Area Covered (Lakh hectare)	Sum Insured (Rs. Crore)	Total Insurance Charges (Rs. Crore)	Claims Paid (Rs. Crore)	Loss Ratio* (per cent)
Rabi 1995-96	8.8	12.8	379.7	6.9	16.6	240.6
Kharif 1996	48.5	80.7	1973.4	30.4	151.3	497.7
Rabi 1996-97	10.0	14.0	493.2	8.9	20.7	232.6
Kharif 1997	51.4	83.5	2229.6	34.3	173.0	504.4
Rabi 1997-98	8.7	13.5	400.3	7.2	13.9	193.1
Kharif 1998	52.9	82.1	2444.2	38.3	—	—

*: Loss ratio is claims paid as ratio of total insurance charges (premium).

Source: Report on Currency and Finance, various issues, Reserve Bank of India.

Recently, government introduced a new Scheme titled 'National Agricultural Insurance Scheme' from Rabi 1999-2000. The scheme envisages coverage of all the food crops (cereals and pulses), oilseeds and annual horticultural/commercial crops. The premium rates vary from 1.5 per cent to 3.5 per cent (of sum insured) for food crops and cereals. Small and marginal farmers will be entitled to subsidy of 50 per cent of the premium. However, the government propose to phase out the premium subsidy over a period of 5 years. The Government has also decided to set up an exclusive organisation for implementation of the new scheme in due course.

Fixation of insurance premium at realistic level is essential for the commercial viability of any programme of agricultural insurance. However, in view of the poor financial position of small and marginal cultivators, most of the developing countries are providing subsidy on the premium to be paid by them. Depending upon the fiscal situation, government can give some amount of subsidy for small and marginal farmers. But it needs to be paid directly to the insurance agency so that the agency can work on commercial basis. The subsidy element can be gradually removed once the insurance programme becomes successful. Ideally, along with the privatisation of the insurance sector, private participation in crop insurance has to be encouraged so that it would not create a burden on the government. In countries like Mexico and Venezuela private insurance companies have been successful in crop insurance. While privatising, to ensure fairness, government can fix the premium and other related conditions without discouraging the interest of the agency. The advantage of private insurance is their operational flexibility to deal with the needs of the sector and to evolve or modify product design to meet the demands of the farmers. The experience of various countries in agricultural insurance reveals that delivery and servicing costs are high and it in turn inhibiting its expansion. Therefore, it is essential to evolve strategies to minimise the cost. One of the ways to reduce the administrative costs could be to establish links with other agencies such as credit institutions, trade associations and marketing boards so that their infrastructural facilities could be used for servicing the insurance provided.

Here it may be noted that crop insurance is not a panacea for the problems of the agricultural sector. It can not increase productivity and is not a substitute for effective network of extension services, supply of inputs, provision of storage and marketing facilities (UNCTAD, 1994). Crop insurance need to be considered as only one among the various alternatives available for reducing the difficulties of the farming community. A long-term solution for the instabilities in farm income has to be found in diversification of cropping pattern, development of non-farm sector, which is integrated with the farm sector, and provision of adequate extension services to tackle calamities at the earliest without much damage to the crops. In this context, farm co-operatives can take care of some of the adversities and, hence, they need to be promoted. Here it may be mentioned that Crop insurance covers only production risk and not market risk arising out of fluctuations in prices and unremunerative prices. Therefore, direct government intervention is needed to tackle the problem of price fluctuations. Development of futures market also can impart some element of stability to market prices (UNCTAD, 1994).

On crop insurance, the following priority tasks are identified:

- Enhance the coverage of agricultural insurance scheme to the entire production process including post-harvest storage and processing.
- Integration of agricultural insurance with credit institutions.
- Encourage private participation in crop insurance

2.5 Globalisation

We now come to the role of the government in the context of opening up of Indian agriculture to global markets. At the theoretical level, globalisation of a sector of an economy means its total integration with the rest of the world without any controls/restrictions. Globalisation encompasses both free imports and exports (total outward orientation) and the convergence of domestic prices with the international prices. The objectives of globalisation are to improve the allocative efficiency of resources and orient production based on the comparative advantage of the country. In Indian context, globalisation involves reduction of import duties on the highly protected manufacturing sector and freeing agricultural exports and imports. It is argued that this process will turn the terms of trade in favour of agriculture and improve the relative incentive environment for agriculture and thereby inviting higher private investments (Gulati, 1998). From a historical perspective, it can be observed that till the late eighties agricultural sector in India was relatively closed as the export orientation was confined to only some commercial crops like spices, tea, coffee, etc. and imports were largely restricted. However, during the period since then the degree of export orientation increased considerably with the removal of some of the restrictions/controls on export of commodities. Till recently, imports of agricultural commodities have been largely restricted with quantitative restrictions and high level of tariffs. As on April 1, 2000, import of around 700 items belonging to the agricultural sector were subjected to quantitative restrictions. However, a significant step has been taken for the liberalisation of imports in the Export-Import Policy of 2000-01 with the removal of QRs on 228 agricultural items. The important items on which the QRs have been removed are dairy products, flours of cereals, coffee, tea and tobacco. Here it may be noted that even after the removal of QRs, India can restrict the import of agricultural commodities by fixing higher import duties, as tariff commitment on most of these agricultural items, which India has submitted to the WTO, are very high, except in case of some items like rice, skimmed milk powder, etc. (Mehta, 2000, NCAER, 2000).

The share of agricultural exports in GDP (both in total GDP and GDP originated in agriculture) would indicate three major aspects, namely, i) the degree of openness or outward-orientation of the agricultural sector in regard to the export activity; ii) the nature of agricultural trade strategies adopted in the country; and iii) supply capacity of the agricultural sector as regards exports. An analysis of these aspects is carried out based on Table 12.12. It can be noted from the Table that after a marginal rise in the shares of agricultural exports in total GDP and in GDP originated through the agricultural sector during the seventies, the

TABLE – 12.12

Share of Agricultural Exports in GDP in India

(Rs.crore at current prices)

	1970-71	1980-81	1990-91	1995-96	1998-99
1. GDP (Total)	39708	122427	477814	1006286	1612383
2. GDP in Agriculture*	16821	42466	135162	255613	428680
3. GDP-Rest of the Economy@	22887	79961	342652	750673	1183703
4. Total Exports	1535	6711	32558	106353	141604
5. Agricultural Exports	487	2057	6019	20344	25225
6. Exports-Rest of the Economy@@	1048	4654	26539	86009	116379
Per cent Share					
a) % of Agri.Exports in GDP (Total)	1.2	1.7	1.3	2.0	1.6
b) % of Agri.Exports in GDP Agri.	2.9	4.8	4.5	8.0	5.9
c) % of Total Exports in GDP (Total)	3.9	5.5	6.8	10.6	8.8
d) % of Exports from the rest of Economy in GDP Agriculture	4.6	5.8	7.7	11.5	9.8

Note: * : GDP originated in agriculture, forestry and fishery
@ : Total GDP minus the GDP originated in agriculture.
@@ : Total Exports minus the export of agricultural products.

Source: 1. National Accounts Statistics, various issues, CSO, New Delhi.
2. Economic Survey, various issues, Government of India, New Delhi.

shares were on the decline in the eighties. However, since the beginning of the nineties there is a perceptible rise in the shares: the share in total GDP rose from 1.3 per cent in 1990-91 to 2.0 per cent in 1995-96 but since then it declined to 1.6 per cent in 1998-99. In case of the share of agricultural exports in GDP originated from the agricultural sector, the rise was from 4.5 per cent to 8.0 per cent and then decelerated to 5.9 per cent, during the above period. From the above observations, it can be inferred that the degree of openness or outward orientation of the agricultural sector, with regard to exports, has increased in recent times, albeit a marginal decline occurred since 1995-96. It reflects the effects of the liberalisation of agricultural exports and improvement in the supply capacity of the economy in recent times (Chart 12.7). Table 12.5 further reveals that agricultural sector is less outward-oriented than the economy as a whole. This is evident from the share of total exports from India in GDP (total). The share was 8.8 per cent in 1998-99, which is higher than the share of agricultural exports in GDP originated from the agricultural sector at 5.9 per cent.

CHART – 12.7

Per cent of Agri. Exports in GDP

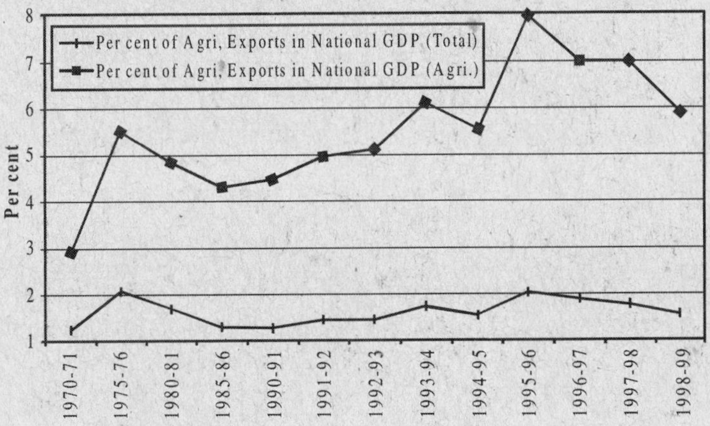

From a phase of gradual export orientation, the agricultural sector in India is likely to enter into a new phase of globalisation with the implementation of the various provisions of WTO (as and when they are made applicable to India). Here it is worthwhile to note that there is no country in the world which has globalised its agricultural sector in the true sense of the term. Even in the advanced market economy countries, agricultural sector is relatively protected. However, with the implementation of the various provisions of WTO agreement, especially the provisions relating to removal of quantitative restrictions, it is expected that a beginning will be made in this direction.

What will be the implication of globalisation of agriculture sector? To find an answer to the above question, here we offer the findings from empirical studies on the subject: A study by Subramanian (1993) revealed that with the liberalisation of trade the movement of terms of trade against agricultural can be moderated. Trade liberalisation will lead to higher price transmission elasticities for all unprocessed commodities except coarse cereals. The author, however, cautioned against extending trade liberalisation to commodities such as edible oils, sugar and processed food as they are highly protected and in cases of those commodities whose per capita availability is low. Parikh, et al., (1995) revealed the following: i) trade liberalisation in the medium run increases allocative efficiency within the agriculture sector and between agricultural and non-agricultural sectors, ii) agricultural liberalisation increases output of all agricultural commodities except coarse grains and other foods, iii) liberalisation leads to higher volume of exports of all agricultural goods, except coarse grains and iv) prices of several agricultural commodities, which were disprotected, would rise with trade liberalisation. Gulati and Sharma (1997), in terms of resource use efficiency (RUE), found that area and production of rice, wheat, maize, sorghum, chickpea and cotton are likely to expand when the international trade in agriculture is completely liberalised. On the other hand, groundnut, rapeseed-mustard and sunflower may have to face deceleration in their future expansion if trade is opened up (there may even be a contraction). Chand (1998) found that imports to India would not be attractive in case of rice, tea, sunflower oil and cotton. There was a strong possibility of rise in imports of sugar and edible oils after the removal of QRs. The study observed that dismantling the trade barriers on imports would increase volatility of Indian prices and farm incomes. On the positive side, the removal of QRs would promote competition in the domestic market, which in turn would be beneficial to the consumers. Gulati (1998) found that globalisation of the economy, including agriculture, offers an opportunity to correct the anti-agriculture bias in Indian trade policies that have been in existence since 1950s. The study further revealed that agriculture could move on to a higher growth trajectory if supply side bottlenecks are freed, and a protective cover is accorded to the poor. Bharadwaj, et al, (1998) found that opening up of the economy was likely to benefit the agriculture and agro-based industries.

In the light of the findings of the above studies, we identify the following issues to be addressed in the context of globalisation of the agricultural sector. They are: i) self-sufficiency in production, ii) price stability, iii) cropping pattern iv) adverse effects on weaker sections and v) WTO commitments. These issues are examined below.

Theoretically, if a country globalises its agricultural sector, it cannot achieve the objective of self-sufficiency in production. This is because of the fact that with globalisation, countries will be forced to concentrate on production of those commodities in which they have comparative advantage in production. For countries like India, with large population and lower purchasing power, the impact of globalisation on availability of food at relatively lower prices is of concern both politically and ethically. Hence, food self-sufficiency at the national level, not necessarily 100 per cent, is desirable so that the reliance on trade can be kept within limits (Parikh, 1999). Undue concentration on production of some agricultural commodities in the long-term may create serious consequences for the quality of land, ecológical balance and employment opportunities. The experience of Punjab and Haryana on account of undue specialisation in the production of rice and wheat is an example in this respect (ICAR, 1998). In view of the likely consequences, it may not be desirable to globalise the sector entirely. Rather, we need to judiciously globalise the sector so as to avoid the undesirable outcomes.

Another issue related to globalisation is the likely price instability in the domestic market due to the convergence of domestic prices with the international prices. Literature indicates that given the high level of instability of commodity prices in the international market, mainly due to variations in crop production and speculative nature of the market, it is quite likely that prices of commodities in the domestic market will be highly unstable which will adversely affect both the producers and the consumers. Hence, dismantling of trade barriers is likely to increase volatility of domestic prices and farm incomes (Nayyar and Sen, 1994). Further, domestic prices will be more volatile when there is an incidence of dumping by countries having bumper harvest (Chand, 1998). Therefore, due precaution has to be taken in case of large-scale import of agricultural commodities.

Freeing trade in agricultural commodities is likely to change the cropping pattern in the country depending upon the level of comparative advantage in the production of commodities. As India has comparative advantage in production of commodities like rice, wheat, maize, sorghum, chickpea and cotton (Gulati, et al, 1994), trade liberalisation will increase their exports, which in turn may lead to expansion of area under these crops. At present, these crops are disprotected or indirectly taxed due to the restriction on exports. However, with liberalisation of trade these commodities will be able to get higher prices and that may promote larger cultivation. However, in case of oilseeds there may be a deceleration in their future expansion as they are not having comparative advantage and they have been getting much higher level of incentives than what they are likely to get under a free-trade scenario (Gulati and Sharma, 1997). With liberalisation of agricultural trade the country can import oilseeds at lower price than the domestic price. Hence, achieving self-sufficiency in oilseeds production may not be desirable given the huge cost involved in it.

Globalisation of the sector may have its adverse effects on certain areas, some crops and some group of people. It has been indicated in the literature that with export promotion and globalisation, the benefits will be accrued to only some areas which are well endowed in terms of resources, some crops which are having comparative advantage in production and some sections of the population who are producing the exporting commodities. Other areas, crops and people are unlikely to be benefited from the globalisation process (Rao, 1994). In other words, the benefits of globalisation process may not be neutral to areas, crops and people. Further, as globalisation may raise the prices of some of the essential commodities, it will have adverse welfare consequences for the people who are not engaged in the agricultural sector.

The country's commitment to WTO, which in a way may facilitate the process of globalisation, is likely to have some consequences for the sector. Currently, the commitment for reduction of subsidy may not affect the quantum of subsidy given to the farmers. However, once the exemptions provided to the developing countries are withdrawn, there can be some pressure for reduction of subsidy, especially the subsidy for food procurement and its distribution through the PDS. The commitments for removal of QRs and reducing the import duty and also for increasing the quantum of imports are likely to increase imports and depress the domestic prices, especially of those commodities in which India does not enjoy comparative advantage.

Despite some of the trade liberalisation measure, foodgrains sector still remains largely controlled and insulated from the global markets, in view of the food security objective. In case of cash crops, exports are allowed when there is enough surplus and are imported when there is a net deficit. Hence, there is a view that agricultural trade is still taking place as a 'residual' between domestic demand and supply rather than as a policy instrument to integrate domestic agriculture with the world agriculture (Gulati, 1998). Ideally, agricultural export and import policies should move in tandem so as to avoid any distortions in domestic prices. However, during the last few years while the agricultural exports have been liberalised, restriction/controls on imports have remained more or less unchanged (Jeromi, 1999). While the liberalisation of exports resulted in rise in domestic prices of some of the commodities (example, onion and potato), the restriction on imports denied access to commodities from abroad. This miss-match in agricultural export-import policy was on account of the undue obsession to remain self-sufficient in all agricultural commodities. However, given the fact that no country in the world can have comparative advantage in production of all the commodities required by it, the restrictions on imports in the face of liberalisation of exports will not be beneficial in a liberalised economic environment (Chand, 1998). Hence, there is a need to continue with the liberalisation of trade in agricultural commodities so as to provide a level playing field for the agricultural sector with the industrial sector. The removal of QRs on some of the agricultural commodities announced in the Export-Import Policy 2000-01 would greatly reduce the miss-match in the policies.

The following priority tasks are identified for the government to help Indian agriculture adjust to globalisation:

- Food self-sufficiency at the national level is desirable so that the reliance on trade can be kept within limits.
- Safetynets are needed to protect the interests of crops, people and regions which are likely to be affected by globalisation.
- Precautions on imports in view of the removal of quantitative restrictions.
- Agricultural export policies need to be synchronised with the import policies to avoid price fluctuations. There is a need for sequencing of measures. In view of the removal of quantitative restriction in the coming days, tariffication process needs to be done judiciously.

2.6 Watershed Development

According to Planning Commission (1997b) about 9.6 million hectares of arable land and 6.9 million hectares of non-arable land have been treated under various watershed programmes. There are still about 60 million hectares of arable land and 15 million hectares of non-arable land which remain to be covered. Studies reveals that watershed development programmes undertaken thus far, have a mixed story of success and failure. The impact assessment shows a great degree of variation in achievement from project to project, depending on location, level and nature of community participation, caste and class structure, land tenure, nature of technology propagated, institutional arrangements, infrastructure, research, as well as extension and training support, etc. Several watershed projects have helped improve soil moisture, cropping intensity, crop yields and employment. [Nagaraja (1996), Deshpande and Reddy (1991)].

The experience of some successful watershed projects in India and abroad shows that people's effective participation in the planning, execution, monitoring and maintenance of project is essential for success. The government should create a proper legal and political environment for people's effective participation, including those of women and the landless. But it should be basically a people's programme, the role of government being limited to providing only technical guidance, basic infrastructure and limited finance, if necessary. Women have an important role in maintaining the household livelihood system. In poor families, they are largely responsible for collection of food, fuel & fodder. Therefore, involvement of women in Watershed Development Programme would be crucial. Further, NGOs are generally considered better than bureaucracies for enlisting people's participation in watershed development. Their role is to organise training for self-help groups and also to create awareness among the people for watershed management for sustainable development. Ralegaon Siddhi, MYRADA and several other voluntary organisations have effectively demonstrated the positive role of NGO's in watershed development. Panchayat Raj Institutions can play a vital role in watershed development. However, Panchayat Acts of various states do not specifically assign any role to the panchayats for implementation of watershed projects. There is need for an effective devolution of responsibilities, finances and administrative powers to panchayats for the purpose. Particularly, the assets and infrastructure created in watersheds must be maintained by Panchayats (Planning Commission, 1997b).

At present watershed development and soil conservation have been treated as a sectoral activity of erosion control. This need to be changed and follow a holistic approach, encompassing land, water, animal and human resources to meet the water and bio-mass needs of the people on sustainable basis. The emphasis should change from mere soil conservation to land husbandry. The potentials of all farm and non-farm activities for the creation of adequate livelihood, income and employment opportunities in each watershed should be explored and utilised. Besides, the watershed development programmes would gradually shift from Centre to State or even local bodies and ultimately the people themselves should plan, execute and maintain them (Planning Commission, 1997b).

Planning Commission (1997b) estimates show that the area available for treatment in the next 25 years would be 60 million hectares of arable land and 15 million hectares of non-arable land. Hence, to cover the entire treatable area of 75 million hectares in about 25 years in a phased manner, about 12 million hectares of arable land and 3 million hectares of non-arable land to be treated in each Five Year Plan. This would require the Government to spend at least Rs. 7,780 crore and another Rs.13,070 crore by the people at constant prices (Table 12.13).

It is necessary to point out here that although the short term objectives of different watershed programmes vary widely, the overall long-term objective of all such programmes is to improve the livelihood system of rural people in rainfed areas through i) improvement in environment/ ecology by conserving and developing natural resources namely, land, water, perennial vegetation etc., ii) improvement in production and productivity of crops, animals, trees etc. and iii) improvement in income and employment opportunities for the people, particularly the landless poor and women.

TABLE – 12.13

Physical and Financial Targets of Perspective Plan for Watershed Development

Plan Period	Area to be covered by (Million hectare)		Cost Per Hectare (Rs.)	Total Cost at 1994-95 Prices (Rs. Crore)		
	Govt.	People's Initiative		Govt.	People	Total
9th Plan	10	5	3000	3000	1500	4500
10th Plan	7	8	3000	2100	2400	4500
11th Plan	5	10	2800	1400	2800	4200
12th Plan	3	12	2600	780	3120	3900
13th Plan	2	13	2500	500	3250	3750
Total	27	48	—	7780	13070	20850

Source: Planning Commission (1997b).

In case of watershed development, the following aspects need to be considered:

- Development and diffusion of appropriate location specific technologies and infrastructure, with people's participation in various rainfed areas.
- Watershed programmes should be more people oriented and panchayats should be actively encouraged with financial and administrative powers.

2.7 Research and Development

Besides land and water resources, one of the major issues relating to overcoming limits to growth is the low productivity of Indian agriculture. There is a view that productivity levels in India have reached a plateau, especially in the green revolution areas (Rao and Gulati, 1994). To an extent this is evident from the deceleration in the growth rates of yields of most of the crops during the nineties. This has serious implications for the future growth of agricultural production, especially in view of the almost stagnation in area under cultivation and the resultant deceleration in production growth during the nineties (Table 12.14).

TABLE – 12.14

Trend Growth Rate of Area, Production and Yield of Important Crops*

(Per cent per annum)

Crops	Area		Production		Yield	
	80's	90's	80's	90's	80's	90's
I. All Crops	0.1	0.4	3.2	2.2	2.6	1.4
II. Foodgrains	-0.2	-0.1	2.9	1.8	2.7	1.4
III. Non-Foodgrains	1.1	1.5	3.8	3.3	2.3	1.4
i. Rice	0.3	0.5	3.6	1.9	3.2	1.3
ii. Wheat	0.5	1.7	3.6	3.1	3.1	1.6
iii. Coarse Cereals	-1.4	-1.8	0.4	0.2	1.7	2.0
iv. Pulses	-0.1	-0.2	1.5	1.0	1.6	1.7
v. Oilseeds	2.4	0.8	5.5	3.4	2.9	2.6
vi. Sugarcane	1.5	1.8	2.7	2.5	1.2	0.7
vii. Cotton	-1.3	3.3	2.8	1.7	4.1	-2.0

Notes: *: Estimated based on semi-log regression equation.
-: 80's cover the period 1980-81 to 1989-90.
-: In case of production, 90s cover 1990-91 to 1999-2000. In case of area and yield 90's cover the period 1990-91 to 1998-99.

Though India is one among the major producers of agricultural commodities in the world, the yield levels, here, for a number of commodities like paddy, wheat, groundnut, cotton, jute, etc., are far lower than the yield levels in major producing countries and in case of some crops it is even lower than the world average (Table 12.15).

Since there is hardly any scope for further expansion of area under cultivation, the future production prospects depends largely on the improvements in the yield levels. Here what we need is to break the yield barrier and bridge the gap between the potential and actual yield through research and development (R&D) efforts. ICAR studies reveals that there is vast unexplored technological potential for improvement in the yield of crops. In this context, Swaminathan (1999) noted that the "low yield phenomena" in India should be considered as a "yield reservoir" and it should be treated as an asset for future development of the sector. Exploiting the "yield reservoir", inter alia, require substantial investment and development and deployment of high yielding seed varieties. So far the emphasis has been on the use of HYV seeds, but it loses it vigour with time. Therefore, new varieties need to be developed periodically to expand production possibilities. However, agricultural research establishment could not come up with improved varieties of seeds, which are suited to different regions of the country, especially in drought prone areas. Therefore, the country has to built up a vital research system which is responsive to the changing needs and circumstances (Parikh, 1999). Compared to other countries, India's efforts in this direction, in terms of provision of resources, is insufficient. India is investing only around 0.3 per cent of GDP in agriculture for agricultural research, as against 0.7 per cent in the developing countries and 2-3 per cent in case of developed countries (Evenson, et al, 1999). Expenditure on agricultural research and education accelerated during the post-green revolution period of the 1970s, but slowed down since the mid-80s and it hovered around 0.49 per cent of agricultural GDP in the early 1990s, which was lower than the requirement of 1.0 per cent projected by the ICAR. Further, the level of research expenditure was sub-optimal or significantly lower than desired in states like Bihar, Orissa, Madhya Pradesh, Uttar Pradesh and West Bengal where productivity is low. Crop-wise, research expenditure was low in case of rice, certain coarse cereals, pulses and oilseeds (Pal, *et al*, 1997).

In India research support for the agricultural sector is provided by i) governmental agencies, ii) international agricultural research centres, iii) imported technology and iv) private Indian research. India is considered as having the largest public agricultural research establishments in the world (Evenson, et al, 1999). Indian Council of Agricultural Re-

TABLE – 12.15

Yield of Important Crops in Major Producing Countries in 1997

(Kg./ha.)

Paddy		Wheat		Groundnut		Sugarcane		Cotton		Jute	
Country	Yield	Country	Yield	Country	Yield	Country	Yield	Country	Yield	Country	Yield
China	6331	China	4087	China	2574	Brazil	69021	China	943	Banga.	1577
Indonesia	4561	France	6530	Nigeria	1124	China	75982	USA	769	China	2517
Pakistan	2827	USA	2673	USA	2828	Thailand	55878	Pakistan	552	Thailand	3548
Philippi.	2933	Australia	1712	Indonesia	1519	Mexico	72734	Turkey	1065	Myanmar	939
Thailand	2143	Canada	2128	Sudan	762	Australia	97337	Argentina	368	Brazil	1714
India	2915	India	2654	India	988	India	69737	India	321	India	1830
World	3827	World	2686	World	1273	World	63324	World	584	World	1734
India % Of World	76.2		98.8		77.6		110.1		55.0		105.5

Source: Production Yearbook, Food and Agricultural Organisation, 1997.

search (ICAR) and agricultural universities constitute the main part of governmental agencies. However, they suffer from several weaknesses like i) uneven progress of varietal improvement across crops and regions, ii) neglect of crop systems research, iii) unimpressive results of local adaptive research, iv) inadequacy of collaborative multi-disciplinary research, v) weak interaction between researchers, extension workers and farmers; vi) excessive centralisation of planning and monitoring, vii) lack of accountability for performance, etc. (Vaidyanathan, 2000). Studies show that public research and extension have been the major sources of increase in the total factor productivity in Indian agriculture during the post-green revolution period. Estimates indicate a very high return to investment in public research (Rao and Gulati, 1994, and Evenson, et al, 1999). Therefore, for achieving greater gains, public investment in research and extension needs to be increased.

Along with public sector, private sector also engages in extensive research and development. It has been reported that expenditures on agricultural research and development in the private sector are approximately half of those expenditures in the public sector. Crop management (mainly in plantations) and processing technology has been the areas on which the private sector research concentrated (Evenson, et al, 1999). Along with public sector, private sector needs to be encouraged to take up R and D activities in the frontier areas like biotechnology. However, the associated issues like threat to sustainable agriculture, access and sharing of genetic resources, and the larger issue of importance of agriculture for eradication of poverty by providing nutritional security are to be addressed while encouraging private participation (Sharma, 2000). Two major areas on which R&D efforts needed are i) genetic resource management and biotechnology, and ii) natural resource management and agro-ecology. World over the focus is on biotechnology. On the need for bio-technology, Rao and Gulati (1994) observed that the tool of bio-technology, including genetic engineering and tissue culture offer possibilities for breaking the yield barriers, especially in the unfavourable agro-climatic regions.

In the light of the discussion in this section, we identify the following priority tasks for research and development.

- Greater public investment in R&D.
- Encourage private sector participation in frontier areas like natural resource management and biotechnology.

2.8 Development of Non-Farm Sector

Till seventies, the significance of Non-Farm Sector (NFS) in generating employment and income to the rural households did not receive adequate attention in India. This is mainly due to the excessive focus on the growth of formal sectors and relegated the informal sector to the background. In the seventies, however, it was realised that the development of formal sectors could not take care of the increasing rural unemployment and underemployment and development economists and policy makers started looking for solutions inside the rural areas themselves. As a result, development of NFS received the attention of policy makers as an alternative strategy for rural development (Chadha, 1993).

It is being pointed out that the future impetus for development of the rural economy has to come from an expanding rural non-farm activities (Mahajan, 1993). Therefore, NFS need to be developed for creation of employment opportunities and earnings for the rural households, especially the weaker sections. According to the agriculture-led -growth theories, another role of NFS is to stimulate agricultural growth through inter-sectoral linkages. A vibrant modern agricultural sector is based on strong forward and backward linkages with the industry and the NFS (Mellor, 1976). Besides, rural non-farm activities can also play an important role in containing large-scale rural-urban migration (Chadha, 1993).

Recent expansion of the non-farm sector in India is influenced by the rising commercialisation in the rural economy. This is evident from the changing proportion of non-farm employment more and more in favour of wage-paid labourers indicating shift in production/service activities from the households to non-household ventures. It has been found that landless labourers and sub-marginal cultivating households, which account for 55 per cent of total rural households, are the prominent job seekers in the NFS due to their assetlessness or near assetlessness (Chadha 1993). The proportion of male workers in non-agriculture is more than females in all the states except in Punjab where the participation of females in non-farm activities is much more than that of males (Balasubramanian, et al, 1994). It may be noted that besides the above three broad category of factors, the growth of NFS in India is also contributed by the various government programmes like IRDP, Nehru Rozgar Yojana, etc. for employment generation and poverty alleviation.

Strong backward linkages with the agricultural sector and forward linkages with the modern manufacturing sector are imperative for the growth and prosperity of the non-farm sector. Literature on Indian experience reveals that there exist weak production inter- linkages, the reason being the surplus labour in the economy (Vaidyanathan, 1986). The reasons for the weak production linkages can be found in (a) production of most of the modern inputs except perhaps repair services are in the urban areas and (b) agro-processing units may not be operating in the rural areas, even if they are working they may not provide much employment due to high capital intensity.

Credit is one of the most important inputs required for the activities in the NFS but its availability both for fixed and working capital has been a problem area both in terms of cost and availability. Within the overall scenario of rural credit, credit needs of the NFS received some attention in recent years. Nevertheless, because of the limited reach of the formal financial institutions especially to interior villages and small producers, private channels of credit continue to play an important role in spite of high cost (Eapen, 1996). Therefore, increasing attention needs to be given by bankers to the requirements of the NFS (Vyasulu and Kumar 1994). Experiences of other countries have shown that rural financial institutions are shifting their focus to non-farm activities as they are found to be more viable. SHGs can be a feasible intermediaries to finance non-farm activities.

Given the development of agriculture and allied activities, infrastructure availability, institutional set up and availability of credit, NFS in India has the promise of becoming the most dynamic part of the economy, which can take care of the ill effects of marginalisation process in the sector. To develop this sector on a sustainable basis appropriate policies need to be formulated, institutions needs to be revamped, credit needs to be met and marketing and technological skills upgraded.

From the above discussion, we suggest the following priority tasks for a policy agenda for agriculture to counter the marginalisation process operating in agriculture.

- Development of a sound and enduring non-farm sector is needed for creation of employment in the rural sector.
- Credit requirements of NFS need to be met by financial institutions. SHGs can be feasible intermediaries to finance non-farm activities.

MODERNISATION OF AGRICULTURE: THE PRIORITIES AT A GLANCE

Towards Self-regulation

- The constitution of the District Planning Committees (DPC) should be completed as soon as possible and the DPCs should commence the work allotted to them. Even in a state like Karnataka which has been keen to activate and support PRIs, DPCs have not been constituted so far.
- Once the DPCs become active, there will be pressure at the state level to make the necessary changes in the planning system. Meanwhile, internalisation of ACRP into state plans may be completed in all the remaining states.
- Change over from the MSP operations to market intervention operations undertaken by an autonomous organisation having the necessary market expertise and freedom to operate on commercial principles without political/administrative interference.
- Promotion of exports would need improvements in infrastructure, modernisation of facilities, rationalisation of rules and procedures and a stable export policy rather than the stop-go type familiar in cases like cotton. We expect that these promotional measures would get implemented in the course of adoption of ACRP approach to stimulate agricultural growth.
- As regards conflicts and clashes of interest with other governments given rise to by arrangements like WTO, the government would have to remain vigilant, make maximum use of opportunities to negotiate for mutually beneficial terms and conditions for trade and take appropriate action to counter or pre-empt hostile moves by other governments or large market operators like multinationals.

Overcoming Limits to Growth

- Building up and maintaining an updated data base on the extent of land and water resources, their location, present status, potentialities, ownership, use, regulation and control. PRIs should be given the primary responsibility for collecting, recording and verifying data. Remote sensing and other advanced technologies should be used to explore the potentialities of the resources and to complement the collection of data at the ground level.

- Preparing a detailed perspective plan to extend irrigation as quickly as possible to make full use of the ultimate potential.
- Ensuring that the market, institutional and policy environment, are conducive to conservation-oriented and judicious use of land and water resources. Economic sanity should be restored to administered pricing, user charges and government operations like procurement, storage and distribution of foodgrains. Micro-level decision-makers like producers and consumers should get signals consistent with the social objective of conservation and economic use of valuable but scarce resources like land and water.
- It is hoped that, given the right environment, schemes for improving degraded lands in green revolution areas and the watershed development strategy in the drought-prone areas would be able to take rapid strides provided the problems of institutional arrangements, procedures and personnel are tackled in right earnest.
- As we approach the limits of land and water resources, search for a technology appropriate to the emerging situation should be intensified. Experts suggest that biotechnology would be a promising field to explore. Attention must also be paid to technologies available in research stations but not reaching farms.

Promoting Human Development

- Broad based agricultural growth and diversification would stimulate value-adding activities like processing and preparing specialist items with large demand. There would be growth in productive employment opportunities but the workers in agriculture would have to be trained for the new skills and occupations. In the light of the experience gained so far in programmes like TRYSEM run by the government and similar activities of NGOs, attempt should be made to look ahead to identify the promising opportunities in different areas and to anticipate in advance the training and other assistance which could help the workers in agriculture to benefit from these emerging employment opportunities.
- Rise in rural incomes and the formation of a relatively better off middle strata in the rural communities would generate wide ranging demands for goods and services. The consequential rise in employment opportunities needs to be kept in mind while

planning the training and other assistance to be given to the workers in agriculture.

- There is a trend towards the rural-urban continuum becoming more connected with quicker and smoother flow of people and goods. This trend needs to be supported so that village economies remaining relatively isolated from the mainstream get more firmly linked with it. Ideally, rural communities should have bustling commuting zone around them for employment, for marketing their products and for purchasing inputs. This would check the flow of migrants to urban slums and flight of talent from villages. It would also help in obtaining a more even and balanced spatial spread of economic and other social activities.

Critical Policies: Capital Formation

- Capital formation in the public sector should be augmented. Money saved from the reduction in subsidy for agricultural inputs should be utilised for this purpose.
- In view of the resource constraints, capital formation requirements need to be prioritised. As ACRP gets operationalised, it would be possible to do prioritisation in a rational manner.
- Inter-state variations in capital formation need to be reduced.
- Delays in disbursement of funds under RIDF should be eliminated.

Agricultural Credit

- Increase the outreach of the formal financial institutions, especially to the small and marginal farmers.
- Continuation of credit targeting for ensuring adequacy of credit in the agricultural sector.
- Progressively link SHGs with formal credit institutions for reducing transaction cost and high recovery.

Agricultural Insurance

- Enhance the coverage of agricultural insurance scheme to the entire production process including post-harvest storage and processing.
- Integration of agricultural insurance with credit institutions.
- Encourage private participation in crop insurance

Globalisation

- Food self-sufficiency at the national level is desirable so that the reliance on trade can be kept within limits.
- Safetynets are needed to protect the interests of crops, people and regions which are likely to be affected by globalisation.
- Precautions on imports are necessary in view of the removal of quantitative restrictions.
- Agricultural export policies need to be synchronised with the import policies to avoid price fluctuations. There is a need for sequencing of measures. In view of the removal of quantitative restriction in the coming days, tariffication process needs to be done judiciously.

Watershed Development

- Watershed programmes should be more people oriented and panchayats should be actively encouraged with financial and administrative powers.
- Development and diffusion of appropriate location specific technologies and infrastructure, with people's participation in various rainfed areas.

Research Development

- Greater public investment in research and development.
- Encourage private sector participation in frontier areas like natural resource management and biotechnology.

Non-Farm Sector

- Development of a sound and enduring non-farm sector for creation of employment in the rural sector.
- Credit requirements of NFS need to be met by financial institutions. SHGs can be feasible intermediaries to finance non-farm activities.

References*

ACRPU (1999), *Proceedings of the Tenth Annual Meeting of the Agro-climatic Regional Planning Project*, Agro-climatic Regional Planning Unit, Sardar Patel Institute of Economic and Social Research, Ahmedabad.

Ahluwalia, D. (1992), "*Public Distribution of Food in India: Issues and Evidence*", Mimeo, SAUNA, World Bank, Washington.

Alagh, Yoginder K. (1997), "Agricultural Investment and Growth", Inaugural Address to the 56th Annual Conference of the Indian Society of Agricultural Economics, Kerala Agriculture University, Trichur.

——— (1997), "Agricultural Development in India: Issues, Policies and Projects", Rajiv Gandhi Institute for Contemporary Studies, New Delhi.

——— (1999), "Agricultural Policy in the Ninth Plan", Hans E. Karl and B.J. Nanjundappa Memorial Endowment Lecture, April, Bangalore.

Aziz, Sartaj (1990), *Agricultural Policies for the 1990s*, Development Centre of the Organisation for Economic Co-operation and Development, Paris, pp.45-73.

Balasubramanian N., *et al*, (1994), *Rural Industrialisation in India - Structure and Determinants of Non-Farm Employment in Rural India*, (monograph), RBI Endowment Unit, Institute for Social and Economic Change, Bangalore.

Balakrishnan, Pulapre (2000), "Agriculture and Economic Reforms-Growth and Welfare", Economic and Political Weekly, March 18, pp.999-1004.

Bhalla, G.S. (1994), "*Globalization and Agricultural Policy in India*", Presidential Address, 54th Annual Conference of Indian Society of Agricultural Economics, *Indian Journal of Agricultural Economics*, Vol.50, No.1, January-March, pp.7-26.

Bhalla, G.S., *et al*, (1999), "*Prospects for India's Cereal Supply and Demand to 2020*", Discussion Paper 29, International Food Policy Research Institute, Washington.

Bhatia, M.S. (1999), "Rural Infrastructure and Growth in Agriculture", *Economic and Political Weekly*, March 27, pp. A-43-48.

Bharadwaj, R. *et al.*, (1998), The Impact of the Uruguay Round on Growth and Structure of Indian Economy, Study No.17, *Development Research Group*, Reserve Bank of India, Mumbai, pp.1-80.

Bhende, M.J. and V.S. Satyapriya (1996), Farming System Approach in the Context of ACRP in Karnataka, Institute for Social and Economic Change, Bangalore.

Bhide, Shashanka, *et al*, (1998), "India's Agricultural Dynamics- Weak Links in Development", *Economic and Political Weekly*, September 26, pp. A-118-127.

Blarcom, Bonni van, *et al*, (1993), "The Reform of Public Expenditures for Agriculture", *World Bank Discussion Paper*, No.216, World Bank, Washington.

Chand, Ramesh (1998), "Removal of Import Restrictions and India's Agriculture, The Challenge and Strategy", *Economic and Political Weekly*, April 11, pp.850-854.

——— (1999), "Emerging Crisis in Punjab Agriculture- Severity and Options for Future", *Economic and Political Weekly*, March, 27, pp. A-2-10.

---

* Besides the literature cited in the text of the paper, there are several recent writings which could be of interest to researchers and policymakers. An attempt is made here to cover this wider ground.

Chadha G.K. (1993), Non-farm Employment for Rural Households in India: Evidence and Prognosis, *The Indian Journal of Labour Economics*, Vol.36, No.3.

——— (1996), Wastelands in Rural India: Policy Initiatives and Programmes for their Development, *Occasional Paper-2*, National Bank for Agriculture and Rural Development (NABARD), Mumbai.

Deshpande, R.S. and V. Ratna Reddy (1991), *Watershed Development Approach in Fragile Resource Region: An Analytical study of Maharashtra*, Agro-Economic Research Centre, GIPE, Pune, December.

Deshpande, R.S. and Thimmaiah, G. (1999), "Watershed Development Approach and Experience of National Watershed Development Programme in the Country", *Journal of Rural Development*, Vol.18, No.3 (Special Issue on Watershed Development Part-1).

Dhawan B.D. and Yadav, S.S. (1995), "Private Fixed Capital Formation in Agriculture", *Economic and Political Weekly*, Vol.30, No.39, September 30.

Dhawan, B.D. (1996a), "Trends and Determinants of Capital Investments in Agriculture", *Indian Journal of Agricultural Economics*, Vol.51.No.4, October-December.

——— (1996b), "Relationship Between Public and Private Investment in Indian Agriculture with Special Reference to Public Canals", Indian Journal of Agricultural Economics, Vol.51.No.1 and 2, January-June.

Dhawan, B.D. and Yadav, S.S. (1997), "Public Investment in Indian Agriculture: Trends and Determinants", *Economic and Political Weekly*, April 5.

Eapen, Mridul (1996), Rural Non-Farm Employment. Some Reflections on Petty Production, *Economic and Political Weekly*, June 29.

Evenson, Robert E., et al., (1999), *Agricultural Research and Productivity Growth in India*, Research Report 109, International Food Policy Research Institute, Washington.

Food and Agricultural Organisation (1996), *World Food Submit, Technical Background Documents 1-5*, Volume I, FAO, Italy, pp.1-49.

——— (1997), *Production Yearbook*, FAO, Rome.

George, P.S. (1999), "Some Reflections on Food Security in India", Presidential Address delivered at the 59th Annual Conference of the Indian Society of Agricultural Economics, *Indian Journal of Agricultural Economics*, Vol.54.No.4, October-December.

Government of India (1998), *Agricultural Statistics at a Glance*, Directorate of Economics and Statistics, Ministry of Agriculture, New Delhi.

Government of India, *Economic Survey*, various issues, Ministry of Finance, New Delhi.

Guha, G.S. (1997), *Agro-climatic Regional Planning Project, Planning Commission - A Profile*, Agro-climatic Documentation and Dissemination Centre, Agro-climatic Regional Planning Unit, Ahmedabad.

Gulati, Ashok (1998), "Indian Agriculture in an Open Economy: Will it Prosper?", *in India's Economic Reforms and Development,* Essays for Manmohan Singh, Isher Judge Ahluwalia and I.M.D. Little (eds.), Oxford University Press, Delhi, 1998, pp.122-146.

Gulati, Ashok and Anil Sharma (1994), "Agriculture under GATT: What it Holds for India", *Economic and Political Weekly*, July, pp.1857-1863.

Gulati, *et al*, (1994), "*Export Competitiveness of Selected Agricultural Commodities*", NCAER, New Delhi.

Gulati, Ashok and Sharma, Anil (1997), "Freeing Trade in Agriculture: Implications for Resource Use Efficiency and Cropping Pattern Changes", *Economic and Political Weekly*, December 27, pp. A155-164.

Gulati, A. and Kelley T. (1999), *Trade Liberalisation and Indian Agriculture*, Oxford University Press, New Delhi.

Gulati A and Chopra K. (1999), *Reform of the Subsidy Regime: Implications for the Agricultural Sector*, Institute of Economic Growth, Delhi.

Hanumappa, H.G. and Bhende, M.G. (1994), *Planning for Full Employment: Strategies for the Small Farmers Agri-business Consortium - Dharward District* (UNDP Project IND/91/096), M.S.Swaminathan Research Foundation, Chennai and Institute for Social and Economic Change, Bangalore.

Hanumappa, H.G. (1997), Agro-climatic Regions, Decentralisation at District Level: Karnataka Experiment, *IASSI Quarterly*, Vol.15, No.4.

——— (1999), *Watershed Management for Sustainable Development* (a paper presented to National Seminar on Watershed Management for Sustainable development, Department of Economics, S.V. University, Tirupati, March, 11-12).

ICAR (1998), *Declining Crop Productivity in Haryana and Punjab: Myth and Reality*?, Report of the Fact Finding Committee, Indian Council of Agricultural Research, New Delhi.

IIMA (1999), *Impact of WTO Agreement on Indian Agriculture*, Indian Institute of Management, Ahmedabad.

Jeromi, P.D. (1997), "Determinants of India's Agricultural Exports", *Reserve Bank of India Occasional Papers*, Vol. 18, No.1, March, pp.61-81.

——— (1999), *Export Competitiveness of Indian Agriculture*, Ph.D. Thesis (unpublished), Indian Institute of Technology Bombay, Mumbai.

Knudsen, Odin, *et al*, (1990), " Redefining the Role of Government in Agriculture for the 1990s, *World Bank Discussion Papers*, No.105, World Bank Washington.

Kurien, C.T. (1981), *Dynamics of Rural Transformation: A Study in Tamil Nadu 1950-1975*, Orient Logman Ltd., Madras.

Lester Brown (2000), State of the World, 2000, the Hindustan Times Website, January 15.

Lokur, Vasudha (undated), *Ralegaon Siddhi - Rural Transformation through People's Participation*, Sant Yadav Baba Shikshan Prasarak Mandal, Ralegaon Siddhi, Dist. Ahmednagar, Maharashtra.

Mani, K.P., *et al*, (1996), "Some Reflections on the Capital Formation in Indian Agriculture", *Indian Journal of Agricultural Economics*, Vol.51.No.4, October-December.

Mahendra, Dev, S. (1998), "Regional Variations in Agricultural Performance in the Last Two Decades", *Indian Journal of Agricultural Economics*, Vol.53.No.1, January-March.

Mallik, J.K. (1997), "Growth of Agriculture in Independent India: 50 Years and After", *Reserve Bank of India Occasional Papers*, Vol.18, Nos.2 & 3, June-September, pp.145-172.

Mahajan, Vijay (1993), "Non-Farm Development in Rural India Through Institutional Interventions: Do's and Dont's", *The Indian Journal of Labour Economics*, Vol.36, No.3.

Mehta, Rajesh (2000), "Removal of QRs and Impact on India's Imports", *Economic and Political Weekly*, Vol. 35, No.19, May 6-12, pp.1667-1671.

Mellor, J.W. (1976), *The New Economics of Growth: A Strategy for India and the Developing World*, Cornell University Press, Ithaca.

Mishra, S.N. and Ramesh Chand (1995), "Public and Private Capital Formation in Indian Agriculture: Comments on Complementarity Hypothesis and Others", *Economic and Political Weekly*, July, 24, pp. A-64-79.

Mishra, S.N. (1996), "Capital Formation and Accumulation in Indian Agriculture Since Independence", *Indian Journal of Agricultural Economics*, Vol.51, No.1 and 2, January-June.

Mishra, V.N. and Hazell B.R. Peter (1996), "Terms of Trade, Rural Poverty, Technology and Investment: The Indian Experience 1952-53 to 1990-91", *Economic and Political Weekly*, Vol.XXXI, No.13, March 30.

Misra, V.N. (1998), "Economic Reforms, Terms of Trade, Aggregate Supply and Private Investment in Agriculture", *Economic and Political Weekly*, August 1.

Mujumdar, N.A. (1999), "Reviving Rural Credit", *Economic and Political Weekly*, June 19, pp.1577-1579.

NABARD (1999a), *Annual Report 1998-99*, National Bank for Agriculture and Rural Development, Mumbai.

——— (1999b), *Report of the Task Force on Supportive Policy and Regulatory Framework for Microfinance in India- Summary and Recommendations*, Reserve Bank of India Bulletin, December.

Nadkarni, M.V. (1993), "Agricultural Policy in India: Context, Issues and Instruments", Study 5, *Development Research Group*, Department of Economic Analysis and Policy, Reserve Bank of India, December.

Nadkarni M.V. and Govindaru, V. (1995), "Nobody's Child: The Economic and Institutional Aspects of Soil Conservation in India", *Journal of Environment and Development* 4, 1 (winter 1995).

Nagaraja, N. (1996), "People's Participation in Karnataka *Watershed Development Project*", in Watershed Development, edited by Jensen, *et al,* WDCU Publication, 1, 1996.

National Institute of Rural Development (1999). Seminar on Tenancy Reforms: Recommendations of the Seminar.

Nayyar, Deepak and Sen, Abhijit (1994), "International Trade and the Agricultural Sector in India", *Economic and Political Weekly*, May 14, pp.1187-1203.

NCAER (2000), *Review of the Economy*, April 2000, National Council of Applied Economic Research, New Delhi.

NSS (1997), *All-India Debt and Investment Survey, 1991-92- Indebtedness of Rural Households As on 30.6.1991*, Report 2 (Part-1),, NSS Forty-Eighth Round, National Sample Survey Organisation, Government of India.

Pal, Suresh, *et al, (1997), Agricultural Research and Extension in India: Institutional Structure and Investments*, National Centre for Agricultural Economics and Policy Research, New Delhi.

Parikh, K.S., *et al,* (1988), *Towards Free Trade in Agriculture*, Matinus Nijhoff Publishers, Netherlands, pp.1-26.

Parikh, S. Kirit, *et al,* (1995), *Strategies for Agricultural Liberalization: Consequence for Growth, Welfare and Distribution*, Indira Gandhi Institute of Development Research, Bombay.

Parikh, Kirit (1999), "Food and Agricultural Policy: The Challenges Ahead", *Vikalpa*, Vol.24, No.2, April-June, pp.3-10.

Patnaik, Prabhat (1996), "Should Domestic Prices be Equated to World Prices", *Economic and Political Weekly*, Special Number, September, pp.2425-2428.

Pattanaik, Sitikantha (1994), "Hike in Procurement Prices of Agricultural Commodities- View Point", *Reserve Bank of India Occasional Papers*, Vol.15, No.3, September.

Patra, Michael Debabrata (1994), "Hike in Procurement Prices of Agricultural Commodities- View Point", *Reserve Bank of India Occasional Papers*, Vol.15, No.3, September.

Pasha S.A. (1999), *Forest Use and Management: A Comparative Perspective from India and Canada*, Working Paper 49, Institute for Social and Economic Change, Bangalore.

Planning Commission (1997a), *Ninth Five Year Plan, Volume I and II,* Planning Commission, Government of India, New Delhi.

——— (1997b), *Report of the Committee on Twenty Five Years' Perspective Plan for the Development of Rainfed Areas*, Government of India, New Delhi.

——— (1998), *Ninth Five Year Plan 1997-2002, Executive Summary*, Planning Commission, Government of India, New Delhi.

Purohit, B.C. and V. Ratna Reddy (1999), *Capital Formation in Indian Agriculture: Issues and Concerns*, Occasional Papers-8, NABARD, Mumbai.

Rangarajan, C. (1996), "Rural India: The Role of Credit", First Ravi Matthai Memorial Lecture, IIM, Ahmedabad, published in *Reserve Bank of India Bulletin*, May.

Rao, V.M. (1993), "Government Interventions in Agriculture -A Review of Studies in Developing Countries", *Indian Journal of Agricultural Economics*, Vol.48, No.4, October-December, 1993

——— (1994), "Agriculture and Liberalisation: Some Implications for Development Policies", *Economic and Political Weekly*, April 16-23, 1994.

——— (1994), "Farmers in Market Economy: Would Farmers Gain through Liberalisation?", Indian Journal of Agricultural Economics, Vol.XLIX, No.3, July-September.

——— (1995), "Planning for Liberalisation: ACRP in the Changing Context", A paper presented to the Annual Meeting of ACRP, Planning Commission, held in Shimla, May, 1994; *Economic and Political Weekly*, June 24, 1995; also included in Agro-climatic Regional Planning in India,Vol.1, Concept and Applications (eds.), D.N.Basu and G.S.Guha, Concept Publishing Company, New Delhi, 1996.

——— (1996), "Agricultural Development with a Human Face -Experiences and Prospects", *Economic and Political Weekly*, Vol.XXXI, No. 26, June 29.

——— (1997), Agricultural Price Policy: Issues for the Next Phase; included in *Agricultural Development Paradigm for the Ninth Plan under New Economic Environment*, (ed.), Bhupat M.Desai, Oxford & IBH, New Delhi, 1997.

——— (1999), "Policymaking for Agricultural Development: Why it Misses the Poor", V.B.Singh Memorial Lecture delivered at 40th Conference of the Indian Society of Labour Economics, *Indian Journal of Labour Economics*, Vol.42, No.1, January-March, 1999.

Rao, V.M. and H.G.Hanumappa (1999), "Marginalisation Process in Agriculture: Indicators, Outlook and Policy Implications", *Economic and Political Weekly* (Review of Agriculture), Vol.XXXIV, No.52, December 25, 1999.

Rao, C.H. Hanumantha (1995), "Liberalisation of Agriculture in India: Some Major Issues", *Indian Journal of Agricultural Economics*, Vol50, No.3, July-September, pp.468-471.

——— (1994), *Agricultural Growth, Rural Poverty and Environmental Degradation in India*, Oxford University Press, New Delhi.

——— (1998), "Agricultural Growth, Sustainability and Poverty Alleviation, Recent Trends and Major Issues of Reform", *Economic and Political Weekly*, July 18.

Rao, C.H. Hanumantha and Ashok Gulati (1994), "Indian Agriculture: Emerging Perspectives and Policy Issues", *Economic and Political Weekly*, December 31, pp.A-158-169.

Ravallion, Martin (2000), "What is Needed for a More Pro-Poor Growth Process in India?", *Economic and Political Weekly*, March 25.

Ray S.K. (1998), *Sources of Change in Crop Output*, Institute of Economic Growth, Delhi.

Reserve Bank of India, *Report on Currency and Finance*, various issues, Reserve Bank of India, Mumbai.

Reserve Bank of India (1971), *Report of the Committee on Differential Interest Rates*, RBI, Mumbai.

——— (1991), *Report of the Committee on the Financial System*, (Chairman: M. Narasimham), Reserve Bank of India, Mumbai.

——— (1997): *Report of the High-Level Committee on Agricultural Credit Through Commercial Banks*, (Chairman: R.V. Gupta), Reserve Bank of India, Mumbai.

——— (1999a), *Handbook of Statistics on Indian Economy*, RBI, Mumbai.

——— (1999b), "Some Aspects and Issues Relating to NPAs in Commercial Banks", *Reserve Bank of India Bulletin*, July.

——— (2000a), *Statement of Monetary and Credit Policy for 2000-2001*, Reserve Bank of India, April 27, Mumbai.

——— (2000b), *Report on Micro Credit*, Micro Credit Special Cell, Reserve Bank of India, Mumbai.

Saggar, Mridual (1994), "Hike in Procurement Prices of Agricultural Commodities-View Point", *Reserve Bank of India Occasional Papers*, Vol.15, No.3, September.

Sawant, S.D. and Achutan, C.V. (1995), "Agricultural Growth Across Crops and Regions", *Economic and Political Weekly*, Vol.30, No.18.

Schiff, Maurice and Valdes, Alberto (1995), "The Plundering of Agriculture in Developing Countries," *Finance and Development*, March, pp.44-47.

Sehgal, J., and I.P. Abrol (1994), *Soil Degradation in India: Status and Impact*, Oxford and IBH, New Delhi.

Shariff A. (1999), *India-Human Development Report*, National Council of Applied Economic Research and Oxford University Press, New Delhi.

Sharma V.P., Gajja B.L., Shah D. (1995), "Managing Land and Water Resources for Sustainable Agricultural Development: Issues and Options", *Artha Vijnana*, Vol.37, No.1.

Sharma, Devinder (2000), "Politics of Agricultural Research", *Business Line*, June 3.

Shetty, S.L. (1990), "Investment in Agriculture: Brief Review of Recent Trends", Economic and Political Weekly, February 17-24.

Singh, Manmohan (1995), Inaugural Address delivered at the 54th Annual Conference of the Indian Society of Agricultural Economics, *Indian Journal of Agricultural Economics*, Vol.50, No.1, January-March, pp.1-11.

Stiglitz, Joseph E. (1987), "Some Theoretical Aspects of Agricultural Policies", *The World Bank Research Observer*, Vol.2, Number 1, January, pp.43-60.

Subramanian, Shankar (1993), *Agricultural Trade Liberalization and India*, Development Centre of the Organization for Economic Co-operation and Development, Paris, pp.1-116.

Swaminathan, M.S. (1999), Speech Delivered at the Ministry of Agriculture, Government of India, New Delhi April.

Swaminathan, Madhura (1999), "Understanding the Costs of the Food Corporation of India", *Economic and Political Weekly*, December 25, pp. A-121-132.

Thamarajakshi, R. (1999), "Agriculture and Economic Reforms", *Economic and Political Weekly*, Vol.XXXIV, No.33, August 14-20, pp.2293-2295.

UNDP (1997), *Human Development Report 1997*, Oxford University Press, New York.

UNCATD (1994): *Agricultural Insurance in Developing Countries*, A study by the UNCATD Secretariat, June.

Vaidyanathan, A. (1986), "Labour Use in Rural India: A Study of Spatial and Temporal Variations", *Economic and Political Weekly*, December 27.

——— (1994), "The Employment Situation: Some Emerging Perspectives", *Economic and Political Weekly*, Vol.29, No.50.

——— (1998), "Strategy for Agricultural Growth: Emerging Policy Issues", *in The Poor in a Hostile Society*, (ed.) V.M.Rao, Vikas, New Delhi.

——— (2000), "India's Agricultural Development Policy", *Economic and Political Weekly*, Vol.35, No.20, May 13-19, pp.1735-1741.

Visaria, Pravin (1995), "Rural Non-Farm Employment in India: Trends and Issues for Research", *Indian Journal of Agricultural Economics*, Conference Number, Vol.L, No.3, July-September.

Visaria, Pravin and Basant Rakesh (1994), *Non-Agricultural Employment in India - Trends and Prospects*, (eds.), Sage Publications, New Delhi.

Vena S. (1998), Article in Deccan Herald, May 8, 1998.

Vyasulu Vinod and Kumar Arun A.V. (1994), *Rural Industrialisation in India - A Review of Policies*, (monograph), RBI Endowment Unit, Institute for Social and Economic Change, Bangalore.

Vyas, V.S. (1994), "Agricultural Policies for the Nineties- Issues and Approaches", *Economic and Political Weekly*, Vol.XXIX, No. 26, June 25, pp. A-54-71.

——— (1999), "Agricultural Trade Policy and Export Strategy," *Economic and Political Weekly*, Vol.XXXIV, No.13, March 27, pp. A 27-33.

World Bank,(1986), *World Development Report 1986*, Oxford University Press, New Delhi, pp.61-168.

——— (1995), *Report on Financial Services for the Rural Poor & Women in India: Access and Sustainability*, March.

——— (1997), *The Indian Oilseed Complex: Capturing Market Opportunities*, Vol.1 - Main Report (Report No.15673-IN), Rural Development Sector Unit, South Asia Region.

Development Research Group, RBI, Study No. 21, Modernising Indian Agriculture, Part II, August 29, 2000.

13

Farm Sector Performance and the Reform Agenda

Rip Landes, Ashok Gulati

I

Introduction

During 1991-93, India introduced major reforms to industrial, trade, and exchange rate policy that helped spark India's emergence as one of the fastest growing developing countries. Since 1990, annual GDP growth has averaged 5.6 per cent and consumer price inflation has averaged just 8 per cent, with performance on growth and price stability even stronger in more recent years. External accounts, previously a chronic weakness of the Indian economy, have turned robust, with rising exports and current account surpluses pushing foreign reserves to more than $100 billion. Most importantly, the share of the population in poverty has dropped from 39 per cent in 1987-88 to 26 per cent in 1999-2000 [Government of India, 2003a].

The 1991-93 reforms, and the growth they have spawned, have created pressures for change in agricultural policy. Food demand is growing and diversifying, in turn placing new demands on market infrastructure and institutions. Long-standing production, procurement, and distribution programmes focused on foodgrains are increasingly expensive and out of step with market demand. Burgeoning subsidy outlays are constraining public investment in transforming institutions and market infrastructure, while a thicket of regulation appears to be restricting private agribusiness investment. And, despite improved growth in the overall economy, growth in farm output and, particularly, rural employment is slowing.

There have been some important changes in agricultural policy since the early 1990s, including removal of quantitative trade restrictions required by the Uruguay Round Agreement on Agriculture (URAA), and initial steps to pare down regulation of domestic input and output markets. The recent elections have sharpened the focus on the performance of agriculture, but political consensus for fundamental reform in agriculture has, in the past, been elusive. The goals of this paper are to survey the performance of agriculture and agricultural policy since the 1991-93 reforms, and identify key areas where achievement of consensus on reform could have positive impacts on the performance of agriculture.

II

Impact of Non-Agricultural Reforms on Agriculture

The macroeconomic reforms of 1991-93 have had at least two important impacts on the agricultural sector. First, deregulation of industry, more open trade, and devaluation are widely agreed to have stimulated a significant improvement in the rate of economic growth, thus strengthening and diversifying food demand. Second, although domestic and border policies directly affecting agriculture were not included in the reforms, reduced levels of industrial protection have improved incentives for investment in agriculture through improvements in the sector's domestic terms of trade.

An additional impact of the reforms may stem from the strengthening of the balance of payments and its influence on policy priorities. Comfortable reserve levels and a much more resilient balance of payments have probably allowed policy-makers to be less focused on agricultural self-sufficiency and more amenable to the modest, mostly unilateral, opening of trade in agricultural goods that came later in the 1990s.

Rising Incomes and Agriculture

The most important impact of the 1991-93 reforms on Indian agriculture has been the strengthening and diversification of food demand resulting from faster growth in per capita incomes. The Indian economy has now expanded at an annual rate of 5.8 per cent (4 per cent per capita) since the early 1990s, ranking it among the fastest growing developing economies during the period. As important, faster growth was achieved while maintaining price stability. Per capita income is now about $2,530 at purchasing power parity [World Bank, 2003] and middle- and high-income households including more than 200 million consumers now comprise the fastest growing components of the population [Bijapurkar, 2003].

Rising incomes, particularly in lower- and middle-income households where the marginal propensity to spend on food is high, are having important impacts on food demand in India. Middle- and upper-income consumers, as well as urban consumers, are upgrading and diversifying their diets, and changing the pattern of growth in food consumption. Growth in demand for staple foods, particularly wheat and rice, which have been the focus of agricultural development policy, institutions, and spending is now slowing (Figure 13.1). By contrast, demand for other foods, including fruits, vegetables, fats and livestock products are now showing relatively high, even accelerating growth.

Figure – 13.1

Growth of Food Consumption in India

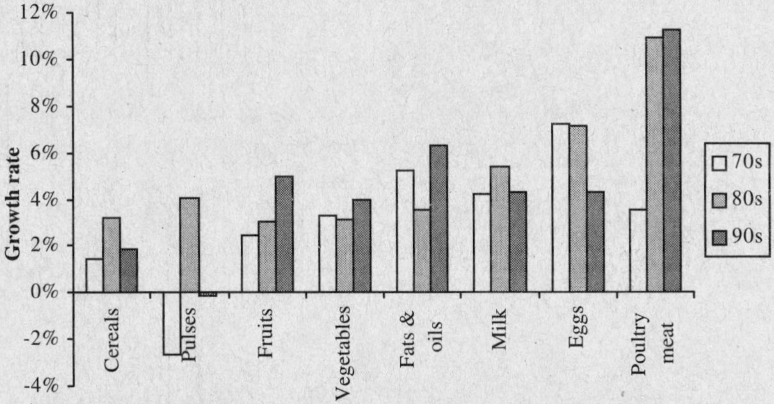

Note: Food consumption based on national production, supply and distribution estimates.

Source: Food and Agriculture Organisation of the UN, FAOSTAT database.

Stronger and more diverse food demand is placing new pressures on agricultural policy, ranging from research priorities to the development of public and private market institutions and facilities to efficiently meet these demands. Shifting demand patterns, when combined with official price and input policies and institutional inertia favouring cereals, provide the context for the costly build-up of wheat and rice surpluses beginning in 1997-98. In contrast to the extensive public sector intervention associated with the achievement of self-reliance in staple cereals, efficiently serving India's increasingly diverse food markets is likely to involve a primary role for private markets, processing and investment.

Improved Relative Prices for Agriculture

An improvement in the relative prices facing agriculture associated with the 1991-93 reforms has also had important impacts, even without major agricultural reforms. Through the mid-1980s, policies that protected industry and taxed agriculture meant relative prices were biased against agriculture. After 1990, however, relative prices turned in favour of agriculture.[1] Although farm policy changes later in the 1990s, primarily higher wheat and rice support prices, likely played a role in this reversal, reduced industrial protection was the key factor.

Improved relative price incentives in agriculture have corresponded with an increasing role for private investment in the sector (Figure 13.2). This appears to have had some impact on several sub-sectors, such as poultry and horticulture, where demand and investment incentives have been particularly strong. Total investment in agriculture, however, remains low and has shown little dynamism. Compared with the average economy-wide level of gross fixed capital formation (GFCF) of about 26 per cent of GDP in 2000-02, agricultural GFCF was only 16 per cent of agricultural GDP. Within this total, on-farm GFCF was about 6 per cent of agricultural GDP, while estimated GFCF in agriculture-related activities was about 10 per cent [Government of India, 2003b]. Burgeoning subsidy outlays appear to be curbing public investment in agriculture. And, despite rising and diversifying food

Figure – 13.2

Relative Agricultural Prices and GFCF in India

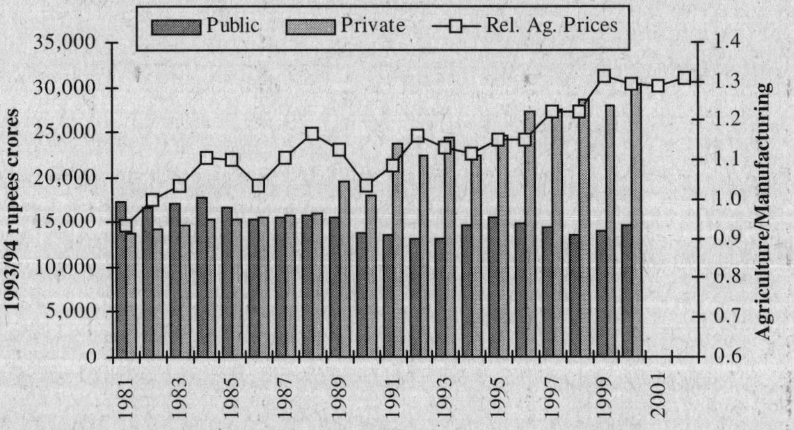

GFCF = Gross fixed capital formation in and for agriculture.

Source: Economic Survey, GoI; Ministry of Agriculture.

product demand, private agribusiness investment that could strengthen rural employment remains largely unattractive compared with other sectors.

Agricultural Performance

Although economic performance has strengthened since the early 1990s, and large foodgrain surpluses accumulated for much of the period, growth in the farm sector has weakened (Table 13.1). In the years immediately following reforms (1992-97), agricultural GDP grew about 3.4 per cent annually, but then slowed to about 2.3 per cent (1997-01). The exact cause of this slump remains a matter of debate and research, and it is difficult to separate the impacts of monsoon performance from other factors. But, sluggish farm sector growth and the sharp slowdown in rural employment gains in the latter half of the 1990s is a constraint to sustaining high rates of overall economic growth, and to achieving rural-urban and regional balance in economic gains. Well-endowed regions, including those with better infrastructure and governance, have tended to register relatively strong growth compared with some others, including heavily populated states such as Uttar Pradesh and Bihar. These disparities may stem less from reforms that have been undertaken, rather than those that have not, but regional imbalances are a concern in India's democratic polity that, perhaps paradoxically, becomes an argument to slow further reform.

Factors on both the supply and demand sides have contributed to sluggish farm sector growth. Looking first at the demand side, we have seen that domestic demand has certainly been there to support stronger performance by the sector. Agricultural exports, which now account for 6-7 per cent of farm output, also strengthened during the 1990s compared with the 1980s, driven largely by gains in non-traditional items, such as cereals, oil cakes, cotton, and marine products (Table 13.2). These exports, however, weakened substantially during 1997-98–2001-02, reflecting internal supply and demand conditions, as well as competition and declining prices in world markets. But, even if declining world prices – resulting partly from policies in other countries – have had a dampening influence on Indian exports, the domestic market dominates demand and has provided a strong impetus for expansion.

On the supply side, sluggish growth in farm output has been associated with conflicting trends in productivity and investment. On the one hand, growth in productivity (yields) has slowed and, on the other, relative price incentives for agriculture have improved and there has been somewhat faster growth in private agricultural investment. But, despite

TABLE – 13.1

Agricultural Supply and Demand Indicators for India

(in per cent)

Period	Real GDP in Agriculture	Demand Indicators		Supply/Investment Indicators						Real Prices (WPI)	
		Real GDP/ Capita	Real Agriculture Exports	Yield Index[1]	Relative Prices[2]	GFCG in/for Agriculture			Total GFCF	Agriculture	Foodgrains 1981-82=100
						In	For	Total			
Growth Rate[3]											
1982-92	3.2	3.1	5.2	2.5	1.3	1.2	2.0	1.6	6.0	1.1	0.3
1992-2001	2.9	4.0	7.3	1.2	1.6	2.3	3.0	2.7	6.9	0.5	1.7
1992-97	3.4	4.2	14.7	1.4	1.2	2.0	3.2	2.8	7.8	0.7	1.4
1997-01	2.3	3.9	–1.3	1.0	2.0	2.6	2.7	2.6	5.9	0.3	2.0
	Share of GDP (Per Cent)	Period Average	Share of Ag GDP (Per Cent)	Period Average	Period Average	Share of Ag GDP (Per Cent)	Share of Ag GDP (Per Cent)	Share of Ag GDP (Per Cent)	Share of GDP (Per Cent)	Period Average	Period Average
1981-83 (average)	39.0	5,987	3.9	104.2	0.99	8.3	10.7	19.0	22.8	99.9	100.0
1991-93 (average)	31.7	8,136	4.2	134.0	1.13	6.8	9.5	16.3	24.2	111.4	102.6
1996-98 (average)	27.6	9,972	6.6	143.7	1.20	6.4	9.4	15.8	26.0	115.5	110.1
2000-02 (average)	24.2	11,614	5.4	149.4	1.30	6.4	9.6	16.0	26.1	116.7	119.2

(1) 1981-82 = 100. (2) Agriculture/Manufacturing, base 1981-82 = 100. (3) Growth rates between 3-year averages centred on years indicated (1982 = 1981-83 average, etc)

Source: Economic Survey, GoI, various issues; Ministry of Agriculture, GoI; *Handbook of Statistics*, Reserve Bank of India, 2002.

TABLE – 13.2

Trends in India's Agricultural Exports

Period	Real Agricultural Exports (Per Cent)		
	Total	Comp[1]	Other
Growth rates			
1982-92	5.2	5.9	4.7
1992-01	7.3	7.3	7.2
1992-97	14.7	19.1	11.0
1997-01	–1.3	–5.8	2.7

Note: [1]. Exports competitive with developed countries (cereals, cotton, tobacco, meats and preps, oilmeal, animal and vegetable oils, and other food and live animals).

Source: Economic Survey, GoI, various issues.

the somewhat higher investment growth, perhaps the key points to be taken from these data are that private investment in agriculture remains noticeably lower than in the rest of the economy and growing much more slowly. Another important issue, of course, is the generally weak performance in public agricultural investment in the 1990s, implying a decline in historically productive investment in surface irrigation systems. Private investment, while growing faster than public investment and now accounting for the larger share of capital formation in the sector, also slowed compared with the 1980s (Table 13.3).

TABLE – 13.3

Trends in Public and Private GFCF in and for Agriculture

(Per cent)

Period	Public	Private	Total
Growth rate*			
1982-92	–2.5	5.2	1.6
1992-99	0.8	3.5	2.3
1992-97	1.5	4.2	2.8
1997-99	–1.1	1.8	1.1
Shares of agricultural GDP			
1981-83 average	10.3	8.6	19.0
1991-93 average	5.9	10.4	16.3
1996-98 average	5.4	10.4	15.8
1998-2000 average	5.0	10.3	15.3

* Growth rates between 3-year averages centred on years indicated.

Source: Ministry of Agriculture, GoI.

Price trends in the domestic market suggest that price policy has also played a role in sector performance. In concert with higher support prices, Indian foodgrain prices rose in real terms during the 1990s, shifting from the historical pattern of constant or declining real prices and holding resources in foodgrain production. In contrast, growth in real prices for the sector as a whole actually slowed in the 1990s, suggesting that, apart from foodgrains, the sector may be doing a reasonable job of adjusting to diversifying demand. But, India's rising real commodity prices, whether for foodgrains or other foods, are sharply at odds with long term global trends. Real world prices for commodities such as wheat, rice, corn, oilseeds, and cotton have all declined 4-6 per cent annually during 1982-2001. Global domestic support, export subsidy, and market access policies have contributed to the declines in world prices, and some hikes in India's cereal support and market prices may have been justified by India's earlier bias against agriculture. But, broad global price trends are fundamentally driven by productivity and marketing efficiency gains in other parts of the world that are not being matched in India.

These sector indicators suggest that, despite the strengthening of demand and improvements in the sector's terms of trade, growth in agricultural productivity has slowed and investment remains weak. A potential explanation for these apparently contradictory trends lies in the performance of India's agricultural policies.

III

Major Agricultural Policies

India's major domestic agricultural policy instruments include a system of minimum support prices for major crops, input subsidies on fertiliser, power, and irrigation water, and public investments in surface, and to a lesser extent, groundwater irrigation. Historically, these interventions have been accompanied by border measures, including quantitative restrictions on imports and exports, import tariffs, and state trading. The border measures were applied in various combinations to different commodities but, except for traditional export crops such as tea, coffee, cashews, and spices, traditionally isolated Indian markets from world markets. In addition, until the 1991 devaluation, an overvalued rupee imposed roughly a 20 per cent tax on domestic production.

The impacts of these policies on Indian agriculture have been documented in a number of studies [Gulati and Narayanan, 2003; Gulati and Kelley, 1999; US Department of Agriculture, 1999] which indicate that, when all commodities are treated as imports, aggregate farm output has been taxed by this policy regime during 1986-2002 (Figure 13.3).[2] Outlays on price supports and input subsidies are large, but the impacts of these measures have typically been more than offset by relatively low domestic farmgate prices that prevail due to quantitative import and export restrictions and high marketing costs. Although some commodities, particularly oilseeds, have been fairly consistently protected (subsidised), and others have been protected in occasional market conditions, the sector as a whole has been taxed, even following the 1991 devaluation. More recent protection estimates show that, through a combination of rising budgetary subsidies and smaller gaps between domestic and world prices, the taxation of Indian agriculture has declined significantly. When the major commodities are treated as exportables – and relative prices are compared at the border rather than the farmgate – protection even turns positive for 2001 and 2002.

Figure – 13.3

Aggregate Producer Support Estimates for India

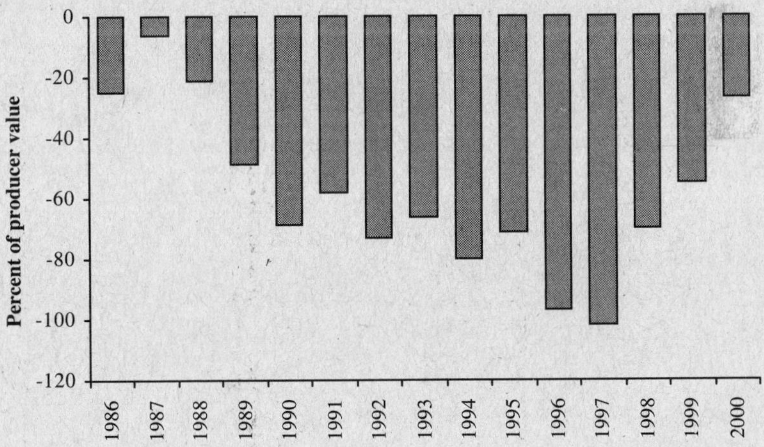

Source: Gulati and Narayanan, 2003.

An additional set of domestic policies affecting agriculture is, however, not directly accounted for in the above protection measures but are, perhaps, increasingly important in their impact on the sector's adjustment to expanding demand. A partial list.

- The Essential Commodities Act (ECA), enacted after the Bengal Famine but still in force in the 1990s, empowers central and state governments to impose restrictions on the storage and movement of commodities, such as foodgrains, pulses, and edible oils, thus limiting the scope for private investment in these markets.
- Until recently, all food-processing industries were limited to small-scale capacities and, despite deregulation, small-scale, low technology firms established under the old laws still dominate the industry. Some products are still restricted to small-scale firms, and food-processing units still require approval from eight central government ministries.
- Agricultural Produce Marketing Committee (APMC) regulations require agricultural sales to occur only in regulated markets, limiting private investment in market activities, as well as integration of producers with the marketing chain.
- Weak laws providing insufficient protection for lessors and lessees limit use of land leasing to assemble larger, more efficient operational units, and limit private investment to improve agricultural land.

Although most of these issues have been the target of discussion and some action by the central government, there has been little actual implementation of reform. State governments, which must accept and implement any changes, have been reluctant to act on central government reform recommendations. These regulations impose costs on the agricultural marketing and processing industries and additional taxes on farm output, as well as weakening the environment for private investment that could boost efficiency and employment.

IV

Agricultural Policy Performance

None of India's domestic support policies faced discipline as a result of the Uruguay Round Agreement on Agriculture. As notified to the WTO, India's Aggregate Measure of Support (AMS) shows negative aggregate support through the 1990s. Input subsidies are notified by India as support to small, resource poor farmers that is exempt under the URAA. Similarly, expenditures under the "foodgrain subsidy" are notified as domestic food aid and not counted as producer support.

The market access disciplines of the URAA that required "tariffication" of agricultural imports, together with India's loss of its WTO balance of payments waiver in 1997, did lead to changes in India's border policies for agricultural products. Changes, completed in April 2001, included the removal of quantitative import restrictions and establishment of tariffs for all agricultural imports. For major commodities, however, tariff bindings are sufficiently high to prevent imports, although some imports of high-value and processed items (fruits, nuts, canned goods, etc.) are now occurring at bound rates. In most cases where significant imports have occurred, such as edible oils, pulses, and cotton, it is because of a unilateral GoI decision to set applied rates below bound rates. For a few commodities, including oilseeds (phyto-sanitary regulation) and corn (tariff rate-quota administration), non-tariff barriers likely prevent trade at bound rates even when market price conditions are favourable.

There are several important areas of agricultural policy during the 1990s that are instructive to analyse in terms of performance and alternatives for reform.

- Grain producer price policy
- Removal of export restraints
- Protection of oilseeds and oils
- Market and regulatory reform

Grain Producer Price Policy

The most observable recent development in Indian agriculture was the accumulation of large government surpluses of wheat and rice, including the emergence of significant – and subsidised – exports of these commodities. The stockpiles and exports occurred alongside rising real domestic wheat and rice prices and actual declines in per capita consumption, even as roughly 260 million Indians continue to live in poverty. Addressing this perverse set of outcomes is a major challenge to Indian policy-makers.

The surpluses emerged in the context of secular changes in consumer demand, together with changes in producer price and public distribution policies. There is good evidence that aggregate demand is shifting away from wheat and rice. Although there is controversy on this issue, analyses of consumer demand based on National Sample Survey data [Kumar, 2001a] suggest that, while low income groups still show positive income elasticities of demand for cereals, but those for the population as a whole are near zero.

National minimum support prices (MSPs) for foodgrains and other major commodities are recommended by the Commission for Agricultural Costs and Prices (CACP), but are actually set by a committee chaired by the Prime Minister. CACP recommendations are based on several factors, but assessments of costs of production (CoP) and domestic and global market conditions appear key. Historically, the MSPs for wheat and rice were generally increased at rates below inflation, and remained well under import parity prices. Although intended to be a national programme covering all major crops, the MSPs are generally defended by GoI purchases only for wheat and rice in the major surplus areas of Punjab, Haryana, western Uttar Pradesh, and Andhra Pradesh (rice only).

Beginning in the late-1990s, the MSPs set for wheat and rice became increasingly out of step with domestic market conditions. One key factor was (and still is) that the CoP concept used in setting the price became a "full cost" measure that, in addition to variable input costs, included the rental value of land, the imputed value of family labour, and a return to management. Another was pressure to compensate farmers for the price swings associated with changes in India's rice and wheat export policy during 1995 and 1996. For rice, higher market prices resulting from the initial removal of export restraints later created pressure for higher MSPs when world prices fell. Similarly for wheat, lower market prices following the re-imposition export restraints led the government to compensate farmers with higher MSPs. With these developments, the

Figure – 13.4

Indian Wheat Support Price, Production Costs, and World Price

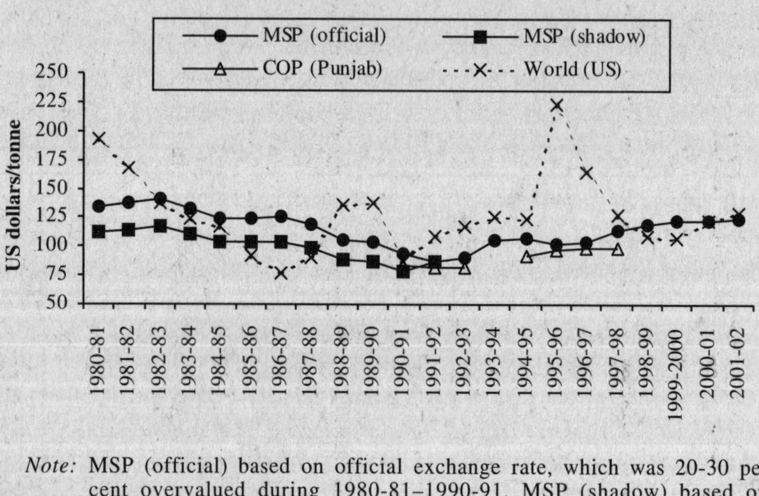

Note: MSP (official) based on official exchange rate, which was 20-30 per cent overvalued during 1980-81–1990-91. MSP (shadow) based on shadow exchange rates.

Sources: Ministry of Agriculture, GoI; US Department of Agriculture, Economic Research Service.

MSPs became disconnected from domestic market conditions and – when world prices fell from a temporary spike in 1996-97 – from competitive world market prices (Figure 13.4). The tendency for MSPs to be increased has likely been compounded as MSP benefits boost land rental, labour, and management costs, thus leading to higher CoP.

An important factor affecting MSP policy in the 1990s concerns the changing political dimensions of the policy when India entered an era of coalition governments and the farm lobby became more influential. During 1995-96 – 2001-02, just before and during the accumulation of surpluses, the government set MSPs above the CACP recommendation in four out of seven years for rice and five out of seven years for wheat [Parikh 2002, *et al.*]. Another key dimension is that the MSP mechanism is one of the few levers available to Indian policy-makers and there is a tendency to try to use it to achieve multiple policy goals, including both price stabilisation and income support.

The failure of price policy to successfully adapt to the new environment has had a number of impacts. First, breaking with the historical pattern, domestic wheat and rice prices have tended to strengthen relative to both world and domestic prices, and to move above domestic market clearing levels (Figure 13.5). While benefiting

Figure – 13.5

Trends in Wholesale Prices in India

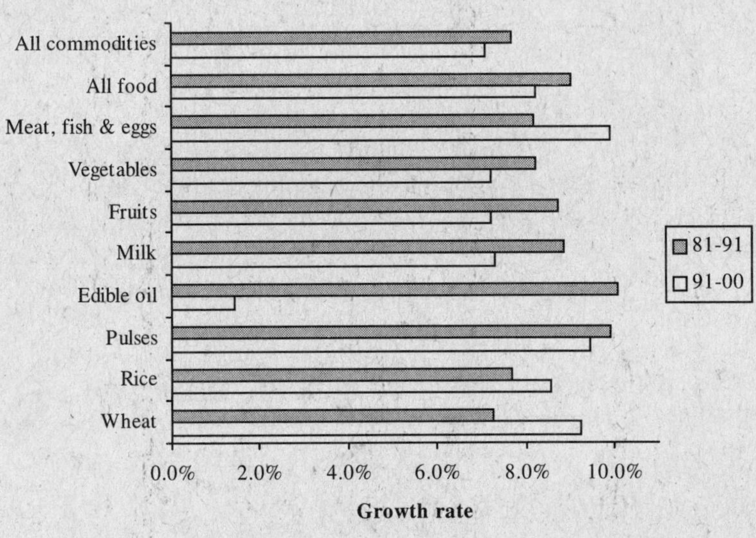

Source : Ministry of Commerce, GoI.

the relatively few producers receiving wheat and rice MSPs, higher consumer prices have undoubtedly had negative impacts. Per capita wheat and rice consumption has actually declined in recent years, as higher procurement and prices contributed to decline in consumption of open market supplies that have not been offset by subsidised distribution. A recent study of the economy-wide impacts of increasing the wheat and rice MSPs when they are above market clearing levels found that reduced consumption and investment associated with higher prices actually reduced incomes, both in aggregate and for most rural and urban income groups [Parikh *et al.*, 2002].[3]

Second, by maintaining high prices, the government has become responsible for the storage and transport of most of the marketed surplus of FAQ-grade wheat and rice in the country – what some observers have termed a "de facto nationalisation" of grain trade. In addition to raising budgetary costs, the policy provides little incentive for private investment in grain storage, handling or distribution, with the exception of the fees traders can earn in the export of subsidised grain allocated by the government.

Third, by focusing on supporting relatively high prices only for wheat and rice in a few regions, MSP policy has not been made an effective tool for stabilising producer prices for other crops and supporting the diversification of agriculture.

Fourth, the budgetary cost of FCI operations under current policies has now reached about $5.5 billion. When policies support domestic prices above market clearing, much of this subsidy accrues to producers rather than consumers. Combined with the cost of subsidies on fertiliser and other inputs, the subsidy bill has burgeoned to about $15 billion annually, far exceeding both public ($1 billion in 2001-02) and private ($2.8 billion) capital formation in agriculture. Subsidy outlays are crowding out new investment needed to boost productivity and marketing efficiency.

Finally, the policy of maintaining high wheat and rice prices has contributed to emergent environmental problems, particularly associated with the intensive wheat-rice cropping system in northern India. When combined with the low cost of irrigation water – much of which is either free, stolen, or subsidised – the strong price incentives for wheat and rice are contributing to the rapid deterioration of groundwater resources, and rising concern with deteriorating soil fertility in some areas.

Removal of Export Restraints

Through the 1980s and early 1990s, Indian agriculture was burdened with export restrictions and overvalued exchange rates that resulted in net taxation of the sector. Exports of agricultural goods were restricted through myriad controls, including prohibitions, licenses, quotas, marketing controls and minimum export prices, for the sake of domestic food security. For a number of products, the quantitative controls on exports were administered through trading enterprises in the public and cooperative sectors.

Agricultural export policies began to change in 1994 and, barring the occasional reversal, have been progressively liberalised. The ministry of commerce, through the director general of foreign trade, imposes or removes export restrictions in order to promote exports while also ensuring 'adequate' domestic supplies of essential commodities at 'reasonable' prices. Reforms have included reductions in products subject to state trading, relaxation of export quotas, the abolition of minimum export prices, and increased credit availability for exports. In 2000, India also began to provide significant budgetary subsidies to support exports of surplus cereals when the combination of declining world prices and higher domestic prices make Indian wheat and rice uncompetitive in world markets.

Developments in the Indian rice market since the removal of export restraints may be indicative of the impacts of this type of reform

Figure – 13.6

Rice Trade and Protection in India

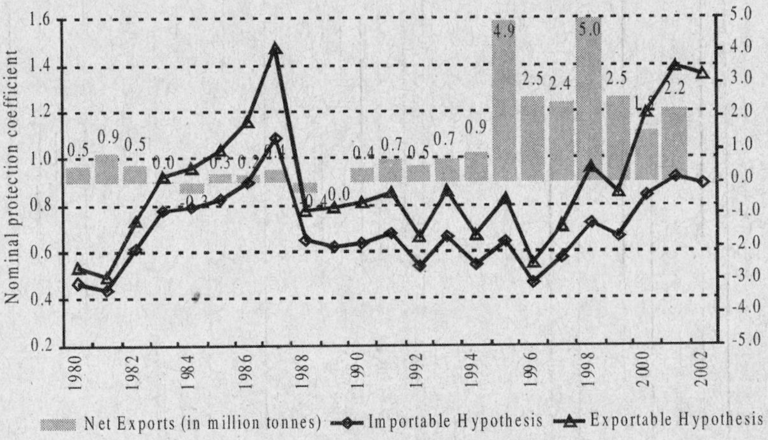

Source: Gulati and Mullen, 2003.

(Figure 13.6). Private traders were permitted to export common rice beginning in 1994-95 and, although exports remain small relative to production, India immediately became a major player, selling primarily into the lower end of the international market. Since 2000-01, however, the combination of lower world prices and firm domestic prices has made Indian rice exports less price-competitive, leading to GoI subsidies for rice exports.

Rice exports have helped moderate the growth of surplus rice stocks and, together with higher MSPs and lower domestic distribution of subsidised rice, contributed to a strengthening of domestic prices. The growth in exports, along with relaxation of earlier policies limiting rice milling to small-scale enterprises, are stimulating investment in modern rice milling and grading equipment. The opening up of exports exposed the inefficiency of domestic rice marketing and processing infrastructure, and the absence of quality and grading standards, needed to compete in world markets. Although the bulk of India's rice continues to be processed in inefficient, small-scale mills with no formal grading standards, the basmati rice export business, in particular, has sparked investment in better technology for processing and grading. In some cases, the basmati export business is also beginning to stimulate market integration or coordination between exporters, millers, and contract producers in order to ensure quality [Bhatt, 2004; Roy, 2002].

With these potentially positive impacts on investment and competitiveness, the removal of export restraints opens up a new set of policy issues concerning the impacts of global price changes on the domestic market. First, the removal of rice export restraints initially benefited producers and traders when it pulled domestic prices above the MSP. But, when world prices retreated, the MSPs became disconnected from market realities, leading to increases in domestic and export subsidy costs. Thus, with the removal of export restraints, it becomes important to have an MSP setting mechanism (and discipline) that keeps MSPs connected with domestic and world prices.

Second, since an important rationale for restraining exports was to ensure stable domestic consumer prices, the removal of export restraints may increase periodic demands on domestic distribution programmes to stabilise supplies for lower-income consumers. The recent higher domestic prices and declines in per capita rice consumption suggest that at least some consumers have been adversely affected. However, since global rice prices have been declining since the mid-1990s, these impacts are more likely driven by high MSPs and declines in distribution associated with implementation of the Targeted Public Distribution System, than by the removal of export restraints.

Import Protection: Case of Oilseeds and Oils

Although the 1991-93 economic reforms substantially liberalised India's external trade regime for many non-agricultural goods, progress in phasing out quantitative restrictions on agricultural products remained slow. Except for the liberalisation of import licensing on sugar and cotton in 1994, most agricultural products remained subject to import controls. In 1997, following the loss of the balance-of-payments waiver, India phased out quantitative import restrictions and QRs were finally lifted in April 2001. Despite the fears of Indian policy-makers, the large anticipated surge in farm imports did not materialise. Imports increased in some categories, including high-value and processed items with tariffs of 50-100 per cent, but not to levels that posed significant threats to domestic producers.

Oilseeds and products are a major sector of domestic production and consumption that has, perhaps, been the most affected by import liberalisation policy during the 1990s (Figure 13.7). Trade policy changes in the sector have, however, been mostly unilateral, rather than mandated by URAA disciplines. Until 1993-94, all edible oil imports were controlled by the State Trading Corporation, which based import

Figure – 13.7

Edible Oil Imports and Tariffs in India

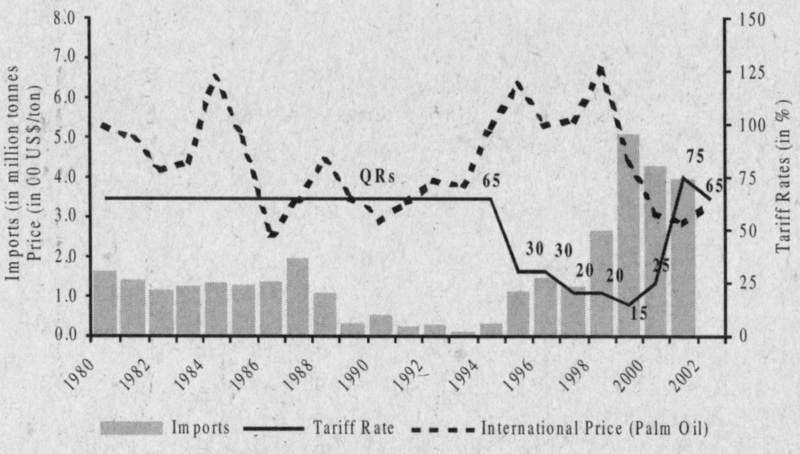

Source: Gulati and Mullen, 2003.

decisions on domestic market conditions and other policy goals. Imports were reduced sharply during 1987-93, as the government attempted to boost production incentives and adoption of modern technology.

In 1993-94, the government abandoned this approach and opened imports to private traders, subject only to tariffs which were set well below bound rates. Imports picked up slowly at first, but surged in the late 1990s, eventually making India the world's largest importer. Tariffs for most oils have now been raised to 65-85 per cent, but are still well below the bound rates of 300 per cent. Hikes in the tariff on palm oil, the major imported oil, as well as rapeseed and sunflower oils, are constrained by the relatively low 45 per cent bound rate for soybean oil, the second largest imported oil. Despite the tariffs, oil imports have continued to expand, now accounting for 45-50 per cent of domestic oil consumption.

The swings in edible oil import policy have clearly had an impact on domestic production, consumption, and prices of oilseeds and oils. Import restraints during 1987-93 led to higher domestic oil and oilseed prices, leading to increases in planted area and yields. Since 1994, with reduced protection for oils, and the lack of a procurement mechanism to defend MSPs for oilseeds, oilseed area has tended to decline and yield growth to stagnate [Kumar, 2001b; Gulati and Kelley, 1999]. Also, chronically low capacity utilisation rates in the oilseed processing industry have fallen even lower. On the consumption side, however, consumers have benefited from lower real domestic oil prices and significant gains in per capita consumption since 1993.

The overall welfare implications of the changes in oil import policy have not been analysed. Farmers and oilseed processors regularly lobby for restrictions on oil imports, and some policymakers have been looking for non-tariff restrictions to get around the low 45 per cent bound rate for soyabean oil so that they can have more flexibility to raise the rates for palm and other oils [Chandrashekhar, 2002]. Oilseed processors also lobby periodically for freer imports of oilseeds and lower duties on crude *vs* refined oils, in order to boost capacity utilisation in crushing and refining.

Largely unanalysed are various policy options for improving the competitiveness of the domestic oilseed and products industry. One option is to shift from reliance on oil import tariffs as the tool for intervention, to an MSP programme that defends oilseed prices through government purchases and, thus, assures remunerative and stable prices directly to growers. There is evidence that the current approach of taxing oil imports primarily benefits oilseed processors and traders, with only a portion of the protection actually benefiting oilseed growers [Gulati and Kelley, 1999; Figure 13.8]. Even in a very efficient and fully integrated market the benefit to oilseed growers of a tariff on oils is limited to the rate of oil extraction from the seed, ranging from about 18 per cent in the case of soyabean to about 45 per cent for sunflower seed. With the domestic processing industry operating for only three-four months of the year, oilseed procurement operations would entail only short-term government stockholding.

Figure – 13.8

Competitiveness of Oilseed Production and Oil Processing in India

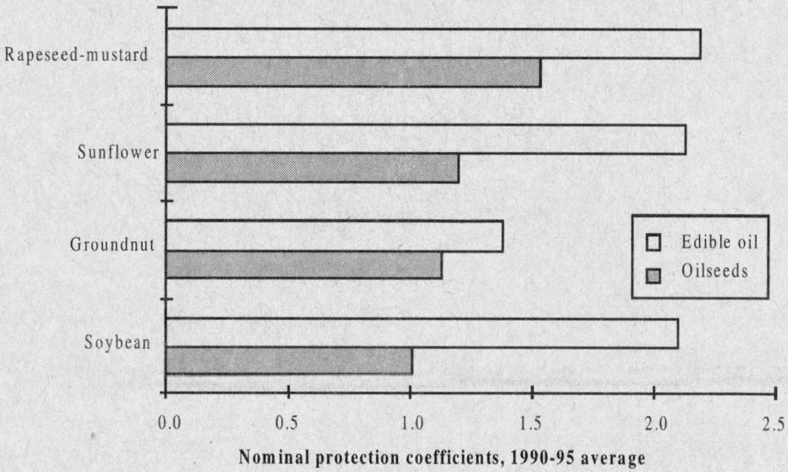

Source: Gulati and Kelley, 1999.

Another option is to ease restrictions on oilseed imports and on the scale of domestic processing facilities to foster the development of a more efficient, vertically integrated domestic processing and marketing industry. Inadequate scale, poor technology, and low potential to boost capacity utilisation from domestic raw materials now make most of India's processing capacity fragmented, inefficient by world standards, and incapable of producing quality oil and feed protein. An alternate scenario, requiring coordination of oilseed and oil tariffs and a solution to current non-tariff barriers to oilseed imports, might allow processors to import oilseeds and boost capacity use, thus making investments in more efficient, integrated units more economically viable. A more efficient and dynamic industry would yield benefits for both producers and consumers, as well as an environment more conducive to private investment to boost local oilseed production.

Market and Regulatory Reform

India's domestic agricultural markets and processing industry have, historically, been subject to a virtual thicket of regulation, initially intended to protect consumers and promote labour-intensive industry, but also severely limiting the viability of employment-generating private investment. Several of these regulatory issues are listed in the above discussion of agricultural policy. Recently, however, initial steps have been taken to liberalise domestic agricultural markets. Among these changes are:

- The temporary removal of licensing requirements, stocking limits, and movement restrictions for wheat, paddy/rice, coarse grains, edible oilseeds and edible oils under the ECA by some, but not all, state governments.
- GoI removal of plant scale restrictions and licensing requirements for most food processing activities.
- GoI removal of the restrictions on futures trading on 54 commodities, including wheat, rice, oilseeds and pulses.
- GoI reform of the milk and milk products order to no longer restrict large-scale investments in new processing capacity.

In addition, the GoI has proposed, for the consideration of the states, revisions to the APMC Act that would permit the development of private markets and is, reportedly, working on legal changes to facilitate land leasing and contract farming. Another important reform under consideration is to streamline food safety laws, including consolidation of responsibilities and jurisdiction, as well as closer alignment with international standards.

These proposed reforms are likely to help improve the environment for private investment, structural change, and efficiency gains in agribusiness that could yield substantial benefits streams to Indian producers and consumers, and boost rural employment. Estimates of current marketing costs in the agricultural sector indicate the potential for efficiency gains:

- In the case of vegetables, most of which are marketed with little grading, packaging, processing or other form of value addition, farmers receive about 25 per cent of the consumer price, and losses in the supply chain are roughly 40 per cent (McKinsey).

- For wheat, most of which is sold to consumers without value addition, producer-to-retail marketing costs also appear high, particularly if the costs of government operations are included. Estimates based on GoI, FCI, and World Bank data indicate total producer-to-consumer margin for wheat of about Rs. 4,850 per tonne, or 80 per cent of the producer price (USDA).

- In southern and western India, vertically integrated broiler operations are reducing production costs among contract growers, and efficiency gains in the form of reduced producer-consumer margins appear significant. Producers are benefiting from reduced marketing risk and assured returns, while consumers gain from lower prices (USDA; Figure 13.9).

Figure – 13.9

Poultry Producer Prices and Retail Margins in India

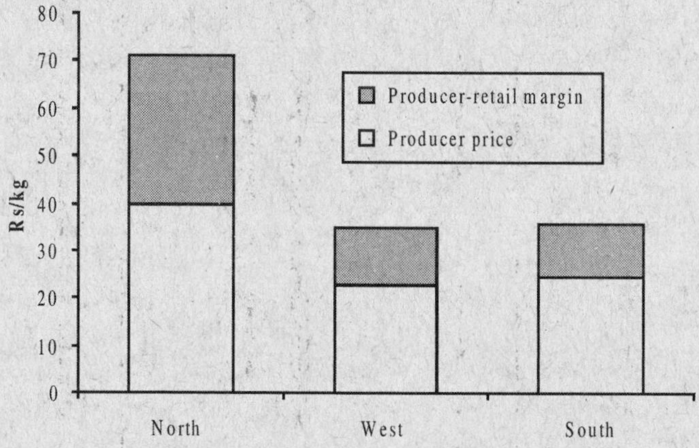

Source: Landes and Persaud.

- Since the removal of quantitative import restrictions, imported processed foods are now seen in many urban stores, despite tariffs of 50-60 per cent. Typically, however, the bulk of the margin between the port and the consumer is not due to the tariff, but to the high margins taken by importers, wholesalers and retailers (USDA).

Following through on marketing and regulatory reform appears to be critical to the emergence of a more dynamic and efficient agribusiness sector driven by private investment. Another potentially significant change now occurring in some urban areas is the emergence of large scale, chain wholesaling and retailing enterprises with investment from either domestic or foreign firms. In other countries, the emergence of large scale and chain retailing has been a key to the development of more efficient, vertically integrated supply chains. This phenomenon has the potential to be an important development in India, as well, although current rules against FDI in retailing is likely to slow its growth. It is unclear whether the recent and proposed reforms will be sufficient to spark increased private domestic and foreign investment, or if additional reforms and/or public infrastructure investments will be needed to improve the investment climate.

V

Shaping Reform Agenda

Consensus-building for change in agricultural policy has been very difficult in India. There is a great deal of inertia in current policies and institutions, in part because of the belief that these policies have served India well in achieving foodgrain self-sufficiency, but also because they have created powerful vested interests. Perhaps more importantly, with the farm sector the source of 25 per cent of GDP, and of income for about 65 per cent of the population, there is a deep-rooted belief that the welfare of the poor is linked closely to the protection of agriculture. In India's era of coalition governments, it has been increasingly difficult for policy-makers to take risks on agricultural policy reform that would entail short-run adjustment costs – either economic or political. Although there is a significant and growing reform-minded constituency, there is little doubt that the largely defensive positions taken by India in the recent Cancun ministerial have been popular in India.

To move forward, it would appear important to forge recognition and agreement on several broad directions for the reform agenda:

Price policy: As long as producer price policy attempts to meet both income and price stabilisation goals, it will be difficult to contain its costs, or to serve the efficient allocation of resources in the sector. In the context of market-oriented reform and a more open trade regime, it will be important for price policy to take more explicit account of domestic and world price conditions, rather than a measure of production costs. Extension of effective producer price stabilisation to crops other than wheat and rice could help promote both sector diversification and income stability. For income support, other policy instruments, including targeted food distribution and actuarially sound crop insurance products, may provide support with lower cost and less market distortion.

Export restraints: The removal of restraints on exports is an important step in reducing the traditional implicit taxation of the agricultural sector. The removal of such constraints can promote beneficial private investment and employment in the supply chain for internationally competitive commodities. To be sustained, however, free exports will require consumer and business acceptance of the influence of world price fluctuations in the domestic market, and in adjusting policy prices. In the case of food staples, low-income consumers may need continued protection from any upswings in world and domestic prices through current or enhanced food distribution programmes.

Import liberalisation/protection: Concerns with the market distorting policies of other countries should not prevent implementation of economically beneficial import liberalisation measures. The removal of quantitative import restrictions has generally had negligible impact on producers, while providing benefits to consumers. In some sectors, such as oilseeds, liberalisation could lead to additional gains for consumers, producers, and processors – not to mention employment gains – by facilitating development of more efficient processing and marketing. Import liberalisation and domestic deregulation have benefited many non-agricultural industries and consumers since 1991-93, why not agriculture?

Public investment: The inability to reform price policy and contain input subsidies has led to a decline in public investment in agriculture at a time when investment in new technology, infrastructure, and institutions is needed. Even though India's subsidies have not been challenged under current WTO rules, their withdraw would provide a large pool of resources with which to compensate producers for price policy reform through higher return investments in technology, markets, and infrastructure.

Private investment: Public investment cannot be expected to fill the investment gap in agriculture. Improving the climate for private investment and employment in markets for agricultural inputs and outputs is, therefore, essential for boosting the growth and competitiveness of an increasingly diverse agricultural sector. Stimulating private domestic and foreign agribusiness investment will require public investments in market infrastructure, supportive import and export policies, and comprehensive 'behind the border' reforms of market regulations and institutions.

VI

Analytical Needs

To help push forward a consensus on reform, there appear to be several important analytical gaps to be filled. First, while policies largely maintained low and stable cereal prices through the 1970s and 1980s, current farm policy has relied on the proposition that higher administered producer prices will have positive long run benefits for employment and income generation among the poor. Even in a country where the average consumer spends about 55 per cent of their income on food, and the poor spend upwards of 70 per cent, it is rare to find an advocate of the potential long run benefit of lower food prices. In a further departure from historical practice, recent policies have embodied the proposition that larger current subsidies on inputs have a higher economic return than public investments in agriculture. More research and analysis within economywide frameworks may be effective in evaluating the growth and equity impacts of these alternative policy options, and in provoking debate and consensus on development strategy.

Second, much of Indian agricultural policy, and fear of market-oriented reform, is based on the perception that reducing import barriers will increase domestic price volatility and threaten producer livelihood and consumer welfare. Thus, Indian WTO positions typically strive to maintain bound rates at levels that will prevent trade, and to also have the right to introduce QRs through safeguard or other mechanisms. Research should be able to play a role by providing objective analysis of the extent to which concerns with volatility may be true, and by examining options for providing producer and consumer price stability with less market distortion and more scope for beneficial import and export competition.

Finally, border reforms that have occurred have tended to expose inefficiency in India's domestic agricultural markets stemming from heavy regulation, poor technology, and substantial under investment – both public and private. While some initial steps have been taken to reduce the web of regulation that has deterred private investment, and private investment has increased, much more is needed. Research should be able to play a role in examining the climate for private investment and identifying additional reforms, beyond those already identified, which may be needed to help stimulate domestic and foreign investment in the sector.

Notes

1. The terms-of-trade for agriculture, that is the ratio of prices received to prices paid in the sector, also improved during the period. Relative prices for agriculture and manufacturing are used here because the data are more current.
2. When commodities are treated as exports, aggregate support becomes marginally positive in 2001 and 2002.
3. Given this evidence, one could hypothesise that more poverty reduction might have occurred in the 1990s had foodgrain price policy maintained its historical balance of producer and consumer interests, rather than tilting towards a small subset of producers.

References

Ahluwalia, M (2002), "Economic Reforms in India since 1991: Has Gradualism Worked?" *Journal of Economic Perspectives*, vol 16, no 3 (Summer): pp 67-88.

Bhatt, D (2004), "KRBL Acquires Integrated Rice Milling Plant in Punjab",. *The Hindu Business Line* (Online). http:www.blonnet.com/2004/02/03/stories/2004020301521100.htm, February 3, 2004.

Bijapurkar, R (2003), "The New Improved Indian Consumer" *Business World* (Online). Available at http//:www.businessworldindia.co/Dec0803/ coverstory01.asp, December 8, 2003.

Chandrashekhar, G (2002), "Trade Perturbed over Proposed Curbs on Soya Oil Inflow", *The Hundu Business Line*, (Online) Available at www.blonnet.com/2002/03/28/stories / 2002032800461.htm March 28, 2004.

Diao, Xinshen, E Diaz-Bonilla, and S Robinson (2003), *How Much Does it Hurt?: The Impact of Agricultural Trade Policies on Developing Countries.* International Food Policy Research Institute, August, p 8.

Dohlman, E, S Persaud and R Landes (2003), *India's Edible Oil Sector: Imports Fill Rising Demand,* Market and Trade Economics Division, Economic Research Service, US Department of Agriculture, OCS-0903-01, November, p 20.

Government of India (2001), *Economic Reforms: A Medium-Term Perspective*. Prime Minister's Economic Advisory Council, New Delhi, January.

——— (2002a), *Agricultural Statistics at a Glance*, Department of Agriculture and Cooperation, New Delhi, June.

——— (2002b), *High Level Committee Report on Long-Term Grain Policy*, Ministry of Consumer Affairs, Food and Public Distribution, New Delhi, Online. Available at http://fcamin.nic.in/hlc_contents.htm May 9, 2003.

——— (2002c), *Report of Inter-Ministerial Task Force on Agricultural Marketing Reforms*, Department of Agriculture and Cooperation, New Delhi, May 27.

——— (2003a), *Economic Survey 2002-03,* Ministry of Finance, New Delhi, (Online). Available at http://indiabudget.nic.in/ May 12, 2003.

——— (2003b), *Report of the Committee on Capital Formation in Agriculture*, Department of Agriculture and Cooperation, New Delhi, (Online). Available at http://agricoop.nic.in/statistics2003/FinalReport.doc March 2003.

Gulati, A and S Bathla (2002), Capital Formation in Indian Agriculture: Trends, Composition, and Implications for Growth, Occasional Paper 24, National Bank for Agriculture and Rural Development, Mumbai.

Gulati, A and T Kelley (1999), *Trade Liberalisation and Indian Agriculture,* Oxford University Press, New Delhi.

Gulati, A and K Mullen (2003), *Responding to Policy Reform: Indian Agriculture During the 1990s and After,* paper prepared for the Fourth Annual Conference on India Economic Policy Reform, The Centre for Research on Economic Development and Policy Reform, Stanford University, Palo Alto, June.

Gulati, A and S Narayanan (2003), *Subsidy Syndrome in Indian Agriculture,* Oxford University Press, New Delhi.

Gulati, A, G Pursell and K Mullen (2003), Indian Agriculture Since Reforms: Performance, Policy Environment, and Incentives (Mimeo, International Food Policy Research Institute).

Joshi, P K and A Gulati (2003), "From Plate to Plough: Agricultural Diversification in India", paper presented at the 'The Dragon and the Elephant: A Comparative Study of Economic and Agricultural Reforms in China and India', New Delhi, India, March 25-26.

Kapila, R and U Kapila (eds) (2002), *Indian Agriculture in the Changing Environment,* Vols 1 and 2, Academic House, Ghaziabad, India.

Kumar, P (2001a): 'Food Demand Projections for India', Agricultural Economics Policy Paper 98-01, IARI, New Delhi.

——— (2001b), "Agricultural Productivity and Performance" in S S Acharya and D P Chaudhri (eds), *Indian Agricultural Policy at the Crossroads*, Rawat Publications, Jaipur and New Delhi, India, pp 353-475.

Landes, M R (2002), "India: Potential Benefits of Wheat Marketing Reform", International Seminar on Wheat and Wheat Products, Hyderabad, India, September 27-28.

Landes, M R and S Persaud (2004), *India's Poultry Sector: Development and Prospects*, Market and Trade Economics Division, Economic Research Service, U S Department of Agriculture. ATR WRS-04-03, January.

Parikh, K S, A Ganesh Kumar and G Darbha (2002), "Growth and Welfare Consequences of Rise in MSP", *Economic and Political Weekly,* Vol XXXVIII, No 9, March 1-7, pp 891-95.

Pursell, G (1996), "India: Trade Policy, the Exchange Rate and the Domestic Terms of Trade for Agriculture", Mimeo, World Bank, Washington, DC.

Roy, A S (2002), "Induss Food in Talks to Upgrade Rice Mills", *The Hindu Business Line*, (Online), http:www.blonnet.com/2002-05/10/stories/2002051000131.htm [May 10, 2002].

US Department of Agriculture (1994), "Estimates of Producer and Consumer Subsidy Equivalents: Government Intervention in Agriculture, 1982-92", Economic Research Service, *Statistical Bulletin,* No 913, December, p 452.

——— (2001), *The Road Ahead: Agricultural Policy Reform in the WTO – Summary Report,* Market and Trade Economics Division, Economic Research Service, AER No 797, January 2001, p 26.

World Bank (2003), *World Development Report*, IBRD, Washington, p 250.

Economic and Political Weekly, August 7, 2004.

14

Food Policy in India:
Some Longer Term Issues

Mihir Rakshit

Abstract

Any long-term food policy needs to have two components. The first consists of measures best suited under prevailing institutional and economic conditions. The second constitutes a package for enduring improvements in income distribution, agricultural productivity and functioning of the market so that the need for large scale public intervention for improving the nutritional intake of the poor comes down sharply over time. So far as the first set of policies is concerned, we share the High Level Committee's (HLC's) perception that at this stage the government has to rely on universal public distribution system (UPDS) along with buffer stocking for promoting its primary objectives. However, measures adopted in this connection seem seriously flawed due to wrong priorities; quite misleading estimates regarding the benefits of food subsidy enjoyed by different groups; and inadequate appreciation of the short and medium term impact of various policy instruments. In light of these inadequacies we have suggested that (a) minimum support prices (MSP) should be based on marginal cost, not average cost (inclusive of returns on farmers' own inputs), of targeted output; (b) while setting the policy instruments it is important to recognise their inter-dependence and the relative efficacy of attaining the basic objectives; (c) MSP should be higher in deficit than in surplus regions; and (d) judicious use of export or import of foodgrains reduces the cost of running PDS as also of buffer stocking. Reliance on direct public intervention in the food market can be reduced significantly if (a) the government ensures full employment of resources; (b) raises the income earning ability of the poor through provision of education and health services on a priority basis; (c) enhances agricultural productivity through investment in irrigation and other infrastructural services; and (d) promotes efficient trading through development of transport, communication, storage facilities and sources of short and long term finance.

We examine in Section I the merits of the widely recommended proposal for dismantling the public distribution system and seek to dispel some official misconceptions regarding the basic objectives of food policy. Section II discusses the short and medium run measures, relating to the minimum support price (MSP), public distribution system (PDS) and buffer stocks, for attaining the objectives in a closed economy. Taking into account the responsiveness of international prices of foodgrains to India's exports and imports, we indicate in Section III how best to exploit the trading opportunities for efficient running of PDS. Section IV takes a broader perspective and focuses on measures other than PDS or FCI's buffer stocking. These measures are mostly long term and should reduce over time FCI's role in raising the nutritional standard of the poor and ensuring food security. The final section provides a summary of our findings and suggestions.

I

SOME BASIC QUESTIONS

Before discussing the features of an optimal food policy, it appears useful to clear the deck and address some basic questions answers which tend to differ widely and are often not based on close reasoning or structural characteristics of the country.

Why not dismantle PDS and all that?

Over the last quinquennium there has been persistent "excess supply" situation in the foodgrains market; the gap between FCI's actual stocks and their stipulated norms registered a sharp rise despite the fall in output in two out of five years[1] during 1997-02; international prices of wheat and rice have come down below the domestic prices;[2] and food subsidies have become onerous for the Treasury.[3] This has prompted an influential group of economists to advocate:

- Dismantling of the system of minimum support price (MSP), PDS and buffer stocking;

- Removal of all restrictions on private foodgrains trade, both domestic and international;
- Holding of sufficient foreign exchange reserves to ensure food security; and
- Provision of direct income support or food stamps[4] to the poor.

The measures, it is argued, will raise efficiency through allocation of agricultural resources in line with the country's comparative advantage, reduce substantially the quantum of food subsidy, and enable the government to support an increase in investment in agriculture or other productive lines of activity.

Despite the apparent attractiveness of the scheme, implementational hurdles and market related problems make it a non-starter for alleviating poverty and promoting allocative efficiency. In light of the experiment with the Targeted Public Distribution System (TPDS), it is quite clear that any programme seeking to provide *direct subsidy* to the poor by way of cash grants or food stamps,[5] is apt to exclude a large number of deserving families, open the floodgates of corruption and leave the intended beneficiaries with only a fraction of the subsidy earmarked for them.[6] Again, there are considerable variations over time in the number as well as composition of BPL families and keeping track of these changes by the concerned authorities is next to impossible.

Second, woefully inadequate network of transport linking rural and urban areas in different parts of the country, severe shortage of storage facilities, significant credit constraints limiting private traders' investment in working capital and long-term capital stocks like godowns — all these tend to make the grain market highly imperfect. The implication is that, contrary to the presumption behind the scheme proposed, under laissez faire in food trade, distress sales in times of harvesting tend to be widespread; inter-regional as well as intertemporal foodgrains prices are characterised by large disparities; and crop failures, even of local nature, very often produce acute hunger and malnutrition.

It is also important to recognise that significant economies of scale in purchase, storage, transport and sale enable the big trader[7] to acquire a high degree of monopsony-cum-monopoly power. This results in a yawning gap between the consumer and producer prices, depresses the level of food output, and lowers the incentive for agricultural investment or adoption of new technology (Rakshit, 1993).

The policy conclusions from the foregoing are fairly robust. Because of identification problem of the poor and infrastructural-cum-credit constraints faced by private traders, some variant of universal public distribution system (UPDS) is essential in the short and medium run.[8] Even when the current impediments to private trading are removed over time, public intervention in the food market may remain necessary as a countervailing force to curb monopoly and monopsony power of large or collusive traders. Recall in this context the observation of none other than the prophet of free trade:

"People of the same trade seldom meet together, even for merriment and diversion, but the conversation ends in a conspiracy against the public, or in some contrivance to raise prices". (Smith, 1776)

What should the Food Policy try to Secure?

The objectives of the government's food policy have so far been to ensure "remunerative" prices for farmers and "affordable" prices for consumers; reduce intra- as well as inter-year variability of foodgrains prices; and provide security against food shortage due to successive harvest failures along with severe disruptions in international sources of supply. These objectives are sought to be attained through high enough minimum support prices (MSPs) for major crops[9] announced well in advance of the sowing season; weekly supply of some rationed quantity through PDS at subsidised prices; and maintenance of some minimum food stocks by FCI for running PDS and providing food security.

The important point to appreciate in this connection is that there is no rational ground for subsidising producers *per se* unless (a) they are poor; and (b) the subsidy is such that it permanently raises their incomes and can be withdrawn within a few years.[10] If the second condition is not satisfied, low incomes alone should not qualify particular groups for special support as producers. So far as the prevailing MSP system is concerned, none of the two conditions is in fact satisfied: the major beneficiaries of procurement at MSP are the big, not marginal or submarginal farmers; nor can the increase in farmers' income due to a rise in MSP (and related policies) be maintained over time unless the rise is of a permanent nature. The *primary* objective of PDS and all that has to be subsidisation of poor consumers;[11] though in the process farmers and relatively well-off consumers may receive some benefit, this cannot be a basic goal and needs to be avoided as far as possible.

In view of gross imperfections of private trading and absence of an insurance market for farmers, intra- and inter-year price stabilisation also constitute a valid objective of food policy. The economic case for reducing large inter-temporal price disparities is quite open and shut: consumers gain through a more even food intake over time; at the same time reduction of market risk promotes use of inputs on the basis of their expected returns and hence raises productivity in the food sector.

II

DESIGNING AN OPTIMAL SYSTEM OF PUBLIC INTERVENTION

We have explained the need for some variant of UPDS in the short and the medium run, if not in the long run, and also indicated why, contrary to the near universal presumption, subsidising farmers should not be a basic goal of food policy; the primary objective should rather be to ensure some minimum food intake by the poor and intertemporal price or consumption smoothing. Before designing a policy package suggested by these considerations, it is useful to appreciate the behaviour of the food market in a closed economy when public intervention takes the form of procurement at pre-stipulated MSP; steady supply of rationed quantity to consumers at below market prices; and buffer stocking and open market sales or purchases for sustenance of PDS and curbing large price increases or decreases in the open market.

Policy Instruments and Behaviour of the Food Economy

The first thing to be noted in this connection is that, given the way the foodgrains market is affected by public intervention, the government cannot set all the policy instruments independently. Thus, a higher minimum support price needs to be accompanied with larger FCI accumulation of food stocks, an increase in the quantity issued through PDS, or a reduction in ration prices.[12] The reason is that if at the higher MSP there are no changes in ration prices and quantities, open market prices will tend to go below MSP unless FCI's stock accumulation is large enough.[13] The unsustainable nature of food policy pursued over the last four to five years may thus partly be traced[14] to inadequate appreciation of such policy constraints.

Apart from the misplaced concern for farmers' fortunes, official perception regarding how PDS benefits producers and consumers has also made food policy distortionary. There is a systematic and considerable overestimation of consumer subsidy and underestimation of producer subsidy. While the first is supposed to be given by the economic cost of running PDS[15] minus the revenue realised from consumers, the second is taken to equal the cost on account of FCI's holding of "excess" stocks (GoI, 2000). There are two sources of bias in official estimate of benefits accruing to consumers. First, FCI's economic cost (inclusive of

MSP) is necessarily higher than the free market price (without public intervention) so that the gap between the former and the ration price overestimates consumer subsidy through rationing. Second, since the open market price under PDS is higher than the free market price, the consumer's net gain is less than the (true) subsidy he gets from rationing.[16]

Again, since the price received by farmers is higher under PDS than under the free play of market forces, producers' gain is always positive and can be quite significant even when FCI does not hold any excess stock (Rakshit, 2002a).

There are also serious difficulties with the way MSP is recommended by CACP[17] and these appear to be ill appreciated in official quarters. MSP, as we have seen, is fixed on the basis of current or expected average costs (including actual or imputed wages, rent, etc.), not for attaining some targeted production[18] to promote the basic objectives of food policy. Again, cost estimates from data collected from individual farmers and fixing prices on that basis involve a fallacy of composition and lead to a rise in MSP over time. The reason is that supply of inputs like land especially suited for cultivation of (say) rice or wheat may be elastic to individual farmers, but not to all producers of the crop taken together in a particular region. In this case the rental on land itself will be driven by food prices — something which has been known since Ricardo's days (Ricardo, 1817). The CACP method of fixing MSP, it is thus clear, raises production along with rental in the ensuing year, requiring an upward revision of costs and MSP in the subsequent year, and so on.

Finally, the food policy has so far been characterised by both PDS-related measures with buffer stocking and a plethora of various kinds of input subsidies. The problem is that, unlike support for extension of irrigation or adoption of new technology, most of these subsidies (e.g., on electricity, water or fertiliser) are not of an once-for-all nature and hence do not cause an enduring increase in productivity. In general, for attaining a targeted increase in output, input subsidies are much less efficient than production subsidies, remembering that the latter leave it to farmers to choose inputs on the basis of their relative costs and productivity.

Instruments and Objectives

We are now in a position to suggest the modalities of public intervention. Ignore for the moment issues relating to inter-regional and international trade as also the seasonality of foodgrains production. The policy instruments the government has then to decide on are per capita rationing, MSP, ration price and buffer stocks to be held.[19] Our earlier analysis suggests that the optimum value of the policy parameters should depend on the following factors:

- price-responsiveness of foodgrains production;
- inter-year variability of output due to climatic or other random factors;
- pattern of income distribution, food demand and extent of the calorie gap among the poor; and
- degree of efficiency or nature of private trade in the foodgrains market.

Given these factors, the choice of MSP and other instruments depends on relative weights attached to the two basic objectives and the government's (inter-temporal) budget constraint.[20] Before characterising the policy package suggested by this approach a few words on how the factors listed above affect policy measures for attaining some given goal are in order. It is not very difficult to see that a larger price responsiveness of foodgrains output requires a smaller increase in MSP in order to support a higher level of rationing. Again, the greater the uncertainty and variability of food production, the larger is the average buffer stock requirement for food security or inter-year price stability. Finally, while a fall in the incidence of poverty and malnourishment reduces the need for large-scale rationing through PDS, improvement in the efficiency of private trade permits FCI to rely more on indirect means, e.g., open market sales or purchases, to promote the basic objectives of food policy.

Inter-year Consumption Smoothing

In order to appreciate the main features of optimal public intervention in the food market let us take the food subsidy bill over a crop cycle as given and see how best to attain the objectives. If the goal is limited to reducing inter-year disparity in calorie intake and prices of foodgrains, FCI operations would be similar to that of informed and efficient competitive traders: consumption and price smoothing take place through stock accumulation in times of bounteous harvest and decumulation in draught years. When part of the carrying costs of stocks can be met through subsidy, inter-temporal smoothing by FCI can go further than under competitive trading.[21]

However, even the most efficient, competitive trading cannot guard against periodic famines and large-scale hunger under some dismal scenario.[22] It is to tackle such situations that FCI requires subsidy for "food security" stocks, not so much for price-consumption smoothing over regular crop cycles.

Policy conclusions of the foregoing are fairly simple. First, buffer stocks should differ from one year to another depending on the deviation of the actual from the average output (over a typical crop cycle). In other words, while in the longer run food stock norms require adjustments on the basis of population growth, changes in the riskiness of agricultural production or other factors, in the medium run rules relating to consumption smoothing imply pro-cyclical inter-year variations in FCI's stock holding. In fact, once the stipulated "food security" stocks have been built up, net addition to stock over a crop cycle should be zero.

Again, while prevention of periodic famines and large-scale hunger has to be a major objective of the government, food stocks required for such purposes cannot be set without any consideration for its carrying costs or alternative modes of providing different degrees of food security and their relative costs. This consideration, as we shall presently discuss, assumes especial significance in the context of international trade and framing of overall economic policy in the long run.

Minimum Support Price, Rationing and Buffer Stocking

Our analysis regarding the objectives of food policy and the relation among policy instruments and other variables suggest some general principles for setting MSP and other policy parameters. Remembering that in equilibrium the open market price cannot but approximate MSP,[23] it needs to be fixed on the basis of targeted output and producers' supply response (or marginal cost at the targeted level of production[24]). Since deviation of actual output from its average over the crop cycle depends on random factors, the government has to go by supply response in a "normal" year while fixing MSP. Again, when FCI has already been holding stocks for purposes of food security, there is no need for accumulation of stocks in such a year and consumers buy the entire output from ration shops and the open market taken together.

An important implication of the foregoing is that out of the three policy parameters,[25] MSP, rationed quantity, and issue price, the government can fix only two.[26] A given MSP, it is worth noting, supports some level of total food consumption, but its inter-family distribution is crucially affected by the quantity of rationing (or issue price): larger the amount disbursed through PDS, less the disparity in per capita consumption of food across different families. The bias in intra-family consumption also suggests the desirability of guaranteeing some minimum food intake per head through PDS even if it involves some increase in the issue price.[27]

Ensuring an enhanced minimum consumption generally requires a higher MSP and larger food subsidy so that the choice in this regard cannot be independent of other objectives and costs of their attainment. However, even with a food subsidy bill that is not too onerous to the Treasury, there is considerable scope for improving nutritional standard of the poor through reformulation of the food policy package along with some supplementary measures.[28]

Consider the major reason for the rise in food subsidy bill from 0.42 per cent of GDP in 96-97 to 0.84 per cent in 01-02 (GoI, 2002). Our analysis suggests that the combination of high MSP, low quantity of rationing and the dual issue prices for BPL and APL families tended to drive open market prices below MSP, caused sharp increases in FCI's addition to stocks, led to a quantum jump in its carrying costs, and made the system non-viable in the medium run. Quite clearly, families other than those fortunate enough to be registered as BPL and to receive the stipulated quotas were worse off under TPDS than under the free market.[29] There are reasons to believe that under the system in force consumers, instead of being subsidised, were heavily penalised for the benefit of producers! Indeed, experience over the last five years illustrates how absence of an appropriate theoretical framework can not only make the policy package unsustainably costly, but defeat the very objectives of such measures.[30] It should thus be possible to ensure at least the 1996 per capita PDS quotas at subsidised prices without adding to the government's budgetary woes. Let us consider in the present section the relatively short-term changes suggested by our analysis.

First, abandonment of the price fixing principle followed so far[31] and making MSP based on producers' supply response for attaining some targeted output will go a long way in reducing the food subsidy bill in the short run and (what is no less if not more important) in putting a brake on its rising trend in the long run. The reason is that MSP can be brought down significantly below its present level without impairing FCI's ability to keep per capita rationing and (real) issue prices at their 1996 levels.[32]

Second, remembering that input subsidies reduce allocative efficiency and raise production costs (in real terms), withdrawal of these subsidies, even when coupled with an upward revision of MSP to keep the targeted output level unchanged, reduces the total subsidy bill and helps in furthering the primary objectives of food policy.

Third, while there may not be much scope in the short or medium run for reducing stocks for purposes of food security,[33] FCI's carrying costs can be brought down significantly if its accumulation of stocks during years of above normal output is balanced by decumulation over periods of below average harvest.

Fourth, in sharp contrast to the widely held view,[34] we have noted: (a) why providing a boost to farmers' income should not be an objective of food policy; and (b) how the lion's share of benefits from PDS go to big and medium farmers. Thus, both equity and medium run budgetary viability strongly suggest the need for instituting an effective system of agricultural income tax or land revenue so that the overall fiscal balance improves and there is a fall in the government's net subsidy bill on account of MSP and associated measures.

Finally, the PDS can be made more cost effective by setting higher MSP in deficit than in surplus regions.[35] The differential, as the perceptive reader must have surmised, should approximate the transport and associated costs of moving grains from the surplus to deficit States. Adoption of the scheme reduces FCI's total costs, as the saving due to lower volume of transport more than outweighs the increase in FCI's procurement cost.[36]

III

FOOD POLICY IN AN OPEN ECONOMY

Our analysis has so far been conducted without any reference to possibilities of exports or imports of foodgrains. It is time we consider whether or how far international trade in cereals can promote the basic objectives of food policy. Since in this regard our approach differs significantly from that of HLC, we may explain first why the Committee's recommendations relating to trade do not seem appropriate from the viewpoint of cost effectiveness in running PDS or of ensuring food security.

Behind HLC's recommendations lies the perception that "India must continue to plan for cereals self-sufficiency" (GoI, 2002), since not only the country, with around 15 per cent of world cereals output, cannot be a price taker in the international market, but reliance on trade may pose a threat to our food security due to monopolistic power of rich countries in world grain trade. It is also suggested that since international prices of wheat and rice are much more volatile than their domestic counterparts, trade will expose farmers to greater risk and make FCI's task of inter-year price stabilisation more difficult. Hence the Committee is in favour of adjusting tariffs to changing international prices so that MSPs, fixed on the basis of domestic costs, could be sustained.[37]

For our part we believe that international tråde, suitably used, can be a potent means of furthering the objectives noted in Section I in both the short and the long run. The reasons behind our perceptions may be worth summarising at this stage.

First, conventional analysis suggests that cost of ensuring some minimum per capita consumption of cereals through the public distribution system will be less with than without international trade in foodgrains.[38]

Second, when domestic and international production and prices are not fully correlated, the cost of consumption smoothing and guaranteeing food security is also less with appropriate buffer stocking backed by purchases or sales in the two markets.

Third, while measures for raising agricultural productivity are extremely important, their purpose should be to raise efficiency of resource use and making agriculture less dependent on the monsoon, not to attain cereals self sufficiency *per se*. Nor will reliance on trade, with an efficient agricultural sector capable of responding to changing market conditions, undermine national security in the long run.

Now for an extension of our earlier analysis in the context of an open economy.

Policy Instruments

While framing the policy package with possibilities of imports or exports we need to take cognisance of two factors which make complete free trade a sub-optimal solution. First, international prices of foodgrains (especially of rice) are not insensitive to the levels of India's exports or imports. Second, both the average (or normal) external market conditions and their variability now become important in the government's choice of policy instruments. In this context let us see how best to exploit trading opportunities to promote the objectives of food policy.

Consider first the policy instruments relevant for a year when supply and demand conditions are normal in both domestic and international markets.[39] Assume further that FCI is already in possession of stocks for ensuring food security so that there would be no net addition to stocks in such a year.[40] Note finally that, as in the closed economy, MSP has to approximate domestic open market price.

The most efficient mode[41] of supplying a given quantity of foodgrains for domestic users, it is easy to see, involves equality of domestic marginal cost and the cost of import at the margin.[42] The implication is that once the government chooses the quantity of rationing and the issue price, the other policy parameters (for the average year), viz., MSP and the tariff rate,[43] are automatically determined. A few words on the nature of instruments and objectives are perhaps in order at this stage.

The larger the quantity of rationing or lower the issue price under PDS, the larger is the aggregate consumption of food. Under our policy package part of the increase is secured through additional output through a higher MSP, but part also comes from enlarged imports, with adjustments in tariffs to keep marginal cost of imports equal to the enhanced MSP. It is also worth noting that agricultural income tax proposed under our scheme along with the import tariff produces a moderating influence on the food subsidy bill.

Given some targeted consumption and issue price, even in a normal year cost minimisation may involve imports in some areas while exports from others, remembering that we have advocated higher MSP in deficit than in surplus regions. Thus, part of the demand for foodgrains in peninsular India may perhaps be met through imports from Thailand, while rice and wheat are exported from Northern India to the Middle East.

If exports are required in a normal year to meet the basic objectives of food policy, market conditions suggest the need for a tax on exports as well. The reason is basically the same as in the case of imports: only with an appropriate tax will the marginal earnings from export equal the marginal cost of domestic production. Thus, subsidising exports or imports can never be a sensible policy when domestic supply is not completely insensitive to price changes.

Finally, whether the country should be a net exporter or importer of foodgrains depends not only on internal and external demand-supply conditions, but also on the nutritional standard targeted by the government. Though domestic prices of wheat and rice are now higher than international prices, the reason lies in FCI's accumulation of stocks and subsidised exports. Free trade with no FCI intervention is likely to drive domestic prices below the international level and India could emerge as an exporter of foodgrains sans subsidy. But this will by no means be a desirable outcome since the basic reason for relatively low domestic prices is inadequate income or low purchasing power of a large number of consumers. The least cost policy of ensuring them some minimum level of food intake is likely to involve imports rather than exports in a normal year. It is only when agricultural productivity has risen sufficiently can India become an exporter of foodgrains after meeting the nutritional needs of her citizens.

Buffer Stocking and Food Security

So far we have dealt with the nature of policies to be pursued in a normal year when there is no net accumulation of stocks and FCI holdings of stocks are just sufficient to provide (the desired degree of) food security. For purposes of inter-year consumption smoothing, it is necessary to add to or reduce stocks when there are deviations in domestic and international supply conditions from their averages. However, while this principle of stock variation is quite easy to appreciate, some remarks on application of the principle seem useful, since the precise phasing of domestic and international crop cycles are not generally the same. Thus, in any year both the magnitude and sign of departures of actual domestic and international supply of foodgrains from their respective averages may be different. Instead of going into all possible combinations of these departures we illustrate the nature of policy requirements under one or two situations.

Note first that since departures from the average are due to random factors, MSP, as in a closed economy, should be left unchanged over the crop cycle.[44] However, with deviations of actual from average supply conditions in the two markets, tariff rate, domestic procurement, imports and accumulation of stocks need to be different from those in a normal year. Thus, when the domestic situation is normal but international supply is above average, there should be addition to stocks through increase in imports with appropriate adjustment in tariffs.[45] It is also not very difficult to see that if in a particular year both domestic and international supply conditions are below normal, stocks are to be reduced, procurement and imports lowered, and tariffs adjusted suitably (in line with the cost minimisation principle). What if a domestic bountiful harvest is coupled with a sharp fall in international supply? In this situation the objectives of food policy are served best through enhanced procurement, along with export of foodgrains.[46] However, even in this case it is necessary to impose an export tax, not provide a subsidy.[47]

Before taking up some issues of a general nature in the next section we draw attention to three features of the scheme suggested for an open economy. First, with no inter-year changes in domestic and external market conditions, the food subsidy bill for providing some targeted public distribution at given issue prices will be less in this scheme than under autarky.

Second, since domestic and international supply conditions are not perfectly correlated, average stocks to be carried for consumption smoothing and provision of food security will be less with reliance on trade.

Third, for cost effectiveness and guarding against exchange rate risk, it is generally necessary to hold food stocks along with some foreign exchange reserves, with the two serving as substitutes (though imperfect substitutes) for one another.

IV

ON HOW TO MAKE PDS REDUNDANT

The PDS related measures form part of an overall policy package for attaining some basic economic and social goals. However, there are three important limitations of the measures which need to be taken note of while formulating other policies. First, even with an extensive coverage PDS by itself may leave a large number of people malnourished — people who are too poor to draw their full ration from fair price shops. Second, in the absence of other short and long term measures, the food subsidy bill can prove extremely burdensome to the Treasury. Third, a major problem with PDS and all such special schemes is that they tend to create vested interests (in both official and non-official circles) which produce their own dynamics and distort government policies. An important criterion for judging the success of these schemes is thus the rapidity with which they can be scaled down significantly, if not dismantled altogether, without compromising on the primary objectives of food policy.

The problems noted above call for two types of measures, some relatively short or medium term, others long term. The period 1995-02, we have emphasised elsewhere (Rakshit, 2002), was marked by a sharp increase in underutilised industrial capacity, rising rate of unemployment and fall in per capita consumption of foodgrains — features which were not unrelated to one another.[48] Full utilisation of labour and non-labour resources, apart from serving other objectives, will be a most potent instrument of raising the nutritional standard of the poor. For pockets of widespread and endemic poverty identified through NSS data, PDS has to be backed up by supplementary measures like food-for-work programmes. In view of considerable slack in the economy and excess stocks being carried by FCI, these programmes as also public investment in infrastructural facilities, we have explained in our earlier paper on food policy (Rakshit, 2001), will, contrary to popular perception, in fact strengthen the government's fiscal balance in the short and medium run.

The most effective and enduring means of eliminating hunger and making PDS redundant in the long run is to raise the income earning capacity of the poor. Remembering that malnutrition leads to morbidity or disability and that inadequate diet of expectant mothers and children retards the latter's mental as well as physical development, ensuring some minimum food intake for the needy through PDS, mid-day meals at schools or other schemes, should be regarded as investment in human resources as well as a means of helping vulnerable groups escape the (inter-generational) poverty trap. This would over time go a long way in effecting significant cuts in public expenditure on support schemes for the indigent. Similarly, especial efforts to extend educational and health services to these groups on a priority basis should help speed up the overall growth process, effect an enduring improvement in income distribution, and provide a boost to the country's quality of life.

While the importance of raising productive capacity of the indigent can hardly be overemphasised, it is also necessary to ensure that this capacity is properly utilised or there is an adequate increase in fruitful employment opportunities. It is beyond the scope of the paper to produce a comprehensive blueprint for development in all spheres. However, in the context of the present enquiry we cannot avoid adding a few words on some measures relating to agriculture that would make food policy more effective and cost efficient in the long run.

While we do not agree with HLC's thrust on self-sufficiency in food production irrespective of costs, it is extremely important to reverse the declining trend in agricultural growth and reduce its volatility observed over the last twelve years, particularly since 1994. This trend has occurred, it is worth noting, despite sharp year-to-year increases in MSPs, generally much in excess of what were recommended by CACP (GoI, 2002). The basic reason behind the slow growth and its volatility, as we have detailed elsewhere (Rakshit, 2002), was fall in public investment in agriculture, especially in irrigation. This, thanks to the crowding in effect, has also brought down private capital accumulation in the farm sector so that performance of this sector has become heavily dependent on climatic factors, and agricultural productivity in India lags behind that in countries like China, Thailand or Vietnam. Hence, the need for stepping up agricultural investment in general and extension of irrigation facilities[49] in particular. At the same time, it is necessary to put in place an effective institutional arrangement to supply credit to farmers for long-term investment and working capital.

The proposals are not for attaining self reliance in food production as such, but to realise the production potential of the farm sector and make agriculture less dependent on vagaries of the monsoon. Under the changed scenario whether the country is to become a net importer or exporter of foodgrains will depend on the relative efficiency of production of different crops.[50] Even if the country becomes an importer, food security is not compromised, remembering that:

(a) an increase in agricultural income (with enhanced overall productive capacity of farms and efficient cropping pattern) raises the purchasing power of the large majority of the poor (the greater part of whom live in rural areas);

(b) improvement in irrigation, credit and other facilities enable farmers to diversify and switch from one crop to another on the basis of changing market conditions;

(c) fall in volatility of food output reduces the need to hold large buffer stocks; and

(d) enhanced trade in agricultural products under a regime of optimal import and export tariffs, raises tax proceeds and the government's ability to support, if necessary, an increase in stocks for purposes of food security.

Finally for policies aimed at development of efficient trading in farm products — a development which provides a boost to agricultural productivity;[51] brings down inter-regional disparity in food consumption and greatly reduces the need for public intervention in the foodgrains markets. Improvement in marketing network requires two types of policies. The first consists in investment in infrastructural facilities like trading centres, transport, godowns and communications including easy access to and means of transmitting information. Because of co-ordination problem among private investors[52] and public goods character of many of these facilities, the government has to play the major role in investing for market development. Second, one of the most important sources of inefficiency and distortion in private trading is lack of adequate credit facilities. This causes post-harvest distress sales, local monopsony-cum-monopoly in foodgrains market and large intra- as well as inter-year variations in consumption of food. Easy access to trading capital along with development of marketing facilities can greatly reduce the role of FCI in buffer stocking and correcting for regional imbalances in cereal intakes. However, given the economies of scale in trading, FCI will still have to act as a countervailing agent to neutralise the monopoly power of big traders.

V

CONCLUSIONS

1. The proposal for dismantling PDS and relying on food stamps is unlikely at the present juncture to meet some minimum nutritional requirement of the poor. The reason lies in difficulty of identifying the poor; likely misuse of the stamps in view of their liquidity and ease of forgery; and gross underdevelopment of private trading in foodgrains, characterised by monopoly-cum-monopsony of traders in many a locality.
2. There have been considerable distortions in food policy pursued so far because of wrong priorities, poor perception of the extent of benefits accruing to different groups and inadequate apprcciation of the limits the government faces in wielding simultaneously the policy instruments at its disposal. Apart from the fact that providing subsidy to (mostly big and medium) farmers should not be an objective of food policy, it is not realised that over the last five years in particular the major beneficiary under PDS has been producers, while subsidy to consumers, properly measured, has mostly been negative.
3. MSP needs to be fixed on thc basis of the targeted output and the producers' supply response, i.e., at the marginal (not average) cost of targeted production. It is also important to recognise that a higher MSP requires for its sustenance a larger PDS quota, a lower ration price or a higher rate of addition to food stocks. Absence of such perceptions has been a major factor behind the FCI's woes in recent years.
4. For attaining some given objective relating to rationing and food security, there is considerable scope for reduction in the subsidy bill. The most important of the cost saving measures are marginal cost based MSP; setting higher MSP for farmers in deficit than in surplus states; judicious use of imports or exports for economising on use of resources; addition to or decumulation of stocks depending on whether the supply conditions in domestic and international markets are above or below normal; and imposition of an agricultural income tax or land revenue.
5. Special measures for raising incomes in areas identified as pockets of endemic poverty are needed side by side with PDS. In the long run reliance on PDS can be reduced significantly and food policy objectives better met through an enduring increase in human

resource development of the poor on a priority basis; enhancement of agricultural productivity through provision of irrigation facilities along with diffusion of knowledge relating to farming practices; and investment in storage, transport and communication for development of private trading.

Notes

1. Foodgrains output fell in 97-98 and 00-01. Even so, procurement recorded substantial increases in each year. So did FCI's excess stocks (over buffer norms), from 1.9 million tonnes in April, 97 to 35.2 million tonnes in April, 02, despite the disposal of more than 17 million tonnes during 01-02 through (subsidised) exports and food-for-work and related schemes outside PDS.
2. Indeed, the open market prices will nosedive were FCI to offload its excess stocks.
3. As we have emphasised before (Rakshit, 2001), proper valuation of FCI stocks will make the food subsidy bill much larger than its official figure.
4. Food stamps serve as a means of payments for buying food.
5. Cash grants, *a la* the text book theory of consumer behaviour, is the best form of subsidy. Even when food stamps can be traded, because of transactions costs they are considered less utility enhancing. For a given amount of government outgo, price subsidy, because of its distortionary effects on the consumer's choice on the one hand and composition of GDP on the other, is taken to be the least efficient.
6. As the CAG report (GoI, 2000) notes, a large number of States and Union Territories made little effort to identify below poverty line (BPL) families; and what is most disconcerting, in States with large concentration of BPL families, the performance of TPDS was abysmal. This is apart from the fact that the official poverty line criterion, even when applied efficiently for purposes of identification, would leave out around 45 per cent of population suffering from endemic nutritional deficiency and spending more than 60 per cent of their consumption outlay on food (GoI, 2002).
7. Who can manage to garner sufficient funds. Note also that credit market imperfections, transport difficulties and low density of buyers and sellers tend to produce local monopoly-cum-monopsony.
8. The High Level Committee (HLC), it is gratifying to note, also favours going back from the Targeted Public Distribution System (TPDS) to UPDS. HLC also observes how TPDS has undermined viability of fair price shops and deprived BPL families easy access to PDS, even where they have been officially identified (GoI, 2002).
9. The MSP recommended by the Commission on Agricultural Costs and Prices (CACP) is designed to yield a "fair" return over costs inclusive of inputed costs of family labour, owned capital and rental on land.
10. The other and familiar ground for government support is positive externality, as in the case of introduction of new technology, which raises overall productivity through learning and diffusion.

11. The case for supporting the poor's food intake is buttressed by what economists call consumption-productivity nexus: improved nourishment reduces the incidence of disease and disability, and raises the income earning ability of the poor in the short as well as the long run.

12. Ignoring international trading possibilities for the moment.

13. It is not very difficult to see that aggregate demand for food (including that in the open market) can be boosted sufficiently to avoid stock accumulation if there is a large enough increase in the quantum of rationing or cutback in ration prices. See Rakshit (2002a) for a rigorous formulation of the argument in terms of interdependence between PDS and open market equilibrium.

14. Though the more important factors behind unsustainability, as elaborated in Rakshit (2001), seem macroeconomic.

15. i.e., the cost of procurement, storage and distribution of the quantity sold through PDS.

16. In fact, with large enough accumulation of stocks by FCI, the consumers' net gain can be negative under PDS, even though the ration price is considerably less than the open market price (Rakshit, 2002a).

17. Even if we ignore the fact that MSPs set by the government have been persistently higher than those recommended by CACP.

18. For realising some targeted output, MSP needs to be fixed on the basis of marginal costs. Estimation of such costs is no doubt difficult; but for its recommendations to make good economic sense, CACP has to conduct serious studies on supply response of agricultural crops.

19. Only three out of the four policy instruments, as we have seen, can be set independently.

20. Remembering that deficits in some years may be balanced through surpluses in others.

21. Though complete inter-year equality of consumption cannot in general be optimum, since attainment of such equality involves use of scarce resources (reflected in carrying costs).

22. e.g., a succession of crop failures, a relatively rare phenomenon. Since private traders are guided solely by profit motive and the probability of such an event is quite low, food stocks carried by them will be quite inadequate to meet such contingencies. The problem is compounded when traders act in collusion and trigger off a scarcity psychosis to set prices sky rocketing.

23. When MSP is less than the open market price, procurement cannot be sustained; in the opposite case FCI has to lift the entire output so that unless this amount is sold through rationing, PDS will collapse due to unabated accumulation of stocks.

24. We have already explained why the CACP method of setting MSP should be abandoned.

25. Relevant for the average year.

26. Thus, once the first two are fixed, the issue price has to be such that in a normal year open market demand at the price equaling the stipulated MSP totals output less PDS sales (or procurement).

27. Malnutrition among children is in fact more widespread in India than in Sub-Saharan Africa, notorious for famines and acute poverty. Note however that (given MSP and the associated output) the higher issue price corresponding to a larger PDS quota may force some poor families to reduce their purchase from ration shops and hence defeat the objective of food policy. Hence, arises the need for (a) striking a balance between a large enough quota and a low enough issue price; and (b) supplementary measures to relieve the hardship of poor families. We shall discuss the nature of these measures in Section IV.

28. HLC (GoI, 2002) has made a number of recommendations for reducing FCI's operational costs. Our focus is more on removing the structural inefficiencies of the system.

29. With no public intervention by way of MSP, PDS, etc.

30. In this instance there were two proximate sources of policy failure. First, the official measures of consumer and producer subsidies, we have already noted, were quite misleading. Second, there was an inadequate appreciation of how policy instruments were related with one another and how they impacted on relevant variables like the food subsidy bill or benefits accruing to different groups.

31. In fact the government has for quite a while been fixing MSP much above the CACP's recommended price.

32. HLC (GoI, 2002) also suggests a reduction in MSP; but in order to make its recommendations acceptable to big farmers' lobby, the committee suggests the reduction to be coupled with compensation to losing farmers. It also seems that the committee's recommendations are not backed by a rigorous analytical framework. However, this does not detract from the fact that many of HLC's recommendations are quite sensible, and their observations on some of the relevant issues pertinent.

33. Ignoring international trade for the moment.

34. Thus, even HLC (GoI, 2002) suggests that through its MSP policy the government should "assure growers an adequate return on their cost".

35. Something which HLC, subscribing to the prevailing view that "the MSP should truly be a national level floor price", does not recommend, even though the Committee recognises that the current practice produces a bias in favour of farmers in surplus States and against those in deficit regions. However, in view of our concern for nutritional status of the poor we suggest uniform ration quotas and prices throughout the country, since there is no alternative scheme which serves this basic objective better, and is not too difficult to implement at the same time.

36. On account of higher prices paid to farmers in deficit areas.

37. "Import tariffs", HLC suggests, "should be varied with world prices to ensure that the tariff inclusive c.i.f. cost of imports does not fall below the economic cost of supplying peninsular India with grain purchased at MSP in North and East India". When world prices are high, HLC favours import subsidy, provided this does not push open market prices "below their normal levels determined on the basis of economic cost". Similar principles are suggested for export tariffs or subsidies to keep domestic prices in line with MSP.

38. Remembering that total costs can be brought down by switching, at the margin, from domestic to foreign sources of supply or vice versa, depending on the

relative marginal costs of procurement from the two sources. More on this while spelling out our policy package.

39. When these conditions are subject to random factors and it is possible to segregate the two markets through tariffs or subsidies.

40. Unless the country is already facing an extraordinary situation in relation to stocks.

41. Implying minimisation of cost to the country. Note that cost of import at the margin will be higher than the c.i.f. price of import when the country's purchase from the rest of the world affects the international price.

42. Which is higher than the c.i.f. import price, remembering that the country's trade in the particular market is not insignificant. In case the equality condition is not satisfied, cost of meeting domestic demand can be reduced through substitution at the margin of supply from the dearer by that from the cheaper source.

43. At the tariff inclusive import price the amount imported is such that its marginal cost to the country equals MSP. See footnote 41 in this connection.

44. This may be difficult to implement in an outlier case characterised by periods of successive and synchronised adverse supply shocks in the international as well as the domestic market.

45. So that the marginal import cost in that year equals MSP. The tariff rate, it is interesting to note, may be higher or lower than in a normal year, and depends on the relative responsiveness of international prices to the quantity of imports.

46. So that costs of PDS and buffer-stocking are minimised.

47. The reason, let us recall, is that under the presumed conditions, international prices are negatively related to exports.

48. They were also related to huge accumulation of food stocks in FCI granaries.

49. Which now cover only 38 per cent of total area under food production.

50. Given the improved infrastructural facilities and availability of credit, whether farmers produce more of food or of other crops will be governed by their relative rates of return. The government can induce larger food production through a higher MSP; but this, as we have seen, may not promote the objectives of food policy. However, our analysis in the earlier section suggests that even under the changed scenario trade in foodgrains should be managed, not left entirely to market forces.

51. Through efficient cropping pattern across regions and an increase in the ratio of retail prices going to farmers.

52. Remembering that to be effective most of these facilities have to be provided simultaneously.

References

Government of India (2000), *Expenditure Reforms Commission's Report on Food Subsidy*, July, New Delhi.

Government of India, Comptroller and Auditor General of India (2000), *Food Security and Nutritional Support*, December, New Delhi.

Government of India, Union Ministry of Consumers Affairs, Food and Public Distribution (2001), *Interim Report of the High Level Committee on Long-term Grain Policy*, May, New Delhi.

———. (2002), *Final Report of the High Level Committee on Long-term Grain Policy*, July, New Delhi.

Rakshit, M. (1993), *Trade, Mercantile Capital and Economic Development*, Orient Longman.

———. (2001), "Some Public Economics of Food Subsidy and Buffer Stock Operations in India: Part I", *Money & Finance*, January-June.

———. (2002), "Some Macroeconomics of India's Reforms Experience", paper presented at Cornell University Conference, April.

———. (2002a), "Long Term Food Policy: Some Analytical and Policy Issues", *Economic and Political Weekly*.

Ricardo, David (1817), *Principles of Political Economy and Taxation*, Everyman, London, 1949.

Smith, Adam (1776), *An Enquiry into the Nature and Causes of the Wealth of Nations*, Modern Library, New York.

ICRA Bulletin, Money & Finance, April-Sept., 2002.

15

Growth and Welfare Consequences of Rise in MSP

Kirit S. Parikh, A Ganesh Kumar & Gangadhar Darbha

I

INTRODUCTION

The mounting food stocks amidst substantial poverty and under-nutrition raise questions on our agricultural policy. Government food stocks were 59.1 million tonnes as of November 30, 2001. With the bumper crop in the agricultural season July 2001 to June 2002, food stocks reached a high of 64.72 million tonnes as of June 1, 2002. The existence of such large stocks in a country with 200 million persons below poverty line is an absurdity. The question is why are the stocks mounting? What is wrong with our policy?

The main reason for increase in food stocks is related to the government procurement price policy. The problem is the level at which the government sets procurement prices, which have become minimum support prices (MSP) over the years. For many years now these prices have been higher than what free market prices would have been. The government, through Food Corporation of India (FCI) buys up whatever is offered at procurement prices ensuring that the harvest price for a particular commodity does not fall below its procurement price. Under the pressure of the farm lobby the prices are set high. At these prices, what farmers produce consumers do not demand for want of adequate purchasing power.

The procurement prices are set by the government on the recommendation of committee on agricultural costs and prices (CACP). The CACP's recommendations are based on costs of cultivation and adequate return to farmers. Table 15.1 shows the CACP recommended prices and the prices set by the government. For a number of recent years, the government has set prices particularly of wheat, at higher levels than recommended by the CACP.

TABLE – 15.1

Procurement Prices for Fair Average Quality Wheat and Paddy

(Rs/Quint)

Crop Year	Paddy		Wheat	
	CACP	Government	CACP	Government
1990-1991	205	205	200	215
1991-1992	235	230	225	225
1992-1993	260	270	245	250
1993-1994	310	310	305	330
1994-1995	340	340	350	350
1995-1996	355	360	360	360
1996-1997	370	380	380	380
1997-1998	415	415	405	475
1998-1999	440	440	455	510
1999-2000	465	490	490	550
2000-2001	510	510	550	580
2001-2002	520	530	580	610

What happens when government increases procurement prices? High procurement price gives farmers an incentive to produce more. They will use more fertilisers and increase yield. But higher price would also reduce demand. To support price, FCI would have to procure more. Stocks would rise further. The government will have to finance the addition to stock. This is done by cutting some other expenditure. The easiest to cut is investment. Less would be invested in agriculture. Irrigation capacity would not grow as much. In a year or two the cumulative impact of lower irrigation would reduce growth rate of agricultural output despite higher procurement price. Farmers themselves could be worse off compared to what they could have been had investment in irrigation not reduced.

Apart from that consumers and particularly the poor consumers may also be hurt. The poor consisting of landless labour, small and marginal farmers are net purchasers of food. They are able to buy less food even when one accounts for increase in wage rate that may follow higher procurement price.

In order to appreciate better the consequences of a procurement price hike, it would be instructive to analyse the exact quantitative impact of a price hike on the growth and welfare of producers and consumers. To undertake such an exercise in a credible way, we need a numerical simulation model that accounts for the inter-sectoral interactions that one finds in a modern economy, price determination and income distribution mechanisms. This note summarises the findings of a recently completed study [Parikh et al, 2002] that explores in an integrated way the consequences of increasing MSP of wheat and rice by 10 per cent.

II

AN APPLIED GENERAL EQUILIBRIUM MODEL FOR INDIA

For this purpose we built a dynamic applied general equilibrium model for India. The model parameters are estimated and the model itself is calibrated for the base year to match the social accounting matrix (SAM) for 1996-97. A detailed discussion of the SAM can be found in Ganesh Kumar and Darbha (1998). The SAM, besides accounting for all the intersectoral and agent transactions for a given year, is made consistent with a demand system estimated over various consumption and commodity classes.[1] Other notable features of the model are: endogenous determination of level of stocks within the model without imposing any arbitrary stock limits, self or home grown consumption possibilities and consumption out of ration shops for some household classes. The later two features are of crucial importance for the purpose on hand as the impact of a price hike on different population classes would differ depending upon whether they are net producers or consumers of the food commodities, which is determined by the proportion of their total consumption they buy from 'home' and ration shops. If a large proportion of their consumption is 'home' grown and comes from 'ration' shops, an increase in market prices cannot affect their real consumptions and welfare significantly. However, the levels of home grown and ration consumption would themselves be affected by the equilibrium prices prevailing in the economy and hence a model that attempts to capture the welfare impacts of a price hike must explicitly account for the endogenous determination of different components of household consumption. Our model accounts for these [for the technical details see Parikh et al, 2002].

In the model the economy is characterised by 65 commodity producing sectors and 10 types of households classified first by their location of residence into two broad groups – rural and urban and within each of them into five classes based on their annual per capita real expenditure (Table 15.2). The model is sequentially dynamic in the sense that it is solved for every year in a sequential manner with the previous year's solution providing a starting value for the next year. The policy shock that we analyse is a one time 10 per cent hike in procurement price of wheat and rice.

TABLE – 15.2

Classification in the Model

A: List of Commodities

Fixed-output Commodities

1 Rice
2 Wheat
3 Other Cereals
4 Pulses
5 Sugarcane
6 Jute
7 Cotton
8 Tea and Coffee
9 Rubber
10 Other Crops
11 Animal Husbandry
12 Forestry and Logging
13 Fishing
14 Coal and Lignite
15 Crude Petroleum and Natural Gas
16 Iron Ore
17 Other Metallic Minerals
18 Non Metallic Minor Minerals
19 Sugar
20 Khandsari
21 Edible Oils

Flexible-output Commodities

22 Other Food and Beverages
23 Cotton Textiles
24 Woolen Textiles
25 Silk Textiles
26 Art Silk and Synthetic Textiles
27 Jute Hemp Mesta Textiles
28 Readymade Garments
29 Other Textiles
30 Wood and Wood Products
31 Paper and Paper Products
32 Leather and Leather Products
33 Rubber Products
34 Plastic Products
35 Petroleum Products
36 Fertilisers*
37 Pesticides
38 Synthetic Fibre and Resin
39 Paints Drugs Cosmetics
40 Other Chemicals
41 Cement
42 Other Non Metallic Mineral Products
43 Iron and Steel
44 Non Ferrous Metals
45 Tractors and Other Agricultual Machinery
46 Other Non Electrical Machinery
47 Electrical Machinery
48 Communication and Electronic Equipment
49 Rail Equipment
50 Motor Vehicles
51 Motorcycle Scooter and Bicycles
52 Other Transport Equipment
53 Other Manufacturing
54 Construction
55 Electricity*
56 Gas
57 Water Supply
58 Rail Transport Service*
59 Other Transport Service
60 Communication
61 Trade
62 Financial Services
63 Social Services
64 Public Administration
65 Other Services

B: Agents

Households and Government.

> Households classified based on location into Rural and Urban.

Within Rural and Urban – five household classes based on annual per capita real expenditure.

Class limits: 0 to 1,800; 1,801 to 3,600; 3,601 to 7,200; 7,201 to 21,600; 21,601 and above.

Notes: * These commodities have administered prices for all type of transactions.

III

THE SCENARIOS

Policy analysis using a model requires specification of the prevailing and changed policy regimes. To facilitate comparison a base/reference scenario is first generated and the outcomes of policy scenarios are compared with that of reference scenario.

The reference scenario, labelled 'REF', against which policy scenarios are compared, is a business-as-usual scenario in which the policy environment specified in the model corresponds to the actual policies observed during the base period, 1996-97. The policy scenario is designed as a one time increase by 10 per cent in the support price of these two commodities in the second year, with all other parameters kept at their base scenario levels. That is, the government assures the producers of rice and wheat a 10 per cent higher price by committing to buy whatever amounts of these two commodities that they may offer for sale. Given fixed rates of trade and transport margins and indirect tax/ subsidies on these two commodities, this hike in procurement price and hence producer price will translate into a commensurate rise in both their market price and the ration price.

IV

RESULTS

Macro Impacts

A hike in procurement prices of rice and wheat results in a marginal decline in total GDP (at constant prices) in the first year of the price hike, because of a fall in GDP non-agriculture (Table 15.3). Agricultural GDP is marginally higher. This increase in agricultural GDP is, however, insufficient to compensate for the fall in non-agricultural GDP and consequently, total GDP is lower in all the years.

The fall in non-agricultural GDP is attributable to the decline in aggregate demand due to rise in the overall price indices and decline in total fixed investments in the economy. The rise in overall price indices to the tune of 1 to 1.5 per cent leads to a general reduction in real incomes and hence demand. Non-agricultural output being demand determined consequently declines. The decline in fixed investments is due to the additional expenditure that the government incurs to support the hike in procurement prices. This additional expenditure arises due to both an increase in procurement prices as well as the quantity procured. Given the overall resource constraint, the additional expenditure on building up stocks comes at the cost of a decline in fixed investments.

While the additional expenditure on stocks favours only rice and wheat, the decline in fixed investments adversely affects the demand for many non-agricultural sectors, and hence the decline in non-agricultural GDP.

TABLE – 15.3

Macro Indicators

	1997	1998	1999	2000
GDP at factor cost (Rs. million)				
REF	11497726	12235821	12923826	13561795
MSP10_LLA	0.00	-0.11	-0.07	-0.33
GDP agriculture (Rs. million)				
REF	3085217	3298892	3457717	3575781
MSP10_LLA	0.00	0.00	0.46	0.03
GDP non-agriculture (Rs. million)				
REF	8412509	8936930	9466110	9986014
MSP10_LLA	0.00	-0.15	-0.26	-0.45
GDP at market prices (Rs. million)				
REF	12767350	13524401	14293975	15028997
MSP10_LLA	0.00	-0.09	-0.08	-0.35
Total savings (Rs. million)				
REF	3479866	3512898	3729888	4017305
MSP10_LLA	0.00	0.83	0.66	-0.42
Total fixed investments (Rs. million)				
REF	3325974	3349796	3538453	3861674
MSP10_LLA	0.00	-0.12	-0.83	-1.88
Net stock purchase (Rs. million)				
REF	153918	163101	191438	155612
MSP10_LLA	0.00	20.30	28.29	35.65
Consumer price index				
REF	100.0	92.4	92.9	101.6
MSP10_LLA	0.00	1.64	1.70	0.94
Producer price index				
REF	100.0	92.3	94.3	105.6
MSP10_LLA	0.00	1.63	1.71	0.99
Agricultural investments share in total investments (per cent)				
REF	8.57	8.57	8.45	8.43
MSP10_LLA	0.00	0.00	0.40	0.49
Agricultural investments (Rs million – at current prices)				
REF	285041	282577	296916	343508
MSP10_LLA	0.00	0.02	-0.28	-4.56
Gross irrigated area (000 hectares)				
REF	73275	75075	75385	77852
MSP10_LLA	0.00	0.00	0.01	-0.14
Gross cropped area (000 hectares)				
REF	189543	189517	190011	191762
MSP10_LLA	0.00	0.00	0.00	-0.03

Notes: 1 The figures for REF are in levels (units for each variable indicated in brackets).
2 All rupee valued variables are at constant prices unless mentioned otherwise.
3 The figures for MSP10_LLA are percentage change over REF levels.
4 Agriculture's share in total fixed investments are at current prices.

The decline in overall investments results in decline in agricultural investment also despite the higher relative price of agriculture. This is felt in terms of virtually insignificant growth in gross irrigated area and gross cropped area, and hence agricultural GDP and in the later years, despite a favourable shift in relative prices towards agriculture.

Thus from a macro perspective, the results indicate that the policy to hike procurement prices of rice and wheat has an adverse impact on overall growth, raises the level of inflation, reduces investment, and has a minuscule impact on agricultural GDP.

Impact on Agricultural Production, Consumption and Stocks

With the hike in prices of rice and wheat, the output of these sectors increase by 1.6 and 2.6 per cent, respectively, only in the year immediately following the price hike (Table 15.4). This increase in output is not sustained over time because of the fall in agricultural investments and irrigated area seen earlier. The hike in procurement prices results in increase in all prices – producer, ration as well as consumer prices, as explained earlier. This in turn, leads to a significant decline in total private consumption of these two commodities by around 3 to 3.5 per cent. Indeed self-consumption of both these commodities is higher while the ration and the market consumption are lower in response to increase in prices. The increase in output along with a decline in consumption results in a build up of stocks of these two commodities. For rice, stocks are larger by 12.9, 28.6 and 43.4 per cent for the years 1998, 1999 and 2000, respectively compared to the REF. For wheat these are larger by 11.0, 23.3 and 25.8 per cent, respectively. The combined stocks of rice and wheat at the end of three years come to around 66.6 million tonnes compared to 50.1 million tonnes in the REF. The effects of an increase in relative prices of rice and wheat on output, consumption and stocks of other agricultural commodities are quantitatively marginal.

Welfare Impacts

The cross-sectional impact of the price hike in terms of distribution of population, income and welfare is instructive. There is a significant increase in the population in the poorer classes, both in rural and urban areas (Table 15.5). Willig-Bailey comparison[2] of the two income distributions under assumptions of Pareto principle, anonymity and aversion to regressive transfers, clearly indicates a significant worsening of welfare of 80 per cent of population in rural areas and all persons in urban areas with higher MSPs (Table 15.6). Further, the welfare loss is in general larger for urban population than for rural population across classes and over time. The welfare loss is in general regressive in the

TABLE – 15.4
Agricultural Commodities

	Rice		Wheat		Other Cereals		Grams and Pulses		Other Crops	
	REF	MSP10_LLA	REF	MSP10_LLA	REF	MSP10_LLA	REF	MSP10_LLA	REF	MSP10_LLA
Private consumption – total (million quintal)										
1997	625.0	0.0	521.4	0.0	307.2	0.0	103.5	0.0	5526.2	0.0
1998	646.5	–3.4	539.3	–3.4	365.5	0.0	108.1	0.1	6299.0	0.0
1999	675.1	–3.1	563.2	–3.1	375.9	0.0	112.9	0.0	6707.1	0.1
2000	712.2	–3.6	594.2	–3.6	390.1	–0.2	113.3	0.3	7245.0	0.1
Private consumption – subsistence (million quintal)										
1997	154.9	0.0	148.3	0.0	91.5	0.0	20.2	0.0		
1998	339.9	0.0	335.0	0.0	54.2	0.0	59.6	0.0		
1999	355.6	4.3	364.2	2.9	54.3	3.0	59.1	1.9		
2000	364.7	2.6	379.1	1.9	56.2	3.0	59.6	2.4		
Private consumption – ration (million quintal)										
1997	70.5	0.0	36.7	0.0	21.5	0.0				
1998	99.4	–5.9	73.8	–15.6	15.5	0.0				
1999	92.3	0.7	54.7	–30.2	15.2	–0.7				
2000	92.9	3.2	53.7	–26.6	14.8	0.7				
Private consumption – market (million quintal)										
1997	399.5	0.0	336.4	0.0	194.2	0.0	83.3	0.0	5526.2	0.00
1998	207.2	–7.7	130.5	–5.2	295.7	0.0	48.6	0.0	6299.0	0.04
1999	227.2	–16.2	144.3	–8.3	306.4	–0.5	53.8	–2.0	6707.1	0.07
2000	254.6	–14.9	161.4	–8.9	319.0	–0.8	53.6	–1.9	7245.0	0.05
Final stocks (million quintal)										
1997	166.9	0.0	147.7	0.0	70.2	0.0	0.9	0.0	2262.5	0.0
1998	170.2	12.9	167.5	11.0	72.3	0.0	3.2	0.0	2288.9	0.0
1999	196.0	28.6	234.3	23.3	74.3	0.0	2.3	0.0	2315.2	0.0
2000	205.7	43.4	295.2	25.8	75.6	0.9	2.3	0.0	2341.5	0.0

Contd.....

...Contd...

	Rice		Wheat		Other Cereals		Grams and Pulses		Other Crops	
	REF	MSP10_LLA	REF	MSP10_LLA	REF	MSP10_LLA	REF	MSP10_LLA	REF	MSP10_LLA
Domestic production (million quintal)										
1997	817.7	0.0	694.0	0.0	340.9	0.0	142.5	0.0	11181.2	0.0
1998	846.5	0.0	733.1	0.0	401.3	0.0	150.4	0.0	12303.7	0.0
1999	908.4	1.6	819.7	2.6	413.2	0.0	151.9	0.0	12990.8	0.0
2000	931.8	0.0	853.3	0.0	428.2	0.1	153.5	0.3	13826.8	0.0
Producer price (Rs. per quintal)										
1997	1014.0	0.0	584.0	0.0	549.0	0.0				
1998	1014.0	10.0	584.0	10.0	384.6	0.2				
1999	1014.0	10.0	584.0	10.0	385.0	0.1				
2000	1014.0	10.0	584.0	10.0	388.8	–0.6				
Consumer ration price (Rs. per quintal)										
1997	1096.6	0.0	631.8	0.0	593.7	0.0				
1998	1093.9	8.4	630.3	8.4	444.3	0.1				
1999	1095.0	8.4	630.9	8.4	445.2	0.2				
2000	1108.1	7.6	638.1	7.7	456.0	–1.3				
Clearing price (Rs. per quintal)										
1997							1906.6	0.0	100.0	0.0
1998							1857.0	0.0	77.3	0.1
1999							1857.0	0.0	71.0	–0.1
2000							2203.6	–4.2	63.2	–0.8
Consumer price (Rs. per quintal)										
1997	1198.0	0.0	690.2	0.0	648.6	0.0	2114.7	0.0	134.1	0.0
1998	1195.3	8.5	688.7	8.5	482.7	0.2	2062.1	0.0	108.7	0.1
1999	1196.4	8.5	689.3	8.5	483.7	0.2	2063.4	0.0	101.8	0.0
2000	1209.5	7.8	696.5	7.9	494.9	–1.3	2424.8	–4.1	95.0	–1.5

*Notes:*1 The figures for REF are in levels (units for each variable indicated in brackets).
2 The figures for MSP10_LLA are percentage change over REF levels.
3 For Other Crops, the units for consumption, stocks and production are in 100 million rupees @ 1996-97 prices.

sense that the lower classes seem to lose more than the upper classes. Only the top 20 per cent of the rural population experience welfare increases in the third year. It should be emphasised that rural population get part of their income from non-agricultural activities. Thus the decline in non-agricultural output affects adversely the income of rural population also; which to some extent neutralises the gains from increase in agricultural prices. The top quintile of rural population has a larger marketable surplus of wheat and rice and they also get a relatively larger share of non-agricultural income.

TABLE – 15.5

Distributional Changes

Class	Population (million)				Per Capita Equivalent Income (Rs.)			
	1997	1998	1999	2000	1997	1998	1999	2000
Rural								
≤ 1800								
REF	17.6	14.1	6.7	2.8	1473	1502	1305	1110
MSP10_LLA	0.0	0.0	34.3	78.6	0.0	-0.9	4.5	8.7
≤ 3600								
REF	108.9	97.9	64.0	38.1	2835	2884	2499	2138
MSP10_LLA	0.0	0.0	13.3	35.2	0.0	-0.7	4.2	9.0
≤ 7200								
REF	258.1	255.5	224.6	185.7	5352	5410	4701	4058
MSP10_LLA	0.0	0.0	-0.5	6.7	0.0	-0.5	2.6	7.0
≤ 21600								
REF	278.0	303.5	368.0	422.9	11542	11587	10304	9158
MSP10_LLA	0.0	0.0	-3.8	-6.4	0.0	-0.2	0.2	3.2
≤ 21600								
REF	23.7	29.0	50.8	78.9	29412	29070	25666	22772
MSP10_LLA	0.0	0.0	8.1	-1.3	0.0	0.2	-1.8	0.9
Urban								
≤ 1800								
REF	2.1	1.5	0.7	0.2	1494	1476	1272	1077
MSP10_LLA	0.0	0.0	42.9	150.0	0.0	-1.8	6.4	12.6
≤ 3600								
REF	18.5	15.4	9.0	4.7	2920	2854	2459	2089
MSP10_LLA	0.0	0.0	22.2	51.1	0.0	-1.7	4.8	10.4
≤ 7200								
REF	65.1	60.7	47.3	34.4	5468	5408	4684	4028
MSP10_LLA	0.0	0.0	3.6	15.7	0.0	-1.5	2.5	7.1
≤ 21600								
REF	123.8	131.2	141.2	145.8	12293	12287	10910	9685
MSP10_LLA	0.0	0.0	-3.8	-4.0	0.0	-1.2	-0.8	2.1
≤ 21600								
REF	24.2	29.5	44.9	62.9	31460	31388	28096	25246
MSP10_LLA	0.0	0.0	3.3	-3.8	0.0	-0.9	-2.1	0.3

Notes: 1 The figures for REF are in levels, units for each variable indicated in brackets.
2 The figures for MSP10_LLA are percentage change over REF levels.

While thc immediate welfare loss due to a general price hike (procurement, ration and market price) is obvious, the welfare loss over time can be explained in terms of the decline in overall GDP attributable to a decline in non-agricultural GDP and mild growth in agriculture output as the decline in fixed investments almost completely offsets the incentive effects of higher MSPs.

TABLE – 15.6

Willig-Bailey Welfare Comparisons

Population Proportion	1998		1999		2000	
	REF Rs. Per Capita	MSP10_LLA % Change over REF	REF Rs. Per Capita	MSP10_LLA % Change over REF	REF Rs. Per Capita	MSP10_LLA % Change over REF
Rural						
0.2	2915	-0.69	2951	-0.39	2988	-0.59
0.4	3944	-0.57	4071	-0.69	4243	-1.29
0.6	5135	-0.47	5383	-0.77	5468	-0.57
0.8	6595	-0.35	6709	-0.57	6692	-0.11
1.0	8636	-0.23	8851	0.00	8934	0.12
Urban						
0.2	3793	-1.61	3951	-2.02	4109	-1.48
0.4	5459	-1.48	5635	-1.73	5691	-1.40
0.6	7162	-1.36	7259	-1.63	7274	-1.35
0.8	8865	-1.29	8882	-1.57	9333	-2.07
1.0	12222	-1.14	12532	-1.19	12696	-1.34

V

CONCLUSIONS

We have seen that a 10 per cent increase in minimum support prices of wheat and rice leads to decline in overall GDP by 0.33 per cent, increase in aggregate price index by 1.5 per cent, reduction in investments by 1.9 per cent and a minuscule impact on agricultural GDP by the third year. What is more important to note is that in terms of welfare the bottom 80 per cent of the rural and all of urban population is worse off.

The results are easy to understand. Higher minimum support prices reduce demand and lead to larger stocks. Thus, the stocks of wheat and rice are larger by 16.5 million tonnes after three years and reach 66.5 million tonnes compared to a reference scenario. We have assumed that a government under hard budget constraints can finance the expenditure on additional stocks only by reducing its investment expenditure, including investment in irrigation. We consider this to be a realistic assumption. This leads to lower agricultural output overtime and even the farmers get hurt.

Thus, the minimum support prices at levels much above market clearing prices are not desirable. One should emphasise here that the adverse impact of increases in MSP is related to the level of MSP to begin with. Only when the increases push up prices above the market clearing prices that the problems arise. Thus, we conclude that government should announce minimum support prices that remain below the market clearing prices in a normal or modal year. In an exceptionally bumper year the market clearing prices would be lower than the announced MSPs. This, however, is fine as in such years the farmers need support which should be provided.

Notes

1 In the model, households' consumer behaviour is characterised by linear expenditure demand systems (LES). The demand system parameters are estimated separately for each of the rural and urban expenditure classes from the underlying commoditywise Engel curves following the procedure of Fischer et al (1988) as modified by Ganesh Kumar and Darbha (1996). An additional restriction is specified to ensure that the commodity demands projected from the classwise LES are consistent with the observed total private consumption demand in the SAM. For more details see Ganesh Kumar and Darbha (1996) and Ganesh Kumar et al (1998).

2 The Willig and Bailey (1981) approach takes into account changes in both the population proportions and equivalent incomes across classes and permit us to compare alternative income distributions, under assumptions of Pareto principle, anonymity and aversion to regressive transfers. They compare the average per capita equivalent incomes of bottom X per cent of the population for all X from 0 to 100. When one policy scenario shows higher equivalent incomes for all values of X, we can say that it represents a superior welfare situation.

References

Fischer, G, K Frohberg, M A Keyzer and K S Parikh (1988), *Linked National Models: A Tool for International Food Policy Analysis*, Kluwer Academic Publishers, Dordrecht.

Ganesh Kumar, A and G Darbha (1996), "Engel Curve Based Linear Expenditure Demand System", paper presented at the 32nd Indian Econometric Society Conference, Bangalore, March 21-23.

Ganesh-Kumar, A, G Darbha and K S Parikh (1998), "Impact of a Hike in the Administered

Prices of Petroleum Products: Analysis Using an Applied General Equilibrium Model for India", Discussion Paper No 150, Indira Gandhi Institute of Development Research, Mumbai.

Parikh, Kirit S, A Ganesh-Kumar and G Darbha (2002), "Growth and Welfare Consequences of a Rise in Minimum Support Prices: An Applied General Equilibrium Analysis for India", report submitted to the Department of Economic Affairs, Ministry of Finance, Government of India.

Willig, R D and E E Bailey (1981), "Income Distribution Concerns in Regulatory Policy Making" in Fromm G (ed) *Studies in Public Regulation*, University of Chicago Press, Chicago.

Economic and Political Weekly, March 1, 2003.

16

Report of the High Level Committee on Long Term Grain Policy

SUMMARY AND RECOMMENDATIONS

India's system of grain management is in crisis. Huge public stocks have been built up, foregoing consumption in the past few years. These stocks are deteriorating because of shortage of storage space, but to hold these the Centre is spending more than what it expends on Agriculture, Rural development and on Irrigation and Flood control taken together. In this situation, this Committee's Terms of Reference required it to examine Long-term grain policy. We have done this keeping in view a horizon of about twenty years.

Our approach was based on the understanding that, although large distortions exist and rapid changes are occurring in the economy, policies to encourage and assist the production and distribution of food grains, especially cereals, remain integral to the development strategy of the country. The objectives of the present public food security system - price stability, price support to farmers, and making grain "affordable", through distribution from surplus to deficit regions and to the poor - cannot be ignored even in the future.

Cereals demand in the country has grown at less than population over the past decade, and is now less than production. From this, it is sometimes concluded that India has moved from deficits to permanent surplus. We have examined this, and conclude that the present excess stocks are more accurately attributed to a fall in consumption than to increased production. We have also examined estimates of cereal demand in 2020. To meet these, yield growth has to increase and production effort be at least similar to that during the past decade.

We believe that India should be able to maintain self-sufficiency in cereals with adequate production effort. But there can be no complacency regarding this effort. Future demand-supply outcomes are uncertain both in India and abroad, and long term policy should be able to cope with this uncertainty. The current situation (which reflects less than ideal distributive conditions and massive increases in cereals prices during the 1990s) cannot be used to infer demand-supply balances in future. It is at best uncertain and at worst unlikely that India will be a major surplus producer two decades from now.

We are of the firm view that India must continue to plan for cereals self-sufficiency. This is a strategic necessity since India accounts for about 15 per cent of total world consumption of cereals and since world production and trade is highly distorted by policies of rich countries. These countries are subsidising grain production heavily at present, but may push prices up if they acquire monopoly in world trade. In this situation of future uncertainty, and India's still low calorie intake compared to other countries, continued food self-sufficiency is an indispensable component of national security.

This implies that the nation cannot afford to give up its emphasis on continued production effort for foodgrains and that, therefore, ensuring reasonable and stable prices through Minimum Support Price (MSP) operations will remain an important element of the food security strategy even in future. After careful deliberation, we conclude that the MSP system with open-ended purchase should continue. It is important to note that this system is WTO-compatible.

A salient feature of India's cereals situation is that most States are deficit. Only five States produced surpluses of rice and wheat over consumption in 1999-2000. The remaining States were deficit by more than a third of consumption. We expect deficits to enlarge in Southern and Western regions of India during the next two decades. If surpluses decline in Punjab-Haryana, it will be essential to realise the potential for production surpluses in Central and Eastern India where presently prices are below full costs of production.

A basic focus of policy should therefore be to ensure effective price support in States and areas with future production potential. In other words, the MSP should truly be a national level floor price, rather than remaining confined to established surplus regions. However, we know that dietary patterns and tastes are changing, and also that there are ecological and environmental issues associated with particular cropping patterns. This means that MSPs should be based strictly on costs of production and balanced across crops.

The existing MSP system was developed with reference to a closed economy, and must obviously adapt to the context of liberalised trade. While there are potential long-run benefits, freer international trade can increase farm income variability. MSP policy will have to be supplemented by variable import and export tariff policies for effective price stabilisation, and MSPs would have to be reasonable in order to allow a workable structure of flexible tariffs.

All these imply that MSPs must be effective but as no more than floor prices. To ensure this, MSPs should have some statutory basis. Also, MSP operations should not be subject to arbitrary levies by State governments.

It is still possible, however, that market prices and procurement may become more variable. It is, therefore, necessary to adopt measures to supplement MSP policy, e.g. market-based insurance against price and income fluctuation and a system of negotiable warehouse receipts. Also, procurement at MSP need not always be sufficient to meet requirements of public distribution. Procurement agencies will need to develop the capacity to procure at market prices, eschewing devices such as levy procurement of rice which discourage private investment in milling without providing direct price support to farmers.

On the consumer side, too, there can be no complacency about a system to protect consumers from possible domestic shortages which might coincide with high world prices. Cereals account for around 60 per cent of total calorie intake, and it is unlikely that this will fall below 50 per cent by 2020. This, and our prognosis that interstate imbalances between production and consumption will widen in future, means that the second aim of the food security system should be the original objective of the Public Distribution System (PDS), to ensure price stabilisation by responding rapidly to situations of temporary shortage and through assured transfer of grain from surplus to deficit regions.

The Targeted Public Distribution System (TPDS), adopted in 1997, introduced the objective of income redistribution by providing food cheaper to the poor than to the non-poor. But this may have served to blunt the efficacy of the PDS in meeting its original goal of price stabilisation, while not delivering fully in terms of the new concern to focus subsidies to the poor.

By excluding a large number of families, the TPDS undermined the viability of Fair Price shops and increased scope for distortion and leakage. It penalised States with relatively low incidence of income poverty but relatively high incidence of calorie deficiency. At the same time, it did not reach the poor in States where the PDS was weak prior to its introduction. We feel that it is essential to go back to an universal PDS, which involves one Central Issue Price for each item that is sought to be procured and distributed.

Welfare/distributive measures are important and were ignored in previous designs of the food security system. However, separate schemes already exist for the poor and other vulnerable groups. Some of these may be linked to grain, and special attention is necessary towards the disabled and the aged who have no regular income support. But delivery of such benefits may be more effective if it is served independently of an income criterion within the PDS. Although the PDS may be adequate to deliver grain in some cases, there may be better delivery systems in other cases.

An important social security measure in the Indian context is provision of employment on public works. While a food component can and should be part of such employment generation in the short run or in periods of local food shortages, in the long run, employment generation should be distinct from the food delivery system. This should not, however, undermine the importance of employment and income generation in eliminating hunger and malnutrition.

In the TPDS, a large subsidy component is additional to the costs of the food security system proper, on account of lower prices for those identified as poor as compared to the non-poor. The redistribution objective would be better met if this additional subsidy component is transferred as cash assistance from Centre to States depending upon levels of poverty and linked to actual food distribution, but allowing States to develop their own food schemes for poverty alleviation while retaining centralised MSP and issue prices.

For foodgrain management proper, what is most necessary is an environment which offers reasonable predictability and stability. MSP policy should extend to all regions, all States must have guarantee against shortage or unduly high prices and private trade should be able to function without threat of arbitrary action. Consumers should not face sudden cuts in commitments, or trade sudden impositions, in situations of shortage; and future situations of surplus should not involve public pricing which puts undue burden on farmers or disrupts normal private trade. Stabilisation should aim to contain prices within a band. For this, there must be adequate commitment to the Central Pool.

This will also necessitate continuation of the Food Corporation of India (FCI). There is considerable scope to improve FCI's performance, to lower its costs of operation and, most importantly, to raise the quality of the grain it supplies. Nonetheless, on the basis of our analysis of FCI costs and market prices and views expressed by the States, we conclude that the FCI has performed reasonably well in maintaining the Central pool, in long-distance movement, and in direct interventions when producer prices have fallen below MSP or there have been particular regional shortages. Our view is that the FCI should develop these areas of core competence, concentrating on rice and wheat.

While the FCI must remain the main agency for procurement and distribution, State government agencies, co-operatives and private trade may also handle these operations in the future. However, the FCI must play a developmental role by starting procurement centres where they do not exist, and become a "buyer of last resort" in case of decentralised procurement. Moreover, for successful decentralisation, and in particular for co-operatives and private agencies to play a credible part, would require disbursement of part of the food subsidy as cash to States. Also contractual arrangements must be devised to legally bind the agencies involved to provide MSP and assure supplies as laid down by the Central government.

We recognise that the idea of decentralisation is at the moment unacceptable to most States. Their concerns are essentially fiscal, that the Central government may thereby withdraw from its existing commitment. Some of our recommendations, specifically reduction of statutory levies, may heighten these concerns. It will be essential to reassure the States that the Central government will not reduce its fiscal commitment. For such reassurance it might be necessary to convene jointly with the States a review of its existing commitments and their functioning.

Over time, we visualise an expanded role for the larger private sector in grain trade, not only in areas like exports and storage, including warehouse receipts for producers, but even as part of the public food management system. This will require greater freedoms, but also safeguards against violation of obligations undertaken on public behalf. Legal reforms are needed to liberalise trade and marketing. The scope of the Essential Commodities Act should be focussed in a manner which, rather than threaten the conduct of normal trade, opens up avenues for the private sector to participate in the public space.

In accordance with these long-term goals, there are strategies to be pursued on a medium and long term basis. For several objectives including development of private trade, greater integration of markets, and prevention of distress sales, we require massive investment in rural infrastructure, particularly rural roads and markets.

However, clearly it is the case that there is an immediate and severe problem with respect to the grain economy of the country. This needs to be addressed in such a way as to be compatible with long term policies. Accordingly, we present recommendations for long term grain policy, some of which should be initiated immediately, as well as specific short-term measures to deal with the current situation of excess public stocks.

We are convinced that no long run policy can be effective unless present imbalances, specifically, the large excess holding of public stocks, are corrected. For the adjustment of stocks, we have outlined a two year Plan of Action which includes immediate steps to lower procurement inflows on the one hand, and to raise outflows, on the other hand, by several means including a large Food for Work programme, a revitalised universal PDS and other grain-based welfare schemes.

Our approach to the present situation is informed by our analysis of why it occurred and possible consequences of different measures to deal with it. We are convinced that the main reason for the present situation are high levels of MSP fixed during the 1990s, and that a significant role was also played by the decision to target the entire food delivery system on the basis of poverty criteria. Besides political compulsions flowing from Andhra Pradesh, Haryana and Punjab, a significant part was played by two assumptions - that world prices of cereals were likely to be higher than Indian prices and that there was significant scope to cut the fiscal involvement of the Central government in the food security system. Both these assumptions proved false. Relatively high cereal prices and inadequate purchasing power among a significant proportion of the population has kept consumption low.

We have in the course of our discussions heard suggestions that the high food stocks require cessation of open-ended procurement and also that this may be an opportunity to dismantle what many believe to be an expensive and outdated food security system. We have considered these views very seriously, and are forced to reject these. End of open-ended procurement at this stage would deal a severe, possibly a crippling, blow to farmers which may be followed by a blow to consumers in about two years time. Despite the many sources of inefficiency which we have identified, particularly in the functioning of the FCI and the PDS, we are convinced that it is reform and not annulment of the existing system that should be on the agenda.

Our recommendations on reducing stocks include many measures to increase offtake, but its linchpin is reduction of the MSP. Our calculations show that "business as usual" will not permit stock reduction. A freeze on MSP will eventually reduce stocks, but not only will this involve longer and more costly adjustment, farmers may be worse-off compared to the package of MSP reduction plus compensation we propose. In addition we consider it vital that three other steps be taken immediately: extend effective MSP to all farmers by shifting FCI's focus to East and Central India; restore consumer confidence in the quality of public stocks by segregating for early commercial disposal all old and relaxed quality grain from the Central Pool and from the PDS; and expand demand through larger public works to strengthen rural infrastructure.

We call upon government not to view these stocks simply as a burden which when reduced will reduce the fiscal deficit. We believe that the present juncture is one where the nation should commit itself to eradication of destitution and chronic malnutrition and rethink many aspects of food policy. With declining importance of cereals in their diets, many in the urban middle classes have almost lost interest in what happens to cereals prices. Nonetheless, the poor still spend about a third of their budget on cereals and derive almost three-fourths of their nutrition from this. Also, three-quarters of India's cereals consumption is in rural areas and grain policy will be critical as rural India diversifies its sources of income, and regions specialise. Not only will demand for grain in surplus regions depend on the extent to which incomes in other regions can be increased by shifting from staple production, the pace of income diversification in these latter regions will depend on whether those who can diversify are reasonably sure of assured and affordable food supply. The main requirement is for much improved rural infrastructure.

LONG TERM RECOMMENDATIONS

In line with the Terms of Reference of this Committee, the following are our views and recommendations regarding policy to be undertaken in the medium to long-run.

A. Focussing Food For Welfare: the Unemployed, the Destitute and Children

India's existing food security system has succeeded relatively well in preventing gross failures of food supply in almost every region, but it has not done enough for the poor and the vulnerable. Certain schemes such as Food for Work and the Antyodaya Anna Yojana have been expanded recently as part of the effort to reduce stocks. In the longer run it should be possible, with resources currently being spent on holding stocks, to eliminate hunger, make a significant dent on the current appalling levels of malnutrition among India's children, and augment the future quality of our human resources.

Social security programmes with some food component in India broadly fall into three groups: employment programmes for the able-bodied, welfare programmes or social assistance for specific vulnerable groups (including infants, pregnant and lactating women, disabled and old age persons) and programmes for basic education and nutrition of children. Once the current high stocks are reduced, we recommend that the resultant savings should be used for:

- Employment schemes, for which there is a strong felt need and which can be used to develop rural infrastructure. We have recommended a major food-based employment programme for the short run. This fiscal commitment should continue after stocks have returned to normal. This should be in the form of a food-linked employment guarantee component in the SGRY which is purely self-targeted, i.e. not linked to prior identification as poor. While direct food provision may be necessary in situations involving local food shortage such as in the case of droughts or floods, we see this scheme as also being relevant to cope with extreme seasonal unemployment. Linkage with food in such cases could be through the existing PDS system (by issuing coupons, or other food entitlement as part of wages).
- Expanding the existing Antyodaya scheme of food support to become a food security system for the entire destitute population. In particular, we recommend:
    - To include other destitute persons, covering those without regular income or economic support, in particular: old people, widows and other single women without regular support; disabled persons and terminally ill persons in BPL families; homeless and other households in extreme poverty. Identification should be by Panchayati Raj Institutions.
    - Where identification has already taken place and where the PDS works reasonably well, Antyodaya persons/families can continue to be supplied grain through the PDS. However, in areas where there are problems with current Antyodaya offtake, grain may be made available to Panchayats or other alternative channels to distribute to the identified persons.

- Central support to States to the extent of 50 per cent for moving to a cooked Mid-day Meal scheme for all school-going children. In moving from provision of dry rations to cooked meals, the scope for production and distribution of processed foods may be explored.
- Supporting and strengthening programmes for infants, children, pregnant and lactating women such as in the Integrated Child Development Services (ICDS).

B. The Public Distribution System

The above presuppose the existence of a food distribution system which can reach every part of the country in the most adverse of circumstances and allocate a part of national production according to requirement rather than consideration of the cost of delivery. This was the main role played by the PDS historically. In the Targeted Public Distribution Scheme (TPDS) an effort was also made to target benefits to the poor. However, the principle of allocating subsidised grain across States on the basis of their poverty ratios has led to imbalances between the resulting allocations and what is necessary to meet the difference between cereals production and requirement. Also, the stabilising role played by the universal PDS has weakened. Given these problems in TPDS functioning, we recommend that:

- A system of universal PDS be reintroduced with uniform Central Issue Prices (CIP), one each for rice and wheat respectively, for all consumers in all parts of the country. In this:
  - There should be a single price for rice, and no distinction between varieties;
  - The uniform CIPs should be the FCI's all-India average acquisition cost at MSP of the relevant grain. In exceptional circumstances of low market prices, this pricing formula may be relaxed to ensure that CIPs remain sufficiently low to facilitate continued offtake; and
  - At these uniform prices, the Centre should allocate grain to States based on population and a monthly per capita quota to be specified from time to time. Actual lifting will be less than allocation, and past lifting should be the basis for decisions regarding grain movement.

This recommendation should restore inter-State grain allocations to the pre-TPDS situation and bring back some of the non-poor but with more discipline on the subsidy, which in universal PDS should be normally limited only to distribution cost. However, in order to retain the main thrust of TPDS, we recommend that:

- An additional subsidy meant for poor consumers or persons in relatively backward regions should be given in cash to States:

  This cash component should be used only for food related schemes for the poor, but States should be free to formulate any food security scheme. Specifically, the following should be allowed:

  - food coupons to the poor and near poor, entitling them to discounts in PDS outlets;
  - differential pricing for the poor and near poor, as in existing TPDS;
  - differential quotas for the poor and near poor, at a uniform price; and
  - strengthening the food distribution system to reach the poor more effectively, either through measures to improve PDS working or on alternative delivery mechanisms, for example, grain banks.

  Payment of the cash component should be conditional on actual grain lifting, including lifting from the scheme of decentralised procurement.

  There should be a ceiling on how much lifting will be eligible for this cash component. This ceiling should be the State's population of the poor and near poor (i.e. a further 10 percentage points of population to minimise errors of exclusion of the poor) multiplied by the specified per capita quota.

  The cash subsidy amount per unit of lifting should correspond to the excess of the FCI's acquisition cost (i.e. the new uniform CIPs) over half FCI's economic cost (i.e. the current norm for the BPL price).

  Where a State wishes to utilise its cash eligibility to strengthen the system for delivery to the poor, and the proposed programme is time bound, it should be allowed to draw cash up to its eligible allocation without necessarily lifting grain, on condition that this will be adjusted in future as lifting improves.

  Conversely, if a State requires extra grain to start up new grain banks or to replenish existing ones in the event of crop failure, it should be allowed to commute its cash component to obtain more grain at CIP than its allocation.

Besides meeting the Central concern of the TPDS without either reducing existing entitlements of the poor or increasing the Centre's fiscal burden unduly, the above proposals are expected to enhance significantly the ability of States to reach the poor. This cash subsidy to poorer consumers or backward regions should, however, not necessarily be linked permanently with either the PDS or the grain management system. Its logical place is with the other proposals in Section A. However, transfers in cash are more fungible than grain. To ensure proper use, we recommend:

- The setting up of an independent Central watchdog body, comprising officials, experts and others, to monitor the use of these cash grants as well as grants under the food for welfare schemes to ensure that they reach the poor.

In addition, to improve the effectiveness PDS at the retail level, we recommend:

- Restrictions on eligibility to be a licensed Fair Price Shop (FPS) dealer, and on the functioning of such shops, should be relaxed significantly by:
  - Making NGOs and village-level private grain retailers eligible to undertake licensed PDS distribution, and encouraging women in this activity.
  - Removing all restrictions regarding the range of commodities which can be sold in a FPS.
  - Allowing registered associations of licensed FPS dealers to purchase the grain allocated to their members directly from the FCI.
  - In border areas of Jammu and Kashmir, the North east, Kutch and Rajasthan, the Ministry of Defence may be requested to involve the Army Supply Corps to make PDS supplies available to civilians.
- These steps to liberalise participation in the PDS network should be accompanied by effective implementation of the PDS Control Order, 2001.
- Greater responsibilities should be given to Panchayati Raj Institutions (PRI), particularly elected women members, in design,

implementation and monitoring of location-specific food security schemes. Also, PRIs should be responsible for initiating action under the PDS Control Order, 2001.

The above constitute a package. Restoration of universal PDS will correct imbalances in regional grain availability and widen the sense of ownership in it. Shifting the differential subsidy to the poor from grain to cash will give cash-constrained States greater flexibility to reach the poor and also simplify FCI accounting. Legal backing and financial provision for effective PRI oversight and initiative will allow simplified rules and better FPS functioning.

In the long run, as markets get better integrated, the PDS function need not remain restricted to designated fair-price shops, and a food coupon system valid even outside PDS outlets may become possible. Food coupons may allow wider choice to consumers in terms of commodities and outlets. In the Committee's view, this is a course which should be followed with considerable caution in view of the experience of other countries, and the possibility of counterfeiting. However, the most important reason food stamps have not been successful elsewhere has been the erosion in the value of the coupons where it was fixed in nominal terms. If the coupon system is to succeed the PDS suggested above, we recommend that the value of the coupon should be indexed to food inflation. The coupon system should not lead to a dilution of the Central government's commitment to food security.

If decentralisation has to proceed to its logical conclusion in the long-term, the entire subsidy in the PDS has to be devolved to the States. This can be done by giving States in cash the difference between the full State-specific economic cost and the CIP on their entire PDS distribution, in addition to the cash component already provided for the poor. States can then either lift from FCI's OMSS, carry out their own procurement or place orders with other State governments directly. In this case, there would also be a large space for the private sector as intermediaries between the States. However, in keeping with our recommendations, this should be subject to legal obligation and not compromise the sanctity of the Central Pool.

C. Minimum Support Prices and Procurement

Minimum Support Price (MSP) policy was critical in India's achievement of foodgrains self-sufficiency but is now grossly distorted. Nonetheless, we are convinced that MSP policy should continue, but with immediate correction. We recommend:

- The Central Government should announce its MSP policy before the sowing season on recommendations of the Commission for Agricultural Costs and Prices (CACP).
  - The CACP should be made an empowered statutory body.
  - In recommending MSPs, which should apply only to FAQ grain, the CACP should go strictly on the basis of C_2 cost of production (i.e. all costs including imputed costs of family labour, owned capital and rental on land) in more efficient regions.
  - The CACP should also indicate its estimate of A_2+FL cost (i.e. costs actually paid plus imputed value of family labour) for relatively high cost regions.
  - The CACP should recommend only a single MSP for paddy.
  - The MSP, set at a floor price on the recommendations of the CACP, should have a statutory status. In particular, the responsibilities of the Central government and obligations of State governments should be defined clearly.
  - All agencies, Central, State, Co-operative or Private, which are part of public grain management should be legally bound by the MSP policy.
  - If the present situation continues, where some States impose excessive levies on MSP purchase, the Central Government may announce its MSP policy by declaring a procurement price inclusive of an uniform 4 per cent allowance for such levies over the MSP. This should be the maximum price payable for MSP purchases by all agencies acting on behalf of the Central Government.

These recommendations regarding MSP policy and its announcement format should come into force immediately. However, in the long-term, effective implementation of MSP policy is even more important than its announcement. On this, we emphasise that:

- Once it announces MSP policy, Central government should underwrite open-ended purchase of FAQ grains to assure growers an adequate return on their cost. It should be the responsibility of the Central government to make the fiscal and banking provisions necessary to enforce MSP throughout the country.

MSP policy is currently implemented on behalf of the Central Government by the Food Corporation of India (FCI) or by State governments agencies acting as agents of FCI. This role is devolved to the States in the scheme of decentralised procurement. In future, if decentralisation proceeds, this might involve more States or even the private sector acting as agents of State governments. However, we recommend that:

- FCI should continue to be the sole agency managing Central Pool stocks for the Central government. In this capacity, the FCI should be at least the "buyer of last resort" for all MSP operations. The Centre should also retain the right of pre-emptive acquisition, through the agency of FCI, of all grain purchased by States or their agents in Centrally-funded MSP operations which is in excess of their PDS requirement.

At present the Central government's main responsibilities in MSP implementation are to guarantee the open-ended provision of credit which is necessary for open-ended MSP purchase, and to defray FCI expenditure. Currently, State agencies in surplus States act as FCI agents, receive a service charge over the actual cost of MSP operations, and are obliged to deliver all their grain to FCI. Our recommendations above imply that in future, even if there is full-fledged decentralisation, the Centre must retain a pre-emptive right over support purchases, it must continue to extend credit guarantee and defray FCI expenditure, and it must assure States that FCI will lift grain acquired in MSP operations on terms which does not involve loss. However, except when the Centre exercises its pre-emptive right, decentralisation would give surplus States the opportunity to make profit. This is relevant since State agencies already do most of the procurement in Punjab and Haryana. Given the proven capacity of State agencies in these States to carry out procurement operations, we visualise less need for FCI in procurement operations in these States. On the other hand, State agencies in certain other States have virtually no capacity to carry out support operations to prevent widespread distress sales. We therefore recommend that:

- FCI should withdraw from procurement in States like Punjab and Haryana where this is handled capably by State agencies. In other States, where distress sales occur and State governments have been unable to provide adequate price support, the Central government should intervene to start-up price support by ensuring that FCI opens procurement Centres in areas of distress sale. There should be substantial redeployment of FCI's procurement capabilities towards price support in Eastern and Central India while retaining its infrastructure to evacuate surplus grain procured by State agencies in Punjab and Haryana.

This recommendation should also be implemented immediately since the largest losers in the present situation of high stocks are farmers in those regions of marginal surplus where MSP policy is ineffective and prices are below costs of production.

Decentralised Procurement

In the Interim Report, we had suggested that decentralised procurement may be considered. However, the response from many States has been that they would prefer the Central government to undertake procurement. While the Centre has to continue to take the primary responsibility for procurement, we believe that as production is dispersed (with diversification along the lines indicated), procurement should also become more dispersed and this process can definitely save on costs of transportation and meet consumer needs more adequately. However, for this certain problems of the present scheme of decentralised procurement must be addressed. In particular:

- Grain procured under the Decentralised Scheme must be treated as part of the Central Pool, with the FCI, in its capacity as buyer of last resort, guaranteeing the lifting of any stock in excess of the State's own PDS offtake at the MSP-linked acquisition cost, provided that this meets FAQ requirements. The acquisition cost above should be equivalent to the norms of the FCI.
- Based on this guarantee of Central purchase at MSP linked price, there should be open-ended bank credit on the same lines as provided to FCI.
- The subsidy provided by the Centre on States lifting from own procurement should be at the same rate as provided on States lifting from the FCI. The subsidy here refers to the difference between the State-specific economic cost of the FCI (the normal OMSS price defined later) and the Central Issue price.
- There should be an adequate system of auditing of actual procurement and offtake by the State government.
- State agencies may continue to be used by the Centre to undertake operations in different States, if they are found to be performing more efficiently than the FCI.
- All procurement and disposal of coarse grains under the MSP operations should be decentralised to State governments with full financial support from the Centre.

Levy on Millers

Another area for immediate action relates to the levy on rice mills, through which the major part of rice procurement currently occurs. This serves as an indirect tax in periods of shortage, which is neither relevant in today's situation nor desirable. In fact, the Committee has reason to believe that the levy route is not helping most farmers in the present situation and is also being misused. Although some expert bodies have recommended the use of levy because this is a cheaper alternative for the FCI than custom-milling of paddy procured directly, we believe that there is a strong case for regular price support operations in paddy. In the long-term, however, we envisage that most of the rice purchased for the PDS will be either through open tender purchase or from prior contracts from mills. We therefore recommend that:

- All compulsory levy orders on rice millers under the Essential Commodities Act (ECA) should be removed with immediate effect, and be replaced by orders requiring mills to custom mill the paddy procured under MSP and give delivery of the resultant rice to the Central pool on a priority basis. Custom milling rates should be fixed by the Central government at realistic rates for different States.

- For rice mills which voluntarily undertake not to buy paddy below MSP, the FCI should offer a prior contract offering to buy any amount of FAQ rice at a price equal to the MSP for paddy plus the contract milling rate fixed, with provision for escalation if paddy price is higher. It should be an offence under the ECA if a contracting mill tries to avail this offer of FCI after having bought paddy below MSP.

Quality Issues in Procurement

A major problem in the present system is the visible decline that has taken place in the quality of grain that has been purchased for the Central Pool in recent years. Quality norms exist, but the Committee notes with concern attempts by various producing State governments to have these relaxed from time to time. Many consuming State governments have refused to accept such grain for PDS distribution. We therefore recommend, also for immediate implementation, that

- FAQ (Fair-average quality) norms should be adhered to strictly in all purchases of grain by the FCI. In fact, in our opinion, the specifications for FCI purchase should be tightened.

- An empowered Technical committee may be constituted, comprising experts for the implementation and review of FAQ specifications.
- In case of natural disaster and lowering of crop quality, compensation may be paid directly to farmers on the recommendation of the Technical Committee.
- In unforeseen circumstances, below FAQ grain may be purchased by State governments as part of support operations at a price no higher than the A_2+FL cost indicated by CACP. This grain should not be taken to the Central pool, and should be disposed of at commercial terms. The cost of this should be part of Central support operations.
- Grain of below FAQ if purchased should be segregated for commercial disposal as soon as possible. Under no circumstance should Central pool stocks contain below FAQ grain.
- All procuring agencies should sort and grade different qualities of grain. The identity of grain by location, date of purchase and quality should, as far as possible, be preserved from the point of procurement to sale.

Alternative Price and Income Stabilisation Measures

Since our recommendations imply that MSPs will only be floor prices in the long run, some additional instruments to stabilise and improve prices are desirable. We have identified two such market based instruments: warehouse receipts, which are discussed below, and insurance against income loss caused not only by crop failure but also by prices declining below their normal past levels. Such insurance would be prohibitively expensive if it is made an income support scheme with indemnity linked to current levels of MSP. However, if MSP policy is effective at the C_2 level that we have proposed, and indemnity is linked not to this but to actual average prices received in past years, this will be quite affordable. This is so even if the "normal" prices insured are above MSP, as for example is likely in the case of Grade-A paddy if our recommendation to have only a single MSP for all grades of paddy is accepted. Insurance can also form part of the transition package of income support that we have recommended to move from present high MSP levels to a future situation where market prices are likely to be higher than MSP. We recommend that:

- The Central government should explore expeditiously with the insurance sector the commercial viability of insurance, devised strictly on actuarial principles, against shortfalls not only of yield but also of prices from their past averages computed on an area basis. Any start-up subsidy required for this should be only in the form of subsidy to farmers on their premium and this should be phased out within a stipulated period for all except poor and marginal farmers.

Dealing with Deficits

A different problem likely to arise as a result of lower MSPs is that there will be higher probability for market prices to exceed MSP and, therefore, quantities offered for sale at MSP may fall short of PDS and buffer stocks requirements. Clearly, if this occurs, there will be a need for FCI to purchase at market rates to maintain adequate stocks in the Central Pool. However, in the past, such situations have led to permanent increases in MSP or to announcements of "bonus" which have eventually been incorporated in MSP. In fact, the present situation of high MSP and high stocks is the result of such an episode. To prevent this in future, we recommend:

- In situations where market conditions are such that MSP purchases fall short of PDS requirements, Government would need to make purchases on the basis of best commercial terms. This may include:

Imports

- Open market Purchases from secondary markets or through open tender purchases.

- Purchase from farmers at a market determined price above MSP. Ideally, this price should be determined by the FCI itself on the basis of its own market assessment. If required, a maximum procurement price higher than MSP but lower than the import price can be announced along with a procurement target which once reached would cause the premium over MSP to be withdrawn. The premium should in no way form part of the basis on which subsequent MSPs are fixed.

Inter Crop Parity

Crop diversification is very important at the current stage of India's agricultural development, given the changing dietary patterns. One consequence of recent MSP policy has been to disturb inter-crop price parities, leading to shift of area towards cereals even as there are huge stocks, often from crops such as oilseeds when there are huge edible oils imports. In this context, there are suggestions that there be special packages for diversification. However, although there are cases such as the paddy-wheat rotation in North-West India which need to be discouraged in view of environmental problems, long-term policy should not be unduly interventionist in this matter. In cases where intervention is necessary this should be through direct subsidies rather than through MSP policy. We recommend that :

- In order to preserve inter-crop parities, differences in MSP across crops should bear roughly the same relationship as differences in costs and returns. The principle for fixation of MSP for all crops should be similar. MSP for paddy and wheat should not be given undue advantage relative to other crops.
- If diversification is to be encouraged, there should be effective MSP operations for other crops and areas. Central government in consultation with State governments should identify a set of crops to be promoted in specific regions for diversification and MSP operations for these should be undertaken with adequate institutional and financial support.
- If insurance schemes are devised to protect incomes from paddy and wheat, similar schemes should be extended to all major crops to ensure that this does not discourage diversification.
- The Government of India should prepare a plan for integrated development of processing, storage and market infrastructure including post-harvest infrastructure, as these are essential for diversification to be successful.

D. Open Market Sales, Exports And Imports

Open market operations are vital for price stabilisation, but have in the past been used in an arbitrary manner. There should be a stable and predictable policy regarding open market sales.

- The prices in the Open Market Sale Scheme (OMSS) may be based on the corresponding Central Issue Prices (which should normally be the acquisition cost of grain) plus the full cost of transport and storage involved in the sale at a specific location and period from harvest, as well as market conditions. In normal conditions, this would ensure that OMSS carries no subsidy and does not distort markets. There should be open-ended sales at these prices to stabilise markets.

- An exception to the principle above, of minimising subsidies on OMSS, can be made for old or otherwise below quality grain. Such stocks should be segregated and sold as such through OMSS as speedily as possible at the best commercial terms. During periods of high stocks, disposal of such old and below quality grain should have priority over sales of better stock, and price differentials should be higher.
- For stabilisation, when world prices are very high, OMSS prices will need to take account of import prices. In such situations imports may also need to be subsidised, provided this does not reduce OMSS prices below their normal levels determined on the basis of economic cost. Also, situations when high world prices threaten domestic price stability should be handled through export tariffs rather than a ban on exports.

The Committee is in favour of an automatic and transparent policy of variable tariffs on both agricultural imports and exports linked to the deviation of spot international prices from their long run trends. This is required for stabilisation of prices in an open economy. The Committee recommends that

- The system of exports and imports of foodgrains should be based on a system of variable tariffs.
- Import tariffs should be varied with world prices to ensure that the tariff inclusive c.i.f cost of imports do not fall below the economic cost of supplying peninsular India with grain purchased at MSP in North and East India. If MSP reflects costs of production, India could make a strong case on grounds of "injury" to initiate safeguard measures if world prices fall so much that the required import tariffs exceed tariff bindings in the WTO.
- Exports should be entirely on private account. Private exporters can, of course, source their grain from the OMSS. The price for exports should therefore follow the same principle as other OMSS sales. Subsidies on this, if any, should, as far as possible, be at the point of export rather than at the point of sale from public stocks and not be higher than on PDS sales. Subsidies should be given only if domestic stocks are sufficiently high and world prices are less than the domestic OMSS price. The only exception to this may be to honour long-term grain contracts that government may offer as incentive to the private sector to develop infrastructure and market presence for future exports.

E. Encouraging Private Trade

We believe that barriers to private trade, economic as well as legal, should be eased. Our recommendations regarding Open Market Sales and tariff policy should, if implemented, bring about a predictable regime of public intervention in grain pricing. The Committee also welcomes the recent removal of stock limits, and movement restrictions on foodgrains. The Committee further recommends that:

- The Essential Commodities Act should in normal circumstances apply only to situations of natural disasters or other contingencies which disrupt normal functioning of civil society, with the exception of some remote regions and possibly certain border areas. Orders under this Act should be reviewed to ensure further facilitation of private trade, keeping in mind that there are ECA provisions which protect consumers without threatening normal trade.
- However, a new set of orders may be required, on the lines of the PDS Control Order (2001), to facilitate the voluntary entry of private agents into activities encompassed in public procurement and distribution. For example, if private millers act as agents of the FCI or of State governments directly in supplying grain to the PDS, they should be required not only to adhere to delivery but also to MSP. In other words, wherever private trade acts on behalf of the FCI or competes with it in the public management of the food economy, and obtains payments based on requirements such as MSP and statutory levies, these requirements should be legally enforceable.
- For better functioning of trade, an uniform upper limit needs to be set to the taxes and statutory levies that can be imposed by States on agricultural produce.
- Acts governing existing regulated markets, and the Agricultural Produce Marketing Committees which manage these, should be amended to require that markets which do not provide certain minimum services will cease to be covered by the Act. Wherever such Acts prohibit trade outside regulated markets, there should be substantial relaxation of the procedures for establishment of new regulated markets. These amendments would allow bulk buyers, be it the public or the private sector, to set up their own procurement Centres outside the regulated market yards.
- To create a viable environment where the private sector can offer storage and warehousing facilities and farmers can benefit, we

recommend that the system of negotiable warehouse receipts should be simplified and expanded. A scheme of certification of warehouses needs to be devised so that not only the quantity but also quality of the produce can be certified and banks should treat this as acceptable collateral for loans.

- All investment for bulk handling of grain for exports should be reserved for the private sector. Rather than guarantee storage by the FCI, any incentive for this should take the form of assured supply for 5 to 6 years at a discount (say, 5 to 10 per cent) from the prevalent world price.
- To encourage the growth of markets, investment should be made in rural roads and market infrastructure.

F. Food Corporation of India Related Issues

Role of FCI

The Committee is of the opinion that the FCI has performed its role in its core functions reasonably well and should continue to do so. However, at the moment, its predominant role is in procuring from a few surplus States rather than ensuring price support to cultivators throughout the country and developing markets for grain in relatively underdeveloped regions.

F.1. Since State governments have been unable to provide these services, we recommend that the Central government intervenes to take an initiative to start-up these services by ensuring that FCI opens procurement centres to provide MSP in areas of distress sale. This role is envisaged under Section 13 of Chapter II of the Food Corporations Act. However, budgetary provision for this should be treated as additional to the normal food subsidy.

Management

While the Committee does not envisage any basic change in the structure of the FCI, there is clear need for the FCI to change the way in which it does business. Changes are called for to enable faster, commercially oriented decision making. Suggestions are given in the body of the Report as well as the Appendix 3 for giving FCI greater operational flexibility; for strengthening the market intelligence set-up and for improving FCI's management practices in procurement, storage and quality control.

F.2. A single line of command has been accepted as the proper form of organisation for public sector organisations. Division of responsibility at the apex of the organisation affects the speed and quality of decision making and weakens the management structure. As recommended a decade ago by the BICP the posts of Chairman and Managing Director may be merged.

F.3. It would greatly help the FCI to operate autonomously, accountably and cost-effectively, in areas within its decision making ambit if a Memorandum of Understanding becomes a standing feature of the FCI-Government nexus.

F.4. FCI's market intelligence set up is at present extremely rudimentary and does not cater to data requirements on domestic and international prices for open market sales, purchases and release of stocks for export. The Committee recommends that FCI strengthen its market intelligence set up.

Quality

F.5. Over the years, the objective of maximising the satisfaction of the consumer seems to have receded. It is important to once again create the awareness that every one of FCI's tasks is part of a customer-supplier relationship. There has to be a work culture of total quality management.

F.6. There should be an overall quality control exercise targeting Punjab, Haryana and western UP, from the farm level to the mandi and godown levels, preserving identity of grain throughout, on the lines given in Appendix 3.

F.7. Quality control assumes added importance when, as at present, abnormally heavy stocks are held being held. The prescribed drills for prophylactic treatment have lost much of their efficacy because of the much longer duration of stock-holding and the inordinately large volumes stored in the open. The drills will, therefore, have to be revised taking the current circumstances into account. Entrusting prophylactic measures to private agencies on contract basis could also be considered.

F.8. The FCI has been given full powers to dispose of substandard stocks of foodgrains. In the current situation of excessive stocks, these powers need to be exercised speedily and comprehensively.

Procurement

F.9. It is desirable that the FCI's role is confined to procurement of the major cereals for the PDS and that price support operations in coarse cereals are handled by State agencies. There have been very large storage losses in FCI's procurement of jowar, maize, bajra and other coarse cereals because of limited shelf life. This adds to the economic costs of the FCI. Experience of the last thirty years indicates that coarse cereals are not demanded for the PDS. We recommend that the coarse cereals support should not be undertaken by FCI.

F.10. In States like Punjab and Haryana, where the bulk of the procurement is being handled by State agencies, there is no reason why FCI should open any procurement Centres. In other States, where distress sales occur and uneconomic Centres have to be opened, a recommendation has been made in F1 above.

F.11. The nature of FCI operations are such that certain purchase Centres are opened not so much for procurement as for preventing distress sales. The costs of operating such distress Centres should be taken into account while benchmarking FCI's costs, and preferably should be reported separately in FCI budget and accounts.

Cost Control

F.12. We recommend that the FCI maintain estimates of unit costs at least at the regional level, preferably at depot level. This will be necessary to calculate the subsidies actually received by States in the case of decentralisation of the food subsidy or any sub-components. It will also help the FCI to identify areas of cost control.

F.13. The normating of FCI's costs done by the BICP in 1989 provides a useful method for assessing FCI's cost-efficiency. However, the BICP norms will have to be recalculated taking prevalent levels of capacity utilisation, current transport leads and new features like conversion of contract labour to departmental labour in the depots. The updated norms should be the basis for the MOUs entered into between FCI and government. The updating of norms should be an annual feature. These norms should be used as the benchmarks for assessing FCI's performance in the annual performance budgets.

F.14. The reports of the Internal Audit and Physical Verification Wing of the FCI should serve as instruments of cost control. The IA & PV reports should cover core issues like manpower, subsidy, budgetary control, construction management, port operations, import and export, open market sales, procurement incidentals and gunny accounts.

F.15. Under the present system, underloading by the FCI at the despatch point and theft of stock while unloading by the FCI at the destination can be easily camouflaged and shown as rail-transit losses. Suggestions are given in Appendix 3 for review of the existing system.

F.16. Furthermore, there is scope for reducing the economic cost in respect of procurement, quality control, transport, storage, inspection, audit and physical verification and financial management. This is discussed in Appendix 3.

Storage

The task of the FCI in the present situation is to tackle the serious diseconomies which have set in because of abnormal stock levels. Certain lines of action have been suggested in the Appendix 3.

F.17. In considering proposals for bulk handling and storage, FCI should enter into guarantees, if at all, only on those projects which have direct bearing on its operations relating to supply grain for the PDS. Such proposals should be carefully evaluated against other existing alternatives.

F.18. To improve utilisation of storage space, it would be feasible to increase stack height taking into account requirements of stack stability and alley space for fumigation. The principle of first-in first-out in respect of stocks must be followed rigorously especially given the growing size of stocks.

F.19. There are large losses in stocks held in the East and North-east and physical verification must be done more frequently in these locations.

F.20. In the current situation, we urgently need a more realistic assessment of storage losses as well as the status (in respect of quality) of currently stored grain. For this, the Committee recommends

- 100 per cent weighing of stocks in one compartment each from a representative selection of godowns selected by a random sample.

- 100 per cent weighing of a random sample of CAP stacks.
- Wholesale killing of all stacks in selected godowns even if this involves extra expenditure on transport of stocks to issue points.
- For lustre loss wheat, there should be an immediate assessment of the quantity available and its shelf life.

F.21. For the present, this Committee does not wish to recommend that use of jute bags by the FCI be stopped. However, there are specific suggestions for tightening of specifications and more rigorous inspection procedures by the jute industry is clearly called for, and recommendations for this may be seen in Appendix 3.

Transit Losses

Under the present system, FCI depot shortages and pilferage at the stage of FCI loading and unloading can be easily camouflaged and shown as transit losses. Safeguards against this are discussed in detail in the Appendix 3.

None of the 34 weigh bridges introduced by the FCI is operational. These electronic in-motion weigh bridges should be made functional immediately.

The FCI had prepared a 15-point Action Plan in 1987 and the BICP in 1990 had given 25 recommendations for controlling storage and transit losses. These cover adherence to quality specifications at the time of procurement, packing in standardised bags, machine stitching of bags, proper weighment, installation of in-motion weigh-bridges, reduction of spillage, regular prophylactic treatment, priority liquidation of stocks in CAP storage, special vigilance over depots which been registering heavy losses, sending escorts with wagons on routes where transit losses have been heavy, frequent squad checking at loading and unloading points, intensive depot inspections and induction of the Central Industrial Security Force. These plans should be fully operationalised, and targets for implementation of these measures should be incorporated in the FCI's MOU with Government.

Credit Management

Open ended procurement requires open-ended bank credit but this makes it all the more necessary to have a clear discipline regarding the relationship between banks, the FCI and the Government of India. We therefore recommend the following.

- The current system envisages that stocks be valued at their acquisition cost up to a period of three months, after which they be valued at the lower average sales prices. This requires the government to make prompt settlement of the subsidies implied by its decision on MSP and CIP. This should be adhered to strictly. In addition the following may be considered:

  i) Banks should develop procedures for third party verification of stock.

  ii) As grain below FAQ should not be procured by FCI for the Central pool, credit for such purposes should not be treated as part of food credit.

  iii) A credit limit for FCI should be fixed at say twice the minimum buffer norms. If the stock situation requires that FCI have more financial accommodation, this should be borne by government not the banks.

  iv) Bank credit should be based on the MSP/procurement price recommended by CACP. Any credit requirement over and above this should be met through the Budget.

- There are good commercial grounds for negotiating with the RBI for a lower rate of interest, not more than one per cent above the average cost of credit, at least for credit up to minimum buffer norms.

Many of the recommendations for the FCI for the long term will need to be initiated in the immediate future.

SHORT RUN RECOMMENDATIONS

Given the present crisis in the food grain management system in India, we need some immediate bold initiatives to set right the present imbalances, and specifically to reduce the level of stocks held by the Central and State governments. Existing measures taken by the government to reduce stocks have pertained only to disposal and distribution and have not addressed the critical issue of procurement. In fact, our assessment is that it is very unlikely that domestic offtake, excluding Food for Work, can exceed 30 million tonnes except for one or two years unless there is a rise in incomes. This implies a maximum total annual offtake of 40 million tonnes, even on the generous allowance of 10 million tonnes for exports. Since procurement is currently about 40 million tonnes, there cannot be any significant stock reduction without reducing procurement.

Procurement

For the above reason, MSP should not be increased or even left at the same rate in the present situation. For example, if the MSPs are frozen at their current nominal values, it will at current inflation rates require about 7 years for it to fall to the level of the C_2 cost of production. On the other hand, cutting the MSP immediately to the C_2 level is likely to reduce rice and wheat procurement to around 15 and 13 million tonnes respectively. The larger the reduction in MSP, the greater the flexibility for food policy. The number of years required for reducing excess stocks will depend on the MSP. The expansion of private trade will also depend on the MSP, as will the extent of crop diversification. For this reason the Committee recommends that there be quick and immediate movement towards several goals of long-term policy:

- The MSP must be lowered immediately from present levels to levels of average C_2 cost, as determined by the Commission for Agricultural Costs and Prices, and there should be only one MSP for paddy.
- Steps should be initiated to give statutory status to MSP.
- All levy orders on rice millers should be removed forthwith.
- Quality specifications should be strictly maintained in respect of procurement. If there is genuine quality loss because of natural weather conditions, cultivators may be compensated separately but not through procurement of lower grade cereals.

However, this will require a compensation package to be given to State governments for compensating cultivators. The Committee recommends that

- The amount to be made available to each State government for this purpose should be the difference between the MSP fixed for 2001-02 and the actual MSP declared on the basis of C_2 cost, multiplied by its average procurement in the preceding three seasons.

Thus, given that average procurement of wheat was 18.6 million tonnes in the past three years, a cut in the MSP of wheat, for example, from Rs. 620 to Rs 500 per quintal, will require a total compensation of Rs. 2232 crore (120*18.6). Similarly, rice procurement has averaged 18.7 million tonnes in the last three years, and a reduction in MSP of paddy, for example, from Rs. 560 to Rs 500 per quintal will involve a compensation of Rs. 1683 crore (60*1.5*18.7). Or a total of Rs 3915 crore.

- This formula should continue till the actual procurement price (i.e. MSP or MSP plus premium, in case a premium is required for adequate procurement) crosses the past highest MSP.
- State governments must offer this compensation to farmers, but may do this in any one or combination of the following:
  - i) Direct per hectare transfer to farmers
  - ii) Subsidising premiums on insurance schemes on crop incomes/ prices
  - iii) Specific crop diversification schemes
  - iv) Other credit/input linked schemes to offset cost, including electricity.
- However, States should not be allowed to offer a bonus on MSP, and as far as possible direct transfers should be on total cropped area, not just area under paddy and wheat; and insurance should also not be limited to paddy/wheat.
- In addition to the above, the Centre should accept a modified version of the Punjab Government's proposal made to the Committee to reduce on environmental grounds the area under paddy by 1 million hectares. For this, Punjab Government can be given an additional package of up to Rs. 300 crores on condition of a limit on procurement of rice/paddy. This should be a time bound programme of 2 to 3 years, during which NAFED should be instructed to ensure support operations in oilseeds and pulses.

The Committee also believes that there is need for immediate implementation of the long-term recommendation to reduce taxes on food grain, an essential commodity which provides the bulk of calories to most of our population, a large proportion who are poor.

- The FCI and its appointed agencies should pay a uniform procurement price comprising the MSP plus 4 per cent in lieu of all statutory taxes, commission agent charges, mandi charges, etc.

Since this will significantly affect finances of some States, another appropriate compensation package should be offered.

- This package should be conditional on an undertaking by the State government that it will reduce all statutory levies to a maximum of 4 per cent, not only for FCI and its agents but for all private buyers as well. So long as the State government maintains this discipline, the Central Government should give the State government a cash transfer equal to the difference between the statutory levies which would have been payable by FCI and its appointed agents at rates in force on 1.4.2002 and what the State receives on implementation.

This package would cost the Centre Rs. 1200 - Rs. 1800 crore. The total compensation to both farmers and State governments would thus be at most Rs. 6000 crore in the first year, and declining from this subsequently. As against this, the savings on acquisition and carrying costs on the reduced procurement, envisaged at about 10 million tonnes, will be about Rs. 10,000 crore in the first year, Rs. 12,500 crore in the second year, Rs. 15,000 crore in the third year and so on, assuming that the entire reduction in procurement will save on additional stockholding. There may be further savings in subsidies which would have been required to dispose additional stocks.

However, none of the recommendations made in this report will have credibility unless MSP becomes reality all over the country. A further immediate procurement related recommendation for the short-run is:

- The FCI should immediately begin to focus its procurement effort in assistance to State Governments in East and Central India to ensure that there is effective price support at these reduced MSP levels.

- All existing bottlenecks in the decentralised procurement scheme should be removed at the earliest, especially in respect of bank finance. Failing this, States may be allowed to opt out of decentralised procurement and FCI required to undertake procurement with the Central Government ensuring all credit and subsidy for this purpose.

This is essential since these regions will receive very little compensation and yet face declining prices as result of stock reduction measures which follow.

Stock Reduction Measures

We suggest that the following recommendations be undertaken as a Special Two Year Programme of Action (this is roughly the minimum time which would be needed to bring stocks back to normal levels).

Disposal of Old and Relaxed Quality Stock

This is essential to restore consumer confidence in the quality of Central Pool stocks. If this is accomplished quickly and transparently, it will also increase offtake from the PDS. Our recommendations are:

- All stocks of three years age and more and all grain bought under relaxed specification, including lustre loss, should be taken out of Central pool food stocks and not be offered to the PDS and other welfare schemes.
- The grain identified above should be sold immediately, in a phased manner, at commercial terms. The lustre loss wheat acquired in 2001 should be liquidated by March 31, 2003. A suitably high differential should be maintained for all domestic open sales and exports of sound grain, especially that acquired in the immediate harvest.
- For sound quality grain of less than three years, current sale prices should not be reduced till the above-identified stocks have been disposed.
- To protect the quality of grain fit for human consumption, we recommend that all possible steps be taken to segregate available stocks by age and quality in order to separate grain that is likely to deteriorate quickly, and plan their disposal on priority basis.
- All grain unfit for human consumption should be disposed of as animal and poultry feed at formula rates, which if necessary may be reviewed downwards.
- Physical verification of stocks for identification of losses (missing stocks) is very important. There should be an agreed method of physical verification within three months, keeping in view the sampling method proposed by the Indian Statistical Institute, and implementation should begin forthwith.

Exports

In view of reports regarding diversion of grain meant for exports, suitable steps have to be taken to tighten procedures to prevent leakages into the domestic market.

The current export drive should be reviewed as soon as stocks come down to 17 and 22 million tonnes for rice and wheat respectively. After which, steps should be taken to move towards the long term recommendation.

Public Distribution

The Committee endorses an immediate shift to a unified PDS as recommended for the long run. Although this would be another change in a system that has seen frequent changes over the last few years (in prices, in quantities, in categories of entitlement), we believe there are significant benefits. Most importantly, this would bring back many of the poor and near poor who have been excluded from the BPL category. The bringing-back of a larger section of the population is critical given the huge stocks remaining with the FCI and can also revive the delivery system that has become non-viable on exclusion of a large part of the population from the PDS. Although in the long run, we recommend the principle of pricing PDS grain close to the acquisition cost, and although today even APL prices are below acquisition cost, a sudden and large price increase for BPL households cannot be justified in the present situation. Also raising the prices of grain does not make commercial sense for the FCI. Further, given the poor quality of grain supplied at present in the PDS, we believe that an improvement in quality should precede a rise in prices. We therefore recommend:

- Immediate unification of the PDS at uniform Central issue prices (CIP) .
- The common issue price for all consumers can be set at Rs 4.50 per kg of wheat and Rs 6 per kg of rice. (this is the weighted average of the current BPL and APL price, weighted by offtake, and also around the acquisition cost net of carrying costs).
- This is to be accompanied by a transfer of 35 paisa per kg of grain offtake as cash incentive to State governments, conditional on lifting and accounting. Alternatively, if the State governments so prefer, the transfer may be in grain, valued at the unified Central issue price. The cash transfer can be used by State governments in any manner for strengthening the PDS and expanding offtake including offering all consumers the old BPL prices. The grain transfer could be used for any poverty alleviation/employment scheme.
- The CIPs should be raised, in a phased manner, moving towards acquisition cost, conditional on

Improvement in quality of stocks

  - Reduction in stocks to 17 and 22 million tonnes for rice and wheat respectively
  - Providing cash transfers, as per our long-run recommendation, when CIPs are raised.

- A definite sequence of phasing the CIP increase should be announced, based on the above, as early as possible to avoid consumers facing a sudden and unanticipated large price increase. Also, it is necessary to increase the CIPs to above MSP as soon as market conditions allow to remove the incentive for recycling.

- Revival of the delivery system is very important for the PDS to function effectively. For this, the network of fair-price shops must be revitalised and extended, particularly in relatively backward areas such as hill regions, drought-prone and drought-affected regions, and regions populated mainly by adivasis. We recommend:
    - Immediate implementation of our long-term recommendations.
    - Provision of Rs. 500 a month to Fair Price Shop dealers in villages and towns outside municipal areas, as an interim measure to restore viability. Assuming there are 2,50,000 shops in such areas, this may cost the Central government Rs. 150 crores annually.

Employment Programmes and Welfare

In the present situation of low demand for almost all agricultural commodities, and the associated need for better rural connectivity to enlarge markets, there is a crying need for a massive public works programme to improve rural infrastructure. Implementation of such a programme would not be inflationary given the present high stocks of grain and large foreign exchange reserves. This would not only reduce the costs of agricultural production and marketing, but also inject demand into the rural economy, which accounts for 60 per cent of demand for all agricultural produce. Most importantly, this could make a significant dent on unemployment and poverty. Ideally, the programme should be such as to offer 30 days employment during the lean season to each agricultural labourer. This amounts to 3090 million person days of employment for the 103 million agricultural labourers, as per the Census of 2001.

In fact, a fairly large increase in demand will be required for stocks to reduce to normal levels within two years even with the measures recommended earlier. On the basis of actual offtake during the past twelve months, it is expected that exports will be around 10 million tonnes and domestic offtake in the region of 28-33 million tonnes. At current procurement levels, this would either leave stocks constant or lead to their decline by at most 5 million tonnes over the next twelve months. However, for stocks to reduce to normal levels in two years requires annual stock reduction of 15 million tonnes. MSP reduction can reduce procurement by about 10-12 million tonnes. But, even allowing for drop in production and rebuilding of private stocks, this would involve increased availability in the market which would tend to depress market prices. Unless accompanied by demand injection, this price decline would restrain offtake and prevent full reduction of procurement, causing adjustment to be more prolonged. In our view, a quick increase in demand is possible only by increasing the incomes of the poor. The additional cash outlay proposed below should be seen primarily in terms of assets that can thereby be created, but this will also lead to corresponding savings in acquisition and carrying costs if it enables a reduction in the adjustment period by one or two years. A two-year horizon for reducing stocks to normal levels is extremely unlikely without such demand injection:

- The present SGRY scheme should be expanded, and at least doubled. This implies doubling grain allocation, from 5 to 10 million tonnes, and also an increase in cash allocation to States by at least Rs. 5000 crore.

On present accounting practice, where grain purchases for SGRY by the Ministry of Rural Development from FCI are at economic cost, this would require doubling of the financial allocation for grain purchase under SGRY from the earlier commitment of Rs. 5,000 to Rs. 10,000 crore. However, to reflect opportunity costs better, we propose:

- The Central government should make allocations of grain for all grain-related welfare/development schemes at the same formula as for PDS (that is, unified Central issue price plus cash subsidy). This should apply also to any such scheme proposed by State governments.

To initiate our vision for Food for Welfare, we further recommend that:

- The expansion and re-orientation of Antyodaya Anna Yojana envisaged in recommendation for the long-term should begin immediately.
- Central support to States to the extent of 50 per cent for a cooked Mid-day Meal scheme, i.e. recommendation for the long run, can be initiated.

In recommending these, we anticipate being accused of pandering to populism and of tying the Government to unsustainable future expenditure. We plead not guilty.

Currently, about half of the food subsidy is being spent on holding stocks in excess of the buffer stock levels necessary for food security. As these stocks are reduced to normal levels, very large fiscal resources of around Rs. 10,000 crore annually will become available. With these resources, which will be in addition to the normal TPDS subsidy including on the BPL, a massive thrust is possible, both directly on destitution and hunger through a comprehensive but flexible system of public food distribution; and through public works on better integration of rural India. That this will still be possible after compensating farmers who lose from immediate MSP reduction and without putting further fiscal burden over what is already being spent on food subsidies is at the same time a comment on the magnitude of past errors and an assertion of our faith in future opportunities.

Union Ministry of Consumer Affairs, Food and Public Distribution, Report of the High Level Committee on Long Term Grain Policy (Chairman: Abhijit Sen), July 22, 2002.

Part III

Industry & Infrastructure

Editorial Notes

17

Industrial Development and Policies Since Independence

This part (Chs. 17 to 23) is devoted to the issues of industrial development and policies. It deals with aspects relating to policies for regulating the pattern of investment in the private and public sectors, policies towards the small scale sector, and the rate and pattern of industrial growth since independence.

The growth and diversification in Indian industry has been covered in the paper by K.L. Krishna (Ch. 18). Structural transformation in industry, a comparative picture of the 80's and 90's also covering the recent policy initiatives and small scale industry is covered in Ch. 17 in the editorial notes. The Industrial policy and performance and fall in organised manufacturing employment are discussed by R. Nagraj's in (Ch. 19 & 20). Public versus private sector is discussed in Ch. 21 by B..S. Minhas. Issues relating to disinvestment are discussed in Ch. 22 (Disinvestment commission report I) and also in the editorial notes (Ch.17). The issues relating to infrastructure development and the necessary regulatory framework are discussed in Ch. 23.

The Industrial Scene at Independence

For understanding the policies for regulating the pattern of investment in private and public sector in industry, one must appreciate the industrial scene at independence characterised as below*:

(i) The industrial sector was extremely underdeveloped with a very weak infrastructure.

(ii) The lack of government intervention in favour of the industrial sector was considered as an important cause of under-development.

(iii) Export orientation had been against the country's interests.

(iv) The structure of ownership was highly concentrated and

(v) Technical and managerial skills were in short supply.

As a result, the national consensus was that economic sovereignty and economic independence lay in rapid industrialization including particularly the promotion of industrial infrastructure.

Organized thinking concerning the direction of industrial development in India may be traced to the Statement of Industrial Policy, 1945, the Industrial Policy Resolution of 1948, the enactment of the Industries (Development and Regulation) Act, 1951, the First and Second Five Year Plan documents, and the Industrial Policy Resolution of 1956. The 1945 Statement of Industrial Policy of the then Government of India (GOI) is remarkable as a precursor of all the thinking that became enshrined in the key industrial policy resolutions after independence. The statement also mentioned the concept of industrial licensing. Special importance was given to the development of steel, heavy engineering, machine tools and heavy chemicals industries. This emphasis has been characteristic of Indian industrial policy thinking ever since. The idea that the government should actively participate in the setting up of certain important industries, either directly or by subscribing shares in such industrial undertakings, was also mooted in this industrial policy statement. The idea of licensing, it seems, was mainly thought to be an instrument for the dispersal of industries and to prevent the establishment of excess capacity in industries 'which promise quick returns'. The list of industries which were proposed to be brought under central controls bears a resemblance to the original schedule of industries brought under the control of the central government through the Industries Development and Regulation (ID&R) Act of 1951. Thus there was significant continuity in thinking between the pre-independence and post-independence government as reflected in the Industrial Policy Resolutions of 1948 and 1956.

The First Five Year Plan stated that the objective of industrial planning was to make good the deficiencies in production of key industrial items and to initiate development which would enable the cumulative expansion of such basic production. The scope and need for the development of India's industries was felt to be so great that it was necessary for the public sector to develop those industries 'in which private enterprise is unable or unwilling to put up the resources required and to run the risk involved.' The idea was that the rest of the field could be left free for private enterprise. The Industrial Policy Resolution of 1948 had identified a small number of industries to be reserved for production by the public sector. The production of arms and ammunition, production and control of atomic energy and ownership and management of railways were to be the sole preserve of the central government. However, coal, iron and steel, aircraft manufacturing, shipbuilding, manufacture of telegraph and wireless equipment (except radios) and minerals were reserved for production by central or state government undertakings. The 1956 list of industries reserved for the public sector is obviously based on this 1948 list but includes a number of additional industries. The thinking concerning the public sector had changed during the course of the 1950s. As far as can be ascertained, the original thinking was concerned with the use of the public sector investment in industries which the private sector would find difficult to invest in. By 1956 this had changed towards an explicit preference for state ownership of industries that were termed as capturing the 'commanding heights of the economy'.

Although the Second Five Year Plan is always seen as the conceptual basis of Indian planning, a close reading of the First Five Year Plan suggests that the difficulty of directing a mixed economy was better appreciated by the earlier planners and policy makers. There was better appreciation of the need for indicative planning in the First Plan and the need for coordination of industrial planning with the formulation of other economic policies such as customs and excise tariff structure, import and export policy, investment and technology policy, monetary and financial policy. The Second Plan and later plans have been increasingly concerned with the allocation of public resources and much less with indications and policies to direct the whole economy in desired directions. (Rakesh Mohan, 1992).

Industrial Control Regime

The system of Indian industrial licensing, therefore, has its origins in a combination of thinking resulting from the exigencies and requirements of a war situation, Indian nationalistic aspirations and the socialistic leanings of some of the founding fathers of the country. The leaders of the private sector of the time were also in favour of strong governmental assertion. The industrial licensing system has operated in the country with the simultaneous operation of other schemes of governmental allocations and controls such as:

(i) Five Year Plan documents

(ii) Import and export controls

(iii) Control of capital issues

(iv) Control of foreign exchange

(v) Transport controls including allocation of raw materials

(vi) Price controls

(vii) Allocations of credit

This suggests that the planners and policy makers in India understood the need for using a wide variety of instruments and controls to steer Indian industrial development in a desired direction. However, there has always been a mismatch between the intentions expressed and the licensing instruments available for realizing these planning intentions. It should also be noted that, whereas the original intention of licensing was to use this power selectively for the promotion of selected important industries, it was later used to control almost all industries with the result that regulation rather than development became the more important feature of the system.

Performance of the Industrial Licensing System

Until the recent industrial and trade policy reforms, the establishment and operation of an industrial enterprise in India required approvals from the central government at almost every step (see Paranjape, 1988). Before making an investment, an entrepreneur had to first obtain approval in principle from the Ministry of Industry. The granting of this approval resulted in the issuance of a Letter of Intent (LOI). Armed with this LOI, the entrepreneur could then tie up other requirements for setting up the project. If he needed to import a capital good, he had to obtain a capital goods import licence from the Chief Controller of Imports & Exports (CCI&E) in the Ministry of Commerce. The approval for the import, however, was given by a committee set up in the Ministry of Industry. If there was also need for a foreign technology collaboration agreement, the entrepreneur had to obtain a specific approval for this (a Foreign Collaboration–FC–approval) from a committee chaired by the Finance Secretary but serviced by the Ministry of Industry. In order to raise funds for the project, if an entrepreneur wanted to go to the capital market, he needed separate approval from the Controller of Capital Issues in the Ministry of Finance. For imports of raw material and components, separate licences had to be obtained on an annual basis from the CCI&E. In each case, an 'essentiality' and indigenous non-availability clearance had to be given by the technical wing of the Ministry of Industry (the Directorate General of technical Development – DGTD). Once everything was tied up and the unit was about to go into production, the entrepreneur had to go back to the Ministry of Industry for an 'Industrial Licence'.

In addition to these approvals, since the enactment of the MRTP Act in 1969, the firms covered under this needed to obtain separate MRTP clearances from the Department of Company Affairs. Further, resulting from the desire to promote small-scale industries, 836 items have been reserved for production in small-scale enterprises. Since 1956, there has also been a list of industries reserved for exclusive production in the public sector. Since 1977, there has also been a ban on the location of industries in the largest twenty to thirty cities. In 1988, this ban was extended to include municipal areas of all towns and cities and to specified areas of influence around the largest twenty-one cities.

That this system was unsuited for directing investments has been well understood since the early 1960s. The most comprehensive description, evaluation and indictment of this system is that by Bhagwati and Desai (1970). The government appointed one committee after another in the 1960s to examine the industrial licensing system (The Swaminathan Committee, 1964; the Mahalanobis Committee, 1964; the Hazari Report, 1967; the Dutt Committee Report, 1969; and the Administrative Reform Commission, 1969). Despite the findings of most of these early committees, that the licensing mechanism was not serving its purpose of channelizing investments into desired directions, there seems to have been a continuing inability of the government, until recently, to bring any substantative changes to the industrial licensing system.

Some of the Hazari Committee's conclusions were:

- That industrial licensing has served to channelize investment into desired directions appears extremely doubtful.
- The gains in terms of balanced regional development and wider distribution of entrepreneurship were at best moderate.
- There is very little follow-up of licensing to see that approved projects fructify in time.
- In attempting to cover almost the whole range of large-scale industrial development licensing, the Act inevitably loses sight of the relative importance of different projects/products, i.e. whether critical to the economy or otherwise, all applications will undergo similar processing.

In respect of Licensing, the system had failed practically on all counts, whether it was regional dispersal, import substitution, or preventing concentration of economic power. Licensing would not even ensure the development of industries mainly according to Plan priorities. Moreover, the licensing system could not attain even its specific objectives. Licences were issued in excess of capacity targets even in non-essential industries. Influential parties and large houses were permitted to pre-empt capacities. The follow-up of licences was unsystematic and licences remained unimplemented for long periods... (Paranjape, 1988).

Even with such adverse comments, it is instructive to examine what this committee recommended. The committee concluded that 'with all its defects the industrial licensing system did have a useful role to play though its limitations needed to be borne in view.' The committee recommended that:

- There should be a list of reservations for small scale industry production.
- Bans on further capacity creation should be utilized to prevent the creation of 'undesirable industries', particularly the production of 'non-essential luxury goods'.

The committee went on to recommend a whole host of other measures which would lead to more detailed rather than reduced control of industry.

Thus despite all the evidence gathered very laboriously there was a persistent reluctance to learn from experience and change course.

It seems the promotion of a sheltered home market had a common appeal to the bureaucratic authoritarian state, urban manufacturers, and multinationals that supplied technology and capital. Protection also met the state's objectives pursuing revenue and expenditure maximising activities through maximum revenue tariffs and export tariffs.

Thus the interests of politicians, bureaucrats, multinationals, as well as domestic industrial houses all coincided to keep Indian industry sheltered through the operation of the industrial control system.

The stagnation of Indian industrial production between the mid-1960s up to the late 1970s induced some serious new thinking. Towards the end of the 1970s and by the early 1980s there emerged a growing consensus that Indian industry was exhibiting a slow-down in industrial growth due to low productivity, high costs, low quality of production and obsolete technology (Ahluwalia, 1985). Three important committees were set up in the early 1980s – the Abid Hussain Committee on trade policy, the Narasimham Committee on the shift from physical to fiscal controls and the Sengupta Committee on the public sector. These committees clearly recommended an easing up of trade policy, the substitution of physical and quantitative controls by fiscal and other means of macroeconomic management, the promotion of greater public sector autonomy in business and operating decisions and the need for measures for enhancing productivity efficiency and modernization.

The result of such thinking was that there was some progress in the process of de-regulation during the 1980s, though perhaps not as significant as is often believed. Two kinds of delicensing activity took place. First, thirty-two groups of industries were delicensed without any investment limit. Second, in 1988, all industries were exempted from licensing except for a specified negative list of twenty-six industries. This exemption from licensing was, however, subject to investment and location limitations. As has often been done in the past, this announcement also contained further restrictions which reduced significantly the effectiveness of exemption from licensing that was provided in this announcement. On the trade policy front, the key change was increasing access of exporters to inputs at international prices. However, it seems that tariff protection to industry increased significantly during the 1980s relative to previous decades.

While the industrial licensing system underwent some changes in terms of threshold levels and types of products, it formed an essential part of Government policy until the end of the 1980s.

New Economic Policy

As Rangarajan (2003) has rightly stated, the year 1991 is an important landmark in the economic history of post-Independent India. The country went through a severe economic crisis triggered by a serious balance of payments situation. The crisis was converted into an opportunity to introduce some fundamental changes in the content and approach to economic policy. The response to the crisis was to put in place a set of policies aimed at stabilisation and structural reform. While the stabilisation policies were aimed at correcting the weaknesses that had developed on the fiscal and the balance of payments fronts, the structural reforms sought to remove the rigidities that had entered into the various segments of the Indian economy. The structural reforms introduced in the early 1990s broadly covered the areas of industrial licensing, foreign trade, foreign investment, exchange rate management and the financial sector. From the point of view of industrialisation, changes in the areas of licensing and foreign trade and investment had important implications.

Even before the onset of reforms, the problems associated with industrial licensing were well recognised. The approach document of the Eighth Plan (1991-1996) submitted in May 1990 had remarked: "A return to the regime of direct, indiscriminate and detailed controls in industry is clearly out of question. Past experience has shown that such control system is not effective in achieving the desired objective. Also the system is widely abused and leads to corruption, delays and inefficiency" (Government of India: 1990). One early step that was undertaken as part of the structural reform process was to dispense with licensing. Changes in foreign trade policy focussed on reducing the tariff rates and dismantling quantitative controls over imports. The tariff rates have been brought down in stages. Some caution in this regard had become necessary to enable the Indian industries set up behind high protective tariff walls to adjust to the changed situation. The policy towards foreign investment underwent a significant change with foreign investors given the freedom to own majority shareholding over a wide spectrum of industries.

Without going into details, the common thread running through the various policy measures introduced since 1991 has been the improvement of the efficiency of the system. The thrust of the New Economic Policy has been towards creating a more competitive environment in the economy as a means to improving the productivity and efficiency of the system. This was to be achieved by removing the barriers to entry and the restrictions on the growth of firms. While the Industrial Policy of 1992 sought to bring about a greater competitive environment domestically, the counterpart Trade Policy set out in the same year, sought to improve international competitiveness subject to the degree of protection offered by the tariffs. The private sector was to be given a larger space to operate in as much as some of the areas, reserved exclusively earlier for the public sector were now to be opened to the private sector. In these areas, the public sector would have to compete with the private sector, even though the public sector might continue to play the dominant role in the foreseeable future. What was sought to be achieved was the improvement in the functioning of the various entities, whether they were in the private or in the public sector.

In the New Industrial Policy 1991, industrial licensing will henceforth be abolished for all industries except these specified irrespective of level of investment.

These specified industries will continue to be subject to compulsory licensing for reasons related to security and strategic concerns, social reasons, problems related to safety and overriding environmental issues, manufactures of products of hazardous nature and the articles of elitist consumption. The exemption from licensing will be particulary helpful to the many dynamic small and medium entrepreneurs who had been unnecessarily hampered by the licensing system.

Industrial Growth

Having looked into the industrial control regime and the performance of the industrial licensing system. Let us now look at the industrial growth since independence – the rate and pattern of growth and the structural changes.

Since independence, the share of industry has increased substantially from 11.8 per cent of GDP in 1950-51 to 24.6 per cent in 1990-91. Secondly, the composition of industry has undergone great transformation. The share of Capital Goods in industrial value added increased steadily at a high pace from 4.7 per cent in 1956 to 23.7 per cent in 1990. The share of Basic Goods increased relatively moderately, from 22.3 per cent to 38.4 per cent. Consumer Goods group declined considerably in relative importance, with the share in industrial value added falling from 48.4 per cent in 1956 to 20.5 per cent in 1990. (K.L. Krishna Ch. 18).

Phases of Industrial Growth

One can identify three distinct phases of industrial growth in India since the planning era. The first phase of rapid growth ends from 1956-1965. The second phase of slow growth or deceleration extends from 1965-66 to 1979-80. The third phase is a phase of recovery and revival of growth since 1980s. Krishna has summarised the various explanatory hypotheses and has also reviewed the available empirical evidence bearing upon the alternative hypotheses (Krishna, Ch. 18)

During the period 1959-60 to 1965-66, value added in organised industry grew at the rate of 8.0 per cent per annum. The growth rate declined to 5.7 per cent in the period 1966-67 to 1989-90. The corresponding growth rates for the registered manufacturing were 7.6 and 5.5 per cent. In capital goods and basic goods the decline was very pronounced from 15.4 to 6.6 and 11.0 to 5.0 per cent per annum, respectively. Consumer goods and its sub-category consumer non-durables experienced slight acceleration. In Intermediate goods and consumer durables, there was mild deceleration. Thus deceleration was largely confined to heavy industry which accounted for about 50 per cent of value added in industry in 1979-80.

Ahluwalia (1985) after empirically examining different hypotheses identified four factors:

(i) slow-down in public investment
(ii) poor management of the infrastructure sector
(iii) slow growth of agricultural incomes, and
(iv) restrictive industrial and trade policies.

However, Ahluwalia did not carry out any econometric exercise to establish her thesis. Rangarajan (1982), Lahiri et al (1984), Ray (1991) Mukhopadhyay (1992), Kavita Rao (1993) and Balakrishnan (1995) conducted econometric exercises to verify the various hypotheses. These exercises established that one or more of the following factors, public investment, agricultural performance, infrastructure, the policy of import substitution and domestic terms of trade turned out to be significant for the different industry groups. The over all inference from the various studies is that the demand constraints were more important than supply constraints (Krishna Ch. 18).

In the 1980s, the industrial sector fared impressively in this decade, compared to the preceding 15-year period. The annual rates of growth for manufacturing, registered manufacturing and unregistered manufacturing were 7.0, 8.1 and 5.8, respectively.

In the first six years of the eighties, consumer durables recorded a growth rate of 14.2 per cent, while capital goods recorded a relatively modest growth of 7.8 per cent per annum.

Empirical evidence suggests that the explanations for the resurgence of growth in the 1980s are similar to those for the deceleration after the mid-sixties.

Industrial Growth in the 90s

The manufacturing sector witnessed an upward trend in growth rates registering growth rate of 8 to 9 per cent in the second half of 80s. In the 90s, the period immediately following the reforms was marked by low growth rates. However, the growth rates quickly recovered. After a decline of 0.8 per cent in 1991-92, the rate of growth climbed to 2.2 per cent in 1992-93, 5.5 per cent in 1993-94, 8.6 per cent in 1994-95 and an estimated 12 per cent in 1995-96. However since 1996-97, deceleration in industrial sector has set in.

The major policy changes initiated in the industrial sector since July 1991 viz removal of entry barriers, reduction of areas reserved exclusively for public sector, rationalisation of the approach towards MRTP, liberalisation of foreign investment policy, far reaching liberalisation of import policy with respect to intermediates and capital goods may have all contributed to the upsurge in industrial growth.

Industrial production registered a higher growth of 6.6 per cent in 1997-98 compared to the 5.6 per cent in 1996-97. The improvement in 1997-98 was due to better performance of mining and electricity generation, which recorded higher growth rates of 5.9 per cent and 6.6 per cent compared to 2.2 per cent and 4 per cent respectively in 1996-97. Higher growth of mining could be attributed to improved performance of crude oil (2.9 per cent in 1997-98 compared to -6.5 per cent in 1996-97) and that of electricity generation to improved performance of hydro-electricity (8.2 per cent in 1997-98 compared to -5.4 per cent in 1996-97). The growth of manufacturing in 1997-98 at 6.6 per cent remained almost at the level of the previous year. In 1998-99 year, industrial production has registered a growth rate of 3.9 per cent during April-December 1998, lower than the 6.8 per cent growth in April-December, 1997. The low growth is noticeable in mining and manufacturing sectors. Electricity generation has posted a higher growth in the current year (Table–17.1).

After a relatively modest performance in 1998-99, the Indian industry experienced a turnaround. Several macro-economic and business indicators were showing signs of a broad-based industrial recovery. The cumulative growth of industrial production, as measured by the Index of Industrial Production (IIP), was 6.2 per cent for April-December 1999, significantly higher than the 4.0 per cent of April-December 1998. The higher growth in the 1999-2000 has been largely contributed by the 7.0 per cent growth in manufacturing and the 7.7 per cent growth in electricity. (Table 17.1)

After a turnaround in 1999-2000, Industrial growth (measured by the Index of Industrial Production) has again slowed down during the year 2000-01 and in 2001-02 registered 2.1 per cent rate of growth against 6.2 per cent in 2000-01.

The industrial deceleration was due to a number of structural and cyclical factors such as normal business and investment cycles, a lack of both domestic and external demand, continuing high real interest rates, infrastructure bottlenecks in power and transport, lack of reforms in land and labour markets, inherent adjustment lags resulting from industrial restructuring through merger and acquisitions, and delays in establishing appropriate institutional and regulatory frameworks in some key sectors.

TABLE – 17.1

Annual Growth Rates of Industrial Production in Major Sectors of Industry

(Based on the index of Industrial production)*

Base: 1993-94=100

(per cent)

Period	Mining & Quarrying	Manufacturing	Electricity	Overall
Weight	**10.4**	**79.4**	**10.2**	**100.0**
1995-96	9.7	14.1	8.1	13.0
1996-97	-1.9	7.3	4.0	6.1
1997-98	6.9	6.7	6.6	6.7
1998-99	-0.8	4.4	6.5	4.1
1999-00	1.0	7.1	7.3	6.7
2000-01	2.8	5.3	4.0	5.0
2001-02	1.2	2.9	3.1	2.7
2002-03	5.8	6.0	3.2	5.7
2003-04	5.2	7.4	5.1	7.0
2004-05 (April-December)	4.8	9.0	6.4	8.4

* Revised index of industrial production

Source: Economic Survey 2004-05.

The difficulties caused by internal constraints were exacerbated by the slow growth in the world economy, which contributed to a substantial slowdown in manufactured exports. While the government was in the process of seeking a consensus for further reforms, external factors such as the attack on the World Trade Centre in September 2001 and related events slowed down the recovery through lack of external demand and adverse impact on air transport, communications and tourism.

Comparative Growth Rates in the '80s and the '90s

The average growth rate of Industrial sector (measured by the Index of Industrial Production) during the period 1992-93 to 1999-2000 was lower than that observed during the period 1980-81 to 1991-92. The growth rate was lower in all the three sectors i.e. manufacturing, mining and electricity. In terms of use-based classification also there was a lower growth rate in basic and capital goods. However, the GDP from manufacturing sector at constant prices showed higher growth rates during the period 1992-93 to 1999-2000 when compared to the period 1980-81 to 1991-92 at the aggregate (total) level and amongst both registered and unregistered segments (Table 17.2).

TABLE – 17.2

Comparative Growth Rates in the Industrial Sector 1980-2000

Parameter	Avg. Annual growth rate (1980-81 to 1991-92)*	Avg. Annual growth rate (1992-93 to 1999-2000)*
Index of Industrial Production		
General	7.8	6.0
Manufacturing	7.6	6.3
Mining	8.4	3.3
Electricity	9.0	6.6
Use-based classification		
Basic goods	7.4	6.1
Capital goods	9.4	5.9
Intermediate goods	4.9	9.1
Consumer goods	6.0	6.3
of which		
(i) Consumer durables	10.8	11.2
(ii) Consumer non-durables	5.3	5.1
GDP-Manufacturing at 1993-94 prices		
Total	6.1	7.4
Registered	6.8	8.1
Unregistered	5.0	6.2

* Simple average of the annual growth rates.
Source : Economic Survey, 2000-01.

The use-based classification, shown in Table 17.3, shows that in addition to capital goods, consumer non-durables were also an area showing sharp growth: an acceleration from 3.2 per cent in 1999-2000 to 12 per cent in 2002-03, the growth rate after declining to 5.7 per cent in 2003-04 rose again to 9.8 per cent in 2004-05.

TABLE – 17.3

Growth Rates of Industrial Production by Use-based Classification

(per cent)

Sectors	*(Weight)*	*1996-97*	*1997-98*	*1998-99*	*1999-2000*	*2000-01*	*2001-02*	*2002-03*	*2003-04*	*Apr.-Dec. 2004-05*
Basic Goods	35.5	3.0	6.9	1.6	5.5	3.7	2.6	4.9	5.4	5.9
Capital Goods	9.3	11.5	5.8	12.6	6.9	1.8	-3.4	10.5	12.7	13.3
Intermediate Goods	26.5	8.1	8.0	6.1	8.8	4.7	1.5	3.9	6.2	6.7
Consumer Goods	28.7	6.2	5.5	2.2	5.7	8.0	6.0	7.1	7.1	11.2
of which										
Consumer Durables	5.4	4.6	7.8	5.6	14.1	14.5	11.5	-6.3	11.6	15.3
Consumer Non-Durables	23.3	6.6	4.8	1.2	3.2	5.8	4.1	12.0	5.7	9.8
IIP (Index of Industrial Production)	100.0	6.1	6.7	4.1	6.7	5.0	2.7	5.7	6.9	8.4

Note : The indices are based on revised itemwise weights.
Source: Economic Survey 2004-05.

This recovery in industrial output appears to reflect a variety of factors, including: the lagged effect of the strong rabi harvest of the previous year, improvements in infrastructure, the demand impact of public investment, and improvement in exports through the recovery of the US and EU markets after the September 11, 2001 incidents in the United States.

Revision of IIP

The index of industrial Production (IIP) is published as a monthly series since 1950. Revisions of IIP are carried out from time to time by shifting the comparison base to a more recent period by reviewing coverage of items/industries for reflecting changes in the structure of industry. The last revision was effected in 1980-81. The Department of Statistics set up in June 1995 a Technical Advisory Committee (TAC) to examine all technical issues relating to comparable state level IIPs and make recommendations thereon. Subsequently in November 1996, the TAC was entrusted with the responsibility to examine all issues and provide technical guidance in the matter of shifting the base period of IIP. On the recommendations of the TAC, IIP base has been shifted to a more recent period (1993-94). The new series was released on May 26,1998. The features of the revised IIP series are captured in Box 17.1.

BOX – 17.1

Revision of IIP Series

The Background

- The IIP, a measure of the trends of industrial production, is being published as a monthly series since 1950.
- IIP has been revised from time to time by shifting the base year to a more recent period, by reviewing the coverage of items and by effecting improvements in the technique of construction with a view to appropriately reflect the pattern of industrial growth.
- At the time of commencement of the Index in India, the base year was 1946. The base year was subsequently revised at various points of time to 1951, 1956, 1960, 1970 and 1980-81.
- The number of items covered in the monthly series of IIP increased from 35 in 1946 to 88 in 1951 and further to 201, 312 and 352 respectively in 1956, 1960 and 1970. The 1980-81 base series retained the number of items at 352.
- Based on the recommendations of the Technical Advisory Committee (TAC) set up by the Department of Statistics in June 1995, the base year of IIP has now been shifted to 1993-94.

Salient Features of the New IIP Series

— Items have been selected on the basis of results of ASI (1993-94), as has been the practice in the past.

— The new series includes 18 items from the small scale sector which also belonged to the 1980-81 series.

— The new series follows NIC 1987 classification as compared to NIC 1970 followed in 1980-81 series.

— A comparative illustration of the number of items and the weighting diagrams for broad sectors (mining, manufacturing and electricity) of IIP for the 1980-81 and 1993-94 series is provided below:

Broad Sector	No. of Items		Weights	
	1980-81	1993-94	1980-81	1993-94
Manufacturing	290	478	77.11	79.36
Mining	61	64	11.46	10.47
Electricity	1	1	11.43	10.17
Total	**352**	**543***	**100.00**	**100.00**

* Clubbed into 287 groups: Manufacturing-285, Mining-1 and Electricity-1.

Contd...

...Box 17.1 Contd...

— Due to adoption of NIC 1987 classification, erstwhile groups 30 (Rubber, plastic, petroleum and coal products) and 31 (Basic chemical products except products of petroleum and coal) of IIP 1980-81 have interchanged places in the revised series. One new group (24: wool, silk and man-made electrical machinery) and 36 (Electrical machinery, apparatus, appliances and supplies and parts) have been amalgemated under the heading 'Machinery and equipment other than Transport equipment'.

In terms of the Index of Industrial Production, a slowdown in the rate of growth of production had set in from 1991-92 to 1998-99, which is generally identified as a period of wide-ranging reforms in the industrial sector. The decline in the rate of growth of production during the 'nineties is clearly visible in different sectors of industry, especially in case of mining and quarrying (Table 17.4).

TABLE – 17.4

Annual Average Growth Rate of Industrial Production

(Per cent)

	Sector	1981-82 to 1998-99	1981-82 to 1990-91	1991-92 to 1998-99
	1	2	3	4
	General Index	**6.9**	**7.8**	**5.8**
a)	Manufacturing	6.9	7.6	5.9
b)	Electricity	8.0	9.0	6.8
c)	Mining and Quarrying	6.0	8.3	3.0

Table 17.4 shows that while the basic and capital goods sectors grew at a faster rate during the 'eighties, it was the intermediate goods sector which recorded faster growth in the 'nineties. The relative decline in the rate of growth of basic, capital and consumer goods sectors in the 'nineties is mainly due to restructuring taking place in the industrial sector.

Relative Contribution of Sectors to Total Production

Changes in the relative contribution of different sectors to the general Index of Industrial Production reflect another dimension of the structural changes in industrial production. Data presented in Table 17.5 reveal that the relative contribution of the manufacturing sector rose from 70.0 per cent during the 'eighties to 81.6 per cent during the 'nineties. However, in case of mining and quarrying, there was a no-

TABLE – 17.5

Relative Contribution of Sectors to the Industrial Production

(Per cent)

Sector	1981-82 to 1990-91 (Average)	1992-93 to 1998-99* (Average)
1	2	3
i) Manufacturing	70.0	81.6
ii) Electricity	14.4	14.4
iii) Mining and Quarrying	15.6	4.0
General Index	100.0	100.0

* The data relating to 1991-92 were excluded in this period because production was almost stagnant.

ticeable decline. This was reflected in the changes in the weights assigned to different sector in the construction of IIP series. The weight for the manufacturing sector rose from 77.1 per cent in the earlier series of IIP with base 1980-81=100, to 79.36 per cent in the current series with base 1993-94=100. Correspondingly, the relative weights of mining and quarrying and electricity sectors declined from 11.46 per cent and 11.43 per cent in the old series to 10.47 per cent and 10.17 per cent, respectively, in the new series (Table 17.6).

TABLE – 17.6

Sector-wise Weighting Pattern

NIC Division	Sector	Base: 1970=100	Base: 1980-81=100	Base: 1993-94=100
1	2	3	4	5
Division 1	Mining & Quarrying	9.69	11.46	10.47
Division 2&3	Manufacturing	81.08	77.11	79.36
Division 4	Electricity	9.23	11.43	10.17
Total	**General Index**	**100.0**	**100.0**	**100.0**

During the 'nineties, while the relative contributions of basic and capital goods sectors declined, there was a rise in those of intermediate and consumer goods sectors (Table 17.7). In the new series (Base: 1993-94=100), the weights of basic and capital goods sectors were reduced and those of intermediate goods and consumer goods sectors were raised.

TABLE – 17.7

Relative Contribution of Sectors to Industrial Production (Use-based Classification)

(Per cent)

Sector	1981-82 to 1990-91 (Average)	1992-93 to 1998-99* (Average)
1	2	3
i) Basic Goods	43.6	35.8
ii) Capital Goods	25.0	7.1
iii) Intermediate Goods	14.6	35.2
iv) Consumer Goods	16.8	21.9
General Index	**100.0**	**100.0**

* The data relating to 1991-92 were excluded in this period because production was almost stagnant.

The relatively low contributions of the basic and capital goods sectors to overall industrial output in the 'nineties reflect, among others, the impact of trade liberalisation, particularly imports, and of financial liberalisation that enabled the corporate sector to make financial gains through 'other income', as also the lack of competitiveness requiring industrial restructuring and modernisation of technologies in a number of industries.

Profile of Industrial Growth

As per the analysis given in RBI Report on Currency and Finance 2001-02 the actual industrial growth during the latter phase of the reform period fell below the potential growth, indicating a decline in the capacity utilisation over the medium-term. Besides, there have been distinct signs of the potential growth itself slowing down compared with the first phase of the reform period and the latter half of the preceding decade. This can be attributed to a deceleration in growth across all sub-sectors, i.e., registered manufacturing, mining and quarrying as well as electricity, gas and water supply. An analysis of industrial slowdown as per the use-based classification reveals that while the consumer goods industries sustained growth momentum to some extent during the latter part of the reform period, substantial decline in growth was witnessed in basic and intermediate goods segments. The demand for these goods in the face of sustained consumption demand in the latter period of the reforms implies that industry may be undertaking inventory adjustment created by the initial phase of capacity creation and overproduction. Although production of capital goods witnessed an improved average growth during the latter phase of the reform period, a rapid decline was observed from 2000-01 onwards, indicating the impact of weakening investment demand in the economy.

Shift in Favour of Registered Manufacturing

The 1990s witnessed a shift in the production structure in favour of the registered manufacturing as against the unregistered one. While the share of registered manufacturing in industrial GDP increased from 38.6 per cent in 1990-91 to 41.5 per cent in 2001-02, the share of unregistered manufacturing declined from 22.5 per cent to 21.6 per cent during the same period. Even within registered manufacturing, traditional industries such as textile, jute and other vegetable fibre textiles witnessed a decline in their respective shares in the reform period while the modern segments like metal products and electrical machinery forged ahead. The relatively low growth in productivity, lack of technological improvements and reduced access to credit have, inter alia, possibly acted as a more binding constraint in respect of the traditional segment vis-a-vis the modern one.

Decline in Employment Growth in Organised Manufacturing

During the 1980s, although the average growth in value added in the manufacturing sector was relatively high at 7.3 per cent, it was not reflected in the commensurate growth in employment mainly on account of reduction in employment in cotton textiles and jute textiles, which were high employment generating industries. The employment growth in the organised manufacturing sector rose to 2.3 per cent in the first half of the 1990s from 0.8 per cent in the 1980s. This may be attributed to increased employment in small and medium size factories as a result of liberalisation of industrial and trade policies (Goldar, 2000). The deceleration in the manufacturing growth rate in the latter half of the 1990s had, however, adverse implications on employment growth. This was visible in employment growth turning negative (-2.1 per cent) in the latter half of the 1990s.

The Stagnant Share of Manufacturing Sector

While the emerging production structure of industry bodes well for the economy, the stagnant share of manufacturing at around 17 per cent of GDP during the 1990s is a matter of concern. Other emerging market economies have exhibited a rising share of manufacturing and industry at similar levels of developments, with these sectors being the lead growth centres. The contribution of industry to GDP in such developing countries is placed in the range of 28 per cent to 51 per cent in 2000, much higher than 25 per cent in India. As a matter of fact, the fast growing East Asian countries witnessed a rise in the share of industry in GDP between 1990 and 2000 (Table 17.8). The differences in the nature of industrial policy and their implementation are found to be critical to the industrial success of such countries. Important elements of industrial policy in these countries included flexibility of labour use, build up of large and efficient social infrastructure, favourable attitude towards international technology transfer, substantial investment in public technology institutions and competitive pressures resulting from exports. Given the stagnating share of industry in GDP in India, the issues of manufacturing slowdown, productivity and competitiveness need further examination, which is attempted next.

TABLE – 17.8

Share of Industry in GDP: Cross-Country Comparison

(Per cent)

Country	1990	2000
	1	2
India	24	25
China	42	51
Indonesia	38	47
Korea, Rep.	43	43
Malaysia	42	45
Thailand	37	40
Brazil	39	29
Argentina	36	28
Mexico	28	28

Source : World Development Indicators 2002, World Bank.

The Manufacturing Slowdown

The loss of momentum in manufacturing growth, which occured in the latter part of 1996, has since continued during the second phase of the reform period. At the disaggregated two-digit level, the manufacturing sector witnessed substantial deceleration in 11 industry groups with a combined weight of 64 per cent in the manufacturing production (Table 17.9). Six industry groups with a combined weight of 36 per cent withstood the slowdown and posted an accelerated growth during 1996-2002. However, in view of their relatively low weight, the manufacturing sector, as a whole, registered a slowdown.

TABLE – 17.9

Growth of IIP-Manufacturing at Two-Digit Level

(Per cent)

Industry Group	Weight	1992-93 to 95-96	1996-97 to 01-02
	1	2	3
1. Food products	9.08	4.5	2.7
2. Beverages, tobacco and related products	2.38	10.9	11.6
3. Cotton textiles	5.52	6.1	2.4
4. Wool, silk and man-made fibre textiles	2.26	14.6	9.0
5. Jute and other vegetable fibre textiles (except cotton)	0.59	4.3	-0.2
6. Textile products (including wearing apparel)	2.54	2.3	3.8
7. Wood and wood products, furniture & fixtures	2.70	7.7	-4.3
8. Paper and paper products and printing, publishing and allied industries	2.65	8.7	5.4
9. Leather and leather & fur products	1.14	3.2	8.3
10. Basic chemicals and chemical products (except products of petroleum & coal)	14.00	7.5	8.0
11. Rubber, plastic, petroleum and coal products	5.73	4.5	6.7
12. Non-metallic mineral products	4.40	9.6	9.0
13. Basic metal and alloy industries	7.45	15.6	3.1
14. Metal products and parts (except machinery and equipment)	2.81	-1.0	6.4
15. Machinery and equipment other than transport equipment	9.57	9.4	6.4
16. Transport equipment and parts	3.98	10.1	7.6
17. Other manufacturing industries	2.56	8.4	4.8
Overall Manufacturing	**79.36**	**11.6**	**5.6**

Note : The category of wool, silk and man-made fibre is available since 1993-94 onwards.

Source : Central Statistical Organisation.

Factors Causing the Industrial Slowdown: Some Hypotheses[1]

A number of hypotheses in terms of cyclical and structural factors have been put forward to explain the slowdown in the manufacturing activity during the latter phase of the reform period. The explanations provided, however, fall short of giving a satisfactory answer to what has led to the manufacturing slowdown and its persistence. The onset of slowdown is often attributed to the satiation of the pent-up domestic demand of 'once-for-all' nature for a host of import-intensive goods, which could be domestically assembled or produced following trade liberalisation (Chandrasekhar and Ghosh, 2002). The short-run increase in domestic demand was seemingly facilitated by easy access to credit, including consumer credit in the wake of financial liberalisation. Once that pent-up demand of transitory nature was satisfied, industry entered the phase of slowdown in the absence of demand support - domestic or exports. However, the huge capacity-build up noticed in the first phase of the reform period runs counter to the momentary surge in demand that was not likely to be sustained in the long run.

Another hypothesis on the onset of slowdown relates to the 'credit crunch' which, it is argued, triggered off the manufacturing slowdown (Sen et al, 1997 and Desai, 2001). The unexpected and temporary tightening of liquidity in money markets during 1995-96, resulting from large dollar sales by the Reserve Bank to contain volatility in the forex market, was mistaken to be an expression of deflationary credit policy (Acharya, 2002).

Yet another factor was the role of the corporate sector. The proportion of corporate funds locked up in inventories and receivables went up steadily, leading to a scarcity of working capital (Sen et al, 1997). Further, the proportion of funds invested in financial instruments, which had hovered around 5 per cent during 1985-1993, crossed the level of 10 per cent subsequently. The depressed stock market conditions in 1995-96 inhibited the redemption of financial instruments. The rising interest rates may also have been prohibitive for new projects and investment, particularly, in the informal sector which has limited access to funds (Shetty, 1997a and 2001b). Reinforced by the increased borrowings by the Government, the weighted average lending rate of scheduled commercial banks rose to 17.1 per cent in 1995-96 from 16.1 per cent in 1994-95. In real terms, the rate shot up to 8.5 per cent in 1995-96 from an all-time low (for the 1990s) of 3.9 per cent in the preceding year.

Given below is an account of these cyclical and structural factors which have impacted upon industrial growth in recent years.

---

1 This section draws from RBI Report on Currency and Finance 2001-02.

Cyclical Factors in Industrial Slowdown

Cyclical factors have generally been recognised as an important source of industrial slowdown. In this context, the significant fall in Government capital investment especially since 1995, has been recognised as the key contributor to the slowdown (Nayyar, 1996). It is, however, important to underscore that while the contraction in Government expenditure does have adverse implications for the manufacturing growth, it declined even during the manufacturing boom (1992-93 to 1995-96). Thus, decline in Government expenditure per se does not provide a satisfactory explanation of the slowdown.

The manufacturing slowdown can also be seen in terms of decline in fixed investment in industry in the context of over-expansion of capacities during the manufacturing boom, slump in the capital market for new issues and rise in real interest rates in 1995-96 (Acharya, 2002). The increase in real fixed investment in manufacturing from 6.8 per cent of GDP in 1990-91 to 13.0 per cent in 1995-96 and the subsequent decline to 7.9 per cent by 2000-01 seems to have mirrored the pattern of manufacturing growth.

Among the other cyclical sources of demand, the lagged effect of the negative agricultural growth in 1995-96 seems to have worked towards slowing down the growth of rural demand for consumer durables and non-durables subsequently (Government of India, 2000). As the demand for industrial products, particularly the consumer durables, is significantly influenced by the rural demand, fluctuations in the agricultural production seem to have adversely impacted the industrial growth.

The cyclical downswing was not confined to the domestic sources of demand but was also clearly visible in manufacturing exports. In anticipation of high potential demand in the wake of reforms, the manufacturing sector built up huge capacity through imports of capital goods during 1994-97 (Table 17.10). Such capacity build-up was not sustainable on the basis of normal growth in domestic demand, and the only feasible outlet was the exports market. However, signs of exports slowdown were visible in 1995-96 when manufacturing exports decelerated. Subsequently, with slowdown in the world trade, sluggishness in the global manufacturing prices and variations in the cross-currency exchange rates, manufacturing exports growth declined to a meagre 3.6 per cent by 1996-97. The real appreciation of Rupee between 1993 and 1995 and the Asia-wide slowdown in exports following the loss of market share to China also contributed to the slowdown in exports.

TABLE – 17.10

Production and Imports of Capital Goods and IIP Growth

(Per cent)

Year	IIP (Manufacturing)	Capital Goods Production	Capital Goods Imports
	1	2	3
1990-91	9.0	16	10.1
1991-92	-0.8	-8.5	10.4
1992-93	2.2	-0.1	-27.5
1993-94	6.1	-4.1	7.1
1994-95	9.1	9.2	37.8
1995-96	14.1	5.4	22.4
1996-97	7.3	11.4	35.2
1997-98	6.7	5.8	-4.0
1998-99	4.4	12.6	-1.3
1999-00	7.1	6.9	2.7
2000-01	5.3	1.8	-10.9
2001-02	2.9	-3.4	-0.3

Sources : 1. Central Statistical Organisation.
2. Directorate General of Commercial Intelligence and Statistics.

As is evident from the foregoing analysis, the growth momentum in manufacturing slackened towards the end of 1996, largely under the influence of factors outside the realm of public policy in the short-run. The movement in major indicators of aggregate demand, viz., domestic capital formation, Government capital expenditure, capital goods production, import of capital goods, manufacturing exports and private final consumption expenditure, all witnessed deceleration during the latter phase of the reforms.

Structural Factors

To the extent the slowdown is prolonged and protracted, it seems to have its origin in structural factors, including, inadequate industrial restructuring undertaken in the face of growing openness of the economy and the associated external competitive pressure. The inadequacy of institutional and structural reforms, which held back the industrial restructuring, has, thus, emerged as a binding constraint on manufacturing growth in the liberalised trade regime.

Infrastructure Constraints in the Industrial Sector

The industrial performance continues to be hampered by physical infrastructure bottlenecks with the demand-supply imbalances persisting and growing during the reform period. A worrisome feature of infrastructure development has been the declining trend in potential output of a number of basic activities such as steel, coal, cargo handling and freight loading. There are, however, signs of improvement for a few sectors, like power and communication. With the initiation of power sector reforms, the demand-supply gap for power has witnessed a decline to 7.9 per cent during the reform period from 8.9 per cent during the pre-reform period. Notably, the power deficit remained high at around 9 per cent during the mid-1990s when the industrial sector was growing at a faster rate. The downtrend in demand-supply gap for telecommunications accompanied by a decline in unit cost reflects the regulatory reforms and increased competition arising from private sector participation.

The deteriorating infrastructure services represent a direct fall out of shrinkage in infrastructure investment in the context of grossly inadequate internal resources of public infrastructure entities and dwindling Plan outlay for infrastructure. The real capital formation in electricity, gas and water supply declined to 2.6 per cent of GDP during the 1990s from 2.9 per cent during the preceding decade (Table 17.11). A similar trend was observed for railways. Within the 1990s also, there was a decline in the real gross capital formation in sectors like electricity, gas and water supply, and the railways between the first and the second half. In contrast, communication witnessed an improvement in the reform period following the market based pricing of services and better regulatory framework. The investment in infrastructure sector as a whole has shown clear decline of one percentage point of GDP between the first and the second halves of the 1990s. This decline can be attributed to declining government investment on infrastructure – a fall out of the prevailing fiscal situation – which was a major contributing factor for the economic slowdown in the latter part of the 1990s.

The pace of public investment in infrastructure slowed down substantially during the reform period on account of rising fiscal imbalances of the Government, both at the Centre and the States. As a result, public investment in major infrastructure sectors declined in real terms during the reform period. The rates of return from infrastructure services extended by the Government continue to be abysmally low, constraining the ability to generate internal resources for investment. For instance, the rate of return on investment for the State power sector deteriorated from (-)12.7 per cent in 1991-92 to (-)32.8 per cent in 2001-02. These essentially indicate lack of required structural reforms in the power sector in India, notably the near absence of market based pricing.

TABLE – 17.11

Real Gross Capital Formation in Infrastructure Sectors

(Per cent of GDP)

Period Averages	Electricity Gas and Water Supply	Construction	Transport, Storage and Communication	Of which: Railways	Communication	Total Infrastructure	Total Gross Capital Formation
	1	2	3	4	5	6	7
1980-81 to 1984-85	2.8	0.5	2.5	0.6	0.4	5.8	25.5
1985-86 to 1989-90	3.1	0.4	2.9	0.7	0.5	6.4	25.4
1990-91 to 1994-95	2.9	0.4	3.0	0.6	0.7	6.3	24.7
1995-96 to 1999-00	2.3	0.4	2.6	0.4	0.7	5.3	25.8
1980-81 to 1989-90	2.9	0.5	2.7	0.7	0.4	6.1	25.4
1990-91 to 1999-00	2.6	0.4	2.8	0.5	0.7	5.8	25.2

Source : National Accounts Statistics, Government of India.

Contemporaneously, response of the private sector to the reform process has not been adequate to offset the declining public investment on account of inadequate institutional reforms, lack of clarity regarding infrastructure development priorities, non-transparency in project outsourcing processes, and numerous time consuming clearances. In the absence of rationalisation of user charges, the infrastructure sectors such as railways, public transport, power continue to suffer from the levy of inadequate user charges, thereby putting off potential private participation. Keeping in view the long gestation period for infrastructure projects, the issue of initial risk sharing by the Government assumes importance, given the inability of the private sector to assess the long-term risks.

The cost of power and energy is an important element in the total cost of manufacturing in India and a higher cost structure of power for the industrial sector adversely affects its price competitiveness. During the 1990s, electricity tariff charged from industrial/commercial users is significantly higher than the average cost of supply. During the 1990s, the tariff charged from the industrial sector, on an average, remained 26 per cent above the average cost of supply of State Electricity Boards (SEBs) and electricity departments, reflecting on the higher input costs for the industry (Table 17.12). The higher cost of electricity is also borne out by the fact that annual variation in WPI for electricity has been higher than that of WPI for manufacturing for the entire period. During latter phase of the reforms, the cost of power for the industry has risen at a rate much faster than the rise in the prices of manufacturing products. For instance, during the period 1996-97 to 2001-02 (i.e., the period of industrial slowdown), while the average tariff charged from industry increased on an average by 7.7 per cent, the manufacturing prices rose by 2.9 per cent. Thus, the distinct rise in the cost of power for the industry has impacted on industrial competitiveness.

TABLE – 17.12

Average Electricity Tariff for Industry

(Paise/Kwh)

Year	Average Cost of Supply of Electricity	Average Tariff Charged from Industry	Index for Average Tariff for Industries	WPI for Manufacturing
	1	2	3	4
1992-93	128.2	171.50	86.5	97.8
1993-94	149.1	198.20	100.0	100.0
1994-95	163.4	219.90	110.9	112.2
1995-96	179.6	245.50	123.9	121.9
1996-97	215.6	276.89	139.7	124.4
1997-98	239.7	314.63	158.7	128.0
1998-99	263.1	324.33	163.6	133.6
1999-00 (P)	305.1	343.37	173.2	137.2
2000-01(RE)	327.3	368.37	185.9	141.7
2001-02(AP)	349.9	381.14	192.3	144.3

P = Provisional Estimates, RE = Revised Estimates,
AP = Advance Estimates.
Source : Planning Commission, Government of India, 2002.

In the context of reducing the unit cost of power to the industry as also to ensure stable supply in the event of rising industrial demand, the issues of pricing, cross subsidy, ownership and the regulatory issues have emerged to the forefront. The major challenges to the sustainable growth of power sector in India continue to emanate from poor recovery of SEBs' dues and transmission and distribution losses, subsidies to the agricultural and domestic sectors, and a lack of restructuring. As the financing of power projects poses a daunting task and requires a long-term solution, resource generation within the sector through prompt and efficient collection of appropriate user charges across the consumer categories should precede the efforts at attracting private investments. The poor response of the private sector is indicated by the fact that even after a decade of opening up of the power sector, private sector accounts for only 10 per cent of the present generating capacity. More recently, regulatory reforms and reforms in the transmission and distribution sectors have been emphasised to improve the efficiency of the power infrastructure and raise the level of revenue realisation. In the Indian context, as power is in the Concurrent List of the Indian Constitution, measures for reforming this sector have been undertaken by a number of State Governments.

The above developments reveal that there has been compression in investment on infrastructure leading to inadequate availability and deterioration in the quality. At the same time, cost of infrastructure, particularly the cost of power for industry, has relatively risen in the late 1990s. Further, there has been a relative increase in the real interest cost for the industrial sector. These factors together, have reduced the competitiveness of the industry and caused the persisting slowdown.

Industrial Performance and Credit Growth

The provision of credit is considered an essential input to industrial activities. The credit delivery mechanism plays an important role, especially in developing economies with credit market imperfections. A major finding of the literature in this regard is that small firms are largely dependent on bank credit to meet their financing requirements while the big firms have alternative sources of finance (Gertler and Gilchrist, 1993; Olinear and Rudebusch, 1995). Therefore, small firms usually get affected more on occasions of tightening of bank credit. Not only the credit availability, but also the cost of credit has a significant impact on the production decisions of firms. Contextually, credit delivery system continues to be a major focal point of the on-going financial reforms in India since the early 1990s. The objective is to meet the credit requirements of the productive sectors and, more so, of the weaker bidders in the credit market.

The credit off-take from scheduled commercial banks to the commercial sector indicated a declining trend during the 1990s, barring an uptrend in the mid-1990s. At the disaggregated level also, there was a slowdown in credit growth for the various segments such as exports, Small Scale Industries (SSIs), medium and large industries, particularly in the second phase of the reform period. Export credit growth declined substantially to about 6.5 per cent during the second half of the 1990s from 31.3 per cent in the first phase. The deceleration in export credit while reflecting the slowdown in exports, can also be attributed to other forms of financing by exporters, such as, Exchange Earners' Foreign Currency Account and availability of funds at sub-PLR.

The slowdown in the credit growth was more pronounced for the SSIs vis-a-vis the medium and large industries. The credit needs of SSIs were largely met in the 1980s and earlier as part of the promotional policies for the SSIs under the priority sector lending by banks. During the period 1990-91 to 2001-02, the growth in credit to SSIs decelerated to 11.6 per cent from 19.4 per cent in the 1980s (Table 17.13). Moreover, credit to SSIs as a percentage of non-food gross bank credit indicated a decline from 14.4 per cent in 1995-96 to 11.8 per cent in 2001-02. It may be noted that while the concessional element in lending rates for the SSIs stands largely withdrawn during the 1990s, financial vulnerability of State level institutions in view of poor recovery and other inherent inefficiencies also raises concerns regarding the prospects of credit flows to the SSI sector. This decline in credit flow to the SSI sector has to be seen in the context of falling productivity in the SSI sector as a whole in the 1990s as against the 1980s with the index declining to 34 in 1994-95 from 50 in 1984-85 (SIDBI, 2001). However, within the SSI sector the productivity in the modern segment remained higher than the traditional/tiny segment. Thus, a key issue for the SSI reforms is to enhance the credit assessment capability of the financial institutions so that the small scale as a whole is not equated with high risk for credit disbursement.

TABLE – 17.13

Growth in Sectoral Non-Food Credit

(Per cent)

Period	SSIs	Medium and Large Industries	Exports
	1	2	3
1980-81 to 1989-90	19.4	16.7	18.8
1990-91 to 2001-02	11.6	13.7	15.7

An analysis of credit to major industrial subgroups within the manufacturing sector reveals that during the reform period a substantial shift has taken place in favour of industries such as iron and steel, electricity, food processing, cement, gems and jewellery and petroleum (Table 17.14). Infrastructure sector improved its share to 6.5 per cent in March 2002 from 2.0 per cent in March 1998. The industries that recorded a decline in their respective shares were metal and metal products, engineering, cotton, jute and other textiles, paper and paper products, chemicals, leather and leather products and construction. The highest decline was noticed for the engineering industry with its share in gross bank credit declining from 22.6 per cent in 1991 to 10.5 per cent in 2002. The cotton, jute and other textiles together also witnessed shrinkage in their share from 13.2 per cent in 1991 to 11.3 per cent in 2002, reflecting partly the rising incidence of sickness in such industries.

TABLE – 17.14

Industry-wise Deployment of Gross Bank Credit – Share of Major Groups

(Outstanding as on Last Reporting Friday of March)

Industries	1985-86 to 1990-91	1991-92 to 1995-96	1996-97 to 2001-02
	1	2	3
Iron and Steel	5.1	6.4	9.2
Other Metals and Metal Products	3.5	3.5	3.2
All Engineering	23.9	21.4	12.6
Electricity	2.0	1.9	3.5
Cotton, Jute, Other Textiles	14.2	12.7	12.5
Sugar	1.5	2.0	2.0
Food Processing	1.9	2.1	2.8
Paper and Paper Products	2.5	2.1	1.7
Rubber and Rubber Products	1.6	1.5	1.2
Chemicals, Dyes, Paints etc.	12.3	12.7	11.3
Cement	1.5	1.5	1.6
Leather and Leather Products	1.5	1.7	1.4
Gems and Jewellery	0.7	2.2	2.5
Construction	1.6	1.9	1.6
Petroleum	0.4	0.5	4.0
Infrastructure	–	–	4.1

Note : Infrastructure has been included as a separate category from 1998 onwards.

Another important source of finance for industry is the financial assistance disbursed by the All India Financial Institutions (AIFIs) mainly for investment operations in medium to long-term horizon. In keeping with the trend in bank credit, the growth in disbursements by AIFIs increased from 21.8 per cent in the pre-reform decade to 24.7 per cent in the first phase of the reform period. Subsequently, however, disbursements witnessed a distinct slow down to 7.9 per cent in the second phase of the reform period. This is indicative of a slow down in the investment demand, particularly for the green-field projects and expansion activities in the industrial sector.

The slowdown in the credit flows from banks and financial institutions may be evaluated in the context of the behaviour of the prime lending rates (PLRs) charged by them. In real terms, the PLR of AIFIs (IDBI) ruled, on an average, 9.11 per cent during 1995-96 to 2001-02, which was higher than 5.52 per cent prevailing during the period 1990-91 to 1994-95 (Table 17.15). The real PLR of banks (weighted average lending rates of Scheduled Commercial Banks) also increased to 12.5 per cent from 6.8 per cent over the same period. Such high real interest rates on medium to long-term borrowings for the industrial sector work as a constraint in undertaking investment decisions. Persistence of high interest cost adversely impacts on the capacity buildup and upgradation. Over a medium-term, the high interest rate effect is ultimately reflected in lower output growth. An assessment of the present trends in the real interest rates for the industrial sector and the real output growth seems to indicate weakening sustainability of the investments. While during the period 1996-97 to 2001-02 growth of real output from industrial sector averaged to 4.9 per cent, the real PLRs remained distinctly high at around 9 per cent. Given the downward rigidity of medium and long-term real interest rates, industrial investment is rendered unviable when such rates are higher than the rate at which the industry is growing.

TABLE – 17.15

Average Real Lending Rates of Select Term Lending Institutions

(Per cent)

Period	IDBI	IFCI	ICICI
	1	2	3
1980-81 to 1984-85	4.71	4.71	4.71
1985-86 to 1989-90	7.34	7.34	7.34
1990-91 to 1994-95	5.52	5.82	5.67
1995-96 to 2001-02	9.11	9.99	8.38

Note : Represent ex-post real interest rates. The real rates are computed by subtracting the Inflation rate (WPI) from nominal Prime Lending Rates.

The decelerated credit off-take by industry from banks and AIFIs needs to be interpreted keeping in mind the alternative sources of finance that are available to industry in the reform period. A comparative analysis of financing patterns of select non-financial public limited companies indicates an increasing recourse to internal sources of financing as against the borrowed sources of funds, particularly since the late 1990s. Among the borrowed sources of funds, financing through debentures, and loans and advances declined from 11 per cent and 13.5 per cent, respectively, during the period 1985-86 and 1989-90 to 5.7 per cent and 11.5 per cent during the second phase of the reform period (Table 17.16). The declining share of credit from banks and financial institutions has been evident particularly in the second phase of the reform period when their share in total sources of funds raised by the corporate sector declined to 17.4 per cent in 2000-01 from 23.8 per cent in 1995-96.

TABLE – 17.16

Sources of Funds of Selected Public Limited Companies

(Percentage share in total funds raised)

Period	Internal Sources	External Sources						
		Paid-up Capital	Borrowings				Trade Dues & Other Current Liabilities	Total
			Debentures	Loans and Advances				
				Banks	FIs	Total		
	1	2	3	4	5	6	7	8
1985-86 to 1989-90	31.8	7.2	11.0	13.5	8.7	37.9	22.8	68.2
1990-91 to 1994-95	29.9	18.8	7.1	8.2	10.3	32.7	18.4	70.1
1995-96 to 2000-01	41.2	12.1	5.7	11.5	9.2	32.1	14.2	58.9

Source : Selected Financial Statistics - Public Limited Companies, RBI.

The reduced role of conventional financing for the corporate sector such as bank credit and financial assistance from AIFIs should be seen in the context of increasing recourse to private placements of debt and equity on account of less stringent disclosure norms, low cost of issuance, ease of structuring instruments and reduced time lag in issuance. Resource mobilisation through this route increased sharply from Rs.13,361 crore in 1995-96 to Rs.64,950 crore in 2001-02. Nevertheless, the high cost of credit in real terms from banks and AIFIs seems to have gone against the conventional sources of financing, inhibiting the growth of investment demand and capacity build-up in industry. The reduced industrial credit can also be seen as an outcome of the riskbased prudential requirements, such as capital adequacy and provisioning norms implemented for banks and financial institutions as part of the financial sector reforms (Nag and Das, 2002). As a result, bank funds have been largely deployed in Government securities, relatively risk free assets, which account for around 39 per cent of their net demand and time liabilities, far exceeding the minimum statutory liquidity requirement of 25 per cent.

It may be difficult to clearly distinguish as to what extent the lower credit growth to the commercial sector from banks and the financial institutions is attributable to the sluggishness in demand or to the heightened risk aversion arising from tighter supervisory/regulatory norms. While the present slowdown in the industrial demand seems to have contributed to the slowdown in the credit growth, both for working capital requirements and long-term investments, the possibility of high lending rates impacting on the credit demand of certain segments, particularly small enterprises having limited access to alternative sources of funds has been a matter of concern. Since large corporates can access alternative cheaper sources of funds, the burden of adjustment in the financial sector seems to have fallen relatively more on small and medium enterprises due to segmentation of credit markets. The problem seems to have been accentuated on account of lack of adequate credit risk assessment regarding small and medium enterprises emanating from poor credit information base on such enterprises. In view of these concerns, the credit delivery system has been a major focus of reforms since the 1990s with the objective of augmenting the total volume of institutional credit while securing an equitable distribution of credit, particularly for weaker bidders in the credit markets, including small enterprises. Besides improving the volume and terms of credit, policy efforts have been directed towards simplifying the procedures.

Productivity Trends in the Manufacturing Sector

Productivity plays a major role in sustaining the industrial growth since it is the principal determinant of cost, price and trade competitiveness of firms and industries. Notwithstanding the differences of views on measurement issues, there is a near unanimity in the empirical literature on productivity growth in the Indian manufacturing sector. It is recognised that there was a decline in total factor productivity growth (TFPG) till 1980, with a turnaround taking place in mid-1980s following the reoriented trade and industrial policies and improved infrastructure performance (Brahmananda, 1982; Ahluwalia,

1985, 1991). In fact, the significant shortfall in the target for industrial output till about the Sixth Plan can be attributed to the negligible TFPG in manufacturing. The later studies covering the period up to mid-1990s have found evidence of a positive TFPG (Balakrishnan and Pushpangadan, 1994; Majumdar, 1996; Rao, 1996; Pradhan and Barik,1999). Thus, there seems to be turnaround in the productivity growth in the mid-1980s.

The role of the reform process in terms of its impact on manufacturing productivity continues to be debatable. While a positive rate of growth in productivity is noticed in the post-1985 period, the level of labour productivity is found to be abysmally low and its convergence to the international standards seems to be a difficult proposition in the near future (Trivedi et al, 2000). The low labour productivity appears to have offset the comparative advantage in terms of low labour cost (CII-World Bank, 2002). NCAER (2001) has observed a decline in productivity growth in 1990s (up to 1997-98) in relation to the 1980s. Besides, the mean technical efficiency of all firms taken together seems to have declined in 1990s as compared to the pre-reform period. Unni et al (2001) also provide evidence of a declining productivity growth in the first half of 1990s. Productivity growth in the SSIs also witnessed a decline, with the labour productivity growth decelerating to 3.7 per cent during 1990-96 from 6.2 per cent during 1980s and the capital productivity growth declining to (-)1.6 per cent from 2.6 per cent during the same period (SIDBI, 2000). Regarding trend in productivity in the unorganised manufacturing sector, Unni et al (2001) have observed a rapid decline in the TFPG to (-)3.1 per cent during the reform period (1990-95) from 11.4 per cent in the latter half of 1980s. The TFPG for the entire period of study, i.e. 1978-95 is estimated at (-)2.5 per cent. This reflects, *inter alia*, low technological change in the unorganised sector in the reform period.

Broad assessment of partial factor productivity for the industry can be based on an analysis of the changes in input intensities. The material intensity of the manufacturing sector which remained high during the 1980s and the first half of the 1990s, witnessed a sharp decline in the latter half. This is indicative of a shift away from material inputs as also the rationalisation of the production process, ensuring efficiency in use of material inputs. The labour intensity index (at constant prices), in contrast, witnessed almost a secular decline from the peak of 114.5 per cent in 1980-81 to 73.6 per cent in 1990-91 and further to 40.8 per cent in 1999-2000. A similar trend is discernible in the labour intensity index at current prices, though the extent of decline has been less. This can be attributed to the relatively high increase in the CPI of industrial workers than in the prices of manufacturing goods. On the other hand, the capital intensity has significantly risen during the 1990s as compared with the 1980s.

The productivity growth in the manufacturing sector seems to have declined during the 1990s and, more so, in the latter phase of the reform period, primarily as a sequel to the faltering pace of implementation of structural reforms, the binding infrastructure constraints, and the lack of required industrial restructuring – all impinging on the competitiveness of the Indian industry. The input intensity indices show that the production process in the manufacturing sector has become more capital intensive, possibly in view of the adoption of capital-intensive new technologies in response to the inflexibilities that characterise the labour market. The efficiency in use of material inputs has, however, shown improvement in the latter part of 1990s.

Recovery in Industrial Growth since 2002-03

The industrial recovery in 2002-03, which consolidated during 2003-04, has gathered momentum during the current year. The dramatic decline in interest rates and the significant turnaround in public investment through the infrastructure development programme have been two critical drivers of the recovery. Low interest rates fuelled the housing, automobiles and consumer durable booms, which were instrumental in the acceleration of industrial growth. Although the momentum in these sectors has slowed down, they still continue to provide the necessary support to the process of industrial growth.

The current year conforms to the normal historic pattern of industrial buoyancy following a good agricultural year. Industrial growth of 8.4 per cent during April – December, 2004-05 is the highest after 1995-96. Robust growth of 9.0 per cent in manufacturing – a sector with a weight of 79.4 per cent in IIP – in the first three quarters of the current year not only came in succession to the high growth in the two previous years, but also contributed significantly to the satisfactory performance of IIP overall (Table 17.1). In April-December, 2004, mining and electricity grew by 4.8 per cent and 6.4 per cent, respectively.

In terms of use-based classification, in the first three quarters of the current year, continuation of double-digit growth in the capital goods industry observed in the previous two years was an encouraging sign (Table 17.3). The significant growth acceleration in capital goods production to 13.3 per cent in April-December from 10.1 per cent in the same period of the previous year indicates a possible step-up in investment activity. Machinery and equipment, with a growth rate of 21.9 per cent, remained the major contributor to the impressive growth in the capital goods sector. Growth in consumer goods sector, after being moderate during the initial months of the current year, picked up momentum subsequently to register a double-digit growth of 11.2 per cent during April-December, 2004-05. Growth in consumer durables at 15.3 per cent was particularly pronounced. Low interest rates may have partly fuelled this growth of consumer goods. Growth in basic and intermediate goods was moderate.

The present trend indicates a positive outlook for industrial growth due to improved capacity utilisation, improved industrial climate, expanding external and domestic demand and ease in availability of credit. The strong performance of the capital goods sector coupled with increased imports of capital goods also augur well for domestic capacity expansion in a large number of industries.

The double-digit growth since 2003-04 in capital goods sector indicates the capital formation taking place in the industrial sector, which can help in strengthening the upswing. Industrial buoyancy is expected to continue during the remaining period of 2004-05 with the strong growth of machinery and equipment sub-sector (21.9 per cent during April-December) and the major components of non-oil imports like machinery and other inputs needed for exports and industrial activity. This is also reflected in the resurgence of exports of manufactured goods with double digit growth during April-October, 2004-05. The ongoing growth process, which is investment-led and fairly evenly spread within manufacturing sector, reflects the medium and long-term optimism on the part of investors.

The strong and positive outlook of both foreign and domestic investors indicates that India is ready for the big push as the growing interest of foreign investors is coinciding with the rising confidence of domestic private investors. The increasing efficiency and competitiveness of domestic producers, liberalised trade, and deregulated interest rate regime are critical contributors to both growth acceleration and macro-economic stability.

The outlook for the industrial sector will further brighten if constraints like infrastructure bottlenecks and shortages, labour market rigidities, entry and exit barriers and land acquisition, and multiple stages and levels of approvals/clearances are removed.

Industrial Policy: Recent Policy Initiatives

The basic framework for the overall industrial policy of the Government of India is contained in the Statement on Industrial Policy, 1991. The Government has been constantly reviewing the policy framework to bring about improvements to suit the emerging situation. Some of the major policy developments which have taken place in recent years are outlined below:

Industrial Licensing

During the year 1998-99, three industries, viz., i) coal and lignite, ii) petroleum (other than crude) and its distillation products and iii) sugar were delicensed. Accordingly, there are only six industries now under compulsory licensing (Box 17.2). Two industries, viz., coal and lignite and mineral oils were taken out from the list of industries reserved for the public sector. At present there are only four industries reserved for the public sector (Box 17.3). Nine items (six from 'farm implements and tools' and three from 'leather') were removed from the list of industries reserved for exclusive manufacture by the Small Scale Industry (SSI). Entries on toys now excludes electronic toys from the purview of reservation. During the year 1998-99, the number of items reserved for the SSI sector stood at 812.

BOX – 17.2

List of Industries Requiring Compulsory Industrial Licensing

1. Distillation and brewing of alcoholic drinks
2. Cigars and cigarettes of tobacco and manufactured tobacco substitute
3. Electronic aerospace and defense equipment; all types
4. Industrial explosives including detonating fuses, safety fuses, gun powder, nitrocellulose and matches
5. Hazardous chemicals
6. Drugs* and pharmaceuticals (according to the modified Drug Policy issued in September, 1994 and subsequently amended in February, 1999).

* Bulk drugs industry has been delicensed.

Notes: The compulsory licensing provisions would not apply in respect of the small scale units taking up the manufacture of any of the above items reserved for exclusive manufacture in small-scale sector.

BOX – 17.3

List of Industries Reserved for the Public Sector

1. Arms and ammunition and allied items of defence equipment, defence aircraft and warships
2. Atomic energy
3. Railway transport

Location Policy

At present, there is no requirement of obtaining industrial approvals from the Central Government (except for the industries under compulsory licensing) for locations not falling within 25 kms. of cities having population of more than one million. However, industries of no-polluting nature such as electronics, computer software and printing can be located within 25 kms. of the periphery of cities with more than 1 million population. Other industries are permitted only if they are located in Industrial Areas designated prior to July 25, 1991. Further, zoning and land use regulations as well as environmental legislation continue to regulate industrial locations.

Foreign Direct Investment

Foreign direct investment (FDI) directly impacts on output growth in India by augmenting the available investible capital. However, a far more important impact of FDI is through externalities leading to higher efficiency and productivity. FDI typically serves to increase competition in markets, bring new technology into India, and foster skill acquisition amongst domestic labour. FDI by international corporations is also central to the process of India being utilised as a platform for global production chains, which would pave the way for strong exports growth.

The Government is committed to promoting increased flow of Foreign Direct Investment (FDI) for better technology, modernisation, exports and for providing products and services of international standards. Therefore, the policy of the Government has been aimed at encouraging foreign investment, particularly in core infrastructure sectors so as to supplement national efforts. Towards this, the Government has been striving not only to provide greater transparency in the policy and procedures but also to enable a more dynamic and investor-friendly policy framework. At the same time, to provide a level playing field to the domestic industry and also to protect national interests, on the basis of sectoral sensitivities, simultaneous measures have been introduced in the form of dividend balancing, foreign exchange neutrality, foreign equity capital, etc. The salient features of the FDI policy are:

Box 17.4 summarises the initiatives taken in fostering FDI, which constitute a part of the ongoing effort from 1991 onwards at steadily opening access to India for FDI flows.

BOX – 17.4

Major initiatives to attract Foreign Direct Investment (FDI)

- In pursuance of Government's commitment to further facilitate Indian industry, Government has permitted access to FDI through automatic route, except for a small negative list. Latest revision to further liberalise the FDI regime are as under:
- Increase in the FDI limits in "Air Transport Services (Domestic Airlines)" up to 49 per cent through automatic route and up to 100 per cent by non-resident Indians (NRIs) through automatic routes. (No direct or indirect equity participation by foreign airlines is allowed).
- Further, reviewing the guidelines pertaining to foreign/technical collaborations under automatic route for foreign financial/technical collaborations with previous ventures/tie- ups in India as per Press Note No. 18 (1998), it has been decided that new proposals for foreign investment/technical collaborations would henceforth be allowed under the automatic route, subject to sectoral policies as per the following guidelines:
  – Prior approval of the Government would be required only in cases where the foreign investor has an existing joint venture for technology transfer/trade mark agreement in the 'same' field.
  – Even in the above mentioned cases, the approval of the Government would not be required in respect of the following:
    i) Investments to be made by venture capital funds registered with SEBI;or
    ii) Where the existing joint venture investments by either of the parties is less than 3 per cent; or
    iii) Where the existing venture/collaboration is defunct or sick.
  – In so far as joint ventures to be entered after the date of Press Note dated January 12, 2005 are concerned, the joint venture agreement may embody a 'conflict of interest' clause to safeguard the interest of joint venture partners in the event of one of the partners desiring to set up another joint venture or a wholly owned subsidiary in the 'same' field of economic activity.
- Foreign investment in the banking sector has been further liberalised by raising FDI limit in private sector banks to 74 per cent under the

Contd...

...Box 17.4 Contd...

automatic route including investment by FIIs. The aggregate foreign investment in a private bank from all sources will be a maximum of 74 per cent of the paid up capital of the bank and at all times, at least 26 per cent of the paid up capital held by residents except in regard to a wholly owned subsidiary of a private bank. Further, the foreign banks will be permitted to either have branches or subsidiaries, not both. Foreign banks regulated by a banking supervisory authority in the home country and meeting Reserve Bank's licence criteria will be allowed to hold 100 per cent paid up capital to enable them to set up wholly-owned subsidiary in India.

- FDI ceiling in telecom sector in certain services (such as basic, public mobile radio trunked services (PMRTS), global mobile personal communication service (GMPCS) and other value added services), has been increased from 49 per cent to 74 percent, in February 2005. The total composite foreign holding including but not limited to investment by FIIs, NRI/OCB, FCCB, ADRs, GDRs, convertible preference shares, proportionate foreign investment in Indian promoters/investment companies including their holding companies etc., will not exceed 74 per cent.
- In January 2004, guidelines on equity cap on FDI, including investment by NRIs and Overseas Corporate Bodies (OCBs) were revised as under:
  - FDI up to 100 per cent is permitted in printing scientific and technical magazines, periodicals and journals subject to compliance with legal framework and with the prior approval of the Government.
  - FDI up to 100 per cent is permitted through automatic route for petroleum product marketing, subject to existing sectoral policy and regulatory framework.
  - FDI up to 100 per cent is permitted through automatic route in oil exploration in both small and medium sized fields subject to and under the policy of the Government on private participation in exploration of oil fields and the discovered fields of national oil companies.
  - FDI up to 100 per cent is permitted through automatic route for petroleum products pipelines subject to and under the Government policy and regulations thereof.
  - FDI up to 100 per cent is permitted for Natural Gas/LNG pipelines with prior Government approval.

Source: Economic Survey 2004-05.

Government has put in place a liberal, transparent and investor friendly FDI policy, wherein FDI up to 100 per cent is allowed under automatic route for most of the sectors/ activities, where the investor does not require any prior approval (Box 17.4). Only notification to the Reserve Bank of India within 30 days of inward remittance or issue of shares to nonresidents is required. Cases requiring prior Government approval are considered by the Foreign Investment Promotion Board (FIPB) in a time-bound and transparent manner. The FDI policy in India is considered as one of the most liberal, with very few barriers. The Global Competitiveness Report 2003-04 by the World Economic Forum ranks India at 41st place on barriers to foreign ownership, against 67th for Malaysia, 75th for Thailand and 81st for China.

Investors are showing their growing confidence in the immediate and medium term prospects of the Indian economy. A recent confidence survey by global consultancy AT Kearney rated India as the third most favoured FDI destination, next only to China and United States. Moreover, for the first time, manufacturing investors surveyed by AT Kearney considered India as a superior manufacturing location than even the US.

According to the World Investment Report, 2004 of United Nations Conference on Trade and Development (UNCTAD), Global FDI Inflows have declined significantly from the peak of US$ 1.4 trillion in 2000 to US$ 560 billion in 2003. FDI inflow to India, on the contrary, has shown a rise, particularly in 2003, to reach US$ 4.27 billion.

FDI inflows have increased in the first eight months of the current year reaching US$ 2.5 billion, which is more than double, compared to the corresponding period last year and is very near to the total FDI inflows in 2003-04 (Table 17.17). Sector-wise FDI inflows from August 1991 until November, 2004, indicates that the highest shares of FDI inflows have gone to the data-processing software and consultancy services, followed by pharmaceuticals and automobile industry (Table 17.18).

Country-wise, FDI inflows to India (Table 17.19) are dominated by Mauritius (34.49 percent), followed by the United States (17.08 percent) and Japan (7.33 percent).

Five States/Union Territory – Maharashtra, Delhi, Tamil Nadu, Karnataka, and Gujarat – which were the top recipients of FDI approvals, secured more than 48 per cent of such approvals in the country (Table 17.20).

TABLE – 17.17

Foreign Direct Investment Approval and Inflows

Sl. No.	Financial Year	Amount in rupees in crore		Amount in US$ No. in million	
		Approvals	Inflows	Approvals	Inflows
1	1991-1992 #	1,345	408 527	165	
2	1992-1993	5,546	1,094	1,976	393
3	1993-1994	7,469	2,018	2,428	654
4	1994-1995	9,971	4,312	3,178	1,374
5	1995-1996	36,608	6,916	11,439	2,141
6	1996-1997	40,206	9,654	11,484	2,770
7	1997-1998	40,033	13,548	10,984	3,682
8	1998-1999	30,324	12,343	7,532	3,083
9	1999-2000	17,976	10,311	4,266	2,439
10	2000-2001	25,207	12,645	5,754	2,908
11	2001-2002	14,465	19,361	3,160	4,222
12	2002-2003	7,904	14,932	1,654	3,134
13	2003-2004	6,224	12,117	1,353	2,776
14	2004-2005 *	6,784	11,726	1,475	2,549
Total		**250,062**	**131,385**	**67,210**	**32,290**

Notes: 1. # Aug.-March; * Up to November 2004

2. As most of the sectors/activities have been placed under automatic route in recent years, which do not require any approval, the FDI approvals statistics are not a true reflection of the FDI approved.

TABLE – 17.18

Sector-wise FDI Approvals and Inflows (Cumulative from August 1991 to November 2004)

Amount rupees in crore (US $ in million)

Rank	Sector	No. of approvals	Amount approved	percentage approved Amount in rupee terms	Amount Inflows	Percentage of total Inflows in rupees terms*
1.	Fuels					
	• Power	371	43,687 (11,888)	17.47	-	-
	• Oil Refinery	338	26,079 (7,185)	10.43		
	TOTAL (power + oil refinery)	709	69,766 (19,073)	27.90	10,433 (2,459)	9.78
2.	Telecommunications (radio paging, cellular mobile, basic telephone services)	805	41,371 (11,441)	16.54	11,231 (2,674)	10.53
3.	Transportation industry	1,105	21,110 (5,427)	8.44	12,123 (2,909)	11.36
4.	Electrical equipments (including computer software & electronics)	4,746	18,947 (4,888)	7.58	16,093 (3,793)	15.09
5.	Metallurgical industries	428	15,412 (4,212)	6.16	2,043 (481)	1.92
6.	Services sector (financial, non-financial & others)	1,332	16,917 (4,417)	6.77	8,752 (2,174)	8.20
7.	Chemicals (other than fertilizers)	1,074	12,618 (3,492)	5.05	6,405 (1,653)	6.00
8.	Food-processing industries	784	9,562 (2,746)	3.82	4,481 (1,128)	4.20
9.	Hotel and tourism	537	4,909 (1,353)	1.96	981 (232)	0.92
10.	Paper and pulp (including paper products)	137	3,116 (832)	1.25	1,282 (336)	1.20
11.	Other sectors (total of remaining sector excluding above)	7,078	36,334 (9,330)	14.53	57,561 (14,451)	30.80
	Total for all sectors (August 1991 to November 2004)	19,444	2,50,062 (67,211)	100.00	1,31,385 (32,290)	100.00

Note: 1. As most sectors/activities have been placed under automatic route in recent years, which do not require any approval, the FDI approval statistics are not a true reflection of the FDI approved.

2.* Percentage figures do not take into account the amount of FDI Inflows for RBI's-NRI Schemes, acquisition of existing shares (upto 1999), stock swapped & advance pending for allotment of shares, as these are not categorized, Sectorwise.

TABLE – 17.19

Share of Top Investing Countries in FDI Inflows (from August 1991 to November 2004)

Amount in rupees crore (millions of US$)

Rank	Country	August 1991 to March 2000	2000-01	2001-02	2002-03	2003-04	2004-05 (up to Nov.)	Total inflows	percent-age of total inflows
1	Mauritius	13,272 (3,608)	4,111 (942)	10,063 (2,182)	3,766 (788)	2,609 (567)	3,730 (811)	37,551 (8,898)	34.49
2	USA	8,956 (2.450)	1,544 (356)	1,748 (382)	1,504 (319)	1,658 (360)	2,401 (522)	17,811 (4,389)	17.08
3	Japan	3,314 (898)	977 (224)	809 (178)	1,971 (412)	360 (78)	466 (101)	7,897 (1,891)	7.33
4	Netherlands	2,260 (628)	706 (162)	890 (196)	836 (176)	2,247 (489)	906 (197)	7,845 (1,847)	7.16
5	UK	2,286 (670)	303 (70)	1,673 (366)	1,617 (340)	769 (167)	361 (78)	7,009 (1,692)	6.56
6	Germany	2,396 (672)	540 (123)	519 (113)	684 (144)	373 (81)	553 (120)	5,066 (1,254)	4.86
7	France	1,002 (280)	455 (104)	499 (108)	534 (112)	176 (38)	165 (36)	2,822 (679)	2.63
8	South Korea	2,094 (572)	90 (21)	5 (1)	188 (39)	110 (24)	115 (25)	2,601 (682)	2.64
9	Singapore	1.244 (344)	502 (117)	251 (54)	180 (38)	172 (37)	225 (49)	2,573 (639)	2.48
10	Switzerland	948 (269)	71 (16)	180 (40)	437 (93)	207 (45)	287 (62)	2,130 (525)	2.04
TOTAL FDI INFLOWS *		60,604 (16,701)	12,645 (2,908)	19,361 (4,222)	14,932 (3,134)	12,117 (2,634)	11,726 (2,549)	1,31,385 (32,290)	-

Source : SIA, FDI Data Cell, Ministry of Commerce & Industry, Department of Industrial Policy and Promotion.

Note : * Includes inflows under NRI Schemes of RBI, stock swapped and advances pending issue of shares.

TABLE – 17.20

State-wise FDI approvals

(from August 1991 to November 2004)

Rank	State	Approvals			Amount of FDI approved		percentage of total FDI
		Total	Tech.	Financial	Rupees in crore	US$ in million	approved
1	Maharashtra	5,037	1,318	3,719	37,020	9,621	14.80
2	Delhi	2,810	307	2,503	30,519	8,445	12.20
3	Tamil Nadu	2,681	618	2,063	22,642	5,894	9.05
4	Karnataka	2,639	502	2,137	19,075	4,833	7.63
5	Gujarat	1,236	568	668	12,437	3,273	4.97

Note : RBI provides regional office wise information based on the intimation of investment received from investors under the automatic route. Consequently, the above table may not necessarily indicate state-wise investment intentions of investors.

Regarding FDI in India, the Mid-term Appraisal of the 10th Plan states "when a foreign investor considers making any new investment decision, it goes through four stages in the decision making process and action cycle, namely, (a) screening, (b) planning, (c) implementing and (d) operating and expanding".

The biggest barrier for India according to MTA is at the first, screening stage itself in the action cycle. "Often India looses out at the screening stage itself" (BCG). This is primarily because we do not get across effectively to the decision-making "board room" levels of corporate entities where a final decision is taken. Our promotional effort is quite often of a general nature and not corporate specific. India is, moreover, a multi-cultural society and a large number of multi-national companies (MNC) do not understand the diversity and the multi-plural nature of the society and the different stakeholders in this country. Though in several cases, the foreign investor is discouraged even before he seriously considers a project, 220 of the Fortune 500 companies have some presence in India and several surveys (JBIC, Japan Exim bank, A T Kearney) show India as the most promising and profitable destination.

On the other hand China is viewed as 'more business oriented,' its decision-making is faster and has more FDI friendly policies (ATK, 2001). Despite a very similar historical mistrust of foreigners and foreign investment arising from colonial experience, modern (post 1980) China differs fundamentally from India. Its official attitude to FDI, reflected from the highest level of government (PM, President) to the lowest level of government bureaucracy (provinces) is one of consciously enticing FDI with a warm welcome. They recognise the multi-faceted and mutual benefits arising from FDI.

All investments, foreign and domestic are made under the expectation of future profits. The economy benefits if economic policy fosters competition, creates a well functioning modern regulatory system and discourages 'artificial' monopolies created by the government through entry barriers. A recognition and understanding of these facts can result in a more positive attitude towards FDI.

Small Industry*

Rationale for Supporting Small Scale Enterprises

The arguments advanced in the literature for promotion of small scale enterprises involve both certain desirable characteristics of such enterprises and also a common belief that under normal market conditions many such enterprises would not be able to survive in the economy. A list of desirable characteristics of such enterprises include, inter alia, higher labour intensity and related positive income distribution effects, their potential for balanced regional development through greater decentralisation, their contribution to the promotion of entrepreneurship, their flexibility in operation, and their ability to export. If these positive characteristics are seen to be important and if there is reason to believe that market failures inhibit the growth of small scale enterprises then it would be appropriate to frame policies that attack these market imperfections.

It is believed that small scale enterprises are hampered in their growth because of imperfections in factor markets, in labour, capital and land. Typically, the factor market most focussed on is the capital market, distortions in which are seen to especially discriminate against small scale enterprises. Similarly, imperfections in the labour market lead to factor price distortions causing larger than justifiable wage differences between large and small enterprises. It can be argued, however, that the higher wages facing large firms can generally be compensated by higher efficiency of the work force so that the wage cost difference per efficiency unit of labour is much less than the observed difference in the prices of capital. Thus it can be argued that distortions in the capital

* This section draws from Rakesh Mohan's paper *Small Scale Industry Policy in India: A Critical Evaluation*, Conference on "Indian Economic Prospects: Advancing Policy Reforms" Centre for Research on Economic Development and Policy Reform, Stanford University, May 31-June 1, 2000.

market are much more important than those in the labour market. Large firms are able to compensate the higher wages through higher efficiency, but small firms are not able to compensate for the high cost of capital through higher efficiency of the capital used. Similarly in the land market small enterprises could face greater regulatory hurdles in achieving appropriate access to land.

The economic argument would then be that in the face of factor market distortions special support policies for small scale industries would tackle the problems at their source. The best solution would be to enact policies that remove the various factor market distortions that are observed at their source. In practice, it is found that it is difficult to remove such factor market distortions through direct interventions. The result is that a whole plethora of other supportive policies for small scale enterprises are observed. India has been no different from other countries in its concern for supporting small scale enterprises. In fact, amongst developing countries, India was the first to display special concern for small scale enterprises, before it became fashionable to do so. A basic focus of Indian government thinking has been that employment generation is of paramount importance in a labour surplus economy. Small enterprises manufacturing labour intensive products make economical use of capital and absorb abundant labour supply which characterises an under developed economy. The belief has been that large enterprises are capital intensive and reward only a small minority of labour which is skilled and urban. Indian concern and support for small scale enterprises has focussed excessively on small scale industries as distinguished from small scale enterprises in general.

All Industrial Policy Statements since independence have provided some special attention to the problem of small scale industries.

The basic structure of institutional promotion of small scale industries was put in place in the 1950s. This institutional structure had aimed to provide for a development programme for small scale industries through the establishment of organisations for providing technical assistance and industrial extension.

The basic idea then was promotion of small scale enterprises through positive technical and marketing support.

A policy of reserving items for the exclusive manufacture in the small scale sector was begun in 1967 when 47 items were reserved. This number rose gradually to 180 by 1976. With the 1977 Industrial Policy Statement a major expansion took place in the number of items reserved for small scale sector. A major shift in small scale industry policy took place with the promulgation of the Industrial Policy Statement of 1977. It was then decided that the sole criterion for reservation of products in the small scale sector would be merely its ability to physically manufacture them. It was stated in the policy that "whatever can be produced on a small scale must be so produced". The regime for small scale industry developed has remained virtually unchanged after that.

The key elements of India's policy for the support of small scale industries have been small scale industry reservations, fiscal concessions by way of lower excise duties, preferential allocation of and subsidisation of bank credit, extension of business services by the government, and preferential procurement by the government. Thus small scale industry has been sought to be protected from the competition of large companies both through reservations as well as fiscal concessions. Extension of business services by the government was considered necessary in the absence of equivalent services being available in the private sector.

In his study Rakesh Mohan has argued that this support structure may have reflected well the needs of the 1950s, 1960s and 1970s. The argument is that these policies have now become obsolete and are now likely to be harmful to the development of small scale industries and of industrial development in general. There has been vast growth of small units over the years. Thus, the governmental structure for technical support of small scale industries has become both obsolete and inadequate. There is now much greater availability of private sector business and technological support service which should be fostered. Second with the opening of the economy the reservation policy has become counter productive. Third, the fiscal concessions can also be operating so as to discourage growth into large units. Thus, it is argued that a whole new approach for supporting small scale industries has to be adopted in India to serve the changing needs of the new open economy.

Definition of Small Scale Industries

Most countries define small scale industries or enterprises in terms of employment levels. Usually small scale industries are taken to be those units which employ more than 5 but less than 50 or 100 workers. India is among the few countries that has used investment ceilings to define small scale industries. Further, in India itself, different definitions are used for different purposes. The Factories Act defines a factory as one which employs 10 workers or more if the unit uses power, or 20 workers or more if it does not use power. All such units have to be registered under the Factories Act and are subject to various labour laws including the provision of medical insurance and some social security. This is known as the registered sector. Within this definition, those units which employ more than 50 workers (if using power) or more than 100 (if not using power) have to compulsorily register themselves with the state governments in order to operate. The main source of data for manufacturing is the Annual Survey of Industries (ASI). The coverage of this survey is limited to those factories which are registered under the Factories Act. The third definition is that used for giving fiscal concessions. At present units which have less than Rs. 3 million turn over are fully exempted from the excise taxes and there is a sliding scale of concessions available for small scale enterprises which have turn over of upto Rs. 30 million.

In 1950, the investment limits was upto Rs. 0.5 million in fixed assets employing less than 50/100 persons with or without power. From 1960 onwards, there are no conditions regarding employment but investment limit has been raised to keep up with inflation and hence to preserve the real value of investment limits. In 1966 Investment limit was raised to 0.75 million in plant and machinery then 1 million in 1975, 2 million in 1980, 3.5 million in 1985, upto 6 million in 1991 and upto 30 million in 1997. A curious development took place in 1999 when, for the first time, a reversal in investment limit was put in to effect by lowering the investment limit to 10 million. The current definition is therefore more restrictive in real terms relative to 1991.

The current status of the investment ceilings for small scale industries is provided in the following Statement.

STATEMENT

Investment Ceilings for Small Scale Industry (December 1999)

Type of Small Scale Industry	Investment Limit	Remarks
Small Scale Industry	Rs. 10 million	Historical cost of plant and machinery
Ancillary	Rs. 10 million	At least 50 per cent of its output should go to other industrial undertakings
Export Oriented	Rs. 2.5 million	Obligation to export 30 per cent of production
Tiny Enterprise	Rs. 0.5 million	No location limits
Service and business enterprise	Rs. 10 million	No location limit
Women Enterprise	Rs. 10 million	51 per cent equity holding by women

Small Scale Reservation Policy

The policy of small scale reservations was initiated in 1967 as a promotional and protective measure for the small scale sector vis-a-vis the large scale sector. Under this policy selected products are identified for exclusive production in the small scale sector. The overwhelming consideration for reservation is whether it is technically feasible to produce that item in the small scale sector, the manufacturing process is of a simple nature i.e. is essentially labour intensive, and whether the small scale units can meet the requirements of consumers both in terms of quantity and quality. The rationale for reservation was based on the advantages of the small scale sector like labour intensity and adaptability to a semi-urban and rural environment. Another objective was to make SSI products competitive with those of the large scale by offsetting the disadvantage of mass scale production, economies of scale, wider marketing network, better credit availability and publicity through mass media and advertisements.

In April 1967 there were only 47 items in the reserved category which increased to 504 by April 1978. In 1978 it was decided to recast the reserved list by following codes adopted in the NIC and in this process, the list of reserved items expanded from 504 to 804. The number had increased to 873 in October 1984 and in 1989 after some dereservation it came down to 836.

Throughout this whole period of reservation there has been little analysis of the effects of this policy. The government has conducted two small scale industries censuses so far; one in 1972 and the other in 1987-88. The share of production in the reserved categories was 25 per cent in total small scale industry production in 1972 and 28 per cent in 1997-98. This small increase in the share was surprising given the large scale expansion of products under reservation that took place in 1977. In both cases capacity utilisation in units producing reserved items was 47 to 48 per cent on average, whereas the average level of capacity utilisation was over 50 per cent in units producing unreserved items. It was also found in 1987-88 that a large number of reserved items were not produced at all in any unit.

The second census of small scale industries provides persuasive evidence of the misplaced importance given the policy of reservation. Out of a total of 200 products leading in value of output produced by the small scale sector, it was found that reserved products accounted for only 21 percent. Only 210,000 small scale units, less than half out of a total of 5,82 000 units, manufactured the reserved products at all. No less than 233 reserved items out of a total of 1,076 (when expanded at a lower level of aggregation in the NIC code) were found not be manufactured at all according to the census. Although further inquiries have revealed that many of these products are found to be manufactured by some units, the fact remains that their production is in negligible quantities.

Conversely, very few of the reserved products attracted significant levels of participation from small scale units. As many as 90 products were found to be manufactured by just one company each. The sum total of the value of production of all small scale companies in as many as 692 items was a low of Rs. 100 million or less. Just 68 reserved items accounted for 81 percent of the total value of production of reserved products and 83 percent of the units.

In recent years, with the opening of Indian trade almost 75 per cent of all reserved items are now already importable with the removal of quantitative restrictions (QRs) in the last few years. India is also committed to remove the remaining QRs by April 2001. We, therefore, now have a curious situation that the reserved items can be produced by large foreign enterprises and imported into India whereas Indian large enterprises are not allowed to produce the same items! Even this change in the external environment has so far not persuaded the authorities to change this policy of small scale industry reservation.

Reviewing the framework of Indian policies protecting and supporting small scale industries Rakesh Mohan remarks, "that these policies and programmes are thinly spread thereby leading to relative ineffectiveness. Many of the policies are such that discourage growth of small scale units into larger ones and thereby are likely to have a stunting effect on manufacturing employment and output growth. Some of these policies may have been useful in the earlier stage of Indian industrialisation and in the context of a highly controlled and closed economy. With all the changes in economic environment that have taken place in the 1990s the indication is that future policies for the promotion of small scale industries must be more growth oriented and more general rather than being sector oriented. It would be more useful if such policies are designed to promote entrepreneurial entry, growth of enterprises technology upgradation and labour productivity in a pervasive manner regardless of specific sectors."

Size of the SSI Sector: Value Added

The share of the unregistered sector has been falling consistently throughout the last two decades, from about 43 per cent in 1980-81 to about 32 per cent in 1997-98. Adding the SSI estimate from the factory sector to the total unregistered sector to form the total share of "Village and Small Scale Industries" (SSI), that share is seen to fall from about 47.3 per cent of manufacturing value added in 1984-85 to about 44 per cent 10 years later in 1994-95. The trend is consistent with the data that can be pieced together from the Annual Survey of Industries (ASI) and Economic Census though the proportions come out to be different. The fall in share of the unregistered sector is much more drastic according to this source. Once again, this demonstrates the poor quality of data in this area.

Size Structure within the Small Scale Sector

One criterion of excessive development of inefficient units in a sector is a strikingly unequal development of the distribution of enterprises. In a dynamic sector, one would naturally expect a large number of very small units which are newly born and struggling to make there way upwards. But if the proportion of such units is excessive, then the natural conclusion is that artificial protection or other measures of subsidy are supporting a host of inefficient units which show little ability to grow. The unequal distribution of units of small and large sizes in terms of contribution to production is quite striking in the SIDO 1987-88 census Report. In 1987-88, at the upper end of the distribution (Investment in plant & machinery Rs.40 lakh and above) 0.004 percent of units, employing 0.08 percent of the total employed in the SIDO sector, accounted for 1.43 percent of total production. At the lower end (Investment in plant & machinery upto Rs.2 lakh) 83 percent of the units employing 54 percent of the workers, managed to produce only 28 percent of the output.

Sandesara also compared the change between the two Censuses. There is a clear increase in concentration of output in larger units and a more unequal distribution of enterprises in terms of production levels within the sector. Between 1972 and 1987-88 the group of enterprises with investment of more than Rs.300000 (at 1972-73 constant prices) increased its share of production from 21 to 52 percent, but the percentage of units went up from only 2 to 7. This represents an increase in the "concentration ratio" from 10.5 to 13 (using data given by Sandesara, 1993). To look at it from the lower end of the distribution, the relative production per unit, in the group with less than Rs.300000 investment (at 1972-73 prices), fell from 0.81 to 0.52. (The percentage of units in this group fell only marginally from 97 to 93).

The NCAER Survey of 657 small-scale enterprises in 1992 also commented on the highly skewed distribution of the units in terms of their output, particularly in some of the industries. In garments, 14 units (17 percent) employing more than 50 persons accounted for no less than 82 percent of production in the units. In electrical components, the share of two units employing more than 50 workers was 36 percent, and in detergents four units in the same size group accounted for 37 percent of production (NCAER, 1993 Table 3.23).

Evidently, the market structure within the SSI sector has been showing clear indications of monopolistic competition, with an excessive number of tiny units crowding in to share in the rent created through policy of protection and subsidisation, while success is achieved by a mere handful.

Trends in Employment, Investment and Productivity in the SSI Sector

The Census of Small Scale Units (CSSO) of 1972 and 1987-88 have been compared by Sandesara for assessing the nature of growth in the SIDO. Substantial growth was recorded in production and fixed assets (at constant prices), but some of this growth is due to increase in the scope of the industries sampled at the two dates.

More interesting is the change in factor ratios over time. The average size of the unit (enterprise) fell in terms of all factors - but most dramatically in terms of employment— from 12 to 6 - while investment in plant and machinery (at 1972-73 prices) fell by 12 percent, and net value added by 8 percent. The smaller employment size of the average enterprise was thus accompanied by an increase in capital intensity (K/L) and also by an increase in the productivity of both labour and capital. To summarize, net value added/ employment (V/L) increased by 73 percent, investment in fixed assets/ employment (K/L) by 66 percent, net value added/ Investment in fixed assets (V/K) by 38 percent.

The data show increased capitalization of the average unit, together with significant economies of scale (or total factor productivity growth). They are consistent with a more skewed distribution of enterprises, in which the more capitalized units achieve a high level of productivity, while a large number of units of low employment size crowd the lower part of the distribution.

Spatial Distribution of SSEs

One of the aims of India's SSI policy was the dispersed development of units in rural areas and in less developed "backward" areas. There has been only limited success in attaining this objective.

The SIDO figures suggest that 85 districts with more than 2,000 units in each account for 51 percent of the total. More than 81 percent of SSEs are concentrated in 204 districts, and more than 50 percent of the districts do not have any significant number of small enterprises (NCAER, 1993 3.7.6, p.81).

Rakesh Mohan argues, the objective of dispersal might be in conflict with the dynamic growth of modern and efficient growth. There has been important spatial concentration of SSEs in "clusters" in particular product lines. The external economies which these clusters generate in terms of easy availability of raw materials, skilled labour, markets etc. have been known to have been instrumental in the growth of SSEs in many countries, including Italy and Germany. India is proving no exception to this basic economic impulse. It is appropriate that these trends might be more emphatically encouraged in official policies and objectives. A closer look needs to be taken at the methods for fostering development in "backward areas" through such methods as tax concessions and special allotment of scarce materials.

Impact of SSI Reservation on Exports

According to Rakesh Mohan, the policy of small scale industry reservations has had a very deleterious effect on the growth of both manufacturing employment and exports. An important feature of industrialisation of the fast growing East Asian countries during the last three decades or so has been high growth in manufactured exports accompanied by high growth in manufacturing employment. The Indian experience has been different. Our record of growth in manufacturing employment has been poor and so has our export growth. The share of exports in Indian GDP has barely reached 10 per cent now. Although this is a significant improvement over the 3 per cent share of 1970 and 5 per cent in 1980, the Indian economy remains the least open among major countries in Asia, including China. While Chinese exports grew from about US $ 18 billion in 1980 to about US $ 120 billion in 1994 Indian exports during that period grew from US $ 8.6 billion to US $ 25 billion. Given that the composition of exports of industrialising countries is largely labour intensive, one of the reasons behind slow employment growth in manufacturing in India is clearly related to the slow growth in exports.

In order to substantiate this assertion Rakesh Mohan examines the commodity composition of exports of key newly industrialising Asian countries over the last three decades or so. It is useful to classify the export commodity groups into five broad categories on the basis of skill, technology, capital and skill. Group I consists of primary commodities including processed foods; Group II consists of labour intensive and resource based industries requiring low levels of technology (textiles, clothing and footwear, toys and sports equipment, wood and paper products and non metallic mineral products). Group III consists of sectors that require low to medium levels of technology sophistication (iron and steel, fabricated metal products, transport equipment, other than motor vehicles and aircraft and sanitary and plumbing equipment). Group IV consists of industries with medium to high levels of technology sophistication (rubber and plastic products, non electrical machinery and motor vehicles). Finally, the sectors with the highest levels of technology sophistication are contained in Group V (chemical and pharmaceuticals product), computerization and office equipment, semi conductors, aircraft and aeronautical equipment, and scientific instruments, watches and photographic equipment). This classification helps us to observe the changing export product composition over time in order to examine whether technology upgradation has been taking place or not. What is expected is that as countries industrialise they would gain in technology sophistication and the export share of Group IV and V would rise.

The pattern of change in export composition of the so called Asian tigers is remarkably uniform. In the first stage of change the share of group I exports i.e. primary products, falls drastically and the share of group II products tends to increase. Second, the share of group III starts rising at the expense of group II and I, and finally in the last stage the share of group IV start rising at the expense of group I, II, and III. Similar patterns can be seen in the changing export composition of countries such as Indonesia, Malaysia and Thailand. In all these cases the initial kick in export growth is provided by group II products, particularly the categories of textiles, clothing and footwear, and to some extent toys and sports equipment. Among group IV products it is the export of relatively simple kinds of electrical machinery (e.g. radios and other domestic electrical appliances) that are exported by industrialising countries. Finally, it's the sophisticated items such as electronic equipment, computers and telecommunications equipment which start to get exported. It is the initial kick given by the group II items that provides the reputation for quality which then enables the export of other more sophisticated goods. It is within these groups also that consistent quality upgradation take place and unit values rise as better quality clothing, footwear etc. begin to get exported. The profits made from these exports provide the surpluses necessary for companies to diversify into more sophisticated areas of exports.

As against this in India there has been relatively unchanging structure of Indian exports since the early 1980s. Like other countries, India also diversified away from primary products quite successfully. But after, this initial diversification its export structure has remained stagnant throughout the period, relative to other Asian countries. In particular the shares of textiles, yarn and clothing has remained stationary as has the share of machinery and transport equipment. No other country exhibits such a stagnant picture of export product composition.

It would be observed that the very high proportion of items in group II are reserved for small scale industries in India. In addition, some of the simpler items (like radios and domestic electrical appliances, some motor vehicle and bicycle parts, extruded plastic products and the like) in groups III and IV are also reserved. It is therefore likely that India's policies on small scale reservation have had a particularly strong impact on Indian export performance.

It is possible that the damage caused by such policies was not very high in the 1970s, when competition in exports of low technology products was not as high as it is now. Furthermore, changing industry structure and demand patterns in the developed world now place a much higher premium on both product quality and service quality with the inexorably rising incomes there. The average quality demanded for products such as clothing, footwear, toys and sports equipment and the like is getting higher and higher. Furthermore, the integration of information technology in even these industries also requires greater investment and greater labour sophistication. Such products are no longer seen as free standing products but are increasingly becoming parts of long value chains with the share of value added in plain manufacturing perhaps falling. Higher quality requires high level designing upstream even for simple products. Downstream marketing involves linkages with large organisations which buy such products in bulk. Small enterprises sandwiched between such high level organisations find it increasingly difficult to operate and be competitive. Thus, apart from the loss that India has suffered over the last 2-3 decades it is likely that the future scenario will become even more difficult for Indian small enterprises to survive, particularly in the reserved sector. Another issue of note is the prospective dismantling of the Multi Fibres Agreement. Paradoxically, although it may have seemed that textile quotas were inhibiting Indian exports, it is likely that we were actually protected through the MFA mechanism. This is shown in Somnath Chatterjee and Rakesh Mohan (1993) who documented the fact that Indian clothing exports went primarily to quota countries and were almost absent in the markets of non quota countries. Thus, the removal of small scale reservation is especially necessary in the items affected by the removal of MFA.

Looking at the record of Indian exports in comparison with East Asian countries, it is difficult to avoid the conclusion that Indian exports have been heavily constrained by the policy of SSI product reservation.

Conclusions

The major conclusions of Rakesh Mohan's study are as below:

- We may distinguish the 'small scale modern' sector - consisting of units employing 6 or more workers and the 'tiny' sector including household enterprises. In terms of employment around 1990, the former accounted for roughly 20 percent of all manufacturing employment, but nearly a half of employment in the modern manufacturing sector. The tiny and household sector is 2.5 to 3 times as large, depending on whether or not we include secondary workers in the labour force. The contribution of SSI in terms of value added is, of course, much smaller - only a third as for as the modern manufacturing sub-sector is concerned and no more than 40 percent of all manufacturing value added. The last point emphasises the enormous difference in labour productivity between the different sub-sectors of manufacturing.
- As in other countries, the household sub-sector has declined slowly over the last two or three decades. A more surprising finding is that in spite of the vigorous policy of protecting the small scale, this decline has not been fully compensated for by the growth of non-household production in the small scale sector. The SIDO figures of high growth rates of SSI's under their purview seem to be grossly exaggerated.
- Inspite of the vast increase in the number of reserved items, much of the growth in the SSI sector seems to have been in product lines outside the reserved list. It is possible that the policy of reservation might be merely protecting inefficient units in stagnant industries.
- A finding of some concern is the unequal distribution of units of small and large sizes within the SSI sector. There seems to be an increase in the concentration of output in larger units over the last two decades. A comparison of the data from the two SIDO censuses of 1972 and 1987-88 show a sharp fall in the mean employment size but an increase in capital-intensity of the SIDO

units-which is consistent with a more skewed distribution of enterprises, and increased contribution of the more productive units.

- The claim that there has been substantial dispersal of units to backward and rural areas under the SSI policy might be exaggerated. As far as the modern SSI's are concerned there is considerable evidence of spatial concentration of SSE's in 'clusters' in specific product groups. We have already emphasised in earlier chapters that there is a need for policies of decentralization to come to terms with the economic logic of external economies which 'clusters' provide.
- All the evidence suggests that the Indian manufacturing sector is likely to have been constrained by the various, anti-growth policies promoting the small scale sector, particularly that of product reservation. Indian manufacturing employment growth has been the lowest among large Asian countries over the past three or four decades.
- A particular casualty of SSI product reservations has been growth in Indian manufacturing exports. A large number of categories in which India exhibits comparative advantage have been reserved for SSI. Consequently, Indian industry is unable to upgrade quality on a continuous basis and is also not able to diversify to higher technology and higher value added item, thereby stunting export growth.

New Policy Directions

A strong rationale already exists for exceptional state support for fostering small scale enterprises. This has always been recognised in India. Now, in order to keep in step with the changing domestic and international environment, it is imperative that a new approach for promoting the small scale sector be developed. The state must increasingly use its scarce resources to act as a facilitator rather than as a direct provider of services. The past policies have also concentrated excessively on small scale industry to the exclusion of other activities. It must be recognized that enterprise exists in a whole host of activities, and in many areas such as software development and other industrial support services, the distinction between industry and service sector activities is increasingly getting blurred. Consequently, the new approach is a must for the support of small scale enterprises (SSEs) as a whole.

The focus on new policies for promotion of small scale industries must be on facilitating new entrepreneurial entry into SSI, facilitation of their growth in terms of output employment, productivity and exports. The new approach for supporting SSI that needs to be designed must use mechanisms that are market related in order to promote the growth of enterprises in the SSI sector. Unlike the previous approach of seeing SSI in competition with large scale industries, and hence protecting them from this competition, the new approach must recognise the many different kinds of relationship that exist emphasizing complementarily between large and small enterprises. Avenues for partnership and cooperation through outsourcing, sub contracting, cross holdings and the like must be encouraged actively to the mutual benefit of both industry segments. Thus, regulations such as the 24 per cent limit on equity holding by both foreign and domestic large enterprises must be abolished. In contrast to the current approach of technical and business services being provide directly by government institutions, the new approach must promote public private partnerships for providing such services, where necessary. Otherwise the promotion of private business and technical services would itself foster the growth of service SSEs. The NCAER (1993) study found that of those SSI units utilising external technical consultancy services, less than a quarter utilised government institutions while others paid private service providers. Thus SSI units are willing and often able to pay for the services they need.

The new approach must focus on improving the competitive ability of SSI units through forging improvements in their efficiency and quality levels, rather than protecting them from competition. In view of the externalities involved in R&D and training assistance, some element of government subsidy is essential. The new approach must look for public private partnerships through tie-ups with business associations, R&D associations, technical colleges and the like, common mechanisms for forging such partnerships include that of providing matching funds. Existing policy mechanisms that provide incentives to units against growth must be abolished or redesigned. Such policies include the existing system of fiscal concessions: one way of doing this would be to permit the fiscal concession for a fixed period even after graduation from the SSI status.

The first policy action that must be taken is the immediate abolition of the product reservation of small scale industries. Second, the specific focus must be on the use of clusters for the facilitation of services to SSI enterprises. Third, a new approach must be adopted for improving the credit flow to SSI enterprises.

The 1991 New Small Enterprises Policy, provides for various financial support measures, infrastructural facilities, marketing and export facilities modernisation, technological and quality upgradation, promotion of entrepreneurship and simplification of rules and procedures.

The policy initiatives announced for the SSI sector in the year 1999-2000 are given in Box 17.4. In order to ensure that credit is available to all segments of SSI sector, RBI has issued instructions that out of the funds normally available for the SSI sector, 40 per cent be given to units with investment in plant and machinery upto Rs. 5 lakhs, 20 per cent to units with investment between Rs. 5 lakhs and Rs. 25 lakhs and remaining 40 per cent for other units. Banks have been asked to operationalise more specialized SSI branches. The single window scheme of SIDBI is also being extended to all districts.

The Government has been taking various measures from time to time in order to enhance the productivity, efficiency and competitiveness of the SSI sector. In pursuance of the comprehensive policy package announced in 1999-2000, the major developments that have taken place in the SSI sector during 2001-02 are briefly outlined in the Box 17.5.

BOX – 17.5

Developments that have taken place during the year 2001-02 for the SSI Sector

1. The investment limit for units in hosiery and hand tool sub sectors was enhanced from Rs. 1 crore to Rs. 5 crore.
2. The corpus fund set up under the Credit Guarantee Fund Scheme has been raised to Rs. 200 crore from Rs. 125 crore.
3. Credit Guarantee cover against an aggregate credit of Rs. 22.88 crore was provided till the end of December, 2001.
4. 14 items were dereserved on June 29, 2001 related to leather goods, shoes and toys.
5. A new scheme named Market Development Assistance Scheme was launched exclusively for the SSI sector.
6. Under the Cluster Development Programme, 4 UNIDO assisted projects have been commissioned during the year.

Source: Economic Survey, 2001-02.

BOX – 17.6

Details of Comprehensive Policy Package on SSI & Tiny Sector announced by the Prime Minister on 30th August, 2000

(i) Raising the exemption for excise duty limit from Rs. 50 lakh to Rs. One crore to improve the competitiveness of small scale sector.

(ii) Providing Credit Linked capital subsidy of 12 per cent against loans for technology upgradation in specified industries.

(iii) Conducting of the third census of small scale industries by the Ministry of SSI & ARI after a gap of 12 years. This census would also cover sickness and its causes.

(iv) Raising the limit of investment in Industry related service and business enterprise from the present level of Rs. 5.00 lakh to Rs. 10 lakh.

(v) Continuation of the ongoing scheme of granting Rs. 75,000 to each small scale enterprise for obtaining ISO 9000 certification till the end of the X Plan.

(vi) SSI associations encouraged to develop and operate testing laboratories. One time capital grant of 50 per cent will be given on reimbursement basis to such associations after detailed examination of each case.

(vii) Raising of the limit for composite loans from Rs. 10 lakh to Rs. 25 lakh.

(viii) Constitution of group under the Cabinet Secretary to suggest/ recommend streamlining of inspection and repeal of redundant laws and regulations applicable to the sector.

(ix) Increasing the coverage of ongoing Integrated Infrastructure Development (IID) scheme to progressively cover all areas in the country with 50 per cent reservation for rural areas and 50 per cent of plots will be earmarked for tiny sector.

(x) Raising the family income eligibility limit of Rs. 24,000 to Rs. 40,000 per annum. Under the Prime Minister's Rozgar Yojana (PMRY) which finances setting up of micro enterprises and generates employment for the educated unemployed.

Source: Economic Survey, 2000-01.

Box 17.7 summarises policy initiatives on the SSI sector in 2003-04.

BOX – 17.7

Policy Initiatives on Small-scale Industries in 2003-04 and 2004-05

2003-04

- 75 items reserved for exclusive manufacture in the SSI Sector consisting of chemicals and their products, leather and leather products, laboratory reagents etc. were dereserved in June, 2003.
- Selective enhancement of investment in plant and machinery from Rs. 1 crore to Rs. 5 crore carried out in respect of 13 items in stationery sector and 10 items of drugs and pharmaceutical sector from June 5, 2003.
- The Union Budget 2003-04 announced that banks would provide credit to SSI sector within an interest rate band of 2 per cent above and below their Prime Lending Rates (PLR). All public sector banks have adopted this norm.
- The composite loan limit for SSI units was enhanced from Rs. 25 lakhs to Rs. 50 lakhs.
- In its Mid-term Review of Monetary and Credit Policy 2003-04, the RBI announced that banks may enhance the limit of dispensation of collateral requirement for loans from the existing Rs. 15 lakh to Rs. 25 lakh on the basis of good track record and financial position of the units.
- The lower limit of Rs. 5 lakh on loans covered under the Credit Guarantee Scheme has been removed. All loans up to Rs. 25 lakh made eligible for guarantee cover under the Credit Guarantee Scheme.
- 417 SSI specialised bank branches made operational throughout the country.
- The Final Results of Third All India Census of Small Scale Industries were released on January 17, 2004.
- 60 clusters identified in the First Phase (July, 2003) for focused development, by including their credit requirements in the respective State Credit Plans.
- Setting up of a Small and Medium Enterprise (SME) Fund of Rs. 10,000 crore under SIDBI, to *inter alia*, address the problem of inadequacy of financial resources at highly competitve rates for small scale sector.

Contd...

...Box 17.7 Contd...

- Laghu Udyami Credit Card scheme liberalized with enhanced credit limit of Rs. 10 lakh (up from 2 lakh) for borrowers with satisfactory track records.

2004-05

- The National Commission on Enterprises in the Unorganised/Informal Sector was set up in September 2004. The Commission will, *inter-alia*, recommend measures considered necessary for improvement in the productivity of these enterprises, generation of large scale employment opportunities on a sustainable basis, linkage of the sector to institutional framework in areas like credit, raw material supply, infrastructure, technology upgradation, marketing facilities and skill development
- 85 items reserved for exclusive manufacture in the SSI sector were dereserved in October 2004. The total number of reserved items now stands at 605
- To facilitate technology upgradation and enhancing competitiveness, the investment limit (in plant and machinery) has been raised in October 2004, from Rs. 1 crore to Rs. 5 crore, in respect of 7 items of sports goods, reserved for manufacture in the small scale sector
- The Small and Medium Enterprises (SME) Fund of Rs. 10,000 crore was operationalised by the SIDBI since April 2004. Eighty per cent of the lending from this fund will be for SSI units, at interest rate of 2 per cent below the prevailing PLR of the SIDBI.
- The Reserve Bank of India enhanced the composite loan limit for the SSI sector to Rs. 1 crore from Rs. 50 lakh.
- With a view to integrate small and medium enterprises, facilitating their growth and enhancing their competitiveness (including measure for freeing the sector from "Inspector Raj"), a suitable legislation is being finalised.
- A new "Promotional Package for small enterprises" is being formulated. This would include measures to provide adequate credit, incentives for technology upgradation, infrastructural and marketing facilities, *etc*.

Source: Economic Survey, 2003-04 & 2004-05.

TABLE – 17.21

Performance of Small Scale Sector

Year	No. of units (in lakhs)	Production (Rs. crore) (at current prices)	Production (Rs. crore) (at constant prices) (1993-94)	Employment Nos. in lakh	Exports (Rs. crore) (at current prices)
1994-95	25.71 (7.66)	2,98,886 (23.69)	2,66,054 (10.10)	146.56 (5.15)	29,068 (14.86)
1995-96	26.58 (3.88)	2,62,656 (21.34)	2,96,385 (11.40)	152.61 (4.13)	36,470 (25.46)
1996-97	28.03 (5.46)	4,11,858 (13.57)	3,29,935 (11.32)	160.00 (4.84)	39,248 (7.61)
1997-98	29.44 (5.03)	4,62,641 (12.33)	3,57,749 (8.43)	167.20 (4.50)	44,442 (13.23)
1998-99	30.80 (4.62)	5,20,650 (12.54)	3,85,296 (7.70)	171.58 (2.62)	48,979 (10.21)
1999-00	32.12 (4.29)	5,72,887 (10.03)	4,16,736 (8.16)	178.50 (4.03)	54,200 (10.66)
2000-01	33.12 (3.11)	6,39,024 (11.54)	4,51,033 (8.23)	185.64 (4.00)	69,797 (28.78)
2001-02	34.42 (3.91)	6,90.316 (8.03)	4,78,456 (6.08)	192.23 (3.55)	NA (10.66)
2002-03 (Projected)	35.72 (3.8)	742021 (7.5)	514292 (7.5)	199.65 (3.9)	NA

Notes : Figures in the brackets show percentage growth over previous year.
Source: Economic Survey, 2002-03.

Public Sector

The Industrial Policy 1991 provides a new approach to public enterprises. The new policy emphasises that measures must be taken to make these enterprises more growth oriented and technically dynamic. According to the New Industrial Policy the priority areas for growth of public enterprises in the future will be the following: Essential infrastructure goods and services; exploration and exploitation of oil and mineral resources; technology development and building of manufacturing capabilities in areas which are crucial in the long term development of the economy and where private sector investment is inadequate; manufacture of products where strategic considerations predominate such as defence equipment.

Government will strengthen those public enterprises which fall in the reserved areas of operation or are in high priority areas or are generating good or reasonable profits. Such enterprises will be provided a much greater degree of management autonomy through the system of memoranda of understanding.

Competition will also be induced in these areas for private sector participation. In the case of selected enterprises, part of government holdings in the equity share capital of these enterprises will be disinvested in order to provide further market discipline to the performance of public enterprises common detriment, control of monopolies, and prohibition of monopolistic and restrictive and unfair trade practices.

Portfolio of public sector investments will be reviewed with a view to focus the public sector on strategic, high tech and essential infrastructure. Whereas some reservation for the public sector is being retained there would be no bar for areas of exclusivity to be opened up to the private sector selectively.

Public enterprises which are chronically sick and which are unlikely to be turned around will, for the formulation of revival/rehabilitation schemes, be referred to the Board for Industrial and Financial Reconstruction (BIFR), or other similar high level institutions created for the purpose. A social security mechanism will be created to protect the interests of workers likely to be affected by such rehabilitation packages.

In order to raise resources and encourage wider public participation, a part of the governments shareholding in the public sector would be offered to mutual funds, financial institutions, general public and workers. Boards of public sector companies would be made more professional and given greater powers.

There will be a greater thrust on performance improvement through the memorandum of understanding (MoU) system through which managements would be granted greater autonomy and will be held accountable. Technical expertise on the part of the government would be upgraded to make the MoU negotiations and implementating more effective.

Public Enterprise Policy

The Government's strategy towards the public sector, continues to encompass a judicious mix of strengthening strategic units, privatising non-strategic ones through gradual disinvestment or strategic sale and devising viable rehabilitation strategic for weak units.

The main elements of Government Policy towards Public Sector Undertakings (PSUs) are :

- Bring down Government equity in all non-strategic PSUs to 26 per cent or lower, if necessary;
- Restructure and revive potentially viable PSUs;
- Close down PSUs which cannot be revived; and
- Fully protect the interest of workers.

To make PSEs more efficient and competitive, the Government has granted autonomy, of varying degrees, to select profit making PSEs. Depending upon the degree of autonomy granted, the select industries are called as *Navratnas* and *Mini-Ratnas.*

Navratnas

The Government has selected 11 PSEs for the Navratnas category up to 1998-99 (Box 17.8). These enterprises, subject to certain guidelines, have full freedom to make capital expenditure, decision regarding joint ventures and setting up of subsidiary offices abroad for technological and strategic alliance.

BOX – 17.8

List of Navratnas

1. Indian Oil Corporation (IOC).
2. Indian Petrochemicals Corporation Limited (IPCL)
3. Oil and Natural Gas Corporation (ONGC)
4. Bharat Petroleum Corporation Limited (BPCL)
5. Hindustan Petroleum Corporation Limited (HPCL)
6. National Thermal Power Corporation (NTPC)
7. Steel Authority of India Limited (SAIL)
8. Videsh Sanchar Nigam Limited (VSNL)
9. Bharat Heavy Electrical Limited (BHEL)
10. Gas Authority of India Limited (GAIL)
11. Mahanagar Telephone Nigam Limited (MTNL)

Mini-Ratnas

The Government has also granted enhanced financial, managerial and operational autonomy to other profit - making enterprises, called *Mini-Ratnas*. These enterprises should have earned profits continuously for the last three years, have positive net worth, do not seek budgetary support or guarantees from the Government and have not defaulted in the repayment of loans/interests to the Government. These enterprises can incur capital expenditure, enter into joint ventures, set up technological and strategic alliances, formulate schemes of human resources management, etc., subject to certain stipulations and guidelines.

In order to give thrust to the process of disinvestment in PSUs, a new Department of Disinvestment has been set up. The Department is responsible for all matters related to disinvestment of Central Government equity in Central Public Sector Undertakings, implementation of disinvestment decisions and recommendations of the erstwhile Disinvestment Commission.

Privatisation

Through the decade of the 1990s, there has been an increasing consensus on the merits of privatisation. The aggregate balance sheet assets of all public sector companies amounts to roughly Rs.22 lakh crore, This suggests that relatively modest improvements in the efficiency of their functioning would have a significant impact upon GDP growth. Hence, policies on privatisation are an important component of policies for efficiency and productivity.

The privatisation process began in 1991-92 with sale of minority stakes in some PSUs. From 1999-2000 onwards, the focus shifted to strategic sales. Table 17.22 highlights the actual disinvestment proceeds as compared with targets for the year.

TABLE – 17.22

Disinvestment in Public Sector Undertakings

Year	Target (Rs. crore)	Proceeds (Rs. crore)
1991-92	2,500	3,038
1992-93	2,500	1,913
1993-94	3,500	-
1994-95	4,000	4,843
1995-96	7,000	362
1996-97	5,000	380
1997-98	4,800	902
1998-99	5,000	5,371
1999-00	10,000	1,860
2000-01	10,000	1,871
2001-02	12,000	5,632#
2002-03	12,000	3,348
2003-04	14,500	15,547
2004-05	4,000	2,765@

Figures inclusive of amount realized by way of control premium, dividend/dividend tax and transfer of surplus cash reserves prior to disinvestment etc. @ Up to December 2004.

Source: Ministry of Disinvestment.

Table 17.23 summarises the transactions which have taken place in 2003-04, which have given proceeds of Rs.15547 crore.

TABLE – 17.23

Disinvestment Proceeds during 2003-04

(Rs. crore)

Sl. No.	Name	Type of Sale	Percentage of equity disinvested	Proceeds realisation to be realized
1.	Maruti Udyog Ltd.	Offer for sale	27.5	993.34
2.	Jessop & Co. Ltd.*	Strategic Sale	72.0	18.18
3.	HZL**	Call option	18.9	323.88
4.	ICIL	Limited Auction	9.2	77.10
5.	IBP	Offer for Sale	26.0	350.66
6.	IPCL	Offer for Sale	28.9	1202.85
7.	CMC	Offer for Sale	26.3	190.44
8.	DCIL	Offer for Sale	20.0	221.20
9.	GAIL	Offer for Sale	10.0	1627.36
10.	ONGC	Offer for Sale	9.9	10542.40
Total				**15547.42**

* Amount has been received by Bharat Bhari Udyog Ltd., the holding company of Jessop & Co. Ltd.

** Excise of Call Option by the Strategic Partner.

Source : Ministry of Disinvestment.

It is interesting to note that while much is made of the likely adverse impact of disinvestments on employment, in fact, over the last 10 years, as reported by the PSE Survey 2000-01, public sector undertakings have seen a net reduction in employment from a level of 2,179 million employees in 1991-92 to a level of 1,742 million in 2000-01, or a reduction of 20 percent over this period. Till March 31, 2001, 3.69 lakh employees had opted for VRS. In comparison, the retrenchment of employees after disinvestment has been marginal.

In eight disinvested PSUs and five disinvested ITDC Hotels, against an initial employee strength of 27,967 at the time of disinvestments, only 2,119 employees were retrenched through VRS, and another 910 for other reasons. As against a total of 3,029 post disinvestment separations, 855 fresh appointments have been made resulting in a net reduction of 2,174 employees or about 7.8 percent employees, compared to the employment level at the time of disinvestments.

As per the Common Minimum Programme (CMP), the United Progressive Alliance (UPA) Government is committed to a strong and effective public sector whose social objectives are met by its commercial functioning. But for this, there is need for selectivity and a strategic focus. The UPA is pledged to devolve full managerial and commercial autonomy to successful, profit-making companies operating in a competitive environment. Generally profit-making companies will not be privatised.

All privatisations will be considered on a transparent and consultative case-by-case basis. The UPA will retain existing "navaratna" companies in the public sector while these companies raise resources from the capital market. While every effort will be made to modernise and restructure sick public sector companies and revive sick industry, chronically loss-making companies will either be sold-off, or closed, after all workers have got their legitimate dues and compensation. The UPA will induct private industry to turn-around companies that have potential for revival.

The Government has enacted a new law, the Competition Act, 2002, for upholding competition in the Indian market. The main objectives of the Act are to provide for the establishment of a Commission to prevent practices having adverse effect on competition, to promote and sustain competition in markets in India, to protect the interests of consumers, and to ensure freedom of trade carried on by participants in market in India and for related matters. The Competition Act provides for the establishment of a Competition Commission of India, which was established on October 14, 2003.

The Government has approved the constitution of a National Investment Fund comprising of proceeds from disinvestment of public sector units. The broad objective of the fund will be to make investments in social sector projects and capital investment in selected profitable or revivable PSEs that yield adequate returns, in order to enlarge their capital base to finance expansion/diversification. The fund will come into effect from April 1, 2005.

The Government has also given 'in principle' approval for listing of currently unlisted profitable PSEs each with a net worth in excess of Rs. 200 crore, through an initial public offer (IPO), either in conjunction with a fresh equity issue by the PSE concerned or independently by the Government on a case by case basis, subject to the residual equity of the Government remaining at least 51 per cent and the Government retaining management control of the PSE. (Economic Survey 2004-05).

Industrial Sickness

According to information compiled by RBI from scheduled commercial banks, as on March 31, 2001, there were 2,52,947 sick/ weak units consisting of 2,49,630 units in the SSI sector and 3,317 units in the non-SSI sector. Among the 3,317 units, the private sector, public sector and joint/ co-operative sector accounted for 2,942 units, 255 units, and 106/14 units, respectively. The total number of sick SSI units has decreased from 3,04,235 units to 2,49,630 units but the number of sick/ weak units in the non-SSI sector has increased from 3,164 to 3,317. The total bank credit blocked in sick units has increased from Rs 23,656 crore (as on March 31, 2000) to Rs 25,775 crore (as on March 31, 2001). The small scale sector has Rs 4,506 crore (17.5 per cent) blocked in its units while the non-SSI sector has Rs. 21,270 crore (82.5 per cent). Bank credit blocked in the non-SSI sector in private, public and joint/ co-operative units was Rs 17,705 crore, Rs 2,986 crore, and Rs 537 crore/Rs. 42 crore, respectively.

Since its inception in May 1987 and till the end of August 2004, the Board for Industrial and Financial Reconstruction (BIFR) has received 6,457 references under the Sick Industrial Companies (Special Provisions) Act, 1985 (SICA). The gross disposal of cases by BIFR declined from 188 in 1997 to 141 in 1998. However, it rose to 385 in 2000. As on March 31, 2003, the gross disposal of cases was 2867. During the current year, as on August 31, 2004, the gross disposal of cases reached to 3318.

Policies for Faster Industrial Growth: Mid-term Appraisal of the Tenth Five Year Plan

Industrialisation and Development

Given the low levels of industrial growth in the Ninth Plan period, there is some pessimism on whether the country can ever become a significant industrial power. The rapid growth of the tertiary sector has raised the question whether India should, in its development strategy, leapfrog from an agricultural to a service economy, skipping the middle phase of industrialisation. However, a number of factors need to be kept in mind when taking a view on the long-term prospects for Indiaís manufacturing sector.

The manufacturing sector has shown some buoyancy in the Tenth Plan period, after languishing at less than 5 per cent growth during the Ninth Plan period, with the growth rate rising to 8.7 per cent in April-February, 2004-05. Despite the steep reduction of tariffs and the elimination of quantitative restrictions, the much-feared flood of imports has not happened. On the other hand, Indiaís exports of manufactures have been rising consistently at more than 20 per cent per annum over the past two years. Although handicapped by policy, procedural and infrastructure constraints, India has maintained its status as a competitive supplier to the world of such labour intensive products as apparel, footwear, jewellery, leather and textiles.

More significantly, the country has, in recent years, emerged as an important supplier of skill-intensive products such as auto components and pharmaceuticals. Some recent assessments suggest that India has the potential to share the top two positions with China in exports of apparel, leather, jewellery, pharmaceuticals, power transmission and distribution equipment, auto components, iron and steel, aluminium and speciality chemicals. In any case, it should be emphasised that no other developing country in Asia has achieved economic growth without a substantial industrial base (Table 17.24).

TABLE – 17.24

Manufacturing Value Added as % of GDP in Asian Economies

Country	1985	1990	1995	2000
India	16.3	17.2	17.8	15.8
China	34.9	32.9	34.7	34.5
Indonesia	15.8	18.3	24.1	26.0
Malaysia	19.3	24.2	26.4	32.8
Singapore	23.3	27.1	24.7	26.5
Thailand	21.9	27.2	28.4	31.9

Source: World Development Report, various issues

The Indian work force consists of labour at different levels of skills, with a large proportion in the unskilled category. A vibrant manufacturing sector is essential for providing job opportunities to this category. Rapid industrialisation is the sine qua non for any diversification of the labour force.

World Class Infrastructure

Improving the quality of infrastructure, especially infrastructure related to electric power and transport facilities, is a prerequisite for realising the potential for industrialisation. Transport infrastructure includes railways, roads, ports and airports. Comparative surveys such as those conducted by the World Competitiveness Yearbook 2003 clearly reflect the fact that such infrastructure is deficient in India compared to Malaysia, Thailand, China and Mexico. On a ten-point scale (0 for least favourable and 10 for most favourable), India scores 3.8 in infrastructure for distribution of goods and services. China scores 5.4 and Malaysia 8. In the case of infrastructure maintenance and development, India scores 2.3 as compared to 5.3 for China and 7.2 for Thailand.

While steps have been taken to increase investment in the physical infrastructure a possible short-term strategy could be to develop six to eight special economic regions (SERs), where manufacturing industries could be encouraged to establish new units. The regions should be of large size (around 5,000 hectares each) and should have their own modern industrial townships in order to attract large-scale investment, including foreign direct investment (FDI). For such SERs to be successful, they must have world-class internal and peripheral infrastructure. The airport and sea-port serving the SER could be upgraded to provide world class services. Each of the SERs could be anchored around one or two big players.

Labour Laws

Both domestic and foreign investors cite rigidity of labour laws as one of the factors affecting the competitiveness of the manufacturing industry, especially the labour intensive sectors. Some of the labour laws may appear to improve the position of labour in the organised sector, but these may also reduce new employment in the organised sector by imposing labour rigidity, especially in the industries where scope for expanding employment is linked to export possibilities and competing producers in other countries benefit from greater labour flexibility.

A case in point is the poor performance of textiles and garment exports after the abolition of quota for textile exports with effect from 1.1.2005, exports of textiles and clothings were expected to sky rocket from India. Exports during January – March, 2005 from China are reported to have increased over 500 per cent. However, exports from India are said to have increased by about 1 per cent in value terms. The Industry has asserted that this insignificant growth of textiles and garments exports against the large potential is to a great extent owing to the rigidity in the prevalent labour regime. There is an urgent need to relax labour legislation.

Examples of provisions which impose rigidity are Chapter V-B of the Industrial Disputes Act, 1947 that requires companies with more than 100 workers to obtain state governmentís approval to retrench their work force, and the Contract Labour (Regulation & Abolition) Act, 1970, which restricts outsourcing of core activities.

These laws make it difficult for employers to respond flexibly to changes in demand when necessary and have the net effect of discouraging the growth of strong labour absorbing sectors. However, there is as yet no consensus on labour reforms. Given the vital need for such reforms to foster industrial development, it is imperative that the search for consensus must continue. In the meantime, on the request of state governments, selective exemption from the applicability of the above two laws could be considered for special economic zones (SEZs) and export-oriented units (EOUs) and even in the larger SERs.

References

Acharya, Shankar (2003), *India's Economy: Some Issues and Answers*, Academic Foundation.

Ahluwalia, Isher J. (1985), *Industrial Growth in India: Stagnation Since the Mid-Sixties*, Oxford University Press.

——— (1991), *Productivity and Growth in Indian Manufacturing*, Oxford University Press.

Bhagwati, Jagdish, and Desai, Padma (1970), *India: Planning for Industrialization*, Oxford University Press.

Desai, Ashok V. (2002), "*A Decade of Reforms*" in A Decade of Economic Reforms in India: The Past, The Present and The Future (ed.) Raj Kapila and Uma Kapila, Academic Foundation.

Govt. of India, *Economic Survey*, various years including 2004-05.

Mohan, Rakesh (1992), *Industrial Policy and Controls* in Bimal Jalan (Ed.): The Indian Economy, Problems and Prospects, Viking Penguin India.

——— (2000), *Small Scale Industry Policy in India: A Critical Evaluation*, NCAER, (June).

Nagaraj, R. (2004), "Fall in Organised Manufacturing Employment: A Brief Note", *Economic and Political Weekly*, Vol. 39, No. 30, July.

Nayyar, Deepak (1996), *Economic Liberalisation in India: Analytics Experiences and Lessons*, R C Dutt Lectures, Orient Longman.

Planning Commission (2001), Approach Paper to Tenth Five Year Plan (September).

——— (2002), Tenth Five Year Plan (2002-07) (December).

——— (2005), Mid-Term Appraisal of the Tenth Five Year Plan (June).

——— (2002), Report of the Steering Group on FDI (August).

Rangarajan, C. (2003), *Select Essays on Indian Economy (Vol.1)*, Academic Foundation.

Reserve Bank of India, Report on Currency and Finance, 1998-99, 2000-01, 2001-02 and 2003-04.

18

Industrial Growth and Diversification

K.L. Krishna

1. Introduction

Since independence industrial policy in India has stressed rapid industrial growth with diversification of the industrial structure as one of the important objectives of industrialisation. There is general agreement that while India has achieved a very diversified industrial structure, her growth performance leaves much to be desired, both with regard to the magnitude of the growth rate and its stability over time. Three phases of growth have been distinguished: a phase of rapid growth from the early 1950s to the mid-1960s; a phase of deceleration from the mid-1960s to late-1970s; and a phase of revival in the late 1970s followed by rapid growth in the 1980s. Several explanations have been offered in the literature to account for the deceleration/stagnation in the second phase and for the resurgence of growth in the third phase. This essay seeks to examine the empirical evidence on growth and diversification over the 40-year period 1951-90. It reviews the attempts at verification of the explanatory hypotheses put forth to account for the deceleration in the second phase and revival/resurgence in the third phase.

The plan of the essay is as follows:

The nature and the quality of the data for the study of industrial growth and diversification are assessed in section 2.

In section 3, we present the growth trends in the industrial sector and its sub-sectors over the period 1951-90, and attempt an overall assessment of the growth performance. Section 4 deals with diversification of the industrial structure; it has been shown that Indian record is quite creditable in this respect. The issue of deceleration in growth in the second phase is the subject matter of section 5. Here we summarize the evidence and review the various attempts to explain the phenomenon of deceleration. The growth experience of the 1980's is studied in section 6, where apart from presenting the growth rates for the 1980's for the registered and unregistered segments of manufacturing at the aggregate level, we study the growth rates and shares for two-digit industry groups in the two segments. Section 7 provides the summary and conclusions of the essay.

2. Sources of Data on Industrial Output/Value Added

It will be useful to indicate briefly the nature and quality of the data on output and value added for the different subsectors of the industrial sector.

The industrial sector consists of three broad subsectors: (i) Manufacturing, (ii) Mining and Quarrying, sometimes referred to as Mining sub-sector and (iii) Electricity, Gas and Water Supply, sometime, referred to as Electricity sub-sector. The manufacturing sub-sector with a value added share of about 80 per cent in the industrial sector has two broad sub-divisions; (a) the Factory Sector, referred to as Registered or Organized Manufacturing Sector, consisting of all manufacturing enterprises registered under the Indian Factories Act of 1948, and (b) the Non-Factory Sector or Unregistered Manufacturing Sector consisting of all manufacturing enterprises which are not registered under the Indian Factories Act. It covers all manufacturing units employing less than 10 workers, if using power, or less than 20 workers if not using power. Thus it includes household enterprises and small-scale non-household enterprises. This sector has considerable overlap with the so-called Modern Small Scale Sector.

There are two distinct sources of output/value added data for the industrial sector: (1) National Accounts Statistics (NAS) and (2) the Index of Industrial Production (IIP), both compiled and published by the Central Statistical Organisation. The revised (or new) series of National Accounts Statistics with 1980-81 as the base year are available for the fiscal year 1950-51 onwards. The concepts, definitions, sources of basic data and methods used in the preparation of National Accounts with base 1980-81 are described in detail in the publication, Central Statistical Organization (1989), *National Accounts Statistics: Sources and Methods*.

The current IIP with the base 1980-81=100, covers 352 items.

The first index of industrial production (IIP) had the base 1950-51=100. The number of items included was quite small, 88, in relation to the total number of items produced in the industrial sector in the post-independence era. There was a progressive increase in the number of items included in the subsequent IIPs (201 for the IIP with base 1956, 312 for the IIP with base 1960, 352 for both the IIP's with bases 1970 and 1980-81). Soon after the introduction of the IIP with 1980-81 as base, a view was expressed that it exaggerated the true industrial growth. Nagaraj (1990) has demonstrated that this criticism was unfounded. He has shown that compared to the Annual Survey of Industries (ASI) data, IIP (1980-81=100) under estimated output growth in several branches of industry. Until July 1991, IIP (1980-81=100) was based on production data received largely from the DGTD (Directorate General of Technical Development) and the weighting diagram, based on the value added data for 1980-81 was derived from the Annual Survey of Industries (ASI). The production data of the DGTD were based on voluntary response from the producers. There have been some slippages in data reporting after the delicensing of most industries since July 1991 and subsequent winding up of the DGTD. Furthermore, the small scale industries (SSI) sector which makes a substantial contribution to manufacturing value added (MVA) in the Indian industrial economy remains under-represented in the weighting diagram due to non-availability of data. Several researchers have highlighted the inadequacies of the IIP data and expressed their preference for the National Accounts data. An advantage of the index is that it is available on a monthly basis and with a time lag of only a few months. Government of India's Economic Survey for different years reports IIP data.

National Accounts data for registered manufacturing, based on the Annual Survey of Industries, appear to be of reasonable quality. However, the estimates of GVA (Gross Value Added) at constant prices are obtained by single deflation method, rather than the double deflation method. For unregistered manufacturing, the estimates of value added for a bench mark year are extended to other years on the basis of suitable indicators of physical output/input. In the new series with 1980-81 as the base year, estimates for this sector have been revised on the basis of data on the production of cloth in the decentralised sector and changes in the bench mark estimates using data from NSSO (National Sample Survey Organization). The periodic surveys provide data on input and output once in five years only and the problem of preparing estimates for intervening years remains to be addressed. This limitation of the data for unregistered manufacturing has to be kept in mind while using the data.

The data for the sub-sectors Mining and Quarrying and Electricity, Gas and Water Supply are also of relatively good quality.

3. Growth Trends in the Era of Planning

The growth rates of GVA in the sub-sectors of the industrial sector, in the agricultural sector and in the entire economy over the period 1950-51 to 1989-90 are presented in Table 18.1. It may be observed that over the 40-year period, 1950-89, as well as over the two sub-periods, 1950-1980 and 1980-1989, each of the sub-sectors within the industrial sector grew faster than the economy as a whole and the agricultural sector. Within the industrial sector, the electricity sub-sector displayed the highest growth of 8.8 to 9.5 per cent per annum throughout. The sub-sector, registered manufacturing, out-performed unregistered manufacturing in each period. The growth rate in the 1980s was far above that in the earlier three decades, in all subsectors of industry, except Electricity. The average rate of growth of MVA increased impressively from 5.1 per cent in 1950-80 to 6.8 per cent in 1980-89. MVA in the factory sector increased from 6.0 to 7.5 per cent, while that in the non-factory sector increased from 4.2 to 5.7 per cent per annum. Thus the decade of the 1980s was characterized by relatively high growth rates in the two broad divisions of manufacturing. This aspect will be considered further in one of the sections later.

TABLE – 18.1

Sectoral Growth Rates of GDP at Factor Cost (1980-81 prices)

(percent per annum)

Sector	1950-51 to 1989-90	1950-51 to 1980-81	1980-81 to 1989-90
(1)	(2)	(3)	(4)
1. Agriculture, Forestry and Fishing	2.3	2.1	2.9
2. Mining and Quarrying	4.9	4.5	6.4
3. Manufacturing	5.2	5.1	6.8
3.1 Registered	5.8	6.0	7.5
3.2 Unregistered	4.3	4.2	6.7
4. Electricity, Gas and Water	8.8	9.5	8.8
Total GDP	**3.7**	**3.5**	**5.2**

Source : Dandekar (1992)
Note : The growth rates have been obtained from semi-log trend regressions.

The rising value added shares of industry and its major branches over the period 1950-51 to 1989-90 are described in Table 18.2. The share of industry increased substantially over the 15 year period 1950-51 to 1965-66, from 12.8 to 19.1 per cent. The increase was marginal over the sub-sequent 15 year period, 1965-66 to 1980-81, from 19.1 to 20.8 per cent. The structural change in favour of industry again gained momentum in the 1980's. At the end of that decade, industry accounted for a little more than one quarter (25.1 per cent) of total GDP.

TABLE – 18.2

Sectoral Shares in GDP at 1980-81 Prices: 1950-51 to 1989-90

(Percent)

Sector	1950-51	1965-66	1980-81	1985-86	1989-90
1. Agriculture, Forestry and Fishing	54.7	43.2	38.0	34.1	31.4
2. Mining and Quarrying	1.1	1.5	1.5	1.7	1.9
3. Manufacturing	11.4	16.7	17.7	20.0	21.0
3.1 Registered	5.4	9.5	10.0	12.3	13.1
3.2 Unregistered	6.0	7.2	7.7	7.6	7.0
4. Electricity, Gas and Water	0.3	0.9	1.6	2.0	2.2
5. Industry = (2)+(3)+(4)	12.8	19.1	20.8	23.7	25.1
6. Services	32.5	37.4	41.2	42.2	43.5
Total	**100.0**	**100.0**	**100.0**	**100.0**	**100.0**

Source: CSO, National Accounts Statistics, various issues.

The share of registered manufacturing in GDP increased impressively from 5.4 to 13.1 per cent over the forty-year period. The increase in the case of unregistered manufacturing was not striking, its share increasing from 6.0 to around 7.5 per cent.

The contribution of manufacturing to industrial value added showed a progressive decline from about 89 per cent in 1950-51 to a little less than 84 per cent in 1989-90. (See Table 18.3) This decline is a reflection of the consistently higher growth achieved in the Electricity sub-sector. Within the manufacturing sector, the large scale (or registered) sub-sector improved its share from 49.4 to 62.4 per cent over the four-decades under review.

To sum up, over the 40 year period 1950-90, both the factory and non-factory branches of manufacturing, displayed higher growth rates of value added than the agriculture sector and the Indian economy at large, with the factory sub-sector performing much better. The growth record of the two branches improved considerably during the 1980s. The four-decades under review witnessed significant structural change in favour of industry and factory sector, in particular, in terms of value added.

TABLE – 18.3

Share of Manufacturing in Industrial GVA and Share of Registered Manufacturing in Total Manufacturing GVA

	1950-51	1965-66	1980-81	1985-86	1989-90
Share of Manufacturing in Industry (%)	89.1	87.4	85.1	84.4	83.7
Share of Registered Manufacturing in Total Manufacturing (%)	47.4	56.9	56.5	62.0	62.4

Source: CSO, National Accounts Statistics, various issues.

However, the growth performance of the industrial/manufacturing sector in India cannot be regarded as satisfactory in comparison with that in several other economies such as China, South Korea, Thailand, Pakistan and Malaysia (See Table 18.4). The performance of South Korea, China and Thailand was very impressive throughout the period 1965-90.

TABLE – 18.4

Average Annual Growth Rate (percent) of GDP in Industry and Manufacturing in India and some other Developing Countries: 1965-80 and 1980-90

Country	Industry		Manufacturing	
	1965-80	1980-90	1965-80	1980-90
(1)	(2)	(3)	(4)	(5)
India	4.2	6.6	4.1	7.1
China	10.0	12.5	8.9	14.4
Pakistan	6.4	7.3	5.7	7.7
Thailand	9.5	9.0	11.2	8.9
S. Korea	16.4	12.2	18.7	12.7
Turkey	7.2	6.2	7.5	7.2
Malaysia	—	7.1	—	8.8
Indonesia	11.9	5.6	12.0	12.5

Source: World Bank, World Development Report, 1992, Table 2, pages 220-21.

The industrial growth rates actually achieved invariably fell short of the targets set in the successive Five Year Plans (see Table 18.5). The target was marginally exceeded only in the First Five Year Plan. In the Seventh Plan spanning the second half of the 1980's, the target of 8.7 per cent was nearly achieved, reflecting the improvement in the performance during the 1980s.

TABLE – 18.5

Growth Rates of Industrial Production

(Percent per annum)

Five Year/Annual Plan (s)	Target	Actual
(1)	(2)	(3)
I 1951-52 to 1955-56	7.0	7.3
II 1956-57 to 1960-61	10.5	6.6
III 1961-62 to 1965-66	11.0	9.0
Annual Plans 1966-67 to 1968-69	—	2.0
IV 1969-70 to 1973-74	12.0	4.7
V 1974-75 to 1978-79	8.0	5.9
Annual Plan 1979-80	—	1.4
VI 1980-81 to 1984-85	8.0	5.9
VII 1985-86 to 1989-90	8.7	8.5

Source: Ahluwalia (1991), Table 1.1, page 11.

4. Diversification of the Industrial Sector

The most striking feature of Indian industrialisation is the extent of diversification it achieved in a relatively short period. Self-reliance through the building of heavy industry was emphasized in the strategy formulated by Mahalanobis in the mid-fifties and India launched a major drive for industrial diversification. Steps were taken for the establishment of machine tool industries, heavy electricals, machine building and other branches of heavy engineering industries. With a substantial increase in the output of basic chemicals coupled with the introduction of new chemical products, chemical industry grew rapidly. In spite of certain setbacks after 1965, progress in regard to diversification of the industrial structure was maintained. Table 18.6 depicts the progress over the period 1951-90 in respect of structural transformation.

TABLE – 18.6

Diversification within the Industrial Sector

(Weights of use-based sectors in the Index of Industrial Production)

	1956	1960	1970	1980	1990
Basic Goods	22.3	25.1	32.3	39.4	38.4
Intermediate Goods	24.6	25.9	20.9	17.5	17.5
Capital Goods	4.7	11.8	15.2	16.4	23.7
Consumer Goods	48.4	37.2	31.5	23.7	20.5
Non-durables	—	(31.6)	(28.1)	(21.1)	—
Durables	—	(5.7)	(3.4)	(2.6)	—
Industry	**100.0**	**100.0**	**100.0**	**100.0**	**100.0**

Sources: (1) Sandesara (1992), Table 3.2
(2) Mohan (1992), Table 3

The share of Capital Goods in industrial value added increased steadily at a high pace from 4.7 per cent in 1956 to 23.7 per cent in 1990. The share of Basic Goods increased relatively moderately, from 22.3 per cent to 38.4 per cent. Consumer Goods group declined considerably in relative importance, with the share in industrial value added falling from 48.4 per cent in 1956 to 20.5 per cent in 1990. Much of the structural change in favour of Capital and Basic Goods industries was achieved by 1965-66. Table 18.7 relating to the growth rates according to use-based and input-based classifications of industries in registered industry shows that the growth in Capital Goods and Basic Goods during 1959-60 to 1965-66 far exceeded that during 1966-67 to 1979-80. This pattern of growth is reflected in the high growth rate of 14.1 per cent per annum during 1959-60 to 1965-66 achieved in the metal-based industries.

In Table 18.8, we compare the structure of manufacturing value added (MVA) in India and some other countries in the years 1970 and 1989. In 1970, India had higher shares of MVA in Machinery and Transport Equipment group and Chemicals group of industries than S. Korea, Pakistan, Thailand and Turkey. India retained this supremacy even in 1989 in the chemicals sector. However, S. Korea attained a higher share (30 per cent) in Machinery and Transport Equipment than India (26 per cent). In the year 1989 the structure of manufacturing value added in India was quite similar to that in China. During 1970-89, heavy industry

TABLE – 18.7

Diversification in Organized Industry: Annual Growth Rates of NVA according to Use-based and Input-based Classifications 1959-60 to 1965-66, 1966-67 to 1979-80, 1959-60 to 1979-80

(Percent per annum)

Industry group	1959-60 to 1965-66	1966-67 to 1979-80	1959-60 to 1979-80
A: Use based classification			
Total organised industry	8.0	5.7	5.6
1. Basic goods	11.0	5.9	6.2
2. Intermediate goods	5.7	4.5	4.2
3. Capital goods	15.4	6.6	8.1
4. Consumer goods	4.7	5.0	4.9
(a) Durable	11.5	10.8	10.7
(b) Non-durable	4.2	5.0	4.3
B: Input-based classification			
1. Agro-based	3.7	4.4	3.2
2. Metal based	14.1	6.5	7.8
3. Chemical based	8.2	8.1	8.6

Source: Ahluwalia (1985), Tables 2.5 and 2.6

Notes: (1) Growth rates are based on semi-log trend regressions. Data are in 1970-71 prices.

(2) Electricity, Gas and Water sub-sector is excluded.

consisting of Machinery and Transport Equipment sector and Chemicals Sector improved its share from 34 to 43 per cent. The share of light industry consiting of Food, Beverages and Tobacco sectors and Textiles and Clothing sector declined from 34 to 23 per cent.

5. The Deceleration Debate

5.1 Introduction

Nagaraj (1990) found that total GDP and GVA in the major sectors including the industrial sector grew much faster between 1980-81 and 1987-88 than in the earlier three decades. Bhargava and Joshi (1990) documented that growth in VA in the registered manufacturing sector between 1980-81 and 1986-87 was significantly higher than that during the preceding two decades. Ahluwalia (1991), after a systematic search

TABLE – 18.8

Structure of Manufacturing in India and Some Other Countries: 1970 and 1989

Country	Value added in manufacturing (millions of current dollars)		Distribution of MVA (per cent; current prices)									
			Food, Beverages, & Tobacco		Textiles and Clothing		Machinery & Transport Equipment		Chemicals		Others	
	1970	1989	1970	1989	1970	1989	1970	1989	1970	1989	1970	1989
(1)	(2)	(3)	(4)	(5)	(6)	(7)	(8)	(9)	(10)	(11)	(12)	(13)
India	7,928	44,445	13	11	21	12	20	26	14	17	32	33
China	27,555	1,45,646	—	12	—	14	—	26	—	12	—	36
S. Korea	1,880	66,215	26	12	17	14	11	30	11	9	36	36
Pakistan	1,462	5,923	24	30	38	19	6	8	9	16	23	27
Thailand	1,130	17,635	43	29	13	18	9	13	6	7	29	33
Turkey	1,930	18,030	26	17	15	15	8	14	7	14	45	41
U.S.A.	2,54,115	—	12	12	8	5	31	31	10	11	39	40

Source: World Development Report, 1992, Table 6, Pages 228-229.

using data on VA in the registered manufacturing sector for the years 1965-66 to 1985-86, concluded that significant revival in growth began in 1980-81.

Thus three distinct phases of industrial growth in India in the planning era can be identified. The first phase of rapid growth ends in around 1964-65. The second phase of slow growth or deceleration extends from 1965-66 to 1979-80. The decade of the 1980s was characterized by recovery and revival of growth.

The issue of deceleration in industrial growth engaged the attention of several economists for more than two decades. Nayyar (1994) has put together in a volume a number of important papers published in Economic and Political Weekly all dealing with industrial growth and stagnation and he contributed a perceptive introduction to the volume.

In the next sub-section we shall outline the various explanatory hypotheses offered to account for the deceleration and in sub-section 5.3 we shall review the available empirical evidence bearing upon the alternative hypotheses.

5.2 The Nature of Deceleration

Ahluwalia (1985) documented with meticulous care the facts about deceleration in the various branches of industry. She presented average annual growth rates in value added and value of output in constant (1970-71) prices at different levels of industrial aggregation for the entire period 1959-80 and for the two sub-periods 1959-65 and 1966-80. On the strength of careful painstaking research, Ahluwalia drew attention to the shortcomings of the industrial production (index) data which were made use of in most of the earlier studies of industrial deceleration. She relied upon the Annual Survey of Industries (ASI) data and the National Accounts data, the latter being the same as ASI data adjusted for variations in coverage. The growth rates calculated from the National Accounts data were in most cases found to be different from those calculated from the industrial production data. The National Accounts data revealed that deceleration was confined to capital goods and basic goods industries, while the industrial production data indicated deceleration in almost all industry groups. Reference may be made to Table-2.10 in Ahluwalia (1985), for details.

Average annual growth rates of net value added for the period 1959-60 to 1979-80 and for the sub-periods 1959-60 to 1965-66 and 1966-67 to 1979-80 for industry groups according to use-based and input-based classification calculated by Ahluwalia (1985) are presented in Table 18.8.

During the first sub-period, net value added in the registered industrial sector grew at an average rate of 8.0 per cent per annum. In the post-1965 period the growth rate was substantially lower at 5.7 per cent. The corresponding growth rates for registered manufacturing were 7.6 and 5.5 per cent. In capital goods industries and basic goods industries, the decline was very pronounced, from 15.4 to 6.6 per cent and 11.0 to 5.0 per cent, respectively. However, consumer goods and its main subcategory consumer non-durables experienced mild acceleration. Intermediate goods and consumer durables too experienced only mild deceleration. Thus, deceleration was largely confined to heavy industry, consisting of basic and capital goods industries. These two groups together accounts for about 50 per cent of the total value added in the industry in 1979-80.

In the input-based classification, only the metal-based category suffered marked deceleration from a growth rate of 14.1 per cent in the pre-1965 period to 6.1 per cent in the subsequent period.

Ahluwalia's results for the 2-digit level industries showed that significant deceleration in growth occured only among industries which had grown at an annual rate of 5 per cent or more during 1959-65. These medium or fast growth industries together had a value added share of 63 per cent in total registered manufacturing. Of these, industries with a value added share of 47 per cent suffered significant decelerations.

It is important to note that earlier studies using production data came to the conclusion that deceleration in growth was across the board. Ahluwalia's results using National Accounts data showed that deceleration was concentrated in heavy industries and in high or medium growth industries. This finding has important implications for the empirical plausibility of the alternative explanations offered to account for the decelerations.

5.3 Alternative Explanatory Hypotheses and Empirical Evidence

The spectrum of explanatory hypotheses is rather wide. The important ones are:

(a) Performance of the agricultural sector (Chakravarty, 1974; Raj 1976; Mitra 1977; and Vaidyanathan (1977). The unsatisfactory performance of the agriculture sector has an impact on industrial growth via the demand-supply linkages between the two sectors.

(b) Income distribution

As pointed out by Ahluwalia (1985), the hypotheses focussing on income distribution are of two types:

(i) those relating to pattern of demand (Mitra, 1977, Nayyar, 1978)

(ii) others relating to the level of demand and therefore savings (Bagchi, 1970, Chakravarty, 1979)

(c) Slowdown in public investment and the infrastructural constraint (Srinivasan and Narayana, 1977, Patnaik and Rao, 1977; Rangarajan, 1982)

(d) Slowdown in import substitution (Ahluwalia, 1985)

(e) Industrial and foreign trade policies in India (Bhagwati and Srinivasan, 1975; and Ahluwalia, 1985)

Several economists have tried to empirically verify some of the above explanatory hypotheses. Some of them have tended to believe that there is a single explanation to account for the observed pattern of industrial growth. Some of the explanations offered and tested may not be relevant in the light of Ahluwalia's finding that deceleration was confined to the group of heavy industries.

Here, we shall outline the findings of Ahluwalia and make a brief reference to a test by Rangarajan (1982), and then draw attention to the findings of studies by Lahiri et al (1984), Ray (1991) Mukhopadhyay (1992) and Kavita Rao (1993).

On the basis of detailed empirical analysis, Ahluwalia concluded that four factors contributed to the observed deceleration since the mid-sixties:

(i) slowdown in public investment and the resulting inadequate infrastructure investment.

(ii) poor management of the infrastructure sector;

(iii) slow growth of agricultural incomes and the resulting slow growth in demand for industrial products and

(iv) restrictive industrial and foreign trade policies leading to high-cost industrial structure.

She found no empirical support for the important hypothesis that deceleration was due to deterioration in income distribution. Similarly, there was no support for the hypothesis of wage goods constraint. The evidence in regard to import substitution as an explanatory factor was found to be mixed.

However, it must be added that Ahluwalia did not test the explanatory hypotheses in a suitable methodological framework. The fact that a given possible explanatory factor, say infrastructure investment, displayed inter-temporal variations, does not necessarily imply that this factor explained the variations in industrial output. Such issues should be investigated with the help of suitable econometric exercises. Ahluwalia's conclusions would have carried better conviction had they been derived from suitably estimated quantitative relationships.

Rangarajan (1982) estimated a model from data for the period 1960-72 to study the impact of agricultural growth on industrial growth and showed that a 1.0 per cent growth rate in agriculture could by itself generate a rate of growth of 0.5 per cent in industry. The effects of agricultural growth on the output of capital and basic goods industries are found to be less strong than the effects on the output of consumer goods industries.

Lahiri et al (1984) estimated an econometric model of the price-quantity adjustment mechanism in the factory sector of Indian industry with specific attention to the role of government policies and international trade in the determination of output and prices. A disaggregated four-sector framework with industries classified on the basis of end use-consumer goods, capital goods, basic goods and intermediate goods-was adopted. The model was estimated from annual data for 1961 to 1977 by ordinary least squares. The major determinants of output were found to be (i) real government expenditure (ii) real exports (iii) real income of the primary sector and (iv) availability of credit. The study provided evidence in support of the hypothesis emphasized by Raj (1976) and Chakravarty (1979) about real income of the agricultural/primary sector as a source of demand for the industrial sector. Significant differences were found in the behaviour patterns of the four sub-sectors. The model formulation emphasized the role of demand factors. The authors believed that supply bottlenecks were not very important in this context. This should have been tested in the model framework.

Ray (1991) made a useful contribution in testing the different explanatory hypotheses. He examined the supply demand linkages between agriculture and industry and also availability of power as determinants of the rate of growth of manufacturing output during 1951-84. The nature of the dynamic relationship between manufacturing output growth rate, the internal terms of trade, availability of foodgrains, agricultural, income and availability of power was studied through time series methodology. Ray's empirical results suggest that increase in food availability stimulated manufacturing output growth with a two-year lag by relaxing the wage goods constraint. Increase in agricultural income had an immediate impact through demand stimulation. Slow growth in power supply had been a serious impediment in the growth of manufacturing output.

It would be worthwhile to apply Ray's methodology to the analysis of output growth in individual sectors such as capital goods, consumer goods and intermediate goods. The role of public investment should be explored in the same methodological framework.

Mukhopadhyay (1992) estimated a demand-supply model for the industrial sector and found that industrial stagnation was due to the demand constraint. However, the relative importance of the different demand side factors could not be assessed. Mukhopadhyay carried out a separate analysis of the capital goods sector and concluded that slowdown in public investment was the cause of deceleration.

Kavita Rao (1993) attempted a study of industrial output determination over the four decades 1951-1990 in the "dual economy" framework. The reduced form of a model of output determination was estimated separately for consumer goods group, capital goods group and intermediate goods group of industries. On the basis of the empirical results, the author concluded that demand side variables, namely, public expenditure and income accruing to agricultural sector, provided a reasonably satisfactory explanation. In the equation for the capital goods group of industries, the policy of import substitution was found to be a relevant factor. The omission of infrastructure, which was found to be relevant in Ray's (1991) study, is a limitation of the Kavita Rao study. Exclusive reliance on the IIP as a measure of output was not justified, because the item coverage of the index was partial and it varied over the four decades. Data from the Annual Survey of Industries (ASI) and National Accounts Statistics should have been used to supplement the analysis based on the IIP data.

Balakrishnan (1995) applied the new time series methodology to analyse the daterminants of industrial output in India during 1952-80. His results indicated that three variables, namely, agricultural production, public investment and domestic terms of trade, together explained the short run variations in industrial output.

Econometric models of the kind estimated by Rangarajan (1982), Lahiri et al. (1984), Ray (1991) Mukhopadhyay (1992), Kavita Rao (1995) and Balakrishnan (1995) provided useful empirical evidence as to what were the causal factors behind slowdown in industrial growth. One or more of the following factors, public investment, agricultural performance, infrastructure, the policy of import substitution and domestic terms of trade turned out to be significant for the different industry groups. On the whole, demand side factors were found to be more important than supply side factors.

6. Growth Experience of the 1980s

6.1 Pattern of Growth

The industrial sector in India fared quite impressively in the 1980s in terms of growth of output/value added, compared to the earlier period 1966-79. There has been much discussion in recent literature on the pattern of growth in the 1980s and the factors behind the observed pattern. In this section we shall look at the available empirical evidence in some detail and review the explanations offered to account for the improved growth performance. The re-orientation of industrial and trade policies initiated in the mid-1970s received a fillip in 1985 with the introduction of some major policy reforms. It would be instructive to see whether the growth performance in the second half of the 1980s was superior to that in the first half.

Table 18.9 presents average annual growth rates in GVA for the entire economy, the agriculture sector and the different sub-sectors of the industrial sector for the 1970s, 1980's and the two halves of the 1980s. It will be observed that there was appreciable increase in the growth rate in the 1980s in all the sectors/sub-sectors for which comparable figures are given in the table. The growth rate of manufacturing value added (MVA) increased from 4.9 in 1970s to 7.0 per cent per annum in 1980s and contributed much to the rise in the overall growth rate of the economy. Within the manufacturing sector, the registered segment grew at 8.1 per cent while the unregistered segment grew much less impressively at 5.8 per cent per annum.

Comparing the two halves of the 1980s, we observe that with the exception of registered manufacturing, all sectors/sub-sectors shown in Table 18.9 fared better in the second half. The unregistered manufacturing sub-sector improved its growth rate considerably from 4.1 to 7.5 per cent per annum and this improvement alone is responsible for the observed increase in the growth rate of the manufacturing sector from 6.2 to 7.8 per cent. The expectation that the policy changes undertaken in 1985 would have a direct positive impact on the growth performance of the registered manufacturing sector was belied, the growth rate of this sub-sector being the same in the two halves of the 1980s. However, it must be noted that the growth rate of this sub-sector accelerated from 0.5 per cent in 1986-87 to 7.1, 10.6 and 13.8 in 1987-88, 1988-89 and 1989-90, respectively. The year 1986-87 appears to be an exceptionally bad year for this sub-sector.

TABLE – 18.9

Sectoral Average Annual Rates of Growth of GVA: 1970-80, 1980-90 (at 1980-81 prices)

(per cent per annum)

Sector	1970-71 to 1979-80	1980-81 to 1989-90	1980-81 to 1984-85	1985-86 to 1989-90
Agriculture, forestry and fishing	1.7	2.4	1.2	3.6
Mining and quarrying	4.6[a]	8.5	8.2	9.0
Manufacturing	4.9[a]	7.0	6.2	7.8
Registered	—	8.1	8.1	8.1
Unregistered	—	5.8	4.1	7.5
Electricity, Gas and Water	7.4[a]	8.7	7.9	9.5
Industry	—	7.6	7.2	8.0
Total GDP	**3.4[a]**	**5.9**	**5.6**	**6.2**

Notes: Figures with superscript (a) are growth rates based on semi-log trend regressions.

Sources: (1) Dandekar (1992)
(2) CSO, National Accounts Statistics, various issues.

Table 18.10 provides the trend growth rates for the period 1980-81 to 1985-86 for consumer goods, capital goods and intermediate goods groups within registered manufacturing, and compares the growth rates for this period with those for the earlier periods 1959-65 and 1966-79. There was an all round increase in the growth rate during 1980-81 to 1985-86, compared to the growth rates in the deceleration phase, 1966-67 to 1979-80. The increase from 8.0 to 14.2 per cent was very steep in the case of consumer durables, while the increase was quite moderate for the other three sub-sectors; in the case of capital goods the increase was from 6.7 to 7.8 per cent, whereas during 1959-60 to 1965-66 this vital sector displayed the highest growth rate of 15.6 per cent. These features of growth in the 1980s have received much comment from several economists. Some were sceptical about the sustainability of the high rates of growth. It was argued that both demand and supply factors would work to slow down the growth in later years. The rise in real incomes of people in the middle income categories in the 1980s gave rise to large demand for consumer durables. Once the repressed demand from previous years was met, rates of growth would come down. Since industrial growth of the 1980s was import and energy intensive with little potential for employment generation, it would face severe resource constraints. [See Patnaik (1988, 1989), Kurien (1989) and Mundle (1989)]. Kelkar and Kumar (1990) argued that policy changes of the 1980s tended to give wrong signals, creating a bias in favour of chemical based industries as opposed to metal based industries in which the country had a comparative advantage; by relying on non-tariff forms of protection in conjunction with liberalised entry the policy resulted in "excessive entry, high costs of production and lack of competitive quality in domestic industries". Ahluwalia's (1991) findings showed that in registered manufacturing employment declined by 0.7 per cent and capital intensity increased by 8.4 per cent per annum during 1980-81 to 1985-86.

TABLE – 18.10

Growth rates of Value Added in Registered Manufacturing: Modified use-based classification

Sector	Share in VA in 1980-81	Annual Growth Rate		
		1959-60 to 1965-66	1966-67 to 1979-80	1980-81 to 1985-86
Intermediate goods	36.8	10.9	4.4	6.5
Capital goods	21.6	15.6	6.7	7.8
Consumer non-durables	35.1	5.0	4.8	7.6
Consumer durables	3.9	14.0	8.0	14.2
Registered Manufacturing	**100.0**	**9.1**	**5.0**	**7.5**

Source : Ahluwalia (1991)

Note : The growth rates were calculated through semilog trend regressions.

Before analysing the pattern of growth at a disaggregated level, let us consider the structure of the manufacturing sector at the beginning of the 1980s. The shares of the different 2-digit industry groups in manufacturing value added (MVA) in 1980-81 are given in col. 3 of Table 18.11. Three largest industry groups, namely, Textiles (with a share of 24.0%) chemicals (9.2%) and Basic Metals (7.6%) together accounted for more than two-fifths of MVA. Transport equipment (6.9%), Repair Services (6.7%), Non-electrical machinery (6.4%), Food Products (6.2%) Metal Products (5.2%) and Electrical Machinery (5.0%) had shares ranging between 5 and 7 per cent. The other six industry groups shown in col. 2 of Table 10 had a combined share of about 23 per cent only.

Let us now comment on the growth performance of the different industry groups. The figures are given in the last column of Table 18.11. Electrical machinery had a growth rate of 20.1 per cent. Rubber, Petroleum etc (11.6%), Chemicals etc (10.8%), Non-metallic mineral products (9.9%), Non-electrical machinery (9.3%), Food products (9.2%), Paper and Printing (9.2%), and Transport Equipment (8.6%) displayed above average growth rates. Among important industries, Textiles (4.9%), and Basic Metals (3.9%) grew slowly. High growth was registered in several industries belonging to either metal-based or chemical-based industry groups. Thus industrial growth in the 1980's was quite broad-based.

TABLE – 18.11

Shares in 1980-81 and Growth Rates Over the Period 1980-81 to 1986-87 of Two-digit Industry Groups in Manufacturing

NIC Code	Industry group	Share in MVA in 1980-81	Trend Growth Rate Over the Period 1980-81 to 1986-87 (per cent p.a.)
(1)	(2)	(3)	(4)
20-21	Food products	6.2	9.2
22	Beverages, Tobacco etc	2.6	3.3
23-26	Textiles	24.0	4.9
27	Wood, Furniture etc	4.5	– 3.0
28	Paper & Printing	3.3	9.2
29	Leather and Products	1.4	6.5
30	Rubber, Petroleum etc	3.2	11.6
31	Chemicals etc	9.2	10.8
32	Non-metallic mineral products	1.7	9.9
33	Basic Metals	7.6	3.9
34	Metal Products	5.2	5.7
35	Non-electrical machinery	6.4	9.3
36	Electrical machinery	5.0	20.1
37	Transport Equipment	6.9	8.6
38	Other manufactures	4.3	15.0
39	Repair Services	6.7	11.0
	Total Manufacturering	**100.0**	**8.3**

Source: (1) CSO, National Accounts Statistics
(2) Nagaraj (1989)

We shall now attempt a comparative study the registered and unregistered segments of the manufacturing sector. The percentage shares of the registered segment in manufacturing for the different 2-digit industry groups for the years 1980-81 and 1990-91 are given columns (3) and (4) of Table 18.12.

TABLE – 18.12

Industry Group Wise Shares of Registered Manufacturing in 1980-81, 1990-91 and Growth Rates of VA in Registered and Unregistered Segments of Manufacturing Over the Period 1980-81 to 1986-87

NIC Code	Industry Group	Share (%) of Regd. Manufacturing in Total Manufacturing		Trend Growth Rate (% p.a.) 1980-81 to 1986-87	
		1980-81	1990-91	Regd. Manuf.	Unregd. Manuf.
(1)	(2)	(3)	(4)	(5)	(6)
20-21	Food products	62	81	13.1	3.2
22	Beverages, tobacco etc.	43	59	9.9	– 0.8
23-26	Textiles	46	47	3.3	5.8
27	Wood, furniture etc.	07	15	6.1	– 4.4
28	Paper & printing	71	73	9.5	8.7
29	Leather & leather products	25	43	16.6	3.2
30	Rubber and Petroleum etc	86	91	12.3	7.5
31	Chemicals etc.	91	73	11.1	8.2
32	Non-metallic mineral products	62	75	16.2	2.1
33	Basic Metals	62	92	4.1	4.9
34	Metal Products	32	25	6.8	4.9
35	Non-elec. Machinery	69	71	10.3	5.5
36	Electrical Machinery	82	72	20.6	16.9
37	Transport Equipment	66	66	9.1	6.4
38	Other Manufacture	48	42	20.6	9.0
39	Repair Services	14	16	13.3	9.9
	All Industry Groups	**57**	**63**	**10.4**	**5.3**

Source: (1) CSO, National Accounts Statistics
(2) Nagaraj (1989)

In 1980-81, the registered segment had a value added share of 57 per cent in aggregate manufacturing and a share of at least 60 per cent in all the major industry groups except Textiles, Repair Services and Metal Products. The registered segment was particularly dominant in Chemicals, Electrical Machinery, Non-electrical Machinery and Transport Equipment. The unregistered segment had a dominant share in Wood, Furniture etc., Repair Services, Leather and Leather products and Metal products industries.

By 1990-91, the share of the registered segment in aggregate manufacturing rose to 63 per cent, and its share in most of the individual industry groups too increased, the exceptions being Metal Products, Electrical Machinery and other Manufacturing. Thus the relative importance of the unregistered segment declined in the aggregate and in most of the industry groups including Food products, and Beverages, Tobacco etc. However, in Textiles there was little change in the position of the unregistered segment.

The industry wise trend growth rates for the two segments for the period 1980-81 to 1986-87 are given columns 5 and 6 of Table 18.12. In all industries (industry groups) excepts Textiles and Basic Metals, the unregistered segment of manufacturing recorded lower growth rates than the registered segment. The relative slow down or decline of the unregistered segment was in evidence even in light industries like Food products, Wood, Furniture etc., Leather and Leather products, Repair services and Beverages, Tobacco etc. Such slow down occured in spite of the continuation of several promotional and protective measures for small industry. The observed relative slow down of this labour intensive segment of manufacturing during 1980s is cause for concern.

6.2 Factors Behind the Resurgence of Growth in the 1980s

Nagaraj (1990) and Ahluwalia (1991) have offered some explanations for the improved growth performance in the 1980's. These explanations are quite similar to those advanced for the decleration in growth after the mid-sixties.

Nagaraj presents some empirical evidence to show that (i) improvement in the rate and pattern of gross domestic capital formation in general and public investment in particular, (ii) better performance of infrastructure as a consequence, (iii) less adverse trends in intersectoral terms of trade in favour of non-agriculture, and (iv) increase in the use of manufactured inputs in crop production, in addition to changes in industrial and trade policies could have contributed to the revival of growth.

Drawing upon suitable data, Ahluwalia attributes the improvement in growth rate to (i) step-up in infrastructure investment and more efficient management of the infrastructure sectors, (ii) growth of per capita agricultural incomes, and (iii) reforms in the industrial and trade policies. According to her, as a consequence of (i) and (iii), there was improvement in Total Factor Productivity which contributed significantly to growth in value added. However, it may be noted that neither Nagaraj nor Ahluwalia tried to quantify the impacts of the different explanatory factors on the growth of value added or output.

The credit for quantifying the impacts of selected explanatory factors on output growth goes to Kavita Rao (1993) who, as mentioned in section 5, estimated output determination equations from data for the period 1951-52 to 1989-90 for three broad industry groups: Consumer Goods, (ii) Capital Goods and (iii) Intermediate Goods.

In the case of consumer goods group, Kavita Rao found that the response of output to a given increase in autonomous expenditure was greater in the 1980's than in the preceding three decades. A test of Nagaraj's (1990) hypothesis that growth in public investment contributed to output growth, was carried out for the capital goods sector. The results indicate that a given increase in the level of public investment brought about a higher increase in the level of output in the 1980s than in the earlier years. Imports of capital goods had a negative impact on the domestic production of capital goods during the period 1960-80, while during the early period of industrialisation 1951-59 capital good imports had no significant impact on domestic production.

Kavita Rao's study produced some useful evidence on important issues in a suitable analytical framework. While the exercise is notable for a careful econometric analysis of the issues, it suffers from three limitations: (i) It was based on index of industrial production (IIP) data, which has been found to be less accurate than the data from the Annual Survey of Industries or National Accounts (2) it did not examine the role of infrastructure, and (3) it did not take into account the possible non-stationarity of the data series.

7. Summary and Conclusion

This paper has attempted to study industrial growth and diversification during the four decades 1951-1990. The focus of the study is on the manufacturing sub-sector and its two branches, registered manufacturing and unregistered manufacturing. In section 2, we have commented on the nature and quality of the two main data sources for the study of growth of industrial output/value added: Index of Industrial Production (IIP) and National Accounts Statistics (NAS). IIP data are available on a monthly basis with a time leg of only few months; however, IIP does not cover small industries adequately and the data are perhaps less accurate than the National Accounts data. NAS provides information separately for registered manufacturing and unregistered manufacturing. The data for registered manufacturing, based on Annual Survey of Industries (ASI), is more accurate than that for unregistered manufacturing. In recent years, National Accounts data are being brought out with shorter time lags. In view of the better quality and coverage of National Accounts data, we have relied on this source of data, as far as possible.

We have considered in section 3 the broad trends in industrial growth in relation to trends in GDP growth and agricultural growth over the period 1951-90. Both the registered and unregistered branches of manufacturing displayed higher growth rates than the agriculture sector and the Indian economy at large, with the registered sub-sector performing much better. The four decades under review witnessed significant structural change in favour of industry and particularly registered manufacturing. However, the growth performance of Indian industry was inferior to that of China, Sourth Korea, Thailand, Malaysia and even Pakistan.

Section 4 deals with the most striking feature of Indian industrialisation, namely, diversification in favour of heavy industry. During 1970-89, heavy industry consisting of machinery, transport equipment and chemicals improved its share from 34 to 43 per cent of manufacturing value added (MVA); there was a corresponding reduction in light industry from 34 to 23 per cent.

Section 5 is devoted to the issue of deceleration in industrial growth. This issue was extensively debated for two decades or more. Deceleration had set in the mid-sixties and stagnant growth persisted till about the end of the seventies.

During the period 1959-60 to 1965-66, value added in organised industry grew at the rate of 8.0 per cent per annum. The growth rate declined to 5.7 per cent in the period 1966-67 to 1989-90. The corresponding growth rates for the registered manufacturing were 7.6 and 5.5 per cent. In capital goods and basic goods the decline was very pronounced from 15.4 to 6.6 and 11.0 to 5.0 per cent per annum, respectively. Consumer goods and its sub-category consumer non-durables experienced slight acceleration. In Intermediate goods and consumer durables, there was mild deceleration. Thus deceleration was largely confined to heavy industry which accounted for about 50% of value added in industry in 1979-80.

Ahluwalia (1985), who made a significant contribution to the debate, after empirically examining different hypotheses identified four factors:

(i) slow-down in public investment
(ii) poor management of the infrastructure sector
(iii) slow growth of agricultural incomes, and
(iv) restrictive industrial and trade policies.

However, Ahluwalia did not carry out any econometric exercise to establish her thesis. Rangarajan (1982), Lahiri et al (1984) Ray (1991) Mukhopadhyay (1992) Kavita Rao (1993) and Balakrishnan (1995) conducted econometric exercises to verify the various hypotheses. These exercises established that one or more of the following factors, public investment, agricultural performance, infrastructure, the policy of import substitution and domestic terms of trade turned out to be significant for the different industry groups. The over all inference from the various studies is that the demand constraints were more important than supply constraints.

The growth experience of the 1980's is the subject matter of section 6. The industrial sector fared impressively in this decade, compared to the preceding 15-year period. The annual rates of growth for manufacturing, registered manufacturing and unregistered manufacturing were 7.0, 8.1 and 5.8, respectively.

While there was increase in growth rate from 4.1 to 7.5 per cent in unregistered manufacturing in the second half of the 1980's compared to the first half, there was no improvement in the case of registered manufacturing.

In the first six years of the eighties, consumer durables recorded a growth rate of 14.2 per cent, while capital goods recorded a relatively modest growth of 7.8 per cent per annum.

Empirical evidence suggests that the explanations for the resurgence of growth in the 1980s are similar to those for the deceleration after the mid-sixties.

Our review of trends in industrial growth and diversification shows that in terms of growth the progress of industrialisation in India has been far below expectations and targets. While within the industrial sector a good measure of diversification has been achieved, the share of industry in aggregate GDP at the end of the 1980s was a meagre 25 per cent. In recent decades capital intensity in organised manufacturing increased to such an extent that the employment in organised manufacturing showed a decline.

In spite of special incentives and protection, unregistered manufacturing (small scale industry) grew much more slowly than organised manufacturing, in most industry groups. The long term viability of unregistered manufacturing appears to be in doubt.

It is hoped, thanks to the reform measures introduced since July 1991, that in the coming years Indian industry will contribute more substantially to overall growth and structural transformation of the economy.

Several aspects of Indian industrialisation other than growth and diversification have been studied in the literature. These aspects include labour absorption in the industrial sector, capacity utilization, total factor productivity, technological capability industrial competitiveness and growth of manufactured exports. There is need to review afresh the evidence on some of these aspects. Some have been covered in a volume recently edited by Mookherjee (1985).

References

Ahluwalia, I.J. (1985), *Industrial Growth in India*: Stagnation since the Mid-Sixties, Delhi, Oxford.

——— (1991), *Productivity and Growth in Indian Manufacturing, Delhi, Oxford.*

Bagchi, A.K. (1970), "Long-Term Constraints on India's Industrial Growth" in Robinson E.A.G. et al (ed.) *Economic Development in South Asia.*

Balakrishnan, P. (1995), "Industrial Prices and Output" in D. Mookherjee (ed.) *Indian Industry*, Delhi, Oxford.

Bhagawati, J.N. and Srinivasan, T.N. (1975), *Foreign Trade Regimes and Economic Development; India*, NBER, Columbia University Press.

Bhargava, S. and Joshi, V. (1990), "Increase in India's Growth Rate : Facts and a Tentative Explanation" EPW, December 1-8.

Chakravarty, S. (1974), "Reflections on the Growth Process in Indian Economy," Lecture at Administrative Staff College of India, Hyderabad.

——— (1979), "On the question of Home Market and Prospects for Indian Growth", EPW, Special Number, August.

Dandekar, V.M. (1992), "Forty Years After Independence" in Jalan, B. (ed.) *The Indian Economy: Problems and Prospects* Delhi, Viking Penguin India.

Central Statistical Organisation (1989a), National Accounts Statistics 1980-85 to 1986-87 New Delhi, Government of India.

——— (1989b), National Accounts Statistics (New Series) 1950-51 to 1979-80, New Delhi, Government of India.

——— (1989c), National Accounts Statistics: Sources and Methods, New Delhi, Government of India.

——— (1994), National Accounts Statistics 1994, New Delhi, Government of India.

Government of India, *Economic Survey,* various issues.

Kathuria, S. (1995), "Competitiveness of Indian Industry" in D. Mookherjee (Ed.) *Indian Industry*, Delhi, Oxford.

Kavita Rao, R (1993), Evaluating in a Dual Economy Framework The Indian Industrial

Performance During 1951-52 to 1989-90, Ph.D. Dissertation, Indian Statistical Institute, Calcutte.

Kelkar, V.L. and Kumar, R (1990), "Industrial Growth in the Eighties: Emerging Policy Issues", EPW, January 27.

Kurien, C.T., (1989), "Indian Economy in the 1980s and on to 1990s", EPW, April 15.

Lahiri, A.K. et al. (1984), "The Industrial Sector in India: A Quantitative Analysis", Economic and Political Weekly, Annual Number, August.

Mohan, Rakesh (1992), "Industrial Policy and Controls" in Jalan, B. (Ed.) *The Indian Economy: Problems and Prospects*, Delhi, Viking Penguin, India.

Mookherjee, D. (Ed.) (1995), *Indian Industry*, Delhi, Oxford.

Mukhopadhyay, H. (1992), An Analysis of Industrial Deceleration from the Mid-Sixties, Ph.D. dissertation, Jawaharlal Nehru University.

Mundle, S. (1989), "Growth, Acceleration and Fiscal Constraint", *Mainstream*, September 9.

Nagaraj, R. (1989), "Growth in Manufacturing Output since 1980: Some Preliminary Findings", EPW, July 1.

——— (1990), "Industrial Growth : Further Evidence and Towards an Explanation and Issues" EPW, October 13.

Nayyar, D. (1978), "Industrial Development in India: Some Reflection on Growth and Stagnation" *Economic and Political Weekly*, Special Number.

——— (Ed.) (1994), *Industrial Growth and Stagnation: The Debate in India*, Delhi, Oxford.

Patnaik, P. and Rao, S.K. (1977), "1975-76: Beginning of the End of Stagnation", *Social Scientist*, January-February.

Patnaik, P. (1987), "Recent Growth Experience of the Indian Economy: Some Comments", EPW, Annual Number, May.

——— (1988), "A perspective on the Recent Phase of India's Economic Development", *Social Scientist*, February.

Raj, K.N. (1976), "Growth and Stagnation in Indian Industrial Development" EPW, Annual Number.

Rangarajan, C. (1982), "Agricultural Growth and Industrial Performance in India" Research Report 33, International Food Policy Research Institute.

Ray, S.C. (1991), "Growth of Manufacturing Production in India: A Time Series Analysis", *Journal of Quantitative Economics* Vol 7, No. 1.

Sandesara, J.C. (1992), Industrial Policy and Planning : 1947-91, Delhi, Sage.

Sanjaya Lall (1991), "Explaining Industrial Success in the Developing World" in Balasubramanyam, V and Lall, S. (eds.) *Current Issues* in *Development Economics*, London, Macmillan.

Shetty, S.L. (1978), "Structural Retrogression in the Indian Economy since the Mid-Sixties" EPW, Annual Number.

Srinivasan, T.N., and Narayana, N.S.S. (1977), "Economic Performance in India since the Third Plan and its Implications for Policy" E.P.W. Annual Number, February.

Srivastava, V. (1994), The Impact of Liberalization on Productivity and Competition: A Panel Study of Indian Manufacturing, 1980-89, Ph.D. dissertation, Boston university.

Vaidyanathan, A. (1977), "Constraints on Growth and Policy Options", EPW, September 17, and December 17.

Weiss, J. (1988), *Industry in Developing Countries, London*, Croom Lem.

World Bank (1992), World Development Report 1992.

19

Industrial Policy and Performance since 1980

Which Way Now?

R. Nagaraj

India's manufacturing sector currently accounts for about 17 per cent of real (measured) GDP, 12 per cent of total workforce, and close to 80 per cent of merchandise exports. Over the past half century, this sector has grown at nearly 6 per cent per year; at over one-and-a-half times the growth rate of domestic output – representing a major break from the colonial past.[1]

The annual trend growth rate of total manufacturing gross value added (output, for short, hereafter) during the last two decades (1980-2000) is close to 7 per cent. While this represents a turnaround compared with the preceding period of 'relative stagnation' (1965-1980), the record is modest in contrast to China's (official) double-digit growth during this period, as also most other industrialising Asian economies (Table 19.1).

I

Evolution of Policy since 1980

Industrial Upturn in the 1980s: Around 1980, the initial year of our study period, there was considerable gloom about the immediate prospects for industrial growth, despite having a surplus of food and

I am grateful to K.V. Ramaswamy, C. Rammanohar Reddy and M.H. Suryanarayana for their comments and suggestions on an earlier draft of this study. None of them are responsible for the erros that remain.

foreign exchange stocks for a few years in the late 1970s – widely regarded as long-term constraints on India's economic growth. For a variety of reasons, lack of industrial demand, especially for investment goods, was widely accepted to be the principal reason for the relative stagnation since the mid-1960s. However, there was also an argument that the controls on output, investment and trade – popularly called the 'permit licence raj' – were stifling private initiative and wasting meagre public resources. Reportedly the controls led to widespread inefficiency in resource use, as reflected in poor total factor productivity growth, or in the economywide rise in incremental capital output ratios in the 1970s [Ahluwalia, 1985; Rangarajan, 1982]. The gloom was perhaps accentuated by the oil price and agricultural supply shocks in the late 1970s, together with political uncertainty as the Indian democracy entered the coalition era at the national level for the first time in 1977.

TABLE – 19.1

Industrial Growth in Asian Perspective, 1980-2000

(Per cent per year)

Country	Growth Rate
India	6.8
China	12.8
Indonesia	10.2
Korea	9.4
Malaysia	11.2
Singapore	7.7
Thailand	9.8

Note: Data are in constant (1996) dollar terms.
Source: World Development Indicators, 2002.

However, from 1980 onwards, after the domestic political uncertainty had ended, industrial policy witnessed greater pragmatism with a gradual loosening of controls, and a greater willingness to import technology and foreign private capital to modernise the manufacturing sector. Greater realism in policy-making also included stepping up of public investment in infrastructure and energy production (to insulate the economy from external shocks), rural development for diffusion of green revolution technology, and for a 'direct' attack on poverty. As the second oil shock was successfully met by increasing domestic oil production and import substitution in fertilisers in a short time, the second half of the 1980s witnessed considerable de-licensing and relaxation of import controls to upgrade the industrial technology – as reflected in Rajiv Gandhi's political slogan of taking the country to the 21st century! To achieve these, there was a greater reliance on the private corporate sector with fiscal incentives provided for stock market-based financing of industrial investment, as government faced a growing resource constraint to meet the ambitious planned investment target.

In the 1980s, many branches of manufacturing like automotive industry, cement, cotton spinning, food processing, and polyester filament yarn, witnessed modernisation and expansion of scales of production. Industrial export growth also improved in the second half of the 1980s as import restrictions moved from quotas to tariffs (as a first phase of trade reforms) although at very high levels, and a steady depreciation of the currency in nominal terms. The turnaround in industrial output growth in this decade has been variedly attributed to liberalisation, improvement in public investment and public sector performance [Ahluwalia, 1992; Nagaraj, 1990].

Speeding Up of Reforms in the 1990s: As part of the orthodox initiatives since 1991, industry and trade policy reforms were accelerated, while public investment contracted sharply to reign in the fiscal imbalance. Financing of industrial development changed considerably as part of the financial sector reform that cut directed lending, and abolished subsidised credit for the identified sectors since development banks' access to long-term credit from the Reserve Bank and SLR funds were terminated. Although formal changes in industrial labour laws were avoided due to lack of political consensus, there were adequate signals to employers that the government would not come in the way of restructuring industrial relations, layoffs and retrenchments of organised workers – giving up the implicit *compact* that had bound capital and labour together in the previous four decades. While reforms appeared like a 'big bang' by Indian standards, the pace was gradual compared with, say, China, let alone Russia and the east European economies.

Proponents expected the reforms to accelerate domestic output and industrial growth, taking it close to those achieved by the successful Asian economies. 'Uncaging the tiger', the metaphor that *The Economist*'s Clive Crook coined, caught the imagination of the policy-makers and public alike – just as the new government was about to be formed in 1991 amidst an external payment crisis.[2] Expectedly, the policy initiatives drew considerable criticism, apprehending deep retrenchment of output and employment as had happened in Latin America, and towards 'dependent development'.

How did the industrial sector really perform in the 1990s? How does it compare it with the previous decade?

II

Industrial Performance, 1980-81 to 2001-02

Quite unlike Latin America, where the manufacturing sector's share in GDP declined sharply over the last two decades, in India the share in the 1990s has remained broadly the same, with a marginal rise (Table 19.2). As Figure 19.1 shows, the manufacturing sector's share in workforce has remained roughly constant at around 12 per cent. Registered manufacturing employment – in factories regularly employing 10 or more workers constituting about one-fifth of total manufacturing employment – has steadily risen from around the mid-1980s for over a decade, without a trace of the effect of the 1991 reforms in the trend (Figure 19.2). Thus, in the aggregate, the worst fears did not come true (more about this later).[3]

Figure – 19.1

Share of Employment, Output and Investment in Total Manufacturing

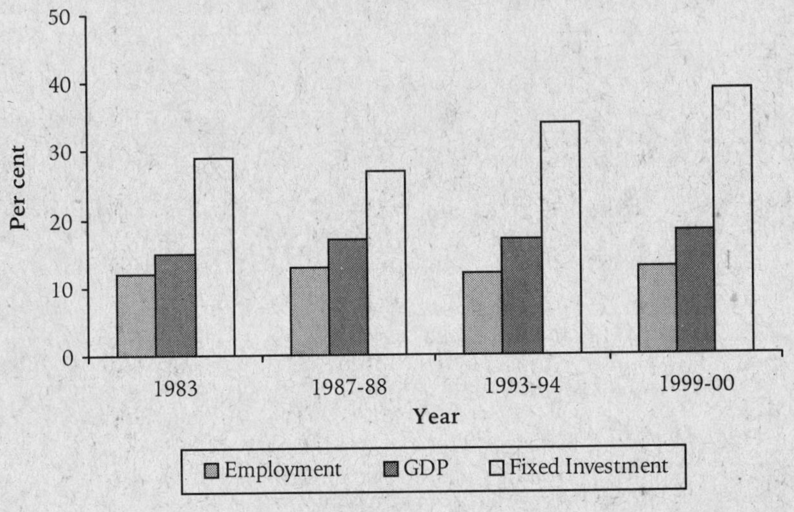

TABLE – 19.2

Share of Manufacturing in GDP, 1980 to 2000

Country	1980	1990	2000
Argentina	29.5	26.8	17.6
Brazil	33.5		24.0
Chile	21.5	19.6	15.9
Mexico	22.3	20.8	20.7
Memo: India	13.8	16.6	17.2

Source: World Development Indicators, 2002; NAS, various issues.

Figure – 19.2

Employment in Registered Manufacturing

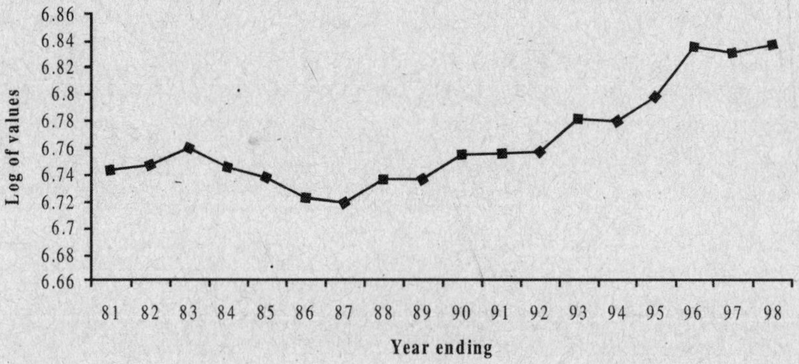

Trend Analysis: Table 19.3 provides the trend growth rates of output for the total and registered manufacturing for varying time periods between 1980-81 and 2001-02. Evidently, the growth rates are, in general, lower in the 1990s compared with those in the previous decade. However, a dummy variable to test for a break in the series in 1991-92 does not show any statistically significant change in the growth rates. Thus, industrial growth during the last two decades have remained roughly the same, both for total and registered manufacturing.

Results of a similar exercise for disaggregated (2-digit) industry groups are reported in Table 19.4. During the two-decade periods, in total manufacturing, chemicals (NIC 30), rubber and petroleum (NIC 31), and electrical machinery (NIC 36) have grown at above average growth rates by a reasonable margin. The same is true separately for each of the two decades. Similarly, textile products (NIC 26), leather, chemicals, rubber and petroleum, (NIC 29-31), and repair services (NIC 39+97) grew faster than the average in registered manufacturing.

TABLE – 19.3

Manufacturing Sector Growth, 1980-81 to 2001-02

(Per cent per year)

Period (Year Ending)	Total Manufacturing	Registered Manufacturing	Dummy Variable Test	
			Sign	Statistical Significance
1981-02	6.7		+	Not significant
1981-91	7.4	8.2		
1992-02	6.3			
1981-01		7.4	+	Not significant
1993-01		6.6		
1981-00	6.9			

Source: NAS, various issues.

TABLE – 19.4

Growth by 2-digit Industry Groups, 1980-81 to 1999-2000

Industry Group (NIC)	Total Manufacturing			Registered Manufacturing		
	1981-91	1992-00	1981-00	1981-91	1992-00	1981-00
20-21	7.0	4.9	6.1	9.5	5.2	7.3
22	2.9	10.8	5.2	8.5	8.4	7.8
23-26				5.5	3.7	4.9
23				5.6	6.3	3.2
24				5.8	13.8	7.6
25				1.9	4.4	0.9
26				12.8	1.6	14.8
27	(–) 2.7	2.0	(–) 0.8	7.3	4.7	0.9
28	9.1	4.3	6.2	9.2	0.6	5.3
29	3.8	5.1	6.0	9.7	3.7	10.4
30	9.3	10.4	10.0	9.4	10.6	10.3
31	14.7	5.5	9.9	17.6	5.5	11.4
32	9	9.9	7.4	11.8	7.7	7.9
33	5.7	8.1	7.4	5.4	8.4	7.2
34	6.0	6.9	4.3	6.5	7.9	6.2
35	6.0	8.7	6.1	6.0	8.5	6.0
36	12.5	12.3	10.0	10.7	13.0	9.6
37	5.5	6.3	5.3	5.4	5.5	6.5
38	11.1	7.6	7.1	7.7	7.0	7.3
39+97	7.1	8.3	5.4	15.3	6.8	13.2
Total	**7.7**	**7.5**	**7.2**	**8.5**	**7.4**	**8.0**

Source: NAS, various issues.

Growth by Use-based Industrial Groups: Many believe, the sharp reduction in tariffs for capital goods in the 1990s has severely affected their domestic output – 'massacre of machine building', to use Ashok Desai's (2001) graphic description. Initial assessments, based on the index of industrial production (IIP) with different base years gave conflicting evidence in this regard. We now have a better basis to assess this proposition using the ASI data for the period 1980-81 to 1997-98 (Table 19.5).[4] The capital goods sector has grown at 6.7 per cent per year during 1981-98, and at 5.7 per cent per year during 1992-98; but there is no statistically significant break in the trend growth rate in 1991-92. The same is true for all the use-based industrial groups. Thus, the trend in output growth in the decades of the 1980s and the 1990s are broadly similar – in the aggregate, by 2-digit industry groups as well as by use-based classification of output.

TABLE – 19.5

Growth in Registered Manufacturing According to Use-Based Classification of Output, 1980-81 to 1997-98

(Per cent per year)

Use-Based Group	1980-81/ 1997-98	1980-81/ 1990-91	Dummy Variable Test
1 Basic goods	8.3	8.0	(–) Not Sig
2 Intermediate goods	10.7	11.2	(–) Not Sig
3 Capital goods	6.7	5.3	(+) Not Sig
4 Consumer goods	9.1	8.9	(–) Not Sig
4.1 Consumer durable goods	12.5	12.0	(+) Not Sig
4.2 Consumer non-durable goods	8.5	8.3	(–) Not Sig

Source: EPW Research Foundation (2002).

However, these trends seem to hide significant variations across specific products and industries. Within capital goods, production (in numbers) of passenger car – a widely accepted indicator of conspicuous consumption in a poor country –went up from about 31,000 in 1980-81 to about 5.8 lakhs in 2000, representing an annual growth rate of 15 per cent during the two decades.

Its contrast with machine tool industry – the heart of domestic machine building capability – is telling. Gross value added in this industry grew at a mere 1.7 per cent per year during 1981-97, witnessing a negative growth thereafter. Indian Machine Tool Manufactures' Association says, "Output by domestic metalworking machine tool manufacturers in 2001 calendar year declined by 14 per cent to Rs. 5,137 million marking fourth year of decline, since 1997, for the Indian machine tool industry" (http://imtma.org/aimti.htm). Domestic machine tool production stagnated at a time when industrial investment really boomed (discussed later). Evidently, much of the incremental demand was met by imports, as the import-to-consumption ratio nearly doubled from 29 in the 1990s, to 56 per cent in 1995.[5]

Due to the differing growth rates over nearly two decades, the relative weights of use-based industrial groups have changed considerably. To discern their long-term changes in registered manufacturing, we have looked at their shares in every decade since 1960-61 (Table 19.6). During nearly three decades since 1970-71, the share of consumer goods has gone up by 7 percentage points from 35 per cent to 42 per cent – mainly on account of consumer durable goods. Shares of basic and intermediate goods have gone down, while that of capital goods increased marginally by about one percentage point.

TABLE – 19.6

Changes in the Use-Based Classification of Registered Manufacturing Output, 1960-61 to 1997-98

Use-Based Groups	1960-61	1970-71	1980-81	1990-91	1997-98
1 Basic goods	27.5	30.7	21.3	23.7	23.0
2 Intermediate goods	21.0	19.0	16.3	16.8	17.0
3 Capital goods	10.7	15.2	21.2	17.5	16.3
4 Consumer goods	40.8	35.1	41.1	42.0	43.6
4.1 Consumer durable goods	2.5	2.8	4.8	6.8	8.8
4.2 Consumer non-durable goods	38.3	32.6	36.4	35.2	34.8

Note: Data for the years 1960-61 and 1970-71 are from Ahluwalia (1985:9).

Though informative, the above findings are incomplete, as they exclude the unregistered sector, which constitute one-third of the total manufacturing value added. Moreover, with the diffusion of technology and skills, spread of electricity, and in response to a variety of policies to encourage small enterprises, many industries have got diffused in the unorgainsed sector in this period. While such a process is more likely in consumer goods industries, it is probably true to a lesser extent in machinery manufacturing, since technology in these industries is amenable to division of labour and specialisation. But we cannot satisfactorily capture these changes, as use-based classification of unorganised sector output is not available.

However, as a proxy for capital goods, we take the share of NIC 35 to NIC 37 in total manufacturing output (Figure 19.3). Expectedly, the capital goods' share in total manufacturing is smaller than that in registered manufacturing. The two shares move in parallel, though there seems to be some narrowing of the gap between the two, suggesting a notable diffusion of capital goods production in the unorganised sector.

Figure – 19.3

Machinery Sector's Share in Manufacturing Output

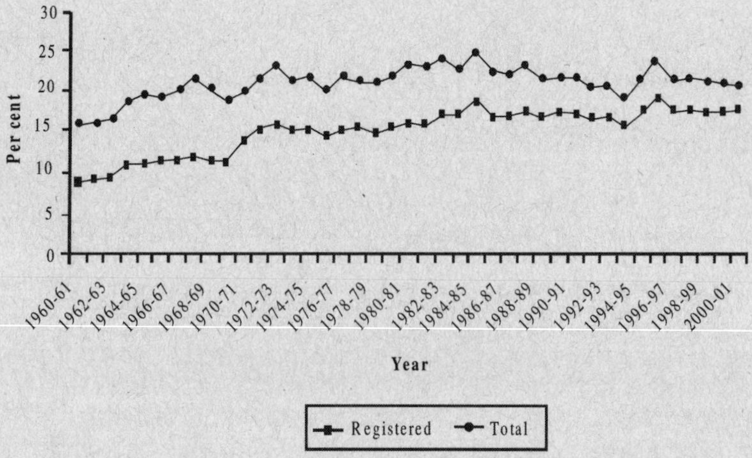

But strikingly, capital goods' share in total manufacturing, after peaking at about 18 per cent in 1984-85 has stagnated in the following decade-and-a-half. Thus, reforms have severely affected the sector – at least in the aggregate. Arguably, the steep rise in imports reflects poor capability of the domestic industry and its high prices. While there may be some merit in such an argument, it is hard to believe that such an outcome was inevitable, with policy reforms.

Capital Goods Prices: But the flip side of this is that, the real price of capital goods – the ratio of prices of capital goods to the GDP deflator – has steadily come down during the last two decades with the decline in tariffs, especially since 1993-94 (Figure 19.4). The same holds true for the real price of construction – a positive effect of gradual decontrol of the cement industry since 1982 leading to substantial capacity creation, entry of new firms and technological upgradation (moving from wet to dry process, thus lowering of the energy intensity of output). As the real price of fixed investment has gone down, and the share of machinery in gross fixed capital formation (GFCF) has risen steadily, the additions to the capital stock are much more productive. This, in principle, would have economywide effects on potential output and productivity growth.

Figure – 19.4

Real Price of GFCF by Type of Assets

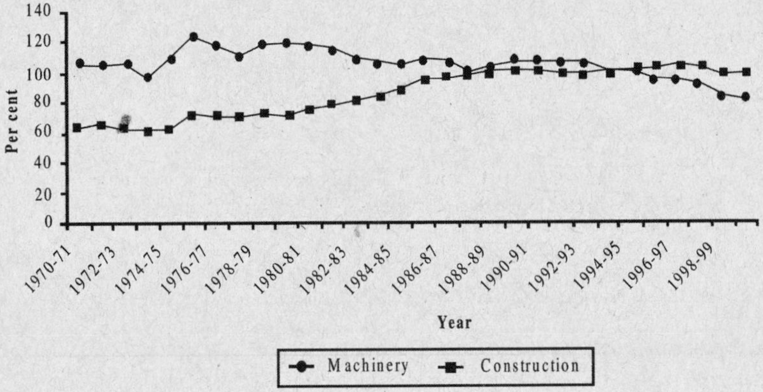

Growth of Construction Sector: With the relaxation of supply constraints on cement and steel, and a fall in their real prices, there seems to have been a steady growth in the construction sector. Though not evident from domestic output estimates, employment figures seem to show a clearer picture.[6] The employment (usual status) share in construction for all India has nearly doubled from 2.3 per cent of the total workforce in 1983, to 4.4 per cent in 1999-2000 [Chadha and Sahu, 2002]. Therefore, quite contrary to the popularly held view, the employment share of the industrial sector (mining, manufacturing, construction and utilities) shows a moderate increase in the last two decades, despite stagnation in manufacturing's share (Figure 19.5).

Better Functioning of Industrial Market: Undoubtedly, economic reforms have increased domestic and external competition, providing greater consumer choice. A relative cheapening of capital goods under pressure from import competition has made fixed investment more productive, the gains of which are increasingly passed on to consumers by price reduction, or quality improvement. Firms can no longer implicitly operate on a 'cost plus' pricing principle. The shift in market conditions is perhaps best reflected in manufacturers' growing use of consumer credit to induce sales of durable goods.

Figure – 19.5

Workforce Distribution, 1983-2000

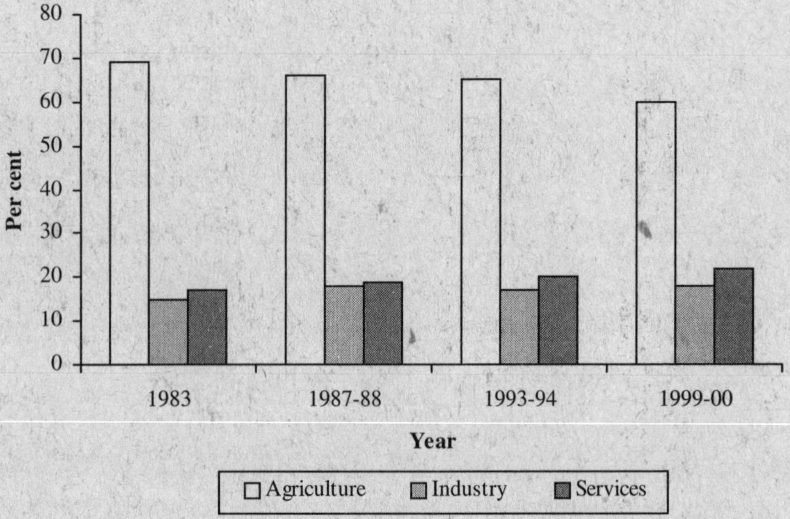

Moreover, the widely commented corruption in the industrial licensing system at the level of the central government has got largely eliminated, as entrepreneurs now have to merely register their proposed project with the concerned ministry, while state governments compete with each other for private investment with incentives. These are certainly significant gains of the gradual reforms over the last two decades.

On a close look, however, there are many causes for concern.

III

A Closer Look at the 1990s

While the trend growth rate in the 1990s is the same as in the previous decade, the yearly growth rates show an interesting pattern

(Figure 19.6). After an expected contraction in response to the external payment crisis in 1991-92, industrial output rebounded rapidly in the following four years, peaking in 1995-96. In fact, the annual growth rate of output of over 14 per cent in that year is perhaps the highest ever recorded in India. The sharp upturn is widely credited to policy reforms, with the expectation of further acceleration with more reforms.

Figure – 19.6

Manufacturing Output Growth, 1991-2002

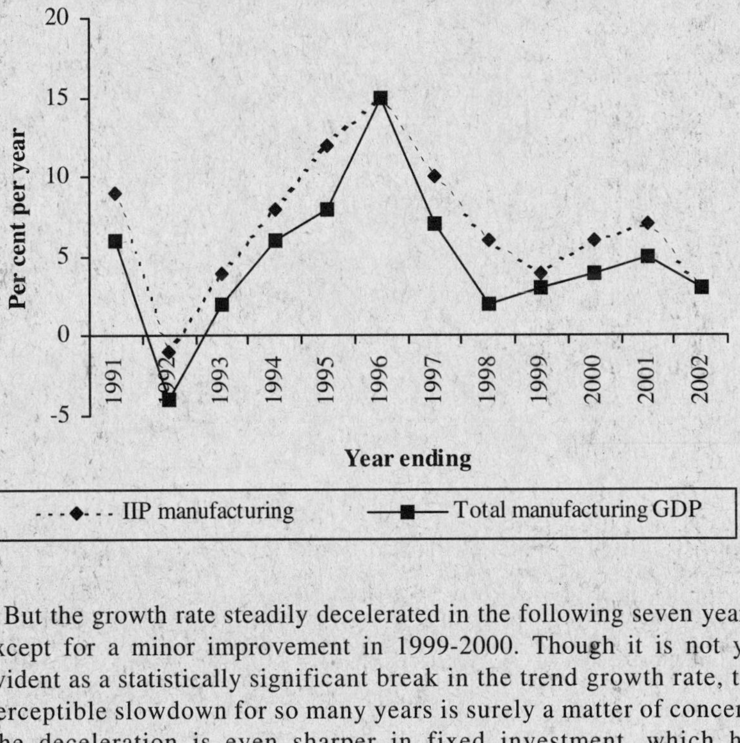

But the growth rate steadily decelerated in the following seven years, except for a minor improvement in 1999-2000. Though it is not yet evident as a statistically significant break in the trend growth rate, the perceptible slowdown for so many years is surely a matter of concern. The deceleration is even sharper in fixed investment, which has turned negative in recent years (Figure 19.7). As there was an investment boom in manufacturing without a corresponding rise in output growth, there is now a huge excess capacity, especially in consumer durable goods, the automotive industry – and more generally in capital goods.

Figure – 19.7

Fixed Investment Growth in Total Manufacturing

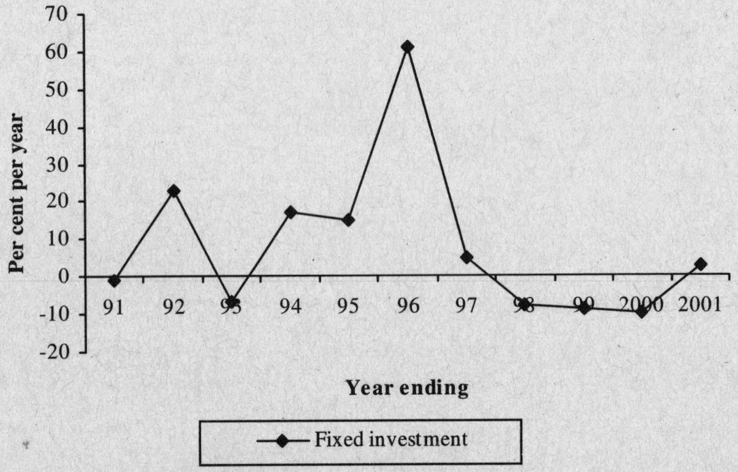

Divergence in Performance: By doing away with the reported import substitution bias in industrial policy, reforms were expected to boost output and exports of labour intensive manufactures. If we accept the distinction of registered and unregistered sectors as proxies for import competing and export-oriented manufacturing respectively (as is widely done in the literature), then the experience of the 1990s seems to be at variance with the priori expectation.

While there was an investment boom in the registered sector, the unregistered sector has suffered. The unregistered sector's share in total manufacturing GFCF has nearly halved, from around 45 per cent in the mid-1980s to less than 20 per cent by the end of the 1990s (Figure 19.8). What explains this? Investments seem to have been driven by the potential size of the domestic market, and the expectation of its growth in the liberalised regime.[7] This is particularly true of consumer durable goods and the automotive industry, largely driven by a surge in foreign direct investment [Nagaraj, 2003]. Many incumbent domestic firms responded to the threat of new entry by modernisation, expansion and strengthening the distribution network, thus contributing to the investment boom. However, this did not translate into output growth as the size of the market was found to be much smaller than projected.

Figure – 19.8

Unregistered Sector's Share in Manufacturing Fixed Investment

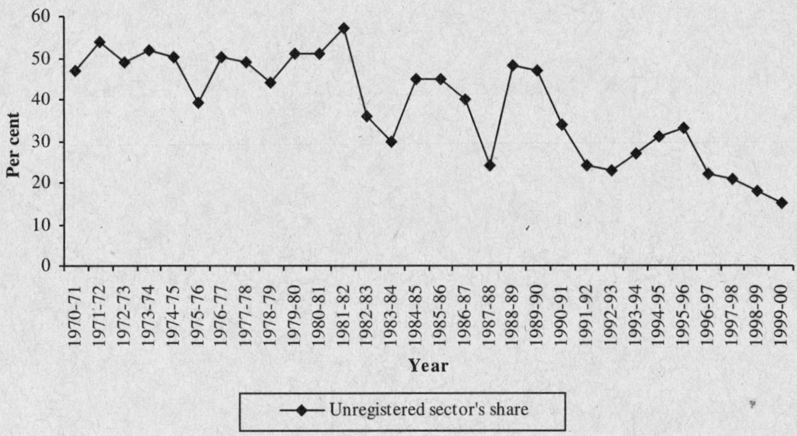

Investment in unregistered manufacturing was probably hurt by high interest rates in the initial years of reforms.[8] While interest rates came down in the second half of the 1990s, commercial banks have resisted lending for productive sector as they found it profitable to invest in risk-free government securities. As a proxy for access to fund investment, bank credit to the small-scale sector in unregistered manufacturing – as proportions of (i) total non-food credit, and (ii) net bank credit – has declined from over 16 per cent in the late 1980s to less than 12 per cent a decade later (Figure 19.9). In other words, in the liberalised regime and without a change in the legal environment, commercial banks had little incentive to lend to small enterprises.

Thus, after over two decades of 'creeping' liberalisation – to borrow Pranab Bardhan's (1998) phrase – there is now widespread gloom, with decelerating growth for nearly seven years since the mid-1990s with a huge excess capacity in many industries. This is in sharp contrast to the euphoria that marked the initiation of the orthodox economic reforms a little over a decade ago.

Figure – 19.9

Bank Credit to SSI, 1980-81 to 2000-01

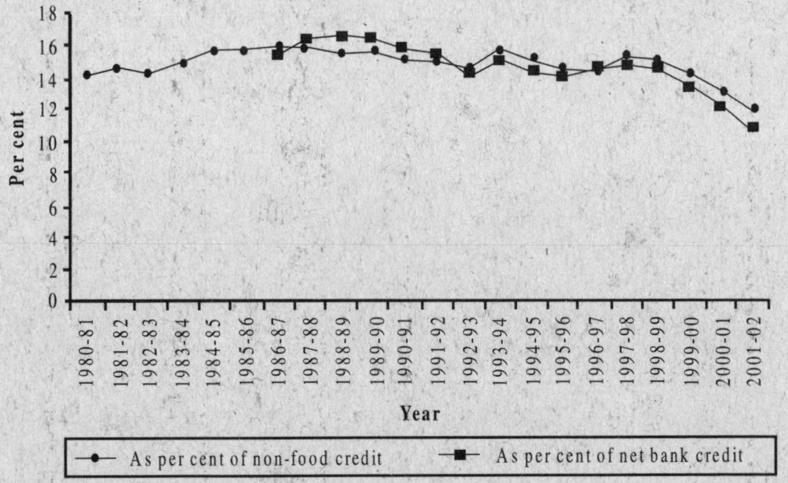

Evidently, there is an uncanny resemblance of the current industrial outlook with that around 1980, which we described at the beginning. Why did reforms not lead to an acceleration of output growth with a greater share of labour-intensive manufactures and exports? More pertinently perhaps, why has growth tapered off after the mid-1990s, although there were no significant policy reversals? If anything, regardless of the political dispensation in power, successive governments have sought to iron out the wrinkles in the reform process. Is it a question of the reforms being too little, too late? Or is it a mere failure of implementation of a sound design (political and bureaucratic inertia)?

These are serious questions that have a bearing not just on industrial performance, but also perhaps on the validity of the analytical model that underpins much of the current policy discourse.

IV

Towards an Explanation

The policy initiatives of the 1990s were based on considerable support from the mainstream economics. They were, in principle, expected to set right what was widely believed to have been wrong with India's industrialisation effort. As T N Srinivasan argued, "They (the reforms) were solidly based on an understanding of what went wrong with Indian development strategy since 1950 that delivered neither rapid growth nor appreciably greater equity" [Srinivasan, 1993:258]. In Jagdish Bhagwati's view, the three main elements of India's policy framework that stifled growth and efficiency were: "extensive bureaucratic controls over production, investment and trade; inward looking trade and foreign investment policies, and a substantial public sector, going well beyond the conventional confines of public utilities and infrastructure" [Bhagwati, 1993:48]. Joshi and Little (1994:3) contended, that "India's control system was not only microeconomically inefficient but macroeconomically perverse", implying that the industrial policy was responsible for persistent fiscal deficits and periodic balance of payment crises.

Broadly, none of these features of the policy framework remain any more after 1991. Why, then, has manufacturing sector growth slowed down so precipitously since the mid-1990s? Why haven't the budgetary imbalances disappeared with the doing away of the allegedly worst features of the policy framework?

Desai (2001), among others, has argued that the credit squeeze in 1996 and rise in interest rates throttled the boom of 1993-96. While it might have been true in the short run, why has industry not revived despite the steady loosening of credit constraint and the fall in interest rates over the past seven years?

Many attribute the slowdown (lack of sustained improvement in the 1990s) to the stalled reforms. They believe a quick and sharp reduction in tariffs to the average levels of many Asian economies, pulling down the remaining restrictions on foreign direct investment, and removal of policy-induced rigidities in the industrial labour market would deliver the desired fruits of reforms. These arguments merit closer examination.

If such an argument is valid, then the hastening of the reforms in the 1990s, compared with the previous decade, ought to have improved industrial growth rate, which evidently did not happen. Moreover, in comparative experience, there is little evidence to suggest an unambiguous positive association between the scope (and speed) of reforms and economic outcomes. If one can cite cases from Asian economies as successful examples of following the orthodoxy, there are equally compelling cases from Latin America with adverse outcomes.

Thus, there are no clear signals as to how to reverse the trend of decelerating industrial growth, except for the fond hope that further relaxation of rules governing the use of capital (domestic and foreign) and labour would somehow do the trick.[9] Moreover, the view that 'reforms have not gone far enough' resembles the arguments in earlier times when repeated failure of the five-year plans to meet targets was attributed to 'not enough planning' or 'lack of political will', despite the growing evidence of the economy's structural weaknesses, or the heavy hand of bureaucracy. Therefore, such arguments in favour of more reforms do not seem to be based on an application of economic reasoning and examination of the evidence. Thus, there is a reason for us to look for an alternative explanation.

It is perhaps useful to start with the classical economic view. As Arthur Lewis once asked, "What limits the size of the manufacturing sector?" His preliminary answer was, "productivity of farmers whose marketable surplus will exchange for manufactures" [Lewis, 1984:121]. As India is still a large and poor agrarian economy with 3/5th of workforce still dependent on agriculture (in Bihar it is close to 3/4th), with land productivity being one-third of China's, per capita value added in manufacturing is the lowest among the newly industrialising economies; and one-fourth of China's (Table 19.7).

TABLE – 19.7

Manufacturing Value Added Per Capita in Selected Industrialising Economies

Countries	Value Added Per Capita in Manufacturing in US$ in 1998
Argentina	1253
Brazil	1078
Mexico	821
Hong Kong	1738
Korea	2142
Singapore	6064
India	70
China	286
Malaysia	946
Indonesia	115
Thailand	582
Turkey	501
Memo: High income economies	5344

Source: Weiss (2001): 15.

If we accept, following Chenery's stylised fact, that large countries in general have low trade ratios, and that India does not have abundant natural resources for exports, then industrial growth lrrgely boils down to the size (and growth) of the domestic market. This, in turn, yet largely depends on how agriculture performs. The rich discourse on India's industrialisation experience has shown that in a poor agrarian economy lack of demand could be a binding constraint on industrial growth. To quote K N Raj:

> Private consumer demand in a country such as India depends to a large extent, ... on how things go in the agricultural sector. If output and income in this sector are rising rapidly, consumer demand for both agricultural and non-agricultural products can also be expected to increase rapidly, the latter being even more than the former since higher proportions are generally spent on non-agricultural products as levels of income rise. Output and incomes in the agricultural sector need not of course always rise together since the effect of sharp increases in output could well be to lower the prices of agricultural products more than proportionately; this is in fact an important factor governing agricultural income in some regions of the country characterised by serious year-to-year variation in climatic conditions and water supply [Raj, 1986:225i]

Without denying that long-term constraint in a developing economy is one of supply of savings and investment, Sukhamoy Chakravarty argued that under specific circumstances that India faced, lack of aggregate demand could become a binding constraint [Chakravarty, 1979 and 1984].

From a variety of analytical perspectives, it is widely accepted that autonomous public investment in a developing economy helps create large demand for industrial goods as well as relieve infrastructure supply constraint [Narayana and Srinivasan, 1978; Patnaik and Rao, 1978]. Pandit's (1995) survey of macroeconometric evidence seems to unambiguously support the view that public investment 'crowds-in' private investment. International evidence also suggests that public investment in infrastructure does not displace private investment, but crowds it in [Serven, 1996].

Combining the above arguments, one can perhaps contend that industrial growth in India is largely run on the twin engines of agriculture productivity and public investment. Apparently, neither of these was functioning well in the 1990s.

Agricultural Performance: In the aggregate, there are no signs of a statistically significant slowdown in the growth of GDP in agriculture in the 1990s [Nagaraj, 2001]. However, there are other pieces of evidence, mainly based on physical output growth, at the disaggregated level, that seem to suggest a different tendency.

A comparison of land productivity of all major crops (and crop groups) between the 1980s and the 1990s shows a distinctly lower trend growth rate in the latter decade, except for wheat (Figure 19.10).[10] If this evidence has any merit, then poorer agricultural performance could have adversely affected the demand for industrial goods.

Figure – 19.10

Trends in Agricultural Production, 1980-81 to 1999-2000

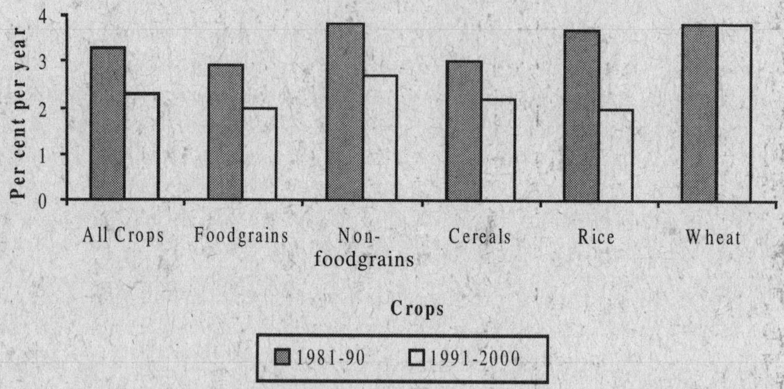

The indifferent agriculture performance in the 1990s is perhaps associated with the much-commented slowdown in public investment in this sector. Although an improvement in private investment seems to have partially compensated for the decline in public investment, there is an undeniable decline in total agricultural investment growth [Roy and Pal, 2002; Gulati and Bathla, 2001].

Poor agricultural performance seems to be also evident in lower labour demand in rural areas. Chadha and Sahu (2002) show that between 1993 and 2000, unemployment rates have gone up, while it had come down in the previous decade. This is found to be true by all measures of unemployment.

Thus, piecing together the above evidence seems to suggest a deterioration of agricultural performance in the 1990s that could perhaps have adversely affected industrial output growth.

Public Investment: It is widely accepted that as part of economic reforms, public investment – over one-half of which is in infrastructure

– was deliberately reduced.[11] Figure 19.11 shows the share of infrastructure (mining, utilities and transport) and manufacturing in GFCF for the period since 1970-71. Evidently, the decline in infrastructure's share started in the second half of the 1980s and became sharp in the mid-1990s. Interestingly, its mirror image can be found in the manufacturing sector's increasing share in GFCF. If we take a longer time-period (not shown here), we discover that the share of public investment in the late 1990s, at about 30 per cent of total GFCF, has fallen close to the level it was in the early 1950s when India initiated planned economic development. In physical terms, the decline in public investment is perhaps best captured in the precipitous fall in the growth of electricity generation capacity from 8-10 per cent per year in the 1980s to 4-6 per cent in the 1990s (Figure 19.12). The fall in public investment has been so drastic that it is now – to rephrase Bhagwati's earlier quote – well *behind* the conventional confines of public utilities and infrastructure.

Figure – 19.11

Share of Manufacturing and Infrastructure in GFCF

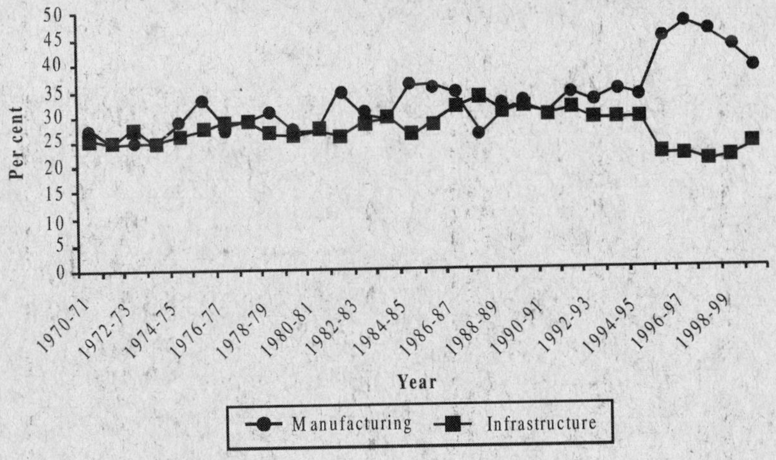

While some may applaud this 'achievement' at dismantling the public sector's role in the provision of social overhead capital, this has not led to a surge in investment and employment in labour-intensive manufactures. But the fall in infrastructure investment seems to have constrained industrial output and export growth, and also perhaps the inflow of foreign direct investment.

Figure – 19.12

Annual Growth in Electricity Generating Capacity, 1981-2001

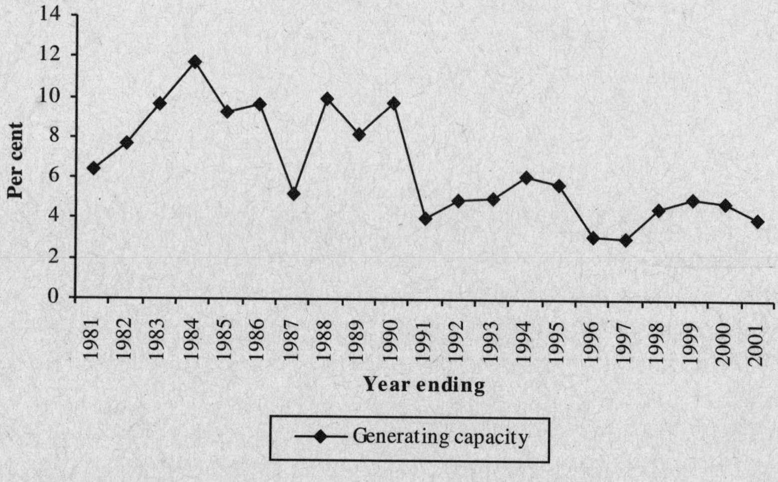

Economic theory seems fairly clear that when markets fail, as often happens in the industrial sector which has considerable externalities, economies of scale, scope and network, state intervention, in principle, improves social welfare. Such a view is increasingly countered by arguing that in developing economies, the costs of 'state failures' due to inefficiency, waste and corruption could outweigh the costs of market failure.

As such disputes cannot be resolved analytically, we have to look at evidence on market failure versus state failure in the course of industrialisation. The experience of successful industrialisation in the 20th century does not seem to support the state failure hypothesis in the aggregate: if anything, the sustained ability at acquisition of technical capability in late industrialising economies has gone hand in hand with substantial, yet responsive, state action [Amsden, 2001]. On the other hand, leaving more and more economic decisions to markets uncritically during the past two decades seems to have led to deindustrialisation, as measured by workforce distribution [Weiss, 2002]. Chile is probably the prime example of Latin America's most industrialised nation getting transformed into a primary producer of exotic (counter seasonal) agricultural produce.

V

Policy Options and Constraints

If the foregoing discussion has any merit, then what should be done for industrial revival? There is widespread support from diverse analytical perspectives for stepping up public infrastructure investment, but the question is how to finance it. Financing by increasing user charges and cutting down delays and waste in public sector (reducing X- inefficiency) are obviously the first-best solution, but it is a gradual and politically difficult – but perhaps not an insurmountable – process in a democratic set-up. Probably the best practical option in the medium-term is to use the available food and foreign exchange reserves for stepping public infrastructure investment – perhaps on the lines that Shetty (2001) suggested. Given the overflowing food stocks and considerable excess capacity in industry, the inflationary potential of such a stance is likely to be modest. But what if such a policy accentuates the existing fiscal imbalance? But it need not necessarily happen, as is often believed. As Mihir Rakshit argued:

> Even in mainstream economics it is recognised that the fiscal deficit cannot be a primary policy parameter, but is the outcome of the working of the entire system...[in] India almost all industrial units producing heavy machinery, equipment and basic metals belong to the public sector; and the wage bill in the large majority of these enterprises constitutes a fixed rather than a variable cost in the short and medium run. This implies that (i) an increase in the demand for fixed capital goods met from domestic sources raises public sector savings by an almost identical amount; and (ii) the value of the investment multiplier is close to unity. Thus even the short-run effects of public consumption and investment on aggregate demand are quite different [Rakshit, 1994:269-70].[12]

Within mainstream economics there are many who argue that after reforms the markets may be less imperfect, but may not 'naturally' lead to improved growth performance. Dornbusch famously argued, "Stabilisation may be inevitable, but it is not a ticket for prosperity...One should not presume that the market automatically solves the coordination problems..." [Dornsbusch, 1990:42-43]. A large and credible public investment programme – besides creating the well known economywide supply and demand linkages – could go a long way in stabilising the private sector's business expectations, and provide powerful signals on the broad direction of the economic policy, and the commitment of policy-makers to it. Further, it would perhaps not be incorrect to argue that in a poor and inequitous, agrarian economy like ours public infrastructure investment contributes towards efficiency as well equity.[13]

Agriculture has received less policy attention in recent years as food stocks have risen well beyond the needs of safe levels for food security. But such a policy overlooks the fact that what is procured and distributed by the public distribution system forms a small part of total food production and consumption; and a sizeable (though declining) share of food output is not marketed at all. Therefore, what share of rural income is left for non-food consumption depends on food production (and its prices), as poor and marginal farmers are net buyers of food.

VI

Summary and Conclusions

To sum up, industrial output growth during the last two decades has improved compared with the previous period of 'relative stagnation'. But contrary to both the euphoria and apprehension, with the acceleration of reforms there has been little change in the trend growth rate of output in the 1990s compared with the previous decade. Moreover, since the mid-1990s, there are distinct signs of a slowdown in growth for seven years now.

Gradualism in industry and trade policy reform during the last two decades has some notable achievements to its credit. Industrial markets have become more competitive, and product quality and variety have improved substantially. A relative cheapening of machinery and construction have made fixed investment more productive. An improved supply of cement and steel, and a fall in their real prices, has spurred the construction sector whose share in total workforce has nearly doubled – increasing industrial sector's share in the total workforce.

Contrary to many apprehensions, the trend growth rate of capital goods in the registered manufacturing has not declined during 1992-98 from that in 1981-91. While the capital goods sector's share in registered manufacturing has increased by about one percentage point in the 1990s, the share in total manufacturing has virtually stagnated since the mid-1980s, clearly suggesting the negative effect of reforms on this sector. Moreover, the aggregate performance seems to hide more than it reveals. To illustrate, the number of passenger cars produced has increased at 15 per cent per year for two decades now. But the machine tool industry – making the mother machines – has barely grown with imports to consumption ratio nearly doubling in the 1990s.

The much expected restructuring of production away from domestic market orientation, and towards labour intensive manufactures and their exports has not happened – at least not as yet. If anything, import competing organised manufacturing has been strengthened by the investment boom, while unregistered manufacturing suffered in the 1990s. Much of the boom went into production for the home market. Quite contrary to Joshi and Little's (1994) contention, elimination of the import substitution bias and the decline in the public sector's role in manufacturing have not resulted in a decline in macroeconomic perversity, as evident from persistent fiscal imbalances even after a decade of economic reforms.

Why did industrial and export growth not accelerate in the 1990s with the speeding up of the orthodox reforms? More precisely, why did the growth momentum of the 1980s taper off so sharply after a mere four-year boom in the early 1990s? The experience seems to suggest that the much argued positive association between reforms and growth seems suspect, or overdone. What, then, should we do to revive industry?

'Stalled' reforms since the mid-1990s are widely believed to be responsible for the industrial deceleration. Such a view presumes a positive association between speed (and depth) of reforms and output growth – a view sustainable neither in principle nor in comparative experience. Successive governments in the 1990s have, by and large, sought to operationalise the reforms and remove various bottlenecks rather than go back on them – but with little effect.

Therefore, it needs to be recognised that the industrial sector currently suffers from a lack of demand especially of investment, and not of supply – constrained by policy. In a poor, agrarian economy there are many structural features that can constrain industrial demand, although low capital stock per head continues to be the long-term constraint. Lack of demand seems to be on account of poor to indifferent agricultural performance in the 1990s and a deep cut in public infrastructure investment since the late 1980s.

Following the classical economic precepts, there is an urgent need to refocus policy on stimulating agricultural productivity that creates rural demand. With growing capital intensity of crop production, such a move will not only augment demand for consumer goods but also for capital and basic goods. Stepping up public infrastructure investment would not only generate investment demand but also ease the constraints on infrastructure supply that could bring in domestic investment, and probably the much sought after foreign investment as well. Given the structural features of the Indian economy, a carefully crafted strategy of financing such investment may not worsen the budgetary imbalance as widely apprehended – on the contrary it may improve it, if the utilisation of excess capacity stimulates internal savings of enterprises.

Notes

1. Unless mentioned otherwise, the growth rates in this paper refer to loglinear trend growth rates, and all economic aggregates are measured at constant prices.
2. Clive Crook wrote, "India is a caged tiger. The tiger, set free, can be as healthy and vigorous as any in Asia. ... What needs to be done is clear. ... The government must dismantle an unbelievably complicated system of restraints and rewards that, over the past four decades, has securely enclosed every aspect of Indian life. The first and necessary step is to see these restraints and rewards as the cage that they are" (*The Economist*: India Survey, May 4, 1991:5).
3. Reportedly, there have been large-scale retrenchments in older industries and locations like Mumbai, though the official estimates do not seem to reflect the reality as the system of reporting of labour statistics has deteriorated. Howell and Kambhampati (1999) give a grim picture of textile workers in Ahmedabad.
4. The latest ASI data are available up to 1999-2000. We are unable to use the information for the last two years of the 1990s as there is, once again, a change in the industrial classification, and the census and sample sectors within the factory sector have also been redefined. We believe the broad trends reported in this study are unlikely to change by adding the data for the latest two years. In this study we have used the consistent time series compiled by EPW Research Foundation (2002).
5. High level of import-to-consumption ratio in machine tools would not have mattered if their exports were also growing rapidly. Machine tools are a highly traded goods, even among countries like the US, Germany and Japan, with considerable economies in specialisation.
6. While output has boomed since cement decontrol in 1982, neither fixed capital formation in construction nor domestic output in construction shows a corresponding increase, suggesting a growing underestimation of value addition in this sector [Nagaraj 2001].
7. Much of this investment was predicated on the estimated size of the domestic market for consumer durable goods to be around 200 million – based on private market research and consumption surveys.
8. Many believe the reservation policy for small scale industries (SSIs) is responsible for the lack of investment in the unregistered sector. While de-reservation surely merits attention, the policy cannot perhaps explain the fall in investment, as the reservation is restricted to a small number of industries, with a modest share in SSIs' output.
9. This view is well reflected in the official *Economic Survey* since the early 1990s.
10. I owe an earlier version of this graph to G S Bhalla.
11. Usually infrastructure includes mining, utilities, transport and communications. However, if investment in major irrigation and flood control were also included, keeping in view the agrarian nature of the economy, its share would be even higher.
12. The Economic advisory committee's report (1987) under the chairmanship of Sukhamoy Chakraverty had worked out numerical exercises to examine the effects of stepping up investment in infrastructure on domestic output and public saving.
13. Bardhan said, "... there are many projects which by relieving the severe constraints faced by poor and improving their conditions can help economic growth in the process. This runs somewhat contrary to the preoccupation of mainstream economics with equity-efficiency tradeoffs, with its emphasis on the various costs of redistribution in terms of reduced economic incentives and performance.... "Then there are important dynamic externalities which can arise from community or neighbourhood -specific characteristics. These may refer to physical infrastructure (like roads, communications, irrigation and power systems) improving the productivity of private investment..." [Bardhan, 1996:1346-47].

References

Ahluwalia, Isher (1992), *Productivity and Growth in Indian Manufacturing*, Oxford University Press, Delhi.

——— (1985), *Industrial Growth in India: Stagnation Since the Mid-Sixties*, Oxford University Press, Delhi.

Amsden, Alice H (2001), *The Rise of 'The Rest': Challenges to the West from Late-Industrialising Economies,* Oxford University Press, New York.

Bardhan, Pranab (1998), *The Political Economy of Development in India*, Expanded edition with an Epilogue on the Political Economy of Reform *in India*, Oxford University Press, Delhi

——— (1996), "Efficiency, Equity and Poverty Alleviation: Policy Issues in Less Developed Countries", *Economic Journal*, Vol 106, September.

Bhagwati, Jagdish (1993), *India's Economy: The Shackled Giant*, Clarendon Press.

Chadha, G K and P P Sahu (2002), "Post-Reform Setbacks in Rural Employment", *Economic and Political Weekly*, Vol 37, No 22, May 25.

Chakravarty, Sukhamoy (1984), "Aspects of India's Development Strategy for the 1980s" reprinted in Chakravarty's, *Selected Economic Writings*, Oxford University Press, Delhi, 1993.

——— (1979), "On the Question of Home Market and Prospects for Indian Growth", *Economic and Political Weekly*, Vol 14, Nos 30-32, August, Annual Number.

Desai, Ashok (2001), "A Decade of Reforms", *Economic and Political Weekly*, Vol 36, No 50, December 15.

Dornsbusch, Rudiger (1990), "Policies to Move from Stabilisation to Growth", Proceedings of the World Bank Annual Conference on Development Economics, World Bank, Washington, DC.

Economic Advisory Council (1987), *Public Enterprises in India: Some Current Issues*, Economic Advisory Council, New Delhi.

EPW Research Foundation (2002), *Annual Survey of Industries, 1973-74 to 1997-98 – A Data Base on the Industrial Sector in India, EPW* Research Foundation, Mumbai.

Gulati, Ashok and Seema Bathla (2001), "Capital Formation in Indian Agriculture Revisiting the Debate", *Economic and Political Weekly*, Vol 36, No 20, May 19.

Howell, Jude and Uma Kambhampati (1999), "Liberalisation and Labour: The Fate of Retrenched Workers in the Cotton Textile Industry in India", *Oxford Development Studies*, Vol 27, No 1, February.

Joshi, Vijay and I M D Little (1994), *India: Macroeconomics and Political Economy, 1961-1991*, Oxford University Press, Delhi.

Lewis, W Arthur (1984), "Development Economics in the 1950s", Gerald Meier and Dudley Seers (eds), *Pioneers in Development*, Oxford University Press, New York.

Nagaraj, R. (2003), "Foreign Direct Investment in India in the 1990s: Trends and Issues", *Economic and Political Weekly*, Vol 38, No 17, April 26.

——— (2001), "National Income and Balance of Payments Statistics: A Review" in C P Chandrasekhar and Jandhyala B G Tilak (eds), *India's Socio-Economic Database: Surveys of Selected Areas*, Tulika, New Delhi.

——— (1990), "Industrial Growth: Further Evidence and Towards an Explanation and Issues", *Economic and Political Weekly*, Vol 15, No 41, October 13.

Narayana, N S S and T N Srinivasan (1977), "Economic Performance since the Third Plan and Its Implications for Policy", *Economic and Political Weekly*, Vol 12, Nos 6-8, February, Annual Number.

Pandit, V. (1995), "Macroeconomic Character of the Indian Economy: Theories, Facts and Fancies" in Prabhat Patnaik (ed), *Macroeconomics*, Oxford University Press, Delhi.

Patnaik, Prabhat and S K Rao (1977), "Towards an Explanation of a Crisis in a Mixed Underdeveloped Economy", *Economic and Political Weekly*, Vol 12, Nos 6-8, February, Annual Number.

Raj, K N (1986), "Growth and Stagnation in Indian Industrial Development", *Economic and Political Weekly*, Vol 11, Nos 5-7, February, Annual Number.

Rakshit, Mihir (1994), "Issues in Structural Adjustment of Indian Economy" in Edmar L Bacha (ed), *Economics in a Changing World: Development, Trade and Environment*, Vol 4, St Martin Press, London.

Rangarajan, C. (1982), "Industrial Growth: Another Look", *Economic and Political Weekly*, Vol 17, Nos 14-16, April, Annual Number.

Roy, B C and Suresh Pal (2002), "Investment, Agricultural Productivity and Rural Poverty in India: A State-Level Analysis", *Indian Journal of Agricultural Economics*, Vol 57, No 4, October-December.

Serven, Luis (1996), *Does Public Capital Crowds Out Private Capital? Evidence from India*, Policy Research Working Paper No 1613, World Bank, Washington, DC.

Shetty, S L (2001), "Reviving the Economy: Some Explorations", *Economic and Political Weekly*, Vol 36, No 30, July 28.

Srinivasan, T N (1993), "Demand Deficiency and Indian Industrial Development" in Pranab Bardhan *et al.*, (ed), *Development and Change: Essays in Honour of K N Raj*, Oxford University Press, Delhi.

Weiss, John (2002), *Industrialisation and Globalisation: Theory and Evidence from Developing Countries*, Routledge, London.

Economic and Political Weekly, August 30, 2004.

20

Fall in Organised Manufacturing Employment

A Brief Note

R. Nagaraj

In 1999-2000, organised (registered or formal) manufacturing sector employed about eight million people – about three-fourth of them 'workers', the rest were supervisors and managers (supervisors, for short).[1] They represented close to 2 per cent of the economy's workforce producing about 11 per cent of domestic output, using 25 per cent of renewable capital stock. Many laws protect and promote interests of workers employed in this sector – like their health and safety, minimum wages and their timely payment, maternity leave for women, bonus, provident fund, gratuity and so on. The larger the factory, the greater is the workers' entitlements. Though any seven workers can form a trade union, such association of workers usually tends to be more durable only in larger factories. About four million workers employed in factories with 100 or more workers have job security under Chapter V-B of the Industrial Disputes (ID) Act, 1947. It means that an employer in these factories has to seek the state's permission to retrench even a single worker (after the amendments in 1976 and 1982). Reportedly such permissions are rarely granted, as the state is, in principle, committed to workers' welfare. However, the protection is not available to supervisors as they are considered part of management.[2]

I am indebted to K.V. Ramaswamy and C. Rammanohar Reddy for their comments and suggestions on an earlier draft of this paper. The usual disclaimers apply.

These labour laws in general, the job security regulation in particular, have been a bone of contention since the economic reforms were initiated in 1991. Many economists and policy-makers believe that the nature and extent of state intervention of industrial labour market is excessive, increasing labour costs and reducing flexibility to respond to vagaries of business in an increasingly open and competitive economy. The lack of managerial freedom to (use the popular term) 'hire and fire' is widely believed to adversely affect output and employment growth [for a recent example, Burgess and Beseley, 2004]. Lack of adaptable labour market is said to have become a binding constrained on expansion of labour-intensive manufacturings and their export, holding back India's ability to effectively compete with east Asia in general, and China in particular. Such an analysis has been widely disputed.[3] However, the Second Labour Commission that was set up a few years ago to examine this contentious issue has broadly endorsed the reformist's view.

In this context, we look at the employment scene in the recent years. To provide a perspective, during 1981-2002, real gross value added (output, for short) in registered manufacturing has grown at 7.4 per cent per year, without any acceleration after the reforms in 1991. However, output and investment boomed in the first half of the 1990s, followed by deceleration that has since persisted [Nagaraj, 2003].

I

Facts

Figure 20.1 shows, there was practically no increase in employment during the 1980s – a period of jobless growth. But the 1990s witnessed a boom for four years during 1992-96, followed by a retrenchment. Between 1995-96 and 2001-02, 1.3 million employees (13 per cent of workforce) lost their jobs. Thus, employment in 2001-02 is roughly same as it was eight years earlier.[4]

It is mostly workers who have lost over 1.1 million jobs (15 per cent) (Figure 20.2). But employment of supervisors increased more or less steadily, though they too experienced job losses. Between 1980-81 and 2000-01, employment of workers increased by 4.3 per cent (0.24 million), while that of supervisors rose up by 39 per cent (0.55 million). On a trend basis, however, the annual growth rates are 0.9 per cent and 2.2 per cent for workers and supervisors respectively.

Figure – 20.1

Number of Employees

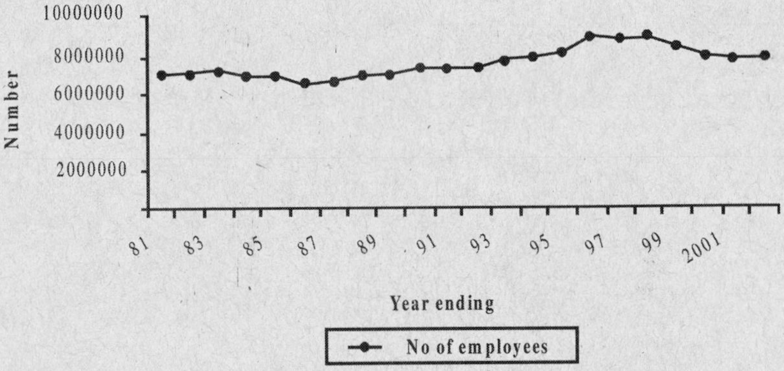

Figure – 20.2

Employment in Organised Manufacturing

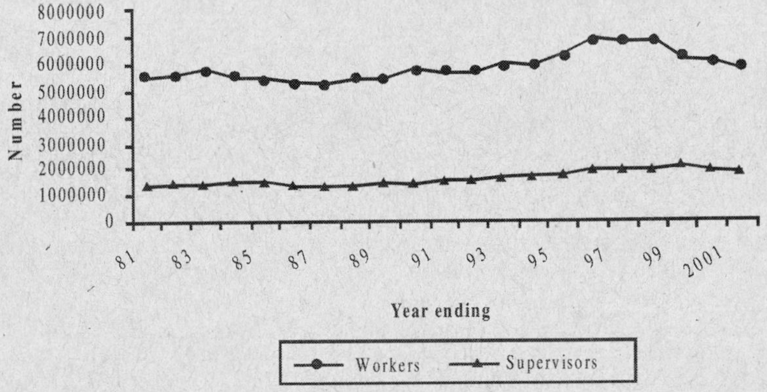

The job losses are widespread across industries and states. Of 15 major industry groups, 11 representing about 80 per cent of the workforce, witnessed a fall in employment during 1996-01 (Table 20.1). Similarly, employment declined in 13 out of 17 major states, constituting close to 90 per cent of the workforce (Table 20.2). The exceptions are industry groups, beverage and tobacco, textile products, chemicals and other manufacturing (NIC, 22, 26, 29 and 38); and the states are Himachal Pradesh, and Kerala. There was no change in Haryana and Punjab. Much of the contraction is likely in larger factories and in public sector enterprises, but we cannot verify it for lack of disaggregated data for the recent years.[5]

TABLE – 20.1

Employment of Workers in Organised Manufacturing by 2-digit Industry Group, 1991-92 to 2000-01

NIC Code	Industry Group	Employment Share in 1991-92	Index Number of Employment with 1991-92 as 100	
		(Per Cent)	1995-96	2000-01
20-21	Food products	15.7	117.0	111.1
22	Beverages, tobacco	8.7	103.3	107.5
23-25	Textiles	19.9	116.1	86.8
26	Textile products	2.7	189.4	287.9
27	Wood, furniture	0.9	120.3	109.3
28	Paper, printing	4.0	119.5	98.0
29	Leather	1.6	121.7	128.5
30	Chemicals	7.3	127.9	136.1
31	Rubber, petroleum	3.4	129.3	124.8
32	Non-metallic products	6.7	104.0	94.2
33	Basic metals	8.1	123.8	94.0
34	Metal products	3.1	123.1	118.4
35-36	Machinery	10.1	116.3	97.1
37	Transport equipment	6.6	125.4	88.7
38	Other manufacturing	1.3	149.4	157.0

Source: Annual Survey of Industries, various issues.

TABLE – 20.2

Employment of Workers in Organised Manufacturing by Major States, 1991-92 to 2000-01

States	Employment Share in 1991-92 (Per Cent)	Index Number of Employment with 1991-92 as 100	
		1995-96	2000-01
Andhra Pradesh	12.4	119.2	107.4
Assam	1.8	112.2	93.2
Bihar	4.5	91.3	73.1
Gujarat	9.1	124.7	109.5
Haryana	3.1	129.2	129.0
Himachal Pradesh	0.3	146.8	174.7
Jammu and Kashmir	0.2	167.2	159.2
Karnataka	5.2	121.5	120.5
Kerala	3.9	117.8	122.2
Madhya Pradesh	4.3	137.3	100.6
Maharashtra	14.4	125.2	99.2
Orissa	1.6	128.7	107.5
Punjab	4.1	121.6	121.0
Rajasthan	2.7	122.6	112.5
Tamil Nadu	13.4	128.3	123.0
Uttar Pradesh	9.1	105.6	83.3
West Bengal	9.7	111.8	83.4

Note: Newly formed states of Chhattisgarh, Jharkhand and Uttaranchal have been merged with the states they were part of before their formation.

Source: Annual Survey of Industries, various issues.

What about the wages, as a measure of welfare? Real wages per worker – nominal wages deflated by consumer price index – has roughly stagnated in the 1990s, while real emoluments for supervisors went up by 77 per cent between 1992 and 2001 (Figure 20.3).[6] Education, skill and experience probably explain the divergence in earnings of workers and supervisors, reflecting the industrial sector's growing technological complexity. Abolition of ceiling on managerial pay in 1991 could also have added to the widening gap.

Figure – 20.3

Real Wages and Emoluments

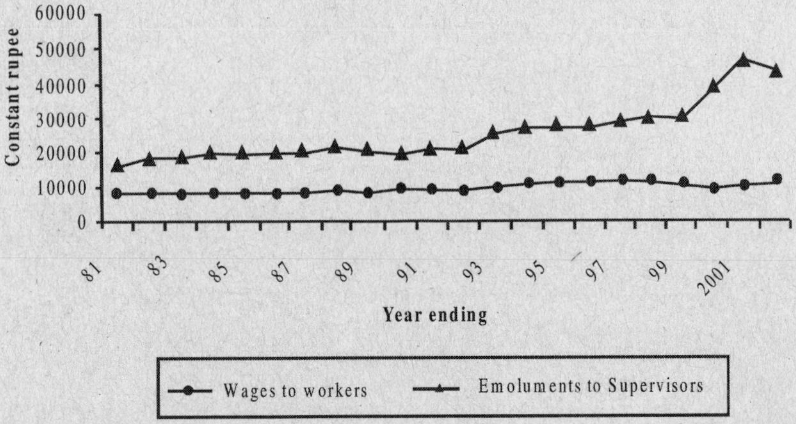

II

An Explanation

What explains the unprecedented job losses? Perhaps setting up of the National Renewal Fund – to finance mainly retrenchment of workers in public sector enterprises – was a signal of the government's tacit support for similar initiatives in the private sector. Although the labour laws remained the same, their enforcement was diluted or government ignored their evasion by employers. In effect, it was reform by stealth.[7] Some of it was perhaps unavoidable with the growing domestic and external competition. Introduction of information technology could also have contributed to workers' displacement.

In the initial years, these adjustments at the factory floor were not evident in the aggregate, as the output and investment boom during 1992-96 created sizeable new job opportunities (Figures 20.4 and 20.5). As the boom petered out, net job creation turned negative since retrenchments and lay-offs continued apace. In principle, these job losses should get reflected in the Labour Bureau's data in 'lay-offs and retrenchments', but they do not, due to increasing under-reporting.

Admittedly, some of the jobs shed are likely to have reappeared in the unorganised (informal) sector with growing subcontracting of production and shedding of auxiliary services like transport, security, cleaning,

Figure – 20.4

Manufacturing Output Growth, 1991-2002

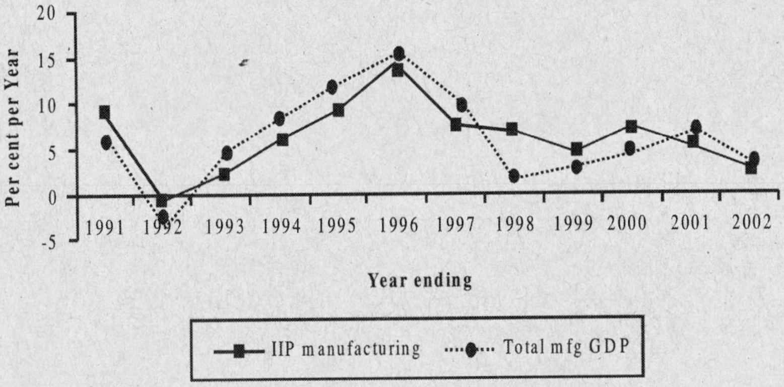

Figure – 20.5

Growth in Fixed Investment

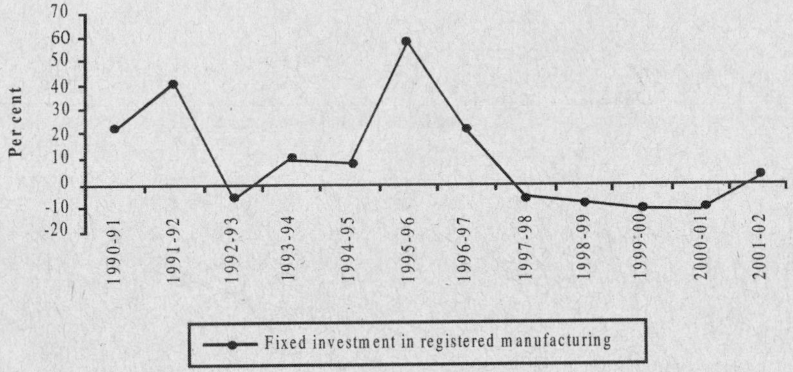

and provision of food at workplace. Hence, in the aggregate, the extent of job losses may not be severe as it appears in the first instance. Some of it may also represent natural attrition of workers in older firms and factories, where employers may not replace the retiring workers but reorganise the work among the remaining ones with suitable incentives.[8] Undoubtedly, these changes in labour use represent a fall in quality of employment with stagnant real wages and greater job insecurity.

What does the job losses imply for the economy? Greater productivity per worker, the gains of which have accrued mainly to employers, since the real wages have remained stagnant. However, with increased competition in product market, some of these gains are likely to have been passed on to consumers in terms of lower prices, or improved quality. Due to a thorough restructuring, (shedding of labour is one of its element) the organised manufacturing has largely withstood the policy shocks of the early 1990s, which apparently has helped some firms and factories to emerge internationally competitive.[9] Whether the greater efficiency implies faster output growth is a moot point. Moreover, if we reckon that workers are also consumers then the stagnation of real wages could have contributed to the shrinking of consumption demand, and to the deceleration of output growth. Similarly, whether investment in information technology secures sustained improvement in productivity is also debatable.[10]

III

Implications

As noted earlier, the labour market is widely believed to suffer from excessive intervention leading to substituting of capital for labour, and hurting employment growth. Job security clause is claimed to have further accentuated the rigidity. Labour market reforms have therefore mainly meant a reduction of the extent of protection and repealing of the job security clause – or simply, to permit 'hire and fire' with minimal interference from government and courts.

Is this view consistent with the experience of the 1990s? Probably not. There has been reform by stealth that has led to 15 per cent fall in employment in six years, without inviting large-scale resistance from the organised labour. It really exposes the ineffectiveness of the job security laws. The fact that real wages have remained stagnant for much of the 1990s despite over 3 per cent growth in per capita income suggests how weak is the organised labour's bargaining power *vis-à-vis* employers. It strengthens the argument that labour laws in India, as in many developing countries, tend to be aspirational with limited enforcement.[11]

Table 20.3 provides a summary of the organised manufacturing sector's performance since 1980-81. Evidently, employment growth is marginal and wage growth is modest (in fact, the wages have relatively declined). However, output has grown at over 7 per cent per year, which is reflected in significant rise in labour productivity, which is largely due to the increase in capital per worker. This is unlikely to represent a substitution of capital for labour, since wage-rental ratio has declined quite steeply, suggesting massive modernisation and diversification of the production structure.

TABLE – 20.3

Performance of Organised Manufacturing Sector, Some Selected Indicators, 1980-81 to 2000-01

	1980-81	1990-91	2000-01	Percentage Change	
				1981-91	1991-01
No of workers (million)	5.5	5.7	5.7	3.6	—
Real wages/worker (index)	100.0	118.2	134.0	18.2	13.1
Product wage/workers (index)	100.0	165.4	210.0	65.4	27.2
Wage-rental ratio (index)	100.0	80.6	60.6	(–) 19.4	(–) 24.8
Labour productivity (index)	100.0	219.1	395.7	119.1	80.6
Capital stock/worker (index)	100.0	183.3	423.8	83.3	131.2
Memo: per capita net national product	145.2	198.5	278.1	36.7	40.1

Notes: All relevant variables are at constant process. Capital stock refers to net fixed capital stock at 1993-94 prices for total manufacturing. Product wage per worker divided the deflator for machinery and equipment (proxy for cost of capital) is the wage-rental ratio. In principle, it is perhaps more appropriate measure of relative cost of labour than the widely product wage per worker.

Sources: ASI, various issues; capital stock is from *National Accounts Statistics*, per capita net national product is from the *Economic Survey, 2001-02.*

Could a rigid labour market have permitted rapid output and productivity growth, with stagnant employment and modest real wage increase? Probably not, for the following reasons. Intuitively, the situation resembles Lewisian 'modern' sector with unlimited supply of labour at constant wages (in terms of food), and the output being inside the marginal productivity curve. Under the threat of increased competition after 1991, employers were able to augment output by work intensification that pushes output towards the marginal productivity curve; at the same time extending the frontier outwards by augmenting capacity. Such a process was perhaps possible only when the labour market is flexible enough to accept the terms and conditions laid down by employers. That the labour, in general, has been docile is evident from the fact that number of days of work lost due to industrial strife has fallen in absolute terms during this period (Figure 20.6).[12]

Figure – 20.6

Mandays Lost by Disputes

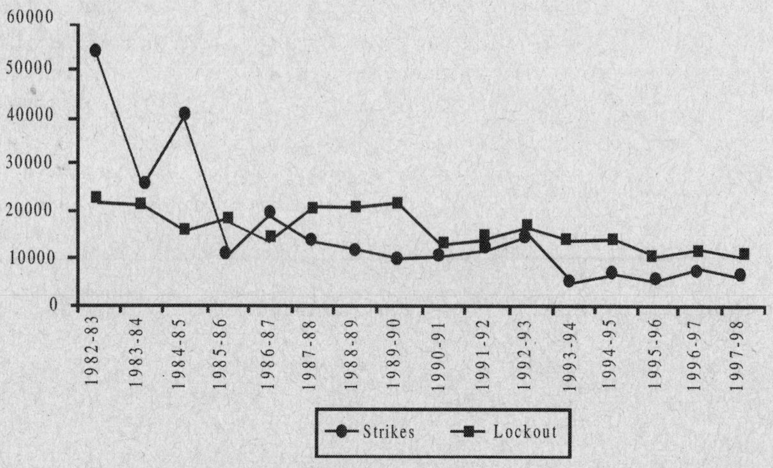

If above arguments and evidence has any merit, it suggests that much publicised labour market rigidity does not seem to hold any more, if it ever did. There now seems little basis to argue for greater freedom for employers to hire and fire. If anything, there is perhaps a need to ensure that workers losing jobs (i) are getting their legitimate dues from their employers and public institutions, (ii) are provided with an opportunity to retrain themselves in more marketable skills, and (iii) have access to financial assistance for self-employment.[13]

These suggestions are in no way an endorsement of the *status quo*. On the contrary, there is a need to rationalise the labour laws to encourage cooperative behviour among workers and employers. Probably we have to move towards income security (in place of job security) safeguarding workers' earnings, in return for more flexible use of their labour time by their willingness to perform a variety of functions [Bardhan, 2000].[14]

It is widely acknowledged that plethora of labour laws do not necessarily improve workers' bargaining position, in the absence of a credible enforcement mechanism. These laws with numerous built-in loopholes seem to offer rent seeking opportunities for some, and lengthy litigations for the bulk of the workers, who bear the brunt of the disputes in the absence of minimal social security.[15]

IV

Conclusions

Between 1995-96 and 2000-01, about 1.1 million workers, or 15 per cent of workers in the organised manufacturing sector lost their jobs. These losses have been widespread across major states and industry groups. Real wages have practically stagnated, when per capita income grew close to 3 per cent per year during the 1990s. However, employment of supervisors rose steadily, and their earnings accelerated in this period.

What explains the unprecedented employment contraction? Setting up of the National Renewal Fund as a component of structural adjustment programme in 1991 to finance VRS in public sector enterprises seems to have provided the initial impetus. Taking cues from it, private sector retrenched and laid off workers, as enforcement of labour laws was relaxed, which can be considered reform by stealth. Shedding of excess labour was perhaps one of the initiatives of industrial restructuring in the face of increased domestic and external competition under changed policy regime.

Up to the mid-1990s, job losses did not show up in the aggregate, as there was considerable job creation due to the boom in industrial output and investment. As the boom went bust, and the lay-offs sustained, there was a steep fall in employment in the second half of the 1990s. Relative cost of labour did not seem to matter in employment decisions, as the wage-rental ratio declined secularly.

The extent and spread of the job losses witnessed suggest that the much discussed inflexibility in industrial labour market seems over done – at least in the aggregate. Productivity gains have largely accrued to employers, as real wages were practically stagnant. The real need of the hour, therefore, is perhaps not greater freedom to employers to hire and fire at will, but to ensure that those losing jobs during industrial restructuring get their legitimate dues from their employers and public institutions. They require retraining to acquire marketable skills, and financial assistance to become self-employed.

There is perhaps also a need to move towards income security with workers accepting multi tasking and flexible use of their labour. Reforms should perhaps be seen as an effort to rationalise labour laws to make them simpler, yet strictly enforceable. In other words, it is imperative to work towards a new compact where workers accept income security and flexible labour use, while employers offer better work and productivity sharing agreements. Such efforts alone could put a human face to the otherwise harsh reality of today's labour market.

Notes

1. *Annual Survey of Industries* (*ASI*), the main data source for this study, defines worker as: "Workers are defined to include all persons employed directly or through any agency whether for wages or not, and engaged in any manufacturing process or in cleaning any part of the machinery or premises used for manufacturing process or in any other kind of work incidental to or connected with the manufacturing process or subject of the manufacturing process. Labour engaged in the repair and maintenance or production of fixed assets for factory's own use or labour employed for generating electricity or producing coal, gas, etc, are included. However, persons holding positions of supervision or management or employed in administrative office, store keeping section and welfare section, sales department as also those engaged in the purchase of raw materials, etc., and in production of the fixed assets for the factory and watch and ward staff are excluded."
2. Overlooking this distinction, as many recent studies have done, could yield misleading results, since there is a growing divergence between employment and earnings of workers and supervisors.
3. For a brief literature review, see Nagaraj (2004).
4. Data for 2001-02 is from the Central Statistical Organisation's (CSO) web site.
5. With the revision of tabulation scheme since 1998-99, CSO has ceased to provide data by size of factories, by type of ownership and organisation, severely restricting the quality of analysis.
6. *ASI* underestimates emoluments to supervisors since it cannot fully capture various perks granted to senior managers, but recorded as part of operating expenses.
7. Jenkins (1999) provides many instances of how powerful regional political leaders have persuaded state governments to make subtle changes in labour laws by administrative orders, yielding substantial leeway for employers.
8. Such a shift, in principle, should get reflected in higher employment growth in unregistered sector, but it is not evident yet [Chadha and Sahu 2002].
9. For instance, Tata Steel halved its workforce to 40,000 and doubled its output to 4 million tonnes in the 1990s, to emerge as the world's second most efficient steel mill, according to World Steel Dynamics (*Far Eastern Economic Review*, February 12, 2004).
10. Even in the US economy that has witnessed most rapid increase in IT related investments, their contribution to productivity growth is hard to measure. See, for instance, symposia on 'Computers and Productivity' in *Journal of Economic Perspectives*, Vol 14, No 4, Fall 2000.
11. Most of the studies by mainstream economists have sought to highlight the strengths of the organised labour and the growing rigidity of the labour market using selected aggregate statistics. They have ignored descriptive, disaggregated, fieldwork based and sociological accounts of the labour market that document problems like the ineffectiveness of the labour laws due to poor enforcement, and inability of workers to get justice in courts and labour departments. For a recent review of this genre of literature, see Chapter 2 of Harris-White (2003).
12. This graph is taken from Uchikawa (2003).
13. Apparently NRF was intended for retraining and relocating workers adversely affected by structural adjustment programme. But it was effectively turned into a source for VRS in public sector enterprises.
14. My reading of industrial disputes suggests that workers and their unions usually accept flexible use of labour and work intensification as long as there is a reasonable assurance of continuity of employment and reasonable sharing of productivity of gains.
15. With detailed documentation, Mathur (1991) shows how the seemingly rigid labour laws contain escape clauses that vitiate the very purpose of such legislations.

References

Bardhan, Pranab (2000), "Social Justice in Global Economy", *Economic and Political Weekly*, Vol 36, Nos 5-6.

Besley, Timothy and Robin Burgess (2004), "Can Labour Regulation Hinder Economic Performance? Evidence from India", *Quarterly Journal of Economics*, Vol 119, No 1, February.

Chadha, G K and P P Sahu (2002), "Post-Reform Setbacks in Rural Employment", *Economic and Political Weekly*, Vol 37, No 22, May 25.

Harris-White, Barbara (2003), *India Working: Essays on Society and Economy*, Cambridge University Press, Cambridge.

Jenkins, Rob (1999), *Democratic Politics and Economic Reform in India*, Cambridge University Press, Cambridge.

Mathur, Ajeet N (1991), *Industrial Restructuring And Union Power*, ILOARTEP, Delhi.

Nagaraj, R, *Labour Market Issues in India: A Note*, http://ctool.gdnet.org/conf_docs/Rayaprolu_paper.pdf

——— (2003), "Industrial Policy and Performance Since 1980: Which Way Now?", *Economic and Political Weekly*, Vol 38, No 35, August 30.

Uchikawa, Shuji (2003), "Employment in Organised Manufacturing Sector: Rise of Medium Scale Units" in Shuji Uchikawa (ed), *Labour Market and Institutions in India*, Manohar, Delhi.

Economic and Political Weekly, July 24, 2004.

21

Public Versus Private Sector

Neglect of Lessons of Economics in Indian Policy Formulation

B.S. Minhas

"The choice between the public sector enterprises and private firms is not a simple either/or question. While there may be eminently good reasons for promoting public sector production under certain circumstances, nevertheless there is no basis whatever for the doctrine of the so-called commanding heights. The Indian economy is struggling in the deep swamps of inefficiency. Its deliverance from this inefficiency trap can be vastly facilitated if both the public sector and private firms are exposed more and more to global competition and the arbitrary bureaucratic controls for the regulation of entry and freedom of exit of firms are substantially rolled back." (Minhas)

— Written in 1991, the analysis in this paper is very much relevant today. (ed.)

1. Introduction

People derive satisfaction/welfare from consuming goods, services and leisure. Other things being equal, the more of any good/service a person has, the greater that person's welfare. The firms and enterprises produce goods and services and try to maximise their profits/surplus by selling them. In this world of welfare and surplus maximisers, if a set of prices of goods and factors of production emerges, such that each producer, with his given production technology, is unable to increase his profits/surplus at the prevailing set of prices and each consumer is unable, within his budget constraint, to increase his welfare, and provided that all markets are cleared in the sense that quantities demanded exactly equal the quantities supplied, then this set of prices, inputs and outputs constitutes a situation of competitive equilibrium. According to a basic theorem[1] of neoclassical economics, a competitive equilibrium is a Pareto optimum - a configuration in which it is not possible to find a reallocation of resources that makes at least one person better off without making anyone else worse off.

The first important thing to note is the "if-then" nature of the above mentioned statement of a competitive equilibrium. Strictly speaking, this formal characterisation only describes the properties of an equilibrium. It does not address the question whether the profit-maximising behaviour of producers and welfare-maximising behaviour of consumers, taking the prevailing set of prices as given, will somehow lead the economy to a competitive equilibrium. Secondly, a situation of Pareto optimality does not imply that it meets some ethical notion of distributive justice, except in the sense of a purely formalistic, distributional compatibility with production efficiency in the context of maximisation of a Social Welfare Function, embodying in it some considerations of a distributional justice.

In case a competitive equilibrium somehow comes into existence, the question of conditions under which it might be sustained has been investigated in the neoclassical literature. Another justly famous theorem of Welfare Economics, for instance, asserts that (under strong assumptions relating to technology, consumer preferences, absence of externalities, etc.) associated with any Pareto Optimum (that maximises social welfare) is a set of prices that will sustain it as a competitive equilibrium provided appropriate redistribution of resource endowments or income through lump sum transfers is feasible. This result presumes a complete set of smoothly functioning markets for commodities, factors of production and insurance and strict observance (enforceability) of trading contracts.

One must note that these two theorems have nothing to say about the virtues or vices of a free market economy[2]. As a formal description of the informationally efficient decentralisation of decisions brought about by price-guided allocation, these theorems are just as applicable to a capitalist system as to the Lange-Lerner world of socialist planning. However, because of the much longer association and closer familiarity of the economists with the model of a competitive market economy, the outcome associated with an idealised market economy is often used as the efficiency benchmark - a touchstone to evaluate and compare different price-output configurations resulting from alternative economic arrangements. In view of the Pareto-efficient property of a competitive equilibrium, its use as the efficiency benchmark is easily understandable, provided it is also clearly recognised that the maximising behaviour of individual economic agents may not generate the prices and other relevant information which will somehow lead the economy into a situation of competitive equilibrium.

At a particular stage of the development of an economic system, the price-market arrangements for some goods and factors of production may not emerge. Aside from this absence of certain markets (such as future markets for many goods), some other markets may suffer from incompleteness. Markets for insurance and capital, for instance, in most less-developed countries are notoriously incomplete. And even if markets do exist, they may fail. In other words, in those situations where markets are absent or incomplete, or when markets fail, the autonomous system of horizontal coordination and parallel processing of economic information, implied in the competitive price-market solution, breaks down. Fortunately, the aetiology of such breakdowns[3] and approaches towards mending them are fairly well known: Economic Science has developed an articulate and fairly convincing theory of market failure - a theory whose scope and practical policy relevance is (unfortunately) not properly appreciated by the politicians and bureaucrats.

2. Reasons for Market Failure

Aside from the phenomenon of public goods, the dominant reasons for market failure arise because of the presence of (a) natural monopoly conditions, (b) externalities, and (c) informational deficiencies/ asymmetries.

A monopoly may come into being quite naturally when the fixed costs of providing a good are high relative to the variable cost, leading to decline in the average cost of production over the relevant range of demand. In such a case, a single firm can produce the particular output at a lower cost than any other market arrangement, including competition. The price elasticity of demand for such a good would determine whether or not the natural monopoly should invite public intervention. Whenever the price elasticity of demand is less than one, an increase in price will increase total revenue. A natural monopoly in this case would result in higher prices and lower output than under competitive conditions. In other words, in a situation of monopoly, the system of production would suffer from allocative inefficiency and loss of social welfare. Public utilities, such as electric power and telecommunications, are common examples of natural monopolies.

Externalities

An externality (external economy or diseconomy) is any valued impact (benefit or cost; positive externality or negative externality) resulting from any action that affects someone who did not fully consent to it. The presence of such externalities in any sector may not lead to the emergence of self-policing economic arrangements. Although discussions on externalities of different kinds have been in the folk-lore of welfare economics since times immemorial, and the literature is littered with examples, yet a rigorous analysis of the subject did not become available until the early 1950s. In the framework of competitive equilibrium analysis, Scitovsky[4] demonstrated that while the current production problems of an economy could be satisfactorily mediated through the market mechanism, but the externalities arising from intertemporal dependence among firms in different sectors (the presence of "pecuniary external economies", as he called them) could cause severe impediments to growth of investment in an underdeveloped economy, if it were to be guided solely by the prevailing price system. His analysis established a presumption that pecuniary external economies could be better mediated through investment planning by public authorities and the outcome associated with this interventionist policy may, under certain circumstances, be superior to the private market solution.

Informational Deficiencies/Asymmetries

If the economic agents can determine the characteristic of every good with certainty prior to its purchase, then the information contained in the prevailing set of prices is likely to lead to an appropriate allocation of resources. However, if the economic agents can determine the characteristics of a good only after its purchase and use then the informational asymmetry is likely to lead to allocative inefficiency. Also there may be some goods and investment actions, whose quality and consequences are difficult to determine without long experience with their use; and often it may be too late for economic agents/consumers to apply correctives to their behaviour, or to undo the adverse consequences of their earlier use or neglect. The presence of such informational asymmetry can lead to failure of price-market arrangements and sub-optimal outcomes. Diffidence of Indian peasants in relation to consolidation of their fragmented land holdings and the consequent sub-optimal investments in land and water development[5] are outstanding examples of informational deficiencies. The attitude of consumers towards the use of certain drugs, neglect of education and medical care of children, etc., are other manifestations (among many others) of the informational asymmetry between different groups in society.

Market Failure and Government Intervention

Acquisition of diagnostic skills to detect the presence of market failure may, perhaps, be considered an easy matter, nevertheless the task of prescribing curative policy interventions is indeed complicated. Administrative costs and harmful side effects of policy interventions are often difficult to fathom in advance. Faced with conditions of endemic market failure in a sector, the dilemma is often sought to be resolved through direct entry of the government in the production/provision of goods and services produced by such a sector. However, such direct involvement of the government, just as often, may turn out to be a mistake, as in many such cases market failure can be better addressed with much less-intrusive policies. In the perspective of sound economic principles, the presence of market failure in a sector provides only a necessary condition for some form of government intervention, nevertheless the sufficient conditions for undertaking its production in the public sector need to be carefully investigated and separately established.

3. Bureaucratic Failure

As indicated earlier, we have a reasonably well worked out and fairly convincing theory of market failure. However, an equally convincing theory of bureaucratic (government) failure has not come into existence yet. Nonetheless, bureaucratic inefficiencies and cases of government failure are not less rampant than the cases of price-market failure. The real source of confusion, which creates most problems in the discussions on public versus the private sector, however, arises from the fact that we have no over-reaching theory that can facilitate the analysis of trade-offs between market failure and bureaucratic failures.

In the absence of a widely accepted theory of bureaucratic failure, it is almost impossible to predict/estimate with confidence the costs and benefits of direct production of goods by public agencies. The social costs of market failure, condoned through government in-action, cannot, therefore, generally be weighed up against the uncertain costs and harmful side effects which bureaucratic activism in the market might entail. This makes it difficult to figure out and evaluate the pay-offs associated with different combinations of market outcomes and direct government intervention in policy formulation.

4. Market Failure and Public Sector Production

It has been said earlier that the presence of an endemic market failure may call for public intervention in some form but not necessarily through government production/provision of the relevant goods. In order to decide the question whether public intervention should be in the shape of direct production/provision of certain goods by the government or through other policies, it is prudent to use the so-called "Double Market Failure Criterion". First one must establish sound evidence of market failure or a consensus for the acceptance of some distributional goal. Second one must also search for evidence that a less intrusive policy cannot be utilised, or effective contracts for private production of public provisions cannot be devised. Whenever double-market failure criterion is fulfilled, the case for public sector production/provision of such goods is usually strong.

The need for public sector production is more or less well established when moral hazards and opportunistic/strategic behaviour are strongly indicated. The most common examples of double-market failure and opportunistic behavior arise in the production of public goods, defence (which is itself a public good), collection of taxes, printing of money, administration of justice, etc. To illustrate the meaning of opportunistic behaviour one can easily conceive of private armies. In fact, private armies have been raised in the course of history and many such armies were involved in the THIRTY YEAR WAR in Europe. The difficulty with the private armies is precisely the opportunistic behaviour of the solders. Private armies cannot be trusted to carry out the contracts because the governments do not have an independent mechanism of enforcement of such contracts. Soldiers can be lured from one side to another because of higher wages or better spoils system devised by the enemy. Notice that the failure here is the failure of the market twice over: My enjoyment of security from a given level of defence is not diminished by the enjoyment of security by millions of others. Defence, as a public good, is non-competitive and non-excludable among the citizens. It is almost impossible to envisage price-market arrangements for national security and further the contracts between the private armies and governments are unenforceable.

5. Private Versus Political Firms

The crucial differences between the private firms and political firms (Public Sector Agencies) is that ownership in the latter is not transferable. In consequence, this lack of transferability of ownership inhibits the capitalisation of future consequences of the actions of public sector bureaucracy into current transfer prices (net worth of the public sector enterprises) and this reduces the incentives of political firms to monitor their own behaviour. One must also quickly add that even in private firms where share holdings might get highly dispersed and the management moves away from primary entrepreneurs to professional managers, the result may be higher costs and lower profitability. In other words, in such a situation allocative inefficiencies also emerge under the price-market arrangements. Nevertheless, the capitalisation of these inefficiencies in the networth of the private firm, and its adverse impact on share prices, is likely to invite drastic corrective action.

Corrective action to mend and improve the behaviour of political firms is often delayed and, in fact, such action may never be taken, except in some special cases after an incumbent government gets thrown out through the normal practices of democracy. In other words, the checks and balances available to a democratic system of governance may provide some occasional correctives to the inherent inefficiencies of some political firms (public sector enterprises), nevertheless there is no guarantee that these democratic correctives would come forth as and when necessary for sustaining the economic health of these enterprises[6].

We have noted that in the presence of incomplete markets, informational deficiencies and externalities, the market equilibrium is in general not Pareto-efficient. Economic theory, on the other hand, tells us that, under these circumstances, one can devise schemes of government intervention which can lead to Pareto-superior outcomes. However, a large body of experience also tells us that the government agencies charged with the responsibility of managing public enterprises often fail to design suitable economic organisations and systems of incentives and punishments to induce dynamic technological and market adaptations, prevent over-manning and promote necessary control of cost and quality in public sector firms. In other words, the dilemma between the private and public sectors looks like one of Hobson's choice under certain circumstances.

All said and done, the following practical question still remains: Are public sector firms less efficient than private firms? There is no categorical answer to this practical question. The evidence all over the world is quite mixed[7]. There is sufficient evidence to support both sides of the question. However, one thing is quite clear. Unmistakably, in practical terms, the degree of competition in a market is a better predictor of efficient performance than the question of ownership (public versus private) per se. While public firms have more often been found to be less efficient than private firms in globally competitive markets, nonetheless, there are many instances of successful and efficient public sector corporations having been established even when there was no evidence of an endemic market failure. France, for instance, produces machine tools, automobiles, watches and certain types of airplanes in state enterprises and sells them in world markets. Instances of efficient public enterprises in India as well as in many other mixed economies and capitalist countries can also be given.

6. Public Sector in India

Aside from the expansion of public sector operations in certain sectors of infrastructure, such as roads, communications, drainage, river basin and certain natural resource developments, agricultural research and extension and public services, where direct government intervention can be justified because of the public good character of these activities, the government in India in the last forty years has vastly expanded its direct operations in a vast variety of sectors with little regard for lessons of economic theory, or its own administrative and management resources. From tourism to road transport, from production of steel, aluminium heavy machinery, drugs, chemicals, fertilizers and cloth to commercial banking and public sector monopoly in airline services, public sector firms/agencies have been established in all manner of manufacturing and trading activities.

These vast public sector investments in manufacturing and commercial enterprises have on the whole failed to produce the surpluses which they were expected to generate for the further growth of the public sector. Instead, large losses have been made which, year in and year out, are simply financed by drawing on the limited budgetary resources of the country. The justification for these losses is not clearly possible to establish in terms of the distributional goals achieved by public sector production.

The growth of public sector in India has generated a fairly large volume of employment, which has often been cited as an example of the fulfillment of some important distributional goals of the government. In other words, employment generation in itself has been seen as a justification to condone large public sector losses. Although it is difficult to prove whether more employment could have been generated elsewhere in the economy with the same volume of funds invested in the public sector during the past forty years, nevertheless the more important question that still remains to be asked is this: Is the current volume of public sector employment sustainable in a dynamic sense? In view of the serious fiscal crisis facing the country - a crisis that has been becoming deeper and deeper since the mid-1980s, the answer to this question would seem to be in the negative. Further, the maintenance of the current levels of employment in many near-sick public sector enterprises would surely jeopardise the possibilities of the creation of many more new jobs in future.

7. State as a Private Trading Post

One final point, which might facilitate more discussion on the question of public sector versus private firms, relates to the nature of the State. To put it differently: can one always take a public interest view of the government? Do our political masters and bureaucrats in their actions always give priority to public interests over their own self-aggrandisement and private gratification? When a government becomes a private trading post[8] in which jobs, favours, policies and contracts are freely traded for money and private gains, and rents of political and bureaucratic power are collected in most transactions, it is imprudent to be optimistic about the efficiency and effectiveness of massive government intervention in the production and provision of goods through public sector firms and agencies.

Undoubtedly, the venality of the predatory state in India gets somewhat restrained by its occasional search for political legitimacy. Nevertheless, the notion of legitimacy itself has gradually been denuded of its rigour and coherence because of the predominance of the single party rule since 1947. The electoral processes of the Indian democracy did throw up some alternatives in 1977 and 1989. However, the creative and dynamic potential of these political events (1977-1979 and 1989-1990) evaporated before any clear and meaningful agenda for policy reform could even emerge, much less being implemented. In other words, the Indian people have not failed in expressing their anger against continuance of the venal and inefficient state of affairs. Nevertheless, a coherent and viable coalition of groups, deriving its legitimacy from the national aspirations and true developmental needs of the Indian people has this far failed to materialise. The forthcoming (May 1991) mid-term elections to Parliament would seem to offer yet another opportunity for some credible policy alternatives to emerge. It is difficult to predict the results of the forthcoming elections. Nevertheless, one hopes that we are not churning water once again as we did less than 18 months ago.

8. Commanding Heights of the Economy or Deep Swamps of Inefficiency

The most obvious economic-theoretic, distributive justice and national security considerations, which might call for some strategic regulation of the price-market system, have briefly been indicated in this note. However, the author has failed to come across any convincing theory (or a generally valid practical case having been made) in support of the political doctrine of State control of the "Commanding Heights of the Economy" through expansion of the public sector. The origin of this phrase, commanding heights, is attributed to Lenin, nevertheless, its popularity and misplaced (over-drawn) policy relevance in India is associated with the name of Jawaharlal Nehru.

Leaving aside the worn-out ideological appeal of the doctrine of expanding state power through public sector production, and also ignoring its dubious gains in terms of redistributive justice, the bureaucratic management of the overall environment of economic policy in India has turned the system into a fast-breeder reacter for the generation of inefficiency, industrial sickness and corruption, both in the public as well as private sector. Instead of climbing to the Commanding Heights, the bureaucratic command system has succeeded in trapping the economy in the deep swamps of inefficiency, very fast growth in government expenditures, unmatched by increases in tax revenues, and the emergence of large fiscal deficits, which currently stands at around 9 per cent of national product. Its main salience today is comprised of higher and higher levels of inflation, a very large and growing trade deficit, and a big mountain of public debt, both internal and external.

9. Ideology and Competition as Tools of Discipline

It is quite easy to appreciate that ideological considerations are important in the affairs of a government. However, as we have argued earlier, under a variety of circumstances, the policy choices between the public sector and private enterprise would appear to have much less to do with ideology than is often made out in public debate in India. The main difficulty with the bureaucratic command system in the public sector is that it rarely succeeds in devising an effective organisational structure and incentive system for the horizontal coordination of the infinitely diverse and multiple decisions which comprise an efficient and dynamic economy. The bureaucratic system of command and controls (which are essentially protective or basically restrictive in operation) scuttles competition and possibilities of learning and creative adjustment.

The competitive order, on the other hand, is generally more efficient because it breeds insecurity and almost instantaneous accountability through the ever-present threat of other competitors and the ultimate fear of exit. In a competitive environment, information gets automatically processed in a parallel manner at a variety of levels. There is little red tape to cut through: long reaction times and delays in adjustment invite loss of business and ultimate accountability through failure. We must therefore promote in India a more competitive order and a far less discretionary policy environment for the efficient operations of private as well as public sector firms. This is the most basic policy lesson which can be drawn from the fundamental theorems of Economics and principles of good government.

10. Some Concluding Remarks

The choice between the public sector enterprises and private firms is not a simple either/or question. While there may be eminently good reasons for promoting public sector production under certain circumstances, nevertheless there is no basis whatever for the doctrine of the so-called commanding heights. The Indian economy is struggling in the deep swamps of inefficiency. Its deliverance from this inefficiency trap can be vastly facilitated if both the public sector and private firms are exposed more and more to global competition and the arbitrary bureaucratic controls for the regulation of entry and freedom of exit of firms are substantially rolled back.

In view of the persistence of a large fiscal deficit, one often comes across suggestions for the privatisation of public sector firms in India. In our considered opinion, privatisation is an exaggerated issue as its scope would seem to be very limited. The perpetual loss-making public sector enterprises, which are very many in numbers, may not find any buyers. On the other hand, selling-off the well-managed, profit making public sector firms will certainly increase the fiscal deficit of the government in the future. The reduction of the fiscal deficit can be brought about only by drastic reductions in government expenditures and raising government revenues. The money gathered from the disposal of public sector enterprises can finance the current deficit but it cannot reduce it. However, the principle that the "by-gones are forever by-gones" is a good one to follow: The loss-making enterprises, which are incapable of being nursed back to good economic health, are better allowed to perish and their salvage value in alternative uses recovered to aid the fiscal operations of the government.

In the current Indian situation, it is not certain whether the private owners of the public sector units will turn out to be better managers than their public sector counterparts. Industrial sickness has also been rampant in the Indian private sector. Thousands of sick units from the private sector have been taken over by the government to add to the burden in the public sector. Under our over-reaching licensing system, the private industrialists and business managers have learnt to manage their competitors through bribing the Executive, rather than through their production skills and marketing acumen. In consequence, the culture of production efficiency and entrepreneurship has largely been stultified[9]. The real answer to our ills should consist in evolving a policy framework, which permits only selective intervention but breeds a more honest and effectively competitive economic order, maintaining conditions of easy entry and allowing the terminally sick units to exit and die. The virtues of fear of failure and freedom of exit can hardly be over-emphasised in sustaining dynamic efficiency and conditions supportive of creative learning and change in an economy.

One can strongly argue that, in consequence of the mindless over-extension of public sector operations in manufacturing and commerce, the Government of India have been able to spare inadequate financial and administrative resources for the development of certain items of infrastructure and essential social services, which because of their public good character legitimately belong in the public sector. This inadequate and deteriorating infrastructure and poor availability of social services, in turn, have had their share in raising costs and lowering the competitiveness of Indian goods in world markets. To put it differently, the case for strengthening public sector activity in certain sectors of infrastructure, such as roads, bridges, communications, drainage and river basin development, agricultural research and extension and basic social services, is indeed strong and by concentrating its administrative and financial resources in the development of infrastructure, the Government of India can facilitate quicker expansion of economic activity in the country in a more cost-effective manner.

One must nevertheless note that the public, or collective, good character of infrastructure and basic social services, arising out of their non-competitiveness or non-excludability in use, furnishes a necessary condition for the existence of a public-good-market-failure which however satisfies only the first part of the double market failure criterion. There are important differences among the great variety of items of infrastructure and public services in terms of the nature of market failure - the differences which may call for appropriate variations in the design of public policy response in different cases. While planning (scale and level) and financing of the provision of infrastructure and basic public services by the public authorities can be shown to led to a Pareto-superior outcome, nevertheless the question of their construction and delivery directly by the government needs to be separately investigated (case by case) with respect to the second part of the double market failure criterion. We have enough empirical evidence to suggest that contracting out to private firms is frequently more efficient than direct supply by government departments and agencies, particularly when a variety of these facilities have to be provided to a large number of distinct locations and geographical areas. While the emergence of opportunistic behaviour in some cases cannot be ruled out, nevertheless it is likely to be limited in nature, particularly when the item of infrastructure or the social service in question yields measurable output and monitoring the quality of output is relatively straightforward.

In summary, both economic theory and developmental experience suggest that aside from a clear role for the public sector in the direct provision of public goods and certain items of infrastructure and basic social services, there may exist strong grounds for public sector activity to protect the interests of future generations in certain areas, such as environmental preservation, which are often poorly reflected in private preferences of the contemporaries. The existence of cases of market failure in the industrial and commercial sectors, suspected to arise out of imperfect information and pecuniary externalities, on the other hand, does not necessarily imply indiscriminate expansion of government ownership, or the imposition of a regime of blanket controls and draconian regulations on the private sector. The experience in India and many other countries suggests that the informational deficiencies and externalities, which might impinge on sectors producing tradable goods and services, are better addressed through the selective use of less intrusive policies rather than through direct government ownership and extensive public regulation of the private sector. The government can play a more positive and catalytic role in the development of industry and commerce by funding research and information dissemination activities relating to technological choices and market intelligence, by facilitating the emergence of better-functioning markets as well as cooperative institutions and, most of all, by enhancing the competitiveness of the tradable goods sector. The incidence of bureaucratic failure in public sector enterprises in India can also be considerably reduced if public sector managers are exposed to the discipline of market competition and market incentives to induce creative learning and prompt responses to new commercial opportunities.

Notes

1. T.C. Koopmans, (1957), *Three Essays on the State of Economic Science*, New York, McGraw Hill.
2. On all this and more, see, T.N. Srinivasan, (1985), "Neoclassical Political Economy, the State and Economic Development", *Asian Development Review*, Vol.3, No.2, pp. 38-55.
3. A fairly intelligent statement of the common causes of market failure, for instance, is available in Francis M. Bator (1958), "The Anatomy of Market Failure", *Quarterly Journal of Economics*, Vol.72, No.3, pp. 351-379.
4. T. Scitovsky, (1954), "Two Concepts of External Economies", *Journal of Political Economy*, Vol.62, pp. 143-151.
5. The interested reader may wish to consult B.S. Minhas (1970), "Rural Poverty, Land Redistribution and Development Strategy", *Indian Economic Review*, Vol.5, April 1970, pp. 97-126.
6. If a part of the equity of political firms is sold in the open market, this would be a way of marketising the public sector. However, the issue under consideration in this paper is different: It is the public sector versus private firms.
7. A large body of empirical evidence on the relative efficiency of public corporations and private firms is listed in David L. Weimer and Aidan R. Vining (1989), *Policy Analysis: Concepts and Practice,* Prentice Hall, Englewood Cliffs, Appendix 5A, pp. 174-75.
8. For an elaboration of this characterisation of the Indian State and its general implications for the design of public policy, the reader may refer to author's "Leadership, Public Policy and Socio-Economic Development", *Economic and Political Weekly*, Vol.23, No.37, September 10, 1988, particularly pp. 1901-05.
9. See, B.S. Minhas, (1988), *op. cit.*

References

Bator, F.M. (1958), "The Anatomy of Market Failure", *Quarterly Journal of Economics*, Vol.72, No.3, pp. 351-79.

Koopmans, T.C. (1957), *Three Essays on the State of Economic Science,* New York, McGraw Hill.

Minhas, B.S. (1970), "Rural Poverty, Land Redistribution and Development Strategy", *Indian Economic Review*, Vol.5, April 1970, pp. 97-126.

—— (1988), "Leadership, Public Policy and Socio-Economic Development", *Economic and Political Weekly*, Vol.23, No.37, pp. 1901-05.

Scitovsky, T. (1954), "Two Concepts of External Economics", *Journal of Political Economy*, Vol.62, No.1, pp. 143-51.

Srinivasan, T.N. (1985), "Neoclassical Political Economy, the State and Economic Development", *Asian Development Review*, Vol.3, No.2, pp. 38-55.

Weimer, D.L. and Vining, A.R. (1989), *Policy Analysis: Concepts and Practice,* Englewood Cliffs, Prentice Hall, pp. 174-75.

Text of Rao Bahadur R.R. Kale Memorial Lecture delivered at the Gokhale Institute of Politics and Economics, Pune, April 27, 1991.

22

Disinvestment Commission (Report I, February, 1997)

PART – A

1. PUBLIC SECTOR – AN OVERVIEW

1.1 Evolution of Public Sector Policy

Historically, public sector undertakings (PSUs) have played an important part in the development of the Indian industry. At the time of independence, it was felt that political independence without economic self-reliance would be detrimental to the country's sovereignty and autonomy in policy-making. Hence, the basic objectives of starting the public sector were :

- To build infrastructure for economic development and promote rapid economic growth and industrialisation of the country;
- To create employment opportunities and promote balanced regional development;
- To create a self-reliant economy through the development of local industries for import substitution and by encouraging and promoting exports;
- To generate investible resources for development by earning suitable returns; and finally
- To prevent/reduce concentration of private economic power.

In the sixties and seventies the Public Sector policy has been largely guided by the Industrial Policy Resolution of 1956 which gave the public sector a strategic role in the economy. Massive investments have been made over the past four decades to build a public sector which had a commanding role in the economy. Many key sectors of the economy are today dominated by the mature public enterprises that have successfully expanded production, opened up new areas of technology and built up a reserve of technical competence in a number of areas.

As a result, the country's ranking in terms of industrialisation with other developing countries is quite high. India's comparative advantages such as a large pool of well-trained work-force, technical skills in manufacturing and chemical industries primarily stem from the public sector.

However, after the initial exuberance of the public sector entering new areas of industrial and technical competence, a number of problems began to manifest themselves in many enterprises. Problems were observed in terms of low productivity, poor project management skills, overmanning, lack of technological upgradation, inadequate attention to R&D and low priority to human resource development.

1.2 New Orientation

These problems and other economic compulsions led to the adoption of a new approach towards the public sector. In July 1991, the Government issued a Statement on Industrial Policy which had the following decisions[1]

- Portfolio of public sector investments will be reviewed with a view to focus the public sector on strategic, high-tech and essential infrastructure. Whereas some reservation for the public sector is being retained there would be no bar for areas of exclusivity to be opened up to the private sector selectively. Similarly the public sector will also be allowed entry in areas not reserved for it.
- Public enterprises which are chronically sick and which are unlikely to be turned around will, for the formulation of revival/rehabilitation schemes, be referred to the Board for Industrial and Financial Reconstruction (BIFR), or other similar high level institutions created for the purpose. A social security mechanism will be created to protect the interests of workers likely to be affected by such rehabilitation packages.
- In order to raise resources and encourage wider public participation, a part of the Government's share-holding in the public sector would be offered to mutual funds, financial institutions, general public and workers.

- Boards of public sector companies would be made more professional and given greater powers.
- There will be a greater thrust on performance improvement through the Memoranda of Understanding (MoU) system through which management would be granted greater autonomy and will be held accountable. Technical expertise on the part of the Government would be upgraded to make the MoU negotiation and implementation more effective.
- To facilitate fuller discussion on performance, the MoU signed between Government and the public enterprises would be placed in Parliament. While focusing on major management issues, this would also help place matters on day to day operations of public enterprises in their correct perspective.

The impact of these policy decisions on the performance of the PSUs is, as yet, debatable. As regards the private sector, the Government has granted freedom to add new capacities, delicensed some industries and has allowed investments in certain sectors. The public sector has to still obtain multi-level and time consuming clearances for such decisions and is accountable to multiple agencies. This lack of autonomy has created a somewhat unequal playing field for the PSUs in an increasingly competitive environment.

1.3 Common Minimum Programme

The Common Minimum Programme has stressed that PSUs will continue, to be an important component of Indian industry. In a competitive and technology-driven economy, the public sector should conduct its business on commercial lines. For this, it has been acknowledged that the public sector requires to be reformed and restructured. Those PSUs which have comparative advantages to be global giants will be identified and supported. Other profit making PSUs will have to be further strengthened. The management of these PSUs will be professionalised and encouragement would be given to worker's participation in management. As regards sick or potentially sick PSUs, they will have to be rehabilitated through different options including handing over management to professional groups or worker's co-operatives.

1.4 Profile of PSUs

An overall profile of the central PSUs is presented in the table below.

TABLE – 22.1

Profile of PSUs

(Rs. '00 crores)

	FY 95	FY 94	FY 93	FY 92	FY 91	FY 90
Operation Units (No)	241	240	239	237	236	233
Net Profits	72.2	45.5	32.7	23.6	22.7	37.9
Profitable Units (No)	130	121	131	133	123	131
Net Profits	121.2	97.7	73.8	60.8	53.9	57.5
Dividend	14.4	10.3	7.9	6.9	4.1	3.2
Loss making Units (No)	109	117	104	102	109	96
Overall Losses	49.1	52.9	39.5	36.7	30.4	19.6

1.5 Composition of Public Sector Plan Outlays

An important aspect relating to the performance of the PSUs has been the incidence of budgetary support. Till the nineties, PSUs in general, had access to funds from the government in the form of budgetary support. Widening fiscal deficits since the early nineties has however led to a sudden withdrawal of budgetary support for PSUs as is evident from the following table.

TABLE – 22.2

Composition of Public Sector Plan Outlays

(%)

	FY 95	FY 94	FY 93	FY 92	FY 91	FY 90
Net Internal Resources	46	34	41	39	34	34
Extra Budgetary Resources	41	52	45	42	42	34
Total Budgetary support	13	14	14	19	24	32
Plan Outlay	100	100	100	100	100	100

Budgetary support as a percentage of the total Plan outlay on the public sector has declined considerably from 32 per cent in FY 90 to 13 per cent in FY 95. This has been offset by the increased component of extra budgetary resources from sources other than the government which has grown from 34 per cent to 41 per cent during the same period.

In addition, increasing levels of deregulation and globalisation have ushered in an era of intense competition in the economy, the effects of which have been felt on certain PSUs. In some cases, even profitable PSUs have been adversely affected, while in some other cases, the losses of the loss making PSUs have compounded. This and the effect of sudden withdrawal of budgetary support have led to increased level of overall losses from about Rs. 1960 crores in FY 90 to about Rs. 4910 crores in FY 95 as shown in the table below:

TABLE – 22.3

Profile of Loss Making Units

(%)

	FY 95	FY 94	FY 93	FY 92	FY 91	FY 90
Total No. of Units	109	117	104	102	109	96
Total Loss (Rs. '00 Cr)	49.1	52.9	39.5	36.7	30.4	19.6
% Loss in taken Over Units	20	24	24	15	16	24
% Loss in Other Units	80	76	76	85	84	76

The composition of the overall losses reveals that almost three-fourths of the overall losses are cash losses (as opposed to book losses). The percentage of cash losses have remained more or less constant over the five years and the extent of depreciation provision has also remained more or less constant (Table 22.4).

TABLE – 22.4

Composition of Net Losses

(%)

	FY 95	FY 94	FY 93	FY 92	FY 91	FY 90
Cash Losses (a)	71	81	73	73	71	77
Depreciation (b)	33	23	34	30	40	39
Cash Profits (c)	4	4	7	3	11	16
Net Losses (a+b+c)	100	100	100	100	100	100

In the future, increasing globalisation and the orientation towards a market driven economy will bring more competitive pressures on these loss making PSUs. Thus, it would be quite reasonable to conclude that unless a viable and a rational strategy is evolved for these companies, they will continue to be an increasing draft on the budget.

Further, it is interesting to study the composition of the losses in terms of the major sectors. As can be seen from Table 22.5, major losses were accounted in Fertilisers, Heavy Engineering and the Consumer Goods sector in FY 95. These industries are characterised by the presence of a large number of players, most of them being in the private sector. The fully contestable nature of these markets has ensured fair competition and also provided a fair degree of protection to the consumer's interest.

TABLE – 22.5

Sectoral Composition of Losses

(% of total losses)

Sector	FY 95		FY 94		FY 93		FY 92		FY 91		FY 90	
	No	%	No	%	No	%	No	%	No	%	No	%
MANUFACTURING												
Fertilisers	3	16	6	15	5	18	2	15	3	14.9	4	18.3
Consumer Goods	15	14	15	14	15	9.5	14	6.1	14	7.2	13	13.3
Heavy Engg.	8	11	8	9.6	9	6.2	8	7.4	8	5.5	7	3.9
Textiles	13	9	14	12	12	15	11	8.4	11	7.5	11	11.6
Steel	5	8.2	5	13	4	16	4	28	2	20.4	3	7.5
Coal	4	8.1	2	2	3	2.9	2	1.9	5	9.4	3	3.3
Medium Engg.	11	4.9	9	3.9	8	1.4	11	3	12	1.7	8	1.5
Transport Equip.	6	4.7	7	5.6	7	6.7	7	6.6	6	4.1	8	10.9
TOTAL	**65**	**75.9**	**66**	**75.0**	**63**	**75.7**	**59**	**76.4**	**61**	**70.7**	**57**	**70.3**
SERVICES												
Trans. Serv.	3	11	3	11	4	12	3	12	4	10.1	4	8.5
Contact & Const.	7	4.6	8	4.8	5	3.6	5	3.5	6	4.5	5	7.1
TOTAL	**10**	**15.6**	**11**	**15.8**	**9**	**15.6**	**8**	**15.5**	**10**	**14.6**	**9**	**15.6**
Others	34	8.5	40	9.1	32	8.7	35	8.1	38	14.7	30	14.1
GRAND TOTAL	**109**	**100**	**117**	**100**	**104**	**100**	**102**	**100**	**109**	**100**	**96**	**100**
Total Net Losses (Rs. '00 Crores)	**49.1**		**52.9**		**39.5**		**36.7**		**30.4**		**19.6**	

Thus, it may be worthwhile to determine whether public sector presence is required in markets which are fully mature. This understanding will, in turn, help determine areas in which public sector needs to have a strong presence.

1.6 Budgetary Support in 1996-97

According to the Expenditure Budget document of 1996-97, the Plan outlay for public sector amounted to Rs. 50,400 crores of which about Rs. 46,700 crores would come by way of internal accruals and extra budgetary resources and the balance of about Rs. 3700 crores by way of budgetary support. It is necessary to examine this figure in order to segregate the support for profitable and loss making PSUs. The Expenditure Budget classifies budgetary support to PSUs under two heads: Plan Investments and non-Plan outlays. Plan investments are taken up by both profitable and loss making PSUs while non-Plan loans are primarily meant for the latter.

1.7 Support to Loss Making PSUs in 1996-97

The following table lists loss making units which have been provided with both Plan assistance and non-Plan loans in 1996-97.

TABLE – 22.6

Support to Loss Making Units

(Rs. Crores)

Sl.No.	Name of PSU	Plan Assistance			Non Plan Loan	Total Assistance
		Equity	Loan	Total		
1.	Nuclear Power Corp.	325		325		325
2.	Fert. Corp. of India	19	20	39	277	316
3.	National Text. Corpn.				243	243
4.	Hindustan Fertilisers	4	5	9	144	153
5.	National Jute Mfg. Corp				80	80
6.	Delhi Transport Corp.		10	10	53	63
7.	HEC	15	15	30	18	48
8.	Cent. Inland Water Transpt.	6	7	13	8	21
9.	Food Corporation	18		18		18
10.	Cement Corp. of India	7	8	15	2	17
11.	Hindustan Shipyard	8	7	15		15
12.	HMT	5	4	9		9
13.	Others	70	54	124	203	327
14.	Naptha Jakri Power*	179	254	433		433
15.	Tehri Hydro Electric*	170		170		170
	Total	**826**	**384**	**1210**	**1028**	**2238**

* Enterprise yet to be commissioned.

The support from the budget in the form of Plan investment to loss making PSUs in the form of equity and loans amounted to about Rs. 1210 crores and on account of non-Plan outlays amounted to about Rs. 1028 crores. Thus, the total assistance provided to loss making units aggregated to Rs. 2238 crores.

1.8 Budgetary Support to Profitable PSUs in 1996-97

The budgetary support provided as Plan assistance to profitable PSUs is as under.

TABLE – 22.7

Support for Profitable Units

(Rs. Crores)

Sl. No.	Name of PSU	Equity	Loan	Total
1.	PFC		550	550
2.	PGCIL*	8	313	321
3.	NHAI		250	250
4.	FACT*		240	240
5.	NTPC*	70	152	222
6.	NHPC*	50	99	149
7.	NLC*		126	126
8.	Singerani Collieries		119	119
9.	IREDA		115	115
10.	Coal India		100	100
11.	HUDCO		51	51
12.	Airport Authority		50	50
13.	REC		50	50
14.	MFL*		37	37
15.	Paradip Phosphates		33	33
16.	SCI*		30	30
17.	DVC		20	20
18.	Uranium Corp.		15	15
19.	Semi Conductor		12	12
20.	HLL*		1	1
21.	MFIL*		1	1
	TOTAL	**128**	**2364**	**2492**

* Referred to the Disinvestment Commission.

1.9 Analysis of Budgetary Support in 1996-97

The following table summarises the position of budgetary support to PSUs in 1996-97.

TABLE – 22.8

Composition of Budgetary Support

(Rs. Crores)

Category	Plan			Non Plan	G. Total
	On lending	Direct	Total		
Profitable	1114	1378	2492		2492
Loss Making	254	956	1210	1028	2238
Total	1368	2334	3702	1028	4730

- It would emerge from the above table that support to profit making PSUs is limited to two counts. Firstly, external loans from multi-lateral agencies were on-lent to PSUs through the central budget. These PSUs were NTPC, NLC, Power Grid, PFC and the total amount of on-lending was about Rs. 1114 crores. It can therefore be concluded that these loans are not a draft on the budget. Thus, out of the total budgetary support of about Rs. 2492 crores to the profitable PSUs, the net draft on the budget is limited to Rs. 1378 crores. This support has been provided to PSUs where normally, external assistance is not available.
- The budgetary support to loss making PSUs is about Rs. 2238 crores out of which Rs.254 crores is on-lend support to Naptha Jakri Power Ltd. Thus, the actual draft on the budget Rs.956 crores on the Plan account and Rs. 1028 crores on the non Plan account. The total budgetary support to loss making PSUs is Rs. 1984 crores which constitutes about 60 per cent of the total direct support to the PSUs.

1.10 Conclusions

The following conclusions can be drawn from the above study:

- *The losses of loss making PSUs have increased in the nineties due to withdrawal of budgetary support as well as increased competition. Most of these losses are cash losses and occur in sectors which have become fully competitive and where perhaps, PSUs have no special role.*

- Losses in loss making PSUs account for about 60 per cent of the total direct budgetary support and will in all probability, keep increasing each year. This will be a recurring draft on the budget.

Keeping these conclusions in mind, the Commission has evaluated the likely consequences of the future support to be provided to loss making units and recommendations in this regard follow in Part B.

2. DISINVESTMENT: STRATEGY, PRINCIPLES AND CRITERIA

2.1 Need for a Long Term Disinvestment Strategy

The public sector in India continues to be an important component of the Indian industry even after liberalisation unlike the experience in many other countries which went in for wholesale privatisation. Therefore, the Commission reiterates that the PSUs in general, must be managed on sound commercial lines and must generate adequate surpluses and make contributions commensurate with the quantum of public resources invested in them. Specifically, in the strategic sector, the public sector is expected to have a commanding presence. PSUs will be called upon to play an important role in certain core sectors of the economy. However, this should be achieved with minimum dependence on budgetary resources while government policies should provide a level playing field for PSUs to compete with the private sector.

Government's withdrawal from non-core sectors is indicated on considerations of long-term efficient use of capital, growing financial unviability and the compulsions for these PSUs to operate in an increasingly competitive and market oriented environment. A large number of PSUs in these sectors is either marginally profitable or loss making. Budgetary support to these loss making PSUs has been a recurring feature over the last several years. Increased competitive pressures have adversely affected some PSUs which were earlier profitable. Growing financial stringency will reduce the capacity of Government to support them and consequently lead to their closure with loss of employment in large numbers. Thus, in all probability, loss making PSUs will continue to be an increasing drain on the budget unless a viable policy of disinvestment is evolved and implemented for them.

Viewed in this scenario, disinvestment has larger implications than just selling government equity at the best price in profitable enterprises, as this alone may not provide long term budgetary benefit unless the question of recurring budgetary support to loss making PSUs is also addressed. The essence of a long term disinvestment strategy should therefore be not only to enhance budgetary receipts, but also minimise budgetary support towards loss making units while ensuring their long term viability and sustainable levels of employment in them.

Disinvestment as a strategy should also aim at wide dispersal of Government shareholding in the domestic market and broadbase ownership in the process. This of course, will be subject to limitations of the capital market in its capacity to absorb the proposed disinvestment and the private sector's capital requirements from the same market. Sale of shares in the foreign markets may, therefore, also become necessary and the extent would be determined on a case to case basis depending on the market conditions etc.

2.2 Long Term Disinvestment Strategy

Accordingly, the Commission's long term strategy on disinvestment would revolve around four long-term objectives:

- Strengthen PSUs where appropriate in order to facilitate disinvestment;
- Protect Employee Interests;
- Broadbase ownership; and
- Augment Receipts for Government

The resulting long term strategies that arise out of the above objectives are:

Strengthen PSUs

- Strengthen profitable PSUs to promote greater competitiveness and profitability to enable payment of higher dividends to the Government and to enhance share values
- Strengthen other marginally profitable PSUs and reduce their future dependence on the budget
- Financially restructure and revive loss making PSUs to invite private capital for long term turn around

Protect Employee Interest

- sustaining long term employment by financial turn around of loss making PSUs
- Providing adequate and fair compensation through VRS to surplus work force
- Provide for employee participation in management.

Broad Base Ownership

- Enhance retail reach of PSU shares to small investor and offer at suitable price discount as compared to the institutional investor

Augment Receipts for Government

- Enhance Government receipts by disinvestment in profitable PSUs
- Eliminate the need for budgetary support for loss making PSUs

2.3 Approach to Disinvestment of Loss making PSUs

The approach to disinvestment in profitable PSUs is fairly straightforward, subject of course, to restructuring where appropriate. The question of eventual disinvestment in loss making PSUs raises the issue of the funds required for revival and restructuring. As analysed earlier, the direct draft on the budget on account of loss making PSUs during 1996-97 is around Rs. 1984 crores under both Plan assistance and non-Plan outlays. This constitutes about 60 per cent of the total direct support to PSUs under the budget. Assuming conservatively that this current draft remains constant over the next five years, the total budgetary support would work out to Rs. 9920 crores. The net present value of Rs. 9920 crores discounted at 12 per cent works out to around Rs.7200 crores.

This figure needs to be compared with the one-time upfront expenditure which will be required to restructure and revive loss making but potentially viable PSUs and the cost of VRS in order to enable closure of other unviable PSUs after taking into account sale of assets, if any. If this one-time expenditure to be incurred in this process in the aggregate is less than Rs.7,200 crores, it may be financially prudent for the Government to initiate this process. this will eliminate the need for recurring budgetary support for the loss making PSUs.

Considering the above, it may therefore be worthwhile to undertake a comprehensive study of all loss making PSUs to classify them as follows:

- Those in which Government could disinvest as a going concern on an as-is-where-is basis;
- Those which could be restructured and turned around before disinvestment; and
- *Those which may need closure.*

In all cases, it will be important to protect the interests of affected labour by devising suitable schemes either for retraining, redeployment or for voluntary retirement with adequate compensation. The costs of such schemes could be met to varying degrees by the sale of assets of the companies concerned. The balance where necessary could be met from the Disinvestment Fund (suggested later in this Report) supplemented if needed in any particular year by a provision in the budget.

Since only 40, mostly profitable PSUs, out of the 245 have so far been referred to the Commission it is unable to undertake this detailed exercise. This exercise is however, urgently needed for evolving a rational strategy for all the loss making PSUs. The Commission will apply these principles with respect to disinvestment in the PSUs referred to it.

The advantages of the above long term strategy are:

- *This holistic view of disinvestment will tackle the larger problem of the drain on the budget from losses in PSUs which need as much attention as the profit making PSUs.*
- The saving in recurring budgetary provisions towards loss making PSUs can then be released for investments in sectors like infrastructure, education and health. Retirement of debt from disinvestment proceeds can also be an option.
- *Dispersal of ownership will exert necessary pressure on the PSUs to improve the performance, earn profits and declare dividends.*

2.4 Approach to Disinvestment Process

The approach to the disinvestment process is to evolve general principles and criteria encompassing all PSUs and apply them across different PSUs as and when they are referred. This will enhance the transparency of the disinvestment process.

In this regard, the Commission has evolved principles for the extent of disinvestment in PSUs by categorising them as strategic, core and non-core. The Commission has taken note of the Government policies and statements on this issue. The criteria for disinvestment will be based on these principles and the analysis of each PSU.

2.5 Principles for Extent of Disinvestment

The extent of eventual disinvestment in a particular PSU will depend on the classification of the PSUs as strategic, core and non-core. Since public sector units were set-up with objectives relevant at different times, it has become necessary to review whether their continuation in public sector is justified at present.

In this context, it may be useful to trace the evolution of the policy relating to Public Sector since independence.

2.6 Evolution of Public Sector Policy

In the 1948 Industrial Policy Resolution, the manufacture of arms and ammunition, production and control of atomic energy, ownership and management of railways became the State monopoly. Six basic industries viz., iron & steel, coal, aircraft manufacture, ship building, mineral oils, manufacture of telephone, telegraph and wireless apparatus were to be developed by the State. All other areas were left open to private initiatives.

Within a decade of laying down the policy parameters in 1948, another policy statement was issued in April, 1956 by the Government to give a new orientation to the "mixed economy" concept. This Policy Resolution categorised industries into three groups.

- Industries exclusively reserved for development by the State viz., arms and ammunition, iron & steel, heavy castings and forging, heavy plant & machinery required for iron and steel production and mining, heavy electrical plant, coal and lignite, zinc, copper, lead, aircraft, ship building and telecommunication equipment.
- Industries which would progressively be State owned and in which the State will therefore, generally take the initiative in establishing new undertakings but in which private enterprise will also be expected to supplement the efforts of the State. These include aluminium, fertilisers, other minerals, machine tools, ferro-alloys and tools, basic and intermediate products required by chemical industries, antibiotics and other essential drugs, synthetic rubber, carbonisation of coal, chemical pulp, road transport and sea transport.
- The remaining industries were left open for private sector initiatives.

In the context of the significant changes in fiscal, monetary, trade and industrial policies, the need for a review of the continued presence of the public sector in a wide range of activity was felt in the nineties. A new strategy for the public sector was spelt out in the policy statement in July 1991 which marked a turning point in the policy guidelines as far as public sector was concerned. The philosophy behind the New Economic Policy (NEP) was that the State should, by and large, leave industry and commerce to the private sector and concentrate on those areas where it had a special or unique responsibility.

The list of industries reserved for public sector was reduced from 17 included in the Industrial Policy Resolution of 1956 to only eight by the

July 1991 policy statement. Subsequently in March 1993, two more items were dereserved. The six industries for exclusive operation in public sector are (i) arms and ammunitions and the allied items of defence equipment, defence aircrafts and warships, (ii) atomic energy, (iii) coal and lignite, (iv) mineral oils, (v) minerals specified in the schedule to Atomic Energy (Control of Production and use) Order 1953, and (vi) railway transport.

Other developments since then are:

- De reservation of mining activity; as a result of which coal extraction has been permitted for captive use by user industries.
- Invitation has been extended to private sector to invest in oil exploration and refining which is otherwise reserved for public sector as well as in infrastructure projects like roads, ports, telecom etc.
- Private sector venture in power generation even with 100 per cent foreign equity has also been allowed.

In the post 1991 scenario, it is necessary to refer to the Rangarajan Committee report on Disinvestment of Shares of Public Sector enterprises wherein targets level of disinvestment has been recommended. The Committee concluded that the percentage of equity to be disinvested should be generally under 49 per cent in industries reserved for the public sector and over 74 per cent in other industries.

2.7 Classification of Industry Groups

The perusal of public sector policy statements and other documents reveals that there is considerable amount of flexibility with respect to the definitions of strategic, core and non-core sectors and the extent of disinvestment in the corresponding sector. In the context of rapid globalisation and the significant investments by the private sector in many areas hitherto reserved for the public sector, a need to clearly demarcate these sectors has been felt.

The analysis of the public sector policy statements reveal that the emphasis of public sector investments has been in areas which are considered important from a national view point or where private sector would find it unremunerative and thus can not be expected to take the lead in promoting investments. Accordingly, some industries have been exclusively earmarked for public sector is expected to supplement the efforts of the State in promoting economic development.

2.8 Strategic Group

At present as per the policy statements of Government, only four industries viz., (i) arms and ammunitions and the allied items of defence equipment, defence aircrafts and warships, (ii) atomic energy, (iii) minerals specified in the schedule to Atomic Energy (Control of Production and use) Order 1953, and (iv) railway transport are the exclusive preserve of the public sector. A perusal of the above list would imply that these industries are important from the national security angle. Thus, it may be more appropriate to term these four industries as "Strategic". The question of disinvestment in such industries does not arise.

2.9 Core Group

In sectors which are capital or technology intensive, the most prevalent market structure may be an oligopoly. With the entry of private sector into these capital intensive areas, there may be a tendency towards an oligopolistic market structure. Examples are telecom, power generation and transmission or petroleum exploration and refining industries. It has been felt that the presence of the public sector will be necessary for sometime as a countervailing force and prevent concentration of private economic power. At the same time a proper regulatory mechanism should be put in place in order to regulate industries particularly in a non-competitive market for protecting interests of consumers.

In addition, it may be appropriate to look at basic industries with extensive and dispersed forward linkages. In some of these sectors, PSUs have a considerable market presence and the private sector is yet to mature fully. Hence it may be desirable to continue public sector presence in these basic industries till such time that the market becomes fully competitive.

By this analysis, such industries may be classified as "core" and public sector disinvestment be limited to a maximum of 49 per cent. However, it may be noted that the composition of "core" industries may change over a period of time as further private investments make the market fully competitive and PSUs may not be required to play a special role. In addition, it is expected that a proper regulatory mechanism would be in place to protect the interest of consumers. The question of disinvesting beyond 49 per cent may be considered at that time.

2.10 Non-Core Group

Over the last four decades, private sector investments have grown considerably in many industries. The presence of a large number of players including matured private sector players, and the forces of competition in these industries have made these markets fully contestable. These would ensure that the consumer's interests are well protected. It can therefore be concluded that the initial objectives of the public sector in such industries have been met. Further investments in such industries will be driven more by demand - supply imbalances and Public investment may no longer be necessary. It may be useful to categorise such industries as non-core. The existing public sector in these industries may not have any unique or special responsibilities. Therefore, it would be desirable to disinvest upto 74 per cent or more in such cases.

2.11 Industry Grouping

With this framework in place, the Commission has classified the 40 referred PSUs. These appear in the table below. The classification of Bharat Electronics Ltd. (BEL), Garden Reach Shipbuilders & Engineers Ltd. (GRSEL), Hindustan Aeronautics Ltd. (HAL), Rail India Technical & Economic Services Ltd. (RITES) and Engineers India Ltd. (EIL) will be considered by the Commission at a later date.

2.12 Framework for Analysing PSUs

In addition to the above, the approach to the disinvestment process will also centre on the analysis of specific PSUs. While the framework is outlined below, the actual analysis is available in Tables 10 to 17 in Annexure 3 of the Report.

TABLE – 22.9

Grouping of PSUs

Group	Name of the PSUs
Core	ONGC, OIL, BRPL, SAIL, MTNL, GAIL, AI, CONCOR, PHL, NLC, NCL, SECFL, WCFL, BALCO, NALCO, IBP, NTPC, PGCIL, NHPC, KIOCL, (20 PSUs)
Non-Core	SCI, ITDC, IPCL, FACT, NFL, MFL, HCIL, HTL, ITI, MFIL, HLL, BEML, HCL, HZL, MOIL (15 PSUs)

2.13 Analysis based on Net Profits

A useful starting point for analysis would be to segregate the PSUs on the basis of reported net profits or losses during the preceding five years. However, it has to be borne in mind that profits are determined by the accounting policies adopted. While PSUs in general have relatively more conservative accounting policies than their counterparts in the private sector, it will still be necessary to examine the extent of profitability by analysing the trend in gross margins and that of return on capital employed. In addition, a comparison of the return on capital employed with the company's cost of capital will help understand whether the company has earned adequate returns. Given the fast-changing economic scenario and the emerging competition, the past performance of a given PSU may not be necessarily sustainable. Therefore, in addition, it may be useful to add other analytical criteria, like the company's competitive position and the prospects for future growth in sales and net profits.

The above analysis will help classify PSUs into two broad categories. The first category of PSUs consists of *Strong Performers,* i.e, those which have reported consistent profits and are well positioned to grow strongly in the future. The second category of Moderate Performers would include those which have demonstrated profitability, but are positioned to grow moderately in the future.

2.14 Analysis by Industry Classification

The objective of the industrial classification is to understand the attractiveness of the industry in which the PSUs operate, as it is expected that the competitive and regulatory scenario in an industry will determine the interest of investors - especially institutional investors - in PSU stocks. This is especially true of PSUs which operate in commodity sectors such as metals and whose profitability is directly impacted by changes in international prices.

It may be noted that the PSUs referred have a presence in industries some of which may be attractive and some of which may not be currently attractive. Therefore, it may be necessary to further classify the industries on the basis of current attractiveness. Accordingly, the Commission has classified PSUs into three categories: those with *High, Medium or Low Potential.* This classification is based on the assessment of current and expected levels of business profitability, competitive nature of the market and impact of Government policies on the operations of the company.

The classification of a PSU may change over a period of time depending on changes in the business environment. It may be cautioned that the categorisation of a PSU as "High Potential" does not necessarily mean that there is no scope for further share value enhancement.

2.15 Analysis based on Paid-up Capital

Size is a criterion for classifying a group of companies. In the context of disinvestment size may be appropriately measured in terms of the paid-up share capital. The level of paid-up share capital and the current share holding of the Government will be important considerations in determining the phasing of the disinvestment programme.

2.16 Analysis based on Accumulated Reserves

In some cases, it may be necessary to understand the extent of accumulated reserves *vis-à-vis* the paid-up share capital. By capitalising reserves, companies can issue bonus shares to the government, which can then be disinvested. This has to be balanced with the dilution in the earnings per share and the increased dividend payout.

2.17 Analysis based on Listing & Trading

It is possible that in some of the PSUs referred to the Commission disinvestment has already occured and the shares are listed on the stock exchanges. It may be useful to classify the PSUs as under:

- Disinvested & Listed : In case of liquid stocks, the stock price can provide a basis for valuation. In cases where trading volumes are insignificant, stock prices may not be appropriate for valuation.
- Disinvested & not yet Listed : These comprise those stocks which have been disinvested and which have still not yet been listed. In these cases, it may be necessary to ensure that this does not act as an impediment to the process of further disinvestment.
- Not Disinvested so far.

2.18 Criteria for Disinvestment

As a general principle the Commission recommends that where appropriate, PSUs should be restructured before disinvestment in order to enhance enterprise and the intrinsic share values. Given the rapidly changing economic scenario, it is possible that some PSUs may already have initiated such changes. In some other cases it is possible that the extent of restructuring required may be minimal.

2.19 Based on the above principles and specific analysis of PSUs, the Commission's recommendations for disinvestment will be based on the following considerations :

- Extent of Restructuring required and the potential for improving share values;
- The permissible extent of disinvestment with reference to the classification of industry as core or non-core;
- The size of the company and the phasing of disinvestment;
- Equity fund raising programme of the concerned PSU;
- Categorisation of the Industry as High, Medium or Low Potential;
- Alternative modalities of disinvestment.

23

Infrastructure and Economic Developments

The Need for a New Approach

The availability of adequate infrastructure facilities is vital for the acceleration of the economic development of a country. Governments have traditionally been well aware of this and have accorded high priority to investment in sectors such as railways, roads, power, telecommunications, ports, water supply, sanitation and sewerage and airports.

Infrastructure services are often monopolistic in nature: they usually involve high upfront costs and long payback periods: and investments are typically bulky and lumpy. They are also characterised by the existence of externalities which make it difficult for infrastructure entities to recoup investment costs and operational expenses through the levy of user charges.

Consequently, infrastructure services have been predominantly provided by the public sector in almost all countries for most of the 20th century.[1]

Commercialisation: A New Wave, A New Necessity

A wave of privatisation and deregulation has been sweeping infrastructure sectors around the globe over the last decade or so. These bold new approaches promote improvement in efficiency and service

1. National Council of Applied Economic Research, The India Infrastructure Report, Volume I, New Delhi, 1996.

quality. Whereas the specific motivations and circumstances vary by countries, and in countries by sectors, there are five basic pragmatic and non-ideology-related factors that are leading economies all over the world to consider enhanced commercialisation of infrastructure provision:

- The massive investment requirements arising from sharply rising economic growth rates are pushing countries to look for additional sources of financing against the backdrop of fiscal stringency in most countries.
- The rising awareness of the importance of efficiency in investment and delivery, in the context of tight fiscal conditions, is leading to rethinking on the ability of government-owned entities to supply infrastructure services in a business like manner.
- Changes in technology now make it easier to charge for marginal use of infrastructure services. Such technological changes are making possible the introduction of competition horizontally and unbundling of services vertically.
- The increasing need for countries to compete in the global marketplace is putting additional pressure on countries to provide efficient infrastructure services to their businesses in a cost-effective and competitive manner. Higher infrastructure costs in terms of both price and time delays can make the difference between firms being globally competitive or otherwise.
- The new dynamism and integration of world capital markets have vastly increased the possibility of raising large funds for infrastructure investment on a commercial basis whereas, earlier, it was governments which had better access to resources. In many cases, it is now the private sector which has the capability of sourcing large funds internationally.

While these forces are pushing most countries towards the commercialisation of infrastructure investment services, there is also increasing understanding of the social dimension of infrastructure. In poor countries, in particular, the state bears a responsibility to provide the impoverished adequate access to basic services such as health, education, water supply, sanitation and sewerage. Moreover, despite the new possibilities of competition mentioned above, most infrastructure services retain very strong monopolistic elements. As such, the state continues to be responsible for providing appropriate regulatory framework which assist investors and infrastructure entities on the one hand and protect consumers from monopolistic exploitation on the other.

The commercialisation of infrastructure and unbundling also lead to a considerable increase in transaction costs which have to be mitigated through transparent and appropriate regulation.

The general conclusion is that whereas the possibility of commercialisation of infrastructure investment and services has increased tremendously over the last decades, the role of the public sector in investment, delivery of services and in regulation will continue to be vital. The future therefore suggests the introduction of a new framework for public-private partnerships in different forms so that appropriate infrastructure investment can fructify.

The Necessary Regulatory Frameworks

The fact that there is now a market for providing infrastructure services has two implications. One, that such services can be provided by the private sector and second, that private capital would have to be accessed on competitive terms. To meet the twin objectives, regulation must primarily be viewed as a mechanism which brings about risk allocation between the service providers and various other entities in the process, making it easy to access capital. When risk allocation becomes easier, it results in reducing the cost of capital. Hence it is necessary to have an articulate regulatory framework, which is radically different from the existing legal framework in terms of transparency, clarity of obligations, duties, and responsibilities between the participants in the infrastructure projects. The new framework must reduce the layering of approvals or bring about a greater degree of certainty in obtaining them within a definite time frame. Such a regulatory framework is very critical if private sector participation is to be encouraged.

There must be certainty that the 'rules of the game', once set, would not be changed too frequently and without notice, so that providers of infrastructure services may be afforded reasonable planning horizons. However, these changes, to occur, will need a demonstrable political and bureaucratic will for the process and this may not be easily achievable.

Rakesh Mohan Committee Report on Indian Infrastructure recommends a Simple Regulatory Framework

- Existing sector-specific enactments be unified into a single statute.
- An autonomous regulatory body be set for each infrastructure sector, on the lines of SEBI.
- The roles of the regulator and the operator must be separated in every sector.

- Mechanisms to settle disputes quickly must be set up.
- An overarching legislation be made for project formats such as BOT, BOO and the like governing projects across all sectors, on the lines of the BOT Law of the Philippines.
- An Infrastructure Coordination Committee be constituted on the same lines as the Foreign Investment Promotion Board which will clear projects on a national level based on broad principles.
- The present restrictions in FII guidelines be removed for investment in infrastructure projects, or separate guidelines similar to FII guidelines without investment limits be issued. Similar guidelines and tax regime should govern any offshore fund set up by a domestic asset management company registered with SEBI, or by a domestic institution.
- Special Purpose Vehicles (SPVs) be used for funding infrastructure projects. Such SPVs should be able to vary their capital with ease; they should be easy to wind up; they should be tax-transparent.

The Government has recognized that private sector participation including foreign investment is required to supplement the public sector efforts. Various reforms have been made in infrastructure sectors, and rules and procedures for investment have been liberalized in order to provide an enabling environment conducive for private participation. The role of the Government has changed from 'owner' and 'sole provider' to that of a 'facilitator', and of safeguarding the interests of the vulnerable sections of the community by legal and institutional framework.

BOX – 23.1

Infrastructure Sector in the Report of the PM's Economic Advisory Council*

The council's report on economy laid emphasis on investments in economic infrastructure if India is to achieve a growth target of 8 per cent during the Tenth Five Year Plan. Private sector investments were muted because the pre-conditions for successful large scale entry of the private sector were not yet met. Two main reasons provided in the report were inadequate user charges and regulatory uncertainty.

Contd...

* India Infrastructure Report 2002, 3i Network.

...Box 23.1 Contd...

While infrastructure remains an exclusive public sector monopoly, the rationalization of user charges in infrastructure is absolutely vital. A

regulatory regime that is seen to be fair to consumers and also sensitive to the legitimate needs of investors, is absolutely essential.

Power

'The flaw in the policy with regard to electricity was the failure to recognize that the root of the problem lies in the financial unviability of the state electricity boards. This has made independent power projects (IPPs) look for temporary solutions such as escrow arrangements and central government guarantees which simply do not address the core problem.'

It suggested that the huge transmission and distribution losses could be brought down through privatization of distribution as the privatized areas would help achieve better efficiency from the distribution system.

The central government should play a pivotal role in the reform of SEBs (State Electricity Boards) as large parts of these dues are to the central government organizations, such as NTPC, Coal India, Railways, and NHPC.

In view of the rapid convergence of telecom, IT and media, a new comprehensive statute, which creates the framework of single license for multiple services, needs to replace the Indian Telegraph Act of 1885.

The government must levy fees to meet administration and regulatory costs, along with universal service obligation charges, through revenue sharing, and not as an avenue to raise resources for the government. Increasing competition within the sector will ensure benefits of reduction in license fees is passed on to consumers. The only area where government should collect rent is in the allocation of spectrum, which is a scarce resource.

Roads

The council suggested that the private sector be encouraged to participate in road projects through the BOT (build, operate, transfer)/Annuity system as 'EPC (engineering, procurement and construction), and O&M (operations and maintenance) contracts be merged and given to the same contractor who would be responsible for construction and maintenance of the road during the concession period.

According to the committee, private sector made little progress for so long because the government found it more attractive to raise money cheaply

Contd...

...Box 23.1 Contd...

through riskless gilt-edged debt, rather than paying the private sector's capital costs with their risk-premium.

Ports

The existing port trusts should be corporatized and turned into landlord ports that would then invite different operators, both public and private, to invest in cargo handling and port infrastructure services. The ports as such should concentrate on the development of common user general cargo facilities. Rather than fresh ports it suggested existing ports be optimally utilized through efficiency enhancing investments. Tariff fixing is no longer necessary as intra-port and inter-port competition will ensure competitive pricing of services.

Railways

The council strongly recommended depoliticization of Railways, rationalization of user charges and corporatization of production units. Railways have a key role in initiating development of the key inter- and trans-modal facilities.

Civil Aviation

The council recommended leasing the major airports (Delhi, Mumbai, Chennai and Calçutta), and inviting private sector management of airports. An independent regulatory framework for ensuring economic regulation in the sector was suggested as there are many operators.

The inland air travel tax and foreign travel tax should be converted into a common 'civil aviation cess' to ensure sufficient flow of funds to develop civil aviation facilities in other parts of the country.

Performance of the Infrastructure

Average Annual Growth Rates 1980-81 to 1999-2000

Trends in the average growth rates of infrastructure sectors for the period 1992-93 to 1999-2000 reflect a slowing down in some of the sectors as compared with the period 1980-81 to 1991-92. (Details in Box 23.2).

BOX – 23.2

Performance of the Infrastructure in 1980-81 to 1999-2000
Average Annual Growth Rates

(per cent)

	Sectors	1980-1981 To 1991-92	1992-1993 To 1999-2000
1.	**Power**		
	Electricity Generation	8.8	6.7
2.	**Railways**		
	a. Railway revenue-earning goods traffic	4.8	3.9
	b. Passenger kilometers	3.9	4.1
3.	**Ports**		
	Cargo handled at major ports	6.1	7.1
4.	**Civil Aviation**		
	a. Cargo handled at AAI Airports	6.5	15.1
	b. passengers handled at AAI Airports	6.0	10.2
5.	**Roads**		
a.	Length of roads	3.6	0.7
b.	Length of National Highways	0.5	0.6
6.	**Telecommunications**		
	New telephone connections provided (Direct Exchange Lines)	19.0	27.1

- Power sector performance during the period 1992-93 to 1999-2000 has been disappointing despite significant reforms in the sector, such as setting up of a regulatory authority and opening power generation to private investment, both domestic and foreign.
- Operation of Indian Railways in terms of passenger kilometers as well as rate of growth of revenue earnings goods traffic has slowed down during the period 1992-93 to 1992-2000. Since railways are less energy intensive and more environment friendly there is need for appropriate policies aimed at capacity augmentation and rationalisation of rail tariffs to reduce cross subsidisation.
- Performance of major ports has improved, in terms of the indicator 'cargo handled at ports' during the period 1992-93 to 1999-2000 compared with the growth in 1980-81 to 1991-92.
- Performance of civil aviation sector, has improved both in terms of cargo and passengers handled at AAI airports during the period 1992-1993 to 1999-2000 compared with the performance during the period 1980-81 to 1991-92.
- There has been a rapid growth in the telecommunications sector in terms of new telephone connections over the last decades.

Source: Economic Survey 2000-01.

TABLE – 23.1

Trends in Growth Rates of Infrastructure Sectors (in per cent)

Items	Unit	2000-01	2001-02	2002-03	2003-04	April-December* 2003-04	April-December* 2004-05
I. Energy							
1 Coal Production	Mn.tonnes	3.5	4.2	4.6	5.1	3.9	6.8
2 Electricity generated (Utilities only)	Bn. Kwh	3.9	3.1	3.2	5.0	3.4	6.5
(a) Hydel	,,	-7.6	-0.7	-13.7	15.6	10.5	17.6
(b) Thermal (incl.nuclear)	,,	7.4	2.5	6.2	3.5	2.4	4.7
3 Petroleum							
(a) Crude oil production	Mn.tonnes	1.5	-1.2	3.2	1.0	-0.5	2.9
(b) Refinery throughput	,,	20.3	3.7	4.9	8.2	7.2	6.7
II. Steel	**Mn.tonnes**	**6.4**	**3.6**	**10.1**	**6.9**	**12.2**	**3.8**
III. Cement	**Mn.tonnes**	**-0.9**	**7.4**	**8.8**	**6.1**	**5.6**	**6.9**
Weighted Average growth I to III		*5.1*	*3.2*	*5.6*	*5.4*	*5.8*	*5.4*
IV. Transport and communications							
1. Railway revenue-earning Goods traffic	,,	3.7	4.0	5.3	7.5	7.0	7.7
2. Cargo handled at major ports	,,	3.4	2.3	9.0	9.9	7.5	11.1
3. Telecommunications-new telephone connections Provided (Direct Exchange Lines)**	'000Nos.	27.2	23.9	21.5	40.1	29.1	21.4
4 Civil Aviation							
(a) Export cargo handled	000 tonnes	5.1	4.1	13.3	1.0	0.0	11.8
(b) Import cargo handled	,,	3.6	-1.0	18.6	13.8	9.7	30.1
(c) Passengers handled at International Terminals	Million	4.6	-5.0	4.8	6.5	4.7	15.7
(d) Passengers handled at Domestic Terminals	,,	7.7	-5.7	9.6	13.1	10.4	25.9

* Provisional ** WLL, Fixed and Cellular.

Source : Item no. I to III Ministry of Commerce & Industry, IV.1 Ministry of Railways, IV.2 and 4 Ministry of Statistics and Programme Implementation and IV.3 Ministry of Communication.
Economic Survey 2004-05.

New Initiatives for Infrastructure Development

Given below is a summary list of the measure/initiatives that have been undertaken for infrastructure Development.

BOX – 23.3

Major Initiatives for Infrastructure Development

Fiscal Incentives

- Ten-Year tax holiday for the core sector of infrastructure, namely, roads, highways, water-ways, water supply, sanitation and solid waste management systems, which may be availed of during the initial twenty years.
- In the case of airports, ports, inland ports, industrial parks and generation and distribution of power, which also become commercially viable only in the long run, a tax holiday of ten years has been allowed to be availed of during the initial fifteen years.
- The five-year tax holiday and 30 per cent deduction for next five years available to the telecommunication sector till March 31, 2000 was reintroduced for the units commencing their operations on or before March 31, 2003. These concessions will also be extended to Internet service providers and broadband networks.
- Tax incentives have also been provided for the investors providing long-term finance or investing in the equity capital of the enterprises engaged in infrastructure facility. Any income by way of interest, dividends or long-term capital gains from such investments in fully exempt.

Viability Gap Funding for Infrastructure (MTA)

Infrastructure projects have long gestation periods and, in most cases, are not financially viable on their own. It may not be possible to fund the very large investment requirements of these projects fully from the budgetary resources of the Government of India alone. In order to remove this shortcoming and to bring in private sector resources and techno-managerial efficiencies, the Government is promoting Public Private Partnerships (PPP) in infrastructure development through a special facility envisaging support to PPP projects through 'viability gap funding'. Primarily, this facility is meant to reduce capital cost of the projects by credit enhancement, and to make them viable and attractive for private investments through supplementary grant funding. Provisions for this facility is made on an year to year basis.

Criteria

The criteria for eligibility for funding are:

(i) The project must be implemented, i.e. constructed, maintained and operated during the project term, by an entity with at least 40 per cent private equity.

(ii) The project must belong to one of the following sectors:

a. Roads, railways, seaports, airports;

b. Power;

c. Water supply, sewerage and solid waste disposal in urban areas; and

d. International convention centers.

(iii) The projects should have been vetted/ endorsed by the concerned line ministries in the Government of India.

(iv) All central projects should have received requisite Government approval at the appropriate level.

(v) The total Government support required by the project, including support from the Government of India under this facility, or any other sources of the Government of India and its agencies, must not exceed twenty per cent of the total project cost as estimated in the preliminary project appraisal, or the actual project cost, whichever is lower.

(vi) The implementing agency must be selected through a transparent and open competitive process. The main criterion for selection will be the extent of viability gap funding required by the private partner to successfully implement the project. The extent of viability gap funding shall be determined on the basis of the net present value of the actual viability gap funding required. For this purpose and for all calculations under these guidelines, the rate of discount shall be the rate of interest on 10-year gilts on the date of submission of the bid.

Appraisal and Approval Procedures

An Empowered Committee has been set up in the Department of Economic Affairs under the Additional Secretary (EA) to consider and authorize sanction of funds up to Rs. 50 crore beyond which approval of the Finance Minster will be required. The projects may be posed by any (a) public agency at the center, state or urban local body which owns the underlying assets; (b) private agency, with sponsorship from the relevant central or state government agency. Project proposals must be accompanied by a preliminary project appraisal (covering (a) techno-economic viability of the project, (b) financial appraisal and project financing arrangements, and (c) extent and nature of viability gap funding proposed) and a commitment letter on behalf of the lending institutions. After approval of the project by the Committee within 30 days of submission, the project will be put to bid by the public agency concerned through transparent and open competitive bidding indicating the extent of viability gap funding that is actually required. The lead financial institution will present its detailed appraisal of the technical and economic viability of the project as proposed by the successful bidder, for the consideration of the Committee. The transfer of viability gap funds and the schedule of such transfers will be approved by the Committee. The lead financial institution will undertake regular monitoring and evaluation of project compliance with agreed milestones and performance levels.

Outlook

There is considerable consensus that improvements in infrastructure will have a strong impact upon GDP growth and poverty alleviation. International experience shows that there are many subtle difficulties in finding the right infrastructure policy framework. A delicate system of checks and balances is required, with careful calibration of incentives, so as to give the private sector the right incentives to invest adequately while at the same time preventing it from extracting monopoly rents. A key part of this is establishing a framework of rules, and limiting arbitrary State power, to give the private sector confidence in embarking upon the multi-decade horizons of these projects.

The most striking success is visible in telecom. Tele-density has risen dramatically, an entire industry with private players has come about, privatisation has begun with VSNL, and new technologies have come about. Telecom, where competition has delivered benefits, can serve as a role model for most infrastructure sectors of the economy. Looking forward, the telecom sector will feature lively competition between multiple private firms, with a strong role for TRAI for establishing pro-competitive policies. The sharp drop in broadband telecom prices in late 2004 may represent the beginning of a phase of hectic expansion of the broadband telecom sector. This may have an even bigger impact upon the economy as compared with the growth in ordinary voice telephony. An important area requiring a fresh policy impetus is that of reducing the extent to which a Stateled planning approach is used in the utilisation of the electromagnetic spectrum.

In the area of roads, substantial portions of the Golden Quadrilateral have been completed, and are already fueling the growth of productivity in the country. For completed stretches, the focus needs to shift from construction to corridor management, i.e. for optimally utilising the capital assets to deliver the maximum throughput and world class levels of road safety. At the same time, a continuous, competition driven process needs to be in place for upgradation from four-lane highways to expressways in high-density stretches, and for construction of new links, such as a highway from Mumbai to Kolkata.

The ports sector has obtained sharp improvements in efficiency parameters through new kinds of contracting. It has benefited from vigorous levels of inter-port and intra-port competition. However, as the recent problems at JNPT have demonstrated, much more work needs to be done in crafting an adequate policy framework. This requires a fresh examination of questions of port-connectivity through rail and road, and international benchmarking on performance parameters and price. India has experienced, and will continue to experience, high growth rates of international trade. The growth of ports needs to be planned in a futuristic way, reflecting projections for traffic rather than meeting existing needs, so as to ensure that India's needs are adequately met.

The railways remain an extremely important area, given the fact that transportation by rail has the highest energy efficiency as compared with the options. This suggests that if the institutional mechanisms come about, then the cost of transportation by rail could be much lower than that seen in the road sector. However, this will require substantial reforms in the functioning of the railways. The experiences with the transformation of telecom, roads and ports can serve as role models for the scale of transformation that may be required.

The civil aviation sector is an area where major progress has been achieved in 2004. It is increasingly clear that there are two very distinct aspects of the civil aviation sector. On one hand is the airline industry, which is analogous to the shipping industry, where the only goal of public policy is to have low entry barriers and high levels of competition. On the other hand are the airports, which have 'public goods' characteristics, and there is a case for a bigger role for the State. In recent months, limited progress has been obtained on both fronts. In particular, improvements in the degree of competition have helped deliver lower prices and a sharp increase in both domestic and international traffic.

In the area of power, there is clarity on the separate issues in generation, transmission and distribution. Generation does not pose problems of public goods, and it can be a normal private industry, provided the downstream buyers are operating in a sound institutional framework. Once reforms in transmission and distribution are in place, it will not be difficult to attract private investments in generation. The Electricity Act and recent reforms in distribution have served to revitalise investments in this area. The 'unscheduled interchange' (UI) market is a major advance in moving towards a normal spot market for electricity, comparable with spot markets for other commodities and financial products in the economy. However, policy bottlenecks continue to inhibit supply of power into the UI market from the private sector.

The losses in power distribution in the country are enormous. They are important from a different perspective: that of obtaining a fiscal correction. Improvements in distribution alone could account for over 1 per cent of GDP of fiscal correction.

Finally, the most important frontier in Indian infrastructure consists of urban infrastructure. The techniques and strategies which worked for national public goods cannot be directly applied to local public goods. Here, the focus has to be on the 74th amendment to the Constitution, on empowering cities, on supporting institutional reforms at cities, and directing fiscal transfers for paying transition costs and poverty targeting.

Part IV

The External Sector

24

Foreign Trade and Balance of Payments

Chs. 24 to 27 are devoted to India's external sector: foreign trade performance, structural change and policies, implications for growth, the new exim policy 2002-07, balance of payments, issue of foreign direct investment, globalisation and its impact on Indian economy.

Indian economic development strategy, particularly relating to industrialization has been driven by perceived foreign exchange scarcities and the desire to ensure that scarce foreign exchange is used only for purposes deemed "essential" from the perspective of development. Industrialization and self-sufficiency in essential commodities have been important objectives of policy in no small part because of the fear that dependence on other, more powerful countries, for imports of essential commodities would lead to political dependence on them as well. Nearly a decade before independence, in 1938, the National Planning Committee was set up by the Indian National Congress (the political party that led the struggle for independence) under the chairmanship of the future prime minister Jawaharlal Nehru. This committee viewed, "... the objective for the country as a whole was the attainment, as far as possible, of national self-sufficiency, International trade was certainly not excluded, but we were anxious to avoid being drawn into the whirlpool of economic imperialism."

Later the First-Year Plan went further :

Control and regulation of exports and imports, and in the case of certain select commodities state trading, are necessary not only from the point of view of utilising to the best advantage the limited foreign exchange resources available but also for securing an allocation of the productive resources of the country in line with the targets defined in the Plan.[1]

India adopted an 'inward looking' strategy of industrialisation. This strategy relied on encouraging domestic production for the domestic market behind high tariffs and high degree of effective protection to the domestic industry. This resulted in an uncompetitive domestic industrial structure. T.N. Srinivasan has argued that the development strategy based on import substituting industrialisation and the system of controls that were implemented failed to produce rapid growth, self-reliance, and eradication of poverty, but instead led to lackluster growth, an internationally uncompetitive industrial structure, a perpetually precarious balance of payments, and, above all, rampant rent seeking and the corruption of social, economic, and political systems.

Far from viewing foreign trade as an engine of growth, Indian planners sought to minimize import demand and viewed exports more or less as a necessary evil mainly to generate the foreign exchange earnings to meet that part of the import bill not covered by external assistance. They created an elaborate administrative regulatory machinery in an attempt to control investment and resource allocation in the economy and ensure their consistency with five-year plan targets. Controls over imports and exports were also part of this regulatory system.

Trade Policy

Reflecting the change in the perception towards the external sector and its role in the overall strategy of development, the policies relating to India's foreign trade have, over the years, undergone significant changes. Though the process of trade liberalisation in India has been underway for over two decades, the trade policy measures initiated since 1991 as a part of the economic reform process have been more comprehensive. Some of the important features of the changes in India's trade policy are discussed in the following paragraphs.

With the realisation of the drawbacks of the excessively inward-looking trade strategy on the one hand and the need for modernisation and technology upgradation of the Indian industry on the other, certain policy measures in the direction of trade liberalisation were initiated in the late 'seventies. The strategy towards a greater integration of the Indian economy with the rest of the world has been pursued since then. The liberalisation process remained somewhat slow during the first-half of the 'eighties and it gathered momentum during the second-half of the decade.

The policy changes have been influenced, *inter alia*, by the recommendations of a number of Committee, which were set up during the 'seventies and the 'eighties. In this context, mention may be made about two prominent Committee Reports – the Report of the Committee on Import Export Policies and Procedures (Chairman: P.C. Alexander, 1978) and the Report of the Committee on Trade Policies (Chairman: Abid Hussain, 1984). The Alexander Committee recommended simplification of the import licensing procedure and provided a framework involving a shift in the emphasis from 'controls' to 'development'. Following the recommendations of the Alexander Committee, selective import liberalisation measures were initiated in the late 'seventies primarily aiming at making the import of capital goods easier. Imports of certain raw materials that were not available indigenously were also placed under the Open General License (OGL) List. The emphasis of the policy efforts was also to simplify the procedures governing India's foreign trade. During this period, special measures were initiated to boost the export of project goods.

The Abid Hussain Committee envisaged "growth-led exports" rather than "export-led growth" and stressed upon the need for harmonisation of foreign trade policies with other economic policies arguing for a phased reduction of effective protection. The Committee also favoured announcement of trade policies for longer periods in order to impart a degree of continuity and facilitate long-term planning of export business. In line with these recommendations, long-term trade policy was introduced with the announcement of an import export policy covering the period 1985-88. The policy was formulated with the aim of boosting exports and encouraging efficient import substitution. Following the announcement of two more such three-year Import Export Policies, these policies are being announced for a longer period of five years beginning with the Export Import (EXIM) Policy for 1992-97.

The trade policy changes in the post 1991 period sought to minimise the role of quantitative restrictions and substantially reduce the tariff rates on the lines suggested by the Tax Reforms Committee (Chairman: Raja J. Chelliah). The developments in India's trade policy during this period needs to be viewed in conjunction with policy reforms initiated in other spheres of the economy. The devaluation of the Rupee in July 1991 and the transition to the market-based exchange rate regime deserve mention in this regard. These measures were aimed, *inter alia*, at enhancing the price competitiveness of exports. The policies governing foreign investment and foreign collaboration also have undergone significant change, which have a bearing on trade performance. Apart from unilateral measures, the liberalisation of India's trade policies also reflects the multilateral commitments of the country to the World Trade Organisation (WTO).

The focus of these reforms has been on liberalization, openness, transparency and globalization with a basic thrust on outward orientation focusing on export promotion activity and improving competitiveness of Indian industry to meet global market requirements. In early 2002, the Government presented a Medium Term Export Strategy (MTES) for 2002-07 providing a vision for creating a stable policy environment with indicative sector-wise targets, with a mission to achieve one percent of global trade by 2007. The new Export and Import (EXIM) Policy framed for the period 2002-07 and unveiled on 31 March, 2002 also seeks to usher in an environment free of restrictions and controls (Box 24.1). Synergy between these policies/ strategies is expected to realize India's strong export potential and enhance the overall competitiveness of its exports.

BOX – 24.1

Export Import (EXIM) Policy 2002-07

The Special Economic Zone (SEZ) scheme has been strengthened by permitting the setting up of offshore Banking Units, hedging of commodity price risks and sourcing of short term External Commercial Borrowings. Supplies by domestic units to SEZs would entitle the former to avail of Duty Entitlement Passbook Scheme benefit. The policy has also ensured procedural simplification in the process of subcontracting carried out by the SEZ units. To ease the power situation in and around the SEZs, units for generation and distribution of power have been permitted to be set up in the SEZs.

The Policy gives a major thrust to agricultural exports by removing export restrictions on designated items. The efforts to promote exports of agro and agro-based products in the floriculture and horticulture sector have been sustained with the notification of 32 Agri-Export Zones across the country. Non-actionable subsidies such as transport subsidy have been provided for the export of fruits, vegetables, floriculture, poultry and dairy products. All Quantitative restrictions on exports (except a few sensitive items) have been re-

Contd...

...Box 24.1 Contd...

moved with only a few items being retained for export through State Trading Enterprises. To improve the productivity and export competitiveness of small scale, cottage and handicrafts sector, the Policy provides a package of incentives, including exemption from maintaining the average export obligation under the Export Promotion Capital Goods (EPCG) scheme, permission to achieve a lower threshold level for achieving the Export House status, preferential access to Market Access Initiative funds and duty free access to trimming and embellishment for achieving value added exports. The towns of export excellence (such as Tirupur for hosiery, Panipat for woolen blanket and Ludhiana for woolen knitwear) are intended to be regional rural motors of economic development for the small scale sector, focusing on plugging critical infrastructural bottlenecks and enhancing quality of support services for industrial development.

To provide the necessary impetus to star achievers, EXIM Policy provides a strategic package for status holders comprising of new/special facilities like issuance of Licence on self-declaration basis, fixation of input-output norms on priority, exemption from compulsory negotiation of documents through banks, cent per cent retention of foreign exchange in Exchange Earners' Foreign Currency account, enhancement in normal repatriation period from 180 days to 360 days and not mandating exports in each of the three licensing years for achieving the status. The Policy has operationalised the procedure for duty free import of fuel under the Advance Licensing Scheme, provided the license holder has a captive power plant.

In view of phasing out of all restrictions on textile products by 2005 under the Agreement on Textile and Clothing (ATC), the EXIM Policy has focused on measures to encourage value added exports in the garment sector. Electronic Hardware Technology Park (EHTP) scheme has been modified to enable hardware sector to face the zero duty regime under Information Technology Agreement (ITA-1), mandating only a positive net foreign exchange as a percentage of exports criteria and obviating any other export obligation for units in Electronic Hardware Technology Parks. The changes carried out in the gems & jewelry scheme include abolition of the licensing regime for the import of rough diamonds, reduction in the value addition norms for export of jewelery and permitting personal carriage of jewelery.

Contd...

...Box 24.1 Contd...

The medium term Policy continues with all the duty exemption/remission schemes, along with existing dispensation of not having any value caps. Procedural simplifications introduced in the policy include abolition of DEEC Book and withdrawal of Annual Advance License under the Advance License scheme, dispensation with technical characteristics for audit purposes under the Duty Free Replenishment Certificate scheme, 12 years export obligation period with 5 years moratorium for Export Promotion Capital Goods licenses of Rs.100 crore or more and supplies under deemed exports to be eligible for export obligation fulfillment along with deemed export benefits.

Procedural simplifications have been made in the EXIM policy to further reduce transaction costs covering Directorate General of Foreign Trade, customs and banks. These include adoption of 8 digit commodity classification for imports which would eliminate the classification disputes, reduction of maximum fee limit for electronic filing from Rs.1.5 lakhs to Rs.1 lakh, introduction of same day licensing, new norms for reduction in percentage of physical examination of export cargo, introduction of the simplified brand rate of drawback scheme and permitting direct negotiation of export documents. Other salient features of the EXIM Policy 2002-07 include widening of the scope of the Market Access Initiative scheme to include activities considered necessary for a focused market promotion of exports, setting up of "Business Centre" in India missions abroad for visiting Indian exporters/businessmen for ensuring a facilitatory environment for exporters, transport subsidy for exports to units located in North East, Sikkim and J&K and introduction of Focus Africa with Focus CIS to follow, to diversify markets.

Policy measures announced in the Union Budget 2002-03 included a comprehensive package for development of Special Economic Zones (SEZ) including entitlement by these Zones to procure duty free equipment, raw materials, components, etc. whether imported or purchased locally, further decontrol and deregulation of agriculture sector to encourage higher exports of farm products (with measures like decanalisation of export of agricultural commodities, phasing out of remaining export controls, setting up of more Agri-Export Zones in various states and enhanced incentives for export of food grains), dereservation from small scale industry (SSI) provisions for over 50 items (of knitwear, selected agricultural implements, chemical & drugs and others) to facilitate higher investment, technology upgradation and exports from these sectors and fiscal measures for strengthening certain key industries (including textiles, steel, non ferrous metals and IT industry) for improving their competitiveness and exports. The Budget announced a reduction in peak customs duty from 35 percent to 30 percent and also provided an indication of further reductions/ rationalization in these duties into only two slabs of 10 percent (for raw material, intermediate and components) and 20 percent (for final products) by 2004-05. A detailed roadmap has been recommended by the Finance Ministry Task Force on Indirect taxation for, inter alia, further reforms in areas related to customs tariffs, rationalization of export promotion schemes, trade facilitation and other changes in tax administration.

World Trade Organisation (WTO) Related Issues

As per the Doha mandate, modalities for negotiations in agriculture are to be established by 31 March 2003 and schedule of commitments, based on these modalities, by September 2003. India has submitted its comprehensive proposals with a view to safeguarding the food and livelihood security of large subsistence level farming community and maximizing export opportunities for Indian agricultural products by seeking a reduction in high tariffs and subsidies prevalent in developed countries. Following the work programme, dedicated sessions were held in 2002 on export competition, market access and domestic support. The discussions revealed a clear divide between the protectionist group led by the European Union and the pro-liberalization group led by Cairns Group (and the USA) on these crucial issues. While the pro-liberalization group favours substantial reduction in tariff and domestic support and reduction in export subsidies, the protectionist group supports gradual tariff reduction. Another group consisting of newly acceded countries (like China and Croatia) does not favour any tariff cuts for themselves while pressing for substantial market access commitments from others. The net food importing countries oppose any substantial reduction in export subsidies while small economies based on single commodity exports prefer maintenance of preferential market access into major markets.

India has repeatedly stated its support for the WTO and the Doha Development Agenda but considers that if further progress is to be made, the onus remains on the developed countries to keep the promises made in Doha (Box 24.2). The progress of the Doha work programme would be reviewed in the Fifth Ministerial Conference of the WTO, to be held at Cancun (Mexico) during September 10-14, 2003.

BOX – 24.2

Third Trade Policy Review of India in WTO

Under the Trade Policy Review Mechanism of the WTO, the trade policies of all the members are subject to periodic review. India's trade policy is subject to review every four years. Its third review of trade policy, practices and measures took place on June 19 and 21, 2002.

The WTO Secretariat Report on Trade Policies and Practices in India, highlighting the progress made by the Indian economy in different sectors, has pointed out that the Indian economy has grown rapidly over the past decade, with real GDP growth averaging some 6 percent annually. Social indicators, such as poverty and infant mortality have improved during the last ten years. Higher growth during this period was, in part, due to continued structural reforms, including trade liberalization, leading to efficiency gains. Major developments since the last review include simplification and rationalization of tariff, reduced licensing, removal of QRs on balance of payments grounds, reduced export restrictions, decline in number of activities reserved for public sector and significant reforms in services (especially telecommunications, financial services and infrastructure such as power and transport). Internal reforms have concentrated on improving efficiency and competition in the economy. To redress the fiscal balance, steps are being taken to rein in expenditure and to improve tax collection, through legislations like Fiscal Responsibility and Budget Management Bill and expenditure reforms as on food subsidy (public distribution system) and administered prices for petroleum. India's foreign direct investment policy has also been liberalized since its previous review. However, the tariff regime continues to be complex, given the numerous end-use based exemptions, with the level of protection remaining relatively high. The report concludes that India's economic reform programme has resulted in strong economic growth throughout the 1990s.

The Policy Statement by the Government of India also highlighted India's sustained economic growth and improvement in its social indicators. Besides giving an overview of key developments in trade and economic policies, it also underlined impediments to growth of India's international trade, which included restrictive import policy regimes

Contd...

...Box 24.2 Contd...

of developed countries, unrealistic standards, testing, labeling and certification including phytosanitary standards, export subsidies (including agricultural export subsidies, preferential export financing schemes), barriers on services, Government procurement regimes and other barriers including anti-dumping and countervailing measures.

During the review, India was commended for its initiative to simplify the tariff, but members voiced concern over the persistence of high rates, escalation, complexity and the gap between applied and bound rates. Concerns were expressed about increased use of contingency measures, notably anti-dumping, and measures such as labeling, certification and sanitary and phytosanitary requirements. The country was commended for its efforts to enforce protection of intellectual property rights both through the adoption of new legislation and through education campaign. It was, however, stressed that further efforts were required in this regard, especially in view of India's need to attract more foreign direct investment. Expressing concern over subsidies for agricultural products and inputs, which have contributed to large grain stocks and to export restrictions on agricultural goods, further liberalization of the agricultural sector was emphasized. Some members also urged liberalization of the Indian textile sector, noting that protection through high tariffs and small scale reservations had hindered its competitiveness. India's progress in reforming services sectors were also appreciated, the success of software sector being an indicative of its ability to compete globally. The concerns of the members and other clarifications were responded to by the Indian delegation.

In conclusion, India was complimented for its reform process, including liberalization and simplification of trade and investment regimes. The need for accelerating the reforms was, however, emphasized given the ambitious growth targets to be achieved. It was stressed that India's efforts would be greatly enhanced by steps on the parts of India's trade partners to reduce, if not remove, the impediments to India's exports, especially in the context of ongoing negotiations in the Doha work programme. While India reiterated its support for WTO and the Doha work programme, it was added that if further progress was to be made, the onus remained on the developed countries to keep the promises made in Doha. This view was endorsed by many other members, who look to India for leadership in these negotiations.

Foreign Trade: Performance and Structural Change

Responding to such policy changes, India's foreign trade exhibited considerable buoyancy during the period 1993-94 to 1995-96 with both exports and imports recording, on an average, an increase of around 20 per cent per annum. The growth in India's foreign trade, however, decelerated during the next three years i.e., during 1996-97 to 1998-99. A review of India's trade performance over the years reveals the influence of a variety of factors – both external and internal. While exact quantification of the relative impact of policy measures vis-a-vis other factors on India's trade performance may not be possible, it would be worthwhile to explore whether the major structural indicators of India's foreign trade have undergone noticeable changes during the 'nineties as compared with the 'eighties.

For the purpose of analysis at the aggregate level, India's trade performance during 1992-93 to 1998-99 (referred to here as the 'nineties) has been compared with that during 1980-81 to 1990-91 (the 'eighties). The year 1991-92 witnessed considerable strain on the balance-of-payments. To meet the crisis, severe restrictions were placed on imports and the Rupee was adjusted downward in July 1991. Being an exceptional year, 1991-92 should be excluded in any time series based analysis of trade developments. The periodisation of the analysis captures the structural shifts in the growth of exports and imports during the sub-periods. For instance, on an average annual basis, export growth during 1992-93 to 1998-99 at 9.8 per cent was higher than that of 8.2 per cent registered during 1980-81 to 1990-91.[2] Similarly, the average import growth observed during the 'nineties at 12.0 per cent remained substantially higher than that of 7.8 per cent recorded during the 'eighties (1980-81 to 1990-91).

The world trade has undergone significant changes since 1996 due to a host of developments including a sharp fall in international prices for manufactured products and the emergence of economic crises in certain parts of the world. In addition, protectionist policies and practices adopted by various industrialised countries during the recent years in the form of sanitary and phytosanitary measures, technical standard requirements and perhaps most importantly anti-dumping and countervailing measures seriously affected the export efforts of the developing countries (Stiglitz, 1999). These unfavourable factors have had their impact on the developing countries including India's trade performance.

In the light of the above factors, it would be appropriate to examine the trade performance of India during the two sub-periods of the 'nineties; the first sub-period covering the first four years following the introduction of reforms (i.e., 1992-93 to 1995-96) and the second sub-period consisting of the subsequent three years (i.e., 1996-97 to 1998-99). During the first sub-period, on an average basis, India's exports and imports increased by 15.7 and 17.5 per cent, respectively, which were significantly higher than the growth rates during the 'eighties. Broadly in line with the unfavourable external developments, between 1996-97 and 1998-99, growth in India's exports and imports, on an average basis, decelerated to 2.0 per cent and 4.5 per cent, respectively. India's share in world exports, which had declined from 0.52 per cent to 0.47 per cent between 1984 and 1987, improved to 0.53 per cent in 1992. Notwithstanding the slowdown in India's export growth since 1996, reflecting the relatively better performance by India vis-a-vis rest-of-the-world, its share in global exports reached 0.62 per cent during 1997 (IMF, 1998).

India's trade-GDP ratio showed substantial improvements during the 'nineties as compared with the 'eighties. The export-GDP ratio declined from 4.9 per cent in 1980-81 to 4.2 per cent in 1985-86 and thereafter it gradually improved and reached 6.1 per cent in 1990-91. During the 'nineties, the ratio reached its highest level at 8.7 per cent in 1995-96.[3] The ratio declined, *albeit* marginally, during the next three years and was at 8.1 per cent in 1998-99. On an average basis, export-GDP ratio increased from 5.0 per cent to +8 per cent between the 'eighties and the 'nineties. Between these two periods, on an average basis, India's import-GDP ratio increased from 7.7 per cent to +10 per cent. The noticeable improvements in the export-GDP and import-GDP ratios point to the increasing openness of India's foreign trade regime to global trade.

Along with the increase in trade-GDP ratio, there has been a decline in India's trade deficit-GDP ratio between the two periods. This is borne out by the fact that the difference between export-GDP and import-GDP ratio on an average basis, declined from 2.7 per cent in the 'eighties to 1.2 per cent in the 'nineties. This indicates that the divergence between export and import performance was more pronounced during the 'eighties than in the 'nineties. Similarly, the export-import ratio (on an average basis) increased substantially from 64 per cent during the 'eighties to 87.0 per cent during the 'nineties. reflecting thereby the increasing alignment between India's export and import performance during the 'nineties as compared with the 'eighties.

TABLE – 24.1

Selected Indicators of External Sector

								(April-Sept.)	
	1990-91	*1998-99*	*1999-00*	*2000-01*	*2001-02*	*2002-03*	*2003-04*	*2003-04*	*2004-05*
1 Growth of Exports-BOP (%)	9.0	-3.9	9.5	21.1	-1.6	20.3	20.4	9.0	23.2
2 Growth of Imports-BOP (%)	14.4	-7.1	16.5	4.6	-2.8	14.5	24.4	23.6	39.0
3 Exports/Imports-BOP (%)	66.2	72.1	67.8	78.5	79.4	83.4	80.7	74.9	66.4
4 Import cover of FER (No of months)	2.5	8.2	8.2	8.8	11.5	14.2	16.9	14.8	13.8
5 External Assistance (net) /TC %	26.2	10.2	8.2	4.8	13.4	-29.4	-13.1	-1.8	3.6
6 ECB (net) /TC %	26.8	55.5	3.1	50.6	-19.0	-15.9	-7.3	1.4	20.9
7 Non-Resident deposits/ TC %	18.3	12.2	14.2	27.2	33.0	27.99	17.5	18.5	-12.3
As % of GDPmp									
8 Exports	5.8	8.3	8.4	9.9	9.4	10.6	10.8		
9 Imports	8.8	11.5	12.4	12.7	11.8	12.7	13.3		
10 Trade balance	-3.0	3.2	-4.0	-2.7	-2.4	-2.1	-2.5		
11 Invisibles balance	-0.1	2.2	2.9	2.2	3.1	3.3	4.3		
12 Current Account Balance	-3.1	-1.0	-1.0	-0.5	0.7	1.2	1.8		
13 External Debt	28.7	23.6	22.1	22.6	21.2	20.3	17.8		

Notes :

(i) TC: Total capital flows (net).
(ii) ECB: External Commercial Borrowing.
(iii) FER: Foreign Exchange Reserves, including gold, SDRs, and IMF reserve tranche.
(iv) GDPmp: Gross domestic product at current market prices.
(v) As total capital flows are netted after taking into account some capital outflows, the ratios against item no. 5, 6 and 7 may, in some years, add up to more than 100 per cent.
(vi) Rupee equivalents of BOP components are used to arrive at GDP ratios. All other percentages shown in the upper panel of the table are based on US dollar values.

Source: Economic Survey 2004-05.

TABLE – 24.2

India's Foreign Trade Ratios

(Per cent)

Period Average	X/GDP	M/GDP	T/GDP	X/M
	1	2	3	4
1980-81 to 1989-90	4.6	7.2	11.8	64.0
1990-91 to 1999-00*	8.0	9.5	17.4	84.1
1990-91 to 1994-95 *	7.3	8.4	15.7	86.9
1995-96 to 1999-00	8.5	10.4	18.9	81.8
2000-01 to 2001-02	9.4	10.8	20.2	86.7

* Excluding 1991-92.

Note : X=Exports, M=Imports, T=Exports+Imports, GDP=Gross Domestic Product at current market prices in rupees.

Sources : 1. Directorate General of Commercial Intelligence & Statistics.
2. Economic Survey, Government of India.

Trends in Merchandise Trade

The impact of trade reforms is evident from the changing structure of India's foreign trade in terms of diversity of markets and products and also in the form of higher degree of trade openness (resulting from higher export growth and the associated increase in the capacity to import). Following the various policy initiatives taken by the Government, there was a perceptible improvement in India's export performance in the initial phase of the reform period - both at the overall level and across commodities. The commodity composition of India's export basket has changed in favour of technology intensive and industrial products such as, engineering goods, besides high-value agricultural products. The destination profile of India's exports shows that the developing countries have gained considerable prominence over the years. The commodity composition of imports is affected by various factors such as impact of trade policy, domestic demand and international prices. The sourcing pattern of imports has also changed, mostly in favour of the developing countries.

Structural Changes in India's Foreign Trade

The foregoing discussion on India's foreign trade policy brings out certain distinctive features of the policy changes introduced since early-'nineties. In the first place, there has been a clear shift in emphasis from import-substitution to export-promotion. Secondly, the reach of the export incentives has been broadened to cover a large number of non-traditional and non-manufactured export items. Thirdly, the policy stance marks a move away from the provision of direct export subsidy to indirect promotional measures. Apart from the discernible change in trade policy, the 'nineties was also characterised by the introduction of market-based exchange rate regime. All these developments put together contributed to a distinct change in the structure of India's trade, at the disaggregated levels between the 'eighties and the 'nineties.

At the outset, it may be mentioned that due to change in the commodity classification used by the Directorate General of Commercial Intelligence and Statistics (DGCI&S), data on India's foreign trade before and after 1987-88 are not strictly comparable. It may also be pointed out that due to balance-of-payments constraints, India's imports were subjected to certain restrictions during 1991-92. Exports, however, were not subjected to similar restrictions. Against this background, the disaggregated analysis in the context of India's exports during the 'eighties has been done on the basis of data for the five-year period covering 1987-88 to 1991-92, while the year 1991-92 has been excluded from the scope of discussion on structural change in India's imports. The disaggregated analyses in the context of both exports and imports for the 'nineties are based on data covering the period 1992-93 to 1998-99.

The average import growth in India which was 7.2 per cent (in US dollar terms) during the 1980s increased to 12.9 per cent during the 1990s. Imports during the period 1990-91 to 1995-96 (excluding 1991-92) experienced an average growth rate of 16.7 per cent, reflecting largely the strong industrial growth during the period. Subsequently, in the remainder of the 1990s the average growth rate fell drastically to 8.0 per cent and further to 1.7 per cent during both 2000-01 and 2001-02, due to the slowdown in economic activity (RBI, 2002). The slow growth in imports is a cause for concern as it has a direct bearing on the exports of capital-intensive goods. Interestingly, India's import growth during the 1990s was lower than that of China but higher than that of the other East Asian countries.

The ratio of exports to GDP increased from an average of 4.6 per cent during the 1980s to 8.0 per cent during the 1990s (excluding the year 1991-92) which represents an increase in export orientation of the economy by 3.4 percentage points of GDP over one decade. Similarly, imports as a proportion of GDP increased from 7.2 per cent during the 1980s to 9.5 per cent during the 1990s. India's total merchandise trade, an indicator of the degree of openness of an economy, increased from about 11.8 per cent of GDP in the 1980s to 17.4 per cent during the 1990s (Table 24.2).

The average export-import ratio, an indicator of the import financing capacity of exports, improved sharply from 64.0 per cent to 84.1 per cent, between the 1980s and 1990s and further increased to 85.2 per cent in 2001-02 (Table 24.2). During the 1980s, the export-import ratio was as high as 115.5 per cent for Malaysia and 93.4 per cent for China. During the 1990s, the ratio for these countries – at 112.0 per cent for China and 106.8 per cent for Malaysia – was still higher than that for India. The exports of these countries thus, more than compensated for higher imports.

India's net terms of trade, which measure the relative change in export and import prices have been generally fluctuating during the 1990s. Import purchasing power of exports as measured by the income terms of trade have consistently improved during the 1990s on account of strong export, growth in volume terms.[4] The income terms of trade, increased on an average from 141.5 in the 1980s to 439.4 in the 1990s and further to 743.2 in 2001-02.

Diversification of exports constitutes an important element of India's export promotion strategy. Reflecting the policy thrust as also the evolving pattern of industrial development, India has gradually transformed from a predominantly primary products exporting country into an exporter of manufactured goods. However, it may be noted that this was more prominent in the 1970s. The progress has, however, stalled thereafter. Aided by various export promotion measures, the share of 'manufactured goods' in India's total exports increased from 70.7 per cent during 1987-90 to 75.3 per cent during 1992-97 and further to 77.4 per cent during 1997-2002.[5] Exports of petroleum products have also increased in the recent years. The commodity composition within the major groups has also undergone a considerable transformation. Within the 'primary products' group, the share of 'ores and minerals' in total exports has declined while the share of 'agricultural and allied products' remained almost unchanged at around 18 per cent between 1990-91 and 1998-99 but declined thereafter to 13.4 per cent in 2000-01. The falling share of 'ores and minerals' has been offset by the increase in share of 'engineering goods' within the manufactured products group – an indication of upward movement of India's exports in the value-addition chain. Similarly, exports of processed agricultural products also showed marked improvement in the post-reform years whereas the shares of traditional export items such as tea, coffee, cereals, handicrafts and carpets declined. Among other major manufactured products, the share of 'chemicals and allied products' has improved while that of 'leather and manufactures' has declined between the years 1990-91 and 2001-02 (Table 24.3).

TABLE – 24.3

Average Share of Exports of Selected Commodities

(Per cent)

Category	1987-90	1990-91	1992-97	1997-02
	1	2	3	4
Primary Products	24.2	23.8	21.9	18.5
Manufactured Goods	70.7	71.6	75.3	77.4
of which:				
Leather and Manufactures	7.5	8.0	5.8	4.6
Chemicals and Allied Products	5.9	7.2	7.2	9.1
Engineering Goods	11.0	12.4	13.8	14.7
Readymade Garments	11.2	12.3	12.0	12.2
Textile Yarn, Fabrics, Made-ups	8.0	8.5	10.9	11.2
Handicrafts including Gems and Jewellery	22.6	18.9	19.7	20.1
Petroleum Products.	3.1	2.9	1.8	2.1

Source : Directorate General of Commercial Intelligence and Statistics.

The areas in which South-East Asian countries have achieved their highest export growth during the 1980s have been typically labour intensive, relatively low technology products such as textiles, clothing, shoes, toys, sport goods and the like. Subsequently, during the 1990s they have graduated up to somewhat higher technology consumer goods and then even higher technology and capital-intensive sectors such as capital goods and petro-chemicals. Over the same period, the Indian export pattern has remained stationary with persistent dominance of labour-intensive low technology products such as clothing, textiles, shoes and other leather goods. Adequate quality upgradation has been absent and unit prices have stagnated. The attainment of both higher volume growth and of higher unit value realisation will require both larger scale of operation and higher quality. It is, therefore, essential to loosen constraints in these sectors so that they can grow freely in volume, utilise better machinery, graduate up to higher technology levels, and utilise better international marketing channels. What is observed in other countries in Asia is that production of such consumer goods may be achieved through final assembly operations that are large in scale, but where a great deal of out-sourcing to small enterprises is undertaken to preserve their competitiveness. Consequently, freeing of restrictions on the size of small-scale industries through dereservation is likely to lead to the growth of many more small-scale enterprises than is currently the case, along with a much higher potential for growth in manufacturing employment (Mohan, 2002).

Destination-wise analysis of the Indian exports indicates an unchanged position in respect of the Organisation for Economic Cooperation and Development (OECD) group being the largest market, increasing prominence of the Organisation of Petroleum Exporting Countries (OPEC) and the developing countries (Asia, Africa and Latin America), and a steep erosion in the relative position of the Eastern Europe. With the break-up of the Soviet Union, the share of the East European countries fell dramatically from 17.9 per cent in 1990-91 to just 2.9 per cent in 2001-02, primarily on account of the termination of Rupee trade and its adverse impact on exports of agricultural products such as tea, tobacco and spices to this region. The loss of this market share was, however, made up by increasing the shares in developing countries and the OPEC region, both of which doubled between the years 1987-88 and 2001-02 (Table 24.4).

TABLE – 24.4

Direction of India's Foreign Trade - Share in Total Exports

(Per cent)

Group/Country	1987-1988	1990-1991	1995-1996	1999-2000	2000-2001	2001-2002
	1	2	3	4	5	6
I. OECD Countries	**58.9**	**56.5**	**55.7**	**57.3**	**52.7**	**49.3**
of which:						
a. EU	25.1	27.5	27.4	25.5	23.4	22.5
b. North America	19.7	15.6	18.3	24.4	22.4	20.8
of which: USA	18.6	14.7	17.4	22.8	20.9	19.4
c. Asia and Oceania	11.6	10.4	8.3	5.8	5.1	4.5
d. Other OECD Countries	2.5	3.0	1.6	1.6	1.9	1.6
II. OPEC	**6.1**	**5.6**	**9.7**	**10.6**	**10.9**	**11.9**
III. Eastern Europe	**16.5**	**17.9**	**4.2**	**3.5**	**3.0**	**2.9**
IV. Developing Countries	**14.2**	**17.1**	**28.9**	**28.4**	**29.2**	**30.9**
a. Asia	11.9	14.4	23.0	22.3	22.5	23.6
b. Africa	2.0	2.2	4.8	4.2	4.4	5.2
c. Latin American Countries	0.3	0.5	1.2	1.9	2.3	2.1

Source : Directorate General of Commercial Intelligence and Statistics.

India's export share in world trade has increased perceptibly during the recent period. India's exports as a percentage of world exports improved to 0.56 per cent during 1991-96 and further to 0.65 per cent during 1996-2002 from 0.48 per cent in the 1980s. The ratio was 0.71 per cent in 2000-01, the highest achieved so far since the 1970s. Nonetheless, India's share in world exports is still very low and appears unimpressive when compared with the other major trading Asian countries, such as, China and other East Asian economies like Malaysia, Thailand, Singapore, Korea and Indonesia (Table 24.5). China demonstrated the most dramatic change as its share in world exports more than doubled in a decade from 2.0 per cent in 1991 to 4.4 per cent in 2001. Group-wise, India's share in the imports of industrialised countries in the 1990s declined as compared to that in 1986. In respect of the developing countries as a group, however, it has increased from 0.5 per cent in 1986 to 1.1 per cent during 1996-2000 (Table 24.6).

TABLE – 24.5

Share of Select East Asian Countries in World Exports

(Per cent)

Country	Annual					Average	
	1991	1995	1999	2000	2001	1991-1995	1996-2000
	1	2	3	4	5	6	7
India	0.5	0.6	0.6	0.7	0.7	0.6	0.6
China	2.0	2.9	3.5	4.0	4.4	2.5	3.4
Indonesia	0.8	0.9	0.9	1.0	0.9	0.9	0.9
Korea	2.0	2.4	2.6	2.7	2.5	3.0	2.5
Malaysia	1.0	1.4	1.5	1.6	1.4	1.2	1.5
Singapore	1.7	2.3	2.0	2.8	2.0	2.0	2.3
Thailand	0.8	1.1	1.0	1.0	2.0	1.0	1.0

Source : International Financial Statistics, February 2003.

TABLE – 24.6

India's Share in World Imports and in Imports of Major Trading Partners

(Per cent)

Group/Country	Annual 1981	Annual 1986	Annual 1990	Average 1991-1995	Average 1996-2000
	1	2	3	4	5
World	**0.5**	**0.7**	**0.6**	**0.6**	**0.7**
Industrial Countries	**0.4**	**0.6**	**0.5**	**0.5**	**0.5**
of which:					
United States	0.5	0.6	0.7	0.8	0.9
Japan	0.7	1.0	0.9	0.9	0.8
Belgium	0.3	0.4	0.6	0.6	0.8
Italy	0.2	0.2	0.4	0.5	0.6
Germany	0.3	0.3	0.5	0.5	0.5
United Kingdom	0.6	0.5	0.6	0.8	0.8
Developing Countries	**1.1**	**0.5**	**0.9**	**0.8**	**1.1**
of which:					
Malaysia	0.7	0.8	0.7	0.8	0.9
Singapore	0.5	0.6	0.6	0.7	0.7
Thailand	4.0	0.6	1.6	1.3	1.0
Bangladesh	0.3	2.2	4.6	9.6	12.9

Source : Direction of Trade Statistics, IMF various issues.

The commodity-structure of India's imports has also shown marked changes, reflecting, inter alia, the impact of trade policy, the movements in international prices and the pattern of domestic demand. The share of oil imports in India's total imports increased from 17.1 per cent during 1987-90 to 23.9 per cent during 1992-97 and further to 27.2 per cent in 2001-02. While the share and absolute value of these imports showed sharp fluctuations over the years mainly on account of the large movements in international crude prices, the volume of such imports has grown significantly on account of increase in domestic consumption and the stagnation in domestic crude oil production. Given the large swings in international crude prices, as also a trend rise in the oil import bill, there is a need for a comprehensive review of energy policy of the country covering the demand-supply aspects, as well as the price policy. Renewed efforts to improve energy supply from domestic sources by encouraging explorations, and stepping up of production and refining capacities are necessary to bring about a structural change in this area.

Reflecting the impact of a series of policy measures undertaken in the post-reform years starting with the repeal of the Gold Control Order in 1991 for liberalising the imports of gold and silver, these imports showed a sharp pick-up from 1992-93. The imports of gold and silver (including passenger baggage) rose from a meagre US $ 6 million in 1991-92 to US $ 1.3 billion in 1992-93 and further to US $ 5.9 billion in 1997-98. A large part of the increase in these imports could be due to a switchover from the unofficial channel to the official channel, initially through the Non-Resident Indian (NRI) baggage route and subsequently through the OGL route. In the subsequent years, however, these imports have stabilised and, in fact, declined to US $ 4.6 billion in 2001-02.

Imports of capital goods registered sharp increases in the initial reform years from US $ 4.5 billion in 1992-93 to US $ 10.3 billion in 1995-96, but exhibited a declining trend thereafter. The share of these imports, which had declined from 29.5 per cent in 1987-88 to 24.2 per cent in 1990-91, rose in the post-reform period to 28.2 per cent in 1995-96 but dropped to 18.1 per cent in 2001-02, reflecting the lack of investment demand associated with the sluggish pace of domestic industrial activity. Among other import items, the relative shares of fertilisers, non-ferrous metals, 'metalliferrous ores and metal scrap' and 'iron and steel' generally showed a declining trend.

There are noticeable changes in the sources of India's imports and in country shares. The share of the OECD countries and the Eastern Europe in India's imports declined between the years 1987-88 and 1999-2000 while that of the developing countries and the OPEC group increased during the same period. The share of India's imports from the OPEC region rose significantly to 25.9 per cent in 1999-2000 from 16.3 per cent in 1990-91, mainly on account of the increase in the oil imports.

The Ministry of Commerce and Industry, Government of India has set an export target of 1 per cent share of world exports by 2006-07 for the medium-term which would be co-terminus with the Tenth Five Year Plan. This target is based on historical trends, current prospects and the requirement of a compound annual growth rate of about 12 per cent for exports till the year 2006-07 (Government of India, 2002a). The export performance is known to depend on price competitiveness, as well as non-price factors. As regards the price competitiveness, a number of earlier studies have emphasised that real exchange rate may be an important variable influencing the price competitiveness of India's exports. In India, large exchange rate misalignment has not occured in the last one decade as the market itself has corrected the misalignment gradually over different episodes. The strong performance of the software exports, however, has created concerns about a possible "Dutch disease" effect which may erode the competitiveness of traditional exports. The export performance across commodity groups shows that most of the export groups have performed well so far, and apparently have not been affected by any "Dutch disease" effect. In a market determined exchange rate regime, exchange rate cannot be used as an instrument of export promotion, even though, at times, nominal appreciation could be prevented consistent with the overall exchange rate policy of the country. If the exporters retain the depreciation induced profits, they cannot improve their price competitiveness and therefore, exports may not increase despite a depreciation. In the Indian context, studies show that there has been an upward movement in exchange rate pass-through for India's exports. While Patra and Pattanaik (1994) estimate the co-efficient (during 1970-71 to 1992-93) at 43 per cent, Dholakia and Saradhi (2000) placed this figure at 30 per cent prior to 1991 and at 70 per cent after 1991.

Some of the recent studies have analysed the role of non-price factors vis-a-vis the price factors. Studies analysing the factors contributing to the competitiveness of India's exports have observed that non-price factors play a more important role (Marjit and Raychaudhuri, 1997). Another study observed an inverse relationship between depreciation of exchange rate of rupee and trade competitiveness, and also emphasised the role of other factors like quality, product design, reliability and after sales service in raising trade competitiveness (Bhatt, 2000).

India's export performance is affected by domestic as well as external impediments. The domestic factors inhibiting India's export growth, as mentioned earlier, inter alia are infrastructure constraints, high transactions cost, small-scale industry reservations, inflexibilities in labour laws, lack of quality consciousness and constraints in attracting FDI in the export sector. High levels of protection in relation to other countries also explain why FDI in India has been much more oriented to the protected domestic market, rather than as a base for exports (Ahluwalia, 2002). The exports of developing countries like India are facing increasing difficulties by emerging protectionist sentiments in some sectors in the form of technical standards, environmental and social concerns besides non-trade barriers like anti-dumping duties, countervailing duties, safeguard measures and sanitary and phyto-sanitary measures. Indian products which have been affected by such barriers include floriculture products, textiles, pharmaceuticals, marine products and basmati rice exports to the European Union and mushroom and steel exports to USA and also grapes, egg products, gherkins, honey, meat products, milk products, tea, and spices. Differential tariffs against developing countries have also adversely affected market access into these countries (Government of India, 2002b; WTO, 2002). According to the WTO, exports from India are currently subject to 40 anti-dumping and 13 countervailing measures mainly for agricultural products, textiles and clothing products and chemicals and related products. This brings into focus the importance of non-price factors like quality, packaging and the like mentioned earlier, where India still seems to be lacking as compared to the international standards. This has adversely affected India's export performance vis-a-vis other developing countries which may have an improved standing in these non-price factors.

To sum up, India's external trade reforms have been quite comprehensive. The protection given to domestic industries has been reduced by way of the reduction in tariff levels. However, the pace of tariff reduction needs to be accelerated (subject to revenue constraints). The tariff levels in India are still among the highest in the world. The evidence from 1991-97 and 2001-2003 suggests that faster tariff reduction is good for industry. India has completely dismantled its quantitative restrictions except for a few items. Various export promotion schemes have been put in place. In the area of multilateral commitments the progress has been satisfactory. The concerns of developing countries as voiced by India in the WTO are being considered. India is making progress on the negotiations on Services and on several issues which are in the process of study. Reforms in the trade sector have also been notable as clearly seen from the increase in India's trade-GDP ratio. There has been a steady increase in the growth rate of exports and imports as compared with the 1980s. The export-GDP ratio has almost doubled from that in the 1980s. The rising export-import ratio is indicative of the improvement in financing capacity of exports. India's share in world exports has been rising and in 2001, this ratio was the highest achieved so far since the 1970s. There has been a discernible shift in India's composition of exports with overall diversification of exports. The share of manufactured goods has shown an improvement driven by the increasing share of chemical and allied products, engineering goods, textiles and handicrafts including gems and jewellery. Imports have been driven by an increase in the imports of mainly export-related items like pearls, precious and semi-precious stones and electronic goods. India has also been successful in diversifying its export market increasingly to the developing countries alongwith the OECD emerging as the largest market for India's exports. A notable feature is that despite the loss of the East European market after the break-up of the Soviet Union, India made a safe transition to other markets like developing countries of Asia and to the OPEC.

Trends in Invisibles

One of the most significant developments in the current account of balance of payments in the 1990s was the remarkable growth in services transactions with the rest of the world, which was made possible by the revolution in information and communication technology. The information and communication related services (services relating to computer software, hardware, internet, e-commerce and telecommunication sector) experienced unprecedented growth during the last decade, outstripping the growth in merchandise trade. Reflecting the growing importance of trade in services, the General Agreement on Trade in Services (GATS) was adopted in 1993 to extend multilateral rules and discipline to services trade, with particular emphasis on non-discrimination and prohibition of quantitative restrictions. The Reserve Bank has undertaken several measures to relax payments restrictions on transactions pertaining to trade in services and other invisible transactions.

With the shift in the competitiveness towards services, in particular the technology related services, India has emerged as one of the fastest growing exporters of services in the world outstripping the growth rate of industrial countries as well as all countries taken together (RBI, 2002a). Reflecting this, gross invisible receipts (comprising services, transfers and income) increased from US $ 7.5 billion (29 per cent of total current receipts) in 1990-91 to US $ 35.6 billion (44 per cent of total current receipts) in 2001-02. Among the various items of invisible receipts, services increased from US $ 4.6 billion (18 per cent of total current receipts) in 1990-91 to US $ 20.3 billion (25 per cent of total current receipts) in 2001-02. Within services, miscellaneous services receipts, which encompasses communication services, construction services, financial services, software services, news-agency services, royalties, copyright and license fees, management services and others, increased from US $ 2.0 billion in 1990-91 to US $ 14.7 billion in 2001-02, representing 41.2 per cent of invisible receipts in 2001-02. Software services have shown spectacular growth while also emerging as the most important source of miscellaneous services earnings. Software exports increased from US $ 0.3 billion in 1993-94 to US $ 1.8 billion in 1997-98 and further to US $ 7.2 billion in 2001-02, with its share rising from 2.9 per cent to 20.1 per cent of total invisibles receipts during this period.

The high skill-intensity of the Indian workforce has imparted a decisive comparative advantage to Indian software services exports and has helped the country in carving out a niche in the global market for software and IT-enabled services. Besides, in recent years, India has emerged as one of the most preferred destinations for offshoring of IT services from advanced economies. While software and services exports have more than trebled between 1998-99 to 2002-03, exports of IT-enabled and business process outsourcing (BPO) services have increased significantly in recent years.

TABLE – 24.7

Invisibles by Category of Transactions

(Per cent of GDP)

	Items	1990-91	1995-96	1999-00	2000-01	2001-02
		1	2	3	4	5
	Invisibles Receipts	**2.4**	**5.0**	**6.8**	**7.5**	**7.4**
	Invisibles Payments	**2.4**	**3.5**	**3.8**	**4.9**	**4.5**
	of which					
I.	Non-Factor Services Receipts	1.4	2.1	3.5	4.1	4.2
	Non-Factor Services Payments	1.1	2.1	2.6	3.6	3.3
	of which:					
	i) Travel Receipts	0.5	0.8	0.7	0.7	0.6
	Travel Payments	0.1	0.3	0.5	0.6	0.5
	ii) Transportation Receipts	0.3	0.6	0.4	0.4	0.4
	Transportation Payments	0.3	0.6	0.5	0.7	0.5
	iii) Insurance Receipts	—	0.1	0.1	0.1	0.1
	Insurance Payments	—	—	—	—	0.1
	iv) G.n.i.e. Receipts	—	—	0.1	0.1	0.1
	G.n.i.e. Payments	0.1	0.1	0.1	0.1	0.1
	v) Miscellaneous Receipts	0.6	0.7	2.3	2.8	3.0
	Miscellaneous Payments	0.6	1.1	1.5	2.2	2.3
II.	Income Receipts	0.1	0.4	0.4	0.5	0.6
	Income Payments	1.3	1.3	1.2	1.3	1.1
III.	Private Transfers Receipts	0.7	2.4	2.8	2.8	2.5
	Private Transfers Payments	—	—	—	—	—
IV.	Official Transfers Receipts	0.1	0.1	0.1	0.1	0.1
	Official Transfers Payments	—	—	—	—	—

Note : G.n.i.e. - Government not included elsewhere. — : Negligible.

Miscellaneous : 1. Communication Services, 2. Construction Services, 3. Financial Services, 4. Software Services, 5. News Agency Services, 6. Royalties, Copyright and Licence Fees, 7. Management Services, 8. Other Services (Advertising, Rentals, Office Maintainance, Prizes, Exhibition and other services not enumerated elsewhere).

Sustainability of Current Account

One of the factors underlying the external payments crisis of 1991 was the high levels of current account deficit (CAD) maintained during the 1980s which at the time of the crisis had reached 3.1 per cent of GDP, well above the sustainable level for India (Cerra and Saxena, 2002). Concerted efforts directed at imparting strength and stability to the external sector emphasised a policy of maintaining the CAD within a sustainable level of about 2 per cent. This is broadly in line with the recommendations of the High Level Committee on Balance of Payments (RBI, 1993), which recommended that CAD-GDP ratio could be sustainable at 1.6 per cent. The current account deficit averaged only about 1.0 per cent of GDP during the last decade (1992-2002), as compared with 1.8 per cent in the 1980s, and recorded a surplus in 2001-02 after a period of 23 years. Among the components of current account, while the trade deficit (BoP basis) declined marginally from 3.2 per cent of GDP during the 1980s to 3.0 per cent during 1992-2002, the invisibles surplus increased significantly from 1.4 per cent of GDP to 2.1 per cent over the same period . With the narrowing of the current account deficit in the recent years, there is a need for revisiting the issue of sustainability of current account in the Indian context.

It has been noted that developing countries typically run CAD in their early stages of development to supplement their domestic saving to achieve higher level of investment and growth. This process enables recipient countries to achieve higher growth without cutting their current consumption; at the same time, higher productivity of capital in developing countries benefits foreign lenders by earning higher returns on their capital. This raises the question of an optimal CAD level for a country which, however, needs to be circumscribed by a sustainable level of capital flows. The external payments problems faced by India in 1991 and the East Asian crisis in 1997 have highlighted, inter alia, the role of large current account deficits and the consequent build-up of external debt, in precipitating the crisis (Rangarajan, 1993; RBI, 1999 and 2002a).

The current account sustainability depends upon external as well as domestic macroeconomic factors (Ghosh and Ostry, 1994; Milesi-Ferretti, Gian and Razin, 1997). Accordingly, a sustainable level of CAD would have elements of time and country specificity. Ultimately it is determined by the foreign investors' confidence in the domestic economy, depending upon the various external and domestic factors identified above. While a ratio of CAD-GDP of 8 per cent or so turned out to be unsustainable in the case of Thailand, the same ratio continues to remain sustainable in the case of New Zealand. This level of deficit need not be a cause for alarm as long as transparent and consistent policies remain (Brash, 1998).

In the Indian context, as mentioned before, it was recommended that the CAD be contained at 1.6 per cent of GDP, given the level of normal capital flows. The Report of the Committee on Capital Account Convertibility, 1997 (Chairman: S.S. Tarapore) felt that a sustainable CAD-GDP ratio cannot be static for all times. It, therefore, recommended that the CAD-GDP ratio could be varied in line with the servicing capacity of the economy proxied by trends in current receipts/ GDP ratio. The actual outcome of CAD-GDP ratio averaging just over 1 per cent in the 1990s so far could be reflective of the limited absorptive capacity and infrastructural and other bottlenecks in the economy that hamper higher levels of investment (RBI, 1999).

In recent years, the current account deficits have been progressively narrowing and now turning into a modest surplus in 2001-02 and first two quarters of 2002-03, which reflects the underlying conditions of weakening aggregate demand. The target growth path in the Tenth Five Year Plan would presage a greater recourse to higher imports and enlarged capital flows. At the same time, there remains considerable degree of concern regarding the sustainable level of the current account deficit for an economy of India's size and diversity. Clearly, exports hold the key to achieving a sustainable balance between the requirements of higher growth and the imperative of ensuring viability in the external sector. The projections of import growth underlying the growth rate of 8 per cent for the Tenth Plan have to be modulated and conditioned by the achievement of export targets along the course charted by the Medium-Term Export Strategy, 2002-07 (RBI, 2002b).

Against this background, financing of an average current account deficit of about 2.8 per cent of GDP as projected in the Tenth Five Year Plan may require a two-fold increase in the size of annual capital flows from the current levels. From a policy perspective, international investor confidence is critical to mobilise capital flows of this order. For this purpose, accumulation of reserves at a high level is an important pre-requisite.

In sum, during the decade of 1990s, the reform measures coupled with sound macroeconomic management succeeded in reducing the current account deficit well within the sustainable level for India. Given the sluggish export performance, the moderate current account deficit experienced in the recent years, including the condition of modest surplus recorded in 2001-02 can be largely attributed to sustained buoyancy in invisibles receipts. This reflects sharp rise in software service exports and subdued non-oil import demand, which in turn is symptomatic of a slowdown in industrial growth. There is, thus, a need for concerted policy efforts to raise the CAD-GDP ratio in line with the Tenth Plan projections so that higher growth is feasible over the medium term.

CAPITAL ACCOUNT, EXTERNAL DEBT AND EXCHANGE RATE: APPROACH, DEVELOPMENTS AND ISSUES

Reflecting the inward oriented economic policies in pursuit of self-reliance through export bias and import substitution, the role of the capital account during the 1980s was basically that of financing the current account deficits (RBI, 1999). The widening of the current account deficit during the 1980s coupled with the drying up of traditional source of official concessional flows necessitated a recourse to additional sources of financing in the form of debt creating commercial borrowings, non-resident deposits and exceptional financing in the form of IMF loans.

The external payment crisis of 1991 brought to the fore the weaknesses of the debt-dominated capital account financing. Recognising this, structural reforms and external financial liberalisation measures were introduced during the 1990s. The policy shift underscored the need for gradually liberalising capital account recognising that this is a process rather than a single event (Jalan, 1999). Throughout the 1990s the role assigned to foreign capital in India has been guided by the consideration of financing a level of current account deficit that is sustainable and consistent with absorptive capacities of the economy (Rangarajan, 1993; Tarapore, 1995; Reddy, 2000). In India, the move towards full capital account liberalisation has been approached with extreme caution. Taking lessons from the international experience, the Committee on Capital Account Convertibility, 1997 (Chairman: S.S. Tarapore) suggested a number of pre-conditions, attainment of which was considered necessary for the success of the capital account liberalisation programme in India (Box 24.3). The need for supplementing debt capital with non-debt capital with a clear prioritisation in favour of the latter has characterised the policy framework for capital inflows in the 1990s. The High Level Committee on BoP had recommended the need for achieving this compositional shift. Keeping in line with the policy thrust, capital flows have undergone a major compositional change in the 1990s in favour of non-debt flows.

BOX – 24.3

Committee on Capital Account Liberalisation
(Chairman: S.S. Tarapore)

With the growing role of private capital flows and the possibility of occasional sharp reversals, the issue of capital account liberalisation and convertibility has spurred extensive debate since 1992 - the period which witnessed a series of currency crises; in Europe (1992-93), Mexico (1994-95), East Asia (1997-98), Russia (1998), Brazil (1999), Turkey (2000) and Argentina (2001-02). These crises have raised the question of desirability of liberalisation and whether it is advisable to vest the IMF with the responsibility for promoting the orderly liberalisation of capital flows. The IMF in its study (1998) stated that "as liberalised systems afford opportunities for individuals, enterprises and financial institutions to undertake greater and sometimes imprudent risks, they create the potential for systematic disturbances. There is no way to completely suppress these dangers other than through draconian financial repression, which is more damaging." The view of IMF itself has changed over time (RBI, 2001). While opening up of the capital account may be conducive to economic growth as it could make available larger stocks of capital at a lower cost for a capital-deficient country, the actual performance of the economy, however, typically depends on a host of other factors. For a successful liberalised capital account, emerging market countries could: (i) pursue sound macroeconomic policies; (ii) strengthen the domestic financial system; (iii) phase capital account liberalisation appropriately and (iv) provide information to the market. At the international level, there is also the role of surveillance to consider, including the provision of information and the potential need for financing (Fischer, 1997).

In India, the move towards full capital account liberalisation has been approached with extreme caution. The Report of the Committee on Capital Account Convertibility, 1997 (Chairman: S.S.Tarapore) taking into account lessons from international experience suggested a number of signposts, the attainment of which are a necessary concomitant in the move towards capital account convertibility. Fiscal consolidation, lower inflation and a stronger financial system were seen as crucial signposts for India.

TABLE – 24.8

Various Recommendations for Capital Account Convertibility (Tarapore Committee)

Recommendations	Developments
Fiscal Consolidation	
1. Reduction in gross fiscal deficit as percentage of gross domestic product from budgeted 4.5 in 1997-98 to 4.0 in 1998-99 and further to 3.5 in 1999-2000.	1. Gross fiscal deficit as a percentage of gross domestic product stood at 5.9 during 2002-03.
Mandated Inflation Rate	
1. The mandated rate of inflation for the three-year period 1997-98 to 1999-2000 should be an average of 3 to 5 per cent.	1. Annual inflation rate based on WPI (base 1993-94=100) averaged at 4.7 per cent during the three years period 1999-2000 to 2001-02.
2. The Reserve Bank should be given freedom to attain mandated rate of inflation approved by the Parliament.	2. Although inflation is an important determinant of monetary policy, in India there is no target/mandated rate of inflation approved by Parliament.
Strengthening of Financial System	
1. Interest rates to be fully deregulated in 1997-98 and any formal or informal interest rate controls to be abolished.	1. All interest rates (except savings bank deposit rate) have been deregulated.
2. CRR to be reduced in phases to 8 per cent in 1997-98, 6 per cent in 1998-99 and to 3 per cent in 1999-2000.	2. CRR was reduced to 4.75 per cent in 2002-03.
3. Gross Non-Performing Assets (NPA) as percentage to total advances to be brought down in phases to 12 per cent in 1997-98, 9 per cent in 1998-99 and to 5 per cent in 1999-2000.	3. Gross NPA of the public sector banks as a percentage to total advances has come down from 16 per cent in end-March 1998 to 11.1 per cent in end-March 2002.

Contd...

...Table 24.8 Contd...

Recommendations	Developments
Fiscal Consolidation	
4. 100 per cent marked to market valuation of investments for banks.	4. The concept of 100 per cent marked to market valuation has been done away with. The modern concept works on the basis of banks classifying their entire portfolio into three categories 'Held to Maturity', 'Available for Sale' and 'Held for Trading'. While in the first category, the investment should not exceed 25 per cent, in the other two categories the banks have a freedom to decide the proportion that would be marked to market.
5. Best practices for forex risk management by banks.	5. Risk management guidelines were issued in October 1999, broadly covering areas of credit risk and market risk.
6. Banks to follow international accounting disclosure norms.	6. The range of disclosures as 'Notes to Accounts' in bank's balance sheet in 'Schedule 17' has been gradually expanded over the years.
7. Capital prescription be stipulated for market risks.	7. In March 2000, standard assets were given a risk weight of 0.25 per cent.
Important Macroeconomic Indicators	
1. A monitoring band of +/-5 per cent around the neutral Real Effective Exchange Rate (REER) to be introduced and intervened by the Reserve Bank when REER is outside the band.	1. No such band is maintained in India.
2. Debt service ratio to be reduced to 20 per cent from 25 per cent.	2. Debt Service ratio has steadily declined from 19.5 per cent in 1997-98 to 14.1 per cent in 2001-02.
3. The foreign exchange reserves should not be less than 6 months imports.	3. As of end-February 2003, foreign exchange reserves covers more than a year's imports.

India followed a gradualist approach to liberalisation of its capital account. India did not experience reversal of its policies towards the capital account as was the case with some emerging market economies that had followed a relatively rapid liberalisation without entrenching the necessary preconditions. This is particularly important since cross-country studies do not provide clear evidence of increase in capital flows resulting from capital account openness across all developing countries, with only 14 developing countries accounting for about 95 per cent of net private flows to developing countries in the 1990s. Besides, empirical evidence on the positive effects of financial capital flows on economic growth is not yet conclusive (Edison et al, 2002).

Foreign Investment

During the first three decades after independence, foreign investment in India was highly regulated. In the 1980s, there was some easing in foreign investment policy in line with the industrial policy regime of the time. The major policy thrust towards attracting foreign direct investment (FDI) was outlined in the New Industrial Policy Statement of 1991. Since then, continuous efforts have been made to liberalise and simplify the norms and procedures pertaining to FDI. At present, FDI is permitted under automatic route subject to specific guidelines except for a small negative list. In the recent period, a number of measures have been taken to further promote FDI. These include: raising the foreign ownership cap to 100 per cent in most of the sectors, ending state monopoly in insurance and telecommunications, opening up of banking and manufacturing to competition and disinvestment of state ownership in Public Sector Undertakings (PSUs). Though the FDI companies have generally performed better than the domestic companies, FDI to India has been attracted mainly by the lure of the large market (RBI, 2002b).

Responding to the policy efforts, foreign investment inflows to India (direct and portfolio investments taken together) picked up sharply in 1993-94 and have been sustained at a higher level with an aberration in 1998-99, when global capital flows were affected by contagion from the East Asian crisis. Total foreign investment has averaged at US $ 5.4 billion during the three year period 1999-2000 to 2001-02 as against negligible levels of the 1980s. Foreign portfolio investment (FPI) on the other hand, has shown larger year-to-year variations, moving in the range of a net inflow of US $ 3.8 billion in 1994-95 to a net outflow of US $ 61 million in 1998-99.

An industry-wise breakup reveals that the direction of FDI inflows has undergone a structural change over the reform period in line with the policy efforts. During the year 2001-02, computers, electronics and electrical equipments accounted for 34 per cent while services accounted for around 38 per cent of total FDI (excluding NRI investment). A country-wise breakup of FDI inflows reflects the increasing importance of Mauritius as the source of FDI in India during the recent years. This pattern highlights, in a sense, the role of tax policies in influencing the pattern of FDI flows at the global level.

Although India took significant steps towards inviting FDI in pursuance of its policy of emphasising non-debt creating capital inflows during the reform period, the actual FDI inflows did not pick up on the expected lines. FDI inflows in India remained low in comparison to other emerging market economies. An international comparison of annual average FDI and FPI inflows for the period 1997-2001 shows that such inflows to India were lower than those to emerging market economies like Argentina, Brazil, China, Korea, Mexico, Thailand and Malaysia. India's failure to attract enhanced inflows of FDI strongly underlines the need for further reforms in this context (Bhagwati, 2001). Given the projected need for financing infrastructure projects, on a rough and ready estimate, about 15 per cent of the total infrastructure financing may have to come from foreign sources. Since the ratio of infrastructure investment to GDP is projected to increase from 5.5 per cent in 1995-96 to about 8 per cent by 2006, with a foreign financing of about 15 per cent, foreign capital of about 1.2 per cent of GDP has to be earmarked only for the infrastructure sector to achieve the GDP growth rate of about 8 per cent (RBI, 2001b).

While inward FDI has been actively pursued, the policy framework has also been substantially liberalised in regard to direct investment from India to other countries during the 1990s. Overseas investment in Joint Ventures (JVs) or Wholly Owned Subsidiaries (WOS) have been recognised as important instruments for promoting global business by Indian entrepreneurs. Continuing with the direction of liberalisation of the capital account, companies have been allowed to invest abroad in JVs or WOS with limits which have been relaxed from time to time. At present, the complete use of American Depository Receipts (ADR)/ Global Depository Receipts (GDR) proceeds and the EEFC account balance for this purpose is also permitted. Taking advantage of the policy, the Indian investment abroad has increased from very meagre amounts in early 1990s to US $ 190 million in 1995-96 and further to US $ 639 million in 2001-02. The current levels, however, do not reflect the full potential of the Indian business and its improved competitiveness after a decade of wide-ranging reforms.

Like FDI, the environment for FPI was also made more congenial through procedural changes for investment and by offering more facilities for investment in equity securities as well as in debt securities to a select category of portfolio investors, viz., the Foreign Institutional Investors (FIIs). Furthermore, the sectoral limits for FIIs in the Indian companies were progressively increased over time; these limits have been done away with altogether, except in select specified sectors. The NRIs, Overseas Corporate Bodies (OCBs) and Persons of Indian Origin (PIOs) are also permitted to invest in shares and debentures of Indian companies, government securities, commercial papers, company deposits and mutual funds floated by public sector banks and financial institutions.

Foreign Direct Investment

Aggregate FDI inflows declined by more than US $ 1 billion in 2002-03 to US $ 3.6 billion from US $ 4.7 billion in 2001-02. Net FDI inflows are sum total of FDI inflows into India and FDI outflows from India. A category-wise analysis reveals that net FDI inflows into India were lower by US $ 1.5 billion in 2002-03, compared with 2001-02. According to the revised system of data reporting for FDI inflows adopted recently by the RBI in line with the international best practices (Box 24.4), FDI inflows comprise equity inflows, reinvested earnings and other capital. The overall decline in 2002-03 was principally on account of a sharp drop in net equity inflows. The analysis points to a slackening of fresh equity injected through FDI in the year 2002-03, which might be indicative of a commensurate deline in new investment projects. FDI outflows from India, which reflect the long term investment commitments of Indian multinationals in foreign markets, showed a decline of US $ 0.34 billion in 2002-03, reflecting lower interests on part of Indian companies in direct investment abroad.

According to the data on monthly inflows of foreign investment compiled by the RBI, FDI inflows for the full year of 2003-04 have been estimated at US $ 4.5 billion, which are slightly lower than US $ 4.7 billion recorded during 2002-03.

BOX – 24.4

Revised FDI Definition

A Committee was constituted by the DIPP in May, 2002 to bring the reporting system of FDI data in India into alignment with international best practices. Accordingly, the RBI has recently revised data on FDI

Contd...

...Box 24.4 Contd..

flows from the year 2000-01 onward by adopting a new definition of FDI. The revised definition includes three categories of capital flows under FDI: equity capital, reinvested earnings and other direct capital. Previously, the data on FDI reported in the balance of payments statistics used to include only equity capital.

Conceptually, the main difference between FDI and portfolio investment is in the (lasting interest) expressed by a non-resident direct investor in a resident enterprise of the domestic economy. The *lasting interest* underlines a firm desire on part of the non-resident investor to be associated with the long-term business activities of the resident enterprise by exerting significant influence on the management of the enterprise. Accordingly, the international best practice systems have focused on recording of FDI data in balance of payments statistics in terms of three main categories as mentioned below:

1. equity flows (equity in branches, shares in subsidiaries and other capital contributions).
2. reinvested earnings (retained earnings of foreign subsidiaries and affiliates), and
3. inter-company debt transactions (inter-corporate debt transactions between associated corporate entities).

There are, however, considerable variations among countries as far as their reporting systems of FDI flows are concerned. China and India are good examples in this regard. The Chinese system of reporting FDI is much more broad-based. Apart from equity capital, reinvested earnings, inter-corporate debt transactions, China includes short-term and long-term loans, trade credits, bonds, grants, financial leasing, investment by foreign venture capital funds, earnings of indirectly held enterprises, non-cash equity acquisition, control premium and non-competition fee within FDI. It also includes project imports as FDI flows, which, in India, are recorded as imports. As compared to China, it is clear that till some time back, the reporting of FDI in India's balance of payments statistics, which was confined only to equity capital, represented a much narrower coverage of FDI flows.

It is interesting to note that adoption of a broader coverage system for FDI flows has resulted in upward revision of annual FDI inflows into India for the years 2000-01 and 2001-02 by US $ 1.7 billion and US $ 2.2 billion respectively, representing on average, a 70 per cent increase over previously reported data. While this is not to suggest that the difference between volume of FDI inflows into China and India is attributable only to the disparities in coverage of data, comparisons between the two nations in terms of their abilities to attract FDI, should take note of this point.

Portfolio Investment

Aggregate portfolio investment inflows exhibited a declining trend between 2000-01 and 2002-03. From a net inflow of US$ 2.6 billion in 2000-01, such inflows declined to US$ 2.0 billion in 2001-02, and dropped further to US$ 0.9 billion in 2002-03. The decline is attributable to a steady fall in portfolio inflows into India, as a result of which the difference between portfolio inflows into India and outflows from India have gradually become smaller, leading to lower levels of aggregate portfolio investment.

The declining trend of portfolio investment observed during 2000-01 to 2002-03, however, witnessed a sharp reversal in 2003-04. During the first three quarters of 2003-04, net portfolio investment stood at US$ 7.6 billion with aggregate portfolio inflows at US$ 17.3 billion. The turnaround from the corresponding period of the previous year (April-December 2002-03), when net portfolio investment was only US$ 0.4 billion, and aggregate inflows were around US$ 5.2 billion, is indeed remarkable. The month-wise statistics compiled by RBI on foreign investment indicates that total portfolio investment inflows during the year 2003-04 amounted to around US$ 11.4 billion, which is far higher than around US$ 1 billion recorded during 2002-03.

NRI Deposits

NRI deposits in the form of Non-Resident (External) Rupee Account (NR(E)RA) and Foreign Currency Non-Resident Account (FCNR(A)) emerged as a steady flow of foreign capital in India from the 1970s, following the labour migration boom in West Asia in the wake of the first oil shock. The onset of the 1990s saw the introduction of as many as five NRI deposit schemes [Foreign Currency Bank and Ordinary (FC(B&O)), Foreign Currency Ordinary Non-Resident (FC(ON)), Non-Resident Non-Repatriable Rupee Deposit (NR(NR)RD), Non-Resident Special Rupee Account (NR(S)RA) and Foreign Currency Non-Resident Bank (FCNR(B))] between 1990 and 1993 designed to attract foreign exchange in the face of external payments crisis of 1991. With the recovery of the external sector, taking into account the lessons of the experience of various NRI deposit schemes during the 1980s and their contribution in aggravating the payments imbalance of 1990-91, the policies with regard to NRI deposits during the 1990s have been aimed at attracting stable deposits. This has been achieved through: (i) a policy induced shift in favour of local currency denominated deposits; (ii) rationalisation of interest rates on rupee denominated NRI deposits; (iii) linking of the interest rates to LIBOR for foreign currency denominated deposits; (iv) de-emphasising short-term deposits (up to 12 months) in case of foreign currency denominated deposits; and (v) withdrawal of exchange rate guarantees on various deposits. The Reserve Bank has also made an active use of reserve requirements on these deposits as an instrument to influence monetary and exchange rate management and to regulate the size of the inflows depending on the country's requirements. Continuing with the policy of progressive liberalisation of capital account, the NR(NR)RD scheme was discontinued with effect from April 1, 2002 and the maturity proceeds of NR(NR)RD can be credited to the account holder's NRE account only on maturity.

The NRI deposits have emerged as a major source of capital inflows during the 1990s. Apart from the size, the success of the policy towards NRI deposits is also reflected in an increase in the proportion of local currency denominated deposits (from around one-fourth in 1991 to almost two-third by 2002) and a substantial decline in short-term NRI deposits.

External Commercial Borrowings

Commercial debt capital includes a whole range of sources of foreign capital where the overriding consideration is commercial. External commercial loans include bank loans, buyers' credit, suppliers' credit, securitised instruments such as Floating Rate Notes and Fixed Rate Bonds, commercial borrowings and the private sector window of multilateral financial institutions.

The policies towards External Commercial Borrowings (ECBs) since the reform programme have been guided by the overall consideration of prudent external debt management by keeping the maturities long and cost low. ECBs are approved within an overall annual ceiling. Over time, the policy has been guided by a priority for projects in the infrastructure and core sectors such as power, oil exploration, telecom, railways, roads and bridges, ports, industrial parks, urban infrastructure and for 100 per cent Export Oriented Units (EOUs). To allow further flexibility to borrowers, end-use and maturity prescriptions have been substantially liberalised. Moreover, corporates have been allowed to borrow upto a certain limit under the 'automatic route'. Apart from these, special bonds (India Development Bonds (IDBs), Resurgent India Bonds (RIBs) and India Millennium Deposits (IMDs)) were issued by the State Bank of India aimed at NRIs. The success in mobilising foreign exchange resources through such exceptional schemes reflected the confidence of the global investor community in the Indian economy and imparted an element of stability to the external sector and the overall balance of payments position.

At times, the rationale behind raising such high cost debt capital has been questioned. Experience, however, would suggest that each time this option was resorted to, it helped in strengthening the confidence in the Rupee and the ability of the country to honour its obligations. The costs of an exchange rate crisis are too severe in relation to cost of debt capital. In a situation of moderate debt-service ratio, such debt capital makes more sense than allowing the exchange rate to fall under pressure. As in the event of payments crisis such as that in 1991, servicing of short-term debt can become difficult, the policies in the 1990s have regulated build-up of short-term debt by allowing short-term credits only for trade-related purposes. Until recently, suppliers' credits of more than 180 days and buyers' credit of all maturities required prior approval from the Reserve Bank. Effective September 2002, with a view to simplify and liberalise the exchange control procedures, the prior approval of the Reserve Bank has been dispensed with for amounts not exceeding US $ 20 million per import transaction.

Over the same period, official aid has waned in importance. This reflected mainly growing amortisation payments in the face of sluggish disbursements of external assistance as also availability of alternative private capital flows. Unlike aid, the share of ECBs in total capital flows have increased from around 31 per cent in 1990-91 to around 40 per cent in 1997-98. This has been mainly on account of the higher appetite for ECBs in view of the strong import demand and industrial growth. Subsequently, the increase in ECBs was entirely on account of RIBs and IMDs in 1998-99 and 2000-01, respectively, as the demand for ECBs remained low on account of weak investment demand.

The impact of the continuum of reforms initiated in the aftermath of the balance of payments crisis of 1991 on India's current account and capital account resulted in an accumulation of foreign exchange reserves of over US $ 70 billion as at end-February 2003. Capital account surplus increased from US $ 3.9 billion during the 1980s to US $ 8.6 billion during 1992-2002 with a steadily rising foreign investment. As a proportion of GDP, capital flows increased from 1.6 per cent during 1980s to 2.3 per cent during 1992-2002. The significant increase in capital flows during the 1990s raises the issue of their determinants as well as their impact on growth. Granger-causality tests indicate a unidirectional causation from net capital flows in the Indian context to growth in GDP over the 1970-2000 period. On the other hand, a component-wise analysis suggests that non-debt creating flows seem to

Granger cause GDP growth. Capital flows, both debt and non-debt, have also been found to crowd-in investment. Non-debt creating flows are discouraged by a higher fiscal deficit and exchange rate depreciation while greater openness and higher reserves have a positive effect on such flows (RBI, 2002b).

The sustained increase in capital inflows as discussed above, coupled with the moderate current account deficit, resulted in a surplus from 1993-94 onwards (excepting 1995-96) in the overall balance of payments (Table 24.9). The surplus amounted to US $ 11.8 billion in 2001-02 as against a deficit of US $ 0.6 billion in 1992-93.

TABLE – 24.9

Balance of Payments - Key Indicators

(Per cent)

Item	1990-91	1995-96	1999-00	2000-01	2001-02
	1	2	3	4	5
1. Trade					
i) Exports/GDP	5.8	9.1	8.4	9.8	9.3
ii) Imports/GDP	8.8	12.3	12.4	12.9	12.0
iii) Trade Balance/GDP	-3.0	-3.2	-4.0	-3.1	-2.7
2. Invisibles Account					
i) Invisible Receipts/GDP	2.4	5.0	6.8	7.5	7.4
ii) Invisible Payments/GDP	2.4	3.5	3.8	4.9	4.5
iii) Invisibles (Net)/GDP	-0.1	1.6	3.0	2.6	2.9
3. Current Account					
i) Current Receipts@/ GDP	8.0	14.0	15.1	17.2	16.7
ii) Current Receipts Growth@	6.6	18.2	12.9	17.1	1.4
iii) Current Receipts@/ Current Payments	71.5	88.8	93.0	96.4	101.2
iv) CAD/GDP	-3.1	-1.7	-1.0	-0.5	0.3
4. Capital Account					
i) Foreign Investment/GDP	–	1.4	1.2	1.1	1.2
ii) Foreign Investment/ Exports	0.6	14.9	13.8	11.4	13.2
5. Others					
i) Debt-GDP Ratio	28.7	27.0	22.2	22.3	20.8
ii) Debt Service Ratio	35.3	24.3	16.2	17.3	14.1
iii) Liability Service Ratio	35.6	24.7	17.0	18.3	15.3
iv) Import Cover of Reserves (in months)	2.5	6.0	8.2	8.6	11.3

@ Excluding official transfers. – Negligible.

The evolution of capital flows over the 1990s reveals a shift in emphasis from debt to non-debt flows with the declining importance of external assistance and ECBs and the increased share of foreign investment - both direct and portfolio. Apart from financing the current account gap, capital flows have played a significant role in India's growth performance.

Evidence of strong complementarity with domestic investment suggests that capital flows brighten the overall investment climate and stimulate domestic investment even when a part of the capital flows actually gets absorbed in the form of accretion to reserves. The growth-augmenting role of foreign capital, particularly FDI, however, seems to have been constrained by the low levels of actual and planned absorption of foreign capital in India (RBI, 2001). The key indicators of balance of payments as explained in Table 24.9 show considerable improvement in India's balance of payments since 1991.

External Debt Management

Efforts towards prudent management of external debt, keeping in view sustainability, solvency and liquidity were put in place in most of the countries in response to the Latin American debt crisis of 1982. Subsequently, the financial crisis of Mexico in 1994-95 and Indonesia, Korea, Malaysia, Thailand and other Asian countries in 1997 highlighted the need for a sound macroeconomic policy for managing short term private capital flows, particularly the debt creating ones. The East Asian crisis emphasised the need for monitoring: (i) both public and private debt; (ii) the size as well as the composition and maturity structure of external debt; (iii) inter company debt between direct investors and subsidiaries, branches and associates; (iv) trade credits, buyers and suppliers credits; (v) money market instruments; (vi) loans from foreign financial institutions for normal inter bank transactions and other commercial purposes; and (vii) foreign currency denominated deposits held by non-residents (Kappagoda, 1999). The East Asian crisis not only highlighted the need for monitoring the short-term debt, but it also emphasised the need for compilation of external debt (both long-term and short-term) on residual maturity basis, rather than original maturity basis. The former gives a better picture of the scheduled foreign exchange drain in the coming years on account of amortisation payments. In addition, the need for greater transparency and accountability, particularly in information disclosed by the private sector, has also been recognised as essential for avoidance of payments crisis (Kumar, 1999; Das, 1999; Williamson, 1999; Mohanty et al, 1999; Patra et al, 1999).

Apart from the need to contain current account deficit to sustainable level, one of the lessons from the external payment crisis of 1991, was to avoid excessive reliance on commercial debt especially of short-term maturity to finance the current account deficit. The approach to the external debt management was broadly based on the recommendations of the Rangarajan Committee, 1993. Following these recommendations, the strategy for external debt management during the 1990s has been guided by: (i) the continuation of an annual cap, minimum maturity restrictions and prioritising the use of ECBs; (ii) LIBOR based ceilings on interest rates and minimum maturity requirements on foreign currency denominated NRI deposits to discourage the volatile component of such deposits; (iii) reduction of short-term debt together with controls to prevent its undue increase in future; (iv) retiring/ restructuring/ refinancing of more expensive external debt; (v) measures to encourage non-debt creating financial flows such as FDI and FPI; (vi) incentives and schemes to promote exports and other current receipts; and (vii) conscious build-up of foreign exchange reserves to provide effective insurance against external sector uncertainties.

Key indicators of debt sustainability point to the continuing consolidation and improved solvency in the 1990s. Although, in nominal terms, India's total outstanding external debt increased from US $ 83.8 billion at end-March 1991 to US $ 98.5 billion at end-March 2002, external debt to GDP ratio declined sharply from 28.7 per cent at end-March 1991 to 20.9 per cent at end-March 2002. Prudent external debt management is also reflected in the proportion of short-term debt to total debt declining from 10.2 per cent in 1991 to 2.8 per cent in 2002 and in the ratio of short-term debt to foreign exchange reserves from a high of 146.5 per cent in the crisis period of 1991 to only 5.1 per cent in 2001-02. Debt service ratio declined from 35.3 per cent in 1990-91 to 14.1 per cent in 2001-02 (Table 24.10). Interest payments to current receipts ratio declined from 15.5 per cent in 1990-91 to 5.4 per cent in 2001-02.

The decade of 1990s witnessed a steady move towards consolidation of India's external debt statistics in terms of size, composition and indicators of solvency and liquidity. Containing the increase in the size of external debt to a modest level in the face of a tremendous growth in foreign exchange reserves during the decade definitely points towards the success of India's debt management strategy. Reflecting this, in terms of indebtedness classification, the World Bank has categorised India as a less indebted country since 1999. Among the top 15 debtor countries of the world, India improved its rank from third debtor after Brazil and Mexico in 1991 to ninth in 2000 after Brazil, Russian Federation, Mexico, China, Argentina, Indonesia, Korean Republic and Turkey. Moreover, among them, key external debt indicators such as short-term debt to total debt and short-term debt to forex reserve ratios are the lowest for India; the concessional to total debt ratio is the highest, while debt to GNP ratio is the second lowest after China.

TABLE – 24.10

Major Indicators of External Debt (as at end-March)

(Per cent)

Items	1991	1996	2000	2001	2002
	1	2	3	4	5
I. Total Debt to GDP	28.7	27.0	22.1	22.4	20.9
II. Short-term Debt (original maturity) to GDP	2.9	1.4	0.9	0.8	0.6
III. Concessional Debt to Total Debt	45.9	44.7	38.9	35.5	36.0
IV. Short-term Debt (original maturity) to Foreign Exchange Reserves	146.5	23.2	10.3	8.6	5.1
V. Short-term Debt (original maturity) to Foreign Currency Assets	382.1	29.5	11.2	9.2	5.4
VI. Non-Debt Liabilities and Short-term Debt to Reserves	148.2	92.3	99.9	100.8	88.4
VII. Short-term Debt and Non-debt Reversible Liabilities to Reserves	146.6	71.1	59.0	58.5	48.1
VIII. Debt Service Ratio	35.3	24.3	16.2	17.5	14.1
IX. Debt to Current Receipts	328.9	188.9	145.6	126.2	122.5
X. Liability Service Ratio	35.6	24.7	17.0	18.3	15.3

Exchange Rate Management

In the context of globalisation and currency crises, recent years, particularly, have seen a renewed interest on the issues relating to exchange rate regime, which is evident in the large and growing body of theoretical and empirical literature on the subject. Nevertheless, both in theory as well as in practice, the state of the debate is unsettled. A worldwide consensus is still evolving in search of an appropriate and credible exchange rate regime. Contemporaneously, in India also, discussion and debate on issues relating to the appropriate exchange rate system, policies on intervention, capital control and foreign exchange reserves figure very prominently. This is especially relevant with the introduction of a market-based exchange rate system in March 1993 and in the context of global currency crises, particularly the East Asian Crisis.

In India the exchange rate system has undergone a paradigm shift from a system of fixed exchange rate (until March 1992) to a market determined regime in March 1993. Since the switchover to a market determined exchange rate regime in March 1993, the behaviour of the exchange rate has remained largely orderly, interspersed by occasional episodes of pressures, which were relieved through appropriate intervention operations consistent with the stated policy of avoiding undue volatility in the exchange rate without reference to any target, whether explicit or implicit. The financial crises encountered by the emerging markets in the last decade have brought to the fore the importance of an appropriate exchange rate policy. The present Indian regime of managed flexibility that focuses on managing volatility without reference to any target has gained increasing international acceptance and well served the requirements of the country in the face of significant liberalisation of external sector transactions. This is particularly so in the context of the series of exchange rate crises experienced by several emerging economies undertaking similar macroeconomic reforms.

In the post-Bretton Woods period, the Rupee was effectively pegged to a basket of currencies of India's major trading partners from September 1975. This system continued through the 1980s, though the exchange rate was allowed to fluctuate in a wider margin and to depreciate modestly with a view to maintain competitiveness. However, the need for adjusting exchange rate became precipitous in the face of the external payments crisis of 1991.

As a part of the overall macroeconomic stabilisation programme, the exchange rate of the Rupee was devalued in two stages by 18 per cent in terms of the US dollar in July 1991. The transition to market determined exchange rate system took place in two stages and the sequencing was based on the Report of the High Level Committee on Balance of Payments, 1993 (Chairman: C. Rangarajan). The Liberalised Exchange Rate Management System (LERMS) instituted in March 1992 was a dual exchange rate arrangement under which 40 per cent of the current receipts were required to be surrendered to the Reserve Bank at the official exchange rate while the rest 60 per cent could be converted at the market rate. The 40 per cent portion surrendered at the official rate was for meeting the essential imports at a lower cost. Although the experience with the dual exchange rate system in terms of volatility in the market determined segment of the forex market was satisfactory, it involved an implicit tax on exports and other invisibles receipts and thereby emerged as a source of distortion. As a system in transition, the LERMS performed well in terms of creating the conditions for transferring an augmented volume of foreign exchange transactions on to the market.

The unified market determined exchange rate regime replaced the dual regime on March 1, 1993 and since then "the objective of exchange rate management has been to ensure that the external value of the Rupee is realistic and credible as evidenced by a sustainable current account deficit and manageable foreign exchange situation. Subject to this predominant objective, the exchange rate policy is guided by the need to reduce excess volatility, prevent the emergence of destabilising speculative activities, help maintain adequate level of reserves, and develop an orderly foreign exchange market" (Jalan, 1999). In order to reduce the excess volatility in the foreign exchange market, the Reserve Bank has undertaken market clearing sale and purchase operations in the foreign exchange market to moderate the impact on exchange rate arising from lumpy demand and supply as well as leads and lags in merchant transactions. Such interventions, however, are not governed by any predetermined target or band around the exchange rate.

The experience with the market determined exchange rate regime has been satisfactory, although the exchange rate management had to occasionally contend with a few episodes of volatility. The period from March 1993 till August 1995 was a phase of significant stability. Capital inflows coupled with robust export growth exerted upward pressure on the exchange rate. However, the Reserve Bank absorbed the excess supplies of foreign exchange. In the process, the nominal exchange rate of the Rupee vis-a-vis the US Dollar remained virtually unchanged at around Rs.31.37 per US Dollar over the extended period from March 1993 to August 1995. The real appreciation that resulted from the positive inflation differentials prevailing during this period triggered off market expectations and resulted in a market led correction of the exchange rate of the Rupee during September 1995 - February 1996. In response to the upheavals, the Reserve Bank intervened in the market and also resorted to monetary tightening so as to restore orderly conditions in the market after a phase of orderly correction for the perceived misalignment (RBI, 1996).

The period since 1997 has witnessed a number of adverse internal as well as external developments. The important internal developments include the economic sanctions imposed in the aftermath of nuclear tests conducted during May 1998 and the border conflict during May-June 1999. The external developments included, inter alia, the contagion from the Asian crisis, the Russian crisis during 1997-98, sharp increases in international crude oil prices in the period beginning with 1999, especially May 2000 onwards, and the post-September 11, 2001 developments in the US. These developments created a large degree of uncertainty in the foreign exchange market at various points of time, leading to excess demand conditions in the market. The Reserve Bank responded through appropriate intervention supported by monetary and other administrative measures like variations in the bank rate, repo rate, cash reserve requirements, refinance to banks, surcharge on import finance and minimum interest rates on overdue export bills. These measures helped in curbing destabilising speculation, while at the same time allowing an orderly correction in the value of the Rupee (Pattnaik, Kapur and Dhal, 2002).

A related issue that has figured in the literature is whether the exchange rate should be managed by monitoring Nominal Effective Exchange Rate (NEER) or Real Effective Exchange Rate (REER). "From a competitive point of view and also in the medium term perspective, it is the REER, which should be monitored as it reflects changes in the external value of a currency in relation to its trading partners in real terms. However, it is no good for monitoring short term and day-to-day movements as 'nominal' rates are the ones which are most sensitive of capital flows... Thus, in the short run, there is no option but to monitor the nominal rate" (Jalan, 2002).

Since the introduction of the market determined regime in March 1993, the Rupee has depreciated by 35 per cent upto February 2003 against the US dollar, i.e., from Rs.31.52 to Rs.48.73 per US dollar. In terms of effective exchange rates, the NEER depreciated by 31.1 per cent, while the REER (5 country trade based index) recorded a depreciation of 2.2 per cent during the period 1993-94 to 2002-03 (up to February 2003) (Table 24.11). A notable feature of the exchange rate in the recent years has been the two-way movement that has increased the risk profile of such market players who maintain open positions guided by the perception that the exchange rate can move only one way in India.

TABLE – 24.11

Exchange Rate and the REER and NEER of the Indian Rupee

Year	Rupees per US Dollar	REER	NEER
		(5 country trade weights with 1993-94=100)	
	1	2	3
1990-91	17.94	141.69	175.04
1991-92	24.47	116.48	131.54
1992-93	30.65	112.31	117.81
1993-94	31.37	100.00	100.00
1994-95	31.40	105.81	96.09
1995-96	33.45	102.29	87.69
1996-97	35.50	103.43	86.38
1997-98	37.16	105.84	86.43
1998-99	42.07	97.79	76.45
1999-00	43.33	96.74	74.22
2000-01	45.68	100.76	73.77
2001-02	47.69	102.09	73.18
2002-03 (up to Feb '03)	48.46	97.77	68.88

The Indian Rupee depreciated against all the other major currencies during the 10-year period 1993-94 to 2002-03 (up to February 2003). The Rupee depreciated against the Pound Sterling and the Japanese Yen by 37 per cent and 27 per cent, respectively, during this period. It depreciated against the Euro by 6 per cent between 1999-2000 and 2002-03 (up to February 2003).

As a whole, India's current exchange rate policy seems to have stood the test of time. It has focused on the management of volatility without fixed rate target, while underlying demand and supply conditions are allowed to determine the exchange rate movements in an orderly way. The Reserve Bank will continue to follow the approach of watchfulness, caution and flexibility by closely monitoring the developments in the domestic and financial markets in home and abroad. It will co-ordinate its market operations carefully, particularly in regard to forex market with appropriate monetary, regulatory and other measures as considered necessary from time to time (RBI, 2002c).

FOREIGN EXCHANGE RESERVES: APPROACH, DEVELOPMENTS AND ISSUES

Approach

The subject of foreign exchange reserves has received renewed interest in recent times in the context of increasing globalisation, acceleration of capital flows and integration of financial markets. The debt-banking-financial crises in several countries have also necessitated the need for an international financial architecture in which the management of foreign exchange reserves has emerged as one of the critical issues.

Contextually, the subject of foreign exchange reserves may be broadly classified into two inter-linked areas, viz., the theory of reserves and the management of reserves. The theory of reserves encompasses issues relating to institutional and legal arrangements for holding reserve assets, conceptual and definitional aspects, objectives for holding reserve assets, exchange rate regimes and conceptualisation of the appropriate level of foreign reserves. In essence, a theoretical framework for reserves provides the rationale for holding foreign exchange reserves. Reserve management is mainly guided by the portfolio management consideration, i.e., how best to deploy foreign reserve assets subject to statutory stipulations? The portfolio considerations take into account inter alia, safety, liquidity and yield on reserves as the principal objectives of reserve management. The institutional and legal arrangements are largely country specific and these differences should be recognised in approaching the critical issues relating to both reserve management practices and policy-making (Reddy, 2002).

The motives for holding reserves may be broadly classified under three categories, viz., transaction, speculative and precautionary. International trade gives rise to currency flows, which are assumed to be handled by banks driven by the transaction motive. Similarly, speculative motive is left to individuals or corporates. Central bank reserves, however, are characterised primarily as a last resort stock of foreign currency for unpredictable flows, which is consistent with precautionary motive for holding foreign assets. Precautionary motive for holding foreign currency, like the demand for money, can be positively related to wealth and the cost of covering unplanned deficit, and negatively related to the return from alternative assets. Furthermore, foreign exchange reserves are instruments to maintain or manage the exchange rate, while enabling orderly absorption of international capital flows. Official reserves are mainly held for precautionary and transaction motives keeping in view the aggregate of national interests, to achieve balance between demand for and supply of foreign currencies, for intervention, and to preserve confidence in the country's ability to carry out external transactions.

The objectives for maintaining reserves are: (i) maintaining confidence in monetary and exchange rate policies; (ii) enhancing capacity to intervene in foreign exchange markets; (iii) limiting external vulnerability by maintaining foreign currency liquidity to absorb shocks during times of crisis including national disasters or emergencies; (iv) providing confidence to the markets, including credit rating agencies, that external obligations can always be met (thus reducing the overall costs at which foreign exchange resources are available to all the market participants); and (v) adding to the comfort of the market participants, by demonstrating the backing of domestic currency by external assets.

India's approach to reserve management, until the balance of payments crisis of 1991 was essentially based on the traditional approach, i.e., to maintain an appropriate level of import cover defined in terms of number of months of imports equivalent to reserves. For example, the import cover of reserves shrank to three weeks of imports by the end of December 1990, and the emphasis on import cover constituted the primary concern say, till 1993-94. The approach to reserve management, as part of exchange rate management, and indeed the overall external sector policy underwent a paradigm shift with the adoption of the recommendations of the High Level Committee on Balance of Payments, 1993 (Chairman: C. Rangarajan). The Committee had recommended that the foreign exchange reserve targets be fixed in such a way that they are generally in a position to accommodate imports of three months. In the view of the Committee, the factors that are to be taken into consideration in determining the desirable level of reserves are: (i) the need to ensure a reasonable level of confidence in the international financial and trading communities about the capacity of the country to honour its obligations and maintain trade and financial flows; (ii) the need to take care of the seasonal factors in any balance of payments transaction with reference to the possible uncertainties in the monsoon conditions of India; (iii) the amount of foreign currency reserves required to counter speculative tendencies or anticipatory actions amongst players in the foreign exchange market; and, (iv) the capacity to maintain the reserves so that the cost of carrying liquidity is minimal.

With the introduction of market determined exchange rate, a change in the approach to reserve management was warranted and the emphasis on import cover had to be supplemented with the objective of smoothening out the volatility in the exchange rate, which has been reflective of the underlying market condition (RBI, 1996). Against the backdrop of currency crises in East-Asian countries and in the light of country experiences of volatile cross-border capital flows, there emerged a need to take into consideration a host of factors. The shift in the pattern of leads and lags in payments/receipts during exchange market uncertainties brought to the fore the fact that besides the size of reserves, the quality of reserves also assumes importance. Unencumbered reserve assets (defined as reserve assets net of encumbrances such as forward commitments, lines of credit to domestic entities, guarantees and other contingent liabilities) must be available at any point of time to the authorities for fulfilling various objectives assigned to reserves (RBI, 1998). As a part of prudent management of external liabilities, the policy is to keep forward liabilities at a relatively low level as a proportion of gross reserves (RBI, 1999).

The overall approach to management of foreign exchange reserves reflected the changing composition of balance of payments and liquidity risks associated with different types of flows and other requirements. The policy for reserve management is built upon a host of identifiable factors and other contingencies, including, inter alia, the size of the current account deficit and short-term liabilities (including current repayment obligations on long-term loans), the possible variability in FPI and other types of capital flows, the unanticipated pressures on the balance of payments arising out of external shocks and movements in repatriable foreign currency NRI deposits (RBI, 2000).

An important issue which has figured prominently in the current debate on foreign exchange management is the question of appropriate policy for management of foreign exchange reserves. In a regime of free float, it can be argued that there is no need for reserves. In the light of volatility induced by capital flows and self-fulfilling expectations that this can generate, there is now a growing consensus among emerging market economies to maintain 'adequate' reserves (Jalan, 2002). Therefore, while focusing on prudent management of foreign exchange reserves in recent years, the 'liquidity at risk' associated with different types of flows has come to the fore (RBI, 2001). With the changing profile of capital flows, the traditional approach to assessing reserve adequacy in terms of import cover has been broadened to include a number of parameters which take into account the size, composition, and risk profiles of various types of capital flows as well as the types of external shocks to which the economy is vulnerable. A sufficiently high level of reserves is necessary to ensure that even if there is prolonged uncertainty, reserves can cover the liquidity at risk on all accounts over a fairly long period. Taking these considerations into account, India's foreign exchange reserves have reached a very comfortable level. The current thinking in this regard has been clearly articulated: "The prevalent national security environment further underscores the need for strong reserves. We must continue to ensure that, leaving aside short-term variations in reserves level, the quantum of reserves in the long-run is in line with the growth of the economy, the size of risk-adjusted capital flows and national security requirements. This will provide us with greater security against unfavourable or unanticipated developments, which can occur quite suddenly" (RBI, 2002c). In the context of the uncertain ramifications of the current developments in Iraq, the relevance of a comfortable reserve level appears particularly important. Unlike 1990-91, implications of such developments in the Gulf region for the external sector appears modest and manageable, mainly due to the comfortable reserve level.

The foregoing discussion points to the evolving considerations and a paradigm shift in India's approach to reserve management. The shift has occurred from a single indicator to a menu or multiple indicators approach. Furthermore, the policy of reserve management is built upon a host of factors, some of which are not quantifiable, and in any case, weights attached to each of them do change from time to time.

Developments

In India, reserves have been steadily built up by encouraging non-debt creating flows and de-emphasising debt creating flows, particularly short-term debt. This strategy, coupled with the maintenance of an acceptable level of current account deficit and market determined exchange rate regime was the cornerstone of the policy of external sector management. In the context of the changing interface with the external sector and the importance of the capital account, reserve adequacy is now evaluated by the Reserve Bank in terms of several indicators and not merely through conventional norms, such as, the import cover. As a matter of policy, as far as possible, foreign exchange reserves are kept at a level which is adequate to withstand both cyclical and unanticipated shocks (RBI, 1999).

In the context of increasing cross-border linkages and the growing importance of the capital account, it became necessary to evaluate reserve adequacy in terms of both conventional indicators and non-conventional norms (Reddy, 1997). The Report of the Committee on Capital Account Convertibility, 1997 (Chairman: S. S. Tarapore) suggested four alternative measures to assess reserve adequacy: (i) import cover of six months; (ii) import cover of three months plus 50 per cent of annual debt service payments plus one month's imports and exports to take into account the possibility of leads and lags; (iii) ratio of short-term debt and stock of portfolio investment related non-debt liabilities to reserves at not more than 60 per cent; and (iv) the net foreign exchange assets to currency ratio (NFA/currency ratio) at around 70 per cent with a minimum of 40 per cent for this ratio to be stipulated by the RBI Act. In recent times, Pablo Guidotti has suggested that emerging market economies must maintain usable forex reserves exceeding scheduled amortisation of foreign currency debts falling due (assuming no roll-overs) during the following year. The concept of 'usable reserves' merits particular attention in view of the developments experienced by Korea and Thailand during the 1997 crisis. A large part of the gross reserves was not available to the authorities to defend the falling exchange rates. Greenspan (1999) suggested a 'liquidity-at-risk' rule and observed that "countries could be expected to hold sufficient liquid reserves to ensure that they could avoid new borrowing for one year with a certain *ex ante* probability, such as 95 per cent of the time".

India is amongst the top ten reserve holding emerging market nations (Table 24.12). India's foreign exchange reserves increased from US $ 4.7 billion in June 1991 to US $ 73.9 billion as on March 13, 2003. The predominant component of foreign exchange reserves is in the form of foreign currency assets that increased from US $ 1.1 billion to US $ 71.7 billion during the same period. The gold holdings of the Reserve Bank remained broadly stable at around US $ 3-4 billion during the same period. SDR holdings of the Government came down from US $ 63 million in June 1991 to US $ 4 million as on March 13, 2003. The movement in India's foreign exchange reserves since 1993-94 can be divided into three phases: (i) the period March 1993 to March 1995, when reserves increased sharply from US $ 9.8 billion to US $ 25.2 billion, (ii) the period March 1995 to March 1999, when reserves increased moderately to US $ 32.5 billion, and (iii) finally since 1999-2000, when there was a phenomenal increase in reserves - as much as US $ 41.3 billion cumulatively (by US $ 5.5 billion in 1999-2000, US $ 4.2 billion in 2000-01, US $ 11.8 billion in 2001-02, and US $ 19.8 billion during 2002-03 (up to March 13, 2003)).

TABLE – 24.12

Total International Reserves *minus* Gold

(SDR billion)

Countries/Country Groups	1963	1973	1983	1993	2002 (Nov)
	1	2	3	4	5
1. All countries	26.6	116.8	362.3	797.7	1837.3
2. Industrial countries	19.2	79.9	206.2	413.4	727.0
3. Developing countries	7.5	36.9	156.1	384.3	1110.3
4. Asia	2.7	8.6	54.6	220.3	703.8
of which:					
i. China, People's Rep.	–	–	14.3	16.3	204.2@
ii. Hong Kong	–	–	–	–	83.8
iii. India	0.4	0.7	4.7	7.4	48.5
iv. Indonesia	0.0	0.7	3.6	8.2	21.9
v. Korea, Republic of	0.1	0.7	2.2	14.7	89.3
vi. Malaysia	0.4	1.1	3.6	19.8	25.7
vii. Philippines	0.1	0.8	0.7	3.4	9.8
viii. Singapore	0.4	1.9	8.9	35.2	60.6
ix. Thailand	0.5	1.0	1.5	17.8	27.8

@ Data refer to October 2002.

Source : International Financial Statistics, Yearbook 2002 and December 2002.

The traditional trade-based indicator of reserve adequacy, i.e., the import cover of reserves (foreign currency assets), which fell to a low of two weeks of imports in June 1991 improved to 11.3 months of imports as at end-March 2002. Import cover of reserves further increased to nearly 14 months of imports by March 2003. In terms of the money-based indicators, the ratio of net foreign exchange assets of the Reserve Bank to currency in circulation sharply increased from 14.4 per cent at end-March 1991 to 105.2 per cent at end-March 2002 while that of net foreign exchange assets to broad money increased from 3.0 per cent to 17.6 per cent over the same period. The debt-based indicators of reserve adequacy also steadily improved in the 1990s. The ratio of volatile capital flows (defined as cumulative portfolio flows and short-term debt to reserves), which was 71.1 per cent as at end-March 1996 fell to 48.1 per cent as at end-March 2002. The ratio of short-term debt to reserves declined from 146.5 per cent in 1990-91 to 5.1 per cent in 2001-02. Taking these factors into account, India's foreign exchange reserves are at present comfortable and consistent with the rate of growth, the share of external sector in the economy and the size of the risk adjusted capital flows (RBI, 2002c).

As a part of prudent reserve management policy, the net forward liabilities have been kept at relatively low levels. The proportion of forward liabilities declined from 6.1 per cent of gross reserves at end-March 1998 to 0.3 per cent at end-August 2002. In the subsequent months, these have been fully retired and the Reserve Bank held net forward assets of US $ 2.6 billion in February 2003.

While the significant accretion to foreign exchange reserves has provided comfort on external sector management, two contentious issues have come to the fore. These are the trade-off between costs and benefits accruing from the reserves accretion and the associated monetary impact that emanates from it.

International Reserves and Optimality

The policy of accretion to reserves to meet the transactions and precautionary needs generally involves both financial and economic cost to the country. In the absence of any unique definition of the opportunity cost, one comes across several interpretations in the literature, the applicability of which depends on the particular economic context. When an economy is both foreign exchange and saving constrained, the opportunity cost could be the rate of return on domestic investment (assuming that the foreign exchange used to finance unsatiated investment demand would have fetched the return on domestic investment). When an economy is only foreign exchange constrained, the opportunity cost could be in terms of foregone consumption. When an economy is not foreign exchange constrained (i.e., all productive forex demand are met before the reserves are built up), the opportunity cost would depend on the difference between the cost of borrowing and the return on reserve assets. If high cost borrowings are used to build reserves on which modest returns are obtained because of the emphasis on safety and liquidity of reserve assets, such reserve build-up policies may prove more costly. Another form of cost - often known as the quasi-fiscal cost - arises from the higher rate of return on domestic assets vis-a-vis foreign assets. Since sterilised intervention gives rise to an offsetting change in the domestic asset holding of a central bank when its foreign assets increase, the overall profits arising from the total asset portfolio of the central bank's balance sheet may decline. As a result, the profits transferred to the Government – which represents a major source of non-tax revenue for the Government – may decline. For countries operating with large fiscal imbalances, such a decline in non-tax revenue could prove more costly, forcing a higher mobilisation of tax revenue or a cut in expenditure that may affect growth and development.

Capital Inflows, Foreign Exchange Reserves and Growth

The coexistence of slowdown in the growth rate of the Indian economy in the recent period and the sharp build-up of foreign exchange reserves, has fuelled the debate on their possible inter-relationship and has called into question, in some quarters, the extant policy of reserve accretion. A recent study by Lal Bery and Pant (NCAER) for example, has contended that India could have attained a higher growth trajectory had capital inflows been allowed to be absorbed by the economy (instead of accumulating them as foreign exchange reserves of the central bank) and had fiscal deficits not been incurred. According to the study, the entire foreign capital can be absorbed by allowing the real exchange rate to appreciate. The real appreciation could be engendered either by allowing the nominal exchange rate to appreciate or by allowing prices to increase (i.e., non-sterilised reserve build-up which will increase the money supply and thereby give rise to both higher inflation and lower interest rates – both of which can increase absorption). An econometric exercise shows that the growth rate could have been higher by about 1 to 6 per cent in different years in the 1990s. The study makes the following policy recommendations: (i) the reserve management policy should be replaced by appropriate monetary and exchange rate policies that could boost growth; (ii) have a tighter fiscal policy (to contain the crowding out effect) and an easier monetary policy (by nonsterilisation of reserves – that could increase prices and lower interest rates); (iii) high reserves and low domestic inflation provide the right environment against which the Rupee can be made fully convertible on the capital account; and (iv) replace on the managed exchange rate regime by full float.

The above results and policy prescriptions, however, need to be viewed with a great deal of circumspection. First, it needs to be recognised that high reserves reflect the lack of absorption/demand, and prescribing real appreciation as a means to raise domestic absorption completely disregards the importance of the trade-off between growth and stability and the role of a central bank in ensuring stability as a means to higher growth.

Second, the experience of the emerging market crises in the last decade shows that with low reserves and appreciated real exchange rate, India would have also faced a similar (or even more severe) crisis. On an average, the crisis years witnessed a sizeable growth reversal of the order of 6 to 7 per cent in all the crisis affected countries which could have offset the perceived 'first round' gains to the growth rate.

Third, it also needs to be recognised that even if REER appreciation is allowed to ensure full absorption of foreign capital, it is important to examine whether the full absorption (i.e. higher current account deficit) would result from an increase in imports or a major fall in exports. Given the asymmetric response of exports and imports to price changes brought about by REER appreciation, it is possible that a higher CAD would be attained more by a fall in exports than an increase in imports. It needs no emphasis that the external sector sustainability hinges critically on the performance of the export sector, and in the face of zero incremental reserves resulting from full absorption, weak export growth could be a strong source of vulnerability to crisis. On the other hand, even if imports increase in response to exchange rate appreciation, it is possible that import demand may just replace domestic demand, and as a result aggregate demand may remain unaltered. In other words, when imports are not driven by overall demand conditions (as is the case now) but are encouraged through a policy of exchange rate appreciation, imports may only compete with domestic supply and in the face of no increase in aggregate demand, the higher absorption through cheaper imports could displace some of the domestic manufacturers and thereby lower growth. Thus, growth gained through full absorption could be offset by lower growth resulting from displacement of domestic producers.

Fourth, the contention that full absorption of capital flows would significantly reduce the extent of crowding out by allowing a larger part of the fiscal deficit to be monetised, ignores the possibility of 'crowding in' effects by certain types of government expenditure which at times may dominate the crowding-out effects.

Finally, it needs to be recognised that foreign capital should not be allowed either to give rise to excessive consumption or excessive investment just to ensure full absorption. When foreign capital finances consumption demand (as in Mexico) or sustains an investment driven overheating (as in South East Asia), higher growth can be obtained only at the cost of a severe financial crisis. High reserves, a flexible exchange rate regime, and cautious liberalisation of the capital account, together aim at preventing a crisis. Sterilisation is a strong instrument to regain monetary independence that allows a policy of reserve build-up without any adverse monetary implications. Sterilisation has been used successfully so far in India and limits to sterilisation are yet to be reached.

The need for raising domestic absorption is well recognised and the Tenth Plan document already envisages a current account deficit of 2.8 per cent of GDP to attain a growth target of about 8 per cent. In the context of the Tenth Plan requirements, current levels of reserves and capital flows appear to be inadequate. Even if large capital flows materialise in future to meet the financing gap of 2.8 per cent of GDP as envisaged in the Tenth Plan document, the flows need to be regulated so that the CAD does not expand beyond the sustainable level. Hence, even though expanding absorption of foreign capital is a major policy challenge in the short-run, the overall medium to long-run policy strategy demands that the CAD be necessarily maintained within the sustainable level. This has been the most important lesson from the balance of payments crisis in 1991. Rather than engendering real appreciation, other counter-cyclical policies can be applied to revive aggregate demand, which in turn can improve absorption of foreign capital.

Summing Up

The external sector reform programme initiated in the wake of the balance of payments crisis of 1991 was all encompassing. Even though the reforms were largely crisis led, the policy initiatives were unique in terms of their gradual, cautious and country specific approach. As against balance of payments problems of varying intensities experienced during 1956-1991, India's balance of payments position strengthened over the 1990s even as the period coincided with the liberalisation of external account, external currency crises and domestic political uncertainties.

Prudent exchange rate management, low current account deficit, steady flow of non-debt creating capital flows, particularly in the form of FDI, a significant reduction in the external debt to GDP ratio and containment of short-term debt to manageable and prudent limits have been some of the positive outcomes of policy reform in the external sector. Resilience of the external sector has helped India successfully avert the contagion effects of the East Asian crisis.

There are, however, a few areas, which require further efforts. India's competitiveness in exports would require to be strengthened to achieve a sustained export growth of at least 12 per cent per annum in order to achieve the medium-term goal of increasing India's share in world exports to 1 per cent by 2006-07. India also needs to make the transition from exports of labour-intensive low technology goods to a wider variety of goods, including technology intensive goods. India's tariff levels continue to be high; accelerated pace of reduction of tariffs and removing the constraints on the small-scale industries would be conducive to industrial growth and exports. Rapid growth in exports would also require addressing the domestic constraints of supply bottlenecks and inadequate infrastructure.

A sustained surge in capital flows in the recent past has implications for monetary and inflation management although, the Reserve Bank has so far been able to sterilise the monetary impact of foreign exchange reserves through large open market sales of government securities. The financial cost of additional reserve accretion in the recent period is low.

There has been a debate that high accretion to forex reserves has resulted in a substantial output loss in the 1990s. It needs to be recognised, however, that the steady growth path is functionally related more to macroeconomic constraints of saving and investment than to the reserve management policy *per se*. The reserve management policy, coupled with the exchange rate management and monetary policy pursued by the Reserve Bank has created an atmosphere of softer interest rate regime, which is conducive to higher economic growth. In addition, the recent policy initiatives have created an investment atmosphere where foreign investment supplements domestic investment, which in a medium-term perspective would ensure a higher growth trajectory.

India's Export Performance *vis-a-vis* Other Developing Countries*

In a recent study Suresh D Tendulkar* (Dec., 2000) has pointed out that although India had a head-long start in industrialisation well-ahead of the rapidly growing economies of East and South East Asia (South Korea, Taiwan, Thailand, Indonesia, Malaysia and (mainland) China which started around more or less the same level of per capita GDP as India in the 1950s but today enjoy much higher living standards than those in India.

Tendulkar has studied the Indian economic performance in respect of exports and rate of economic growth in an Asian perspective over the period from 1980 to 1996 and examined the association between export performance and the rates of economic growth experienced by the selected Asian economies. For providing the Asian perspective nine countries have been selected besides India. They include the Republic

---

* This section draws from S.D. Tendulkar study (Dec. 2000) *Indian Export & Economic Growth Performance in Asian Perspective*, Working Paper No. 54, Indian Council for Research on International Economic Relations (ICRIER), New Delhi.

of (mainland) China with similar factor endowments to those of India, early industrialising countries of South Korea and Taiwan, India's immediate neighbours Pakistan and Bangladesh and South East Asian members of ASEAN: Thailand, Malaysia, Indonesia and the Philippines.

For an examination of export performance the period 1980-96 has been divided in to three sub period: 1980-86, 1987-90 and 1993-96. Covering two overlapping decades (1980-90) and (1987-96) in intertemporal comparisons. These overlapping decades have been referred as the first and the second period in subsequent discussion. The choice of subperiods is derived mainly from the Indian context of the study although it turned out to have other equally important and compelling justifications too.

In India the decade (fiscal years) 1980-81 to 1990-91 was marked by the emergence of the Indian economy out of the low growth syndrome of the previous three decades. The average of the annual growth rates of gross domestic product (GDP) at factor cost (at 1993-94 prices) had been stuck around 3.5 per cent per annum (pcpa henceforth) during the three decades 1950-51 and 1980-81 (calculated from NAS (2000)). It rose by more than two percentage points per annum to 5.8 pcpa during the decade of the nineteen eighties. This step up was partly fuelled by selective, hesitant and partial deregulation of industrial and trade policies but was associated with rising and unsustainable fiscal deficits financed by internal (public) and external (commercial) borrowings. The political instability and the Gulf war towards the end of the decade also contributed to rising current account deficits, pressure on the exchange rate, capital flight and dwindling foreign exchange reserves. The resulting crisis forced a major fiscal adjustment in the 1990s and wide ranging policy reforms involving liberalisation of industrial and trade policies since 1991. The average of the annual growth rate of GDP dipped to 3.8 pcpa during the three year period of fiscal contraction 1990-91 to 1992-93. This was followed by a spurt in the average aggregate growth rate at 6.6 pcpa during 1993-94 and 1998-99 which was higher than that during the decade of the 1980s. Tendulkar's analysis of export performance omits the period of fiscal contraction in making intertemporal comparisons over the overlapping decades 1980-90 covering the period of deregulation and a consequent step-up in the aggregate growth rate and 1987-96 covering the period of economic reforms. It also stops in 1996 in order to avoid the distortions in value of exports caused by the Asian currency crisis that followed.

It so happened that the world trade growth went through two distinct phases during the selected period. Following a crash in primary commodity prices after the second oil price hike in 1979, there was a virtual stagnation in the value of world exports during the seven year period 1980-86. This was followed by a spurt in growth rate of value of exports to 8 pcpa during 1987-96. The growth rate of the volume of world merchandise exports, too, slowed down from 3.68 pcpa (1973-80) to 3.48 pcpa (1980-87) before recovering to 5.70 pcpa (1987-96). The subperiods enable us to examine how the export performance of the selected Asian economies was affected by the changes in world trading environment.

Growth in Exports: 1980-96

The period is divided into two sub periods: The period 1980-87 of depressed world trade and 1987-96 of renewed spurt in world trade. The export performance is analysed in terms of growth in U.S. Dollar earnings for total exports (all SITC categories), extended manufacturing exports (SITC 4 to 8) which, in turn, are divided into the following 6 broad categories:

1. Resource-intensive exports.
2. Labour-intensive exports.
3. Scale-intensive exports.
4. Differentiated exports.
5. Science-based exports
6. Miscellaneous (not classified elsewhere)

Broadly, resource intensive exports are based on primary agricultural or mineral raw material and labour intensive category covers light manufacturing mostly consumer goods. The scale intensive (homogenous) and differentiated categories of products are expected to be technologically more sophisticated than the first two categories whereas the science based products belong to the hi-tech variety. The UN-ESCAP study indicates that usually most countries started with either resource or labour-intensive exports depending on initial relative factor endowments and the relocation of entire manufacturing activity from developed to developing countries. Their progress to more sophisticated manufactures was observed to be varied and expected to be a function of both physical and human capital accumulation, pace of adaptation to new technologies, the quality control that they exercise and the access and ability to participate in international (buyer or seller driven) production chains in more sophisticated manufactured products.

The major findings of Tendulkar's empirical analysis are:

(1) During 1980-96 period, growth of Indian export earnings turned out to be above the world average for all the broad categories of Extended-Manufacturing (E-Mfg) exports including double digit growth rates in labour and scale intensive products. However Indonesia, Malaysia and Thailand posted much higher and more stable growth rates than India. India had a head-long start in industrialisation in the 1950s well ahead of these countries, but the persistently autarchic character of Indian industrialisation not only made it internationally non-competitive but wasteful in scarce capital and foreign exchange, thereby slowing down the rate of economic growth.

(2) Faster than world average export growth in E-Mfg over 1980-96 resulted in a rise in India's share in world E-Mfg exports from an average of 0.3 per cent (1980-86) to 0.5 per cent (1993-96). By itself, this was remarkable because the World E-Mfg exports tripled over this period. However, much smaller countries like South Korea and Taiwan as also other late entrant smaller economies like Malaysia and Thailand more than doubled their shares in E-Mfg. China, too, doubled its higher share over a shorter period from 1987-90 to 1993-96.

(3) Turning to the commodity composition of country specific export basket, India improved the share of E-Mfg significantly from 56 per cent (1980-86) to 71 per cent (1987-90) in total exports (all SITC codes) during the first period but only marginally further to 75 per cent during 1993-96. The first period 1980-90 was marked by a rise in the share of scale-intensive exports. Share of labour intensive exports remained constant around 40 per cent. Other early trade liberalising and rapidly growing economies changed their export-basket increasingly towards differentiated and science-based products. This diversification reflected corresponding changes in their factor endowments and domestic production structure thereby reducing their vulnerability to volatile world trading environment in resource intensive exports and slower growing world exports of labour intensive products.

(4) Analysis of incremental average annualised exports between 1980-86 and 1993-96 for nine countries excluding China showed that these countries accounted for 21 per cent of corresponding incremental world exports in labour intensive manufacturing products. Four countries (Thailand, Indonesia, Taiwan and South

Korea) had more than two thirds of the regional share with India (2.5 per cent) coming fifth. Ten countries including China over the shorter period between 1987-90 and 1993-96 had 42 per cent share in world incremental labour-intensive exports more than half of which was claimed by China. India with 4.5 per cent share occupied the fourth position after China, Indonesia and Thailand.

(5) Analysis of competitiveness at 3-digit SITC level showed that India had sustained presence only in certain labour-intensive products in some of which South Korea and Taiwan too, had maintained their competitiveness. These two countries along with Indonesia, Thailand and Malaysia had established competitiveness in technologically more sophisticated differentiated and science-based products.

(6) Better export-performance than India by smaller economies like Thailand and Malaysia as well as large economies (in terms of population) like Indonesia and China was attributable to their earlier start than India, not in industrialisation but in unilateral trade liberalisation. Possibly realising the limited size of their domestic markets at low levels of per capita incomes, these countries had switched from import-substitution to export-orientation fairly early in their development process. India was the first in initiating industrialisation but the last in trade liberalisation. This difference got reflected in the more rapid growth rates of aggregate GDP (between 6 to 10 pcpa compared to 5 pcpa by India over (1980-96)) recorded by these countries. The difference in the aggregate performance would be sharper over the entire post-Second World War period. the powerful instrumental role of international trade that these Asian countries exploited needs to be emulated by India with great urgency because it has lagged behind these countries technologically, industrially and in terms of per capita GDP in purchasing power parity dollars.

"The rapidly growing East and South-East Asian neighbours of India have clearly established that economies, whether small or large, (in terms of population) have improved their living standards by aggressively participating in the global division of labour and interacting with the global economy under expanding as well as fluctuating and volatile conditions of the world trading environment. The critical factor has been not the state of the international trading environment but the functioning of the domestic mainsprings of the growth process (such as competent governance, incentive structure for technological and organisational innovations, improvements in the quality of human resources, reliable and cost effective transport and communication facilities and stable and responsible macroeconomic management) which requires proactive approach on the part of the society, polity and economy. The basic point is that international trading opportunities can act as a powerful instrument in stepping up the rate of economic growth provided the internal mainsprings of the growth process are maintained and continually strengthened. There is, thus, an inextricable and indispensable link between progressive global integration of the Indian economy and the now widely accepted social objective of achieving and maintaining rapid economic growth in India. Rapid economic growth, in turn, has proved to be the tried and tested device for making a lasting dent on the long standing problem of abject poverty. It does so through a rapid generation of gainful employment opportunities at progressively rising levels of productivity per worker. If India wishes to get out of the dubious distinction of hosting the largest number of world's poor population, rapid growth is an absolute necessity and so is the imperative need for progressive integration with the global economy along with internationally competitive production structure in tradables. Progressive export orientation of the economy would yield not only very obvious efficiency gains in resource utilisation but also two other benefits which have not been so widely noted: One, because of the expansion of domestic market beyond international borders it would enhance and maintain the rate of return on productive investment and raise the rates of domestic savings and investment essential for rapid growth. Two, it would also impart resilience to the economy to successfully overcome external shocks.

It is also important to emphasise that the process of shedding more than four-decade long protectionist past would require reallocation of resources away from the inefficient import-substitution-oriented and towards export oriented activities. This process of major structural adjustment is bound to be painful. Adequate safety nets are clearly essential for alleviating and minimising the pains of adjustment in the form of dislocation, unemployment and earnings disparities. But if these painful adjustments are necessary for putting the Indian economy on the higher growth path, the society and polity will have to evolve socially fair and credible mechanisms of cost-sharing and conflict resolution. Failure to do so would condemn the Indian economy to a low growth path and persistence of abject poverty. This is the challenge of globalisation. How the Indian society, polity and economy manage to grapple with it, only time can tell."

APPENDIX TABLES

TABLE – 24.1

India's Trade Sector Performance Since the 1950s

Annual Average	Growth Rate: In Rupee Terms		Growth Rate: As per cent to GDP		
	Exports	Imports	Exports	Imports	(Exports+ Imports)@
1	2	3	4	5	6
1950-51 to 1959-60	3.6	6.1	5.1	6.7	11.8
1960-61 to 1969-70	8.9	6.3	3.4	5.5	8.9
1970-71 to 1979-80	16.8	20.7	4.5	5.3	9.8
1980-81 to 1989-90	16.4	14.9	4.6	7.2	11.8
1990-91 to 1995-96	25.3	23.4	7.5	8.5	16.0
1992-93 to 1995-96	24.7	26.8	8.1	9.0	17.1
1996-97 to 2002-03	13.6	13.6	8.9	10.8	19.7
1990-91 to 1999-2000	19.5	20.1	7.8	9.3	17.1

@ Figures may not add-up due to rounding off.

Source: 1 Directorate General of Commercial Intelligence and Statistics, Government of India.

2. International Financial Statistics, CD ROM, IMF, 2003.

TABLE – 24.2

Different Types of Non-Tariff Barriers on India's Imports, 1996 to 2003* (Number of tariff lines, 10 digit level#)

Type of NTB	1996	1997	1998	1999	2000	2001	2002	2003
1	2	3	4	5	6	7	8	9
Prohibited	59	59	59	59	59	59	52	52
Restricted	2,984	2,322	2,314	1,183	968	479	554	484
Canalised/STE	127	129	129	37	34	29	33	32
SIL	765	1,043	919	886	226	-	-	-
Free	6,161	6,649	6,781	8,055	8,854	9,582	11,032##	11,103
Total	**10,096**	**10,202**	**10,202**	**10,220**	**10,141**	**10,149**	**11,671**	**11,671**

* As on April 1.

As per Harmonised System of India Trade Classification, HS-ITC classification of export & import.

This includes 148 items with conditions.

Note: 1. STE: State Trading Enterprises.

2. SIL: Special Import License.

3. —: Nil

Source: 1. Economic Survey, Government of India, 2001-02.

2. Ministry of Commerce and Industry, Government of India.

TABLE – 24.3

India's Leading Exports

Commodity	Export Share (Per cent)			Destination	Major Competitors
	1990-91	1995-96	2002-03		
1	2	3	4	5	6
1. Gems and Jewellery	16.1	16.6	16.8	USA (36.6), Hong Kong (19.2) Belgium (11.5);	Israel Belgium China (studs), Italy (plain gold) Thailand (gemstones)
2. Readymade Garments	12.3	11.6	10.2	USA (31.3), UK (8.9), Germany (7.7), UAE (7.0), France (6.8)	China, Korea, Taiwan, Indonesia, Thailand, Malaysia, Bangladesh
3. Basic Chemicals, Pharmaceuticals and Cosmetics	6.8	6.8	8.3	USA (14.1), Germany (5.6), China (4.4), UK (3.7), UAE (2.8)	China, Brazil (in castor oil)
4. Cotton Yarn, Fabrics, Made-ups etc.	6.4	8.1	6.2	USA (18.4), Korea (5.4), UK (4.7), Italy (4.6), Bangladesh (4.6)	China, USA, Australia (for yarn and made-ups), China, Pakistan, Bangladesh (for fabrics)
5. Petroleum Products	2.9	1.4	4.6	NA	NA
6. Machinery and Instruments	3.8	2.6	3.5	USA (13.9), Germany (7.5), UAE (6.8), UK (5.8), Nigeria (3.2)	Germany, Japan, Italy, China, Taiwan, Korea
7. Iron and Steel	0.9	2.2	3.4	China (27.5), USA (15.8), UAE (4.9), Bangladesh (3.7), Taiwan (3.5)	Indonesia, Korea, Malaysia, Australia, Brazil, South Africa
8. Manufactures of Metals	2.5	2.6	3.3	USA (23.6), UAE (10.8), UK (9.9) Germany (3.6),	Russia, South Africa, Korea
9. Marine Products	2.9	3.2	2.6	USA (27.9), Japan (22.6), China (7.6)	Indonesia, Thailand, Vietnam, Bangladesh
10. Man-made yarns, Fabrics, Made-ups etc.	1.2	2.4	2.5	UAE (19.7), Saudi Arab (5.3), Turkey (5.2), UK (4.7), USA (4.7)	Korea, China, Mexico, Bangladesh, Pakistan

N A: Not Available.
Note : Figures in parenthesis indicate the share of exports, as on 2002-03, directed to the respective countries in total exports of that commodity.
Source : Directorate General of Commercial Intelligence and Statistics, Government of India.

ANNEXURE – 24.1

Main Issues in WTO

Agenda for Discussion	Main Issues	India's Position
1. Agriculture		
a. Export Subsidies	• Reductions of, with a view to phasing out, all forms of export subsidies.	• Removal of all forms of direct and indirect export subsidies, by developed countries, in a time-bound manner. • For developing countries, retention of Article 9.4 of the Agreement on Agriculture, thereby enabling grant of marketing and transportation subsidies on exports listed in Article 9.1 (d) and (e).
b. Market Access	• Substantial improvements in market access for agricultural products of developing countries, while allowing them to retain the necessary flexibility.	• Any reduction in tariffs by developing countries should be based on an approach that secures an overall average reduction in bound rates for them which is significantly lower than that by developed countries. • To provide the flexibility of minimal tariff cuts or exemption from tariff cuts by developing countries in respect of Special Products towards food and livelihood security and rural development, based on self-declaration. • To establish for developing countries a new Special Safeguard Mechanism (SSM) applicable to all agricultural products, based on price and volume triggers, to safeguard against import surge and price volatility. • To achieve substantial reductions in tariff peaks and tariff escalation, and to improve disciplines on Tariff Rate Quota administration, in products of export interest to developing countries.

Contd...

...Contd. ...

Agenda for Discussion	Main Issues	India's Position
c. Domestic Support	• Substantial reductions in trade-distorting domestic support.	• Towards meeting the Doha mandate for substantial reductions in trade-distorting domestic support, the Amber Box support reduction should permit steeper reductions by developed country Members providing higher levels of support. The *de minimis* for developed countries should be reduced from the existing level of 5 per cent of the value of agricultural production. Blue Box support should be capped and brought under reduction disciplines, and disciplines on direct payments under the Green Box should be strengthened. To prevent circumvention of reduction commitments through the shifting of support between one box and another, trade-distorting Amber Box, Blue Box, and the *de minimis* should be brought under an overall reduction discipline.
		• Retain and enhance the provisions of Article 6.2 for low-income and resource poor farmers for developing countries towards addressing food and livelihood security and rural development concerns.
	• Special and Differential Treatment for developing countries	• The negotiated mandate agreed at Doha is for extending undifferentiated special and differential treatment to developing countries as an integral part of all aspects of negotiations. Developing countries can be expected to reciprocate in market access, subject to their economic and social conditions, development needs, food and livelihood security and rural development, only if they get adequate concessions and commitments by developed countries in all the three pillars of Agreement on Agriculture, namely, domestic support, export subsidies and market access.

Contd...

... *Annexure 24.1 Contd.* ...

Agenda for Discussion	Main Issues	India's Position
2. GATS		
• Professional Services • Computer Related Services • Audio Visual Services • Distribution Services • Education and Training Services • Environment Services • Financial Services • Telecommunication Services • Tourism Services • Transport Services • Postal Services • Recreational, Cultural and Sporting Services	• Under GATS, India has taken commitments in the areas of its economic interests, which include services like financial, telecommunication, health, business, construction, tourism and travel-related. India's commitments are based on its domestic policy and has been taken mainly in Mode 3 (i.e. commercial presence), which are in consonance with the policy on FDI.	• Liberalisation of certain sectors is essential to accelerate growth in developing countries. However, there are certain sensitive sectors that needs to be treaded with caution. • For the developing countries including India, the balance of benefit in the negotiations will accrue to the extent to which their service providers are allowed to supply services in important overseas markets either from remote locations or through temporary movement of natural persons. • In case the resistance among developed countries for agreeing to the request of developing countries for enhanced market access under Modes 1 and 4 continues, this would substantially erode India's flexibility to make commitments in sectors of interest to developed countries.
3. Market Access for Non-Agricultural Products		
a. Finalisation of modalities for the actual tariff negotiations, i.e., the tariff reduction method and the extent of tariff reduction to be offered by different countries.	• A formula to be applied to all tariff lines of all Members coupled with a mandatory sectoral tariff elimination proposal on seven sectors of export interest to developing countries.	• The formula proposed by the Chairman of the Negotiating Group have merits as it incorporates adequate special and differential provisions by incorporating an element of tariff average in the formula. It thus recognises the principle of less than full reciprocity in the core modality of reduction commitments.

Contd...

...*Contd.* ...

Agenda for Discussion	Main Issues	India's Position
	• The formula requires all members to reduce their tariffs on all industrial products.	• Amending any aspect of the formula or the formula itself would negate the entire work done so far. The suggestion for mandatory tariff harmonisation and elimination would be most iniquitous to developing countries. There is no mandate for harmonisation of tariffs under the Doha Ministerial Declaration. For developing countries, the initiative for sectoral tariff elimination should be voluntary rather than mandatory and should also incorporate the principle of less than full reciprocity. • Being at different stages of development, developing countries may not have the capacity to undertake binding obligations on all the proposed sectors. • Some of the highest tariffs are found in developed countries in these sectors, namely, in textiles and clothing; leather and footwear; marine products; and gems and jewellery.
b. How to deal with non-tariff barriers	• The main issue is to clearly identify what is the measure, who is imposing it, how it affects trade and an estimation of the trade restricting	• Several WTO members including India have notified existing NTBs faced by their goods during exports to various markets. Discussions are going on as to how to address these NTBs. impact of the measure.
c. Special treatment if any, of environ-mental goods in these negotiations.	• Members are not clear as to what constitutes an 'environmental good' and thereafter what should be the special treatment.	• In the list of environmental goods, goods of export interest for developing countries should also be included.

Contd...

Annexure 24.1 Contd. ...

Agenda for Discussion	Main Issues	India's Position
4. TRIPS		
a. TRIPS and Public Health	• How to ensure patent protection for pharmaceutical products does not prevent people in poor countries from having access to medicines while at the same time maintaining the patent system's role in providing incentives for R&D into new medicines.	• TRIPS Agreement under Article 31 provides for compulsory licensing procedure to make available patented medicines and drugs at affordable prices. Doha Declaration on TRIPS and Public Health adopted in November 2001 provides that the TRIPS Agreement does not and should not prevent Member countries from taking measures to protect public health and that each Member has the right to grant compulsory licenses and the freedom to determine the grounds upon which such licenses are granted as well as the right to determine what constitutes a national emergency or other circumstances of extreme urgency referred to under Article 31. Further, General Council has taken a decision on August 30, 2003 to waive obligations under Article 31(f) and 31(h) of TRIPS Agreement, with certain conditions. This decision would ease the problem being faced by the developing countries and Least Developed Countries having little or no manufacturing capacities in the pharmaceutical sector, in using the flexibility of compulsory license. This decision would enable manufacture and export of pharmaceutical products under compulsory license to countries with limited or no manufacturing capacities in the pharmaceutical sector. This would further improve accessibility of patented medicines at reasonable prices in poor countries. India has not taken any decision on all of these issues.

Contd...

...Contd. ...

Agenda for Discussion	Main Issues	India's Position
b. Geographical indications	• Geographical indications are place names used to identify origin and quality, reputation or other characteristics of products. • Whether to extend the 'higher level of protection' beyond 'wines and spirits' to a wide range of other products, including food and handicrafts.	• India has proposed that the proposed multilateral register should be extended for products other than wines and spirits. From India's point of view, the most important issue is the legal obligations of the Register on non-participating Members. Consensus among the Members could not be reached so far on this issue. • India has been demanding extension of protection available under Article 23 of TRIPS Agreement to products of geographical indications other than wines and spirits.
c. Bio-diversity and traditional knowledge	• How to deal with patentability or non-patentability of plant and animal inventions and the protection of plant varieties. • Whether discussions on these subjects have developed far enough to be handled immediately in the WTO or whether they should wait for technical discussions.	• Draft Cancun Ministerial Text (Second Revision) under para 13 regarding implementation issues, while reaffirming the mandates given under para 12 of Doha Ministerial Declaration and Decision on Implementation-Related Issues and Concerns, instructed the TNC and other negotiating bodies to redouble the efforts to find appropriate solutions as a priority and requested the Director General to continue the consultations undertaken by him on issues including extension of the protection of geographical indications provided for in Article 23 of the TRIPS Agreement to products other than wines and spirits. However, since there was no consensus among the Member countries on the draft Cancun Ministerial Text, the above draft language could not be agreed to.
d. Non-violation complaints	• The purpose of allowing 'non-violation' cases is to preserve the balance of benefits struck during multilateral negotiations. The issue is to decide whether 'non-violation complaints' should be allowed in intellectual property and if so, to what extent and how (scope and modalities) they could be brought to the WTO's Dispute Settlement procedures.	• However, the draft language as suggested by India and other like-minded countries on implementation issues was different. India alongwith other like-minded Member countries such as Cuba, Egypt, Indonesia, Jamaica, Kenya, Malaysia, Pakistan, Sri Lanka, Tanzania, Uganda and Zimbabwe, reaffirmed that negotiations on outstanding implementation issues shall be an integral part of the Doha Work Programme.

Contd...

Appendix 24.1 Contd. ...

Agenda for Discussion	Main Issues	India's Position
5. Singapore Issues		
a. Trade and Investment b. Trade and Competition Policy c. Trade Facilitation	• Whether there is 'an explicit' consensus on modalities that would allow negotiations to go ahead, leading to new WTO rules on these four issues.	• WTO is not the right forum and that the traditional WTO principles of non-discrimination particularly national treatment are not appropriate for a development policy-related issues like investment. • There are significant and deep differences in views of Members on many elements of these issues. India is not entirely convinced of the appropriateness of taking a decision on modalities as it does not give any idea of the substance and direction of obligations that agreements in this area may require the country to undertake.
d. Transparency in Government Procurement	• Members also take position that, negotiation will commence after the Fifth Ministerial and results of negotiations would be part of 'single undertaking' to be concluded by March 31, 2005.	• Negotiations on these issues may commence only after 'explicit consensus' on modalities among all members of the WTO and that each of the four Singapore issues should be considered separately and not covered under a single set of modalities. • The need for a multilateral agreement on investment itself is not clear. Although it can neither promise additional investment flows nor reduce transaction costs for investors significantly, such agreement will certainly curtail the policy space of developing countries. • There exists a wide divergence in views on various elements of 'investment' including scope and definition, transparency, dispute settlement, performance requirement, etc. • Further work needs to be done on understanding elements in 'competition' such as core principles, cooperation mechanisms and the coverage and prohibition of hardcore cartels through appropriate mechanisms before India can start comprehending the implications of any multilateral discipline. • Multilateral rules, binding in nature, in respect of trade facilitation and transparency in government procurement would entail high costs for developing countries.

Contd. ...

...*Contd.* ...

Agenda for Discussion	Main Issues	India's Position
6. Trade Rules		
a. Anti-Dumping	• Improve and clarify the anti dumping Agreement	• India has made three submissions to the negotiating group on Rules. The first submission has sought Special and Differential treatment for developing countries during anti-dumping and countervailing duty investigations. The second submissions has identified specific provisions of the anti-dumping agreement which require amendments. The third submission highlights provisions that require amendments to the Subsidies Agreement.
b. Subsidies	• Improve and clarify disciplines in the Subsidies Agreement.	
c. Regional Trade Agreements	• How to interpret the phrase 'substantially all the trade'; regulations that could restrict trade such as rules of origin under preferential schemes; how regional agreements relate to development and the primacy of the multilateral trading system and the negative effect regional agreements can have on other countries.	
7. Dispute Settlement	• Clarify and improve provisions of the Dispute Settlement Understanding (DSU). The Doha Declaration stated that these negotiations will not be part of the single undertaking. i.e. that they will not be tied to the success or failure of the other negotiations mandated by the declaration. All members, however, expressed a readiness to continue work beyond May 31, 2003 towards an agreement.	• A comprehensive set of proposals was tabled by India alongwith certain other countries in the special session of Dispute Settlement Body (DSB).

Contd...

Annexure 24.1 Contd. ...

Agenda for Discussion	Main Issues	India's Position
8. Trade and Environment	• The need to clarify the relationship between existing WTO rules and specific trade obligations set out in multilateral environmental agreements (MEAs); exchange of information between the WTO and MEA secretariats; criteria for granting observer status to other international organisations and liberalisation of trade in environmental goods and services.	• India has submitted a paper on "the effect of environmental measures on market access" to the Committee on Trade and Environment (CTE). (WT/CTE/W/207 dated 21/5/2002) and another paper on "Relationship between Specific Trade Obligations set out in MEA and WTO Rules" (TN/TE/W/23 dated 20/2/2003).
9. Trade, Debt and Finance	• Durable solution to the problem of external indebtness of developing countries and to strengthen the coherence of international trade and financial policies with a view to safeguarding the Multilateral Trading System (MTS) from the effects of financial and monetary instability.	• It is necessary to make significant progress in the areas of great importance to developing countries.
10. Trade and Technology Transfer	• Recommend on steps to be taken within the mandate of WTO to increase flows of technology to developing countries.	• Need to move to stage of identification of elements of a possible agreement and agree on start of negotiations.
11. Electronic Commerce	• The main issues are (i) classification of the contents of certain electronic transmissions, (ii) development-related issues, (iii) fiscal implications of e-commerce, (iv) relationship (and possible substitution effects) between ecommerce and traditional forms of commerce, (v) imposition of customs duties on electronic transmissions, (vi) competition, and (vii) jurisdiction and applicable law/ other legal issues	

Source: Reserve Bank of India, Report on Currency and Finance, 2002-03.

References

Bhagwati, J. (2001), "The Design of Indian Development", In *India's Economic Reforms and Development: Essays for Manmohan Singh*, I.J. Ahluwalia and I.M.D. Little (eds.), New Delhi: Oxford University Press, pp. 23-39.

Das, T. (1999), "East Asian Economic Crisis and Lessons for Debt Management". In *External Debt Management-Issues, Lessons and Preventive Measures*, Reserve Bank of India, Mumbai.

Edison, H.H., et.al (2002), "Capital Account Liberalisation and Economic Performance, Survey and Synthesis", NBER Working Paper No. 9100, (August).

Jalan, B. (1999), "International Financial Architecture: Developing Countries' Perspective", *RBI Bulletin*, Reserve Bank of India, Mumbai (October).

——— (2002), "India's Economy in the New Millennium: Selected Essays", New Delhi: UBS Publishers and Distributors.

Kumar, R. (1999), "Debt Sustainability Issues: New Challenges for Liberalising Economies". In *External Debt Management - Issues, Lessons and Preventive Measures*, Reserve Bank of India, Mumbai.

Lal, D., S. Bery and Pant, D.K. (2003), "The Growth Slowdown: Real Exchange Rate misalignment, Fiscal Deficits and Capital Flows". Mimeo, New Delhi: NCAER, (January).

Mohanty, D., et.al (1999), "Short Term and Volatile Capital Flows: The Indian Experience". In *External Debt Management-Issues, Lessons and Preventive Measures*, Reserve Bank of India, Mumbai.

Patra, M.D., et.al (1999), "External Debt Management: The Indian Experience". In External Debt Management - Issues, Lessons and Preventive Measures, Reserve Bank of India, Mumbai.

Pattnaik, R.K., et.al (2002), "Exchange Rate Policy and Management: An Assessment of the Indian Experience", Mimeo, Reserve Bank of India, (December).

Rangarajan, C. (2003), "Select Essays on Indian Economy", Academic Foundation, New Delhi.

Reddy, Y.V. (1997), "Exchange Rate Management: Dilemmas", in *RBI Bulletin*, (September).

——— (2000), "Operationalising Capital Account Liberalisation: Indian Experience", *RBI Bulletin*, (October).

——— (2002), "India's Foreign Exchange Reserves: Policy, Status and Issues", *RBI Bulletin*, (May).

Srinivasan, T.N. and Tendulkar, S.D. (2003), Reintegrating India with the World Economy (OUP).

Tarapore, S.S. (1995), "Financing of Indian Industry in an Open Economy", Address at the Seminar Organised by the Indo-American Chamber of Commerce.

Tendulkar, S.D. (2000), "Indian Export & Economic Growth Performance in Asian Perspective", Working Paper No. 54, Indian Council for Research on International Economic Relations (ICRIER), New Delhi.

Vasudevan, A. (2003) (ed.), *Money and Banking: Select Papers by the Economists of Reserve Bank of India*, Academic Foundation.

Williamson, J. (1999), "Implications for East Asian Crisis for Debt Management". In *External Debt Management-Issues, Lessons and Preventive Measures*, Reserve Bank of India, Mumbai.

25

Foreign Trade Policies and India's Development

T.N. Srinivasan

Indian economic development strategy, particularly relating to industrialization has been driven by perceived foreign exchange scarcities and the desire to ensure that scarce foreign exchange is used only for purposes deemed "essential" from the perspective of development. Industrialization and self-sufficiency in essential commodities have been important objectives of policy in no small part because of the fear that dependence on other, more powerful countries for imports of essential commodities would lead to political dependence on them as well. Nearly a decade before independence, in 1938, the National Planning Committee was set up by the Indian National Congress (the political party that led the struggle for independence) under the chairmanship of the future prime minister Jawaharlal Nehru. This committee viewed that

> In the context of the modern world, no country can be politically and economically independent, even within the framework of international interdependence, unless it is highly industrialized and has developed its power resources to the utmost. Nor can it achieve or maintain high standards of living and liquidate poverty without the aid of modern technology in almost every sphere of life. An industrially backward country will continually upset the world equilibrium and encourage the aggressive tendencies of more developed countries. Even if it retains its political independence, this will be nominal only and economic control will tend to pass to others (Nehru 1946: 413).

> The objective for the country as a whole was the attainment, as far as possible, of national self-sufficiency, International trade was certainly not excluded, but we were anxious to avoid being drawn into the whirl-pool of economic imperialism (p. 403).

Later the First Five-Year Plan went further:

> Control and regulation of exports and imports, and in the case of certain select commodities state trading, are necessary not only from the point of view of utilising to the best advantage the limited foreign exchange resources available but also for securing an allocation of the productive resources of the country in line with the targets defined in the Plan (Planning Commission 1950: 42).

Indeed, an elaborate system of government control over production investment, technology and locational choice, prices and foreign trade was instituted in the mid-1950s. In what follows, I argue that the development strategy based on import-substituting industrialization and the system of controls that were implemented failed to produce rapid growth, self-reliance, and eradication of poverty, but instead led to lackluster growth, an internationally uncompetitive industrial structure, a perpetually precarious balance of payments, and, above all, rampant rent seeking and the corruption of social, economic, and political systems.

Five Year Plans: Objectives and Policy Instruments of Implementation

India gained its independence on August 15, 1947. After extensive debate in the constituent assembly, a constitution was adopted, and India became a republic on January 26, 1950. Not entirely coincidentally, the Planning Commission was established almost immediately, in, March 1950, as an advisory body with no executive functions. There had been a broad consensus on the need for planning for national development even during the struggle for independence from Britain. Indeed, soon after the National Planning Committee was established in 1938, a group of private businessmen produced the so-called Bombay Plan. Even the colonial government had put together development plans for postwar India. The adoption of the constitution, however, gave a particular impetus to planning.

The constitution enunciated a set of guiding principles for the formulation of government policy, called the Directive Principles for State Policy. They enjoined the state to strive to secure "a social order in which justice – social, economic and political – shall inform all the institutions of national life" and "to minimize inequality in income, status, facilities and opportunities, amongst individuals and groups." Further, the state was required to ensure "that the ownership and control of the material resources of the community are so distributed as best to subscribe to the common good; that the operation of the economic system does not result in the concentration of wealth and means of production to the common detriment" (Basu-1983). The constitution also protected rights to work, to education, and to public assistance in case of unemployment, disability, or sickness. It is evident that these principles envisaged a dominant role for the state in achieving an egalitarian society through state intervention in economic activity.

Besides the overarching goal of poverty alleviation, the three broad objectives of the Indian development strategy are economic growth, self-reliance, and social justice. Even though the state was assigned a dominant role in developing the economy, leaders across the political spectrum recognized to varying degrees that India had a mixed economy with a significant private sector, and more important, that the private sector had a vital political role in ensuring social stability and in the functioning of the democratic framework of the constitution.

Indian planning was influenced by Soviet planning, with which Prime Minister Nehru and Professor P.C. Mahalanobis (the author of the Second Plan) were familiar. Although Soviet planning operated with totalitarian political control of the society and state ownership of the means of production, India's mixed economy and democratic policy ruled out planning by command. Instead, the policy framework had to create incentives for the private sector to conform to the priorities of the plan. In designing such a framework, the Indian policy makers opted in most cases for direct, discretionary, nonmarket, quantitative controls over indirect, rule-based, market-mediated controls operating through the price mechanism. Unfortunately this choice adversely affected economic growth, efficiency, and equity. Above all, it corrupted the political system.

Agriculture dominated the economy, accounting for nearly 60 percent of gross domestic product (GDP) and providing employment to over 70 percent of the labour force when the first plan was initiated in 1950.[1] Its share in GDP drastically declined to less than 30 percent by 1990/91. Yet over 60 percent of the labour force still depends on agriculture for employment. This fact, more than anything else, demonstrates that the Indian industrialization strategy failed to generate significant productive employment opportunities outside of agriculture for a growing labour force. No significant redistribution of land emerged from the land reform legislation of the 1950s. Concentration of land ownership, however, has not meant that a large proportion of farms are operated on a large scale. In 1982, the year of the most recent sample survey of land holdings, only 20 percent of the farm area was operated in holdings exceeding ten hectares. Early planners showed some enthusiasm for cooperative farming. The National Commission on Agriculture, reporting in 1976, concluded that under Indian conditions, small peasant-owned farms cultivated mainly with family labour should be the preferred mode of organization of production rather than large Soviet-style collective farms or large capitalist farms cultivated with farm machinery and hired labour. This preference has not hindered mechanization in some regions and the emergence of large capitalist farms, particularly in the fast-growing agricultural regions of Punjab and western Uttar Pradesh, Small owner-operated farms, however, continue to be the dominant mode of operation.

State intervention in agriculture, while significant, has been different in nature from state intervention in industry. In agriculture the state has made substantial investments in irrigation, fertilizer production, and infrastructure. Other state interventions affected the prices that farmers paid for their inputs and received for their outputs. Irrigation, water from public reservoirs, and electricity for private irrigation pumps were subsidized. Prices paid for the part of output that was purchased by the government for its subsidized public distribution system were regulated. There were some quantitative restrictions, such as the ban on interstate movement of foodgrains on private account, but these were abandoned early on. Policies that placed quantitative restrictions on millions of individual producers were obviously infeasible, although access to subsidized credit is an exception. Remarkably, India has maintained a constant trend growth in agricultural output of about 3 percent per year over nearly four decades despite slow growth in cultivated area. This trend reflects the superiority of the largely market-mediated interventions in agriculture, unlike the discretionary interventions in industry.

The government's industrial policy resolution of 1948 (amended and elaborated in 1956) divided industries into three broad groups: those to be developed exclusively by the public sector, those reserved for the private sector, and those open to development by either or both sectors. The development of key industries, such as railways, tele-communications, and electricity generation, was assigned to the public sector. In addition, industries producing key industrial raw materials and equipment, such as steel, petroleum, and heavy machinery, including electric generators, were also in the public sector. The philosophy behind the resolution was that by controlling the "commanding heights" of the industrial landscape – that is, the infrastructure and industries supplying key raw materials – the state could cause the development of all industries, in the private and public sectors, to follow socially desirable directions. Goods and services produced and supplied by the public sector could be priced appropriately for generating surpluses to be used for investment in the public sector and to finance other public expenditures. Also, the state hoped to promote the development of backward regions through the location of public sector projects. Finally, the public sector was to be model for the private sector to follow with respect to the wages and working conditions of workers.

The public sector did not evolve as planned. A major share of investment in the five-year plan was appropriated by the public sector. Yet the enterprises created by the investment and others acquired through nationalization (such as major commercial banks) performed poorly in supplying key services and inputs at a reasonable cost, in appropriate amounts, and at the time and place where demands arose. The public sector therefore acted as a brake on private sector development rather than promoting and channeling it in socially desired directions. Policy making with respect to location, technology, employment, and pricing in the public sector became politicized. Inefficiency and waste in resource use, overmanning, and mounting losses were the results. Far from generating resources, the public sector became an albatross around the neck of the taxpayers.

The system of industrial licensing and exchange controls was the favored tool for making the private sector conform to the plans. Its broad features remained essentially unchanged from the late 1950s until the 1991 reforms, though its severity waxed and waned. The system was meant to achieve several goals. First, capacity created in the private sector had to be made consistent with plan targets. Second, the location of private sector plants had to be such that they did not overload the infrastructure, particularly in cities and other areas to which they would naturally gravitate. The system induced plant owners to move to backward regions with a potential for development. Third, the objective of self-reliance had to be promoted; that is, domestically available technology, equipment, and raw materials were to be used rather than imports. Fourth, concentration of economic power was to be prevented. Given the perennial shortage of foreign exchange, the state looked at every investment proposal from the point of view of its demand for foreign exchange for imports of equipment at the time of investment and for imports of raw materials and spares during the lifetime of the plant.

An industrial license was required to invest in capacity creation if the quantity of investment or the value of equipment imports exceeded specified limits. For importation of equipment, a capital-goods license was needed. If foreign collaboration was involved, a separate clearance was required. In particular, foreign equity participation was limited to under 50 percent, with some exceptions. If foreign technology imports involving royalty payments were to be undertaken, yet another clearance was mandated. If part of the equity was to be obtained by selling shares in the domestic capital market, permission had to be obtained from the controller of capital issues. Even the investment projects of public enterprises required many of these permits, in addition to clearances from the ministry or department in charge of the enterprise and from other relevant ministries (such as finance). In sum, several hurdles had to be crossed before a single rupee was spent on any project in the private or public sector. Even though success in obtaining all the required clearances was by no means assured, entrepreneurs had to expend considerable time and resources pursuing them.

The licensing mechanism was designed to approve (often with many modifications) or deny an application for license. The criteria for evaluation of applications were sufficiently broad that the licensing authorities had substantial discretion in granting or denying a license. The licensing bureaucrats and their political bosses were under constant pressure from interested parties. It should cause no surprise that the exercise of their discretionary power led to their corruption and the politicization of decisions.

Obviously a private entrepreneur would apply for a license to invest in a project only if he expected it to be profitable. The license could be denied, of course, if the project was deemed socially unworthy. But licensing authorities could not induce a private sector entrepreneur to apply for a license and invest in a socially worthy project if he did not find it privately profitable. The grant of license did not necessarily mean that the capacity licensed came on stream, and even if it did, that it came on stream, at the time specified in the application. Since the processing of a license application often took so long and restrictive conditions were often attached to accepted applications, it was possible that the project for which a license was granted would no longer be profitable from the applicant's perspective and hence he would choose not to implement it. Further, given that licenses were granted only to the extent of capacity expansion called for in the relevant five-year plan, firms had a built-in incentive to take out a license and then fail to invest, essentially to foreclose competition by preventing other firms from getting it. An information system to keep track of the licenses granted and their implementation did not exist, so the link between capacity increases targeted in the plan and their actual realization through licensing was tenuous. In the final analysis, the procedure for license granting became ad hoc and followed rules of thumb rather than any economic rationale. It degenerated into an exercise in dispensing political and other kinds of patronage and a source of rents for personal and political use rather than a guidance mechanism for directing the private sector to conform to the plans.

Table 25.1 compares some performance indicators of the Indian economy under planning with those of other developing countries. It is clear that Indian performance is relatively poor. India's average annual rate of growth of per capita GNP from 1965 to 1990 is the lowest of the five countries and would have been even lower had the data for the 1980s been excluded. In 1965 India's manufacturing industry was more than five times the size of Korea's in terms of value added at current U.S. dollars. But by 1990 Korea's manufacturing industry had grown to exceed India's in size and its manufactured exports were nearly five times that of India. Only China, which also followed an inward-oriented development strategy until recently, had a greater share of the labour force in agriculture than India.

The Foreign Trade Regime: Analytical Phases and Changes over Time

J. Bhagwati and A. Krueger, in their comparative analysis of the impact of foreign trade regimes and economic development in a number of countries, defined a set of analytical phases in which an exchange control regime may be found (Bhagwati and Srinivasan 1975: 248). A country does not necessarily pass through all the phases, and the numbering of the phases does not indicate a chronological sequence. These phases were

1. *Phase I*: During this phase, quantitative restrictions (QRs) on international transactions are imposed, generally in response to an unsustainable balance of payments deficit, and then, after a period, are intensified. The period during which reliance upon QRs for containing the balance of payment deficit is increasing is Phase I.
2. *Phase II*: While QRs continue to be intense, various measures are undertaken to offset some of the undesired results of the system. Heightened tariffs, surcharges on imports, rebates for exports, special tourist exchange rates, and other price interventions are

TABLE – 25.1

Selected Indicators for India and other Developing Countries

	India	China[a]	Brazil	Mexico[a]	Korea[a]
Population, mid-1990 (millions)	850	1,134	150	86	43
GNP per capita, 1990 (US$)	350	370	2,680	2,490	5,400
Average annual GNP per capital growth rate, 1965-1990 (%)	1.9	5.8	3.3	2.8	7.1
Inflation rate, 1980-1990 (%)	7.9	5.8	284.3	70.3	5.1
Share in GDP, 1990 (%)					
Agriculture	31	27	10	9	9
Industry	29	42	39	30	45
Value added in manufacturing, 1989 (billions of US$)	44	146	121	51	66
Gross domestic investment/GDP, 1990 (%)	23	39	22	20	37
Gross domestic saving/GDP, 1990 (%)	20	43	23	19	37
Life expectancy at birth, 1990 (years)	59	70	66	70	71
Total fertility rate, 1990	4.0	2.5	3.2	3.3	1.8
Labour force in agriculture, 1986-1989 (%)	63	74	29	23	18
Merchandise exports, 1990 (billions of US$)	18	62	31	27	65
Manufactured exports, 1990 (billions of US$)	13	45	16	12	61
Merchandise imports, 1990 (billions of US$)	24	53	22	28	70
Aggregate net resource flow, 1990 (billions of US$)	3.6	10.1	1.2	8.4	-0.2
Total outstanding external debt, 1990 (billions of US$)	70.1	52.6	116.2	96.8	34.0
Total debt service/exports, 1986 (%)	29	10	21	28	11
Overall central government deficit, 1990 (% of GNP)	-7.3	—	-16.6	0.8	-0.7

a GDP, GNP, and related ratios are at purchaser's prices.

Source: For labour force in industry and agriculture, United Nations Development Programme, *Human Development Report* 1992 (New York: Oxford University Press, 1992). For all other data, World Bank, World Development Report 1991 (New York: Oxford University Press, 1992).

used. However, QRs continue to be relied upon as the primary means for controlling the balance of payments deficit.

3. *Phase III*: An attempt is made to systematize the changes introduced during Phase II. This phase often starts with a formal exchange rate change and may be accompanied by removal of some of the surcharges and other special measures imposed during Phase II and by reduced reliance upon QRs. Phase III may end up being little more than a tidying-up operation, in which case the chances are high that the country will re-enter Phase II. The country may also move beyond tidying and signal the beginning of withdrawal from reliance upon QRs, in which case it enters Phase IV.
4. *Phase IV*: If the response to changes introduced in Phase III are encouraging enough for the continuation and extension of liberalization, the country is said to enter Phase IV. A favourable response in the form of increased foreign exchange earnings would encourage a gradual relaxation of QRs. The relaxation may take the form of either changes in the nature of QRs or increased foreign exchange allocations, and thus reduced premiums, under the same administrative system.
5. *Phase V*: The exchange regime is fully liberalized. There is full convertibility on current account, and QRs are no longer employed as a means of regulating the ex ante balance of payments.

Bhagwati and Srinivasan (1975) provide a phase chronology of the Indian foreign trade regime for the period 1950-1970. An unpublished oxford doctoral thesis of Narahari Rao (1985) and private communication from an ongoing study by Gary Pursell at the World Bank have helped me extend it beyond 1970. The following phase chronology covers the entire period 1950-1992.

1950-1956 (Phase IV)

The period 1950-1956 included the First Five-Year Plan. It was a period of good harvests and a rough equilibrium in the balance of payments, with import demand more or less equaling export earnings that were stagnant once the Korean War boom was over. The machinery of import control inherited from the World War II period was not used in any systematic way to impose QRs.

1956-1962 (Phase I)

The ambitious, heavy industry-oriented Second Five-Year Plan was initiated in 1956, and promptly led to a severe balance of payments crisis in 1957. Instead of adopting appropriate macroeconomic policies including making exchange rate adjustments, the government imposed a regime of QRs on imports. The QRs and the industrial licensing system were both selective rather than across-the-board. Besides containing the demand for foreign exchange, the selectivity of QRs served the objective of the development of particular industries through import substitution. The QR regime was used to provide automatic and custom-made protection to any domestic activity that substituted imports. Foreign aid flows increased substantially from less than 0.5 percent of net national product in the pre-1956 period to over 3 percent in 1960-61.

1962-1966 (Phase II)

While the QR regime for imports initiated in 1957 continued, export subsidization was introduced in 1962 primarily to offset the penalties that the QR regime was in effect imposing on exports. Two exogenous events in this period had major economic consequences: the Indo-Pakistan War in late 1965 and the consequent suspension of foreign aid; and a major drought in the agricultural year 1965-66, which affected traditional exports adversely and increased the need for food imports.

Increasing use was made of import duties, in part to mop up the premia on imports that license receivers were realizing. Export subsidization and increasing import duties could be viewed as a *de facto* devaluation of the exchange rate although unlike in a de jure devaluation, the impact was selective. Some efforts to loosen up the industrial licensing system were made toward the end of the period.

By early 1966 the combined effects of the drought and suspension of aid caused import premia to rise to unprecedented levels. The donors of bilateral and multilateral (the World Bank and the International Monetary Fund) external aid made resumption of large-scale aid and access to short-term credit conditional on the liberalization of the economy.

1966-1968 (Phase III)

The first step in the liberalization was the devaluation of the rupees by 57.5 percent (from Rs. 4.76 to Rs. 7.50 per U.S. dollar) announced in June 1966. Since this was also accompanied by the elimination of export subsidies and reduction of import duties, the net devaluation after allowing for these changes was on average less than the gross devaluation of 57.5 percent and varied among commodities. According to Bhagwati and Srinivasan (1975), the total net devaluation on the trade account was 21.6 percent for exports and 42.3 percent for imports. On the current account, the total net devaluation was 22.3 percent for receipts and 44.8 percent for payments. In 1966-67 another disastrous drought followed that of 1965-66. The two severe droughts in succession resulted in price increases, adverse effects on traditional exports, and an industrial recession induced by shortage of agro-based raw materials. Economic liberalization, of which devaluation was a major component, was stalled in part for economic reasons related to the drought. More important, the economic difficulties were accentuated by political problems: the fact that devaluation was seen as capitulation to pressure from donors of external aid made liberalization politically suspect, not only among the opposition but also within the ruling Congress party led by the newly installed and politically insecure Prime Minister Indira Gandhi. The 1967 general elections saw considerable erosion of support for the Congress party. To compound this loss of support, the external aid promised at the time of devaluation, which was meant to ease the short-run costs of adjustment to a liberalized economy, did not materialize. Under the circumstances, it was not surprising that the hesitant steps towards liberalization introduced with devaluation were soon abandoned.

1968-1975 (Phase II)

With the abandonment of liberalization, import premia rose, though not as high as immediately before devaluation. Export subsidies were reinstated and augmented. Industrial licensing reverted to its severely restrictive mode.

The economy experienced several exogenous shocks during this period. First, the Bangladesh War in 1971 and the refugee inflow that preceded it created severe economic strains. Second, adverse weather conditions during the 1972-1975 period led to stagnant agricultural output and double-digit inflation for two years in a row in 1972-73 and 1973-74. Third, the Bretton Woods system of fixed exchange rate parties collapsed in 1971. Following the collapse, India linked the rupee initially to the floating British pound and in 1975 to a basket of currencies. Between 1971 and 1975 the pound depreciated against the U.S. dollar and other major currencies, leading to a gradual and modest depreciation of the rupee against the U.S. dollar in that period. This depreciation provided across-the-board incentives for exports and import substitution. But with the rupee linked to a basket of currencies, its "vicarious" devaluation was halted (Bhalla 1989). Fourth, in 1973 the first oil shock occurred.

In this period "import policy became increasingly restrictive and complex. Scarcity of foreign exchange became even more acute – a new set of restrictive measures was introduced every year. Import allocation criteria became more complex and subject to marginal conditions. Tariff rates were gradually escalated (to absorb partially the increasing import premia generated by the tighter QR's)" (Rao 1985).

1975-1985 (Phase III)

Foreign exchange availability improved dramatically during the early part of the 1975-1985 period. Net reserves of foreign exchange went up from a low of US$758 million in 1974-75 to a high of US$7579 million in 1979-80, fueled in part by the dramatic increase in remittances from Indians working in West Asia. The decline in public investment and the slowing of industrial growth after the mid-1960s also contributed to reducing the pressure in the balance of payments. With dramatic increases in the output of wheat, and to a smaller extent of rice, during the green revolution, the public stock of foodgrains mounted and foodgrain imports ceased. The net result was a relaxation in the severity of the QR regime. Rao (1985) points out that "import allocation rules were made simpler and most non-competing `essential' imports were liberalized. Protective quotas, however, remained intact and domestic industry continued to be completely shielded from import competition.

Interestingly, the second oil shock in 1979 did not lead to a tightening of the QR regime, partly because of the substantial increase in worker remittances and partly because of the fortuitous discovery and development of significant offshore oil deposits (the Bombay High Field) in the Arabian Sea. Output of crude oil more than doubled, from 8.4 million tons in 1975-76 to 21.1 million tons in 1982/83.

1985 to Mid-1991 (Phase III Continued)

In April 1985, in a significant departure, the government announced that the import and export policy was to cover a period of three years (1985-1988) rather than six months or a year as in the past. This innovation was meant to bring some stability to the policy and thereby reduce the uncertainty about year-to-year changes that exporters and importers faced. Yet the government could not resist introducing changes almost every week to the statement issued in April 1985, and a revised statement had to be issued in October 1986. Until 1988, there were 250 public notices regarding changes in the policy. The subsequent policy statement for the period 1988 – 1991, announced in April 1988, candidly recognized that changes have to be announced within the three-year period and stated, "It is proposed to issue a revised version of the import and export policy at the beginning of each year." So much for stable policy!

Although the complexity of the scheme of QRs had not diminished substantially, the two three-year policies did represent some major simplifications. In particular the number of items in the category of open general license (OGL) – that is, a license to import but with no quantitative restrictions – for capital goods imports had increased from nil in 1975 to over 1,100 items in the 1988-1991 policy. Similarly, many intermediate goods were put in the OGL category. Lest this give the impression that QRs had largely been abandoned, it should be pointed out that many of the items put under the OGL were noncompetitive imports; that is, there was no substitute for them from domestic production. Therefore, lifting QRs on their import had little effect on import competition with domestic production. Also, the import of some items formally in the OGL category was restricted on other grounds. For example, the value of equipment imports had to conform with licensed investment capacity. Although tires had been in the OGL category since 1978, no imports took place, in part because of high tariffs, in part because the firms in the replacement market did not qualify as "actual users" to whom OGL applied, and in part because actual users such as car and truck manufacturing firms were under "phased manufacturing programmes" through which they were under an obligation to replace imports by domestic substitutes over time in a progressive manner. The share of the value of imports covered by OGL in total imports appeared to be modest (perhaps less than a fifth), though no official information is available.

Mid-1991 to Present (Phase IV?)

In July 1991 the newly installed minority government of Prime Minister Narasimha Rao announced a set of major economic reforms. In announcing the reforms to the Indian Parliament, Finance Minister Manmohan Singh declared with some hyperbole that "Let the world hear it loud and clear. India is now wide awake. The emergence of India as a major economic power in the world....is an idea whose time has come." The proximate reason for these policy changes was a crisis in the economy that was both acute and different from anything experienced in the postindependence era: a drastic fall in the foreign exchange reserves to a level not even enough to pay for three weeks of imports, a near default in the colossal external debt of over US$71 billion, and a fiscal deficit of nearly 9 percent of GDP. But the deeper reason for the changes was the realization that India's economic development strategy since 1950 and the regulatory framework created to implement it had failed miserably. The policy reforms were further extended in scope and coverage in 1992.

The chief elements of Rao-Singh reforms of 1991-92 are devaluation of the rupee: abolition of import licensing replacement of cash subsidies for exports, initially by the so-called exim scrips (free salable rights to imports linked to exports) and later by partial convertibility of the rupee under which exporters could sell 60 percent of their foreign exchange receipts at a market-determined exchange rate: abolition of industrial licensing except for investment in eighteen industries and for locational reasons in cases of "polluting" industries; relaxation of restrictions on large industrial houses under the Monopolies and Restrictive Trade Practices Act; easing of entry requirements (including equity participation) for direct foreign investment; and allowance of private investment in some industries hitherto reserved for public sector investment. A National Renewal Fund for assisting workers employed in enterprises that will have to be scaled down or closed altogether has been estblished, although without the support of the political barons of the labour aristocracy in the organized sector such scaling down is unlikely. The government has contemplated reform of the financial sector but has not yet implemented it.

It is obvious that these reforms are systemic and go beyond liberalizing the more irksome controls at the margin that earlier economic liberalizations attempted. Besides, authorities apparently realize that the benefits from reforming one sector would be limited if other related sectors are not also reformed. The needed reforms are conceived as a package of mutually supporting and consistent elements that call for coordinated action in several areas.

The elimination of import licensing and the introduction of partial convertibility of the rupee are certainly indicative of Phase IV. Since the reforms have been in place only since July 1991, however, a period which saw a recession in the industrial countries as well as the collapse of the Soviet Union, with which India had barter trading arrangements, the favourable potential of the reforms is yet to be seen. But as significant growth resumes in the industrial world and as Eastern Europe and the states of the former Soviet Union complete their transition to market economies, Indian reforms may begin to pay rich dividents. If the full convertibility of the rupee for current account transactions in the not-too-distant future (a declared objective of the government) is in fact realized, there is a good chance that the economy will enter the nirvana of Phase V.

The Anatomy of the Pre-1991 Exchange Control System

The pre-1991 exchange control system divided imports into three broad categories: consumer goods, capital goods, and intermediate goods (raw mateials, components, spares, and suplies). Consumer goods imports, other than those canalized and imported by state agencies (such as foodgrains, edible oils, sugar, and certain drugs and medicines) were not permitted. Other imports were divided into the following licensing categories: nonpermissible, limited permissible, automatic permissible, and recently, OGL.

The allocation of permissible imports by sector of use (private and public), by type of good (consumer, capital, and intermediate), by indutry, and by firm within industries was carried out by an elaborate administrative machinery. For example, Volume 1 of the 1988-1991 policy statement relating only to import policy consists of 387 pages, divided into twenty-three chapters and seventeen appendixes! Broadly speaking, the complex system described in Bhagwati and Srinivasan (1975) and reproduced in the Appendix to this chapter held away during the 1957-1991 period, although some categories and authorities changed names, others ceased to exist (for example, the category of established importers), and some new categories of both import and export licenses appeared. OGL became an increasingly important category. Canalized imports also grew in importance: the 1988-1991 statement listed nearly sixty items, the import of which were canalized through public sector agencies, ranging from paraffin wax to steel, petroleum products, fertilizers, and fatty acids.

The import control regime inevitably led to a lower effective exchange rate for exports than for imports on the average and for each industry. The scheme of export subsidization, initiated in 1962 in an attempt to redress this bias against exports, was extremely complex, with little or no economic logic to support its complexity. Subsidies took essentially two major forms: (1) direct subsidies through fiscal measures and (2) indirect subsidies through import entitlement schemes that entitled exporters to scarce and restricted imports. Some other relatively minor promotional activities included budgetary allocations for market development.

Before turning to the specific subsidy schemes, it is worth mentioning that analogous to the category of nonpermissible and restricted imports, there were also nonpermissible and restricted exports. As of 1988, there were 172 such products, 67 of which could simply not be exported. An important difference, however, was that exports of items not on this list could be made without a license, while a license was required for the import of any item other than personal baggage.

Turning to export-assistance, the major fiscal measures were tax drawback schemes (that is, refunds of indirect taxes including import duties on inputs used in exports), exemptions from sales taxes, cash compensation schemes, and rail freight concessions. Import replenishment licenses, previously called import entitlement certificates, allowed the exporter to import certain restricted raw materials and components. Whereas under the import entitlement certificate scheme the value of the entitlement equaled twice the import content, under the import replenishment license scheme the value of the license was supposed to equal the actual import content of exports. Between July 1991 and February 1992 such licenses were called exim (export-import) scrips.

Import entitlements as a proportion of the f.o.b. values varied widely across different products. Since it was virtually impossible to assess the actual import content, such variation was more a reflection of arbitrary assignment by policy makers than of variation of actual import contents. There were fifty-eight pages in Appendix 17 and its annexes to the 1988-1991 policy statement on import replenishment licenses! The rates varied from a low of 3 percent to a high of 80 percent. For example, wheat bran exporters were given import replenishment licenses at the rate of 3 percent and permitted to import under those licenses only silk and nylon bolting cloth! Unlike actual user licenses, import replenishment licenses could be sold and transferred subject to certain conditions. Exporters were registered and classified under various categories such as manufacturer exporter, merchant exporter, export house, and "deemed" exporter (the last category refers to those domestic producers of intermediates who sell part of their output to exporters). Figures 25.1 and 25.2 taken from Rao (1985), illustrate the complexity of the import control mechanism and the transfer restrictions on import replenishment licenses as of 1975-76. The exim scrips of 1991-92 were however freely salable.

It is easily shown that it was not economically efficient to assist exporters through the import replenishment scheme. There was no compelling economic logic either for confining the scheme, at least in the early years, to certain categories of exports such as engineering goods or for the enormous variation across commodities in import replenishment rates.

The compensatory cash support scheme was intially introduced to compensate for taxes not refunded under the duty drawback scheme and for any excess of short-run marginal cost of production over f.o.b. realization. It was later extended to compensate for a whole host of factors, including losses incurred on exports when domestic demand was inadequate to use installed capacity fully. The rates of compensatory cash support also varied significantly across products with no

Figure 25.1. India's Import Control Mechanism, 1975-1976

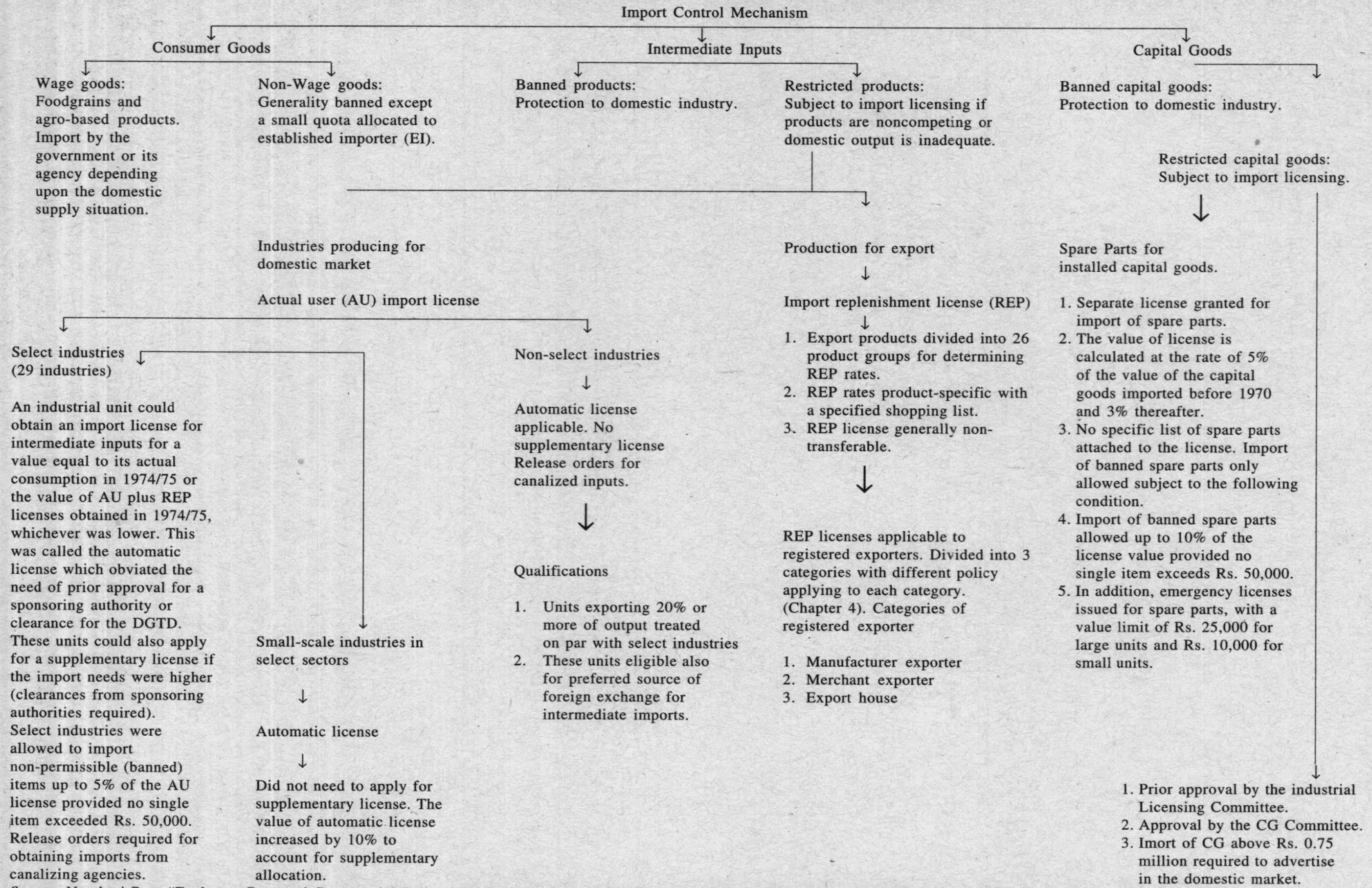

Source: Narahari Rao. "Exchange Rate and Commercial Policy in a Controlled Trade Regime: A Case Study opf India." PhD. dissertation, Oxford University, 1985, Chapter 2.

Figure - 25.2

Transfer Restrictions on India's Replenishment Licenses, 1975-1976

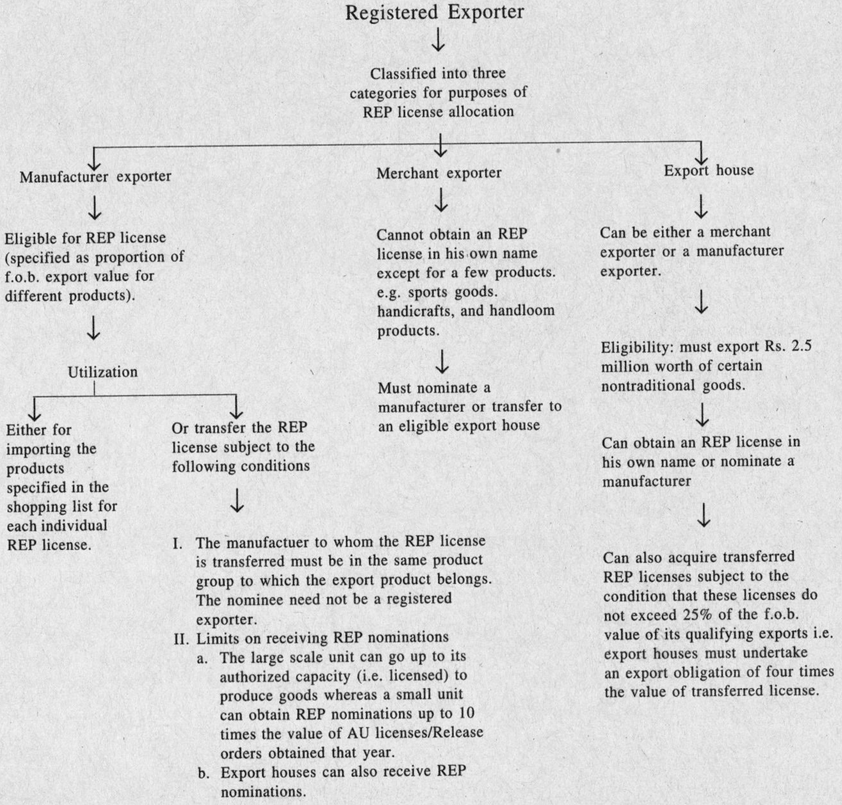

Source: Narahari, Rao. "Exchange Rate and Commercial Policy in a Controlled Trade Regime: A Case Study of India." Ph.D. dissertation, Oxford University, 1985, Chapter 2.

apparent rationale.

The rationale for most of the export assistance schemes was that Indian exporters should be compensated for the excess costs they incurred compared with their competitors because of other distortions in the Indian economy. Since these excess costs were hard to quantify, there was no way to establish that the total assistance received under various incentive schemes to which a potential exporter was entitled was more or less than necessary to induce him to export. The bureaucratic requirements to be met in order to claim the assistance available under these schemes were complex, time consuming, and costly. Small-scale exporters often did not find it worthwhile to claim the incentives to which they were entitled. As is the case of import controls, export incentives schemes were made complex without any functional need for such complexity. By eliminating import licensing and introducing partial convertibility of the rupee, the 1992 reforms eliminated at one stroke the maze of complexity and variance in incentives across commodities of the import replenishment and compensatory cash support schemes.

The Political Economy of the Foreign Exchange Regimes

The political economy of India's foreign trade and exchange control regimes before reforms were initiated in 1991 can be understood from the implications of its selective, discretionary, and non-market-oriented character. First, macroeconomic instruments, including most importantly the exchange rate of the rupee, were never used to address balance of payments problems except for the rupee devaluation of 1966. Given that QRs on imports were substantially below market demand, the domestic price of an imported commodity far exceeded its landed cost inclusive of tariff duties and other taxes. As such there were rents associated with a license to import. Thus the power to grant a license meant power to confer the right to the rent involved. Since the domestic price of an imported commodity, and hence the rent to be earned per unit of import, would depend on the total quantity of imports allowed in, the licensing authority not only conferred the right to the rent but also determined its amount.

It hardly requires much imagination to realize that if rents could be created and allocated, individuals and groups would spend resources in influencing their creation and allocation in their favour. The analytics of lobbying for trade policies that create rents and for the allocation of rents once created have attracted the attention of trade theorists. Bhagwati, Brecher, and Srinivasan (1984) surveyed this literature, and it is still growing. More recent analysis appears in Meier (1991). Without delying into this literature, I will note some of the manifestations of rent seeking and their political and economic implications in the Indian context.

It should be evident even to a casual observer of the Indian scene that a significant amount of scarce talents and material resources that could have been used for producing goods and services were spent instead on seeking and dispensing rents. Senior bureaucrats who wielded power spent much of their time in meetings that decided individual cases rather than set broad policies. In a large country with an abysmal telephone system, businessmen from far corners of the country frequently flew to the seat of power at Delhi to influence decisions. Larger enterprises that had continuing business with the government maintained "embassies" in Delhi. Even if there had been no corruption resources spent on such activities would have resulted in significant deadweight losses since those resources generated no material output. But there was certainly alleged to be corruption! Indeed, the point has been made that with a ban on corporate contributions to political parties, politicians gained resources for electoral campaigns through kickbacks from rents conferred. Of course, if adoption of favorable decisions and the prevention of unfavorble decisions had to be bought, so to speak, only those who could afford to pay the price would enter the market. Clearly entrepreneurs with relatively few material resources and contacts at crucial decision-making agencies were unlikely to enter the market.

Bardhan (1984) has suggested that there are essentially three proprietary classes in India: the industrial capitalists, the rich farmers, and the public sector professionals. He argues, "In the context of economic growth it is rather the capacity of the system to insulate economic management from political processes of distributive demands, rent-seeking and patronage disbursement that makes the crucial difference – a lack of political insulation from conflicting intersts, coupled with the strong power base of the white-collar workers in public bureaucracy that keeps the Indian state, in spite of its pervasive economic presence, largely confined to regulatory functions, avoiding the hard choices and politically unpleasant decisions involved in more active developmental functions" (Bardhan 1984: 72-73). Indeed one could go further and argue that any effort to reform the system (or more accurately, to revolutionize the system) by "making a bon-fire of controls," as Dr. I.G. Patel, a distinguished ex-bureaucrat and controller, called for long after leaving office, would be stymied by the same constellation of forces: It would clearly not be in the interest of the members of the industrial capitalist class, who enjoy and oligopolistic if not monopolistic position in domestic markets by virtue of the QR regime, to support its dismantling. On the one hand, the rich farmers, who receive subsidies doled out by the system, would be interested in the demand stimulus for agriculture that more rapid growth would generate and in the availability of a large range of less-costly and better-quality industrial goods that reform might bring. On the other hand, they might fear that the dismantling of industrial protection would soon be followed by the dismantling of various agricultural subsidies. They are likely to perceive the certain loss of subsidies more clearly and concretely than the uncertain potential benefit of more rapid growth and better-quality goods. The professionals in the public sector certainly have a vested interest in the continued expansion of the public sector, which a market-oriented reform might threaten. Thus, the three proprietary classes would collude, implicitly or explicitly, in stalling, if not preventing altogether, any reform. Of course, the usually unthinking leftist intellectuals in India have always identified controls and regulation with socialism and a market economy with imperialism. Unsurprisingly, they would fulminate against any liberalization. The interesting and vital question is whether the Rao-Singh reforms will be thwarted by these forces.

Foreign Trade Performance

Surjit Bhalla (1989) presents a simple econometric analysis of the determinants of India's aggregate exports and imports as well as some of their components. A satisfactory structural model of India's exports and imports, taking into account the full direct impact of the selective system of import controls and export incentives, the indirect impact of the industrial licensing system, restrictions on foreign collaboration and investment, and the performance of the public sector in the supply of key inputs and infrastructure for export supply and import demand is next to impossible to construct given the complexity of the systems involved and the paucity of available data. Bhalla's analysis, while insightful, must be viewed with caution. Instead of summarizing his analysis, this section is devoted to an analytical description of foreign trade performance.

Since the purpose of the import control regime was to confine imports to essential consumer goods, raw materials, and investment goods needed for domestic production and exports, it is not surprising that changes in the commodity composition of India's imports (Tables 25.2 and 25.3) reflected this. For example, foodgrains and edible oils accounted for about 16 percent of total imports in 1960-61 and about 1 percent in 1990-91. Imports of gems, which were negligible in 1960-61, accounted for US$2.079 million or nearly 8 percent of imports in 1990-91, reflected the fact that gems and jewellery exports at S1.667 million comprised nearly a sixth of total exports. The share of crude petroleum, oils, and lubricants in total imports rose from about 6 percent in 1960-61 to a high of roughly 40 percent in 1980/81 only to fall to about 23 percent in 1990-91, reflecting in part the rise and fall of crude petroleum prices and in part the rapid growth of domestic crude output from the Bombay High Field.

Turning to exports, Table 25.4 shows that India's share of world exports has fallen steadily from about 2 percent in 1950 to less than 0.5

TABLE – 25.2

India's Merchandise Imports, 1950-51 - 1978-79 (US$ Million at Current Prices)

	1950/51	1955/56	1960/61	1965/66	1966/67	1968/69	1970/71	1973/74	1974/75	1975/76	1976/77	1977/78	1978/79
Foodgrains	n.a.	n.a.	378.4	670.3	854.0	443.0	271.8	597.0	951.3	1,537.3	958.7	121.2	114.4
Petroleum, Oils, and lubricants	116.4	116.7	144.0	143.2	84.1	177.1	181.2	719.1	1,450.5	1,416.5	1,581.1	1,811.2	2,043.4
Fertilizers	25.9[a]	4.7	22.3	82.1	132.2	228.7	100.9	242.8	617.6	609.5	214.4	301.4	451.8
Fertilizer raw materials[b]	n.a	n.a.	10.8	26.8	34.6	40.5	32.4	52.0	134.2	102.2	101.1	139.5	144.7
Iron and steel	42.0	118.8	257.3	205.7	130.4	114.9	196.1	320.2	531.2	360.4	245.5	306.9	572.1
Non-ferrous metal	59.4	51.6	99.4	144.4	114.2	118.7	159.2	180.1	224.0	116.0	175.7	224.4	301.6
Metal ores and scrap	0.9	1.0	7.0	4.3	7.2	8.2	14.6	17.1	7.5	23.3	34.8	52.7	82.2
Edible Oils	n.a.	n.a.	7.4	14.8	14.9	12.9	30.6	72.8	15.0	15.8	111.7	829.0	649.3
Non-edible oils	n.a.	n.a.	2.7	13.7	4.7	12.9	20.7	10.5	28.4	3.5	20.0	31.5	5.2
Oilseeds	4.8	16.8	24.4	18.5	6.4	4.7	8.5	9.5	12.6	9.1	3.7	15.6	54.9
Cotton (raw)	211.6	120.4	171.7	97.0	75.3	120.3	131.8	66.8	34.4	32.6	144.9	232.2	35.4
Other fibers	n.a.	n.a.	18.8	65.1	91.4	42.3	37.2	52.4	49.7	51.8	80.6	270.8	294.5
Cashew nuts (raw)	6.0	10.2	20.2	31.6	26.1	41.8	39.2	37.0	45.9	38.8	20.5	21.0	11.2
Diamonds	n.a.	n.a.	0.7	0.2	1.9	30.0	25.2	84.7	59.9	90.5	193.1	375.3	557.8
Pulp and paper	22.2	38.4	39.5	40.7	41.9	38.3	49.8	49.4	87.0	85.2	76.4	120.4	178.8
Chemicals	n.a.	n.a.	157.7	138.4	140.9	149.3	155.5	212.3	285.6	240.8	250.6	405.9	514.2
Precision equipment	14.0	24.2	22.9	29.4	22.9	23.0	32.5	38.9	43.1	46.9	62.3	105.2	145.3
Machinery	192.0	273.2	547.3	885.4	685.2	596.8	437.5	714.4	707.7	898.4	980.9	1,033.6	1,166.0
Transport equipment	73.4	133.4	152.0	148.1	83.0	88.4	88.7	121.9	164.5	181.6	191.0	263.1	329.6
Other imports	n.a.	n.a.	306.9	198.1	219.6	253.0	165.5	194.3	215.4	224.1	229.0	369.6	616.0
Total Imports	1,365.4	1,425.6	2,393.4	2,957.9	2,771.1	2,544.8	2,178.9	3,793.2	5,665.5	6,084.3	5,676.0	7,030.5	8,269.5
Revised total													4,272.8

n.a. = not available.

a Includes crude fertilizers.

b Rock phosphate, sulphur and unroasted Iron pyrites , phosphoric acid, and ammonla.

Source: World Bank (private communication)

TABLE - 25.3

India's Merchandise Imports, 1980-81 - 1991-92

	Value (US$ millions at current prices)											Growth rate (percentage)		
81	1980/ 82	1981 83	1982/ 84	1983/ 85	1984/ 86	1985/ 87	1986/ 88	1987/ 89	1988/ 90	1989/ 91	1990/ 1990[a]	1985/ 91	1990/ 92[b]	1991/
Food	1,348	1,474	1,065	1,716	1,394	1,321	1,068	1,292	1,203	714	713	-11.6	-0.1	-53.6
Foodgrains	127	389	388	784	204	90	37	25	437	227	84	-1.4	-63.0	-27.5
Edible Oils	865	700	399	705	775	600	479	709	503	127	180	-21.4	41.9	-54.3
Other	356	385	278	227	415	631	552	557	263	361	450	-6.5	24.7	-61.8
Other consumer goods	378	354	306	385	315	452	594	600	700	800	853	13.5	6.6	n.a.
Petroleum, oils, and lubricants	6,669	5,591	4,734	3,492	3,236	4,054	2,187	3,148	2,938	3,766	5,726	7.1	52.0	-13.5
Crude petroleum[c]	4,243	3,964	3,095	2,240	1,571	3,013	1,672	2,395	1,891	2,455	3,238	1.4	31.9	n.a.
Petroleum products	2,426	1,627	1,639	1,252	1,665	1,041	515	753	1,047	1,311	2,488	19.0	89.8	n.a.
Capital goods	2,307	2,219	2,672	3,078	2,546	3,337	4,910	4,732	3,656	4,189	4,292	5.2	2.5	-26.9
Intermediate: primary	1,277	1,460	1,620	2,058	1,886	2,156	2,474	2,997	3,800	4,488	4,184	14.2	-6.8	-10.4
Fertilizer raw materials	210	212	170	213	286	313	218	243	301	329	338	1.5	2.7	-10.9
Gems	528	445	757	1,065	868	899	1,170	1,538	1,984	2,546	2,079	18.3	-18.3	1.8
Other	539	803	693	780	732	944	1,087	1,217	1,515	1,613	1,766	13.4	9.5	-26.0
Intermediate: manufactures	3,920	3,923	3,343	3,430	3,722	4,744	4,564	4,504	7,167	7,295	7,790	10.4	6.8	n.a.
Fertlizer manufactures	826	571	212	199	847	860	387	132	341	737	608	-6.7	-17.5	5.6
Iron and steel	1,080	1,348	1,217	1,017	792	1,140	1,134	982	1,341	1,383	1,231	1.5	-11.0	-32.4
Non-ferrous metals	605	445	358	379	346	443	324	444	544	752	618	6.9	-17.9	-48.5
Other		1,409	1,559	1,556	1,835	1,737	2,301	2,719	2,946	4,941	4,423	5,333	18.3	20.6
n.a.														
Total[c]	15,899	15,020	13,741	14,159	13,100	16,064	15,798	17,273	19,464	21,252	23,557	8.0	10.8	-20.5
Statistical discrepancy	-7	532	646	623	2,324	1,231	1,930	2,539	3,875	3,162	2,870	18.4	-9.2	n.a.
Total[c]	15,892	15,552	14,387	14,782	15,424	17,295	17,728	19,812	23,339	24,414	26,427	8.8	8.2	n.a.

n.a.= not available

a Compound growth rate between 1985/86 and 1990/91.

b Based on April-February data for aggregate imports, and April-January data for components.

c Net of crude oil exports.

percent in 1990. Since world export grew rapidly between 1950 and 1973 and somewhat more slowly thereafter, India's exports grew in absolute terms in spite of a declining share. But the dramatic fall in share reflects the fact that other countries were able to take greater advantage of growing world trade.

TABLE – 25.4

India's Share in World Exports, 1950-1990

(Percentage)

Year	Bhagwati and Desai	Economic Survey	GATT
1950	2.0		
1955	1.5		
1960	1.2		
1965	1.0		
1966	0.9		
1967			
1970		0.6	
1973		0.5	
1975		0.5	
1977		0.6	
1978		0.5	
1979		0.5	
1980		0.4	
1981		0.4	
1982		0.5	
1983		0.5	
1984		0.5	
1985		0.5	
1986		0.4	
1988			0.5
1989			0.5
1990			0.5

Source: J.N. Bhagwati and P. Desai, *India: Planning for Industrialization* (London: Oxford University Press, 1970).Table 18.1. p. 370, India, *Economic survey* (New Delhi: Government Printing Press, 1983 through 1992); GATT, *Intenational Trade*, Vol. 2 (Geneva; GATT, 1985 through 1991).

A crude index of terms of trade based on indexes of unit value of exports and imports shows no distinct trend but significant fluctuations

TABLE – 25.5

Unit Value and Volume Indexes of Exports and Imports and India's Terms of Trade 1950-51 - 1980-81

Year (April-March)	Exports		Imports		Terms of trade
	Volume index	Unit value index (in US$)	Volume index	Unit value index (in US$)	
1950/51	73	99	50	187	53
1951/52	58	145	63	123	118
1952/53	65	102	47	121	84
1953/54	65	93	44	112	83
1954/55	68	99	52	109	91
1955/56	75	91	55	106	86
1956/57	71	96	65	110	87
1957/58	77	96	74	120	80
1958/59	70	94	66	112	84
1959/60	75	94	73	104	90
1960/61	70	104	85	107	97
1961/62	74	104	80	110	95
1962/63	79	101	87	106	95
1963/64	89	99	89	109	91
1964/65	93	101	97	110	92
1965/66	87	107	102	117	91
1966/67	84	102	99	106	96
1967/68	86	102	110	96	106
1968/69	100	100	100	100	100
1969/70	100	104	84	100	104
1970/71	106	106	87	100	106
1971/72	107	109	105	94	116
1972/73	120	117	99	94	124
1973/74	125	141	114	133	106
1974/75	133	172	100	225	76
1975/76	147	171	99	243	70
1976/77	174	176	97	233	76
1977/78	168	207	130	218	95
1978/79	180	214	140	238	90
1977/80	199	219	135	334	66
1978/81	194	241	199	322	75
	Average compound growth rate (% per year)				
1950/51-1976/77	3.4	2.2	2.6	0.8[b]	
1970/71-1980/81	6.2	8.6	8.6	12.4	
1979/80	10.6	2.3	-3.6	40.3	
1980/81	-2.5	10.0	47.4	-3.6	

Note: The indexes available on four different base periods have been converted to the base 1968-69 by the chain base method.

a Relates to the period June-March.

b Note that for the base year 1950-51, the unit value index for imports was exceptionally high.

Source: World Bank (private communication).

(Tables 25.5 and 25.6). The volume of India's exports grew at an average annual rate of 3.0 percent during 1965-1980 and 6.5 percent during 1980-1990. During 1965-1980 the volume of world exports grew at an average annual rate of 6.6 percent and that of low-income developing countries grew at 5.1 percent per year during the same period. In the period 1980-1990 Indian export growth was faster than that of the world (4.3 percent per year) and that of low-income developing countries (5.4 percent per year).

TABLE – 25.6

Unit Value and Volume Indexes of Exports and Imports and India's Terms of Trade 1981-82 - 1990-91 (1980/81 = 100)

Year (April-March)	Exports		Imports		Terms of trade
	Volume index	Unit value index (in US$)	Volume index	Unit value index (in US$)	
1981/82	101	100.0	101	93.3	107.6
1982/83	97	98.0	94	92.3	106.2
1983/84	97	101.1	101	88.1	114.8
1984/85	103	98.5	95	87.1	113.1
1985/86	106	97.7	119	85.2	115.0
1986/87	118	97.1	124	80.3	121.0
1987/88	135	106.0	116	93.6	114.0
1988/89	154	107.8	130	93.8	115.0
1989/90	178	110.3	135	99.2	111.0
1990/91	186	115.2	140	106.0	100.0

Source: World Bank (Private communication).

The composition of India's exports (Tables 25.7 and 25.8) has, as expected, shifted moderately away from primary products to manufactured goods, whose share rose from about 45 percent in 1950/51 to 79 percent in 1990-91. In recent years, however, primary exports have been virtually stagnant, and manufactured products have accounted for almost the entire growth in total exports (Table 25.9). Among manufactured products, just four items leather, gems, garments, and textiles – account for most of the growth in recent years. In contrast, the export of engineering goods, which rose by over 20 percent per year in value terms between 1950-51 and 1975-76 and between 1970-71 and 1978-79, declined between 1980-81 and 1985-86. From the low point of US$780 million in 1985-86, the value of

TABLE – 25.7

India's Merchandise Exports, 1950-51 - 1978-79

Commodity	Value (US$ millions at current prices)											Annual compound growth rate (percentage)			
												1950/51-1975/76	1970/71-1978/79		
	1950/51	1955/56	1960/61	1965/66	1968/69	1970/71	1973/74	1975/76	1976/77	1977/78	1978/79	1975/76	1978/79	1977/78	1978/79
Agricultural products	328.8	380.9	420.7	497.0	478.5	519.3	858.6	1,393.3	1,362.5	1,639.5	1,471.7	5.9	13.9	20.5	-10.2
Tea	168.9	229.2	259.6	241.2	208.6	197.7	187.4	273.8	327.9	665.3	414.9	2.0	9.7	102.9	-37.6
Oil cakes	0.1	11.1	30.0	72.8	66.0	73.9	228.7	111.5	262.2	155.6	141.1	32.4	8.4	-40.7	-9.3
Coffee	2.8	3.2	15.2	27.2	24.0	35.5	59.1	77.0	141.0	227.0	175.6	14.2	23.0	61.0	-22.6
Sugar	0.8	2.0	5.1	22.0	13.5	56.8	55.0	545.9	165.7	22.7	160.8	29.8	20.2	-86.3	608.4
Spices	53.4	22.4	34.9	48.5	33.5	51.8	70.7	82.7	85.9	160.1	180.4	1.8	16.9	90.8	12.7
Fish	5.2	7.9	9.7	14.3	30.3	41.7	114.5	147.0	202.0	203.6	278.2	14.3	26.8	0.8	36.6
Cashew	18.0	27.3	39.7	57.5	81.2	69.4	95.5	111.1	118.7	174.6	97.8	7.6	4.4	47.1	-44.0
Vegetable oils[a]	53.0	72.1	17.9	8.6	15.6	9.4	39.6	39.8	56.4	24.2	16.5	-1.1	7.3	-57.1	-31.8
Essential oils	26.6	5.7	8.6	4.9	5.8	5.1	8.1	4.5	4.7	6.4	6.4	-6.9	2.9	36.2	-
Raw materials	78.3	138.0	135.4	196.8	217.2	252.7	335.8	641.1	637.2	539.0	595.2	8.8	11.3	-15.4	10.4
Raw cotton	10.4	62.3	18.2	20.4	14.8	18.6	41.6	47.7	30.2	0.8	19.5	6.3	0.6	-97.4	2337.5
Unmanufactured tobacco	29.6	22.4	30.7	41.1	44.2	41.9	87.8	107.6	108.3	132.2	134.9	5.3	15.7	22.1	2.0
Iron ore	0.5	13.2	35.8	88.4	117.8	152.9	170.5	247.1	266.8	281.3	283.8	28.2	8.0	5.4	0.9
Mica	21.0	17.6	21.2	23.7	18.0	20.7	16.7	16.9	19.4	20.2	23.1	-0.9	1.4	4.1	14.4
Manganese	16.8	22.5	29.5	23.2	18.0	18.6	12.1	20.2	21.4	12.7	18.8	0.7	0.1	-40.7	48.0
Silver	n.a.	n.a.	n.a.	n.a	4.4	n.a.	7.1	201.6	191.1	91.8	115.1	n.a.		-52.0	25.4

Contd...

...Contd...

Manufactured items	568.8	457.3	571.7	782.4	977.2	976.3	1,543.7	1,992.4	2,848.6	3,300.1	3,801.7	5.1	18.5	15.8	15.2
Jute															
manufactures	239.0	248.3	283.8	384.0	290.6	253.9	292.0	290.0	225.0	285.9	203.0	0.8	-2.8	27.1	-29.1
Cotton textile															
Millmade	225.4	101.2	110.8	98.5	87.3	90.0	208.8	140.5	238.4	167.4	169.4	-1.9	8.2	-29.8	1.2
Handloom	22.8	17.8	10.0	17.5	6.7	10.4	41.6	45.8	60.6	95.0	74.4	2.8	27.9	56.8	-21.7
Coir															
manufactures	22.8	20.2	18.2	22.5	18.4	17.3	19.7	22.0	26.8	27.9	32.1	-0.1	8.0	4.1	15.1
Clothing	0.8[b]	n.a.	1.8	13.4	19.6	40.3	127.9	234.6	372.7	386.8	518.5	25.5[c]	37.6	3.8	34.0
Cotton yarn and thread	4.2	9.5	9.3	14.6	19.1	29.6	14.6	7.4	31.5	35.3	18.9[a]	2.3	n.a.	12.1	n.a.
Leather and leather															
manufactures	54.5[c]	48.3	56.6	72.6	206.5	108.8	239.5	263.6	264.4	317.6	430.4	6.5	18.8	20.1	35.5
Gems	n.a.	n.a.	0.3	31.0	59.7	55.8	137.2	171.6	321.1	637.4	865.9	n.a.	40.9	98.5	35.8
Other															
handicrafts	n.a.	n.a.	n.a.	21.4	32.4	37.3	85.6	119.6	188.7	240.5	294.6	n.a.	29.5	27.5	22.5
Iron and steel[f]	3.3[b]	n.a.	20.3	26.5	105.2	121.6	33.6	78.6	325.0	216.6	140.2	13.5[c]	1.8	-33.4	-35.2
Engineering goods[f]	1.2[b]	n.a.	37.8	41.6	89.8	155.3	258.9	477.3	633.5	721.0	852.3	27.1[c]	23.7	13.8	18.2
Chemicals[g]	17.9	12.0	7.2	19.2	25.8	39.2	64.6	98.6	124.0	136.3	178.3	7.1	20.8	9.9	30.8
Mineral fuels	n.a.	n.a.	15.6	19.6	16.1	16.8	19.7	42.8	36.9	32.5	23.7	n.a.	4.4	-11.9	-27.1
Other	285.4[b]	302.7[b]	258.7	215.6	137.6	298.6	500.8	645.3	904.8	836.8	1,107.6	3.3	17.8	-7.5	32.4
Total	1,261.3	1,278.9	1,386.5	1,691.8	1,810.5	2,046.9[i]	3,238.9	4,672.1	5,753.1	6,315.4	6,976.2	5.4	16.6	9.8	10.5

n.a. = not available.
a Edible oils excluding vanaspati.
b Relates to 1951/52.
c Relates to the period 1951/52 to 1975/76.
d Excluding cotton thread.
e Excludes footwear.
f In accordance with the classification followed by the Ministry of Commerce. In 1972 several manufactured items formerly included under iron and steel were reclassified as engineering goods. Data from 1973/74 onward follow the new classification and hence are not comparable with data for earlier years.
g Excluding essential oils and plastics.
h Includes items listed above for which data are not available.
i Unadjusted total. Because of a change in recording technique, the data from the Directorate General of Commercial Intelligence and Statistics probably overstate exports by about 5% in 1970/71.

Source: World Bank (private communication).

TABLE – 25.8

India's Merchandise Exports, 1980-81 - 1991-92

	Value (US$ millions at current prices)											Growth rate (percentage)		
	1980/81	1981 82	1982/83	1983/84	1984/85	1985/86	1986/87	1987/88	1988/89	1989/90	1990/91	1985/1990[a]	1990/91	1991/92[b]
Primary exports	3,400	3,308	3,110	3,093	3,102	3,108	3,237	3,125	2,905	3,428	3,740	3.8	9.1	2.0
Fish	270	314	378	353	321	334	421	405	437	412	535	9.9	29.8	3.2
Rice	284	412	226	110	142	160	154	250	230	256	245	8.9	-4.3	22.5
Cashews	178	203	141	146	151	184	256	236	192	221	249	6.2	12.8	7.1
Coffee	271	164	194	176	177	216	232	203	193	206	141	-8.2	-31.4	-6.3
Tea	539	443	384	500	645	512	451	457	414	543	599	3.2	10.3	-25.5
Spices	141	111	98	113	174	227	218	238	173	148	130	-10.6	-12.2	14.2
Iron ore	384	394	395	389	387	473	427	419	464	557	585	4.3	5.1	5.7
Other primary	1,333	1,267	1,294	1,306	1,105	1,002	1,078	917	803	1,086	1,257	4.6	15.7	9.4
Manufactured Exports	5,067	5,214	4,931	5,187	5,462	5,684	6,501	9,013	11,105	13,185	14,383	20.4	9.1	-4.2
Chemicals	298	420	362	317	406	406	456	635	1,058	1,759	1,781	34.4	1.2	7.6
Leather and leather goods	478	454	408	449	568	629	721	886	1,028	1,171	1,423	17.7	21.5	-10.8
Textiles	1,292	1,155	988	921	1,171	1,026	1,079	1,483	1,044	1,214	1,705	10.7	40.5	-1.3
Garments	717	737	628	719	827	872	1,040	1,382	1,449	1,935	2,252	20.9	16.4	-4.2
Gems and Jewellery	783	909	1,054	1,255	1,040	1,228	1,622	2,016	3,038	3,178	2,903	18.8	-8.7	-3.6
Engineering goods	1,010	1,043	892	782	803	780	886	1,105	1,630	1,993	1,978	20.5	-0.8	-7.2
Petroleum products	10	28	178	346	215	425	327	488	349	418	523	4.2	25.1	-29.8
Other manufactures	479	468	421	-398	432	318	370	1,018	1,509	1,517	1,819	41.7	19.9	n.a.
Total[c]	8,467	8,522	8,041	8,280	8,564	8,792	9,738	12,138	14,010	16,613	18,123	15.6	9.1	-1.9
Statistical discrepancy	-135	175	348	810	1,205	669	722	506	252	237	362			
Total[c]	8,332	8,697	8,389	9,090	9,769	9,461	10,460	12,644	14,262	16,850	18,485	14.3	9.7	n.a.

n.a. = not available.

a Compound growth rate between 1985/86 and 1990/91.

b Based on April-February data for aggregate exports, and April-January data for components.

c Net of crude petroleum exports.

Source: Ministry of Commerce, Directorate General of Commercial Intelligence and Statistics; Reserve Bank of India.

engineering goods exports grew at an average annual rate of 20.5 per cent during the period 1985-1990. Chemical exports show a similar pattern.

TABLE – 25.9

Composition of Recent Export Growth in India, 1980-81 - 1990-91

	Average annual value (US$ millions at current prices)			
	1980/81-1985/86	1986/87-1990/91	Increase	Contribution to growth (%)
Manufactured exports	5,296	10,837	5,542	97
Consumption goods	3,408	6,514	3,106	55
Leather	502	1,046	544	10
Gems (gross)	1,097	2,551	1,454	26
Garments	757	1,612	855	15
Textiles	1,052	1,305	253	4
Investment goods[a]	860	1,518	658	12
Intermediate goods	1,028	2,805	1,777	31
Chemicals	382	1,138	756	13
Petroleum products	238	421	183	3
Other[b]	407	1,247	839	15
Primary exports	3,144	3,287	143	3
Fish	340	442	102	2
Rice	210	227	17	0
Cashews	165	231	66	1
Coffee	185	195	9	0
Tea	497	493	-4	0
Spices	145	181	37	1
Iron ore	408	490	83	1
Other primary exports	1,195	1,028	-167	-3
Total exports (Customs)[c]	8,440	14,124	5,685	100
Discrepancy	641	416	-226	
Total exports (BOP)[c]	9.081	14,540	5,459	
Memo				
Gems(net)[d]	290	688	398	

a Refers to engineering goods.
b Including unclassified exports.
c Total exports, f.o.b., net of crude oil.
d Exports less imports of gems and jewellery.

Source: Ministry of Commerce. Directorate General of Commercial Intelligence and Statistics: Reserve Bank of India.

The export of gems has grown rapidly since the early 1970s. This export is heavily dependent, however, on the import of uncut small gems, the cost of which is determined in large part by the South African monopoly De Beers. The exports of garments and textiles are governed by India's quotas under the multifiber arrangement (MFA). Bhalla (1989) points out that until the 1980s India did not fully use its quotas, and India's competitors did better in quota, as well as nonquota, countries. It is possible that the recent spurt in India's garment and textile exports reflects better use of quotas and higher prices realized on the average. Whether India will be able to compete in the textile and apparel market in the absence of the MFA is debatable, particularly in view of the fact that the Indian textile industry has fallen behind technologically in the past four decades primarily because of the government's textile policy. A recent study by Trela and Whalley (1989) suggests that the general equilibrium welfare effects of removing bilateral MFA quotas and tariffs on textiles and clothing for all countries are on the order of a modest US$15.5 billion in 1986 U.S. dollars, of which US$7.97 billion accrue to the developing countries. India gains an extremely modest US$0.08 billion. China (US$1.72 billion), Korea (US$1.62 billion), Brazil (US$0.92 billion), and Taiwan (US$0.89 billion) account for most of the gains to developing countries. The Trela and Whalley simulation, however, is a static exercise and assumes that all countries have the same technology but differing labour productivity and product quality. It is not clear whether the results will stand up if changes are made in these assumptions. The fact that a relatively narrow range of product groups accounted for the recent growth in India's exports and that their growth may not be sustained in the future if the external environment changes is disturbing.

Conclusion

India's growth performance in the four decades since planning for national development was initiated in 1950 has been unspectacular. In the 1950s, 1960s, and 1970s the average annual growth rate of real GDP was 3.7 percent, 3.3 percent, and 3.4 percent. The 1980s saw some modest improvement in the growth rate to 5.3 percent. India's development strategy was inward oriented, and self-reliance was an important objective. The pursuit of this objective has resulted in a diversified industrial structure. Most of India's industries, however, are not internationally competitive in terms of either cost per unit or product quality.

Far from viewing foreign trade as an engine of growth, Indian planners sought to minimize import demand and viewed exports more or less as a necessary evil mainly to generate the foreign exchange earnings to meet that part of the import bill not covered by external assistance. They created an elaborate administrative regulatory machinery in an attempt to control investment and resource allocation in the economy and ensure their consistency with five-year plan targets. Controls over imports and exports were also part of this regulatory system. The system was exceedingly complex, and its rules of operation had no discernible economic rationale. Above all, it was selective and discretionary and relied on quantitative restrictions rather than on policy instruments that affected market prices. The integrity of the administrative and political structure was increasingly eroded by the enormous opportunities for rent seeking and the corruption this spawned.

India's share in world trade declined steadily from 2 percent in the 1950s to 0.5 per cent in 1990. Most of the growth in exports in the 1980s was accounted for by just four product groups: leather, gems and jewellry, textiles, and garments. Exports of engineering goods and chemicals, which were once dynamic, suffered a decline in the first half of the 1980s and recovered somewhat in the second half. A diversified and dynamic export sector has yet to emerge.

It is clear that to achieve sustained, rapid, equitable, and efficient growth, India must abandon its inward-oriented, capital-intensive, and inefficient development strategy implemented through an administrative allocation system based on QRs. In its stead a system of economic management must be put in place that relies largely on market forces and that confines state intervention in the economy to investment in some infrastructure sectors such as transport, communication, and major irrigation and to those areas where there are no efficient private sector alternatives, including services such as primary education, primary health care, and agricultural extension and research. The Rao-Singh reforms are vital initial steps in these directions. They must be consolidated and extended. Above all, the credibility of the government's commitment to the reforms must be firmly established.

Because the reforms are solidly based on an understanding of what went wrong with the Indian development strategy that delivered neither rapid growth nor appreciably greater equity and because they constitute a package of mutually supporting and consistent elements, they are not as easily opposed on analytical grounds as earlier piecemeal efforts at economic liberalization. The collapse of the socialist economies of Eastern Europe and the realization that India has been left behind in development by other Asian economies have generated widespread support for reforms in the national press. The coherence of the reform package and support of the press, however, are not enough to convince producers in India and abroad that the government is committed to carrying out the package and that the short-run economic, social, and political costs of adjustment to a liberalized economy are manageable. Although the prime minister and the finance minister continue to stand by the reforms and proclaim that they are irreversible, concrete actions have been slow in coming. *The New York Times* (August 15, 1992) reports that "a year after the new policies were announced by Prime Minister P.V. Narasimha Rao far less has been accomplished than promised bureaucratic red tape still hamstrings new investment, both foreign and domestic and not a single one of India's huge, bankrupt state controlled industries has been shut." It adds that Motorola, "which intended to invest $14 billion in India over the next decade has decided to move some of those investments to China. In the first three months of this year, China received $6.5 billion in foreign investment in contrast to [India's] $300 million."

To be fair to Rao and Singh it should be pointed out that four decades of dirigisme is not easily replaced by market-friendly economic management in one year. Moreover, the government does not have an absolute majority in Parliament, though the divisions within the opposition and its reluctance to face another general election soon after the last one in 1991 give the government some room to maneuver. If India uses this narrow window of political opportunity effectively, with the support of expanded aid from the donor community abroad to ease the short-run costs of adjustment, the reforms would indeed become irreversible and their fruits would be realized.

Some actions, if taken promptly, could enhance credibility. For instance, the government could announce a phased programme to reduce excessively high tariffs and their variance across commodities. If the announced reductions are bound with the General Agreement on Tariffs and Trade (GATT) so that they acquire the force of an international agreement, their credibility would be enhanced considerably. Another step would be successful negotiations with the labour unions in the public and organized private sectors to persuade them to change their focus from seeking protection of their existing jobs in inefficient industries that have to be scaled down or closed altogether to seeking better jobs in a liberalized economy in which employment opportunities would be rapidly growing and plentiful. With the National Renewal Fund (established in 1991) financing voluntary retirement opportunities for older workers and retraining opportunities for younger workers laid off from enterprises that are to be scaled down adjustment costs should be manageable as long as productive employment grows more rapidly than in the past. For rural workers, a more efficient version of the existing employment creation programmes could serve well. And a limited but better-targeted and managed public distribution system for essential commodities would provide a social safety net for the poor.

Full convertibility of the rupee for current account transactions should be instituted as soon as possible. This step should enable the government to considerably scale down export subsidies, if not eliminate them altogether. With a better-functioning infrastructure and freer availability of imported inputs industrial efficiency should improve, thereby reducing unit costs of production. In particular, reduced production costs for fertilizers should allow for the phasing out of fertilizer subsidies. With the exist of inefficient public sector units dependent on budgetary support, yet another source of the public sector deficit would disappear. With improvements in the revenue side of the budget (in particular, a wider tax base, reduced tax rates, and more efficient tax administration), the fiscal deficit would be brought within safe limits. With the reforms credibly enforced and extended, it should not take India as long as it took other such formerly inward-oriented economies, such as Mexico, to climb out of the unavoidable adjustment phase and move onto a path of sustainable, rapid, efficient, and equitable growth.

References

Bardhan. P.K. (1984), *The Political Economy of Development in India* Oxford: Basil Blackwell.

Basu, D.C. (1983), *Introduction to the Constitution of India*. 10th edition. New Delhi: Prentice-Hall.

Bhagwati, J.N., and P. Desai. (1970), *India: Planning for Industrialization*. London: Oxford University Press.

Bhagwati, J.N., and T.N. Srinivasan. (1975), *Foreign Trade Regimes and Economic Development: India*. New York: Columbia University Press.

Bhagwati, J.N., R. Brecher, and T.N. Srinivasan. (1984), "DUP Activities and Economic Theory." In D.C. Colander, ed., *Neo-classical Political Economy*. Cambridge: Ballinger.

Bhalla, S. (1989), "Indian Exports, Imports and Exchange Rates: A Comparative Quantitative Analysis." (Processed).

General Agreement on Tariffs and Trade (GATT). *International Trade*. Vol. 2. Geneva: GATT.

India. (1986), *Economic Survey* 1985-86. New Delhi: Government Printing Press.

——— (1988). *Import and Export Policy*. Vol. 1. New Delhi: Government Printing Press.

Meier. Gerald M., ed. (1991), *Politics and Policy Making in Developing Countries*. San Francisco: ICS Press for the International Center for Economic Growth.

Nehru, Jawaharlal. (1946), *The Discovery of India*. New York: John Day Company.

Planning Commission. (1951), *The First Five Year Plan*. New Delhi: Government Printing Office.

Rao, Narahari. (1985), "Exchange Rate and Commercial Policy in a Controlled Trade Regime: A Case Study of India." Ph.D. dissertation, Oxford University.

Srinivasan, T.N. (1992), "Planning and Foreign Trade Reconsidered." In Subroto Roy and William E. James, eds., *Foundations of India's Political Economy*. New Delhi: Sage Publications.

Trela, I., and J. Whalley. (1989), "Unraveling the Threads of the MFA." Centre for the Study of International Economic Relations, University of Western Ontario, London, Ontario. Processed.

United Nations Development Programme. (1992), *Human Development Report 1992*. New York: Oxford University Press.

World Bank. (1991), *World Development Report 1991*. New York: Oxford University Press.

Agriculture and Trade in India and China, Ch.5, International Centre for Economic Growth, (ICEG), San Francisco, U.S.A. 1994. Reprinted with permission from the author and ICEG.

26

Foreign Direct Investment in India in the 1990s

Trends and Issues

R. Nagaraj

Introduction

Compared to most industrialising economies, India followed a fairly restrictive foreign private investment policy until 1991 – relying more on bilateral and multilateral loans with long maturities. Inward foreign direct investment (FDI, or foreign investment, or foreign capital hereafter) was perceived essentially as a means of acquiring industrial technology that was unavailable through licensing agreements and capital goods import. Technology imports were preferred to financial and technical collaborations.

Even for technology licensing agreements, there were restrictions on the rates of royalty payment and technical fees. Development banks largely met the external financial needs for importing capital equipment. However, foreign investment was permitted in designated industries, subject to varying conditions on setting up joint ventures with domestic partners, local content clauses, export obligations, promotion of local R&D and so on – broadly similar to those followed in many rapidly industrialising Asian economies.

Foreign Exchange and Regulation Act (FERA), 1974 stipulated foreign firms to have equity holding only up to 40 per cent, exemptions were at the government's discretion. Setting up of branch plants was usually disallowed; foreign subsidiaries were induced to gradually dilute their equity holding to less than 40 per cent in the domestic capital market. The law also prohibited the use of foreign brands, but promoted hybrid domestic brands (*Hero-Honda*, for instance). However, pragmatism prevailed to ensure stable domestic supply at reasonable prices.

Such a restrictive policy is believed to have retarded domestic technical capability (as reflected in the poor quality of Indian goods); it also meant a loss of export opportunity of labour-intensive manufactures – in contrast to many successful east Asian economies. Moreover, such a policy is said to have encouraged 'rent seeking' by domestic partners on imported technology – with little efforts to improve product quality, undertake innovation, and seek export markets [Ahluwalia 1985]. This popular perception was perhaps best illustrated by the passenger car industry that produced obsolete (and fuel-inefficient) models of the 1950s at very high costs in small numbers.

Without denying some of these arguments and evidence, others have shown that the regulation reduced costs of technology imports [Subramaniam 1991], and promoted export of goods with relatively stable technologies where domestic firms had the opportunity of 'learning by doing' by catering to the large domestic market – as illustrated by successful firms like TELCO (commercial vehicles) and BHEL (heavy electrical equipment) [Lall 1982]. The recent international achievements of some Indian pharmaceutical firms (Cipla, Ranbaxy, Dr. Reddy's Laboratories, for instance) is also attributed to the regulatory and promotional policies, and the patent laws [Chaudhari 1999] that sought to encourage domestic production to reduce drug prices.

However, the 1980s witnessed a gradual relaxation of the foreign investment rules – perhaps best symbolised by the setting up of Maruti, a central government joint venture small car project with Japan's Suzuki Motors in 1982. It was followed by Pepsi's entry in the second half of the decade, to primarily export processed food products from Punjab and also to bottle its well known beverages for the domestic market.

Reforms in the 1990s

All this changed since 1991. Foreign investment is now seen as a source of scarce capital, technology and managerial skills that were considered necessary in an open, competitive, world economy. India sought to consciously 'benchmark' its policies against those of the rapidly growing south-east Asian economies to attract a greater share of the world FDI inflows. Over the decade, India not only permitted foreign investment in almost all sectors of the economy (barring agriculture, and, until recently, real estate), but also allowed foreign portfolio investment – thus practically divorcing foreign investment from the erstwhile technology acquisition effort. Further, laws were changed to provide foreign firms the same standing as the domestic ones.[1]

What are the trends in the quantum and composition of the FDI inflow; and what are their benefits and costs to the economy? This paper seeks to provide a preliminary answer for these questions. To do so, we first discuss, very briefly, the recent literature on foreign investment and economic development (Section I). The limitations of the available data to test the propositions following from the analytical literature are discussed in Section II. As a first step in our assessment, Section III describes the trends in FDI in the 1990s. Section IV contains a brief comparison of foreign investment in India and China – an issue that has a bearing on the current policy discussion. Based on the available, limited and preliminary, information, Section V makes an initial assessment of foreign investment by raising some issues for further work. Section VI suggests a more realistic policy on the basis of the analytical discussion and comparative experience. Section VII concludes by summarising the study's main findings.

I

A BRIEF ANALYTICAL REVIEW

Much of the currently held perceptions of foreign investment's role essentially take a macroeconomic view: it is a source of additional external finance (and of risk capital), augmenting fixed investment, potential output and employment.[2] Such a positive view gained currency mainly after the crises in Latin America in the early 1980s, more recently in east Asia, when other forms of capital inflows quickly dried up (or reversed), accentuating the macroeconomic vulnerability of these economies. As against portfolio investment, FDI is also seen as a source of technology and managerial skills, creating tangible (and intangible) assets in the host economy. Foreign firms seek not only the domestic market, but also provide access to external markets by sourcing manufactured products (and services) from domestic firms.

The crux of the policy, therefore, is how the benefits of such investments are distributed between the foreign firms and the host country, as also between the various factors of production within the host country. In other words, the real question is the cost of foreign capital to the host economy: is it too high, compared to the alternative sources of external finance and technology, in the short and the long run?

However, in a microeconomic perspective, a different set of questions is usually asked: What does FDI do to the working of the domestic markets, and their effect on output and productivity growth [Caves 1996]. If, as is often the case, the entry of a foreign firm results in the creation of a domestic monopoly, then the benefits of such investment may be limited, unless accompanied by a sound anti-trust law (or competition policy). Similarly, if FDI inflow results in the displacement of domestic monopolies with the foreign ones, then again, social benefits of such investments may be marginal (if any), as any monopolist, regardless of its origin, would maximise profits either by varying price or output (or both). Moreover, the host government may have considerable difficulty in enforcing domestic laws adequately, as foreign firms often seek protection under complicated legal structures.[3]

In industrial organisation literature, from a variety of analytical perspectives, foreign firms are seen as having firm-specific advantages – including significant market power that they seek to exploit in many countries.[4] Availability and costs of these resources for the host economy depend on the relative bargaining strength of the foreign firms vis-à-vis the domestic firms (and the host government). While the foreign firms' advantages lie in their size, control over technology and marketing strength worldwide, the host country can use its domestic market, access to cheap labour, location and quality of infrastructure (all of which go to reduce the cost of production to service the international market) to bargain with the foreign firms.

Thus, a social cost benefit approach is perhaps a meaningful method to assess the potential effects of FDI. If such a view is valid, then what countries should do is perhaps not to maximise foreign investment inflow per se, but to channel it in the desired directions to maximise long-term returns to the economy. From the development economics perspective, the questions one asks could get even deeper. In a world with unequal resources and technological capabilities (including brand names), how does FDI affect the ownership and control of industrial firms? In the market for industrial technologies that is invariably oligopolistic, does foreign capital inflow augment or reduce access to technology and domestic R&D efforts? Does foreign capital improve exports (and export capability) from the host country? What is the cost of FDI over a long period; is it necessarily lower than that of external debt [Helleiner 1989]?[5]

It is perhaps worth reiterating that markets for industrial technologies continue to be imperfect and probably have got accentuated with the recent international agreements like the TRIPS. Moreover, the experience of the last half a century clearly suggests that countries with liberal FDI and technology import policy are not necessarily the examples of successful industrialisation [Bruton 1989]. They may have become either outposts of foreign firms servicing regional markets (like Singapore), or partners in the international division of labour with limited mastery over production technology and generation of domestic brand names (Brazilian automobile industry, for example).

In the development literature, well reflected in the Indian discourse, there is a wide consensus that regulation reduces costs of imported technology [Lall 1989]. One of the ways to acquire the disembodied technology is to 'unbundle' the package that foreign firms offer, and to buy the technology outright, while providing for capital investment by the domestic financial system. This has been the time-tested method of all the successful late industrialising economies [Amsden 2001].[6]

II

DATA ON FDI AND THEIR LIMITATIONS

To understand how the recent changes in foreign investment policy have influenced the economy, quantitative information is needed on broad dimensions of the investment (and its distribution) across industries, regions and by size of projects; firm and industry level production accounts, and audited financial statements. However, such information is scarce. The most easily available (and widely used) data in India are on FDI approvals (contracted), by broad industry group (1-digit ISIC), by country of origin, and by states (regions) of destination. This represents mere intentions of investment. The actual (or realised) foreign investment is not available by the same classification, but according to the administrative and institutional channels of the inflow. Therefore, it is not possible to compare the realised with the intentions, in any meaningful manner. Apparently, even the concerned official agency does not seem to know – let alone monitor – how the actual inflows are translated into capital formation, transfer of assets or change in managerial control.

The actual FDI inflow is recorded under five broad heads: (i) Reserve Bank of India's (RBI) automatic approval route for equity holding up to 51 per cent, (ii) Foreign Investment Board's discretionary approval route for larger projects with equity holding greater than 51 per cent,

(iii) acquisition of shares route (since 1996), (iv) RBI's non-resident Indian (NRI) schemes, and (v) external commercial borrowings (ADR/GDR route). Reportedly, the Indian definition of FDI differs from that of the IMF, as well as of the UN's *World Investment Report*. IMF's definition includes external commercial borrowings, reinvested earnings and subordinated debt, while the *World Investment Report* excludes external commercial borrowings.[7]

Ideally, FDI inflow should get reflected in (i) capital formation (ii) formation of new firms and factories, (iii) increase in foreign equity holding in the existing firms, and (iv) mergers and acquisitions of existing firms and factories (or parts of them). However, the availability of information on them depends on their legal status. We know very little about those registered outside the country, and in tax shelters, like Mauritius. For instance, Enron's Dabhol Power Company – the largest foreign investment project yet – is incorporated in India as an unlimited liability company. But it is a shell company that Enron controls through at least six holding companies registered in various offshore locations [Mehta 1999].[8]

Similarly, fully owned private limited companies of foreign firms (or branch plants) reveal very little information about their investment and output. An increasingly large proportion of foreign firms have set up fully owned subsidiaries that have become manufacturers (and distributors) by acquiring domestic firms. They provide very little audited financial information to assess the impact of the firms on the industry, and the corporate sector.[9] Considering these legal problems, many of their operations do not seem to get recorded in the RBI's survey of financial performance of foreign controlled companies – a valuable data source in the earlier times.

Therefore, the assessment of foreign investment reported in this study remains preliminary. However, based on the preceding discussion, the issues raised below can perhaps be taken as working hypotheses for further research.

III

THE TRENDS

FDI Approvals and Its Composition

Approved FDI rose from about Rs 500 crore in 1992 to about Rs 55 thousand crore in 1997 [*Economic Survey*, 2001-02] (Figure 26.1). Cumulative approved foreign investment during 1991 and 2000, in dollar terms, is about $ 67bn – at an average exchange rate of Rs 40 to a dollar. A fifth of it is from the US (Table 26.1). Mauritius is the second largest source; reportedly a conduit for many US based firms, as India has a tax avoidance treaty with it since 1982. In Asia, South Korea has emerged as a new source of foreign investment.[10] A quarter of the approved FDI is for power generation (Table 26.2), followed by telecommunications (mobile phone firms) at 18.5 per cent, and electrical equipment (mainly software) at 10 per cent. While the proportion of projects with investment up to Rs 5 crore is high, their share is less than 5 per cent in value. At the other end of the distribution, larger projects with Rs 100 crore and above account for over two-thirds of the total value of approvals (Table 26.3). Evidently, very little of the FDI has gone to augment exports that are mostly from labour-intensive unregistered manufacturing. The economically advanced states of Maharashtra, Delhi, Karnataka, Tamil Nadu and Gujarat have attracted one-half of the approved foreign investment (Table 26.4).

TABLE – 26.1

Top 10 Investing Countries in India, 1991-2000

Country/Region	Share (in Per Cent)
U.S.	20.4
Mauritius	11.9
U.K.	6.4
Japan	4.0
South Korea	3.9
Germany	3.4
Australia	2.7
Malaysia	2.3
France	2.1
Netherlands	1.9

Note : In addition to the countries, external commercial borrowings and non- resident Indians (NRIs) contributed 17.2 and 3.9 per cent of the FDI approvals.

Source: Handbook of Industrial Policy and Statistics, 2001.

TABLE – 26.2

Sectoral Distribution of FDI Approvals, 1991-2000

Sector	No. of Approvals	Approved Investment (Rs.Billion)	Share (in Per Cent)
Power and fuel	541	634531.2	25.7
Telecommunications	579	458845.0	18.5
Services sector	790	152389.0	6.2
Chemicals (other than fertilisers)	809	123016.2	5.0
Food processing	648	87574.9	3.5
Transport sector	722	184467.6	7.5
Metallurgical industries	304	143796.8	5.8
Elec. equipment (incl. software)	2491	245791.5	10.0
Textiles	548	33617.8	1.4
Paper and paper products	111	31580.6	1.3
Industrial machinery	530	22438.5	0.9
Others	2404	348976.2	14.2
Total	11965	2467025.3	100.0

Note : Data is for the period, August 1991 to March 1998.
Source: Handbook of Industrial Policy and Statistics, 2001.

TABLE – 26.3

Distribution of FDI by Size of Investment, 1991-97

Investment	No of FDI Approvals		Quantum of FDI Approved	
(Rs. Crore)	Number	Share (in Per Cent)	Amount	Share (in Per Cent)
0-1	3040	49.2	919.4	0.9
1-5	1686	27.3	3800.8	3.6
5-25	906	14.7	10046.0	9.5
25-50	212	3.4	7503.5	7.1
50-100	128	2.1	8828.4	8.4
100-500	173	2.8	38699.0	36.6
Over 500	38	0.6	35992.4	34.0

Note : This distribution is for the approvals during August 1991 and May 1997.
Source : Rao and Murthy (1999).

TABLE – 26.4

Top Five Destinations of Approved FDI among the Indian States

State	No. of Financial Collaborations Approved	Approved FDI ($ Million)	Share (in Per Cent)
Maharashtra	2015	11135.9	16.9
Delhi	1226	9226.7	13.1
Karnataka	1078	5247.1	8.1
Tamil Nadu	1223	5073.8	7.7
Gujarat	458	3129.6	4.5
State not indicated	3119	19476.4	27.9

Source : Handbook of Industrial Policy and Statistics, 2001.

Table 26.5 provides the actual FDI inflow as estimated by four different agencies, for 1991 to 2000. IMF's and the *World Investment Report*'s estimates of the cumulative inflow during the 1990s are roughly the same – at about $17bn. The *Economic Survey* estimate is about $ 22bn, while that by RBI is $17.3bn. The difference between the last two estimates is mainly on account of ADR/GDR inflows. While the *Economic Survey* classifies them as FDI, RBI records them under foreign portfolio investment.

TABLE – 26.5

Alternative Estimates of the Actual FDI, 1991-2000

Year	Economic Survey (Rs. crore)	RBI (Rs. Crore)	International Financial Statistics (Million $)	World Investment Report (Million $)
1991	351	316		155
1992	675	965	276.5	261
1993	1787	1836	550.1	586
1994	3289	4126	973.3	947
1995	6820	7172	2143.6	2144
1996	10389	10015	2426.1	2591
1997	16425	13220	3577.3	3613
1998	13340	10358	2634.7	2614
1999	16868	9338	2168.6	2154
2000	19342	10686	2315.1	2315
Total	89286	68034	17065.3	17080

Sources: Economic Survey, various issues; RBI's Handbook of Statistics on Indian Economy, 2001; IMF's International Financial Statistics CDROM; UN's World Investment Report, various issues.

As there has been a gradual improvement in the actual inflow from a low base, and a slow down in the approvals after 1997, there is an increase in the ratio of the actual-to-approved FDI in the last few years. On average, it is a little over one-third in the 1990s (Figure 26.1). India's share in world foreign investment increased from 0.5 per cent in 1992, to 2.2 per cent in 1997 (Figure 26.2).

Figure – 26.1

FDI into India, 1992-2000

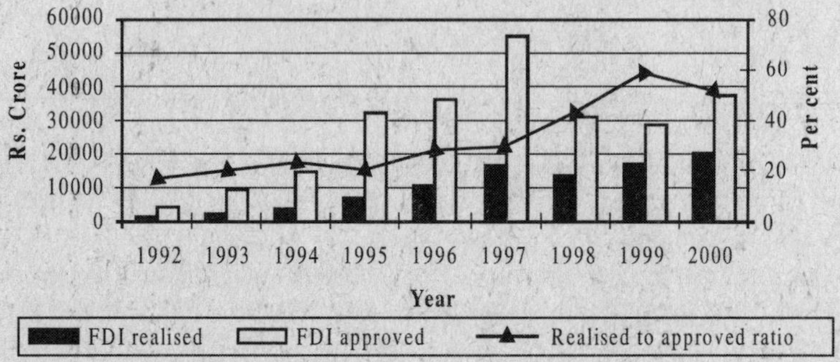

Figure – 26.2

India's Share in World FDI

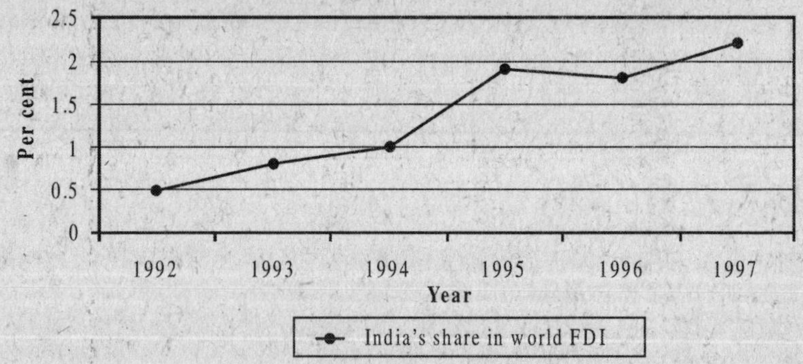

Figure 26.3 describes the actual inflow by various routes discussed in the previous section. The FIPB route – representing larger projects requiring the government's discretionary approval – accounts for the bulk of the inflow, though its share is somewhat declining. Automatic approval route via RBI meant for smaller sized investments received

modest inflow; and the NRI route's share has declined sharply. Proportion of the inflow to acquire shares in the domestic firms, and flotation of ADRs/GDRs have gained in prominence in the second half of the 1990s.

Figure – 26.3

Actual FDI by Different Routes

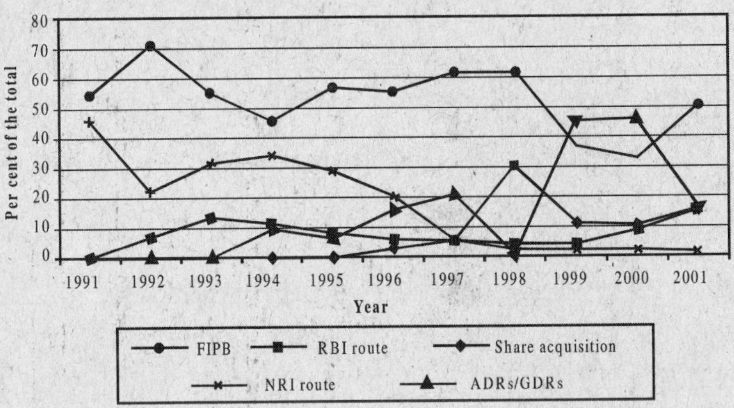

Interpreting the Trends

Though it is not possible to compare the actual with the approved FDI for the reasons discussed earlier, some broad generalisation can perhaps be made based on the available qualitative information. While the bulk of the approvals is for infrastructure, the actual inflow seems to be largely in registered manufacturing – more precisely, in consumer durable goods and automotive industries; very little of it has gone into capital goods industries. The inflow in telecommunication industry is probably to get licences for mobile phone operations, not for manufacturing equipment. The investments in electrical machinery industry are apparently to set up local offices to produce computer software.

Much of the realised FDI has also come in as fully owned subsidiaries (or branch plants) of their parents abroad. Table 26.6 provides an illustrative list of such foreign entities. Most of them have not issued IPOs in the domestic bourses, hence are not quoted companies. Quite contrary to the earlier period, the government has so far not insisted on enforcing its policy in this respect (more about this later).

TABLE – 26.6

Illustrative List of Foreign Firms Not Listed in the Domestic Stock Market

Product Group	Foreign Firms
Automobiles and allied products	GM, Ford, Mercedes Benz, Honda, Hyundai, Fiat, Toyota, Volvo, Yamaha, Cummins, Goodyear
Food and beverages	Coca-cola, Cadbury Schweppes, Kellogg, Heinz, Seagram, Hiram Waker, United Distillers, Perfitti, Wrigley, KFC, McDonalds
Consumer durable goods	Daewoo, Samsung, Sony, General Electric, LG Electronics, Black and Decker, Kimberley Clark
Personal care products	Revlon, L'Oreal, Cussons, Unilevers

Source : Rao, Murthy and Ranganathan (1999).

About 40 per cent of the inflow seems to have been used for acquiring existing industrial assets, and their managerial control (Table 26.7 (i)); and, there seems to be a gradual increase in such merger and acquisitions in the 1990s (Table 26.7 (ii)). Further, Table 26.8 provides an illustrative list of plants (and divisions) of Indian controlled firms acquired by foreign firms in the 1990s. This is also evident from the fact that foreign firms seem to use a larger proportion of their total funds for such acquisition than for capital formation, compared to Indian owned firms in the private corporate sector, the ratio of fixed capital formation to total uses of funds by foreign firms is lower than that by the domestic companies [Nagaraj 1997].

TABLE – 26.7 (i)

Share of M and A as in FDI Inflows in India

Year	FDI Inflow ($ Million)	M and A Fund ($ Million)	Share of M and A Fund in FDI Inflow (Per Cent)
1997	3200	1300	40.6
1998	2900	1000	34.5
1999 (Jan-Mar)	1400	2800	39.4

Source : Kumar (2000: 2852).

TABLE – 26.7 (ii)

Foreign Firms Related M and A in India

Year	Mergers	Acquisitions	Total
1993-94	4	9	13
1994-95	-	7	7
1995-96	-	12	12
1996-97	2	46	48
1997-98	4	61	65
1998-99	2	30	32
1999-2000 (Up to Jan 2000)	5	74	79
Total	17	239	256

Source : Kumar (2002: 2852).

TABLE – 26.8

Illustrative List of Units/Divisions Transferred to Foreign Firms

Units to be Transferred/Transferred	Remark
A par Lighting Division	Transferred to the joint-venture (JV) GE-Apar Ltd.
Compressor unit of Kirloskar Brothers	Transferred to Kirloskar Copeland
Compressor unit of SIEL and Kelvinator	Taken over by Tecumseh Venture
Engine valve division of Oil Engines	Proposed to be transferred to a JV Kirloskar with MWP, subsidiary of Mahel Germany.
Halol Plant of Hind Motors	Transferred to a JV with GM, of the US
Hinditron Computers	Acquired by Digital Equipment Corp
India Linoleum	Transferred to a JV with DLW of Germany
Premier Auto	Taken over by Fiat
Luxar Pen	Transferred to a JV with Gillette
Electricmeters of VXL Ltd	Transferred to VXL Landys Gys Ltd
Motor cycle division of Escorts	Transferred to Escorts Yamaha Ltd
Oral Care Division of Parle	Acquired by Gillette
Refrigerator division of Godrej & Boyce	Transferred to Godrej-GE appliances
Specialty chemicals div of Max India	Transferred to Max-Atotech
Stabiliser division of Jan Auto	Taken over by NHK Jai suspensions Ltd
Sugar machinery div. of KCP Ltd	Transferred to FCB-KCP Ltd
Ceat's Two-and three-wheeler tyre plant	Transferred to South Asia with Goodyear Tyres Ltd

Source: Rao, Murthy and Ranganathan (1999)

Predominance of acquisitions in India as a route to FDI is similar to the trends in many developing economies. For instance, in Brazil, the ratio is as high as 70 per cent, mainly fueled by privatisation drive in the 1990s.[11] Foreign firms seem to find it a quick and cheaper route to enter a new market, and secure a sizeable market share.

Of late, taking advantage of the changes in the rules governing the stock market listing, in a situation of low share price level, many existing foreign firms are re-purchasing their equity to exit from the domestic bourses. Table 26.9 provides an illustrative list of such firms. This represents a reversal of the positive effect that the foreign firms' domestic listing has had on the development of the primary stock market since the late 1970s [Nagaraj 1996].

TABLE – 26.9

An Illustrative List of Foreign Firms Moving to De-List from Domestic Bourses

Sl No	Company	Acquirer's Current Holding (Per Cent)	Offer Price (Rs)	Post-offer Holding (Per Cent)
1	Cabot	60	100	92
2	Cadbury	51	500	90
3	Carrier Aircon	51	100	86
4	Centak Chemicals	75	200	93
5	Hoganas	51	100	85
6	Otis	69	280	79
7	Philips	51	105	83
8	Reckitt & Colman	51	250	Yet to open
9	Sandvik	73	850	89

Source: Business India, April 1-14, 2002:118.

IV

A COMPARISON OF FDI IN INDIA AND CHINA

Though the actual FDI inflow in India in the 1990s increased significantly over the past, it is modest compared to many Asian economies (Figure 26.4); and, it pales into insignificance in comparison to China (Figure 26.5).[12,13] UNCTAD's ranking of countries in terms of foreign investment (relative to the size of the economy) for the period 1998-2000 is 119 for India, and 47 for China. The ranking a decade ago

Figure – 26.4

FDI in Selected Asian Economies, 1991-2002

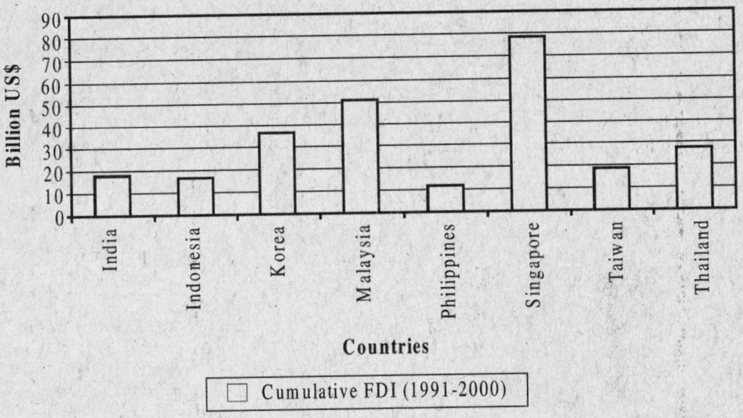

Figure – 26.5

FDI in India and China

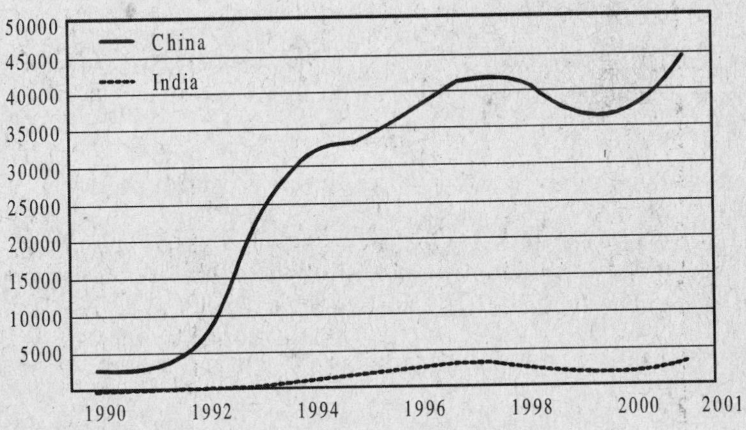

was 121 and 61 respectively *(The New York Times*, August 28, 2002). It shows that even at the start of the reforms, China's ranking was way ahead of India's; China moved up in the ranking much faster than India did in the 1990s.

These statistics are widely seen as an evidence of the failure of India's reforms, since greater inflow of foreign capital in China is believed to be largely responsible for its exceptional growth and export performance. As this perception is much discussed in the current policy discourse, we examine the quality of the Indian and the Chinese estimates, and the evidence on the role of FDI on economic performance in the recent years.

According to IFC (2002), India does not follow the standard IMF definition as it excludes (i) external commercial borrowings, that is ADRs/GDRs, (ii) reinvested profits and (iii) subordinated debt.[14] IFC is probably right, but only partially. As noted earlier, the *Economic Survey* estimates include external commercial borrowings, but not the remaining two items. Thus, notwithstanding the underestimation of FDI in the Indian statistics, there is little doubt that foreign investment inflow in India is negligible as compared to China.

However, it is well recognised that a large share of the investment inflow in China represents 'round tripping' – recycling of the domestic saving via Hong Kong to take advantage of tax, tariffs and other benefits offered to non-resident Chinese. This is estimated to be in the range of 40-50 per cent of the total FDI (IFC, *Global Financial Report, 2002*).

Further, about a quarter of the inflow in China is invested in real estate [Tseng and Zebregs 2002]. Some of the Chinese coastal cities have attracted considerable speculative capital in this sector in the 1990s after the collapse of the property prices in Hong Kong. It is widely accepted, especially after the east Asian financial crisis, that foreign investment in real estate is inherently problematic, as this sector can easily give rise to financial bubbles, with potentially adverse macroeconomic consequences.

Of the remaining, only a small fraction has gone into large-scale manufacturing that can potentially augment domestic capability and exports. In fact, FDI from the advanced economies that could bring in newer technology and managerial practices are limited, as the Chinese still seem to have a fairly strict regulation on such inflows. Reportedly, in 31 industries China does not allow wholly foreign owned enterprises; and in 32 others, Chinese partners must hold majority share holding.[15]

Based on the foregoing, the International Finance Corporation's study of business environment, in fact, places India marginally ahead of China – from the viewpoint of foreign investors [IFC 2002]. The study also found that the quantum of FDI inflow in China and India, as proportions of their respective GDP, is roughly comparable. Thus, the widely held view of China's ability to attract enormous foreign capital needs to be taken with considerable circumspection.

Do countries that attract larger FDI inflow necessarily grow faster? In other words, is there a positive association between foreign investment inflow and GDP growth? Evidence is far from unambiguous. If China's exceptional performance is believed to be largely on account of the foreign capital inflow, then one also has to contend with the recent Brazilian experience that proves the contrary. It has probably attracted the largest FDI from the industrialised economies since 1994. As noted earlier, much of it has gone to acquire domestic assets that were privatised on a large scale. But neither Brazil's growth or its export performance improved in the recent years.

Firm level studies also do not show any evidence that foreign investments improve output and productivity growth [Caves 1996]. There are, however, numerous cross-country studies that provide conflicting evidence on this issue. But, they often suffer from serious methodological problems. A recent study that seeks to address many of the concerns associated with such exercises, seems to find no evidence of a positive association between FDI inflow and output growth [Carkovic and Levine 2002].[16]

Thus, the quantum of FDI inflow into China, and its positive effect on the economy are perhaps overstated. Without getting into simplistic comparisons, what we need to appreciate from the Chinese experience is perhaps how to take advantage of the openness to investment and trade, to expand domestic capability and get access to external markets for its labour intensive manufactures.

V

A PRELIMINARY ASSESSMENT

Focus on Domestic Market

As noted earlier, India's seemingly large (and growing) domestic market is probably the main attraction for foreign firms. For instance, international soft drinks producers and fast food chains that were unknown a decade ago have acquired a visible presence in the metropolitan cities, though their quantitative significance may yet be marginal. These firms have brought with them the oligopolistic market structures and firm rivalries that are evident in the developed economies. While such market structures may have some desirable properties, if they lead to tacit collusion to bar new entry, then it may not be a positive development in the long run.

Similarly, almost all major international automobile companies have set up assembly and manufacturing facilities in varying extent. The same probably holds true for washing machines, refrigerators, and entertainment electronics. Such large-scale entry of firms has resulted in increased price and non-price competition, leading to a greater choice and quality improvement – a desirable outcome for consumers.

Initially, there were considerable apprehensions that international firms with their superior technology, marketing skills and financial strength would wipe out domestic firms (and brand names) in many of these industries. To some extent this has indeed happened – in the aerated drink market, for instance. The same is partly true in the automotive industry as well: Fiat gradually acquired Premier Auto (its erstwhile licensee); Hindustan Motors (an erstwhile GM licensee) has largely become a sub-contractor for GM and Ford, producing engines and transmission equipment.

But many technologically strong and financially sound domestic firms seem to have withstood the growing competition – at least so far. In some cases, domestic firms have severed their ties with their foreign collaborators to assert their managerial independence after some years of association, though such cases are only a few.[17] Further, contrary to many early apprehensions, bulk of the domestic firms (and brand names) have not been displaced from the market. Dominant domestic firms have sought to protect their market shares by expanding capacity and distribution networks, contributing, among other factors, to the boom in fixed investment in registered manufacturing in the 1990s [Nagaraj 2002].

Though foreign firms have acquired a visible presence in consumer durable goods industries, by and large, it has apparently not been an easy entry for them. While, again, no definitive estimates are available, popular reports suggest many of them overestimated the size (and the growth) of the domestic market, and the appeal of international brands, and thus now suffer from excess capacity and poor profits (*Financial Times*, April 25, 2002). Foreign firms seem to have realised the smallness of the domestic market, and price sensitivity of its consumers.[18] Reportedly, a few foreign firms have left India, while many others have staggered their investment and expansion plans.[19]

However, realising the narrowness of the domestic market, many foreign firms are discovering the way out is to indigenise production to reduce costs and secure economies of scale. Moreover, there seems to be a growing appreciation of the cost advantage of domestic manufacturing for exports. For instance, discovering that their car was too expensive for the domestic market, Ford has now found it profitable to use its Indian facilities for the external market. Reportedly, it has exported 30,000 CKD kits to China and South Africa last year [*Business World*, December 2, 2002]. *Samsonite* is apparently expanding its Indian operations for exports, while closing down its Europe plants. There are similar reports from ABB (electrical equipment manufacturer) and Cummnis (Diesel engine manufacturer) as well. If such a tendency gathers momentum, India could possibly emerge as a competitive manufacturing base in these firms' global production networks.

Problems with Infrastructure Investment

Foreign investment in power generation that attracted the largest approved FDI was predicated on securing a high and assured rate of return on invested capital – modeled after Enron's DPC. It was the first of its kind, offering exchange rate guaranteed 16 per cent rate of return on investment on power purchase by the Maharashtra State Electricity Board. The agreement was not based on competitive bidding, violating many established norms of investment planning for a project of that size and scope. This was apparently done in the early years of the reforms to signal India's eagerness to invite foreign investment.

Most of these power projects did not fructify, as they were based on unrealistic assumptions regarding the profitability and the market size. Moreover, as the Enron's Indian saga unraveled, most foreign firms discovered the state governments' inability to ensure the guaranteed return, hence cancelled their investment plans. The speed and secrecy, with which the Enron project was launched, ignoring the checks and balances in public decision-making, invoked considerable debate in the press, parliament and academia. In retrospect, many of the criticisms seem valid, denting foreign investment's popular image (and the credibility of its exponents).

However, there are probably other reasons as well. Much of the projected demand for power that formed the basis for inviting such a large FDI in this sector was apparently inflated.[20] After the industrial slow down since the mid-1990s, the demand-supply gap was found to be relatively modest [Nagaraj 2002]. Moreover, cost of production of the thermal power plants of many state electricity boards using domestic raw material and capital equipment were found to be lower than that of the proposed FDI (invariably using imported feedstock). With hindsight – consistent with much of what the critics maintained – the problem with the power sector was not so much the inefficiency of generation, but pricing and recovery of the user charges. Despite the much publicised reforms in the 1990s, the average revenue-to-cost ratio in the power sector has not improved.

Net Foreign Exchange Inflow

For long it has been held that foreign firms bring in limited net resources in the host economy, as they usually take a large surplus out of the country as dividends and royalties [Chandra 1991]. This, to some extent, is probably true of what happened in India in the early 1990s, though it may be hard to substantiate. One of the earliest changes in the foreign investment rules after the reforms was to remove the restriction on the foreign equity holding in the existing foreign firms – reversing the policy initiatives of the earlier period. Foreign firms were quick to seize the opportunity to issue large equity to themselves at a fraction of the market prices (when the stock market was booming). This meant, in principle, a substantial FDI inflow in the book of accounts during 1991-94, but in reality it was simply a book transfer without any fresh capital inflow. With a larger proportion of equity held by the parent firms, it is now possible for them to take out an ever-larger share of surplus in perpetuity.[21] Table 10 provides an illustrative list of the foreign firms that followed such a practice, and their gains due to the discount on the issue price of the fresh equity.

It only goes to show how sensitive foreign firms are about the managerial control. In the absence of suitable regulations, they would like to retain an absolute control that may not be desirable for the host country. However, it is often argued that majority equity holding is necessary for international firms to be assured enough to bring in the latest technology that could potentially have positive spillover in the host economy. This view seems suspect. There is some evidence to show it is not the majority control, but the market structure that determines innovation and the introduction of new technology. Mani (1983), in a case study, showed that in the 1970s when the world's leading firms dominated the Indian automotive tyre industry, it was the new Indian entrants like Apollo and Vikrant Tyres that introduced innovations, and not the incumbent firms. Faced with such a threat, foreign firms quickly followed suit to protect their market shares.

Technology Spillovers

As noted earlier, one of the arguments in favour of FDI is the potential positive externality of technology into the host economy. However, in reality, the process may not be that simple. We have seen, that foreign investment does not necessarily lead to fixed capital formation; moreover, technical spillovers depend on the extent of value addition that is carried out in the host economy. For instance, assembly operations or production of simple consumer products is likely to have marginal externality.

For instance, most automobile firms – barring Hyundai and to a less extent Ford – have essentially set up minimal facility to assemble and paint their imported CKD kits, leading to a proliferation of firms and models with modest rise in domestic production and technological capability.[22,23]

In other durable goods industries too, foreign firms have acquired dormant domestic firms and/or resorted to contract manufacturing with the existing firms rather than set up green field plants.[24] While these may be efficient strategies for the firms concerned, the social benefit of such arrangements may remain modest. Our contention is consistent with Richard Caves's observation:

...While productivity spillovers from foreign subsidiaries to local firms are apparently widespread, they are neither ubiquitous nor independent of firms' market ambient structure. ... Spillovers may be a justification for LDC government policies to encourage flow of foreign direct investment. ... Justification is likely to be conditional on the country's state of development and the structure of particular industries in which foreign subsidiaries might alight [Caves 1999: 17].

Decline in Competition

FDI, in principle, brings in greater market discipline on the incumbent firms by increasing competition. But, as we have seen, foreign firms often acquired dominant positions by taking over domestic firms (and brands). This, again, is best illustrated by Coca Cola's acquisition of the dominant domestic competitor, Thums Up; and Hindustan Lever's – Indian subsidiary of Unilever – acquisition of its largest domestic rival, and the second largest firm in the industry, TOMCO, and the largest cosmetics firm, Lakme.

In principle, in a well functioning market economy such acquisitions would have attracted the provisions of the competition law. But they went unchallenged in India as the MRTP Act – the anti-trust law – was practically abolished as part of the economic reforms. Further, the government ignored the public and academic criticisms of such acquisitions, as it was keen to signal a positive outlook towards FDI. Thus, our examples show, the widely held view of foreign investment per se leading to greater competition needs to be taken with caution.

Foreign Exchange Earnings

One of the common apprehensions against foreign investment is the net drain of foreign exchange in the host countries. Many countries seek to overcome this problem by imposing foreign exchange neutrality clauses. Reportedly even the UK applied such a clause while permitting Japanese automotive firms in the early years of conservative reforms in late 1970s and the early 1980s. Many states in the US apply conditions of job creation while offering incentives for Japanese automotive firms. Though we do not have data to examine net foreign exchange outgo on account of foreign firms that came into India in the 1990s, the government, reportedly, has been lax in enforcing this clause or has diluted it.[25] This could be a serious matter, especially with many automotive firms that have set up are largely limited assembly plants.

Brand Names

In consumer goods industries intangible assets like brand names matter most; and, it takes a long time and effort to create them. A large home market is widely accepted to be advantageous in building such assets before 'exporting' them. India followed a prudent policy in this respect up to the 1980s. However, in the 1990s, as mentioned earlier, in soft drink industry, Coca Cola bought rival brand Thumps Up; Gold Spot and Limca; Pepsi purchased Mongola, Dukes and so on. The foreign firms destroyed many of the purchased brands that competed with their international ones. Coca Cola "killed" all competing brands except Thums Up, as it was too uneconomical to do so. Reportedly, even now, this cola drink sells four times as much as the worldwide brand of Coke. It only seems to show how 'path dependent' brand loyalty can be in consumer goods. Therefore there seems to be considerable merit in promoting indigenous brands that have the potential to compete in the world market. Such hasty policy changes could prove a costly mistake in the long run for India, as consumer goods are nothing but their brand names.[26]

Loss of Bargaining Power in the Technology Market

It is well accepted that dominant international firms have substantial market power, and many developed countries widely intervene in the technology market to protect and promote interests of their firms.[27] Indian policy, after the reforms, practically ceased to intervene in the technology market, significantly weakening domestic firms' bargaining position.

TABLE – 26.10

An Illustrative List of Foreign Companies that Issued to Themselves Shares at a Concession

Sl. No.	Company	No. of Shares Allotted (in million)	Preferential Issue Price (in rupees)	Market Price on Allotment Date (rupees)	Gain to the Company (in million rupees)
1	Colgate	11.3	60	700	7227.5
2	Castrol	3.5	110	1050	3325.7
3	Sesa Goa	3.3	120	1025	2968.4
4	Asea Brown Boveri	4.8	60	325	1260.0
5	Bata	4.7	35	325	936.7
6	Coats Viyella	7.5	65	260	1444.7
7	Alfa Lavel	3.4	73	290	738.8
8	Nestle	4.8	70	285	1021.6
9	Glaxo	4.5	75	255	808.0
10	Hoechst	2.2	70	370	645.3
11	Lipton	3.5	105	380	972.4
12	Proctor & Gamble	4.8	70	285	1021.6
13	Proctor & Gamble	1.9	225	340	223.1
14	Philips	7.7	40	205	340.0
15	Reckitt & Colman	3.0	100	380	848.4
	Total gain to the foreign firms				24737.0

Source: Jain (2001:219).

With the increasing role of financial collaborations, foreign technical agreements as a source of technology have steadily dwindled in the 1990s – both in absolute and relative terms (Figure 26.6) [*Economic Survey, 2001-02*]. Evidently, foreign firms do not want to part with their technology, as they can now come into India without a domestic partner.

Considering their superior financial and technical strengths, many foreign firms in the capital goods industry seem to have wrested managerial control in the existing joint ventures in the 1990s. For example, Caterpillar bought out Birla's stake in their joint venture manufacturing earthmoving equipment although the firm was doing well in the market. Many automotive firms started as joint ventures, but gradually foreign partners increased their financial stake by buying out domestic partners, as Indian partners were unable to bring in the resources to make up for the losses in the early years of the firms' operations. This happened at a time when the domestic interest rates were higher than the international rates. Foreign partners found it an inexpensive way to acquire a greater managerial control, especially as the currency was steadily depreciating.

Figure – 26.6

Decline in Technical Collaborations Agreements

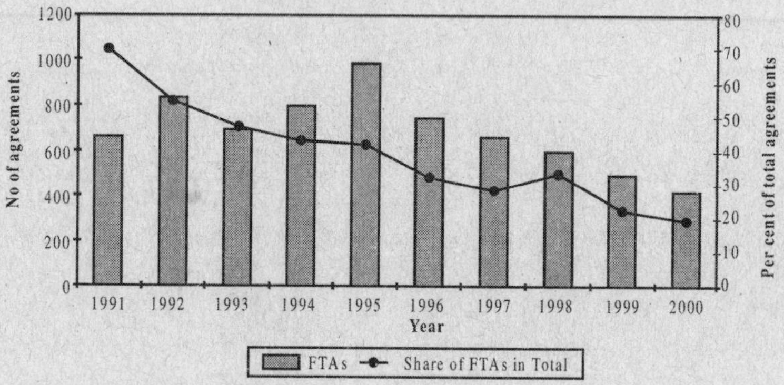

For instance, Honda bought out the Sriram group, and Ford acquired Mahindra's stake in their joint venture car projects. However, more recently, there are instances of the converse, where Indian firms have bought out their foreigner partners; for instance, TVS Motors and Suzuki, Kinetic motors and Honda, and LML and Piaggio. But such instances seem far fewer.

Arguably, the above examples illustrate the virtues of a market driven process for corporate control that is best left to it. Such a benign view may not necessarily favour developing countries and their consumers in the long run. For instance, the demise of Spanish automotive firms with its integration in the European Union, and the lack of technological and market dynamism in the Brazilian auto industry – despite substantial investment and output growth – probably suggests that strategic intervention to support domestic firms and industry are not incompatible with securing dynamic comparative advantage and export competitiveness.

In sum, while the entry of foreign firms has increased competition and improved the variety and quality of consumer goods, there are some disturbing signals. Foreign investment in infrastructure is a failure. Gradual loss of managerial control in many industrial firms, decline in competition in some industries, extinction of some leading domestic brand names and limited improvement in domestic production capability seem to be signs of concern.

VI

TOWARDS A REALISTIC FDI POLICY

It is widely believed that India has not done enough of policy reforms to attract substantially more foreign investment. Moreover, it is not the financial incentives but the lack of adequate infrastructure, bureaucratic delays and above all, the rigid industrial labour laws that have come in the way of attracting more investments [Sachs and Bajpai 2001]. This view seems to have many limitations. For instance, there is no evidence of a positive association between the extent of market oriented reforms and FDI inflows across developing economies [Easterly 2001]. Moreover, as discussed earlier, greater foreign investment inflow does not necessarily mean faster output and export growth. What, then, should guide India's foreign investment policy?

If history is any guide, foreign investment in infrastructure is potentially problematic. Latin America witnessed a wave of foreign infrastructure investment from the US in the 1930s, only to leave with the bitter experience of nationalisations in a couple of decades. It bears repetition that infrastructure is inherently capital intensive with long gestation lags, and low (but stable) returns over a long period. Market failures are ubiquitous in these industries, with considerable network economies necessarily inviting wide and deep state intervention. In a world consisting of politically independent nations with a growing number of democracies, the pricing of infrastructure is bound to be a political decision. Foreign firms with short pay back periods invariably find it hard to stay on, as it conflicts with the goals of developing economies caught in an increasingly uncertain world economy.[28]

There are also perhaps some India specific factors for the relatively small foreign capital inflow. It seems worth reiterating that India is still largely an agrarian economy, with land productivity being a third of China's, where the average disposable income after meeting food and clothing (wage goods) requirement is still relatively small. Price-income-ratio of most consumer goods that foreign firms usually sell is high by domestic standards, accentuated perhaps by cultural factors and regional heterogeneity of markets [*Financial Times*, April 25, 2002].

In infrastructure industries, the rupee cost of electricity supply by foreign firms seems high. Given India's fairly diversified industrial capability, and low labour costs, foreign firms may not have a cost advantage over the domestic producers – especially with the currency depreciating in nominal terms. This is perhaps best illustrated, again, by the Enron's DPC. With imported capital goods and fuel, and high operating cost due to international norms of costing, Enron's cost of production was found to be higher than the comparable new plants using domestic capital equipment [Morris 1996].

At the same time, Hyundai's large investment with consciously built-in high domestic content secured through economies of scale has succeeded in producing a small car that seems competitive both in price and quality. Reportedly, Hyundai proposes to use its Indian plant as a global hub for its small car [*The Economic Times*, January 2, 2003]. Thus, the key to increasing FDI inflow seems to lie in industries (and products) with relatively high technology that have large economies of scale, with substantial domestic content.

However, the foregoing reasoning still does not explain why foreign investment does not come to use cheap labour and skills for export of labour intensive manufactures – as it has happened in China. We are inclined to believe that the foreign investment policy lacks a clear focus. Unlike China, India has not invested in export infrastructure. In fact, as is widely accepted now, the share of infrastructure in fixed capital formation has declined sharply for nearly one and half decade now [Nagaraj 1997]. Further, what is needed is perhaps not large investment but suitable inducement to international marketers – trading houses and retail chains – to set up purchase offices and testing facilities to tap the potential of the domestic manufacturers.[29] It is widely acknowledged that China's export success largely lies in marrying its low cost manufacturing capability in Town and Village Enterprises (TVEs) with Hong Kong's highly developed trading houses and other long-established commercial organisations catering to international trade. While it is out of question for India to replicate the locational and historical advantage of Hong Kong for China, investment in export infrastructure in strategic locations and carefully tailored incentives to international trading houses (and retailers) merit a serious consideration. Similarly such investments are perhaps equally necessary to tap the growing potential for using India's labour cost advantage for doing back office jobs – business processes outsourcing – for international firms [*The Economist*, May 5, 2001].

Realistically, what is it that India expects from foreign investment, and how to secure it? In principle, openness to foreign investment should be strategic, not passive (or unilateral). History does not seem to support such an uncritical international integration as a proven route to growth and efficiency. If the recent experience is any guide, foreign capital is far from a major provider of external savings for rapid industrialisation of any large economy. It can only supplement the domestic resources, wherever they necessarily come bundled with technology, and access to international production and distribution networks. The terms of foreign investment will depend on the relative bargaining power of the foreign firm vis-à-vis domestic firms, backed by the state. Indian advantages are the availability of skilled workforce, cheap labour, and the size of the domestic market, which it should leverage as most successful countries have done. A telling instance of it is perhaps Korea's big leap in semiconductor and telecom equipment manufacturing in the recent years, as it seems to have tied liberalisation of domestic market to sharing of production technology.

If this view has any value, then how should we go about inviting FDI that is consistent with the economy's long-term interests? Foreign investment should be allowed mainly in manufacturing to acquire technology, and to establish international trading channels for promoting labour intensive exports.

VII

SUMMARY AND CONCLUSION

Ending its long held restrictive foreign investment policy in 1991, India sought to compete with the successful Asian economies to get a greater share of the world's FDI. Cumulative approved foreign investment since then is about $67 bn, but the realised amount is about a third of it – the ratio roughly comparable to China's. While the foreign investment inflow represents a substantial jump over the 1980s, it is modest compared to many rapidly growing Asian economies, and miniscule compared to China. While the bulk of the approved FDI is for infrastructure, the realised investment is largely in manufacture of consumer durable goods and the automotive industry seeking India's seemingly large and growing domestic market. Foreign investment in telecom and software industries has also been significant. Approved FDI has largely gone to a few developed states – similar to its concentration in the southern coastal provinces in China. A sizable part of the foreign investment seems to represent a gradual increase in foreign firms' equity holding (hence managerial control) in the existing firms, and acquisition of industrial assets (and brand names).

China's ability to attract a phenomenal amount of foreign investment is a puzzle for many. About 40-50 per cent of China's FDI represents its domestic saving recycled as foreign investment via Hong Kong to take advantage of economic incentives – popularly called the "round tripping". Another 25 per cent or so, seems to represent investment in real estate by overseas Chinese that is potentially problematic, as such investments could easily give rise to property bubbles. Thus, the quantum of foreign investment from the advanced economies that could improve domestic production capability is perhaps not very different from that in India, in relation to its domestic output. Contrary to the popular belief, China's foreign investment regime is said to be more restrictive than India's. Therefore, what India should be concerned about is not so much the absolute quantum of the inflow, but how effectively it uses its external openness to augment the domestic capability, and access foreign markets for its labour intensive manufactures.

For a careful economic analysis of the effects of foreign investment, considerable detailed statistical information is required – both at the aggregate and at the firm or industry level. In their absence, much of our analysis is indicative in nature, raising questions for further enquiry.

As the 1990s' experience shows, quite contrary to the popular perception, the size of India's domestic market is relatively small, given the low levels of per capita income. After meeting the needs of food and clothing (wage goods), income left for spending on products that most foreign firms offer seems small; their price-income ratio too high for Indian consumers. Therefore, many of them seem to be making efforts to indigenise production to reduce costs and secure economies of scale. In this process, many foreign firms are discovering the potential of low cost of manufacturing for exports.

Much of the approved FDI in infrastructure did not fructify, as the rupee cost of electricity supply by foreign firms is much too high for Indian consumers. This seems true for two reasons: one, prices of goods like electricity are widely subsidised, and cannot be increased without inviting public opposition; second, India produces much of these services at lower cost using domestic raw material and capital equipment.

Foreign investment in consumer goods industries has increased domestic competition, resulting in greater choice and quality improvement. While FDI inflow displaced some domestic firms (and brand names), the bulk of them have – at least yet – largely been able to withstand the competition by making large capital investment, and in expanding distribution networks.

However, in industrial goods there have probably been sizable acquisitions of domestic firms (and factories) whose details are not known. There are many instances of foreign firms gradually acquiring controlling interests, edging out domestic partners. Whether these firm-level changes get reflected in industrial efficiency in the aggregate – as many expected – is a moot point.

What should be done to increase foreign investment? It is popularly believed that a more liberal policy regime, industrial labour market reforms, and infrastructure investment are needed. While infrastructure improvement surely merits a close attention, one is not so sure if the extent of the reforms and the quantum of foreign investment inflow are positively related. Moreover, there is little evidence that greater FDI inflow ensures faster output and export growth. Such simplistic associations, usually based on cross-country analysis, seem to have support neither in principle nor in comparative experience.

What is needed is a strategic view of foreign investment as a means of enhancing domestic production and technological capability, and as also to access the external market for labour intensive manufactures – as China has precisely done. It seems valuable to reiterate what K N Raj, a perceptive observer of comparative economic development, noted early on in China's liberalisation drive, "It is certainly not without good reason that China has chosen to be hospitable even to multinationals with world-wide ramifications like IBM, evidently in the expectation of securing the know-how for building up semi-conductor industry of its own. Those who do not realise the implications of all this for India are living in a dream world of their own..." [Raj 1985].

Such interventions need selectivity, and strategic intent. Comparative experience seems to clearly favour such a policy stance.

Notes

[This is a revised version of a paper presented at the Conference on Foreign Direct Investment – Opportunities and Challenges for Cambodia, Laos and Vietnam organised by the State Bank of Vietnam and the IMF in Hanoi in August 2002. Following the usual disclaimers, the author gratefully acknowledges the comments and suggestions that he received on this study from K V Ramaswamy, C Rammanohar Reddy and M H Suryanarayana. The author is also indebted to Pradyumna Kaul for sparing time to discuss some issues on foreign infrastructure investment.]

1. For a chronological account of the policy reforms, see appendix of Bajpai and Sachs (2001). For detailed official statements on the policy changes, refer to the ministry of industry's annual publication, *Handbook of Industrial Statistics*.
2. There is some evidence to support this view. For instance, using crosssection data for 58 developing countries during 1978-95, Bosworth and Collins (1999) show that a dollar of FDI translates into an equivalent domestic investment, while no such association was found with respect to foreign portfolio investment.

3. For a long time developing countries have complained about foreign firms, as they seemed to hide their true operations from the host country rules. But in the recent years under easier capital flow regime the same legal maze seems to have begun to hurt tax compliance in the developed countries as well. Recently a report in the *New York Times* sought to unveil the legal maze of such operations [Johnston 2002].
4. Though largely ignored in the mainstream economic writings, much of the literature on the behaviour of international firms builds on Stephen Hymer's (1976) original contribution that focused on firm specific characteristic, including their market power.
5. It has long been held in the development literature that while short run cost of foreign debt is high, the long-term costs of FDI could be even higher [Lewis 1953]. In fact, it is such a view that prevailed in the successful industrialisation efforts of Japan, Korea and Taiwan that carefully regulated foreign investment inflow.
6. However, some recent literature in mainstream economics has argued that while the state may have succeeded in steering these economies in the past, there is little guarantee that in the developing countries today the state has similar capability to repeat the performance [World Bank 1993].
7. "*Flow of FDI* comprises capital provided (either directly or through other enterprises) by a foreign direct investor to an FDI enterprise or, capital received from an FDI enterprise by a foreign direct investor. There are three components in FDI: equity capital, reinvested earnings, and intracompany loans." (*World Investment Report*, 2001: 275).
8. Apparently, there is a discrepancy in Enron's declaration of its equity holding in the Indian entity. To the US bankruptcy court it has declared that it holds 50 per cent, but here it has declared that it owns 65 per cent equity.
9. The law requires all closely held (private limited) companies to submit their annual audited accounts to the department of company affairs that are, in principle, available to the public. But practice seems different as the law enforcement seems poor.
10. Korean firms have aggressively moved in to India, since they perceive it as their only chance to get into the last unexplored market, to beat their established corporate rival from Japan and the US.
11. Assessing the Brazilian reforms, Rocha (2002) said, "Mergers and acquisitions of private firms have been equally central to the restructuring of the Brazilian economy...A recent study shows that between 1995 and 1999 there were 1,233 mergers and acquisitions in which multinational corporations acquired control or participation in Brazilian industries – the devaluation of the real since 1999 making such purchases cheaper. A KPMG survey reveals that 70 per cent of all acquisitions in Brazil during the same period were undertaken by multinationals, to the tune of some $50 billion of FDI inflows" [Rocha 2002: 23].
12. Data for this graph is from the various issues of the UN's *World Investment Report*.
13. Figure 5 is from IFC (2002). In this graph, x-axis represents years, and y-axis measures FDI in million US dollar.
14. I am grateful to Cherian Samuel for providing this unpublished study.
15. Quoting an OECD study, *China in the World Economy*, Srinivasan (2002) reports that majority Chinese equity holding is mandatory in coal mining, design and manufacture of aircraft, oil and gas, printing and publishing, agricultural production in grains, cotton and oil seeds, domestic commerce, foreign trade, medical instruments and repairs, design and manufacture of ships.
16. I am grateful to Edward Graham for this unpublished paper.
17. For instance, in the two-wheeler industry, TVS, Kinetic and LML have terminated their technical and/or financial collaboration with Suzuki, Honda and Piaggio respectively to introduce indigenously developed motorcycle/scooter models that have been well re-

ceived in the market. Bajaj has stopped making motorcycles in joint brand name with Kawasaki for the domestic market, to introduce its own brand of motorcycles. In consumer products, Godrej, a leading domestic firm, terminated its comprehensive ties with Proctor and Gamble, and repromoted own brands to regain its lost market share. In wristwatch industry, Titan industries ceased its collaboration with Timex to expand internationally.

18. External liberalisation was predicated on the proposition that India has a core of about 200 million consumers with purchasing power close to that in the developed economies. After a decade's experience, many market research agencies have reportedly pruned the estimate to a quarter of the original.

19. For instance, BMW (motorcycles), Piaggio (scooters), Nine Gold (broadcasting), Kokna and Haier (Chinese electronics firms), Roche, Merck (pharmaceuticals), Blue Bunnies (ice cream) and so on have left India (*Business Standard*, October 28, 2002).

20. During the earlier policy regime, the Central Electricity Authority – an autonomous body – was responsible for looking into the techno-economic feasibility keeping in view the network externality of power generation and distribution system. Apparently after the deregulation, such official scrutiny was largely ignored in the belief that, 'markets know the best'. Hence, based on power demand projections drawn up by private consultants, large numbers of projects were approved.

21. Admittedly, the share of foreign controlled firms in the private corporate sector is, by most reckoning, small. However, they account for a substantial share of total profits and dividend in this sector.

22. In fact, considering the fragmented nature of the market, many automotive firms view their Indian operations as mainly distribution and 'brand building' exercises, rather than manufacturing ones. Therefore, it is hard to expect such operations to have significant positive spillovers.

23. According to knowledgeable sources, the Indian auto industry now is as fragmented as the Brazilian industry was when it liberalised its industry some 30 years ago. While Brazil failed to climb up the technology ladder, it was strategic technology importing countries like Japan and Korea that produced world-class automotive manufactures. If the present trend persists it seems likely that India will follow the Brazilian path, rather than the Japanese and the Korean one.

24. To illustrate, Hyderabad Allwyn, acquired by Voltas, after privatisation, has been engaged in contract manufacturing for the Korean firm Samsung [*Business Standard*, November 11, 2002].

25. Reportedly, Coca Cola has repeatedly refused to comply with the law in diluting its equity in the domestic capital market for the past six years [Guha 2002].

26. Apparently, the US tax laws provide tax credit for promotion of American brands abroad. We do not have evidence to substantiate this claim.

27. The US protection of the super computers manufacturer, Cray, despite competing products by Japan's Hitachi and Fijitsu being much cheaper is a well known case. Recently when, for the first time, the US department of agriculture bought a Fujitsu super computer, *The New York Times* considered the decision news worthy to report it (June 14, 2002).

28. Writing at the height of the foreign infrastructure investment boom in the 'emerging markets' in the mid-1990s, Wells and Gleason (1995) cautioned the American businessman against rushing into such investment precisely on the above arguments.

29. In fact, it was Mrinal Datta Chaudhuri (1981) who long ago emphasised the role of large domestic and international trading houses as market institutions in promoting manufactured exports from Korea and Taiwan.

References

Ahluwalia, Isher (1985), *Industrial Growth in India – Stagnation since the Mid-Sixties*, Oxford University Press, Delhi.

Amsden, Alice (2001), *The Rise of 'The Rest': Challenges to the West From Late-Industrialising Economies*, Oxford University Press, New York.

Bajpai, Nirupam and Sachs, Jeffery D (2001), "Foreign Direct Investment in India: Issues and Problems", HIID, Development Discussion Paper No 759, March.

Bosworth, Barry P and Collins, Susan M (1999), "Capital Flows to Developing Countries: Implications for Savings and Investment", *Brooking Papers on Economic Activity*, No 1.

Bruton, Henry (1989), "Import Substitution" in *Handbook of Development Economics*, Vol 2, edited by Hollis Chenery and T N Srinivasan, North Holland, London.

Carkovic, Maria and Levine, Ross (2002), "Does Foreign Investment Accelerate Economic Growth?" Finance Department, University of Minnesota, Mimeo.

Caves, Richard E (1999), "Spillovers from Multinationals in Developing Countries: The Mechanisms at Work", Working Paper No. 247, Department of Economics, Harvard University.

——— (1996), *Multinational Enterprise and Economic Analysis*, 2nd Edition, Cambridge University Press, London.

Chandra, Nirmal (1991), "Growth of Foreign Capital and importance in Indian Manufacturing", *Economic and Political Weekly*, Vol 26, Nos 11-12.

Chaudhuri, Sudip (1999), "Growth and Structural Change in the Pharmaceutical Industry in India", Indian Institute of Management, Calcutta WP No 356/99.

Datta Chaudhuri, M K (1981), "Industrialisation and Foreign Trade: The Development Experiences of South Korea and Philippines" in E Lee (ed) *Export Led Industrialisation and Development*, ILO, Geneva.

Easterly, William (2001), "The Lost Decades: Developing Countries Stagnation in spite of Policy Reforms 1980-1998", *Journal of Economic Growth*, Vol 6, June.

Guha Thakurta, Paranjoy (2002), "Coke: Arrogance of a Multinational", www.rediff.com, July 20.

Helleiner, G K (1989), "Transnational Corporations and Direct Foreign Investment" in *Handbook of Development Economics*, Vol 2, edited by H Chenery and T N Srinivasan, Elsevier Science Publishers B V.

Hymer, Stephen (1976), *The International Operations of National Firms: A Study of Direct Foreign Investment*, MIT Press, Massachusetts.

International Finance Corporation (2002), "Business Environment and Surveys", (mimeo), Washington DC.

Jain, Virendra (2001), *Investors Beware*, Macmillan India, Delhi.

Johnston, David Cay (2002), "Tax Treaties with Small Nations Turn into a New Shield for Profit", *The New York Times*, April 16.

Kumar, Nagesh (2000), "Mergers and Acquisitions by MNEs: Patterns and Implications", *Economic and Political Weekly*, August 5.

Lall, Sanjaya (1989), *Learning to Industrialise*, Macmillan, London.

——— (1982), *Developing Countries as Exporters of Technology*, Macmillan, London.

Lewis, W Arthur (1953), *Aspects of Industrialization*, Bank of Egypt, Cairo.

Mani, Sunil (1983), *Industrial Concentration and Economic Behaviour: Case Study of Indian Tyre Industry*, Centre for Development Studies, Trivandrum.

Mehta, Abhy (1999), *Power Play: A Study of the Enron Project*, Orient Longman, Hyderabad.

Morris, Sebastian (1996), "Political Economy of Electric Power in India", *Economic and Political Weekly*, Vol 31, No 21, May 25.

Nagaraj R (2002), "Performance of India's Manufacturing Sector in the 1990s: Some Tentative Findings" in Shuji Uchikawa (ed) *Economic Reforms and Industrial Structure in India*, Manohar, Delhi.

——— (1997), "What has Happened Since 1991? Assessment of India's Economic Reforms", *Economic and Political Weekly*, Vol 32, No 44-45.

——— (1996), "India's Capital Market Growth: Trends, Explanations and Evidence", *Economic and Political Weekly*, Vol 31, Nos 35-37 (Special Number), 1996.

Rao, K S Chalapati, Murthy, M R and Ranganathan, K V K (1999), "Foreign Direct Investment in the Post-Liberalisation Period: An Overview", *Journal of Indian School of Political Economy*, Vol 11, No 3, Jul-Sept.

Rao, Chalapati K S and Murthy, M R (1999), "Foreign Direct Investment" in *Alternative Economic Survey, 1991-98: Seven Years of Structural Adjustment*, Alternative Survey Group, New Delhi.

Reserve Bank of India (2001), *Handbook of Statistics on Indian Economy*, Mumbai.

Rocha, Geisa Maria (2002), "Neo-Dependency in Brazil", *New Left Review*, No 16, July-August.

Srinivassan, G (2002), "Secret of China's FDI Riches", *Business Line*, December 6, 2002.

Subramaniam, K K (1991), "Technological Capability under Economic Liberalism: Experience of Indian Industry in the Eighties", *Economic and Political Weekly*, Vol 26, No 35, August 31.

Tseng, Wanda and Harm Zebregs (2002), "Foreign Direct Investment in China: Some Lessons for other Countries", IMF Policy Discussion Paper (PDP/02/03), Washington DC.

Wells, Louis T and Gleason, Eric S (1995), "Is Foreign Infrastructure Investment Still too Risky?", *Harvard Business Review*, September- October.

World Bank (1993), *The East Asian Miracle: Economic Growth And Public Policy*, Oxford University Press, New York.

Economic and Political Weekly, April 26, 2003, (with permission from the author).

27

Globalisation and Its Impact

C. Rangarajan

Introduction

Globalisation has become an expression of common usage. Unfortunately, it connotes different things to different people. To some, it represents a brave new world with no barriers. For some others, it spells doom and destruction. We need to have a clear understanding of what globalisation stands for, if we have to deal with a phenomenon that is willy-nilly gathering momentum.

As we begin analysing the implications of globalisation, several questions arise. What is globalisation? Is it purely an economic concept? Is this a new phenomenon? What are the benefits of globalisation? Who gets hurt in the process of globalisation? Is globalisation intrinsically inequitous? Is it possible for individual countries to isolate themselves from globalisation? What are the complementary institutions and policies that countries can build to protect themselves or to gain maximum benefits? Where does India stand in this race for globalisation? Is she a potential gainer or loser?

Broadly speaking, the term 'globalisation' means integration of economies and societies through cross country flows of information, ideas, technologies, goods, services, capital, finance and people. The essence of globalisation is connectivity. Cross border integration can have several dimensions — cultural, social, political and economic. In fact, some people fear cultural and social integration even more than economic integration. The fear of "cultural hegemony" haunts many. However, we use the term globalisation in this article in the more limited sense of economic integration which can happen through the three channels of (a) trade in goods and services, (b) movement of capital and (c) flow of finance. Besides, there is also the channel through movement of people.

Historical Development

Historically, globalisation has been a process with highs and lows. During the Pre-World War I period of 1870 to 1914, there was rapid integration of the economies in terms of trade flows, movement of capital and migration of people (Tables 27.1, 27.2 and 27.3). The 19th century had witnessed some revolutionary breakthroughs in communication and transport with the emergence of railroad, steamship and telegraph (Frankel, 2000). Keynes wrote in 1920 "What an extraordinary episode in the progress of man that age was which came to an end in August 1914!.... The inhabitant of London could order by telephone, sipping his morning tea in bed, the various products of the whole earth..... he could at the same time and by the same means adventure his wealth

TABLE – 27.1

World Trend in Trade 1876-1959

Index No. 1913=100

Period	Trade Volume	
	Manufacturing	Primary Produce
1876-80	31	31
1896-1900	54	62
1911-13	94	97
1926-30	113	123
1931-33	81	116
1934-35	84	114
1936-38	100	125
1948-50	132	116
1951-53	178	133
1954-56	216	156
1957-59	251	182

Source: Maizels (1970)

Original Sources: 1. Industrialisation and Foreign Trade, League of Nations, Geneva, 1945

2. W.A. Lewis - World Production, Prices and Trade, 1870-1960, Manchester School, Vol. 20, No. 2, 1952.

TABLE – 27.2

Net Capital Flows as Percentage of GDP

Period	US	UK	Japan	France	Germany	Canada	Australia
1870-89	0.7	4.6	0.6	2.4	1.7	7.0	8.2
1890-1913	1.0	4.6	2.4	1.3	1.5	7.0	4.1
1914-18	4.1	3.1	6.8	**	**	3.6	3.4
1919-26	1.7	2.7	2.1	2.8	2.4	2.5	4.2
1927-31	0.7	1.9	0.6	1.4	2.0	2.7	5.9
1932-39	0.4	1.1	1.0	1.0	0.6	2.6	1.7
1940-46	1.1	7.2	1.0	**	**	3.3	3.5
1947-59	0.6	1.2	1.3	1.5	2.0	2.3	3.4
1960-73	0.5	0.8	1.0	0.6	1.0	1.2	2.3
1974-89	1.4	1.5	1.8	0.8	2.1	1.7	3.6
1990-96	1.0	2.0	2.2	0.7	1.9	4.1	4.0

Source: Obstfeld (1998).
Note : The figures refer to mean absolute value of current account as percentage of GDP.
** : Not Available.

TABLE – 27.3

Intercontinental Migration, 1801 to 1955

in millions

Items	1801-20	1821-50	1851-80	1881-1910	1911-40	1946-55
1. Emigration from Europe						
Total Flow per Decade						
(a) Gross	0.12	0.98	2.89	8.49	5.39	na
(b) Net	0.12	0.90	2.37	5.89	3.32	4.36
As Percentage of Population						
(a) Gross	0.1	0.4	1.0	2.2	1.1	na
(b) Net	0.1	0.4	0.8	1.5	0.7	0.8
2. Immigration into US						
(a) Gross	0.12	0.82	2.57	5.91	3.46	1.95
(b) Net	0.12	0.75	2.11	4.10	2.13	1.70
As Percentage of Population						
(a) Gross	1.7	5.5	7.2	8.5	3.0	1.3
(b) Net	1.7	5.9	5.9	5.9	1.9	1.1

Source: Kuznets (1972).

in the natural resources and new enterprise of any quarter of the world...". The Pre-World War I period witnessed the growth of globalisation mainly led by the technological forces in the fields of transport and communication. There were less barriers to flow of trade and people across the geographical boundaries.[1] Indeed there were no passports and visa requirements and very few non-tariff barriers and restrictions on fund flows (Streeten, 1998). The pace of globalisation, however, decelerated between the First and the Second World Wars. The inter-war period witnessed the erection of various barriers to restrict free movement of goods and services (Maizels, 1970 and Frankel, 2000). Most economies thought that they could thrive better under high protective walls. After World War II, all the leading countries resolved not to repeat the mistakes they had committed previously by opting for isolation. Although after 1945, there was a drive to increased integration, it took a long time to reach the Pre-World War I level. In terms of percentage of exports and imports to total output, the US could reach the pre-World War level of 11 per cent only around 1970. Most of the developing countries which gained Independence from colonial rule in the immediate Post-World War II period followed an import substitution industrialisation regime. The Soviet bloc countries were also shielded from the process of global economic integration. However, times have changed. In the last two decades, the process of globalisation has proceeded with greater vigour. The former Soviet bloc countries are getting integrated with the global economy. More and more developing countries are turning towards outward oriented policy of growth. Yet, studies point out that trade and capital markets are no more globalised today than they were at the end of the 19th century.[2] However, there are more concerns about globalisation now than before because of the nature and speed of transformation. What is striking in the current episode is not only the rapid pace but also the enormous impact of new information technologies on market integration, efficiency and industrial organisation.

Gains and Losses from Globalisation

The gains and losses from globalisation can be analysed in the context of the three types of channels of economic globalisation identified earlier.

Trade in Goods and Services

According to the standard theory, international trade leads to allocation of resources that is consistent with comparative advantage. This results in specialisation which enhances productivity. While the classical theory of comparative advantage was based on assumptions of perfect competition, constant returns to scale and fixed technology, the "new trade theory" which takes into account imperfect competition, increasing returns to scale and changing technology also comes to the conclusion that openness leads to improved rates of growth (Frankel, 2000). The new trade theory talks of dynamic gains from international trade. It is accepted that international trade, in general, is beneficial and that restrictive trade practices impede growth. That is the reason why many of the emerging economies which originally depended on a growth model of import substitution have moved over to a policy of outward orientation. Obviously, even in relation to trade in goods and services, there is one concern. Emerging economies will reap the benefits of international trade only if they reach the full potential of their resource availability. This will probably require time. That is why international trade agreements make exceptions by allowing longer time to developing economies in terms of reduction in tariff and non-tariff barriers. Special and differential treatment has become an accepted principle.

Movement of Capital

Capital flows across countries have played an important role in enhancing the production base. This was very much true in 19th and 20th centuries. Capital mobility enables the total savings of the world to be distributed among countries which have the highest investment potential. Under these circumstances, one country's growth is not constrained by its own domestic savings. The inflow of foreign capital has played a significant role in the development in the recent period of the East Asian countries. The current account deficit of some of these countries had exceeded 5 per cent of the GDP in most of the period when growth was rapid. In fact, at the peak, the foreign capital inflow into Malaysia in 1993 was 17.4 per cent of its GDP, while in Thailand in 1995 it was 12.7 per cent of the GDP (Rangarajan, 2000a). Capital flows can take either the form of foreign direct investment or portfolio investment. For developing countries the preferred alternative is foreign direct investment. Portfolio investment does not directly lead to expansion of productive capacity. It may do so, however, at one step removed. Recent events have shown that portfolio investment can be volatile particularly in times of loss of confidence. That is why countries want to put restrictions on portfolio investment. However, in an open system such restrictions cannot work easily. Even in relation to foreign direct investment, two aspects have raised concerns. First, there is always the fear that some part of the domestic economy will be controlled by external factors. In India, it is very often referred to as the "East India Company Syndrome". However, there is an increasing realisation on the part of transnational companies also not to act in a manner inconsistent with the policies of countries in which investment is made. Even in recent East Asian crisis it was found that foreign direct investment was a stable element. While to some extent fresh capital inflow was moderated, there was no outflow of foreign direct investment (Rangarajan, 2000b). The second aspect of concern in relation to foreign direct investment has been the fact that a significant part of foreign direct investment has been in the form of cross border mergers and acquisitions[3]. It is felt that FDI entry through the take over of domestic firms is less beneficial because such foreign acquisitions do not add to the productive capacity but simply transfer ownership and control from domestic to foreign hands. While this is correct, it overlooks the fact that the funds released to the domestic entrepreneurs because of the acquisition can be utilised for expanding capacity by the domestic entrepreneurs. Whether or not mergers and acquisitions lead to technological upgradation in the short-term is not clear. However, it is reported that over the longer term, effects could be different. Cross border mergers and acquisitions can be followed by transfer of new or better technology, when acquired firms are restructured to increase the efficiency of their operations. As recent events in India have shown while foreign direct investment is beneficial, public policy will have to be extremely careful in setting the conditions under which private capital is invited. Seeking guarantees and providing guarantees are inconsistent with an open system. Risk taking is the basic element of entrepreneurial spirit.

Financial Flows

The rapid development of the capital market has been one of the important features of the current process of globalisation. While the growth in capital and foreign exchange markets have facilitated the transfer of resources across borders, the gross turnover in foreign exchange markets has been extremely large. It is estimated that the gross turnover is around $ 1.5 trillion per day worldwide (Frankel, 2000). This is of the order of hundred times greater than the volume of trade in goods and services. Currency trade has become an end in itself. The expansion in foreign exchange markets and capital markets is a necessary pre-requisite for international transfer of capital. However, the volatility in the foreign exchange market and the ease with which funds can be withdrawn from countries have often created panic situations. The most recent example of this was the East Asian crisis. Contagion of financial crises is a worrying phenomenon. When one country faces a crisis, it affects others. It is not as if financial crises are solely caused by foreign exchange traders. What the financial markets tend to do is to exaggerate weaknesses. Herd instinct is not uncommon in financial markets. When an economy becomes more open to capital and financial flows, there is even greater compulsion to ensure that factors relating to macro-economic stability are not ignored. This is a lesson all developing countries have to learn from East Asian crisis. As one commentator aptly said "The trigger was sentiment, but vulnerability was due to fundamentals" (Reddy, 2000). In this context, it has been emphasised that opening of the capital account need not preclude moderate controls, either price based or regulatory, on capital flows. Controls should be selective, designed to achieve the specific objective of containing speculative capital. While there is, no doubt, that countries benefit by capital flows, the need to keep a watchful eye on foreign exchange markets becomes essential. What applies to trade may not necessarily apply to finance in full measure. However, while stringent capital controls may be adopted as a temporary shield as part of crisis management, they cannot be a permanent solution (Rangarajan, 2000b).

Concerns and Fears

On the impact of globalisation, there are two major concerns. These may be described as even fears. Under each major concern there are many related anxieties. The first major concern is that globalisation leads to a more inequitous distribution of income among countries and within countries. The second fear is that globalisation leads to loss of national sovereignity and that countries are finding it increasingly difficult to follow independent domestic policies. These two issues have to be addressed both theoretically and empirically.

The argument that globalisation leads to inequality is based on the premise that since globalisation emphasises efficiency, gains will accrue to countries which are favourably endowed with natural and human resources. Advanced countries have had a head start over the other countries by at least three centuries. The technological base of these countries is not only wide but highly sophisticated. While trade benefits all countries, greater gains accrue to the industrially advanced countries. This is the reason why even in the present trade agreements, a case has been built up for special and differential treatment in relation to developing countries. By and large, this treatment provides for longer transition periods in relation to adjustment. However, there are two changes with respect to international trade which may work to the advantage of the developing countries. First, for a variety of reasons, the industrially advanced countries are vacating certain areas of production. These can be filled in by developing countries. A good example of this is what the East Asian countries did in the 1970s and 1980s. Second, international trade is no longer determined by the distribution of natural resources. With the advent of information technology, the role of human resources has emerged as more important. Specialised human skills will become the determining factor in the coming decades. Productive activities are becoming "knowledge intensive" rather than "resource intensive". While there is a divide between developing and the advanced countries even in this area — some people call it the digital divide — it is a gap which can be bridged. A globalised economy with increased specialisation can lead to improved productivity and faster growth. What will be required is a balancing mechanism to ensure that the handicaps of the developing countries are overcome.

Apart from the possible inequitous distribution of income among countries, it has also been argued that globalisation leads to widening income gaps within the countries as well. This can happen both in the developed and developing economies. The argument is the same as was advanced in relation to inequitous distribution among countries. Globalisation may benefit even within a country those who have the skills and the technology. The higher growth rate achieved by an economy can be at the expense of declining incomes of people who may be rendered redundant. In this context, it has to be noted that while globalisation may accelerate the process of technology substitution in developing economies, these countries even without globalisation will face the problem associated with moving from lower to higher technology. If the growth rate of the economy accelerates sufficiently, then part of the resources can be diverted by the state to modernise and re-equip people who may be affected by the process of technology upgradation.

The second concern relates to the loss of autonomy in the pursuit of economic policies. In a highly integrated world economy, it is true that one country cannot pursue policies which are not in consonance with the world wide trends. Capital and technology are fluid and they will move where the benefits are greater. However, this is not a new phenomenon. For example, in the days of gold standard, maintenance of the external value of the currency in terms of gold content became paramount. Domestic monetary policy actions were subordinated to this overriding consideration. In fact, the fixed exchange rate system under the Bretton Woods arrangement also imposed similar constraints. In a more or less fixed exchange rate regime, no country can allow its inflation rate to be out of alignment with the inflation rate in the rest of the world. Of course, the flexible exchange rate regime which is now prevalent, gives a little more autonomy in the pursuit of domestic monetary policy. It is, however, impossible for any country to have domestic autonomy, fixed exchange rate and free capital flows. This is the famous impossible trinity. Similar to the limitations of monetary policy in an open economy, the process of globalisation imposes some constraints on fiscal policies of countries as well. Multilateral commitments have led many developing countries to reduce import duties which traditionally have been a major source of revenue. Free capital mobility results in tax competition among countries. At any rate, no country wants its tax regime to be less attractive for investment. While fiscal autonomy in this sense is reduced, the overall fiscal impact will depend on the elasticity of revenues to GDP and the impact of globalisation on growth of GDP and the tax base. As the nations come together whether it be in the political, social or economic arena, some sacrifice of sovereignty is inevitable. The constraints of a globalised economic system on the pursuit of domestic policies have to be recognised. However, it need not result in the abdication of domestic objectives.

Another fear associated with globalisation is insecurity and volatility. When countries are inter-related strongly, a small spark can start a large conflagration. Panic and fear spread fast. The only hope here is that despite integration, different parts of the world economy can be at different phases of the business cycle. In fact, until recently there had been a lag between the time the US reached the peak of the cycle and the European Union reached it. Such non-synchronised movements have had a beneficial effect. However, we are now facing for the first time since the 1980s the first synchronised downturn. There is greater insecurity because of the constant drive towards efficiency and competition. The downside to globalisation essentially emphasises the need to create countervailing forces in the form of institutions and policies at the international level. Global governance cannot be pushed to the periphery, as integration gathers speed.

Empirical evidence on the impact of globalisation on inequality is not very clear. The share in aggregate world exports and in world output of the developing countries has been increasing. In aggregate world exports, the share of developing countries increased from 20.6 per cent in 1988-90 to 29.9 per cent 2000 (IMF, 2001 and Table 27.4A). In fact, in comparing the share of the developing countries over time, care has to be taken to compare the share of the same set of countries over the entire time frame. In fact, four of the countries which are now classified as newly industrialised Asian economies, are excluded from developing countries when data on developing countries are presented in the various documents. We have included these four countries in the category of developing countries while computing the share and comparing the trend. Similarly the share in aggregate world output of developing countries has increased from 17.9 per cent in 1988-90 to 40.4 per cent in 2000 (IMF, 2001 and Table 27.4B). The growth rates of the developing countries both in terms of GDP and per capita GDP have been higher than those of the industrial countries. These growth rates have been in fact higher in the 1990s than in the 1980s. All these data do not indicate that the developing countries as a group have suffered in the process of globalisation. In fact, there have been substantial gains. But within developing countries, Africa has not done well and some of the South Asian countries have done better only in the 1990s.[4]

TABLE – 27.4A

Share in Aggregate World Exports

per cent

Year	Major Industrial Countries*	Developing Countries**	Asia	Africa
1988-90	55.5	20.6	10.8	2.0
1995	50.0	26.9	17.5	1.8
2000	47.7	29.9@	19.1	2.1

Note : * Major Industrial Countries include US, Japan, Germany, France, Italy, UK and Canada.

** Developing Countries also includes Newly Industrialised Asian Economies.

@ Excluding share of Israel which is shifted to Industrial Countries group.

Source: Various Issues of World Economic Outlook, IMF.

TABLE – 27.4B

Share in Aggregate World Output

per cent

Year	Major Industrial Countries*	Developing Countries**	Asia	Africa
1988-90	62.7	17.9	7.2	1.7
1995	46.2	41.2	24.4	3.3
2000	45.4	40.4@	25.0	3.2

Note : * Major Industrial Countries include US, Japan, Germany, France, Italy, UK and Canada.

** Developing Countries also includes Newly Industrialised Asian Economies.

@ Excluding share of Israel which is shifted to Industrial Countries group.

Source: Various Issues of World Economic Outlook, IMF.

While the growth rate in per capita income of the developing countries in the 1990s is nearly two times higher than that of industrialised countries (Table 27.5), in absolute terms the gap in per capita income has widened.[5] As for income distribution within the countries, it is difficult to judge whether globalisation is the primary factor responsible for any deterioration in the distribution of income. We have had considerable controversies in our country on what happened to the poverty ratio in the second half of 1990s. Most analysts even for India would agree that the poverty ratio has declined in the 1990s. Differences may exist as to what rate at which this has fallen. Nevertheless, whether it is in India or any other country, it is very difficult to trace the changes in the distribution of income within the countries directly to globalisation.

India and the External Sector

India's economic policy towards foreign trade and foreign investment in the first four decades after India's Independence was restrictive. Import substitution constituted a major element of country's foreign trade and industrial policies. The approach to foreign investment was equally constrained. The deficit on the current account was met mainly by borrowing and particularly from official sources. India's share in world exports which stood at 1.85 per cent in 1950 fell to 0.58 per cent in 1992.[6] In the wake of the economic crisis that overtook the

TABLE – 27.5

Key Average Growth Rates

Items Industrialised Countries*	Major Countries**		Developing		Asia		Africa	
	1982-91	1991-2001 $	1982-91	1991-2001 $	1982-91	1991-2001 $	1982-91	1991-2001
GDP Growth Rate	3.1	2.8	4.3	4.5	6.9	7.4	2.2	2.8
Per Capita GDP Growth Rate	2.3	2.0	2.0	3.8	5.0	6.0	-0.7	0.3
Exports Growth Rate (Volume)	5.1	5.9	4.2	8.7	8.4	11.3	2.8	2.9
Imports Growth Rate (Volume)	5.8	6.7	1.9	8.2	6.6	9.3	1.2	3.5

Note : * Major Industrial Countries include US, Japan, Germany, France, Italy, UK and Canada.

** Developing Countries does not include Newly Industrialised Asian Economies and Israel in the group of developing countries since 1997.

$ figures for 1991-2001 are based on the projections for the year 2000 and 2001.

Source: World Economic Outlook, May 2000, IMF.

country in 1991, the approach to and content of economic policy underwent a far reaching change. This change was reflected in trade and investment policies. An outward orientation began to emerge. Tariff rates have been steadily brought down while quantitative controls have been dismantled. Foreign investment policy has become proactive. Majority ownership by foreign investors is allowed over a wide spectrum of industries. Authorised foreign institutions are allowed to invest in Indian stock markets. The exchange rate of the rupee is by and large determined by the forces of supply and demand, although the central bank does intervene to avoid instability and volatility.

How has the Indian economy fared as a result of the steady opening up? India's growth rate has definitely been higher in the period following 1992-93, even though there are concerns about falling growth rate in the last two years. In relation to the external sector, the situation has been comfortable. The current account deficit which peaked to 3.2 per cent of GDP in 1990 has been declining and is remaining around only one per cent of GDP in the last few years. The foreign exchange reserves of the country has been increasing and stands today at $ 55.6

billion. The import growth rate has not shown any alarming rise. The increasing integration has not resulted in a jolt to the economy. On the contrary, the broad macro-economic indicators have shown an improvement. However, many concerns have been raised in relation to the impact of globalisation on Indian industries, agriculture in general and food security in particular and on the stability of the financial sector.

While recognising the fact that the Indian economy in the last decade has become more open, it is also necessary to note that the Indian economy is much less open than many other economies. Taking the most commonly used indicator of openness which is the proportion of import and export of goods and services to GDP, it is seen that this ratio has increased from 15 per cent in 1980 to 25 per cent in 1998[7]. However, this ratio of 25 per cent is much smaller than many other countries. For small countries like Malaysia and Singapore with a high outward orientation, this ratio exceeds 200 per cent. Among the industrially advanced countries, the United States is the only country which has a ratio similar to that of India (Table 27.6). Tariff levels are another indicator of openness. Here again, while India's weighted mean tariff rate has come down from 49.8 per cent in 1989-90 to 29.5 per cent in 1999, it is still high compared with many other countries (Table 27.7).

TABLE – 27.6

Foreign Trade as Percentage of GDP

Country	1970	1999
US	11	24
Canada	43	84
Japan	20	19
UK	44	53
France	30	50
Germany	**	57
Italy	32	49
EU	3.6	2.7
HongKong	181.0	261.0
Singapore	232	**
Korea	37	77
India	8	27

Note : Foreign Trade refers to exports and imports of goods and services.

Source: World Development Indicators, 2001, World Bank.

While the weighted average tariff rate is nil for Hong Kong and Singapore, it is as low as 2.7 per cent in European Union countries and 2.8 per cent in the US. However, it is of significance to note that the standard deviation of the tariff rates in US is high at 11.4 per cent which means that the rates on certain products are very high (World Bank, 2001).

TABLE – 27.7

Tariff Barriers in Different Countries

Country	Weighted Mean Tariff (All)		Standard Deviation		Weighted Mean Tariff (Primary)		Weighted Mean Tariff (Manfd.)	
	1988/89/90	1999	1988/89/90	1999	1988/89/90	1999	1988/89/90	1999
US	4.1	2.8	6.7	11.4	2.1	2.0	4.5	2.9
Canada	6.5	3.2	7.0	22.3	2.4	5.9	7.2	2.9
Japan	3.3	2.3	8.0	7.3	3.7	4.0	2.9	1.4
EU	3.6	2.7	5.6	5.0	2.8	1.8	4.1	3
HongKong	0.0	0.0	0.0	0.0	0.0	0.0	0.0	0.0
Singapore	0.5	0.0	2.2	0.0	0.0	0.0	0.6	0.0
Korea	13.8	5.9	8.1	5.9	8.1	5.5	16.9	6.1
India	49.8	29.5	43.8	12.4	26.0	24.9	69.9	32.3

Source: World Development Indicators, 2001, World Bank.

Framework of Policy

What should be India's attitude in this environment of growing globalisation? At the outset it must be mentioned that opting out of globalisation is not a viable choice. There are at present 142 members in the World Trade Organisation (WTO). Some 30 countries are waiting to join the WTO. China has recently been admitted as a member. What is needed is to evolve an appropriate framework to wrest maximum benefits out of international trade and investment. This framework should include (a) making explicit the list of demands that India would like to make on the multilateral trade system, (b) measures that rich countries should be required to undertake to enable developing countries to gain more from international trade and (c) steps that India should take to realise the full potential from globalisation.

Demands on the Trading System

There is considerable concern about the next round of negotiations in the WTO. Developing countries including India should project strongly their viewpoint. Without being exhaustive, the demands on the multilateral trading system should include (1) establishing symmetry as between the movement of capital and natural persons, (2) delinking environmental standards and labour related considerations from trade negotiations, (3) zero tariffs in industrialised countries on labour intensive exports of developing countries, (4) adequate protection to genetic or biological material and traditional knowledge of developing countries, (5) prohibition of unilateral trade action and extra territorial application of national laws and regulations, and (6) effective restraint on industrialised countries in initiating anti-dumping and countervailing action against exports from developing countries (Ganesan, 1999).

Concerns have been expressed about the impact of present WTO arrangements on Indian agriculture. However, under the present provisions, the degree of protection enjoyed by Indian agriculture is below what is permissible. In fact, in relation to some agricultural products, very recently the import duty was increased considerably. On the contrary, Indian agricultural products can gain greater market access in the advanced countries, as the tariff barriers come down in those countries. This expectation has not been fulfilled so far. The developed countries have played a clever game by taking recourse to 'Green Box' and 'Blue Box' provisions. But possibilities do exist for expanding the market for Indian agricultural products.

Negotiations are not that easy. We have to give in some areas to gain in others. The manoeuvering abilities of developed countries to steer the international trading system in the direction of meeting their own needs and concerns cannot be underestimated. They have shown themselves to be crafty in this area. However what is important is the approach. We must stay and fight whether they be intellectual property rights or public policy considerations. Doha showed some success in this direction. But the benefits of being part of the larger system should not be lost sight of.

Rich Country Initiatives

The purpose of the new trading system must be to ensure "free and fair" trade among countries. The emphasis so far has been on "free" rather than "fair" trade. It is in this context that the rich industrially advanced countries have a role to play. They have often indulged in "double speak". While requiring developing countries to dismantle barriers and join the main stream of international trade, they have been raising significant tariff and non-tariff barriers on trade from developing countries. Very often, this has been the consequence of heavy lobbying in the advanced countries to protect 'labour'. Although average tariffs in the United States, Canada, European Union and Japan — the so called Quad countries — range from only 4.3 per cent in Japan to 8.3 per cent in Canada, their tariff and trade barriers remain much higher on many products exported by developing countries. Major agricultural food products such as meat, sugar and dairy products attract tariff rates exceeding 100 per cent. Fruits and vegetables such as bananas are hit with a 180 per cent tariff by the European Union, once they exceed quota. Even in the case of dismantling the Multi-Fibre Agreement (MFA), it is stretched up to 2005 and has been back loaded so that much of the benefits will accrue to countries like India only towards the end (Stern, 2001). In fact, these trade barriers impose a serious burden on the developing countries. It is important that if the rich countries want a trading system that is truly fair, they should on their own lift the trade barriers and subsidies that prevent the products of developing countries from reaching their markets. It is important that these issues are brought to the forefront of the discussions at all international fora.

Actions by India

The third set of measures that should form part of the action plan must relate to strengthening India's position in international trade. India has many strengths, which several developing countries lack. In that sense, India is different and is in a stronger position to gain from international trade and investment. India's rise to the top of the IT industry in the world is a reflection of the abundance of skilled manpower in our country. It is, therefore, in India's interest to ensure that there is a greater freedom of movement of skilled manpower. At the same time, we should attempt to take all efforts to ensure that we continue to remain a frontline country in the area of skilled manpower. India can attract greater foreign investment, if we can accelerate our growth with stability. Stability, in this context, means reasonable balance on the fiscal and external accounts. We must maintain a competitive environment domestically so that we can take full advantage of wider market access. We must make good use of the extended time given to developing countries to dismantle trade barriers. Wherever legislations are required to protect sectors like agriculture, they need to be enacted quickly. Infact, we had taken a long time to pass the Protection of Plant Varieties and Farmers' Rights Bill. We must also be active in ensuring that our firms make effective use of the new patent rights. South Korea has been able to file in recent years as many as 5000 patent applications in the United States whereas in 1986, the country filed only 162

(Bergsten, 1999). China has also been very active in this area. We need a truly active agency in India to encourage Indian firms to file patent applications. In effect, we must build the complementary institutions necessary for maximising the benefits from international trade and investment.

TABLE – 27.8

India's Exports Performance Since Independence

per cent

Year	Share in World Exports	Year	Share in GDP
1950	1.85	1950s	6.0
1960	1.03	1960s	4.0
1970	0.64	1970s	6.0
1980	0.42	1980s	6.0
1990	0.52	1990-91	5.7
1995	0.63	1995-96	9.0
2000-01	0.67	2000-01	10.1

Sources: 1. Fifty Years of Indian Parliamentary Democracy, 1997, Lok Sabha Secretariat, New Delhi.

2. Economic Survey, 2001-2002, Government of India.

3. Medium Term Export Strategy, 2002-2007, Government of India.

Conclusion

Globalisation, in a fundamental sense, is not a new phenomenon. Its roots extend farther and deeper than the visible part of the plant. It is as old as history, starting with the great migrations of people across the great land masses. Only recent developments in computer and communication technologies have accelerated the process of integration, with geographic distances becoming less of a factor. Is this 'end of geography' a boon or a bane? Borders have become porous and the sky is open. With modern technologies which do not recognise geography, it is not possible to hold back ideas either in the political, economic or cultural spheres. Each country must prepare itself to meet the new challenges so that it is not bypassed by this huge wave of technological and institutional changes.

Nothing is an unmixed blessing. Globalisation in its present form though spurred by far reaching technological changes is not a pure technological phenomenon. It has many dimensions including ideological. To deal with this phenomenon, we must understand the gains and losses, the benefits as well as dangers. To be forewarned, as the saying goes, is to be forearmed. But we should not throw the baby with bath water. We should also resist the temptation to blame globalisation for all our failures. Most often, as the poet said, the fault is in ourselves.

Risks of an open economy are well known. We must not, nevertheless, miss the opportunities that the global system can offer. As an eminent critic put it, the world cannot marginalise India. But India, if it chooses, can marginalise itself. We must guard ourselves against this danger. More than many other developing countries, India is in a position to wrest significant gains from globalisation. However, we must voice our concerns and in cooperation with other developing countries modify the international trading arrangements to take care of the special needs of such countries. At the same time, we must identify and strengthen our comparative advantages. It is this two fold approach which will enable us to meet the challenges of globalisation which may be the defining characteristic of the new millennium.

Notes

1. According to Streeten (2001), there were much less barriers to immigration during 1870-1913, and that sixty million Europeans moved to Americas, Australia or other area for new settlement. According to Kuznets (1972), "...through most of the nineteenth and in the early twentieth century emigration from Europe was essentially voluntary, unrestricted, and in response to greater economic opportunities in the country of destination... During the nineteenth and early twentieth centuries, when intercontinental emigration was high and unimpeded by legal restrictions either at origin or at destination, the identity of the countries in Europe with high migration proportions changed continuously."
2. The share of exports in GDP for 16 major industrial countries was 18.2 in 1900 and 21.2 in 1913. In 1992, the share was still lower at 17 per cent for the industrial countries (Streeten, 1998). While international investment flows as measured by absolute value of current account exceeded 3 per cent of GDP before 1914, they slumped to less than half that level in 1930s and only after 1970 began to move decisively upward — reaching 2.3 per cent in 1990-96 (Obstfeld, 1998).
3. The ratio of the value of cross border M&As to FDI inflows in developing countries has risen from one-tenth in 1987-89 to more than one-third in 1997-99. Among developing regions, the ratio is the highest in Latin America and the Caribbean: it increased from 18 per cent to 61 per cent between these two periods, while in developing Asia it increased from 8 per cent to 21 per cent between the same periods (United Nations, 2000).
4. It is not easy to answer the question whether globalisation has led to a more unequal distribution of income in the world. Even if one were able to establish that the distribution of income globally had become more unequal in the 1990s, it is difficult to trace this

purely to globalisation. Apart from this, there are two other issues. First, there is the issue whether incomes of countries should be measured by actual exchange rates or purchasing power parity rates. Second, there is the issue whether all countries should be treated equal or given weights according to their respective population. Inequality measured by deciles, indicates that, between 1988 and 1993, the share of world income going to the poorest 10 per cent of the world's population fell from 0.88 per cent to 0.64 per cent, whereas the share of richest 10 per cent rose from 63.7 per cent to 66.9 per cent (Wade, 2001). However, the limitation of the measure of deciles is that, it focuses only on the extreme 20 per cent observations of the population. This measure ignores the improvement in economic performance of developing countries of Asia and western hemisphere, which lie in the middle of the distribution. In fact, the worsening of the income distribution may be due to the extremely low growth of certain countries particularly in the Sub-Saharan Africa. However, even according to the study by Wade, the Gini coefficient which takes into account the entire spectrum of distribution of income shows no deterioration, if countries are weighted by respective population and purchasing power parity exchange rates are used. There are also studies which show that the number of people in extreme poverty as measured by people below a certain poverty line has declined.

5. The level of GDP per capita in developing countries has increased from US $ 2,170 in 1990 to US $ 3,260 in 1998 with a compound growth rate of 5.2 per cent. In between the same periods, the level of GDP per capita in OECD countries has increased from US $ 16,040 to US $ 20,360 registering a compound growth rate of 3.0 per cent. These figures show that, although the growth rate of per capita income of developing countries is much higher than that of OECD countries during 1990-98, the gap between the respective levels of per capita income has widened from US $ 13,870 in the year 1990 to US $ 17,100 in the year 1998 (UNDP, 2000).
6. India's share in world exports experienced a declining trend since 1950 up to 1980. Afterwards, the share started increasing slowly from 0.4 per cent in 1980 to reaching 0.67 per cent in 2000-01 (Table 8). It can also be noted that, India's share in the world trade was as high as close to 4 per cent during 1860-1889 (Kuznets, 1972). During the first four decades since Independence, India's exports share in the GDP remained almost constant, where as India's share in world exports witnessed a declining trend (Table 8). This phenomenon is due to the fact that, the world exports were increasing at a faster rate than the growth rate of India's GDP.
7. Compared to this, the ratio of sum of merchandise exports and imports to NDP in India was 18.83 per cent and 19.57 per cent in the year 1894 and 1899, respectively (Brahmananda, 2001).

References

Bergsten, C. Fred (1999), "India and the Global Trading System", Fourteenth EXIM Bank Commencement Day Annual Lecture delivered at Mumbai on 10th March.

Bhalla, A.S. (ed.) (1998), *Globalisation, Growth and Marginalization*, IRDC, Ottawa.

Brahmananda, P.R. (2001), *Money, Income, Prices in 19th Century India*, Himalaya Publishing House, Mumbai.

Debroy, Bibek (1996), *Beyond the Uruguay Round: The Indian Perspective on GATT*, Response Books, New Delhi.

Dunning, John H. (1994), "Globalisation, Economic Restructuring and Development", 6th Raul Prebisch Lecture, UNCTAD, Geneva.

Feldstein, Martin (2000), "Aspects of Global Economic Integration", *NBER Working Paper*, September.

Frankel, Jeffrey A. (2000), "Globalisation of the Economy", *NBER Working Paper*, August.

Ganesan, A.V. (1999), Presidential Address delivered at the Fourteenth EXIM Bank Commencement Day Annual Lecture, Mumbai on 10th March.

Government of India (2002), *Economic Survey, 2001-2002*, Ministry of Finance, New Delhi.

——— (2002), *Medium Term Export Strategy*, 2002-2007, Ministry of Commerce and Industry, New Delhi.

IMF (2000), *World Economic Outlook*, May, Washington DC.

——— (2001), *World Economic Outlook*, October, Washington DC.

Keynes, John Maynard (1920), *The Economic Consequences of Peace*, Harcourt Brace and Howe, New York.

Kuznets, Simon (1972), *Modern Economic Growth: Rate, Structure and Spread*, Oxford and IBH Publishing Co., New Delhi.

Lok Sabha Secretariat (1997), *Fifty Years of Indian Parliamentary Democracy,* New Delhi.

Maizels, Alfred (1970), *Growth and Trade,* NIESR Students' Edition, Cambridge University Press, London.

Nayyar, Deepak (1995), "Globalisation: the Past in Our Present", Presidential Address at the Seventy-Eighth Annual Conference of Indian Economic Association, 28-30 December.

Obstfeld, Maurice (1998), "The Global Capital Market: Benefactor or Menace", *Journal of Economic Perspective*, Vol. 12, No. 4, PP.9-30.

Panitchpakdi, Supachai (2001), "If You Are in WTO Fold, You'll be Heard", interview with *The Economic Times* on 25th September.

Raghavan, Chakravarthi (1996), "What is Globalisation?", *Third World Resurgence*, No. 74.

Rangarajan, C. (2000a), "Understanding the East Asian Crisis" in *Perspective on Indian Economy: A Collection of Essays* by C. Rangarajan, UBSPD, New Delhi.

——— (2000b), "Capital Account Liberalisation and Control: Lessons from the East Asian Crisis", in *Perspective on Indian Economy: A Collection of Essays* by C. Rangarajan, UBSPD, New Delhi.

Reddy, Y.V. (2000), "The Asian Crisis: Asking the Right Questions" in *Monetary and Financial Sector Reforms in India* by Y.V. Reddy, UBSPD, New Delhi.

——— (2001), "Globalisation and Challenges for South Asia", B.P. Koirala India-Nepal Foundation Lecture at Kathmandu, *RBI Bulletin*, June.

Ricupero, Rubens (1997), "Is there Life after Globalisation? — Prospects for Development in the 21st Century" *Southern Economist*, June.

Sen, Amartya (2001), "A World of Extremes: Ten Theses on Globalisation", *The Times of India*, 16th July.

Stern, Nicholas H. (2001), "Globalisation, the Investment Climate, and Poverty Reduction", Lecture at ICRIER, New Delhi on 27th March.

Streeten, Paul (1998), "Globalisation: Threat or Salvation?", in Globalisation, Growth and Marginalization edited by A.S. Bhalla, IRDC, Ottawa.

——— (2000), "Integration, Interdependence, and Globalisation", *Finance & Development*, IMF, Washington DC.

UNDP (2000), *Human Development Report*, 2000, OUP, New Delhi.

United Nations (2000), *World Development Report 2000 — Cross-border Mergers and Acquisitions and Development*, New York.

World Bank (2001), *World Development Indicators*, 2001, Washington DC.

Economic Developments in India (2002), Vol.58, Academic Foundation.

Part V

Growth & Structural Change Since 1950 and Assessment of the Growth Experience

28

Growth and Structural Change Since 1950

The Indian economy has undergone a gradual transformation during the post-independence period, the pace of such transformation, however, being relatively rapid since the last decade. The present chapter discusses the nature, depth and genre of the transformation based on movements in some key macroeconomic parameters such as national income, saving and investment, their sectoral composition and industrial and occupational structure of workforce.

With the Indian economy shifting to a high growth path during the 'eighties, it was evident that the economy has emerged from a phase of stagnation, which had set in since the mid-'sixties (Table 28.1). However, the impressive growth performance of the 'eighties was also associated with a steady deterioration in a number of macroeconomic indicators. The crisis of 1991 had cast serious doubts about the sustainability of the growth experience of the 'eighties. Following the major shift in macroeconomic policy, oriented towards liberalisation and globalisation, in the wake of the 1991 crisis, the economy has once again been set on a high growth trajectory. Similar trends are also noticeable in the case of other key macroeconomic variables like saving and investment.

Long-Term Trends in Real GDP

The structural transformation that occurred in the Indian economy over the decades is a consequence of the development process witnessed since the beginning of planning in 1951. This is reflected, *inter alia*, in the growth rate and in the changing sectoral composition of the Gross

Domestic Product (GDP). In the 'eighties (1980-81 through 1990-91), GDP has recorded a trend growth rate of 5.5 per cent; the average rate of growth at 5.8 per cent being slightly higher than the trend rate of growth. However, there was considerable volatility in the annual growth rate, and for a number of years during this period, GDP grew by less than 5 per cent. The volatility in real growth rate is most reflected in case of GDP originating in agriculture. However, the high growth phenomenon of the 'eighties associated with a widening of the saving-investment gap and rising fiscal deficits, could not be sustained, as the experience of the crisis year of 1991-92 revealed, when the annual GDP growth rate declined to a low of 0.8 per cent.

TABLE – 28.1

Average Annual Growth Rate in GDP

(Per cent)

Period		Growth rate
First Plan	: 1951-56	3.6
Second Plan	: 1956-61	4.1
Third Plan	: 1961-66	2.5
Annual Plans	: 1966-69	3.8
Fourth Plan	: 1969-74	3.3
Fifth Plan	: 1974-79	5.0
Annual Plans	: 1979-80	-6.0
Sixth Plan	: 1980-85	5.4
Seventh Plan	: 1985-90	5.8
Annual Plans	: 1990-92	3.3
Eighth Plan	: 1992-97	6.8
Ninth Plan	: 1997-02	5.6
Annual Average	: 1997-98	4.8
Annual Average	: 1998-99	6.5
Annual Average	: 1999-00	6.1
Annual Average	: 2000-01	4.4
Annual Average	: 2001-02	5.8
Annual Average	: 2002-03 (P)	4.0
Annual Average	: 2003-04 (Q)	8.5
Annual Average	**: 2004-05 (A)**	**6.9**

Source: Planning Commission, *Indian Planning Experience: A Statistical Profile*, January, 2001 and CSO Estimates (Revised and Quarterly Estimates, June 28, 2002), CSO, June 30, 2005, Economic Survey 2004-05.

P : Provisional Q : Quick Estimates A : Advance Estimates

A comparison of the more recent period of the 'nineties (1992-93 to 1997-98) with the 'eighties (i.e., 1980-81 through 1990-91) reveals some notable features. In terms of average rate of growth, the performance in the 'nineties (6.5 per cent) was better than that recorded in the 'eighties (5.8 per cent). While both the industrial and the services sectors experienced *high* growth rates during the recent period, agriculture and allied activities, registered a relatively *low* order of growth as compared with the 'eighties.

The contrast between the 'eighties and the 'nineties is also sharp if the trend growth rates are considered at 1993-94 prices (i.e., during 1993-94 through 1998-99). This underlines a major structural shift in the Indian economy during the recent period, with economic growth becoming less vulnerable to agricultural performance and to vagaries of the monsoon. While the improvement in growth has emerged from both the industrial and services sectors, there is a marked difference in the sectoral composition of growth as between these two major sectors. Within the industrial sector, the major impetus to growth has come from manufacturing, while both 'mining and quarrying', and 'electricity, gas and water supply' registered lower rates of growth. The services sector, on the other hand, experienced higher growth in a more uniform and consistent manner with sectors like 'trade, hotels, restaurants, storage and communication', and 'financing, insurance, real estate, and business services', experiencing high trend growth rates. A possible interpretation of this phenomenon could be an upsurge of industry-related services sector in recent years.

Sectoral Composition of Real GDP

In developed and mature economies, the industrial and services sectors contribute a major share in GDP, with agriculture accounting for a relatively lower share. During the process of growth over the years, the Indian economy too experienced an improvement in the shares of industry and services sectors in overall GDP. The sectoral composition of real GDP at 1980-81 prices shows that the share of the agricultural sector in GDP gradually declined from 36.4 per cent in the 'eighties to 28.6 per cent in the 'nineties (1990-91 to 2000-01) (Table 28.2). In contrast, the shares of industry and services increased from 25.0 per cent to 27.1 per cent and from 38.6 per cent to 44.3 per cent, respectively during the same period.

Thus, there was a surge in the growth of the services sector since the early 'eighties, with the trend rate of growth being more pronounced in recent years. The recent years' experience shows that the growth of the services sector has imparted much of the resilience to the economy, particularly in times of adverse agricultural shocks.

TABLE – 28.2

Sector-wise Average Shares, Growth Rates and Contribution to GDP Growth

(Per cent)

Period	Services			Industry#			Agriculture		
	Share in GDP	Growth Rate	Contribution to GDP Growth	Share in GDP	Growth Rate	Contribution to GDP Growth	Share in GDP	Growth Rate	Contribution to GDP Growth
1	2	3	4	5	6	7	8	9	10
1950-51 to 1959-60*	28.2	4.1	32.2	16.0	5.7	25.3	56.0	2.3	42.5
1960-61 to 1969-70	31.4	4.9	38.1	21.1	6.5	32.9	47.8	2.5	29.2
1970-71 to 1979-80	34.4	4.5	52.7	22.8	3.7	28.7	42.8	1.3	18.6
1980-81 to 1989-90	38.6	6.6	43.6	25.0	6.8	28.9	36.4	4.4	27.5
1990-91 to 2000-01	44.3	7.6	57.6	27.1	5.9	27.6	28.6	2.9	14.8
1999-00	53.2	9.4	79.2	21.6	4.2	15.1	25.2	1.3	5.7
2000-01	53.7	5.0	67.4	22.1	6.2	34.1	24.2	-0.2	-1.4
2001-02	54.1	6.2	61.1	21.6	3.3	13.6	24.3	5.7	25.4

\# Inclusive of construction

* 9 year data for growth and weighted contribution since data for 1949-50 are not available. Due to rounding off, sectoral data may not add up to 100.

Source : National Accounts Statistics, CSO.

The RBI report on Currency and Finance (2000-01) states, the compositional shift in favour of services has been brought about by accelerated expansion in the services sector output at a rate of 7.6 per cent in the period 1990-91 to 2000-01 compared with 6.6 per cent during 1980-81 to 1989-90. While the growing contribution of the services sector to GDP is in line with the development experiences of a number of countries of the world, it is, however, not yet clear whether it is the comparative advantage that is driving up the share of the services sector in GDP or whether the sector also derives strength from the policies that are being pursued since the early 'nineties.

There has been a relative deceleration in the performance of agriculture during the 'nineties despite favourable monsoons, increase in net irrigated area and positive terms of trade. The decline in public investment and the limited infusion of new technologies may have contributed to the poor performance of agriculture.

However, Indian economy attained and maintained a high GDP growth in the 'nineties despite substantial deceleration in agricultural growth. For example in 1995-96 when the economy achieved a record 8.6 per cent growth in GDP, the agricultural sector witnessed a negligible 0.2 per cent growth over the previous year. In fact, as the RBI report on Currency and Finance states, "the recent years' experience shows that the growth of services sector has imparted much of resilience to the economy particularly in times of adverse agricultural shocks."

Thus, economic growth is becoming less vulnerable to agricultural performance and to vagaries of the monsoon. While the improvement in growth has emerged from both the industrial and services sectors, there is a marked difference in the sectoral composition of growth as between these two major sectors. Within the industrial sector, the major impetus to growth has come from manufacturing, while both 'mining and quarrying', and 'electricity, gas and water supply' registered lower rates of growth. The services sector, on the other hand, experienced higher growth in a more uniform and consistent manner with sectors like 'trade, hotels, restaurants, storage and communication', whereas 'financing, insurance, real estate, and business services' are experiencing high trend growth rates. A possible interpretation of this phenomenon could be an upsurge of industry-related services sector in recent years.

The phenomenal expansion of services world-wide led to services being regarded as an engine of the growth and even as a necessary concomitant of economic growth. Development economics suggest that development is a three-stage process. The dominance of the services sector in the growth process is usually associated with the third stage of growth. During the 1980s and 1990s, services accounted for a share of close to or above 70 per cent of GDP in industrialised countries and about 50 per cent in developing countries. In India, services accounted for 38.6 per cent of the GDP in the 1980s and 44.3 per cent in the 1990s.

Sustainability of Services Growth

Since the 1980s, growth process in India has been marked by a robust performance of services sector. While this is partially in line with the experience of developed countries, the Indian experience is somewhat unique in the sense that the sectoral shift in favour of services sector accompanied almost stagnant share of industry and reduced share of agriculture. The momentum continued during the 1990s; in fact, it was the growth performance of the services sector that provided a modicum of resilience to the overall growth of the economy, particularly in times of adverse agricultural shocks and industrial slowdown.

The set of economic reform measures initiated since 1991 also impacted on the performance of the services sector. First, reforms in the domestic industrial environment which resulted in rising manufacturing growth provided synergies to the services sector in the form of increased demand for producer services. Second, the liberalisation of the financial sector provided an environment for faster growth of the financial services. Third, reforms in certain segments of infrastructure services also contributed to the growth of services. Consequently, the services sector posted a much higher growth during the reform period as compared with the prereform period with its share touching nearly the 50 per cent mark. Finally, the rapid growth in services sector appears to have benefited from external demand; the typical example of which is the software industry and call centres. Interestingly, the decelerating trend in manufacturing and overall GDP seems to have been much less pronounced in case of services. Nevertheless, there are apprehensions about its sustainability in view of the contribution of "public administration and defence" to growth in services.

Against the above backdrop, the present section broadly looks into the following two issues: First, the performance of the services sector and second, the sustainability of services growth. After analysing the relative performance of the services sector in the reform period, the supply-side sources of services growth are examined followed by a discussion on the decomposition of services into three segments, viz., Producer services, Consumer services and Government services.

Performance of the Services Sector

Since the 1980s, services sector has come to occupy a position of dominance in the composition of GDP. The average share of services sector increased to 45.4 per cent during the reform period as against 38.9 per cent in the pre-reform period. In terms of growth, services sector posted a higher growth of 7.8 per cent during the reform period as against 6.7 per cent during the preceding period. However, services sector is actually an amorphous entity; on the one hand, it includes sectors like 'public administration and defence', largely independent of the level of economic activity, and on the other, it has sectors like 'trade, hotels and restaurants'. At the sub-sector level, 'trade, hotels and restaurants' continued to be the major segment in terms of its share in services. The growth performance improved for all segments during the reform period barring 'financing, insurance, real estate and business services'. However, the 'financing, insurance, real estate and business services' improved its share during the reform period when all other segments witnessed shrinkage in their respective shares, which seems to be the result of the financial sector reforms that led to emergence of new participants, instruments and markets. The poor performance of the non-banking sector, among others, has been the cause for the deceleration in growth of this sector. Nevertheless, the relative contribution of this sub-sector to the services growth has been maintained across the periods (Table 28.3).

TABLE – 28.3

Share and Growth of Sub-Sectors of Services

(Per cent)

Sector	1981-82 to 1990-91		1992-93 to 2001-02		Growth during the three phases of 1992-93 to 2001-02		
					1992-93 to 1993-94	1994-95 to 1996-97	1997-98 to 2001-02
	1	2	3	4	5	6	7
	Share	Growth	Share	Growth	Growth	Growth	Growth
Trade, hotels and restaurants	32.2	5.9	30.7	8.1	6.6	10.9	7.1
Transport and communication	16.1	5.6	15.8	8.9	5.9	9.7	9.6
Financing, insurance, real estate and business services	21.0	9.9	26.1	7.8	9.6	6.9	8.1
Community, social and personal services	30.7	6.1	27.3	7.1	4.0	5.8	9.1
Services	100.0 (38.9)	6.7	100.0 (45.4)	7.8	6.5	8.2	8.1

Note : Figures in brackets are share of services in GDP.

Source : Central Statistical Organisation.

Factors underlying the Services Growth

Growth of services stemming from capital productivity/total factor productivity could be seen as an encouraging development in a capital scarce economy like India. The gross value added from services registered a higher growth in the reform period even though the trend growth of Gross Capital Formation (GCF) in services decelerated to 5.7 per cent from 5.9 per cent in the pre-reform period. This could imply an improvement in capital productivity and/ or total factor productivity in services. There is a broad consensus that the recent surge in services has been contributed, among others, by the skill-intensive and high productivity activities such as Information Technology (IT) services, which have emerged as one of the fastest growing segments in the 1990s. The labour productivity in software services is estimated to be twice that of the manufacturing sector (Arora and Athreye, 2001). The ascendancy of services can also be seen as an outcome of the economic liberalisation and encouragement of private investment in industry and infrastructure (Government of India, 2002c). Besides, increased expenditure on public administration and defence, social services and rural extension services has had a positive impact on the services growth in the 1990s.

Given the inter-sectoral linkages of services sector with other sectors, particularly industry, performance of the commodity producing sectors has implications for the growth performance of services sector. To explore such inter-linkages, a demand function for services sector has been estimated using GDP from industry, exports of services and prices of services as explanatory variables. The estimates reveal a significant positive impact from the industrial sector as is evident from its elasticity at 0.11. Export of services also has a positive effect on the services demand with its elasticity at 0.02 while the impact of services prices turns out to be negative, as expected.

Composition of Growth in the Services Sector

(i) Intermediate versus Final Consumption of Services

For a meaningful analysis, the issue of absorption of services as intermediate vis-a-vis final consumption is examined by classifying them into Producer, Consumer and Government services. Their relative roles can provide insights as regards the sustainability of services growth. Activities like 'trade', 'transport, storage and communication', 'financing, insurance, real estate and business services', which are more of intermediate nature, are taken as producer services. Activities like 'hotels and restaurants' and 'other services', having the nature of final consumption, are classified as consumer services whereas 'public administration and defence' (PAD) are treated as Government services.

While producer and consumer services have recorded a higher growth in the reform period, the Government services have witnessed a marginal decline. This has implications for growth dynamics, not only for services sector but also for the overall growth process.

(ii) Producer Services

The increased share of producer services in total services in the reform period can be explained by, inter alia, the phenomenon of increasing relevance of outsourcing by the Indian industry. Peripheral service-oriented activities, which were carried out earlier in-house, are being contracted out to the outside agencies in order to focus on core competencies in an increasingly competitive environment in the reform period. Furthermore, the increasing share of producer services reflects the growing complementarity between services and manufacturing (RBI, 2002). The expansionary potential of services can be viewed from the fact that 50 per cent of the industries are directly or indirectly services-intensive (Bhowmik, 2000). The major demand for producer services emanates from the manufacturing sector as well as exports. The estimates of demand function for the producer services show that a rise in manufacturing output drives up the demand for producer services (elasticity 0.18). The export growth also leads to a rise in demand for producer services (elasticity 0.06). Increase in the price of producer services expectedly has a negative impact on demand (elasticity-0.24). However, as some of the producer services such as 'transport, storage and communication' are used as input for industrial production, a bi-directional relationship between industry and services sector cannot be ruled out.

Consumer Services and Private Final Consumption Expenditure

An upward trend was observed in consumer services, which recorded a growth of 8.0 per cent in the reform period as compared with 5.8 per cent in the preceding period. The increased growth in consumer services in the reform period has been accompanied by a similar growth pattern in private final consumption expenditure (PFCE) on services. The share of services in PFCE has moved up to 24.9 per cent in the reform period from 18.0 per cent in the preceding period. A disaggregated analysis of PFCE on services shows that medical care and hotels have recorded significant increases in growth during the reform period while growth in transport and communication has slowed down over the same period.

(iii) Government Services

Government services, comprising PAD is often singled out for the high growth in services since increased expenditure of the Government in the form of wage bill gets directly reflected in its value added even without any addition to services. An examination of the issue of faster growth of this sub sector in the 1980s showed that the tertiary sector growth was not solely due to increase in the growth of GDP originating from PAD (Nagaraj, 1990; Kumar, 1992). The steep wage hike in 1990s in line with the Fifth Pay Commission's recommendations brought back the issue into focus once again (Acharya, 2003). According to Shankar Acharya, a part of the services growth in the last four years is "spurious" in the sense that it simply reflects the revaluation of the subsector 'Public Administration and Defence' because of higher pay scales resulting from decisions on the Fifth Pay Commission. It is a peculiarity of national income accounting procedures that value added in this subsector of non-marketed services is estimated on the basis of cost. Thus higher salaries lead to faster growth here even when consumers of government services may not vouch for any increase in value added! These Pay Commission effects were spread mainly over three years, 1997/98 to 1999/2000 for the Centre and States. Allowing for trend growth, the "spurious" component of growth from this subsector to account for about half a per cent of GDP growth in each of these three years.

It is also observed that one percentage point of growth of 5.0 per cent in GDP for 1997-98 is attributed to the 20 per cent increase in real value added in the PAD sub sector arising chiefly from pay increases to Government servants (Government of India, 1999).

The growth in PAD, during the period 1997-98 through 1999-2000, has been far higher than growth in services excluding PAD and therefore PAD undoubtedly contributed to the overall growth of services. During the reform period as a whole, an assessment of services excluding PAD, however, contradicts the perception that PAD alone is responsible for higher services growth. Although the Fifth Pay Commission related pay increases might have distorted estimates of GDP originating from services for a few years, they do not affect the trend growth which remains at 8.2 per cent during the reform-period even if Government administration is excluded altogether. The log-linear trend growth of services with and without PAD has been broadly the same during the reform period (Table 28.4). On the whole, the services sector growth appears to have accelerated in the reform period, with the impetus coming from sources other than PAD.

TABLE – 28.4

Growth in Public Administration and Defence (PAD)

Year	PAD	Services Sector without PAD	Services Sector
	1	2	3
1992-93	4.9	5.4	5.1
1993-94	2.6	8.5	7.1
1994-95	1.3	8.0	6.6
1995-96	6.8	11.0	9.5
1996-97	4.1	7.6	6.7
1997-98	14.5	9.1	8.9
1998-99	10.3	7.9	7.6
1999-00	12.2	9.3	8.8
2000-01	2.5	6.9	6.5
2001-02	2.9	7.3	6.8
1992-93 to 2001-02*	7.2	8.2	8.0
1981-82 to 1990-91*	7.4	6.7	6.8

* Log-linear trend rate of growth.

Source : Central Statistical Organisation.

External Demand for Services

The growing role of tradable services in international trade and exchange has come to be recognised with the General Agreement on Trade in Services (GATS). India's share in world exports of commercial services has doubled from 0.6 per cent in 1990 to 1.2 per cent in 2000, while the share in world merchandise exports has gone up marginally from 0.5 per cent to 0.7 per cent during the same period. Interestingly, there has been a consistent surplus on account of trade in services. The compositional shifts in foreign trade in favour of services in the reform period has helped in the emergence of new sources of earnings in India's balance of payments. Earnings from software exports have increased from negligible levels in early 1990s to a level of US $ 7.5 billion in 2001-02. These are likely to surge by 30 per cent during 2002-03 as per the NASSCOM estimates. Thus, while the 1980s was dominated by tourism earnings, the second half of 1990s witnessed an unprecedented jump in India's earnings from new economy activities like software services exports and other information technology related skill intensive exports. The services exports thus, provided some element of stability to the external balance of the country and also positively impacted on the overall demand in the services sector.

Summing Up

The services sector has exhibited a strong trend component that has provided an element of stability to the growth process. The sector seems to have grown in the reform period, sustained by an increasing demand for producer and consumer services coupled with the external demand. The role of public administration and defence appears to have been limited in the growth process. The emergence of producer services as an important source of services growth reflects strong interlinkage with commodity producing sectors of the economy. Apart from providing inputs, services contribute to the outward shift of the industrial sector's production frontier by enhancing productivity growth. Conversely, services growth could be sustained provided adequate demand impulses are generated in industry or agriculture. Given India's comparative advantage in information technology, services growth momentum can be sustained by exploiting new opportunities in international trade in services, particularly, in the area of communication and information services, technology transfer and software.

Growth Rates in the 90's — Problem of Comparability

It needs to be mentioned at the outset that there is some problem of comparability of growth rates during the 'nineties. The real GDP numbers are available only up to 1996-97 with 1980-81 as the base year, while the GDP figures for the period 1993-94 to 1998-99 are available with 1993-94 as the base (consequent to the adoption of 1993-94 as the new base year by the Central Statistical Organisation (CSO) since February 1999). However, such changes in the base year emanating from the necessity of adapting the statistical system to the changing structure of the economy (Box 28.1), for the purpose of compiling the estimates of real GDP had been a regular feature in the past. Keeping those methodological changes in view and with a view to developing a more meaningful analytical framework for analysing the developments in the 'nineties, growth rates of real GDP and its components have been taken with 1980-81 as the base year for the period 1991-92 through 1993-94, and with the base year 1993-94 for the period 1994-95 through 1998-99.

BOX – 28.1

Evolution of Official National Accounts Statistics in India

In August, 1949, the Government of India set up a High Powered Expert Committee popularly known as the 'National Income Committee' under the chairmanship of Professor P.C. Mahalanobis. Based on the methodology

Contd...

...Box 28.1 Contd...

and the pattern of presentation recommended by this Committee, the first official estimates of national income with 1948-49 as the base year were prepared by the Central Statistical Organisation (CSO) and published in the *Estimates of National Income* in 1956. Ever since, the CSO has regularly continued to undertake a review of the methodology and the database used in the estimation of various aggregates. In the past, national accounts were revised decennially, changing the base to a year coinciding with the decennial population census. This was primarily because in the base year estimates, the information on work force played an important role and the work force estimates were obtained from the population census conducted decennially. Accordingly, the base years of the National Accounts Statistics series have been shifted from 1948-49 to 1960-61 in August 1967, from 1960-61 to 1970-71 in January 1978 and from 1970-71 to 1980-81 in February 1988.

The national income series with 1948-49 as the base commonly known as the 'conventional series' continued till 1966. The special feature of the revised series of national income with 1960-61 as base was the estimate of 'capital formation' and 'saving'. Accordingly, in 1969, two special Brochures viz., *National Income Statistics-Estimates of Capital Formation in India-1960-61 to 1965-66* were published. Subsequently, the aggregates of capital formation and saving formed an integral part of the national income series published annually by the CSO. In course of time, the coverage was further extended to include private consumption expenditure, factor incomes, and consolidated accounts of the nation and detailed accounts of the public sector. Accordingly, with effect from January 1975, the title of the publication on national income was changed to *National Accounts Statistics (NAS)* to depict the expanded scope of the publication. The revised series with 1970-71 as the base was published in *NAS 1978*. These estimates had the same scope, coverage and methodology as in the earlier estimates included in NAS. In 1988, CSO released a new series of national accounts with 1980-81 as the base year. This series, besides making use of the latest available data, undertook, *inter alia*, revision of estimates of consumption of fixed capital stock using the Perpetual Inventory Method. The coverage of the series was enlarged to include the state of Sikkim.

In February 1999, the CSO released a *New Series of National Accounts Statistics* with 1993-94 as the base year replacing the earlier series with 1980-81 as the base year. The CSO has used for the first time work force estimates based on National Sample Survey Organisation (NSSO)'s quinquennial survey on employment and unemployment (1993-94) instead of the work force estimates based on population census. This deviation was necessitated because in the population census, the work force (especially female work force in the rural areas) was not adequately captured.

Source: Report on Currency & Finance, 1998-99.

Trends in the Share of the Public Sector

The share of government sector in gross domestic product was 7.6 per cent in 1950-51, which rose to 14.9 per cent in 1970-71, 19.7 per cent in 1980-81 and 26.2 per cent in 1995-96. The increase in the share of the government sector has been due to the expansion of the economic activities of the State — enlarging administrative services as well as increasing productive activities in public enterprises. The factors contributing to the increase in the share of non-departmental enterprises are — setting up of new enterprises existing over, nationalisation of coal mining, banks and insurance and the like.

TABLE – 28.5

Share of Public Sector in Gross Domestic Product at Current Prices

	1970-71	1980-81	1995-96
Gross domestic product of public sector	14.9	19.7	26.2
(i) Government administration	6.5	7.3	8.4
(ii) Departmental enterprises	4.1	3.2	3.8
(iii) Non-departmental enterprises	4.4	9.2	14.0

Source: CSO, National Accounts Statistics, 1986 and 1998.

Share of Organised and Unorganised Sector in NDP

There has been a shift in the composition of NDP from the unorganised to the organised sector which is due to the process of development. The share of organised sector has risen from 30 per cent in 1980-81 to 40.3 per cent in 1995-96, thus resulting in a fall in the share of unorganised sector from 70 per cent in 1980-81 to 60 per cent. The change in the share of organised sector has mainly been brought about in the mining, manufacturing and services sector. On the other hand, in agriculture, forestry and fishing, the contribution of the unorganised sector instead of declining increased marginally from 95.2 per cent in 1980-81 to 95.9 per cent in 1995-96.

Inter-regional Variations of National Income

A study by Montek Ahluwalia on Economic Performance of the States in the post reform period brings out that there is considerable variation in the performance of individual states, with some states growing faster than the average and others slower. What is important is that the degree of dispersion in growth rates of SDP (State domestic product) across states increased significantly in the 1990s. The range of variation in the growth rate of SDP in the 1980s was from a low of 3.6 per cent per year in Kerala to a high of 6.6 per cent in Rajasthan. In the 1990s the variation was much larger, from a low of 2.7 per cent per year for Bihar to a high of 9.6 per cent for Gujarat.

TABLE – 28.6

Percentage Share in Net Domestic Product by Organised and Unorganised Sectors

	1980-81		1995-96	
	Organised	Unorganised	Organised	Unorganised
1. Agriculture, Forestry and fishing	4.8	95.2	4.1	95.9
2. Mining manufacturing, etc.	56.8	43.2	62.5	37.5
3. Services	39.9	60.1	48.7	51.3
4. Total	30.0	70.0	40.3	59.7

Source: CSO, National Accounts Statistics (1998)

The differences in performance across states become even more marked when we allow for the differences in the rates of growth of population and evaluate the performance in terms of growth rates of per capita SDP (Table 28.7). The variation in growth rates in the 1980s ranged from a low of 2.1 per cent for Madhya Pradesh to a high of 4.0 for Rajasthan, a factor of 1:2. In the 1990s it ranged from a low of 1.1 per cent year in Bihar and 1.2 per cent in U.P., to a high of 7.6 per cent per year in Gujarat, with Maharashtra coming next at 6.1 per cent. The ratio between the lowest (Bihar) and the highest (Gujarat) is as much as 1:7.

The increased variation in growth performance across states in the 1990s reflects the fact that whereas growth accelerated for the economy as a whole, it actually decelerated sharply in Bihar, Uttar Pradesh and Orissa, all of which had relatively low rates of growth to begin with and were also the poorest states. There was also a deceleration in Haryana and Punjab, but the deceleration was from relatively higher levels of growth in the 1980s, and these states were also the richest.

Six states showed acceleration in growth of SDP in the 1990s. The acceleration was particularly marked in Maharashtra and Gujarat, both of which were among the richer states, but there was also acceleration in West Bengal, Kerala, Tamil Nadu and Madhya Pradesh all belonging to the middle group of States in terms of per capita SDP.

TABLE – 28.7

Annual Rates of Growth of Gross State Domestic Product (SDP)

		1980-81 1990-91 % p.a.	1991-92 1997-98 % p.a.
1.	Bihar	4.66	2.69
2.	Rajasthan	6.60	6.54
3.	Uttar Pradesh	4.95	3.58
4.	Orissa	4.29	3.25
5.	Madhya Pradesh	4.56	6.17
6.	Andhra Pradesh	5.65	5.03
7.	Tamil Nadu	5.38	6.22
8.	Kerala	3.57	5.81
9.	Karnataka	5.29	5.29
10.	West Bengal	4.71	6.91
11.	Gujarat	5.08	9.57
12.	Haryana	6.43	5.02
13.	Maharashtra	6.02	8.01
14.	Punjab	5.32	4.71
	Combined SDP of 14 States	**5.24**	**5.94**
	GDP (National Accounts)	**5.55**	**6.89**

Notes: States are ranked in ascending order of per capita SDP in 1980-81. The growth rates have been estimated by fitting log linear trends to the State SDP data in constant 1980-81 prices obtained from the CSO and the GDP data from the national accounts.

It is important to note that the high growth performers in the 1990s were not concentrated in one part of the country. The six states with growth rates of SDP in the 1990s above 6.0 per cent per year are fairly well distributed regionally i.e. Gujarat (9.6 per cent) and Maharashtra (8.0 per cent) in the West, West Bengal (6.9 per cent) in the East, Tamil Nadu (6.2 per cent) in the South and Madhya Pradesh (6.2 per cent) and Rajasthan (6.5 per cent) in the North.

The performance of Kerala deserves special attention. Kerala has justly celebrated for its achievements in human development but it has also been criticised for under performance in economic growth. It is important to note that its performance in the 1990s showed a marked improvement compared with the 1980s. From an SDP growth rate much below the 14 States average in the 1980s it accelerated to a growth rate only marginally below the average in the 1990s. However, because of the low population growth, its performance in per capita SDP growth in the 1990s was actually much better then the average (Table 28.7).

The fact that Gujarat and Maharashtra grew at rates normally associated with "miracle growth" economies also deserves special mention. It should be emphasised that if these States have benefited the most in the post reforms period, their superior performance was not the result of any conscious policy of limiting the benefits of liberalisation to these States, as was the case for example in China, where liberalisation was deliberately limited to designated coastal zones. The superior performance of Gujarat and Maharashtra must therefore be attributed to the fact that the States were able to provide an environment most conducive to benefiting from the new policies.

Implications of Inter-State Inequality

The differences in per capita income and other indicators of social development across States have long attracted attention and for good reasons. Punjab, the richest State has a per capita SDP which is 5 times that of Bihar at the other end of the spectrum and although our Plans have never explicitly fixed targets for reducing these differences, there has always been an unstated assumption that inter-State differences would narrow with development. This can only happen if the poorer States actually grow faster than the richest States but the pattern of growth witnessed in the 1990s has been quite different, generating concern that we may be witnessing an increase in regional inequality, with the poorer States being left further behind.

According to Montek Ahluwalia, while inter-State inequality as measured by the gini-coefficient has clearly increased, the common perception that the rich States got richer and the poor States got poorer is not entirely accurate. A closer look at Table 7 shows a slightly more complex pattern of behaviour.

i. It is not true that all the richest States got richer relative to poorer States. Punjab and Haryana were the two richest of the 14 States in 1990-91. The growth rates of per capita SDP of these two States in the 1990s were not only lower than in the 1980s, but in both cases actually fell below the national average. Except for Bihar, UP and Orissa, all the other States therefore narrowed the per capita income gap with the two richest States.

ii. Maharashtra and Gujarat, which were just below Punjab and Haryana in terms of per capita income levels and therefore in the richer group, accelerated very significantly in the 1990s and grew at rates much higher than the national average.

iii. It is important to note that not all the poorer States lagged behind. Rajasthan, which was also one of the poorer States, experienced much stronger growth in per capita SDP, more than double that of the other poor States. Rajasthan's performance in terms of SDP growth is actually better than the average of the 14 States (see Table 28.7) but it slips below the average in per capita SDP growth because of higher rates of population growth.

iv. Performance of six middle income States (Tamil Nadu, Kerala, West Bengal, Madhya Pradesh, Andhra Pradesh and Karnataka) was clustered around the average rate. All six of these States grew faster in terms of per capita GDP than they did in the 1980s, though in some cases the difference was very marginal.

Implications for Policy

What are the policy implications that follow from the pattern of growth observed in the 1990s? First, it is important to emphasise that the mere fact that States grow at different rates should not be viewed as a failure of policy. Given our size and diversity, it is unrealistic to expect that all States will grow at the same rate. Some may grow faster than others at certain times because they may be particularly well placed to exploit some new opportunity that arises. For example, the green revolution technology was peculiarly well suited to conditions in Punjab and Haryana and led to a spurt of growth in these States in the 1970s. Coastal States may have a locational advantage in a globalising world because they suffer less from the disadvantage imposed on hinterland States by our poor transport infrastructure. Finally, differences in growth may arise because some States are better managed and therefore able to create an environment which generates higher growth. Since the "pay off" from superior management has also increased because of liberalisation it is very likely that variations in the quality of economic management will lead to greater inter-State variation in management performance than was the case earlier.

It needs to be clearly understood that the objective of balanced regional development should not be pursued by following policies which seek to achieve equality through a process of "leveling down" by preventing States from reaching their full growth potential. On the contrary, well managed States must be encouraged to reach their full growth potential, if only to show what is possible in Indian conditions. The lessons learnt from their superior performance could then serve as a model for others to emulate. This process is bound to generate some differences in growth performance across States, but such differences can have a healthy demonstration effect with best practice being spread through emulation.

Accepting differences in growth performance across States does not however mean that we should passively accept the pathologically low growth rates witnessed in Bihar, UP and Orissa. Continuation of such low growth rates into the future for a group of States representing almost a third of the total population, while the rest of the country enjoys robust growth has alarming implications. It means that inter-State inequality would continue to increase and poverty would become even more regionally concentrated than it is today, an outcome which would be socially and politically explosive. It would not only affect the politics of these parts of the country but, because of their size, it would undoubtedly have a debilitating impact on the politics of the country as a whole.

It is therefore necessary to increase the rate of growth of per capita SDP in these States from around 1.5 per cent experienced in the 1990s to somewhere between 3.5 and 4 per cent. This requires the rate of growth of SDP to increase from a little over 3 per cent per annum observed in the 1990s to at least 6 per cent per annum. This doubling in the growth rate of SDP is clearly necessary to deal with regional inequality since, by definition, inequality will increase if the poorer States do not grow at least as fast as the national average. However the acceleration in growth is also needed to tackle the problem of poverty in these States. Because they account for a large proportion of national poverty there is a tendency to think that the solution to the poverty problem in these States lies in intensifying anti-poverty programmes. This approach misses the point that a sufficiently broad based expansion in income earning opportunities, of the kind needed to achieve a sustainable reduction in poverty can only come from a substantially higher rate of growth, including especially faster growth in the agricultural sector. It is true that high growth by itself may not be enough. It needs to be broad based and it also needs to be supplemented by targeted poverty alleviation schemes to take care of groups which are left out of the growth process. However, these schemes can only be a supplement to a high growth strategy and not a substitute for it.

The Role of the Central Government

Given the severe resources problem of the poorer States, it is natural to ask whether the Centre can provide additional financial help to the weaker States? The Centre's own fiscal position is also far from comfortable and this makes it difficult to envisage any significant expansion in these flows.

While the scope for providing additional resources from the Centre to help the poorer States is very limited, an issue which has not received the attention it deserves is whether the Centre should introduce mechanisms which might improve the effectiveness of the resources it provides to the States. At present, Central assistance in support of State Plans is transferred by the Planning Commission as a "block transfer" without any significant linkage to actual performance. This system of unconditional transfer could be replaced by a system in which a substantial part of the Central assistance to the States is made available with a more explicit linkage to performance conditions.

Structural Transformation of Saving and Investment

Long-Term Trends in Saving and Investment

Sector-wise Saving and Investment Rates

The periodisation scheme for discerning the long-term trends in saving and investment is similar to that adopted for assessing the real growth performance. This is done for the sake of uniformity and for discerning the links between the structural changes in saving and investment, on the one hand, and the process of economic growth, on the other.

The rates of savings and capital formation (GDCF) showed a gradual increase from 20.4 per cent and 22.5 per cent, during the 'eighties (1980-81 to 1990-91) to 24.3 per cent and 25.7 per cent, respectively, during the 'nineties (1992-93 to 1996-97). The gross capital formation (GCF) too increased from 23.0 per cent to 24.6 per cent during the comparable period. The same outcome is obtained even if one considers the more recent period, viz., 1993-94 to 1997-98 (i.e., the 1993-94 series). A look at the period-wise average of sectoral saving and investment rates (as percentage of GDP at current market prices) reveals certain interesting features as outlined below :

(a) There has been a steady increase in the household sector savings with the financial savings outstripping the physical savings in the 'nineties (with the sole exception of 1995-96, when the rate of financial saving turned out to be *lower* than that of physical saving of the household sector). The household saving rate, which was 15.7 per cent during the 'eighties, increased substantially to 19.1 per cent during 1992-93 through 1996-97 (18.4 per cent during 1993-94 through 1997-98). This rise is primarily on account of substantial increase in the rate of household financial saving, notably in bank deposits, provident and pension funds, and claims on Government, supported by a marginal increase in the physical saving (investment).

(b) A sharp jump in the saving and investment rates of the private corporate sector was witnessed during the 'nineties. The private corporate savings, which remained below 2 per cent during the 'eighties, rose to 3.6 per cent during 1992-93 through 1996-97 (3.9 per cent during 1993-94 through 1997-98). The investment (GCF) rate of this sector, which was 4.4 per cent during the 'eighties rose sharply to 7.4 per cent during the 'nineties. In fact, the saving rate of the private corporate sector exceeded that of the public sector for the first time in 1988-89. The continued persistence of this behaviour has led to the widening of the gap between the two sectors during the subsequent period. The improved investment rates recorded in the 'nineties can be attributed to the liberalisation measures introduced in the economy and the consequent impetus afforded to the private sector in the successive budgets in the 'nineties.

(c) The public sector saving rates declined in both the 'eighties and the 'nineties. The investment (GCF) rates of this sector also declined in the 'nineties. The rate of public sector saving declined from 2.8 per cent during the 'eighties to 1.6 per cent during 1992-93 through 1996-97 (1.3 per cent during 1993-94 through 1997-98). The declining trend in the rate of public sector saving since the 'eighties is on account of increased dis-saving of Government administration. The investment (GCF) rate recorded by the public sector declined from 10.3 per cent in the 'eighties to 8.4 per cent during 1992-93 through 1996-97 (7.5 per cent during 1993-94 through 1997-98).

TABLE – 28.8

Share of Public and Private Sectors in Gross Domestic Saving

(Plan Period Averages at Current Prices)

Average for Plan Period	% Share in Total Saving		As % of GDP at Market Prices		
	Public Sector	Private Sector	Public Sector	Private Sector	Total
First Plan: 1951-56	16.2	83.8	1.7	8.6	10.3
Third Plan: 1961-66	23.7	76.3	3.1	10.1	13.3
Fifth Plan: 1974-78 #	21.8	78.2	4.3	15.5	19.8
Seventh Plan: 1985-90	10.8	89.2	2.3	18.6	20.9
Eighth Plan: 1992-97 *	6.9	93.1	1.7	23.0	24.7

Note : i) # : The Fifth Plan was terminated in 1978.
ii) * : Figures with old series data only.

Source : National Accounts Statistics, CSO.

Physical and Financial Saving of the Household Sector

The household sector saving has been the most important component of India's domestic savings performance. It is influenced by several factors like growth in income, macroeconomic stability, inflation, interest rates, financial intermediation, working population, insurance, pension and safety net, and tax benefits, etc. The financial savings of the household sector recorded an impressive growth from 7.4 per cent of GDP during the 'eighties to 10.3 per cent during 1992-93 through 1996-97 (10.1 per cent during 1993-94 through 1997-98). The rate of physical saving of this sector increased marginally from 8.3 per cent to 8.8 per cent during the comparable period; however, there had been a reduction in the rate of physical saving of the household sector to 8.2 per cent in the recent period of 1993-94 through 1997-98. The share of financial saving surpassed, on a sustained basis, that of physical saving during the 'nineties (the year 1995-96 is, however, an exception). The uptrend in financial saving of the household sector is indicative of increased financial intermediation, widening and deepening of the financial system as well as the movement of relative rates of return on assets of the household sector's portfolio.

Saving – Investment Gap

In a closed economy, domestic saving and investment must be equal *ex post*. In an open economy, however, such equality does not hold even *ex post*. The difference between the two is accounted for by the net capital inflow from abroad that gives a measure of a country's dependence on foreign saving for sustaining its economic development. Thus, definitionally, the saving-investment gap indicates the extent of indebtedness of a sector (economy) on other sectors (economies). Hence, this serves as a measure of macroeconomic balance (or its absence) with important implications for the growth potential of an economy (Box–28.2).

In a growing economy like India, as expected, investment has always outstripped domestic saving. However, the implied dependence on foreign saving (i.e., Saving – GDCF gap) has been, on an average, within 1.8 per cent of GDP for the entire period of the study – 1980-81 to 1996-97. Such dependence amounted to 2.1 per cent during 'eighties and then declined to 1.4 per cent during 1992-93 through 1996-97 (1.3 per cent during 1993-94 through 1997-98). However, immediately preceding the crisis year (i.e., 1991-92), the reliance on foreign saving rose to 3.4 per cent of GDP. Subsequent macroeconomic stabilisation measures led to a fall in the saving-investment gap to less than 2 per cent of GDP.

The important issues from a macro-economic viewpoint, however, are not only the level of saving-investment gap but also the nature and composition of investment. The end-use of saving into fixed capital formation or changes in stocks and inventories, thus, has important ramifications for the growth process. While technical considerations and the structure of production would require certain level of inventories, excessive inventory build-up withdraws resources from circulation and locks up funds. The changes in stock (unadjusted) came down from 2.2 per cent of GDP during the 'eighties to 1.6 per cent during 1992-93 through 1996-97 (0.7 per cent during 1993-94 through 1997-98), indicating perhaps better inventory management. The trends remained similar even after adjusting the numbers for changes in stocks.

The behaviour of the saving-fixed investment gap over the two periods also presents interesting results. The domestic saving has just managed to keep pace with fixed investment (adjusted) during the 'eighties. While the saving – fixed investment (adjusted) gap becoming mildly positive during 1992-93 through 1996-97 (0.3 per cent), in the more recent period (1993-94 through 1997-98) there had been worsening of the saving-fixed investment (adjusted) gap. The divergence becomes pronounced if the saving – fixed investment (unadjusted) gap is considered. Sectorally, the saving – fixed investment (adjusted) gap of the public sector showed a marginal deterioration from 6.9 per cent in the 'eighties to 7.0 per cent during 1992-93 to 1996-97; the deterioration would have been sharper but for some improvement recorded in the said gap during the recent period, viz., 1993-94 through 1997-98.

A sector-wise analysis of saving-investment gap reveals that the household sector was in surplus and the deficit of the public sector was higher than that of the private corporate sector. Similar trends are also recorded if the saving – investment (unadjusted) gap is considered. The saving-investment (adjusted) gap for the private corporate sector witnessed a steady increase from 2.4 per cent of GDP during the 'eighties to 4.1 per cent during 1992-93 through 1996-97 (4.0 per cent during 1993-94 through 1997-98). Such saving-investment (adjusted) gap for the public sector, which could be interpreted as an indicator of public sector's borrowing requirements at the macro level, remained unaltered at 7.2 per cent of GDP during the 'eighties and during 1992-93 to 1996-97; in recent years (1993-94 to 1997-98) there had been, however, some improvement in the saving-investment (adjusted) gap of this sector (at 6.8 per cent). The household sector, however, reported a steady improvement in its surplus position over the years.

Tenth Plan

The Tenth Plan has been prepared against the backdrop of the performance of the Indian economy during the Eighth and Ninth Plan periods, during which many of the commonly held beliefs regarding the potentialities and constraints governing the operation of the economic system have been brought into question. Although much of this has been covered in some detail in the Ninth Five Year Plan document and the Mid-term Appraisal of the Ninth Plan, it is nevertheless useful to briefly outline a few of the developments that have taken place in the Indian economy during the past decade in order to lay the groundwork for the macroeconomic strategy being proposed for the Tenth Plan and beyond. There are indeed four major features of the experience of the immediate past, which need to be highlighted.

First and foremost, there is now clear evidence that the growth rate of the Indian economy may no longer be constrained by the availability of savings or, more generally, investible resources. All previous Plans have been based on the implicit, and often explicit, assumption of a binding savings constraints. In other words, it has been assumed that the demand for investible resources always exceeds the supply, which implies a belief that the total level of investment in the economy is determined uniquely by the availability of savings. This assumption was questioned for the first time in the Ninth Five Year Plan, where it was pointed out that there was a strong likelihood that investment demand in the country may not be able to fully absorb the resources available. For this reason it was proposed that public investment may have to be increased sufficiently to make up for this lack of private investment demand, if growth opportunities were not to be missed. Subsequent experience during the course of the Ninth Plan appears to have borne out this contention.

The clearest evidence that savings or investible resources have not been the primary limitation on investment in the country is given by the persistent difference between the external capital inflows and the current account deficit (CAD) that has existed through much of the 1990s. Theoretically, the CAD represents the excess of total investment in the country over domestic savings, while external capital flows represent the inflow of potential savings from abroad. The excess of the latter over the former is therefore an indication of the failure of investment demand to absorb foreign savings. The position in this regard is shown in Table 28.9.

TABLE – 28.9

Absorption of External Resources

(US$ billion)

	Current Account Balance	Capital Account (Net)	Foreign Investment	Reserves to Imports Ratio (Months)
1990-91	-9680	7188	103	2.51
1991-92	-1178	3777	133	5.25
1992-93	-3526	2936	557	4.85
1993-94	-1158	9695	4235	8.64
1994-95	-3369	9156	4807	8.42
1995-96	-5910	4689	4805	5.96
1996-97	-4619	11412	6153	6.48
1997-98	-5500	10011	5390	6.88
1998-99	-4038	8260	2312	8.20
1999-2000	-4698	11100	5117	8.24
2000-01	-2579	8435	4588	8.56
2001-02	1351	10406	5286	11.27

The literature offers a number of alternative constraints to growth and investment. In brief, there are six : (a) the foreign exchange constraint, or the adequate availability of foreign exchange for ensuring balance of payments (BoP) sustainability; (b) the agricultural constraint, which arises from the insufficiency of 'wage goods', on one hand, and the lack of a widely dispersed distribution of purchasing power, on the other; (c) the fiscal constraint, or the availability of sufficient resources with the government to meet the development objectives in a fiscally sustainable manner; (d) the infrastructural constraint, which arises from the lack of adequate infrastructure for sustaining a high level of capacity utilisation in the rest of the economy; (e) the financial intermediation constraint, where weaknesses in the financial system prevents savings from being translated into investment; and of course (f) the general aggregate demand constraint in which there is a basic imbalance between the productive capacity of the economy and the level of aggregate demand.

Although each of these constraints is conceptually distinct, it is difficult to identify what exactly is the binding constraint with any degree of quantitative precision on the basis of ex-post data. The reason for this is that most of these constraints eventually manifest themselves either as an investment rate lower than the total savings rate (inclusive of foreign savings) or a rising rate of inflation. Nevertheless, it is important to identify at least which are the proximate constraints, since it has a crucial bearing on the macroeconomic strategy and conduct of policy. From the recent economic experience it is evident that neither the foreign exchange constraint nor the agricultural constraint provides an adequate explanation, since both foreign exchange reserves and foodstocks have been rising steadily and the rate of inflation has come down significantly. All the other four are, however, candidates, and none can be excluded on a-priori grounds. Therefore, the strategy has to address the likelihood of each of them being a contributory factor to the lower than potential growth performance.

The second issue that needs to be highlighted is the fact that the growth rate of the economy is no longer being driven entirely by the level of investment activity in the country. The most compelling proof of this assertion is available from the observed growth rates during the Eighth and Ninth Plan periods. A statement of the year-wise investment rates and the associated rates of private savings is given in Table 28.10. It may be seen that the real investment rate has been consistently higher during the Ninth Plan period as compared to the Eighth, with the exception of one year (1995-96). On the average, the Ninth Plan recorded a real investment rate of 26.3 per cent of GDP as compared to 24.9 per cent during the Eighth Plan. Nevertheless, the rate of growth during the Eighth Plan was significantly higher at 6.7 per cent per annum on the average as against 5.3 per cent during the Ninth Plan.

Although it is tempting to infer a dramatic fall in the efficiency of capital from these figures (Table 28.10), the real explanation lies elsewhere. This is the third feature which needs to be noted. It may be seen from the second column of the table that the investment ratios, when measured in nominal terms, actually declined during the Ninth Five Year Plan. A further point of interest that should be noted is that in four of the five years of the Ninth Plan period, the nominal investment rate has been at or below the private savings rate. This has never happened before in India. The inference that can be drawn from the differential behaviour of the investment rate when measured in real terms and in nominal terms is that while the pace of capacity creation in the economy actually rose during the Ninth Plan period, the role of investment as a component of aggregate demand actually declined. As a consequence, the evidence suggests that the Ninth Plan period was characterised by a steady decline in the levels of capacity utilisation. This conclusion is borne out by exercises carried out in the Planning Commission which indicate that the capacity utilisation in a number of sectors did decline in the Ninth Plan period, especially in manufacturing in which the assessed level of excess capacity at the end of the Ninth Plan was about 21 per cent of the actual production.

TABLE – 28.10

Investment and Private Savings Ratios

(as % of GDPmp)

Years	Investment Real*	Ratios Nominal	Private savings
1991-92	22.0	22.6	20.1
1992-93	22.9	23.6	20.2
1993-94	23.1	23.1	21.9
1994-95	26.4	26.0	23.2
1995-96	27.2	26.8	23.1
1996-97	25.1	24.5	21.5
1997-98	26.4	25.0	22.0
1998-99	25.4	23.0	23.0
1999-2000	26.7	24.3	24.1
2000-01	26.3	24.0	25.0
2001-02	26.4	24.4	25.2
Eighth Plan (1992-97)	24.9	24.8	22.0
Ninth Plan (1997-02)	26.3	24.3	23.6

* at 1993-94 prices

The fourth feature of the change that has taken place in the Indian economy over the years and which needs to be factored into the growth strategy is the role of agriculture. In the past, when the share of agriculture in the Indian economy was high, the growth rate of GDP was strongly influenced by the growth of agriculture through its direct contribution to the GDP. Over the years, however, the share of agriculture in GDP has fallen significantly and, as a result, the aggregate GDP has become relatively less sensitive to fluctuations in agricultural performance. This factor is of course well recognised, but the role of agriculture, and particularly agricultural incomes, in influencing GDP growth indirectly through the demand side is less well understood. Table 28.11 presents the share of agriculture in GDP and the share of nonfood consumption in rural expenditures over the last three decades. As can be seen, while the share of agriculture in GDP has fallen from 44 per cent in 1973-74 to 27 per cent in 1999-2000, nonfood expenditure has risen from 25 per cent in 1973-74 to nearly 41 per cent in 1999-2000. In other words, a 1 per cent change in the growth rate of agriculture would have affected the GDP growth rate by 0.44 per cent in 1973-74 but only by 0.27 per cent in 1999-2000. On the other hand, the indirect effects of change in agricultural growth through the demand for non-agricultural goods and services has actually gone up from a little under 12 per cent of total aggregate demand in 1973-74 to nearly 14 per cent in 1999-2000. In the future, as average agricultural incomes increase, this indirect effect of agricultural incomes on nonagricultural growth will become progressively stronger as the bulk of the incremental income in rural areas will be spent on non-agricultural goods and services and not on food.

TABLE – 28.11

Role of Agriculture in Growth

(per cent)

	Share of Agriculture in GDP	Share of Non-food in Rural Expenditures
1973-74	44.0	25.1
1983	38.7	34.4
1993-94	32.9	36.8
1999-2000	26.9	40.6

Keeping in mind these features of the Indian economy as they obtain at the end of the Ninth Plan, the growth strategy for the Tenth Plan period has to be decided. The most important feature that needs to be taken into account is the existence of large excess capacities, especially in the manufacturing sector. The existence of such unused capacity presents both an opportunity and a problem for accelerating the growth in the Tenth Plan. On the one hand, if much of these capacities can be brought into productive use, it would be possible to accelerate the rate of growth significantly without a commensurate increase in the rate of capacity creation through fresh investment. Thus, the aggregate investment rate can be significantly lower than would have been otherwise. On the other hand, the existence of large unutilised capacities is likely to curb the desire to invest by the private sector. Thus, the strategy will have to be developed in a manner in which these idle capacities are progressively brought into production during the early years of the Plan on the basis of demand generated from the non-private investment components of aggregate demand, with strong growth of private investment driving the growth process in the later years.

In stepping up the pace of public investment, it is necessary to take into account two important facets of the role of public investment and public borrowings on the economy. On the one hand, efforts to increase the share of public expenditure in GDP through enhanced borrowings tend to reduce private investment by pre-empting investible funds and causing what is known as 'crowding out'. On the other hand, as has been argued above, private investment can be positively influenced by public investment, both through its demand-generating role and through creation of infrastructure. Thus, under certain circumstances, public investment can actually lead to 'crowding in' of private investment. An objective appraisal of the Indian economy suggests that the danger of crowding out is practically non-existent at the present time. The excess of ex ante savings over investment demand implies that not only will public borrowing not lead to an effective reduction in resources available to the private sector, but that it may actually be necessary to absorb the excess savings and thereby prevent the emergence of deflationary pressure. Over the longer run, however, as private investment demand begins to grow strongly, the danger of "crowding out" can come into existence unless appropriate measures are taken. It is, therefore, extremely important that the increase in public investment that is being proposed during the latter half of the Plan be financed to the extent possible through corresponding increases in public savings.

Growth Targets, Investment Needs and Resources

Taking into account the above factors, the macroeconomic requirements for achieving the target rate of growth have been projected on the basis of the planning model that is used for such purposes. The parametric requirements of the economy are presented in Table 28.12. As can be seen, the achievement of the Tenth Plan targets hinges critically upon an expected reduction in the incremental capital output ratio from 4.53 during the Ninth Plan to 3.58 in the Tenth Plan.

TABLE – 28.12

Macro Parameters for the Tenth Plan (2002-2007)

		IX Plan	X Plan	Post Plan
1	Domestic Savings Rate (% of GDPmp)	23.31	26.84	33.01
2	Current Account Deficit (% of GDPmp)	0.91	1.57	3.13
3	Investment Rate (% of GDPmp)	24.23	28.41	36.14
4	ICOR	4.53	3.58	3.84
5	GDP Growth Rate (% per annum)	5.35	7.93	9.40
6	Export Growth Rate (% per annum)	6.91	12.38	******
7	Import Growth Rate (% per annum)	9.80	17.13	******

In order to appreciate the magnitude of the efforts that will be required to attain the Tenth Plan growth target, it may be more instructive to examine the macroeconomic aggregates as percentages of GDP. This information is presented in Table 28.13. As may be seen, the average investment requirement of 28.4 per cent of GDP involves a sharp acceleration in the investment rate from 24.4 per cent in the base year to 32.3 per cent in the terminal. Of this nearly 8 percentage points increase, more than five would be in the private sector and about 2.6 in the public. In order to finance an increase in the investment rate of this magnitude, domestic savings would have to rise by about 6 percentage points and the current account deficit by nearly 2 percentage points of GDP. Over the course of the Tenth Plan the size of the external sector is expected to expand substantially from under 27 per cent of GDP in 2001-02 to over 35 per cent by the end of 2006-07.

One of the most significant features of the Eighth Plan period was the sharp increase that occurred in domestic private savings. In the Seventh Plan, the private savings rate was 18 per cent, and it was expected to improve to 19.6 per cent. In actuality, however, it turned out to be around 22 per cent. This upward trend in the private savings rate continued in the Ninth Plan, albeit at a slower pace, with the average for the period being 24.1 per cent. Domestic private savings can be divided into two main components: (a) savings by household sector; and (b) savings by the private corporate sector.

TABLE – 28.13

Macro Economic Aggregates for the Tenth Plan (2002-2007)

(Per cent of GDPmp)

		IX Plan	2001-02	2006-07	X Plan
1	Gross Domestic Savings	23.31	23.52	29.41	26.84
	of which:				
	1a. Private	24.13	25.22	27.33	26.40
	1b. Public	-0.82	-1.71	2.08	0.44
2	Total Consumption	78.53	78.19	72.60	75.06
	of which:				
	2a. Private	65.32	63.98	60.50	62.00
	2b. Public	13.20	14.21	12.10	13.06
3	Gross Capital Formation	24.23	24.42	32.26	28.41
	of which:				
	3a. Private	17.08	17.09	22.36	19.97
	3b. Public	7.15	7.32	9.90	8.44
4	Public Borrowings	7.97	9.03	7.82	8.00
5	Current Account Deficit	0.91	0.90	2.85	1.57
6	Exports of Goods & Non Factor Services	12.34	12.43	15.11	14.24
7	Imports of Goods & Non Factor Services	15.09	15.04	19.98	17.71

It may be noted that in the classification used by the Indian statistical system, the household sector comprises not only of households in the common understanding of the term, but also of all unincorporated enterprises. Thus, the savings behaviour of the household sector is determined both by the level and growth of personal disposable income, and by the profitability and share in GDP of unregistered enterprises. Much of the increase in the savings rate of this sector during the Eighth and Ninth Plans has been the consequence of a higher growth in disposable incomes than of GDP arising out of the steady reduction in the tax/GDP ratio. In addition, during the Ninth Plan, the share in GDP of the unincorporated sector has gone up. During the Tenth Plan period, however, fiscal imperatives demand that the tax/GDP ratio be stepped up significantly, which would tend to reduce household savings. On the other hand, the rapid increase in incomes arising from higher growth will tend to raise it. On the balance, therefore, it is expected that the household savings rate will tend to decline during the Tenth Plan period.

The gross savings of the private corporate sector primarily comprises the depreciation reserve and retained earnings of corporate entities. The savings rate of this sector, therefore, depends upon its share in GDP, its profit rate and its capital intensity. This rate has registered a steady and sustained increase since the 1970s, and accelerated during the 1990s, particularly during the Eighth Plan. In the Ninth Plan, however, due to severe compression in profit rates during the later years, the savings rate of the corporate sector has shown a decline. During the Tenth Plan, as capacity utilisation in this sector increases and thereby improves both profitability and GDP share, it is expected that the savings rate of this sector will rise strongly.

The overall picture regarding the magnitude and pattern of domestic savings during the Tenth Plan is presented in Table 28.14. On the basis of the savings behaviour of households and the corporate sector as discussed above, private savings are projected to rise by just over 2 percentage points of GDP. Thus, as can be seen, in order to meet the domestic savings rate target, a fair proportion of the additional savings required will have to come from the public sector, which would be required to increase its savings rate from -0.8 per cent to 0.4 per cent, i.e. an increase of over 1.2 per cent of GDP. The required degree of correction is, however, much larger. As can be seen from Table 28.13, public savings has to rise from – 1.7 per cent of GDP in the base year to nearly 2.1 per cent in the terminal – a total turn around of 3.8 per cent of GDP.

TABLE – 28.14

Composition of Domestic Savings

(per cent of GDPmp)

		VIIIth Plan	IXth Plan	Xth Plan
1.	Public Sector Of which:	1.57	-0.82	0.44
	1.1 Government Sector	-1.50	-4.29	-2.41
	1.2 Public Enterprises	3.06	3.47	2.85
2.	Private Corporate Sector	3.95	4.90	6.10
3.	Household Sector	18.11	19.23	20.30
4.	Gross Domestic Savings	23.63	23.31	26.84

It may further be seen that the overall improvement in the public savings rate obscures the nature of the correction that is to be effected. The savings rate of public enterprises is actually expected to decline quite significantly during the Tenth Plan period. This is the result of two conflicting forces. On the one hand, the share of public enterprises in GDP is expected to decline due to the disinvestment process; and, on the other hand, the profitability of the remaining enterprises, particularly the State Electricity Boards, is expected to improve. It should be noted, however, that it was not possible to fully take into account the impact of disinvestment on the share of public enterprises in GDP because of the uncertainties involved in the process, and therefore, these are only indicative calculations. This should not create too many problems in the macroeconomic sense since any additional disinvestment will only result in a further decline in the share of public enterprises, which is exactly balanced by an increase in the share of the private corporate sector.

The more important issue that emerges is that the government sector will be required to reduce its dissavings by nearly 2 percentage points of GDP over the Tenth Plan period in order to meet the aggregate domestic savings target. In the absence of such an improvement, it is very unlikely that the growth target for the Plan will be achieved primarily due to a resource constraint towards the latter part of the Plan.

The most critical, and perhaps the most contentious, element of the macroeconomic projections made for the Tenth Plan is the investment requirement that has been specified. After the experience of the Ninth Plan, there may be some scepticism about the possibility of raising the growth rate of the economy by nearly 2.6 percentage points with an increase in the investment rate of just above 4 percentage points. These figures taken in isolation would appear to indicate that the incremental capital-output ratio (ICOR) being used for the additional growth is only about 1.6. Such an interpretation would, however, be completely wrong. It may, therefore, be desirable to spell out with some clarity the nature of the relationship between growth and investment that is being contemplated for the Tenth Plan.

The incremental capital-output ratio (ICOR) is a summary expression for the existing technical conditions and structural configuration of the economy which captures the relationship between investment and additional productive capacity. The first point that needs to be made is that the ICOR relates investment to capacity and not to output. The difference between the two is the level of capacity utilisation. Although ICORs are usually estimated by using output data, it is implicitly assumed that the level of capacity utilisation remains unchanged or appropriate corrections are made. Second, the ICOR is an a-priori technical construct, and not a figure that arises in an ex-post sense. It is therefore meaningless to refer to increases or decreases in the ICOR on the basis of short-period changes in growth rates or investment rates. Third, the aggregate ICOR for the whole economy is a weighted average of sectoral ICORs, which can be very different from sector to sector. Indeed, for anything other than discursive purposes, it makes more sense to estimate ICORs at the sectoral level than for the GDP as a whole. Thus, the aggregate ICOR depends crucially upon the sectoral composition of growth and investment. The sectoral structure of growth, in turn, depends upon a number of factors such as pattern of demand, the nature of inter-sectoral linkages, and the possibilities offered by trade. These complexities are best handled by the use of planning models which are designed to capture the linkages and constraints.

Recent theoretical research suggests that the relationship between the investment rate and the growth rate of capacity is not constant (see Box 28.2). As a result, rates of growth that are significantly higher than experienced in the past require investment rates which are proportionately not as high. In addition, adjustment has to be made for the availability of excess capacities, which can be brought into use to raise the growth rate, which further reduces the required investment. As has already been mentioned, there is substantial excess capacity available in the Indian economy, particularly in manufacturing, in the base year of the Tenth Plan. These factors have been taken into account while working out the sectoral structure of growth during the Tenth Plan and the sectoral ICORs. This information is presented in Table 28.15. As may be seen, the implicit sectoral ICORs, which have been computed as the ratio of actual sectoral investment rates to actual sectoral growth rates, have varied significantly between the Eighth and the Ninth Plans. Neither of the two sets of ICORs represents the true underlying technical relations because in the Eighth Plan capacity utilisation went up sharply, while in the Ninth it declined in most sectors. The ICORs for the Tenth Plan, by and large, lie between these two sets, and represent a possibly more justifiable estimate of the true ICORs, suitably corrected for the improved capacity utilisation that is expected during the Tenth Plan period.

It should perhaps be mentioned that the ICORs computed for the Tenth Plan period do not capture the significant improvement in efficiency that is sought to be brought about by policy and procedural reforms, and through better governance. It is expected, therefore, that if the policy and the governance imperatives that have been detailed in the Plan are carried out, there could be a further reduction in the ICORs.

BOX – 28.2

Incremental Capital Output Ratio : An Alternative Interpretation

The Incremental Capital Output Ratio is commonly measured as the ratio of investment rate to growth rate for a particular period. Some of the standard assumptions in the traditional Harrod-Domar framework of calculating ICOR included, inter-alia, (a) the economy is on a steady growth path, (b) there is no lag between investment and setting up of additional capacity, i.e. investment instantaneously translates into additional capacity, (c) there is a continuous full capacity utilization, (d) unchanging sectoral structure of the economy.

These are rather strong assumptions and are often violated in real life situation. For the Tenth Plan, an attempt was made to overcome some of these problems by computing the investment requirement of the economy based on what has been termed as 'net ICOR'. The long-term net ICOR have been estimated taking into account the lag structure of Investment, the average capital output ratio and the deprecation of capital stocks. From this approach, it follows that the investment requirement is lower for growth rates higher than the historical growth rates and vice-versa for lower growth rates.

Net ICORs were used to compute the potential output of each sector. The difference between actual and the potential output give the slack in the system for each sector for the base year, 2001-02. It was found that the slack varied across sectors and was 8 per cent in the aggregate. Sectors with slack implied that investment has already been made and capacity had been created. This existence of excess capacity could be used to generate higher output if utilised efficiently.

As far as the sectoral growth rates are concerned, specific mention needs to be made of four sectors that are critical for generating the desired growth in employment with relatively low capital investment requirements. These are agriculture, construction, other transport, and other services. The targeted growth rate in agriculture is significantly higher than in the Ninth Plan, but not as high as was recorded during the Eighth Plan. The reason for this is that the public investment rate in agriculture has dropped steadily over the past two decades and, as a result, this sector continues to be sensitive to weather-related fluctuations. It is hoped that the strategy and measures detailed in the Plan will reduce the vulnerability of the sector during the course of the Tenth Plan and set the stage for higher growth in the future. The growth rate of the construction sector has improved significantly during the Ninth Plan, and this acceleration is expected to continue into the Tenth. Even faster growth can possibly be achieved if the various land-related suggestions made in the Plan are implemented expeditiously. It is realised, however, that these are sensitive issues, and progress may not be as rapid as desired. The growth rate of other transport too is targeted to be significantly higher than in the Ninth Plan, although not as high as in the Eighth. In this case as well, even faster growth can be achieved if the requisite policy changes permitting greater involvement of the private sector are implemented. The potential of tourism has not been adequately harnessed by India, and it is expected that progress will be made in this direction during the Tenth Plan. This, coupled with expected high growth rates in the information, communication and entertainment (ICE) sectors, should lead to an acceleration in the growth of other services, of which these sectors are a part. Finally, there are segments within manufacturing which are also important as far as employment generation is concerned. Encouragement to these segments is an integral component of the Plan, without which the target growth rate of the manufacturing sector is unlikely to be achieved.

TABLE – 28.15

Sectoral Growth Rates and ICORs

	SECTORS	Eighth Plan		Ninth Plan		Tenth Plan	
		Growth	ICOR Rate (%)	Growth	ICOR Rate (%)	Growth	ICOR Rate (%)
1	Agriculture & Allied activities	4.69	1.59	2.06	4.05	3.97	1.99
2	Mining & Quarrying	3.59	10.74	3.81	5.44	4.30	7.99
3	Manufacturing	9.77	6.67	3.68	18.37	9.82	7.77
4	Elect, Gas & Water Supply	5.50	18.00	6.46	15.43	7.99	14.97
5	Construction	3.56	1.74	6.82	1.00	8.34	0.99
6	Trade	9.06	0.54	5.86	1.09	9.44	0.91
7	Rail Transport	1.95	27.94	4.70	9.87	5.40	14.66
8	Other Transport	8.42	4.41	5.63	6.09	7.54	5.37
9	Communication	14.31	7.25	17.14	5.28	15.00	8.33
10	Financial Services	10.21	2.23	8.93	1.35	11.69	1.56
11	Public Administration	3.91	7.82	9.21	4.09	6.43	5.45
12	Other Services	6.22	4.19	8.19	3.70	9.26	3.53
	Total GDPfc	6.54	3.43	5.35	4.53	7.93	3.58

The sectoral structure of the Indian economy that will emerge from these targeted growth rates is shown in Table 28.16. As may be seen, despite the higher growth rate targeted for agriculture, its share in GDP is expected to fall over this period. The sectors, which are expected to record an increase in the share of GDP, are manufacturing and some of the services, especially other services for reasons mentioned above.

The sectoral target growth rates and the estimated ICORs yield the investment requirements of each sector for achieving the growth targets. The main challenge facing the planning and economic administration system of the country is to devise strategies by which the investment programme envisaged in the Plan are realised. Even in the past, when there was considerable degree of governmental control over the pattern of investment through a high share of public investment, on the one hand, and industrial licensing, on the other, the sectoral pattern of investment tended to be somewhat different from the planned. With the substantial reduction in the share of public investment in recent years and the almost complete deregulation of private investment, the uncertainties involved in determining the likely pattern of investment have increased manifold.

TABLE – 28.16

Sectoral Structure of GDP at Factor Cost

(per cent)

	SECTORS	Ninth Plan	2001-02	2006-07	Tenth Plan
1	Agriculture & Allied Activities	25.7	24.7	20.5	22.2
2	Mining & Quarrying	2.4	2.3	1.9	2.1
3	Manufacturing	15.5	15.3	16.7	16.1
4	Elect, Gas & Water Supply	2.8	2.8	2.8	2.8
5	Construction	6.0	6.0	6.1	6.1
6	Trade	12.8	12.7	13.6	13.3
7	Rail Transport	0.9	0.9	0.8	0.8
8	Other Transport	4.8	4.9	4.8	4.8
9	Communication	1.4	1.7	2.3	2.1
10	Financial Services	6.2	6.3	7.5	7.0
11	Public Administration	6.4	6.6	6.1	6.4
12	Other Services	15.0	15.8	16.8	16.4
	Total	100.0	100.0	100.0	100.0

Conclusion

The process of development of the economy gained momentum during the 'nineties with the initiation of major economic reforms in 1991. The economy has since then been successfully launched on to a higher growth trajectory and has registered an improvement in a number of macroeconomic indicators in a short span of less than a decade. The sectoral composition of GDP has undergone a change in the 'nineties. The services sector has come to occupy a place of prominence in terms of relative contribution to GDP. The higher contribution of the services sector to GDP has a number of implications for the economy, the most important being the increased resilience of the economy, particularly, in times of adverse agricultural shocks. Further, the saving – investment gap has declined from 2.1 per cent of GDP during the 'eighties to 1.4 per cent during the 'nineties (1.3 per cent if the more recent period is considered). The reduction in the saving – investment gap was facilitated by strong net saving of the household sector, particularly, in the financial assets.

The available evidence shows that the differences in performance across states is enormous. Some states have done exceptionally well, several others show a strong performance, while some are doing poorly. These differences according to Montek Ahluwalia may be on account of state-specific characteristics which may be economic, institutional, socio-economic or even socio political. Accordingly, strategies have to be devised that can help break the specific constraint that prevent the present poorly performing states from replicating the success of the better performers.

Structural Change in terms of Industrial Distribution of Work Force and Occupational Structure*

The structural change in Indian economy is also reflected in the industrial distribution of work force and occupational structure over the period 1961-99-2000.

A recent study by K. Sundaram brings out that for the total work force, there is a 16 percentage point decline in the share of the Agriculture, Forestry & Fishing sector. This decline is greater than the 10 percentage point decline in the share of this sector in the rural work force and reflects the effect of a shift in the rural-urban composition of the work force towards the latter.

Of this 16 percentage point decline in the share of the agriculture sector, less than 3 percentage points represent the gain in the share of

---

* This section draws from K. Sundaram's study *Employment & Poverty in India in the Nineteen Nineties,* Working Paper No., 95, Centre for Development Economics, Delhi School of Economics, Delhi, July 2001.

the Manufacturing (and repair services) sector, with the Construction sector recording a 3 percentage point gain in its share in the work force.

It is the Services sector, as a group, that recorded a 10 percentage point gain in its (collective) share in the work force - with half of this being accounted for by the Trade, Hotels & Restaurants Sector. The Transport, Storage and Communications, and, the Community, Social and Personal Services sectors each gained 2 percentage points in their (respective) shares in the work force.

Focusing on the 1990s, the pace of decline in the share of the agriculture sector in the total work force has been faster: nearly twice as fast as that realised over the 33 year period between 1961 and 1994. Parallelly, the gains in the shares of the other sectors have also taken place at an equally accelerated pace during the 1990s - except that, in the case of the Manufacturing (and repair services sector), this acceleration, though present, has been much less marked (from 0.6 per cent per annum between 1961 and 1994 to 0.8 per cent per annum in the 1990s).

Within the broad Agriculture and Allied Activities Sector, crop production has recorded a reduction in the size of its work force of 1.5 million in the aggregate but not in the rural areas - where, in fact, there has been a marginal increase in the number of workers in crop production. Significantly, the reduction in the number of female workers, both in the broader agricultural and allied activities sector and in the crop-production sub-sector, has been much greater than in the total work force. The reduction in the size of the work force in the livestock sector is almost totally among female workers but is somewhat more evenly split across the rural-urban divide.

Moderating the decline in the size of the work force in the agriculture and allied activities sector in the total work force and among female workers (and contributing to the increase in the rural work force in this sector) is the increase of about 2 million workers engaged in providing agricultural support services in the aggregate which is concentrated, almost exclusively, in the rural areas.

The addition of a little over 5 millions to the work force of the Manufacturing and Repair Services sector between 1994 and 2000 is more or less evenly split across the rural-urban divide. However, across the gender divide, only 20 per cent of the additional work force in this sector are female workers.

TABLE – 28.17

Industrial Distribution of Total (Rural plus Urban) Work Force: All India: 1961, 1993-94 and 1999-2000

Industry Division/Group	1961		1993-94		1999-2000	
	No. of Workers ('000)	Share (per 1000)	No. of Workers ('000)	Share (per 1000)	No. of Workers ('000)	Share (per 1000)
0. Agriculture, Forestry & Fishing	**143,282**	**759**	**238,682**	**638**	**237,786**	**599**
00-01. Crop production & Plantations	138,637	735	217,220	581	215,751	543
02. Livestock	3,684	20	16,936	45	16,141	41
03. Agricultural Services	NIL	NIL	1,850	5	3,769	9
04-06. Logging, Forestry & Fishing	952	5	2,696	7	2,125	5
1. Mining & Quarrying	**919**	**5**	**2,676**	**7**	**2,263**	**6**
2+3+97. Mfrg+Repair Services	**17,906**	**95**	**43,218**	**116**	**48,296**	**122**
Of which: Food Products	2,126	11	4843	13	5,409	14
Beverages & Tobacco	1,124	6	4,410	12	4,925	12
Textiles & Products	6,553	35	10,335	28	10,480	26
Wood, Products & Furniture	2,175	12	4,295	11	5,367	14
Leather, fur & Products	704	4	730	2	1,081	3
Non-metallic Mineral Products	1,504	8	3,134	8	3,485	9
Metal Products & Parts	944	5	1,638	4	2,276	6
Repair Services	366	2	3,362	9	4,203	11
4. Electricity, Gas & Water	**257**	**1**	**1,394**	**4**	**1,048**	**3**
5. Construction	**2,768**	**15**	**12,127**	**32**	**17,618**	**44**
6. Trade, Hotels & Restaurants	**8,171**	**43**	**28,459**	**76**	**37,128**	**94**
Retail Trade	6871	36	21,384	57	28,887	73
Hotels & Restaurants	805	4	3,436	9	4,600	12
7. Transport Storage + Communication	**3,262**	**17**	**10,757**	**29**	**14,757**	**37**
8. Finance, Insurance, real estate & Business Services	**542**	**3**	**3,653**	**10**	**4,924**	**12**
9. Community, Social & Personal Services	**11,571**	**61**	**32,866**	**88**	**33,200**	**84**
Of which: Public Admn. + Defence	3,394	18	10,349	28	10,589	27
Education + Research	1,811	10	6,513	17	8,554	22
Medical & Health	645	3	1,966	5	2,522	6
Community Services	593	3	1,125	3	1,055	3
Personal Services	4,490	24	10,654	28	9,429	24
Total Work Force	**188,676**	**1000**	**373,832**	**1000**	**397,018**	**1000**

Reproduced from K. Sundaram, CDE Working Paper No. 95, July 2001, P. 27, Table 4.

In contrast to the rising share of the manufacturing sector as a whole, a major sub-sector namely, textiles and textile products has suffered a sizeable decline in its share in the total, rural and the female work force over the entire period. In the case of the total work force, the share of this sector has declined from 35 per 1000 in 1961 to 26 per 1000 in 2000. In terms of absolute number of workers, between 1994 and 2000 less than 1.5 lakh workers have been added in the Textiles & Products Sector. Further, all the increase in employment in this sub-sector has taken place in the rural areas with the employment in urban areas in this sector actually declining by about 93,000. Also, taking both the rural and urban areas together, employment of women workers in the textiles and products sector has declined by 143,000 between 1994 and 2000.

Two other non-agricultural sectors where the absolute number of workers has actually declined over the 1990s are the Mining & Quarrying (over 400,000) and the Electricity, Gas and Water (over 300,000) sectors.

Construction is one of the sectors that has shown a sizeable addition to its work force - by close to 5.5 million. Of this increase, over 60 per cent has been in the rural areas. However, less than 10 per cent of the incremental work force in this sector were women workers.

The expansion of the work force in the Construction sector outstripped the growth in gross value added originating in the Construction sector resulting in an absolute reduction in labour productivity or gross value-added per worker. The changes in the size of the work force in the Construction sector relative to the changes in GDP originating in that sector highlight a more general point: elasticity of employment with respect to value-added (in this case >1) and changes in labour productivity (in this case a reduction in the absolute size of value-added per worker) are obverse sides of the same phenomenon. Focusing exclusively on employment elasticity one can easily lose sight of the consequences for labour productivity.

On a comparable basis, the number of workers in the "Hotels and Restaurants" sector have grown from 3.4 million in 1993-94 to 4.6 million in 1999-2000. Compared to this, the work force in the Manufacturing and Repair Services has grown by a little over 5 million (from 43.2 to 48.2 million) over the same period. Even within the broader Industry Division, Trade, Hotels and Restaurants, the Hotels and Restaurants sub-sector accounted for less than 15 per cent of the incremental work force in this Industry Division. Among women workers too, the

Hotels and Restaurants sub-sector has added less than 3 lakh workers over the six year period. So that, while "McJobs" have indeed expanded in the 1990s, such jobs accounted for just about 5 per cent of the incremental work force. And, assuredly, with a share of a little over one per cent in the total work force and about half that in the rural work force and the female work force for the Hotels and Restaurants sub-sector, India is in no imminent danger of becoming a "restáurant and bar economy", remarks Sundaram !

With 4 million workers added to its work force, Transport, Storage and Communication is another sector which has absorbed over 15 per cent of the increase in the total work force between 1993-94 and 1999-2000. Of this addition of 4 million workers in the TCS-sector, a little over half has taken place in the rural areas. However, women workers have contributed only marginally (0.1 million) to the additions to the work force in this sector.

Community, Social and Personal Services is another sector which has suffered an erosion in its share in the total work force and in the rural work force - but not in the female work force - between 1994 and 2000.

Within the broader group of Community, Social and Personal Services (Industry Division 9 as per NIC 1987) two developments are noteworthy.

First, there has been a rise in both the absolute number of workers and of the share in work force in the two social sectors: Education and Research and Medical and Health Services. Some of this increase in employment in both the social sectors has taken place in rural India also.

Another significant change over the 1990s is the reduction in the absolute number of workers in personal services by over 1.2 million in the aggregate with a decline of over half a million for women workers. Given that this segment has been traditionally a low-productivity - low income-per-worker sector, a reduction in the size and share of the personal services sector must be viewed as a positive development in the employment situation in the nineteen nineties.

Occupation Structure

Estimates of the Occupational distribution of the work force, separately for the rural, urban and the total work force, for three time points: 1961, 1993-94 and 1999-2000 are presented at the broader Occupation-division level in Table 28.18 and for identified 2-digit occupation groups in Table 28.19.

TABLE – 28.18

Occupational Distribution of Work Force by Rural-Urban Residence: All India, 1961-1999-2000

(in '000s)

	NCO 1968 Divisions	1961			1993-94			1999-2000		
		Rural	Urban	Total	Rural	Urban	Total	Rural	Urban	Total
0-1.	Professional & Technical and Related Workers	1689 (10)	1547 (59)	3236 (17)	6516 (22)	7191 (87)	13707 (37)	5984 (20)	8590 (89)	14574 (37)
2.	Administrative, Executive & Managerial Workers	764 (5)	1048 (40)	1812 (10)	2415 (8)	4717 (57)	7132 (19)	4179 (14)	8039 (84)	12218 (31)
3.	Clerical & Related Workers	1046 (6)	2820 (107)	3866 (21)	3497 (12)	7573 (92)	11070 (30)	4053 (13)	8480 (88)	12533 (32)
4.	Sales Workers	3244 (20)	3632 (138)	6876 (37)	11635 (40)	13681 (166)	25316 (68)	11716 (39)	15856 (165)	27572 (69)
5.	Service Workers	2815 (17)	2743 (104)	5558 (30)	5331 (18)	7421 (90)	12752 (34)	7117 (24)	9219 (96)	16336 (41)
6.	Farmers, Fishermen, Hunters, Loggers & Related Workers	134329 (830)	3261 (124)	137590 (731)	227763 (781)	10152 (123)	237915 (636)	226762 (753)	8885 (92)	235647 (594)
7,8,9:	Production and Related Workers, Trspt Eqpt. Operators and Labourers	18052 (111)	11234 (427)	29286 (156)	34370 (118)	31564 (384)	65934 (176)	41148 (137)	36993 (385)	78141 (197)
	All Occupations	161,939	26,285	188,224	291,529	82,299	373,826	300,959	96,061	397,021

Figures within brackets relate to share (per 1000) of the occupation-group to the corresponding total workers in all occupations.

Reproduced from K. Sundaram's Working Paper No. 95, Page 29, Table 6.

TABLE – 28.19

Number of Workers in Identified 2-digit Occupation-groups by Location: All-India: 1961-1999-2000

(in '000s)

NCO 1968 : Occupation Groups	1961			1993-94			1999-2000		
	Rural	Urban	Total	Rural	Urban	Total	Rural	Urban	Total
08: Nursing & other Medical & Health Technicians	143	180	323	298	469	767	414	728	1142
15: Teachers	959	623	1582	3258	3082	6340	3717	3739	7456
30-35: Clerical Workers & Supervisor, Stenographers, Bookkeepers etc.	738	2459	3197	2831	6800	9631	3265	7539	10804
36-39: Trsp & Communications Workers & Supervisors	308	361	669	666	767	1433	788	941	1729
40: Merchants & Shopkeepers	2449	2241	4690	8493	8424	16919	8244	9313	17559
51-54: House keepers, Cooks, Maids etc.	1000	1590	2590	1687	3813	5500	1632	2338	5970
55-56: Launders, Hair dressers, Beauticians etc.	1352	476	1828	2124	1105	3229	2906	1278	4184
60-61: Cultivators	97,889	1732	99621	117,669	3895	121564	111,701	3343	115,044
63: Agricultural Labourers	30,603	919	31522	86413	3535	89948	91,747	3029	94,776
64: Plantation Workers	990	67	1057	3106	299	3405	3115	249	3364
71: Miners, Quarrymen etc.	546	126	672	960	360	1320	802	327	1129
72: Metal Processors	46	103	149	189	407	596	198	405	603
75: Spinners, Weavers, Knitters, Dyers etc.	3002	1959	4961	3723	3409	7132	3136	2710	5846
77: Food & Beverage Processors	1346	491	1837	1458	1070	2528	1918	1269	3187
79: Tailors, Dressmakers etc.	634	574	1208	2625	2824	5449	2720	3247	5967
82-89: Machines & Workers, Tool makers & operator	1828	2043	3871	5333	6480	11813	3472	7707	13179
95: Brick layers & other Construction Workers				3910	2707	6617	6276	4177	10,453
98: Trspt Eqpt. Operators	375	832	1207	2641	3608	6249	4160	4973	9133
99: Labourers not elsewhere classified	6020	2621	8641	5351	4028	9379	7182	4676	11858

Reproduced from K. Sundaram's Working Paper No. 95, Page 30, Table 7.

Reflecting the declines in the share of the agriculture and allied activities in the industrial distribution of the work force, the share of the occupation category: Farmers, Fishermen, Hunters, Loggers and Related workers also falls from 73 per cent in 1961 to a little under 60 per cent in 2000. Over the 1990s, not only the share but also the absolute number of workers in this category has declined - by over 2 million workers, equally divided between the urban and the rural areas. Also during the 1990s, while the number of cultivators has declined sharply - by over 6.5 million - this has been partially offset by an over 3 million increase in the number of agricultural labourers.

Over the entire period 1961-2000, the share of the two top-end occupation categories (Professional & Technical and Related workers; and Administrative, Executive and Managerial Workers) has increased by about 2 percentage points in each case. Over the 1990s, however, while the share of the first category has stagnated that of Division 2 has increased from 19 per 1000 to 31 per 1000.

In the Professional and Technical workers category, the 2 identified 2-digit groups are: Nursing and other Medical and health Technicians; and, Teachers. In the former category, (i.e. Nursing & Medical), the growth in the number of workers has sharply accelerated over the 1990s: from about 2.7 per cent per annum between 1961-1994 to 6.9 per cent per annum between 1994 and 2000. In contrast, there has been a slow down in the growth of teachers - from 4.3 per cent per annum (1961-1994) to 2.7 per cent per annum between 1994 & 2000.

It is significant that the share of clerical and related workers in the urban work force has fallen over the entire period as also over the two sub-periods. The share of sales workers has decreased in both rural and urban work force - *albeit* marginally - and the equally marginal rise in its share in the total work force merely reflects a rise in the share of urban work force in the total.

Also noteworthy is the significant rise in the share of Production and Related workers in the rural work force between 1994 and 2000 with close to 7 million additional workers, the share of this mixed category has risen by 19 points (per 1000) over the six years of the 1990s compared to a 17 point rise over the 33 years between 1961 and 1994.

At the 2-digit detail, three developments are noteworthy. First, is the decline over the 1990s, in the absolute number of workers in the category, "Spinners, Weavers, Knitters, dyers etc." from 7.1 million in 1994 to 5.8 million in 2000. This decline is partially offset by a rise of about half a million workers - in the category of Tailors, dress-makers etc.

The second, is the decline over the 1990s in the absolute number of workers in the occupation category 82-89 in the rural work force - from 5.3 million in 1994 to 3.5 million in 2000.

Thirdly, we have a sharp increase in rural India, in the number of construction related workers (from 3.9 million in 1994 to 6.3 million in 2000) and of Transport equipment operators (from 2.6 to 4.2 million) between 1993-94 and 1999-2000.

The broad conclusion of Sundaram's study is that overall, despite a sizeable reduction in the share of such workers in the total work force, India still remains a land of Farmers, Fishermen, Hunters and Loggers. At the other end of the skill spectrum, Professional and Technical workers and Administrative, Executive and Managerial workers together formed less than 7 per cent of the total work force at the beginning of the year 2000. Production process workers too accounted for less than 20 per cent of the workers in 1999-2000.

References

Acharya, Shankar (2003), *India's Economy: Some Issues and Answers*, Academic Foundation.

Ahluwalia, S. Montek (2000), *Economic Performance of the States in Post Reform Period* (NCAER, Golden Jubilee Lecture).

C.S.O. (1999), New Series on National Accounts Statistics (base year 1993-94), Govt. of India.

Planning Commission (2001), Indian Planning Experience, January.

——— (2002), Tenth Five Year Plan (2002-07), December.

Reserve Bank of India, Reports on Currency and Finance 1998-99 and 2000-01, 2001-02.

Sundaram, K. (2001), *Employment and Poverty in the Nineteen Nineties*, Working Paper No. 95, (July), Centre for Development Economics, Delhi School of Economics, Delhi.

29

The Growth Rate Mystery

K.B.L Mathur

Three major studies on growth rate of Indian economy by three 'Arvinds' have appeared in the first three months of the year. Arvind Virmani (February 2004), Arvind Panagariya (March 2004)[1] and Arvind Subramanian, with Rodrik Dani (March 2004) ('three studies' and 'Arvinds' henceforth). Broadly, all the three studies explore explanations of the change of trajectory in the long-term growth rate of the Indian economy particularly in the context of post-reform period. Conclusions drawn in all the three studies are based on dispassionate analysis of trends through most rigorous statistical tests. No doubt these are valuable additions to the existing rich literature on the subject a sample of which is illustrative from the list of references here.

Instead of making a rather uncomfortable attempt to summarise these comprehensive and technical studies so also essentially to escape from the possibility of the likely allegations of misinterpretation and consequential emergence of non-issues we indicate a few issues emerging out of the conclusions in the studies under reference with the help of other relevant studies wherever found necessary. Thus, this small piece is neither a 'yet another' study on India's economic growth story nor is it a review of earlier studies. The only provocation for this piece is that while the 'Arvinds' in their studies resolve a few 'puzzles' and 'mysteries' of India's economic growth story over a longer term, they also leave a few messages which are contradictory (not uncommon with the economist fraternity), if not confusing, and thereby creating new mysteries.

Regardless of the degree of gains achieved consequent upon the all pervasive and remarkable changes in the economic policy there is hardly any dispute over the fact that the 1991 crisis was converted into an opportunity to change the direction of the economy. What could then be the points at issue? Some of these emerging out of the recent studies particularly the three cited above relate to liberalisation during 1980s, shift of growth trajectory during 1990s, 'fragility' of growth rate during 1980s and 1990s and finally the prospects now onwards, i.e., beyond 2002-03.

Liberalisation or Something Else?

According to Panagariya's study two broad factors account for much of the spurt in growth rate during 1980s, especially the sub period 1988-91. "First, liberalisation played a significant role. On the external front, policy measures such as import liberalisation, export incentives, and a more realistic real exchange rate contributed to productive efficiency. On the internal front, freeing up of several sectors from investment licensing reinforced import liberalisation and allowed faster industrial growth. Second, both external and internal borrowings allowed the government to maintain high levels of public expenditure and thus boost growth through demand." While accepting the fact of some 'liberalisation' during 1980s, Rodrik and Subramanian do not quite find the similar factor as in Panagariya's study for increase in productive efficiency leading to spurt in growth during the second half of 1980s. According to Rodrik and Subramanian, reforms in 1980s were not pro-liberalisation but pro-business in the important sense that they served to boost the profits of existing business without threatening them with real competition. The shift in policy was only 'attitudinal' one, having to do with the government's attitude towards business and the private sector, rather than as policy reform per se. In fact, Rodrik and Subramanian's study finds factors like 'external liberalisation', 'exchange rate changes' and even 'internal liberalisation' amongst those 'explanations that don't work' in explaining the improved productivity and growth rate in 1980s. In support of the explanation that trade liberalisation during 1980s resulted in productivity increase in the manufacturing sector Chand and Sen (2002) study has been referred to by Panagariya where it is found that protection level had declined over the sample period (1984-88) in intermediate and capital goods sector. Rodrik and Subramanian study, however, refers to a study by Das (2003) which shows that the effective rate of protection had increased during 1986-90 over 1980-85 as given in Table 29.1.

TABLE – 29.1

Measures of Trade Protection, 1980-2000*

(In per cent)

	1980-85	1986-90	1991-95	1996-2000
All industries	115.1	125.9	80.2	40.4
Intermediate goods	147.0	149.2	87.6	40.1
Capital goods	62.8	78.5	54.2	33.3
Consumer goods	101.5	111.6	80.6	48.3

Note : * Average effective rate of protection.

Source: Based on Table 6 in Rodirk and Subramanian, Arvind (March 2004).

Virmani finds yet other different and elaborate explanations for the accelerated growth during 1980s. Apart from the 'incremental (tinkerisation) rather than revolutionary individual policy reforms, Virmani's study also includes 'credibility' of reforms and 'output gap' factors. According to the 'credibility' factor, there were politically credible signals of the intent to reform failed policies: "This had an impact on the investment environment leading to more private investment and a shift from building of structures towards machinery and equipment". Under the 'output gap' hypothesis the explanation is that for almost the 15 year period prior to 1980s the economy had under-performed increasing thereby the gap between the potential and actual GDP. The policy reforms during 1980s "provided an opportunity for catch-up growth or an upturn in the growth cycle".

What then could be the explanation? One way to answer this is to simply accept a combination of all the explanations except where they contradict. The debate over non-economic factors like 'attitude', 'credibility', etc, can hardly be conclusive, except that they do create mysteries.

Going strictly by the numbers alone one may not find a significant improvement in the growth rate average during the post-reform period over the pre-reform period. The numbers, at times, differ depending on the period covered. Convention has grown where most studies use the period as 1980s and 1990s representing pre-reform period and post-reform period without being precise at times about the starting or ending year covered. The convenience of using the '1990s' to refer to post-reform period has continued to the extent that even 2001-02 and 2002-03 are also being included in the period referred to as '1990s'. Also it depends on the timing of the study and availability of data at that time. It is in this context that Panagariya draws special attention[2] to this aspect of period covered to compare growth rates during 1980s and 1990s and specifically defines the years included for 1980s and 1990s while referring to post-1991 reform period. Thus in Panagariya's study "the post-1991 reform period is defined to start in 1992-93 and last until the latest year for which data are available, 2002-03". Virmani also refers to this aspect of comparisons being made between the pre-crisis and post-crisis years but does not pursue this issue because the objective of the study is to analyse the growth trends over 50 years period (1950-51 to 2001-02).

It is interesting to find the variations in the period covered in different studies and the consequential differing numbers of growth rate to compare pre-reform and post-reform or 1980s and 1990s (Table 29.2).

What is, however, important here is that regardless of a year or two included or excluded in referring to pre-reform and post-reform periods the increase in the average growth rate during post-reform period over the average growth rate during the pre-reform period is not more than 0.6 percentage points[3] in any of the studies (included in Table 29.2).

A limited point being made here is that it is difficult to find a definitive conclusion regarding a significant shift in the post-reform growth average over the pre-reform growth average as is usually claimed. The only statement one may have to contend with is that during the post-1991 reform period there is a "slight upward shift in the mean growth rate" (Panagariya) or the "growth record is only slightly better" (Ahluwalia). But these are only parts of the statements and it is necessary to complete the sentences to know the full conclusion. Most studies have qualified the 'slight growth rate shift' by claiming that the growth during 1980s when compared to 1990s was 'fragile' and 'unsustainable' resulting in the 1991 crisis.

Is Post-1991 Reform Growth Less Fragile?

Recognising well that it is not numbers alone that matter for the assessment of the outcome of reforms the other facets including the 'fragility' and 'sustainability' of the growth rates during the pre-reform and post-reform period have been emphasised.

One of the conclusions in Panagariya's study is that "the variance of growth rates during the 1980s is statistically significantly higher than that in the 1990s. In this sense, growth during the first period was fragile relative to that in the second and, indeed, culminated in the June 1991

TABLE – 29.2

Indian Economy: Growth Rates during 1980s/Pre-reform and 1990s/Post-reform

Study *	Growth Rate (Period Covered)		Remarks
	1980s/Pre-reform	1990s/Post-reform	
Acharya, Shankar (April 27, 2004)	5.6 (1981-82 to 1990-91)	6.1 6.7 (1992-93 to 1996-97) 5.5 (1997-98 to 2001-02)	
Arvind, Panagariya (March 2004)	5.8 (1980-81 to 1990-91) or 5.4 (1980-81 to 1991-92)	5.9 (1992-93 to 2002-03)	1991-92 taken as the dividing line between the two points.
Rodrik, D and Arvind Subramanian (March 2004)	5.85 (1980-91)	5.59 (1990-99)	Based on average Annual Growth Rate of output as given in Bosworth - Collins.
Arvind Virmani (March 2004)	5.5 (1980-81 to 1990-91)	6.1 (1992-93 to 2001-02)	Prefers to omit 1991-92 from both periods.
Acharya S, Cassen R and McNay K (2004)	5.6 (1981-82 to 1990-91)	5.6 (1991-92 to 2000-01) 6.1 (1992-93 to 2000-01)	
Rakshit, Mihir (2004)	5.81 (1980-81 to 1989-90)	6.10 (1992-93 to 2000-01) 5.61 (1990-91 to 2000-01)	
Gorden J and Gupta P (Nov 2003)	5.8 (1981-90)	5.8 (1991-2000)	Years not specifically mentioned
RBI (August 2003)	5.8 (1980-81 to 1989-90)	6.0 (1993-94 to 2002-03)	10 years for each period.

Contd...

...Table 29.2 Contd...

Study *	Growth Rate (Period Covered)		Remarks
	1980s/Pre-reform	1990s/Post-reform	
World Bank (July 2003)	5.6	5.8	Years not specifically mentioned.
Planning Commission	5.8 (1980-81 - 1989-90)	6.0 (1992-93 to 2001-02)	
Government of India	5.54 (1980-81 - 1984-85)	6.68 (1992-93 to 1996-97)	
Tenth Five-Year Plan (2003)	6.02 (1985-86 - 1989-90)	5.35 (1997-98 to 2001-02)	
IMF (September 2002)	5.6	6.1	
		6.7 (Mid-1990s) 1990-91 to 1996-97	
		5.3 (Late-1990s) 1996-97 to 2001-02	
RBI (January 2002)	5.8 (1980-81 to 1989-90)	5.8 (1990-91 to 1999-00)	
Ahluwalia, Montek S (Summer 2002)	5.7 (1981-82 to 1990-91)	6.0	
		6.7 (1992-93 to 1996-97)	
		5.4 (1997-98 to 2001-02)	

* With apologies to all other studies which could not be included inadvertently.

crisis". Further, "the conclusion that growth in the 1980s was more fragile than in the 1990s received unequivocal support in the data". Virmani also found the coefficient of variation in GDP growth rate fell to 20 per cent during 1990s (1992-2001) from 50 per cent during 1980s (1980-91). In the backdrop of international comparison Rodrik and Subramanian (March 2004), however, come out with the following result:

> Between 1980 and 1999, [however] India's growth exhibits the lowest variation in terms of both the standard deviation and the coefficient of variation. Thus, India outperformed all regions, save east Asia, in terms of average growth, and outperformed all regions, including East Asia, in terms of stability of growth. Interestingly, and contrary to some claims, Indian growth was more stable in the 1980s than in the 1990s. (emphasis added)

Earlier an RBI (2003) study did report a reduction in 'variability' (measured by coefficient of variation, i.e., CV) of overall GDP growth to 23.0 per cent during the 'period of reforms' (1992-93-2002-03) compared to 39.1 per cent during the decade preceding reforms (1981-82 to 1990-91). But the same study also finds that for 'industry' the variability in growth rates had doubled from 24.1 per cent to 53.5 per cent during a similar period. For the manufacturing sub-sector the increase in CV was from 28.9 per cent to 62 per cent. Table 29.3 shows the sharp increases in CVs of growth rates of different sectors/sub-sectors as given in the RBI study.

If a decline in variability is considered as a positive outcome of reforms, should it not be a matter of concern that the variability in the growth rates of a critical sector of the economy, i.e., manufacturing has doubled along with a reduced level of growth rate during the post-reform period. Significantly increased variability is found in several other sub-sectors including 'electricity, gas, water supply, finance, insurance', etc.

As per the RBI study, it is the agriculture and allied activities sector which mainly contributed to the decline in the variability in the overall GDP. But, going by Virmani's results, it is difficult to feel confident that the agriculture sector provided better stability during 1990s compared to 1980s. As the study concludes: "Conventional wisdom has been that Indian agriculture and the economy has become less dependent on the weather since the 1980s. This has been based on the fact that share of GDP from agriculture has declined and that of services has increased. *The results... ...contradict this conclusion and imply that there is no change in the impact of rainfall fluctuations on the Indian economy"* (emphasis added).

TABLE – 29.3

Sectoral Trend Growth Rates of Real Gross Domestic Product

	Sector	Decade Preceding Reforms (1981-82 to 1990-91)		Crisis Year (1991-92)	Period of Reforms (1992-93 to 2002-03)	
		Growth	CV (%)	Growth	Growth	CV (%)
		1	2	3	4	5
1	Agriculture and allied activities	3.1	150.7	-1.5	2.5	130.2
2	Industry	7.6	24.1	1.2	6.2	53.5
	Mining and quarrying	7.5	59.3	3.7	4.2	84.7
	Manufacturing	7.4	28.9	-3.6	6.6	62.0
	Electricity, gas and water supply	9.4	21.2	10.4	6.0	46.4
3	Services	6.7	18.0	4.5	8.0	22.7
	Construction	4.8	102.5	2.1	6.0	51.0
	Trade, hotels and communication	5.9	18.9	2.5	8.6	22.0
	Financing, insurance, real estate and business services	10.1	16.3	12.0	7.8	40.2
	Community, social and personal services	6.6	30.9	2.6	8.0	44.7
4	GDP at factor cost	5.6	39.1	1.3	6.1	23.0

Notes: (1) Trend growth rates have been calculated using semi-logarithmic regression.
(2) CV refers to coefficient of variation of growth.

Source: RBI (March 2003).

In fact CVs during a broken period as analysed by Rakshit (2004) show an increase at 297.8 per cent during 1997-98 to 2000-01 from 80.8 per cent during 1992-93 to 1996-97 and there is no difference in the CVs of agriculture growth rate between the two periods of 1980-81 to 1989-90 and 1992-93 to 2000-01, these being 125.6 per cent and 125.1 per cent respectively. A limited point being made here is that if the degree of fragility in the growth rate during 1980s is considered an important factor leading towards crisis then this very factor during the post-reform period hardly provides any comfort. A more than 100 per cent increase in CV in a reduced level of growth rate of industry and in particular of manufacturing during the post-reform period can hardly be overlooked. Even though it can be argued that the relative level of 'variability' in manufacturing and sub-sectors of services (relative to agriculture sector) is much lower, the fact remains that with the increasing share of services sector in the economy if several of its sub-sectors show increased variability the 'fragility' factor in growth rate remains as valid as in 1980s. Perhaps a better alternative explanation could be that during 1980s the Indian economy had much less resilience compared to what it gained during the post-reform period to meet the 'fragility' in growth rate which can lead to a crisis situation.

What Next?

Economists are at their best while making projections particularly on macroeconomic variables. But the scope of the studies by 'Arvinds' was limited to exploring the explanations for the past long-term trends in the growth rates. The only limited observation for future made by Virmani is that "with the cyclical recovery of the economy to a predicted 8 per cent plus growth in 2003-04 and a forecast of 6 per cent growth rate in 2004-05, the economy is returning to the 'Bhartiya' rate of growth trend of 5.8 per cent per annum". Rodrik and Subramanian (April, 2004), in a separate study following the one included in the 'three studies' came out with explanations on 'Why India Can Grow at 7 Per Cent a Year or More' and based on a simple growth accounting framework, projected India's future potential output growth rate close to 7 per cent through 2025. The study provides the basis for this forecast, discusses the factors that might make this an underestimate as also the downside risks. It was around the same time (March-April, 2004) that there was an upbeat mood to make growth rate projections for the Indian economy partly because 'advance estimates' of GDP growth rate for the third quarter (October-December) of 2003-04 were at 10.4 per cent and for the full year the 'advance estimate' of GDP growth rate during 2003-04 was placed at 8.1 per cent. Several economists and of course politicians (particularly that being the election period) started projecting 8 to 10 per cent GDP growth rate for next several years. To find the seriousness of all these claims Acharya (April, 2004) came out with 'a reality check' and asked a straight question: "Has the Indian economy really attained the new trajectory of sustained 8 per cent growth? Through the major reasons indicated in brief in the study, he replied rather convincingly why India's medium term (five years) growth is far more likely to be constrained to 6 per cent or below than to rip along at 8 per cent". Based on hard facts and of his own earlier studies containing in-depth analysis of macroeconomic trends over a longer period as also the one Acharya S, Cassen Robert, and Mc Nay Kirsty (2004), the results of the 'reality check' were sufficient for any reader to believe that constraints for 8 per cent growth in the medium term were stronger than perhaps the facilitators.

However, Kelkar (April, 2004) in his study on 'India : On the Growth Turnpike' found India at the threshold of 'a golden age of growth' and concluded that "India - riding the wave of growth fundamentals such as demographic transition, human capital accumulation, improved incentive structures, diffusion of new technologies such as IT, total factor productivity accelerators through "network industries", and an improved security environment - will be growing at growth rates which can be above 10 per cent per annum, *i e*, double digit growth rates". Apart from the logically established factors likely to contribute towards a double-digit growth in the next two decades, it would appear as if it was more a result of Kelkar's deep-rooted conviction and wish for the Indian economy to achieve double-digit growth. In his earlier [Kelkar 1999] paper he had illustrated for the need of it by saying that "when a satellite is put into orbit, it requires high velocity to ensure exit from the earth's gravitational force; similarly, if our economy is to exit from the gravitational pull of poverty, it requires an exit velocity of double-digit growth rate over the next two decades". Interestingly, Kelkar in his paper (April, 2004) includes amongst the non-economic factors India's democratic framework as a key growth fundamental. But even on such fundamentals there are caveats. In the context of 'credibility of reforms' as an important factor impacting the growth rate, Virmani finds that 'the enormous growth potential of the Indian economy is not being realised because of the constraints placed on it by the Indian political system'. Basu (2004: 19), has the following to say on the contradictions, if not mysteries of a democratic system: "Advisers from Washington, DC, and many economists recommend that third world nations must have democracy and must open up their economy and privatise, oblivious to the fact that to ask for a democracy and then to insist what the democracy should choose amounts to a contradiction". It is perhaps under such contradictions that the real mystery of India's economic growth would remain.

Notes

1 An expanded version of the paper 'India in the 1980s and 1990s: A Truimph of Reforms' has since appeared in *Economic and Political Weekly*, June 19-25, 2004.

2 A few other studies also do mention this aspect but either in a passing reference or in a 'foot note'.

3 It may deserve mention here that the GDP estimates at times undergo revisions even up to 0.3 per cent in one year, even though the difference being referred to here is in the average of growth rates of a decade or so. The revisions made in GDP growth estimates,

for example, between quick estimates of GDP for 2002-03, and the provisional final estimates for the year 2001-02 as released at the end of Jan 2004 had shown the change from 5.6 per cent to 5.8 per cent for 2001-02 and 4.3 per cent to 4.0 per cent for 2002-03. The changes in the estimates for different sectors have been systematically summarised in the ICRA Bulletin on 'Money and Finance' October 3-March 4 (pp 21-22).

References

Acharya, Shankar (2004), "Growth Prospects: A Reality Check", *Business Standard*, April 27.

Acharya, Shankar, Robert Cassen and Kirsty McNay (2004), "The Economy - Past and Future" in Dyson Tim, Robert Cassen and Leela Visaria (eds), *Twenty First Century India*, Oxford.

Ahluwalia S, Montek (2002), "Economic Reforms in India since 1991: Has Gradualism Worked?", *Journal of Economic Perspectives*, Volume 16, Number 3, Summer 2002.

Basu, Kaushik (2004), "The Indian Economy up to 1991 and Since" in Kaushik Basu (ed), *India's Emerging Economy*', MIT Press.

Gordon, Jim and Poonam Gupta (2003), "Understanding India's Services Revolution", Paper presented at the IMF-NCAER Conference, November 14-16, New Delhi.

Government of India (2003), "Tenth Five-Year Plan 2002-2007", Planning Commission.

IMF (2002), "India: Selected Issues and Statistical Appendix", IMF Country Report No 02/193, September.

Kelkar, L Vijay (1999), "India's Emerging Economic Challenges", *Economic and Political Weekly*, August 14-21.

——— (2004), "India: On the Growth Turnpike: 2004 Narayan Oration", Australian National University Canberra, April 27, Mimeo.

Panagariya, Arvind (2004), "India in the 1980s and 1990s: A Triumph of Reforms", IMF Working Paper WP/04/43, March.

Rakshit, M (2004), "Some Macroeconomics of India's Reform Experience" in Kaushik Basu (ed), *India's Emerging Economy*, MIT Press.

Reserve Bank of India (2002), "Report on Currency and Finance 2000-01", January.

——— (2003), "Report on Currency and Finance, 2001-02", March.

——— (2003), "Annual Report 2002-03", August.

Rodrik, Dani and Arvind Subramanian (2004), "From 'Hindu Growth' to Productivity Surge: The Mystery of the Indian Growth Transition", NBER Working Paper 10376, http://www.nber.org/papers/w10376 March.

——— (2004), "Why India Can Grow at 7 Per Cent a Year or More: Projections and Reflections", *Economic and Political Weekly*, April 17.

Virmani, Arvind (2004), "India's Economic Growth' from Socialist Rate of Growth to Bharatia Rate of Growth", Indian Council for Research on International Economic Relations, February.

World Bank (2003), "India Sustaining Reform, Reducing Poverty", Report No. 25797-IN, July 14.

Economic and Political Weekly Commentary, July 17, 2004.

30

Growth of SDP and Structural Changes in State Economies

Interstate Comparisons

S.L. Shetty

The objective of this study is to make a comparison of economic growth across states based on the key results that are discernible from the data base for over four decades on SDP. The data is the first of its kind in India and has just been published by the Economic and Political Weekly Research Foundation (EPWRF). No doubt, state income and per capita income have their limitations in any wholesome study of interstate comparisons of progress and development experiences. In this respect, the history of literature is full of studies, which have supplemented SDP data with other social and economic indicators, to analyse the comparative picture of states' development [Roy and Dutta 1996]. Interstate comparison of SDP is also hampered by the quality of statistics produced by different states,[1] apart from interstate price differentials. However, in recent years, considerable progress has been made by the Central Statistical Organisation (CSO) in achieving uniformity in the use of concepts and definitions as well as data sources by different states for SDP estimation purposes. Be that as it may, undoubtedly SDP, per capita SDP and the sectoral composition of SDP constitute the most crucial set of indicators to measure the economic performance of states. Hence, this note concentrates on these above indicators for analysis, following the tradition set by many other studies.

I

STUDIES ON CONVERGENCE AND DIVERGENCE

In the array of research studies on the subject, a theme which has dominated the literature relates to interstate disparities in income growth. The logical question that arises is whether there has been inter-regional convergence in income growth and whether income differentials have narrowed over specified periods. These studies can be broadly placed under two opposing camps, that is, (i) those that have found that there was a marked reduction in income differentials or that they have seen a noticeable tendency for convergence of long-term SDP growth rates; and (ii) those that have noted a widening of regional disparities amongst states or have depicted a picture of interstate divergence. It must be clarified here that the results of these studies may have been period-specific, based as they are on the data sets then available or covered. The studies that have seen a positive sign of convergence are: Gupta (1973); Dholakia (1994); Cashin and Sahay (1996); Sarkar (1996); and Ahluwalia (2001). On the other hand, those that have discerned tendencies of divergence are: Nair (1971); Chaudhury (1974); Majumdar and Kapoor (1980); Bajpai and Sachs (1996); Marjit and Mitra (1996); Rao *et al* (1999); Dasgupta *et al* (2000) and Sachs *et al* (2002). However, two studies which depart somewhat from these clear-cut strands are those by Nagaraj *et al* (2000) and Dasgupta *et al* (2000). Nagaraj *et al* provide an empirical analysis of conditional convergence across Indian states they assess the extent to which differences in core, social and economic infrastructure endowments give rise to differences in steady-state levels of output, and therefore, to differences in their long-run growth performance. Dasgupta *et al* use the per capita SDP data up to 1995-96 and find "a clear tendency for the Indian states to have diverged during the period in question as far as per capita SDP goes". However, in terms of sectorwise composition of SDP, they discern a tendency for overall convergence towards the national average.

Studies on the Post-Reform Period

In this respect, the most-illuminating studies are those that have covered the recent post-reform period. Two noteworthy ones in this category are Sachs *et al* (2002) and Ahluwalia (2001). The study by Sachs *et al* reviews studies in both the opposing strands of thought and concludes that "Most papers, like ours, find a tendency towards divergence rather than convergence" (p 3). Using different measures of convergence, the authors find that India, like China, does not show any signs of even conditional convergence, let alone unconditional convergence. In the list of studies cited by them is the one by Ahluwalia (2001) which, however, has a distinctly different interpretation of its own statistical results as well as those of others. Both Sachs *et al* (2002) and Ahluwalia (2001) are the latest in a series of studies that use more recent data and seem to belong to the genre of 'political economy'. The former deals with growth performances of states against the backdrop of the newer policy environment of economic reforms. The latter addresses "the differential economic performance of India's states, especially under the forces of globalisation in the 1990s". Both review the extant studies of others, but come to somewhat different conclusions. Again, insofar as SDP data are concerned, both use the same set of statistics up to 1997-98-1998-99, but provide interestingly different interpretations of their results.

In reviewing the existing studies, Ahluwalia (2001) finds that in studies which deal with long-term trends, the general conclusion "seems to be that there is no evidence of unconditional convergence but there is evidence of conditional convergence" (p 6). That is, after allowance is made for differences across states in some of the initial conditions that affect growth rates (such as share of agriculture and some measure of infrastructure development) the long-term time paths of per capita gross state domestic product (GSDP) across states show convergence. He argues that conditional convergence is of course quite consistent with divergence in per capita GSDP over certain periods. Ahluwalia explains that his paper is not concerned with convergence in the sense of underlying long-term trends, but rather, with the actual behaviour of per capita GSDP in the post-reform period compared with pre-reform behaviour. He argues that though interstate inequality as measured by Gini coefficient clearly increased, the common perception that "the rich states got richer and the poor states got poorer" was misleading. Punjab and Haryana, which were the richest states, have not only faced slower per capita GSDP growth in the 1990s than in the 1980s, but have also lagged behind the national average. Except for Bihar, Uttar Pradesh and Orissa, which have grown even more slowly, all other states have narrowed the distance between themselves and Punjab and Haryana. Apart from Maharashtra and Gujarat, the other two high-income states, which have experienced the fastest rates of growth in per capita GSDP, Rajasthan and Madhya Pradesh, have broken ranks from BIMARU states and performed reasonably well. Analysing further the increased regional inequality in growth performance during the 1990s, which his results confirm, Ahluwalia finds that the states, which have achieved strong growth in GSDP in the 1990s, are fairly well-distributed regionally.

They are: Gujarat and Maharashtra in the west, Madhya Pradesh and Rajasthan in the north, West Bengal in the east and Tamil Nadu, Karnataka and Kerala in the south. Ahluwalia also questions the role of geography such as coastal locations determining growth performance – a theme which Jeffrey Sachs *et al* (2002) have been canvassing. Madhya Pradesh and Rajasthan are both heartland states but have performed reasonably well, and better than Orissa which is a coastal state. The southern states as a group have done well, though they are by no means the only ones to achieve an acceleration in growth during the 1990s.

Nagaraj (2002), examining the effects of economic reforms on output, investment and employment, singled out the distribution of net state domestic product (NSDP) originating in the manufacutring sector across states. This is because economic reforms in India have essentially focused on the manufacturing sector. Nagaraj's analysis shows no statistically significant improvement in the growth performance of states that have initiated market-oriented policies. On the other hand, four states, namely, Bihar, Haryana, Punjab and Uttar Pradesh, have experienced a statistically significant slowdown in their manufacturing growth rates after the reforms, thus, implying growing inequality in the pattern of manufacturing growth. However, this in turn may "imply a greater efficiency as the production decisions are increasingly driven by private profitability considerations" (p19).

II

GROWTH PERFORMANCE OF STATES AS SEEN THROUGH SDP DATA

Interstate Comparisons of Growth Performance

Using data presented in the data base, four different measures of growth performance of states based on SDP and per capita SDP data at constant prices have been worked out and presented in Tables 30.1 and 30.2. The nature of data availability has necessitated these four different measures. First, separate growth measures have been worked out for gross and net SDP in real terms and for real per capita SDP in both gross and net terms. Second, an attempt has been to estimate annual growth rates during the decades of the 1980s and 1990s, as the concerned literature has recognised the qualitative differences in economic management and policy perspectives in India between the two decades [RBI 2002, RBI 2003, Ahluwalia 2001 and Sachs *et al* 2002]. Finally, with the availability of the new series of SDP from 1993-94 as the base year, the period of study had to be broken into two blocks of periods

1980-81 to 1993-94 and 1993-94 to 2000-01. However, it is also found that in some cases, the measured average growth rate in the two decades is sensitive to the specific years included in a set. Thus, it is found that the measured growth rate for the period 1990-91 to 2000-01 is found to be significantly different for some states from the rate for the period 1993-94 to 2000-01, using the 1993-94 series of SDP (though with splicing method is used for a brief period from 1990-91 to 1992-93 to the 1993-94 series backwards). In doing so, some of the smaller or newer states for which 1980-81 series did not exist had to be excluded in working out the growth rates (e g, Jharkhand, Chattisgarh, Mizoram and Chandigarh). The annual growth rate has been worked out for the comparable time series of SDP and per capita SDP, using the measure of compound growth rate derived from a semi-log regression equation with respect to time (see Tables 30.1 and 30.2). The following paragraphs summarise the results.

First, though there are differences in growth rates, as there are differences between gross SDP and net SDP – total as well as per capita, they are not so significant as to alter the sequential order of states, arranged in descending order of growth rates, except for a very few cases. Therefore, the discussion being carried on here is based on gross SDP (Table 30.1), though some references are made to the growth rates based on net SDP (Table 30.2) too, whenever they are warranted.

Second, all measures of SDP growth suggest that there has been an overall acceleration in the 1990s period from the 1980s. All states growth together has roughly improved to about 5.50-5.70 per cent per annum in the 1990s, from about 5.20-5.30 per cent per annum in the 1980s, in terms of aggregate NSDP or GSDP. Per capita estimates have improved to 3.60-3.80 per cent per annum in the 1990s, from 3.00-3.10 per cent per annum in the 1980s (Tables 30.1 and 30.2). Also, the number of states whose annual growth rates have been higher than the average growth for all states together, have risen somewhat in gross as well as net total SDP. The rise has been much sharper in terms of per capita SDP, which combined with the acceleration in overall growth, portrays a situation of greater inequality in the 1990s (More of it in the later period). The difference between total SDP growth and per capita SDP growth arises from the relative differences in the population growth of states. For instance, Kerala's total SDP growth at about 5.30 per cent has been below the all-states growth rate, 5.70 per cent, during the 1990s. However, in per capita SDP, Kerala's annual growth of 4.10 per cent in the same decade has upstaged the average per capita growth for all states of about 3.80 per cent per annum. On the other hand,

Maharashtra, which has experienced near 6 per cent annual growth in total GSDP during the 1990s and has remained above the all-states growth of about 5.70 per cent, slipped below in rank and come closer to the average growth in terms of per capita SDP. The change though is fractional, and stands at 3.82 per cent against the all-states average growth of 3.78 per cent. This is understandable, for Kerala experienced, a population growth of 9.42 per cent between the 1991 and 2001 Censuses, while Maharashtra saw a population expansion of 22.57 per cent. This is, slightly higher than even the nation's overall population increase of 21.35 per cent during the decade.

Third, in terms of both SDP and per capita SDP growth, all-states with a few exceptions (Uttar Pradesh, Assam and Punjab) have shown accelerated growth during the 1990s. Many major states like Gujarat, West Bengal, Himachal Pradesh and Kerala have moved up the ladder to reach above or near the all-states average SDP growth. In this respect, amongst the major states that have shown outstanding performance in the 1990s are Karnataka, West Bengal, Rajasthan, Tamil Nadu and Gujarat, which belong to different regions in the country. At the same time, deceleration in the growth of high-income states of Punjab, Haryana and Maharashtra stands out. It should be noted here in parenthesis that Punjab has remained as the state with the highest per capita NSDP throughout the past two decades, but has persistently experienced reduced growth rates. Looking at it differently, 16 states and UTs or eight major ones have shown average GSDP growth of over 6 or near 6 per cent per annum in the 1990s.

Fourth, at the other end, the low-income and poorly-performing major states of Uttar Pradesh, Madhya Pradesh, Bihar, Orissa, and Assam, have not only persisted with their low growth syndrome, but have also experienced further deceleration in growth rates in the 1990s (except Bihar and Orissa which have shown some differing trends between per capita GSDP and per capita NSDP). It is for this reason that, despite the improvement in growth rates of many middle-income states, the degree of dispersion in growth rates, as measured by the coefficient of variation (cv), has become widened in the 1990s. CV (in percentages) of GSDP growth rates has increased from 29.6 per cent in the 1980s to 41.1 per cent in the 1990s, and that of NSDP from 33.4 per cent to 46.0 per cent (Tables 30.1 and 30.2).

Fifth, with the general phenomenon of relatively higher population growth in low-income and low-growth states, the growth of per capita incomes in such states is found to be relatively lower than the growth of total state incomes. The per capita incomes growth of high-income and middle-income states is comparatively higher than the growth in their total incomes. This phenomenon is reflected in not only a substantially higher CV for growth rates of per capita incomes in both the periods, but also in a sizeable increase in CV for per capita GSDP and NSDP. For instance CV increased from 51.1 per cent in the 1980s to 68.0 per cent in the 1990s in respect of per capita GSDP, and from 58.6 per cent to 74.6 per cent in respect of per capita NSDP. These suggest that fluctuations in the growth rates of per capita SDP are much steeper than those in total SDP growth.

Sixth, as explained earlier, the measure of the annual average of incomes seems to become sensitive to the years covered in the period of the study. To be specific, if the period of 1993-94 to 2000-01 is expanded to cover the whole decade of 1990-91 to 2001-01 (by a reasonably acceptable method of splicing to extend the 1993-94 series backward, the measure of dispersion in growth rates of both total SDP and per capita SDP gets considerably reduced. Consequently, the picture of increasing regional inequality in growth rates gets corrected and there in fact arises a small fall in CV, from 30.5 per cent in the 1980s to 28.1 per cent in the 1990s, of growth rates of GSDP. For growth rates of per capita GSDP, the CV rises only fractionally from 50.2 per cent to 52.2 per cent. Incidentally, it is found that the disparity in growth rates of 16 major states (covering over 90 per cent of the total population in the country) turned out to be considerably less than the CV in growth rates of all states together (see Tables 30.1 and 30.2).

Finally, the inclusion of the first three years in the decade of the 1990s, by extending the 1993-94 series backward through splicing, alters the relative growth rates of various states. This gives a clue regarding the possible differences in the growth rates of SDP and per capita SDP between the initial years of the decade and its later years. To examine this phenomenon, we have split the decade into two halves and presented different measures of growth rates for the periods 1990-91 to 1995-96 and from 1995-96 to 2000-01 (Table 30.3). These results reveal certain interesting features. Overall, the difference in growth as between the two quinquennia has been negligible; while all-states total GSDP shows a fractional deceleration in growth from about 5.60 per cent in the first half of the decade to about 5.50 per cent in the second half, all-states per capita GSDP sustains a growth of about 3.60 per cent per annum throughout the two quinquennia. But, growth differences at individual state levels are significant. While a number of major states like Karnataka, West Bengal, Punjab, Haryana, Andhra Pradesh and Rajasthan have shown acceleration in growth in the second half, some crucial ones, on the other hand, namely, Maharashtra, Gujarat, Madhya Pradesh, Orissa and Assam, have experienced deceleration. The loss in the growth momentum of Maharashtra and Gujarat between the two five-year in terms of GSDP periods is indeed steep – from 9.2 per cent to 4.2 per cent in the case of Gujarat and from 8.2 per cent to 5.3 per cent for Maharashtra. Though, Kerala's growth in total GSDP shows a decline in the second half of the decade, its performance nevertheless remains above the national average in terms of per capita income growth.

Evolving State Ranks Measured by GSDP Per Capita

In Tables 30.4(A) and 4(B) Graph A, 16 major states are ranked in descending order of their per capita NSDP and GSDP for the four sample periods of the early 1980s and the early 1990s, based on 1980-81 series and for the middle and end of the 1990s, based on 1993-94 prices. The rankings have been done on the basis of three-yearly averages of per capita NSDP and per capita GSDP. An amazing impression imparted by these data is that there has been little change in the relative position of states in terms of rankings during the past two decades. In particular, the composition of the top five states and of the bottom six states have generally remained unchanged (choice of five and six is based on roughly unchanged positions). Significantly, even the relative ranks of the top five – Punjab, Maharashtra, Haryana, Gujarat and Tamil Nadu in that order – have stayed the same in the early 1990s and at the end of the decade (except for a interchange between Punjab and Maharashtra in the top position of per capita GSDP). In the early 1980s too, the first four out of the top five were the same states and in the same order; it is just that West Bengal, which held the fifth rank in that early period steadily and steeply slipped thereafter and was replaced by Tamil Nadu in the subsequent three periods. Likewise, it is equally revealing that at the bottom end, the same six states, namely, Rajasthan, Madhya Pradesh, Assam, Uttar Pradesh, Orissa and Bihar, have remained stuck at the bottom position during the four period intervals except for some minor shuffling (like Assam and Uttar Pradesh exchanging their 14th and 15th positions in per capita GSDP in the last two periods.

TABLE – 30.1

Annual Compound Growth Rate in GSDP and Per Capita GSDP during 1980s and 1990s

(In per cent per annum)

GSDP at 1980-81 Prices		GSDP at 1993-94 Prices		Per Capita GSDP at 1980-81 Prices		Per Capita GSDP at 1993-94 Prices	
1980-81 to 1993-94		1993-94 to 2000-01		1980-81 to 1993-94		1993-94 to 2000-01	
(1)		(2)		(3)		(4)	
Sikkim	10.65	Pondicherry	13.76	Sikkim	8.05	Pondicherry	11.65
Arunachal Pradesh	8.79	Chandigarh	9.60	Arunachal Pradesh	5.51	Goa	7.91
Delhi	7.40	Goa	9.45	Goa	4.53	Tripura	6.84
Nagaland	6.92	Sikkim	8.97	Maharashtra	4.18	Karnataka	6.63
Maharashtra	6.57	Delhi	8.89	Tamil Nadu	4.10	Chandigarh	5.88
Rajasthan	6.24	Karnataka	8.24	Rajasthan	3.67	Sikkim	5.64
Goa	6.12	Tripura	8.19	Karnataka	3.67	Manipur	5.54
Tripura	6.10	Manipur	7.98	Andhra Pradesh	3.53	West Bengal	5.46
Haryana	6.01	West Bengal	7.12	Haryana	3.50	Tamil Nadu	5.15
Andhra Pradesh	5.75	Meghalaya	6.82	**All-India GDP (CSO)**	**3.17**	Himachal Pradesh	4.96
Karnataka	5.61	Rajasthan	6.80	Gujarat	3.17	Delhi	4.87
Meghalaya	5.60	Himachal Pradesh	6.79	Punjab	3.14	Gujarat	4.48
A and N Islands	5.52	**All-India GDP (CSO)**	**6.32**	Delhi	3.12	**All-India GDP (CSO)**	**4.32**
Tamil Nadu	5.51	Tamil Nadu	6.23	Himachal Pradesh	3.10	Rajasthan	4.16
All-India GDP (CSO)	**5.35**	Gujarat	6.16	Tripura	3.08	Kerala	4.13
All States GSDP	**5.27**	Maharashtra	5.92	**All States GSDP**	**3.08**	Andhra Pradesh	4.12

Contd...

...Contd...

Manipur	5.14	Haryana	5.73	Kerala	2.88	Maharashtra	3.82
Gujarat	5.13	**All States GSDP**	**5.72**	West Bengal	2.69	**All States GSDP**	**3.78**
Punjab	5.12	Andhra Pradesh	5.46	Meghalaya	2.63	Haryana	3.75
Himachal Pradesh	5.06	Kerala	5.28	Nagaland	2.54	Meghalaya	3.23
West Bengal	4.93	Punjab	5.07	Manipur	2.52	Punjab	3.10
Madhya Pradesh	4.68	Jammu and Kashmir	4.79	Uttar Pradesh	2.33	Madhya Pradesh	2.25
Uttar Pradesh	4.61	Madhya Pradesh	4.29	Madhya Pradesh	2.25	Jammu and Kashmir	2.21
Kerala	4.27	Uttar Pradesh	4.25	Orissa	1.94	Uttar Pradesh	2.06
Orissa	3.82	Bihar	4.13	Assam	1.39	Orissa	2.03
Assam	3.63	Nagaland	4.02	Bihar	1.36	Jharkhand	1.77
Bihar	3.53	A and N Islands	3.96	A and N Islands	1.35	Bihar	1.33
Jammu and Kashmir	3.35	Jharkhand	3.56	Jammu and Kashmir	0.78	Chhattisgarh	1.25
Pondicherry	3.22	Orissa	3.27	Pondicherry	0.28	Assam	1.00
		Arunachal Pradesh	3.06			Arunachal Pradesh	0.56
		Chhattisgarh	2.88			A and N Islands	0.37
		Assam	2.63			Nagaland	-1.12
Coefficient of Variation (percentage)							
For all states	29.61		41.09		51.06		68.04
For 16 major states*	18.12		27.17		29.99		43.25

Contd...

TABLE – 30.1 *(Contd...)*

Annual Compound Growth Rate in GSDP and Per Capita GSDP during 1980s and 1990s

(In per cent per annum)

GSDP at 1980-81 Prices		GSDP at 1993-94 Prices		Per Capita GSDP at 1980-81 Prices		Per Capita GSDP at 1993-94 Prices	
1980-81 to 1990-91		1990-91 to 2000-01		1980-81 to 1990-91		1990-91 to 2000-01	
(5)		(6)		(7)		(8)	
Sikkim	11.64	Pondicherry	10.09	Sikkim	8.76	Pondicherry	8.11
Arunachal Pradesh	8.35	Goa	8.38	Arunachal Pradesh	5.00	Goa	6.75
Delhi	7.59	Sikkim	8.12	Goa	3.91	Karnataka	5.89
Nagaland	7.42	Karnataka	7.56	Rajasthan	3.91	Tripura	5.60
Rajasthan	6.60	Gujarat	7.35	Haryana	3.89	Gujarat	5.56
Haryana	6.43	Tripura	7.31	Tamil Nadu	3.88	Tamil Nadu	5.52
Maharashtra	6.02	West Bengal	6.84	Maharashtra	3.63	West Bengal	5.10
Tripura	5.75	Maharashtra	6.83	Andhra Pradesh	3.39	Sikkim	4.80
Andhra Pradesh	5.65	Delhi	6.83	Punjab	3.35	Maharashtra	4.70
A and N Islands	5.64	Tamil Nadu	6.62	**All-India GDP (CSO)**	**3.32**	Kerala	4.58
All-India GDP (CSO)	**5.55**	Manipur	6.33	Karnataka	3.25	Himachal Pradesh	4.45
Meghalaya	5.51	Himachal Pradesh	6.31	Delhi	3.19	**All-India GDP (CSO)**	**4.08**
Goa	5.49	A and N Islands	6.17	Himachal Pradesh	3.12	Andhra Pradesh	3.92
Tamil Nadu	5.38	**All-India GDP (CSO)**	**6.10**	Nagaland	3.11	Manipur	3.91
Punjab	5.32	Rajasthan	6.07	Gujarat	3.04	**All States GSDP**	**3.83**
Karnataka	5.29	Kerala	5.82	**All States GSDP**	**3.02**	Rajasthan	3.54
All States GSDP	**5.26**	**All States GSDP**	**5.82**	Tripura	2.69	Haryana	2.94
Gujarat	5.08	Meghalaya	5.62	Uttar Pradesh	2.57	Delhi	2.92
Manipur	5.06	Andhra Pradesh	5.44	Meghalaya	2.55	Punjab	2.89

Contd...

...Contd...

Himachal Pradesh	5.03	Nagaland	5.28	Bihar	2.45	Madhya Pradesh	2.67
Uttar Pradesh	4.95	Haryana	5.06	West Bengal	2.44	A and N Islands	2.49
West Bengal	4.71	Punjab	4.85	Orissa	2.42	Orissa	2.28
Bihar	4.66	Jammu and Kashmir	4.81	Manipur	2.39	Jammu and Kashmir	2.21
Madhya Pradesh	4.56	Madhya Pradesh	4.78	Kerala	2.15	Meghalaya	2.19
Pondicherry	4.39	Arunachal Pradesh	4.74	Madhya Pradesh	2.12	Arunachal Pradesh	2.18
Orissa	4.29	Uttar Pradesh	3.95	Pondicherry	1.43	Uttar Pradesh	1.86
Assam	3.58	Orissa	3.75	Assam	1.38	Assam	0.93
Kerala	3.57	Bihar	2.87	A and N Islands	1.15	Nagaland	0.80
Jammu and Kashmir	2.99	Assam	2.76	Jammu and Kashmir	0.40	Bihar	0.12
Coefficient of Variation (percentage)							
For all states	30.52		28.14		50.20		52.19
For 16 major states*	17.12		27.94		25.36		48.02

* For the list, see Table 4(A) and 4(B).

Notes: (i) All states GSDP represents the summation of GSDP for all states at constant prices for individual years and the compound growth rate has been estimated from them.

(ii) Growth rate in all-India GDP (CSO) represents the compound growth rate based on the CSO's estimates of GDP as per national accounts statistics.

(iii) All SDP measures at 1993-94 prices for the period 1990-91 to 1992-93 have been derived by a method of splicing using the available 1980-81 series.

(iv) Data with respect to Chhattisgarh, Jharkhand, Nagaland, Sikkim and Andaman and Nicobar Islands are available only upto 1999-2000; their series have been extended upto 2000-01 by certain assumed growth rates: the previous year growth for three, A and N Islands, Chhattisgarh and Jharkhand; for the other two, growth rates of neighbouring states, Tripura for Nagaland and Arunachal Pradesh for Sikkim, have been applied.

(v) The annual compound rate of growth has been worked out applying the log-linear model for SDP with respect to time (t): log SDP = a + bt, where b is said to represent instantaneous rate of growth. To derive the compound growth rate, we take the antilog of b, subtract 1 from it, and multiply the difference by 100. This is achieved by transforming the compound growth formula $SDP = A(1+r)^t$ into a regression equation log SDP = a + bt, where b = log (1+r) and the growth rate r = [(antilogb) - 1] where b represents the regression coefficient.

TABLE – 30.2

Annual Compound Growth Rate in NSDP and Per Capita NSDP during 1980s and 1990s

(In per cent per annum)

NSDP at 1980-81 Prices		NSDP at 1993-94 Prices		Per Capita NSDP at 1980-81 Prices		Per Capita NSDP at 1993-94 Prices	
1980-81 to 1993-94		1993-94 to 2000-01		1980-81 to 1993-94		1993-94 to 2000-01	
(1)		(2)		(3)		(4)	
Sikkim	10.45	Pondicherry	14.80	Sikkim	7.85	Pondicherry	12.67
Arunachal Pradesh	8.89	Goa	9.73	Arunachal Pradesh	5.63	Goa	8.20
Delhi	7.86	Chandigarh	9.64	Goa	5.19	Tripura	7.08
Nagaland	7.58	Delhi	9.01	Maharashtra	4.20	Karnataka	6.53
Goa	6.78	Sikkim	8.88	Tamil Nadu	4.06	Sikkim	6.29
Maharashtra	6.59	Tripura	8.42	Haryana	3.60	Manipur	5.93
Rajasthan	6.15	Manipur	8.39	Karnataka	3.58	Chandigarh	5.92
Haryana	6.11	Karnataka	8.14	Rajasthan	3.58	West Bengal	5.52
Tripura	5.89	Meghalaya	7.25	Delhi	3.56	Tamil Nadu	5.01
Andhra Pradesh	5.76	West Bengal	7.17	Andhra Pradesh	3.54	Delhi	4.99
Karnataka	5.52	Rajasthan	6.79	Punjab	3.18	Himachal Pradesh	4.69
Tamil Nadu	5.47	Himachal Pradesh	6.52	Nagaland	3.09	**All-India NDP (CSO)**	**4.20**
All-India NDP (CSO)	**5.25**	**All-India NDP (CSO)**	**6.20**	**All-India NDS (CSO)**	**3.07**	Rajasthan	4.15
All States NSDP	**5.19**	Tamil Nadu	6.08	**All States NSDP**	**3.01**	Andhra Pradesh	4.12

Contd...

...*Contd*...

Punjab	5.17	Haryana	5.57	Gujarat	2.98	Kerala	3.92
Meghalaya	5.04	**All States NSDP**	**5.52**	Himachal	2.92	Meghalaya	3.64
Gujarat	4.95	Maharashtra	5.46	Tripura	2.88	Gujarat	3.63
A and N Islands	4.90	Andhra Pradesh	5.46	Kerala	2.66	Haryana	3.59
Himachal Pradesh	4.87	Gujarat	5.30	West Bengal	2.57	**All States NSDP**	**3.57**
Manipur	4.87	Kerala	5.06	Manipur	2.26	Maharashtra	3.37
West Bengal	4.80	Punjab	4.88	Uttar Pradesh	2.23	Punjab	2.92
Uttar Pradesh	4.51	Jammu and Kashmir	4.57	Meghalaya	2.09	Jharkhand	2.19
Madhya Pradesh	4.28	Nagaland	4.21	Madhya Pradesh	1.87	Madhya Pradesh	2.16
Kerala	4.05	Madhya Pradesh	4.20	Orissa	1.61	Jammu and Kashmir	1.99
Orissa	3.49	Uttar Pradesh	4.01	Bihar	1.16	Uttar Pradesh	1.77
Assam	3.38	Jharkhand	3.98	Assam	1.14	Orissa	1.30
Bihar	3.33	Bihar	3.97	A and N Islands	0.75	Bihar	1.17
Pondicherry	2.83	A and N Islands	3.55	Jammu and Kashmir	0.05	Assam	0.81
Jammu and Kashmir	2.60	Arunachal Pradesh	2.76	Pondicherry	-0.09	Chhattisgarh	0.44
		Orissa	2.53			Arunachal Pradesh	0.28
		Assam	2.44			A and N Islands	-0.01
		Chhattisgarh	2.05			Nagaland	-0.56
Coefficient of Variation (percentage)							
For all states	33.43		45.99		58.60		74.55
For 16 major states*	20.69		29.93		34.79		48.09

Contd...

TABLE – 30.2 *(Contd...)*

Annual Compound Growth Rate in NSDP and Per Capita NSDP during 1980s and 1990s

(In per cent per annum)

NSDP at 1980-81 Prices		NSDP at 1993-94 Prices		Per Capita NSDP at 1980-81 Prices		Per Capita NSDP at 1993-94 Prices	
1980-81 to 1990-91		1990-91 to 2000-01		1980-81 to 1990-91		1990-91 to 2000-01	
(5)		(6)		(7)		(8)	
Sikkim	11.44	Pondicherry	10.31	Sikkim	8.54	Pondicherry	8.34
Arunachal Pradesh	8.34	Delhi	8.70	Arunachal Pradesh	5.03	Goa	6.97
Delhi	7.60	Goa	8.60	Goa	4.43	Karnataka	5.73
Nagaland	7.59	Sikkim	8.12	Haryana	4.00	Tripura	5.68
Rajasthan	6.58	Karnataka	7.41	Rajasthan	3.89	Tamil Nadu	5.36
Haryana	6.55	Tripura	7.40	Tamil Nadu	3.77	Sikkim	5.24
Goa	6.02	West Bengal	6.87	Maharashtra	3.60	West Bengal	5.13
Maharashtra	6.00	Gujarat	6.86	Punjab	3.40	Gujarat	5.07
Andhra Pradesh	5.66	Maharashtra	6.50	Andhra Pradesh	3.39	Delhi	4.72
Tripura	5.53	Manipur	6.49	**All-India NDP (CSO)**	**3.25**	Kerala	4.56
All-India NDP (CSO)	**5.47**	Tamil Nadu	6.46	Nagaland	3.23	Maharashtra	4.37
Punjab	5.37	A and N Islands	6.13	Delhi	3.20	Himachal Pradesh	4.12
Tamil Nadu	5.27	Himachal Pradesh	5.97	Karnataka	3.14	Manipur	4.05
Karnataka	5.18	**All-India NDP(CSO)**	**5.95**	Himachal Pradesh	2.97	Andhra Pradesh	3.88
All States NSDP	**5.17**	Rajasthan	5.95	**All States NSDP**	**2.94**	**All States NSDP**	**3.67**
A and N Islands	5.10	Kerala	5.80	Gujarat	2.84	**All-India NDP(CSO)**	**3.65**
Uttar Pradesh	4.95	Meghalaya	5.78	Uttar Pradesh	2.58	Rajasthan	3.42
Meghalaya	4.95	**All States NSDP**	**5.65**	Bihar	2.56	Haryana	2.76
Gujarat	4.88	Andhra Pradesh	5.39	Tripura	2.46	Punjab	2.62

Contd...

...Contd...

Himachal Pradesh	4.87	Nagaland	5.27	West Bengal	2.32	Madhya Pradesh	2.52
Bihar	4.76	Haryana	4.87	Orissa	2.12	A and N Islands	2.41
Manipur	4.74	Madhya Pradesh	4.64	Manipur	2.10	Meghalaya	2.35
West Bengal	4.58	Punjab	4.58	Meghalaya	2.01	Arunachal Pradesh	2.02
Pondicherry	4.29	Arunachal Pradesh	4.57	Madhya Pradesh	1.73	Jammu and Kashmir	1.93
Madhya Pradesh	4.17	Jammu and Kashmir	4.52	Kerala	1.71	Orissa	1.68
Orissa	3.99	Uttar Pradesh	3.60	Pondicherry	1.31	Uttar Pradesh	1.43
Assam	3.33	Orissa	3.14	Assam	1.14	Nagaland	0.74
Kerala	3.13	Assam	2.52	A and N Islands	0.61	Assam	0.69
Jammu and Kashmir	2.17	Bihar	2.42	Jammu and Kashmir	-0.39	Bihar	-0.31
Coefficient of Variation (percentage)							
For all states	33.28		32.00		57.09		56.39
For 16 major states*	20.06		30.60		30.27		53.82

* For the list, see Table 30.4(A) and 30.4(B).

Notes: (i) All states NSDP represents the summation of GSDP for all states at constant prices for individual years and the compound growth rate has been estimated from them.

(ii) Growth rate in all-India NDP (CSO) represents the compound growth rate based on the CSO's estimates of NDP as per national accounts statistics.

(iii) All SDP measures at 1993-94 prices for the period 1990-91 to 1992-93 have been derived by a method of splicing using the available 1980-81 series.

(iv) Data with respect to Chhattisgarh, Jharkhand, Nagaland, Sikkim and Andaman and Nicobar Islands are available only upto 1999-2000; their series have been extended upto 2000-01 by certain assumed growth rates: the previous year growth for three, A and N Islands, Chhattisgarh and Jharkhand; for the other two, growth rates of neighbouring states, Tripura for Nagaland and Arunachal Pradesh for Sikkim, have been applied.

(v) The annual compound rate of growth has been worked out applying the log-linear model for SDP with respect to time (t): log SDP = a + bt, where b is said to represent instantaneous rate of growth. To derive the compound growth rate, we take the antilog of b, subtract 1 from it, and multiply the difference by 100. This is achieved by transforming the compound growth formula $SDP = A(1+r)^t$ into a regression equation log SDP = a + bt, where b = log (1+r) and the growth rate r = [(antilogb) - 1] where b represents the regression coefficient.

TABLE – 30.3

Quinquennium Compound Growth Rates of SDP and Per Capita SDP (at 1993-94 Prices) of States During 1990s

(In per cent per annum)

Gross State Domestic Product (GSDP)				Per Capita Gross State Domestic Product (Per Capita GSDP)			
1990-91 to 1995-96		1995-96 to 2000-01		1990-91 to 1995-96		1995-96 to 2000-01	
(1)		(2)		(3)		(4)	
A and N Islands	9.60	Pondicherry	13.51	Gujarat	7.24	Pondicherry	11.41
Gujarat	9.24	Goa	9.72	Tamil Nadu	6.10	Goa	8.14
Maharashtra	8.21	Manipur	9.37	Maharashtra	6.02	Tripura	7.66
Arunachal Pradesh	8.18	Sikkim	9.31	A and N Islands	5.79	Karnataka	7.49
Tamil Nadu	7.25	Karnataka	8.97	Arunachal Pradesh	5.50	Manipur	6.93
Nagaland	6.96	Delhi	8.94	Kerala	5.44	Sikkim	6.21
Kerala	6.82	Tripura	8.75	Karnataka	4.64	West Bengal	5.49
Karnataka	6.40	West Bengal	7.04	West Bengal	4.42	Tamil Nadu	5.01
West Bengal	6.31	Meghalaya	6.79	Goa	4.29	Delhi	4.97
Goa	6.05	Himachal Pradesh	6.55	Nagaland	3.61	Himachal Pradesh	4.72
Sikkim	5.80	Tamil Nadu	6.03	Himachal Pradesh	3.58	Andhra Pradesh	4.36
All States GSDP	**5.63**	**All-India GDP (CSO)**	**5.84**	**All States GSDP**	**3.57**	Kerala	4.35
All-India GDP (CSO)	**5.56**	Haryana	5.84	Andhra Pradesh	3.50	Haryana	4.07
Himachal Pradesh	5.47	Bihar	5.75	**All-India GDP (CSO)**	**3.43**	All-India	3.83
Andhra Pradesh	5.32	Andhra Pradesh	5.58	Orissa	3.06	All States GSDP	3.61
Tripura	5.12	**All States GSDP**	**5.48**	Tripura	2.83	Punjab	3.44
Orissa	4.92	Kerala	5.42	Madhya Pradesh	2.61	Meghalaya	3.27
Madhya Pradesh	4.85	Punjab	5.41	Sikkim	2.56	Maharashtra	3.27
Jammu and Kashmir	4.71	Maharashtra	5.30	Punjab	2.39	Bihar	3.01
Rajasthan	4.65	Rajasthan	5.10	Rajasthan	2.31	Gujarat	2.53
Punjab	4.34	Jammu and Kashmir	4.62	Jammu and Kashmir	1.98	Rajasthan	2.49
Meghalaya	3.68	Gujarat	4.05	Haryana	1.24	Jammu and Kashmir	2.15
Haryana	3.58	A and N Islands	3.90	Uttar Pradesh	1.07	Orissa	2.08
Delhi	3.58	Uttar Pradesh	3.72	Assam	0.92	Madhya Pradesh	1.60
Uttar Pradesh	3.14	Madhya Pradesh	3.52	Manipur	0.66	Uttar Pradesh	1.42
Assam	3.08	Orissa	3.14	Meghalaya	0.54	Assam	1.25
Manipur	3.04	Assam	2.72	Delhi	-0.16	A and N Islands	0.31
Pondicherry	1.54	Nagaland	2.51	Pondicherry	-0.35	Arunachal Pradesh	-0.36
Bihar	-0.54	Arunachal Pradesh	2.10	Bihar	-3.22	Nagaland	-2.85

Contd...

...Contd...

Net State Domestic Product (NSDP)				Per Capita Net State Domestic Product (Per Capita NSDP)			
1990-91 to 1995-96		1995-96 to 2000-01		1990-91 to 1995-96		1995-96 to 2000-01	
(5)		(6)		(7)		(8)	
A and N Islands	10.16	Pondicherry	14.94	Gujarat	7.37	Pondicherry	12.81
Gujarat	9.36	Goa	10.33	A and N Islands	6.21	Goa	8.73
Arunachal Pradesh	8.28	Manipur	10.00	Tamil Nadu	5.95	Tripura	8.11
Maharashtra	8.11	Tripura	9.20	Maharashtra	5.92	Karnataka	7.65
Delhi	7.65	Delhi	9.18	Kerala	5.70	Manipur	7.54
Kerala	7.09	Karnataka	9.13	Arunachal Pradesh	5.61	Sikkim	7.20
Tamil Nadu	7.09	Sikkim	9.07	West Bengal	4.41	West Bengal	5.53
Nagaland	6.99	Meghalaya	7.28	Karnataka	4.40	Delhi	5.20
West Bengal	6.31	West Bengal	7.09	Goa	4.38	Tamil Nadu	4.92
Karnataka	6.16	Himachal Pradesh	6.39	Delhi	3.77	Himachal Pradesh	4.56
Goa	6.14	Tamil Nadu	5.94	**All States NSDP**	**3.46**	Andhra Pradesh	4.29
Sikkim	5.79	Bihar	5.77	Andhra Pradesh	3.35	Kerala	4.09
All States NSDP	**5.52**	**All-India NDP (CSO)**	**5.75**	**All-India NDP (CSO)**	**3.29**	Haryana	3.91
All-India NDP (CSO)	**5.36**	Haryana	5.68	Himachal Pradesh	3.21	Meghalaya	3.75
Andhra Pradesh	5.17	Andhra Pradesh	5.51	Nagaland	3.01	**All-India NDP (CSO)**	**3.75**
Himachal Pradesh	5.09	**All States NSDP**	**5.31**	Orissa	2.75	All States NSDP	3.45
Tripura	4.92	Punjab	5.30	Tripura	2.64	Punjab	3.32
Orissa	4.60	Kerala	5.16	Sikkim	2.64	Bihar	3.02
Madhya Pradesh	4.48	Maharashtra	4.94	Madhya Pradesh	2.24	Maharashtra	2.91
Rajasthan	4.31	Rajasthan	4.93	Punjab	2.00	Rajasthan	2.31
Jammu and Kashmir	4.30	Jammu and Kashmir	4.36	Rajasthan	1.98	Jammu and Kashmir	1.89
Punjab	3.95	A and N Islands	3.56	Jammu and Kashmir	1.58	Madhya Pradesh	1.57
Meghalaya	3.40	Uttar Pradesh	3.56	Haryana	1.02	Gujarat	1.55
Haryana	3.36	Madhya Pradesh	3.49	Assam	0.59	Orissa	1.39
Manipur	2.74	Gujarat	3.06	Uttar Pradesh	0.52	Uttar Pradesh	1.38
Assam	2.74	Assam	2.63	Manipur	0.34	Assam	1.16
Uttar Pradesh	2.58	Nagaland	2.61	Meghalaya	0.27	A and N Islands	0.03
Pondicherry	-0.15	Orissa	2.44	Pondicherry	-1.95	Arunachal Pradesh	-0.65
Bihar	-1.52	Arunachal Pradesh	1.80	Bihar	-4.17	Nagaland	-2.11

Notes and Sources: See Tables 30.1 and 30.2.

TABLE – 30.4(A)

Rank of States in Descending Order of Per Capita NSDP (Three-Yearly Annual Averages)

Rank	State	Per Capita NSDP at 1980-81 Prices: Annual Averages for 1980-81 to 1982-83	Rank	State	Per Capita NSDP at 1980-81 Prices: Annual Averages for 1990-91 to 1992-93	Rank	State	Per Capita NSDP at 1993-94 Prices: Annual Averages for 1993-94 to 1995-96	Rank	State	Per Capita NSDP at 1993-94 Prices: Annual Averages for 1998-99 to 2000-01
	Part A: Per Capita Net State Domestic Product (NSDP)										
1.	Punjab	2818	1.	Punjab	3829	1.	Punjab	12834	1.	Punjab	14881
2.	Maharashtra	2452	2.	Maharashtra	3573	2.	Maharashtra	12521	2.	Maharashtra	14732
3.	Haryana	2419	3.	Haryana	3476	3.	Haryana	11426	3.	Haryana	13681
4.	Gujarat	2011	4.	Gujarat	2704	4.	Gujarat	10993	4.	Gujarat	13163
5.	West Bengal	1727	5.	Tamil Nadu	2290	5.	Tamil Nadu	9686	5.	Tamil Nadu	12315
6.	Himachal Pradesh	1718	6.	Himachal Pradesh	2240	6.	Kerala	8401	6.	Karnataka	11257
	Average for all states	**1595**	7.	West Bengal	2236	7.	Himachal Pradesh	8387	7.	Himachal Pradesh	10529
	All-India NDP(CSO)	**1672**	8.	Karnataka	2193	8.	Karnataka	8101	8.	Kerala	10141
7.	Karnataka	1563		**Average for all states**	**2132**	9.	Andhra Pradesh	7757	9.	Andhra Pradesh	9534
8.	Tamil Nadu	1555		**All-India NDP(CSO)**	**2264**		**Average for all states**	**7694**	10.	West Bengal	9307
9.	Andhra Pradesh	1504	9.	Andhra Pradesh	2078		**All-India NDP(CSO)**	**8234**		**Average for all states**	**9245**
10.	Kerala	1487	10.	Rajasthan	1891	10.	West Bengal	7114		**All-India NDP(CSO)**	**10139**
11.	Assam	1374	11.	Kerala	1858	11.	Rajasthan	6844	11.	Rajasthan	8466
12.	Madhya Pradesh	1369	12.	Uttar Pradesh	1631	12.	Madhya Pradesh	6631	12.	Madhya Pradesh	7520
13.	Uttar Pradesh	1299	13.	Madhya Pradesh	1617	13.	Assam	5737	13.	Assam	5933
14.	Orissa	1265	14.	Assam	1559	14.	Uttar Pradesh	5156	14.	Uttar Pradesh	5633
15.	Rajasthan	1261	15.	Orissa	1463	15.	Orissa	4921	15.	Orissa	5206
16.	Bihar	933	16.	Bihar	1106	16.	Bihar	3045	16.	Bihar	3294

TABLE – 30.4(B)

Rank of States in Descending Order of Per Capita GSDP (Three-Yearly Annual Averages)

Rank	State	Per Capita GSDP at 1980-81 Prices: Annual Averages for 1980-81 to 1982-83	Rank	State	Per Capita GSDP at 1980-81 Prices: Annual Averages for 1990-91 to 1992-93	Rank	State	Per Capita GSDP at 1993-94 Prices: Annual Averages for 1993-94 to 1995-96	Rank	State	Per Capita GSDP at 1993-94 Prices: Annual Averages for 1998-99 to 2000-01
	Part B: Per Capita Gross State Domestic Product (GSDP)										
1.	Punjab	3174	1.	Punjab	4286	1.	Punjab	14405	1.	Maharashtra	16865
2.	Haryana	2705	2.	Maharashtra	3931	2.	Maharashtra	14019	2.	Punjab	16848
3.	Maharashtra	2695	3.	Haryana	3843	3.	Haryana	13021	3.	Gujarat	15779
4.	Gujarat	2280	4.	Gujarat	3118	4.	Gujarat	12661	4.	Haryana	15716
5.	Himachal Pradesh.	1888	5.	Tamil Nadu	2579	5.	Tamil Nadu	10823	5.	Tamil Nadu	13859
6.	West Bengal	1871	6.	Himachal Pradesh	2507	6.	Himachal Pradesh	9454	6.	Karnataka	12619
	Average for all states	**1776**	7.	Karnataka	2462	7.	Kerala	9266	7.	Himachal Pradesh	12027
	All-India GDP(CSO)	**1857**	8.	West Bengal	2448	8.	Karnataka	9054	8.	Kerala	11304
7.	Tamil Nadu	1743		**Average for all states**	**2393**	9.	Andhra Pradesh	8681	9.	Andhra Pradesh	10665
8.	Karnataka	1739		**All-India GDP(CSO)**	**2538**		**Average for all states**	**8672**		**Average for all states**	**10510**
9.	Kerala	1683	9.	Andhra Pradesh	2312		**All-India GDP(CSO)**	**9234**		**All-India GDP(CSO)**	**11433**
10.	Andhra Pradesh.	1673	10.	Kerala	2158	10.	West Bengal	7844	10.	West Bengal	10236
11.	Madhya Pradesh.	1529	11.	Rajasthan	2129	11.	Rajasthan	7749	11.	Rajasthan	9569
12.	Assam	1485	12.	Madhya Pradesh	1882	12.	Madhya Pradesh	7479	12.	Madhya Pradesh	8495
13.	Uttar Pradesh	1449	13.	Uttar Pradesh	1833	13.	Assam	6476	13.	Assam	6762
14.	Rajasthan	1416	14.	Assam	1719	14.	Uttar Pradesh	5877	14.	Uttar Pradesh	6500
15.	Orissa	1371	15.	Orissa	1639	15.	Orissa	5682	15.	Orissa	6236
16.	Bihar	1080	16.	Bihar	1291	16.	Bihar	3349	16.	Bihar	3656

Note: The original data are from the data base in EPWRF 2003.

TABLE – 30.5

Percentage Share of Top Five, Middle Five and Bottom Six States in Terms of Per Capita GSDP (Three-Yearly Annual Averages)

Sl.No.	State	Percentage Share of GSDP at 1980-81 Prices: Annual Averages for 1980-81 to 1982-83	Sl.No.	State	Percentage Share of GSDP at 1980-81 Prices: Annual Averages for 1990-91 to 1992-93	Sl.No.	State	Percentage Share of GSDP at 1993-94 Prices: Annual Averages for 1993-94 to 1995-96	Sl.No.	State	Percentage Share of GSDP at 1993-94 Prices: Annual Averages for 1998-99 to 2000-01
	Top Five States	**28.3**		**Top Five States**	**36.3**		**Top Five States**	**37.5**		**Top Five States**	**38.3**
1	Maharashtra	14.0	1	Maharashtra	15.4	1	Maharashtra	15.3	1	Maharashtra	15.6
2	Gujarat	6.4	2	Tamil Nadu	7.1	2	Tamil Nadu	8.1	2	Tamil Nadu	8.3
3	Punjab	4.4	3	Gujarat	6.4	3	Gujarat	7.2	3	Gujarat	7.4
4	Haryana	2.9	4	Punjab	4.3	4	Punjab	4.0	4	Punjab	3.9
5	Himachal Pradesh	0.7	5	Haryana	3.1	5	Haryana	3.0	5	Haryana	3.0
	Middle Five States	**31.6**		**Middle Five States**	**25.1**		**Middle Five States**	**25.0**		**Middle Five States**	**26.4**
6	West Bengal	8.4	6	West Bengal	8.2	6	Andhra Pradesh	7.8	6	West Bengal	7.9
7	Andhra Pradesh	7.4	7	Andhra Pradesh	7.6	7	West Bengal	7.3	7	Andhra Pradesh	7.8
8	Tamil Nadu	6.9	8	Karnataka	5.5	8	Karnataka	5.6	8	Karnataka	6.4
9	Karnataka	5.3	9	Kerala	3.1	9	Kerala	3.6	9	Kerala	3.6
10	Kerala	3.5	10	Himachal Pradesh	0.6	10	Himachal Pradesh	0.7	10	Himachal Pradesh	0.7
	Bottom Six States	**35.3**		**Bottom Six States**	**33.4**		**Bottom Six States**	**28.0**		**Bottom Six States**	**26.9**
11	Uttar Pradesh	13.3	11	Uttar Pradesh	12.6	11	Uttar Pradesh	10.8	11	Uttar Pradesh	10.2
12	Madhya Pradesh	6.6	12	Madhya Pradesh	6.2	12	Madhya Pradesh	5.0	12	Rajasthan	5.1
13	Bihar	6.2	13	Bihar	5.5	13	Rajasthan	4.8	13	Madhya Pradesh	4.8
14	Rajasthan	4.0	14	Rajasthan	4.6	14	Bihar	3.0	14	Bihar	2.8
15	Orissa	3.0	15	Orissa	2.6	15	Orissa	2.4	15	Orissa	2.2
16	Assam	2.2	16	Assam	1.9	16	Assam	2.0	16	Assam	1.7

GRAPH – A

Ranks of Major States in Descending Order of Per Capita GSDP

(Three-Yearly Annual Averages)

(i) Per Capita NSDP at 1980-81 Prices
(1980-81 to 1982-83)

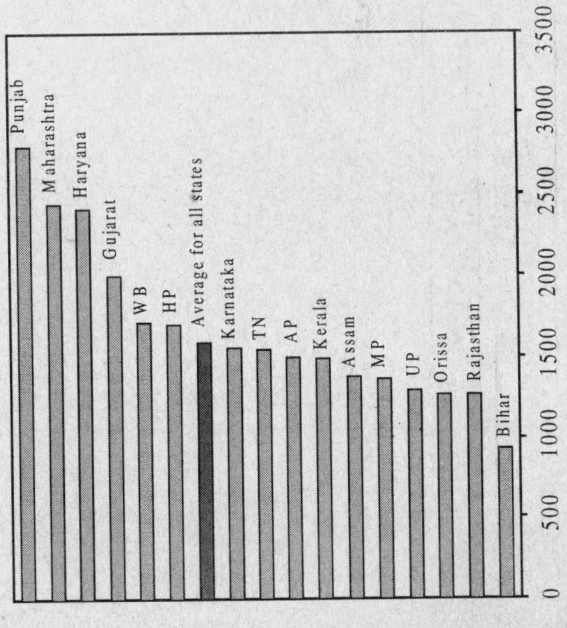

(ii) Per Capita GSDP at 1993-94 Prices
(1989-99 to 2000-01)

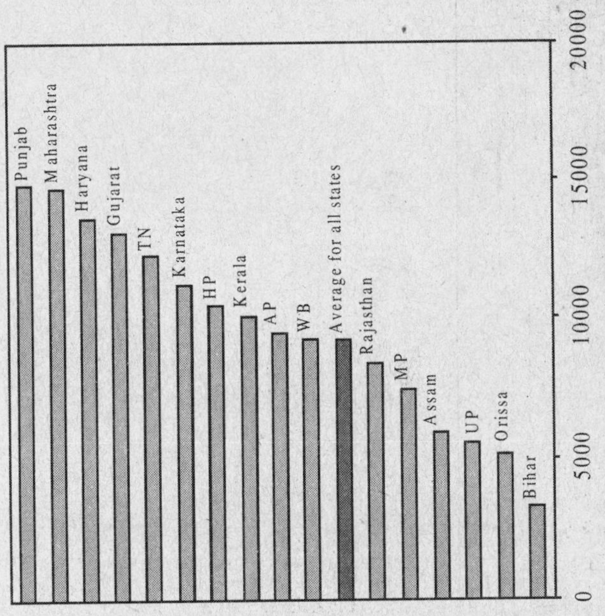

(iii) Per Capita GSDP at 1980-81 Prices
(1980-81 to 1982-83)

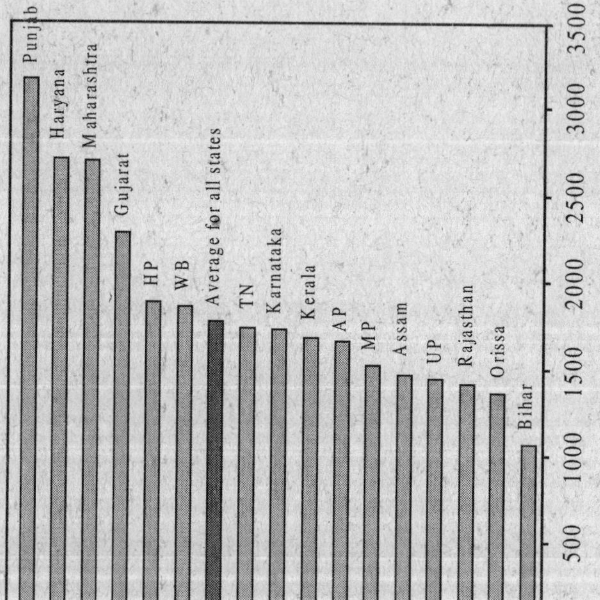

(iv) Per Capita GSDP at 1993-94 Prices
(1989-99 to 2000-01)

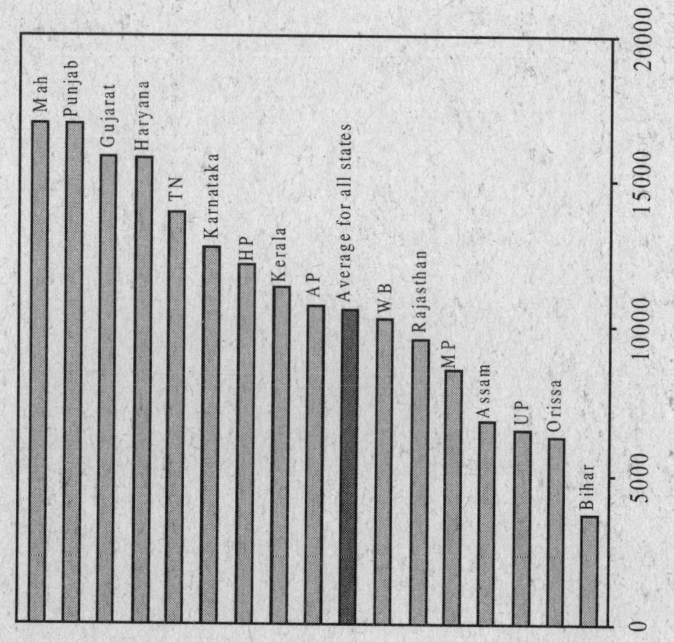

Interestingly, even the spread between the top five and the bottom six states, based on their per capita GSDP, has become widened. To present a crude measure as in Table 30.5, the top five states, which accounted for 24.7 per cent of the country's total population, had a share of 34.6 per cent of all-states GSDP during the early 1980s. This GSDP share increased to 38.2 per cent by the end of the 1990s. On the other hand, the bottom six states which accounted for a 41.6 per cent share in the total population, have suffered a setback in their GSDP share, from 35.3 per cent to 26.9 per cent, between these two periods. Even the middle five states, the composition of which has remained the same, have suffered an erosion in their GSDP share over the last two decades. Furthermore, the spread between the highest (Punjab) and the lowest (Bihar) state, in per capita NSDP terms, became wider in the four periods. The percentage ratio constituting the spread moves up from 302 per cent to 346 per cent and to 421 per cent and finally to 452 per cent, during the periods 1980-81-1982-83, 1991-92-1993-94, 1993-94-1995-96 and 1998-89-2000-01, respectively. As explained earlier, the first two periods are based on the 1980-81 series of real per capita income and the last two are based on the 1993-94 real series.

It must be clarified that the above results are somewhat at variance with the results of Ahluwalia's (2001) study. This is because of the differences in the data used and because there a considerable downward revision of the growth rate of SDP data for Maharashtra has occurred in the revised 1993-94 series. For instance, according to the 1980-81 series, Maharashtra's GSDP per capita grew by 16.5 per cent or by 5.5 per cent per annum between 1993-94 and 1996-97. However, the same measure at 1993-94 prices grew by 11.8 per cent or 3.9 per cent per annum (both simple averages). As indicated in the previous section, Maharashtra's growth rate has suffered a major setback in the second half of the 1990s, according to the 1993-94 series, as compared with the first half of the 1990s for which the average growth rate combines the growth in the 1980-81 and 1993-94 series (Table 30.2). Ahluwalia's study had anticipated such a change in assessment if the SDP figures were revised like the national accounts revisions 1993-94 as the base. To quote him, "we note that if such a revision were to affect some states more than others, it could alter our assessment of the relative performance of states" (p 3).

The picture of unchanged relative positions of states above, or of a widening spread between states with the highest and the lowest per capita SDP, does not mean that state rankings have been totally static. Amongst the southern states, Karnataka and Kerala have moved up in the ladder. Amongst the eastern and northeastern states, West Bengal and Assam have suffered some setback. In relation to the average per capita SDP for all states, the distinction of crossing the threshold has gone to the southern states of Karnataka and Kerala amongst the major states over the two decades (Graph A). No other state, which was below the all-states average earlier, has crossed the average line in the 1990s.

Growing Inequality

Finally, the relative changes in the ranks of different states apart, there is no gainsaying that overall inequality in the levels of real per capita income has risen over the past two decades. This is evident from the year-to-year steadily rising Gini coefficient worked out for the distribution of average per capita GSDP amongst states, separately for the individual years from 1980-81 to 1996-97 based on 1980-81 price series and for those from 1993-94 to 2000-01 at 1993-94 prices (Table 30.6). Three key results that stand out in these measures of Gini coefficients for individual years: (i) both the series show a rise in inequality over the years, though during the 1980s, the coefficients were generally stable up to 1986-87 – a revelation emphasised by Ahluwalia's (2001) study for the major 14 states as well (p 6); (ii) the measure of inequality according to per capita GSDP, based on the revised 1993-94 series, seems to have declined somewhat though the rising trend between 1993-94 and 2000-01 has persisted; and (iii) it is found, based on both the series, that Gini coefficients appear significantly lower for the 16 major states (possessing 90 per cent of the population) than for all the 27 states and union territories, suggesting the presence of wider disparities amongst the smaller states and union territories.

III

STRUCTURAL CHANGES IN STATE ECONOMIES

The mass of SDP data presented by industry of origin in the data base constituting the basis of this study enables us to gauge the nature of structural changes taking place in state economies. To facilitate this, the sectoral compositions of GSDP and NSDP, expressed in percentages, have been worked out for all the four base period series 1960-61, 1970-71, 1980-81 and 1993-94, both at current and constant prices. Apart from depicting the nature of changes taking place in the composition of state incomes, in terms of agriculture, industry and services,[2] the structural ratios also facilitate an assessment of the changes in the relative prices experienced by various sectors. The latter is possible

TABLE – 30.6

Gini Coefficients for the Annual Series of Statewise Real Per Capita GSDP

At 1980-81 Prices			At 1993-94 Prices		
	All States	Major States#		All States	Major States#
1980-81	0.209	0.167	1993-94	0.239	0.201
1981-82	0.202	0.168	1994-95	0.248	0.201
1982-83	0.211	0.171	1995-96	0.250	0.209
1983-84	0.200	0.163	1996-97	0.262	0.213
1984-85	0.205	0.173	1997-98	0.264	0.209
1985-86	0.211	0.181	1998-99	0.276	0.213
1986-87	0.214	0.181	1999-2000	0.278	0.216
1987-88	0.217	0.182	2000-01@	0.292	0.224
1988-89	0.216	0.182	1989-90	0.220	0.190
1990-91	0.224	0.190	1991-92	0.228	0.191
1992-93*	0.244	0.206			
1993-94*	0.237	0.209			
1994-95*	0.250	0.215			
1995-96*	0.251	0.220			
1996-97$	0.258	0.236			

\# 16 Major states as listed in Table 8.3.

* Data with respect to Sikkim and Nagaland are not available.

$ Data with respect to Himachal Pradesh, Sikkim and Nagaland are not available.

@ Data with respect to Andaman and Nicobar Islands, Chhattisgarh, Jharkhand, Nagaland and Sikkim are not available.

Note: Gini Coefficients have been worked out for individual years based on the distribution of real per capita GSDP amongst all states as specified in Exhibits 8.B

The method employed is: $$G = \frac{\sum_{i=1}^{n}(2i-n-1)x_i'}{n^2\mu}$$

(Where 'i' is the rank of a state per capita SDP when arranged in ascending order; 'n' is the number of states; 'x_i' is the observed per capita SDP of state 'i'; 'μ' is the mean per capita income of all states in the sample).

The sample Gini coefficient defined above has been multiplied by n/(n-1) in order to become the *unbiased estimator* for the population coefficient.

Source: Christian Damgaard (2003): www.mathworld.wolfram.com/GiniCoefficient.html (March 11).

from the differences in sectoral shares in the real series and nominal series. Based on these sectoral compositions, the following key results are highlighted.

First, amongst the major states, the share of agriculture in total GSDP remained at one-half or above until the early 1980s in respect of a large number of important states. They are: Bihar, Uttar Pradesh, Madhya Pradesh, Rajashtan, Orissa, Punjab, Haryana and Himachal Pradesh. That was the period when the national share of agriculture in gross domestic product (GDP) was around 40 per cent according to the CSO's National Accounts Statistics (NAS).[3] Thus, the high agricultural share was observed both in agriculturally advanced states, with the highest per capita income in the country (Punjab and Haryana), and in many poorer states, reflecting general backwardness. Towards the end of the 1990s, Punjab is the only state which has retained agriculture as a 40 per cent or over share of GSDP. All other states mentioned above have agricultural share of GSDP of around 35 per cent or less; the national average according to CSO's NAS stands at about 25 per cent in 2000-01. The relatively low national average is due to the fact that a few more industrially advanced states like Maharashtra, Gujarat and Tamil Nadu have an agricultural share far below the national average, hovering at around 15 per cent.

Second, significant structural changes have occurred in the sectoral composition of incomes at the state level, broadly on the pattern observed at the national level. A steady fall in the share of agriculture (to about 25 per cent), a gentle rise in the share of industry (comprising mining, manufacturing, electricity, and construction) to nearly 27 per cent, and a steady rise in the share of services to above 48 per cent has taken place. At one end, even Punjab's agricultural share has fallen from over 50 per cent in the mid-1980s to around 40 per cent by the end of the 1990s. This relatively moderate fall is accompanied by a very moderate rise in the state's share of GSDP, originating in industry and services sectors. In regard to non-agricultural sector shares, what stands out is the niggardly growth of industry share, accompanied by relatively more rapid rise in the share of the services sector. The only exception in this respect has been the state of Gujarat, which has experienced a distinct improvement in the share of industry both in the 1980s and in the 1990s. This share went up from 30.4 per cent in 1980-81 to 37.8 per cent in 1993-94 according to the 1980-81 series (both at current prices), and from 38.8 per cent in 1993-94 to 43.8 per cent in 2000-01 according to the 1993-94 series (also at current prices). Gujarat thus sports the highest share of industry in the states' GSDP. Interestingly, Maharashtra,

Tamil Nadu and West Bengal, all of which had higher industry shares in the early 1980s, have experienced a chequered trend. Maharashtra and Tamil Nadu improved their industry share in the 1980s, but have suffered a setback in the 1990s, whereas West Bengal is yet to recover from the declining trend in industry share that the state began to experience in the early 1980s. As explained earlier, the share of the services sector has risen in all the states, but amongst the major states the most rapid expansion has taken place in Kerala and Maharashtra. Both these states now possess the highest services sector share of 54 per cent each in their respective GSDP at current prices; both of them had begun the decade of the 1980s with the same ratio of around 37-38 per cent. Other major states which enjoy a near or more than 50 per cent share in respect of services are Tamil Nadu, West Bengal, and Bihar. There are of course a number of smaller states like Goa, Tripura and Meghalaya, which have much higher ratios for the services sector.

Finally, there are interstate differences in sectoral shares between the current and constant price series, which have implications for trends in inter-sectoral terms of trade, though in crude form. While analysing the sectoral composition of GDP at the national level, it was said:

> Agricultural sector, for instance, enjoyed relatively better terms of trade between the mid-1960s and mid-1970s but suffered adverse terms during the 1980s, which has been only partially corrected since the beginning of the 1990s. The manufacturing sector has experienced relatively adverse terms of trade in the 1990s as reflected in the fact that the proportion of GDP originating in the sector at current prices has steadily declined from 16.1 per cent in 1993-94 to 15.3 per cent in 2001-02, while it has stayed put at constant prices – a feature which has significant implication for the process of industrialisation [EPW Research Foundation 2002, p 24].

Obviously, this composite national scenario was the sum total of divergent state-level experiences. For instance, the agriculturally advanced state of Punjab has not benefited from improved terms of trade in agriculture in the 1990s, and not even Andhra Pradesh and Madhya Pradesh. In some other states like Haryana, Bihar, Uttar Pradesh, Karnataka and Tamil Nadu, agricutlure has enjoyed some edge with respect to terms of trade. In the industrially advanced states of Maharashtra, Gujarat, West Bengal and Tamil Nadu, the terms of trade have moved in favour of industry, as seen in a relative rise of the sector's share in GSDP, at current prices as compared to constant prices.

Interestingly, such improvement in the terms of trade for the industrial sector seem to have occurred in all the states.

Notes

[An earlier version of this paper appeared as part of the data base study of the EPWRF, *Domestic Product of States of India: 1960-61 to 2000-01*, June 2003. Apart from presenting in respect of all states and Union territories all available statistical series on state domestic product (SDP) for over four decades from 1960-61 through 2000-01 for the first time in India, the data base study dilates a while on the evolution of academic thinking in the international arena on the subject of regional accounts and presents a description of the history of SDP estimation in India and the evolution of its methodology over the decades. It also presents the results of attempts, however sporadically made, at estimating state level gross fixed capital formation by a few states. The study also carries four methodological notes on SDP contributed by Jitender Kumar and his colleagues in the Central Statistical Organisation (CSO), Government of India. Within the EPWRF, a large team consisting of V.P. Prasanth, Sabyasachi Ray, Gauri Shankar Gogoi and Seema Kunte worked on the data base, while L. Thulasamma undertook the required econometric work and S.A. Shetty crtically read through the initial drafts and offered valuable comments. K. Srinivasan and Rema K. Nair worked on typesetting and page-making. The author wishes to offer his sincere thanks to all of them].

1. Such misgivings are found in literature relating to even the most recent period. See Ahluwalia (2001). However, differences probably are the largest in the quality of data sources used rather than in the concepts and definitions employed.
2. SDP originating in different sectors is grouped under these three broad categories:
   (i) Agriculture covers Agriculture, Forestry and Logging and Fishing;
   (ii) Industry covers Mining and Quarrying, Manufacturing, Electricity, Gas and Water Supply and Construction; and
   (iii) Services covers all the other sectors in the GDP distribution by economic activity.
3 Database on and reviews of CSO's National Accounts Statistics are contained in EPWRF (2002).

References

Ahluwalia, M S (2001), "State Level Performance Under Economic Reforms in India", Working Paper No 96, *Centre for Research on Economic Development and Policy Reform*, Stanford University, March.

Bajpai, N and Jeffrey D Sachs (1996), "Trends in Inter-State Inequalities of Income in India", Discussion Paper No 528, *Harvard Institute for International Development*, Harvard University.

Cashin, P and R Sahay (1996), "Internal Migration, Centre-State Grants and Economic Growth in the States of India", *IMF Staff Papers*, Vol 43.

Chaudhury, Mahindar D (1974), "Behaviour of Spatial Income Inequality in a Developing Economy: India 1950-76", Paper presented at the *Ninth Conference of the Indian Association for Research in National Income and Wealth.*

Dasgupta, Dipankar, Pradip Maiti, Robin Mukherjee, Subrata Sarkar, and Subhendru Chakrabarti (2000), "Growth and Interstate Disparities in India", *Economic and Political Weekly*, Vol XXXV, No 27, July 1.

Dholakia, R (1994), "Spatial Dimension of Acceleration of Economic Growth in India", *Economic and Political Weekly*, Vol XXIX, No 35, August 21.

Economic and Political Weekly Research Foundation (EPWRF) (2002), *National Accounts Statistics of India: 1950-51 to 2000-01*, July.

——— (2003), *Domestic Product of States of India*, 1960-61 to 2000-01, June.

Gupta, S (1973), "The Role of the Public Sector in Reducing Regional Income Disparity in India", *Journal of Development Studies*, Vol 9, No 2, pp 243-60.

Majumdar, Grace and J L Kapoor (1980), "Behaviour of Interstate Income Inequalities in India". Paper presented at the *Twelfth Conference of the Indian Association for Research on National Income and Wealth*.

Marjit, Sugata and Sandip Mitra (1996), "Convergence in Regional Growth Rates" Indian Research Agenda, *Economic and Political Weekly*, Vol XXXI, No 33, August 17.

Nagaraj, R, A Varoudakis, and M A Veganzones (2000), "Long-Run Growth Trends and Convergence across Indian States", *Journal of International Development*, Vol 12.

Nagaraj, R (2002), "Performance of India's Manufacturing Sector in the 1990s: Some Tentative Findings", in Uchikawa, Shuji (ed) (2002): *Economic Reforms and Industrial Structure in India*, Manohar.

Nair, K R G (1971), "A Note on Inter-State Income Differentials in India 1950-51 to 1960-61", *Journal of Development Studies*, Vol 7, No 1, pp 441-47.

Roy, Choudhury, Uma Datta (1996), "Pattern of Regional Development As Measured Through Physical and Social Indicators", *The Journal of Income and Wealth*, IARNIW, Vol 18, No 1, January.

Rao, M Govinda, R T Shand, and K P Kalirajan (1999), "Convergence of Incomes across Indian States: A Divergent View", *Economic and Political Weekly*, Vol. XXXIV, No 13, March 27.

Reserve Bank of India (2002), "Regional Dimension of Economic Growth in India", *Report on Currency and Finance 2000-01*, pp III, 45-III, 48, January.

——— (2003), *Report on Currency and Finance 2001-02*, March.

Sachs, Jeffrey D, Nirupam Bajpai and Ananthi Ramiah (2002), "Understanding Regional Economic Growth in India", paper prepared for Asian Economic Panel, Seoul, October 25-26, Presented to the prime minister of India, December 25, New Delhi, *Working Papers Series of Centre for International Development at Harvard University (CID)*, No 88, March.

Sarkar, P C (1996), "Growth Differentials in Incomes of Major Indian States", *The Journal of Income and Wealth*, IARNIW, Vol 18, No 1, January.

Economic and Political Weekly, December 6, 2003.

31

Economic Performance of the States in the post Reforms Period

Montek S. Ahluwalia

There is a very lively debate in the academic world and in the Press on our national economic performance and the success or failure of various aspects of national policies, but there is relatively little analysis of how individual States have performed over time and the role of State Government policy in determining State level performance. This neglect is to some extent the natural consequence of not specifying State specific growth targets in our National Plans which are approved by the National Development Council which includes all the Chief Ministers. The Plan document lays down GDP growth targets for the country as a whole but this aggregate growth is not disaggregated into targets for the growth of State Domestic Product in individual States. The Plan also does not report the growth performance of different States in the past, nor analyse the reasons for differences in performance across States. The Annual Economic Survey brought out by the Finance Ministry is also silent on these issues.

And yet, there are very good reasons why we should pay much greater attention to this subject. We are a federal democracy in which the constitutional division of powers between the Centre and the States makes the States pre-eminent in many areas and co-equal with the Centre in others. Governments at the State level are run by different political parties and competitive politics should make the performance of individual States a matter of high political and electoral interest. Liberalisation has reduced the degree of control exercised by the Centre in many areas leaving much greater scope for State level initiatives. This is particularly true as far as attracting investment both domestic and foreign is concerned. State level performance and policies therefore deserve much closer attention than they receive. It is particularly important to study the differences in performance among States in order to extract lessons about what works and what does not. A better understanding of the reasons for the superior performance of some States would help to spread success from one part of the country to the other.

This lecture is modest contribution towards focussing attention on these issues. I must warn at the outset that I expect to raise more questions than I can hope to answer. I only hope that raising these questions will stimulate others to explore these issues in greater depth.

I. Growth Performance of the States

The growth performance of individual States can be judged from the available data on the Gross State Domestic Product (SDP) for each State. Ideally, the SDP data series for individual States should be fully consistent with the national accounts estimates of GDP but this type of consistency is not possible at present. Information on the State Domestic Product (at constant prices) reported by State Governments is collected by the CSO and is used as one of the inputs for national accounts estimation. In this process the CSO takes note of differences in methods of estimating the SDP in different States, but it does not refine the State SDP series to make them consistent with each other and with the national accounts.

Lack of consistency between the SDP series for different States and the national accounts data is a major lacuna in our statistical system and there is need for a greater effort by the CSO and the State Statistics departments to make the data more comparable in future. However this should not deter us from using State level data for analysing State performance. Most of our States are much larger than most developing countries and the national accounts data of developing countries are also not always fully comparable. Yet this has not deterred development economists from comparing performance across developing countries and drawing lessons from inter-country variations. We should have no hesitation therefore about taking a leaf out of established international practice while offering the usual caveats on data problems.

Because of the special features of the North Eastern and other special category States, and also some gaps in the data for some of these States,

I have excluded them from the analysis. I have also excluded the smaller States such as Goa and also Delhi, the latter having the additional special feature of being the capital, with a large concentration of the Central Government's bureaucracy. The analysis that follows is therefore confined to 14 major States, which together account for 95 per cent of the total population.

TABLE – 31.1

Annual Rates of Growth of Gross State Domestic Product (SDP)

		1980-81 1990-91 % p.a.	1991-92 1997-98 % p.a.
1.	Bihar	4.66	2.69
2.	Rajasthan	6.60	6.54
3.	Uttar Pradesh	4.95	3.58
4.	Orissa	4.29	3.25
5.	Madhya Pradesh	4.56	6.17
6.	Andhra Pradesh	5.65	5.03
7.	Tamil Nadu	5.38	6.22
8.	Kerala	3.57	5.81
9.	Karnataka	5.29	5.29
10.	West Bengal	4.71	6.91
11.	Gujarat	5.08	9.57
12.	Haryana	6.43	5.02
13.	Maharashtra	6.02	8.01
14.	Punjab	5.32	4.71
	Combined SDP of 14 States	**5.24**	**5.94**
	GDP (National Accounts)	**5.55**	**6.89**

Notes: States are ranked in ascending order of per capita SDP in 1980-81. The growth rates have been estimated by fitting log linear trends to the State SDP data in constant 1980-81 prices obtained from the CSO and the GDP data from the national accounts.

a) Growth Rates of SDP

Table 31.1 presents the estimated growth rates of SDP in the 14 major States in the pre-reform period 1980-81 to 1990-91 and in the post-reform period 1991-92 to 1997-98. The growth rate for each State in each period is estimated based on a loglinear trend.[1] We can draw the following conclusions about the growth performances of the States.

i. The growth rate of the combined SDP of all the 14 States taken together has increased from 5.2 per cent in the pre-reform period to 5.9 per cent in the second. This acceleration corresponds to a similar acceleration in GDP growth as reported in the national accounts. GDP shows a very similar growth rate of 5.4 per cent per year in the first period but it shows a much faster acceleration to 6.9 per cent in the second period. The faster acceleration revealed in the national accounts probably reflects the fact that the GDP data were revised for the period from 1993-94 onwards and a similar revision has not yet been done for SDP at the State level. There is a need to revise the State GDP series to reflect the methodological changes made in the national accounts. Since the growth rate of GDP is a full percentage point higher than the growth of SDP of the 14 States, a revision of the SDP series to reflect the changes made in the national accounts could alter out assessment of the relative performance of States if it affects different States very differently. This possibility is ignored in the analysis that follows.

ii. As one would expect, there is considerable variation in the performance of individual States, with some States growing faster than the average and others slower. What is important however, is that the degree of dispersion in growth rates across States increased very significantly in the 1990s. The range of variation in the growth rate of SDP in the 1980s was from a low of 3.6 per cent per year in Kerala to a high of 6.6 per cent in Rajasthan, a factor of less than 2. In the 1990s the variation was much larger, from a low of 2.7 per cent per year for Bihar to a high of 9.6 per cent for Gujarat, a factor exceeding 3.5 !

iii. The differences in performance across States become even more marked when we allow for the differences in the rates of growth of population and evaluate the performance in terms of growth rates of per capita SDP (Table 31.2). The variation in growth rates in the 1980s ranged from a low of 2.1 per cent for Madhya Pradesh to a high of 4.0 for Rajasthan, a factor of 1:2. In the 1990s it ranged from a low of 1.1 per cent year in Bihar and 1.2 per cent in U.P., to a high of 7.6 per cent per year in Gujarat, with Maharashtra coming next at 6.1 per cent. The ratio between the lowest (Bihar) and the highest (Gujarat) is as much as 1:7.

iv. The increased variation in growth performance across States in the 1990s reflects the fact that whereas growth accelerated for the economy as a whole, it actually decelerated sharply in Bihar, Uttar Pradesh and Orissa, all of which had relatively low rates of growth to begin with and were also the poorest States. There was also a deceleration in Haryana and Punjab, but the deceleration was from relatively higher levels of growth in the 1980s, and these States were also the richest.

v. Six States showed acceleration in growth of SDP in the 1990s. The acceleration was particularly marked in Maharashtra and Gujarat, both of which were among the richer States, but there was also acceleration in West Bengal, Kerala, Tamil Nadu and Madhya Pradesh all belonging to the middle group of States in terms of per capita SDP.

vi. It is important to note that the high growth performers in the 1990s were not concentrated in one part of the country. The six States with growth rates of SDP in the 1990s above 6.0 per cent per year are fairly well distributed regionally i.e. Gujarat (9.6 per cent) and Maharashtra (8.0 per cent) in the West, West Bengal (6.9 per cent) in the East, Tamil Nadu (6.2 per cent) in the South and Madhya Pradesh (6.2 per cent) and Rajasthan (6.5 per cent) in the North.

An interesting feature of the performance in the 1990s is that the popular characterisation of the so called BIMARU State (Bihar, Madhya Pradesh, Rajasthan and UP) as a homogeneous group of poor performers, a grouping originally proposed in the context of observed commonalities in demographic behaviour, does not hold as far as economic performance is concerned.[2] Bihar and U.P. performed poorly, growing much more slowly than the average, but the other two members of this group, Rajasthan and Madhya Pradesh have performed reasonably well. Rajasthan actually had a good performance in the 1980s – it was the fastest growing State – and though its growth rate in the 1990s was marginally lower, it remained a strong performer with above average growth. Madhya Pradesh's growth in the 1980s was below the averages for the 14 States but it accelerated significantly in the 1990s.

Similarly, the perception that it is only the coastal States or the southern States have done well in the period of liberalisation is also not valid. Orissa is a coastal State, but its growth performance is very poor while Madhya Pradesh and Rajasthan are both heartland States and have performed reasonably well. The best performers are Gujarat and Maharashtra followed by West Bengal, Rajasthan, Tamil Nadu and Madhya Pradesh.

Of the Southern States only Tamil Nadu is in the top six. The Southern States as a group have done well, but they have not been the only beneficiaries of the growth acceleration harnessed in the 1990s.

The performance of Kerala deserves special attention. Kerala is justly celebrated for its achievements in human development but it has also been criticised for under performance in economic growth. It is important to note that its performance in the 1990s showed a marked improvement compared with the 1980s. From an SDP growth rate much below the 14 States average in the 1980s it accelerated to a growth rate only marginally below the average in the 1990s. However, because of the low population growth, its performance in per capita SDP growth in the 1990s was actually much better then the average (Table 31.2).

TABLE – 31.2

Annual Rates of Growth of Per Capita Gross State Domestic Product

	1980-81 1990-91 % p.a.	1991-92 1997-98 % p.a.
1. Bihar	2.45	1.12
2. Rajasthan	3.96	3.96
3. Uttar Pradesh	2.60	1.24
4. Orissa	2.38	1.64
5. Madhya Pradesh	2.08	3.87
6. Andhra Pradesh	3.34	3.45
7. Tamil Nadu	3.87	4.95
8. Kerala	2.19	4.52
9. Karnataka	3.28	3.45
10. West Bengal	2.39	5.04
11. Gujarat	3.08	7.57
12. Haryana	3.86	2.66
13. Maharashtra	3.58	6.13
14. Punjab	3.33	2.80
15. Combined SDP of 14 States	**3.03**	**4.02**

Source: SDP and population data obtained from the CSO.

The fact that Gujarat and Maharashtra grew at rates normally associated with "miracle growth" economies also deserves special mention. It should be emphasised that if these States have benefited the most in the post reforms period, their superior performance was not the result of any conscious policy of limiting the benefits of liberalisation to these States, as was the case for example in China, where liberalisation was deliberately limited to designated coastal zones. The superior performance of Gujarat and Maharashtra must therefore be attributed to the fact that the States were able to provide an environment most conducive to benefiting from the new policies. Their experience together with the experience of the other strong performance should be subject to State level studies which would help to identify the key ingredients of success in these States, which should be emulated by others.

b) Implications for Inter-State Inequality

The differences in per capita income and other indicators of social development across States have long attracted attention and for good reasons. Punjab, the richest State has a per capita SDP which is 5 times that of Bihar at the other end of the spectrum and although our Plans have never explicitly fixed targets for reducing these differences, there has always been an unstated assumption that inter-State differences would narrow with development. This can only happen if the poorer States actually grow faster than the richest States but the pattern of growth witnessed in the 1990s has been quite different, generating concern that we may be witnessing an increase in regional inequality, with the poorer States being left further behind.

The best way of measuring whether the pattern of growth in the 1990s has led to an increase in inter-State inequality is to construct a gini co-efficient measuring inter-State inequality for each year. This can be done by taking the entire population of the 14 States and by assuming that all individuals within a State have a gross income equal to the per capita SDP. The gini co-efficient for the population using this assumption provides a measure of inequality for the total population of the 14 States which suppresses the effect of intra-State inequality arising out of the unequal distribution within the State. It measures only the degree of inequality in the total population which arises solely because of inequality among States. Table 31.3 presents the resulting estimates of the inter-State gini-coefficient. The coefficient was fairly stable up to about 1986-87, but began to increase in the late 1980s and this trend continued through the 1990s. The increase in the gini-coefficient from about 0.16 in 1986-87 to 0.23 in 1997-98 is a substantial increase and fitting a time trend to the series shows a statistically significant positive slope.

TABLE – 31.3

Trend in Gini Coefficient Measuring Inter State Inequality

1980-81	0.152	1989-90	0.175
1981-82	0.152	1990-91	0.171
1982-83	0.152	1991-92	0.175
1983-84	0.151	1992-93	0.199
1984-85	0.154	1993-94	0.207
1985-86	0.159	1994-95	0.214
1986-87	0.157	1995-96	0.225
1987-88	0.161	1996-97	0.228
1988-89	0.158	1997-98	0.225

While inter-State inequality as measured by the gini-coefficient has clearly increased, the common perception that the rich States got richer and the poor States got poorer is not entirely accurate. A closer look at Table 31.2 shows a slightly more complex pattern of behaviour.

i. It is not true that all the richest States got richer relative to poorer States. Punjab and Haryana were the two richest of the 14 States in 1990-91. The growth rates of per capita SDP of these two States in the 1990s were not only lower than in the 1980s, but in both cases actually fell below the national average. Except for Bihar, UP and Orissa, all the other States therefore narrowed the per capita income gap with the two richest States. The deceleration in growth in these two well off and agriculturally advanced States deserves closer State level study to understand the reasons for the loss of momentum on the basis of which remedial steps can be taken.

ii. Maharashtra and Gujarat, which were just below Punjab and Haryana in terms of per capita income levels and therefore in the richer group, accelerated very significantly in the 1990s and grew at rates much higher than the national average.

iii. Three of the poorest States, Bihar, Uttar Pradesh and Orissa, which together account for over a third of the population of the country, did fare very poorly in 1990s. They did not actually become poorer on average, as they also had positive growth rates of per capita GDP, but these rates were very low. In the case of Bihar and UP they were less than a third of the national average.

iv. It is important to note that not all the poorer States lagged behind. Rajasthan, which was also one of the poorer States, experienced much stronger growth in per capita SDP, more than double that of the other poor States. Rajasthan's performance in terms of SDP growth is actually better than the average of the 14 States (see Table 31.1) but it slips below the average in per capita SDP growth because of higher rates of population growth.

v. Performance of six middle income States (Tamil Nadu, Kerala, West Bengal, Madhya Pradesh, Andhra Pradesh and Karnataka) was clustered around the average rate. All six of these States grew faster in terms of per capita GDP than they did in the 1980s, though in some cases the difference was very marginal.

c) Trends in Poverty in the States

The differences in growth performance of the individual States have important implications for poverty reduction which is a critical objective of national policy. One would expect to find that poverty declined more rapidly in the faster growing States and less so in others. In States where per capita income growth is very low e.g. Bihar, UP and Orissa, it may not have declined at all. Unfortunately, it is difficult to pronounce definitively on what has happened to poverty in the individual States because of data limitations.

The only available estimates of poverty in individual States are those derived from the so called "large sample" surveys, covering about 120,000 households, which are conducted by the NSS every five years. The NSS also conducts annual surveys –the so called "thin sample" covering about 25,000 households – but the sample size is too small to provide reliable estimates of poverty for individual States. Large sample surveys were conducted in 1983, 1987-88 and in 1993-94 and State specific poverty estimates made by the Planning Commission using these surveys are presented in Table-31.4. They show that for the 14 States as a whole, the percentage of the population below the poverty line declined from 43.8 per cent in 1983 to 36.3 per cent by 1993-94. The reduction in poverty of about 7.5 percentage points in ten years is obviously somewhat slow – at this rate it would take 28 years to bring poverty down to around 15 per cent and 38 years to bring it down to 10 per cent.

The State level data in Table 31.4 show that all States experienced a decline in poverty over the ten year period with only two exceptions –

Bihar and Haryana, both of which show an increase. The increase in poverty in Bihar can be explained by the fact that per capita GDP in Bihar grew at less than 0.8 per cent per year between 1983-84 and 1993-94 (Table 31.5). However the observed deterioration in poverty in Haryana is difficult to explain since per capita SDP grew at 3.4 per cent per year over the ten year period. It is of course possible for poverty to increase despite an increase in per capita income if the distribution worsens sufficiently, but it is difficult to believe that distribution in Haryana could have worsened sufficiently to offset an increase of 40 per cent in the per capita SDP over the period. This is especially so since trends in Haryana should be similar to those in Punjab which shows a steady decline in poverty in the same period. As shown in Table 4, the trend in Haryana between 1983 to 1987-88 was similar to that in the rest of the country, with a clear decline in poverty. The reversal occurred only in the second half of the period, when the percentage of the population in poverty is estimated to have increased sharply from 16.6 per cent in 1987-88 to 25.1 per cent in 1993-94. The estimate for Haryana for 1993-94 is clearly somewhat suspect.

TABLE – 31.4

Percentage of Population in Poverty

		1983	1987-88	1993-94
1.	Bihar	52.22	52.13	54.96
2.	Rajasthan	34.46	35.15	27.41
3.	Uttar Pradesh	47.07	41.46	40.85
4.	Orissa	65.29	55.58	48.56
5.	Madhya Pradesh	49.78	43.07	42.52
6.	Andhra Pradesh	28.91	25.86	22.19
7.	Tamil Nadu	51.66	43.39	35.03
8.	Kerala	40.42	31.79	25.43
9.	Karnataka	38.24	37.53	33.16
10.	West Bengal	54.85	44.72	35.66
11.	Gujarat	32.79	31.54	24.21
12.	Haryana	21.37	16.64	25.05
13.	Maharashtra	43.44	40.41	36.86
14.	Punjab	16.18	13.20	11.77
	All 14 States	**43.80**	**39.92**	**36.25**
	All India	**44.48**	**38.86**	**35.97**

Source: Planning Commission.

Estimates of poverty in individual States beyond 1993-94 will only become available when data from the 60th Round of the NSS for 1999-2000, which is currently being conducted, become available. In the absence of estimates based on a comparable survey, we can only speculate about what might have happened to poverty in individual States, on the basis of what we know about economic growth in these States after 1993-94. The all India experience in the 1960s and most of the 70s showed that poverty reduction was negligible when per capita GDP growth was below 2 per cent, but it began to decline when per capita growth accelerated to 3 per cent and more in the late seventies and eighties. Generalising from this experience one should expect that some poverty reduction should have occurred in all the States where per capita growth exceeds 3 per cent or so after 1993-94 unless the nature of growth has changed significantly compared to earlier years.

Table 31.5 presents the growth rate of per capita GDP in the individual States for the period after 1993-94 and compares them with growth rates in the period 1983-84 to 1993-94, which is the period for which State specific poverty data are available. It is evident that growth continued to be low in U.P. and Bihar in the years after 1993-94 and this suggests that the percentage of the population below the poverty line would not have declined significantly in these States. Other States where growth between 1993-94 and 1997-98 was not fast enough to expect a significant decline in poverty are Orissa, Madhya Pradesh, Andhra Pradesh and Punjab. However there were 8 States where per capita SDP grew by 3 per cent or more in this period i.e. Rajasthan, Tamil Nadu, Kerala, Karnataka, West Bengal, Gujarat, Maharashtra and Haryana. These States should have experienced a continuing decline in poverty in the period after 1993-94 unless, as pointed out earlier, the nature of growth in this period changed in a way which made it less poverty reducing.

If poverty did indeed decline significantly in the 8 States which experienced strong growth after 1993-94, and which together account for almost half the population of the 14 States taken together, then even if it did not decline in U.P., Bihar and in some other States, one would nevertheless expect to see a continuing, if somewhat modest decline in poverty in the country as a whole. The lack of progress in reducing poverty in the slow growing States would slow down the decline in poverty for the country as a whole, but not eliminate it entirely. This expectation is not borne out by various studies examining trends in national poverty in the 1990s using the NSS thin samples.[3] According to these studies poverty has not declined in the 1990s despite robust growth and this has naturally raised questions about the nature of the growth process witnessed in this period. Critics of economic reforms have argued that the nature of the growth in the 1990s may have been less distributionally benign than earlier.

TABLE – 31.5

Annual Rates of Growth of Per Capita SDP Between 93-94 and 97-98

		1983-84 1993-94 % p.a.	1993-94 1997-98* % p.a.
1.	Bihar	0.78	2.14
2.	Rajasthan	1.79	5.94
3.	Uttar Pradesh	1.76	1.69
4.	Orissa	1.37	2.61
5.	Madhya Pradesh	2.38	2.71
6.	Andhra Pradesh	3.49	2.40
7.	Tamil Nadu	4.69	4.47
8.	Kerala	4.11	3.79
9.	Karnataka	3.76	3.42
10.	West Bengal	2.69	5.45
11.	Gujarat	2.50	7.62
12.	Haryana	3.39	3.16
13.	Maharashtra	4.96	3.90
14.	Punjab	3.30	2.60
	All 14 States	**3.16**	**3.87**

* Growth rates in this table have been calculated as compound growth rates between the two end years and not as log-linear trends. This is partly because of the limited number of observations in the second period and partly also because these growth rates are being used to explain changes in poverty between the two end years of the first period which makes the calculation of growth rates based on end years more appropriate.

This is certainly an important issue and one that deserves serious attention. However, the results obtained from the NSS thin samples are not necessarily conclusive. They have been questioned on various grounds which can be summarised as follows:

i. The conclusion that poverty did not decline in the 1990s is sometimes questioned because of the size of the thin samples. However, it can be argued that the smaller sample size does not necessarily introduce a systematic bias in the assessment of underlying trends.

ii. It has been argued the price index used to adjust the poverty line for inflation exaggerates the extent of inflation and therefore of poverty. This is because a base weighted Laspeyres index exaggerates inflation over time unless the weights are frequently revised to reflect changes in the pattern of expenditure in response to price changes. The Consumer Price Index for Agricultural Labour (CPIAL), which is the price index used for adjusting the rural poverty line, is based on 1960-61 weights which have not been revised for forty years. Deaton and Tarozzi (1999), have estimated the change in poverty between the 43rd Round (1987-88) and the 50th Round (1993) using a different price index, and their findings show a larger decline in poverty between those years then in the traditional studies especially in rural areas[4]. This seems to confirm the suspicion that the CPIAL exaggerates the extent of rural poverty in later years.

iii. The NSS data also appear to under-estimate consumption compared with the national accounts and the extent of under estimation has been increasing overtime. Whereas at one stage, the underestimation was around 20 per cent it has increased to as much as 40 per cent in the latest data for 1998! This is indeed a serious weakness in the NSS data and Bhalla (2000) has argued that this makes the estimated trends in national poverty in the 1990s derived from the NSS unreliable. The possibility that the NSS has been underestimating consumption is borne out by the results obtained by the NSS when it introduced a second method of estimating consumption in 1994-95. The sample was divided into two and the traditional method, using a reference period of one month to estimate consumption of all items, was used for half the sample while a new method, using different reference periods for different items was used for the other half.[5] The new method yielded an estimate of per capita consumption which waas about 15 to 20 per cent higher than the traditional method. Consumption measured by the new method was also more equally distributed. The percentage of the population in poverty using the new consumption measurement combined with the old poverty line drops to around 20 per cent. However, since consumption estimates based on the new method are available only for the period after 1994-95, one cannot use them to draw conclusions about trends in poverty in the 1990s.

TABLE – 31.6

All India Trends in Poverty: (Percent of Population Below Poverty Line)

	Rural %	Urban %	National %
1983	45.31	35.65	43.00
1986-87	38.81	34.29	37.69
1987-88	39.23	36.20	38.47
1988-89	39.06	36.60	38.44
1989-90	34.30	33.40	34.07
1990-91	36.43	32.76	35.49
1991-92	37.42	33.23	36.34
1992-93	43.47	33.73	40.93
1993-94	36.66	30.51	35.04
1994-95	41.02	33.50	38.40
1995-96	37.15	28.04	35.00
1996-97	35.78	29.99	34.40

Source: Datt (1997) and (1999) quoted in Srinivasan (1999).

iv. Finally, trends in the percentage of low income households reported in the NCAER study by Natarajan (1998) using the NCAER's MISH survey show a steady decline in the percentage of "low income" households both before the reforms and after, in both urban and rural areas (see table 31.7). This is a very different picture from that presented by the NSS.

TABLE – 31.7

Percentage of Households in the Low Income Category According to the NCAER's MISH

	1985-86	1989-90	1992-93	1995-96
Rural	73.6	67.3	65.5	57.2
Urban	42.1	37.1	38.4	27.9
Total	65.2	58.8	58.2	48.9

Source: Natarajan (1998)

It is difficult to pronounce definitively on trends in poverty in view of these data problems. More detailed study is needed which is clearly beyond the scope of this lecture. Hopefully, the results of the large sample survey for 1999-2000 will provide more reliable estimates. In any case we have to wait for the result of the survey before we can pronounces on trends in individual States. When these results become available it will be possible to determine whether the process of declining rural poverty witnessed between 1983-84 and 1993 has continued in the subsequent years at least in those States which experienced strong growth after 1993.

This is not to suggest that we can afford to be complacent about trends in poverty in the 1990s on the basis of what we know. On the contrary, as I have already pointed out, the pace of poverty reduction even between 1983 and 1993-94, when there is no dispute about the direction of change, was modest at best and the slowing down in the rate of growth in the 1990s in some of the poorest States must have halted the process of poverty reduction in these areas. There can be no doubt that we need to do much better in the first decade of the new millennium, especially in the poorer and slow growing States, if the extent of poverty is to be significantly reduced in 10 years.

II. Implications for Policy

What are the policy implications that follow from the pattern of growth observed in the 1990s? First, it is important to emphasise that the mere fact that States grow at different rates should not be viewed as a failure of policy. Given our size and diversity, it is unrealistic to expect that all States will grow at the same rate. Some may grow faster than others at certain times because they may be particularly well placed to exploit some new opportunity that arises. For example, the green revolution technology was peculiarly well suited to conditions in Punjab and Haryana and led to a spurt of growth in these States in the 1970s. Coastal States may have a locational advantage in a globalising world because they suffer less from the disadvantage imposed on hinterland States by our poor transport infrastructure. Finally, differences in growth may arise because some States are better managed and therefore able to create an environment which generates higher growth. Since the "pay off" from superior management has also increased because of liberalisation it is very likely that variations in the quality of economic management will lead to greater inter-State variation in management performance than was the case earlier.

It needs to be clearly understood that the objective of balanced regional development should not be pursued by following policies which seek to achieve equality through a process of "leveling down" by preventing States from reaching their full growth potential. On the contrary, well managed States must be encouraged to reach their full growth potential, if only to show what is possible in Indian conditions. The lessons learnt from their superior performance could then serve as a model for others to emulate. This process is bound to generate some differences in growth performance across States, but such differences can have a healthy demonstration effect with best practice being spread through emulation.

Accepting differences in growth performance across States does not however mean that we should passively accept the pathologically low growth rates witnessed in Bihar, UP and Orissa. Continuation of such low growth rates into the future for a group of States representing almost a third of the total population, while the rest of the country enjoys robust growth has alarming implications. It means that inter-State inequality would continue to increase and poverty would become even more regionally concentrated than it is today, an outcome which would be socially and politically explosive. It would not only affect the politics of these parts of the country but, because of their size, it would undoubtedly have a debilitating impact on the politics of the country as a whole.

It is therefore necessary to increase the rate of growth of per capita SDP in these States from around 1.5 per cent experienced in the 1990s to somewhere between 3.5 and 4 per cent. This requires the rate of growth of SDP to increase from a little over 3 per cent per annum observed in the 1990s to at least 6 per cent per annum. This doubling in the growth rate of SDP is clearly necessary to deal with regional inequality since, by definition, inequality will increase if the poorer States do not grow at least as fast as the national average. However the acceleration in growth is also needed to tackle the problem of poverty in these States. Because they account for a large proportion of national poverty there is a tendency to think that the solution to the poverty problem in these States lies in intensifying anti-poverty programmes. This approach misses the point that a sufficiently broad based expansion in income earning opportunities, of the kind needed to achieve a sustainable reduction in poverty can only come from a substantially higher rate of growth, including especially faster growth in the agricultural sector. It is true that high growth by itself may not be enough. It needs to be broad based and it also needs to be supplemented by targeted poverty alleviation schemes to take care of groups which are left out of the growth process. However, these schemes can only be a supplement to a high growth strategy and not a substitute for it.

Achieving a growth rate of around 6 per cent per annum in these slow growing States is probably also necessary if we are to achieve our declared national target of raising India's rate of growth of GDP from the present level of around 6.5 per cent to around 7.5 per cent over the next decade. Bihar, UP and Orissa together account for 20 per cent of the GDP of the 14 States. Raising their growth rate from a little over 3 per cent observed in the 1990s to say 6 per cent would itself achieve more than half of the projected acceleration of one percentage point in GDP growth. Without this contribution, the achievement of 7.5 per cent growth nationally would require the growth rate in the other States to be raised to implausibly high levels.

Doubling the rate of growth of any large economy is not an easy task and the three States we are concerned with have a combined population of over 300 million ! The simplest growth models – perhaps I should say the simplistic growth models – used to focus on investment as the critical determinant of growth. We know today that both public and private investment are important but that the efficiency of resource use is at least as important as the level of investment. Efficiency in turn depends upon many other factors such as the level of human resource development, the quality of infrastructure, the economic policy environment and the quality of governance. Ideally, we should be able to explain the observed differences in growth across States in terms of differences in these and other causal factors and then try to identify the critical areas in each State where policy can stimulate the determinants of growth, or help to remove the constraints which impede growth, so that the State can move to a higher growth path. Not enough work has been done in this area at the level of individual States, but some broad generalisations can be made.

a) Investment and Growth in Individual States

Although economists regard differences in the rate of investment as one of the critical determinants of growth, we have no reliable information about the total level of investment or gross fixed capital formation in individual States. The national accounts provide data for investment in the country as a whole, but this cannot be broken down into investment in individual States. We do not know therefore whether the low growth rates in Bihar, UP and Orissa reflect low investment ratios (as a % of SDP) or lower levels of efficiency (i.e. higher ICORs). However, it is probably reasonable to assume that both factors are at work and a doubling of growth in the poorer performing States almost certainly needs higher levels of investment.

In the absence of State level data on investment, a great deal of attention focusses on the size of State Plans. State Governments are keen to announce large State Plans at the time of Annual Plan discussions as if the size of the State Plan is the only credible indicator of the scale of the development effort in the State. Plan expenditure is not the same thing as investment. In fact the revenue component of Plan expenditure for all States taken together has increased steadily over the years to reach 51 per cent in 1997-98. Nevertheless, State Plan expenditure is viewed as an important indicator of the level of investment activity in a State and it is therefore useful to examine trends in Plan expenditure in relation to SDP in the 14 States.

Table 31.8 presents the average ratio of Plan expenditure to SDP in the 1980s and compares it with the average ratio in the 1990s. The following features are worth noting.

i. Taking the 14 States together, the percentage of State Plan expenditure to SDP declined from an average of 5.7 per cent in the 1980s to 4.5 per cent in the 1990s. The decline of 1.2 percentage points in State Plan expenditures almost certainly hides an even larger decline in investment for new capacity, because of the increase in the revenue component of the Plan.

ii. The decline in Plan expenditures as a percentage of SDP has occurred in both the better performing as well as the poorer performing States. The drop is the largest in Bihar, but Gujarat and Maharashtra, two of the best performers, also show a significant decline as do a number of good performers such as Madhya Pradesh, Tamil Nadu and West Bengal.

iii. There is considerable variation across States in the ratio of State Plan expenditure to SDP and this variation has increased in the 1990s compared with the 1980s. More importantly, there is no statistically significant relationship between State Plan expenditure as a percentage of SDP and growth performance across States in either decade. Orissa which had the highest ratio of State Plan expenditure to GDP at 7.1 per cent in the 1990s had a SDP growth rate of only 3.25 per cent. West Bengal, with the lowest Plan ratio of 2.7 per cent, had a relatively robust growth of 6.9 per cent. Maharashtra, which was the second fastest growing State, had an average Plan ratio of only 3.97 per cent well below the average. Gujarat

Figure – 31.1

Relationship between Growth of SDP and Ratio of State Plan to SDP (1980-81 to 1990-91)

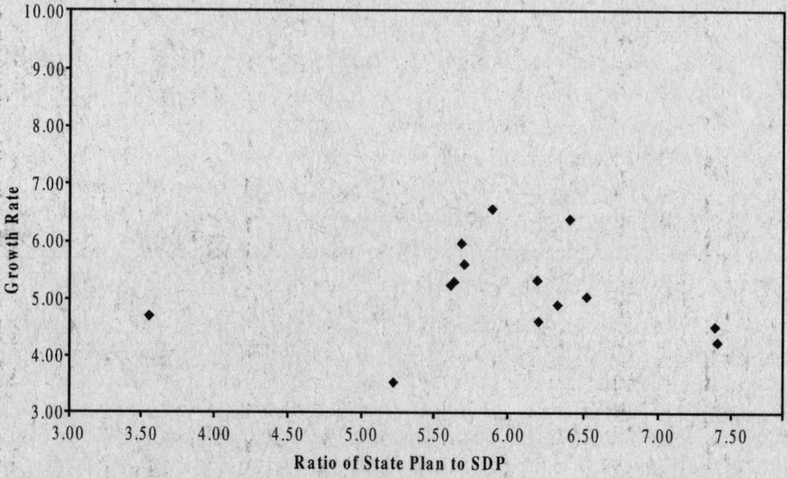

Figure – 31.2

Relationship between Growth of SDP and Ratio of State Plan to SDP (1991-92 to 1997-98)

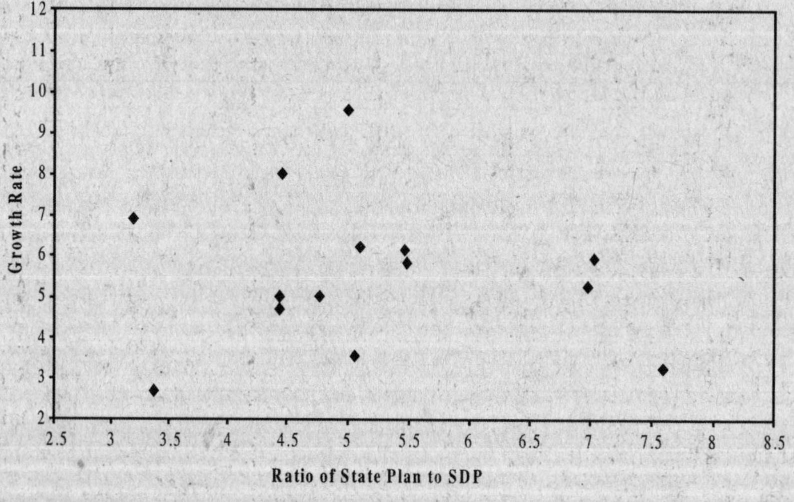

which was the fastest growing State had a Plan ratio only equal to the average. The lack of correlation can also be seen from Figs. 31.1 and 31.2 which plot growth rates of SDP against the ratio of Plan expenditure to State SDP for the 1980s and 1990s respectively.

The lack of correlation between State Plan expenditure and the growth rate of SDP is not in itself surprising because it is total investment which affects growth as State Plan expenditure is a poor indicator of the total volume of investment in the State. As shown in Table 31.8, State Plan expenditure for all 14 States taken together amounted to about 4.5 per cent of SDP in the 1990s and since half of State Plan expenditure accounted for by revenue expenditure, the investment component of State Plan expenditure would amount to only 2.25 per cent of SDP. Since Gross Fixed Investment in the economy 1997-98 was around 25 per cent of GDP, this means that the investment component of State Plans on average account for only about 9 per cent of total investment. Inter-State variations in investments undertaken through State Plan expenditure may therefore be swamped by variations in other components of investment.

TABLE – 31.8

Plan Expenditure as Percentage of SDP

	Average 1980-81 1990-91 %	Average 1990-91 1997-98 %
1. Bihar	6.20	2.87
2. Rajasthan	5.89	6.54
3. Uttar Pradesh	6.33	4.56
4. Orissa	7.41	7.10
5. Madhya Pradesh	7.39	4.97
6. Andhra Pradesh	5.70	4.28
7. Tamil Nadu	6.19	4.60
8. Kerala	5.22	4.99
9. Karnataka	5.61	6.49
10. West Bengal	3.56	2.70
11. Gujarat	6.52	4.51
12. Haryana	6.41	3.94
13. Maharashtra	5.68	3.97
14. Punjab	5.63	3.94
All 14 States	**5.69**	**4.50**

Source: Planning Commission.

In this context, we need to remember that almost three-fourths of the gross fixed investment at the national level comes from the private sector, with private corporate investment accounting for 38 per cent of the total and private household investment about 33 per cent. Public sector investment at the national level is only about 28 per cent of total investment and this includes both the Centre and the States. Public investment by the Centre and States together is therefore about 6.8 per cent of GDP, of which State Plans account for only one third. Any effort to increase the total level of investment in the slower growing States must therefore recognise the importance of private investment, identify the constraints on increasing such investments and devise policies that will deal with these constraints.

The poorer performing States suffer from obvious handicaps in attracting private investment. Private corporate investment is potentially highly mobile across States and is therefore likely to flow to States which have a skilled labour force with a good "work culture", good infrastructure especially power, transport and communications, and good governance generally. The mobility of private corporate investment has increased in the post-liberalisation period since decontrol has eliminated the Central Government's ability to direct investment to particular areas, while competition has greatly increased the incentive for private corporate investment to locate where costs are minimised. Poorer performing States will have to address the underlying factors which attract investors i.e. labour skills, work culture, good infrastructure and good governance if they want to increase the volume of private corporate investment.

Private household investment may appear less mobile across States because it depends largely on internal surpluses of firms, households and farms, but poorer States are at a disadvantage in this area compared to the richer States even in this area because their lower levels of per capita income mean lower savings rates and therefore lower internal availability of funds. The relative disadvantage of poorer States on this score is likely to be compounded by the fact that the more advanced States are much further ahead in the demographic transition. This is likely to reduce dependency rates in these States in the near future, which in turn will increase household savings available for investment in households and farms.

These innate advantages of the more advanced States in achieving higher levels of private investment in the corporate and the household sector are compounded by the fact that an efficient financial system will redirect financial savings towards the better performing, faster growing

States. The fact that this process is taking place is reflected in the enormous variation in the credit-deposit ratios of the banks. The credit deposit ratio for all scheduled commercial banks for the country as a whole at the end of March 1998 was around 55 per cent but it was as low as 27 per cent in Bihar and 31 per cent in UP whereas it ranged between 68 per cent and 72 per cent for Karnataka, Andhra Pradesh and Maharashtra, with Tamil Nadu having an exceptionally high ratio of 90 per cent. Somewhat surprisingly, Gujarat, the fastest growing State, has a credit deposit ratio of only 54 per cent.

In view of the difficulties in attracting private investment to the poorer States it is natural to consider whether more can be done through public investment. However, the limitations of this instrument need to be clearly understood. We know from experience that public investment is a poor substitute for private investment in most commercial sectors where the private sector is likely to be more competitive and efficient. However, it is an appropriate instrument for creating social and economic infrastructure facilities, which are desperately needed. This is especially so in the less developed States which suffer from greater infrastructure deficiencies and are also least likely to be able to attract private investment in this area. Both Central and state sector public investment should therefore be used as much as possible to build economic and social infrastructure in the poorer performing States which would help remove constraints upon growth in these States and help leverage a larger flow of private investment. The extent to which this can be done obviously depends upon resource constraints in the Centre and the States and I will return to this subject later in this lecture.

b) Human Resources

The quality of human resource development is another critical determinant of growth and one would expect to find faster growing States to be the States with superior availability of human skills. Unfortunately, we do not have reliable measures of the educational attainment and skill level of the labour force in different States and the literacy rate of the population is therefore commonly used as a proxy for the quality of human resources. This is clearly a highly unsatisfactory measure of labour skills, but nevertheless it is useful to what can be gleaned from the available data on literacy for individual States. These data are summarised in Table 8 and the following points are worth noting:

i. Literacy levels in the slow growing States are distinctly lower than the average for all States. However there is no statistically significant correlation between growth of SDP and the level of literacy. Although literacy in UP, Bihar and Orissa was very poor, the situation in Madhya Pradesh, Rajasthan and Andhra Pradesh at the start of the decade was only marginally better and yet these States showed a much better performance in the 1990s. The poor performance in UP, Bihar and Orissa cannot therefore be explained solely by the low levels of literacy in these States. However the very low levels of literacy reflect inadequacies in the human resource base of these States which must constrain growth performance.

ii. Literacy rates have risen over time in all States, including the slow growing States in Bihar, UP and Orissa. Literacy in Bihar in 1997 is significantly higher than it was in Madhya Pradesh and Andhra Pradesh in 1991. Similarly the literacy rate in UP in 1997 is about the same as in Karnataka or West Bengal in 1991. However, this improvement in absolute terms still leaves the States much worse in relative terms because other States have also moved ahead. The absolute improvement in literacy (as a proxy for human resource development) should help improve the efficiency of resource use in these States but the continuing relative gap means that poorer States will continue to find it difficult to compete with the more advanced States in attracting investment.

The lack of any statistical correlation between literacy and growth needs some explanation. It probably reflects the fact that literacy is a poor measure of labour skills. There is ample evidence from the development literature that economic growth and indeed development more generally, is favourably affected by improvements in education and skill levels and this suggest that poorer performing States must make special efforts to upgrade the quality of human resources. Education and skill development falls within the sphere of State Governments and there is need for much stronger emphasis on these sectors in State Plans. This calls for larger allocations to these sectors and, equally important, it calls for measures to ensure effective use of resources.

TABLE – 31.9

Total Literacy Rate

	1981 (%)	1991 (%)	1997 (%)
1. Bihar	26.20	38.48	49
2. Rajasthan	24.38	38.55	55
3. Uttar Pradesh	27.16	41.60	56
4. Orissa	34.23	49.09	51
5. Madhya Pradesh	27.87	44.20	56
6. Andhra Pradesh	29.84	44.09	54
7. Tamil Nadu	46.76	62.66	70
8. Kerala	70.42	89.81	93
9. Karnataka	38.46	56.04	58
10. West Bengal	40.94	57.70	72
11. Gujarat	43.70	61.29	68
12. Haryana	36.14	55.85	65
13. Maharashtra	47.18	64.87	74
14. Punjab	40.86	58.51	67
All India	**36.23**	**52.21**	**62**

Note:

a) 1981, 1991 data related to literacy rates are based on census.

b) 1997 data of literacy rates are based on "NSSO Survey".

c) Quality of Infrastructure

It is generally agreed that rapid industrial growth depends critically upon the availability of infrastructure support in the form of electric power, road and rail transportation and telecommunications. Similarly, agricultural growth depends upon rural infrastructure such as the spread and quality of irrigation, land development, extent of rural electrification and the spread of rural roads. As with the level of human skills, good infrastructure not only increases the productivity of existing resources going into production and therefore helps growth, it also helps to attract more investment which can be expected to increase growth further. Although all States suffer from infrastructural deficiencies, the poorer performing States definitely lag behind in this area. Some of these infrastructure needs can be met by the private sector, but the scope for private investment in infrastructure is limited in the less developed States. Most of the infrastructure development needed in these States will have to be met through public investment, either by the Central Government or the State Government.

Some areas are the exclusive responsibility of the Central Government, and infrastructure development in these sectors must come either from the Central Plan or from the private sector responding to Central Government policies in these areas. Examples of such sectors are the national highways, rail transportation, telecommunications, airports and major ports. Investment in these sectors can be crucial for the poorer performing States in the hinterland because these States are especially in need of improvements in the transport infrastructure, which at present puts them at a disadvantage vis-a-vis coastal States. The role of Central Government investment in infrastructure development as an instrument for accelerating growth in the poorer performing States is not given the attention it deserves in the public debate. Too often, the focus is on how the Centre can help the poorer States by transferring resources but this misses the point that it may be able to do more by removing critical infrastructure constraints.

The recently launched National Highways Development Project, which is being funded by a cess on petrol and diesel, is a major Central Government initiative which could help to overcome transport bottlenecks affecting hinterland States. A similar large scale effort is needed to modernise the railway system, with particular emphasis on its freight carrying capacity. Hinterland States would benefit the most from an efficient railway system capable of transporting freight over long distance at attractive rates. It is not generally realised that the pricing policy followed by the railways of subsidising passenger traffic by overcharging freight works against the interest of hinterland States because it increases the cost of rail freight. This has made it cheaper for coastal power plants in the South to import coal rather then transport it from the coal fields of Bihar. It is interesting to note in this context that while it is the freight carrying function of the railways which is most likely to spur development in hinterland States, the visible pressure on the Railways even from these States, is usually for the addition of new railway lines and trains aimed at expanding facilities for subsidised passenger traffic.

Can the Centre significantly increase the volume of central public investment for the development of infrastructure in the poorer States? Unlike the distribution of Central assistance for State Plans, which is constrained by the Gadgil formula under which the poorer States get a proportionally larger share, there is no strict rule determining the distribution of Central public sector investment across States. In principle, therefore, the Central government has considerable flexibility to determine the regional distribution of central public sector investment.

However, the scale on which the Centre can undertake such investment is obviously constrained by the total availability of resources.

One way of overcoming the resources problem would be to accelerate the privatisation of Central public sector undertakings (PSUs) and earmark the proceeds from these sales for the development of much needed infrastructure in the backward States. This would certainly be a much better strategy than pushing existing PSUs to redirect their own investment into backward areas. Experience shows that making PSUs invest in sub-optimal locations, as was often done in the past, does little for the economic development of the area but only increases the chance of sickness of PUSs. This is even more true in today's liberalised environment, when the PSUs are under strong competitive pressure to reduce costs. On the other hand, privatising existing Central PSUs and using the proceeds to build social and economic infrastructure in the backward States is likely to increase the efficiency with which existing PSU assets are used, while simultaneously helping to expand infrastructure in the backward States, which in turn is the best way of leveraging a greater flow of private investment.

State Governments also have a major role to play in developing infrastructure needed for accelerating growth. In fact, many of the critical areas are those where the primary responsibility is that of the State Government. This includes investments in the social sectors i.e. schools and health facilities and also investments in critical economic infrastructure such as the power system including especially rural electrification, the development of irrigation and water management systems, land development, State highways and district and rural roads. Larger investments are needed in all these areas to achieve higher rates of growth.

Most State Governments recognise the importance of investing in such infrastructure in order to achieve higher growth but actual investments have fallen far below the required level, not only in the poorer States but in most States. In fact, it can be argued that the high growth observed in the better performing States in the 1990s may not be sustained in future unless corrective action is taken. The problem has arisen because States are faced by severe resource constraints which have made difficult for them to achieve Plan targets for investment. As pointed out earlier, Plan expenditure as a percentage of GDP has declined in most States. There is an urgent need to increase public investment in critical areas, but this can only happen if the resources problem can be overcome.

d) The Policy Environment and Governance

The overall policy environment and the quality of governance are also important factors determining the growth potential of a State. There are several ways in which good governance affects growth. First, it has a direct impact on the effectiveness with which developmental programmes are implemented. Poor administration and corruption (the two are in fact intimately linked) are now widely recognised as major problems reducing the effectiveness of many Government programmes. There is no objective measure of the quality of governance, but impressionistic assessments suggest that the situation varies across States and the poorer performing States have more problems in this area. Unless these deficiencies are address, Plan schemes will not achieve their stated objective.

Second, the quality of governance can help stimulate growth is by making the policy environment more business friendly through deregulation, decontrol and procedural simplification. Entrepreneurs setting up an industrial unit in most States typically need as many as 30 permissions from various departments, each of which subjects the entrepreneur to the triple vicissitudes of the "inspector-raj harassment", delay and corruption. Sweeping reform of these regulatory systems at the State level is needed to reduce the transaction costs of doing business. Some States have begun to take initiatives in this area and have introduced simplified procedures and one-window arrangements to improve the business climate. The poorer performing States have generally lagged far behind the more advanced States in this dimension. It is important to note that the high transaction costs of cumbersome procedures are borne primarily by small businesses, which is precisely the group which most State Governments are otherwise keen to promote. Unless the local business environment is significantly improved, it is difficult to imagine that larger corporate investment can be attracted from outside the State.

Third, the general conditions for law and order are a reflection of the overall level of governance and are particularly important for stimulating private sector investment. This aspect of governance is usually taken for granted in formulating economic policies, but the fact is that conditions on the ground vary considerably across States. It is extremely difficult to provide an objective assessment of this dimension of governance and to compare the situation quantitatively across States. It is known that some States suffer from disturbed conditions in rural areas in some parts which is bound to have an impact on developmental activity. There are reports of urban mafias engaged in extortion, various types of protection rackets and even kidnapping in parts of some States which must affect the pace of economic activity. Some instances of this type occur everywhere and it is difficult to determine when the problem has reached critical proportions, but impressionistic evidence suggests that the poorer performing States clearly lag behind the others in this dimensions. It is difficult to imagine any significant acceleration in economic growth without a significant improvement in this aspect of governance.

Finally, a neglected area, where State Governments could take an initiative to improve the policy environment for investment, relates to the degree of flexibility allowed with regard to labour laws. It is commonly said that our labour laws are too inflexible in the matter of retrenchment of labour and closure of units, both of which require the permission of the State government which is almost never given. The need to amend the Central legislation to allow flexibility has been pointed out on many occasions. However, this is an area where, even without legislation. State governments could formulate more flexible guidelines within which the State Governments would act on these matters. States suffering from low growth and low investment could try to overcome these deficiencies in other areas by allowing greater flexibility with regard to labour. A transparent statement of circumstances under which retrenchment and closure would be allowed may actually help to attract more investment and expand the total volume of employment. No State government has experimented with this possibility thus far.

e) The Problem of State Finances

This brings me to the problem of State finances which looms ominously large on the fiscal landscape, not only for the poorer performing States but for all States. I have argued that an acceleration in growth almost certainly calls for higher levels of public investment in critical social and economic infrastructure sectors by State Governments. However the financial position of most States is actually forcing a continuing squeeze on Plan investment. As recently as 1990-91, several States had a positive balance from current revenues (BCR) which contributed something to finance the Plan.[6] This balance has now turned negative for almost all States which means that State governments have to borrow to finance the negative BCR, and then borrow even more to finance the Plan.

To be fair it must be recognised that the problem of fiscal imbalance is not limited to the States alone, but applies equally to the Centre. Over the years, both the Centre and the States have seen a burgeoning of non-

Plan expenditure in the face of inadequate buoyancy of revenues. They have responded by resorting to larger and larger volumes of borrowing to finance Plan expenditure, which is shrinking as a percentage of SDP. The process has led to a steady build up of debt, which in turn has generated a rising interest burden.

There is of course nothing wrong with borrowing to finance investments which yield financial returns since the returns form part of current reserve and offset the growth of interest payments. It would even be argued that there is nothing wrong with borrowing to finance development generally even when there is no immediate financial return, if development leads to greater growth, which in turn generates the buoyancy in tax revenues needed to service the debt. Unfortunately, this has not happened. Total revenues of the State Governments are stagnant relative to SDP and continuous resort to borrowing has led to a steadily rising interest burden which is squeezing the ability to finance developmental expenditure and pushing the States into an ever increasing dependence on borrowed funds.[7]

The extent of fiscal stress in the States is reflected in the trends in the ratio of interest payments to total revenues (tax plus non-tax revenues) shown in Table 31.10. For the 14 States as a whole the ratio of interest payments to tax revenues has increased from 7.7 per cent in 1980-81 to 13.1 per cent in 1990-91 and further to 17.6 per cent in 1996-97. The ten percentage point increase in interest payments over 17 years for the 14 States taken together has obviously squeezed the capacity of the States to finance normal developmental expenditure from current revenues. It has made them more dependent upon borrowing even as the level of Plan expenditure as a percentage of GDP has declined. The problem is particularly acute in some States. Both Uttar Pradesh and Orissa have seen interest payments as a percentage of total revenues increase by 17 percentage points over 17 years. Interestingly, the increase is much less for Bihar, mainly because Bihar has not tried to maintain the level of Plan expenditure or development expenditure.

It is interesting to note that it is not the poor performing States alone that have problems. Punjab has seen the largest increase in its interest ratio from 10.9 per cent in 1980-81 to 29.4 per cent in 1996-97 though this is partly due to the burden of loans to handle security related expenditure in the 1980s. There are some States which are in a reasonably good position. This includes Madhya Pradesh, Tamil Nadu, Karnataka, Haryana and Maharashtra. These States also have large current deficits which have worsened recently because of the impact of large civil service salary increases given at the time of implementing the

Fifth Pay Commission. However they do not have such a large accumulation of past debts and as such they are likely to find it easier to finance development expenditure in future.

TABLE – 31.10

Interest Payment as Percentage of Total Revenue

		1980-81	1990-91	1996-97
1.	Bihar	10.84	17.44	17.62
2.	Rajasthan	10.59	13.66	20.54
3.	Uttar Pradesh	8.29	15.38	25.33
4.	Orissa	8.10	16.79	25.17
5.	Madhya Pradesh	6.82	11.28	13.74
6.	Andhra Pradesh	6.45	11.02	16.42
7.	Tamil Nadu	7.11	8.95	12.33
8.	Kerala	7.11	14.17	17.95
9.	Karnataka	6.54	11.19	12.55
10.	West Bengal	9.97	15.25	23.58
11.	Gujarat	6.68	15.72	16.65
12.	Haryana	8.04	12.64	11.83
13.	Maharashtra	5.41	10.12	12.70
14.	Punjab	10.93	16.81	29.35
	All 14 States	**7.74**	**13.12**	**17.56**

Source: RBI data on State budgets.

Unless State finances can be put in order, there is little chance of the poorer States being able to undertake the substantial infrastructure financing needed to raise their rates of growth to reasonable levels. In fact the problem is not limited to the poorer States alone. The financial position of the other States has also deteriorated to a level where it will lead to a slowing down of their growth unless corrective action is taken. What needs to be done to tackle the financial problem of the States is well known, though that does not make it any easier.

i. The volume of direct and indirect subsidies in the system has become unsustainable and most of these subsidies are not specifically targeted at the poor. The major State level subsidies are cheap or free power to farmers, highly subsidized road transport rates, grossly inadequate rates changed by the irrigation departments. Very low user charges in higher education and for hospital services. An increase in user charges in each of these areas to reduce the total volume of subsidies is needed urgently. For example, the average tariff rate for electricity supplied to agriculture is around 30 paise for all States (some States have made it free). The norm proposed by the National Development Council Committee on Power in 1991 was that the minimum rates charged should be brought to 50 paise. At current prices this would require the tariff for agriculture to be raised to around Re. 1 per unit. Irrigation charges at present cover only around 20 per cent of the maintenance costs of the system. Since resources are not available from the budget to make up the deficiency, the result has meant that the irrigation network in most States has been massively neglected. These examples can be multiplied.

ii. The largest single drain on the system is the losses of the SEBs. In 1992-93, SEB losses were Rs. 2725 crores or 9.8 per cent of total State Plan expenditure in that year. They have increased to around Rs. 13,000 crores in 1998-99, which is around 18 per cent of total State Plan expenditure. These large losses are not due to low tariffs alone. Operational inefficiencies are equally important. Transmission and Distribution (T&D) losses of the State Electricity Boards (SEBs) are officially estimated at around 23 per cent, which is itself very high, but the actual figure is much higher. Official estimates of T&D losses are grossly underestimated by inflating the volume of electricity consumed by agriculture, where supply is not metered. In Orissa for example, when T&D losses were re-estimated in the context of unbundling distribution from generation, it was found that actual T&D losses were as high as 46 per cent compared with 22 per cent reported earlier. Similar exercises conducted in other States have yielded similar results. Most of this large loss represents outright theft, often with the full connivance of staff in the distribution segment. Privatising the distribution segment may be the simplest way to eliminate these losses the burden of which is ultimately borne by the system as a whole including consumers especially honest consumers. Since privatisation is likely to be strongly resisted by vested interests, it will be necessary to mobilise public opinion to make people realise that the present system is being massively misused for the benefit of vested interests.[8] At the very least, a part of the distribution system in each State should be privatised so as to provide a benchmark against which performance in the public sector can be monitored.

iii. State governments must make a serious effort to get out of public sector enterprises which have proliferated at the State government level. Many of these State PSUs are little more than vehicles for creating jobs at all levels. In many States, political personalities are appointed as Chairmen of State Corporations and given the rank of a cabinet Minister. Most State PSUs are unlikely to yield significant resources if privatised, though privatisation could help avoid recurring losses. However there are some that could be privatised with an immediate budgetary gain. The various tourism corporations, or public sector sugar mills or cement plants owned by so many State governments are examples of units where a start can be made. Some steps have been taken to privatise PSUs in some States, but the progress as yet is very limited.

iv. State tax administration needs to be massively modernised to provide simple tax systems with transparent administrative procedures and an honest tax administration. In most Centre-States forums, States often complain that they do not have sufficient taxing power but in fact they have not used the powers available in many areas. The taxation of agriculture for example is constitutionally a State subject but States have left this tax base untouched. No State has seen fit to levy an agricultural income tax even on large farmers. Land revenue, which is a form of agricultural taxation, and could be a substitute for agricultural income tax, has been reduced over the years to negligible levels. Urban property taxation is a crucial source of municipal revenue in most countries but our system is hopelessly outdated leading to very poor realisations. And yet our urban areas are desperately short of the resources needed to undertake basic investments in urban infrastructure. A major modernisation in the system of property taxation is urgently needed.

v. Finally, the government bureaucracy has proliferated in most States (as indeed in the Centre). This not only eats up resources but also perpetuates inefficiency and sluggishness in the system. Resources allocated to many government programmes are disproportionately absorbed by salaries of a bloated bureaucracy leaving very little non-salary funds to meet even the minimum non-salary expenditures needed to deliver the services which the programmes are meant to pro-

> vide. Downsizing government as a whole is therefore essential to remedy this problem. The resources released can then be used to increase expenditures, and possibly also employment, in critical areas such as health and education which are currently underfunded. The reluctance to downsize is understandable because of the large unsatisfied demand for government jobs, but we have to recognise that the reluctance to take these hard decisions will lead to a loss of growth which leads to a loss of many more potential jobs.

Progress in these areas is obviously not easy, especially in the poorer States. Many of the problems listed have arisen because of the populist pressures generated by our polity and for that reason are not amenable to purely technocratic solutions. However there is also no obvious alternative which can restore the financial health of the States and unless this is done the poorer States cannot possibly make the substantial investments needed in their social and economic infrastructure. Paradoxically, reforms to restore financial viability are most needed in the poorer performing states, even though they are in some ways the most reluctant to implement them.

f) The Role of the Central Government

Given the severe resources problem of the poorer States, it is natural to ask whether the Centre can provide additional financial help to the weaker States? A detailed discussion of this issue is clearly outside the scope of this lecture. The fact is that the total resources devolved from the Centre to the States through statutory devolution via the Finance Commission mechanism, together with the non-statutory flow of Central Assistance through the Planning Commission, already add up to a substantial amount. The Centre's own fiscal position is also far from comfortable and this makes it difficult to envisage any significant expansion in these flows. In fact, the Central Government needs to take steps urgently to reduce its own fiscal deficit, which reached 5.6 per cent of GDP in 1999-2000. A reduction in the Central fiscal deficit is necessary if real interest rates are to be reduced, an outcome which would benefit the States both directly, through its impact on interest rates, and also indirectly via the effect on private investment.

While the scope for providing additional resources from the Centre to help the poorer States is very limited, an issue which has not received the attention it deserves is whether the Centre should introduce mechanisms which might improve the effectiveness of the resources it provides to the States. At present, Central assistance in support of State

Plans is transferred by the Planning Commission as a "block transfer" without any significant linkage to actual performance. This system of unconditional transfer could be replaced by a system in which a substantial part of the Central assistance to the States is made available with a more explicit linkage to performance conditions.

The idea of introducing performance linkage or conditionality in transfers to States will be strongly resisted by advocates of federal autonomy and decentralization and it must be conceded that their arguments have some merit. One can legitimately argue that Central assistance to the States should be devolved on the basis of some objective criterion of "entitlement" and the accountability in the use of those resources should be left to the normal political process at State level. However, this approach also implies that the Centre can have no particular responsibility to ensure that the specific constraints to growth at the State level are effectively addressed. An alternative approach would be to argue that Central assistance to State should be linked to specific action to be taken by the States to overcome the particular constraints that hold back their performance.

For example, if growth in the poorer States is held back by gaps in infrastructure and social development, then Central assistance should be made available linked to specific investments and policy initiatives in these sectors and the disbursement of these funds should be linked to the achievement of specific milestones in project implementation or policy reform. This would involve introduction of conditionality, but as long as the design of the programmes and the identification of milestones for implementation has the full involvement of the State, there can be no intellectual objection to enforcing these as conditions for disbursement. In the longer run, linking Central transfers to performance, with the relevant performance criteria or conditionality being negotiated by the Planning Commission, with the State government on the basis of a shared assessment of critical constraints affecting the State, may make a greater contribution to the development of the backward States than is possible in the present system.

I would like to conclude by reiterating what I said at the beginning. We need to take much more interest in what is happening in individual States because the available evidence shows that the difference in performance across States is enormous. Some States have done exceptionally well, several others show a strong performance while some are doing very poorly. We need to be able to explain the reasons for these differences on the basis of relevant State specific characteristics which may be economic, institutional, socio-economic or even socio-political. This would help in devising strategies that can help break the specific constraints that prevent the present poorly performing States from replicating the success of the better performers.

Notes

1. Assuming that the underlying relationship is $Y=A(1+r)^t$ we estimate the regression equation in Y=a+bt where b=log (1+r). The growth rate r is then calculated using the regression estimate as r = antilog b-1.
2. The acronym BIMARU, taken from the initial letters for Bihar, Madhya Pradesh, Rajasthan and UP was a pun on the Hindi word Bimar, meaning sick and was first used by Ashish Bose in the context of demographic analysis as these States displayed much higher fertility rates than other States in the country.
3. See for example Datt (1999) and Gupta (1999).
4. They construct a new price index using budget shares from the NSS surveys and unit valves as reported by the NSS and find a much larger decline in poverty between 1987-88 and 1993 than reported in conventional studies using the CPIAL for rural inflation and the Consumer Price Index for Manual Labour (CPIML) for urban areas. The difference is especially large in rural areas where Deaton and Tarozzi report a larger decline in poverty.
5. The alternative method sought information on expenditure on food, tobacco, medicines etc. for the previous week; for fuel, light, miscellaneous goods and services the reference period was the previous month and for education, clothing, footwear and durable goods it was the previous year.
6. The Balance from Current Revenues is the surplus of current revenues over non-Plan current expenditure. When this is positive, it contributes along with borrowed resources to finance the Plan.
7. The Central Government is actually in a worse position because Central government revenues have actually declined as a percentage of GDP.
8. In principle it should be possible to reduce these losses within a public sector framework also by introducing discipline and accountability, but in practice this extremely difficult to achieve and if achieved it is difficult to maintain.

References

Bhalla, Surjit S. (2000), "Growth and Poverty in India – Myth or Reality" Paper prepared for a Conference in Honour of Raja Chelliah, Institute of Economic and Social Change, Bangalore, Jan. 17, 2000.

Datt, Gaurav (1999), "Has Poverty Declined Since Economic Reforms Economic & Political Weekly, Vol. 34 No. 50.

Deaton Angus and Alessandra Tarozzi (1999), "Prices and Poverty in India". Princeton University Mimeo Dec. 13, 1999.

Natarajan, I (1998), "India Market Demographics Report, 1998, NCAER.

Gupta, S.P. (1999), "Trickle Down Theory Revisited: The Role of Employment And Poverty", V.B. Singh Memorial Lecture, Mimeo Nov. 18-20, 1999.

Twelfth NCAER Golden Jubilee Lecture, Economic & Political Weekly, May 6, 2000.

Editorial Notes

32

Assessment of the Growth Experience

Poverty, Unemployment and Inflation

This section is devoted to an assessment of the growth experience in terms of the problem of poverty, unemployment inequality, and inflation (Chs. 32 to 37). Poverty debate, results of 55th round of employment-unemployment survey and 55th round consumer expenditure survey as analysed by K. Sundaram in CDE working paper no. 95 are covered in the editorial notes (Ch.32) Poverty and development policy dealing with conceptional issues, measurement issues, and policy issues are discussed in Chs. 33 & 34 (A. Vaidyanathan & R. Radhakrishna et al.). A re-examination of Poverty and Inequality is available in Ch.35 (Angus Deaton and Jean Dreze). The Employment opportunities as per the Planning Commission Report of the Task Force on Employment Opportunities is covered in Ch.36. Inflation and price stability is discussed in Ch. 37.

Poverty and Unemployment

The problem of poverty and unemployment is considered as the biggest challenge to development planning in India. High poverty levels are synonymous with poor quality of life, deprivation, malnutrition, illiteracy and low human resource development. The slogan of poverty eradication has been adopted by all political parties in one form or another and there is a national agreement for the goal of poverty alleviation. The national consenses on poverty alleviation provided the necessary condition for launching various schemes and programmes aimed at achieving this objective. But the persistence of poverty during all these years suggests that the national consenses on objectives did not and could not provide sufficient conditions for poverty alleviation.

Poverty Estimates

India accounts for about 20 per cent of the global count of those living on less than $ 1 a person per day, so that what happens in India is not only a reflection of worldwide trends, but one of their major determinants[1].

Historically, the Indian statistical system has led the world in the measurement of poverty. The sample surveys that were pioneered by Mahalanobis at the Indian Statistical Institute in Kolkata in the 1940s and 1950s were moved into the government statistical system as the National Sample Survey Organisation (NSSO), whose household surveys are the basis for the regular publications on poverty by the Planning Commission. Following Mahalanobis and India, today, most countries have a recent household income or expenditure survey from which it is possible to make a direct assessment of the living standards of the population (Deaton 2005).

National statistical systems collect more than survey data, and much non-survey information is relevant for the monitoring of living standards. Most important are the National Accounts Statistics (NAS), which provide widely used measures of aggregate performance, particularly GDP and its components, particularly consumption. Although these consumption estimates rely on surveys for several of their components, much also comes from other sources. And although there are important differences in definition between the survey and national accounts concepts of consumption, a well-functioning statistical system uses multiple estimates to cross-check and validate one another. And in India, there is a long and distinguished tradition of empirical work on such cross-checking and validation of the consumption estimates.

The Selection of Poverty Lines

The calculation of poverty measures requires two components, a distribution of household expenditure, and a poverty line or cut-off that separates poor from non-poor households. Although poverty lines are often linked to the amount of money that households need, to be able to buy a minimally satisfactory diet, the use and long-term survival of poverty lines depends on policy makers and others accepting them as useful[2].

The starting point for estimating the number of households below the poverty line is a normative nutritional requirement per person per day at some base point. There is a debate on the minimum calorie requirement, and whether it should be the same for all parts of the country. Most acceptable figures are 2,400 calories per person per day in rural areas, and 2,200 calories per person per day in urban areas. The next step is to translate the nutrient requirement into monetary terms. The expenditure level of households which are able to spend the requisite amount to obtain the desired calories serves as the cut-off point, or the poverty line. To adjust the poverty line over a period of time, price variations have to be considered and an appropriate price deflator has to be selected. The problem arises in deciding upon such a deflator.

Thus, the following elements mainly affect the magnitude of the poverty ratio: (i) the nutrition norm (translated into monetary terms) in the base year; (ii) price deflator used to update the poverty line; and (iii) pro rata adjustment in the number of households in different expenditure classes to determine the number of households below and above the poverty line. Different assumptions and methods are used for these three purposes, which accounts for the different estimates provided by scholars.

For some time the magic number of Rs. 20 per head at 1960-61 prices was used. From late 1970s into the mid-1990s, the Planning Commission used two poverty lines for per capita household expenditure in India, Rs. 49 for rural households, and Rs. 57 for urban households, so that prices were taken to be about 16 per cent higher for urban households. The poverty lines were held constant in real terms, and were converted to current rupees using the implicit price deflator of consumption in the National Accounts. This process had the disadvantage of ignoring interstate differences in price levels, as well as variations from state to state in urban to rural price differential. Furthermore, it might be doubted whether the national accounts consumption deflator was an ideal measure of inflation for households near the poverty line. These problems (and several others) were dealt with by an Expert Group in 1993, whose recommendations for new poverty lines were adopted (in a somewhat modified form) by the Planning Commission, and these 'Expert Group' poverty lines have been used in the official calculations of poverty in India from 1983 (back-casting the methodology) to the present day. According to these procedures, poverty lines are defined at the state level, separately for urban and rural households. Each line is updated by a state-specific price index, the state consumer price index for agricultural labourers (CPIAL) for rural lines, and the state consumer price index for industrial workers (CPIIW) for urban lines. (separate procedures are followed for the small states and territories, sometimes assuming the poverty *line* of a nearby state, and sometimes its poverty *rate*.) There is no countrywide poverty line as such; instead, once the all-India rural and urban headcount ratios have been calculated, the all-India lines are defined implicitly as the lines which, when applied to all households, give the all-India poverty rates.

The Planning Commission has been estimating the incidence of poverty at the national and state level using the methodology contained in the report of the Expert Group on Estimation of Proportion and Number of Poor (Lakdawala Committee) and applying it to consumption expenditure data from the large sample surveys on consumer expenditure conducted by the NSSO at an interval of approximately five years. On this basis, comparable estimates of poverty are available at national and state level from 1973-74 to 1999-2000.

According to Deaton, the Expert Group poverty lines have a serious problem in that the urban to rural price differencials that are implied by them are too large to be credible. It is unclear how this happened, whether there was an error in the calculations, or whether the price indexes that went into the calculations produced the result through some unfortunate cumulative effect.

As per the estimates of poverty by the Planning Commission, based on the 55th round of NSSO covering the period July 1999 to June 2000, in the last two decades there was a significant decline in proportion of people living below poverty line, from 51.3 per cent in 1977-78 to 26.1 per cent in 1999-2000. In absolute terms, the number of the poor declined from 328.9 million in 1977-78 to 260.3 million in 1999-2000 (Table 32.1).

Results of two annual surveys of household consumer expenditure conducted by NSSO for 2000-2001 and 2001-2002 have also become available. As per the results of the 57th NSS round, at the all-India level the proportion of chronically hungry households (not getting enough to eat during any month of the year) has declined to 0.5 per cent in rural areas and 0.1 per cent in urban areas. As for seasonal hunger, 16 per thousand households in rural areas and 3 per thousand households in urban areas reported getting enough food only in some months of the year.

TABLE – 32.1

Estimates of Poverty

Year	All India		Rural		Urban	
	All India Number (Million)	Poverty Ratio (per cent)	Rural Number (Million)	Poverty Ratio (per cent)	Urban Number (Million)	Poverty Ratio (per cent)
1973-74	321	54.9	261	56.4	60	49.0
1977-78	329	51.3	264	53.1	65	45.2
1983	323	44.5	252	45.7	71	40.8
1987-88	307	38.9	232	39.1	75	38.2
1993-94	320	36.0	244	37.3	76	32.4
1999-2000	260	26.1	193	27.1	67	23.6
2007*	220	19.3	170	21.1	49	15.1

* Poverty projection for 2007.

Source: Tenth Five-Year Plan.

Though poverty has declined at the macro-level, there are wide rural-urban and inter-state disparities in the improvement pattern. In 1999-2000 Bihar and Orissa continued to be the two poorest States. In 1999-2000, 20 States and Union territories had poverty ratios below the national average. Significant declines in the incidence of poverty were witnessed in Andhra Pradesh, Gujarat, Haryana, Karnataka, Kerala, Maharashtra, Punjab and West Bengal. Haryana and Punjab have been successful in reducing the incidence of poverty by following a strategy of high agricultural growth, Andhra Pradesh succeeded in implementing its public distribution programme for food grains, West Bengal's success came from empowerment of Panchayats and implementation of land reforms, and poverty was impacted in Kerala by a clear focus on human resource development. The Tenth Plan (2002-07) has set a target of reduction in poverty ratio by five percentage points to 19.3 per cent by 2007 and by 15 percentage points by 2012. The targets for rural and urban poverty in 2007 are 21.1 per cent and 15.1 per cent respectively.

In a study[3] (July 2001) K. Sundaram (Table 32.3) has estimated the proportion of population in households below the poverty line by gender, age and rural-urban location, at the all India level, for 1993-94 and 1999-2000 based on the distribution of population by per capita ccnsumer expenditure size-classes derived from the Employment-Unemployment Surveys for 1993-94 and 1999-2000. Table 32.4, presents

TABLE – 32.2

Poverty Ratio at the State Level

(per cent)

S.No.	State	Rural			Urban			Combined		
		1973-74	1993-94	1999-2000	1973-74	1993-94	1999-2000	1973-74	1993-94	1999-2000
1.	Andhra Pradesh	48.41	15.92	11.05	50.61	38.33	26.63	48.86	22.19	15.77
2.	Arunachal Pradesh	52.67	45.01	40.04	36.92	7.73	7.47	51.93	39.35	33.47
3.	Assam	52.67	45.01	40.04	36.92	7.73	7.47	51.21	40.86	36.09
4.	Bihar	62.99	58.21	44.30	52.96	34.50	32.91	61.91	54.96	42.60
5.	Goa	46.85	5.34	1.35	37.69	27.03	7.52	44.26	14.92	4.40
6.	Gujarat	46.35	22.18	13.17	52.57	27.89	15.59	48.15	24.21	14.07
7.	Haryana	34.23	28.02	8.27	40.18	16.38	9.99	35.36	25.05	8.74
8.	Himachal Pradesh	27.42	30.34	7.94	13.17	9.18	4.63	26.39	28.44	7.63
9.	Jammu & Kashmir	45.51	30.34	3.97	21.32	9.18	1.98	40.83	25.17	3.48
10.	Karnataka	55.14	29.88	17.38	52.53	40.14	25.25	54.47	33.16	20.04
11.	Kerala	59.19	25.76	9.38	62.74	24.55	20.27	59.79	25.43	12.72
12.	Madhya Pradesh	62.66	40.64	37.06	57.65	48.38	38.44	61.78	42.52	37.43
13.	Maharashtra	57.71	37.93	23.72	43.87	35.15	26.81	53.24	36.86	25.02
14.	Manipur	52.67	45.01	40.04	36.92	7.73	7.47	49.96	33.78	28.54
15.	Meghalaya	52.67	45.01	40.04	36.92	7.73	7.47	50.20	37.92	33.87
16.	Mizoram	52.67	45.01	40.04	36.92	7.73	7.47	50.32	25.66	19.47
17.	Nagaland	52.67	45.01	40.04	36.92	7.73	7.47	50.81	37.92	32.67
18.	Orissa	67.28	49.72	48.01	55.62	41.64	42.83	66.18	48.56	47.15
19.	Punjab	28.21	11.95	6.35	27.96	11.35	5.75	28.15	11.77	6.16
20.	Rajasthan	44.76	26.46	13.74	52.13	30.49	19.85	46.14	27.41	15.28
21.	Sikkim	52.67	45.01	40.04	36.92	7.73	7.47	50.86	41.43	36.55
22.	Tamil Nadu	57.43	32.48	20.55	49.40	39.77	22.11	54.94	35.03	21.12

Contd...

...Contd...

S.No.	State	Rural			Urban			Combined		
		1973-74	1993-94	1999-2000	1973-74	1993-94	1999-2000	1973-74	1993-94	1999-2000
23.	Tripura	52.67	45.01	40.04	36.92	7.73	7.47	51.00	39.01	34.44
24.	Uttar Pradesh	56.53	42.28	31.22	60.09	35.39	30.89	57.07	40.85	31.15
25.	West Bengal	73.16	40.80	31.85	34.67	22.41	14.86	63.43	35.66	27.02
26.	A & N Island	57.43	32.48	20.55	49.40	39.77	22.11	55.56	34.47	20.99
27.	Chandigarh	27.96	11.35	5.75	27.96	11.35	5.75	27.96	11.35	5.75
28.	Dadra & Nagar Hav.	46.85	51.95	17.57	37.69	39.93	13.52	46.55	50.84	17.14
29.	Daman & Diu	N.A.	5.34	1.35	N.A.	27.03	7.52	N.A	15.80	4.44
30.	Delhi	24.44	1.90	0.40	52.23	16.03	9.42	49.61	14.69	8.23
31.	Lakshadweep	59.19	25.76	9.38	62.74	24.55	20.27	59.68	25.04	15.60
32.	Pondicherry	57.43	32.48	20.55	49.40	39.77	22.11	53.82	37.40	21.67
	All India	**56.44**	**37.27**	**27.09**	**49.01**	**32.36**	**23.62**	**54.88**	**35.97**	**26.10**

N.A. Not Available

1. Poverty Ratio of Assam is used for Sikkim, Arunachal Pradesh, Meghalaya, Mizoram, Manipur, Nagaland and Tripura.
2. Poverty Line of Maharashtra and expenditure distribution of Goa is used to estimate poverty ratio of Goa.
3. Poverty Line of Himachal Pradesh and expenditure distribution of Jammu & Kashmir is used to estimate poverty ratio of Jammu & Kashmir.
4. Poverty Ratio of Tamil Nadu is used for Pondicherry and A & N Island
5. Urban Poverty Ratio of Punjab used for both rural and urban poverty of Chandigarh
6. Poverty Line of Maharashtra and expenditure distribution of Dadra & Nagar Haveli is used to estimate poverty ratio of Dadra & Nagar Haveli.
7. Poverty Ratio of Goa is used for Daman & Diu.
8. Poverty Ratio of Kerala is used for Lakshadweep.
9. Urban Poverty Ratio of Rajasthan may be treated as tentative.
10. Estimates on a 30 day recall basis for 1999-2000.

Source: Planning Commission.

similar results for the proportion of households below the poverty line for types of rural households differentiated by their principal means of livelihood.

TABLE – 32.3

Proportion of Population in BPL Households by Gender, Age and Rural-Urban Location All-India: 1993-94 - 1999-2000

	1993-94			1999-2000		
	Children (0-14)	Adults (15+)	All Ages	Children (0-14)	Adults (15+)	All Ages
Rural Males	45.43	34.45	38.66	42.31	31.17	35.55
Rural Females	46.85	36.08	39.96	45.64	32.63	37.34
Rural Persons	46.10	35.25	39.36	43.89	31.90	36.35
Urban Males	37.44	25.09	29.14	36.42	23.57	27.68
Urban Females	39.69	27.69	31.69	39.41	25.53	29.83
Urban Persons	38.51	26.33	30.37	37.84	24.51	28.76
Males	43.62	31.95	36.26	40.98	29.07	33.52
Females	45.22	33.96	37.94	44.25	30.76	35.47
Persons	44.37	32.96	37.13	42.54	29.90	34.42

K. Sundaram, Centre for Development Economics, Working Paper No. 95.

Sources: 1993-94: Results on Employment Situation in India, Fifth Quinquennial Survey, NSS 50th Round (July 1993-June 1994), Sarvekshana vol. 20, no. 1, July-September 1996.

1999-2000: Results on Employment-Unemployment in India, 1999-2000, NSS 55th Round, July 1999-June 2000.

Poverty Lines: (Rupees Per capita per month)

1993-94:	Rural: 211.30	Urban: 274.88
1999-2000:	Rural: 335.46	Urban: 451.19

At the all-India level, the results are clear and unambiguous. Except in respect of girl children in urban India, there is a definite and unambiguous decline in the proportion of population in households that lie below the poverty line. The same holds true, in terms of the proportion of households below the poverty, for all the types of households distinguished by reference to their principal means of livelihood. Particularly significant is the 7.5 percentage point decline in the incidence of poverty for agricultural labour households and a 6 percentage point decline for other labour households. This result of a clear and sizeable decline in the poverty prevalence ratios among agricultural labour households and other labour households should survive any adjustment for use of a 365-day reference period for durables etc. in the NSS 55th Round Survey.

TABLE – 32.4

Proportion of Rural Households below the Poverty Line by Livelihood Categories: All-India: 1993-94 - 1998-2000

Percentage of Households Below the Poverty Line

Household/Type	1993-94	1999-2000
Self-Employed in Agriculture	27.81	24.12
Self-Employed in Non-Agriculture	29.68	27.00
Agricultural Labour	54.49	46.96
Other Labour	35.21	29.24
Others	23.64	18.38
All	35.24	31.48

Notes & Sources: 1993-94: Results on Employment Situation in India, Fifth Quinquennial Survey, NSS 50th Round (July 1993-June 1994), Sarvekshana vol. 20, no. 1, July-September 1996.

1999-2000: Results on Employment-Unemployment in India, 1999-2000, NSS 55th Round, July 1999-June 2000.

Poverty Lines: (Rupees Per capita per month)

1993-94: Rural: 211.30 Urban: 274.88

1999-2000: Rural: 335.46 Urban: 451.19

Reproduced from K. Sundaram Working Paper No. 95 (Table 11, P.34).

Overall, at the all-India level, the results of 55th Round the Employment-Unemployment Survey confirms the direction of change: the prevalence of poverty has indeed declined over the 1990s. However, the order of decline is much less than that indicated by the 55th Round Consumer Expenditure Survey.

Is the above conclusion also valid for the major states individually? To answer this question, in Table 32.5, estimates of poverty prevalence ratios for all-India and 15 major States for 1993-94 and 1999-2000 based on the size-distribution now available from the 55th Round Employment-Unemployment Survey have been presented. These estimates are presented separately for the rural and the urban populations in each State.

TABLE – 32.5

Poverty Prevalence Ratios by Rural-Urban Location: All-India and 15 Major States 1993-94 - 1999-2000

Percentage of Population Below the Poverty Line

States	Rural		Urban	
	1993-94	1999-2000	1993-94	1999-2000
All-India	39.36	36.35	30.37	28.76
Andhra Pradesh	27.97	25.48	35.44	32.28
Assam	58.25	61.78	10.13	12.45
Bihar	64.41	58.85	45.03	45.10
Gujarat	28.62	26.22	28.86	21.70
Haryana	30.52	14.86	13.40	13.79
Karnataka	37.73	38.50	32.41	24.55
Kerala	33.95	26.50	28.20	31.89
Madhya Pradesh	36.93	39.35	46.02	46.29
Maharashtra	50.21	50.00	33.52	32.16
Orissa	59.12	62.67	36.99	34.27
Punjab	17.61	14.24	6.79	6.74
Rajasthan	25.92	15.01	30.60	24.36
Tamil Nadu	37.27	39.27	37.83	29.82
Uttar Pradesh	39.08	29.87	34.23	36.39
West Bengal	54.15	56.16	20.97	16.74

Notes and Sources:

State-specific poverty lines for 1993-94 have been adjusted for inflation by reference to the Consumer Price Index for Agricultural Labourers (for rural population) and the Consumer Price Index for Industrial Workers for the urban population.

Poverty Prevalence Rates for 1993-94 have been computed from Table 4.4.1 in Sarvekshana vol. 20, No. 1, July-September 1996 and those for 1999-2000 from Table 4.3.2 in Draft Report No. 458 (55/10/2), Employment-Unemployment Situation in India 1999-2000 Part I, NSS 55th Round (July 1999-June 2000), NSSO, April 2001.

Reproduced from K. Sundaram, op., cit., (Table 12, P.35).

The key results to emerge from Table 32.5 are:[4]

i. In respect of rural areas in six States (Assam, Karnataka, Madhya Pradesh, Orissa, Tamil Nadu and West Bengal) the poverty prevalence ratios in 1999-2000 are higher than in 1993-94 while in Maharashtra, there has been virtually no change in the poverty ratios between 1993-94 and 1999-2000.

At the all-India level, and in eight of the fifteen major States, rural poverty prevalence ratios have declined over the 1990s. Of these eight states, except in three States (Andhra Pradesh, Bihar and Gujarat) where the decline in poverty ratios is less than 10 per cent (of the 1993-94 value), the decline has been sizeable: ranging from 19 per cent in Punjab to 51 per cent in Haryana;

ii. In urban areas, a decline in poverty ratios is seen in eight of the fifteen states - besides all-India. Among these eight states (Andhra Pradesh, Gujarat, Karnataka, Maharashtra, Orissa, Rajasthan, Tamil Nadu and West Bengal) the order of decline was less than 5 per cent in Maharashtra and between 5 and 10 per cent in Andhra Pradesh and Orissa. In the other five states, the decline ranged between 20 and 25 per cent of the 1993-94 levels.

As for the other seven states, the poverty ratios remained more or less unchanged in Bihar, Haryana, Karnataka, and Punjab, while in Uttar Pradesh, the increase was of the order of 6 per cent. In two states, Assam and Kerala, the poverty ratios increased by more than 13 per cent between 1994 and 2000.

Overall, the confirmation obtained from the Employment-Unemployment survey that, at the all-India level the prevalence of poverty in India had indeed declined over the 1990s is not uniformly present across all the major States. While in a majority of the 15 States analysed (*albeit* a majority of one) poverty ratios have indeed declined between 1993-94 and 1999-2000, in both the rural and the urban areas, in seven States poverty ratios have either remained unchanged or have even increased over the 1990s.

This above result is, of course, in sharp contrast to the results of an across-the-board and sharp reduction in poverty obtained from the 55th Round Consumer Expenditure Survey.

The only effective way of resolving this conflict of results from the two Surveys is to track the consequences of the two sources of non-comparability (with the 1993-94 Survey) that remain: (i) the use of an abridged consumer expenditure schedule in the 55th Round Employment-Unemployment Survey; and, (ii) the use of a 365-day reference period in respect of expenditure on durables as well as certain items of miscellaneous expenditure.

Finally, at the all-India level, the results of the 55th Round Employment-Unemployment confirms that the poverty ratios have indeed declined over the 1990s. However, at the level of individual states, the results are more mixed. While in eight out of fifteen major States, poverty ratios have indeed declined over the 1990s, in seven others it has remained either unchanged or have even increased. In all-cases, even at the all-India level, the order of decline (wherever that has materialised) in the poverty prevalence rates revealed by the Employment-Unemployment Survey has been significantly smaller than that revealed by the 55th Round Consumer Expenditure Survey.

Deaton's poverty lines, together with his procedures for correcting the 55th Round data, form the basis for the analysis of poverty and inequality in the paper by Deaton and Jean Dreze, included here as Chapter 35. According to these estimates, there has been a fairly steady poverty decline in India in the 1970s, 1980s and 1990s, with neither acceleration nor deceleration over the last decade. Deaton and Dreze argue that their estimates are broadly consistent with a range of other evidence, including state-level growth rates from state GDP accounts and the growth of agricultural wages. They also note that there has been a marked increase in consumption inequality in the late 1990s, between states, with the already better-off states in the south and west growing more rapidly than the poorer states in the north and east, between rural and urban households, with growth a good deal more rapid for the latter, and within the urban sectors of many states, where consumption has been growing more rapidly among the best off.

According to Deaton the recent debate on Indian poverty has focused primarily on the headcount index, or proportion of people whose per capita consumption falls below the poverty line. But estimates of poverty that rely exclusively on income and consumption measures fail to capture important aspects of deprivation experienced by the poor. Human development is one of these: the Human Development Index (HDI) is based on a multidimensional concept of human development that has been developed under the overall leadership of the United Nations Development Program (UNDP). In India, there are several initiatives being pursued at the national and the state level to build database on human development indicators. Insecurity, including food insecurity, violence, social exclusion, and lack of basic human rights are other important aspects of deprivation in India[5].

As Deaton has rightly remarked "despite an extensive body of empirical work by eminent researchers, the debate on what happened to Indian poverty in the 1990s continues. .... There is little doubt that things have changed in India and in many cases changed for the better. But there are still important concerns, e.g. about differences in opportunities and growing regional disparities, characterised by lagging progress in some states in the face of impressive and uncontestable progress in others. And there are concerns about perceived discrimination and continuing disparities across social, ethnic, and religious groups, all of which contribute to the mixed regional picture. Even with perfect data; there would be no single answer to the question 'what has happened to poverty in India in the 1990s?"[6]

Employment Perspective

Creating adequate employment opportunities to absorb the existing unemployed and underemployed as well as the increase in labour force has been among the important and continuing concerns of Indian development policy throughout the post-independence period.

Full employment at rising levels of productivity and incomes would not in any case be feasible without growth and diversification of economic activity. This called for increasing the investment rate, a modern industrial base to produce equipment and material to complement labour, and improvement of technology all round [GoI, Planning Commission 1953].

The Mahalanobis strategy focused on the requisites for achieving and sustaining a rapid rate of growth in the long term. It recognised that in the transitional period employment may not keep pace with the growth of the labour force. The interests of employment in the medium term was sought to be balanced with those of long-term growth by a deliberate policy of producing mass consumption goods with labour-intensive techniques in the early stages of development. Discriminatory measures (differential taxation, reservation and subsidies) to protect, and positive measures (credit, marketing and technical help) to encourage, traditional and labour-intensive industry has been a continuing feature of policy throughout the last four decades.

By the end of the 50s, demographic growth was found to be much higher than expected even as the overall growth did not show much of an improvement. This led to fears that increases in job opportunities may not keep up with increase in population and labour force and that the problem of unemployment will be aggravated. The plan documents forecast an increasing 'backlog' of unemployment. The apprehensions were strengthened by other developments notably the increasing proletarianisation of rural labour and indications that the new agricultural technology did not increase employment in the same proportion as output. Data from the rural labour inquiries showed that even as dependence on wage labour was rising, employment per worker did not and real wage rates were stagnant or falling. The belief that growth would automatically lead to more employment and higher wages for everyone, was also losing its appeal.

The early 1970s witnessed an extensive debate on the 'trickle down' hypothesis, the nexus between unemployment and poverty and the need for special measures to alleviate the conditions of the poor and the unemployed who are by-passed by growth. There was near general agreement in the country, as indeed international bodies including the World Bank, that growth alone would not suffice to eliminate poverty and that special programmes designed to directly augment income and employment of the poor were essential. A special works programme of a rather modest scale had been included in the Third Plan; but the real fillip to the 'poverty alleviation' programmes came in the early 1970s with Indira Gandhi adopting 'Garibi Hatao' as the centre-piece of the government policy. Special employment schemes were an important component of this new programme. Over the years they have undergone various modifications culminating in the Jawahar Rozgar Yozana (JRY); more importantly the scale of outlays on these programmes has grown rapidly. By 1990-91 outlays on JRY exceeded Rs. 2,600 crore and it was estimated to generate additional employment of nearly 870 million person days a year.

The Eighth Plan aimed at bringing employment into a sharper focus in medium-term perspective with the goal of reducing unemployment to negligible level within the next ten years. Such an approach is now considered necessary also because it is realised that larger and efficient use of available human resources is the most effective way of poverty alleviation, reduction in inequalities and sustenance of a reasonably high pace of economic growth.

While approaching employment as an objective of the Plan, employment generation and economic growth are to be treated as mutually complementary rather than conflicting processes. Employment has, therefore, to be generated in the process of, and contribute to the acceleration of, economic growth. Employment, to be gainful and sustainable, has, therefore to be productive in character; it should be able to yield a reasonable level of income to the worker and also generate surplus for further growth and employment generation (8th Five Year Plan).

Improvement in the productivity of work-force assumes particular significance in our economy where low productivity and low incomes of a large mass of employed persons constitute a problems of much higher dimension than unemployment, measured conventionally in terms of involuntary idleness. Incidence of poverty is much higher than that of unemployment. An overwhelming majority of the poor are thus not apparently unemployed, but are engaged for a major part of their time in some activity, *albeit*, at very low levels of productivity and earnings. Thus the strategy has to focus not only on the creation of new 'jobs', but also on the augmentation of the existing employment in terms of productivity and incomes through suitable technological, market and institutional interventions.

Labour and Unemployment

Data on the labour force and unemployment are collected by the National Sample Survey Organisation (NSSO) through, quinquennial surveys. As per the results of the 55th NSSO Round (1999-2000), the rate of growth of employment, on Current Daily Status (CDS) basis, declined from 2.7 per cent per annum in 1983-1994 to 1.07 per cent per annum in 1994-2000 (Table 32.6). The decline in the rate of growth of employment during the 1990s was associated with a comparatively higher growth in GDP, indicating a decline in the labour intensity of production.

TABLE – 32.6

Employment and Unemployment (CDS Basis)

(person years)

	(Million)			Growth per annum (%)	
	1983	1993-94	1999-2000	1983 to 1993-94	1993-94 to 1999-2000
		All India			
Population	718.20	894.01	1003.97	2.00	1.95
Labour Force	261.33	335.97	363.33	2.43	1.31
Workforce	239.57	315.84	336.75	2.70	1.07
Unemployment rate (%)	8.30	5.99	7.32		
No. of unemployed	21.76	20.13	26.58	-0.08	4.74
		Rural			
Population	546.61	658.83	727.50	1.79	1.67
Labour Force	204.18	255.38	270.39	2.15	0.96
Workforce	187.92	241.04	250.89	2.40	0.67
Unemployment rate (%)	7.96	5.61	7.21		
No. of unemployed	16.26	14.34	19.50	-1.19	5.26
		Urban			
Population	171.59	234.98	276.47	3.04	2.74
Labor Force	57.15	80.60	92.95	3.33	2.40
Workforce	51.64	74.80	85.84	3.59	2.32
Unemployment rate (%)	9.64	7.19	7.65		
No. of unemployed	5.51	5.80	7.11	0.49	3.45

Source: Planning Commission and Economic Survey 2003-04.

Some of the other important findings emerging from the 55th Round (1999-2000) are:

(i) The decline in the rate of growth of employment was associated with a sharp decline in the rate of growth of the labour force.

(ii) The absolute number of unemployed increased from 20 million in 1993-94 to 27 million in 1999-2000. Also, the incidence of unemployment, (expressed in terms of unemployed as a percentage of the labour force) increased from 5.99 per cent in 1993-94 to 7.32 per cent in 1999-2000.

(iii) The decline in the overall growth rate of employment in 1994-2000 was largely attributable to a near stagnation of employment in agriculture. As a result, the share of agriculture in total employment dropped substantially from 60 per cent in 1993-94 to 57 per cent in 1999-2000.

(iv) On the other hand, employment growth in all the sub-sectors within services, such as trade, hotels, restaurant, transport, storage, communication and financial and busines services, (except community, social and personal services having negative growth rate) exceeded 5 per cent per annum (Table 32.7).

(v) As has been the trend in the past, the share of casual labour in total employment went up.

Some estimates of employment available from the Annual Rounds of NSSO for July-December 2002, indicate that on a usual status basis employment in the country increased at the rate of 2.07 per cent per annum during 2000 to 2002 (July-December) as compared to 1.07 per cent per annum during 1994-2000. During 2000 to 2002 (July-December) in absolute terms, again on usual status basis, employment increased by 84 lakh per year, on an average, as against the target of creating approximately 5 crore employment opportunities over the Tenth Plan period i.e. 1 crore employment opportunities per year. However, these estimates are based on thin samples which suffer from large sampling errors.

A Special Group constituted by the Planning Commission on targeting ten million employment opportunities per year over the Tenth Plan period had noted the decline in the rate of growth of population, labour force and workforce, but an increases in the unemployment rate during 1993-1994 and 1999-2000 (Table 32.6) in spite of the improvement in the overall growth performance of the economy from the previous decade.

TABLE – 32.7

Sectoral Employment Growth (CDS basis)

Sector	Employment (in million)				Annual growth (%)			
	1983	1987-88	1993-94	1999-2000	1983 to 1987-88	1987-88 to 1993-94	1983 to 1993-94	1993-94 to 1999-2000
Agriculture	151.35	163.82	190.72	190.94	1.77	2.57	2.23	0.02
Industry								
Mining & quarrying	1.74	2.40	2.54	2.26	7.35	1.00	3.68	-1.91
Manufacturing	27.69	32.53	35.00	40.79	3.64	1.23	2.26	2.58
Electricity, gas and water supply	0.83	0.94	1.43	1.15	2.87	7.19	5.31	-3.55
Construction	7.17	11.98	11.02	14.95	12.08	-1.38	4.18	5.21
Services								
Trade, hotels and restaurant	18.17	22.53	26.88	37.54	4.89	2.99	3.80	5.72
Transport, storage and communication	6.99	8.05	9.88	13.65	3.21	3.46	3.35	5.53
Financial, insurance, real estate and business services	2.10	2.59	3.37	4.62	4.72	4.50	4.60	5.40
Community, social and personal services	23.52	27.55	34.98	30.84	3.57	4.06	3.85	-2.08
All sectors	239.57	272.39	315.84	336.75	2.89	2.50	2.67	1.07

Source: NSSO-Different rounds.

In view of the declining employment elasticity of growth, observed during 1994-2000, the Special Group has recommended that over and above the employment generated in the process of present structure of growth, there is a need to promote certain identified labour intensive activities. These sectors are agriculture and allied activities, small and medium industries, information technology, construction, tourism, financial sector, education and health etc. With proper policy initiatives taken in these labour intensive sectors, an additional 20 million jobs could be created during the Tenth Plan. The Report also identified programs/targets for achieving the ten million employment opportunities per year. Another Task Force on Employment Strategies and Employment Monitoring at state level was set up by Planning Commission under the Chairmanship of the (then) Member, Planning Commission (Dr. S.P. Gupta), with representatives from states and major central Ministries/Departments.

There are large inter-state differentials in unemployment (Table 32.8). During the period 1993-94 to 1999-2000, growth in employment was the highest in Haryana (2.43 per cent) followed by Gujarat (2.31 per cent), while Kerala recorded the least growth of only 0.07 per cent.

TABLE – 32.8

Employment Scenario in States

(CDS basis)

Sl. No.	Selected States	Employment ('000) 1999-00	Employment growth 1993-94 to 1999-00 (% p.a.)	Unemployment rate 1999-00 (%)	Unemployment rate 1993-94 (%)	Employment elasticity 1993-94 to 1999-00	GDP growth (% per annum) 1993-94 to 1999-00
1.	Andhra Pradesh	30614	0.35	8.03	6.69	0.067	5.2
2.	Assam	7647	1.99	8.03	8.03	0.737	2.7
3.	Bihar	30355	1.59	7.32	6.34	0.353	4.5
4.	Gujarat	18545	2.31	4.55	5.70	0.316	7.3
5.	Haryana	5982	2.43	4.77	6.51	0.420	5.8
6.	Himachal Pradesh	2371	0.37	2.96	1.80	0.052	7.1
7.	Karnataka	20333	1.43	4.57	4.94	0.188	7.6
8.	Kerala	8902	0.07	20.97	15.51	0.013	5.5
9.	Madhya Pradesh	28725	1.28	4.45	3.56	0.272	4.7
10.	Maharashtra	34979	1.25	7.16	5.09	0.216	5.8
11.	Orissa	11928	1.05	7.34	7.30	0.262	4.0
12.	Punjab	8013	1.96	4.03	3.10	0.426	4.6
13.	Rajasthan	19930	0.73	3.13	1.31	0.104	7.0
14.	Tamil Nadu	23143	0.37	11.78	11.41	0.052	7.1
15.	Uttar Pradesh	49387	1.02	4.08	3.45	0.185	5.5
16.	West Bengal	22656	0.41	14.99	10.06	0.056	7.3
All India		336736	1.07	7.32	5.99	0.160	6.7

Source: Planning Commission and Economic Survey 2003-04.

Employment in the Organized Sector

Only a small percentage (8 to 9 per cent) of the total workforce of the country is employed in the organized sector. Organized sector employment on March 31, 2002 was 27.2 million of which 69 per cent or 18.8 million was in the public sector. With public sector employment declining by 1.9 per cent in 2002 over 2001, there was a corresponding decrease of 2.1 per cent in employment in the organized sector in 2002. The decline in public sector employment, reflecting a conscious policy decision, was compounded by a decline in organized private sector employment.

The data available from the 945 employment exchanges in the country indicates that in February 2004, the number of jobseekers registered with the employment exchanges (all of whom are not necessarily unemployed), was of the order of 4.11 crore out of which, approximately 70 per cent are educated (10th standard and above). The number of women job seekers registered was of the order of 1.07 crore (26 per cent of total job seekers). The maximum number of job seekers awaiting employment were in West Bengal (67.5 lakh). The placement was maximum in Gujarat, whereas the registration was maximum in Maharashtra. The placement effected by the employment exchanges at all-India level during 2003 was of the order of 1.55 lakh as against 2.56 lakh vacancies notified during this period.

Women in the Workforce

Women constitute a significant proportion of the labour force. Female participation in the workforce, however, varies across rural-urban areas. According to the 58th Round (July-December 2004) Survey of NSSO, the female Workforce participation rate in rural areas declined to 281 per thousand compared to 299 in the 55th Round (July 1999-2000). In Urban areas, it increased marginally from 139 to 140. In rural areas, 85 per cent of women workers are engaged primarily in agricultural activities, and related sectors such as animal husbandry. In urban areas, a significant proportion of women workers are employed in the unorganized sectors such as household industries, petty trade and services and building and construction activities. According to a National Institute of Public Finance & Policy (NIPFP) study on Gender Budgeting the average female wage is almost 80 per cent of the male average in urban areas, while it is less than 60 per cent of the corresponding male rate in rural areas.

Employment of women in the organized sector (both public and private) as on March 31, 2002 at 4.95 million, constituted 18.1 per cent of the total organized sector employment in the country, compared to 17.9 per cent in 2001. The distribution of women employees across industries reveals that community, social and personnel services sectors employed 56.5 per cent of women workers followed by manufacturing (20.6 per cent), agriculture and allied occupation (9.4 per cent) and finance, insurance, real and business (5.2 per cent). The proportion of women in organized sector employment is higher in States with higher female literacy rates.

Improvement in the quality of women's employment depends upon increased access to education and skill-development training.

The various Rounds of Surveys conducted by the National Sample Survey Organisation (NSSO) reveal that the average annual growth rate of overall employment (in both the organised and unorganised sectors) was 2.73 per cent per annum in the period 1972-73 to 1977-78 but declined to 1.54 per cent per annum in 1983 to 1987-88. (Table 32.6). However, the growth rate of employment increased to 2.43 per cent per annum over 1987-88 to 1993-94. As per the 55th Round (July 1999-June 2000) of the Survey on Employment conducted by the NSSO, overall employment grew by about 1 per cent per annum during 1993-94 to 1999-2000. Employment in absolute numbers has risen from 303 million in 1983 to 374 million in 1994 (2.04 per cent) and to 397 million in 2000 (0.98 per cent). (Table 32.9). The labour force participation rate declined in 1999-2000 as compared with 1993-94, which is reflected in a sharp deceleration in the growth of the labour force from 2.29 per cent per annum in 1987-88 to 1993-94, to 1.03 per cent per annum in the period 1993-94 to 1999-2000. The deceleration in employment is therefore also associated with a sharp decline in the growth of the labour force.

Organised sector employment in 1999-2000 was 28.11 million. i.e. about 7 per cent of the total employment of about 397 million. (Table 32.7) Over two-thirds of the total organised sector employment i.e. 19.41 million is in the public sector. Trends in organised sector employment reveal that employment in this sector has been declining. This has been entirely due to the slowing down in employment in the public sector from 1.52 per cent per annum between 1983 to 1994 to a negative growth of (-) 0.03 per cent per annum during 1994-2000. The decline in the rate of growth of public sector employment could be attributed to restructuring programmes of the public sector, and the ban on recruitment in many State Departments/Institutions as part of the 'economy drive' to reduce government expenditure.

TABLE – 32.9

Total Employment and Organised Sector Employment

Sector	Employment (Million)				Growth Rate (per cent per annum)	
	1983	1988	1994	1999-00	1983-94	1994-00
Total Population	718.21	790.00	895.05	1004.10	2.12	1.93
Total Labour Force	308.64	333.49	381.94	406.05	2.05	1.03
Total Employment	302.75	324.29	374.45	397.00	2.04	0.98
Org. Sector Employment	24.01	25.71	27.37	28.11	1.20	0.53
Public Sector	16.46	18.32	19.44	19.41	1.52	-0.03
Private Sector	7.55	7.39	7.93	8.70	0.45	1.87

Note:

1. The total employment figures are on Usual Status (UPSS) basis.
2. The Organised sector employment figures are as reported in the Employment Market Information System of Ministry of Labour and pertain to 1st March of 1983, 1988, 1994 and 1999.
3. The rate of growth of total employment and organised sector employment are compound rates of growth.

Source: Planning Commission and Economic Survey 2001-02.

The annual growth of employment in the organised sector, both public and private, for the period 1991-2000 is listed in Table 32.10. The major contribution in the overall growth of organised sector employment has been made by the private sector after 1995. However, this growth in private sector employment did not offset the effect of the slowdown in public sector employment since the private sector share of employment in the organised sector was only one third. Growth in organised sector employment is now dependent on employment growth in the private sector.

The sector-wise growth of overall employment (Table 32.11) indicates that the employment growth rate decelerated from 1983 – 1994 to 1994-2000, primarily due to slower growth in agricultural employment, with the absolute number of persons employed in agriculture showing a decline for the first time. Employment in sectors like trade, construction, financial services, transport, storage and communication has grown faster than the average, and the share of these sectors in total employment has increased. This reflects the structural changes in product markets in the post-reforms period.

TABLE – 32.10

Growth Rates of Employment in Organised Sector (per cent)

Year	Public Sector	Private Sector	Total Organised
1991	1.52	1.24	1.44
1992	0.80	2.21	1.21
1993	0.60	0.06	0.44
1994	0.62	1.01	0.73
1995	0.11	1.63	0.55
1996	-0.19	5.62	1.51
1997	0.67	2.04	1.09
1998	-0.09	1.72	0.46
1999	-0.02	-0.57	-0.19
2000*	-0.68	0.97	-0.17

* Quick Estimates

Source: Planning Commission and Economic Survey 2001-02.

TABLE – 32.11

Growth of Employment by Sectors (UPSS)

Industry	Employed Workers * (Million)			Annual Growth Rate (Per cent)	
	1983	1993-94	1999-00	1983-94	1994-00
Agriculture	207.23	242.46	237.56	1.51	-0.34
Mining & Quarrying	1.76	2.70	2.27	4.16	-2.85
Manufacturing	34.03	42.50	48.01	2.14	2.05
Electricity, Gas & WS	0.85	1.35	1.28	4.50	-0.88
Construction	6.78	11.68	17.62	5.32	7.09
Trade	19.22	27.78	37.32	3.57	5.04
Transport, Storage & Commn	7.39	10.33	14.69	3.24	6.04
Financial Services	1.70	3.52	5.05	7.18	6.20
Community Social & Pers.Services	23.80	35.13	33.20	2.90	0.55
Total Employment	302.76	374.45	397	2.04	0.98

* The NSS gives the percentage distribution across industries of each of the four categories of workers. We apply this distribution to the absolute numbers of workers of each category for each year and add up the four categories in each industry to derive estimates of total workers in each industry.

Source: Planning Commission and Economic Survey 2001-02.

The level, quality and growth of wages, incomes and employment in the economy is affected by the overall growth in the economy as measured by GDP, as also growth in population and consequent additions to the labour force. A number of specifically designed poverty alleviation programmes are in operation in rural and urban areas in order to encourage self and wage employment. For the year 2001-02 (BE) an outlay of Rs. 9,765 crore has been provided under Plan provisions as compared to Rs. 9,270 crore (BE) made available in 2000-01 to the Ministry of Rural Development for rural development, rural employment and poverty alleviation programmes (excluding Pradhan Mantri Gram Sadak Yojana for which Rs. 2,500 crore have been separately provided in 2000-01 and 2001-02). The performance of the major anti-poverty and employment generating programmes is given in Table 32.12. Details of the programmes are given in Box 32.1. *A Task Force on Employment Opportunities* was set up by the Planning Commission under the Chairmanship of Shri. M.S.Ahluwalia, then Member, Planning Commission to examine the existing employment and unemployment situation in the country and to suggest strategies of employment generation for achieving the target of providing employment opportunities to 100 million people over the next 10 years i.e. 10 million people per year. (for details see ch.36).

The government is presently examining the issues of rigidities in labour legislations, promotion of industrial investment in labour intensive activities and measures for safeguarding the interests of workers. The Second National Labour Commission set up in December 1998 to suggest rationalisation of existing labour laws in the organised sector and also to suggest an umbrella legislation for ensuring a minimum level of protection to the workers in the unorganised sector. Making vide ranging recommendations, submitted its report in 2002.

In a recent study[7] Sundaram has presented estimates of current daily status unemployment rates by gender and rural-urban location for 1993-94 and 1999-2000.

At the all-India level, this widely accepted measure of open unemployment indicates a worsening of the unemployment situation over the 1990s in three out of the four population segments, with urban women as the sole exception. The increase in the daily-status unemployment rate is the steepest for rural males (29 per cent) followed by rural females (21 per cent). For urban males, at 7 per cent the increase is relatively modest. This increase in the unemployment rate for rural males has to be seen in the context of the rise in the share of casual labour (from 338 to 362 per 1,000) and a decline in the share of self-

TABLE – 32.12

Physical Performance of Special Employment and Poverty Alleviation Programmes (in million)

	2002-03		2003-04		2004-05	
	Target	Achieve	Target	Achieve	Target	Achieve
A. Programmes in rural areas						
1) JGSY/SGRY-II - Mandays of employment generated*	-	367.14	-	391.65P	-	401.71P***
2) EAS/SGRY-I – Mandays of employment generated**	-	381.15	-	372.83P	-	-
3) SGSY – Total Swarozgaris assisted	-	0.83	-	0.90	-	0.51 #
4) IAY – Dwelling Units	1.31	1.55	1.48	1.36	1.78	0.63 P
5) ARWSP-Habitation/villages	0.06	0.03^	0.11	0.04	0.75	0.02
6) CRSP- (No. of Sanitary latrines)	-	-	-	4.63	-	2.18
B. Programmes in urban areas						
1) PMRY – (I) Micro enterprises	0.22	0.19	0.22	0.12P		
(II) Employment generated $	0.30	0.29	0.30	0.18P		
2) SJSRY of which						
I USEP-			-	0.51	-	0.66
(i) Beneficiaries	0.08	0.13	0.08	0.10	-	-
(ii) Persons trained	0.10	0.10	0.10	0.12	-	
II UWEP – mandays of employment generated.	-	3.13	-	4.56	-	51.34
3) Beneficiaries covered under community structure component	-	31.70	-	32.56	-	3.25
4) Beneficiaries assisted under DWCUA	-	0.03	-	0.04	-	0.11

- \- Targets are not fixed.
- * JGSY has been merged into SGRY with effect from 2001-02 and is now SGRY-II, SGRY is self-targeting scheme.
- ** EAS has been merged into SGRY with effect from 2001-02 and is now SGRY-I, SGRY is self-targeting scheme.
- *** SGRY I and SGRY II schemes have been merged into a single scheme of SGRY w.e.f. 1-4-2004.
- ^ Upto, January 2003.$ Transferred to State Plan with effect from 2002-03.
- \# upto November, 2004^ Cumulative information since it is a continous process.
- P Provisional.

Source: Economic Survey and Ministry of Rural Development (MORD).

employed among rural male workers on the usual status (principal plus subsidiary). Given that the daily status unemployment rate better captures the unemployment among casual labourers than that among the self-employed (where we could be faced with the phenomenon of work spreading) the rise in the daily status unemployment rate among rural males could well be due to the change in the status-composition of the workforce (Sundaram and Tendulkar 1988).

The tables indicates a reduction in the unemployment rates on the usual principal status for the educated - those with 'secondary and above' level of education as also for the sub-set of those with 'graduate and above' level of education - in almost all the four population segments. The exception was rural females with 'graduate and above' level of education who experienced an increase in usual status unemployment rate from 323 to 351 per 1,000 (Table 32.13, Panel B).

TABLE – 32.13

Dimensions of Unemployment by Gender and Rural-Urban Location, India 1993-94 and 1999-2000

Panel A: Current Daily Status Unemployment Rates

	Rural Males	Rural Females	Urban Males	Urban Females
1993-94	56	56	67	105
1999-2000	72	68	72	98

Panel B: Usual Status Unemployment Rates for the Educated (Per 1,000)

Segment	Secondary and Above		Graduate and Above	
	1993-94	1999-2000	1993-94	1999-2000
Rural Males	89	69	134	107
Rural Females	243	204	323	351
Urban Males	69	66	64	66
Urban Females	207	163	203	163

Source: Table 16, NSS (2000).
Reproduced from K. Sundaram, EPW March 17-23, 2001, P. 935, Table 6.

One of the indicators of underemployment among those classified as workers on the Usual (principal plus subsidiary) status available from the NSS Employment-Unemployment Surveys is the proportion of such workers (adults above 15 years of age) who had sought or were available for additional work - either on most days or on some days of the year. Those who reported themselves as seeking or available for additional work are further classified by reasons for seeking or being available for additional work, with 'to supplement income'; 'not enough work'; and 'not enough work and to supplement income' as the principal rubrics of 'reasons'. In this tabulation, the proportion of usual status workers reporting that they had not sought (nor were available for) additional work may be treated as those who perceive themselves to be fully employed during the 365-day reference period.

Table 32.14 presents for 1993-94 and 1999-2000 the per 1,000 distribution of adult usually working persons as between those who had not sought (nor were available for) additional work, those who had sought or were available for additional work on most days, and those who did so on some days. To focus on the self-perceived underutilisation of

TABLE – 32.14

Per 1,000 Distribution of Adult (15 and above) Usually Working Persons (Principal and Subsidiary) Who had Sought or Were Available for Additional Work by Gender and Rural-Urban Location, All-India, 1993-94 and 1999-2000

Category	1993-94			1999-2000		
	Not Sought	Sought on Most Days	Sought on Some Days	Not Sought	Sought on Most Days	Sought on Some Days
Rural Males						
Self-employed	948	22(8)	30(11)	925	28(10)	47(20)
Casual labourers	887	44(15)	69(27)	829	71(21)	99(46)
All workers	929	29(9)	42(16)	894	43(14)	64(28)
Rural Females						
Self-employed	968	12(5)	20(8)	957	20(5)	23(10)
Casual labourers	912	35(13)	53(21)	874	47(19)	79(35)
All workers	945	22(8)	33(12)	924	31(11)	45(20)
Urban Males						
Self-employed	959	23(11)	19(8)	940	24(11)	37(15)
Casual labourers	890	55(21)	55(18)	861	53(18)	86(38)
All workers	955	24(9)	21(7)	938	25(10)	37(15)
Urban Females						
Self-employed	953	23(10)	24(10)	943	24(10)	33(15)
Casual labourers	903	47(19)	50(12)	884	46(13)	70(23)
All workers	945	29(11)	26(8)	939	27(10)	34(10)

Notes: Figures within brackets relates to the sum of the proportion of persons (per 1,000) who sought or were available for additional work for reasons of (i) 'not enough work' or (ii) 'not enough work and to supplement income'.

Source: 1993-94: NSSO (1996); 1999-2000: NSSO (2000).

Reproduced from K. Sundaram, EPW March 17-23, 2001, P. 936, Table 7.

labour time, we also present the proportion of those who had sought additional work - separately for those who did so on most days and those who did so on some days - who reported either 'not enough work' or 'not enought work and to supplement income' as the reasons. this is presented separately by gender and rural-urban location and within each population segment this information is presented separately for the self-employed workers and casual labourers in addition to all workers.

The key results of Sundaram's study are :

i. An increase in the current daily status unemployment rate in three of the four population segments, with urban women as the sole exception. The increase in the daily status unemployment rate has been the steepest for rural males (29 per cent): an increase which could well be due to a change in the status composition of the work force (a rise in the proportion of casual labourers and a reduction in the share of the self-employed) and a conversion of the underemployment of the erstwhile self-employed into open unemployment of the casual labourers;

ii. a reduction in the unemployment rates on the usual principal status for the educated in almost all the four population segments; and,

iii. an increase in self-perceived underemployment captured by a reduction, over the 1990s, in the proportion of usual status workers who had not sought additional work. However, much of this is reflected in an increase in the proportion of usual status workers who sought additional work on "Some days" rather than on "most days". Also, even among those adding to the proportion of workers who sought additional work on "most days", the principal reasons was the need to supplement income rather than lack of work *per se*.

Educated Employment

The picture of overall employment trends contrasts however with a significant deterioration in educated employment. The estimated number of persons with matriculate level education or better is estimated to have risen more than eight-fold between 1961 and 1988. It is estimated that the total stock of this category has risen from 9.5 million to 79 million [Visaria and Minhas 1991]. The distribution of this stock between rural and urban areas has also shifted in favour of the former. The total number of matriculates and above in rural India has risen more than 10-fold, and its share in the country's stock of this category from 26-27 per cent to 40 per cent.

Educated unemployment in rural areas must have risen considerably faster than in urban areas. At present rural areas have about 40 per cent of the educated, but more than half of the educated unemployed.

There are also indications that as the opportunities for wage salary employment are becoming scarcer relative to supply of job seekers, more and more of the educated persons tend to seek to go into self-employment. Thus among matriculate male workers resident in rural areas, the proportion reporting wage employment has fallen from 40 per cent in 1977-78 to 38 per cent in 1987-88; while in urban areas it has fallen from 69 per cent to 62 per cent. Among male graduates the comparable proportion fell from 63 to 52 per cent in urban areas, and from 78 to 71 per cent in rural areas. The increased incidence of self-employment in rural areas probably reflects the growing number of educated people in farming households. In urban areas on the other hand it probably reflects a genuine shift to self employment. (Vaidyanathan, 1994)

The government has also introduced special programmes to promote self-employment among educated youth and provide them with technical and financial assistance for the purpose. More important, several state governments have sought to accommodate unemployed educated youth by creating temporary jobs in the public sector. Though jobs are created initially on '*ad hoc* temporary' basis, pressures for granting permanent jobs and parity of emoluments with regular staff are generated and sooner or later the governments find it expedient to concede the demands.

Now that the fiscal squeeze has drastically reduced the scope for increasing public employment - if anything the compulsions are to reduce it - the 'market' for public sector jobs may become more active (so long as the differential between the earnings and benefits in public and unorganised sector remains as large as it is currently. However, as fresh recruitment is reduced, if not altogether stopped, the clamour for reservations in public sector jobs will tend to lose their edge. At the same time one may expect more intense agitation on the part of '*ad hoc* temporary' appointees to secure permanence. If liberalisation is sustained and succeeds, we may expect a rapid growth in job opportunities for the educated in the organised private sector. These jobs are currently cornered by the 'elite' among the educated (i.e., those who have the opportunity to get into better staffed, better equipped, more expensive and very likely English medium institutions). If they expand and public sector openings get scarcer, the tension between the educated elite in the urban areas and those who are kept out of this bonanza (mostly from the urban underclass and the rural areas) can be expected to increase.

This tension, as Vaidyanathan rightly points out, can be eased only if economic growth is rapid. If education imparts skills which are needed in the economy and the educated overcome the strong cultural aversion for non-white collar work. A massive expansion of vocational education at the matriculate level and above is desirable. The other way to check potential social disruption - apart from rapid growth - is for those who are left out of wage employment seek to strike out on their own. That there are already signs of this happening is a good augury. It would be prudent for the state to follow policies which encourage this tendency. It is also just conceivable that the slack market for educated will dampen the demand for higher education - especially if higher education is made more expensive. Whether these measures will be taken and whether the effect will be large enough to contain the pressures which are building up among the educated classes is a moot question but it is a question which should worry us deeply.

The only effective and lasting solution, to repeat, lies in policies designed to stimulate faster overall development; in interventions (by way of training, credit, infrastructure support) to help educated people to take more and more to self-employment; and to pay far greater attention to improving the functional content of education both in terms of imparting skills which are needed in the growing economy, and also of equipping people to upgrade the skills or acquire new skill.

Progress during Tenth Plan (MTA)[8]

No fresh quinquennial survey-based data has become available since the formulation of the Tenth Plan. The results of the next round of the quinquennial survey of the National Sample Survey Organisation (NSSO) on employment and unemployment, covering the period 2004-05, will only become available in 2006. The assessment of performance on the employment front, therefore, has to be based on indirect indicators, which have a bearing on employment growth.

Pending the availability of estimates on current daily status (CDS) basis, from the quinquennial 61st round of National Sample Survey (NSS) on employment and unemployment, being undertaken in 2004-05 – the third year of the Tenth Plan the assessment is based on growth in output, and the observed elasticities in the recent past. NSS Annual Rounds do not provide CDS estimates of employment. However, annual estimates of employment are available in NSS Annual Rounds on Usual Status basis; the latest annual round being the 59th Round, covering the January-December, 2003 period.

TABLE – 32.15

Estimates of Labour Force, Work Opportunities and Unemployment in the First Three Years of the Tenth Plan

(Current Daily Status basis)

	Unit	2001-02	2002-03	2003-04	2004-05
Labour force	Million	378.21	385.02	391.95	399.00
Employment	Million	344.68	349.89	356.16	362.64
Unemployment rate	%	8.87	9.12	9.13	9.11
No. of unemployed	Million	33.53	35.13	35.79	36.36

Notes:

1. Employment projections are based on observed sectoral output Elasticity of employment (1994-2000) (CDS Measure)
2. Labour force growth was assumed at 1.8 per cent per annum in the Tenth Plan.

Source: Mid-term Appraisal of the Tenth Five Year Plan.

If employment generation on Usual Status basis is considered, there has been an increase in the rate of growth of employment between 2000 and 2003. However, the magnitude of change in employment should be interpreted with reference to changes in the labour force. Between 1994 and 2000, the labour force increased at 1.08 per cent per annum on Usual Status basis and employment increased at 1.02 per cent per annum, that is, at a pace less than that of the increase in the labour force. In the subsequent period 2000-2003, the labour force increased at 2.85 per cent per annum and employment increased at 2.93 per cent per annum. Thus, the incidence of unemployment appears to have come down in the 2000-2003 period, for which NSSO small sample annual survey provisional data is available.

Employment in the organised sector, however, has decreased in the last three years (Table 32.16).

TABLE – 32.16

Estimates of Employment in Organised Sector

(Lakh persons as on March 31)

Years	Public Sector	Private Sector	Total
2001	191.38	86.52	277.89
2002	187.73	84.32	272.06
2003	185.80	84.21	270.00

Source: Ministry of Labour, DGE&T.

According to Mid-term Appraisal of the Tenth Plan, a more disaggregated level, the process of liberalisation of the economy has thrown up newer opportunities for employment in emerging and dynamic economic activities, and at locations that provide an environment conducive for the growth of such activities.

Poverty Alleviation and Employment Guarantee Programmes

BOX – 32.1

Major Poverty Alleviation and Employment Generation and Basic Services Programmes

National Food for Work Programme

In line with the NCMP, National Food for Work Programme was launched on November 14, 2004 in 150 most backward districts of the country with the objective to intensify the generation of supplementary wage employment. The programme is open to all rural poor who are in need of wage employment and desire to do manual unskilled work. It is implemented as a 100 per cent centrally sponsored scheme and the food grains are provided to States free of cost. However, the transportation cost, handling charges and taxes on foodgrains are the responsibility of the States. The collector is the nodal officer at the district level and has the overall responsibility of planning, implementation, coordination, monitoring and supervision. For 2004-05, Rs.2020 crore have been allocated for the programme in addition to 20 lakh tones of foodgrains.

Swaranjayanti Gram Swarozgar Yojana (SGSY)

SGSY, launched in April 1999, aims at bringing the assisted poor families (Swarozgaris) above the poverty line by organizing them into Self Help Groups (SHGs) through a mix of Bank credit and Government subsidy.

Contd....

...Box 32.1 Contd....

Sampoorna Grameen Rozgar Yojana (SGRY)

SGRY, launched in 2001, aims at providing additional wage employment in all rural areas and thereby food security and improve nutritional levels. The SGRY is open to all rural poor who are in need of wage employment and desire to do manual and unskilled work around the village/habitat. The programme is implemented through the Panchayati Raj Institutions (PRIs).

Rural Housing – Indira Awaas Yojana (IAY)

The Indira Awaas Yojana (IAY) operationalised from 1999-2000 is the major scheme for construction of houses for the poor, free of cost. The Ministry of Rural Development (MORD) provides equity support to the Housing and Urban Development Corporation (HUDCO) for this purpose.

Pradhan Mantri Gramodaya Yojana (PMGY)

PMGY launched in 2000-01 envisages allocation of Additional Central Assistance (ACA) to the States and UTs for selected basic services such as primary health, primary education, rural shelter, rural drinking water, nutrition and rural electrification. For 2003-04 as well as 2004-05, the annual allocation of ACA for PMGY was Rs.2,800 crore.

Rural Employment Generation Programme (REGP)

REGP, launched in 1995 with the objective of creating self-employment opportunities in the rural areas and small towns, is being implemented by the Khadi and Village Industries Commission (KVIC). Under REGP, entrepreneurs can establish village industries by availing of margin money assistance from the KVIC and bank loans, for projects with a maximum cost of Rs.25 lakh. Since the inception of REGP, up to 31 March 2004, 1,86,252 projects have been financed and 22.75 lakh job opportunities created. A target of creating 25 lakh new jobs has been set for the REGP during the Tenth Plan. 8.32 lakh employment opportunities have already been created during 2003-04. For 2004-05, a target of creating 5.25 lakh job opportunities has been fixed.

Prime Minister's Rozgar Yojana (PMRY)

PMRY started in 1993 with the objective of making available self-employment opportunities to the educated unemployed youth by assisting them in setting up any economically viable activity. So far, about 20 lakh units have been set up under the PMRY, creating 30.4 lakh additional employment opportunities. The targets for additional employment opportunities under the Tenth Plan and in 2004-05 are 16.50 lakh and 3.75 lakh, respectively. While the REGP is implemented in the rural areas and small towns (population up to 20,000) for setting up village industries without any cap on income, educational qualification or age of the beneficiary, PMRY is meant for educated unemployed youth with family income of up

Contd....

...Box 32.1 Contd....

to Rs.40,000 per annum, in both urban and rural areas, for engaging in any economically viable activity.

Pradhan Mantri Gram Sadak Yojana (PMGSY)

The PMGSY, launched in December 2000 as a 100 per cent Centrally Sponsored Scheme, aims at providing rural connectivity to unconnected habitations with population of 500 persons or more in the rural areas by the end of the Tenth Plan period. Augmenting and modernising rural roads has been included as an item of the NCMP.

The programme is funded mainly from the accruals of diesel cess in the Central Road Fund. In addition, support of the multi-lateral funding agencies and the domestic financial institutions are being obtained to meet the financial requirements of the programme.

Up to October, 2004, with an expenditure of Rs 7,866 crore, total length of 60,024 km. of road works has been completed. The National Rural Roads Development Agency (NRRDA), an agency of the Ministry of Rural Development registered under the Societies Registration Act, provides operational and technical support for the programme.

Drought Prone Areas Programme (DPAP), Desert Development Programme (DDP) and Integrated Wastelands Development Programme (IWDP)

DPAP, DDP and IWDP are being implemented for the development of wastelands/degraded lands. During 2004-05 allocation of Rs. 300 crore, Rs. 215 crore and Rs. 368 crore were provided for DPAP, DDP and IWDP, respectively. So far, during 2004-05, 2,550 projects covering 12.75 lakh hectares, 1,600 projects covering 8 lakh hectares and 165 projects covering 8.32 lakh hectares, have been sanctioned under DPAP, DDP and IWDP, respectively.

Antyodaya Anna Yojana (AAY)

AAY launched in December 2000 provides foodgrains at a highly subsidized rate of Rs.2.00 per kg for wheat and Rs.3.00 per kg for rice to the poor families under the Targeted Public Distribution System (TPDS). The scale of issue, which was initially 25 kg per family per month, was increased to 35 kg per family per month from April 1, 2002. The scheme initially for one crore families was expanded in June 2003 by adding another 50 lakh BPL families. During 2003-04, under the AAY, against an allocation of 45.56 lakh tonnes of foodgrains, 41.65 tonnes were lifted by the State/UT Governments. Budget 2004-05 expanded the scheme further from August 1, 2004 by adding another 50 lakh BPL families. With this increase, 2 crore families have been covered under the AAY.

Swarna Jayanti Shahari Rozgar Yojana (SJSRY)

The Urban Self Employment Programme and the Urban Wage Employ-

Contd....

...Box 32.1 Contd....

ment Programme are the two special components of the SJSRY, which, in December 1997, substituted for various extant programmes implemented for urban poverty alleviation. SJSRY is funded on a 75:25 basis between the Centre and the States. The expenditure during 2003-04 was Rs.103 crore. For 2004-05, the allocation is Rs.103 crore, out of which Rs. 90.38 crore were utilized by December 31, 2004.

Valmiki Ambedkar Awas Yojana (VAMBAY)

The VAMBAY launched in December 2001 facilitates the construction and upgradation of dwelling units for the slum dwellers and provides a healthy and enabling urban environment through community toilets under Nirmal Bharat Abhiyan, a component of the scheme. The Central Government provides a subsidy of 50 per cent, the balance 50 per cent being arranged by the State Government. Since its inception and up to December 31, 2004, Rs. 753 crore have been released as Government of India subsidy for the construction/upgradation of 3,50,084 dwelling units and 49,312 toilet seats under the scheme. For the year 2004-05, out of the tentative Central Fund allocation of Rs.280.58 crore, up to December 31, 2004, an amount of Rs. 223.66 crore has been released covering 1,06,136 dwelling units and 20,139 toilet seats.

The National Rural Employment Guarantee Scheme

The National Rural Employment Guarantee Bill 2004 was passed in the Lok Sabha on August 23, 2005.

"Now that the Employment Guarantee Scheme (EGS) is a reality, it is time for some serious introspection on the part of the planners and politicians with a view to reversing the ongoing jobless growth as well as for exploring bold and innovative methods for the effective implementation of the EGS", says C.H.H. Rao (2005)[9]. "Provision of employment through public works has never been regarded as the first best option by experts. For a developing economy like ours, labour-intensive or job-oriented growth has always been regarded as the first best alternative for generating productive employment."

According to Rao if our agricultural output had grown at a minimum rate of 4 per cent per annum, as targeted by the successive Five Year Plans, together with large-scale diversification of agriculture into dairying, horticulture, fisheries, etc. and if there was significant growth in the rural non-farm sector, comprising agro-processing and other rural industries, the rural employment growth would have been sufficient to absorb bulk of the growing labour force and there would not have been any need for the EGS[10].

Maharashtra provides a classic illustration of how the introduction of EGS became inevitable in the '70s because the agriculture growth rate there fell persistently short of population growth over a long period. Despite the notable achievements of EGS, the persistence of rural poverty in Maharashtra, even after the implementation of EGS for three decades, underscores the importance of employment-oriented growth for sustainable reduction in poverty.

There has been a sharp deceleration in the growth of crop output in the country in the post-reform period of '90s and a very slow pace of diversification of agriculture and growth of rural non-farm enterprises. This retrogression is attributable to the continued decline in public investment and effort for building up rural infrastructure, e.g. irrigation, rural roads, agricultural research and extension and institutional credit. Also, effective implementation of EGS should be an area of major concern. The objective here should be two-fold; to use the scheme for productive activities which have the potential for sustained employment generation; and to minimise leakages of benefits from the scheme to the non-poor.

According to Rao the best way to ensure high productivity of public works in rural areas is to coordinate and integrate EGS with the ongoing programme for 'Bharat Nirman' involving the development of rural infrastructure like irrigation, roads, water supply, electrification, housing, etc. As it is, under the food-for-work programme, currently in operation in 150 most backward districts until the EGS comes into force, eco-development works such as soil and moisture conservation are to be given a high priority.

Certain features of the scheme, viz., the responsibility for implementation entrusted to panchayats, invoking of social auditing through Gram Sabhas and the possibility of using the newly-enacted Right-to-Information Act hold promise for minimising the leakages. However, since the risk of leakages arises essentially from the top-down nature of the scheme, prevailing hierarchical social structure that is exploitative and competitive politics — unless the political parties rise above partisan considerations and display the same unity of purpose as at the time of passing the Bill — it would be difficult to prevent the scheme from fast degenerating into the likes of the old. (Rao 2005)

While all-out efforts need to be made to reverse this trend, it would be naive to envisage EGS as the main instrument for poverty eradication throughout the country. EGS quickly graduating into a programme for infrastructure development as an integral part of Bharat Nirman provides an efficient and the least risky way for sustainable rural development and poverty eradication. (Rao 2005)

BOX – 32.2

National Rural Employment Guarantee Bill, 2004 – Salient Features

- State Governments to provide at least 100 days of guaranteed wage employment in every financial year to every household whose adult members volunteer to do unskilled manual work.
- Sampoorna Grameen Rozgar Yojana (SGRY) and National Food for Work Programme to be subsumed within the Scheme once the Act is in force.
- Until such time as a wage rate is fixed by the Central Government, the minimum wage for agricultural labourers shall be applicable for the scheme.
- An applicant not provided employment within fifteen days, to be entitled to a daily unemployment allowance as specified by the State Government subject to its economic capacity, provided such rate is not less than a quarter of the wage rate for the first thirty days during the financial year and not less than a half of the wage rate for the remaining period of the financial year.
- Central Employment Guarantee Council to be constituted to discharge various functions and duties assigned to the Council. Every State Government to also constitute a State Council for this purpose.
- Panchayat at the district level to constitute a Standing Committee of its members to supervise, monitor and oversee the implementation of the Scheme within the district.
- For every Block, State Governments to appoint a Programme Officer for implementing the Scheme.
- Gram Panchayat to be responsible for identification of the projects as per the recommendations of the Gram Sabha and for executing and supervising such works.
- Central Government to establish a National Employment Guarantee Fund. State Governments to establish State Employment Guarantee Funds for implementation of the Scheme.
- The Scheme to be self-selecting in the sense that those among the poor who need work at the minimum wage would report for work under the scheme.

Source: Economic Survey 2004-05.

Review of Inflationary Trends in India

The inflation rate (measured by variations in annual average wholesale price index, WPI) over the past five decades averaged 6.6 per cent per annum. However, decade-wise, the inflation rate accelerated steadily from an annual average of 1.7 per cent during the 1950s to 6.4 per cent during the 1960s and further to 9.0 per cent in the 1970s before easing marginally to 8.0 per cent in the 1980s. On the other hand, the volatility in the inflation rate, as measured by the coefficient of variation, which was fairly high in the 1950s (4.4 per cent), moved in a narrow range of 0.4–1.0 per cent in the subsequent decades.

The first half of the 1990s saw a sharp increase in inflation. The decade began with double digit inflation attributable to the large-scale monetisation of fiscal deficits. This was intensified by hikes in procurement prices as well as supply-demand imbalances in essential commodities like pulses, oilseeds and edible oils.

TABLE – 32.17

Annual Average Inflation Rate based on Wholesale Price Index (WPI) Since 1991-92

(Based on 52 week average inflation rates)

Annual average inflation (%)

	All Commodities	Primary	Fuel	Manufactured
1991-92 to 1995-96	10.6	11.3	11.3	10.1
1996-97 to 2000-01	5.1	5.4	13.0	3.1
2001-02 to 2003-04	4.1	3.7	7.0	3.3
2004-05 as on 29-01-2005	6.5	3.9	9.2	6.5
2003-04 as on 31-01-2004	5.5	4.8	6.9	5.3

Source: Economic Survey 2004-05.

The second half of the 1990s was marked by a significant turnaround in the inflation outcome. The inflation rate declined from an average of 11.0 per cent during 1990-95 to 5.3 per cent during the second half of the 1990s.

In recent years, supply side factors have been more instrumental in determining the direction and magnitude of price rise, while the impact of demand side factors on inflation has been relatively weak. The occurrence of drought, decline in agricultural production, increase in global crude oil prices, supply shortages and increased international prices of imported commodities like crude oil, steel and edible oils are some of the factors that have played a crucial role in fueling inflation in the recent past. Imported inflation has therefore, a crucial role to play in setting the direction of domestic inflation.

Overall Behaviour

According to Bhattacharya, "there is no stable relationship between inflation rate and output growth rate. Nor is there a stable relationship between inflation rate and money (whether measured by M_1 or M_3) per unit of output. The overall behaviour of inflation, therefore, corresponds to neither pure monetarist nor pure structuralist models."

Monetarist-structuralist explanation of inflation is perhaps more applicable to Indian economy. Though the approach and presentation of the problem differ in different studies on the subject, most of the studies have emphasised both demand and supply constraints in varying degrees and have studied both general and sectoral prices.

According to these studies, the inflation process starts from public investment financed by government budgetary deficit. Lack of capital coupled with urge for development compels the government to follow deficit budget policy resulting in monetary expansion and simultaneously aggregate demand through multiplier mechanism at disaggregated level. Other aggregative studies (e.g., Raj, 1965) tried to determine foodgrain prices through disequilibrium between aggregate demand and aggregate supply of foodgrains. Keynesian income model is used to predict aggregate demand through a stable autonomous expenditure multiplier. These studies ignore stock-adjustment in relation to price changes. But in Indian economy, changes in stocks are very important in influencing price level, as government's buffer stock operation and public distribution system affect food price significantly, particularly in post-green revolution period.

In Indian economy, money supply is positively related to output and employment growth in the long run to a good extent in the sense that government follows a deliberate deficit financing policy to finance several development projects and public investment programmes. But the basic structural bottlenecks impose a constraint on the aggregate supply to rise in relation to aggregate demand in the face of expanding market size. This leads to a rise in general price level in the economy. The continuous gap between aggregate demand and supply causes a positive price expectation which plays a very important dynamic role in price determination as can be seen in studies of Pandit (1978, 1984) and Bhattacharya (1984). Agricultural supply constraint coupled with price expectations [Pandit (1978), Bhattacharya (1984)] play a key role not only in the inflation process, but also in income distribution. As a consequence, a trade-off between inflation and growth occurs in the economy which can be considered as cost of development in a developing economy with structural imbalances [Bhattacharya and Pandit (1985), Bhalla (1981)]. It is in this context worth noting the Chakravarty Committee (1985) recommendation of having a positive inflation rate to bring in desired changes in relative prices; or in other words, it is implicitly assumed that zero inflation rate is not conducive for balanced growth of the economy.

To sum up, we find that though money is an important determinant of inflation in India, it is not the only factor affecting aggregate and relative prices. More important is to note that money supply itself is growing on account of government budget deficit caused by structural imbalances in the growth process. It appears that a mere reduction in money supply may reduce inflation rate, if at all, only at the expense of income and output growth.

Notes

1. Angus Deaton & Valerie Kozel (ed), The Great Indian Poverty Debate, 2005.
2. Ibid, p. 15.
3. K. Sundaram, *Employment and Poverty in India in the Nineteen Nineties*, Working Paper No. 95, Centre for Development Economics, July 2001.
4. Ibid, p. 19.
5. Angus Deaton & Valerie Kozel (ed), The Great Indian Poverty Debate, 2005, p. 18-19.
6. Ibid, p. 20.
7. K. Sundaram, Economic & Political Weekly, March 2001 and Centre for Development Economics, Working Paper No. 95.
8. Planning Commission, Mid-term Appraisal of the Tenth Five Year, June 28, 2005.
9. C.H. Hanumantha Rao, Rural Jobs Schemes & Tasks Ahead, Economic Times, September 5, 2005.
10. Ibid.

References

Angus Deaton & Valerie Kozel (ed) (2005), "The Great Indian Poverty Debate", Macmillan, New Delhi.

Bhattacharya, B.B. and Lodh, Madhumita, "Inflation in India: An Analytical Survey in Indian Economy Since Independence", (ed. Uma Kapila) 1999-2000 edition.

Economic Survey 2000-01, 2001-02, 2002-03, 2003-04 and 2004-05.

Plan Documents: Eighth Plan, Ninth Plan and Tenth Five Year Plan.

Sundaram, K. (2001), "Employment and Unemployment in the Nineteen Nineties: Results from NSS 55th Round", *EPW*, March 17-23.

33

Poverty and Development Policy

A. Vaidyanathan

I

BACKGROUND

The idea that eradication of abject poverty must be a central concern of public policy has gained wide currency in current academic and public discourse on development. Time was when the focus used to be on the rate and pattern of growth, and on inequalities in distribution of income and wealth. Even as these continue to be important concerns, increasing attention is being given to the extent to which people in individual countries and the world at large are deprived of the minimum requirements for a long, healthy and fulfilling life.

The idea is not new. In India it dates well back into pre-independence era – recall Naoroji's book *Poverty and UN British Rule* – and was prominent in the deliberations of the Congress Party. The National Planning Committee report in fact spelt out in concrete terms the concept and content of minimum living standard. The 15th Indian Labour conference which deliberated on the basis for fixing fair wages also spelt out the constituents of a living wage. A committee on economic policy (headed by Nehru) appointed by the AICC suggested that assurance of a national minimum standard in respect of "all the essentials of physical and social well-being" to every family within a reasonable period of time" should be the practical goal of all schemes of development. The Constitutional provisions on the Directive Principles of State Policy specifically enjoined the government to ensure adequate livelihood and employment, health and nutrition, education and security to the citizens.

However it took a long time for government to define its developmental objectives and policies with reference to these principles. The first three Five-Year Plan documents saw sustained high rates of growth as the principal means to alleviate malnourishment, unemployment, illiteracy and other manifestations of poverty. There was much talk in political rhetoric and in policy pronouncements about reducing inequalities of income and wealth through land reforms, public ownership and control of key sectors, and progressive taxation. But with actual growth proving to be much slower than expected, and redistributive measures proving to be ineffective, the appalling conditions in which the bulk of the population continued to live and the necessity to address their problems seriously came into sharp relief. The late Ram Manohar Lohia dramatised it by calling attention of parliament to the fact that more than half the population subsisted on less than 6 annas per head per day!

In 1962, an unofficial seminar,[1] in which several leading economists, political figures and social activists participated, gave a fresh impetus to the idea that planning should aim at ensuring a minimum standard of living to every one within a reasonable period. They suggested that the national minimum should include a time-bound target of minimum income (Rs 20 per capita per month in rural areas and about Rs 25 in urban areas); expenditure on education and health to be provided by the state according to the Constitution[2] transfers and social welfare expenditure to ensure minimum for the poorest 20 per cent of the population who are not likely, for various reasons, to benefit automatically from growth.

Soon thereafter the implications of planning for this minimum living were worked out in a paper[3] prepared by the perspective planning division of the Planning Commission and further elaborated entitled "Notes on Perspectives of Development India's 1960-61 to 1975-76" [GoI, PC, 1964]. The latter was considered but not formally approved by the Planning Commission. In the event, for a variety of reasons (including Nehru's death, the aftermath of military engagements with China and Pakistan, and the droughts) it was shelved. The Fourth Five-Year Plan did not even mention minimum living standard or basic needs!

The late 1960s witnessed a spurt of interest among economists in the study of poverty both at the conceptual and empirical levels. At the conceptual level, questions began to be raised about the validity of using per capita GDP or per capita consumption as a satisfactory measure of well-being. A strong case was made for a much broader concept of 'quality of life' which would include nutritional status, life expectancy and literacy. Attention was also focused on the possibility – based on the example of Kerala in India and Sri Lanka – that the quality of life in the broader sense is not necessarily contingent on high level of income. The factors – largely social and political – which made this possible have attracted much attention and discussion [United Nations 1975; Sen 1981; Bhalla 1988; Streeten and Burki 1978].

The findings of the Mahalanobis Committee [GoI, PC 1964, 1969] and Hazari's study (1967), as is well known, found no reduction in inequalities in consumption, incomes or in concentration of economic power. A number of researchers took up empirical and theoretical studies focused on absolute poverty and strategies to eradicate it. Dandekar and Rath's (1974) well known monograph 'Poverty in India' argued for defining the poverty line on the basis of the minimum income required for nutritional diet and other essentials, provided estimates of the number of people who fell below this line, and outlined a strategy (based on a massive public works programme) to give them the needed additional incomes to reach the minimum. Around the same time a number of others discussed estimates of inequalities in income distribution, incidence of and trends in poverty, conceptual and measurement problems involved, and strategies for tackling poverty.

This research highlighted significant differences in estimates of mean incomes and consumption, inequality indices and poverty incidence obtained from different sources. There was a major controversy over whether or not poverty incidence had declined during the 1960s. This stimulated serious investigation into theoretical aspects of concepts and measurements, the merits and weaknesses of different sources of relevant data, the interrelation between growth, distribution of assets and income, employment and poverty; and different strategies for rapid reduction of poverty.[4] All these themes continue to figure prominently in the ever growing literature on this subject both nationally and internationally. The discussions have of course become more detailed, technically more refined and wider in scope.

By the early 1970s, development economists, both within the country and abroad as well as in international agencies, had veered round to the view that overall growth, while necessary, would not by itself be able to take care of the needs of the poor. The pace of growth is unlikely to be uniform across regions; all segments of the economy and sections of the population are not integrated into the wider economy; and large sections are not equipped (for a variety of reasons) to take advantage of the opportunities arising from growth. Therefore programmes for 'direct attack' on poverty came to be accepted as desirable even by agencies like the World Bank.

This perception did not long remain a matter of academic interest. In India, the set back to the economy during the late 1960s, (slow growth, cut back in investment, inflation), heightened apprehensions of increased inequalities, growing unemployment and worsening of poverty. It happened to coincide with the struggle for political power in the (then dominant) Congress Party. 'Radical' measures, (like bank nationalisation and abolition of privy purses) ostensibly meant to contain the rich, were tried but they were limited in scope and did not mean much to the poor. In this conjuncture, Indira Gandhi sought to broaden her political base by adopting the 'Garibi Hatao' slogan and launching a number of poverty alleviation schemes.

Apart from a Minimum Needs Programme, a number of other initiatives – notably special schemes for small and marginal farmers (later replaced by Integrated Rural Development, IRDP for short), rural employment schemes, mid-day meals for school children, and subsidised public distribution of food and other essential commodities – were launched. Some were new; others essentially were refurbished versions of older schemes. That they did not remain slogans, but were backed by substantial financial allocations made them politically credible. That it struck a positive chord among the people is evident from the resounding electoral success of Congress Party under Indira Gandhi's leadership.[5]

For the first time, assurance of basic minimum needs found an explicit and prominent place in the Fifth Plan. The concept included not only an assurance of purchasing power sufficient to procure a collection of basic items of consumption deemed to constitute 'basic' or 'minimum' collection, but also elementary education for all children up to 14 years of age; minimum public health facilities integrated with family planning and nutrition for children; protected water supply; amenities for landless labour and slum improvement in larger towns; and rural roads and rural electrification.

The idea of direct, targeted poverty alleviation programmes quickly took root and gained widespread acceptance across the entire political spectrum.[6] Governments, at the centre and in the states, have since vied with each other in increasing allocations and devising new schemes (or the same schemes under different names) under this rubric. Along with the number and variety of schemes, financial allocations have also increased progressively. Motivations were of course not as high minded as the slogans made out. They reflect cold political calculations. That the programmes provided opportunities for large-scale, widespread and diffused patronage as well as opportunities for personal gain for political leaders and cadres obviously made them highly attractive to parties in power.

Having reviewed, briefly, the evolution and acceptance of minimum living standard among the objectives of policy in the agenda of political parties as well as governments, we now turn to a consideration of some important issues concerning concepts and measurement of poverty as well as the design and implementation of policies to tackle the problem.

II

CONCEPTUAL ISSUES

In India, there is a broad consensus that the minimum should include (i) a nutritionally satisfactory diet, a reasonable standard of clothing, housing and other 'essentials'; and (ii) access to a minimum level of education, health care, clean water supply and sanitary environment. Norms for specific elements under both categories have been specified. The income necessary for people to afford the elements constituting the first category defines the 'poverty line'. Ensuring the minimum standards for various social services and amenities are deemed to be the responsibility of the state. These concepts as well as the specific content of the minimum standard have gained wide currency in public discourse on development policy. Minimum living standards and poverty are however deceptively simple notions. Complex and contentious issues are involved in deciding the basis on which the minimum bundle is to be determined and valued; whether the status of individuals or households is to be judged in relation to affordability of the bundle as a whole or on the basis of actual consumption/use relative to the norms for individual items; whether the bundle should be uniform or allowances be made for differences in need and circumstances across space and between classes.

Of the various ingredients entering minimum income consumption, food has received the most attention. The emphasis on food is obviously justified. The fact that nutrition experts have worked out the level of nutrients (calories, proteins, fat, etc) necessary for healthy, active functioning of human beings would appear to give an objective basis for determining minimum norms. The normal practice has been to work out the per capita norm for a reference population of specified composition (in terms of age, sex, body size and activity) in rural and urban areas. The appropriateness of a uniform per capita calorie norm has been questioned on the grounds that the relevant characteristics of the population (age and sex composition, body mass and activity) vary across and even within regions and there are biological mechanisms which enable individuals to adapt to lower intakes, over a sizeable range, without any adverse effects on health or activity.[7] Nevertheless, there is a strong case for such a uniform norm and it rests basically on three grounds:

(1) The purpose of the norm is to help define a standard of consumption which is socially accepted as the minimum desirable. This standard covers not only food but also other items.

(2) A uniform standard provides a common yardstick for comparisons across regions and of directions and relative rates of its change over time. It is also essential for meaningful discussion of the public policy for poverty alleviation and their effectiveness in different regions. This consideration acquires added force when poverty incidence (or the numbers of poor) is used - as it has come to be used - as an important criterion in deciding the sharing of central tax revenues, central government assistance for state plans and also of allocation for poverty alleviation between and (increasingly) within the states.

(3) A standard basket of food products corresponding to the calorie norm also helps comparability. One could in principle estimate the minimum cost food basket taking into account food habits and prices prevailing in different regions. But the practical problems (in terms of information requirement and computational complexity) make it difficult to do so. Reasons of both comparability and convenience therefore argue for using a uniform commodity composition for determining the poverty line. The current practice in India is to use the NSS data on commodity composition of food basket of people whose calorie intake is equal to the nutritional norm. This is done separately for rural and urban area using national level data.[8]

(4) The levels and composition of non-food items included in the minimum standard are taken to be whatever happens to go along with the fulfilment of the calorie norm at the national level. Together they also used to determine the value of per capita consumption expenditure which defines the national poverty line for rural and urban areas. This procedure for determining the non-food components of the minimum is obviously quite arbitrary. Hardly any thought has gone into

> working out norms for clothing, housing and other elements under this category. The necessity to consider explicitly and systematically the basis for determining levels and components of non-food consumption to be included in the minimum and the need to review and revise the specification of the minimum bundle at periodic intervals hardly needs emphasis.

While there are good reasons for adopting a standard commodity basket comprising the national minimum, there are no good reasons to ignore differences in level and structure of prices between states (and also between rural and urban area) as well as their behaviour over time. On the contrary there is a strong case for taking these into account in as much as the income necessary to afford the minimum consumption bundle is a function of price level and structure. There may also be a case for taking regional difference into account in fixing norms for social amenities. Following the recommendations of the Lakdawala Committee [GoI, PC 1993], the earlier practice of using a single national level poverty line and deflator (to adjust for price changes) for state level estimates has been given up. Instead state level poverty lines, adjusting for differences in base year price levels and deflated on the basis of state-specific price indices, are used.

Ensuring that households have sufficient incomes to acquire the minimum consumption standard and that norms for publicly provided schools health care and water supply and connectivity are met, does not automatically ensure that people actually obtain and consume the bundle of goods and services or use the amenities as envisaged in the standard. Actual consumption patterns depend on individuals' decisions which are influenced by numerous personal, familial, environmental and cultural factors. If they choose not to acquire the normative minimum bundle the state can do little about it. Furthermore, consumption data, which usually are obtained for the households do not tell us much about what individual members get and whether it meets the minimum standard for them. The extent to which the poor and the underprivileged actually use and benefit from social services and amenities to be provided by the state also depends to a considerable degree on the decision of individual households which in turn is influenced by the economic circumstances and socio cultural attitudes as well as by the quality and cost of services provided by these public facilities. Because of these factors, the actual position of households, including poor households, may differ substantially from the potential for achieving to minimum living standard even where growth and state policies enable them to do so. Such deficiencies cannot be attributed to failure of government policy except insofar as they are the result of deficiencies in design and implementation of government programmes.

At a more fundamental level, minimum incomes and minimum standards of social amenities are not all desired solely or even mainly for their own sakes but for what they do to peoples' well-being.[9] Amartya Sen, who has done so much to clarifying the complex issues involved in the assessment of well-being and suggesting ways to deal with them in a practical way, has strong and persuasive arguments to show that well-being of persons cannot be judged only on the basis of their incomes or access to education and other amenities or of the volume and composition of goods (and services) they have. While these are indeed important, goods and services are not sought for their own make but as means to achieve desired states of what he calls 'being and doing' (such as leading a well nourished, healthy and long life, being well clothed, mobile, able to take informed part in community life, etc). The particular combination of functionings which individuals choose depends on the resources (income) available to them, the different combinations of goods from which they can choose and the kinds of functioning they make possible. Together they define the domain of choice effectively available to individuals which Sen calls 'capabilities'.

The choice within this domain reflects the valuation which individuals place on different kinds of functioning which in turn depends on their personal and social characteristics. Choices are constrained not just by resources at their command as well as by social conditioning. The availability and quality of education, healthcare, sanitation, transport/communication networks and other facilities – which are not determined solely by individuals but depend to an important degree, on the efforts of society and community, governments and non-government organisations – have a direct bearing on peoples' well-being, the choices open to them as well as their perception of the choices. One must also bear in mind that people often have a tendency to restrain their aspirations within limits of what they consider realistically feasible.

The assessment of well-being in a society needs to take into account not only individuals' choices but also assess different social states. The problems involved in doing this are at the heart of the continuing debate among economists and social philosophers. This debate has highlighted the limitations of the market as the arbiter of social states and the difficulties in arriving at a generally acceptable consensus on desirable social states based on a consistent and complete evaluation of available alternatives.

A satisfactory general solution to this problem remains elusive. However, this is much less of a problem in the context of poor countries where large sections do not have adequate and nutritious food, are prone to disease and relatively low life expectancy and are not equipped to access the knowledge and skills needed to function in a complex economy, take advantage of economic opportunities and participate in community life. Under these conditions, it is not surprising that assurance of adequate food (in quantity and quality), basic education and healthcare facilities and connectivity with the outside world figure prominently in the concept of 'minimum living standard' in India and other similarly placed countries. Though, as noted earlier, concretising this and relating it to well-being is a difficult task.

Moreover, if our concern is 'well-being', conventional indicators such as the proportion of population below the poverty line, mean calorie intake, mortality rates, literacy and school enrolment are inadequate basis to assess progress towards poverty eradication. Important as these are, one needs to supplement them with assessments of nutritional and health status, duration of education as well as quality aspects, and gender and group disparities. This calls for considerably wider and more detailed information through surveys to ascertain people's perceptions of their state as well as direct, non-market observations of access to basic goods and functionings at the individual level. There is also a good case to broaden the scope of 'well-being' to cover such aspects as freedom, fresh air, absence of crime, child and women abuse, social peace.

Broadening the notion of well-being and the indicators used to evaluate it has gained currency thanks to the United Nations' Human Development Reports put out by the UNDP. Even those, like the World Bank, who have reservations about preoccupations with poverty and minimum standard of living as the main focus of policy, now include them in their list of development indicators. Increasingly researchers outside government are also broadening the scope of their investigations. However devising objective and measurable indicators for this purpose is daunting and fraught with great difficulties.[10]

III

MEASUREMENT ISSUES

Conceptual problems are compounded by problems of empirical Measurement. The Indian statistical system generates an extraordinarily vast and rich amount of data on different aspects of economy and society.

The most important and richest source for assessment of poverty and levels of living is the National Sample Survey (NSS). The NSS, which has been in existence for nearly 50 years, has conducted large-scale sample surveys on a variety of subjects relevant for this purpose (ownership of land and other productive assets, household consumption, employment, educational levels, school enrolment, morbidity, health care, access to and the benefit from various programmes meant for the poor and the underprivileged, disability, housing, water supply sources and sanitation). Several of these surveys, particularly those relating to employment and consumption, have been repeated periodically. Published reports provide estimates of mean value of key characteristics and their distributions, as well as their composition for rural and urban areas of the country as a whole and in most cases at the state level. Until recently these were the principal basis for estimation and analysis outside the government. The recent policy decision to make primary household level data available for researchers makes possible vastly more intensive and detailed analyses.

Large-scale sample surveys of household incomes and consumption, education and health have also been done by the National Council of Applied Economics Research (NCAER),[11] though at a lower frequency. The National Nutrition Monitoring Board (NNMB) has been conducting for over 20 years detailed surveys of actual food intake and nutritional status of individuals on a small sample basis in several States.[12] The National Family Health Survey (NFHS) provides detailed information especially on children and women.[13] The ICRISAT survey of 26 villages in semi-arid tropical regions of the country, and a common set of households for a period of 12 years provides a rare and rich body of panel data on practically every aspect of rural economy.[14] In addition, there are a large number of micro studies assessing the impact of government's poverty alleviation programmes and exploring particular aspects of nutrition, health education and social amenities.

Published reports on NCAER surveys are generally less detailed and give less information on design, concepts and comparability compared to NSS. Far more detailed information and analyses based on them is available for the ICRISAT survey and the NFHS. The primary data from both of them are also freely accessible to researchers. The ICRISAT survey data in particular have been extensively used for exploring – in a degree of detail and depth not feasible with published NSS (and more so NCAER) reports – the characteristics of the poor, adaptations to fluctuations and shocks, transient and permanent poverty, participation and impact in employment schemes and other related issues. Of late the

NSS has greatly liberalised access to its primary data which can now be purchased at nominal cost on cd-roms and diskettes. NCAER is also giving researchers access to its primary data.

On the whole, the use of these data have, until recently, tended to focus heavily, if not exclusively, on definition of the poverty line and estimating poverty incidence and its trends. Factors underlying regional and temporal variations in these respects and policy interventions have also been explored but not to the extent one would expect. Other aspects such as gender discrimination, educational participation and attainment, health and nutrition are beginning to greater attention among scholars but do not figure at all in official assessments of the poverty situation.

The methodology of poverty estimates has long been the subject of debate. The first time this came into prominence was in the context of sharply divergent estimates of trends in poverty incidence during the 1960s: one estimate pointing to a significant rising trend in the headcount ratio and another to a falling trend. It was apparent that much of this different was traceable to the different estimates of mean consumption used by them: one relying on the NSS and the other National Accounts estimate. Systematic differences between the two sources in the estimated consumption expenditure, both overall and for major commodity groups, as well as their time profiles was brought out in the course of that debate.

This led to a critical scrutiny of the assumptions and procedures underlying NSS and official estimates of consumption per head [Kansal 1965; Srinivasan et al 1974; Vaidyanathan 1986; and Minhas 1988]. Significant differences in scope, coverage, data sources and basis of evaluation were identified. Minhas and Kansal (1989) attempted a systematic assessment of the effect of these differences and more importantly the relative merits of estimates for various specific items from these two sources verifying them in some cases with other independent data sources. They also offered several important suggestions to reconcile the differences and for ensuring greater comparability in future. Useful as these are, problems remain.

For one thing the differences in scope of methodology and basic data sources are too large to permit reconciliation or even reasonable degree of comparability. To the extent this is possible, it can be done at best for aggregate private consumption for the country as a whole; nothing can be done about rural-urban or state level estimates.[15] Assessing the relative merits of the two-time series in capturing changes over time is problematic; the scope, concept and assumptions underlying NAS and

NSS have both changed over time; and both are prone to errors of observation and estimation of unknown magnitudes.

There have been significant changes in the scope, design and procedure of NSS consumption surveys. The 1950s were a period of experimentation about sampling, questionnaire design, reference periods and the relative merits of single versus multipurpose surveys, which continued into the 1960s when consumption data were for a while compiled through integrated household surveys. There is much greater comparability after the early 1970s when NSS switched to quinquennial consumption-cum-employment surveys. But as we shall see presently, some changes in sampling design and reference periods have raised doubts about comparability of more recent data.

Changes have also been made in the NAS estimates. The changes were no doubt implemented after discussion with experts with a view to ensure firmer empirical base and minimising arbitrary assumptions. While the general consensus is that these have led to significant improvements, serious gaps and weaknesses in basic data remain: the system for obtaining output data for agriculture and even organised industry has visibly deteriorated. State-level estimates suffer from even more serious deficiencies in basic data. The basis for back-casting the series for earlier periods at every revision, though transparent, can hardly be called robust. The arbitrary manner in which estimates for agriculture have been revised recently hardly helps to increase confidence. In view of the above, the revised NAS series cannot be accepted without question and there is certainly no basis to assume that they are better than the NSS.

During the 1970s the Planning Commission - which puts out the official estimate of poverty - reviewed and revised the poverty line essentially by refixing the calorie norms, but did not address the problem of discrepancy between NAS and NSS estimates.[16] Instead it used NAS estimates of consumption expenditure, and NSS estimate of the distribution of population by level of consumption to estimate poverty incidence. That the NAS does not provide separate estimates of consumption for rural and urban areas at the national level or estimate of even total consumption expenditure of the state level, did not deter them from providing disaggregated estimate of poverty. The highly arbitrary and questionable assumptions underlying this procedure were highlighted by the Lakdawala Committee [GoI, PC 1993].

This committee examined the possibilities of cross validation of NAS and NSS estimates. They noted that even if one could find a satisfactory procedure for reconciling the differences in estimates of aggregate consumption and making appropriate adjustments to in the estimate of size distribution, problems arising from '...differences in coverage, time period classification schemes and implicit prices...' will remain. Adjusting NAS to get state-level estimates and estimates for rural and urban areas would involve far too many arbitrary assumptions. They noted that the NSS gives statewise estimates of size distribution and commodity composition of consumption for rural and urban areas separately derived from surveys which are carefully organised, use uniform concepts and procedures across the country and sampling is rigorous. While NSS data are not free from errors and sustained efforts to improve their quality is essential, it remains the best available source for assessing poverty incidence and characteristics of the poor across space and time. They therefore suggested that "if estimates of incidence are to be made with minimum recourse to adjustments based on arbitrary assumptions, the best course would be to base them entirely on the NSS". The Planning Commission has since accepted these recommendations and official estimates of poverty are based entirely on the NSS.

During the 1970s and 1980s the NAS and NSS showed similar, though not identical, time profiles of change in mean consumption at the national level. Using NSS estimates of inequality, both showed a declining trend in the headcount ratio. However, the NSS, whose estimate of mean consumption was lower and its rise considerably slower than the NAS, showed poverty incidence to be higher and declining much more slowly than the official estimate.[17] But since both showed a decline, the relative reliability of the two sources did not figure prominently in the debate.

But after 1987-88 the NSS began providing annual estimates of mean consumption as well. This shows no significant trend in either inequality or mean per capita consumption in rural areas, and therefore in the incidence of poverty. In urban areas, according to NSS, poverty has declined largely because of an increase in per capita real consumption. Overall poverty incidence in the country has not changed significantly. That this happened during the decade of major changes in economic policy and despite the relatively high rate of overall growth indicated by NAS is cited by critics of the reforms as evidence of its anti-poor character. The reliability of NSS data in capturing changes in consumption levels and distribution has, therefore, again become an issue.

While the NAS estimate of consumption no longer enters poverty estimation, the striking difference between the time profile of consumption growth during the 1990s obtained from it and that of the NAS deserves notice. This comparison, which is possible only at the national level, shows that while according to NAS, per capita real consumption expenditure increased progressively at an average annual rate of over 2 per cent during the 1990s, the NSS showed an erratic trend and a much smaller rise.[18] However, using the same deflation procedures, the movement of the two series based on the quinquennial data from 1973-74 to 1993-94 turn out to be more or less similar. Therefore the divergence between two in the 1990s seems unlikely to be due to deflation procedure. We have to look for other explanations, in terms of changing designs, procedures and biases in the NSS itself.

One aspect of the post 1988 NSS series which has attracted notice is that, except for 1993-94, they are based on so-called thin samples. In the quinquennial surveys, whose primary focus is consumption and employment, the sample size is large enough to provide state level estimates at an acceptable margin of sampling error. In other years consumption and employment data are canvassed on a much smaller sample, and subsidiary to the main theme which varies each year. Sampling and survey design being the same, the smaller size of the sample in the annual surveys by itself should not make any difference to the reliability or comparability of their national estimates, with those of large samples. The fact that the primary focus of annual surveys is on other subjects could however affect the quality of consumption data obtained through them: Being secondary themes the investigators and their supervisors may not give as close an attention to this part of the survey as for the primary theme.

While this may increase the scope for non-sampling errors, there is no basis to suppose that they would affect the nature or extent of such bias NSS data may be generally prone to. There is a widespread belief that richer households tend to be less cooperative and tend to underestimate their consumption more than the poor. But we do not have information to test the validity of this supposition and how large its magnitude is. Unfortunately, despite repeated suggestions NSS does not provide information on the relative incidence of non-response or the characteristics of non-responding households, nor the investigator's impressions about the cooperativeness of the respondents and their willingness to provide information. Unless the under reporting bias of richer households in the thin sample rounds is higher for either of these reasons, and has increased over time, there is no reason to question comparability of the series on this ground.

It is also arguable that the underestimates of consumption by the rich does not affect the poverty estimates so long as the not-so-well-to-do people report their consumption correctly. The rich may have an incentive to understate much more than the poor. While this is true, it needs noting that if NAS estimate is correct, and the poor accurately (or at least far more accurately than the better off) report their consumption to NSS, the degree of underestimation by the rich, and therefore inequalities, must have increased. But this is pure conjecture.[19]

Changes in sampling, reference periods, questionnaire design, and interview procedures can however make a difference. A significant change in sampling design allowing for stratification of households according to broad income class, and a higher sampling fraction of richer households, did take place in the 1980s. But this should not affect the comparability of the series from the late 1980s through 1998 unless - let me repeat - the degree of non-response or non-cooperation of the better-off can be shown to have increased.

Another source of non-comparability is changes in reference period. That the length of the reference period affects the respondents' estimate is well known. After some initial experimentation, the NSS decided on a uniform 30-day reference period for all items of consumption and kept to this practice for nearly 30 years. In the 1980s this aspect was again reviewed. The effect of changing reference period from 30 days to one year on the responses re-consumption of clothing and durables was tested by canvassing two independent sets of sample households. The differences were expectedly substantial. Subsequently, from 1991, this experiment was extended to all commodities getting information from two independent subsamples one on the basis of a 30-day reference period for all commodities and another using different reference periods for different commodity groups. This was expected to assess the direction and magnitude of difference in reported consumption with different reference periods. Reference periods did indeed make a difference, more in some commodity groups and less in others. The difference in reported consumption of food, drink and tobacco based on a 30-day reference and seven-day reference period turned out to be quite large, the latter being much higher. In the case of clothing and durables, the figure reported with 30-day reference period was lower, and substantially lower in the case of durables, than for the 365-day reference period. Such exercises are essential to provide a basis, after systematic analysis and, if need be, further experimentation with different sets of reference periods, to improve the survey design. So long as this is done on independent sub-samples we get a comparable series using the prevailing practice and the difference changes make to the magnitude. When the prevailing practice is changed we also have a clear basis to link the earlier and the new series without losing comparability.

While these precautions were taken care of up to 1998,[20] the large sample survey of 1999-2000 made a significant departure by canvassing information on consumption using two different reference periods, on all sample households. This, it has been rightly pointed out, vitiates the estimates obtained from the latest survey and makes it difficult to compare them with those of earlier surveys including the 1993-94 surveys. Those, like me, who believed that a comparison of the 1999-2000 results with those of 1993-94 ratio provide a better basis to assess the impact of reforms on consumption levels, inequality and poverty at the national and state levels are understandably dismayed!

As already mentioned large-scale surveys of household income, consumption and several other aspects have also been done by NCAER. Estimates of mean consumption, inequalities and poverty incidence reported on the basis of these surveys differ significantly from the ones widely in use: For instance 1968-69 survey [Bhatty 1974] found per capita consumption close to the official estimates, but there were large differences compared to NSS rankings of states by levels of consumption expenditure and inequalities. Based on panel survey of rural households at 2 different time points (1970-71 and 1980-82), NCAER concluded that incomes have grown considerably across all classes; (and more so at the lower end) and that poverty had declined substantially more than shown by NSS [NCAER 1987]. There are obvious and large differences in scope, aims design and methods between NSS and NCAER surveys [Bhatty 1974] and between NCAER surveys at different points of time [Bhalla 1988; Pradhan et al 2000].[21] These differences have not attracted the degree of critical scrutiny which one would have expected.

That different sources, using different methods, give quite different estimate is confusing. Much greater attention must be given to assessing the purposes, concepts and methods underlying different data sets, their reliability and suitability for generating reasonably and comparable estimates of mean consumption and inequality. The scope for confusion could be reduced if these details were available for critical scrutiny by scholars and informed analysis of the reasons for differences in the estimates. Better still if different survey organisations get together and agreed on minimum degree of comparability in scope and concepts in the conduct of such surveys.

With the best of efforts, however, these issues cannot be fully resolved. The fact is that here is nothing like perfectly accurate and reliable data. The challenge is to make ingenious use of imperfect, incomplete information subject to sizeable, and often unknown, margins of error, and to squeeze such insights as we can legitimately extract from them. Plurality of data sets is useful as cross checks. If independent sources reveal the same or similar patterns we can be more confident of the patterns they indicate. But it is necessary to recognise and allow for defects and non-comparability and to maintain pressures to ensure the integrity and transparency of the statistical system.

An equally important lesson to be drawn is not to be preoccupied exclusively, or even primarily, on poverty incidence as the sole index of well-being. It is necessary to broaden our inquiries to cover other aspects which affect and reflect well-being; and to pay much more attention to the characteristics of those at the bottom of the socioeconomic pyramid, how their conditions are changing and how effective public interventions are in improving their conditions and opportunities.

It is for these reasons that the Lakdawala Committee recommended that, apart from estimates of the proportion and number of poor, a fuller picture of the living conditions and well-being of the poor must cover the following aspects:

(i) The composition of the poor population in terms of dominant characteristics, i.e., their distribution by region, social group, family characteristics (e g, size, education, age, sex of household head, dependency ratio) and the way this is changing over time. Much of this can be done by appropriate tabulation of NSS employment and consumption survey data.

(ii) Nutritional status of the population; levels of intake of principal nutrients, incidence of malnourishment, anthropometric measurements and activity patterns by age, sex and socioeconomic categories. This can be done by the National Institute of Nutrition.

(iii) Health status: mortality (overall, infant and child, maternal); morbidity; access to and use of health services (public and private) and costs. The quinquennial surveys of public consumption as well as mortality indicators based on the Sample Registration System and the morbidity surveys of NSS need to be put on a systematic and continuing basis.

(iv) Educational status: school enrolment by region, sex and age group and by economic social class; reach and quality of public education services and costs. Here again information from the NSS social consumption enquiries and the all-India Education Surveys suitably restructured would provide the basic data.

(v) Living Environment: distribution by density of settlement: living space per head; type of houses; access to safe drinking water and sanitation; access to amenities (post office, telephones, railway, pucca road, markets, etc).

The committee further suggested the preparation of a 'State of Poverty' report every five years covering the above aspects and highlighting the condition of the poorest 30 per cent of the country's population. Unfortunately there area as yet no signs of these suggestions being implemented by the Planning Commission.

IV

CORRELATES AND DETERMINANTS

Having discussed the problem of data and measurement at length and cautioned about assessments of changes in overall poverty incidence, I would like now to turn to what we have learnt from the available data, and from studies based on them, about incidence of poverty, its characteristics and determinants.

It is indisputably clear that a large proportion of the country's population cannot afford the bundle of good and services including food, education, health which constitute the currently accepted norms of minimum living standard. The deficiencies both in absolute and relative terms are considerably larger in rural India than in urban areas. It is also evident that in rural India asset-poor households, those dependent mainly on wage labour, and those with relatively large families and a high proportion of children relative to adults figure far more prominently among the poor than those with land (especially those with relatively large holdings), self employed in non-agricultural activities and those with better education. Scheduled castes/tribes households, being disadvantaged on all these counts, have a considerably higher incidence of poverty then other groups [Visaria 1978, 1979; Lipton 1981].

Poverty incidence shows large variations across states. In 1993-94, rural poverty incidence varied from about 2 per cent in the Punjab to 58 per cent in Bihar. Broadly speaking the proportion of rural population living below the poverty line is higher than the national average in east and central India and well below the average in the southern states. About two-fifths of the country's rural poor are concentrated in Bihar, Orissa, MP and West Bengal. The NSS data also show the rate of poverty reduction in these states to be much slower than in others. This implies an increase in the geographical concentration of poverty.

Overall poverty incidence in rural areas seem to be largely a reflection of differences in mean per capita incomes across states and less to inequalities within states [Bhattacharya et al 1988]. More detailed analysis using household level data from an NCAER survey [Gaiha 1988] suggests that the likelihood of a household, being poor is influenced by the social and economic infrastructure of the village they live in, some characteristics of agricultural technology and the demographic and other feature of the household. The effect of agricultural technology being the largest followed by household characteristics. Both are seen to have a more marked influence on poverty incidence among cultivator households than other categories. The relative importance of factors varies between different groups.

Tendulkar and Sundaram (1988) constructed and estimated a model to assess the impact of demographic pressure on land (the principal productive resource of rural areas), the value of productive assets per head, and the inequality in their distribution, the productivity of land, wage labour incidence, employment and the interactions among them in accounting for variations in rural poverty. Estimates of the reduced form of the model showed that poverty incidence tends to be lower (to a statistically significant extent) in regions with relatively low demographic pressure (low land man ratio), higher productive assets per head and more equal distribution of these assets. Other things being the same, the higher productivity per unit of land goes with lower poverty incidence. This line of approach to understanding determinant of rural poverty, with refinements to take into account price differentials, the determinants of land productivity, diversification of employment and such other elements seems promising. But not much further work on these lines has been done since.

Attempts to explain trends in rural poverty incidence in terms of trends in agricultural production and prices have given some useful insights. The factors underlying them have also been extensively examined but for reasons already cited the conclusions are much less robust. An early attempt along these lines [Ahluwalia 1978] found that at the all- India level there was a significant negative relation between the value added by agriculture per head of rural population and rural poverty ratio; and that there was also a significant element of secular decline over time on account of other (unspecified) factors. Subsequently Ahluwalia (1986) showed that the price index for the poor relative to the average for the population also has a significant bearing on rural poverty trend: the higher this index, the higher the poverty. But in this case there is no time trend independent of production and prices. At the state level the inverse relation between agricultural production and poverty was found to hold in several but not all states.[22]

The rationale for inclusion of price and its specification has evoked a lively debate [Mellor and Desai (eds) 1988]. The argument for taking the overall inflation rate as an explanatory variable is not clear. Presumably it would impact on poor via the wage rate. But this depends on the extent and rapidity with which rural wage rates adjust to changes in the general price level. Very little is however known about this. Moreover, as many have pointed out, changes in consumer price index for the poor relative to that of the better off may be more relevant than the general rate of inflation. A better specification (and one used in several recent studies)[23] would be the relative price of food to non-food items in as much as food dominates the poor's consumption and accounts for a much higher proportion of expenditure than the better off.

Till recently the debate on rural poverty focused mainly on agriculture and has been marked by an underlying concern that emerging patterns of technology and production tend to increase inequalities and that therefore agricultural growth may not automatically reduce poverty. The HYV-fertiliser-irrigation centred strategy was, and to some degree still is, widely believed to be biased against small and marginal farmers and the growing class of wage labourers. Relatively small farms cannot afford the resources needed to make effective use of the new technology. Also the new technology does not generate fast enough increase in employment opportunities to absorb the growth of labour force particularly for the burgeoning class of wage labourers. This led to predictions of increased unemployment, reduced real wages and worsening inequalities in rural areas. And in the context of relatively slow growth in the rest of the economy, this tendency was expected to spill over into the non-agricultural sector and urban areas as well. The evidence from actual experience is mixed.[24] Access to irrigation has traditionally been relatively higher among small holdings compared to large ones. But during the last three decades irrigated area has increased much faster than average among larger farms. This would tend to accentuate inequalities. There is also evidence of increased inequality in the distribution of operational holdings in some areas due to dispossession of tenants and the spread of 'reverse' leasing. On the other hand the adoption ratio of HYV and fertilisers, which used to be relatively low on small farms compared to large farms in the early stages of their spread, is no longer so. This narrowing difference in adoption of bio-chemical technology offsets the impact of large farmer bias in irrigation, though to what extent remains an open question.

Agricultural employment has increased much slower than agricultural output partly because of the spread of mechanisation. Over time this tendency seem to have intensified. While the share of wage labour in total rural labour force has increased rapidly, agricultural employment has remained virtually stagnant. However, the expected worsening in rural unemployment and in real wage rates has not materialised. On the contrary, non-farm employment has risen at a surprisingly rapid rate during 1970s and 1980s and real wage rates have everywhere risen.

This has led to broadening the scope of the explanatory hypotheses regarding determinants of rural poverty to include the extent of non-agricultural employment (which captures differences in the degree of diversification in the rural economy), commercialisation, real wage rates and public development expenditure. But specifications vary in terms of the variables included without a convincing a priori basis to choose between them. Most of them do well in terms of the proportion of variance explained (R squares exceeding 85-90 per cent) in both national time series and pooled state cross section and time series. The coefficients for individual variables have the expected signs and are statistically significant [Ravillion and Datt op cit and Abhijit Sen op cit].

It is noteworthy, however, that inequality in distribution of productive resources or determinants of labour supply and demand do not figure in these exercises in the manner attempted by Tendulkar and Sundaram. There are also data problems arising from the marked deterioration in the system for compiling official agricultural statistics. The levels and, more importantly, time profiles of change in agricultural output per rural person and NSS estimates of real consumption per capita are often dissimilar. Also as noted earlier, changes in scope, methods and basis of estimation, which affect both NSS and Official estimates, vitiate comparability across different periods and raise questions about the validity of time series analysis especially for long periods as done in some world bank studies.

Poverty studies deal mostly with rural areas. Urban poverty has received comparatively less attention even at a descriptive level.[25] Available surveys show urban areas to have a higher level of mean per capita consumption as well as higher inequality. Mean per capita consumption in urban areas is higher and more unequally distributed than in rural India. Regional variations in both respects are marked: poverty incidence being higher than average in Bihar, MP and Orissa and less than average in Assam, Punjab, Haryana and West Bengal.

There seems to be no significant association, across states, between poverty incidence and mean consumption. However, states where urban poverty incidence is persistently higher than the national average, price levels as well as inequalities are higher than average; the contrary being the case in those where urban poverty rate is persistently below national average. In both cases differences in inequality are more important than price differentials [Minhas et al 1988].

NSS data points to a progressive decline in urban poverty since the early 1970s reflecting a modest rising trend in mean per capita consumption without any significant change in the inequality index [Datt 1999]. The trend towards urban poverty reduction is noticed in all states but in varying degrees. The differences largely reflect differences in the pace of increase in mean per capita consumption; there seems to be no significant urban trend in inequality in most states.

Factors underlying regional and temporal variations in urban poverty have not been explored even to the limited extent attempted in the case of rural areas.[26] Very little is known about the characteristics of the urban poor. There are isolated location specific studies of the informal sector, slum and pavement dwellers. But these need to be considerably expanded in scope and integrated into a wider framework to better understand urban poverty. Here perhaps the focus of comparative studies could be on towns of different sizes and different degrees of economic dynamism. Understanding urban poverty naturally would also require greater attention to the migration patterns and more generally to the nature of rural – urban linkages in terms of commodity, income and labour flows.

Refinement in mapping and analysis of income poverty is necessary but not sufficient. Their scope needs to be widened to include different aspects of the poor's well-being in its broader sense. Also deeper investigations are necessary to understand how the poor and the underprivileged cope with vicissitudes how they adapt to reduction in employment and incomes, how far they are able to take advantage of opportunities opened by the growth of the economy and various poverty alleviation and affirmative action policies of the government.

Some aspects – notably food intake and nutrition, transient and chronic poverty, gender disparities, literacy and educational levels, and access to health care – have been the subject of study based both on macro data and in depth micro-level studies. But there is much room for extending and refining such work and making them an integral part of the effort to better understand the nature and role of socio-economic deprivation. Trends in level and composition of food intake, both overall and for different fractile groups, intra-family allocation of food (especially between males and females), the effectiveness of special nutrition programmes and subsidised food supply and the relation between food intake and nutritional status have attracted much attention.[27] Despite their limitations, the mean level of calorie intake and the proportion of population with intakes below the calorie norm continue to be widely used as an indicator of nutritional status of the population. The NSS data show a trend of decline in calorie intake of the better off and the very low elasticity of calorie consumption even among the poorer groups, whose calorie intake remains well below the norms. There have also been significant shifts in the pattern of consumption, including especially among the poor, from food to non-food items, from cereals to more costly non-cereal foods and, within cereals, from cheaper to more expensive grains.[28] But there has been hardly any serious investigation of the factors underlying these changes or their impact on health and nutritional status.

If the data on food consumption trends of the poorer segments is correct, one must explain why, despite near stagnation of calorie intake, there are no signs of deterioration in height, weight, health or activity indicators even in states, which, by all indicators are very poor.[29] Surprisingly this apparent puzzle has not attracted much attention.

Nutritional status obviously cannot be judged by food intake levels alone. Education, safe drinking water, hygiene, incidence and control of infections – all of which have a bearing on how efficiently food is utilised – must be taken into account. While the standards in all these respects are no doubt far below desired levels, improvements have taken place partly as a result of public policy and partly the spread in availability and use of antibiotics. Both may have contributed to an overall improvement which indicates nutritional status despite stagnation in calorie intake at low levels. This is only a conjecture whose validity (especially for the poorer socio-economic groups) needs much closer investigation.

On other aspects of living standards – eg, clothing, housing, education, water supply/sanitation, and health facilities - considerable amount of information is available in numerous surveys and studies based on them. Literacy rates, enrolment and intention of children in school, mean years of schooling, costs, inter-group disparities and other aspects of education are well documented [PROBE Team 1998; Vaidyanathan and Nair (eds) 2001]. So are mortality rates, morbidity, availability and use of public and private health care facilities in different regions and socio-economic groups. We know that, while considerable improvement has taken place in most of these respects, they are generally inadequate and highly uneven with rural areas and poorer sections of the population invariably reporting lower access and use the facilities and at a higher cost relative to their incomes, than the rich.[30] These data sources, and analytical studies to interpret factors underlying spatial and temporal variations, need to be given a much more prominent place in the study of poverty and well-being. Another example relates to the attempt at differentiating between different types of poverty (seasonal and annual; transient and persistent; poor and ultra poor).[31] Macro surveys can tell us little, if at all, on these matters or of the process underlying them. Only detailed micro-level inquiries and panel type surveys can provide the needed information. We do have some micro studies which give an idea of diverse strategies that poor people adopt to tide over bad years and lean seasons. They include maintaining emergency reserves, borrowing, sale of assets, migration, changing nature, and intensity of activity and altering intra-fairly food allocation. Panel surveys have been used to focus on households who are persistently below the poverty line [Gaiha 1988].

The role of formal and informal social security mechanisms to take care of the aged, disabled and widows among the poor is attracting increasing attention in research and policy discourses. The coverage, organisation and scale of arrangements for the organised sector are best documented. Descriptive accounts of informal and traditional social mechanisms (family, kin networks, charitable institutions) as well as of various government sponsored pension and insurance schemes for the poor are available.[32] But critical studies of their working and impact have not received as much attention.

The nature, extent and manifestations of persistent gender disparities in access to family resources for food, education and health care have been extensively documented and commented on.[33] The deprivations and disadvantages suffered by underprivileged social groups (especially scheduled castes and tribes, artisans) are also well documented. That they figure prominently among the poor and are prone to various forms of 'exclusion' which handicaps them in taking advantage of opportunities generated by growth and that they are specially vulnerable to the introduction of new products and processes is well known.

There is compelling evidence that the position of these groups in terms of practically every indicator of well being remains much below the average. However the evidence also shows that there have been substantial improvements and in some respects at least a substantial narrowing of the gap between them and the rest of the population.[34] The extent of this phenomenon however varies considerably between and within regions. The reasons for these variations in the extent and manner in which some segments of this excluded groups are able to improve their condition while others continue in chronic deprivation; the way affirmative action and other government interventions meant to mitigate their disadvantages actually work; and the reasons why, even when basic amenities are in place, some groups do not make effective use of them deserve far more attention than they have received so far.

V

POLICY

Some people – especially among those who see rapid overall economic growth as both a necessary and sufficient condition for eradicating poverty and who see excessive state intervention as the major impediment to growth – consider this obsession with poverty, and counting the number of poor, as distracting attention and resources from growth promoting policies. The government according to them should confine itself to ensuring law and order, enabling markets to function freely, facilitating free trade and capital movements and providing universal elementary education, health care, water supply, sanitation and essential infrastructure. On the other hand they question the efficacy of various poverty alleviation programmes and, by implication, the justification for spending huge amounts on social programmes. These arguments are fundamentally flawed.

Growth – necessary as it is – does not 'benefit' automatically and in equal proportion to all regions and sections of the population. For a variety of reasons – historical factors, resource endowments, social and political conjunctures and, of course, government policy – growth happens to be very uneven across regions. This fact is beyond dispute. It also happens that regions which are poorly developed to begin with have also grown at a slower rate than average. This tendency cannot be dismissed as an inevitable but transitional phase which will get corrected over time. Nor can one accept the proposition that so long as there is no decline in level of development in any region and all record some improvement, there is no need for intervention. Such a proposition, apart from being questionable on merits, is politically unacceptable in a democracy. Concern for equity and political necessity are compelling arguments for government intervention to correct the imbalance.

This argument acquires even greater force in relation to people: both as a proportion of the population and in absolute terms, those who do not have and cannot afford even the quite modest minimum living standard currently accepted as the norm in the Indian context are very large. And they happen to be concentrated in the poor regions, among sections of the population who suffer the cumulative consequences of systematic exclusion and the attendant social and economic disadvantages. That basic needs and minimum living standards figure so prominently not only in rhetoric of all political parties, but also in the sizeable public resources committed for this purpose is a reflection of both moral and political compulsions.

The evolution of policies and programmes meant to tackle this problem may be haphazard and in some respects even incoherent. Nevertheless one can see a clear pattern in the way they seek to recognise and address differing needs of backward areas with special problems, and of different segments of the poor and underprivileged. Broadly they can be divided into the following groups:

(1) Affirmative action by way of reservations for scheduled castes and tribes in elected bodies, public sector jobs and educational institutions supplemented by special programmes, with earmarked allocations, for their development and welfare.

(2) Programmes (notably IRDP, TRYSEM, DWACRA) designed to help poor segments to acquire or add to their productive assets and enable them to make more productive use of such assets.

(3) Various special programmes to provide additional employment to the poor.

(4) Schemes to ensure that all villages have access to a minimum standard of educational and health facilities, safe drinking water and roads.

(5) Various forms of direct transfers by pension and insurance schemes for aged, disabled and widows, school feeding and child nutrition programmes and subsidised distribution of foodgrains and other essential commodities to the poor.

(6) Special programmes for the development of production potential for hill tracts, deserts and drought prone areas.

For the most part these programmes are conceived and funded by the central government which determines the criteria for allocation between states (and in some cases within states). Actual implementation is left to the state government agencies subject to guidelines (sometimes quite detailed) regarding the scope and content of schemes, and their targeting and implementation procedures. Only a few (notable being the

Maharashtra Employment Guarantee Scheme and Tamil Nadu's Midday Meals Programme for school children) have been taken up entirely at the initiative of states.

Over the years the functioning of these programmes and their impact on the poor has attracted a great deal of attention. Numerous studies - several under the auspices of the government, and many more based on independent surveys, micro studies and analyses of available macro data - have highlighted their achievements as well as weaknesses.[35] A healthy and wholesome feature is the extraordinarily free and open discussion of deficiencies of particular schemes, the relative merits of different interventions and suggestions for restructuring and reorientation.

Official claims of the number of beneficiaries, works carried out, additions to productive assets and employment generated are unreliable and exaggerated. Poor targeting is reflected in the high proportion of non-poor and other non-eligible persons among the beneficiaries. Leakages due to inappropriate works, inefficient implementation and corruption are high. Quality of assets provided/created under these programmes is poor and their impact on income level of beneficiaries dubious. Assets and schemes are frequently not appropriate to the needs and potentials of particular regions or groups. There is little consultation with, not to speak of involvement of local communities generally and target groups in particular, in deciding and implementing schemes. Lack of accountability remains a major problem. The structure, content and funding of these programmes remain mostly in the hands of the central government. There is considerable overlap among these schemes as well as between them and development schemes included under the normal state plans. Typically each programme is administered by a separate agency each with its own line hierarchy and operating independently. These features, taken together with the rigidity of central guidelines, make for fragmentation and duplication of schemes. Coordination is difficult; so is monitoring of accomplishments in terms of efficacy of targeting, quality of works actually completed and impact on the beneficiaries.

The programmes tend to emphasise loans and subsidies and provision of current wage employment rather than ensuring that they are used to augment productive capacity for achieving a higher level of employment and income on a sustained basis. The selection of beneficiaries, the distribution of loans and subsidies, and the recovery of loans offer much scope for patronage and corruption at the political and bureaucratic levels.

The public distribution system (PDS) does not accomplish its ostensible aim of ensuring essential consumer goods to the poor at reasonable prices. Large parts of the country (especially states which have the largest concentration of poor) simply to not have a distribution network to reach the supplies where they are most needed. In states (Kerala, West Bengal, Tamil Nadu) which have such networks, the coverage is not limited to the poor. And attempts to ensure better targeting have been thwarted by administrative difficulties and political opposition. The efficiency of PDS as a poverty alleviation measure and the desirability of continuing it in the present form is being questioned. Supporters of PDS, who see it as a major instrument for ensuring food security for the poor, strongly oppose this prescription even as they recognise the need for restructuring the programme.[36]

These widely known and documented deficiencies have given poverty alleviation programmes a bad name. Critics argue – some explicitly and more by implication – that the effective contribution of these schemes to sustained poverty reduction is not commensurate with the resources spent on them. That given the high level of fiscal deficits and the severe shortage of resources for infrastructural investments needed for overall growth, the country can ill afford this luxury.

It is certainly true that outlays on targeted poverty alleviation programmes have increased rapidly both in absolute terms and relative to total public sector plan outlay. Prior to 1970, these were limited to special schemes for nutrition scheduled castes and tribes, social welfare, backward areas, and a minuscule rural works programme during the Fourth Plan (1969-74). Total outlay for these was Rs 6 billion, or less than 4 per cent of public sector plan. During the Eighth Plan (1992-1997), the outlay on a vastly larger and more varied poverty alleviation programme amounted to Rs 460 billion (about 11 per cent of the total public sector plan).[37] Also, outlays on PA programmes have grown considerably faster than total plan outlay in a period marked by severe infrastructure shortage and bottlenecks. However large these figures might seem, the fact remains that they account for barely 1 per cent of the GDP, and barely a sixth of the gross fiscal deficit of the centre and the states put together. The public sector resource crisis cannot be laid at the door of PA programmes. The more important and deeper causes lie in the falling tax to GDP ratio, the inability to contain runaway increase in revenue expenditures and the huge and burgeoning deficits incurred in providing public services.[38] All of these are due to policies – be it taxation, salaries and allowances of public sector employees, subsidised supply of water and power – which largely benefit the better off segments in fact the top quintile of the population. A disproportionate share of the food and fertiliser subsidies also accrue to the better off. Under these conditions cutting back the allocation for poverty alleviation is no solution to the fiscal problem; and it is certainly not justified morally or politically.

This is not to deny the need and immense scope for improving the efficacy of poverty alleviation programmes by better targeting, reducing waste and corruption, making the programmes more meaningful in terms of relevance to local needs and priorities, and creating institutional conditions for greater accountability. The focus should be on rationalising the approach, organisation and priorities of the PA programmes rather than on cutting back the outlays.[37] The number of PA programmes can, and should, be drastically reduced and streamlined to minimise duplication and fragmentation. We need distinguish only between 3 and 4 basic PA programme categories: (1) Those which are meant to ensure that all communities in the country have a minimum standard of school, primary health care, water supply, sanitation and connectivity. (2) Those which are meant to enable resource poor segments of the population to acquire productive assets and to use them effectively. (3) Programmes to provide additional employment opportunities to those poor who do not have productive assets and depend on wage employment. And (4) programmes to enable scheduled castes and tribes to take advantage of educational and health facilities so that they are better equipped to take advantage of growing opportunities.

There are already accepted norms of minimum standards mainly in terms of distance of each community from each facility as well as physical facilities and personnel at delivery points. The norms may in some cases need review and redefinition. Once this is done, a comparison between existing ground situation and the norms would provide an objective basis for identifying, fairly precisely, the areas and locations which are deficient, as well as quantify the extent and nature of the deficiencies. Investment in physical facilities to make up these deficiencies should of course be part a national Minimum Needs Programme. But creating physical facilities will not suffice. The tasks of ensuring that the prescribed staff are in position, that they function regularly and well, that the underprivileged segments can readily access them and get proper attention are equally important. These will need action in the sphere of administrative reform and social mobilisation.

Category 2 covers the present IRDP and also special area programmes: The former, which provide loans and subsidies for purchase of non-land assets by the poor, has proved to be wasteful and far less effective than expected. The latter are meant to develop productive resources in drought prone, desert and hill areas to facilitate more effective use of resources and open up opportunities for increased production in a variety of activities. These two have not been effective partly because they overlap with schemes which are part of the sectoral programmes and also because of poor design and implementation. All these schemes are in need of drastic change.

IRDP in its present form deserves to be scrapped. Identification of poor, the kinds of assets to be provided, ensuring the back up needed for their programme cannot, as experience has shown, be managed efficiently by government. The difficulties are compounded when they involve heavy subsidies and are implemented by a bureaucracy to political interference. Instead, public investment ought to concentrate on providing infrastructure to facilitate overall development and in each region according to its resource potential thereby opening up greater and more diverse opportunities for employment and entreprenurial activity.

The poor of course need special help by way of information, technical advice and training to take advantage of growing investment opportunities. The government has a key role in providing this help. But it is neither necessary nor desirable for the government to decide what assets are to be provided, to whom and on what terms. These tasks are better left to individual's choices. Those who want to invest in any enterprise can seek credit from financial institutions who must be left free to judge the viability of the loan and the borrowers. The government's role here would be essentially to lay down guidelines (such as priority sector lending) and providing interest subsidies or insurance of loans given to the poor.

There is also a strong case for including land among the assets eligible for institutional credit for the rural landless and land poor. Redistribution of land through conventional approach to land reforms has not worked and seems unlikely to make much headway. However, the spread of education among the bigger farmers is leading to increasing migration to urban areas; they are also seen to be investing their surplus in non-agricultural activities. The resulting weakening of their economic stake as well as their power in the village communities is creating a situation where they are willing to sell their land. This process has already occurred on a significant scale in several parts of the country and seems to be spreading. In such a situation, asset poor households wanting to acquire land – the most important productive resource in rural areas-deserves as much emphasis in poor-oriented credit programmes as for the acquisition of other assets or setting up other enterprises.

The rationale for special area programmes as a separate category is also questionable. Practically all the components of these programmes figure in the sectoral programmes. Scrapping the special area programme and merging them into sectoral and area development programmes will make for more effective use of public funds by eliminating dysfunctional and wasteful fragmentation of resources and effort. From the view point of poverty alleviation, agriculture and related activities are the most important. The scale and content of these programmes should however be tailored to the diverse resource potentials in different regions and constraints impeding their realisation. This is the rationale for watershed development and planning on the basis of agro-climatic regions. But these are at present no more than in name. If these are pursued seriously and the organisational arrangements for planning are recast on that basis, there is really no need for special area (or for that matter special crop specific) schemes.

In implementing integrated regional resource planning, it would be perfectly legitimate to earmark allocations, and even provide special extra funds, for use in regions which rank low in terms of per capita income and employment. The distribution of funds between regions must however be based not only on needs, but also potential for development of land, water and livestock resources as part of integrated area development plans.

Employment schemes can all be merged into one and allocations between and within states determined on the basis of the magnitude of poverty incidence, magnitude of unemployment and development potential. There is considerable room for refinement to get disaggregated estimates of poverty and unemployment (which is feasible with available NSS data by pooling central and state samples and in some cases pooling across years). Information available in the population, agricultural and livestock censuses together with studies of the kind which the agro-climatic regional plans can provide indications of potential for development and interventions needed to exploit them. This would however call for a shift from the current pre-occupation with generating additional employment in the present as the over-riding objective to giving much greater emphasis to creating assets which by augmenting production and improving socio-economic infrastructure can lead to a sustained higher level of employment and incomes.

Within the framework of the above broad approach, it is possible to provide earmarked allocations for schemes to ensure minimum standard of amenities and acquisition of assets for scheduled castes and tribes; and for assistance (by way of subsidies or loans) to enable them to finance higher education and skill acquisition. These would make better sense and be more effective when they are part of an overall regional plan.

Targeting

The other, and in many ways more important, issue is targeting. The search for ways to reduce chances of mistargeting has largely focused on more effective monitoring of beneficiary selection; creating credible checks against mistargeting; and creating incentives for 'self selection'. Incomes are notoriously difficult to ascertain. And once it is known to determine eligibility for benefits, there is a strong general incentive to understate incomes. It is better to rely on more easily verifiable attributes (family size, land holding, caste, etc) associated with poverty. Though this does not eliminate scope for falsification, it certainly reduces the scope for it compared to the income criterion.

Clearly, targeting errors can be reduced if conditions of eligibility and/or the scale of benefits are so defined as to reduce the incentives for those above the poverty line to get into the programme. Insisting on a certain portion of beneficiaries being drawn from poor/vulnerable groups (SC, ST, women) and providing wage employment in employment schemes at wages somewhat below the market/minimum wage rate and at locations away from the residence would be a more effective way of reaching target population than relying on discretionary authority. The reservation idea is now incorporated in the guidelines for all ministry of rural development projects. But the idea of lowering wage rates on works programmes below the legal minimum is not favoured: The government cannot violate its own laws!

Targeting has not only a class/individual dimension, but also a spatial aspect. The poor being unevenly distributed between regions, spatial targeting is an important, but relatively neglected, aspect. Except in Jawahar Rojgar Yojana, allocations of PA programme outlays between and within states are not systematically related to poverty, unemployment or deficiency in basic amenities. Richer states generally tend to have larger resources and plan outlays per capita. One would expect the PA programme allocations to correct this imbalance at least to some degree. Data for the early 1980s [Subbarao 1992] suggest that, if anything, states with low incidence of poverty had higher outlay on PA programmes both in absolute per capita terms and as a proportion of total state plan outlays.

There is thus a strong case for rationalising the criteria for spatial allocation along the following lines. Allocations for all employment and production oriented PA schemes should be pooled and distributed between states, and within states, in proportion to the absolute number of poor or preferably, income deficit and the number of unemployed. Funds for programmes to ensure a minimum standard of basic amenities (elementary education, health care, water supply and access to roads) can be similarly pooled and distributed in proportion to the magnitude of deficiency in relation to the accepted minimum levels of facility. This would greatly add to the transparency of the programme and its effectiveness.

Accountability

Public accountability for ensuring proper choice of beneficiaries and proper use of funds remains a serious problem. Efforts to publicise the scale and nature of PA programmes in a particular block or district, the criteria by which beneficiaries are selected, the specific benefits to which they are entitled under each programme, and the procedures for availing of them have not been effective. Even when the information is available, there are no institutional mechanisms for making complaints or seeking redressal of grievances. Involvement of MLAs, MPs and other local leaders – whether formally as members of advisory committees or because of their ability to exert informal pressure – has not helped. On the contrary, irrespective of their party affiliation, politicians tend to use the opportunity to influence choice of schemes, locations and beneficiaries under these programmes as a source of power, and as instruments for consolidating their political base and often for personal gain. Surprisingly, neither elected representatives nor local cadres of political parties (even when they belong to the opposition) have shown much interest in taking up these issues.

Non-governmental organisations do take up such issues, but they are far too few to make more than a localised impact. Though numerous, they differ greatly in terms of focus, motivation, effectiveness. Some are concentrated on particular activities like education, social welfare and watershed development. Some are concerned with development activities covering several sectors. Funding sources differ. Most use their contacts with sympathetic government officials to secure support and resources for activities in their area. Some get funding from institutional agencies and foreign foundations. Several have innovative programmes to mobilise beneficiaries and building local institutions to make more effective use of government programmes.

NGOs also play a role in making people aware of the various PA programmes and benefits available under them; and interceding with concerned government agencies to secure benefits for eligible people. Some have taken the role of mobilising public opinion to assert people's entitlements under various PA programme or to press the government to allocate more resources and permit greater flexibility in programming to adapt scheme to local conditions. NGOs have played an active role in lobbying for freedom of information concerning details of public development schemes, entitlements to their benefits and the beneficiaries.

All this has contributed to raising people's consciousness of entitlements under government programme, including PA programmes. There is also growing awareness, especially among the poor, of their importance in influencing the outcome of electoral politics. There is greater assertiveness on their part in articulating general demands in the political arena. But there is as yet no organised attempt to see that the choice of beneficiaries and implementation of local programmes in particular communities is improved. This does not seem likely unless both the power and the resources for local development are fully devolved to elected representatives of local governments.

The necessity and the wisdom of democratic decentralisation has been a recurrent theme of debates on the structure of government in India. The Constitution did not recognise or provide for representative local government institutions. By the late 1950s a review of the experience of the community development programme emphasised the need for democratically elected local governments for vigorous and equitable development in rural areas. Legislation to create panchayati raj bodies were passed by most states soon thereafter. However, few are keen to devolve powers and resources, and there was no legal or political compulsion to do so. Many did not even hold regular elections.

But some states (notably Karnataka and West Bengal) have tried to make it work. After a promising start the Karnataka experiment has stuttered. West Bengal's record in holding regular elections is the longest and most sustained though the devolution process has not gone as far as expected. Nevertheless both experiences have demonstrated the benefits of consultation and participation of local communities in making schemes more relevant to local felt needs, reducing duplication, ensuring that schemes are completed on schedule (often below estimated costs) and also in terms of the functioning of schools and PHCs.

The passage of the 73rd and 74th Constitutional Amendments which provides for a three tier system of local government, mandatory elections every five years and devolution development functions with authority and resources from the state to these bodies, has created a space and opportunity for decentralised participatory local development effort with in-built pressures for accountability. Implementation of these provisions is far from complete. Several states have not held local body elections as required by the Constitution. Even those which have, show a strong unwillingness to hand over to the elected bodies the authority and the resources to decide and implement local development. They have no power over the staff assigned to them nor the flexibility to hire any personnel on their own; schemes continue to be decided and implemented by the government and its bureaucracy; practically everywhere opposition state- and central-level politicians and the bureaucracy are resisting the process vigorously and in most places successfully.

This is evident even in Kerala which has made by far the most serious and determined effort to implement the spirit of the 73rd and 74th Amendments in all its essential respects. Legislating a statutory transfer of 40 per cent of state plan resources to local bodies - Kerala is the only state to have done so - is a revolutionary step. Efforts to prepare elected members of local bodies for their new role through mass mobilisation and public education training programmes and innovative ways to promote active and meaningful people's participation have been as impressive as they are unprecedented. The process, however, is being impeded at every step by strong rearguard opposition from those with a vested interest in the current dispensation.[39] That this is being increasingly contested by local leaders cutting across party lines and insisting on effective devolution of resources and power to them gives basis for optimism that this opposition will be overcome in due course.

A number of reasons are advanced to justify the opposition. One is the argument that given the highly stratified and unequal socio-economic structure of Indian villages, the dominant landowning caste elites would effectively control power and that they are unlikely to be concerned about the welfare of the poor and the women. Reservation of a specified, substantial proportion of elected positions for SC/STs and for women is meant to give a secure space for the disadvantaged to articulate their needs in the decision-making bodies. Sceptics doubt whether this space can and will in fact be used effectively in all cases and soon. However pessimism on this account seems unwarranted, at any rate exaggerated, for several reasons.

The growing political consciousness of the so-called lower castes as well as the scheduled castes and tribes is bound to express itself in local government as well. Secondly, villages/blocks differ greatly in caste/ class composition: Some villages are no doubt dominated by better off upper castes, but this is by no means the case everywhere. One must expert the outcome of decentralisation will be far from uniform. Even if initially only a fraction of elected local bodies do well, their superior performance will over a period of time act as spur to improvement in others.

The growing economic differentiation of rural society, the rapid diversification of activity and its commercialisation have loosened traditional social structures. The process will if anything intensify and lead to a significant realignment of the power structure in substantial parts of rural India favouring the disadvantaged groups. Such realignments will not of course to occur in all cases spontaneously and in a manner which gives effective voice to the poor and promote their interests. The process initiated by PR and the potential for change created by it are much more important than the immediate outcomes. Interventions in the process must therefore focus on creating conditions which will facilitate and encourage, the realisation of its potential. In this context three aspects deserve special attention.

First, a great deal of knowledge and expertise is needed to assess local resources and their potential, different ways of exploiting the potential, the costs involved and raising resources. This knowledge, much of it technical in nature, is often not available locally. Strong support from state agencies and/or non-government organisations (including educational institutions) is necessary to make it accessible to the communities and their leaders. A major change in the role of government agencies is also necessary. Instead of planning, deciding and implementing schemes on their own, as they now do, the agencies will have to play a supportive role by providing expertise, helping elected bodies to take informed decision and facilitating coordination between related schemes of different communities and in the larger regional context.

Second, the creation of democratic institutions of local government and assured representation for disadvantaged groups are necessary, but not sufficient conditions to ensure that the latters' interests are safeguarded. The determination of priorities, in the context of limited resources, inevitably involves a process of bargaining between different groups. In order for this to work in favour of the poor/vulnerable, the latter have to articulate their needs and actively persuade and/or pressure the relevant forums to take necessary action to meet their needs. None of these occur easily or automatically. Conscious measures to encourage and strengthen institutions of civil society are essential.

Non-governmental and voluntary organisations have a particularly key role in obtaining and disseminating information on the working of government (including local government), making people aware of their entitlements and obligations, and enabling them to vent their grievances and seek redress. Besides interceding with the concerned authorities to secure benefits for the eligible and minimise leakages, they have a role in motivating and organising local communities to take active interest in the working of specific programmes and persuading bureaucracy to work with the community for improving the effectiveness of programmes. Over time they can help promote a process of more broad-based changes in institutional mechanisms for funding/managing local development activities to meet the specific local conditions. Active encouragement of NGOs and giving them ample public space is therefore highly desirable for healthy evolution of local government.

Third, rising expectations and assertiveness of the people vis-a-vis government and bureaucracy increases pressures on the latter to perform. But better performance often requires a significant change in the relative roles of the three elements involving, among other things, reduced power and increased accountability of bureaucracy. It also involves shifts in the relative power of those who hold political office at different levels and of different segments of the bureaucracy. Reform therefore invariably encounters resistance. Moreover if the elected panchayat raj institutions merely generate demands for larger devolution of resources from the state and central governments there is little stake or incentive for them to address the task of efficient use of resources. It is therefore imperative that local bodies should be required to mobilise their own resources to meet a significant part of the costs of their programmes and given greater control over their staff engaged in various activities.

All this implies a basic change in the relations between the state and local governments, the role of the bureaucracy and the attitudes of local governments. There are no standard blue prints for accomplishing the change. A great deal of experiment and learning from experience is inevitable. The upsetting of existing power balances between the various groups involved creates an opportunity for engineering desirable changes through a combination of sustained pressures on the system as a whole via the general political process along with grass roots efforts to initiate and sustain a discussion of the problem of restructuring among the concerned groups (namely the local and state level politicians, the bureaucracy and its trade unions and non-government organisations).

Notes

[Kale Memorial Lecture delivered at Gokhale Institute of Economics and Politics, Pune, December 10, 2000.]

1 It merits noting that the late Pitambar Pant, who was then personal assistant to Nehru in his capacity as chairman of the Planning Commission, was the moving spirit behind the seminar on Planning for Minimum Living and, as head of PPD, the preparation of a perspective plan based on its recommendations.

2 Interestingly this was followed by a phrase 'in the light of its other commitments' which in effect diluted the force of this commitment.

3 This paper, titled 'Perspective of Development 1961-1976: Implications of Planning for a Minimum Level of Living', is reprinted in Srinivasan and Bardhan (eds) (1974).

4 Much of the work of this period is published in Srinivasan and Bardhan (eds) (1974).

5 Notable subsequent collections include Bardhan and Srinivasan (eds) (1988); Harris et al (eds) (1992); Drese and Sen (1995); Krishnaswamy (ed) (1990); Bhattacharya et al (1990); Rao (ed).

6 For a review of the evolution of these programmes and their problems see Vaidyanathan (1994a).

7 For a comprehensive and detailed discussion of the complex issues involved see Srinivasan (1981); Osmani (ed) (1992); and Sukhatme (ed) (1992).

8 For a detailed and critical discussion of this procedure see Rudra (1974, 1978); Dandekar (1996).

9 The ensuing summary of Sen's arguments is based on Sen (1985).

10 The theoretical and measurement problems involved are discussed in the Development Reports and their background papers published by the UNDP.

11 Noteworthy among these being the All India Household surveys of income, savings and consumption conducted in 1967-68 and 1975-76; panel surveys of sample rural households in 1970-71 and 1981-82; Market Information Surveys of Households (done more or less regularly since 1985); a survey of social indicators (1998); and a household survey to assess macro impact of macro adjustment policies.

12 Reports of NNMB's annual nutrition surveys, which are being conducted more or less regularly since the mid 1970s, are published by the National Institute of Nutrition, Hyderabad. Unfortunately these reports, not to speak of the primary data, are not easily accessible.

13 International Institute of Population Studies 1995.

14 A description of the scope, aims and methodology of the surveys is available in Walker and Ryan (1990).

15 One could compare SDP per capita estimates and per capita weighted mean consumption from NSS at the state level. But output originating is not a good proxy for incomes accruing to the population in a state, which is more relevant for determining consumption. In the case of rural areas SDP in agriculture may not be a good indicator of even total output originating (let alone income accruing) in rural areas. At the all India level, there seems to be a significant positive correlation between official estimates of agricultural GDP per head of rural population and NSS estimates of per capita real consumption (both at constant prices) in the post 1973

period. But at the state level in many cases agricultural GDP per rural population is not strongly correlated with per capita real consumption.

16 For details of these revisions see GoI PC (1993) Ch 3.

17 According to official estimates poverty incidence fell progressively from 51.5 per cent in 1972-73 to 29.9 per cent in 1993-94; while the NSS based estimate showed a decline for 54.9 per cent in 1972-73 to 39.3 per cent in 1993-94 [GoI PC 1993].

18 A point-to-point comparison shows that the mean per capita consumption (in real terms) during the triennium ending 1997 was about 14 per cent higher than during 1989-91 according to NAS and only 3 per cent higher according to NSS.

19 If the conjecture is valid, the criterion that the reforms have accentuated inequalities would stand vindicated.

20 These points are discussed at length by Abijit Sen (2000) and Visaria (2000) and in an as yet unpublished note by Deaton.

21 The aims, scope and design of these surveys vary. Some were focused primarily on household incomes, other or market for branded manufactures and yet others on social indicators. This and the fact that, in some cases, two different surveys give very different estimates raises serious questions as to their comparability and reliability especially for assessing changes in inequality and poverty incidence. Even in the case of the panel survey of 1970-71 and 1981-82, more than one-fourth of the 1970-71 sample could not be traced in 1971-72; and not all the panel responded. The characteristics of the missing households is not indicated.

22 Significantly during the period covered by his study, the rate of decline in poverty is not significantly correlated with the rate of agricultural growth. Punjab and Haryana, which recorded among the highest growth rates in this period, showed no significant fall in poverty.

23 Two recent examples being Ravillion and Dutt (1995) and Abijit Sen (1996).

24 The relevant data are summarised in Vaidyanathan (1994, 1996).

25 For a recent overview see Rakesh Mohan and Pushpa Thottan (1988) and Minhas et al (1988). Also GoI PC 1993.

26 Abhijit Sen's (1996) attempt to explain trends in urban poverty incidence at the all India level in terms of changes in agricultural incomes per head of rural population, per capita non-agricultural incomes, commercialisation, etc, are not as convincing as in the case of rural areas both in terms of the underlying logic and the consistency, significance and stability of the estimated coefficients.

27 On the nature and extent of these shifts use Radhakrishna and Ravi (1992); Suryanarayana (2000) and Meenakshi (2000).

28 State level time series for education and mortality indicators compiled from official sources are collated in Nayyar 1992. Information on morbidity and access to medical care is available from the social consumption surveys conducted by the NSS in 1986-87 and in 1996-97. NNMB surveys give data, for small but representative sample of households in major states, of measured food intake, anthropometric measurements and assessment of clinical signs of nutrition deficiencies. There has been little analysis of the NNMB data. For analysis of nutrition data from the ICRISAT village surveys see Walker and Ryan 1990.

29 See Visaria and Gumber 1996 for a comprehensive and comparative analysis of NSS data on morbidity and health care utilisation and expenditure pattern in different states in 1986-87.

30 See for example Lipton (1983); Chambers (1988); and Sahn (eds) (1989).

31 Notable and pioneering works on this subject include Guhan (1988); Chen (ed) (1998); Dreze and Sen (1989).

32 See for example Lipton (1983); Sen (1988); Bardhan (1988); Walker and Ryan (1992); Kumar and Stewart (1992); Agarwal (1994); Vaidyanathan (1986, 1994).

33 The censuses and the NSS collect and publish data separately for scheduled castes and tribes in respect of demographic features, education, vital rates, employment and land ownership. They show that while their position in all these respects remain well below the average, there have been substantial improvements both in absolute and relative terms. The large variations in these respects between and within regions and in particular the underlying factors (including the effect of affirmative action policies) have received surprisingly little attention.

34 The literature on effectiveness of policy interventions is vast. For useful summaries of current debates and bibliographies on IRDP see Copestake (1988); on employment, Mahendra Dev (1993) and Gaiha (1997), on nutrition, Subba Rao (1988), Osmani (ed) (1992).

35 For a recent and thorough discussion of issues See Krishnan and Krishnaji (eds) (2000) and Swaminathan (2000).

36 The estimate for the Fourth Plan includes outlays on area development, village industries, backward areas, slum improvement, social welfare and special area programme. That for the Eighth Plan includes rural development, scheduled caste and tribes, social welfare, nutrition and village industry. Including outlays on minimum needs programme, for which separate for as figures are available the total is substantially higher bringing the total outlay on targeted PA programmes to 17 per cent of the public sector plan outlay.

37 In 1994-95 unrecovered costs of publicly provided goods and services are estimated at Rs 1,370 billion which exceeds the public sector plan outlay by 30 per cent and overall fiscal deficit by 40 per cent.

38 The subsequent arguments draw heavily than earlier paper of the author, Vaidyanathan (1998).

39 For a detailed, illuminating and self-critical assessment of the Kerala experience see Isaac (2000).

References

Agarwal, Bina (1994), *Field of One's Own: Gender and Land Rights in South Asia*, Sage, New Delhi.

Ahluwalia, M S (1978), "Rural Poverty and Agricultural Performance in India", *Journal of Development Studies.*

——— (1986), "Rural Poverty, Agricultural Production and Prices: A Re-examination" in Mellur and Desai (eds).

Bardhan, Pranab K (1988), "Sex Disparity in Child Survival in Rural India" in Srinivasan and Bardhan (eds).

Bhalla, Surjit (1988), "Is Srilanka An Exception? A Comparative Study of Living Standards" in Srinivasan and Bardhan (eds).

Bhalla, Surjit and Prem Vasishta (1988), "Income Distribution in India: A Re-examination" in Srinivasan and Bardhan (eds).

Bhattacharya, N D Coondoo, P Maiti and R Mukherjee (1991), *Poverty Inequality and Prices in Rural India*, Sage, New Delhi.

Bhatty, I Z (1974), "Inequality and Poverty in Rural India" in Srinivasan and Bardhan (eds).

Chen, Martha Alter (ed) (1998), *Widows in India,* Sage, New Delhi.

Copestake, James (1992), "The Integrated Rural Development Programme" in Harris et al (eds).

Chambers, Robert (1992), "Poverty In India; Concepts, Research and Reality" in Harris et al (eds).

Dandekar, V M (1996), The Indian Economy 1947-1992 Vol 2: *Population, Poverty and Employment*, Chapter 6, Sage, New Delhi.

Dreze, Jean and Amartya Sen (1989), "Public Action for Social Security: Foundations and Strategy", *STICERD, No 20,* London School of Economics.

Gaiha, Raghav (1988), "On Measuring the Risk of Rural Poverty in India" in Srinivasan and Bardhan (eds).

——— (2000), "Rural Public Works and the Poor: A Review of the Employment Generation Scheme in Maharashtra" (mimeo).

GoI, Planning Commission (1962), *Report of the Committee on Distribution of Income and Levels of Living,* 2 Volumes, New Delhi.

——— (1964), *Notes of Perspectives of Development, India: 1960-61 to 1965-66,* New Delhi.

——— (1993), *Report of Expert Group on Estimates of Poverty and Number of Poor,* New Delhi.

Gopala Krishna Kumar and Frances Stewart (1988), "Tackling Malnutrition: What Can Targeted Nutritional Interventions Achieve?" in Harris et al (eds).

Guhan, S (1988), "Social Security in India: Looking One Step Ahead" in Harris et al (eds).

Harris, Barbara, S Guhan and Robert Cassen (eds) (1992), *Poverty in India:. Research and Policy*, Oxford University Press, New Delhi.

Hazari, R K (1967), *The Structure of the Corporate Prive Sector - A Study of Concentration, Ownership and Control,* Asia Publishing Home, Bombay.

International Institute of Population Studies (1995), *National Family Health Survey, 1992-93*, Mumbai.

Issac, Thomas and Richard W Franke (2000), *Local Democracy and Development: Peoples Campaign for Decentralised Planning in Kerala,* Leftword, New Delhi.

Kansal, S M (1965), "Preliminary Estimate of Total Consumption Expenditure in India 1950-51 to 1963-64", Indian Statistical Institute Planning Unit, Discussion Paper 5, Delhi.

Krishnaji N and T N Krishnan (eds) (2000), *Public Support for Food Security: The Public Distribution System in India,* Sage, New Delhi.

Lipton, Michael (1983), "Poverty, Undernutrition and Hunger", World Bank Staff Working Paper, P 23, Washington, DC.

——— (1983), *The Poor and the Ultra Poor: Characteristics, Explanation and Politics,* Development Research Department, CDS, Survey.

——— (1985), "Poor and the Poorest", World Bank Discussion Paper 25, Washington DC

Mahendra Dev, S (1995), "India's Maharashtra Employment Guarantee Scheme: Lessons and Experience" in Frederick Von Braun (ed), *Employment for Poverty Reduction and Food Security*, International Food Policy Research Institute, Washington, DC.

Mellor John and Gunvant Desai (ed) (1986), *Agricultural Change and Rural Poverty*, Oxford University Press, Delhi.

Meenakshi, J V (2000), "Food Consumption Trends in India: A Regional Analysis" in Krishnajis and Krishnan (eds).

Minhas, B S (1985), *Validation of Large-Scale Sample Survey Data in Case of NSS Estimates of Household Consumption Expenditure*, Sankhya: A series B Vol 50 - Part I.

Minhas, B S and S M Kansal (1989), "Comparison of NSS and CSO Estimates of Private Consumption: Some Observation Based on 1983 Data", *The Journal of Income and Wealth,* Vol III-November 1.

Minhas, B S, S M Kansal and L R Jain (1988), "The Incidence of Urban Poverty in States 1970-71 to 1983 in Harris", Guhan and Casen (eds).

National Institute of Nutrition - Annual Reports on the NNMB Nutrition Surveys.

Nayyar, Rohini (1991), *Rural Poverty in India: An analysis of Inter State Differences*, Oxford University Press, Mumbai.

NCAER (1987), *Changes in the Structure of Household Income and Distribution of Gains in the Rural Household Sector: An All-India Inter Temporal Analysis 1970-71, 1981-82.*

Osmani, S (ed) (1992), *Nutrition and Poverty,* Clarendeon, Oxford.

Parikh, K S and T N Srinivasan (1990), "Poverty Alleviation Policies in India: Food Consumption Subsidies, Food Production Subsidies and Employment Generation", mimeo, Indira Gandhi Institute for Development Research, Mumbai.

Pradhan, Basant K et al (2000), "Rural Urban Disparities, Income Distribution, Expenditure Pattern and Social Sector", *Economic and Political Weekly.*

Probe, Team (1999), *Public Report on Basic Education,* Oxford University Press, New Delhi

Rakesh Mohan and P Thottan (1992), "The Regional Spread of Urbanisation, Industrialisation and Urban Poverty" in Harris et al (ed).

Rao, C H H and H Linneman (eds) (1996), *Economic Reforms and Poverty Alleviation in India*, Sage, New Delhi.

Radhakrishna R and C Ravi (1992), "Effects of Growth, Relative Prices and Preferences on Food and Nutrition", *Indian Economic Review.*

Ravillion, Martin and Gaurav Datt (1995), "Poverty in India", Background paper to the 1995 World Development Report, working paper series 1405, World Bank, Washington DC.

Rudra, Ashok (1974), "Minimum Level of Living: A Statistical Examination" in Srinivasan and Bardhan (ed).

——— (1978), *The Basic Needs Concept and Its Implementation in Indian Development Planning,* ILO, ARTEP, Bangkok.

Sahn, David E (ed) (1989), *Seasonal Variability in Third World Agriculture: The Consequences for Food Security* John Hopkins University Press, Baltimore.

Sen, Abijit (1996), "Economic Reforms, Employment and Poverty: Trends and Options", *Economic and Political Weekly.*

——— 2000, "Consumer Spending and its Distribution...", *EPW,* December.

Sen, Amartya (1985), *Commodities, and Capabilities,* North Holland, Amsterdam.

Sen, Amartya K and S Sengputa (1988), "Family and Food: Sex Bias in Poverty" in Srinivasan and Bardhan (eds).

Srinivasan, T N (1981), "Malnutrition: Some Measurement and Policy Issues", *Journal of Developing Economics.*

Srinivasan, T N and P K Bardhan (eds) (1988), *Rural Poverty in South Asia,* OUP, Delhi. Srinivasan, T N, P N Radhakrishnan and A Vaidyanathan (1974).

Streeten, Paul and S J Burki (1978), "Basic Needs: Some Issues", *World Development.*

Sundaram, K and Tendulkar S D (1988), "Towards an Explanation of Inter Regional Variations in Poverty and Unemployment in India" in Srinivasan and Bardhan (eds).

Subba Rao (1992), "Interventions to Fill Nutrition Gaps at the Household Level" in Harris et al (eds).

Sukhatme, P V (ed) (1992), *Newer Concepts in Nutrition and Their Implications for Policy*, Maharashtra Association for Cultivation of Science, Pune.

Suryanarayana, M H (2000), "How Real is the Secular Decline in Rural Poverty", *Economic and Political Weekly.*

Suryanarayana, M H and N S Iyengar (1986), "On Reliability of NSS Data", *Economic and Political Weekly.*

Swaminathan, Madhura (2000), Weakening Welfare: *The Public Distribution of Food in India*, Leftword, New Delhi.

UNDP (2000), "Human Development Report".

——— (various years), "Human Development Papers". United Nations, Department of Economic and Social Affairs, 1975.

Vaidyanathan, A (1986a), "On the Validity of NSS Consumption Data", *Economic and political Weekly.*

——— (1986b), "Food Consumption and the Size of the People: Some Indian Evidence", Economic and Political Weekly.

——— (1992), "On Measurement of Nutrition and Health Status".

——— (1994a), "Political Economy of the Evolution of Anti Poverty Programmes" in Sathyamurthy T S (ed).

——— (1994b), "Second India Series Revisited, Food and Agriculture", mimeo, MIDS, Chennai.

——— (1996), "Employment Situation: Some Emerging Perspectives", *EPW.*

Vaidyanathan, A and P R G Nair (eds) (2000), *Elementary Education in Rural India: A Grass roots View,* Sage, New Delhi.

Visaria, Pravin (1978), "Size of Holdings, Living Standard and Employment in Western India, 1972-73", World Bank Staff Working Paper.

——— (1979), "Poverty and Development in India: An Analysis of Rural Evidence", World Bank Staff Working Paper.

Economic & Political Weekly, May 26-June 1, 2001.

34

Chronic Poverty and Malnutrition in 1990s

R. Radhakrishna, K. Hanumantha Rao,
C. Ravi, B. Sambi Reddy

Malnutrition

The reports from the National Nutrition Monitoring Bureau (NNMB) provide data on the nutritional status of general population as well as certain vulnerable groups in rural areas. The information is based on large scale, periodic diet and nutritional surveys in nine states. These reports use Gomez classification[1] for children and body-mass index (BMI)[2] classification for adults. The NNMB data show that the incidence of under-nutrition among children, even though slowly declining, is still alarmingly high during the late 1990s and their incidence is higher than that of income poverty. About half of the children and slightly over a third of adults were undernourished in 2000-01 [Radhakrishna and Ravi, 2004].

The percentage of malnourished children declined from 61.5 in 1975-79 to 56.2 in 1991-92 and further to 47.7 in 2000-01 which is visible across all NNMB sample states except Madhya Pradesh and Orissa *(ibid)*. The decline is very striking in Kerala and Tamil Nadu – from 56.8 per cent to 28.8 per cent during 1975-2001 in Kerala and from 59.6 per cent to 39.0 per cent in Tamil Nadu. Malnutrition levels in Madhya Pradesh and Orissa in 2000-01 is about the same as in early 1970s.

The authors are thankful to IIPA for sponsoring this study and to Aasha Kapur Mehta and Andrew Shepherd for their comments.

TABLE – 34.1

Undernutrition (Height-for-age) among Poor and Incidence of Chronic Poverty: 1997-98

State	Rural		Urban	
	Percentage of Stunted Children among Poor	Percentage of Chronically Poor	Percentage of Stunted Children among Poor	Percentage of Chronically Poor
Andhra Pradesh	49.6	5.2	34.3	13.5
Assam	52.4	21.1	49.1	3.8
Bihar	57.5	25.3	63.0	19.3
Gujarat	49.5	6.1	51.2	7.3
Haryana	60.5	4.5	64.2	6.1
Himachal Pradesh	58.8	4.4	54.8	2.7
Jammu and Kashmir	59.9	2.8	51.6	1.2
Karnataka	56.5	9.6	49.7	13.9
Kerala	32.4	3.1	30.9	6.5
Madhya Pradesh	57.4	21.4	56.9	22.2
Maharashtra	55.8	13.0	30.9	15.0
Orissa	51.1	24.4	49.1	22.2
Punjab	56.9	3.4	46.4	3.1
Rajasthan	60.1	8.1	57.2	11.7
Tamil Nadu	41.6	8.4	46.5	9.4
West Bengal	60.0	19.0	53.5	8.8
Uttar Pradesh	63.1	19.6	59.6	19.4
Other States	43.1	5.3	46.4	3.9
All-India	**57.1**	**15.1**	**49.6**	**13.7**

Note: Stunted children among the poor and chronically poor are estimated by matching NSS and NFHS at unit level.

There are substantial inter-state variations in the malnutrition levels of children of under-five years; in 2000-01, it varied between 28.8 per cent in Kerala and 63.9 per cent in Madhya Pradesh. In terms of nutritional status of children, middle-income states such as Kerala, Tamil Nadu and Andhra Pradesh performed better than West Bengal and higher-income states like Maharashtra and Gujarat. Not surprisingly, poorer states such as Madhya Pradesh and Orissa showed the worst performance. It is worth noting that, with low food energy intake, Kerala and Tamil Nadu could perform well possibly due to their successful interventions in health and nutrition. The National Family Health Survey (NFHS) estimates of malnutrition based on standard deviation classification also reveal a similar pattern. NFHS-2 shows that north-eastern states performed better [Radhakrishna and Ravi, 2004].

NNMB data for eight sample states show that, in 2000-01, 37.4 per cent of adult females and 39.4 per cent of adult males suffered from Chronic Energy Deficiency (CED) and the extent of malnutrition among the adults was almost as much as that of children. The inter-state variations in CED are similar to those of malnutrition among the children. The CED was found to be lower in Kerala (22.4 per cent for males and 18.7 per cent for females) and Tamil Nadu (26.7 per cent for males and 38.7 per cent for females) and higher in Madhya Pradesh, Maharashtra and West Bengal (above 50 per cent). Gender differences seem to exist in some states, particularly in Tamil Nadu.

The NFHS-2 results show that 36 per cent of ever-married women aged between 15 and 49 have chronic energy deficiency (Arnold *et al.*, 2004). It is more pronounced among rural, illiterate and those with a low standard of living. Those who consume milk or curd daily are less prone to CED than other women *(ibid)*. Chronic energy deficiency levels are higher in higher income states such as Maharashtra (40 per cent) and Gujarat (38 per cent) and middle income state West Bengal (44 per cent) and the levels are closer to that of less developed states like Bihar (40 per cent), Madhya Pradesh (39 per cent) and Orissa (48 per cent). Punjab (17 per cent), Kerala (19 per cent), Arunachal Pradesh (11 per cent), Manipur (19 per cent) and Nagaland (19 per cent) and Sikkim (11 per cent) have lower incidence of feminine malnutrition. Clearly, north-eastern states performed better. Some of them out performed even Punjab and Kerala.

Poverty and Malnutrition

What is the impact of poverty reduction on malnutrition? Is the reduction in malnutrition commensurate with poverty reduction? The NFHS-2 statewise data for rural malnutrition based on weight-for-age is regressed on rural poverty estimates based on NSS 55th round.[3] The results indicate the prevalence of malnutrition even when poverty is completely eradicated. The poverty coefficients, which are positive and significant, show that a 10 per cent reduction in poverty reduces malnutrition by 6 per cent. The malnutrition for 20 fractile classes formed on the basis of standard of living index also revealed that malnutrition declines slowly with improvement in standard of living but persists even among the top fractile classes. For example, 28 per cent of the children of the richest fractile class in the rural areas and 21 per cent of children of the richest fractile class in urban areas suffer from malnutrition.

The NFHS-2 data are analysed to identify the determinants of malnutrition in rural areas using logit regression model. The model is estimated separately for underweight and stunted categories of malnutrition based on standard deviation classification.[4] The standard of living index is one of the independent variables chosen to serve as a proxy for the income level of the household. The other independent variables are: sex of the child, birth order and place of delivery and leafy vegetable consumption – specific to the child; mother's age, mother's body mass index, employment status, education and ante-natal care – specific to the mother; household size, caste and consumption of nutritious food – specific to the household; existence of drainage, fair price shop, '*anganawadi*', '*mahilamandal*', health and education facilities – specific to the village.

In the case of child-specific variables, coefficients are significant for birth order and leafy vegetable consumption. The probability of child malnutrition decreases with the increase in the consumption of leafy vegetables and increases with the birth order. Nutritional status, education, age and working status of the mother have significant impact on malnutrition. Probability of a child falling into malnutrition decreases with increase in mother's body mass index. Probability of malnutrition also decreases with age and ante-natal visits but, on the other hand, increases when the mother is working. The adverse effect of the working status of the mother may be a characteristic among the poor households.

The coefficient of all the household-level variables are statistically significant and are in conformity with our understanding that the risk of malnutrition decreases with the standard of living of the household and increases with household size. However, contrary to our understanding, scheduled tribes have a low probability of malnutrition which may be due to the low incidence of malnutrition in north-eastern states/union territories. None of the village level variables are found to be significant.

Development Experiences and Lessons

Three major conclusions follow from the preceding analysis. The first one is that all the states, with the exception of Assam and Orissa, have experienced poverty reduction between 1993-94 and 1999-00. However, due to uneven poverty reduction across states and social groups, the poor got concentrated in less developed states and among a few vulnerable social groups. In the agriculturally prosperous states, agricultural labour households have accounted for bulk of the rural poor while in the less developed regions, rural poverty has extended to other occupational groups including those self employed in agriculture. In urban areas, poverty was concentrated among casual labour households. The second conclusion is that Assam, Orissa, Madhya Pradesh and Uttar Pradesh have remained laggards in poverty reduction. Structural factors and inadequate growth might be the major causes underlying their poor performance. In this context, it is worth mentioning that Rajasthan, a resource poor state, could perform better in poverty reduction and may have lessons to offer from its experience. The third and final conclusion is that the poor are likely to be vulnerable to risks in labour market and may increasingly suffer more from transient poverty since their dependence on the casual labour market for livelihood is rising fast both in rural and urban areas. Backward regions and disadvantaged social groups are afflicted by chronic as well as transient poverty.

The trends in total expenditure/income and food energy intake over the last three decades do not show strong relationship between them. The food energy intake increased marginally during 1970-1989 and stagnated/declined during the 1990s across all classes. The slow response could be attributed to the shift in consumption patterns – from cereal to non-cereals and from coarse cereals to fine cereals – across all income groups [Radhakrishna *et al.*, 1992, 2004]. The significant increase in the price of food in the 1990s also had an adverse impact on food energy intake [Radhakrishna, Ravi, 2004]. These tendencies should become a major cause of concern since the per capita intake of the bottom 30 per cent at 1,600-1,700 k cal/day falls short of the required nutritional norm (Table 34.2).

TABLE – 34.2

Per Capita Calorie Intake and Its Growth Rates

Expenditure Classes	K Cal/day				Growth Rate (Per Cent)
	1972-73	1977-78	1993-94	1999-00	1972-2000
Rural					
Bottom 30 per cent	1504	1630	1678	1696	0.6
Middle 40 per cent	2170	2296	2119	2116	–0.1
Top 30 per cent	3161	3190	2672	2646	–0.8
All groups	2268	2364	2152	2149	–0.3
Urban					
Bottom 30 per cent	1579	1701	1701	1715	0.4
Middle 40 per cent	2154	2154	2438	2136	–0.0
Top 30 per cent	2572	2979	2405	2622	0.1
All groups	2107	2379	2071	2156	0.1

Source: Computed from NSS Report No 405.

The connection between food energy intake and nutritional status is less illuminating. For instance, Kerala and Tamil Nadu have achieved high levels of nutritional status with low calorie intake. This underscores the impact of factors other than food energy intake on nutritional status. Sukhatme, in his pioneering studies on malnutrition, explained that conversion efficiency of food into energy depends on the access to safe drinking water, health care and environmental hygiene.

Logit regression results show that the risk of child malnutrition decreases with increased standard of living, and increases with household size. The risk of malnutrition also decreases with mothers' nutritional status and education. The risk of malnutrition is greater if the child has a working mother. Birth order and consumption of leafy vegetables are other important factors and so is ante-natal care. It can be inferred from the above findings that social and food security policies, which improve incomes of the poor households as well as access of women to education and health care, would reduce both chronic poverty and malnutrition. The Kerala experience illustrates how these policies have facilitated demographic transition from a high-mortality – high fertility regime to a low one.

Concluding Observations

Over the three decades, severity of poverty reduced faster than extent of poverty. The percentage of very poor, was about 8 per cent in rural areas and 9 per cent in urban areas in 1999-00. The estimated level of chronic poverty (15 per cent in rural areas and 13.7 per cent in urban areas) is greater than the incidence of very poor but lower than the incidence of child malnutrition. In the 1990s, the urban poverty reduced faster than rural due to faster urban economic growth; but inter-quintile urban inequality and rural-urban inequality increased. The poor will increasingly depend on risky labour markets and increasingly will live in poorer states. The profiles of very poor reveal that the presence of socially disadvantaged groups (SCs, STs and female-headed households) is high in very poor households. Similarly, the landless households, dependent mainly on wage earnings and casual labour (vulnerable to changes in land and labour markets), are found in larger proportion in very poor households. In developed regions where poverty levels are low, the very poor generally belong to SCs and STs, and/or casual labour households. Nearly half of the very poor are children. The very poor also suffer from poor housing and hunger.

While India has made considerable progress in poverty reduction, the overall improvement in nutritional status has been rather slow. Economic growth although resulted in decline in income poverty but has not translated into either commensurable increase in food energy intake nor significant reduction in malnutrition. The estimates of undernourishment show that 20 to 21 per cent of rural children are severely malnourished and another 30 to 39 per cent, mild to moderately malnourished (based on weight-for-age criterion) and 25 per cent are severely and another 24 per cent are mild to moderately malnourished (according to height-for-age criterion) [Radhakrishna *et al.,* 2003]. Generally the risk of malnutrition is high among poor households where mothers have poor nutritional levels.

The eradication of severe malnutrition should be the first priority of social policy and the feeding programmes should be targeted towards them, especially, women and children. Liberal use of growth-supplementing, employment-oriented food-for-work programmes should be the principal instruments to eradicate mild to moderate malnutrition. However, efficacy of these programmes depends on targeting, good governance of the delivery system and above all, political commitment.

Notes

1. In Gomez classification, the body weights of pre-school children are expressed as a percentage of National Centre for Health Statistics (NCHS) standards and their nutritional status are identified. Children with weight for age less than 60 are treated as severely malnourished, between 60 and 75 as moderately malnourished, between 75 and 90 as mildly malnourished and above or equal to 90 are treated as normal [NIN, 2002].
2. The Body Mass Index (weight in kg/height in metres^2) is used as an indicator of nutritional status of the adults. Adults whose body mass index is less than 18.5 are considered to suffer from chronic energy deficiency [NIN, 2002].
3. The regression results are given in Radhakrishna and Ravi (2004). The following regression has been estimated using statewise estimates of child malnutrition (NFHS 2) and poverty (55th NSS round) for rural areas: $\log m_1 = 2.08 + 0.026$ HCR and $\log m_2 = 2.85 + 0.012$ HCR, where m_1 is the proportion of children with severe underweight (< median – 3 SD) and m_2 is the children with underweight (< median -2SD) and HCR is the headcount ratio. All coefficients are statistically significant.
4. The results of logit regression estimated for rural areas are given in Radhakrishna *et al.* (2003). Inferences have been drawn from only significant coefficients. Results are similar for underweight and stunted.

References

Fred, Arnold; Parveen, Nangia and Uma, Kapila (2004), "Indicators of Nutrition for Women and Children in India: Current Status and Programme Recommendations", *Economic and Political Weekly*, Vol XXXIX, No 7, February 14-20.

National Institute of Nutrition (NIN) (2002), *Diet and Nutritional Status of Rural Population,* NNMB Technical Report No 21, Hyderabad.

Radhakrishna, R (1991), "Food and Nutrition: Challenges for Policy", *Journal of the Indian Society of Agricultural Statistics*, 43(3), 211-27.

Radhakrishna, R and C Ravi (1990), "Food Demand Projections for India", Centre for Economic and Social Studies, Hyderabad.

——— (1992), "Effects of Growth, Relative Price and Preferences on Food and Nutrition", *Indian Economic Review*, 27 (special number), 303-23.

——— (2004), "Malnutrition in India: Trends and Determinants", *Economic and Political Weekly*, Vol XXXIV, No 7, February 14-20.

——— (2004), "Measurements of Changes in Economic Welfare in India: 1970-2001", *Journal of Quantitative Economics* (forthcoming).

Radhakrishna, R, K Hanumantha Rao, C Ravi and B Sambi Reddy (2003), "Chronic Poverty, Food Security and Malnutrition in the Nineties", Paper presented in the seminar on Chronic Poverty Related Issues, at *Indian Institute of Public Administration*, New Delhi, November.

Radhakrishna R, S Indrakant and C Ravi (2004), "Changing Food Preferences, Nutritional Intake, and Nutritional Status: Emerging Perspectives and Issues", in Aditya Bhattacharjee and Sugata Marjit (ed), *Globalisation and the Developing Economics*, Manohar.

Rao, C H H (2000), "Declining Demand for Foodgrains in Rural India: Causes and Implications", *Economic and Political Weekly*, January 22.

Rao, C H H and R Radhakrishna (1997), "National Food Security: A Policy Perspective for India" in G H Peter and J V Braun (ed), *Food Security, Diversification and Resource Management: Re-focussing the Role of Agriculture*, Ashgate.

Ravi, C (2000), "Complete Demand Systems, Welfare and Nutrition: An Analysis of Indian Consumption Data" (unpublished PhD thesis).

[An earlier version of this paper was presented at the seminar on 'Chronic Poverty and Development Policy in India' organised by the Institute of Public Administration (IIPA), November 4, 2003, New Delhi].

Economic and Political Weekly, July 10, 2004, Excerpts from the article (Sections IV, V & VI).

35

Poverty and Inequality in India

A Re-Examination

Angus Deaton, Jean Dreze

Poverty trends in India in the nineties have been a matter of intense controversy.[1] The debate has often generated more heat than light, and confusion still remains about the extent to which poverty has declined during the period. In the absence of conclusive evidence, widely divergent claims have flourished. Some have argued that the nineties have been a period of unprecedented improvement in living standards. Others have claimed that it has been a time of widespread impoverishment.[2] Against this background, this paper presents a reassessment of the evidence on poverty and inequality in the nineties.

Economic Inequality in the Nineties

Growth, Poverty and Inequality

It is possible to think about poverty decline, as captured by standard poverty indexes, in terms of two distinct components: a growth component and a distribution component. The growth component reflects the increase of average per capita expenditure. The distribution component captures any change that may take place in the distribution of per capita expenditure over households.

This decomposition exercise is pursued in Table 35.3, with reference to the headcount ratio (very similar results apply to the poverty-gap index). The first column repeats the headcount ratio for 1993-94 from Table 35.1. The second column (labelled 'derivative with respect to growth') shows our estimate of the percentage-point reduction in HCR associated with a distribution-neutral, 1 per cent increase in APCE in the relevant state. To illustrate, in rural Andhra Pradesh a 1 per cent increase in APCE in 1993-94, with no change in distribution, would have led to a decline of 0.9 percentage points in the rural headcount ratio.[3] This derivative depends positively on the fraction of people who are at or near the poverty line, which is typically larger in the poorer states. The figures in column 2 vary from –1.27 in rural Assam to –0.15 in urban Jammu and Kashmir. Column 3 reproduces the total percentage growth between 1993-94 and 1999-2000 from Table 35.2.

If we multiply the second column (the derivative with respect to growth) by the third column (the amount of growth), we get an estimate of the amount of poverty reduction that we would expect from growth alone, in the absence of any change in the shape of the distribution. This is an approximation, because the derivative is likely to change as the headcount ratio falls. In column 4, we report a more precise calculation: an estimate of what the headcount ratio would have been in 1999-2000 if the distributions of consumption in each state were identical to those in 1993-94, but had been shifted upwards by the amount of growth in real per capita expenditure that actually took place. This can be readily calculated by reducing the 1993-94 poverty lines by the amount of growth, and re-estimating the headcount ratios from these adjusted lines and the 1993-94 expenditure data. These hypothetical changes can then be compared with the *actual* reductions in the headcount ratios, shown in the final column. The difference between these last two columns is the change in the headcount ratio that is attributable to changes in the shape of the consumption distribution.

It is important to note that the last two columns are highly correlated. The correlation coefficients across the states are 0.97 (rural) and 0.93 (urban), so that growth alone can predict much of the cross-state pattern of reduction in HCRs. Nevertheless, the estimates are far from identical. In particular, the all-India calculations show that 'growth alone' would have reduced the poverty rate by *more* than actually happened, implying that there was an increase in inequality that offset some of the effects of growth, or put differently, that APCE growth among the poor was less than the average. These inequality effects vary somewhat from state to state and are much weaker in rural than in urban areas. In urban India, increasing inequality moderated the decline in the headcount ratio in all states except Delhi, Maharashtra and Jammu and Kashmir. In some cases, such as urban Kerala and Madhya Pradesh, the 'moderating effect' is pronounced, with actual rates of reduction only a little over half those predicted by the growth in the mean.

For the urban sector as a whole (the last row of the table), the actual decline in the HCR is one and a half points lower (5.9 versus 7.4 per cent) than would have been the case had growth been equally distributed within each state. This estimate, which is the population-weighted average of the corresponding numbers for each state, calculates what would have happened if each household in each state had experienced the average growth for that state. An alternative, and equally interesting, counter-factual is what would have happened if, between 1993-94 and 1999-2000, each household in the country had experienced the countrywide growth rate of 10.9 per cent. Such a calculation yields an all-India HCR of 21.4 per cent (for rural and urban areas combined), compared with an actual all-India HCR of 22.7 per cent based on the 55th Round. In other words, the all-India HCR in 1999-2000 was 1.3 percentage points higher than it would have been (with the same growth rate of APCE) in the absence of any increase in inequality.

Aspects of Rising Inequality

Three aspects of rising economic inequality in the nineties have come up so far in our story. First, we found strong evidence of 'divergence' in per capita consumption across states. Second, our estimates of the growth rates of per capita expenditure between 1993-94 and 1999-2000 (Table 35.2) point to a significant increase in rural-urban inequalities at the all-India level, and also in most individual states. Third, the decomposition exercise in the preceding section shows that rising inequality within states, particularly in the urban sector, has moderated the effects of growth on poverty reduction.

Table 35.4 provides more systematic evidence on recent changes in consumption inequality within each sector of each state using two different measures of inequality. We show the logarithm of the difference of the arithmetic and geometric means (approximately the fraction by which the arithmetic mean exceeds the geometric mean), as well as the variance of the logarithm of per capita expenditure.

The table shows that the correction for questionnaire design is critical for understanding what has been happening. (Note that the correction for prices has no effect within sectors and states.) The direct use of the unit record data in the 55th Round, with no adjustment, shows a substantial *reduction* in inequality within the rural sectors of most states, with little or no increase in the urban sectors. With the correction, we see that within-state rural inequality has not fallen, and that there have been marked increases in within-state urban inequality. We suspect that the main reason why the unadjusted data are so misleading in this context is the change from 30 to 365 days in the reporting period for the low frequency items (durable goods, clothing and footwear, and institutional medical and educational expenditures). The longer reporting period actually reduces the mean expenditures on those items, but because a much larger fraction of people report *something* over the longer reporting period, the bottom tail of the consumption distribution is pulled up, and both inequality and poverty are reduced. Whether 365-days are a better or worse reporting period than 30-days could be argued either way, but the main point here is that the 55th and 50th Rounds are not comparable, and that the former artificially shows too little inequality compared with the latter. Once the corrections are made, we see that, in addition to increasing inequality between states, there has been a marked increase in consumption inequality within the urban sector of nearly all states.

Two further pieces of evidence are worth mentioning in this context. First, our findings on rising economic inequality within the urban sector are consistent with recent work by Banerjee and Piketty (2001), who use income tax records to document very large increases in income among the very highest income earners. They show that, in the 1990s, real incomes among the top one per cent of income earners increased by a half in real terms, while those of the top 1 per cent of 1 per cent increased by a factor of three in real terms.

Second, it is interesting to compare the growth rate of real wages for agricultural labourers with that of public sector salaries. As we saw earlier, real agricultural wages have grown at 2.5 per cent or so in the nineties. Public sector salaries, for their part, have grown at almost 5 per cent per year during the same period.[4] Given that public-sector employees tend to be much better off than agricultural labourers, this can be taken as an instance of rising economic disparities between different occupation groups. Since agricultural labourers and public sector employees typically reside in rural and urban areas, respectively, this finding may just be another side of the coin of rising rural-urban disparities. Even then, it strengthens the evidence presented earlier on aspects of rising economic inequality in the nineties.

To sum up, except for the absence of clear evidence of rising intra-rural inequality within states, we find strong indications of a pervasive increase in economic inequality in the nineties. This is a new development in the Indian economy: until 1993-94, the all-India Gini coefficients of per capita consumer expenditure in rural and urban areas were fairly stable.[5] Further, it is worth noting that the rate of increase of economic inequality in the nineties is far from negligible. For instance, the compounding of inter-state 'divergence' and rising rural-urban disparities produces very sharp contrasts in APCE growth between the rural sectors of the slow-growing states and the urban sectors of the fast-growing states (Table 35.2). This is further compounded by the accentuation of intra-urban inequality, which is itself quite substantial, bearing in mind that the change is measured over a short period of six years (Table 35.4).

It might be argued that a temporary increase in economic inequality is to be expected in a liberalising economy, and that this trend is likely to be short-lived. Proponents of the 'Kuznets curve' may even expect it to be reversed in due course. However, China's experience of sharp and sustained increase in economic inequality over a period of more than 20 years, after market-oriented economic reforms were initiated in the late 1970s, does not inspire much confidence in this prognosis.[6] It is, in fact, an important pointer to the possibility of further accentuation of economic disparities in India in the near future.

Qualifications and Concerns

Food Consumption

There have been major changes in India's food economy in the nineties. The eighties were a period of healthy growth in agricultural output, food production, and real agricultural wages. During the nineties, however, productivity increases slowed down in many states. The quantity index of agricultural production grew at a lame 2 per cent per year or so. The growth of real agricultural wages slowed down considerably. And cereal production barely kept pace with population growth.[7]

The virtual stagnation of per capita cereal production in the nineties has been accompanied by a gradual switch from net imports to net exports, and also by a massive accumulation of public stocks. Correspondingly, there has been no increase in estimated per capita 'net availability' of cereals (Table 35.5). If anything, net availability declined a little, from a peak of about 450 grams per person per day in 1990 to 420 grams or so at the end of the nineties. This is consistent with independent evidence, from National Sample Survey data, of a decline in per capita cereal consumption in the nineties. Between 1993-94 and 1999-2000, for instance, average cereal consumption per capita declined from 13.5 kg per month to 12.7 kg per month in rural areas, and from 10.6 to 10.4 kg per month in urban areas.[8] This comparison is based on the 'uncorrected' 55th Round data, and the 'true' decline may be larger still, given the changes in questionnaire design.

The reduction of cereal consumption in the nineties may seem inconsistent with the notion that poverty has declined during the same period. Indeed, this pattern has been widely invoked as evidence of 'impoverishment' in the nineties. If cereal consumption is declining, how can poverty be declining?

It is worth noting, however, that the decline of cereal consumption is not new. A similar decline took place (according to National Sample Survey data) during the seventies and eighties, when poverty was certainly declining. Hanchate and Dyson's (2000) recent comparison of rural food consumption patterns in 1973-74 and 1993-94 sheds some useful light on this matter. As the authors show, during this period per capita cereal consumption in rural areas declined quite sharply on average (from 15.8 to 13.6 kgs per person per month), but rose among the poorest households. The decline in the average is driven by reduced consumption among the higher expenditure groups.[9]

The average decline is unlikely to be driven by changes in relative prices; indeed, there has been little change in food prices, relative to other prices, in the intervening period. Instead, this pattern appears to reflect a substitution away from cereals to other food items as incomes rise (at least beyond a certain threshold). The consumption of 'superior' food items such as vegetables, milk, fruit, fish and meat did rise quite sharply over the same period, across all expenditure groups. Seen in this light, the decline of average cereal consumption may not be a matter of concern per se. Indeed, average cereal consumption is inversely related to per capita income across countries (e.g, it is lower in China than in India, and even lower in the United States), and the same applies across states within India (e.g, cereal consumption is higher in Bihar or Orissa than in Punjab or Haryana).

Food intake data collected by the National Nutrition Monitoring Bureau (NNMB) shed further light on this issue. Aside from detailed information on food intake, the NNMB surveys include rough estimates of household incomes. These are used in Figure 35.1 to display the relation between per-capita income and food intake; for different types of food. The substitution from cereals towards other food items with rising per-capita income emerges quite clearly.[10] This pattern, if confirmed, would fit quite well with the data on change over time.[11] It also implies that the decline of average cereal consumption in the nineties is not inconsistent with our earlier findings on poverty decline.[12]

Figure – 35.1

Food Intake for Different Per Capita Income Groups, as a Proportion (Per Cent) of Average Intake (1996-97)

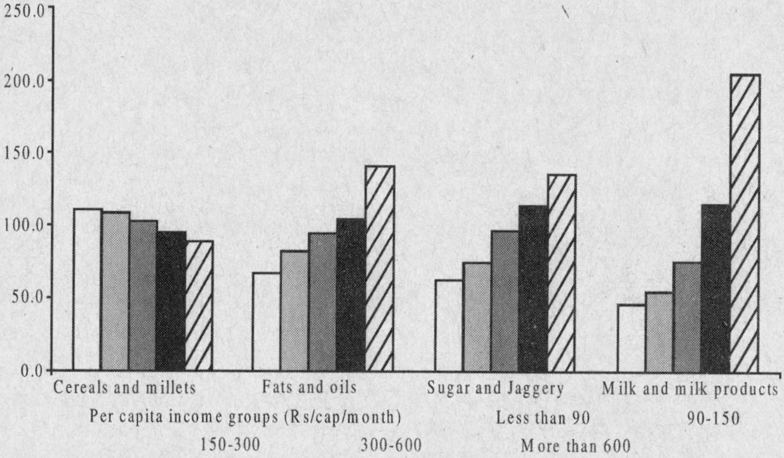

Source : Calculated from National Nutrition Monitoring Bureau (1999), Table 6.9. The data relate to rural areas of eight sample states.

Localised Impoverishment and Hidden Costs

The overall decline of poverty in the nineties does not rule out the possibility of impoverishment among specific regions or social groups. That possibility, of course, is not new, but it is worth asking whether its scope has expanded during the last decade. As the economy gives greater room to market forces, uncertainty and inequality often increase, possibly leading to enhanced economic insecurity among those who are not in a position to benefit from the new opportunities, or whose livelihoods are threatened by the changes in the economy. The increase of economic inequality in the nineties, noted earlier, suggests that tendencies of this kind may well be at work in India today. Adverse trends in living standards could take several distinct forms, including: (1) impoverishment among specific regions or social groups, (2) heightened uncertainty in general, and (3) growing 'hidden costs' of economic development.

In connection with the first point, we have already noted that some of the poorer states, notably Orissa and Assam, have not fared well at all in the nineties. It is quite possible that the poorer regions within these states have done even worse, to the point of absolute impoverishment for substantial sections of the population. In the case of Orissa, there is some independent evidence of localised impoverishment in the poorer districts, due *inter alia* to the destruction of the local environmental base and to the dismal failure of state-sponsored development programmes [Drèze 2001].[13]

Similarly, the overall improvement of living standards may hide instances of impoverishment among specific occupation groups. The nineties have been a period of rapid structural change in the Indian economy, leading in some cases to considerable disruption of earlier livelihood patterns. Examples include a deep recession in the powerloom sector, a serious crisis in the edible oil industry after import tariffs were slashed, periodic waves of bankruptcy among cotton growers, the displacement of traditional fishing by commercial shrimp farms, and a number of sectoral crises associated with the abrupt lifting of quantitative restrictions on imports in mid-2001.[14] The destruction of local environmental resources is another common cause of disrupted livelihoods in many areas.

A related issue is the possibility of 'hidden hardships' associated with recent patterns of economic development. To illustrate, there is much evidence that, in many of the poorer regions of India, further impoverishment has been avoided mainly through seasonal labour migration.[15] The latter often entails significant social costs that are poorly captured, if at all, in standard poverty indexes or for that matter in the other social indicators examined in this paper. Examples of such costs include irregular school attendance, the spread of HIV/AIDS, the disruption of family life, and rising urban congestion.[16] Similarly, involuntary displacement of persons affected by large development projects such as dams and mines tends to have enormous human costs. These, again, are largely hidden from view in income-based analyses of poverty. In fact, the incomes of displaced persons often rise (with 'cash compensation') even as their lives are being shattered.[17] The 'informalisation' of labour markets is another example of economic change with substantial hidden costs (e.g, longer working hours, higher insecurity, lower status, and deteriorating work conditions).[18] These issues are not new, but it is important to acknowledge the possibility that the hidden costs of economic growth have intensified in the nineties.

This acknowledgement helps to reconcile the survey-based evidence reviewed earlier with widespread media reports, in recent years, of sectoral economic crises and localised impoverishment.[19] This issue calls for further scrutiny, based on more focused analysis of survey data as well as on micro-studies.

Beyond Poverty Indexes

The decline of poverty in the nineties, as captured in the indicators examined so far, can be seen as an example of *continued progress* during that period. Whether the rate of progress has been faster or slower than in the eighties is difficult to say, and the answer is likely to depend on how the rate of progress is measured. There is, at any rate, no obvious pattern of "acceleration" or 'slowdown' in this respect.

It is important to supplement the evidence reviewed so far, which essentially relates to purchasing power, with other indicators of well-being relating, for instance to educational achievements, life expectancy, nutritional levels, crime rates, and various aspects of social inequality. This broader perspective reveals that social progress in the nineties has followed very diverse patterns, ranging from accelerated progress in some fields to slowdown and even regression in other respects. The point is illustrated in Figure 35.2, where simple measures of the progress of different social indicators in the nineties are compared with the corresponding achievements in the eighties.

Figure – 35.2

Progress of Selected Social Indicators in the 1980s and 1990s (Per Cent Per Year)

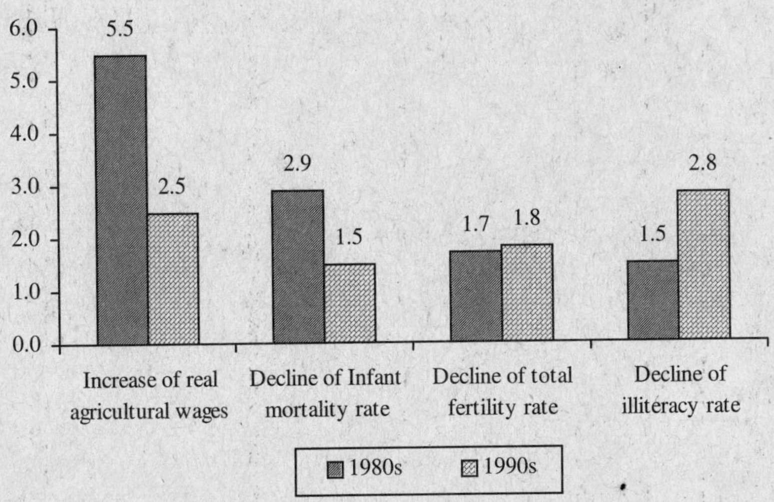

Source : Drèze and Sen (2002), chapter 9.

Elementary education provides an interesting example of accelerated progress in the nineties.[20] This trend is evident not only from census data on literacy rates, but also from National Family Health Survey data on school participation. To illustrate, school participation among girls aged 6-14 jumped from 59 per cent to 74 per cent between 1992-93 and 1998-99.[21] The regional patterns are also instructive. It is particularly interesting to note evidence of rapid progress in Madhya Pradesh and Rajasthan, demarcating them clearly from Bihar and Uttar Pradesh, the other two members of the so-called BIMARU set.[22] There is an important pointer here to the relation between public action and social achievements. Indeed, Madhya Pradesh and Rajasthan are two states where there have been many interesting initiatives in the field of elementary education in the nineties (on the part of government as well as non-government institutions), in contrast with Bihar and Uttar Pradesh where schooling matters continue to be highly neglected. The fact the literacy rates and school participation have surged in the more 'active' states is an encouraging indication of the possibility of effective public intervention in this field.

Turning to instances of 'slowdown', we have already referred to the slackening of the growth rate of real agricultural wages in the nineties. Another important example is the slowdown of infant mortality decline. During the eighties, India achieved a reduction of 30 per cent in the infant mortality rate – from 114 deaths per 1,000 live births in 1980 to 80 per 1,000 in 1990. During the nineties, however, the infant mortality rate declined by only 12.5 per cent – from 80 to 70.[23] In fact, in the second half of the nineties, India's infant mortality rate has remained virtually unchanged. In some states, notably Rajasthan, the infant mortality rate has stagnated for as long as 10 years. These worrying trends have received astonishingly little attention in policy debates, and even in the debate on 'poverty in the nineties'.

Finally, there have also been some areas of 'regression' in the nineties. The increase of economic inequality, discussed earlier, can be seen in those terms. Given the adverse social consequences of economic inequality (ranging from elitist biases in public policy to the reinforcement of other types of inequality), this accentuation of economic disparities is not a trivial matter. Another example of adverse development in the nineties is the decline in the female-male ratio among children, from 945 girls per 1,000 boys (in the 0-6 age group) in 1991 to 927 girls per 1,000 boys in 2001.[24] This decline appears to be driven by the spread of prenatal sex-determination technology and sex-selective abortion, but this does not mean that it is a 'technological' phenomenon, unrelated to other recent economic and social trends. Economic growth, in particular, may facilitate the spread of sex-selective abortion, by making the use of sex-determination technology more affordable. In this connection, it is worth noting that the largest declines of the female-male ratio among children between 1991 and 2001 occurred in five states (Gujarat, Haryana, Himachal Pradesh, Punjab and Delhi) that are relatively well-off economically, and have also experienced comparatively high rates of growth of per capita expenditure in the nineties (Table 35.2).[25]

A detailed assessment of the progress of development indicators in the nineties is beyond the scope of this paper. However, a few general observations can be made on the basis of these illustrations. First, as noted already, poverty is not unidimensional. The poverty indexes used in the first part of this paper are useful indicators of inadequate purchasing power, but on their own do not do justice to the range of deprivations we ought to be concerned with. Following on this, it is important to acknowledge that recent progress in eliminating poverty and deprivation has been quite uneven in different fields. The debate on 'poverty in the nineties' has often overlooked this basic point.

Second, this recognition is also important in assessing the relation between poverty decline and economic growth. As noted earlier, the decline of poverty in the nineties, as captured by conventional indexes such as the headcount ratio or the poverty-gap index, has been overwhelmingly driven by the growth of average per capita expenditure. From this it may seem that the reduction of poverty is mainly a question of economic growth. However, there is an element of circularity in this argument: if poverty is defined as lack of income, it is not surprising that the growth of income plays a key role in reducing it. When the multidimensional nature of poverty is acknowledged, this relation appears in a different light. To illustrate, consider child mortality as an aspect of the deprivations associated with poverty. There is, of course, a significant (negative) relation between child mortality and purchasing power. But child mortality is also strongly influenced by other factors such as educational levels, fertility rates, public health provisions (including clean water and vaccinations), and various aspects of gender relations. Looking at inter-state contrasts in India, the correlation between child mortality and average per capita expenditure (or even poverty indexes) is actually quite weak. Other factors, particularly female literacy, are often more important.[26] Similar comments apply in the context of elementary education: the nineties have demonstrated the possibility of rapid progress in this field through public intervention, with or without rapid economic growth. In short, the standard focus on headcount ratios and other expenditure-based poverty indexes tends to foster a simplistic view of the relation between economic growth and poverty decline.

Third, it is also interesting to re-examine the issue of trends in inequality, in the light of this broader perspective. There is much evidence of rising economic inequality in the nineties, in the form of a widening rural-urban gap, enhanced inter-state disparities, and also growing inequality within urban areas in most states. What about other types of social inequality, involving other dimensions of well-being (e.g, educational levels or life expectancy) and other bases of disadvantage (e.g, gender or caste)? The decline of the female-male ratio among children illustrates the fact that the phenomenon of rising inequality in the nineties is not confined to standard economic inequalities: 'natality inequality' between males and females is also rising.[27] But this is not to say that inequality has risen across the board. Even within the field of gender inequality, there are changes in the other direction, such as the emergence of a substantial gender gap in life expectancy in favour of *women*, overturning India's long history of female disadvantage in this respect. Similarly, it is interesting to note that while economic disparities between rural and urban areas have sharply risen in the nineties, there are trends in the opposite direction as well. The rural-urban gap in life expectancy, for instance, has declined from 10 years or so in the late 1970s to seven years or so today, and rural-urban differentials in school participation have also narrowed.[28] Here again, the picture is more diverse (and more interesting) than it appears on the basis of purchasing-power indicators alone.

Fourth, the broad approach explored here calls for a correspondingly broad reading of the causal influences underlying the identified changes. In the debate on 'poverty in the nineties', there has been a tendency not only to view development trends in unidimensional terms, but also to attribute these trends in a somewhat mechanical manner to the economic reforms initiated around 1991. At one end of the spectrum, it has been claimed that the last decade has been a period of unprecedented improvement in living standards, thanks to liberalisation.[29] At the other end, the nineties have been described as a period of widespread 'impoverishment', attributed to liberalisation.[30] Clearly, these readings fail to do justice to the diversity of recent trends. But in addition, they ignore the diversity of causal influences that have a bearing on these trends. The accelerated progress of elementary education in the nineties, for instance, has little to do with liberalisation, and the same applies to the slowdown of infant mortality decline, not to speak of the decline of the female-male ratio among children. Much else than liberalisation has happened in the nineties, and while issues of economic reform are of course extremely important, so are other aspects of economic and social policy.

TABLE – 35.1A

State-Specific Headcount Ratios

(Per cent)

	Official Methodology			Adjusted Estimates		
	1987–88	1993–94	1999–00	1987–88	1993–94	1999–00
Rural						
Andhra Pradesh	21.0	15.9	10.5	35.0	29.2	26.2
Assam	39.4	45.2	40.3	36.1	35.4	35.5
Bihar	53.9	58.0	44.0	54.6	48.6	41.1
Gujarat	28.6	22.2	12.4	39.4	32.5	20.0
Haryana	15.4	28.3	7.4	13.6	17.0	5.7
Himachal Pradesh	16.7	30.4	7.5	13.3	17.1	9.8
Jammu and Kashmir	25.9	30.4	4.7	15.3	10.1	6.1
Karnataka	32.6	30.1	16.8	40.8	37.9	30.7
Kerala	29.5	25.4	9.4	23.8	19.5	10.0
Madhya Pradesh	42.0	40.7	37.2	43.7	36.6	31.3
Maharashtra	41.0	37.9	23.2	44.3	42.9	31.9
Orissa	58.7	49.8	47.8	50.4	43.5	43.0
Punjab	12.8	11.7	6.0	6.6	6.2	2.4
Rajasthan	33.3	26.4	13.5	35.3	23.0	17.3
Tamil Nadu	46.3	35.9	20.0	49.0	38.5	24.3
Uttar Pradesh	41.9	42.3	31.1	34.9	28.6	21.5
West Bengal	48.8	41.2	31.7	36.3	25.1	21.9
All-India Rural	39.4	37.1	26.8	39.0	33.0	26.3
Urban						
Andhra Pradesh	41.1	38.8	27.2	23.4	17.8	10.8
Assam	11.3	7.9	7.5	13.6	13.0	11.8
Bihar	51.9	34.8	33.5	38.1	26.7	24.7
Gujarat	38.5	28.3	14.8	16.4	14.7	6.4
Haryana	18.4	16.5	10.0	11.8	10.5	4.6
Himachal Pradesh	7.2	9.3	4.6	1.7	3.6	1.2
Jammu and Kashmir	15.0	9.3	2.0	3.8	3.1	1.3
Karnataka	49.2	39.9	24.6	26.0	21.4	10.8
Kerala	39.8	24.3	19.8	21.0	13.9	9.6
Madhya Pradesh	47.3	48.1	38.5	20.7	18.5	13.9
Maharashtra	40.3	35.0	26.7	21.2	18.2	12.0
Orissa	42.6	40.6	43.5	20.8	15.2	15.6
Punjab	13.7	10.9	5.5	6.6	7.8	3.4
Rajasthan	37.9	31.0	19.4	19.8	18.3	10.8
Tamil Nadu	40.2	39.9	22.5	26.2	20.8	11.3
Uttar Pradesh	44.9	35.1	30.8	29.3	21.7	17.3
West Bengal	33.7	22.9	14.7	22.3	15.5	11.3
Delhi	15.1	16.1	9.2	4.7	8.8	2.4
All-India Urban	39.1	32.9	24.1	22.5	17.8	12.0

Source: Authors' calculations based on NSS unit record data from 43rd, 50th and 55th Rounds.

TABLE – 35.1B

State-Specific Poverty-Gap Indexes

	Official Methodology			Adjusted Estimates		
	1987–88	1993–94	1999–00	1987–88	1993–94	1999–00
Rural						
Andhra Pradesh	4.4	2.9	1.8	8.0	5.8	4.8
Assam	7.4	8.3	8.5	6.5	5.7	6.1
Bihar	12.9	14.7	8.7	13.2	10.7	8.5
Gujarat	5.5	4.1	2.2	8.4	6.8	3.8
Haryana	3.6	5.6	1.3	2.8	3.0	0.7
Himachal Pradesh	2.6	5.6	1.0	2.1	3.0	1.5
Jammu and Kashmir	4.5	5.6	0.6	2.4	1.6	0.7
Karnataka	7.9	6.3	2.7	10.5	8.6	6.1
Kerala	6.4	5.6	1.5	4.8	3.9	1.7
Madhya Pradesh	10.6	9.5	7.7	11.2	8.2	6.6
Maharashtra	9.6	9.3	4.4	10.8	11.2	7.6
Orissa	16.3	12.0	11.7	13.0	9.7	10.5
Punjab	2.0	1.9	0.8	1.0	1.0	0.3
Rajasthan	8.6	5.2	2.1	9.2	4.4	3.0
Tamil Nadu	12.6	7.3	3.8	13.7	9.1	4.6
Uttar Pradesh	9.9	10.4	5.8	7.5	5.8	3.9
West Bengal	11.6	8.3	6.5	7.7	4.2	3.5
All-India Rural	9.4	8.4	5.2	9.2	7.0	5.2
Urban						
Andhra Pradesh	10.6	9.3	5.6	4.9	3.4	1.9
Assam	1.5	0.9	1.5	2.0	2.0	1.9
Bihar	13.0	7.9	6.7	8.2	5.6	5.0
Gujarat	8.2	6.2	2.4	2.8	2.6	1.0
Haryana	3.6	3.0	2.0	2.3	1.9	0.7
Himachal Pradesh	0.7	1.2	0.6	0.2	0.5	0.2
Jammu and Kashmir	2.4	1.2	0.2	0.5	0.5	0.2
Karnataka	14.1	11.4	5.6	5.7	4.5	2.1
Kerala	10.4	5.5	3.9	4.5	2.7	1.7
Madhya Pradesh	13.6	13.4	9.5	4.1	3.5	2.6

Contd....

...Table 35.1B Contd...

Maharashtra	12.3	10.1	6.7	5.3	4.6	2.8
Orissa	11.1	11.4	11.1	4.2	3.0	3.0
Punjab	2.3	1.7	0.6	1.0	1.1	0.4
Rajasthan	9.6	7.0	3.4	4.0	3.2	1.7
Tamil Nadu	11.5	10.2	4.8	6.2	4.5	2.0
Uttar Pradesh	12.2	9.0	6.6	6.3	4.6	3.3
West Bengal	7.4	4.5	2.5	4.2	2.9	1.9
Delhi	2.8	3.9	1.5	0.7	1.7	0.4
All-India Urban	10.4	8.3	5.2	4.8	3.7	2.3

Notes to Table 35.1:

Table 35.1a. The headcount ratios labelled "official methodology" are computed from the unit record data using the official poverty lines, as well as the official procedures for assigning poverty rates (or poverty lines) to small states. We have also followed the official treatment of Jammu and Kashmir. The all-India poverty rates are computed by adding-up the number of poor in each state and dividing by the total population. Because the Planning Commission uses interpolation rather than computations from the unit record data, there are minor differences between these numbers and those published in the official releases. The adjusted estimates are computed as described in the text (and more fully in Deaton and Tarozzi, 2001, and Deaton, 2001b); they use price indexes computed from the unit record data, and correct for the changes in questionnaire design in the 55th Round. The final column is a somewhat refined version of the corresponding column in Deaton (2001b). The estimates for Jammu and Kashmir are calculated directly, and not by assuming the poverty line or poverty rate for any other state (as in the official methodology).

Table 35.1b. The poverty-gap indexes labelled "official methodology" are computed from the unit record data using the official poverty lines, and using rules for assigning poverty-gap indexes to small states (and to J and K) that mirror the rules used by the Planning Commission for computing the official headcount ratios. The adjusted indexes use the recomputed price indexes to update the poverty lines, and correct for the changes in questionnaire design in the 55th Round. All numbers are directly computed from poverty lines and unit record data for each state, and the all-India estimates are calculated as weighted averages of the state estimates.

TABLE – 35.2

Growth Rates of APCE and Per Capita SDP, 1993-94 to 1999-2000

	Six-Year Growth of APCE ('Adjusted'), 1993-94 to 1999-2000			Annual Growth Rate of Per Capita SDP, 1993-94 to 1999-2000
	Rural	Urban	Combined	
Assam	0.9	8.8	1.7	0.58
Orissa	1.4	–0.0	3.3	2.34
West Bengal	2.1	11.5	3.3	5.48
Jammu and Kashmir	5.4	8.0	5.3	2.49
Bihar	6.9	4.8	7.1	2.10
Madhya Pradesh	6.6	14.1	7.8	2.78
Andhra Pradesh	2.8	18.5	8.3	3.57
Rajasthan	7.0	15.4	8.6	4.60
Uttar Pradesh	8.3	10.1	9.0	2.99
India	8.7	16.6	10.9	4.36
Karnataka	9.5	26.5	14.0	5.82
Maharashtra	14.1	16.7	15.9	3.53
Gujarat	15.1	20.9	16.8	4.88
Himachal Pradesh	16.2	28.5	17.6	5.06
Tamil Nadu	15.7	25.1	18.9	5.39
Kerala	19.6	18.2	19.6	4.01
Punjab	20.2	17.9	19.9	2.74
Haryana	31.0	23.0	29.2	3.05
Delhi	–	30.7	30.7	5.69

Note : The states are arranged in ascending order of the growth rate of APCE for rural and urban area combined.

Sources: For APCE: Authors' calculations from unit record data for the 50th and 55th Rounds of the National Sample Survey. For SDP: Authors' calculations based on unpublished data kindly supplied by the Planning Commission. The figures in the last column should be taken as indicative, given the significant margin of error involved in SDP estimates.

TABLE – 35.3

Growth and the Headcount Ratio, 1993-94 to 1999-2000

	HCR_{50}	Derivative with Respect to Growth	Six Years Growth	Change in HCR_{55} Inequality Fixed	Change in HCR_{55}, Actual
Rural					
Andhra Pradesh	29.2	-0.90	2.8	-2.5	-3.0
Assam	35.4	-1.27	0.9	-1.4	0.1
Bihar	48.6	-1.06	6.9	-8.2	-7.4
Gujarat	32.5	-0.91	15.1	-12.1	-12.4
Haryana	17.0	-0.63	31.0	-12.9	-11.3
Himachal Pradesh	17.1	-0.75	16.2	-8.3	-7.3
Jammu & Kashmir	10.1	-0.50	5.4	-2.6	-4.0
Karnataka	37.9	-0.91	9.5	-9.0	-7.2
Kerala	19.5	-0.62	19.6	-10.3	-9.5
Madhya Pradesh	36.6	-0.93	6.6	-6.5	-5.3
Maharashtra	42.9	-0.81	14.1	-10.9	-11.0
Orissa	43.5	-1.04	1.4	-1.2	-0.5
Punjab	6.2	-0.34	20.2	-4.0	-3.8
Rajasthan	23.0	-0.78	7.0	-5.5	-5.7
Tamil Nadu	38.5	-0.90	15.7	-13.3	-14.1
Uttar Pradesh	28.6	-0.79	8.3	-6.6	-7.2
West Bengal	25.1	-0.97	2.1	–2.0	–3.2
All-India	33.0	–0.88	8.7	–6.8	–6.7
Urban					
Andhra Pradesh	17.8	-0.62	18.5	-9.0	-6.9
Assam	13.0	-0.64	8.8	-3.1	-1.2
Bihar	26.7	-0.79	4.8	-4.0	-2.0
Gujarat	14.7	-0.55	20.9	-8.7	-8.3
Haryana	10.5	-0.47	23.0	-6.3	-6.0
Himachal Pradesh	3.6	-0.26	28.5	-2.9	-2.4
Jammu & Kashmir	3.1	-0.15	8.0	-0.4	-1.8
Karnataka	21.4	-0.60	26.5	-12.9	-10.6

Contd...

...Table 35.3 Contd...

Kerala	13.9	-0.46	18.2	-7.1	-4.2
Madhya Pradesh	18.5	-0.63	14.1	-8.0	-4.6
Maharashtra	18.2	-0.45	16.7	-6.1	-6.2
Orissa	15.2	-0.54	0.0	0.1	0.4
Punjab	7.8	-0.38	17.9	-4.9	-4.4
Rajasthan	18.3	-0.59	15.4	-8.4	-7.5
Tamil Nadu	20.8	-0.66	25.1	-12.9	-9.6
Uttar Pradesh	21.7	-0.59	10.1	-6.0	-4.4
West Bengal	15.5	-0.56	11.5	-5.8	-4.3
Delhi	8.8	-0.26	30.7	-5.7	-6.4
All-India	17.8	–0.56	16.6	–7.4	–5.9

Source : Authors' calculations from the unit record data of the 43rd, 50th, and 55th Rounds of the NSS. Note that the hypothetical all-India figures are calculated on the counterfactual asssumption that each household received the state growth rate. They therefore do not show what would have happened had growth been more equally distributed across the states: see the text for this alternative calculation.

TABLE – 35.4

Inequality Measures

	logAM¥logGM[a]			Variance of Logs		
	50th Round	55th Round	55th Round Adjusted	50th Round	55th Round	55th Round Adjusted
Andhra Pradesh	0.14	0.09	0.13	0.24	0.17	0.22
Assam	0.05	0.07	0.06	0.10	0.13	0.11
Bihar	0.08	0.07	0.08	0.16	0.13	0.16
Gujarat	0.10	0.09	0.11	0.17	0.18	0.18
Haryana	0.16	0.10	0.23	0.28	0.19	0.31
Himachal Pradesh	0.13	0.10	0.14	0.22	0.17	0.24
Jammu and Kashmir	0.10	0.06	0.07	0.16	0.12	0.14
Karnataka	0.12	0.10	0.12	0.21	0.18	0.22
Kerala	0.15	0.14	0.16	0.26	0.24	0.27
Madhya Pradesh	0.13	0.10	0.12	0.22	0.18	0.22
Maharashtra	0.16	0.11	0.16	0.27	0.20	0.28
Orissa	0.10	0.10	0.12	0.18	0.18	0.21
Punjab	0.13	0.10	0.14	0.22	0.19	0.24
Rajasthan	0.12	0.07	0.10	0.20	0.14	0.18
Tamil Nadu	0.16	0.14	0.15	0.27	0.23	0.24
Uttar Pradesh	0.13	0.10	0.12	0.23	0.18	0.21
West Bengal	0.11	0.09	0.08	0.17	0.15	0.15
All-India Rural	0.14	0.11	0.14	0.23	0.21	0.24
Andhra Pradesh	0.17	0.16	0.17	0.30	0.29	0.33
Assam	0.13	0.16	0.14	0.25	0.30	0.27
Bihar	0.15	0.17	0.17	0.27	0.30	0.30
Gujarat	0.14	0.14	0.14	0.25	0.25	0.26
Haryana	0.13	0.14	0.15	0.24	0.27	0.28
Himachal Pradesh	0.38	0.16	0.42	0.37	0.29	0.40
Jammu and Kashmir	0.13	0.09	0.12	0.24	0.16	0.21
Karnataka	0.16	0.18	0.17	0.31	0.32	0.34
Kerala	0.20	0.17	0.22	0.31	0.32	0.37
Madhya Pradesh	0.18	0.17	0.18	0.29	0.29	0.33
Maharashtra	0.21	0.21	0.21	0.40	0.36	0.40
Orissa	0.15	0.14	0.16	0.29	0.26	0.29
Punjab	0.13	0.14	0.14	0.23	0.25	0.25
Rajasthan	0.14	0.13	0.14	0.25	0.23	0.26
Tamil Nadu	0.21	0.27	0.20	0.39	0.34	0.35
Uttar Pradesh	0.17	0.18	0.19	0.31	0.31	0.34
West Bengal	0.19	0.20	0.19	0.34	0.31	0.35
Delhi	0.29	0.21	0.30	0.43	0.39	0.46
All-India Urban	0.19	0.20	0.21	0.34	0.34	0.37
All-India	0.17	0.18	0.19	0.29	0.29	0.32

Note : a AM is the arithmetic mean and GM is the geometric mean: the difference in their logarithms is the mean relative deviation, a measure of inequality.

TABLE – 35.5

Cereal Availability in the Nineties
(Grams per person per day)

	Net Production	Net Imports	Net Change in Public Stocks	'Net Availability' (1+2-3)
1985-89	422.7	2.0	-5.3	430.1
1990	456.9	0.3	5.0	452.1
1991	447.9	-1.4	0.4	446.1
1992	446.8	1.3	4.2	443.8
1993	446.4	2.5	16.6	432.3
1994	456.3	0.2	16.6	439.9
1995	448.6	-5.9	-2.3	445.1
1996	451.7	-6.9	-11.7	456.4
1997	445.5	-6.7	-4.2	443.0
1998	455.3	-4.7	11.0	439.6
1999	456.3	-5.4	25.3	425.6
2000	452.7	-5.2	30.7	416.8

Note : All figures (except first row) are three-year averages centred at the year specified in the first column.

Source: Calculated from Government of India (2002), p S-21.

Notes

[We are grateful to Suresh Tendulkar for helpful comments]

1. See Datt (1999a), Gupta (1999), Bhalla (2000a, 2000b), Deaton and Tarozzi (2000), Drèze (2000), Lal, Mohan and Natarajan (2001), Nagaraj (2000), Ravallion (2000), Sen (2000), Sundaram and Tendulkar (2000, 2001, 2002), Visaria (2000), Sundaram (2001a, 2001b, 2001c), Chandrasekhar and Ghosh (2002), Datt and Ravallion (2002), among others.

2. On the first position, see, e.g, Bhalla (2000a), Bhagwati (2001), Das (2000). On the other side, see Mehta (2001), Sainath (2001a, 2001b), Shiva (2001a), among others.

3. Note that these derivatives are not elasticities in the usual sense, and are not the same as the elasticities sometimes quoted, which are the derivatives of the logarithm of the headcount ratio with respect to the logarithm of mean per capita expenditure.

4. Calculated from Government of India (2002), p S-51. There have been further major increases in public sector salaries after 1999-2000, with the gradual implementation of the recommendations of the Fifth Pay Commission by many state governments.

5. See Drèze and Sen (2002), Statistical Appendix, Table A.6; also Datt (1999a, 1999b).

6. On rising income inequality in China in the post-reform period, see Bramall and Jones (1993), Griffin and Zhao Renwei (1993), Yao Shujie (1999), Khan and Riskin (2001), among others.

7. On these and related trends, see Drèze and Sen (2002), chapter 9. On the growth of foodgrain production, see Government of India (2002), pp S-21 and S-22.

8. See Shariff and Mallick (1999), Table 5, and National Sample Survey Organisation (2001), pp A-101 and A-134.

9. For similar observations based on a comparison of 1972-73 and 1993-94 NSS data, see Rao (2000).

10. For further evidence, see also National Institute of Nutrition (1997). This pattern, sometimes known as the 'nutrition transition', is familiar to nutritionists [Drewnoski 1999]. It is worth noting that its implications for health are not uncontroversial; some nutrition experts have apparently "pointed to the beneficial health effects of dire poverty, poor diets, and strenuous manual labour", presumably referring to the benefits of a low fat, low sugar, and high fibre diet, rather than low quantities. (Drewnoski, 1999, p 195).

11. Unlike NNMB data, National Sample Survey data suggest that per capita cereal consumption rises monotonically with per capita expenditure. The contradiction between nutritional food intake and expenditure surveys is neither uncommon nor fully understood; for two different interpretations of the Indian case, see Subramanian and Deaton (1996) and Subramanian (2001).

12. Also worth noting in this context is tentative evidence of recent improvement in nutritional indicators based on anthropometric measurements. According to NNMB data, the proportion of adults with a low "body mass index" has declined in the nineties [see Vaidyanathan 2002]. The National Family Health Surveys also suggest that the proportion of undernourished children has declined between 1992-93 and 1998-99 [see International Institute for Population Sciences 1995: xxxiii, and International Institute for Population Sciences, 2000: 267 and 443].

13. It should also be noted, however, that Orissa was hit by a devastating cyclone in October 1999, around the middle of the 55th Round survey period. The 1999-2000 poverty estimates for Orissa are therefore likely to be somewhat 'above trend'.

14. For insightful case studies of localised economic crises in the nineties, see e.g, Roy (1999), Breman (2001a), Krishna (2001), Jhabvala and Sinha (2002), Samal (2002), and Dabir-Alai (2002).

15. See Rodgers and Rodgers (2000), Rogaly *et. al.* (2001), Sharma (2001), Institute for Human Development (2002), among others.

16. On the other hand, labour migration can also have positive roles, such as facilitating the diffusion of knowledge [Maharatna 2001] and enabling the disadvantaged castes to "escape from the clutches of the prevailing caste discrimination in the village" [Sharma 2001: 18].

17. For a telling case study of the human costs of involuntary displacement, see Bhatia (1997).
18. On this, see particularly Breman (2001a, 2001b).
19. See e.g, Sainath (2001a, 2001b, 2001c, 2001d), Breman (2001b), Drèze (2001), Mehta (2001). We are not referring here to media reports of short-term hardship associated with the recent drought (in 2000 and 2001), but to stories of sustained impoverishment.
20. For further discussion, see Drèze and Sen (2002), chapter 5.
21. See Drèze and Sen (2002), p 148; also International Institute for Population Sciences (1995, 2000), for further details.
22. To illustrate, looking at the percentage reduction in illiteracy between 1991 and 2001, Madhya Pradesh and Rajasthan did better than any other major state except Himachal Pradesh; Uttar Pradesh is very close to the all-India average; and Bihar ranks second from the bottom (calculated from census data given in Government of India, 2001b). The comparison is particularly instructive because all four BIMARU states started off with similar (very low) levels of literacy in 1991. On the 'schooling revolution' in Himachal Pradesh (an even more remarkable example of successful promotion of elementary education), see PROBE Team (1999), chapter 9.
23. See Government of India (1999a), Table 1, and *Sample Registration Bulletin*, April 2001; also UNICEF (2001) and Mari Bhat (2002). The comparison with Bangladesh is also instructive: Bangladesh's infant mortality rate was much higher than India's in 1990 (91 and 80 per 1,000, respectively), but by 1999 it had come down to 61 as against India's 71. See *World Development Indicators 2001*, pp 16-17.
24. On this and related issues, see Drèze and Sen (2002), chapter 7.
25. The relevant female-male ratios are given in Government of India (2001b), pp 92-94.
26. Across states, the correlation coefficient between child mortality and per capita expenditure is 0.4 (in absolute value), compared with 0.8 for the correlation coefficient between child mortality and female literacy. After controlling for female literacy, per capita expenditure bears no significant association with child mortality at the state level. For further discussion, see Drèze and Sen (2002), pp 87-89. On the determinants of mortality and fertility in India, see also Murthi, Guio and Drèze (1995) and Drèze and Murthi (2001), and further studies cited there.
27. On 'natality inequality' and its significance, see Sen (2001).
28. See e.g, Government of India (1999), p 16, and Drèze and Sen (2002), p 148.
29. To illustrate: "Economic reforms initiated in 1991 have led to a radical transformation in the well-being of the bottom half of the population. From an approximate level of 38 per cent in 1987, poverty level in India in 1998 was close to 12 per cent" [Bhalla 2000b, p 7].
30. To illustrate: "Both under the World Bank structural adjustment, and from the finance ministry – it's feet might be in India, but it's head is in Washington – and then under the World Trade Organisation obligations, we're basically getting a fundamental destruction of notions of the rights of citizens... Very vital resources we need both for survival – drinking water, all the resources people need for livelihoods – are just disappearing so rapidly that life is becoming impossible...we really have a very, very major crisis of survival at hand...." [Shiva 2001b]. For further contributions on both sides of the debate, see the literature cited in footnote 2.

References

Acharya, Sarthi (1989), "Agricultural Wages in India: A Disaggregated Analysis", *Indian Journal of Agricultural Economics*, 44.

Ahluwalia, Montek S (2000), "Economic Performance of States in Post-reforms Period", *Economic and Political Weekly*, May 6.

Banerjee, A and Piketty, T (2001), "Are the Rich Growing Richer: Evidence from Indian Tax Data", MIT, Cambridge MA, and CEPREMAP, Paris, processed. Available at http://www.worldbank.org/indiapovertyworkshop.

Bhagwati, Jagdish (2001), "Growth, Poverty and Reforms", *Economic and Political Weekly*, March 10.

Bhalla, Surjit (2000a), "Growth and Poverty in India: Myth and Reality", mimeo, Oxus Research and Investments, New Delhi.

——— (2000b), "FAQ's on Poverty in India", mimeo, Oxus Research and Investments, New Delhi.

Bhatia, Bela (1997), "Forced Evictions in the Narmada Valley" in Drèze, J P , Samson, M, and Singh, S (eds) (1997), *The Dam and the* Nation: Displacement and Resettlement in the *Narmada Valley*, Oxford University Press, New Delhi.

Bramall, Chris, and Jones, Marion (1993), "Rural Income Inequality in China since 1978", *Journal of Peasant Studies*, 21(1).

Breman, Jan (2001a), "An Informalised Labour System: End of Labour Market Dualism", *Economic and Political Weekly*, 35(52).

——— (2001b), "The State of Poverty in Urban India at the Beginning of the 21st Century", Sukhamoy Chakravarty Memorial Lecture, Delhi School of Economics, November 16.

Central Statistical Organisation (2001), *National Accounts Statistics 2001,* CSO, New Delhi.

Chandrasekhar, C P, and Ghosh, J (2002), *The Market that Failed: A Decade of Neoliberal Economic Reforms in India,* Leftword Books, New Delhi.

Dabir-Alai, Parviz (2002), "The Socio-Economics of Street Vending: A Case Study of Vulnerability for Delhi in the 1990s", mimeo, Richmond School of Business, London.

Das, Gurcharan (2000), *India Unbound,* Penguin, New Delhi.

Dasgupta, Partha, and Ray, Debraj (1990), "Adapting to Undernourishment: The Biological Evidence and Its Implications" in Drèze and Sen (1990), vol i.

Datt, Gaurav (1999a), "Has Poverty Declined since Economic Reforms?", *Economic and Political Weekly*, December 11-17.

——— (1999b), "Poverty in India: Trends and Decompositions", mimeo, World Bank, Washington, DC.

Datt, Gaurav, and Ravallion, Martin (2002), "Is India's Economic Growth Leaving the Poor Behind?", mimeo, World Bank, Washington, DC.

Deaton, Angus (2001a), "Adjusted Indian Poverty Estimates for 1999-2000", Princeton, Research Programme in Development Studies, processed. Available at http://www.wws.princeton.edu/~rpds.

——— (2001b), "Computing Prices and Poverty Rates in India, 1999-2000", Princeton, Research Programme in Development Studies, processed. Available at http://www.wws.princeton.edu/~rpds.

Deaton, Angus and Tarozzi, Alessandro (2000), "Prices and Poverty in India", Princeton, Research Programme in Development Studies, processed. Available at http://www.wws.princeton.edu/~rpds.

Diewert, W Erwin (1976), "Exact and Superlative Index Numbers", *Journal of Econometrics*, 4.

Drewnowski, Adam (1999), "Fat and Sugar in the Global Diet: Dietary Diversity in the Nutrition Transition" in Grew, R (ed), *Food in Global History*, Westview, Boulder.

Drèze, Jean (2000), "Poverty: Beyond Headcount Ratios", *The Hindu*, September 9.

——— (2001), "No More Lifelines: Political Economy of Hunger in Orissa", *The Times of India*, September, 17.

Drèze, Jean, and Murthi, Mamta (2001), "Fertility, Education, and Development: Evidence from India", *Population and Development Review*, 27.

Drèze, Jean and Sen, Amartya (eds) (1990), *The Political Economy of Hunger*, Clarendon, Oxford.

——— (2002), India: Development and Participation, Oxford University Press, New Delhi.

EPW Research Foundation (1993), "Poverty Levels in India: Norms, Estimates and Trends", *Economic and Political Weekly*, August 21.

Government of India (1993a), *Report of the Expert* Group on Estimation of Proportion and *Number of Poor*, Planning Commission, New Delhi.

——— (1993b), *Sample Registration System: Fertility and Mortality Indicators 1990*, Office of the Registrar General, New Delhi.

——— (1999), *Compendium of India's Fertility and Mortality Indicators 1971-1997*, Office of the Registrar General, New Delhi.

——— (2001a), *Economic Survey 2000-2001*, Ministry of Finance, New Delhi.

——— (2001b), "Provisional Population Totals", Census of India 2001, Series 1(India), Paper 1 of 2001, Office of the Registrar General, New Delhi.

——— (2002), *Economic Survey 2001-2002*, Ministry of Finance, New Delhi.

Griffin, K, and Zhao Renwei (eds) (1993), *The Distribution of Income in China*, Macmillan, London.

Gupta, S P (1999), "Tricle Down Theory Revisited: The Role of Employment and Poverty", V B Singh Memorial Lecture, 41st Annual Conference of the Indian Society of Labour Economics, November 18-20, Mumbai.

Hanchate, A and Dyson, T (2000), "Trends in the Composition of Food Consumption and their Impact on Nutrition and Poverty in India", mimeo, London School of Economics.

Institute for Human Development (2002), "Dynamics of Poverty, Employment and Human Development in Bihar", project report; to be published as a monograph.

International Institute for Population Sciences (1995), National Family Health Survey 1992-93: India, IIPS, Mumbai.

——— (2000), *National Family Health Survey 1998-99 (NFHS-2): India*, IIPS, Mumbai.

Jhabvala, R and Sinha, S (2002), "Liberalisation and the Woman Worker", *Economic and Political Weekly*, May 25.

Jose, A V (1988), "Agricultural Wages in India", *Economic and Political Weekly*, June, 25.

Khan, A R and Riskin, C (2001), *Inequality and Poverty in China in the Age of Globalisation*, Oxford University Press, New York.

Krishna, Sridhar (2001), "Phasing Out of Import Licensing: Impact on Small-scale Industries", *Economic and Political Weekly*, July 7.

Kulshreshtha, A C and Kar, A (2002), "Estimates of Food Consumption Expenditure from Household Surveys and National Accounts", paper presented at the joint Planning Commission/World Bank workshop on poverty measurement, Delhi, January. Available at http://www. worldbank.org/indiapovertyworkshop.

Lal, D, Mohan, R and Natarajan, I (2001), "Economic Reforms and Poverty Alleviation: A Tale of Two Surveys", *Economic and Political Weekly*, March, 24.

Maharatna, Arup (2001), "On the 'Brighter Side' of Seasonal Migration: A Case Study of Fertility Transition in Tribal Population in Rural West Bengal, India", mimeo, Gokhale Institute of Politics and Economics, Pune.

Mari Bhat, P N (2002), "Has the Decline in Infant Mortality Rate Slowed Down? A Review of SRS Evidence", paper presented at a national workshop on 'Infant Mortality: Levels, Trends and Interventions' held at New Delhi on April 11-12.

Mehta, Jaya (2001), "Give Poverty a Face Please!", in *Alternative Economic Survey 2000-2001,* Rainbow Publishers, Delhi.

Murthi, M, Guio, A C and Drèze, J P (1995), "Mortality, Fertility and Gender Bias in India", *Population and Development Review*, 21.

Nagaraj, R (2000), "Indian Economy since 1980: Virtuous Growth or Polarisation?", *Economic and Political Weekly*, August 5.

National Institute of Nutrition (1997), *25 Years of National Nutrition Monitoring Bureau*, NIN, Hyderabad.

National Nutrition Monitoring Bureau (1999), Report of Second Repeat Survey – Rural *(1996- 97),* National Institute of Nutrition, Hyderabad.

National Sample Survey Organisation (2001a), "Level and Pattern of Consumer Expenditure in India 1999-2000", Report 457, National Sample Survey Organisation, New Delhi.

——— (2001b), "Consumption of Some Important Commodities", Report 461, National Sample Survey Organisation, New Delhi.

Osmani, Siddiq R (1990), "Nutrition and the Economics of Food: Implications of Some Recent Controversies" in Drèze and Sen (1990), vol i.

PROBE Team (1999), *Public Report on Basic Education in India,* Oxford University Press, New Delhi.

Rao, C H Hanumantha (2000), "Declining Demand for Foodgrains in Rural India: Causes and Implications", *Economic and Political Weekly*, January 22.

Ravallion, Martin (2000), "Should Poverty Measures be Anchored to the National Accounts?", mimeo, ARQADE, University of Toulouse.

Rodgers, Gerry and Rodgers, Janine (2000), "Semi-Feudalism Meets the Market: A Report from Purnia", Working Paper 6, Institute for Human Development, New Delhi.

Rogaly, B, Biswas, J, Coppard, D, Rafique, A, Rana, K and Sengupta, A (2001), "Seasonal Migration, Social Change and Migrants" Rights: Lessons from West Bengal', *Economic and Political Weekly*, December 8.

Roy, Tirthankar (1999), "Growth and Recession in Small-Scale Industry: A Study of Tamil Nadu Powerlooms", *Economic and Political Weekly*, October 30.

Sainath, P (2001a), "Will the Real National Calamity Please Stand Up?", *The Hindu*, February 25.

——— (2001b), "It's the Policy, Stupid, Not Implementation" (2 parts), *The Hindu*, September.

——— (2001c), "Mass Media: Disconnected from Mass Reality", *The Hindu*, September 2.

——— (2001d), "Where Stomachaches Are Terminal", *The Hindu*, April 29.

Samal, K C (2002), "Shrimp Culture in Chilika Lake: Case of Occupational Displacement of Fishermen", *Economic and Political Weekly*, May 4.

Sarmah, Sasanka (2000), "Agricultural Wages: Trends and Determinants", M Phil thesis, Delhi School of Economics.

——— (2001), "Agricultural Wages in India: An Analysis of Regions and States", mimeo, Centre for Development Economics at the Delhi School of Economics; forthcoming in *Indian Journal of Labour Economics.*

Sen, Abhijit (2000), "Estimates of Consumer Expenditure and its Distribution", *Economic and Political Weekly*, December 16.

Sen, Amartya (2001), "Many Faces of Gender Inequality", *Frontline*, October 27, 2001.

Shariff, A and Mallick, A C (1999), "Dynamics of Food Intake and Nutrition by Expenditure Class in India", *Economic and Political Weekly*, July 3.

Sharma, Alakh (2001), "Agrarian Relations and Socio-Economic Change in Bihar", paper presented at a conference on 'Labour and Capitalist Transformation in Asia' held at the Centre for Development Studies, Thiruvananthapuram, December 13-15.

Shiva, Vandana (2001a), "India: Corporatisation of Agriculture Disastrous", *The Guardian*, March 7.

——— (2001b), "Is Globalisation Killing the Environment?", interview with Frederick Noronha; available at http://www.onweb.org/archive/features/shiva/shiva.html.

Subramanian, A (2001), "Are Income-Calorie Elasticities Really High in Developing Countries? Some Implications for Nutrition and Income", mimeo, National Council of Applied Economic Research, New Delhi.

Subramanian, Shankar and Angus Deaton (1996), "The Demand for Food and Calories", *Journal of Political Economy*, 104, 133-62.

Sundaram, K (2001a), "Employment-Unemployment Situation in Nineties: Some Results from NSS 55th Round Survey", *Economic and Political Weekly,* March, 17.

——— (2001b), "Employment and Poverty in 1990s: Further Results from NSS 55th Round Employment-Unemployment Survey, 1999-2000", *Economic and Political Weekly*, August 11.

——— (2001c), "Poverty in India: Some Issues in Measurement and Database", mimeo, Delhi School of Economics, Delhi.

Sundaram, K and Tendulkar, S (2000), "Poverty in India: An Assessment and Analysis", draft report for the Asia Development Bank; mimeo, Delhi School of Economics, Delhi.

——— (2001), "NAS-NSS Estimates of Private Consumption for Poverty Estimation: A Disaggregated Comparison for 1993-94", *Economic and Political Weekly*, January 13.

——— (2002), "Recent Debates on Data Base for Measurement of Poverty in India", Delhi School of Economics, processed. Presented at joint GoI/World Bank poverty workshop, Delhi, January 2002. Available at http://www.worldbank.org/indiapovertyworkshop.

Tarozzi, Alessandro (2001), "Estimating Comparable Poverty Counts from Incomparable Surveys: Measuring Poverty in India", Research Programme in Development Studies, Princeton University, processed. Available at http://www.wws.princeton.edu/~rpds.

UNICEF (2001), "GOI-UNICEF Country Programme of Cooperation 2003-2007", mimeo, UNICEF, New Delhi.

Vaidyanathan, A (2002), "Food Consumption and Nutrition Status: A Re-examination Based on Indian Evidence", mimeo, Madras Institute of Development Studies, Chennai.

Visaria, Pravin (2000), "Alternative Estimates of Poverty in India", *The Economic Times*, June 27.

Yao Shujie (1999), "Economic Growth, Income Inequality and Poverty in China under Economic Reforms", *Journal of Development Studies*, 35.

Economic and Political Weekly, September 7, 2002 (Excerpts).

36

Report of the Task Force on Employment Opportunities

Planning Commission

The need to ensure adequate growth in employment opportunities to provide productive employment for the continuing increase in the labour force is widely regarded as one of the most important problems facing the country. There is widespread concern that the acceleration in GDP growth in the post reforms period has not been accompanied by a commensurate expansion in employment. Public sector employment is expected to fall as the public sector withdraws from many areas. There are fears that the process of internal liberalisation and globalisation, inevitable though they may be, are creating an environment which is not conducive to expanding employment in the organised private sector. Existing industrial units are shedding excess labour in order to remain competitive and new technology, which is essential to ensure competitiveness, is typically more automated and therefore not job creating. The net result of these forces, it is feared, could be a very slow expansion in employment opportunities in the organised sector, with a rise in unemployment rates and growing frustration among the youth. The problem is perceived to be especially severe for educated youth, who have high expectations about the quality of employment opportunities that should come their way.

1.2 Recognising this problem, the Planning Commission established a Task Force on Employment Opportunities under the Chairmanship of

For complete Report and other reports of Planning Commission, see Planning Commission Reports on Labour and Employment, Academic Foundation, 2002.

Shri Montek S. Ahluwalia, Member, Planning Commission to examine the existing employment and unemployment situation in the country and to suggest strategies for employment generation for achieving the target of providing employment opportunities to 10 crore people over the next ten years, i.e. one crore on average per year. The detailed terms of reference of the Task Force and its composition are given in Appendix I.

1.3 In this chapter we provide an overview of our report and its basic message. The detailed recommendations for policy action proposed in individual chapters are not summarised here but are presented in Chapter 8.

1. Some Dimensions of the Problem

1.4 Our assessment of the employment and unemployment situation in the country along with an assessment of recent trends is presented in Chapter 2. The rate of unemployment, as measured by the NSS surveys appears to have increased in the 1990s with unemployment on the basis of current daily status increasing from 6.03 per cent in 1993-94 to 7.32 per cent in 1999-00. Other measures of unemployment also show an increase.

1.5 The NSS data show that the growth of employment has dropped sharply from about 2.0 per cent per year in the period 1983 to 1993-94 to less than 1 per cent in the period 1993-94 to 1999-00. The deceleration in employment growth has attracted a great deal of attention but it is not adequately recognised that the estimate of employment is derived by applying the unemployment percentage in the NSS Survey to the labour force estimate derived from the Survey. Since the NSS Survey shows a sharp deceleration in the growth of the labour force from 2.3 per cent in the period 1983 to 1993-94 to a little over 1.0 per cent in the period 1993-94 to 1999-00, the employment growth shows a comparable deceleration.

1.6 A basic point which emerges from our review is that the employment objective cannot be defined solely in terms of whether enough job opportunities are created for the projected increase in the labour force. This purely quantitative approach ignores the very important issue of the low "quality" of employment which is the source of much of the current unhappiness with the employment situation. This is evident from the fact that while unemployment according to the CDS measure was only 7 per cent in 1999-00, the percentage of the population in poverty was 26 per cent. In other words, large numbers of those currently employed according to the NSS definition earn income levels which are insufficient to take them above the poverty line. In this situation, an employment strategy which focuses on a mere creation of low quality job opportunities will not address the real nature of the problem.

1.7 Employment policy in future must therefore focus not just on creating new employment opportunities in quantitative terms, but also on improving the quality of employment. One aspect of quality is the income generated by the job opportunity but other aspects are also important. For example there is a strong preference for employment opportunities in the organised sector rather than the unorganised sector and especially for employment in the government sector. Our review of recent trends in Chapter 2 show that organised employment grew at only 1.2 per cent per year in the period 1983-1994 which is much slower than the growth rate of total employment in the same period. If the expectations of the labour force regarding creation of employment in the organised sector are to be met, it will be necessary to generate much faster growth in this sector. Similarly, there is a preference for regular wage employment rather than casual wage employment and for self employment which is economically viable, in the sense of providing an adequate and reliable income level, rather than low income self employment of a residual category subject to high variability and uncertainty.

1.8 Some of these expectations definitely cannot be met in future. Expansion in government employment for example is unlikely to be an important source of future employment growth. There is evidence of excessive employment in the government sector as a consequence of fiscal indiscipline in the past when large number of people have been added the rolls, much beyond what is functionally necessary. In any case, fiscal constraints make impossible to continue in this way. If government employment cannot be expanded the demand for organised sector jobs can only be met by a faster growth in employment in the private organised sector. This may require supportive action in other areas to encourage growth of the organised sector component. One of the steps needed for this purpose is a modification in labour laws.

1.9 The quality of employment is important not only for the new employment opportunities to be created to absorb the new entrants to the labour force, but also for existing employment opportunities, a large part of which are clearly of low quality. A successful employment strategy must bring about a substantial structural change in the pattern of employment over the next ten years, with certain types of traditional low quality, low income, employment opportunities gradually disappearing, and being replaced by higher income, better quality employment. It is therefore important to recognise that a concern with employment should not lead to a desire to protect all forms of existing employment. On the contrary structural change in employment with the disappearance of low quality existing employment should be an important objective of policy.

2. Towards a Strategy for Employment Generation

1.10 The employment strategy needed to achieve our objective of providing sufficient expansion in total employment opportunities to absorb the net addition to the labour force, while also upgrading the quality of existing employment has to extend much beyond any narrow conception of employment policy and employment programmes. To this extent, the employment generation strategy cannot be distinguished from the broader policy thrust for growth and structural change in the economy as a whole.

1.11 We have identified five broad areas of policy which together would constitute an appropriate strategy for employment generation. These are:

- Accelerating the rate of growth of GDP, with a particular emphasis on sectors likely to ensure the spread of income to the low income segments of the labour force.
- Pursuing appropriate sectoral policies in individual sectors which are particularly important for employment generation. These sector level policies must be broadly consistent with the overall objective of accelerating GDP growth.
- Implementing focused special programmes for creating additional employment and enhancing income generation from existing activities aimed at helping vulnerable groups that may not be sufficiently benefited by the more general growth promoting policies.
- Pursuing suitable policies for education and skill development, which would upgrade the quality of the labour force and make it capable of supporting a growth process which generates high quality jobs.
- Ensuring that the policy and legal environment governing the labour market encourages labour absorption, especially in the organised sector.

The main message emerging from our review of each of these areas is summarised below.

3. Role of Growth in Employment Generation

1.12 A central message of our report is that the aggregate employment problem in the country cannot be solved except through a process of accelerated growth which would create additional demand for labour and also provide the increase in labour productivity needed to achieve the much needed improvement in employment quality. The implications of alternative growth rates of GDP for employment generation are explored in Chapter 3. The various projections of employment generated by alternative growth paths are compared with projections of the labour force to come to a broad assessment of the employment situation over the next ten years.

1.13 A sophisticated projection of the labour force over the next ten years requires detailed demographic information from the 2001 census, which will become available only later in the year and this exercise is being attempted as part of the Tenth Plan. For the purpose of our report, we have made a rough projection using available data from the census and the 55th Round NSS survey for 1999-00. An important feature of the 55th Round results is the deceleration in the labour force growth in the period 1993-94 to 1999-00 to 1.03 per cent per year. This low growth rate has emerged because of a sharp decline in the labour force participation rates in 1999-00 compared with 1993-94. However we find that the decline is primarily a reflection of the fact that the participation rates in the 1993-94 survey were unduly high which has exaggerated the extent of the reduction in labour force participation rates between 1993-94 and 1999-00. We cannot therefore assume that the participation rate will decline at the same rate in the next ten years. This means the growth of the labour force will be lower than the growth of the working age population, which is likely to be around 2 per cent per year, but it will not be much lower. Accordingly we have worked with two alternative assumptions with labour force growing at 1.5 per cent and 1.8 per cent respectively.

1.14 These projected growth rates for the labour force growth imply that the expected scale of addition to the labour force, and therefore the need for new employment opportunities, will be significantly less than assumed in our terms of reference. Even if we adopt the higher growth rate assumption of 1.8 per cent, the addition to the labour force in the next ten years will be 8.3 million per year on average and not 10 million as stated in our terms of reference.

However, although the number of additional job seekers is likely to be less than was earlier assumed, the employment prospects remain a matter of concern.

1.15 Our growth simulations suggest that continuation of 6.5 per cent GDP growth is not likely to bring about a significant improvement in the employment situation. The employment elasticities we have used imply that 6.5 per cent GDP growth will only generate additional employment of 5.9 million per year, leading to a continuing worsening in the rate of unemployment. GDP growth of 6.5 per cent with labour force growth of 1.5 to 1.8 per cent will of course bring about a steady improvement in the productivity per person, which can be expected to generate an improvement in the quality of much of the existing employment, but it may not lead to an improvement in open unemployment.

1.16 Acceleration to 9 per cent growth brings about a significant improvement in the employment situation, with a marked tightening of the labour market. In fact, since the supply of labour in our projections is independent of demand, we find that 9 per cent GDP growth actually generates a labour deficit or "negative unemployment". Of course, in practice, we do not expect to see labour deficits because the progressive tightening of the labour market will raise real wages and automatically moderate the demand for labour. However, our projections can be interpreted as implying that growth rates of GDP between 8 per cent and 9 per cent are needed over the next ten years if we want to see a significant improvement in the employment situation.

1.17 The relative importance of accelerated growth in generating employment compared to targeted programmes for employment creation can be seen by comparing the additional employment generated by higher growth with the employment created by specific employment oriented programmes. Our simulations show that a shift from 6.5 per cent growth to 8 per cent growth generates an additional employment of 14.5 million in the terminal year 2012. In contrast, the total volume of employment created by all special employment programmes put together is only about 4.4 million and this level has actually declined over time. Because of severe resource constraints, it is unlikely that the volume of employment provided by special employment programme can be increased significantly in future. Indeed substantial additional resources may be needed simply to maintain the present level of employment while improving the quality of employment created. The role of growth in generating additional employment is therefore overwhelming.

4. Macro Level Policies For Rapid Growth

1.18 If accelerated GDP growth must be the core of any viable strategy for employment creation, the policy framework for achieving rapid growth of GDP must be regarded as essential pre-condition for successful employment generation. We regard the following areas to be critical at the level of macro-economic policy.

i) Higher Rates of Investment

1.19 Accelerated growth requires a combination of higher rates of investment and an improvement in efficiency in resource use. As far as investment rates are concerned, we estimate that it will be necessary to increase the gross domestic investment rate by about 4.5 percentage points of GDP to around 29 or 30 per cent to achieve a GDP growth rate of 8 per cent. The resources to finance this expansion in investment have to come dominantly from an improvement in public savings and from an increase in foreign investment. The required improvement in public savings calls for a major improvement in the revenue deficit of both the Centre and the States.

ii) Improvements in Efficiency

1.20 Investment alone will not suffice unless accompanied by a substantial improvement in the efficiency of resource use. This calls for policies to promote domestic competition and to continue the process of opening the economy to international competition.

iii) Improvements in Infrastructure

1.21 Deficiencies in infrastructure are currently a major constraint on India's ability to achieve 8 per cent growth. This is true for infrastructure in rural areas, especially irrigation and rural roads which are critical for agricultural development, and also social infrastructure especially health and education in rural areas which is very deficient. Infrastructure deficiencies are also a serious problem for the non-agricultural economy. Power, telecommunications, roads, railways and ports are all critical sectors for the competitiveness of the economy, and substantial investments will be needed in these sectors along with an improvement in quality to support 8 per cent growth. This calls for a combination of increased public investment and the evolution of a policy framework in which public private partnership in infrastructure can evolve, with a substantial expansion in the role of the private sector which is essential if total infrastructure needs are to be met.

iv) The Financial System

1.22 An efficient banking system and well functioning capital markets are an essential support structure to achieve 8 per cent growth in the economy. Unless the financial system functions efficiently, channeling resources to productive sector in a manner which supports efficient firms and provides sufficient financial resources to permit investment and expansion, it will not be possible for the real economy to respond to the reform signals aimed at accelerating growth. This emphasises the need for continuing reforms in the banking sector and in the capital markets.

v) Credit for the Informal Sector

1.23 The formal financial system is not well suited to meeting the credit needs of the informal sector and yet this sector is expected to play a major role in expansion of the economy and the provision of employment over the next ten years. It is therefore essential to ensure that the credit needs of the informal sector are adequately addressed. The co-operative system is a potentially important mechanism for providing credit for the informal sector but the system has been greatly weakened in most states. Non-banking financial companies are another potentially important mechanism for reaching the informal sector with several advantages over the formal banking system. It is necessary to find ways of strengthening NBFCs to enable them to perform this intermediation role with suitable prudential safeguards. Micro-finance through self-help groups is another potentially useful channel.

5. Some Critical Sectoral Policies

1.24 In addition to macro-level policies for accelerating growth, it is necessary to focus on policies in specific sectors which are critical for employment generation and for the quality of employment. In Chapter 4 we present a number of policy suggestions for individual sectors which would help to realise the overall growth objective while also helping to create high quality employment.

i) Agriculture and Allied Activities

1.25 This sector now accounts for just under 60 per cent of total employment but we do not expect significant growth in total employment opportunities in this sector because it suffers from considerable under-employment at present. However acceleration of agricultural growth is important to increase labour productivity in this sector and thereby increase the quality of employment for large numbers of the existing labour force. This requires action on several fronts.

- It is necessary to increase public investment in agriculture especially in irrigation. This depends critically upon improving the fiscal position of state governments. There is a case for restructuring the existing allocation of resources by reducing implicit subsidies and increasing public investment.

- Controls on agriculture act as an impediment to the development of a national market and should be removed urgently.
- Laws regarding leasing of land need to be liberalised to allow marginal landholders to lease out agricultural land.

Agricultural exports will support diversification of agriculture and also promote employment in rural areas. Our policies towards agricultural export have not been sufficiently supportive. In particular, control on agricultural exports should be abolished. Other steps also need to be taken to promote agri-exports.

ii) Food Processing

1.26 This sector is highly under-developed compared to its potential. Development of food processing could be an important support for agricultural diversification which is necessary, and it would provide significant non-farm employment in rural areas. Government policy towards this sector has not been adequately supportive and needs to be comprehensively reviewed. There is a case for rationalisation of multiple laws affecting this sector and in particular, modernisation of the Prevention of Food Adulteration Act. The structure of taxation should also be reviewed to remove disincentive for food processing.

iii) Small Scale Industry

1.27 The small scale sector is an important source of industrial dynamism and growth of employment. It needs to be encouraged through multiple initiatives. The following are particularly important.

- Some of the larger issues of reforms in infrastructure development (especially power) and reforms in labour laws, are particularly important for the SSI sector, much more so than they are for large industry. Progress in these areas will therefore help SSI development and the growth of employment in this sector.
- The benefits currently given to the SSI sector in industry should be extended to small scale enterprises in the non-industrial sector, including services.
- Government should provide resources for upgrading infrastructure for industry clusters where there is a sufficient agglomeration of SSI units.

- State governments must undertake concerted efforts, in close consultation with SSI organisations, to reduce the burden of "inspector raj" which is especially heavy on SSI units.
- The policy of reservation has become an impediment to the development of a strong SSI sector capable of competing effectively in the new more open trading regime. We recognise, this is a sensitive subject but after careful consideration of all factors, we recommend phased abolition of reservation over a period of 4 years. This will give existing units time to adjust and will create a healthier and more vibrant SSI sector.

iv) Services

1.28 The services sector will be the major source for employment generation in future providing about 70 per cent of the new job opportunities in the economy. Adequate attention has not been given to the many sectoral policy constraints which hold back employment in services. We have made recommendations in the following areas which we believe are critical for achieving our employment objectives in the next ten years.

- Travel and Tourism
- Information Technology
- Housing and Real Estate Development
- Construction
- Road Transport
- Distributive Trade
- Education and Health Services

Our recommendations in these sub-sectors are designed to remove constraints which prevent rapid growth and modernisation of these sectors. Some of these recommendations will lead to an expansion in total employment. Others may not contribute to an increase in total employment but will accelerate the shift from unorganised modes of production to organised sector modes, which is extremely important if we want to improve the quality of employment. It is important to emphasise that the structural shift in some areas may appear to displace traditional types of employment, but it needs to be encouraged nevertheless.

6. The Role of Special Employment Programmes

1.29 Special employment programmes aimed at providing wage employment or self employment opportunities have been an important element of our employment strategy over the years. In Chapter 5 we have reviewed the experience with these programmes and made an assessment of their potential role in the future. Our review of past experience suggests at best a mixed picture. Many of the major programmes, especially IRDP, suffered from major weaknesses. There was little evidence of success in generating sustainable self-employment opportunities. The wage employment programmes also suffered from weaknesses in design and implementation. The focus on pure employment creation in these programmes led to the specification of excessively high wage components which had the effect that the assets created under the programmes were insufficiently productive.

1.30 Since financial resources with the central government are scarce, and there are competing demands from the social sector and infrastructure, it is difficult to count on any substantial increase in the volume of resources devoted to these programmes. The shift of emphasis from pure wage employment generation to creation of durable infrastructure assets will also reduce the amount of direct employment generated for a given volume of resources. It is therefore unlikely that the total volume of employment created by these programmes can expand significantly in future. However, while special employment programmes may not make a significant contribution to the expansion in total employment in future, they will continue to play an important role in providing supplementary employment, especially to groups of the population that are specially vulnerable and in areas subject to sudden economic stress *e.g.* on account of droughts, floods or other natural calamities.

1.31 There is a case for continued support for programmes like PMRY and the Margin Money Scheme of KVIC which help new entrants into small business and potential village industry entrepreneurs. These programmes are relatively less dependent on budgetary support and rely to a greater extent upon parallel resource flows from the commercial banks. However in implementing these programmes it is important to ensure that the commercial viability of these activities is effectively established.

7. Labour Skills and Training

1.32 While faster GDP growth is necessary to generate a demand for labour, it can only be achieved if the labour force is sufficiently skilled. This is especially so if the growth is to come from expansion of more labour using sectors, which would generate a large demand for skills in all sectors. Unfortunately, the skill endowment of India's labour force leaves a great deal to be desired. Almost 44 per cent of the labour force in 1999-2000 was illiterate and only 33 per cent had schooling of secondary education and above. The latter category includes all those who have some secondary school education even if they did not complete secondary school. The percentage of those who had at least completed secondary school would be significantly lower. The position in relation to vocational skills is even more alarming. Only 5 per cent of labour force in the 20-24 age category have vocational skills compared with 28 per cent in Mexico and as much as 96 per cent for Korea.

1.33 Part of the problem is a strong preference among the young for general education over vocational training because general education has traditionally been seen as a route to acquiring government jobs which are highly valued. This has led to a low demand for vocational training courses. However, there is also a problem with the supply side of vocational training. The physical capacity of the existing training institutes is limited and the quality of the training provided is also not up to the mark. Training courses in government run institutes are often not sufficiently reflective of market demand. There is also a perception among employers that the skill levels acquired by graduates of these institutes are inadequate.

1.34 Correction of these deficiencies calls for action on several fronts. Given the continuing low levels of enrollment and high drop out rates in middle and secondary school, there can be no doubt that a major expansion in general education is necessary. However, efforts should be made to increase the vocational content of education. More generally, the education system must evolve in a manner which lays greater emphasis on acquiring marketable skills. The ITIs in the public sector need to be strengthened by providing additional resources for upgrading their facilities. They also need to be restructured to provide much greater interaction with industry and joint management.

1.35 At the upper end of the educational spectrum, the capacity for producing trained engineers needs to be expanded. Given the heavy demand for graduates of IITs abroad and the likelihood that many future graduates will continue to migrate, we need to expand the capacity of the existing institutes to ensure that our demand for high skills is met. There is a case for substantially expanding the capacity of existing IITs and also the total number of IITs by creating an IIT in each major state.

1.36 The role of the private sector in providing education and training needs to be encouraged as much as possible. Private training institutes have done well in many sectors though there are problems of assuring quality. Existing policies regarding private sector investment in education and training need to be reviewed to remove impediments which hamper the flow of private resources into this sector. The role of the government must change from being a direct provider of services to being a facilitator and source of certification.

8. Regional Dimensions of Employment

1.37 An aspect of employment growth which we have not explicitly addressed in the Report is the regional variation in the employment situation in future. The experience of the 1990s shows that growth rates of State Domestic Product vary considerably across states with the fastest growing state, Gujarat, recording a growth rate of about 8 per cent, while the slow growing states grew at only 3 per cent. Given the importance of GDP growth as a determinant of employment growth in our simulation of employment in Chapter 3, one can assume that continued disparity in regional growth rates will imply corresponding divergence in the rate of improvement of the employment situation. This will be moderated to some extent by migration from the slow growing states to the faster growing states, a trend that is already evident, but large scale migration is not the answer to inadequate availability of employment opportunities, especially for lower skill levels. A regionally balanced employment strategy therefore calls for much faster growth rates of SDP in the poorer states. This in turn points to the importance of policies which can accelerate SDP growth in the poorer states, including, especially in the agricultural sector, as the critical factors for improving the employment situation in these states.

1.38 Many of our recommendations on policy reform at sector level require initiatives by the State Governments, and to the extent it is not uniformly pursued by all States, the impact of our recommendations will differ across States. At the same time, some of the sector level reforms we have recommended will give much better returns in terms of generating employment and improving the qualities of employment in States that have done less thus far.

9. Reform of Labour Laws

1.39 To achieve a significant increase in the proportion of organised sector employment to the total, we will need to address problems with our labour laws which are widely regarded as being too rigid and therefore have the effect of discouraging growth of employment in the organised sector. This issue is examined in Chapter 7. Our assessment is that the existing labour laws, and in particular the way they have been administered and implemented, have this unintended effect of discouraging employers from investing and expanding in labour intensive areas. This has made us uncompetitive in these areas in export markets denying us the possibility of large expansion in organised sector employment. It has also made our producers uncompetitive *vis-a-vis* imports in an environment where the economy is increasingly becoming more open, a trend which is unavoidable and should be continued.

1.40 A comprehensive review of the labour laws will no doubt be undertaken by the Second Labour Commission. However there are some changes that are urgent. It is particularly necessary to introduce flexibility by deleting the provision requiring prior permission of the government for retrenchment and closure. This provision was introduced in 1976 and it has introduced a degree of inflexibility that does not exist in any other country. In a globalised world if we subject our producers to a labour regime which reduces their ability to adjust in the face of changing economic circumstances, the result is not to protect employment but to make production uncompetitive both in export markets and in domestic markets. We have also made a number of other suggestions for amendment of the Trade Unions Act (1926) and the Contract Labour (Regulation and Abolition) Act (1970), which in our view are desirable to make Indian industry competitive.

1.41 Reform of labour laws is a particularly sensitive issue and there is understandable reluctance to proceed with reforms which may appear "anti-labour". For this reason it is necessary to bring about a better appreciation of the negative effects of existing labour laws on total employment in the economy and the potential benefits to labour of introducing greater flexibility. It is also important to implement labour law reform as part of a package which could be seen as putting suitable pressure on inefficient managements. Reform of bankruptcy laws is particularly important in this context. It is also necessary to make a start towards implementing some form of unemployment insurance as a safety net to mitigate the hardship associated with retrenchment. Such a system would have to be based on contributions from labour and employers and should not involve an open ended burden on the state.

1.42 In the chapters that follow, we spell out in detail the policy implications of the broad approach overviewed in this chapter. We wish to reiterate that one most important message is that the employment strategy for the next ten years cannot be dissociated from the process of accelerating economic growth and bringing about structural change in the economy. This acceleration in growth has to be achieved in an environment in which competition, including international competition is inescapable. Our policies must therefore be tailored to ensure that the economy can achieve more rapid growth of output and employment in an enviro in which the process of integrating with the global economy is unavoidable. At a macro level, we need to push the policies which can help to achieve a more rapid rate of growth with an emphasis on the growth of labour using sectors, including especially agriculture and agro-based industries. This will create an environment conducive to growth of total employment and an improvement in the quality of employment. This macro level strategy needs to be supported by policies at the sectoral level which attempt to remove the sector specific constraints which hold back growth.

1.43 Many of the policies that emerge from the strategy proposed in this report may not seem to be directly relevant for employment generation, but they are in fact crucial if we want to achieve rapid growth in total employment with an improvement in the quality of employment of which is equally important. A viable employment strategy for the future must go beyond the limited concern with employment programmes which has dominated the policy debate in the past. It is only a rapidly growing economy, with a structural change in which labour intensive sectors see major modernisation and technological upgradation, that can provide the expansion in productive and high quality employment opportunities that we will need in the next ten years.

Planning Commission Report of the Task Force on Employment Opportunities, Ch.I (Chairman, Montek Ahluwalia).

37

Inflation

Inflation is an important indicator of macro economic stability. The Indian inflation record over the past five decades can be considered satisfactory as compared with many developing economies.

Trends in Wholesale Prices: 1950's to 80's

The inflation rate (measured by variations in annual average wholesale price index, WPI) over the past five decades averaged 6.6 per cent per annum. However, decade-wise, the inflation rate accelerated steadily from an annual average of 1.7 per cent during the 1950s to 6.4 per cent during the 1960s and further to 9.0 per cent in the 1970s before easing marginally to 8.0 per cent in the 1980s. On the other hand, the volatility in the inflation rate, as measured by the coefficient of variation, which was fairly high in the 1950s (4.4 per cent), moved in a narrow range of 0.4–1.0 per cent in the subsequent decades.

The pickup in inflation from 1970s onwards coincided with a sharp rise in M_3 growth, partly reflecting fiscal dominance. At the same time, the inflationary dynamics also reflected supply shocks, such as the two wars (1962 and 1965), hike in crude oil prices (1973-74 and 1979-80) and crop failures. Demand pressures, emanating partly from the widening fiscal imbalances, sustained the inflation in the 1980s.

The Period of 90's

The first half of the 1990s saw a sharp increase in inflation. The decade began with double digit inflation attributable to the large-scale monetisation of fiscal deficits. This was intensified by hikes in procurement prices as well as supply-demand imbalances in essential commodities like pulses, oilseeds and edible oils. The severe foreign exchange shortage that the country faced at the time constrained the ability of the authorities to augment the supply position through imports and also contributed to inflationary pressures. Increases in fuel prices and other administered items also fed higher inflation. The inflationary pressures continued during 1993-94 and 1994-95 in the wake of unprecedented capital inflows and the consequent higher monetary expansion. The focus of monetary policy, therefore, shifted to the moderation of money supply with the objective of containing inflation to create an enabling environment for the process of structural adjustment.

TABLE – 37.1

Annual Average Inflation Rate based on Wholesale Price Index (WPI) Since 1991-92

(Based on 52 week average inflation rates)

Annual average inflation (%)

	All Commodities	Primary	Fuel	Manufactured
1991-92 to 1995-96	10.6	11.3	11.3	10.1
1996-97 to 2000-01	5.1	5.4	13.0	3.1
2001-02 to 2003-04	4.1	3.7	7.0	3.3
2004-05 as on 29-01-2005	6.5	3.9	9.2	6.5
2003-04 as on 31-01-2004	5.5	4.8	6.9	5.3

Source: Economic Survey 2004-05.

The second half of the 1990s was marked by a significant turnaround in the inflation outcome. The inflation rate declined from an average of 11.0 per cent during 1990-95 to 5.3 per cent during the second half of the 1990s.

In recent years, supply side factors have been more instrumental in determining the direction and magnitude of price rise, while the impact of demand side factors on inflation has been relatively weak. The occurrence of drought, decline in agricultural production, increase in global crude oil prices, supply shortages and increased international prices of imported commodities like crude oil, steel and edible oils are some of the factors that have played a crucial role in fueling inflation in the recent past. Imported inflation has therefore, a crucial role to play in setting the direction of domestic inflation.

During the post-reforms period, inflation has had a distinct decelerating trend as liberalisation of both internal and external trade and continual reduction and rationalisation of taxes has led to greater competition and cost-efficiency. Average annual WPI inflation decelerated from 10.6 per cent in the first half of 1990s to 4.1 per cent during 2001-02 to 2003-04 (Table 37.1).

The trend was reversed in 2004-05 with pressures on prices across all groups. Erratic and delayed monsoon in 2004-05 with uneven distribution of rainfall over time and space had an adverse impact on the expectation about the kharif crops and fueled inflation of some agro-based products. Inflationary pressures were further fueled by hardening of international prices of crude oil, minerals and metal related products. With prices of these items shooting up in world markets, imported inflation played a crucial role in domestic inflation in 2004-05.

There are no supply constraints in the domestic market. Domestic production of minerals, coal, POL, and metals group except steel has performed well in the current year. Furthermore, all these products are tradable. Therefore, current high inflation is not of the demand-pull variety, but basically of the cost-push type, driven by a hardening of international prices of oil, minerals and metals.

Box 37.1 highlights the trends in inflation rate since the mid-1950s.

BOX – 37.1

Five Year Average Inflation Rate

Though on an average, inflation based on the WPI remained below the 7 per cent level through the 1950s and 1960s, it accelerated during the first half of the 1970s to touch double digit figures but decelerated in the second half of 1970s as also through the 1980s. Four out of the first five years of the 1990s registered double digit inflation, with a 13.7 per cent peak reached in 1992-93.

5 year average annual inflation rate

(Per cent)

Period	52 week annual average
1956-57 to 1960-61	.3
1961-62 to 1965-66	5.8
1966-67 to 1970-71	6.7
1971-72 to 1975-76	12.0
1976-77 to 1980-81	8.5
1981-82 to 1985-86	6.5
1986-87 to 1990-91	7.8
1991-92 to 1995-96	10.6
1996-97 to 2000-01	5.1

Contd...

...Box 37.1 Contd...

From 1995-96 onwards, there has been a continuous deceleration and the average inflation for the period 1996-97 to 2000-01 is by far the lowest since the mid-1950s in terms of the 52 week average. Though inflation rates may still be higher than those witnessed in some developed economies, India's performance on inflation has improved significantly since the mid-1990s.

BOX – 37.2

Drought and Inflation

Poor Monsoon results in lower agri/foodgrains output, shortages of primary products and uptrend in overall inflation rate triggered by rise in primary product prices.

In the 1970s, double-digit inflation characterised all the three drought/poor rainfall years, with 1974-75 registering a record inflation rate of 25.2 percent (with primary commodities also rising by 25.4 percent), reflecting the effect of not only reduced supplies but also an amplified psychology of shortages.

1974-75 was also the year when the economy was exposed to the most severe oil price shock with the formation of the OPEC cartel. The combined effect of drought and the external oil shock pushed up the inflation rate to record levels. (see table below)

Years of Drought/poor Rainfall in India

Drought/poor rainfall years	All India rainfall (percentage departure from normal)	Average inflation (percent)			Growth rate Agri. prod.	percent change Foodgrain prod.
		All Comm.	Primary	Fuel		
1972-73	(-)24	10.0	13.9	5.0	(-)5.6	(-)7.7
1974-75	(-)12	25.2	25.4	51.1	(-)2.8	(-)4.6
1979-80	(-)19	17.1	14.4	15.5	(-)13.4	(-)16.8
1982-83	(-)14	4.9	3.8	7.5	(-)0.5	(-)2.8
1986-87	(-)13	5.8	5.4	6.7	(-)0.6	(-)4.7
1987-88	(-)19	8.2	9.7	3.7	(-)1.4	(-)2.1
2002-03	(-)19	2.6*	2.8*	4.6*	-	-

* week ended January 18, 2003

There were three poor rainfall years in the 1980s. Agriculture (and foodgrains) growth was negative during these years and inflation rate ranged between 5 to 8 per cent. In recent years, the agricultural economy has by and large moved from a shortage to a surplus situation and is thus more insulated against the vagaries of nature. Therefore, despite the failure of monsoon, average inflation rate remained low thanks to surplus stocks

Contd...

...Box 37.2 Contd...

of foodgrains during the last three years. Reduced dependence of foodgrain production on rainfall has helped reduce the severity of the drought. The impact of the present drought could have been more severe had it not been for the fact that today 55 per cent of foodgrains are being produced in irrigated areas and only the remaining 45 per cent produced in rainfed areas as against only 33 per cent of foodgrains produced in irrigated areas in 1987-88 and about 25 per cent in the early 1970s.

Source: Economic Survey 2002-03.

Factors for Low Inflation Rate since the Second Half of the 90's

The low inflation rate since the second half of the 1990s, (despite an unchanged GFD/GDP ratio, sustained external capital flows and continued double digit fuel price increases) can be attributed to a number of factors (Table 37.2).

TABLE – 37.2

Inflation and Its Major Determinants

(Annual averages in per cent)

Variable/Period	1980-85	1985-90	1990-95	1995-2002	1998-2002
	1	2	3	4	5
WPI Inflation Rate	9.3	6.7	11.0	5.3	5.0
CPI Inflation Rate	10.1	8.0	10.5	7.3	6.2
Food Articles Inflation	10.7	6.4	11.9	6.6	6.0
Increase in Procurement Prices:					
Paddy	7.6	6.3	13.0	6.6	6.3
Wheat	6.1	6.6	11.2	8.3	5.0
Fuel Inflation	12.5	6.0	12.8	11.3	12.5
M_3 Growth @	16.8	17.6	17.5	16.8 (16.3)	17.2 (16.2)
GFD/GDP @@	5.9	7.7	6.3 (5.5)	5.6 (5.1)	5.9 (5.6)
GDP Growth	5.6	6.0	5.0	6.1	5.6
Increase in Unit Value Index of Imports	5.6	8.0	7.6	6.3	5.2

@ : Figures in brackets are growth rates excluding RIBs/IMDs.

@@: Figures in brackets exclude States' share in small savings.

- There was a perceptible deceleration in the M_3 growth rate from 17.5 per cent during 1990-95 to 16.2 per cent during 1998-2002 even as the real GDP growth accelerated from 5.0 per cent to 5.6 per cent over the same period. This was facilitated by the increased flexibility in monetary policy due to the improved monetary fiscal interface. At the same time, (as noted below), monetary policy was able to sterilise the capital flows. This also enabled a deceleration in broad money growth consistent with the objective of containment of inflationary pressures.
- Food articles inflation halved during the period from 11.9 per cent to 6.0 per cent, led by a deceleration in procurement price increases.
- External pressure on domestic prices (as measured by unit value index of imports in rupees) was lower than that in the first half of the 1990s.
- While increased capital flows and higher foreign exchange reserves have inflationary implications through monetary expansion, at the same time, they provide a greater flexibility in supply management in the face of supply shocks.

In brief, the decline in the inflation rate since the second half of the 1990s reflected a confluence of factors. These included better monetary management facilitated by improved fiscal monetary co-ordination, lower pressures from administered procurement price hikes, weakness of domestic aggregate demand, presence of excess capacities, ample food stocks and foreign exchange reserves.

Although the inflation rate witnessed a noticeable deceleration in the second half of the 1990s in India, the volatility of the inflation rate did not see a concomitant decline. This could be attributed to an increased volatility in fuel group inflation - the coefficient of variation of the fuel group increased from 16 per cent in the first half of the 1990s to 32 per cent in the period 1995-2002 reflecting volatile international crude oil prices. The primary articles inflation too was more volatile during the second half of the 1990s.

Developments during 2003-04

After the drought of 2002 and the POL price increases resulting from tension in the Gulf region, the year 2003-04 began with an inflation rate of 6.7 per cent. However, with the ebbing of hostilities in Iraq and the end of the war, the pressure on crude prices gradually eased off, giving temporary relief on the inflation front. The annual point-to-point inflation rate based on the WPI after peaking at a high of 6.9 per cent in the first week of May 2003, decelerated continuously, reaching a low of 3.9 per cent in end-August, 2003.

The interplay of different factors — increase in energy prices, rise in prices of food articles-led to a firming of the inflation rate during September-November 2003, and it hovered around the 6 per cent level in December 2003. A further firming of energy and primary product prices resulted in the inflation rate crossing 6 per cent in January 2004. However, inflation rate softened during March 2004 and fell to below 5 per cent. The year 2003-04 ended with an annual point-to-point inflation rate of 4.6 per cent, while the 52 week average inflation rate was 5.5 per cent. The high point-to-point inflation through much of 2003-04, and its sharp deceleration in March 2004, was partly because of the carry over of the price increase that took place in the last quarter of 2002-03, especially March 2003.

The manufacturing sector is the major contributor to inflation accounting for nearly 80 per cent of the inflation in 2003-04. While the year end point-to-point inflation rate for the primary group in 2003-04 remained below 2 per cent, the same for the manufactured and fuel products groups were 6.7 and 2.5 per cent, respectively. Non-food articles in the primary products group, including fibres, raw cotton, oilseeds and sugarcane, recorded a high price rise during the year 2003-04, consequent to the production shortfalls resulting from the drought of 2002. Within the manufacturing sector, food products, edible oils, textiles, leather and leather products, basic metal and alloys and iron and steel were the prime movers.

Developments in 2004-05 so far[1]

Inflation rates for both manufactured products and primary articles were lower at 5.1 per cent and 1.5 per cent, respectively as on January 22, 2005, compared with 6.6 per cent and 4.1 per cent, respectively on the corresponding date last year. But, there was an acceleration of inflation for the fuel and power group from 7.7 per cent last year to 10.1 per cent this year due to hardening of international prices of oil and minerals and rise in domestic production cost.

Primary Products

Primary products recorded an inflation of 1.5 per cent on January 22, 2005 compared to 4.1 per cent a year ago. Primary items with weights of 22 per cent in WPI contributed 6.2 per cent to overall inflation this year, lower than 14.9 per cent a year ago.

Fuel Power, Light and Lubricants

This group with a weight of 14.2 per cent recorded an inflation rate of 10.1 per cent on January 22, 2005, substantially higher than 7.7 per cent a year ago, and contributed 39.1 per cent to overall inflation in the current year compared to 25.3 per cent a year ago. Major contribution to inflation was made by coal (5.9 per cent) and petroleum products (30.9 per cent) (Table 37.3).

TABLE – 37.3

Annual WPI Inflation Rate (per cent) as on January 22, 2005

Year	Annual point-to-point Inflation rate (per cent)			
	Primary articles	Fuel, power, light, lubricants	Manufactured products	All commodities
Weights (per cent)	22.0	14.2	63.8	100.0
2000-01	1.6	15.2	4.1	5.6
2001-02	3.8	3.8	-0.1	1.6
2002-03	6.1	10.8	5.1	6.5
2003-04	1.6	2.5	6.7	4.6
2004-05 on 22-01-05	1.5	10.1	5.1	5.4
2003-04 on 24-01-04	4.1	7.7	6.6	6.2
	Contribution to annual inflation (per cent)			
2004-05 on 22-01-05	6.2	39.1	54.4	100
2003-04 on 24-01-04	14.9	25.3	59.5	100

Manufactured Products

The Manufacturing group (with total weight of 63.75 per cent in WPI) recorded an annual inflation of 5.1 per cent on January 22, 2005, lower than 6.6 per cent a year ago. The price rise is due to high inflation rates in two groups *viz.* sugar, gur and khandsari (26.7 per cent), and basic metals, alloys and metal products (16 per cent), particularly iron and steel (19.2 per cent). Except these items, price rise of other manufactured items is moderate.

The price rise in the manufacturing group in recent years has helped arrest the erosion in the domestic terms of trade of manufacturing group *vis-a-vis* agricultural products. Thus, the terms of trade of the manufacturing group, which recorded continued deterioration until 2002-03, staged a recovery in 2003-04 and 2004-05 so far.

Essential Commodities

Thirty essential commodities, important for the common person, with a weight of 17.6 per cent in WPI, registered an average annual inflation rate of 6 per cent on January 22, 2005, compared to 3.7 per cent a year ago, and contributed 19.2 per cent to overall inflation compared to 10.6 per cent a year ago.

Inflation Rate based on CPI(IW)/Consumer Inflation

It is generally argued that WPI inflation is not an appropriate index to determine the impact of price rise on the cost of living of the common man. Rather, the Consumer Price Index for Industrial Workers (CPI-IW), which also includes selected services and is measured on the basis of retail prices, and is used to determine the dearness allowance of employees in both the public and private sectors, is the appropriate indicator of general inflation. In sharp contrast to the WPI, CPI-IW inflation has been stable and moderate. This is because food items have higher weights in CPI-IW than in WPI, and in general the price increases of these items have been moderate in the current year.

Consumer Price Index (CPI) reflects changes in the retail prices of selected goods and services on which a homogeneous group of consumers spend a major part of their income. There are three distinct series of CPI - for industrial workers (IW), for agricultural labourers (AL) and for urban non-manual employees (UNME). Of these, the CPI (IW) is the most popular as the Central Government employees' wage compensation (dearness allowance) is calculated on the basis of movement in this index. CPI(IW) is constructed on a monthly basis, with a lag of one month. The base year for CPI (IW) is 1982.

Food items with a weight of 57 percent dominate the CPI(IW), and is therefore sensitive to changes in prices of food articles. (see Box 37.3)

BOX – 37.3

Sensitivity of WPI & CPI – A Comparison

The Wholesale Price Index (WPI) is the most widely used price index in India, and is an indicator of movement in wholesale prices of 435 commodities in all trade and transactions. WPI is the only price index in India, which is available on a weekly basis with the shortest time lag of two weeks. It is due to these attributes that it is widely used in business and industry circles and by Government and is generally taken as an indicator of the rate of inflation in the economy. The base year of the WPI series is 1993-94.

Contd...

...Box 37.3 Contd...

The Consumer Price Index for Industrial Workers - CPI (IW) is constructed on a monthly basis, with a lag of one month. CPI measures changes in retail prices of goods and services covering 260 items of consumption from 70 centres. The base year for CPI (IW) is 1982. WPI and CPI (IW) differ conceptually in terms of purpose and use, commodity coverage, weighting diagram, associated markets and the base year. Therefore, some degree of difference between the two is unavoidable. Differences in market and price behaviour of some uncommon items in the two series are responsible for creating differences in the movements of the two series. A comparison of the weighting diagram of the two series brings out this fact more clearly :

Weighting diagram of WPI and CPI (IW)

WPI		CPI (IW)	
	(Weight)		(Weight)
All commodities	100.00	All commodities	100.00
Primary products	22.02	Food	57.00
Food articles	15.04	Non-food articles	6.14
Pan, Supari, Tobacco	3.15	Minerals	0.48
Fuel group	14.23	Fuel & light	6.28
Coal Mining	1.75	Mineral oils	6.99
Housing	8.67	Electricity	5.48
Manufactured products	63.75	Clothing, Bedding	8.54
Food Products	11.54	Textiles	9.80
Miscellaneous	16.36	Chemicals	11.93
Basic Metals	8.34	Others	21.62

The WPI and CPI (IW) series differ significantly in terms of their weighting diagram. This implies that the degree of importance given to specific commodity groups is not the same in the two series. While food gets the maximum weight of 57 per cent in the CPI (IW) series, food articles in the primary group and food products in the manufactured products group in the WPI series together have a weight of only 27 per cent. The CPI (IW) series is therefore more sensitive to changes in food prices. The fuel group on the other hand gets a much higher weight in the WPI series (14.23) than in the CPI (IW) series (6.28). International price movements of crude oil would therefore have a greater bearing on the WPI series than on the CPI (IW) series in terms of their direct impact. One major sub-group in the CPI (IW) series is the miscellaneous group which includes services like transport, education, health *etc*. Services however do not get reflected in the WPI series. Differences in inflation rate in the two series could therefore also be on account of price movement in the services sector which gets captured in the CPI (IW) based inflation rate.

Consumer Inflation

Retail inflation, as measured by variations in the consumer price index for industrial workers (CPI(IW) or CPI for brevity), by and large, moved in tandem with WPI inflation. Although CPI inflation, at 7.7 per cent, remained lower than WPI inflation during the 1970s, it turned out higher at 9.0 per cent during the 1980s and 9.5 per cent during the 1990s. The divergence between the two inflation indicators widened during the second half of the 1990s with the CPI inflation at 8.6 per cent, almost three percentage points higher.

The wedge between the two inflation indicators largely reflects the larger weight of the food group in the CPI and a differential movement in the inflation rates of various sub-groups. For instance, in the WPI index, the 'primary articles' inflation at 6.5 per cent was higher than that of 4.1 per cent recorded by 'manufactures' in the second half of the 1990s. In addition, the divergence between the CPI and WPI could also reflect the movements in the prices of services, which are included in the CPI.

In view of the divergence between the CPI and the WPI inflation, there may be a need for monitoring a host of other indicators to obtain a more accurate assessment of expectations of inflation for a forward looking monetary policy. Pethe and Samanta (2001), for example, developed a 'composite leading indicator' for inflation and found manufacturing output, money stock, exchange rate, bank credit and raw material prices as possessing predictive capability for future inflation in India. Food prices, exchange rate and real money gap lead inflation expectations by one month each while yield spreads and fuel prices lead by two and six months, respectively (RBI, 2001b).

As the inflation rate in the short-run is often dominated by supply shocks originating from the agricultural sector or fuel prices, the year-to-year headline (*i.e.*, WPI) inflation rate does not necessarily reflect the underlying inflationary pressures in the economy. This brought forth the construction of 'core' measures of inflation to eliminate the noise or transient components of the headline, especially in terms of supply shocks. However, the loss of information content in the construction of core inflation and the relatively greater public acceptability of the headline inflation make the core measures useful only as indicators of the underlying inflationary process rather than as policy targets. Furthermore, in developing countries, a measure of core inflation excluding food items – which can account for more than half of the weight in the index – may not be very meaningful (Jalan, 2002b).

Inflation Targeting

In recent years, particularly given the trend of globalisation, there is increasing debate on the role of inflation targeting as a framework for implementing monetary policy. Box 37.4 introduces the concept of inflation targeting and explores its relevance for developing economies.

BOX – 37.4

Inflation Targeting as a Tool for Containing Inflationary Expectations: Its Relevance for Developing Economies

There is an increasing focus on inflation targeting as a framework for implementing monetary policy. Inflation targeting may be defined as a framework for policy decisions in which the central bank makes an explicit commitment to conduct policy to meet a publicly announced numerical inflation target within a particular time frame. Some countries have adopted point targets while others are following a more flexible approach of targeting inflation within a band. Inflation targeting has been adopted by a number of central banks around the world, including those in New Zealand, Australia, Canada, Finland, Israel, Spain, Sweden, and the U.K.

Rationale for Inflation Targeting

Inflation targets may help provide a clear path for the medium-term inflation outlook, reducing the size of inflationary shocks and their associated costs. Since long-term interest rates fluctuate with movements in inflation expectations, targeting a low rate of inflation would lead to more stable and lower long-term rates of interest.

Important Considerations

Inflation targeting attempts to relate monetary policy implications on inflation. However, concentrating only on numerical inflation objectives may reduce the flexibility of monetary policy, especially with respect to other policy goals. Since monetary policy actions affect inflation with a lag, inflation targeting would mean that the central bank would need to rely on forecasts of future inflation. Given the uncertainties, an inflexible and undue reliance on inflation forecasts can create policy problems. Therefore inflation targets should leave room for a good deal of flexibility and should be adjusted for volatile (supply-side) components. However too flexible a target reduces the credibility of the central bank.

Pre-requisites for Inflation Targeting

Countries adopting inflation targeting need to fulfill some pre-requisites before adopting inflation targeting. It is imperative that the central bank should not be constrained to finance the Government Budget and must have an effective monetary policy instrument like the short-term interest

Contd...

...Box 37.4 Contd...

rate that is fully market determined. Moreover, transparency and accountability of the Central Bank is essential to anchor inflationary expectations. The Central Bank must possess the ability to forecast inflation and to assess the impact of monetary policy on inflationary expectations.

The country adopting inflation targeting has to select the relevant price index that is to be targeted. Most countries have adopted the Consumer Price Index for this purpose. Countries which are susceptible to external shocks and supply side shocks may target their core or underlying inflation rate rather than the headline inflation. The inflation targeting framework should be forward looking as any monetary policy action has a lagged effect.

Scope of Inflation Targeting in Developing Countries

Developing countries generally have relatively higher rates of inflation. Predicting future inflation is often uncertain. Hence, missing inflation targets is more likely in developing economies than in the developed economies. Moreover, in many developing countries, central bank autonomy is more a statutory than a *de facto* situation, because its decisions are still governed primarily by the need to finance the fiscal deficit. Therefore, central banks might hesitate to raise interest rates for fiscal reasons, although they would be required to do so to contain inflation.

Inflation Targeting - Is India ready for it?

Based on the experience of some industrialised countries, there is a view that in India also, monetary policy, to be transparent and credible, should have an explicit narrowly defined objective like an inflation mandate or target. While technically this appears to be a sound proposition, there are several constraints in the Indian context in pursuing a single objective. First, the debt management function gets inextricably linked with the monetary management function while steering the interest rates. Secondly, in the absence of fully integrated financial markets, which remain still imperfect and segmented, the transmission channel of policy is yet to evolve fully. Thirdly, a fully dependent measure of inflation for targeting purposes needs to be developed. Under these circumstances, it is necessary to carefully measure and balance between possible outcomes, after taking into account movements in a variety of monetary and other indicators.

Movement of Agricultural Prices *vis-a-vis* Manufactured Prices

Agriculture accounts for one fourth of the country's GDP. Due to the sheer size of the agricultural economy, gains (and setbacks in a bad year) in agricultural production have significant potential impact on growth and poverty. A good agricultural growth provides demand stimulus for industrial products. In the post-reform period, policy emphasis shifted to liberalising trade in agriculture. Quantitative restrictions (QRs) were dismantled in April 2001. These policy changes now provide an opportunity to farmers and agro-based industries to tap the world markets. The new economic environment has created a conducive environment for improving the terms of trade for agriculture *vis-a-vis* the manufacturing sector. The price index of agricultural products has moved much faster as compared to the manufactured products in recent years. Trade liberalisation and removal of quantitative restrictions have helped promote greater export growth in agricultural commodities.

Issues in Price Stability

There is, by now, an emerging consensus in the literature, that while money is typically neutral in the long run, monetary policy generates short-run real effects in view of price rigidities and expectation errors. Recent research in the context of developed countries suggests that monetary policy should aim at an inflation rate of 1.5-4.0 per cent (Akerlof *et al*, 1996; Krugman, 1996). In view of the possibility of a inflation growth trade-off, a growth-maximising threshold inflation rate has been placed at around 1-3 per cent for industrialised countries and 7-11 per cent for developing countries

The Chakravarty Committee's observation of four per cent inflation rate as being acceptable can be regarded as the first illustrative benchmark on threshold inflation for the Indian economy. A number of studies have subsequently placed threshold inflation in the range of 4-7 per cent (Rangarajan, 1997; Kannan and Joshi, 1998; Vasudevan, Bhoi and Dhal, 1998; Samantaraya and Prasad, 2001; and RBI, 2002a). The estimate of threshold inflation has, however, a shifting perspective. With structural changes in the economy, prolonged price stability at the global level as well as in India and the credible anchoring of inflationary expectations at a lower level, the threshold inflation could also move downwards.

Finally, while there is little disagreement regarding the long-run benefits of low and stable inflation, a number of studies stress the possible short-run costs in the process of reducing inflation. This is discussed in the received literature in terms of the so-called sacrifice ratio, which is defined as cumulative output losses that an economy needs to endure to reduce average inflation, on a permanent basis, by one percentage point. The concept of sacrifice ratio focuses on reducing inflation on a permanent basis by the monetary authority rather than on a temporary reduction in inflation (say, due to beneficial supply shocks like lower food prices). Furthermore, the sacrifice ratio measures cumulative output losses, which could be spread over a number of periods. The output losses refer to deviations of actual output from its trend. Over time, as inflation expectations stabilise at a lower level, actual output gradually converges to its trend path. The sacrifice ratio measures such output losses in the process of disinflation. One study puts the estimate of the sacrifice ratio at around two for India (Kapur and Patra, 2000). It is necessary to emphasise here that for a proper interpretation of the sacrifice ratio, it is crucial to analyse the dynamics and sources of inflation. In particular, a clear distinction must be made between low inflation driven by benign supply factors and a tight monetary policy.

Anti-inflationary Measures

Containment of inflation remains high on the agenda of the Government, as inflation hurts everybody, particularly the poor whose incomes are not indexed to prices. High inflation puts pressure on interest rates leading to a rise in project costs and investment. It also tends to reduce real interest rates, thereby adversely affecting the savings rate. Anti-inflationary policies of the Government include strict fiscal and monetary discipline, rationalisation of excise and import duties of essential commodities so that there is no undue burden on the poor, effective supply-demand management of sensitive items through liberal tariff and trade policies, and strengthening the public distribution system.

Unfavourable monsoon at home and hardening of international prices of minerals, metals, crude oil and related products led to acceleration of WPI inflation since May 2004, which reached 8.7 per cent on August 28, 2004. However, sound macro-economic management by the Government coupled with specific monetary and fiscal measures led to continual deceleration of WPI inflation since then. The current point-to-point WPI inflation is running around 5.2 per cent compared to 5.9 per cent a year ago. In general there is a downward trend of prices particularly for the agro-based products during January-March every year due to seasonality of prices. The current year is no exception to this general trend.

Government of India, Economic Survey 2002-03, 2003-04 and 2004-05 (Excerpts from Ch.5).

Statistical Appendix

APPENDIX TABLE

Selected Economic & Social Indicators 1950-51 to 2003-2004

	1950-51	1960-61	1970-71	1980-81	1990-91	1998-99	1999-2000	2000-01	2001-02	2002-03	2003-04
1	2	3	4	5	6	7	8	9	10	11	12
ECONOMIC INDICATORS											
GDP at factor cost:											
(i) At current prices (Rs. crore)	9547	16220	42222	130176	510954	1598127	1761838	1902999	2081474	2254888[P]	2519785[Q]
(ii) At constant prices (Rs. crore)	140466	206103	296278	401128	692871	1082748	1148367	1198592	1267945	1318362[P]	1430548[Q]
Per capita net national product, at 1993-94 prices (Rupees)	3687	4429	5002	5352	7321	9650	10071	10308	10754	11013[P]	11799[Q]
Index of industrial production[a] (Base: 1993-94=100)	7.9@	15.6	28.1	43.1	91.6	145.2	154.9	162.6	167.0	176.6	189.0
Index of agricultural production (Base: triennium ending 1981-82)	46.2	68.8	85.9	102.1	148.4	177.9	176.9	165.7	178.3	150.5	179.6
Gross domestic capital formation (as per cent of GDP)	8.7	14.4	15.4	20.3	26.3	22.6	25.3	23.8	22.6	24.8[P]	26.3[Q]
Gross domestic savings (as per cent of GDP)	8.9	11.6	14.6	18.9	23.1	21.5	24.2	23.5	23.4	26.1[P]	28.1[Q]
Output:											
(a) Foodgrains (million tonnes)	50.8	82.0	108.4	129.6	176.4	203.6	209.8	196.8	212.0	174.2	212.2
(b) Finished Steel (million tonnes)$	1.0	2.4	4.6	6.8	13.5	24.7	28.5	30.3	31.1	33.4	36.9
(c) Cement (million tonnes)	2.7	8.0	14.3	18.7	48.8	87.9	98.2	97.6	106.9	116.3	123.5
(d) Coal (including lignite)[g] (million tonnes)	32.3	55.2	76.3	119.0	225.5	315.7	322.1	332.6	352.6	367.2	389.1
(e) Crude oil (million tonnes)	0.3	0.5	6.8	10.5	33.0	32.7	31.9	32.4	32.0	33.0	33.4
(f) Electricity generated (utilities only) (Billion KWH)	5.1	16.9	55.8	120.8	264.3	448.5	480.7	499.5	517.4	532.7	565.1
Wholesale price index* average (Base: 1993-94=100)	6.8	7.9	14.3	36.8	73.7	140.7	145.3	155.7	161.3	166.8	175.9
Consumer price index (Base: 1982=100) @@	17	21	38	81	193	414	428	444	463	482	500
Plan outlay (Rs. crore)	260##	1117	2524	15023	58369	151580	160608	185737	186315	210203	243550 (RE)

...Contd...

1	2	3	4	5	6	7	8	9	10	11	12
ECONOMIC INDICATORS											
Foreign Trade											
(i) Exports											
Rs. crore	606	642	1535	6711	32553	139752	159561	203571	209018	255137	293367
US $ million	1269	1346	2031	8486	18143	33218	36822	44560	43827	52719	63843
(ii) Imports											
Rs. crore	608	1122	1634	12549	43198	178332	215236	230873	245200	297206	359108
US $ million	1273	2353	2162	15869	24075	42389	49671	50536	51413	61412	78149
Foreign exchange reserves£ (excluding gold and SDRs):											
Rs. crore	911	186	438	4822	4388	125412	152924	184482	249118	341476	466215
US $ million	1914	390	584	5850	2236	29522	35058	39554	51049	71890	107448
SOCIAL INDICATORS											
Population											
Population (million)[b]	359	434	541	679	839	983	1001	1019	1037	1055	1073
Birth rate (per 1000)[c]	39.9	41.7	41.2	37.2	33.9	26.5	26.1	25.4	25.0	...	...
Death rate (per 1000)[c]	27.4	22.8	19.0	15.0	12.5	9.0	8.7	8.4	8.1	...	...
Life expectancy at birth (in years)[d]											
(a) Male	32.5	41.9	46.4	50.9	58.6	...	...	63.87[h]	...	...	...
(b) Female	31.7	40.6	44.7	50.0	59.0	...	...	66.91[h]	...	...	...
Total	32.1	41.3	45.6	50.4	58.7	...	...	...	...	...	...
Education:											
Literacy rate (percentage)[e]											
(a) Male	27.16	40.40	45.96	56.38	64.1	...	...	75.85	...	...	...
(b) Female	8.86	15.35	21.97	29.76	39.3	...	...	54.16	...	...	...
Total	18.33	28.30	34.45	43.57	52.2	63.1	...	65.38	...	...	...

Contd...

...Contd...

1	2	3	4	5	6	7	8	9	10	11	12
Health & Family Welfare[f]											
Registered medical practitioners (RMP) Allopathic (thousand) (as on 31st Dec.)	61.8	83.7	151.1	268.7	393.6	535.6#	555.1#	575.6#	...	...	...
RMP per 10,000 population	1.7	1.9	2.8	3.9	4.7	5.5#	5.6#	5.6#	...	...	...
Beds (all types)** per 10,000	3.2	5.7	6.4	8.3	9.5	...	...	...	...	...	...

@ Relates to the calender year 1950. # Provisional ## Relates to 1951-52. $ Including secondary producers

@@ Figures for the period up to 1988-89 derived by converting indices on earlier bases into base 1982=100.

* Figures for the period up to 1993-94 derived by converting the indices on earlier bases into base 1993-94.

** Includes beds in hospitals, dispensaries, P.H.Cs, clinics, sanatoriums, etc.

£ As at end-March. RE Revised estimates. ... Not available.

Q Quick estimates P Provisional estimates.

Notes:

a The Index of Industrial Production has been revised since 1993-94.

b Relate to mid-financial year (as on October 1) based on population figures given in the NAS, 2003 of C.S.O. and Revised Estimates 2003-04

c For calendar year. Figure shows against 1990-91 is for calendar year 1990 and so on. Source: Ministry of Health and Family Welfare and Office of R.G.I.

d Data for 1950-51, 1960-61, 1970-71 and 1980-81 relate to the decades 1941-50, 1951-60, 1961-70 and 1971-80 respectively, centred at mid-points of the decade, i.e., 1946, 1956, 1966 and 1976. The estimates for 1990-91 and 1991-92 refer to the periods 1988-92 and 1989-93 respectively.

e Data for 1950-51, 1960-61, 1970-71, 1980-81, 1990-91 and 2000-01 are as per Census of India 1951, 1961, 1971, 1981, 1991 and 2001. The figures for 1951, 1961 and 1971 relate to population aged 5 years and above and those for 1981 and 1991 to population aged 7 years and above. All India literacy rates exclude Assam for 1981 and J&K for 1991. Data for 1995-96 and 1997-98 relate to the years 1996 and 1998 respectively and are based on NSSO survey, 53rd Round upto 1997. For 1998, data is based on National Family Health Survey (1998-99) (+6 years). Data for 2000-01 pertains to Cenus 2001.

f Relate to calendar year e.g., 1950-51 pertains to 31st December, 1951 and so on.

g Coal output includes Meghalaya Coal from 2001-02 onwards.

h. Pertains to 2001-2006.

Source: Government of India, Ministry of Finance, Economic Survey, 2004-2005.